WITHDRAWN
lonely planet

W9-BUG-842

Southeast Asia
on a shoestring

Myanmar
(Burma)
p479

Laos
p314

Thailand
p643

Vietnam
p812

Cambodia
p68

Philippines
p545

Brunei
Darussalam
p56

Malaysia
p380

Singapore
p609

Indonesia
p151

Timor-Leste
p789

THIS EDITION WRITTEN AND RESEARCHED BY

Nick Ray, Isabel Albiston, Greg Bloom, Ria de Jong, David Eimer,
Sarah Reid, Simon Richmond, Iain Stewart, Ryan Ver Berkmoes,
Richard Waters, China Williams

PLAN YOUR TRIP

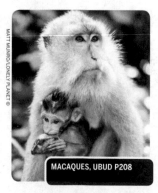

MACAQUES, UBUD P208

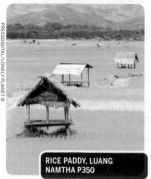

RICE PADDY, LUANG
NAMTHA P350

ON THE ROAD

MATT MUNRO/LONELY PLANET ©

PRESSDIGITAL/LONELY PLANET ©

Contents

ON THE ROAD

Contents

UNDERSTAND

SURVIVAL GUIDE

SPECIAL FEATURES

Welcome to Southeast Asia

Lush landscapes, urban jungles, blissful beaches, brooding volcanoes, ancient temples, modernist architecture, creative cuisine: Southeast Asia seamlessly delivers the accessible, affordable exotic.

Elemental Forces

Water has sculpted many Southeast Asian landscapes. The jungle-topped islands are fringed by coral reefs that calm the ocean into turquoise pools. The languorous Vietnamese coastline greets the South China Sea from tip to tail, while inland dramatic karst mountains soar skywards. The meandering Mekong River winds its way from the densely packed mountains of northern Laos to the pancake-flat Mekong Delta. The traditional 'highways' of Borneo are coffee-coloured, jungle-clad rivers. And the volcanoes of Indonesia and the Philippines provide a glimpse into the earth's volatile heart.

Spiritual Sojourns

Southeast Asia is a spiritual space. As dawn breaks, the smoke of incense wafts from earth to heaven. Barefoot monks embark on their call to alms; the muezzin's call reverberates from mosques; and family altars are flush with fruit and flowers for the guardian spirits. The region's great monuments were wrought from divine inspiration, from Angkor's heaven incarnate to Bagan's shimmering spires. The spiritual side of life is omnipresent and travellers can boost their karmic balance at meditation retreats or by hiking to a golden temple atop a sacred mountain.

Urban Adventures

The cities of Southeast Asia are stepping into the future with one foot dragging in the past. Bangkok is the gateway to many Asian adventures, where Skytrains whisk shoppers from mall to mall and hawkers ply their wares on the steaming pavements below. Singapore is a gleaming testament to Asia at its most efficient. For old meets new, explore the backstreets of Phnom Penh, Hanoi's Old Quarter or downtown Yangon, which have a beguiling blend of traditional architecture, colonial-era gems and a contemporary twist. One thing all the cities have in common is a buzz.

Epicurean Encounters

With a burning sun and cooling rains, the earth here delivers a colourful palette of fruits, spices once as prized as gold, and the Southeast Asia staple, rice. From Indian curries to Chinese dim sum, the regional cuisine tells a tale of migration and mixing. And there is no better way to meet the region's melting pot of people, with their infectious spirit and irrepressible love of life, than with a meal in a market or a drink at a street stall. Despite the rapid development, the street remains the stage for the real-life drama that unfolds each day.

Why I Love Southeast Asia

By Nick Ray, Writer

Six months in Southeast Asia in 1995 sparked a lifelong love affair with the region which shows no sign of abating. Slow boats down the Mekong, motorbike adventures in the jungle and island-hopping in Indonesia were all early highlights, but new frontiers are opening up all the time with Myanmar embracing democracy and Timor-Leste not yet on the traveller radar. The people are irrepressible, the experiences unforgettable and the stories impossible to re-create, but sometime during your journey, Southeast Asia will enter your soul.

For more about our writers, see p976

Above: Boating in the Mekong Delta (p894), Vietnam

Southeast Asia

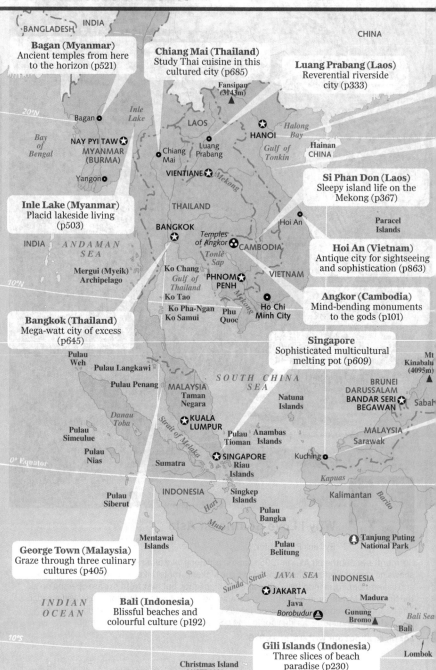

Bagan (Myanmar)
Ancient temples from here to the horizon (p521)

Chiang Mai (Thailand)
Study Thai cuisine in this cultured city (p685)

Luang Prabang (Laos)
Reverential riverside city (p333)

Si Phan Don (Laos)
Sleepy island life on the Mekong (p367)

Inle Lake (Myanmar)
Placid lakeside living (p503)

Hoi An (Vietnam)
Antique city for sightseeing and sophistication (p863)

Angkor (Cambodia)
Mind-bending monuments to the gods (p101)

Bangkok (Thailand)
Mega-watt city of excess (p645)

Singapore
Sophisticated multicultural melting pot (p609)

George Town (Malaysia)
Graze through three culinary cultures (p405)

Bali (Indonesia)
Blissful beaches and colourful culture (p192)

Gili Islands (Indonesia)
Three slices of beach paradise (p230)

BANGLADESH
INDIA
CHINA
Bagan
Inle Lake
NAY PYI TAW
MYANMAR (BURMA)
Yangon
Fansipan (3143m)
LAOS
HANOI
Halong Bay
Hainan CHINA
Gulf of Tonkin
Chiang Mai
Luang Prabang
VIENTIANE
Bay of Bengal
INDIA
ANDAMAN SEA
THAILAND
Mekong
BANGKOK
Temples of Angkor
CAMBODIA
Tonlé Sap
Hoi An
Paracel Islands
VIETNAM
Mergui (Myeik) Archipelago
Ko Chang
Gulf of Thailand
Ko Tao
Ko Pha-Ngan
Ko Samui
PHNOM PENH
Phu Quoc
Ho Chi Minh City
Pulau Weh
Pulau Langkawi
Pulau Penang
MALAYSIA
Taman Negara
SOUTH CHINA SEA
Natuna Islands
Mt Kinabalu (4095m)
BRUNEI DARUSSALAM
BANDAR SERI BEGAWAN
Sabah
Danau Toba
Strait of Melaka
KUALA LUMPUR
Pulau Tioman
Anambas Islands
MALAYSIA
Sarawak
Pulau Simeulue
Pulau Nias
Sumatra
SINGAPORE
Riau Islands
Kuching
Kapuas
0° Equator
Pulau Siberut
INDONESIA
Singkep Islands
Pulau Bangka
Kalimantan
Barito
Hari
Musi
Mentawai Islands
Pulau Belitung
Tanjung Puting National Park
JAVA SEA
INDONESIA
INDIAN OCEAN
Sunda Strait
JAKARTA
Java
Borobudur
Madura
Gunung Bromo
Bali Sea
Bali
Lombok
Christmas Island
AUSTRALIA
100°E
110°E
20°N
10°N
0°
10°S

EAST CHINA SEA

Tropic of Cancer

TAIWAN

Halong Bay (Vietnam)
Limestone towers anchoring
a jewel-coloured bay (p831)

**Phong Nha-Ke Bang
National Park (Vietnam)**
The world's biggest cave (p846)

Batanes
Islands

Luzon Strait

Babuyan
Islands

**Ifugao Rice Terraces
(Philippines)**
Emerald staircases (p565)

Banaue ⊙

Luzon

PHILIPPINE
SEA

Polillo
Islands

MANILA ✪

Catanduanes

PHILIPPINES

Palawan (Philippines)
Rugged, remote and oh-so-
beautiful beaches (p592)

Mindoro

Calamian
Group

Sibuyan
Sea

Samar

Panay

Visayan
Sea

Letye

Cebu

Dinagat

Bohol

Siargao

Palawan

Negros

Bohol Sea

Malaysian Borneo
Jungle adventures
galore (p432)

SULU SEA

Mindanao

PALAU

Basilan

Jolo Sulu
Archipelago

PACIFIC
OCEAN

Tawi-Tawi

Talaud

Semporna
Archipelago

Sangir
Islands

Morotai

CELEBES SEA

Equator 0°

Halmahera

Waigeo

Togean Islands

Pulau
Biak

Teluk
Tomini

MALUKU
SEA

HALMAHERA
SEA

Yapen

Pulau
Bacan

Sula Islands

Obi

Teluk
Cenderawasih

**Komodo & Flores
(Indonesia)**
Idyllic beaches (p239)

Sulawesi

Banggai
Islands

SERAM
SEA

Misool

Sula wesi

Buru

Seram

INDONESIA
Papua

Tana
Toraja

INDONESIA

Ambon

Puncak Jaya
(5030m)

PAPUA
NEW
GUINEA

Teluk
Bone

Butung
(Buton)

Banda
Islands

Kai
Islands

Aru
Islands

BANDA SEA

Selayar

Yos
Sudarso

FLORES SEA

Alor Atauro

Wetar Leti
Islands

Tanimbar
Islands

Sumbawa Komodo

Islands Island

Babar
Islands

ARAFURA
SEA

Flores

Solor
Islands

✪ DILI

TIMOR-LESTE

Timor-Leste
Get off the
beaten trail (789)

Sumba

West
Timor

TIMOR SEA

SAWU SEA

Sawu Rote

AUSTRALIA

20°N

10°N

10°S

120°E

140°E

Southeast Asia's
Top 20

Temples of Angkor (Cambodia)

1 One of the world's most magnificent sights, the temples of Angkor (p87) are so much better than the superlatives. Angkor Wat is the world's largest religious building; Bayon, with its immense four-sided stone faces, is perhaps the world's weirdest spiritual monument; and at Ta Prohm nature has run amok. Siem Reap, a buzzing destination with superb restaurants and bars, is the base from which to explore this collection of temples. Beyond the temples are cultural attractions galore, such as floating villages and cooking classes. Bayon (p103), Angkor Thom

Hoi An (Vietnam)

2 Vietnam's most cosmopolitan and civilised town, this beautiful ancient port (p863) is bursting with gourmet restaurants, hip bars and cafes, quirky boutiques and expert tailors. Immerse yourself in history in the warren-like lanes of the Old Town, wander through the shops and tour the temples and pagodas. Dine like an emperor on a peasant's budget – and even learn how to cook like the locals. Then hit glorious An Bang beach, wander along the riverside and bike the back roads. Yes, Hoi An has it all. Hoi An Old Town (p863)

LUIS CASTANEDA INC/GETTY IMAGES ©

FELIX HUG/GETTY IMAGES ©

MATT MUNRO/LONELY PLANET ©

TERADAT SANTIVIVUT/GETTY IMAGES ©

Bagan (Myanmar)

3 More than 4000 Buddhist temples are scattered across the plains of Bagan (p521), the site of the first Burmese kingdom and an architectural complement to the temples of Angkor. Dating from the 11th and 13th centuries, the vast majority have been renovated, as Bagan remains an active religious site and place of pilgrimage. Yes, there are tour buses and crowds at the most popular sunset-viewing spots, but they can be avoided. Pedal off on a bike and have your own adventure amid the not-so-ruined temples.

Bangkok (Thailand)

4 This superstar city (p645) has it all, and in super-sized proportions: food, shopping, fun and then some. Bangkok may be a pressure cooker for new arrivals, but it will be a needed dose of civilisation after weeks of dusty back roads. Build in plenty of time to load up on souvenirs, refresh your wardrobe, get a much-kneaded massage, and recount tall tales over a cold bottle of beer. Don't forget a sunset river-ferry ride, an evening noodle tour of Chinatown and one final round of temple spotting.

Halong Bay (Vietnam)

5 More than 3000 limestone-peaked islands sheltered by shimmering seas make Halong Bay (p831) one of Vietnam's top tourist draws as well as a Unesco World Heritage Site. An overnight cruise allows you to adore the scenery through the day's dramatic changes of light: rise early for an ethereal misty morn, kayak into the tidal-carved grottoes and lagoons and track the pastel parade of the sinking sun. (If you're still hankering for more karst action, move on to less touristy Lan Ha Bay.)

Luang Prabang (Laos)

6 Hemmed in by the Mekong and Nam Khan rivers, this ancient city (p333) boasts history, religious devotion and natural beauty. Once a royal capital, Luang Prabang is populated by temples and Buddhist monks, best seen on their morning call to alms. In between are forested river views and world-class French cuisine. Hire a bike and explore the backstreets, take a cooking workshop or encounter an elephant, or just ease back with a restful massage at one of many affordable spas. Wat Ho Pha Bang (p333), Royal Palace Museum

SIMON IRWIN/LONELY PLANET ©

CHRISTIANA A. BAUMLE/500PX ©

Bali (Indonesia)

7 Though Indonesia's 17,000 islands offer myriad cultural and exploration adventures, the one island not to miss is Bali (p192). The original backpackers' haven, here you can surf epic breaks and then party till dawn and beyond. Bali has one of Southeast Asia's richest cultures; artistic expression linked to their unique form of Hinduism fills locals' days and nights. Stay at one of the many cool, beachy dives on the coast down to Ulu Watu and you may find it hard to even contemplate moving on. Kuta Beach (p195)

Komodo & Flores (Indonesia)

8 Spot prehistoric dragons at Komodo National Park (p239), dive some of Indonesia's best spots and laze away days on deserted-island beaches, all while enjoying the charms and fun of Labuanbajo, the ever-more-popular waterfront town at the west end of the volcano-studded island of Flores (p241). It's enjoying a surging popularity as the next Indo 'it' spot and offers stunning vistas and ancient cultures. Hop around nearby islands to laze on beaches of varying hues. Komodo dragon (p240)

George Town (Malaysia)

9 Once abandoned by locals and seemingly forgotten by tourists, George Town (p405) has managed to cling to its reign as one of the region's hottest destinations. The 2008 Unesco World Heritage declaration sparked a frenzy of cultural preservation, and the city's charismatic shophouses have been turned into house museums, charming boutique hotels and chic cafes. Aggressive drivers aside, it's also one of the most rewarding cities in Southeast Asia to explore on foot – and also home to some of Malaysia's best food. Bicycle rickshaw, Blue Mansion (p405)

Chiang Mai (Thailand)

10 Bestowed with endless charm, Chiang Mai (p685) is a cultural and artistic magnet for Thais and tourists alike. The old city is framed by a time-preserving moat and chock-a-block with antique teak temples displaying northern Thailand's distinctive art and architecture. Visitors come to study language, massage, meditation or just chat with a monk. Guarding the city is Doi Suthep, a sacred peak bejewelled with a sacred temple; beyond the city limits are high-altitude valleys and mountain vistas.

Talat Pratu Chiang Mai (p693)

Si Phan Don (Laos)

11 The Mekong River sheds its characteristic muddy hue for a more tropical turquoise blue as it eddies around 4000 islands, known collectively as Si Phan Don (p367). This is Laos at its most quintessential: a sleepy, riverside idyll. The villages host a whole lot of hammock-hanging as well as meandering cycling trips and late-night carousing. Kayakers and tubers take to the water, giving this hang-out haven a bit of a pulse – and the rare Irrawaddy dolphins make seasonal appearances.

Timor-Leste

12 Often (unfairly) excluded on a typical Southeast Asian itinerary, the region's newest nation (p789) offers some of its greatest untapped adventures. After learning about Timor-Leste's harrowing history in Dili's museums, use the capital as a base for dive trips to the untouched reefs fringing the north coast, and 4WD excursions to the districts for magical mountain climbs, traditional village visits, and excellent snorkelling off sacred Jaco Island. Cap off your trip with a night on sleepy Atauro Island to get a feel for the Southeast Asia of the 1960s. Independence Day celebration

Inle Lake (Myanmar)

13 Surrounded by an enormous carpet of greenery, Inle Lake (p503) is so awe-inspiring and large that everybody comes away with a different experience. If you're counting days, you'll most likely be hitting the hot spots: water-bound temples, shore-bound markets and floating gardens. If you have more time, consider day hikes or exploring the more remote corners of the lake. The cool weather, friendly folks and that placid pool of ink-like water are bound to find a permanent place in your memory. Traditional fishing on Inle Lake

Singapore

14 The small city-state of Singapore (p609) excels in the art of multi-culti cuisine. Over the generations, descendants from China, Malaysia, Indonesia and India joined together their cooking pots, importing, creating and tweaking dishes from their homelands. In between meals visit Gardens by the Bay, a plant conservatory without the Victorian-era stuffiness, or the Baba House, a restored Straits-Chinese home that provides a free history and culture lesson. If a few hours have passed, it's time for another tasty meal. Supertrees, Gardens by the Bay (p616)

Palawan (Philippines)

15 Rugged and remote, Palawan (p592) has sky-rocketed in popularity as travel magazines rush to add it to their lists of world's best islands. The crown jewel is the Bacuit Archipelago near El Nido, a surreal seascape of brooding limestone cliffs where you can kayak among sea turtles. Further south, the heavenly beaches of Port Barton and Sabang beckon. To the north, make the eerie descent to the sunken Japanese ships in Coron Bay. Island-hopping trips around Coron or El Nido shouldn't be missed. Cadlao Island (p596), El Nido

Malaysian Borneo

16 Part of Malaysia but with a character all of their own, the Bornean states of Sabah (p432) and Sarawak (p450) will fulfil your wildest jungle dreams. Visit longhouse communities in Sarawak, scale Sabah's Mt Kinabalu, dive Sipadan's reefs or spot orangutans swinging between treetops. An astonishing array of cultures, religions and languages thrive here, not to mention cuisines; fuel up on seafood in cosmopolitan Kuching (Sarawak) and grows-on-you Kota Kinabalu (Sabah) between jungle jaunts. Iban longboater, Sarawak

Ifugao Rice Terraces (Philippines)

17 These incredible terraces (p566) were hand-hewn centuries ago by the Ifugao tribe in the remote Cordillera of the northern Philippines: the result was arable land where there had been only vertical impediments. Considered by Filipinos as one of the wonders of the world, the Ifugao rice terraces ring the towns of Banaue and Batad, but adventurous travellers will find terraces ribbing most of the Cordillera. Rice terraces, Banaue (p565)

MARK READY/LONELY PLANET ©

CHRIS HANNANT/LONELY PLANET ©

M. GEBICKI/GETTY IMAGES ©

Phnom Penh (Cambodia)

18 The Cambodian capital (p72) is a chaotic yet charming city that has thrown off past shadows to embrace a brighter future. Boasting one of the most beautiful riverfronts in the region, Phnom Penh is in the midst of a boom, with hip hostels, cool cafes and buzzing bars ready to welcome urban explorers. Experience emotional extremes at the inspiring National Museum and the sobering Tuol Sleng Museum, showcasing the best and worst of Cambodian history. Once called the 'Pearl of Asia', Phnom Penh is fast regaining its shine. Royal Palace (p74)

Gili Islands (Indonesia)

19 One of Indonesia's greatest joys is hopping on a fast boat from busy Bali and arriving on one of the irresistible Gili Islands (p230). Think sugar-white sand; warm, turquoise waters; and wonderful beach resorts and bungalows just begging you to extend your stay. Not to mention the coral reefs, teeming with sharks, rays and turtles. Savour the dining and nightlife on Gili Trawangan, the perfect balance of Gili Air and the pint-sized charms of Gili Meno. Or simply lie back and do nothing at all. Sea turtle

Phong Nha-Ke Bang National Park (Vietnam)

20 With jagged hills shrouded in verdant rainforest and mountain rivers coursing through impressive ravines, above-ground Phong Nha-Ke Bang region is one of Vietnam's most spectacular national parks (p846). A fortunate selection of travellers can head underground to experience the cathedral-like chambers of Hang Son Doong, the world's largest cave. More accessible are the ziplining and kayaking. thrills of Hang Toi (Dark Cave), and the ethereal beauty of aptly-named Paradise Cave.

Need to Know

For more information, see Survival Guide (p929)

Planes
Affordable flights for Indonesian island-hopping or cutting out long-haul buses.

Buses
The region's primary intra-country mode of travel; reliability and road conditions vary.

Trains
Slow but scenic alternative to buses for some destinations.

Ferries
Services connect islands and archipelago nations; quality and safety varies.

Bikes
Either motor or push-bike; easy and convenient for in-town travel.

Cars
Rentals are available in most tourist towns, though road rules are confusing – better to hire a driver.

Local Transport
Taxis and chartered vehicles are plentiful; bargain before getting in.

When to Go

Hanoi
GO Oct–May

Bangkok
GO Nov–Mar

Boracay
GO Jan–Sep

Ko Tao
GO Feb–Oct

Kuching
GO Jun–Sep

Bali
GO Apr–Aug

Tropical climate, rain year round
Tropical climate, wet & dry seasons
Highland areas, warm summers, cool winters

High Season
(Jun–Aug & Dec–Feb)

➡ Dry, cool in winter months

➡ Chilly in mountains

➡ Travel is difficult during Tet in Vietnam

➡ Summer rains across most of the region

Shoulder Season
(Mar & Nov)

➡ Hot, dry season begins in March

Low Season
(Apr–Jun & Sep–Oct)

➡ Travel difficult for April's new year festivals in Cambodia, Laos, Myanmar and Thailand

➡ Easter festivities in the Philippines

➡ Wet season (Sep–Oct); flooding, typhoons, transport cancellations

➡ Indonesia's dry season (Apr–May)

Useful Websites

Lonely Planet (www.lonely planet.com) Read country profiles, share questions with the traveller community on the Thorn Tree forum and make travel reservations.

Travelfish (www.travelfish.org) Popular travel site specialising in Southeast Asia.

Agoda (www.agoda.com) Regional hotel booking website.

Bangkok Post (www.bangkok post.com) In-depth analysis of current events in Southeast Asia.

Time Zones

GMT+6½hr Myanmar

GMT+7hr Thailand, Cambodia, Vietnam, Laos, parts of Indonesia (Sumatra, Java, and West and Central Kalimantan)

GMT+8hr Malaysia, Singapore, Brunei, Philippines, parts of Indonesia (Bali, Nusa Tenggara, South and East Kalimantan and Sulawesi)

GMT+9hr Timor-Leste, parts of Indonesia (Papua, Maluku)

Money

Each country has its own currency. ATMs are widely available in most of mainland Southeast Asia and the Philippines. ATMs are limited to major cities in Indonesia, Laos, Myanmar and Timor-Leste; stock up on local currency or have a supply of US dollars or travellers cheques before travelling to small towns or remote areas. Check with your bank to determine international withdrawal fees and to notify them of your travel plans.

Daily Costs

Budget:
Less than US$50

➡ Cheap guesthouse: US$10–20

➡ Local meal or street eats: US$1–5

➡ Local transport: US$1–5

➡ Beer: US$1–5

Midrange:
US$50–100

➡ Hotel room: US$21–75

➡ Restaurant meal: US$6–10

➡ Motorcycle hire: US$6–10

Top End:
More than US$100

➡ Boutique hotel or beach resort: US$100+

➡ Dive trip: US$50–100

➡ Car hire: US$50

Visas

➡ No visa required for most nationalities in Brunei, Malaysia, Philippines, Singapore and Thailand. Vietnam has 15-day visa-free entry.

➡ Visas on arrival in Cambodia, Indonesia, Laos and Timor-Leste. Most arrival visas are valid for about a month, though there are exceptions. Travel with a ready supply of passport photos for visa applications.

➡ Advance visa required for Myanmar.

➡ Verify that the border offers arrival visas; some land and sea borders do not.

➡ Be aware that overland border crossings are often fraught with minor rip-offs.

Staying in Touch

Most of Southeast Asia is globally wired with modern communication technologies, including internet cafes, wi-fi networks and 3G. Tourist centres have more options, better rates and faster connectivity than remote villages.

Mobile Phones Local, pre-paid SIM cards and mobile phones are available throughout the region. International roaming (ie on your home number) is prohibitively expensive.

Wi-fi & Internet Access Wi-fi is usually free in guesthouses, cafes and restaurants. Internet cafes are common in tourist centres. 3G networks are common in large cities.

Calling Home International calling rates are fairly affordable; to call from a mobile phone, dial + followed by the country code, area code and phone number. Internet cafes are often equipped with headsets and Skype as an alternative. With wi-fi you can also make Skype or Viber calls from a mobile phone.

Arriving In...

Suvarnabhumi International Airport (Bangkok, Thailand) Taxis (one hour) and rail (30 minutes) to the centre.

Changi International Airport (Singapore) Rail (45 minutes) and taxis (one hour) to the centre.

Kuala Lumpur International Airport (Kuala Lumpur, Malaysia) KLIA Ekspres rail (30 minutes) to the centre.

Soekarno-Hatta International Airport (Jakarta, Indonesia) Taxis and buses (one hour) to the centre.

For much more on **getting around**, see p940.

First Time Southeast Asia

For more information, see Survival Guide (p929)

Checklist

➡ Make sure your passport is valid for at least six months past your arrival date.

➡ Apply for an extended visa if visiting a country for longer than the standard visa allows.

➡ Organise travel insurance, diver's insurance and international driving permit (p945).

➡ Visit a doctor for check-up and suggested vaccines (p947).

➡ Inform your bank and credit-card provider of your travel plans.

What to Pack

➡ A week's worth of lightweight clothes

➡ Rain gear (jacket, breathable poncho, dry pack for electronics)

➡ Comfortable sandals

➡ Earplugs

➡ Medicine/first-aid kit

➡ USB drive

➡ GSM mobile phone

➡ Refillable water bottle

➡ Sunscreen and heavy-duty deodorant

Top Tips for Your Trip

➡ Know the scams (p937): border crossings, dodgy transport, touts.

➡ Be prepared for crazy driving; pedestrians have no rights.

➡ Most supplies (mosquito repellent, umbrella) can be bought locally.

➡ Take your cue from the locals when it comes to appropriate dress.

➡ Take digital pictures of important documents and cards in case of theft or loss.

➡ Know your passwords! Extra security measures will be triggered by your new location.

➡ Carry your valuables in a waist pack to prevent theft; keep them secure on overnight journeys, in dorms and in rooms with insufficient locks.

➡ Pay for accommodation first thing in the morning, or the night before if you have an early morning departure.

What to Wear

In general, lightweight, loose-fitting clothes will be the most comfortable options. Bring a jacket for cool temperatures in the mountains and on heavily air-conditioned buses. Wear clothes that cover down to your elbows and knees for visits to temples and rural villages.

Sleeping

Book ahead during high season or around festivals or holidays, when rooms fill up in popular destinations. For more on accommodation in the region, see p934.

➡ **Hotels** From staid to snazzy, hotels have modern amenities (refrigerators, TVs, air-con) and private bathrooms.

➡ **Guesthouses** These backpacker faves have a range of rooms from basic to plush – and loads of local information.

➡ **Homestays** Live like a villager in a family home; set-ups are simple but it's a cultural immersion.

➡ **Hostels** Dormitories provide cheap and social lodging for solo travellers. Amenities sometimes include pool, restaurant or hang-out space.

Money

Most businesses deal only in cash. You can withdraw notes in the local currency directly from your home account through local ATMs. Have a mix of cash and travellers cheques as back-up. Currency exchanges accept US dollars, Australian dollars, British pounds and euros.

➡ Keep your cash in a money belt worn on your person.

➡ Don't use your ATM card for point-of-sale purchases (ie in shops, restaurants etc).

➡ Ask your bank about overseas banking fees. Get a 24-hour international customer-service phone number in case of card loss or theft.

➡ Monitor credit-card activity to avoid missing payments and to protect against fraudulent charges.

➡ Bring cash in crisp, untorn bills. Some money changers will reject old or ripped bills.

➡ Get travellers cheques in large denominations (US$100 or US$50) to avoid per-cheque commissions; record which cheques you've cashed to protect against theft or loss.

For more information, see p936.

Bargaining

It is acceptable to bargain for goods and services when there isn't a posted price. You can't bargain for food, at shopping malls or wherever a price is posted.

Tipping

Tipping is not standard, but it is appreciated as wages are very low. If you hire guides buy them lunch, and tip a little extra at the end.

Selling rice crackers at a village market, Inle Lake (p503), Myanmar

Etiquette

➡ **Modesty** Though fashions are changing in the cities, modesty is still important in traditional areas, especially Muslim-dominated places. Avoid baring too much skin in general – and no topless sunbathing. Cover up when visiting religious buildings.

➡ **Taboos** Politics and religion are often sensitive topics. Always treat both with deference and avoid being critical. Many Southeast Asian cultures are superstitious; it is wise to learn about these beliefs and act accordingly. Muslims don't drink alcohol or eat pork. Women shouldn't touch Buddhist monks or their belongings.

➡ **Save Face** Southeast Asians, especially Buddhist cultures, place a high value on harmonious social interactions. Don't get visibly angry, raise your voice or get into an argument – it will cause you and the other person embarrassment. When in doubt, smile.

➡ **Shoes** Take them off when entering a private home, religious building and certain businesses. If there's a pile of shoes at the door, be sure to follow suit.

Language

Tourist towns are well-stocked with English speakers, though bus drivers, market vendors and taxi drivers tend to be less fluent. Thailand, Laos, Cambodia and Myanmar all have their own written script.

Learn how to say 'hello', 'thank you' and 'how much' in each language. Counting is also helpful. If you like taking pictures of people, learn how to ask their permission.

If You Like...

Fabulous Food

Bangkok (Thailand) Food, glorious food! Fresh, tasty meals are everywhere in this nonstop grazing city. (p661)

Hanoi (Vietnam) Be an urban forager among Hanoi's street-food stalls. (p825)

Luang Prabang (Laos) Cafes and bakeries with a French flair preserve a delicious colonial connection. (p338)

Chiang Mai (Thailand) Learn how to slice and dice like the Thai wok masters at a cooking school. (p693)

Singapore Savour Asia old and new, from 50-year-old chicken-rice stalls to swish international outposts. (p629)

Penang (Malaysia) Malaysia's multi-culti melting pot is an edible journey through Indian curries, Chinese dim sum and Malay desserts. (p408)

Phnom Penh (Cambodia) Dine to make a difference at one of Phnom Penh's many training restaurants to help the disadvantaged. (p75)

Bali (Indonesia) Enjoy some of Asia's most affordable and inventive cuisine at dozens of great restaurants in Kerobokan or Seminyak. (p199)

Temples & Mosques

Temples of Angkor (Cambodia) An architectural wonder of the world built by the Khmer god-kings of old. (p94)

Bagan (Myanmar) Hundreds of ancient temples stretch out towards the horizon on a stupa-studded plain. (p521)

Borobudur (Indonesia) A stunning Buddhist monument ringed by mist and mountains. (p181)

Shwedagon Paya (Myanmar) A golden hilltop temple that gleams with heavenly splendour in the heart of Yangon. (p482)

Wat Phra Kaew (Thailand) A dazzling royal temple and home to the revered Emerald Buddha. (p645)

Wat Xieng Thong (Laos) The jewel in the crown of Luang Prabang's temples, with its roofs sweeping majestically low to the ground. (p333)

Hue (Vietnam) Vietnamese emperors constructed impressive monuments around Hue; don't miss the tombs of Tu Duc and Minh Mang. (p849)

Sukhothai (Thailand) The ancient capital of one of Thailand's first home-grown kingdoms. (p679)

Masjid Jamek (Malaysia) Graceful Mughal-style mosque in the heart of Kuala Lumpur. (p385)

Spectacular Treks

Gunung Bromo (Indonesia) An active volcano hiked up at night for a sunrise view of its moonscape summit. (p187)

Mt Kinabalu (Malaysia) Borneo's highest mountain is a two-day march to the sky. (p440)

Sapa (Vietnam) Dirt paths wind through verdant rice terraces tended by ethnic minorities in this toothy mountainous region. (p838)

Taman Negara National Park (Malaysia) Old-growth rainforest conveniently close to civilisation. (p429)

Gibbon Experience (Laos) Trek up to the canopy at this zipline course outfitted with treetop lodging. (p355)

Cordillera Mountains (Philippines) Ancient hand-hewn rice terraces are carved into jagged mountains. (p562)

Khao Yai National Park (Thailand) Wild patch of jungle close to Bangkok and filled with elephants, birds and monkeys. (p719)

Kalaw (Myanmar) Follow the undulating landscape through forested hills and minority villages to lovely Inle Lake. (p506)

Nam Ha National Protected Area (Laos) Eco-oriented treks through an old-growth forest and high-altitude hill-tribe villages. (p350)

Mondulkiri (Cambodia) Experience 'walking with the herd' at the Elephant Valley Project in Cambodia's wild east. (p136)

Beautiful Beaches

Lombok (Indonesia) A Kuta more beautiful than Bali's, with the iconic Gili Islands just offshore. (p223)

Krabi/Railay (Thailand) Rock-climbers scale the karst cliffs, while kayakers slice the jewel-hued waters. (p768)

Sihanoukville (Cambodia) Good times rule at Cambodia's premier seaside hang-out and the nearby islands of Koh Rong and Koh Rong Sanloem. (p116)

Phu Quoc Island (Vietnam) Picture-perfect white crescents and sandy bays sheltered by rocky headlands seduce sun worshippers. (p897)

Bohol (Philippines) This well-rounded island is a haven for sand and scuba addicts. (p587)

Pulau Tioman (Malaysia) Hollywood stand-in for Bali Ha'i is practically castaway perfection. (p418)

Ko Pha-Ngan (Thailand) This backpacker legend rages during its Full Moon parties, but snoozes alongside gorgeous coves in between. (p743)

Mui Ne (Vietnam) Squeaky sands, towering dunes and kitesurfing galore. (p875)

Top: Noodle dish at Pad Thai Shop (p765), Phuket, Thailand
Bottom: Kitesurfing, Mui Ne (p875), Vietnam

Top Nightlife

Bangkok (Thailand) Bangkok is home to the original 24-hour party people and sleep is still optional. (p666)

Phnom Penh (Cambodia) Cambodia rocks: hit the happy hours, crawl some bar strips and rave on at a nightclub. (p80)

Ko Pha-Ngan (Thailand) Home of the very first Southeast Asia Full Moon parties and the ultimate beach-bum island. (p747)

Nha Trang (Vietnam) Plenty of R&R is available at this lively coastal city. (p873)

Boracay (Philippines) Beach-party paradise in a small package. (p576)

Kuala Lumpur (Malaysia) Petronas Towers look spectacular illuminated at night; there are plenty of drinking options below. (p391)

Bali (Indonesia) Quaff a sundowner on the sand from Kuta north to Canggu, then head out to heaving all-night clubs. (p200)

Siem Reap (Cambodia) Pub St says it all – this temple town is officially a party town as well. (p98)

Singapore Sky-high drinks served at sky-high prices, but oh, what a view. (p632)

Markets & Shopping

Bangkok (Thailand) From the 8000 stalls at Chatuchak Weekend Market to street stalls and glitzy malls, Bangkok is a shoppers paradise. (p667)

Singapore From the bustling markets to luxury malls, shopping is a national pastime. (p635)

Chiang Mai (Thailand) The weekend 'Walking Streets' offer the chance to shop 'til you drop. (p695)

Bac Ha (Vietnam) See the unique costume of the Flower Hmong at one of the most colourful markets in Southeast Asia. (p837)

Luang Prabang (Laos) The candlelit Handicraft Night Market is an endless ribbon of colourful textiles, paper lanterns and ethnic motifs. (p340)

Can Tho (Vietnam) Get up early and experience the Mekong Delta's famous floating markets. (p894)

Jonker Walk Night Market (Malaysia) Melaka's weekly shopping extravaganza offers up trinket sellers, food hawkers and fortune tellers. (p400)

Phnom Penh (Cambodia) The Russian Market is the city's top shopping spot: if it's available in Cambodia, it will be somewhere in here. (p82)

Cultural Encounters

Balinese Dance (Indonesia) The haunting sounds, elaborate costumes and careful choreography add up to a must-see in Ubud. (p214)

Hsipaw (Myanmar) Surrounding this delightful highland town are traditional Lisu, Palaung and Shan villages. (p520)

George Town (Malaysia) Old-town buildings have become canvases for young creatives and their vibrant street art. (p405)

Maubisse (Timor-Leste) Visit an *uma lulik* (traditional sacred house) in the highlands. (p802)

Luang Prabang (Laos) Visit the Living Land farm to learn how to plant and grow sticky rice, the ubiquitous national dish. (p333)

Singapore Modern Southeast Asian art displayed in an architectural landmark at the National Gallery Singapore. (p611)

Chiang Mai (Thailand) The original detox: join a meditation retreat at Wat Suan Dok in Chiang Mai. (p688)

Siem Reap (Cambodia) Roll up, roll up – catch a performance of Phare the Cambodia Circus, an original experience. (p98)

Colonial Classics

Hanoi (Vietnam) The grand old dame of French Indochine has imposing civic buildings and impressive leafy villas. (p816)

Yangon (Myanmar) The former Rangoon has endless streets of British-era shophouses and some epic, abandoned former government buildings. (p482)

Luang Prabang (Laos) It may have been a Mekong outpost, but the French loved it and left some landmark legacies. (p333)

George Town (Malaysia) This ethnic entrepôt has experienced a renaissance in recent years, as dilapidated mansions are reborn as hotels and galleries. (p405)

Hoi An (Vietnam) The Portuguese, Spanish, Japanese, Chinese and French all left their mark on this stunning old port town. (p863)

Vigan (Philippines) Perfectly preserved Spanish colonial jewel under the shadow of an eponymous volcano. (p567)

Battambang (Cambodia) A rich legacy of French-era architecture is evident in the sleepy streets along the banks of the Sangker River. (p106)

Month by Month

TOP EVENTS

Buddhist New Year/ Water Festival, April

Rainforest World Music, August

Ork Phansaa, October

Festival of the Nine Emperor Gods, October

Deepavali, November

January

Peak tourist season, cool and dry weather in mainland Southeast Asia and the Philippines. The east coast of the Malay peninsula (Samui archipelago, Pulau Perhentian) and Indonesia are wet thanks to the northeast monsoon; low season in Bali.

✯✯ Ati-Atihan

The mother of all Filipino fiestas, Ati-Atihan celebrates Santo Niño (Infant Jesus) with colourful, Mardi Gras–like indigenous costumes and displays in Kalibo, on the island of Panay.

✯✯ Prophet Mohammed's Birthday

The birthday of Islam's holy prophet is celebrated in the third month of the lunar-based Islamic calendar (1 December 2017, 21 November 2018) with religious prayers and processions.

✯✯ Myanmar Independence Day

The end of colonial rule in Burma is celebrated as a national holiday on 4 January.

✯✯ Sultan of Brunei's Birthday

Colourful official ceremonies are held on 15 January to mark the birthday of Sultan Hassanal Bolkiah.

✯✯ Bun Pha Wet

This Lao-Buddhist festival commemorates the story of the Buddha-to-be. It's considered an auspicious time to enter the monastery. Festivities are held in villages throughout Laos.

February

Peak season continues in mainland Southeast Asia and the beaches are buzzing. The east coast of the Malay peninsula starts to dry off as the rains move further east; still raining in Bali.

✯✯ Tet

Vietnam's lunar New Year (sometimes occurring in late January) is the country's biggest holiday, recognising the first day of spring. It involves family reunions, ancestor worship, gift exchanges and lots of all-night luck-inducing noise. Travel is difficult; businesses close.

✯✯ Chinese New Year

This lunar festival (sometimes occurring in January) is celebrated in Chinese-dominated towns. In Penang, it's a family affair and businesses close for one to two weeks. In Bangkok, Singapore, Phnom Penh and Kuching, there are dragon-dancing parades, food festivities, fireworks and noise.

LUNAR CALENDAR

Buddhist and Hindu religious festivals follow the lunar calendar, so dates vary each year, typically within a two-week period. Muslim holidays go by the Islamic calendar; dates move forward about 11 days each year.

✨ Makha Bucha

One of three Buddhist holy days, Makha Bucha falls on the full moon of the third lunar month and commemorates Buddha preaching to 1250 enlightened monks. Celebrated at temples across Cambodia, Laos, Myanmar and Thailand.

March

Mainland Southeast Asia is hot and dry; beaches start to empty out. The winds kick up, ushering in kitesurfing season. In Bali, northwest monsoon rains are subsiding to afternoon showers.

✨ Nyepi

Bali's 'Day of Silence' is marked by fasting and meditation; businesses and beach access close. The next day is the Balinese New Year's Day, welcomed with night-time racket.

✨ Easter Week

This Christian holiday (sometimes in April) is observed in Vietnam, the Philippines, Indonesia, Melaka and Timor-Leste. Holy Week (Semana Santa) in the Philippines starts on the Wednesday before Easter Sunday; Spanish-influenced observances, such as fasting, penance rituals and churchgoing, ensue.

April

The hottest time of year in mainland Southeast Asia makes inland sightseeing a chore. Cambodia, Laos, Myanmar and Thailand celebrate their traditional new year – book transport

Top: Loi Krathong (p30), Thailand
Bottom: Nyepi, Bali, Indonesia

in advance. Good shoulder season in Bali.

✨ Buddhist New Year/Water Festival

In mid-April, Buddhist countries celebrate their lunar New Year with symbolic water-throwing and religious observances.

✨ Vietnamese Liberation Day

The day US troops withdrew from Saigon (30 April) as North Vietnamese forces entered the city. Also called Reunification Day.

✨ Hue Festival (Biennial)

Vietnam's biggest cultural event is held every two years (2016, 2018 etc). Art, theatre, music, circus and dance performances, including domestic and international acts, are held inside Hue's Citadel.

May

Still hot in mainland Southeast Asia. May hosts preparations for the upcoming rains and the start of rice-planting season. Northern Vietnam has spring-like weather and Bali is not yet crowded.

✨ Royal Ploughing Ceremonies

In Thailand and Cambodia, this royal ceremony employs astrology and ancient Brahman rituals to kick off rice-planting season.

✨ Rocket Festival

Villagers fire off bamboo rockets *(bang fai)* to provoke rainfall for a bountiful rice harvest. Mainly celebrated in northeast Thailand and Laos; dates vary from village to village.

✨ Visaka Bucha

This Buddhist holy day, the 15th day of the waxing moon in the sixth lunar month, commemorates Buddha's birth, enlightenment and *parinibbana* (death). Activities are held at temples in Cambodia, Laos, Myanmar and Thailand.

✨ Timor-Leste Independence Day

One of the planet's youngest nations, Timor-Leste celebrates Independence Day (20 May) with cultural and sporting events.

June

The southwest monsoon brings rain to most of mainland Southeast Asia and most of the Philippines. Summer in Europe and China brings another high season, especially in Bali.

✨ Gawai Dayak

The end of the rice-harvest season is celebrated the first two days of June in Sarawak (Malaysian Borneo). City-dwelling Dayaks return to their longhouses to socialise, eat and down shots of *tuak* (rice wine).

✨ Ramadan

The Muslim fasting month is observed in Malaysia, Indonesia, Brunei and parts of southern Thailand in the ninth month of the Islamic calendar (May to June 2017 and 2018). Muslims abstain from food, drink, cigarettes and sex between sunrise and sunset. Idul Fitri marks the end of Ramadan.

July

Mainland Southeast Asia prepares for Buddhist Lent, a period of meditation coinciding with the rainy season (southwest monsoon). Despite the drizzle, this is an ideal time for rural sightseeing as rice planting begins. Thailand's Samui archipelago often stays dry during the southwest monsoon.

✨ Asanha Bucha

The full moon of the eighth lunar month commemorates Buddha's first sermon. Buddhists flock to temples to light candles, offer flowers and pray for good fortune. Celebrated at temples across Cambodia, Laos, Myanmar and Thailand.

✨ Khao Phansaa

Marking the rainy season, Buddhist monks retreat into monasteries. This is the traditional time for young men to be ordained. Worshippers offer candles and donations at temples. Ubon Ratchathani (Thailand) celebrates with a parade.

August

Mini high-season still in effect. Afternoon showers in most of mainland Southeast Asia, with a few all-day soakers. Weather in Indonesia (especially Bali) is just right.

☆ Rainforest World Music

Sarawak (Malaysian Borneo) celebrates tribal music from around the world during this three-day music festival.

✯✯ Queen's Birthday

Thailand celebrates its queen's birthday (and Mother's Day) on 12 August.

✯✯ Independence Day (Indonesia)

The country celebrates liberation from the Dutch on 17 August with large parades in Jakarta.

September

One of the wettest parts of the wet season for mainland Southeast Asia – flooding and boat cancellations are common. Occasional typhoons sweep in across Vietnam and the Philippines, wreaking havoc. Shoulder season in Bali.

✯✯ Pchum Ben

In Cambodia, respects are paid to the dead through temple offerings. Many Khmers return to their home villages and try to visit seven temples in seven days. Sometimes celebrated in October.

October

Mainland Southeast Asia prepares for the end of the rainy season and the end of Buddhist Lent. The northeast monsoon (affecting the east coast of the Malay peninsula and Indonesia) begins. Bali has occasional showers.

✯✯ Festival of the Nine Emperor Gods

In Thailand, this Taoist event is called the Vegetarian Festival, marked by abstinence from meat and other purification

rituals. The most extreme is Phuket's parade of entranced and pierced worshippers. Variations occur in Singapore, Malaysia and Myanmar.

✯✯ Ork Phansaa

The end of the Buddhist Lent occurs three lunar months after Khao Phansaa. Merit-makers present new robes to the monks. The Mekong River's mysterious '*naga* fireballs' coincide with Ork Phansaa. Localities in Thailand (such as Nong Khai) and Laos celebrate with traditional boat races.

✯✯ Islamic New Year

This lunar New Year (known as Awal Muharram) in Indonesia and Malaysia is marked by fasting, self-reflection and commemoration of the martyrdom of Hussein ibn Ali.

November

Early in the month is a shoulder season in mainland Southeast Asia, with cool, dry days and a lush landscape. Northern altitudes see chilly nighttime temperatures. The east coast of the Malay peninsula and Indonesia are in the midst of the rainy season.

✯✯ Bon Om Tuk

This Cambodian festival (sometimes held in October) celebrates Jayavarman VII's victory over the Chams in 1177 and the reversal of the Tonlé Sap river. Boat races stir local patriotism; huge crowds descend on Phnom Penh. A smaller event takes place in Siem Reap.

✯✯ Deepavali

The most important festival in the Hindu calendar is this festival of lights celebrating the triumph of good over evil. Tiny oil lamps are ceremoniously lit in Malaysia. Singapore's Little India hosts public festivities. Sometimes occurs in October.

✯✯ Loi Krathong

During November's full moon, Thais launch banana-leaf boats decorated with candles in honour of the river goddess. In Chiang Mai, floating paper lanterns are also made as offerings. A similar tradition is practised in the Shan State of Myanmar during the fire-balloon competitions in Taunggyi.

✯✯ Bun Pha That Luang

Laos pays tribute to its iconic stupa in Vientiane with a week-long festival coinciding with the full moon.

December

This is mainland Southeast Asia's busiest tourism season. The weather is fine; rain is tapering off on the Samui archipelago but still falling in Bali.

✯✯ Lao National Day

On 2 December Laos celebrates the 1975 victory over the monarchy and the establishment of the Lao People's Democratic Republic.

✯✯ King's Birthday

This Thai holiday (5 December) hosts parades and merit-making events in honour of the king; it's also recognised as Father's Day.

Itineraries

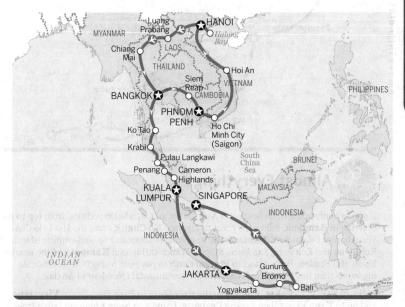

8 WEEKS The Best of Southeast Asia

This Southeast Asia sampler hits the highlights: cool cities, ancient kingdoms, beautiful beaches and smouldering volcanoes. Start in fun-filled **Bangkok**, then bus it to **Siem Reap** for Angkor's magnificent temples. Continue to party HQ **Phnom Penh**, then to Vietnam's bustling **Ho Chi Minh City**. Head north to adorable **Hoi An**, then hit the antique streets of **Hanoi** and dramatic karsts of **Halong Bay.**

Fly out of Vietnam to laid-back **Luang Prabang**, Laos' world-heritage city; fly to chic **Chiang Mai** for hill-tribe adventures and Thai cooking courses.

Head south through Bangkok to **Ko Tao** and learn to dive before hitting the rock-climbing retreat of **Krabi**. Cross the border from Ko Lipe to Malaysia's **Pulau Langkawi**, then on to the food paradise of **George Town** (Penang) and overland to Malaysia's multi-ethnic capital **Kuala Lumpur**, with a stop in the lush **Cameron Highlands**.

Fly from Kuala Lumpur to **Jakarta**, Indonesia's capital; soak up Java's renowned culture in **Yogyakarta**. Bus it to active volcano **Gunung Bromo**, then leapfrog to **Bali** for sun, fun and the island's unique culture. Double back to bustling, multiculti **Singapore** for an onward flight anywhere.

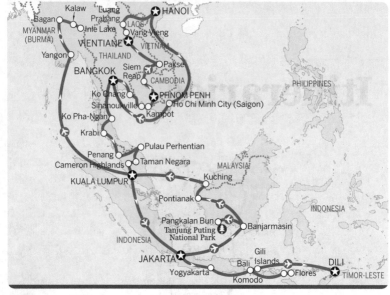

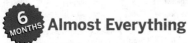

Almost Everything
6 MONTHS

If you're really going to *do* Southeast Asia, go for an extended expedition from top to toe. Starting in **Bangkok**, follow the coast to forested **Ko Chang**, cross the Hat Lek–Cham Yeam border bound for **Sihanoukville's** sublime beaches and up-and-coming islands of Koh Rong and Koh Rong Samloem. Stop in Franco-influenced **Kampot** and the nearby Bokor Hill Station. Turn inland to **Phnom Penh** to pay your respects at its genocide museums then bus it to **Siem Reap** and the monumental splendour of Angkor.

Board a flight to **Pakse**, gateway to the river life of Si Phan Don. Bus to **Vientiane** and on to **Vang Vieng** then **Luang Prabang**; trundle to Nong Khiaw for tribal trekking. Follow the rugged revolutionaries' trail through the Vieng Xai Caves and Na Meo border, a remote, adventurous crossing to **Hanoi**.

Work your way through Vietnam, sampling history, culture and beaches. Fly from **Ho Chi Minh City** to **Bangkok** and travel down the Malay peninsula, swimming and diving around **Ko Pha-Ngan** and **Krabi**.

Slip into Malaysia for the street eats of **Penang**. Hit the peaceful beach retreat of **Pulau Perhentian**, then head for **Taman Negara**, a wilderness preserve. Detour to the mist-shrouded hills of the **Cameron Highlands** and alight in **Kuala Lumpur**.

Fly to **Jakarta** (Java) and immerse yourself in cultural **Yogyakarta** and the Unesco treasure of Borobudur. Bask on the beach in **Bali** or the **Gili Islands**, escape the crowds in **Flores**, and spot dragons on **Komodo**. Catch a flight from Bali to **Dili** in Timor-Leste, a fledgling tourist nation.

Or fly from Jakarta to **Banjarmasin** (Kalimantan) for a jungle excursion into Borneo. Fly to **Pangkalan Bun** for the orangutan research camps of **Tanjung Puting National Park**, then fly from Banjarmasin to **Pontianak** and bus to the border to reach Malaysia's **Kuching**, a gateway to more Borneo nature reserves.

Fly back to **Kuala Lumpur** and connect to **Yangon** (Myanmar) and the beautiful Buddhist temples of **Bagan**. Take a trek to **Kalaw** or relax on the placid waters of **Inle Lake**. Or turn things on their head by starting off in Myanmar.

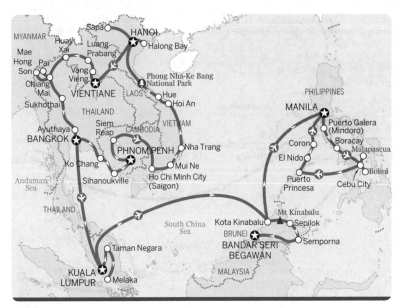

 Mainland to Borneo & the Philippines

Cruise around mainland Southeast Asia, hitting the beaches and the highlands, and then bound over to Borneo and the Philippines to climb into the heavens and dive under the sea. From **Bangkok**, head to **Ko Chang**, then cross the border to **Sihanoukville** for lots of sand and suds. Scoot to shabby-chic **Phnom Penh**. Admire the architectural wonder of the Angkor temples from **Siem Reap**. Fly to full-throttle **Ho Chi Minh City**. Migrate to the beaches of **Mui Ne** or **Nha Trang**, the antique city of **Hoi An**, the imperial capital of **Hue** and the extensive caves of **Phong Nha-Ke Bang National Park**. Rest in mature capital **Hanoi**. Cruise karst-filled **Halong Bay** and detour to **Sapa** and its ethnic highland communities. Return to Hanoi.

Fly to **Vientiane** (Laos), bus to **Vang Vieng** and on to **Luang Prabang**, a sublime world-heritage town. Ride the Mekong River to the Laos–Thailand border at **Huay Xai** and the fabled Golden Triangle.

On to **Chiang Mai**; escape to the mountains of **Pai** or **Mae Hong Son** for stunning mountain vistas and intriguing border cultures. Descend to the lowlands for the ancient capitals at **Sukhothai** and **Ayuthaya** before returning to **Bangkok**.

Budget flight or bus it to **Kuala Lumpur**. Explore **Taman Negara**, an ancient wilderness. Cruise through colonial **Melaka**. Return to KL for a tour of Malaysian Borneo. Fly to **Kota Kinabalu**, Sabah, and ascend Mt Kinabalu, Borneo's highest peak. Head east to **Sepilok**'s orangutan sanctuary, then to **Semporna**, gateway to dive sites. Detour to oil-rich Brunei's unassuming capital, **Bandar Seri Begawan** (BSB), surrounded by pristine rainforests and water villages.

Cheap flights link **Kota Kinabalu** with **Manila** (Philippines). Bus to the incredible Ifuagao rice terraces in the mountains of **North Luzon**, then return to Manila and hit up party isle **Boracay** via dive hotbed **Puerto Galera** (Mindoro). Spend a few days unwinding in Boracay, then fly to **Cebu City** – in easy range of several laid-back beach destinations, including **Malapascua** and **Bohol**. Fly from Cebu to **Puerto Princesa**, Palawan; go north to **El Nido** via the lonely beaches and pristine jungles of Palawan's west coast. Take the all-day boat trip to wreck-diving hotbed **Coron** before flying back to Manila.

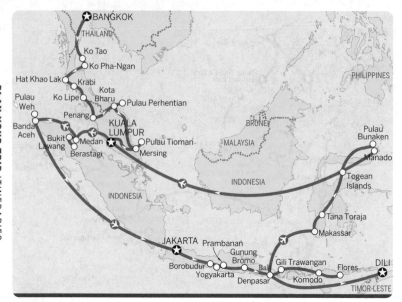

 Mainland Beaches to Indonesia

8 WEEKS

Become a beach connoisseur by tracing the coastline of Thailand, Malaysia and Indonesia. In between grab some culture to keep things balanced. From **Bangkok**, make a beeline for the islands in the Gulf of Thailand: dive-crazy **Ko Tao** and hippy trippy **Ko Pha-Ngan**. Get certified on Tao, then follow the herd to the Andaman coast. **Hat Khao Lak** is the base for dive trips to the world-class Surin and Similan islands. Skip down to adrenaline-charged **Krabi** for rockclimbing and cave exploring, then island-hop to rasta-vibed **Ko Lipe**. Cross the border at Pulau Langkawi for **Penang's** famous hawker centres.

From Penang, take a bus to **Kota Bharu**, jumping-off point for the fabulous jungle islands of **Pulau Perhentian**. Head south to **Mersing**, the mainland port for sleepy **Pulau Tioman**, before returning to **Kuala Lumpur** to pick up a flight to Indonesia.

From Indonesia's tip in **Medan**, Sumatra, visit the orangutan reserve of **Bukit Lawang** and hike a volcano in **Berastagi**. From Medan fly to lovely **Banda Aceh** for divetastic **Pulau Weh**.

Say goodbye to rugged Sumatra and buzz over to Java, touching down in **Jakarta**, Indonesia's intense capital. Explore **Yogyakarta** and its culture trail; day-trip to the giant Buddhist stupa of **Borobudur** or the ancient Hindu temple of **Prambanan**. Continue eastwards to **Gunung Bromo** volcano for a sunrise spectacle over a lunar landscape.

Leapfrog to **Denpasar**, Bali, to nuzzle the sandy beaches of the Bukit Peninsula or get cultured in Ubud. Party in **Gili Trawangan**, spot dragons on **Komodo** and go rustic on the beaches of **Flores**.

Check your visa and apply for an extension back in Denpasar, then fly to **Makassar**, Sulawesi. Pay your respects in **Tana Toraja**, known for ancient funeral rites and effigies standing guard over cliffside burial sites. Travel to the remote and pristine **Togean Islands** and the northern diving destination of **Pulau Bunaken**; it might feel far away, but it's well worth it. Fly from **Manado** to Kuala Lumpur.

Alternatively, from Denpasar hop over to Timor-Leste's capital of **Dili** to tour old colonial towns and uncrowded reefs.

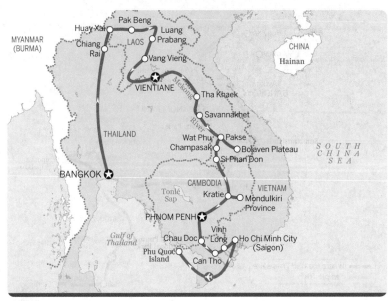

4 WEEKS Mekong River Meander

This trip follows the famous river downstream from northern Laos all the way to its terminus in Vietnam's Mekong Delta. En route you'll encounter a wide range of landscapes and cultures as you slice through all four countries of the Mekong region. Leave behind bustling **Bangkok** and make a beeline for **Chiang Rai**, near the Golden Triangle, where the borders of Laos, Myanmar (Burma) and Thailand converge. Crossing into Laos at **Huay Xai** is like stepping back in time. Take a slow boat down the Mekong to **Luang Prabang**, stopping overnight in **Pak Beng**. Soak up the magic before leaving the river for some relaxation in **Vang Vieng**.

Continue to **Vientiane** and reunite with the mighty waterway. The sleepy Lao capital has some great cafes, restaurants and bars (which you won't be encountering for a while after leaving). Board a bus and follow the river southeast, stopping off in **Tha Khaek** and **Savannakhet** before arriving in **Pakse**. Visit the imposing Khmer sanctuary of **Wat Phu Champasak**; explore the waterfalls and villages of the **Bolaven Plateau**; or enjoy the laid-back islands of **Si Phan Don**.

Cross into Cambodia. If you missed the Irrawaddy dolphins near Si Phan Don, you can see them further south in the laid-back riverside town of **Kratie**. From Kratie, consider a visit to the mountains of **Mondulkiri Province**, home to elephants, hill tribes and pristine nature.

Weeks in rural provinces will have you happy to see **Phnom Penh**, where the Mekong merges with another vital regional waterway, the Tonlé Sap. Take a sunset boat cruise and hit the bars for a well-deserved night out on the town. Recharged, board a fast boat downstream to **Chau Doc**, Vietnam, gateway to the Mekong Delta; check out **Can Tho**, its commercial heart. Hotfoot it to **Ho Chi Minh City** for some fun; delve deeper into the delta with a homestay around **Vinh Long**, or make for the tropical retreat of **Phu Quoc Island**, a well-earned reward. If you still have time and stamina, the rest of Vietnam beckons.

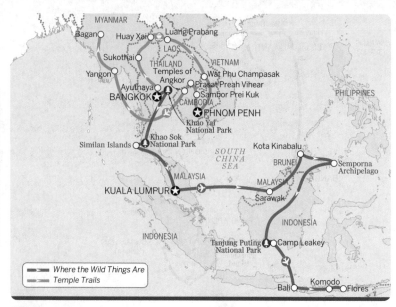

Where the Wild Things Are
Temple Trails

Where the Wild Things Are

6 WEEKS

Southeast Asia is home to diverse wild-life, including tigers, elephants, primates, whale sharks and the Komodo dragon. Start out in **Bangkok**; explore **Khao Yai National Park** to see wild elephants and Asian black bears. Heading south, explore **Khao Sok National Park**, home to gibbons and macaques. Explore the underwater wilds of the **Similan Islands** for the chance to see whale sharks.

Continue to **Kualu Lumpur** to hop a flight to **Sarawak** in Borneo. See rare proboscis monkeys in Bako National Park and the gentle orangutans of Semenggoh Wildlife Centre. Head to **Kota Kinabalu**, Sabah, to explore the Kinabatangan River and perhaps see wild orangutans and rare pygmy elephants. Wind down on the beaches and reefs of the **Semporna Archipelago**, one of Malaysia's top dive sites.

Head south into Kalimantan (Indonesia) and explore the jungle waterways of **Tanjung Puting National Park**. Stay overnight in a *klotok* (boat) and visit **Camp Leakey**, an orangutan research station. Fly to **Bali** and head east to the rocky outcrops of **Komodo** and **Flores**, home to the Komodo dragon and some superb diving.

Temple Trails

6 WEEKS

When it comes to spectacular temples, Southeast Asia is in a league of its own. Start in **Bangkok**, home to the iconic Temple of the Dawn, before heading to the stupa-studded former capital **Ayuthaya**. Further north is the ancient Khmer capital of **Sukothai**.

Cross the Mekong River border at **Huay Xai** and cruise to **Luang Prabang**, a gilded city of active temples and saffron-clad monks. Travel to Laos' deep south to see the Khmer mountain temple of **Wat Phu Champasak**.

Continue into Cambodia, the region's temple heavyweight. Pass through **Phnom Penh** to the pre-Angkorian temples of **Sambor Prei Kuk**. Make an adventurous diversion north to the mountain temple of **Prasat Preah Vihear** before arriving at the **Temples of Angkor** – arguably the most inspired collection of temples on earth, including soaring Angkor Wat.

Hop a flight to **Yangon**, home to the shimmering Shwedagon Paya. Finish at **Bagan**, home to the greatest concentration of temples in the region, where hundreds of stupas stretch into the infinite horizon.

Top: Temple, Bagan (p521), Myanmar

Bottom: Whale shark, Similan Islands Marine National Park (p759), Thailand

ARMIBLUE/GETTY IMAGES ©

Off the Beaten Track: Southeast Asia

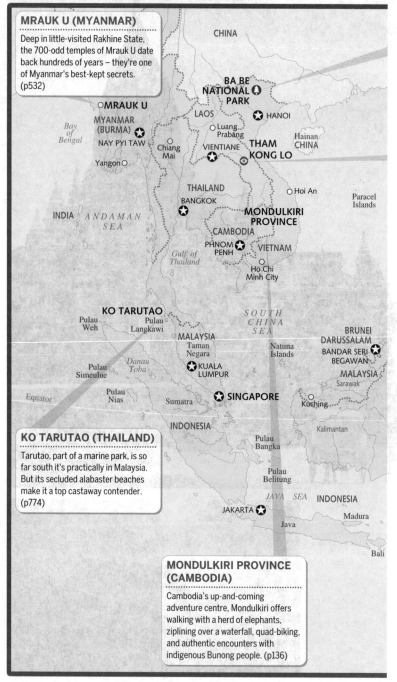

MRAUK U (MYANMAR)

Deep in little-visited Rakhine State, the 700-odd temples of Mrauk U date back hundreds of years – they're one of Myanmar's best-kept secrets. (p532)

CHINA

BA BE NATIONAL PARK

MRAUK U

LAOS

HANOI

MYANMAR (BURMA)

Bay of Bengal

NAY PYI TAW

Luang Prabang

Chiang Mai

VIENTIANE

Hainan CHINA

THAM KONG LO

Yangon

THAILAND

BANGKOK

Hoi An

Paracel Islands

INDIA

ANDAMAN SEA

MONDULKIRI PROVINCE

CAMBODIA

PHNOM PENH

VIETNAM

Gulf of Thailand

Ho Chi Minh City

KO TARUTAO

Pulau Weh

Pulau Langkawi

SOUTH CHINA SEA

MALAYSIA

Taman Negara

Natuna Islands

BRUNEI DARUSSALAM

BANDAR SERI BEGAWAN

Pulau Simeulue

Danau Toba

KUALA LUMPUR

MALAYSIA

Sarawak

Equator

Pulau Nias

Sumatra

SINGAPORE

Kuching

KO TARUTAO (THAILAND)

Tarutao, part of a marine park, is so far south it's practically in Malaysia. But its secluded alabaster beaches make it a top castaway contender. (p774)

INDONESIA

Pulau Bangka

Kalimantan

Pulau Belitung

JAVA SEA

INDONESIA

JAKARTA

Java

Madura

Bali

MONDULKIRI PROVINCE (CAMBODIA)

Cambodia's up-and-coming adventure centre, Mondulkiri offers walking with a herd of elephants, ziplining over a waterfall, quad-biking, and authentic encounters with indigenous Bunong people. (p136)

```
0 ┣━━━━━━━━━ 500 km
0 ┣━━━━━━━━━ 300 miles
```

BA BE NATIONAL PARK (VIETNAM)

A stunning landscape of limestone mountains, sloping valleys, mist-shrouded lakes and evergreen forests provides a full dose of nature exploration. For a cultural hook, ethnic minorities host rustic homestays. (p836)

THAM KONG LO (LAOS)

A watery underworld awaits at this 7.5km-long cave explored by longtail boat. Daylight recedes as you putter deep into the darkness and bulbous-shaped calcified sculptures decorate the vaulted ceiling. (p356)

SIARGAO (PHILIPPINES)

Famous for its surf break, this Catholic island in northern Mindanao is blessed with pretty coves, fine blonde beaches and laid-back villages. Nearby Camiguin has volcano hikes, reef dives and scenic places to wander. (p590)

ULU TEMBURONG NATIONAL PARK (BRUNEI DARUSSALAM)

This pristine tract of primary rainforest, reachable only by boat, is one of the few remaining expanses of the truly wild jungle that once covered all of Borneo. (p64)

TOGEAN ISLANDS (INDONESIA)

The blissful Togean Islands are an unadulterated vision of the tropics. Wander blinding white-sand beaches fringed by coconut palms and enjoy world-class snorkelling and diving on majestic coral reefs. (p288)

ATAURO ISLAND (TIMOR-LESTE)

If you've made it all the way to Timor-Leste, take one more hop over to this blissfully undeveloped isle off Dili for excellent snorkelling, diving, hiking and hammock-swinging. (p798)

Map labels:

Tropic of Cancer
TAIWAN
O Banaue
Luzon
PHILIPPINE SEA
MANILA
Catanduanes
PHILIPPINES
Mindoro
Samar
Panay
Cebu
Bohol
SIARGAO
Palawan
SULU SEA
Mindanao
PACIFIC OCEAN
Mt Kinabalu (4095m)
Jolo
Sabah
Tawi-Tawi
Talaud
ULU TEMBURONG NATIONAL PARK
Sangir Islands
Morotai
CELEBES SEA
Waigeo
TOGEAN ISLANDS
Sula Islands
Misool
Seram
SERAM SEA
Sulawesi
Tana Toraja
INDONESIA
Buru
Puncak Jaya (5030m)
Papua
PAPUA NEW GUINEA
Butung (Buton)
Kai Islands
Aru Islands
BANDA SEA
Selayar
Bali Sea
FLORES SEA
ATAURO ISLAND
Wetar
Tanimbar Islands
Yos Sudarso
Lombok
Flores
DILI
Babar Islands
TIMOR-LESTE
ARAFURA SEA
TIMOR SEA
AUSTRALIA

Plan Your Trip
Big Adventures, Small Budgets

You don't need to be a high-roller in Southeast Asia – in fact you can live like a cheapskate and still bask on beautiful beaches, visit magnificent temples and explore stunning landscapes. But you do need to watch your spending and plan wisely.

Planning & Costs
Planning Timeline

12 months before Calculate a trip budget and start saving.

6 months Pick which countries to visit, when and for how long. Research long-haul flights.

8 to 6 weeks Make passport and visa arrangements as needed.

4 weeks Get vaccinations and travel insurance.

2 weeks Reserve high-season transport and accommodation for popular destinations and activities.

1 week Book accommodation for arrival city; start packing.

Average Costs

Bottle of beer US$1–3

Long-distance bus ticket US$10–30

Food-stall meal US$2–5

Guesthouse room US$5–20

Internet access per hour Free to US$5

Domestic flight US$50–150

Budget Guide

Southeast Asia's cost of living is very reasonable: shoestringers can survive on a daily budget of about US$25 to US$50 a day. This covers the basics: food, shelter, local transport and a few beers. Costs will vary by country, the popularity of the destination and the time of year.

Factor in the costs of long-distance travel by bus, boat or air. Add any special activities, such as diving or rock climbing. Then allow for unexpected expenses, such as increased costs during holidays or needing to get somewhere fast.

Accommodation costs are a big portion of your budget; luckily the region is filled with good-value lodgings. The more creature comforts (air-con, hot water, private bathroom) you can forsake, the more you will save.

Public transport within each country is affordable. Costs rise with boat and air travel and wherever road conditions are rough. Local public transport won't stretch the budget, but hiring private taxis is pricey. Getting around individual islands can often be expensive because of price-fixing or lack of competition. You can save on local transport costs if you know how to ride a motorbike. Much cheaper is bicycle hire, which is a great way to explore.

Tips by Destination

We posed the following question to our authors: What's the cheapest place for the best time in each country?

Brunei Darussalam Tiny, oil-rich Brunei can be a great budget destination if you arrive by bus from Malaysian Borneo. Stay in a hostel, dine in the open-air markets and tour the free cultural sights.

Cambodia You can have a great time living it up on the cheap in Sihanoukville, where you can score dorm beds for around US$5 and a beer for US$0.50. Or pop across to Koh Rong, the new party island in the region, to experience the Thailand of old.

Indonesia Do Bali on the cheap by opting for an Ulu Watu homestay. Enjoy a surfer-chic scene and epic views with enough spare cash to wash it all down with several Bintangs.

Laos Si Phan Don (Four Thousand Islands) is the quintessential lotus-eating country: hammock-hanging, a happening traveller scene, laid-back island life, tubing down the river and dolphin-spotting.

Malaysia Pulau Perhentian is an awesome deal and has some of the cheapest diving in Asia, comparable to Ko Tao. Cherating is another budget-friendly beach.

Myanmar (Burma) It's a little bit of a schlep, but Mrauk U is one of the country's best-value spots: this ancient capital of temples doesn't cost a fortune and has fewer package tourists than Bagan.

Philippines North Luzon and Palawan are inexpensive, off-the-beaten-track options. Sleep amid Batad's rice terraces or beach-camp in Coron or El Nido.

Singapore You can't afford to be a high-flyer in Singapore on a budget, but you can soak up culture with the Singapore Symphony Orchestra's free concerts.

Thailand Ko Tao is still a cheap place for an open-water diving certificate. The east side of Ko Pha Ngan remains a bargain. On the Andaman side, Railay still has cheap digs.

Timor-Leste Catch a *microlet* (local bus) heading to Liquica (US$1) and hop off at the rocky point near the Pope's monument. Welcome to Dili Rock West. Go snorkelling to see amazing coral and fish.

Vietnam With some of the cheapest beer in the region (from US$0.30 a glass), Vietnam might win the budget showdown. Nha Trang is the backpackers' beach, with rocking nightlife and affordable lodging.

Sticking to a Budget: Top 10

➡ Eat like a local at street stalls or markets.

➡ Opt for dorm rooms or share a room with a friend.

➡ Stay in fan (non-air-con) rooms with shared bathrooms.

➡ Travel overland instead of flying.

➡ Snorkel instead of dive.

➡ Hire a bicycle instead of a motorbike.

➡ Be selective about which national parks to visit.

➡ Know the price of local transport and bargain accordingly.

➡ Do souvenir shopping at the end of your trip with surplus funds.

➡ Track your daily expenses so you know your average costs.

PACKING FOR YOUR TRIP

Take as little as possible: you're going to have to carry it everywhere. Pack your bag once and then repack it with a third less stuff. Repeat until your pack is small enough to fit into the aircraft's overhead compartment, which represents the average size of most stowage areas on buses and trains. The smaller your pack the easier it will be to climb on and off public transport and to explore a new place on foot – and you'll look like less of a target for touts and hustlers.

Accommodation Tips

Lodging will be one of your primary expenses. Here are some tips for saving money:

➡ If the price is too high, ask if they have a cheaper room.

➡ Unless it's the low season, most rates are non-negotiable.

➡ Once you've paid for a room, there's no refund.

➡ Pay per day rather than all in advance to allow some flexibility in your planning.

➡ When making bookings, don't rely on agents who charge a commission.

Surfing in Sumbawa (p237), Indonesia

Plan Your Trip
Activities

Mountains high, rivers deep; towering volcanoes, cathedral-like caverns; barrels above, reefs below – the adventures in Southeast Asia are limitless. Trekking, cycling, climbing, caving, surfing, diving: it's all here, as are some of the world's best wellness experiences for relaxing afterwards.

Top Activities

Best Diving
Indonesia & the Philippines When it comes to reefs and drop-offs, these archipelago nations are the undisputed dive capitals of Southeast Asia.

Best Hiking & Trekking
Malaysia Ascend the lunar landscape of Mt Kinabalu, tramp through virgin rainforests or explore the Cameron Highlands – standouts in a region full of top treks.

Best Surfing
Indonesia Barrel through the breaks of Java and Bali to Nusa Tenggara's big waves on Sumbawa and Sumba, or head north to the Mentawai Islands off Sumatra.

Best Wildlife-Watching
Malaysia Borneo is not known as the Amazon of Asia for nothing: meet orangutans, proboscis monkeys and pygmy elephants in the national parks of Sabah and Sarawak.

Best Caving
Vietnam There's no better place to head underground right now than Phong Nha-Ke Bang National Park, where bigger and better caves keep being discovered.

Hiking & Trekking

Hiking is popular throughout the region and ranges from jungle treks to volcano ascents, from one-day jaunts to multiday expeditions. A guide is required as trails are not well marked, transport to the trailhead is difficult to arrange, and you will be unfamiliar with the region's microclimates. Hiring a guide also provides income for local villagers.

You should also be aware of local laws, regulations and etiquette about wildlife and the environment.

Be prepared for a trek with proper clothing: long pants, adequate hiking shoes and leech socks (during and after the rainy season). Bring along rain gear (for yourself and your pack) even if the skies are clear. Carry a torch (flashlight), mosquito spray and a first-aid kit. Drink lots of water and pace yourself: the humidity can make even minimal exercise feel demanding.

Elephant trekking is also popular but standards of the elephant camps vary greatly. Do your homework before signing up for a trek, and opt for a 'walking with the herd' experience (available in Cambodia, Laos and Thailand) rather than an elephant ride, which can be detrimental to the animals' health.

When to Go

Rain, not temperature, is the primary consideration when planning your trip. Just after the rainy season (November to February) is ideal for mainland Southeast Asia, when the forest is lush and flooding is not a concern – although frost is possible at higher elevations, such as Sapa. December to January is high season for international and domestic tourists. January and February are the wettest months of the northeast monsoon in most of Brunei, Indonesia, Malaysia and Timor-Leste. April to June is shoulder season for Indonesia, when the weather is drier. July and August are peak season in many parts of the region. September and October are the wettest months for most of mainland Southeast Asia.

Where to Go

Mt Kinabalu (Malaysia) Hoof it over granite moonscapes for the ultimate Bornean sunrise atop 4095m-high Mt Kinabalu. (p440)

Ifugao Rice Terraces (Philippines) Hiking around the exquisitely carved rice terraces of Ifugao, Bontoc and Kalinga is one of Southeast Asia's top trekking experiences. (p565)

Baliem Valley (Indonesia) The Baliem Valley draws acolytes from around the world for hikes among some of the world's most unique cultures. (p297)

Sapa (Vietnam) Sapa is Vietnam's trekking hub, with spectacular scenery, majestic mountains, impossibly green rice paddies and some fascinating tribal villages. (p838)

Cycling between temples, Bagan (p521), Myanmar

RESPONSIBLE TREKKING IN VILLAGES
....
Tourism can bring many benefits to highland communities: cross-cultural understanding, improved infrastructure, cheaper market goods, employment opportunities and tourist dollars supporting handicraft industries. Negatives can include increased litter, control of the tourism business by the dominant community at the expense of highland minorities, and the tendency of tourists to disregard local customs.

To tour villages responsibly, travel in small groups and hire indigenous guides to ensure your money goes directly to their communities. They also greatly improve your access to highland residents, they understand taboos and traditions that might be lost on non-native guides, and they have an intimate knowledge of the landscape.

Hsipaw (Myanmar) Hike into the hills surrounding laid-back Hsipaw to discover a multitude of timeless, friendly Shan, Palaung and Lisu villages. (p520)

Mt Ramelau (Timor-Leste) Rise at dawn to scale Timor-Leste's highest peak – just in time to watch the sun rise over the glittering ocean. (p802)

Cycling

There's great cycling throughout the region, from urban orienteering on two wheels to upcountry adventures. For hardcore cyclists, the mountains of northern Vietnam and northern Laos are the ultimate destination. For a gentler trip, meandering along Mekong villages is memorable, particularly in the Mekong Delta in Vietnam. Biking around major historic sites such as Angkor, Bagan and Sukothai is a great way to get around. Further south, Thailand and Borneo offer some good mountain biking for adventurous riders. Indonesia is simply too big for many to consider touring, but individual

TOP VOLCANO TREKS

Forming part of the Pacific Ring of Fire, Indonesia and the Philippines are together home to more than 100 active volcanoes, many of which can be climbed all the way to the summit, on anything from short jaunts to multiday expeditions. Some of these volcanoes are active (while others have been dormant for centuries), so enquire with local authorities before setting out.

Gunung Bromo (Indonesia) One of three volcanic cones (one active) that emerge from an other-worldly caldera. Highly recommended. (p187)

Mt Mayon (Philippines) The country's most iconic and postcard-perfect volcano, the conical-shaped Mt Mayon (2462m) is also one of the Philippines' most active – do your homework first. (p568)

Gunung Batur (Indonesia) This Bali volcano's extraordinary scenery almost makes you forget about the hassles at the bottom. (p218)

Mt Pinatubo (Philippines) Hiking around the bizarre lahar formations and up to the serene crater lake of Mt Pinatubo (1450m) is an unmissable experience. (p559)

islands offer great rides, including Bali and Lombok or, for the more adventurous, Flores and Sulawesi.

Throughout the region, basic bicycles can be rented for US$1 to US$5 per day; good-quality mountain bikes cost US$10 to US$20. When it comes to cycling tours, Bangkok-based **Spice Roads** (www. spiceroads.com) is the acknowledged expert on Southeast Asia, but there are good local operators in each country.

When to Go

Cycling in the monsoon rains is no fun, so plan around the dry season. It's particularly important to avoid the wet season in mountain areas, where landslides are a real and present danger. The ideal months to tour mainland Southeast Asia are November to February, when the temperatures are lower and the wind is up.

Where to Go

Temples of Angkor (Cambodia) The temples can get very busy in peak season, so leave the crowds behind and follow local jungle trails. (p94)

Bagan (Myanmar) The temples here are spread far and wide across the Ayeyarwady plain, so getting around by bicycle is the best way to explore. (p521)

Luang Prabang (Laos) Biking is a great way to get around the old town or explore some of the surrounding countryside and minority villages. (p333)

Mekong Delta (Vietnam) The flatlands of the Mekong Delta region are ideal for long-distance rides down back roads. (p894)

Motorcycling

For those with a thirst for adventure, motorcycle trips into remote areas of the region are unforgettable. The mobility of two wheels is unrivalled: motorcycles can traverse trails that even the hardiest 4WD cannot follow, and put you closer to the countryside than a car or bus. Motorbiking is still a main mode of transport, so you'll find repair shops everywhere. Vietnam, Cambodia, Laos and Thailand lead the way in motorcycle adventures.

Motorcycles are widely available for rent. Daily charges start at US$5 to US$10 for 100cc bikes and rise to US$15 to US$50 for 250cc dirt bikes or road bikes. One-way bike rentals are often available for an extra fee. Specialist motorcycle-touring companies can organise multiday trips into remote areas.

Hiring bikes rarely requires a licence in this part of the world, although you might be asked to show one in Brunei, Malaysia or Thailand. You almost always need to leave a passport to hire a bike, though this can cause problems if you get injured in a remote place and need to be evacuated out of the country.

When to Go

It's no fun motorbiking in the rain, so plan the trip around dry-season months. (See the boxed text on p49 for information about monsoons.)

If you are heading off-road in places like Cambodia, Laos and Vietnam, leave the trip a little later into January to give the remote jungle trails time to dry out after the rain.

Where to Go

Sapa (Vietnam) There's glorious mountain scenery, river valleys and tribal villages around Sapa, Bac Ha and Dien Bien Phu. (p838)

Preah Vihear Province (Cambodia) Get your kicks on Route 66, the old Angkor highway that runs from Beng Mealea Temple to Preah Khan Temple. (p112)

Vang Vieng (Laos) Delve deep into the limestone karsts that pepper the west bank of the Nam Song River with this scenically stunning motorcycle ride. (p328)

Mae Hong Son (Thailand) The classic northern route is the Mae Hong Son loop, a 600km ride that begins in Chiang Mai and takes in Pai, Mae Hong Son and Mae Sariang. (p708)

Boat Trips, Kayaking & Rafting

With the Mekong cutting through the region's northern half and the rest made up of island archipelagos, boat trips are a major drawcard here. You can explore small jungled tributaries leading to remote minority villages in Cambodia and Borneo, or cave systems by boat in Laos and Vietnam, as well as experience the bustle of a floating market in the Mekong Delta. Island-hopping is de rigeur in Indonesia and the Philippines, particularly in more remote areas not connected by air.

Kayaking has seen an explosion in popularity in the past few years. Krabi Province in Thailand is the spiritual home of sea kayaking in the region and most Halong Bay tours in Vietnam also now include kayaking through the karsts. River systems in Indonesia, Laos and Malaysia are popular for kayak exploring, offering access to remote tribal villages. Lakes are also popular for kayaking: top spots include beautiful Ba Be National Park in Vietnam, the flooded forests and floating villages of the Tonlé Sap Lake in Cambodia, and Mekong tributaries in northern Laos.

Though white-water rafting here is not as dramatic as that of, say, Nepal, things get a little more vigorous in the wet sea-

THE WEATHER REPORT: PICK YOUR BEACH

BEACH	JAN–FEB	MAR–APR	MAY–JUN	JUL–SEP	OCT–DEC	SEE MORE
Ko Tao (Thailand)	dry, high season	dry, shoulder season	dry, shoulder season	dry until Sep, high season	rain, low season	p748
Phuket (Thailand)	dry, high season	dry, shoulder season	start of rains, shoulder season	rain, low season	dry, shoulder season	p759
Bali (Indonesia)	rain, low season	end of rains, shoulder season	dry, shoulder season	dry, high season	start of rains, shoulder season	p192
Nha Trang (Vietnam)	dry, high season	dry, high season	dry, high season	dry, high season	rain, low season	p869
Sihanoukville (Cambodia)	dry, high season	dry, shoulder season	start of rains, shoulder season	rain, low season	rain, shoulder season	p116
Boracay (Philippines)	dry, high season	dry, high season	dry, shoulder season	rain, low season	end of rains, shoulder season	p573
Timor-Leste	rain, low season	dry, high season	dry, high season	dry, high season	dry, high season	p789

Kayaking in Sabah (p432), Malaysian Borneo

son. Go with the flow and try rafting on the Pai River in Thailand or the Chico or Cagayan Rivers of the Philippines.

Stand-up paddleboarding (SUP) is also growing in popularity around the region as an easy option for beginners to test themselves on calm seas or gentle rivers.

When to Go

Whether you're after a mellow boat cruise on the Mekong or a white-water rafting trip on a raging river, the best time to go is during the rainy season. Rivers are high, lakes are full and the landscape is lush and green.

Where to Go

Halong Bay (Vietnam) Take an overnight cruise among the karsts and paddle into a hidden lagoon, or try stand-up paddleboarding. (p831)

Krabi Province (Thailand) Sea kayaking in Southeast Asia began here with stunning paddling around iconic karst islands. (p761)

Tham Kong Lo (Laos) This river cave might feel like the River Styx, but offers one of the most

memorable underground boat rides on earth. (p356)

Chico River (Philippines) One of the Philippines' best white-water rafting sites, where you can tear down the raging waters of North Luzon. (p564)

Bhamo to Mandalay (Myanmar) Cruise the mighty Ayeyarwady River from remote Bhamo to Mandalay. (p527)

Ulu Temburong National Park (Brunei) Approach this impressive national park by longboat for a river trip to remember. (p64)

Diving & Snorkelling

Southeast Asia is a diving and snorkelling paradise, with inexpensive dive-certificate training and myriad undersea environments. Thailand, Malaysia, Indonesia and the Philippines are all famous dive destinations, while Cambodia, Vietnam and Myanmar are less spectacular options but good for beginners. Advanced divers will find some of the world's top sites in Indonesia and the Philippines.

RESPONSIBLE DIVING

➡ Never use anchors on the reef, and take care not to ground boats on coral.

➡ Avoid touching or standing on living marine organisms or dragging equipment across the reef.

➡ Be conscious of your fins: the surge from fin strokes near the reef can damage delicate organisms. Take care not to kick up clouds of sand, which can smother organisms.

➡ Practise and maintain proper buoyancy control: major damage can be done by divers descending too fast and colliding with the reef.

➡ Take great care in underwater caves. Spend as little time within them as possible – your air bubbles may be caught within the roof and leave organisms high and dry. Take turns to inspect the interior of a small cave.

➡ Resist the temptation to collect or buy corals or shells or to loot marine archaeological sites (mainly shipwrecks).

➡ Ensure that you take home all your rubbish, and any litter you may find. Plastics are a serious threat to marine life.

➡ Do not feed fish.

➡ Minimise your disturbance of marine animals. Never ride on the backs of turtles.

Diving and snorkelling put unique pressures on the natural environment. Select reputable and environmentally conscious operators.

When to Go

Diving depends on visibility, which depends on calm waters and storm-free days. Most diving locations have sub-par conditions during the rainy season; luckily the double monsoon means you'll find high visibility somewhere. You can dive the Gulf of Thailand most of the year.

Where to Go

Komodo National Park (Indonesia) Besides dragons, this national park boasts some of Indonesia's best and most varied diving. (p239)

Bohol (Philippines) The entire island is festooned with wonderful dive sites, but the highlight is undoubtedly Balicasag Island. (p587)

Similan Islands (Thailand) Keep an eye out for whale sharks on a liveaboard diving adventure to this marine national park. (p759)

Semporna Archipelago (Malaysia) The legendary 'Coral Triangle' has wild sea turtles, sharks and multicoloured reefs. (p448)

Atauro Island (Timor-Leste) Dazzling, pristine reefs fringe Timor-Leste's north coast, but arguably the best dive sites lie off Atauro Island. (p798)

Best-Value Places to Learn to Dive

Ko Tao (Thailand) New to diving? Check out Ko Tao, the cheapest and best place to learn the basics. (p748)

Gili Trawangan (Indonesia) Among the best places to get certified worldwide; accessible reefs are within a 10-minute boat ride. (p234)

Perhentian Islands (Malaysia) Sign up for an open-water course with prices rock-bottom when the ringgit is down. (p424)

Moalboal (Philippines) The home of Philippines diving is still one of the best places to learn. (p586)

Water Sports

Surfing and kitesurfing are big draws in Southeast Asia. Indonesia is the region's surfing capital, with the Philippines a close second. Vietnam and Thailand have consistent winds for seasonal kitesurfing; Vietnam also has some accessible surf. Be sure to go with a company with a good safety record, especially if you're a beginner.

Snorkelling in the Philippines

Mui Ne (Vietnam) Mui Ne Beach is fast becoming a windchasers' hotspot in Asia. (p875)

Siargao (Philippines) Home to Cloud Nine, the name of this legendary right-hander says it all: one of the country's best breaks. (p590)

Rock Climbing

Southeast Asia's limestone cliffs have been transformed into climbing routes for vertical challenges and spectacular views. Thailand, Laos and Vietnam boast several rock-climbing centres for beginners and experts. Climb sea karsts in Krabi Province, Thailand and around Cat Ba Island near Vietnam's Halong Bay; try deep-water soloing (DWS), or free climbing with a drop-off into deep water (this should only be undertaken with an experienced guide). Or climb some land karsts around Vang Vieng in Laos, Chiang Mai in Thailand or Phong Nha-Ke Bang National Park in Vietnam.

When to Go

Climbing in the wet season is not advisable as the rocky surfaces are slippery and potentially dangerous. Heavy showers also make visibility a big problem – not good when you're halfway up a rock face.

When to Go

May to September brings prime swells to Indonesia's Lombok and Sumbawa, while Bali always has a good surf spot somewhere. In the Philippines surf season coincides with the typhoons (August to November). Good for beginners, Phuket (Thailand) has swells from April to September, and Cherating (Malaysia) from November to March.

Kitesurfing is popular on Boracay (Philippines), the east and west coast of Thailand (Hua Hin and Phuket), in Mui Ne (Vietnam) and at Hu'u and Lakey Beach on Sumbawa (Indonesia). These beaches tend to have a long windy season through most of the year.

Where to Go

Sumatra (Indonesia) Tough competition in the surf capital of Southeast Asia, but the Mentawai Islands in Sumatra are pure perfection. (p258)

Phuket (Thailand) As one of Thailand's top beach destinations, Phuket offers surfing, kitesurfing and more. (p759)

KNOW YOUR MONSOON

The region's two monsoon rains and the tourist seasons are big factors in determining when and where to plot your adventures. The southwest monsoon (June/July to September/October) brings rain to mainland Southeast Asia and the west coast of the Malay peninsula (Phuket and Langkawi). Following the rains is dry, cool weather (November to February), and then it hots up (March to June). Most of the Philippines follows this weather pattern, so steer clear if there's a typhoon brewing. The northeast monsoon starts in September, bringing rain to the east coast of the Malay peninsula (Ko Samui, Pulau Perhentian), and then migrates east through Indonesia, hitting Timor-Leste by December.

Where to Go

Railay (Thailand) Scaling these limestone crags while surrounded by azure seas and a fabulous beach makes Railay the number-one climbing site in Thailand. (p768)

Cat Ba Island (Vietnam) Instruction for beginners and dedicated trips for rock stars set against the backdrop of Halong Bay. (p832)

Vang Vieng (Laos) More than 200 rock-climbing routes – many of them bolted – up the limestone cliffs. (p328)

Caving

Having fun 'outdoors' in Southeast Asia can also involve exploring its extensive underground network of caves. Definitely not for the claustrophobic, spelunking is an exhilarating adventure involving a combination of swimming through underground rivers, squeezing under crevasses and over ledges to encounter gleaming formations and breathtaking cathedral-like passages.

When to Go

Given you're going underground, to some extent it doesn't really matter. However, access to certain caves can be difficult during the wet season due to slippery trails. Caves with a river running through them are sometimes closed when the water level is too high.

Ziplining at the Gibbon Experience (p355), Laos

> ### ZIPLINING
>
> There are ziplines in Cambodia, Laos, Indonesia, Thailand and Vietnam. Zip between islands in Malaysia and Thailand, over waterfalls in Cambodia and Laos, or into a cave in Vietnam.
>
> The **Gibbon Experience** (p355) in Laos blazed an aerial trail: visitors glide through forest where the gibbons roam, and can stay overnight in a treehouse. In Cambodia, **Flight of the Gibbon Angkor** (p93) offers ziplining near the temples with wild gibbons in the trees. Newcomer **Mayura Zipline** (p137) offers a memorable flight over the Bou Sraa Waterfall in northeast Cambodia's Mondulkiri Province.

Where to Go

Phong Nha-Ke Bang National Park (Vietnam) There are stupendous cave trips at Phong Nha-Ke Bang National Park, many of which involve some hiking, swimming and climbing. (p846)

Vieng Xai Caves (Laos) Explore this underground base and wartime capital of the Pathet Lao communists, set beneath stunning limestone rock formations. (p348)

Gunung Mulu National Park (Malaysia) Explore some of the world's largest and most spectacular caves in this Sarawak national park. (p466)

Sagada (Philippines) Explore fascinating burial caves or slog through underground rivers on the thrilling cave-to-cave connection. (p564)

Watching Wildlife

It may not be as easy to spot wildlife in the steamy jungles of Southeast Asia as it is on the open plains of Africa, but there are some excellent wildlife-watching opportunities here. Encounter large mammals such as wild elephants; meet orangutans in Malaysia and Indonesia; spot rare birdlife around

TIM GERARD BARKER/GETTY IMAGES ©

BIRDWATCHING IN SOUTHEAST ASIA

Tram Chin National Park (Vietnam)
Home to the rare eastern sarus crane, a huge red-headed bird depicted on the bas-reliefs of Angkor. (p896)

Khao Sok National Park (Thailand)
Fish eagles, hornbills and kingfishers are found in this beautiful national park. (p757)

Papua (Indonesia) Encounter the rainbow-hued birds of paradise, many of which are endemic to the island of Papua. (p294)

Jurong Bird Park (Singapore) See almost every major bird under the sun at the world's largest bird park. (p624)

lakes and rivers; and discover an incredible underwater world just off the coastline. Tigers and big cats can be seen at the leading wildlife sanctuaries and zoos in the region.

When to Go

Many of the best wildlife destinations are in protected forests or deep jungle, so plan a visit in the dry season. However, some national parks in the region include boat trips, in which case you can go during wet season. Birdwatching is seasonal due to migratory patterns.

Where to Go

Sungai Kinabatangan (Malaysia) Cruise down this Sabah river to spot orangutans, proboscis monkeys, monitor lizards and even elephants. (p445)

Khao Yai National Park (Thailand) Elephants, monkeys, hornbills, blood-suckers and other creepie-crawlies call this monsoon forest home. (p719)

Cat Tien National Park (Vietnam) Meet primates in the jungles of Cat Tien on a wild gibbon trek and visit the Dao Tien Endangered Primate Species Centre. (p877)

Kratie Province (Cambodia) Spot rare freshwater Irrawaddy dolphins in the Mekong River at Kampi in Kratie Province. (p130)

Tanjung Puting National Park (Indonesia) Anchor along one of Kalimantan's iconic rivers and watch orangutans go about their business just metres away. (p277)

Wellness

Southeast Asia is a leading wellness centre in the world, with a wide range of activities to help you de-stress and unwind. Meditation has long been practised by Buddhists and is a popular activity, as is yoga. Thailand and Bali have some top-notch health retreats.

Accessible for all are massage and spa. Not all massages are as advertised in places like Cambodia, Thailand and Vietnam, but the look of the establishment should give a clear indication of what kind of 'services' the place is really offering. (Red lights or fairy lights usually mean the main business may not be wellness.) But the vast majority of places are legitimate and practitioners in the region are famous for their craft. Some masseurs are stronger than others and some techniques more persecution than pleasure, so only request a strong massage if you were a wrestler in an earlier life.

When to Go

Unless the yoga or meditation is in an outdoor setting, it really doesn't matter when you plan your wellness. Some centres may offer more varied programs during the high season, as resident yoga instructors may move around over the course of the year. Plan ahead if you want a tailor-made experience.

Where to Go

Phuket (Thailand) The island has several top spots offering retreats aimed at foreigners, plus several leading yoga schools. (p759)

Ubud (Indonesia) Ubud is the epicentre of wellness in Bali. Yoga, meditation, massage – this is as chill as it gets here. (p208)

Siem Reap (Cambodia) Foot massages to soothe your soul, yoga classes, meditation retreats and some of the best spas in the country. (p89)

Luang Prabang (Laos) The spiritual soul of Laos, with some excellent spas and a small yoga community. (p333)

Mawlamyine (Myanmar) The Pa-Auk-Taw-Ya Monastery is one of the largest and most welcoming meditation centres in Myanmar. (p499)

Countries at a Glance

Thailand

Culture/History
Beaches
Food

Monarchs & Monuments

Thais are devoted royalists, and Bangkok's glittering royal temples continue the tradition of fusing royalty and religion. In the northeast, the Khmer empire built mini-Angkors, while the Thais crafted their own versions in the central plains.

Coastal Chilling

With their azure waters and shimmering sand, Thailand's southern beaches have tropical-island proportions and a party personality. Samui and Pha-Ngan are the headliners; Krabi is a karst cathedral where diving abounds.

Curries & Chillies

A global culinary legend, Thai food combines four elemental flavours (spicy, sweet, sour and salty) into radioactively coloured curries, vegetable-studded stir-fries and steaming bowls of noodles.

p643

Brunei Darussalam

Food
Outdoor Activities
River Journeys

Culinary Surprises

Bruneian cuisine may not be well known, but we can guarantee you've never eaten anything like *ambuyat* (made from sago starch), or the delicious *kueh* (baked sweets) available in night markets, a perfect complement to a chicken satay.

Between Earth & Sky

Brunei's rainforests are safeguarded as precious natural habitats. You'll experience pristine wilderness and a bird's-eye view of the canopy.

Watery World

Glimpse Brunei's traditional culture in the world's largest stilt village, on the banks of Sungai Brunei, or experience a watery obstacle course aboard a longtail boat.

p56

Cambodia

Culture/History
Community-Based Tourism
Beaches

Heaven & Hell

Visiting the unrivalled Temples of Angkor, an architectural wonder built by ancient kings, is a must. The modern tragedy of genocide and civil war is remembered at Tuol Sleng Prison and the Killing Fields.

Activities for a Cause

Community-based tourism projects are turning former poachers into trekking guides and rural river villages into immersive experiences. Now you can do something good just by being a tourist.

Blissful Beaches

Budget sun-seekers find Thailand's beaches increasingly expensive, but Cambodia has squeaky-clean stretches of sand with young revellers and fewer package tourists.

p68

Indonesia

Culture/History
Outdoor
Activities
Beaches

So Many Spice Islands

A huge archipelago spanning two great oceans, Indonesia is mythical and magical, with smoking volcanoes, deep jungles and vibrant cultures. So many places, too little time.

Smoking Giants

Huff and puff your way up a nearly vertical volcano to its smouldering summit, with foul-smelling gases and entrancing above-the-clouds views. (So what if they sometimes erupt and cause air-travel chaos?)

Beach Buffet

Charming Bali is a cultured beach bum. Just across the channel are the Gili Islands for diving, Sumbawa for surfing, Flores for discovering and Sumba for simply getting lost.

p151

Laos

Culture/History
Outdoor
Activities
River Journeys

Temples & Tribes

The former royal capital of Luang Prabang offers historic temples and remnants of Indochina. In nearby mountains, hill tribes host village homestays, providing a face-to-face cultural exchange.

Leafy Laos

With around 20 protected areas, Laos has an abundance of undisturbed wilderness. Eco-oriented programs like the Gibbon Experience turn trekkers into zipline fliers and treetop sleepers.

River Reverie

The rivers of Laos impart an easy-going pace to daily life. Laze beside the muddy waters, kayak deep into the hinterland or use the river as a highway from Luang Prabang to the Golden Triangle.

p314

Malaysia

Food
Diving
Outdoor
Activities

Laksa Luck

Malaysia is a multi-cultural success story: Chinese and Indian immigrants intermarried with Malays to create a unique cultural offspring. Discover the diversity at hawker stalls, where noodles and dumplings are served with coconut-milk curries.

Below the Surface

Borneo's Semporna Archipelago and Pulau Perhentian are big draws for the scuba crowd. Malaysia's beaches are blessedly less boozy than Thailand's.

Borneo Bound

The fabled jungles of Borneo are sliced by tea-coloured rivers. Mt Kinabalu's granite spire offers a two-day pilgrimage, while orangutan sanctuaries provide refuge for our hairier cousins.

p380

Myanmar (Burma)

Culture/History
Outdoor
Activities
Festivals

History in the Making

Aung San Suu Kyi's National League for Democracy is now in power and people here are smiling. The historic sites – from golden pagodas to ancient cities – are marvellous, but the country's newfound optimism is history you can feel.

Mountain Dew

Inle Lake hugs a rugged mountainous landscape where the water's surface has been transformed into fertile farmland. Boats are more important than wheels and puttering about is a peaceful pastime.

Elemental Celebrations

Myanmar brightens up during Tazaungdaing, its festival of lights, and douses the hot season during Thingyan, the Burmese New Year.

p479

Philippines

Culture/History
Outdoor Activities
Beaches

Maritime Madonna

Foreigners have long been drawn to these shores. Spain planted colonial towns and Catholicism; America left behind cars and the English language – and the Filipinos sewed it all up into an intriguing cultural quilt.

Coughing Cones

Volcanoes create lush and statuesque landscapes, with still-smouldering specimens and dormant peaks that have been carved into rice terraces.

Coastal Jigsaw

The myth of deserted palm-fringed beaches is a reality among the Philippines' 7000-plus islands – a huge playground for divers, kiteboarders and surfers, as well as beachcombers.

p545

Singapore

Culture/History
Food
Outdoor Activities

Super Singapore

The best of East and West formed lovable Singapore. It has a host of well-curated and well-funded museums, atmospheric colonial houses and oh-so-modern shopping malls.

Hawk Me a Meal

Ever-efficient Singapore corralled its roaming vendors into hawker centres, where appetites and meals could be happily united. These open-air pavilions are the centre of a community and meals that turn into nightcaps.

Urban Jungle

Escape the shiny skyscrapers into the wilderness. Leisurely wander the futuristic Gardens by the Bay or lush Botanic Gardens. Adventurers can hike Bukit Timah Nature Reserve or the Southern Ridges.

p609

Timor-Leste

Culture/History
Outdoor Activities
Diving

History in Motion

It might be one of the youngest nations in the world, but Timor-Leste has lived many lives. Colonial-era architecture, hilltop statues of Jesus and habit-wearing nuns embody the Portuguese legacy, while Dili's cemeteries and museums memorialise the struggle for independence from Indonesia.

Vistas

Climb to the top of sacred Mt Ramelau for its Virgin Mary statue and a spectacular sunrise view over two coasts.

Epic Immersions

Though barely a blip on the global dive radar, Timor-Leste boasts excellent diving – much of it just steps from the mainland, and off Atauro Island.

p789

Vietnam

Culture/History
Beaches
Food

Outsized History

Be it neighbouring China, colonial France or anti-communist USA, foreign powers couldn't keep their hands off Vietnam. There are epic tales of occupation, resistance and the home-grown heroes of ancient Hanoi, imperial Hue and entrepreneurial Ho Chi Minh City.

Dunes & Tunes

Vietnam has a voluptuous coastline and a young, sociable vibe in the old R&R haunt of Nha Trang and towering dunes of Mui Ne (to name but two).

Nuoc Mam to You

Vietnam's cuisine is a legend thanks to the zesty dishes of the humid south and the hearty soups of the north. Colonialism's legacy bestowed feisty cups of coffee and crusty baguettes.

p812

On the
Road

Brunei Darussalam

☏ 673 / POP 420,000

Best Places to Eat

➡ Tamu Selera (p62)

➡ Tamu Kianggeh (p62)

➡ Pasar Malam Gadong (p62)

Best Architecture

➡ Kampong Ayer (p59)

➡ Jame'Asr Hassanil Bolkiah Mosque (p59)

➡ Omar Ali Saifuddien Mosque (p59)

Why Go?

The tiny sultanate of Brunei, last remnant of a naval empire that once ruled all of Borneo and much of the Philippines, is best known for its oil wealth. This quiet *darussalam* (Arabic for 'abode of peace') has the largest oilfields in Southeast Asia, and thanks to the money they've generated, Brunei hasn't turned its rainforests into oil palm plantations. Old-growth greenery abounds, especially in verdant Ulu Temburong National Park.

The citizens of the capital, Bandar Seri Begawan (BSB), are mad for food and shopping (booze is banned). Here magnificent mosques contrast with the charmingly haphazard water village, while the nearby mangrove forest is home to proboscis monkeys and crocodiles. This tranquil (sometimes somnolent) nation is the realisation of a particular vision: a strict, socially controlled religious state where happiness is found in pious worship and mass consumption. Visit and judge the results for yourself.

When to Go
Bandar Seri Begawan

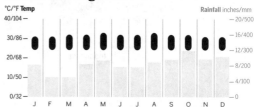

Feb–Mar These are the driest months. National Day is celebrated on 23 February.

Jun The biggest holiday of the year is for Hari Raya Aidil (6 July 2016, 26 June 2017, 15 June 2018).

Jul It's *hot*. The sultan's birthday (15 July) is marked with festivities.

Don't Miss

Spending time surrounded by the rustling, buzzing, chirping rainforests of Ulu Temburong National Park is one of the highlights of a visit to Brunei Darussalam – and the journey there is part of the adventure. After whizzing along palm-lined waterways on a speedboat from BSB, you board a *temuai* (shallow-draft Iban longboat), dodging submerged boulders and hanging vines as you make your way upriver. A steep, slippery climb through virgin jungle takes you to a towering wall of scaffolding: the park's famous canopy walk. Held steady by guy wires, the structure creaks as you make your way up into the jungle canopy for breathtaking views across the virgin rainforest.

ITINERARIES

Two Days
Spend your first day exploring BSB: visit the water village of Kampong Ayer in the morning then explore central BSB, including the splendid Omar Ali Saifuddien Mosque and the Royal Regalia Museum. Take a water-taxi excursion at sunset before checking out the night market in Gadong. Spend your second day on a tour of Ulu Temburong National Park.

Five Days
Take a second day in BSB, visiting the Brunei Museum and more excellent food stalls, followed by a day soaking up the gilded atmosphere of the Empire Hotel & Country Club or diving Brunei's reefs and wrecks. Allow two days for Ulu Temburong, staying overnight in the jungle and doing the canopy walk at dawn.

Essential Food & Drink

Ambuyat This gelatinous porridge-like goo made from the ground pith of the sago tree and dipped in spicy sauces is Brunei's unofficial national dish.

Kueh Garishly coloured and fiendishly sweet local cakes are sold at markets and street stalls.

Ayam Penyet A classic Indonesian dish of fried then smashed chicken served with sambal; it is popular in Brunei.

Teh Tarik Tea and condensed milk poured into the cup from a height; a spectacle not to be missed.

AT A GLANCE

BRUNEI DARUSSALAM

Currencies Brunei dollar (B$), Singapore dollar (S$)

Language Bahasa Malaysia, English

Money ATMs easy to find in towns, but not in Temburong District

Visas Granted on arrival to most nationalities. Free for most nationalities, except Australians.

Mobile phones Prepay local SIM B$30

Fast Facts

Area 5765 sq km

Capital Bandar Seri Begawan (BSB)

Emergency Ambulance 991, police 993, fire 995

Exchange Rates

Australia	A$1	B$1.00
Euro	€1	B$1.54
Malaysia	RM10	B$3.26
Singapore	S$1	B$1.00
UK	UK£1	B$2.16
USA	US$1	B$1.40

Daily Costs

Dorm bed B$10–25

Food-stall meal from B$1

Museum admission free

Coffee B$3–4

Entering the Country

Daily buses link Sabah (KK) and Sarawak (Miri) with BSB. Ferries connect Pulau Labuan with Brunei (Muara).

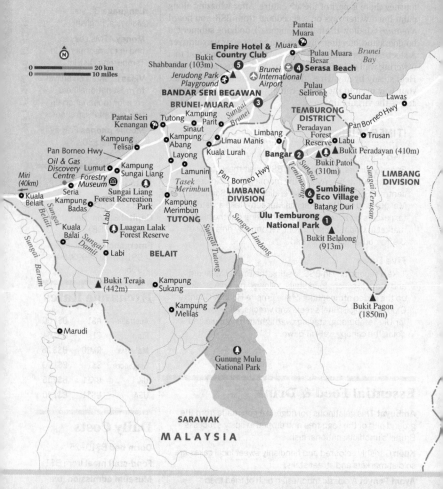

Brunei Darussalam Highlights

1 Climbing high into the rainforest canopy and swimming in a cool jungle river at **Ulu Temburong National Park** (p64).

2 Tearing along mangrove-lined waterways on a **speedboat** (p64) from Bandar Seri Begawan to Bangar.

3 Taking a water taxi to the water village of Kampong Ayer and gorging on the culinary delights of **Bandar Seri Begawan** (p59).

4 Exploring the reefs and wrecks of Brunei's unspoilt dive sites off **Serasa beach** (p61).

5 Enjoying the extravagance of the **Empire Hotel & Country Club** (p62) and cooling off in the pool.

6 Relaxing amid rural greenery at **Sumbiling Eco Village** (p65) in Temburong District.

BANDAR SERI BEGAWAN

POP 241,000

Cities built on oil money tend to be flashy places, but with the exception of a palace you usually can't enter, a couple of enormous mosques and one wedding cake of a hotel, Bandar (as the capital is known, or just BSB) is a fairly understated place. Urban life pretty much revolves around mosques, malls and restaurants, but BSB does have a few museums, the biggest water village in the world and some great food stalls.

◉ Sights

◎ Central BSB

★ Kampong Ayer   WATER VILLAGE

Home to around 30,000 people, Kampong Ayer consists of 42 contiguous stilt villages built along the banks of the Sungai Brunei (Brunei River). A century ago, half of Brunei's population lived here, and even today many Bruneians still prefer the lifestyle of the water village to residency on dry land. The village has its own schools, mosques, police stations and fire brigade. To get across the river, just stand somewhere a water taxi can dock and flag one down (the fare is B$1).

**Kampong Ayer Cultural &
Tourism Gallery**   GALLERY

(south bank, Kampong Ayer; ⊙ 9am-5pm Sat-Thu, 9-11.30am & 2.30-5pm Fri) FREE A good place to start a visit to Kampong Ayer – and get acquainted with Brunei's pre-oil culture – is the Cultural & Tourism Gallery, directly across the river from Sungai Kianggeh (the stream at the eastern edge of the city centre). Opened in 2009, this riverfront complex focuses on the history, lifestyle and crafts of the Kampong Ayer people. A square, glass-enclosed viewing tower offers panoramic views of the scene below.

Omar Ali Saifuddien Mosque   MOSQUE

(Jln Stoney; ⊙ interior 8.30am-noon, 1.30-3pm & 4.30-5.30pm Sat-Wed, closed Thu & Fri, exterior compound 8am-8.30pm daily except prayer times) FREE
Completed in 1958, Masjid Omar Ali Saifuddien – named after the 28th Sultan of Brunei (the late father of the current sultan) – is surrounded by an artificial lagoon that serves as a reflecting pool. This being Brunei, the interior is pretty lavish. The floor and walls are made from the finest Italian marble, the chandeliers were crafted in England and the luxurious carpets were flown in from Saudi Arabia. A 3.5-million-piece glass mosaic overlaying real gold leaf covers the main dome.

Royal Regalia Museum   MUSEUM

(Jln Sultan; ⊙ 9am-5pm Sun-Thu, 9-11.30am & 2.30-5pm Fri, 9.45am-5pm Sat, last entry 4.30pm) FREE When called upon to present a gift to the sultan of Brunei, you must inevitably confront the question: what do you give a man who has everything? At this entertaining museum you'll see how heads of state have solved this conundrum (hint: you'll never go wrong with gold and jewels). Family photos and explanatory texts offer a good overview of the life of the sultan, who is himself depicted in myriad forms (including a hologram) in a series of portraits.

◎ East of Central BSB

Brunei Museum   MUSEUM

(Jln Kota Batu; ⊙ 9am-5pm Sat-Thu, 9-11.30am & 2.30-5pm Fri, last entry 30min before closing; P) FREE Brunei's national museum, with its Islamic-art gallery, exhibits depicting Brunei's role in Southeast Asian history from the arrival of the Spanish and Portuguese in the 1500s, and natural-history gallery, is a decent place to blow an hour of your time. It is situated 4.5km east of central BSB along the coastal road, at Kota Batu; to get here take the 39 bus. At research time the museum was closed for ongoing renovations.

**Brunei Darussalam Maritime
Museum**   MUSEUM

(Muzium Maritim; Simpang 482, Jln Kota Batu; ⊙ 9.30am-4.30pm Sat-Thu, 9am-noon Fri; P) FREE A gleaming building, ship-like in both style and proportion, houses this interesting museum opened in 2015 at Kota Batu, 4.5km east of the city centre (take the 39 bus). On display are some of the more than 13,000 artefacts excavated from a shipwreck discovered by divers in 1997. The ship is believed to have set sail from China sometime in the late 15th or early 16th centuries before being struck by stormy weather as it approached Brunei.

◎ North & West of Central BSB

**Jame'Asr Hassanil
Bolkiah Mosque**   MOSQUE

(Sultan Hassanal Bolkiah Hwy, Kampung Kiarong; ⊙ 8am-noon, 2-3pm & 5-6pm Mon-Wed & Sat, 10.45am-noon, 2-3pm & 5-6pm Sun, closed Thu & Fri; P) FREE Built in 1992 to celebrate the 25th year of the current sultan's reign, Brunei's largest mosque and its four terrazzo-tiled

Bandar Seri Begawan

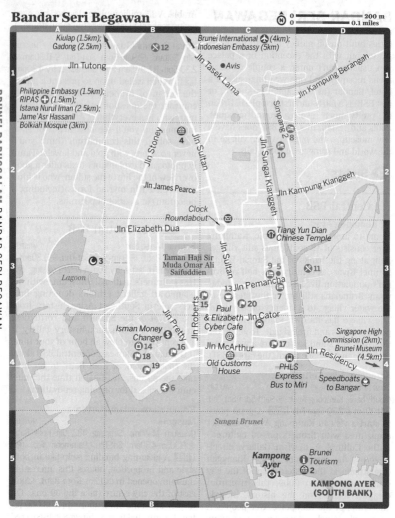

minarets dominate their surroundings. It's impossible to miss as you head towards Gadong, about 3km from the city centre. The number 1 bus goes here.

It's certainly an impressive building; because the sultan is his dynasty's 29th ruler, the complex is adorned with 29 golden domes. At night the mosque is lit up like a gold flame.

Istana Nurul Iman PALACE
(Jln Tutong) Istana Nurul Iman (Palace of the Light of Faith), the official residence of the sultan, is one of the largest habitations of any sort in the world – more than four times the size of the Palace of Versailles (in France).

The palace is open to the public only during the three-day Hari Raya Aidil Fitri festivities at the end of Ramadan. The best way to check it out on the other 362 days of the year is to take a water-taxi cruise.

🏃 Activities

Though it's still relatively new, Brunei's dive scene has the advantage of having some decent dive operators without the downside of crowds. There are several interesting wrecks and plenty of undamaged reef here, including patches that are largely unexplored.

Bandar Seri Begawan

Poni Divers DIVING
(☑ 223 3655; www.ponidivers.com; Seri Qlap Mall, Unit L3/12, Kiulap; 2 fun dives B$150; ⊙9am-5pm) Brunei's largest dive centre offers a full range of PADI certification courses, recreational dives and various water sports including waterskiing and banana boating. Operates from Serasa beach, with a booking office in BSB. Also puts together dive packages including airport transfers and accommodation at the dive centre's homestay.

Water-Taxi Cruise BOATING
(1hr B$30-40) The best way to see BSB's water villages and the sultan's fabled palace, Istana Nurul Iman, is from a water taxi, which can be chartered along the waterfront for about B$30 to B$40 (a bit of negotiating will occur, but at least you know the locals can't claim the petrol is expensive). Finding a boat won't be a problem, as the boatmen will have spotted you before you spot them.

☞ Tours

Borneo Guide TOUR
(☑ 718 7138, 242 6923; www.borneoguide.com; Unit 204, Kiaw Lian Building, Jln Pemancha; ⊙9am-5pm Mon-Thu, 9am-noon & 2-5pm Fri, 9am-1pm Sat & Sun) Excellent service, good prices and a variety of packages around Brunei and Borneo available. A day trip to Ulu Temburong National Park costs B$135 per person from BSB. Also offers overnight trips to Temburong with accommodation at Sumbiling Eco Village (p65) just outside the park (two days and one night from B$185). The office serves as a useful tourism information centre.

🛏 Sleeping

Finding a cheap bed in BSB can be tricky but isn't impossible. Upscale places often offer big online discounts.

Youth Hostel HOSTEL $
(Pusat Belia; ☑ 222 2900, 887 3066; Jln Sungai Kianggeh; dm B$10; ❈ ⊛ ❄) Popular with backpackers, despite the fact that couples can't stay together. The five male and four female sex-segregated dorm rooms with functional furnishings and passable bathrooms are situated at the southern end of the Youth Centre complex, behind the cylindrical staircase. Reception is supposed to be open 7.30am to 4.30pm Monday to Thursday and Saturday, but staffing can be intermittent.

KH Soon Resthouse GUESTHOUSE $
(☑ 222 2052; khsoon-resthouse.tripod.com; 2nd fl, 140 Jln Pemancha; dm B$25, s/d B$40/50, without bathroom B$35/40; ❈) This basic guesthouse, in a converted commercial space with red cement floors, offers budget rooms, huge but spartan rooms, and a central location. The reception-level rooms that share bathrooms (squat toilets only) are probably a better bet than the ones upstairs, which have private facilities positioned awkwardly behind lower than ceiling-height partitions and dodgy-looking electrical wires.

★ Brunei Hotel HOTEL $$
(☑ 224 4828; www.thebruneihotel.com; 95 Jln Pemancha; r/ste incl breakfast B$140-175/240-320; ❈ @ ❄) A chic, dare we say hip, hotel with clean lines, monochromatic colour schemes, geometric patterns and a general up-to-date

SPLURGE

Pharaonic in its proportions and opulence, the 522-room **Empire Hotel & Country Club** (☑241 8888; www.the empirehotel.com; Lebuhraya Muara-Tutong, Jerudong; d B$400-600, ste B$1000-2750, villas B$2200-3500; ❊⊕✿⊠) was commissioned by Prince Jefri at a cost of US$1.1 billion as lodging for guests of the royal family and quickly transformed into an upscale resort. It's worth a visit if only to gawp at the cavernous, glass atrium and US$500,000 lamp made of gold and Baccarat crystal in the lobby. For B$25 you can use the seafront swimming pool complex, and the resort even has its own three-screen **cinema** (☑261 0001; www.timescineplex.com; adult B$4-8, child B$3-8; ⊙11am-2am).

The hotel is 26km northwest of BSB's city centre. To get there, take bus 57 (B$1) from central BSB, or a taxi (B$35 one way).

style that is pretty unexpected in the sultanate. There's a decent breakfast buffet thrown into the deal, served in the downstairs Choices Cafe.

**Capital
Residence Suites** HOTEL $$
(☑222 0067; www.capitalresidencesuites.com; Simpang 2, Kampong Berangan; d/ste incl breakfast B$80/180-280; ❊⊛) This good-value, rather blandly decorated hotel is lifted by friendly, helpful staff and a free shuttle service from 9am to 9pm, which transports guests all around BSB city and to the beaches and attractions beyond. The spacious suites are like small apartments with sofas, a kitchen and washing machine. Standard rooms, though comfortably furnished, are a little cramped.

🍴 Eating

⭐**Tamu Selera** HAWKER $
(cnr Jln Tasek Lama & Jln Stoney; mains B$2-6; ⊙5pm-midnight) At this old-fashioned hawker centre, set in a shady park, diners eat excellent, cheap Malaysian and Indonesian dishes under colourful tarps and ceiling fans. Options include satay, fried chicken, seafood, rice and noodle dishes, and iced drinks. It's 1km north of the waterfront.

Pasar Malam Gadong MARKET $
(Gadong Night Market; Jln Pasar Gadong; ⊙4-10pm) Thanks to its authentic local snacks and dishes, this is Brunei's most popular night market. Unfortunately, it's geared to car-driving locals who take the food away, so there are almost no places to sit. Situated 3km northwest of the city centre. Served by bus 1, but after about 7pm the only way back to town is by taxi (B$15 until 10pm, then B$20).

Tamu Kianggeh HAWKER $
(Kianggeh market; Jln Sungai Kianggeh; mains from B$1; ⊙5am-5pm) The food stalls here serve Brunei's cheapest meals, including *nasi katok* (plain rice, a piece of fried or curried chicken and sambal; B$1) and *nasi lemak* (rice cooked in coconut milk and served with chicken, egg and cucumber slices; also B$1). The market feels endearingly chaotic and messy, something of a rarity in the sultanate.

Aminah Arif BRUNEIAN $$
(☑223 6198; Unit 2-3, Block B, Rahman Bldg, Simpang 88, Kiulap; mains $B4-28; ⊙7am-10pm; ☑) Aminah Arif is synonymous with *ambuyat* (thick, starchy porridge), Brunei's signature dish. If you're up for a generous serving of wiggly white goo, this is a good spot to do so (B$22 for a set meal for two people). Meals can be washed down with iced *kasturi ping* (calamansi lime juice; B$1.50).

🍷 Drinking & Nightlife

A double espresso is the most potent drink you're likely to find in Brunei, as the sale and public consumption of alcohol is banned.

De Royalle Café CAFE
(38 Jln Sultan; ⊙24hr; ☑) With a living-room-style indoor area (complete with leopard-print armchairs) and outdoor pavement tables, this always-open establishment has a supply of perusable English-language newspapers and serves up an international menu (mains B$5.90 to B$15.90) and, of course, freshly brewed coffee. A fine place for a relaxed rendezvous with friends.

🛍 Shopping

The malls of Gadong, Brunei's main shopping district, are about 3km northwest of the city centre. To get there, take bus 1; a cab costs B$15 one way.

Hua Ho Department Store DEPARTMENT STORE
(Yayasan Complex, Jln McArthur; ⊙10am-10pm) A four-floor department store with a decent supermarket on the basement level.

ℹ Information

Banks and international ATMs are sprinkled around the city centre, especially along Jln McArthur and Jln Sultan. The airport has ATMs, too.

Brunei Tourism (☑ 220 0874; www.brunei tourism.travel; Kampong Ayer Cultural & Tourism Gallery; ⊙9am-12.15pm & 1.30-4.30pm Mon-Thu & Sat, 9-11.30am & 2-4.30pm Fri) Free maps, brochures and information about Brunei. The website has oodles of useful information.

Isman Money Changer (Shop G14, ground fl, Block B, Yayasan Complex, Jln Pretty; ⊙10am-8pm) Changes cash. Just off the central atrium.

Main Post Office (cnr Jln Sultan & Jln Elizabeth Dua; ⊙8am-4.30pm Mon-Thu & Sat, 8-11am & 2-4pm Fri) The Stamp Gallery displays some historic first-day covers and blow-ups of colonial-era stamps.

Paul & Elizabeth Cyber Cafe (1st fl, 62 Jln McArthur; per hr B$1.80; ⊙8.30am-8.30pm) Old-style cybercafe with decent connections but a bad soundtrack.

RIPAS Hospital (☑ 224 2424; www.moh.gov. bn; Jln Putera Al-Muhtadee Billah; ⊙24hr) Brunei's main hospital, with fully equipped, modern facilities. Situated about 2km west of the centre (across the Edinburgh Bridge).

ℹ Getting Around

TO/FROM THE AIRPORT
The airport, about 8km north of central BSB, is linked to the city centre, including the bus terminal on Jln Cator, by buses 23, 36 and 38 until about 5.30pm.

A cab to/from the airport costs B$25; pay at the taxi counter. Some hotels offer airport pickup.

BUS
BSB's public bus system is cheap, but buses don't have fixed timetables and routes can be hard to figure out.

Buses (B$1) operate daily from about 6.30am to about 6pm, but after that your options are taking a taxi or hoofing it. Finding stops can be a challenge – some are marked by black-and-white striped uprights or a shelter, others by a yellow triangle painted on the pavement, and yet others by no discernible symbol.

The bus station, on the ground floor of a multi-storey parking complex two blocks north of the waterfront, lacks an information office or a ticket counter, and while the schematic wall map may make sense to BSB natives, it's hard to decipher for the uninitiated. It may be best to ask about transport options at your hostel or hotel before heading out.

CAR
Brunei has Southeast Asia's cheapest fuel – petrol is just B$0.53 a litre and diesel goes for only B$0.31.

Hiring a car is a good way to explore Brunei's hinterland. Prices start at about B$85 a day. Most agencies will bring the car to your hotel and pick it up when you've finished.

Avis (☑ 222 7100; www.avis.com; Radisson Hotel, Jln Tasek Lama 2203; ⊙8am-noon & 1.30-5pm Mon-Thu, 8am-noon & 2-5pm Fri, 8am-noon & 1.30-4pm Sat, 9am-noon &

GETTING TO MALAYSIA

BSB to Miri

Getting to the border Two buses a day link BSB with Miri's Pujut Bus Terminal (B$20, 3½ hours, 7am and 1pm).

At the border Most travellers to Malaysia are granted 30- or 90-day visas on arrival. Border posts are open from 6am to 10pm.

Moving on A taxi from Miri's Pujut Bus Terminal to the city centre (4km) costs RM18.

For information on doing this crossing in the other direction, see p465.

BSB to Pulau Labuan & Kota Kinabalu

Getting to the border One bus a day links BSB with Kota Kinabalu's Jalan Tugu bus station (B$45, eight hours, 8am) via Limbang, Bangar, Lawas and various towns in Sabah. But you can avoid seven border queues and passport stamps by taking a ferry from Muara (20km north of BSB) to Pulau Labuan (B$17, 1½ hours, four a day).

At the border Most travellers to Malaysia are granted 30- or 90-day visas on arrival. Border posts are open from 6am to 10pm.

Moving on From Labuan, twice-daily ferries go to Kota Kinabalu (three hours).

For information on doing this crossing in the other direction, see p449.

1.30-3pm Sun) Also has an office at the **airport** (☑233 3298; ⊗8.30am-5.30pm).

Hertz (☑airport 872 6000; www.hertz.com; Brunei Airport arrival hall; ⊗8am-5pm)

TAXI

Taxis are a convenient, if expensive, way of exploring BSB – if you can find one, that is. There is no centralised taxi dispatcher, and it's nearly impossible to flag one down in the street. Hotels can provide drivers' mobile-phone numbers. Most taxis have yellow tops; a few serving the airport are all white.

BSB's only proper **taxi rank** (Jln Cator) is two blocks north of the waterfront at the bus terminal on Jln Cator. Some taxis use meters, although many drivers will just negotiate a fare with you. Sample daytime fares include Gadong (B$15), Brunei Museum (B$25), Muara (B$40) and the Empire Hotel & Country Club (B$35). Fares go up by 50% after 10pm.

WATER TAXI

If your destination is along Sungai Brunei, water taxis are a good way of getting there. You can hail one anywhere along the BSB waterfront that a boat can dock, as well as along Sungai Kianggeh. Crossing straight across the river costs B$1 per person; diagonal crossings cost more.

TEMBURONG DISTRICT

POP 11,000

This odd little exclave (part of a country physically separated from the rest of the nation) is barely larger than Penang, but happens to contain one of the best preserved tracts of primary rainforest in all of Borneo. The main draw is the brilliant Ulu Temburong National Park, accessible only by longboat.

Bangar

Bangar, a three-street town on the banks of Sungai Temburong, is the gateway to (and administrative centre of) the Temburong district. It can easily be visited as a day trip from BSB.

🛏 Sleeping & Eating

Youth Hostel   HOSTEL **$**
(Pusat Belia; ☑522 1694; Jln Bangar Puni-Ujong, Bangar; dm B$10; ⊗office staffed 7.30am-4.30pm, closed Fri & Sat; ❄) This basic hostel is in a bright-orange building across the road and about 100m downhill from the Bangar ferry terminal. The sex-segregated dorms, each

with six beds (bunks), are clean and have air-con. The office is upstairs.

Food Court   HAWKER **$**
(1st fl, Kompleks Utami Bumiputera; mains B$1-3; ⊗6am or 7am-8pm, closed noon-2pm Fri) Head up the stairs from the small fruit and vegetable market to find half-a-dozen good-value Malay food stalls.

ℹ Information

3 in 1 Services (Shop A1-3, 1st fl, Kompleks Utami Bumiputera; per hr B$1; ⊗8am-5.30pm, closed Sun) Internet access on the 1st floor of the building next to the market (across the pedestrian bridge from the hawker centre).

Bank Islam Brunei Darussalam (⊗8.45am-3.45pm Mon-Thu, 8.45-11am & 2.30-4pm Fri, 8.45-11.15am Sat) The only bank in town's ATM only accepts foreign cards with the Cirrus sign (our Visa card didn't work). Non-account holders cannot change money. On the river 150m north of the bridge.

Chop Hock Guan Minimarket (⊗8am-8pm) Exchanges Malaysian ringgits for Brunei dollars. In the first row of shops to the west of Bangar ferry terminal.

ℹ Getting There & Away

The journey from BSB to Bangar is an exhilarating speedboat ride, though at research time work had begun on a 30km bridge, which will link the districts of Brunei-Muara and Temburong, due to be completed in 2018.

Speedboats (adult B$7, 45 minutes) run from 6am to at least 4.30pm, later on Sunday and holidays. In BSB the dock is on Jln Residency, about 200m east of Sungai Kianggeh. Boats depart at a scheduled time or when full, whichever comes first. Peak-hour departures can be as frequent as every 15 minutes.

The **Jesselton** (☑719 3835, 717 7755, in BSB 718 3838) bus from BSB to Lawas and Kota Kinabalu (B$25) stops in front of Bangar's Youth Hostel sometime around 10am.

Ulu Temburong National Park

Ulu Temburong National Park is in the heart of the pristine rainforests that blanket southern Temburong. Only about 1 sq km of the park is accessible to tourists – in order to protect it for future generations, the rest is off limits to everyone except scientists.

One of the best things about visiting Ulu Temburong is the journey there, travelling upriver in a *tenuai* (shallow-draft Iban longboat) from Batang Duri. The park's main attraction is a delicate aluminium walkway that brings you level with the jungle canopy, up to 60m above the forest floor.

☞ Tours

For all intents and purposes, the only way to visit the park is by booking a tour. BSB-based Borneo Guide (p61) is a good bet.

🛌 Sleeping

★ **Sumbiling Eco Village** CABIN **\$\$**
(☑ 242 6923, 718 7138; www.borneoguide.com/ecovillage; Kampong Sumbiling Lama, Jln Batang Duri; per person incl breakfast & dinner B\$85) ✈ If you're looking for Brunei's version of a jungle camp with basic amenities and a chilled-out atmosphere that encourages slipping into a state of utterly relaxed Zen, come to Sumbiling. This eco-friendly rustic camp in a beautiful riverside location offers tasty Iban cuisine and accommodation in bamboo huts or tents, which have beds, mosquito nets and fans.

UNDERSTAND BRUNEI DARUSSALAM

Brunei Darussalam Today

The implementation of the first of a three-phase process of the introduction of sharia law in Brunei made global headlines in 2014, but more than a year later it has made minimal impact on life in the quiet, law-abiding sultanate. The new penal code applies to both Muslims and non-Muslims and will include corporal punishments for crimes such as theft and adultery.

Brunei's oil and gas wealth affords its citizens one of the highest standards of living in the world, with a GDP per capita of US\$73,200. Literacy stands at 96%, average life expectancy is 77 years, and generous state benefits include free healthcare and education, cheap loans and subsidised housing. It's not surprising that most Bruneians, happy with their lot, prefer not to ponder the question of what will happen when the oil runs out (recent reports suggest that at current rates of extraction it will last only another 20 years).

History

The earliest recorded references to Brunei concern China's trading connections with 'Pu-ni' in the 6th century. Prior to the region's embrace of Islam in the 1400s, Brunei was within the boundaries of the Sumatran Srivijaya empire, then the Majapahit empire of Java. By the late 15th and early 16th centuries, the so-called Golden Age of Sultan Bolkiah (the fifth sultan), Brunei had become a considerable regional power, with its sea-faring rule extending throughout Borneo and deep into the Philippines.

The Spanish and Portuguese arrived in the 16th century and at times confronted the sultanate with force, though in the long term the European powers' disruption of traditional patterns of trade proved more damaging. In the mid- and late 19th century, internal divisions and the policies of Sarawak's first White Rajah, a British adventurer named James Brooke, led to a series of treaties ceding land and power. To save itself, Brunei became a British protectorate in 1888. Despite this, two years later Limbang was lost to Sarawak, dividing the sultanate into two parts.

In 1929 oil was discovered, turning the tiny state into an economic power overnight. The present sultan's father, Sultan Omar Saifuddien, kept Brunei out of both the Federation of Malaya and Malaysia, preferring that his country remain a British protectorate – and that oil revenues stay on home soil.

Saifuddien abdicated in 1967, leaving the throne to his popular son and heir, Sultan Hassanal Bolkiah. In 1984 he reluctantly led his tightly ruled country to complete independence from Britain and later adopted a national ideology known as Melayu Islam

Beraja (MIB; Malay Islamic Monarchy), which stresses Malay culture, Islam (the official religion) and the legitimacy of the sultan.

People & Culture

Ethnic Malays make up two-thirds of the sultanate's 420,000 inhabitants, people of Chinese heritage account for 10%, and Iban, Kelabit and other Dayak groups constitute around 3.4%. Temporary workers make up the rest. The state religion is Islam.

Traditional crafts have almost disappeared in modern Brunei. In its heyday, Brunei produced brassware – gongs, kettles, betel containers and, most famously, ceremonial cannons – that was prized throughout Borneo and beyond. *Jong sarat* sarongs, handwoven using gold thread, are still worn at formal ceremonial occasions.

Environment

Brunei (5765 sq km) consists of two non-contiguous areas separated by Sarawak's Limbang Division. The larger, western part of the country includes the main towns: Bandar Seri Begawan (BSB), the oil town of Seria and the commercial centre of Kuala Belait. The eastern sliver of Brunei, the hilly, mostly forested Temburong District, is much less developed.

SURVIVAL GUIDE

ⓘ Directory A–Z

ACCOMMODATION
The following price ranges refer to a double room with bathroom.

$ less than B$60 (US$40)
$$ B$60–150 (US$40–100)
$$$ more than B$150 (US$100)

ELECTRICITY
Brunei uses 240V, 50Hz AC electricity; power outlets have three flat sockets.

EMBASSIES & CONSULATES
Australian High Commission (☑222 9435; Level 6, Dar Takaful IBB Utama, Jln Pemancha)
British High Commission (☑222 2231; Unit 2.01, 2nd fl, Block D, Yayasan Complex, Jln Pretty)

Canadian High Commission (☑222 0043; www.brunei.gc.ca; 5th fl, Jalan McArthur Bldg, 1 Jln McArthur)
French Embassy (☑222 0960; www.ambafrance-bn.org; 51-55, 3rd fl, Kompleks Jalan Sultan, Jln Sultan)
German Embassy (☑222 5547; www.bandar-seri-begawan.diplo.de; Unit 2.01, 2nd fl, Block A, Yayasan Complex, Jln Pretty)
Indonesian Embassy (☑233 0180; www.kemlu.go.id/bandarseribegawan; Lot 4498, Simpang 528, Jln Muara, Kampung Sungai Hanching)
Malaysian Embassy (☑238 1095-7; www.kln.gov.my/web/brn_begawan; No 61, Simpang 336, Jln Kebangsaan)
New Zealand Consulate (☑222 5880/2422; www.mfat.govt.nz; c/o Deloitte & Touche, 5th fl, Wisma Hajjah Fatimah, 22-23 Jln Sultan) Honorary consul.
Philippine Embassy (☑224 1465/6; www.philippine-embassybrunei.com; Simpang 336-17, Diplomatic Enclave, Jln Kebangsaan)
Singapore High Commission (☑226 2741; www.mfa.gov.sg/brunei; No 8, Simpang 74, Jln Subok)
US Embassy (☑238 4616; http://brunei.us embassy.gov; Simpang 336-52-16-9, Jln Duta) About 5km northeast of downtown BSB.

FOOD
Brunei's cuisine is similar to Malay food, but with some local specialities. Market stalls serve cheap meals.

The following price ranges refer to the cost of the cheapest nonvegetarian main dish on the menu.

$ less than B$6 (US$4)
$$ B$6–16 (US$4–11)
$$$ more than B$16 (US$11)

INTERNET ACCESS
All hotels have internet connections, as do many restaurants and cafes. BSB has a number of internet cafes.

LEGAL MATTERS
There are severe penalties for drug offences in Brunei, including the death penalty.

The sale and public consumption of alcohol is forbidden. Non-Muslim visitors over 17 are allowed to import 12 cans of beer and two bottles of wine or spirits for personal consumption.

During Ramadan, eating, drinking and smoking in public is prohibited for Muslims and non-Muslims alike.

LGBT TRAVELLERS
Homosexual activity is illegal in Brunei.

DRESSING FOR BRUNEI

Bruneians are quite conservative when it comes to what they wear. There is no need for women to cover their hair, but clothing that comes below the shoulders and knees is generally a good idea for both women and men.

MEDIA

The *Borneo Bulletin* (www.borneobulletin.com.bn) and the *Brunei Times* (www.bt.com.bn) cover local and international news, none of it controversial.

MONEY

Brunei dollars (B$ or BND) and Singapore dollars (S$ or SGD) are legal tender and accepted virtually everywhere.

OPENING HOURS

All offices, businesses and shops – including restaurants and food stalls – are required to close from noon to 2pm on Friday, when Muslims go to the mosque to pray. During Ramadan, business hours are shortened. Restaurants and cafes are prohibited from serving eat-in food during fast hours, even to non-Muslims. Standard hours at other times are as follows:

Banks 8.45am to 3.30pm or 4pm Monday to Friday, 8.45am to 11am on Saturday.

Government offices 7.45am to 12.15pm and 1.30pm to 4.30pm Monday to Thursday and Saturday.

Shops 10am to 6pm. Shopping malls generally 10am to 10pm.

TELEPHONE

Prepaid SIM cards (B$30, including B$5 credit) are available at DST stores (www.dst-group.com). Bring your passport.

TOURIST INFORMATION

Brunei Tourism (p63) has an office at the Kampong Ayer Cultural & Tourism Gallery and a useful website.

VISAS

Travellers from the US, the European Union, Switzerland and Norway are granted a 90-day visa-free stay; travellers from New Zealand receive 30 days; Japanese and Canadians get 14 free days.

Australians receive on-arrival visas but have to pay: B$20/30 for a single-/multiple-entry visa and B$5 for a transit visa. Israeli travellers are not permitted to enter Brunei.

WOMEN TRAVELLERS

Women are rarely hassled, and report being able to converse freely with both women and men. Some Muslim women do not shake hands with men.

❶ Getting There & Away

Brunei is an easy stopover if you are travelling between the Malaysian states of Sabah and Sarawak.

AIR

Brunei International Airport (☑233 1747; www.civil-aviation.gov.bn) is about 8km north of central BSB. There are flights with AirAsia (to Kuala Lumpur), Cebu Pacific Air (to Manila), Royal Brunei Airlines (to London, Dubai, Hong Kong, Shanghai, Bangkok, Manila, Melbourne, Singapore, Surabaya, Jakarta and KL) and Singapore Airlines (to Singapore).

BOAT

Passenger ferries from the Terminal Feri Serasa in Muara, about 20km northeast of BSB, to Pulau Labuan (B$17, 1¼ to 1¾ hours) are at 7.45am, 8.30am, 1pm and 4.40pm. There are two ferries a day from Labuan to Kota Kinabalu (three hours).

To get from the bus station in central BSB to the ferry terminal in Muara, you can take bus 38 (one hour) to Muara town and then bus 33. Leave *plenty* of time. A taxi should cost B$40.

BUS

Jesselton Express (☑016-830 0722, 0060 88 751722; www.sipitangexpress.com.my) sends a bus to Kota Kinabalu (B$45, eight hours), via Limbang, Bangar and Lawas, daily at 8am. In the other direction, the bus leaves Kota Kinabalu's Jalan Tugu Bus Station at 8am. Reservations can be made at www.busonlineticket.com. Make sure your passport has plenty of pages – the trip between BSB and Sabah will add eight stamps.

PHLS Express (☑277 1668) links BSB with Miri (B$20 from BSB, RM50 from Miri, 3½ hours) daily at 7am and 1pm; tickets are sold onboard. Departures from Miri's Pujut Bus Terminal, where ticketing is handled by Bintang Jaya, are at about 8.15am and 3.45pm. Booking ahead is not necessary.

Another option for travel between BSB and Miri is to go by private transfer (B$25 or RM70 per person, three hours). To reserve, contact **Mr Foo** on ☑013-833 2231 (Malaysian mobile) or ☑878 2521 (Brunei mobile). Departures from BSB are usually at 1pm or 2pm; departures from Miri are generally at 9am or 10am.

Cambodia

📞 855 / POP 16 MILLION

Best Temples

➡ Angkor Wat (p101)
➡ Bayon (p103)
➡ Ta Prohm (p104)
➡ Banteay Srei (p104)
➡ Prasat Preah Vihear (p112)

Best Places for Culture

➡ Temples of Angkor (p94)
➡ Kampot Province (p124)
➡ Mondulkiri Province (p136)
➡ Battambang (p106)
➡ National Museum of Cambodia (p72)

Why Go?

Ascend to the realm of the gods at Angkor Wat, a spectacular fusion of spirituality, symbolism and symmetry. Descend into the darkness of Tuol Sleng to witness the crimes of the Khmer Rouge. This is Cambodia, a country with a history both inspiring and depressing, a captivating destination that casts a spell on all those who visit.

Fringed by beautiful beaches and tropical islands, sustained by the mother waters of the Mekong River and cloaked in some of the region's few remaining emerald wildernesses, Cambodia is an adventure as much as a holiday. This is the warm heart of Southeast Asia, with everything the region has to offer packed into one bite-sized chunk.

Despite the headline attractions, Cambodia's greatest treasure is its people. The Khmers have been to hell and back, but thanks to an unbreakable spirit and infectious optimism they have prevailed with their smiles and spirits largely intact.

When to Go
Phnom Penh

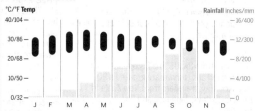

Nov–Feb The best all-round time to visit with relatively cool climes.

Mar–Jun Khmer New Year falls in mid-April and the mercury regularly hits 40°C.

Jul–Oct Green season: rice paddies shimmer, clouds bring some relief and prices plummet.

Don't Miss

Cambodia's nightlife is the stuff of legend. While other cities in the region tuck themselves into bed for the night, thanks to curfews and closing times, Phnom Penh and Siem Reap rumble on from dusk till dawn. Phnom Penh has a vibrant bar and club culture. The riverfront area is a good hunting ground for bars, but as the night wears on it's time to try other haunts such as St 51, home to Pontoon and the Heart of Darkness.

Up in sublime Siem Reap, one street boasts so many bars it's earned itself the moniker 'Pub St'. There is no easier place for a crawl in the region and draught beer is almost a give-away at US$0.50 a glass. Try alternative backpacker bars Angkor What? or Charlie's, or something a little more refined such as Laundry Bar or Asana.

ITINERARIES

One Week

Soak up the sights, sounds and smells of Phnom Penh, Cambodia's dynamic and fast-changing capital. Travel by road to Siem Reap, gateway to the majestic temples of Angkor, passing by the pre-Angkorian temples of Sambor Prei Kuk or taking a longer detour via the charming colonial-era city of Battambang. Explore Angkor in depth, as nowhere does temples quite like Cambodia.

Two Weeks

After exploring Phnom Penh and Siem Reap for a week, hit the provinces. Those heading to Thailand should head south to Cambodia's up-and-coming coastline. Soak up the languid charms of Kampot and Kep, then head to Sihanoukville, where dreamy islands lurk offshore. Try some adrenaline adventures around Koh Kong before exiting the country. Laos- or Vietnam-bound travellers can easily spend a week in the wild east, trekking in Ratanakiri or Mondulkiri and tracking rare Irrawaddy dolphins on the Mekong River around Kratie or Stung Treng.

Essential Adventures

Chi Phat Mountain biking, trekking, kayaking, birdwatching – it's all here at this pioneering ecotourism project.

Mekong Discovery Trail Kayak with rare Irrawaddy dolphins then continue down the Mekong amid enchanting flooded forests.

Veun Sai-Siem Pang Conservation Area Trek deep into the jungle to observe rare gibbons in their element in Ratanakiri.

Koh Kong Island Beachcomb the deserted sands and shores of this tropical island near the city of the same name.

Mondulkiri Province Walk with elephants, quad-bike to jungle viewpoints, and zipline over the Bou Sraa Waterfall in this adventure centre.

AT A GLANCE

Currency Riel (r)

Language Khmer

Money ATMs common in major cities

Visas Available on arrival for most nationalities

Mobile phones Prepaid SIM cards are cheap, but you need a passport to register

Fast Facts

Area 181,035 sq km

Capital Phnom Penh

Emergency Police ☎117

Exchange Rates

Australia	A$1	3580r
Euro	€1	5440r
Thailand	10B	1220r
UK	UK£1	6595r
USA	US$1	3960r
Vietnam	10,000d	1880r

Daily Costs

Budget guesthouse room US$4–10

Local restaurant meal US$1.50–5

Draught beer in backpacker bar US$0.50–1.50

Moto ride US$0.50–1

Entering the Country

Fly into Phnom Penh or Siem Reap. Land borders with Laos, Thailand and Vietnam.

Cambodia Highlights

1 Discovering the eighth wonder of the world, the **temples of Angkor** (p94).

2 Enjoying the 'Pearl of Asia', **Phnom Penh** (p72), with its impressive museums, a sublime riverside setting and happening nightlife.

3 Island-hopping around the **Southern Islands** (p122), Cambodia's next big thing.

4 Delving into the lush **Battambang** (p106) countryside, climbing hilltop temples, exploring caves and riding the 'Bamboo Train'.

5 Exploring wild **Mondulkiri** (p136), a land of rolling hills, thundering waterfalls, indigenous minorities and adrenaline activities.

6 Slipping into the soporific pace of riverside **Kampot** (p124), with French-era architecture, cave temples and pepper plantations.

7 Making a pilgrimage to the awe-inspiring mountain temple of **Prasat Preah Vihear** (p112).

8 Exploring the bucolic Mekong islands and dolphin pools around **Kratie** (p130) by bicycle and boat.

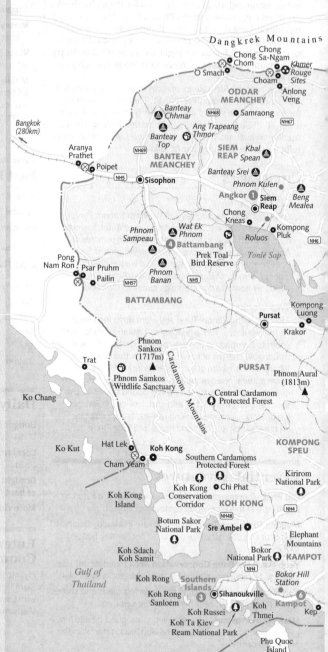

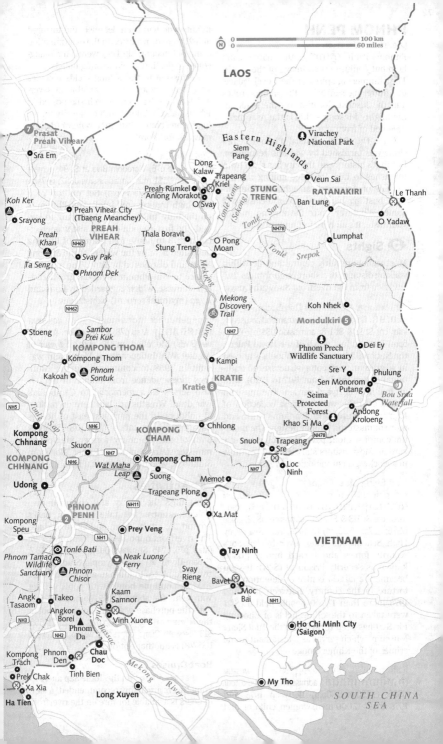

PHNOM PENH

🎵 023 / POP 2 MILLION

Phnom Penh (ភ្នំពេញ): the name can't help but conjure up an image of the exotic. The glimmering spires of the Royal Palace, the fluttering saffron of the monks' robes and the luscious location on the banks of the mighty Mekong – this is the Asia many dreamed of from afar.

Once the 'Pearl of Asia', Phnom Penh's shine was tarnished by war and revolution. But that's history and the city has risen from the ashes to take its place among the hip capitals of Asia, with an alluring cafe culture, bustling bars and a world-class food scene. Whatever your flavour, no matter your taste, it's all here in Phnom Penh.

💿 Sights

Most sights are fairly central and lie within walking distance or a short *remork-moto (tuk tuk)* ride from the riverfront Sisowath Quay.

★ **National Museum of Cambodia** MUSEUM
(សារមន្ទីរជាតិ; Map p76; www.cambodiamuseum. info; cnr St 13 & St 178; admission US$5; ⊗8am-5pm) Located just north of the Royal Palace, the National Museum of Cambodia is housed in a graceful terracotta structure of traditional design (built from 1917 to 1920), with an inviting courtyard garden. The museum is home to the world's finest collection of Khmer sculpture – a millennium's worth and more of masterful Khmer design. The museum comprises four pavilions, facing a pretty garden. Most visitors start left and continue in a clockwise, chronological direction.

Tuol Sleng Museum of Genocidal Crimes MUSEUM
(សារមន្ទីរប្រល័យពូជសាសន៍ទួលស្លែង; Map p78; cnr St 113 & St 350; admission US$2, guide US$6; ⊗7am-5.30pm) In 1975, Tuol Svay Prey High School was taken over by Pol Pot's security forces and turned into a prison known as Security Prison 21 (S-21); it soon became the largest centre of detention and torture in the country. Between 1975 and 1978 more than 17,000 people held at S-21 were taken to the killing fields of Choeung Ek. S-21 has been turned into the Tuol Sleng Museum, which serves as a testament to the crimes of the Khmer Rouge.

Killing Fields of Choeung Ek MUSEUM
(វាលពិឃាតជើងឯក; admission incl audio tour US$6; ⊗7.30am-5.30pm) Between 1975 and 1978 about 17,000 men, women, children and infants who had been detained and tortured at S-21 were transported to the extermination camp of Choeung Ek. They were often bludgeoned to death to avoid wasting bullets.

Admission to the Killing Fields includes an excellent audio tour, available in several languages. The site is well signposted in English about 7.5km south of the city limits. Figure on about US$10 for a *remork* (drivers may ask for more).

Wat Phnom BUDDHIST TEMPLE
(វត្តភ្នំ; Map p76; Norodom Blvd at St 94; temple admission US$1, museum admission US$2; ⊗7am-6.30pm, museum 7am-6pm) Set on top of a 27m-high tree-covered knoll, Wat Phnom is on the only 'hill' in town. According to legend, the first pagoda on this site was erected in 1373 to house four statues of Buddha deposited here by the waters of the Mekong River and discovered by Penh. The main entrance to Wat Phnom is via the grand eastern staircase, which is guarded by lions and *naga* (mythical serpent) balustrades.

Independence Monument MONUMENT
(វិមានឯករាជ្យ; Map p78; cnr Norodom & Sihanouk Blvds) Modelled on the central tower of Angkor Wat, Independence Monument was built in 1958 to commemorate the country's independence from France in 1953. It also serves as a memorial to Cambodia's war dead. Wreaths are laid here on national holidays. In the park just east of here is an impressive **statue** (Map p78; Sihanouk Blvd) of the legendary former king/prime minister/statesman King Father Norodom Sihanouk, who died a national hero in 2012.

🏃 Activities

Don't miss the quirky and colourful **aerobics** sessions that take place in parks around the city at dawn and again at dusk. The riverfront opposite **Blue Pumpkin** cafe (Map p76; 245 Sisowath Quay; mains US$3-7; ⊗6am-11pm; 📶) and Olympic Stadium are two good places to jump in and join the fun.

Most boutique hotels with pools will let you **swim** for about US$5, sometimes free with the purchase of food. The great pool at the **Himawari Hotel** (Map p78; 🎵023-214555; 313 Sisowath Quay; admission weekday/weekend US$7/8) is another option.

Boat Cruises

Sunset boat trips on the Tonlé Sap and Mekong Rivers are highly recommended. A slew of boats is available for hire on the riverfront

Phnom Penh

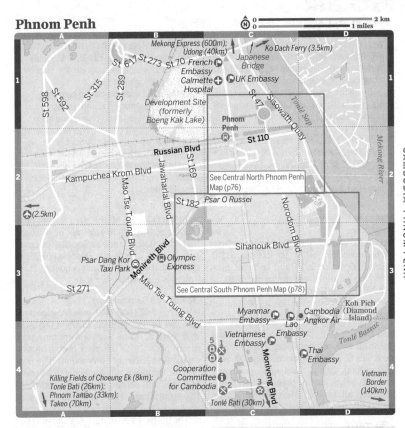

about 500m north of the tourist boat dock. Arrange one on the spot for around US$20 an hour, depending on negotiations and numbers. Bring your own drinks.

Public river cruises are another option. They leave every 30 minutes from 5pm to 7.30pm from the **tourist boat dock** (Map p76; 93 Sisowath Quay) and last about 45 minutes (US$5 per head).

Cooking Classes

Cambodia Cooking Class   COOKING COURSE (Map p78; ☎ 012 524801; www.cambodia-cooking-class.com; booking office 67 St 240; half/full day US$15/23) Learn the art of Khmer cuisine through Frizz Restaurant. Classes are held near the Russian embassy. Reserve ahead.

Cycling

Vicious Cycle   CYCLING (Map p76; ☎ 012 430622; www.grasshopper adventures.com; 23 St 144; road/mountain bike

Phnom Penh

⊗ Eating
1 Café Yejj	C4
2 Super Duper	C4

⊕ Entertainment
3 Sovanna Phum Arts Association	C4

⊟ Shopping
Rajana	(see 1)
4 Rajana	C4
5 Russian Market	C4

per day US$4/8) Plenty of excellent mountain and other bikes available here. Kiddie seats can be attached to your mountain bike for US$3.

Vicious represents well-respected Grasshopper Adventures in Phnom Penh.

ROYAL PALACE

With its classic Khmer roofs and ornate gilding, the **Royal Palace** (ព្រះបរមរាជវាំង; Map p76; Sothearos Blvd; admission incl camera 25,000r, guide per hr US$10; ⊙7.30-11am & 2-5pm) dominates the diminutive skyline of Phnom Penh. It's a striking structure near the riverfront, bearing a remarkable likeness to its counterpart in Bangkok.

Being the official residence of King Sihamoni, parts of the massive palace compound are closed to the public. Visitors are allowed to visit only the throne hall and a clutch of buildings surrounding it. Adjacent to the palace, the Silver Pagoda complex is also open to the public.

From the palace compound you enter the **Silver Pagoda complex** through its north gate. The Silver Pagoda was so named in honour of the floor, which is covered with more than 5000 silver tiles weighing 1kg each, adding up to five tonnes of gleaming silver. You can sneak a peek at some near the entrance – most are covered for their protection. It is also known as Wat Preah Keo (Pagoda of the Emerald Buddha)

Massage

Daughters
SPA

(Map p76; ☑077 657678; www.daughtersof cambodia.org; 65 St 178; 1hr foot spa US$10; ⊙9am-5.30pm Mon-Sat) Hand and foot massages are administered by participants in this NGO's vocational training program for at-risk women. Shorter (15- to 30-minute) treatments also available.

Nail Bar
MASSAGE

(Map p76; www.mithsamlanh.org; Friends n' Stuff store, 215 St 13; 30/60min massages US$4/7; ⊙11am-9pm) Cheap manicures, pedicures, foot massages, hand massages and nail painting, all to help Mith Samlanh train street children in a new vocation.

☞ Tours

Cyclo Centre
TOUR

(Map p76; ☑097 700 9762; www.cyclo.org.kh; 95 St 158; per hour/day from US$3/12) Dedicated to supporting *cyclo* (bicycle rickshaw) drivers in Phnom Penh, these tours are a great way to see the sights. Themed trips such as pub crawls or cultural tours are also available.

🛏 Sleeping

Phnom Penh's traditional backpacker area around Boeng Kak ('The Lake') all but died when the lake was filled in with sand in 2011. Several mini Khao San Rd backpacker colonies have emerged in its wake, with additional options scattered around the centre. St 172 between St 19 and St 13 has emerged as the most popular area for budget accommodation. For walk-in guests, this is a great area to target. South of St 172 and closer to the river, St 258 has a clutch of budget guesthouses.

In the O Russei Market area west of busy Monivong Blvd there is a mix of discount high-rise hotels and backpacker-oriented guesthouses. The trendy Boeng Keng Kang (BKK) district south of Independence Monument is the flashpacker zone.

★ Eighty8 Backpackers
HOSTEL $

(Map p76; ☑023-500 2440; www.88backpackers. com; 98 St 88; dm US$5.25-7.75, r US$18-26; ❄@🛜🏊) A hostel with a swimming pool means party time – this place hosts a big one on the first Friday of every month. The pool and the extensive villa are home to a variety of dorms and private rooms. The courtyard has a central bar, with a pool table and plenty of spots to lounge around the pool.

The dorms come in air-con and fan varieties, plus a female dorm.

★ Mad Monkey
HOSTEL $

(Map p78; ☑023-987091; www.phnompenhhos tels.com; 26 St 302; dm US$4-7, r from US$14-30; ❄@🛜) This colourful and vibrant hostel is justifiably popular. The spacious dorms have air-con and sleep six to 20; the smaller ones have double-width bunk beds that can sleep two. The private rooms are swish for the price but lack TVs and, often, windows. The rooftop bar above quiet St 302 serves free beer on Mondays from 6pm to 8pm.

Top Banana Guesthouse
HOSTEL $

(Map p78; ☑012 885572; www.topbanana.biz; 9 St 278; dm US$5, r US$8-18; ❄@🛜) Fifteen years on, a facelift has greatly improved the rooms and there are some dorms available, including a four-bed female dorm. The main draw is the strategic location overlooking Wat Langka and Golden St, plus the open-air chill-out area. Book way ahead. **One Up**

Banana Hotel (Map p78; ☑023-211344; www.1uphotelcambodia.com; Z9-132 St 51; s/d from US$33/39; ❄@🔊) is its nearby flashpacker upgrade.

Narin Guesthouse GUESTHOUSE $
(Map p78; ☑099 881133; www.naringuesthouse.com; 50 St 125; r with fan/air-con US$12/17; ❄@🔊) One of the stalwarts of the Phnom Penh guesthouse scene (we first stayed here back in 1995). Rooms are smart, bathrooms smarter still and the price is right. There is a super-relaxed, open-air restaurant-terrace where you can take some time out.

Blue Dog Guesthouse HOSTEL $
(Map p78; ☑012 658075; bluedogguesthouse@gmail.com; 13 St 51; dm US$5-6, r US$9-22; @🔊) The location and price are right, plus there's a cosy common area and a popular bar downstairs, so you won't end up spending too much time in the clean but basic rooms. Mains at the bar-restaurant include a free drink.

White Rabbit HOSTEL $
(Map p78; ☑023-223170; www.whiterabbitguesthouse.com; 40A St 294; dm with fan/air-con from US$3/5, r US$6-15; ❄🔊) This convivial hostel is a hidden gem, with an attractive ground-level bar and hang-out area with a thousand movies or Sony PS3 games on a big screen. The private rooms are good value, but most opt for the comfortable dorms with clean bathrooms and wide bunk beds.

Velkommen Backpackers GUESTHOUSE $
(Map p76; ☑077 757701; www.velkommenbackpackers.com; 17 St 144; dm US$5, r US$8-30; ❄🔊) The popular Velkommen has been looking after travellers for the better part of a decade now. Dorms are air-conditioned and rooms come in a pick-and-mix of shapes and sizes. There is a bar-restaurant downstairs and lots of useful travel info. Directly across the road is the **Velkommen Guesthouse** (Map p76; ☑077 757701; www.velkommenguesthouse.com; 18 St 144; r US$18-45; ❄🔊), with smarter rooms.

Tat Guesthouse GUESTHOUSE $
(Map p78; ☑012 921211; tatcambodia@yahoo.com; 52 St 125; s without bathroom US$4, r US$7-15; ❄@🔊) A super-friendly spot with a breezy rooftop hang-out that's perfect for chilling. The rooms aren't going to wow you but they are functional. For US$12 you get air-con. It also owns nearby **Tattoo Guesthouse** (Map p78; ☑011 801000; 62A St 125; r US$5-10; ❄🔊), which has smarter rooms.

Sundance Inn & Saloon GUESTHOUSE $$
(Map p76; ☑016 802090; www.sundancecambodia.com; 61 St 172; r US$23-38; ❄@🔊❄) Sundance is a step above the guesthouse pack on St 172 with oversize beds, designer bathrooms, kitchenettes and computers that hook up to flat-screens in every room. With open-mic Mondays, frequent live music, all-day US$1 cocktails and a pool out back, it is quite the party pad. Free airport pickup with 24 hours notice.

Number 9 Guesthouse FLASHPACKER $
(Map p78; ☑023-984999; www.number9hotel.com; 7C St 258; r from US$15; ❄🔊❄) The first of Phnom Penh's old-school backpacker pads to undergo a transformation into a flashpacker hotel, it is still going strong thanks to great rates, a rooftop pool and a lively bar-restaurant. Worth a splash for backpackers who have been exploring rural Cambodia.

🍴 Eating

For foodies, Phnom Penh is a delight, boasting a superb selection of restaurants that showcase the best in Khmer cooking, as well as the greatest hits from all over the globe.

🍴 North Central

Anjali/Karma Cafe CAFE $
(Map p76; 273 Sisowath Quay; mains US$3-6; ☺7am-late) Twin-sister restaurants practically under one roof. The prices are more than reasonable for this part of town. Anjali has some Indian offerings, but otherwise they share an identical menu – pub grub and some Asian highlights.

Sorya Food Court ASIAN $
(Map p76; 11 St 63; 5000-10,000r; ☺9am-9pm) The top-floor food court is a more sanitised way to experience a variety of local fare,

---

SPLURGE

Blue Lime (Map p76; ☑023-222260; www.bluelime.asia; 42 St 19z; r incl breakfast US$50-85; ❄@🔊❄) offers smart, minimalist rooms and a leafy pool area that invites relaxation. The pricier rooms have private plunge pools, four-poster beds and concrete love seats. The cheaper rooms upstairs in the main building are similarly appealing. No children.

Central North Phnom Penh

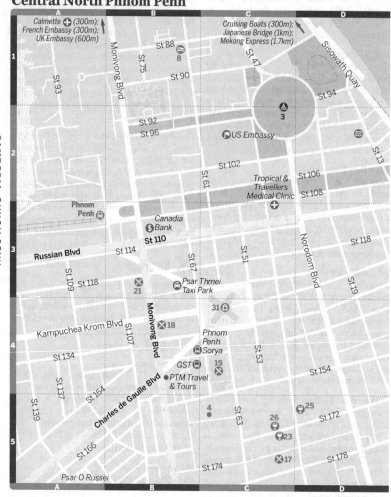

with stalls serving a wide range of affordable Cambodian, Chinese, Vietnamese, Malaysian and Korean dishes. It works on a coupon system.

★ **Boston**   CAMBODIAN **$$**
(Map p76; 54 St 172; mains US$3-10; ⏱7.30am-11pm; 🛜) This sophisticated backpacker cafe is popular with expats and serves a range of Cambodian and international dishes. With enjoyable music, a wine list and some care given to presentation, it's a step above most dining options on the busy St 172 strip. Try the signature beef Wellington.

Happy Herb Pizza   PIZZA **$$**
(Map p76; 📞012 921915; 345 Sisowath Quay; medium pizzas US$6-8.50; ⏱8am-11pm; 🛜) No, happy doesn't mean it comes with free toppings, it means pizza à la ganja. The non-marijuana pizzas are also pretty good, but don't involve the free trip. It's a good place to sip a cheap beer and watch the riverfront action unfold.

Sam Doo Restaurant   CHINESE **$$**
(Map p76; 56-58 Kampuchea Krom Blvd; mains US$2.50-15; ⏱7am-2am) Many Chinese Khmers swear that this upstairs eatery near Central Market has the best Middle King-

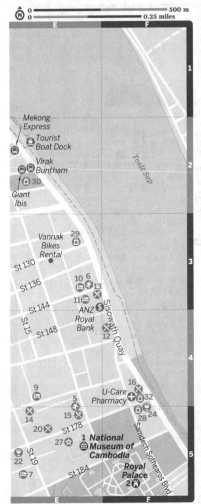

CAMBODIA PHNOM PENH

dom food in town. Choose from its signature Sam Doo fried rice, *trey chamhoy* (steamed fish with soy sauce and ginger), fresh seafood, hotpots and dim sum.

Thai Huot　　　　　　SUPERMARKET $
(Map p76; 103 Monivong Blvd; ⊙7.30am-8.30pm) A good spot for those who wish to self-cater. It's ideal for French travellers who are missing home, as it stocks many French products, including Bonne Maman jam and the city's best cheese selection. Additional location in **BKK** (Map p78; cnr St 63 & St 352; ⊙7.30am-8.30pm).

⟡ South Central

★ **Boat Noodle Restaurant**　　　THAI $
(Map p78; ☏012 774287; 57 Sothearos Blvd; mains US$3-7; ⊙7am-9pm; ☎) Relocated to Sothearos Blvd, this long-running Thai-Khmer restaurant has some of the best-value regional dishes in town. It offers delicious noodle soups and lots of local specialities. In terms of where to sit, you

Central South Phnom Penh

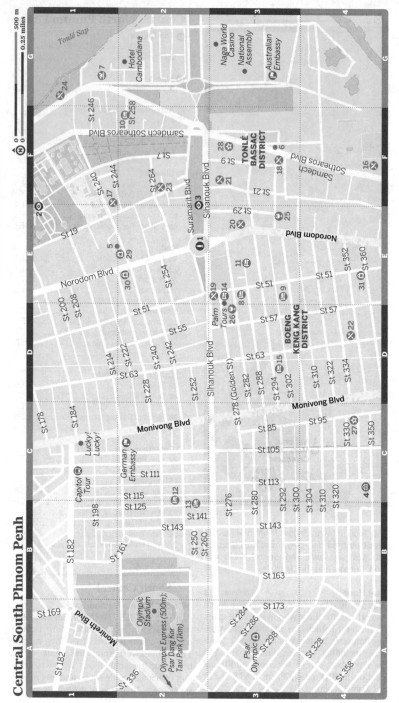

500 m
0.25 miles

Tonlé Sap

Hotel
Cambodiana

Naga World
Casino
National
Assembly
Australian
Embassy

St 246
St 258
St 10
Samdech Sothearos Blvd

St 7
TONLÉ
BASSAC
DISTRICT
St 9
Samdech Sothearos Blvd

St 240
St 244
St 17
St 264
23
Suramarit Blvd
Sihanouk Blvd
St 21

St 19
St 29
Norodom Blvd

St 200
St 208
Norodom Blvd
St 254
St 51
Palm
Tours
St 57
BOENG
KENG KANG
DISTRICT
St 352
St 360
St 51
St 57

St 214
St 222
St 240
St 242
St 55
St 63
St 228
St 282
St 288
St 294
St 302
St 310
St 322
St 334
St 252
Sihanouk Blvd
St 278 (Golden St)
Monivong Blvd

St 178
St 184
Lucky!
Lucky!
German
Embassy
St 111
Monivong Blvd
St 85
St 95
St 330
St 350
St 105

Capitol
Tour
St 115
St 125
St 12
St 13
St 141
St 276
St 280
St 292
St 300
St 304
St 310
St 320
St 113
St 198
St 143
St 250
St 260
St 143

St 182
St 161
St 163

St 169
Monireth Blvd
Olympic
Stadium
Olympic Express (500m);
Psar Dang Kor
Taxi Park (1km)
St 173
St 284
St 286
Psar
Olympic
St 298
St 328
St 358

St 182
St 336

Central South Phnom Penh

can choose from the contemporary but traditionally decorated space at the front or a traditional wooden house behind.

Aeon Mall Food Court   ASIAN $

(Map p78; 132 Sothearos Blvd; US$1-6; ⊙9am-10pm; 🛜) It may be surprising to venture into the country's swankiest mall to find cheap eats, but there are two food courts here covering the best of Asia and beyond. Downstairs is the more local option with noodle soups, fried rice and fresh sushi. Upstairs on Level 2 is the **World Dining Food Court**, with fancier furnishings and live music.

Dosa Corner   INDIAN $

(Map p78; 5E St 51; mains US$1.50-5; ⊙8.30am-2pm & 5-10pm) Fans of Indian dosas will be pleased to discover this place does just what it says on the label – namely, a generous variety of savoury pancakes from the south. Vegetarian thalis (set meals) are US$4.

The Vegetarian   CAMBODIAN, VEGETARIAN $

(Map p78; 158 St 19; mains US$1.75-2.50; ⊙10.30am-8.30pm Mon-Sat; 🖉) This is one of the best-value spots in Phnom Penh. All dishes are US$2.50 or under – and it doesn't skimp on portions either. Noodles and fried rice are the specialities. The leafy setting in a quiet nook off central Sihanouk Blvd is yet another plus.

★Yi Sang   CHINESE $$

(Map p78; Sisowath Quay; US$6-20; ⊙6am-11pm; 🛜) The riverfront location is one of the only places in the city where you can dine right on the riverside, perfect for a relaxing sunset cocktail. The menu here includes a mix of well-presented Cambodian street flavours like *nam ben choc* (rice noodles with curry), plus plenty of dim sum and some international flavours.

ARTillery   CAFE $$

(Map p78; St 240½; mains US$4-6; ⊙7.30am-9pm Tue-Sun, to 5pm Mon; 🛜🖉) Healthy salads, sandwiches, shakes and snacks like hummus and felafel are served in this creative space on an artsy alley off St 240. The menu is mostly vegetarian, and pizza is among the offerings on its small raw-food menu. The daily specials are worth a sample.

✖ Russian Market Area

Café Yejj   CAFE $

(Map p109; www.cafeyejj.com; 170 St 450; mains US$3.50-6; ⊙8am-9pm; 🛜🖉) 🌱 An air-con escape from Russian Market (walk upstairs), this bistro-style cafe uses organic ingredients to prepare pastas, salads and wraps, as well as a few more ambitious dishes such as Moroccan lamb stew and chilli con carne. It also promotes fair trade and responsible employment.

LOCAL FLAVOURS

Khmer Barbecues

After dark, Khmer eateries scattered across town illuminate their Cambodia Beer signs, hailing locals in for grilled strips of meat or seafood and generous jugs of draught beer. Khmer barbecues are literally all over the place, so it won't be hard to find one. Some recommended local eateries:

Sovanna (Map p78; 2C St 21; mains US$2-8; ⊙6-11am & 3-11pm) Always jumping with locals and a smattering of expats who have made this their barbecue of choice thanks to the huge menu. It's as good a place as any to sample the national breakfast, *bei sait chrouk* (pork and rice).

Red Cow (Map p78; 126 Norodom Blvd; mains US$2.50-7; ⊙4-11pm) Grills up everything imaginable – eel, eggplant, frog, pig intestine, quail – along with curries and other traditional Khmer dishes.

Markets

Phnom Penh's many markets all have large central eating areas where stalls serve up local faves like noodle soup and fried noodles during daylight hours. Most dishes cost a reasonable 4000r to 8000r. The best market for eating is Russian Market (p82), with an interior food zone that's easy to find and with a nice variety of Cambodian specialities. Psar Thmei (p82) is another great option with a large food court.

Super Duper SUPERMARKET
(Map p109; www.super-duper.biz; 21 St 488; ⊙24hrs) Phnom Penh's only 24 hour supermarket, this could be very handy if the midnight munchies strike. It has one of the best product ranges in town, as the owners bring in their own containers from the US and Australia.

🍷 Drinking & Nightlife

Phnom Penh has some great bars and clubs and it's definitely worth planning at least one big night on the town. Many venues are clustered around the intersection of St 51 and St 172, where seemingly everybody ends up late at night. 'Golden St' (St 278) is popular and the riverfront also has its share of bars. Another up-and-coming area is St 308 and the adjacent Bassac Lane bar strip. Two-for-one happy hours are a big thing in Phnom Penh, so it pays to get started early.

There are some great hostel bars in Phnom Penh, so keep these in mind if you want to meet other travellers on a big night out. Top Banana (p74) has one of the liveliest rooftop bars. Check out the streetside bar of Blue Dog (p75) or the rooftop bar at Mad Monkey (p74), in the same part of town. Eighty8 Backpackers (p74) has a 'first Friday of the month' party that sees the expat and backpacker worlds collide. Sundance Inn has two lively bars at its two locations on

St 172 (p75) and the riverfront (79 Sisowath Quay).

For the low-down on club nights, check out Phnom Penh Underground (www.phnom-penh-underground.com), an online guide to the club scene.

⭐**FCC** BAR
(Foreign Correspondents' Club; Map p76; 363 Sisowath Quay; ⊙6am-midnight; 🛜) A Phnom Penh institution, the 'F' is housed in a colonial gem with great views and cool breezes. It's one of those must-see places in Cambodia – almost everyone swings by for a drink. Happy hours are 5pm to 7pm and 10pm to midnight. If the main bar is too crowded, head up to the rooftop, which often sees live music at weekends.

⭐**Dusk Till Dawn** BAR
(Map p76; 46 St 172) Also known as Reggae Bar because of the clientele and the music; the rooftop setting makes it a great spot for a sundowner, but the party lasts well into the night. The bar is split over two levels, so continue upstairs if the first level is quiet. Ride the lift to the top floor in the tall building opposite Pontoon Club.

Score BAR
(Map p78; ☑023-221357; www.scorekh.com; 5 St 282; ⊙8am-late; 🛜) With its cinema-sized screen and television banks on every wall, this cavernous bar is the best place to watch

a big game. It's not just the usual footy and rugby – almost all sports are catered for here. Several pool tables tempt those who would rather play than watch.

Red Bar
BAR

(Map p78; cnr St 308 & St 29; ⊙5pm-1am; 🔊) A friendly little local bar in the popular 308 St. The drinks here are so cheap that drinkers find themselves lingering long into the night...or maybe that's just us?

Blue Chili
GAY

(Map p76; 36 St 178; ⊙6pm-late; 🔊) The owner of this long-running, gay-friendly bar stages his own drag show every Friday and Saturday at 10.30pm.

Heart of Darkness
CLUB

(Map p76; www.heartofdarknessclub.com.kh; 26 St 51; ⊙8pm-late) This Phnom Penh institution with an alluring Angkor theme has evolved more into a nightclub than a bar over the years. It goes off every night of the week, attracting all – and we mean *all* – sorts. Everybody should stop in at least once just to bask in the atmosphere of the place.

Pontoon
CLUB

(Map p76; www.pontoonclub.com; 80 St 172; admission weekends US$3-5, weekdays free; ⊙9.30pm-late) After floating around from pier to pier for a few years (hence the name), the city's premier nightclub has finally found a permanent home on terra firma. It draws top local DJs and occasional big foreign acts. Thursday is gay-friendly night, with a 1am lady-boy show. Adjacent **Pontoon Pulse** is more of a lounge-club, with electronica and ambient music.

☆ Entertainment

For news on what's happening in town, *AsiaLife* is a free monthly with entertainment features and some listings. Online, try www.phnompenhweek.com or www.lengpleng.com.

★ Plae Pakaa
PERFORMING ARTS

(Fruitful; Map p76; ☑023-986032; www.cambodianlivingarts.org; National Museum, St 178; adult/child US$15/6; ⊙7pm Mon-Sat Oct-Mar, Fri & Sat May-Sep, closed Apr) Plae Pakaa is a series of must-see performances put on by **Cambodian Living Arts** (CLA; Map p78; ☑017 998570; www.cambodianlivingarts.org; 128 Sothearos Blvd). There are three rotating shows, each lasting about an hour. *Children of Bassac* showcases traditional dance styles. *Passage of Life* depicts the various celebrations and rituals that Khmers go through in their lifetimes (weddings, funerals, etc). *Mak Therng* is a traditional *yike* opera.

★ Meta House
CINEMA

(Map p78; www.meta-house.com; 37 Sothearos Blvd; ⊙4pm-midnight Tue-Sun; 🔊) This German-run cinema screens art-house films, documentaries and shorts from Cambodia and around the world most evenings at 4pm (admission free) and 7pm (admission varies). Films are sometimes followed by Q&As with those involved. Order German sausages, pizza-like 'flamecakes' and beer to supplement your viewing experience.

DINING FOR A CAUSE

These fantastic eateries act as training centres for young staff and help fund worthy causes in the capital.

Romdeng (Map p76; ☑092 219565; 74 St 174; mains US$5-8; ⊙11am-9pm; 🔊) Set in a gorgeous colonial villa with a small pool, Romdeng specialises in Cambodian country fare, including a famous baked-fish *amok*, two-toned pomelo salad and tiger-prawn curry. Sample deep-fried tarantulas or stir-fried tree ants with beef and holy basil if you dare. Part of the Friends' extended family, it is staffed by former street youth and their teachers.

Friends (Map p76; ☑012 802072; www.friends-restaurant.org; 215 St 13; tapas US$4-7, mains from US$6-10; ⊙11am-10.30pm; 🔊) One of Phnom Penh's best-loved restaurants, this place is a must, with tasty tapas bites, heavenly smoothies and creative cocktails. It offers former street children a head start in the hospitality industry.

Sugar 'n Spice Cafe (Map p76; www.daughtersofcambodia.org; 65 St 178; sandwiches US$3.50-7; ⊙9am-6pm Mon-Sat; 🔊) This fantastic cafe on the top floor of the Daughters visitors centre features soups, smoothies, original coffee drinks, cupcakes and fusion-y mains served by former victims of trafficking, who are being trained by Daughters to reintegrate into society.

Flicks
CINEMA

(Map p78; www.theflicks-cambodia.com; 39B St 95; tickets US$3.50; 🎬) Flicks shows at least two movies a day in an uber-comfortable air-conditioned screening room. You can watch both films on one ticket.

Sovanna Phum Arts Association
PERFORMING ARTS

(Map p109; ☎023-987564; www.shadow-puppets.org; 166 St 99, btwn St 484 & St 498; adult/child US$5/3) 🎭 Regular traditional shadow-puppet performances and occasional classical dance and traditional drum shows are held here at 7.30pm every Friday and Saturday night. Audience members are invited to try their hand at the shadow puppets after the 50-minute performance. Classes are available here in the art of shadow puppetry, puppet making, classical and folk dance, and traditional Khmer musical instruments.

🛍 Shopping

An affirmation of identity, the *krama* (chequered scarf) is worn around the necks, shoulders and waists of nearly every Khmer. The scarves make superb souvenirs, as do Cambodia's sculptures and handicrafts.

Bargains galore can be found at Phnom Penh's vibrant markets. Navigating the labyrinths of shoes, clothing, bric-a-brac and food is one of the most enjoyable ways to earn a foot massage.

Psar Thmei
MARKET

(ផ្សារធំថ្មី; Central Market; Map p76; St 130; ⏱6.30am-5.30pm) A landmark building in the capital, the art-deco Psar Thmei is often called the Central Market, a reference to its location and size. The huge domed hall resembles a Babylonian ziggurat – some claim it ranks as one of the 10 largest domes in the world. The design allows for maximum ventilation, and even on a sweltering day the central hall is cool and airy. The market was recently renovated with French government assistance and is looking good.

Russian Market
MARKET

(Psar Tuol Tom Pong; Map p109; St 155; ⏱6am-5pm) This sweltering bazaar is the one market all visitors should come to at least once during a trip to Phnom Penh. It is *the* place to shop for souvenirs and discounted name-brand clothing. We can't vouch for the authenticity of everything, but along with plenty of knock-offs you'll find genuine articles stitched in local factories. You'll pay as little as 20% of the price back home for brands like Banana Republic, Billabong, Calvin Klein, Columbia, Gap and Next.

TOP FIVE: GOOD-CAUSE SHOPPING

The stores here sell high-quality silk items and handicrafts to provide the disabled and disenfranchised with valuable training for future employment, plus a regular flow of income to improve lives.

Daughters (Map p76; www.daughtersofcambodia.org; 65 St 178; ⏱9am-6pm Mon-Sat) Daughters is an NGO that runs a range of programs to train and assist former prostitutes and victims of sex trafficking. The fashionable clothes, bags and accessories here are made with eco-friendly cotton and natural dyes by program participants.

Mekong Blue (Map p76; www.bluesilk.org; 9 St 130; ⏱8am-6pm) This is the Phnom Penh boutique for Stung Treng's best-known silk cooperative to empower women. Produces beautiful scarves and shawls, as well as jewellery.

Rajana (Map p107; www.rajanacrafts.org; 170 St 450; ⏱7am-6pm Mon-Sat, 10.30am-5pm Sun) One of the best all-around handicraft stores, Rajana aims to promote fair wages and training. It has a beautiful selection of cards, some quirky metalware products, jewellery, bamboo crafts, lovely shirts, gorgeous wall hangings, candles – you name it. Also has a **shop** (Map p107; ⏱10am-6pm) at the Russian Market.

Tabitha (Map p78; 239 St 360; ⏱7am-6pm Mon-Sat) A leading NGO shop with a good collection of silk bags, tableware, bedroom decorations and children's toys. Proceeds go towards rural community development, such as well-drilling.

Women for Women (WFW; Map p76; www.womanforwoman.net; 9 St 178; ⏱7am-10pm) Pillows, throws, bags, scarves, jewellery, silver and more, hand-fashioned by women with disabilities.

Night Market
MARKET

(Psar Reatrey; Map p76; cnr St 108 & Sisowath Quay; ⊙5-11pm Fri-Sun) A cooler, alfresco version of Russian Market, this night market takes place every Friday, Saturday and Sunday evening if it's not raining. Bargain vigorously, as prices can be on the high side. Interestingly, it's probably more popular with Khmers than foreigners.

Monument Books
BOOKS

(Map p78; 111 Norodom Blvd; ⊙7am-8.30pm) The best-stocked bookshop in town, with almost every Cambodia-related book available and a superb maps and travel section. There's also a wi-fi-enabled branch of Blue Pumpkin cafe on-site.

D's Books
BOOKS

(Map p76; 7 St 178; ⊙9am-9pm) The largest chain of secondhand bookshops in the capital, with a good range of titles. There's a second branch (Map p78; 79 St 240; ⊙9am-9pm) just east of Norodom Blvd.

ℹ Orientation

Phnom Penh's sequentially numbered streets may be a paragon of logic, but when it comes to house numbering, utter chaos reigns. It's not uncommon to find a row of adjacent buildings numbered, say, 13A, 34, 7, 26. Worse, several buildings on the same street, blocks apart, may have adopted the same house number! When you're given an address, try to get a cross-street, such as 'on St 240 near St 51'.

ℹ Information

EMERGENCY

Ambulance (🖉119, in English 023-724891)
Fire (🖉in Khmer 118)
Police (🖉in Khmer 117)

INTERNET ACCESS

Pretty much all hotels and most cafes, restaurants and bars offer free wi-fi. Internet cafes are less common than they used to be, but usually charge US$0.50 to US$1 per hour.

MEDICAL SERVICES

Calmette Hospital (Map p109; 🖉023-426948; 3 Monivong Blvd; ⊙24hr) The best of the local hospitals, with the most comprehensive services and an intensive-care unit.

Tropical & Travellers Medical Clinic (Map p76; 🖉023-306802; www.travellersmedical clinic.com; 88 St 108; ⊙9.30-11.30am & 2.30-5pm Mon-Fri, 9.30-11.30am Sat) Well-regarded clinic, run by a British general practitioner for over a decade.

ℹ WARNING: BAG-SNATCHING

Bag- and phone-snatching has become a real problem in Phnom Penh. Hotspots include the riverfront and busy areas around popular markets, but there is no real pattern and the speeding motorbike thieves, usually operating in pairs, can strike any place, any time. Countless expats and tourists have been injured falling off their bikes in the process of being robbed. Keep your valuables close or concealed and be prepared to let go rather than be dragged into the road. Keep shoulder bags in front of you when riding on *motos* (motorbike taxis). These people are real pros and only need one chance.

U-Care Pharmacy (Map p76; 26 Sothearos Blvd; ⊙8am-10pm) International-style pharmacy with a convenient location near the river.

MONEY

Phnom Penh's airport has a few ATMs. The city has plenty of banks and exchange services, including the following:

ANZ Royal Bank (Map p76; 265 Sisowath Quay; ⊙8.30am-4pm Mon-Fri, to noon Sat) ANZ has ATMs galore all over town, including at supermarkets and petrol stations, but there is a US$5 charge per transaction.

Canadia Bank (Map p76; cnr St 110 & Monivong Blvd; ⊙8am-3.30pm Mon-Fri, to 11.30am Sat) Has ATMs around town, with a US$4 charge. At its flagship branch you can also change travellers cheques of several currencies for a 2% commission, plus get free cash advances on MasterCard and Visa. Also represents MoneyGram.

POST

Central Post Office (Map p76; St 13 at St 100; ⊙8am-6pm) A landmark – it's in a French colonial classic just east of Wat Phnom.

TOURIST INFORMATION

There is not much in the way of official tourist information in the Cambodian capital, but private travel agencies are everywhere and are usually happy to dispense advice.

The *Phnom Penh Visitors' Guide* (www.canby publications.com) has good maps and is brimming with useful information on the capital.

Pick up the free *Drinking & Dining* and *Out & About* produced by Pocket Guides (www.cambo diapocketguide.com).

CAMBODIA PHNOM PENH

TRAVEL AGENCIES

Reliable travel agencies include the following:

Palm Tours (Map p78; ☏ 023-726291; www.palmtours.biz; 1B St 278; ⊙8am-9pm) Efficient Volak and her team are a great option for bus tickets (no commission) and the like.

PTM Travel & Tours (Map p76; ☏ 023-219268; www.ptmcambodia.com; 200 Monivong Blvd; ⊙8am-5.30pm Mon-Sat) Good place for outgoing air tickets.

ⓘ Getting There & Away

AIR

Many international air services run to/from Phnom Penh. Domestically, **Cambodia Angkor Air** (Map p109; ☏ 023-666 6786; www.cambodiaangkorair.com; 206A Norodom Blvd) flies four to six times daily to Siem Reap (from US$60 one way, 30 minutes), while newcomers **Bassaka Air** (☏ 023-217613; www.bassakaair.com) and **Cambodia Bayon Airlines** (☏ 023-231555; www.bayonairlines.com) have at least one flight a day, from US$40 one way.

BOAT

Between August and March, speedboats depart daily to Siem Reap (US$35, five to six hours) at 7.30am from the tourist boat dock at the eastern end of St 104, but the tickets are overpriced compared with the bus.

Following the river to Chau Doc in Vietnam is a gorgeous way to go; see the boxed text 'Getting to Vietnam: Mekong Delta Borders'.

BUS

All major towns in Cambodia, plus regional hubs Bangkok, Ho Chi Minh City and Pakse, are accessible by air-conditioned bus from Phnom Penh. Most buses leave from company offices, which are generally clustered around Psar Thmei or located near the corner of St 106 and Sisowath Quay.

Not all buses are created equal. Buses run by Capitol Tour and Phnom Penh Sorya are usually among the cheapest; Giant Ibis runs upscale 'VIP' buses with plenty of leg-room and dysfunctional wi-fi, but they are about double the average price. Virak Buntham is the night-bus specialist.

Express vans are an option to most cities. These shave hours off average trip times, but are cramped and often travel at scary speeds.

Main bus companies:

Capitol Tour (Map p78; ☏ 023-724104; 14 St 182) Offers trips all the way through to Chau

BUSES FROM PHNOM PENH

DESTINATION	COMPANY	FARE (US$)	DURATION (HR)	FREQUENCY
Bangkok	Mekong Express, PP Sorya, Virak Buntham	18-23	12	daily per company
Battambang (day bus)	GST, PP Sorya, Virak Buntham	5-10	6	several per company
Ho Chi Minh City	Capitol Tour, Giant Ibis, Mekong Express, PP Sorya	8-13	7	several daily per company
Kampot (direct)	Capitol Tour	6	3	2 daily
Kampot (via Kep)	PP Sorya	6	4	7.30am, 9.30am, 2.45pm
Koh Kong	Olympic Express, PP Sorya, Virak Buntham	7	6	several daily per company
Kratie	PP Sorya	8	6-8	6.45am, 7.15am, 7.30am, 9.30am, 10.30am
Pakse via Don Det (Laos)	PP Sorya	28	12-14	6.45am
Sen Monorom	PP Sorya	9	8	7.30am
Siem Reap (day bus)	most companies	6-15	6	frequent
Sihanoukville	Capitol Tour, GST, Mekong Express, PP Sorya, Virak Buntham	5-6	5	frequent
Stung Treng	PP Sorya	12.50	9	6.45am, 7.30am

GETTING TO VIETNAM: MEKONG DELTA BORDERS

Phnom Penh to Ho Chi Minh City

The original Bavet/Moc Bai land crossing between Vietnam and Cambodia has seen steady traffic for two decades.

Getting to the border The easiest way to get to Ho Chi Minh City (HCMC; Saigon) is to catch an international bus (US$8 to US$13, six hours) from Phnom Penh. Numerous companies make this trip.

At the border Long lines entering either country are not uncommon, but otherwise it's a straightforward crossing.

Moving on If you are not on the international bus, it's not hard to find onward transport to HCMC or elsewhere.

For information on making this crossing in reverse, see p893.

Phnom Penh to Chau Doc

The most scenic way to end your travels in Cambodia is to sail the Mekong to Kaam Samnor, about 100km south-southeast of Phnom Penh, cross the border to Vinh Xuong in Vietnam, and proceed to Chau Doc on the Tonlé Bassac River via a small channel. Chau Doc has onward land and river connections to points in the Mekong Delta and elsewhere in Vietnam.

Various companies do trips all the way through to Chau Doc using a single boat (US$25 to US$35, about four hours) or a cheaper bus/boat combo (US$19). Prices vary according to speed and level of service. Departures are from the tourist boat dock in Phnom Penh.

For information on making this crossing in reverse, see p898.

Takeo to Chau Doc

The remote and seldom-used Phnom Den/Tinh Bien border crossing (open 7am to 5pm) between Cambodia and Vietnam lies about 50km southeast of Takeo town in Cambodia and offers connections to Chau Doc.

Getting to the border Take a share taxi (10,000r), a chartered taxi (US$25) or a *moto* (US$10) from Takeo to the border (48km).

At the border Formalities are minimal here, as international traffic is light.

Moving on On the other side, travellers are at the mercy of Vietnamese *xe om (moto)* drivers and taxis for the 30km journey from the border to Chau Doc. Prepare for some tough negotiations. Expect to pay around US$10 by bike, more like US$20 for a taxi.

For information on making this crossing in reverse, see p898.

Doc using a combination of bus and boat. Capitol Tour services depart at 8am; the trip is about six to seven hours.

Giant Ibis (Map p76; ☑ 023-999333; www.giantibis.com; 3 St 106) This is the 'VIP' bus and express-van specialist. The big bus to Siem Reap has plenty of leg-room and dysfunctional wi-fi. A portion of profits go toward giant ibis conservation.

GST (Map p76; ☑ 023-218114; 13 St 142)

Mekong Express (☑ 023-427518; http://cat mekongexpress.com; 2020 NH5) Has a riverside **booking office** (Map p76; Sisowath Quay).

Olympic Express (Map p109; ☑ 092 868782; 70 Monireth Blvd)

Phnom Penh Sorya (Map p76; ☑ 023-210359; cnr St 217 & St 67, Psar Thmei area)

Virak Buntham (Kampuchea Angkor Express; Map p76; ☑ 016 786270; 1 St 106) Night-bus specialist with services to Siem Reap, Sihanoukville and Koh Kong.

CAR & MOTORCYCLE

Guesthouses and travel agencies can arrange a car and driver for US$25 to US$75 a day, depending on the destination.

SHARE TAXI & MINIBUS

Share taxis serve most destinations. They save time and offer flexible departure times. Local minibuses and pickups tend to be slow and packed, but they will save you a buck or two if you're pinching pennies and offer a true 'local' experience (especially if somebody vomits on you).

Taxis to Kampot, Kep and Takeo leave from **Psar Dang Kor** (Map p109; Mao Tse Toung Blvd), while local minibuses and share taxis for most other places leave from the northwest corner of **Psar Thmei** (Map p76).

ⓘ Getting Around

TO/FROM THE AIRPORT & BUS STATION

Phnom Penh International Airport is 7km west of central Phnom Penh. An official booth outside the airport arrivals area arranges taxis/remorks to anywhere in the city for a flat US$12/7. You can get a remork for US$5 and a moto for US$3 if you walk one minute out to the street. Heading to the airport from central Phnom Penh, a taxi/remork/moto will cost about US$10/5/3. The journey usually takes about 30 minutes to one hour, depending on traffic.

If you arrive by bus, chances are you'll be dropped off near Psar Thmei (aka Central Market), a short ride from most hotels and guesthouses. Figure on US$0.50 to US$1 for a moto, and US$2 to US$3 for a remork. Prices are about the same from the tourist boat dock on Sisowath Quay, where arriving boats from Vietnam and Siem Reap incite moto-madness.

BICYCLE

Simple bicycles can be hired from some guesthouses and hotels from US$1 a day, or contact Vicious Cycle (p73) for something more sophisticated.

MOTO, REMORK & CYCLO

Motos are everywhere and the drivers of those hanging out around tourist areas can generally speak good street English. Short rides around the city cost 2000r rising to US$1 for a longer ride of 2km. At night these prices double. To charter one for a day, expect to pay around US$10 in town. Remorks usually charge double the price of a moto, possibly more if you pile on the passengers. Cyclos can be tougher to find but cost about the same as motos.

MOTORCYCLE

Exploring Phnom Penh and the surrounding areas on a motorbike is a very liberating experience if you are used to chaotic traffic conditions. You generally get what you pay for when choosing a steel steed.

Lucky! Lucky! (Map p78; ☑ 023-212788; 413 Monivong Blvd) Motorbikes are US$4 to US$7 per day, less for multiple days. Trail bikes from US$12.

Vannak Bikes Rental (Map p76; ☑ 012 220970; 46 St 130) Has high-performance trail bikes up to 600cc for US$15 to US$30 per day, and smaller motorbikes for US$5 to US$7.

TAXI

Taxis are cheap at 3000r per kilometre but don't expect to flag one down on the street. Call **Global Meter Taxi** (☑ 011 311888) or **Choice Taxi** (☑ 023-888023, 010 888010) for a pickup.

AROUND PHNOM PENH

There are several sites close to Phnom Penh that make for interesting excursions.

Tonlé Bati, Phnom Tamao and Phnom Chisor are all near each other on NH2 and make a great full-day excursion by car or motorbike.

Koh Dach   កោះដាច់

Known as 'Silk Island' by foreigners, this is actually a pair of islands lying in the Mekong River about 5km northeast of the Japanese Friendship Bridge. They make for an easy half-day DIY excursion for those who want to experience the 'real Cambodia'. The hustle and bustle of Phnom Penh feels light years away here. The name derives from the preponderance of silk weavers who inhabit the islands, and you'll have plenty of chances to buy from them.

Remork drivers offer half-day tours to Koh Dach; US$12 should do it, but be ready to negotiate. Daily boat tours from the tourist boat dock, departing at 8.30am, 9.30am and 1pm, are another option (minimum four people).

Tonlé Bati   ទន្លេបាទី

Locals love to come to this lake (admission US$3) for picnics, as along the way they can stop off at two 12th-century temples: Ta Prohm and Yeay Peau. Ta Prohm is the more interesting of the two and it has some fine carvings in good condition, depicting scenes of birth, dishonour and damnation.

The well-marked turn-off to Tonlé Bati is on the right 33km south of central Phnom Penh. The Takeo-bound Phnom Penh Sorya bus (8000r, four daily – shoot for the 7am or 10.30am one) can drop you here; find a moto to the temples (1.8km from the highway). Returning to Phnom Penh, buy a ticket in advance on Sorya's Takeo–Phnom Penh bus. Otherwise, hire a moto.

WORTH A TRIP

KOMPONG LUONG

Kompong Luong (កំពង់ល្វង) has all the amenities you'd expect to find in a large fishing village – cafes, mobile-phone shops, chicken coops, ice-making factories, a pagoda, a church – except that here everything floats. The result is an ethnic-Vietnamese Venice without the dry land. In the dry season, when water levels drop and the Tonlé Sap shrinks, the entire aquapolis is towed, boat by boat, a few kilometres north.

The way to explore Kompong Luong, naturally, is by boat. The official tourist rate to charter a four-passenger wooden motorboat (complete with life-jackets) is US$10 per hour for one to three passengers. **Homestays** (per person per night not incl boat ride US$4-6; 🛜) are available with local families and meals are available for US$1 to US$2 per person. This is an interesting way to discover what everyday life is really like on the water. You can book a homestay when you arrive at the boat landing.

The jumping-off point to Kompong Luong is the town of Krakor, 32km east of Pursat. From Krakor to the boat landing where tours begin is 1.5km to 6km, depending on the time of year. From Pursat, a *moto/remork* costs about US$10/20 return. From Phnom Penh, take any Pursat- or Battambang-bound bus.

Phnom Tamao Wildlife Sanctuary ភ្នំតាម៉ៅ (សួនសត្វ)

This **sanctuary** (adult/child US$5/2; ⊙8am-5pm) for rescued animals is home to gibbons, sun bears, elephants, tigers, deer and a bird enclosure. All were taken from poachers or abusive owners and receive care and shelter here as part of a sustainable breeding program.

The access road to Phnom Tamao is clearly signposted on the right 6.5km south of the turn-off to Tonlé Bati on NH2. If coming by bus, have the driver let you off at the turn-off, where *motos* await to whisk you the final 5km to the sanctuary.

SIEM REAP & THE TEMPLES OF ANGKOR

☑ 063 / POP 175,000

Siem Reap is the life-support system for the temples of Angkor, the eighth wonder of the world. Although in a state of slumber from the late 1960s until a few years ago, the town has woken up with a jolt and is now one of the regional hotspots for wining and dining, shopping and schmoozing.

The ultimate fusion of creative ambition and spiritual devotion, the temples of Angkor are a source of inspiration and profound pride to all Khmers. No traveller to the region will want to miss their extravagant beauty and spine-tingling grandeur. One of the most impressive ancient sites on earth, Angkor has the epic proportions of the Great Wall of China, the detail and intricacy of the Taj Mahal and the symbolism and symmetry of the Egyptian pyramids, all rolled into one.

Angkor is a place to be savoured, not rushed, and Siem Reap is the perfect base from which to plan your adventures.

ℹ Getting Around

There are endless options when it comes to exploring Angkor. Bicycles are a great way to get to and around the temples, which are linked by flat roads that are in good shape. Just make sure you drink plenty of water at every opportunity.

Another environmentally friendly option is to explore on foot. There are obvious limitations, but exploring Angkor Thom's walls or walking to and from Angkor Wat are both feasible. Don't forget to buy an entrance ticket.

Zippy and inexpensive *motos* (about US$10 per day, more for distant sites) are the most popular form of transport around the temples. Drivers accost visitors from the moment they set foot in Siem Reap, but they often end up being friendly and knowledgeable. Guesthouses are also a good source of experienced driver-guides.

Remorks (around US$15 a day, more for distant sites) take a little longer than *motos* but offer protection from the rain and sun.

Even more protection is offered by cars, though these tend to isolate you from the sights, sounds and smells. Hiring a car in Siem Reap costs about US$30 for a day cruising around Angkor; US$50 to Kbal Spean and Banteay Srei; US$70 to Beng Mealea; and US$90 out to Koh Ker.

Siem Reap

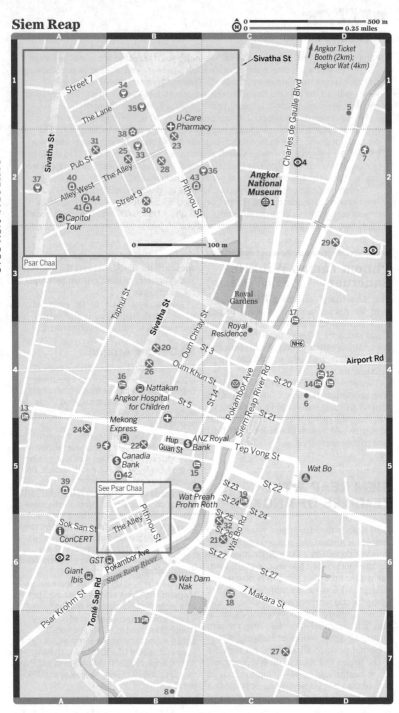

Sivatha St

Angkor Ticket Booth (2km);
Angkor Wat (4km)

Street 7

The Lane

34

35

U-Care
Pharmacy

38

23

Sivatha St

31

Pub St

25 33

28

The Alley

37

40

Alley West

44

41

Capitol
Tour

Street 9

30

43 36

Pithnou St

Psar Chaa

5

7

Angkor
National
Museum

4

1

Charles de Gaulle Blvd

29

3

Taphul St

Sivatha St

Royal
Gardens

17

Royal
Residence

NH6

Airport Rd

20

26

Oum Chhay St

St 3

Oum Khun St

16

Nattakan

Angkor Hospital
for Children

St 5

St 14

Pokambor Ave

Siem Reap River Rd

St 20

10

12

14

6

13

24

Mekong
Express

9

22

Hup
Guan St

ANZ Royal
Bank

St 21

Canadia
Bank

42

15

Tep Vong St

Wat Bo

See Psar Chaa

Pithnou St

The Alley

Wat Preah
Prohm Roth

19

St 23

St 24

St 22

39

Sok San St
ConCERT

2

GST

Giant
Ibis

Pokambor Ave

Siem Reap River

St 25

32

St 26

21

Wat Bo Rd

St 24

St 27

St 27

7 Makara St

Wat Dam
Nak

18

Psar Krohm St

Tonlé Sap Rd

11

8

27

Siem Reap

Siem Reap   សៀមរាប

Siem Reap is the comeback kid of Southeast Asia. It has reinvented itself as the epicentre of the new Cambodia, with more hotels and guesthouses than temples, world-class wining and dining, and sumptuous spas.

At its heart, it remains a charming town with rural qualities. Old French shophouses, shady tree-lined boulevards and a winding river are attractive remnants of the past, while five-star hotels, air-con buses and international restaurants point to a glitzy future.

⊙ Sights

★ **Angkor National Museum**   MUSEUM
(សារមន្ទីរអង្គរ; Map p88; ☑063-966601; www.angkornationalmuseum.com; 968 Charles de Gaulle Blvd; adult/child under 1.2m US$12/6; ⊙8.30am-6pm, to 6.30pm 1 Oct-30 Apr) Looming large on the road to Angkor is the Angkor National Museum, a state-of-the-art showpiece on the Khmer civilisation and the majesty of Angkor. Displays are themed by era, religion

and royalty as visitors move through the impressive galleries. After a short presentation, visitors enter the Zen-like 'Gallery of a Thousand Buddhas', which has a fine collection of images. Other exhibits include the pre-Angkorian periods of Funan and Chenla; the great Khmer kings; Angkor Wat; Angkor Thom; and the inscriptions.

Artisans Angkor – Les Chantiers
Écoles   ARTS CENTRE
(អាទីសង់អង្គរ; Map p88; www.artisansdangkor.com; ⊙7.30am-6.30pm) 🖉 FREE Siem Reap is the epicentre of the drive to revitalise Cambodian traditional culture, which was dealt a harsh blow by the Khmer Rouge and the years of instability that followed its rule. Les Chantiers Écoles teaches wood- and stone-carving techniques, traditional silk painting, lacquerware and other artisan skills to impoverished young Cambodians. Free guided tours explaining traditional techniques are available daily from 7.30am to 6.30pm. Tucked down a side road, the school is well signposted from Sivatha St.

Temples of Angkor

CAMBODIA

ANGKOR THOM

Angkor Thom North Gate

8

Preah Palilay 12

Royal Enclosure & Phimeanakas

Angkor Thom Victory Gate

11

BAYON

6

Angkor Thom East Gate

Angkor Thom West Gate

Bayon 2

Angkor Thom South Gate

Baksei Chamkrong

PHNOM BAKHENG

7

ANGKOR WAT

1

Angkor Wat

Western Mebon

Western Baray

Siem Reap International Airport

NH6

Airport Rd

Dykes

Royal Angkor International Hospital

Angkor Ticket Checkpoint

Tourist Police

13

SIEM REAP

17

18 Charles de Gaulle Blvd

Sivatha St

10

Psar Chaa

Makara St

19 16

See Siem Reap Map (p88)

Dyke

Dyke

Wat Bo Rd

Wat Athvea

Phnom Krom

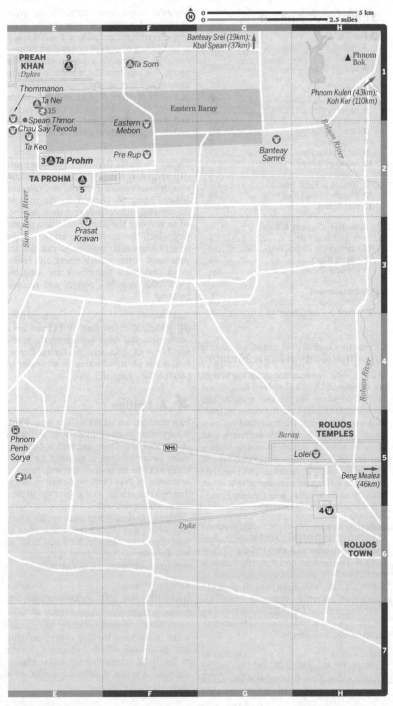

Temples of Angkor

Cambodia Landmine Museum   MUSEUM
(សារមន្ទីរគ្រាប់មីនកម្ពុជា និងមូលនិធិសង្គ្រោះ;
☑ 012 598951; www.cambodialandminemuseum.
org; donation US$3; ☉ 7.30am-5pm) Established
by DIY de-miner Aki Ra, this museum has
eye-opening displays on the curse of landmines in Cambodia. The collection includes
mines, mortars, guns and weaponry, and
there is a mock minefield where visitors
can try to locate the deactivated mines.
Proceeds from the museum are ploughed
into mine-awareness campaigns. It is about
25km from Siem Reap, near Banteay Srei.

Banteay Srei
Butterfly Centre   WILDLIFE RESERVE
(សួនអំពៅបន្ទាយស្រី; ☑ 097 8527852; www.
angkorbutterfly.com; adult/child US$4/2; ☉ 9am-
5pm) ✔ The Banteay Srei Butterfly Centre is
the largest fully enclosed butterfly centre in
Southeast Asia, with more than 30 species of
Cambodian butterflies fluttering about. It is
a good experience for children, as they can
see the whole life cycle from egg to caterpil-
lar to cocoon to butterfly.

Cambolac   ARTS CENTRE
(ខេមប៊ូឡាក់; Map p88; ☑ 097 843 1790; cambol
ac.com; ☉ 8-11.30am & 1-5pm Mon-Sat) **FREE**
Cambodia has a long tradition of producing
beautiful lacquerware, although the years
of upheaval resulted in some of the skills
being forgotten. Cambolac is a social enterprise helping to restore Cambodia's lacquer
tradition and create a new contemporary
scene. You can tour the workshop to learn
more about the perfectionist approach required to produce a piece of lacquerware.
Most of the guides are hearing-impaired
and a tour allows some great interaction
and the opportunity to learn some basic sign
commands.

Khmer Ceramics Centre   ARTS CENTRE
(មជ្ឈមណ្ឌលស្ថាបត្យខ្មែរ; Map p88; ☑ 017 843014;
www.khmerceramics.com; Charles de Gaulle Blvd;
☉ 8am-7.30pm) ✔ Located on the road to
the temples, this ceramics centre is dedicated to reviving the Khmer tradition of pottery, which was an intricate art during the
time of Angkor. It's possible to visit and try
your hand at the potter's wheel, and courses in traditional techniques are available
for US$20, including pottery and ceramic
painting.

Wat Thmei   BUDDHIST TEMPLE
(វត្តថ្មី; Map p90; ☉ 6am-6pm) Wat Thmei has a
small memorial stupa containing the skulls
and bones of victims of the Khmer Rouge.
It also has plenty of young monks eager to
practise their English.

🏃 Activities

Foot massage is a big hit in Siem Reap, hardly surprising given all those steep stairways
at the temples. There are half a dozen or
more places offering a massage for about
US$6 to US$8 an hour on the strip running
northwest of Psar Chaa. Some are more authentic than others, so dip your toe in first
before selling your sole.

For an alternative foot massage, try a **fish
spa**, which sees cleaner fish nibble away at
your dead skin – heaven for some, tickly as
hell for others. Places have sprung up all
over town, including along Pub St.

Krousar Thmey   MASSAGE
(គ្រួសារថ្មី; Map p90; www.krousar-thmey.org;
Charles de Gaulle Blvd; massage US$7) ✔ Mas-
sages here are performed by blind masseurs. In the same location is the free Tonlé
Sap Exhibition, which includes a 'Seeing
in the Dark' interactive exhibition exploring what it is like to be blind, guided by a
sight-impaired student.

Peace Cafe Yoga
YOGA

(Map p88; ☎063-965210; www.peacecafeangkor.org; Siem Reap River Rd; per session US$6) This popular community-centre-cum-cafe has daily yoga sessions at 8.30am and 6.30pm, including ashtanga and hatha sessions.

Seeing Hands Massage 4
MASSAGE

(Map p88; ☎012 836487; 324 Sivatha St; per hr fan/air-con US$5/7) ✪ Seeing Hands trains blind people in the art of massage. Watch out for copycats, as some of these are just exploiting the blind for profit.

Angkor Wat Putt
GOLF

(Map p90; ☎012 302330; www.angkorwatputt.com; adult/child US$5/4; ⊗7.30am-10pm) Crazy golf to the Brits among us, this home-grown mini-golf course contrasts with the big golf courses out of town. Navigate mini temples and creative obstacles for 14 holes. Win a beer for a hole-in-one.

★Flight of the Gibbon Angkor
ZIPLINE

(Map p90; ☎096 9999101; www.treetopasia.com; near Ta Nei Temple, Angkor; per person US$109; ⊗7am-5pm) Angkor provides the ultimate backdrop for a zipline experience, although you won't actually see the temples while navigating the course. Flight of the Gibbon Angkor is inside the Angkor protected area and the course includes 10 ziplines, 21 treetop platforms, four skybridges and an abseil finish. There is a panoramic refreshment stop at the halfway stage and highlights include a tandem line for couples.

Happy Ranch
HORSE RIDING

(Map p90; ☎012 920002; www.thehappyranch.com; 1hr/half-day US$28/59) Forget the Wild West – try your hand at horse riding in the Wild East. Happy Ranch offers the chance to explore Siem Reap on horseback, taking in surrounding villages and secluded temples. This is a calm way to experience the countryside, far from the traffic and crowds.

🍲 Courses

Cooks in Tuk Tuks
COOKING COURSE

(Map p88; ☎063-963400; www.therivergarden.info; River Rd West; per person US$25) Starts at 10am daily with a visit to Psar Leu market, then returns to the River Garden for a professional class.

Le Tigre de Papier
COOKING COURSE

(Map p88; ☎012 265811; www.angkor-cooking-class-cambodia.com; Pub St; per person US$14) ✪

Daily classes are held at 10am and 1pm in English, and at 5pm in French. Classes include a visit to the market.

☞ Tours

KKO (Khmer for Khmer Organisation) Bike Tours
BICYCLE TOUR

(Map p88; ☎093 903024; www.kko-cambodia.org; cnr St 20 & Wat Bo Rd; tours US$35-50) ✪ Good-cause cycling tours around the paths of Angkor or into the countryside beyond the Western Baray. Proceeds go towards the Khmer for Khmer Organisation, which supports education and vocational training.

Quad Adventure Cambodia
ADVENTURE TOUR

(Map p88; ☎092 787216; www.quad-adventure-cambodia.com; sunset ride US$30, full day US$170) The original quad-bike operator in town. Rides around Siem Reap involve rice fields at sunset, pretty temples, and back roads through traditional villages.

🛏 Sleeping

While accommodation is spread throughout town, three areas hold the bulk of budget choices: the Psar Chaa area; the area to the west of Sivatha St; and north of Wat Bo on the east bank of the river. Psar Chaa is the liveliest part of town, brimming with restaurants, bars and boutiques. Staying here can be a lot of fun, but it's not the quietest part of town. The area to the west of Sivatha St includes a good selection of budget guesthouses and midrange boutique hotels. There is a great guesthouse ghetto in a backstreet running parallel to the north end of Wat Bo Rd, which is good for on-the-spot browsing.

CAMBODIA SIEM REAP

SUPPORTING RESPONSIBLE TOURISM IN SIEM REAP

Many travellers passing through Siem Reap are interested in contributing something to the communities they visit as they explore the temples and surrounding areas. ConCERT (Map p88; ☎063-963511; www.concertcambodia.org; 560 Phum Stoueng Thmey; ⊗9am-5pm Mon-Fri) is a Siem Reap–based organisation that is working to build bridges between tourists and good-cause projects in the Siem Reap–Angkor area. It offers information on anything from ecotourism initiatives to volunteering opportunities.

Temples of Angkor

THREE-DAY EXPLORATION

The temple complex at Angkor is simply enormous and the superlatives don't do it justice. This is the site of the world's largest religious building, a multitude of temples and a vast, long-abandoned walled city that was arguably Southeast Asia's first metropolis, long before Bangkok and Singapore got in on the action.

Starting at the Roluos group of temples, one of the earliest capitals of Angkor, move on to the big circuit, which includes the Buddhist-Hindu fusion temple of ❶ **Preah Khan** and the ornate water temple of ❷ **Preah Neak Poan**.

On the second day downsize to the small circuit, starting with an early visit to ❸ **Ta Prohm**, before continuing to the temple pyramid of Ta Keo, the Buddhist monastery of Banteay Kdei and the immense royal bathing pond of ❹ **Sra Srang**.

Next venture further afield to Banteay Srei temple, the jewel in the crown of Angkorian art, and Beng Mealea, a remote jungle temple.

Saving the biggest and best until last, experience sunrise at ❺ **Angkor Wat** and stick around for breakfast in the temple to discover its amazing architecture without the crowds. In the afternoon, explore ❻ **Angkor Thom**, an immense complex that is home to the enigmatic ❼ **Bayon**.

Three days around Angkor? That's just for starters.

Bayon
The surreal state temple of legendary king Jayavarman VII, where 216 faces bear down on pilgrims, asserting religious and regal authority.

Terrace of the Leper King

Preah Palilay

Phimeanakas Temple

Tep Pranam

West Gate Angkor Thom

Baphuon Temple

Terrace of the Elephants

❼

South Gate Angkor Thom

Phnom Bakheng

Baksei Chamrong

❺

Angkor Wat
The world's largest religious building. Experience sunrise at the holiest of holies, then explore the beautiful bas-reliefs – devotion etched in stone.

TOP TIPS

» **Dodging the Crowds** To avoid the hordes, try dawn at Sra Srang, post sunrise at Angkor Wat, and lunchtime at Banteay Srei.

» **Extended Explorations** Three-day passes can be used on non-consecutive days over the period of a week but be sure to request this.

Angkor Thom
The last great capital of the Khmer empire conceals a wealth of temples and its epic proportions would have inspired and terrified in equal measure.

Preah Khan
A fusion temple dedicated to Buddha, Brahma, Shiva and Vishnu; the immense corridors are like an unending hall of mirrors.

Preah Neak Poan
If Vegas ever adopts the Angkor theme, this will be the swimming pool; a petite tower set in a lake, surrounded by four smaller ponds.

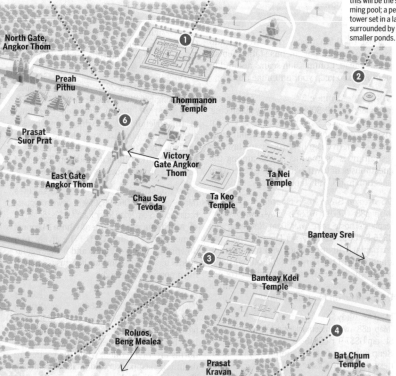

North Gate, Angkor Thom

Preah Pithu

Thommanon Temple

Prasat Suor Prat

Victory Gate Angkor Thom

East Gate Angkor Thom

Chau Say Tevoda

Ta Keo Temple

Ta Nei Temple

Banteay Srei

Banteay Kdei Temple

Roluos, Beng Mealea

Prasat Kravan

Bat Chum Temple

Ta Prohm
Nicknamed the *Tomb Raider* temple; *Indiana Jones* would be equally apt. Nature has run riot, leaving iconic tree roots strangling the surviving stones.

Sra Srang
Once the royal bathing pond, this is the ablutions pool to beat all ablutions pools and makes a good stop for sunrise or sunset.

SPLURGE

A hotel with a heart, promoting local causes to help the community, boutique **Soria Moria Hotel** (Map p88; ✆063-964768; www.thesoriamoria.com; Wat Bo Rd; r US$39-63; ❀@🛜🏊) ✎ has attractive rooms with smart bathroom fittings. There's a fusion restaurant downstairs, sky hot-tub upstairs and a new swimming pool. Half the hotel was transferred to staff ownership in 2011, a visionary move.

Most of these places offer free pickup from the airport, port or bus station: email or call ahead. Commission scams abound in Siem Reap so keep your antennae up.

★ **Ivy Guesthouse 2** GUESTHOUSE $
(Map p88; ✆012 800860; www.ivy-guesthouse. com; Psar Kandal St; r US$6-15; ❀@🛜) An inviting guesthouse with a chill-out area and bar, the Ivy is a lively place to stay. The restaurant is as good as it gets among the guesthouses in town, with a huge vegetarian selection and US$1 'Tapas Fridays'.

Downtown Siem Reap Hostel HOSTEL $
(Map p88; ✆012 675881; www.downtownsiem reaphostel.hostel.com; Wat Dam Nak area; dm US$6-8, r US$12-18; ❀🛜🏊) The rates here are particularly inviting when you factor in the small pool in the garden. Chill out with air-con in the more expensive dorms or rooms. Outside visitors can use the pool with a US$6 spend on food and drink.

Mad Monkey HOSTEL $
(Map p88; www.madmonkeyhostels.com; Sivatha St; dm US$7-9, r US$16-26; ❀@🛜) The Siem Reap outpost of an expanding Monkey business, this is a classic backpacker crashpad with several dorms, good-value rooms for those wanting privacy, and the obligatory rooftop bar, only this one's a beach bar!

Funky Flashpacker HOSTEL $
(Map p88; ✆070 221524; www.funkyflash packer.com; Funky Lane; dm US$7, r US$16-35; ❀@🛜🏊) This upscale backpackers has a funky vibe – the entire downstairs courtyard is taken up with a swimming pool where regular bouts of water polo take place. A great hostel, but not ideal for recovering partyholics as there's always a buzz about the place.

Babel Guesthouse GUESTHOUSE $
(Map p88; ✆063-965474; babel-siemreap.com; 738 Wat Bo Village; r incl breakfast US$18-33; ❀@🛜) ✎ A Norwegian-run guesthouse set in a relaxing tropical garden, where the service and presentation are a cut above the nearby budget places and rates include breakfast. The Babel owners are keen supporters of responsible tourism.

Happy Guesthouse GUESTHOUSE $
(Map p88; ✆063-963815; www.happyangkor guesthouse.com; 134 Wat Bo Village; r US$7-14; ❀@🛜) This place will really make you happy thanks to welcoming owners who speak English well *et un peu de Français*. Great-value rooms start at the price of dorms elsewhere and there's free internet.

European Guesthouse GUESTHOUSE $
(Map p88; ✆012 582237; www.european-guest house.com; 566 Wat Bo Village; dm US$7, r US$22; ❀@🛜🏊) ✎ Rooms are well presented at this friendly place, which now boasts a swimming pool to go with the relaxing garden. The European is a member of local NGO networks Childsafe and ConCERT, and supports projects such as the White Bicycles.

Rosy Guesthouse GUESTHOUSE $
(Map p88; ✆063-965059; www.rosyguest house.com; Siem Reap River Rd; r US$9-35; ❀🛜) ✎ A Brit-run establishment whose 13 rooms come with TV and DVD. The lively pub downstairs has great grub and hosts regular events to support community causes, including a popular quiz night.

Siem Reap Hostel HOSTEL $
(Map p88; ✆063-964660; www.thesiem reaphostel.com; 10 Makara St; dm US$8-10, r incl breakfast US$34-45; ❀@🛜🏊) Angkor's original backpacker hostel is pretty slick. The dorms are well tended, while the rooms are definitely flashpacker and include breakfast. There is a lively bar-restaurant and a covered pool, plus a well-organised travel desk.

✗ Eating

Worthy restaurants are sprinkled all around town but Siem Reap's culinary heart is the Psar Chaa area, whose focal point, the Alley, is literally lined with mellow eateries offering great atmosphere. It is wall-to-wall with good Cambodian restaurants, many family-owned.

Cheap eats can be found in the **small eateries** (Map p88; mains US$1.50-4; ⊗7am-9pm) lining Psar Chaa. For self-caterers, markets sell fruit and veg. **Angkor Market** (Map p88; Sivatha St), a supermarket, can supply international treats.

★**Marum**   INTERNATIONAL $
(Map p88; www.marum-restaurant.org; Wat Polanka area; mains US$3.25-6.75; ⊙11am-10pm Mon-Sat; 🔊🖋) 🖋 Set in a delightful wooden house with a spacious garden, Marum serves up lots of vegetarian and seafood dishes, plus some mouth-watering desserts. Menu highlights include red-tree-ant fritters and ginger basil meatballs. Marum is part of the Tree Alliance group of training restaurants; the experience is a must.

★**Haven**   FUSION $
(Map p88; 🖋078 342404; www.haven-cambodia. com; Chocolate Rd; mains US$3-7; ⊙11.30am-2.30pm & 5.30-9.30pm Mon-Sat; 🔊) 🖋 A culinary haven indeed. Dine here for the best of east meets west; the fish fillet with green mango is particularly zesty. Proceeds go towards helping young adult orphans make the step from institution to employment. It recently relocated to the Wat Dam Nak area, just near Angkor High School.

Khmer Kitchen Restaurant   CAMBODIAN $
(Map p88; www.khmerkitchens.com; The Alley; mains US$2-5; ⊙11am-10pm) Can't get no (culinary) satisfaction? Then follow in the footsteps of Sir Mick Jagger and try this popular place, which offers an affordable selection of Khmer and Thai favourites, including zesty curries.

Bugs Cafe   INSECTS $
(Map p88; 🖋017 764560; www.bugs-cafe.com; Steung Thmei St; US$2-8; ⊙5pm-midnight; 🔊) Cambodians were on to insects long before the food scientists started bugging us about the merits of critters. Choose from a veritable feast of crickets, water bugs, silkworms and spiders. Bee cream soup, feta and tarantula samosas, and pan-fried scorpions – you won't forget this menu in a hurry.

Banllé Vegetarian Restaurant   VEGETARIAN $
(Map p88; 🖋085 330160; www.banlle-vegetarian. com; St 26; US$2-4; ⊙9am-9.30pm, closed Tue; 🔊🖋) Set in a traditional wooden house with its own organic vegetable garden, this is a great place for a healthy bite. The menu offers a blend of international and Cambodian dishes, including a vegetable *amok*, and zesty fruit and vegetable shakes.

Blossom Cafe   CAFE $
(Map p88; www.blossomcakes.org; St 6; cupcakes US$1.50; ⊙10am-5pm Mon-Sat; 🔊) 🖋 Cupcakes are elevated to an art form at this elegant cafe, with beautifully presented creations available in a rotating array of 48 flavours. Creative coffees, teas and juices are also on offer and profits assist Cambodian women in vocational training.

Blue Pumpkin   CAFE $
(Map p88; tbpumpkin.com; Pithnou St; mains US$3-7; ⊙6am-10pm) The original branch of an expanding local chain. Venture upstairs for a world of white minimalism, with beds to lounge on and free wi-fi. The menu includes light bites, great sandwiches, filling specials and divine shakes. The homemade ice cream comes in some exotic flavours.

Curry Walla   INDIAN $
(Map p88; Sivatha St; mains US$2-5; ⊙10.30am-11pm) For good-value Indian food, this place is hard to beat. The thalis (set meals) are a bargain and the owner, long-time resident Ranjit, knows his share of spicy specials from the subcontinent.

Red Piano   ASIAN, INTERNATIONAL $$
(Map p88; www.redpianocambodia.com; Pub St; mains US$3-10; 🔊) Strikingly set in a restored colonial gem, Red Piano has a big balcony for watching the action unfold below. The menu has a reliable selection of Asian and international food, all at decent prices. Former celebrity guest Angelina Jolie has a cocktail named in her honour.

Cambodian BBQ   BARBECUE $$
(Map p88; www.restaurant-siemreap.com/html/ cambodianbbq.php; The Alley; mains US$5-9; ⊙11am-11pm; 🔊) Crocodile, snake, ostrich and kangaroo meat add an exotic twist to the traditional *phnom pleung* (hill of fire) grills. Cambodian BBQ has spawned half a dozen or more copycats in the surrounding streets, many of which offer discount specials.

Le Tigre de Papier   INTERNATIONAL $$
(Map p88; www.letigredepapier.com; Pub St; mains US$2-9; ⊙24hr; 🔊🖋) One of the best all-rounders in Siem Reap, the popular Tigre serves up authentic Khmer food, great Italian dishes and a selection of favourites from most other corners of the globe. It conveniently offers frontage on both Pub St and the Alley, the latter generally a lot quieter.

WORTH A TRIP

FLOATING VILLAGES

The famous floating village of **Chong Kneas** is an easy excursion to arrange yourself. The village moves depending on the season and you will need to rent a boat to get around it properly. Unfortunately, large tour groups tend to take over and Sou Ching, the company that runs the tours, has fixed boat prices at an absurd US$15 per person. Contact **Tara Boat** (☑ 092 957765; www.taraboat.com; per person US$29/36 lunch/dinner) for an all-inclusive trip. The small, floating **Gecko Centre** (www.tsbr-ed.org; ⊙ 8.30am-5.30pm) has displays on the Tonlé Sap's remarkable annual cycle.

To get to Chong Kneas from Siem Reap costs US$3 by *moto* each way (more if the driver waits), or US$15 by taxi. The trip takes 20 minutes. Alternatively, you can rent a bicycle in town, as it's a leisurely 11km ride through pretty villages and rice fields.

More memorable than Chong Kneas, but also harder to reach, is the friendly village of **Kompong Pluk**, an other-worldly place built on soaring stilts. In the wet season you can explore the nearby flooded forest by canoe.

Similar to Chong Kneas, prices have been fixed at US$20 per person for a boat, but again it may be possible to negotiate this as a per-boat cost split between a group.

To get here, either catch a boat at Chong Kneas (US$55 return, 1¼ hours) or come via the small town of Roluos by a 60- to 90-minute combination of road and boat.

Temple Coffee & Bakery INTERNATIONAL **$$**
(Map p88; Siem Reap River Rd; US$3-12; ⊙ 7am-11pm) The latest, greatest offering from the Temple group, this huge place is a mash-up of a bakery, restaurant and cocktail lounge. Downstairs there are vintage motobikes and inviting cakes, or continue up to the rooftop bar with a pool and beanbags, a popular romantic retreat for young Cambodians.

🍸 Drinking & Nightlife

Siem Reap is now firmly on the nightlife map of Southeast Asia. The Psar Chaa area is a good hunting ground, and one street is now known as 'Pub St': dive in, crawl out.

★ Charlie's BAR
(Map p88; www.charliessiemreap.com; 98 Pithnou St; ⊙ 10am-1am; 🖹) A cracking retro Americana bar with cheap drinks and a convivial crowd. This is the missing link between the more sophisticated bars around the alleyways and the madness unfolding nightly on Pub St. Food is optional, shots obligatory.

Laundry Bar BAR
(Map p88; St 9; ⊙ 4pm-late; 🖹) One of the most chilled bars in town thanks to low lighting and discerning decor, this is the place to come for electronica and ambient sounds. It heaves on weekends or when guest DJs crank up the volume. Happy hour until 9pm.

Angkor What? BAR
(Map p88; Pub St; ⊙ 5pm-late; 🖹) Siem Reap's original bar claims to have been promoting irresponsible drinking since 1998. The happy hour (to 9pm) lightens the mood for later when everyone's bouncing along to indie anthems, sometimes on the tables, sometimes under them.

Asana BAR
(Map p88; www.asana-cambodia.com; The Lane; ⊙ 11am-late; 🖹) Also known as the wooden house, this is a traditional Cambodian countryside home dropped into the backstreets of Siem Reap, which makes for an atmospheric place to drink. Lounge on *capok*-filled rice sacks over a classic cocktail made with infused rice wine. Khmer cocktail classes with Sombai spirits are available at US$15 per person.

X Bar BAR
(Map p88; Sivatha St; ⊙ 4pm-sunrise; 🖹) One of *the* late-night spots in town, X Bar draws revellers for the witching hour when other places are closing up. Early-evening movies on the big screen, pool tables and even a skateboard pipe... take a breath test first!

☆ Entertainment

Classical dance shows take place all over the town, but only a few are worth considering.

★ Phare the Cambodian Circus CIRCUS
(Map p90; ☑ 015 499480; www.pharecambodian circus.org; west end of Sok San Rd; adult/child

US$18/10, premium seats US$35/18; ⊘8pm daily) Cambodia's answer to Cirque du Soleil, Phare the Cambodian Circus is so much more than a conventional circus, with an emphasis on performance art and a subtle yet striking social message behind each production. Cambodia's leading circus, theatre and performing arts organisation, Phare Ponleu Selpak opened its big top for nightly shows in 2013 and the results are a unique form of entertainment that should be considered unmissable when staying in Siem Reap.

Beatocello   CLASSICAL MUSIC
(Map p90; www.beatocello.com; Charles de Gaulle Blvd; ⊘7.15pm Thu & Sat) 🕊 Better known as Dr Beat Richner, Beatocello performs cello compositions at Jayavarman VII Children's Hospital. Entry is free, but donations are welcome as they assist the hospital in offering free medical treatment to the children of Cambodia.

Temple Club   DANCE
(Map p88; Pub St; 🕾) Temple Club stages a free traditional dance show upstairs from 7.30pm, providing punters order some food and drink from the very reasonably priced menu.

🛍 Shopping

Siem Reap has an excellent selection of Cambodian-made handicrafts. Psar Chaa is well stocked and there are bargains to be had if you haggle patiently and humorously. **Angkor Night Market** (Map p88; www.angkornightmarket.com; ⊘4pm-midnight) is packed with silks, handicrafts and assorted souvenirs. Up-and-coming **Alley West** is also a great strip to browse socially responsible fashion boutiques.

Several shops – such as the exquisite **Artisans Angkor** (Map p88; www.artisansdangkor.com; ⊘7.30am-6.30pm) 🕊 – support Cambodia's disabled and disenfranchised.

Smateria   ACCESSORIES
(Map p88; www.smateria.com; Alley West; ⊘10am-10pm) 🕊 Recycling rocks here with funky bags made from construction nets, plastic bags, motorbike seat covers and more. Fairtrade enterprise employing some disabled Cambodians.

Rajana   ARTS & CRAFTS
(Map p88; ☑063-964744; www.rajanacrafts.org; Sivatha St; ⊘9am-9pm Mon-Sat) 🕊 Sells quirky wooden and metalwork objects, well-designed silver jewellery and handmade cards. Rajana promotes fair-trade employment opportunities for Cambodians.

Bambou Indochine   CLOTHING
(Map p88; Alley West; ⊘10am-10pm) Original clothing designs inspired by Indochina. A cut above the average souvenir T-shirts.

Senteurs d'Angkor   HANDICRAFTS
(Map p88; ☑063-964860; Pithnou St; ⊘8.30am-9.30pm) 🕊 Opposite Psar Chaa, this shop has an eclectic collection of silk and carvings, as well as a superb range of traditional beauty products and spices, all made locally. It targets rural poor and disadvantaged Cambodians for jobs and training, and sources local products from farmers. Visit its **Botanic Garden** (Map p90; Airport Rd; ⊘7.30am-5.30pm) on Airport Rd, a sort of Willy Wonka's for the senses, where you can sample infused teas and speciality coffees.

Blue Apsara   BOOKS
(Map p88; St 9; ⊘9am-9pm) The longest-running second-hand bookstore in town has a good selection of English, French and German titles.

ℹ Information

Hotels, restaurants and bars can provide the free *Siem Reap Angkor Visitors Guide* (www.canbypublications.com). Or pick up *Dining & Drinking* and *Out & About*, both produced by Pocket Guides (www.cambodiapocketguide.com).

There are ATMs at the airport and in banks and minimarts all over central Siem Reap, especially along Sivatha St. The greatest concentration of internet shops is along Sivatha St and around Psar Chaa. Free wi-fi is available at many of the leading cafes, restaurants and bars, not forgetting most guesthouses and hotels.

Angkor Hospital for Children (AHC; Map p88; ☑063-963409; angkorhospital.org; cnr Oum Chhay St & Tep Vong St; ⊘24hr) This international-standard paediatric hospital is the place to take your children if they fall sick. It will also assist adults in an emergency for up to 24 hours. Donations accepted.

ANZ Royal Bank (Map p88; Achar Mean St) Credit-card advances and can change travellers cheques in most major currencies. Several branches and many ATMs (US$5 per withdrawal) around town.

Canadia Bank (Map p88; Sivatha St) Offers credit-card cash advances (US$4) and changes travellers cheques in most major currencies at a 2% commission.

Main Post Office (Map p88; Pokambor Ave; ⊘7am-5.30pm) Services are more reliable

GETTING TO THAILAND: SIEM REAP TO BANGKOK

The original land border crossing (open from 7am to 8pm) between Cambodia and Thailand is by far the busiest and the one most people take when travelling between Bangkok and Siem Reap. It has earned itself a bad reputation over the years, with scams galore to help tourists part with their money, especially coming in from Thailand.

Getting to the border Frequent buses and share taxis run from Siem Reap and Battambang to Poipet. Buying a ticket all the way to Bangkok (usually involving a change of buses at the border) can expedite things and save you the hassle of finding onward transport on the Thai side. The 8am through-bus to Mo Chit bus station in Bangkok run by **Nattakan** (Map p88; ☑ 078 795333; Sivatha St) in Siem Reap costs an inflated US$28, but is the only bus service that allows you to continue to Bangkok without a change of bus.

At the border Waits of two or more hours are not uncommon, especially in the high season. Show up early to avoid the crowds. You can pay a special 'VIP fee' (aka a bribe) of 200B on either side to skip the lines. There is no departure tax to leave Cambodia despite what Cambodian border officials might tell you. Entering Thailand, most nationalities are issued 30-day entry free of charge.

Moving on Minibuses wait just over the border on the Thai side to whisk you to Bangkok (B300, four hours, every 30 minutes). Or make your way 7km to Aranya Prathet by túk-túk (80B) or *sŏrng·tǎa·ou* (pickup truck; 15B), from where there are regular buses to Bangkok's Mo Chit station (223B, five to six hours) between 4am and 6pm. The 1.55pm train is another option to Bangkok.

For information on making this crossing in reverse, see p732.

these days, but it doesn't hurt to see your stamps franked. Includes a branch of EMS express mail.

Royal Angkor International Hospital (Map p90; ☑ 063-761888; www.royalangkorhospital. com; Airport Rd) This international facility affiliated with the Bangkok Hospital is on the expensive side as it's used to dealing with insurance companies.

Tourist Police (Map p90; ☑ 012 402424) Located at the main ticket checkpoint for the Angkor area, this is the place to lodge a complaint if you encounter any serious problems while in Siem Reap.

U-Care Pharmacy (Map p88; ☑ 063-965396; Pithnou St; ☺ 8am-10pm) Smart pharmacy and shop similar to Boots in Thailand (and the UK). English spoken.

❶ Getting There & Away

AIR

Siem Reap International Airport (Map p90; ☑ 063-761261; www.cambodia-airports.com) is a work of art set 7km west of the centre and offers regular connections to most neighbouring Asian cities, plus domestic flights to Phnom Penh and Sihanoukville.

BOAT

Boats for the incredibly scenic trip to Battambang (US$20, five to nine hours depending

on water levels) and the faster ride to Phnom Penh (US$35, six hours, August to March only) depart at 7am from the tourist boat dock at Chong Kneas, 11km south of town. Tickets are sold at guesthouses, hotels and travel agencies, including pickup from your hotel or guesthouse around 6am.

BUS

All buses arrive in and depart from the bus station, which is 3km east of town and about 200m south of NH6. Upon arrival, be prepared for a rugby scrum of eager *moto* drivers greeting the bus.

Tickets are available at guesthouses, hotels, bus offices, travel agencies and ticket kiosks. Some bus companies send a minibus around to pick up passengers at their place of lodging. Most departures to Phnom Penh are between 7am and 1pm, but there are also lots of night buses available. Buses to other destinations generally leave early in the morning.

Tickets to Phnom Penh via NH6 cost anywhere from US$5 for basic air-con buses to US$15 for the business-class buses run by Giant Ibis.

Several companies offer direct services to Kompong Cham (US$5, five or six hours), Battambang (US$5 to US$8, three hours) and Poipet (US$5 to US$8, three hours). There are no through buses to Ho Chi Minh City, but it is possible to change in Phnom Penh.

Bus companies that serve Siem Reap:

Capitol Tour (Map p88; ☑ 063-963883; www.capitoltourscambodia.com)

Giant Ibis (Map p88; ☑ 023-999333; www.giantibis.com) Smartest operator with daily service to Phnom Penh (US$15) and free wi-fi on board.

GST (Map p88; ☑ 092 905016)

Mekong Express (Map p88; ☑ 063-963662; catmekongexpress.com/) Upscale bus company with hostesses and drinks.

Phnom Penh Sorya (Map p90; ☑ 012 235618; www.ppsoryatransport.com)

SHARE TAXI

Share taxis stop along NH6 just north of the bus station. Destinations include Phnom Penh (US$10, five hours), Kompong Thom (US$5, two hours), Sisophon (US$5, two hours) and Poipet (US$7, two hours).

❶ Getting Around

From the airport, an official taxi costs US$9, while *remork-motos* (US$7) are also available.

From the bus station a *moto/remork* to the city centre should cost about US$1/2. If you're arriving on a bus service sold by a guesthouse, the bus will head straight to a partner guesthouse.

If arriving by boat, a *moto* into town should cost about US$3 from the dock in Chong Kneas.

Short *moto* trips around the centre of town cost 2000r or 4000r, more at night. A *remork* starts from US$2 and up.

Most guesthouses and small hotels can usually help with bicycle rental for about US$2 per day. Look out for guesthouses and hotels supporting the **White Bicycles** (www.thewhitebicycles.org) project, whose proceeds go to local development projects.

Motorbike hire is currently prohibited in Siem Reap.

Temples of Angkor
ប្រាសាទនៅតំបន់អង្គរ

Where to begin with Angkor? There is no greater concentration of architectural riches anywhere on earth. Choose from the world's largest religious building, Angkor Wat, one of the world's weirdest, Bayon, or the riotous jungle of Ta Prohm. All are global icons and have helped put Cambodia on the map as the temple capital of Asia.

Beyond the big three are dozens more temples, each of which would be the star were it located anywhere else in the region: Banteay Srei, the art gallery of Angkor; Preah Khan, the ultimate fusion temple uniting Buddhism and Hinduism; or Beng Mealea, the *Titanic* of temples suffocating under the jungle. The most vexing part of a visit to Angkor is working out what to see, as there are simply so many spectacular sites. One day at Angkor? Sacrilege! Don't even consider it.

The hundreds of temples surviving today are but the sacred skeleton of the vast political, religious and social centre of the ancient Khmer empire. Angkor was a city that, at its zenith, boasted a population of one million when London was a small town of 50,000. The houses, public buildings and palaces of Angkor were constructed of wood – now long decayed – because the right to dwell in structures of brick or stone was reserved for the gods.

Angkor Wat
អង្គរវត្ត

The traveller's first glimpse of **Angkor Wat** (អង្គរវត្ត; Map p90; admission to all of Angkor 1 day/3 days/1 week US$20/40/60; ⊙5am-5.30pm), the ultimate expression of Khmer

TRANSPORT FROM SIEM REAP

DESTINATION	CAR/MOTORBIKE	BUS	BOAT	AIR
Bangkok	8hr	US$12-28, 10hr, frequent		from US$90, 1hr, 8 daily
Battambang	3hr	US$4-8, 4hr, mostly morning	US$20, 7hr, 7am	
Kompong Thom	2hr	US$5, 2½hr, frequent		
Phnom Penh	5hr	US$6-15, 6hr, frequent	US$35, 5hr, 7am	from US$40, 30min, 9 daily
Poipet	3hr	US$5-8, 4hr, regular		

genius, is simply staggering and is matched by only a few select spots on earth, such as Machu Picchu or Petra.

Angkor is heaven on earth, namely the symbolic representation of Mt Meru, the Mt Olympus of the Hindu faith and abode of ancient gods. It is the perfect fusion of creative ambition and spiritual devotion. The Cambodian 'god-kings' of old each strove to better their ancestors in size, scale and symmetry, culminating in the world's largest religious building, Angkor Wat.

Angkor Wat is the Khmers' national symbol, the epicentre of their civilisation and a source of fierce national pride. Unlike the other Angkor monuments, it was never abandoned to the elements and has been in virtually continuous use since it was built.

The temple is surrounded by a moat, 190m wide, which forms a giant rectangle measuring 1.5km by 1.3km. Stretching around the outside of the central temple complex is an 800m-long series of bas-reliefs, designed to be viewed in an anti-clockwise direction. Rising 31m above the third level is the central tower, which gives the whole ensemble its sublime unity.

Angkor Wat was built by Suryavarman II (r 1113–52), who unified Cambodia and extended Khmer influence across much of mainland Southeast Asia. He also set himself apart religiously from earlier kings by his devotion to the Hindu deity Vishnu, to whom he consecrated the temple, built around the same time as European Gothic heavyweights such as Westminster Abbey and Chartres.

The upper level of Angkor Wat is once again open to modern pilgrims, but visits are strictly timed to 20 minutes.

EXPLORING THE TEMPLES

One Day

If you've got only one day to spend at Angkor, that's unfortunate, but a good itinerary would be Angkor Wat for sunrise, after which you can explore the mighty temple before the crowds arrive. From there, drop by Ta Prohm before breaking for lunch. In the afternoon, explore the temples within the walled city of Angkor Thom and the enigmatic faces of the Bayon in the late-afternoon light. Biggest mistake: trying to pack in too much.

Three Days

With three days to explore the area, start with some of the smaller temples and build up to the big hitters. Visit the early Roluos group on the first day for some chronological consistency and try the stars of the Grand Circuit, including Preah Khan and Preah Neak Poan. Day two might include Ta Prohm and the temples on the Small Circuit, plus the distant but stunning Banteay Srei. Then the climax: Angkor Wat at dawn and the immense city of Angkor Thom in the afternoon.

One Week

Angkor is your oyster, so relax, enjoy and explore at will. Make sure you visit Beng Mealea and Kbal Spean. Do at least one overnight trip further afield, to Koh Ker, Banteay Chhmar or Prasat Preah Vihear. For a change of pace, take a boat to the stilted village of Kompong Pluk.

Tickets

The Angkor ticket checkpoint (p100) is on the road from Siem Reap to Angkor. Three-day passes can be used on any three days over a one-week period, and one-week passes are valid over the course of a month. Tickets issued after 5pm (for sunset viewing) are valid the next day. Tickets are not valid for Phnom Kulen, Beng Mealea or Koh Ker. Get caught ticketless in a temple and you'll be fined US$100.

Eating

There are dozens of local noodle stalls just near the Terrace of the Leper King, and a village with a cluster of restaurants opposite **Sra Srang** (ស្រះស្រង់; Map p90; ☺7.30am-5.30pm), the former royal bathing pond. Angkor Wat has full-blown cafes and restaurants.

Try to be patient with the hordes of children selling food, drinks and souvenirs, as they're only doing what their families have asked them to do to survive. You'll find that their ice-cold bottled water and fresh pineapples are heavenly in the heat.

Angkor Thom   អង្គរធំ

It is hard to imagine any building bigger or more beautiful than Angkor Wat, but in Angkor Thom (Great Angkor, or Great City) the sum of the parts add up to a greater whole. It is the gates that grab you first, flanked by a monumental representation of the Churning of the Ocean of Milk, 54 demons and 54 gods engaged in an epic tug of war on the causeway. Each gate towers above the visitor, the magnanimous faces of the Bodhisattva Avalokiteshvara staring out over the kingdom. Imagine being a peasant in the 13th century approaching the forbidding capital for the first time: it would have been an awe-inspiring yet unsettling experience to enter such a gateway and come face to face with the divine power of the god-kings.

The last great capital of the Khmer empire, Angkor Thom took monumental to a whole new level, set over 10 sq km. It was built in part as a reaction to the surprise sacking of Angkor by the Chams. Jayavarman VII (r 1181–1219) decided that his empire would never again be vulnerable at home. Beyond the formidable walls is a massive moat that would have stopped all but the hardiest invaders in their tracks.

⊙ Sights

At the heart of Angkor Thom is the 12th-century **Bayon** (បាយ័ន; Map p90; ☉ 7.30am-5.30pm). The mesmerising if slightly mind-bending state temple of Jayavarman VII epitomises the creative genius and inflated ego of Cambodia's most celebrated king. Its 54 gothic towers are famously decorated with 216 gargantuan smiling faces of Avalokiteshvara that bear more than a passing resemblance to the great king himself.

It's known as the 'face temple' thanks to its iconic visages. These huge heads glare down from every angle, exuding power and control with a hint of humanity – precisely the blend required to hold sway over such a vast empire, ensuring the disparate and far-flung population yielded to the king's magnanimous will.

The Bayon is decorated with 1.2km of extraordinary bas-reliefs incorporating more than 11,000 figures, depicting everyday life in 12th-century Cambodia. You may notice something that looks much like the 'Thai' kickboxing of today depicted in these bas-reliefs; much of Thailand's culture is linked to the Cambodian artisans, dancers, schol-

TOP ANGKOR EXPERIENCES

➡ See the sun rise over the holiest of holies, **Angkor Wat**, the world's largest religious building.

➡ Contemplate the serenity and splendour of the **Bayon**, its 216 enigmatic faces staring out into the jungle.

➡ Witness nature reclaiming the stones at the mysterious ruin of **Ta Prohm**, the *Tomb Raider* temple.

➡ Stare in wonder at the delicate carvings adorning **Banteay Srei**, the finest seen at Angkor.

➡ Trek deep into the jungle to discover the River of a Thousand Lingas at **Kbal Spean**.

CAMBODIA TEMPLES OF ANGKOR

ars and fighters with whom the Thais made off after they sacked Angkor in 1432. The history of Angkor remains a seriously sensitive topic between the two cultures, fuelling a bitter rivalry that's lasted centuries.

Baphuon   HINDU TEMPLE
(បាពួន; Map p90; ☉ 7.30am-5.30pm) Some have called Baphuon 'world's largest jigsaw puzzle'. Before the civil war the Baphuon was painstakingly taken apart piece-by-piece by a team of archaeologists, but their meticulous records were destroyed during the Khmer Rouge regime, leaving experts with 300,000 stones to put back into place. After years of excruciating research, this temple has been partially restored. On the western side, the retaining wall of the second level was fashioned, in the 16th century, into a reclining Buddha 60m in length.

Terrace of Elephants   ARCHAEOLOGICAL SITE
(លានជល់ដំរី; Map p90) The 350m-long Terrace of Elephants was used as a giant viewing stand for public ceremonies and served as a base for the king's grand audience hall. Try to imagine the pomp and grandeur of the Khmer empire at its height, with infantry, cavalry, horse-drawn chariots and elephants parading across Central Square in a colourful procession, pennants and standards aloft. Looking on is the god-king, shaded by multi-tiered parasols and attended by mandarins and handmaidens bearing gold and silver utensils.

DON'T MISS

TA PROHM

The ultimate Indiana Jones fantasy, **Ta Prohm** (តាព្រហ្ម; Map p90; ⊙7.30am-5.30pm) is cloaked in dappled shadow, its crumbling towers and walls locked in the slow muscular embrace of vast root systems. If Angkor Wat is testimony to the genius of the ancient Khmers, Ta Prohm reminds us equally of the awesome fecundity and power of the jungle. There is a poetic cycle to this venerable ruin, with humanity first conquering nature to rapidly create, and nature once again conquering humanity to slowly destroy.

Built from 1186 and originally known as Rajavihara (Monastery of the King), Ta Prohm was a Buddhist temple dedicated to the mother of Jayavarman VII. Ta Prohm is a temple of towers, closed courtyards and narrow corridors. Ancient trees tower overhead, their leaves filtering the sunlight and casting a greenish pall over the whole scene. It is the closest most of us will get to the discoveries of the explorers of old.

Terrace of the Leper King   ARCHAEOLOGICAL SITE
(ទីលានព្រះគម្លង់; Map p90) The Terrace of the Leper King is just north of the Terrace of Elephants. Dating from the late 12th century, it is a 7m-high platform, on top of which stands a nude, though sexless, statue. The front retaining walls of the terrace are decorated with at least five tiers of meticulously executed carvings. On the southern side of the Terrace of the Leper King, there is access to a hidden terrace with exquisitely preserved carvings.

Around Angkor Thom

◉ Sights

Phnom Bakheng   HINDU TEMPLE
(ភ្នំបាខែង; Map p90; ⊙5am-7pm) Located around 400m south of Angkor Thom, the main attraction at Phnom Bakheng is the sunset view over Angkor Wat. For many years, the whole affair turned into a circus, with crowds of tourists ascending the slopes of the hill and jockeying for space. Numbers are restricted to just 300 visitors at any one time, so get here early (4pm) to guarantee a sunset spot. The temple, built by Yasovarman I (r 889–910), has five tiers, with seven levels.

Preah Khan   BUDDHIST TEMPLE
(ព្រះខ័ន, Sacred Sword; Map p90; ⊙7.30am-5.30pm) The temple of Preah Khan (Sacred Sword) is one of the largest complexes at Angkor, a maze of vaulted corridors, fine carvings and lichen-clad stonework. It is a good counterpoint to Ta Prohm and generally has slightly fewer visitors. Like Ta Prohm it is a place of towered enclosures and shoulder-hugging corridors. Unlike Ta Prohm, however, the temple of Preah Khan is in a reasonable state of preservation thanks to the ongoing restoration efforts of the World Monuments Fund (WMF; www.wmf.org).

Preah Neak Poan   BUDDHIST TEMPLE
(ព្រះនាគព័ន្ធ, Temple of the Intertwined Nagas; Map p90; ⊙7.30am-5.30pm) The Buddhist temple of Preah Neak Poan is a petite yet perfect temple constructed by Jayavarman VII in the late 12th century. It has a large square pool surrounded by four smaller square pools. In the middle of the central pool is a circular 'island' encircled by the two *nagas* (mythical serpents) whose intertwined tails give the temple its name.

Bakong   HINDU TEMPLE
(បាគង; Map p90; ⊙7.30am-5.30pm) Bakong is the largest and most interesting of the Roluos group of temples. Built and dedicated to Shiva by Indravarman I, it's a representation of Mt Meru, and it served as the city's central temple. The east-facing complex consists of a five-tier central pyramid of sandstone, 60m square at the base, flanked by eight towers of brick and sandstone, and by other minor sanctuaries. A number of the lower towers are still partly covered by their original plasterwork.

Further Afield

◉ Sights

★Banteay Srei   HINDU TEMPLE
(បន្ទាយស្រី; ⊙7.30am-5.30pm) Considered by many to be the jewel in the crown of Angkorian art, Banteay Srei is cut from stone of a pinkish hue and includes some of the finest stone carving anywhere on earth. Begun in AD 967, it is one of the smallest sites at Angkor, but what it lacks in size it makes up for in stature. A Hindu temple dedicat-

ed to Shiva, Banteay Srei is wonderfully well preserved and many of its carvings are three-dimensional.

Kbal Spean
HINDU SHRINE

(ក្បាលស្ពាន; ⊙ 7.30am-5.30pm) A spectacularly carved riverbed, Kbal Spean is set deep in the jungle to the northeast of Angkor. More commonly referred to in English as the 'River of a Thousand Lingas', the name actually means 'bridgehead', a reference to the natural rock bridge at the site. *Lingas* (phallic symbols) have been carved into the riverbed, and images of Hindu deities are dotted about the area. Kbal Spean was 'discovered' in 1969, when ethnologist Jean Boulbet was shown the area by a hermit.

Phnom Kulen
MOUNTAIN

(ភ្នំគូលែន; US$20) Considered by Khmers to be the most sacred mountain in Cambodia, Phnom Kulen is a popular place of pilgrimage on weekends and during festivals. It played a significant role in the history of the Khmer empire, as it was from here in AD 802 that Jayavarman II proclaimed himself a *devaraja* (god-king), giving birth to the Cambodian kingdom. Attractions include a giant reclining Buddha, hundreds of *lingas*

carved in the riverbed, an impressive waterfall and some remote temples.

Beng Mealea
BUDDHIST TEMPLE

(បឹងមាលា; admission US$5; ⊙ 7.30am-5.30pm) A spectacular sight to behold, Beng Mealea, about 68km northeast of Siem Reap, is one of the most mysterious temples at Angkor, as nature has well and truly run riot. Exploring this titanic of temples is Angkor's ultimate Indiana Jones experience. Built in the 12th century under Suryavarman II, Beng Mealea was built to the same floorplan as Angkor Wat and is enclosed by a massive moat measuring 1.2km by 900m.

Koh Ker
HINDU TEMPLE

(កោះកេរ៍; admission US$10; ⊙ 7.30am-5.30pm) Abandoned to the forests of the north, Koh Ker, capital of the Angkorian empire from AD 928 to 944, is within day-trip distance of Siem Reap. Most visitors start at Prasat Krahom where impressive stone carvings grace lintels, doorposts and window columns. The principal monument is Prasat Thom, a 55m-wide, 40m-high sandstone-faced pyramid whose seven tiers offer spectacular views across the forest. Koh Ker is 127km northeast of Siem Reap.

GETTING TO THAILAND: REMOTE NORTHERN BORDERS

There are a couple of seldom-used crossings along Cambodia's northern border with Thailand. The usual 30-day entry to Thailand and Cambodian visas-on-arrival are available at both borders. For information on making these crossings in reverse, see p732.

Anlong Veng to Chong Sa-Ngam
The remote Choam/Chong Sa-Ngam crossing (open from 7am to 8pm) connects Anlong Veng in Oddar Meanchey Province with Thailand's Si Saket Province.

Getting to the border A *moto* from Anlong Veng to the border crossing (16km) costs US$3 or US$4. Share taxis link Anlong Veng with Siem Reap (20,000r, 1½ hours).

At the border Formalities here are straightforward.

Moving on On the Thai side, find a motorcycle taxi or taxi to take you to the nearest town, Phusing (30 minutes), where buses and *sŏrng·tăa·ou* (pickup trucks) head to Si Saket and Kantharalak. Or try to hop on a casino shuttle from the border to Phusing, Ku Khan or Si Saket.

Samraong to Surin
The remote O Smach/Chong Chom crossing connects Cambodia's Oddar Meanchey Province and Thailand's Surin Province.

Getting to the border Share taxis link Siem Reap with Samraong (30,000r, two hours) via NH68. From Samraong, take a *moto* (US$5) or a charter taxi (US$15) for the smooth drive to O Smach (40km, 30 minutes) and its frontier casino zone. A private taxi from Siem Reap all the way to the border should cost US$60 to US$70.

At the border The crossing itself is easy.

Moving on On the Thai side walk to the nearby bus stop, where regular buses depart to Surin throughout the day (60B, 70km, 1½ hours).

NORTHWESTERN CAMBODIA

Offering highway accessibility and outback adventure in equal measure, northwestern Cambodia stretches from the Cardamom Mountains to the Dangkrek Mountains, with Tonlé Sap lake at its heart. Battambang attracts the most visitors thanks to an alluring blend of mellowness, colonial-era architecture and excellent day-tripping.

Northwestern Cambodia's remote plains and jungles conceal some of the country's most inspired temples, including spectacular Prasat Preah Vihear, declared a World Heritage site in 2008, and the pre-Angkorian temples of Sambor Prei Kuk near Kompong Thom.

Battambang បាត់ដំបង

📞 053 / POP 147,000

The elegant riverside town of Battambang is home to Cambodia's best-preserved French-period architecture. The stunning boat trip from Siem Reap lures travellers here, but it's the remarkably chilled atmosphere that makes them linger. Battambang is an excellent base for exploring nearby temples and villages that offer a real slice of rural Cambodia.

AN EVENING UNDER THE BIG TOP

Battambang's signature attraction is the internationally acclaimed **Phare Ponleu Selpak** (📞053-952424; www. phareps.org; adult/student US$14/7), a multi-arts centre for disadvantaged children. Even though it is now running shows in Siem Reap, it's worth timing your visit to Battambang to watch the amazing spectacle where it all began. Performances are at 7pm on Monday, Thursday and Saturday, with a Friday show added during the high season.

Guests are welcome to join a daytime guided **tour** (US$5; ⊙8-11am & 2-5pm Mon-Fri) of the Phare complex and observe circus, dance, music, drawing and graphic-arts classes.

To get here from the Vishnu Roundabout on NH5, head west for 900m and then turn right (north) and continue another 600m.

◉ Sights

Much of Battambang's charm lies in its early-20th-century French architecture. Some of the finest colonial buildings are along the waterfront (St 1), especially just south of Psar Nath, itself an architectural monument, albeit a modernist one. The two-storey **Governor's Residence**, with its balconies and wooden shutters, is another handsome legacy of the early 1900s. Designed by an Italian architect for the last Thai governor, who departed in 1907, it has imposing balconies and a grand reception room with 5m ceilings.

Phnom Penh-based **KA Architecture Tours** (www.ka-tours.org) has collaborated with Battambang Municipality to create two heritage walks in the historic centre of Battambang, available for free download on its website. This is a great way to spend half a day exploring the city.

Battambang Museum MUSEUM
(សារមន្ទីរខេត្តបាត់ដំបង; St 1; admission US$1; ⊙8-11am & 2-5.30pm) This small and rather dusty museum displays a trove of fine Angkorian lintels and statuary from all over Battambang Province, including pieces from Prasat Banan and Sneng. Signs are in Khmer, English and French.

A mammoth museum enlargement and modernisation project was in the planning stages when we were last in town and may be well under way by the time you visit.

🏃 Activities

Soksabike CYCLING
(📞012 542019; www.soksabike.com; half-day US$23-27, full day US$34-40; ⊙departs 7.30am) 🚲 Based at Kinyei cafe (p107), Soksabike is a social enterprise aiming to connect visitors with the Cambodian countryside and its people. Half-day/full-day trips cover 25km/40km and include stops at family-run industries such as rice-paper making and the *prahoc* (fermented fish paste) factory, and a visit to a local home. Tour prices depend on group size.

Green Orange Kayaks KAYAKING
(📞017 736166; www.fedacambodia.org; Ksach Poy; half-day US$12) 🚣 Kayaks can be rented from Green Orange Kayaks, part of FEDA, a local NGO which runs a community centre in the village of **Ksach Poy**, 8km south of Battambang. Half-day, self-guided kayaking trips begin at Ksach Poy's Green Orange Cafe. From there you paddle back to the city along

the Sangker River. A guide (US$3) is optional. Booking ahead is highly recommended.

Coconut Lyly COOKING COURSE
(☑016 399339; www.coconutlyly.com; St 111; per person US$10) Classes are run by Chef Lyly, a graduate from Siem Reap's Paul Dubrule Cooking School. Half-day classes (start times 9am and 3.30pm) include a visit to Psar Nath, preparing four typically Khmer dishes (recipe book included) and then eating your handiwork afterwards. The excellent restaurant here is open from 8am to 10pm.

Seeing Hands Massage MASSAGE
(☑078 337499; St 121; per hr US$6; ☉7am-10pm) ☞ Trained blind masseurs offer soothing work-overs.

🛏 Sleeping

★Angkor Comfort Hotel HOTEL $
(☑077 306410; www.angkorcomforthotel.com; St 1; r with air-con US$15; ➼🅿🛜) Serious bang for your buck. The huge rooms are sparkling clean and come with white linens on the bed, flatscreen TVs, enough power-points to charge up all your devices at once, and modern bathrooms with walk-in showers – these are mid-range amenities on a backpacker budget.

Here Be Dragons HOSTEL $
(☑089 264895; www.herebedragonsbattambang.com; Riverside East; dm US$3, r US$8-10; 🛜) A funky fun bar, leafy front garden for relaxing, and free beer on arrival make Here Be Dragons a top backpacker base. Six-bed dorms come with lock-boxes, while sunny private rooms are cheerfully decked out with brightly coloured bedding. The quiet location next to the riverside park on the East Bank is a bonus.

Ganesha Family Guesthouse GUESTHOUSE $
(☑092 135570; www.ganeshaguesthouse.com; St 1½; dm US$4.50, r US$11-14; 🛜) The best of Battambang's cheapies, Ganesha has a light-filled dorm with double-wide beds, and small private rooms with bamboo furniture and tiled bathrooms (cold water only). Downstairs is an inviting cafe.

Royal Hotel HOTEL $
(☑016 912034; www.royalhotelbattambang.com; St 115; r with air-con US$20-25; 🅱@🛜) An old-timer on the Battambang scene, the Royal is deservedly popular. Some rooms may be faded but all are decently sized and come with fridge and TV. Staff here are some of the most clued-up in town.

ALL ABOARD THE BAMBOO TRAIN
....

Battambang's **bamboo train** (return ride for 2 or more passengers each US$5, for 1 passenger US$10; ☉7am-dusk) is one of the world's all-time unique rail journeys. From O Dambong, on the east bank 3.7km south of Battambang's old French bridge (Wat Kor Bridge), the train bumps 7km southeast to O Sra Lav along warped, misaligned rails and vertiginous bridges left by the French.

Each bamboo train – known in Khmer as a *norry* – consists of a 3m-long wooden frame, covered lengthwise with slats made of ultralight bamboo, that rest on two barbell-like bogies, the aft one connected by fan belts to a 6HP gasoline engine. Pile on 10 or 15 people or up to three tonnes of rice, crank it up and you can cruise along at about 15km/h.

Senghout Hotel HOTEL $
(☑012 530327; www.senghouthotel.com; St 2; r with fan US$10-15, with air-con US$15-35; 🅱🛜🛏) Known for its on-the-ball staff who are quick to help with traveller queries, the Senghout has a variety of nicely decorated rooms. Some are a bit pokey, so check out a few before deciding. The rooftop pool is a key drawcard.

🍴 Eating & Drinking

Cheap dining is available in and around Psar Nath. There's a **riverside night market** (St 1; mains 4000-8000r; ☉3pm-midnight) opposite the Battambang Museum.

★Lonely Tree Cafe CAFE $
(www.thelonelytreecafe.com; St 121; mains US$4-5.50; ☉10am-10pm; 🛜) ☞ Upstairs from the shop of the same name, this uber-cosy cafe serves Spanish tapas–style dishes and a few Khmer options under a soaring, bamboo-inlaid ceiling. Its mascot is an actual tree on the road to Siem Reap. Proceeds support cultural preservation and the disabled, among other causes.

Kinyei CAFE
(www.kinyei.org; 1 St 1½; coffee US$1.25-2.50, snacks US$1-2.50; ☉7am-7pm; 🛜) ☞ Want to know where we go for our morning coffee in Battambang? This titchy cafe has – hands-down – the best coffee in town. National

Battambang

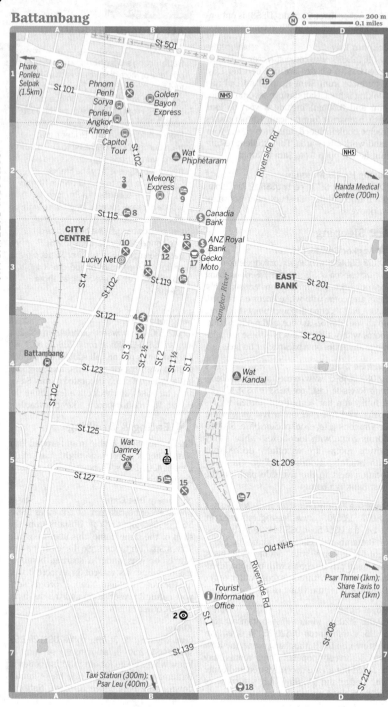

Battambang

0 _____ 200 m
0 _____ 0.1 miles

Phare Ponleu Selpak (1.5km)

St 501

St 101

NH5

NH5

Phnom Penh Sorya

16

Golden Bayon Express

Ponleu Angkor Khmer

Capitol Tour

St 102

Wat Phiphétaram

3

Mekong Express

9

St 115   8

Canadia Bank

CITY CENTRE

10

13

ANZ Royal Bank

Lucky Net @

12

Gecko Moto

17

11

6

St 119

St 4

St 102

St 3

EAST BANK   St 201

Sangker River

St 121

4

14

St 123

Battambang

St 102

St 3   St 2½   St 2   St 1½   St 1

St 203

Wat Kandal

St 125

Wat Damrey Sar

1

St 209

5

15

7

St 127

Old NH5

Psar Thmei (1km); Share Taxis to Pursat (1km)

Riverside Rd

Tourist Information Office

2

St 1

St 139

St 208

Taxi Station (300m); Psar Leu (400m)

St 212

18

Battambang

barista champs have been crowned here. All your espressos, flat whites and cappuccinos are on offer and there's a small menu of breakfast options and light bites.

Choco l'art Café CAFE $
(www.chocolartcafe.com; St 117; breakfasts & mains US$1.50-6; ⊙9am-midnight Wed-Mon; 🛜) Run with gusto by local painter Ke and his French partner Soline, this inviting gallery-cafe sees foreigners and locals alike gather to drink and eat Soline's wonderful bread, pastries and (for breakfast) crêpes. Live music gets going occasionally.

Coconut Water INTERNATIONAL $
(St 119; mains US$2-3.50; ⊙8am-9pm; 🍴) 🌱 Eat in the snug 1st-floor cafe or amid the cushions on the shaded rooftop. There's great breakfast options and a small list of Khmer staples, or you can munch on a caramelised chicken or tofu burger. Profits support various community projects.

Fresh Eats Café INTERNATIONAL $
(www.mpkhomeland.org; St 2½; mains US$2.50-4; ⊙9am-9pm; 🛜) 🌱 Run by an NGO that helps disadvantaged youth, this place complements its Khmer specialities with build-your-own baguettes, great salads and pasta. There's a small handicrafts boutique on-site.

Vegetarian Foods Restaurant VEGETARIAN $
(St 102; mains 1500-3000r; ⊙6.30am-5pm; 🍴) This hole-in-the-wall eatery serves some of the most delicious vegetarian dishes in Cambodia, including rice soup, homemade soy milk and dumplings for just 1000r. Tremendous value.

⭐ **Jaan Bai** FUSION $$
(📞078 263144; jaanbai@cambodianchildrenstrust.org; cnr St 1½ & St 2; small plates US$3, mains US$4-10; ⊙11am-10.30pm Tue-Sun; 🛜🍴) 🌱 Jaan Bai ('rice bowl' in Khmer) is Battambang's foodie treat, with a sleekly minimalist interior offset by beautiful French-Khmer tile work lining the wall. The menu likewise is successfully bold. Order a few of the small plates to savour the range of flavours, or go all-out with the tasting menu: seven plates plus wine for US$15 per person (minimum two people).

Riverside Balcony Bar BAR
(cnr St 1 & St 149; ⊙4-11pm Tue-Sun; 🛜) Set in a gorgeous wooden house high above the riverfront, Australian-run Riverside is Battambang's original bar and a mellow place for a sundowner. The small menu mixes pub grub and Khmer classics (mains US$3.50 to US$7.50).

⊙ Information

For information on what's happening in town, look out for copies of the free *Battambang Buzz* magazine at restaurants, bars and hotels. The city map available at the tourist office details scenic routes to the bamboo train and other attractions outside of town.

Free wi-fi access is the norm at hotels and most cafes and restaurants.

ANZ Royal Bank (St 1; ⊙8.30am-4pm Mon-Fri, ATM 24hr)

Canadia Bank (Psar Thom; ⊙7.30am-3.30pm Mon-Fri, to 11.30am Sat, ATM 24hr)

Handa Medical Centre (📞095 520654; NH5; ⊙clinic 9am-3.30pm, emergency 24hr) Has two ambulances and usually a European doctor or two in residence.

Tourist Information Office (📞012 534177; www.battambang-town.gov.kh; St 1; ⊙8-11am

& 2-5pm Mon-Fri) Moderately useful office with a great map of Battambang.

ℹ️ Getting There & Away

BOAT

The riverboat to Siem Reap (US$20, 7am) squeezes through narrow waterways and passes by protected wetlands, taking from five hours in the wet season to nine or more hours at the height of the dry season. Cambodia's most memorable boat trip, it's operated on alternate days by **Angkor Express** (☑ 012 601287) and **Chann Na** (☑ 012 354344). In the dry season, passengers are driven to a navigable section of the river.

BUS

Most bus companies are clustered in the centre just south of the intersection of NH5 and St 4. For Phnom Penh, Capitol Tour and Phnom Penh Sorya have the most services, but for quicker day travel to the capital, consider express mini-vans run by Golden Bayon Express (US$10, 4½ hours) or Mekong Express (US$12, 4½ hours). Sleeper buses arrive at an ungodly hour so are not recommended.

Capitol Tour (☑ 053-953040; St 102)
Golden Bayon Express (☑ 070 968966; St 101)
Mekong Express (☑ 088 576 7668; St 3)
Phnom Penh Sorya (☑ 053-953904; St 4)
Ponleu Angkor Khmer (☑ 053-952366; St 4)

TAXI

At the **taxi station** (NH5), share taxis to Phnom Penh (40,000r, 4½ hours) leave from the south-east corner, while taxis to Poipet (20,000r, 1¾ hours) and Siem Reap (26,000r, three hours) leave from north of the market out on NH5.

Share taxis to Pailin (20,000r, 1¼ hours) near the Psar Pruhm–Pong Nam Ron border leave from the east edge of Psar Leu.

ℹ️ Getting Around

English- and French-speaking *remork* drivers are commonplace in Battambang, and all of them are eager to whisk you around on day trips.

Figure on US$12 for a half-day trip and US$16 to US$20 for a full day, depending on your haggling skills and the destinations. A *moto* costs about half as much.

A *moto* ride in town costs around 2000r, while a *remork* ride starts from US$1.

Gecko Moto (☑ 089 924260; St 3; ⊗ 8am-7pm) and Royal Hotel (p107) rent out motorbikes for US$7 to US$8 per day. Bicycles are a great way to get around; these can be rented at the Royal Hotel, Soksabike (p106) and several other guesthouses for about US$2 per day.

Around Battambang

The countryside around Battambang is littered with old temples, bamboo trains and other worthwhile sights. Admission to Phnom Sampeau, Phnom Banan and Wat Ek Phnom costs US$3. If you purchase a ticket at one site, it's valid all day long at the other two.

Phnom Sampeau   ភ្នំសំពៅ

At the summit of this fabled limestone outcrop, 12km southwest of Battambang (towards Pailin), a complex of **temples** affords gorgeous views. Some of the macaques that live here, dining on bananas left as offerings, are pretty cantankerous.

Between the summit and the mobile-phone antenna, a deep canyon descends steeply through a natural arch to a 'lost world' of stalactites, creeping vines and bats.

About halfway up the hill, a turn-off leads 250m up to the **Killing Caves of Phnom Sampeau.** An enchanted staircase, flanked by greenery, leads into a cavern where a golden reclining Buddha lies peacefully next to a glass-walled memorial filled with the bones and skulls of some of the people bludgeoned to death by Khmer Rouge cadres, before being thrown through the overhead skylight.

BUSES FROM BATTAMBANG

DESTINATION	COMPANY	FARE (US$)	DURATION (HR)	FREQUENCY
Bangkok	PP Sorya, Mekong Express	15-16	9	10.30am, 11.30am, noon
Pailin	Ponleu Angkor	3-4	1½	1pm, 3pm
Phnom Penh	all companies	5-12	6	frequent
Poipet	PP Sorya	4-4.50	2¼	7.45am, 1pm
Siem Reap	most companies	4-5	4	frequent to 2pm

GETTING TO THAILAND: WESTERN BORDERS

Pailin to Chanthaburi

The laid-back Psar Pruhm/Ban Pakard border (open from 7am to 8pm) is 102km south-west of Battambang and 18km northwest of Pailin via good sealed roads.

Getting to the border From Battambang, the daily Ponleu Angkor buses to Pailin continue on to this border. Alternatively, take a share taxi to Pailin from Psar Leu in Battambang, then continue to the border by *moto* (US$5) or private taxi (US$10).

At the border Formalities are extremely straightfoward and quick on both sides.

Moving on Onward transport on the Thai side dries up mid-morning so cross early. In the morning you should be able to find a motorcycle taxi (50B) to the nearby *sŏrng-tǎa-ou* (pickup truck) station, where two morning minibuses head to Chanthaburi (150B, 1½ hours), offering frequent buses to Bangkok.

For information on making this crossing in reverse, see p731.

Koh Kong to Trat

Getting to the border To cross at the Cham Yeam/Hat Lek border, take a taxi (US$10 plus toll) or *moto* (US$3 plus toll) from Koh Kong across the toll bridge to Cham Yeam at the border.

At the border Departing Cambodia via the Hat Lek border is actually pretty straightforward, as there are no visa scams for immigration to benefit from.

Moving on Once in Thailand, catch a minibus to Trat (120B), from where there are regular buses to Bangkok (from 254B, five to six hours). Arrange onward transport to Ko Chang in Trat.

For information on making this crossing in reverse, see p731.

Phnom Banan   ភ្នំបាណន់

Exactly 358 stone steps lead up a shaded slope to 11th-century **Wat Banan**, 28km south of Battambang, whose five towers are reminiscent of the layout of Angkor Wat. The views are well worth the climb. From the temple, a narrow stone staircase leads south down the hill to three caves, which can be visited with a local guide.

Wat Ek Phnom   វត្តឯកភ្នំ

This atmospheric, partly collapsed, 11th-century **temple** is 11km north of Battambang. A lintel showing the Churning of the Ocean of Milk can be seen above the east entrance to the central temple, whose upper flanks hold some fine **bas-reliefs**. This is a great place for a shady picnic.

Kompong Thom   កំពង់ធំ

☏ 062 / POP 68,000

A bustling commercial centre, Kompong Thom is mainly a base from which to explore dazzling Sambor Prei Kuk.

🍴 Sleeping & Eating

Arunras Hotel   HOTEL **$**
(☏ 062-961294; NH6; s/d with fan US$5/8, d with air-con US$15; ▧ 🛜) Dominating Kompong Thom's accommodation scene, this corner establishment has 58 good-value rooms with Chinese-style decoration and on-the-ball staff. The popular restaurant downstairs dishes up tasty Khmer fare. Operates the slightly cheaper, 53-room **Arunras Guesthouse** (☏ 012 865935; NH6; s/d with fan US$6/8, with air-con US$10/13; ▧ 🛜) next door. Extra bonus for the lazy traveller: buses through town stop literally right outside the door.

Prum Bayon Restaurant   CAMBODIAN **$**
(Prachea Thepatay St; mains incl rice 6000-10,000r; ⏱ 5am-9pm) Lacking English signs but with an English menu, this immensely popular feeding station is where locals come for flavourful Khmer cooking.

★ **Kompong Thom Restaurant**   CAMBODIAN **$$**
(NH6; mains US$3-8; ⏱ 6.30am-9pm; 🛜 🖵) With delightful bow-tied waiters and a pocket-sized terrace overlooking the river, this restaurant is easily Kompong Thom's best. Unique

concoctions featuring water buffalo and stir-fried eel feature on the menu of Khmer classics, which come in generous portions.

ⓘ Information

Canadia Bank (NH6; ⊗8am-3.30pm Mon-Fri, 8-11.30am Sat, ATM 24hr)

ⓘ Getting There & Around

Dozens of buses travelling between Phnom Penh (US$5, four hours) and Siem Reap (US$5, two hours) pass through Kompong Thom and can easily be flagged down outside the Arunras Hotel.

Heading north to Preah Vihear City, share taxis (US$5, two hours) depart in the morning only.

Im Sokhom Travel Agency (☑012 691527; St 3) rents bicycles (US$1 a day) and motorbikes (US$5 a day).

Around Kompong Thom

Sambor Prei Kuk   សំបូរព្រៃគុក

Cambodia's most impressive group of pre-Angkorian monuments, **Sambor Prei Kuk** (សំបូរព្រៃគុក; www.samborpreikuk.com; admission US$3) encompasses more than 100 brick temples scattered throughout the forest. Originally called Isanapura, it served as the capital of Chenla during the reign of the early-7th-century King Isanavarman.

Forested and shady, Sambor Prei Kuk has a serene atmosphere. The main temple area consists of three complexes: **Prasat Sambor**, dedicated to Gambhireshvara, one of Shiva's many incarnations; **Prasat Yeay Peau**, which feels lost in the forest, its east-

---

OFF THE BEATEN TRACK

PRASAT PREAH VIHEAR   ប្រាសាទព្រះវិហារ

This 800m-long **temple** (ប្រាសាទព្រះវិហារ; admission US$10; ⊗7.30am-4.30pm) is the most dramatically situated of all the Angkorian monuments. It sits high atop the Dangkrek escarpment on the Thai border, with stupendous views of Cambodia's northern plains.

Prasat Preah Vihear consists of a series of four cruciform *gopura* (sanctuaries) decorated with exquisite carvings, including some striking lintels. Starting at the **Monumental Stairway**, a walk south takes you to the **Gopura of the Third Level**, with its early rendition of the Churning of the Ocean of Milk, and finally, perched at the edge of the cliff, the **Central Sanctuary**. Stick to well-marked paths, as the Khmer Rouge laid huge numbers of landmines around Prasat Preah Vihear as late as 1998.

Prasat Preah Vihear and the lands surrounding it were ruled by Thailand in the 19th century, but were returned to Cambodia during the French protectorate. In 1959 the Thai military seized the temple from Cambodia, but the International Court of Justice (ICJ) in the Hague recognised Cambodian sovereignty in a 1962 ruling.

In July 2008 Prasat Preah Vihear was declared Cambodia's second Unesco World Heritage site. Thai troops soon crossed into Cambodian territory, sparking an armed confrontation. In July 2011 the ICJ ruled that both sides should establish a demilitarised zone. Then in November 2013 the ICJ confirmed its 1962 ruling that the temple belongs to Cambodia. The border area remains tense, but is considered safe.

Driving in from Sra Em, stop at the **information centre** (Kor Muy; ⊗7am-4.30pm) in the village of Kor Muy. This is where you pay your donation, secure an English-speaking guide (US$15), and arrange transport via *moto* (US$5 return) or 4WD (US$25 return, maximum six passengers) up the 6.5km temple access road, the final 1.5km of which is extremely steep.

Budget lodging is plentiful in the burgeoning town of Sra Em, 23km south of the information centre. Try **Sok San Guesthouse** (☑097 715 3839; s/d with fan US$8/10, with air-con from US$13/15; ❄🛜), 1km west of Sra Em's central roundabout.

With a private car you can get to Prasat Preah Vihear (not to be confused with Preah Vihear City, 110km south) in about three hours from Siem Reap (about US$140 round-trip). It makes more sense to break up the long trip with a night in Sra Em, which is just 30km from the temple. Share taxis (US$10 per person, three hours) link Sra Em with Siem Reap. From Sra Em's central roundabout, you can find a *moto* to the information centre in Kor Muy (US$10 return).

ern gateway smothered by an ancient tree; and **Prasat Tao** (Lion Temple), the largest of the Sambor Prei Kuk complexes, boasting two large and elaborately coiffed stone lions.

Isanborei (☑017 936112; www.samborprei kuk.com; dm/d US$4/6) 🖉 runs a community-based homestay program, offers cooking courses, rents bicycles (US$2 per day) and organises ox-cart rides. It also operates a stable of *remorks* to whisk you safely to/from Kompong Thom (US$15 one way).

You'll find plenty of restaurants (mains US$2 to US$4) serving local fare around the large open-air handicrafts market near the temple entrance.

Sambor Prei Kuk is 30km northeast of Kompong Thom via smooth roads. A round-trip *moto* ride out here should cost US$10, a *remork* about US$20.

SOUTH COAST

Cambodia's south coast is an alluring mix of clear blue water, castaway islands, pristine mangrove forests, time-worn colonial towns and jungle-clad mountains, where bears and elephants lurk. Adventurers will find this region of Cambodia just as rewarding as sunseekers do.

Koh Kong City ក្រុងកោះកុង

☑035 / POP 36,000

Once Cambodia's Wild West, its frontier economy dominated by smuggling, prostitution and gambling, the city of Koh Kong, eponymous capital of the province, is striding towards respectability as ecotourists scare the sleaze away.

◉ Sights & Activities

Koh Kong's main draw is for those seeking adventure in and around the Cardamom Mountains and the Koh Kong Conservation Corridor.

Peam Krasaop
Mangrove Sanctuary　　　　NATURE RESERVE
(ជម្រកសត្វព្រៃបឹងក្រឹយាក ពាមក្រសោប; admission 5000r; ⊗6.30am-6pm) Anchored in alluvial islands – some no larger than a house – this 260-sq-km sanctuary's magnificent mangroves protect the coast from erosion, serve as a vital breeding and feeding ground for fish, shrimp and shellfish, and are home to myriad birds.

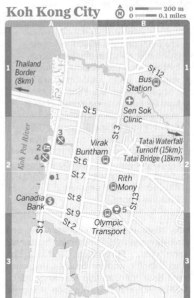

Koh Kong City　　　　Ⓝ　0 ▭▭▭ 200 m
　　　　　　　　　　　　　　　0 ▭▭▭ 0.1 miles

Koh Kong City

🔵 **Activities, Courses & Tours**
　1 Ritthy's Koh Kong Eco Adventure
　　Tours A2

🔵 **Sleeping**
　2 Koh Kong City Hotel A2

🔵 **Eating**
　3 Baan Peakmai A2
　4 Café Laurent A2

🔵 **Drinking & Nightlife**
　5 Fat Sam's B2

🔵 **Transport**
　Phnom Penh Sorya ....(see 5)

To get a feel for the delicate mangrove ecosystem, explore the 600m-long concrete mangrove walk, which wends its way above the briny waters for a 15m observation tower. The entrance is 5.5km southeast of Koh Kong. A *moto/remork* costs US$5/10 return.

☞ Tours

Boat tours are an excellent way to view Koh Kong's many coastal attractions. English-speaking **Teur** (☑016 278668) hangs around the boat dock and can help you

KOH KONG ISLAND

The west coast of Cambodia's largest island shelters seven pristine beaches fringed with coconut palms and lush vegetation, just as you'd expect in a true tropical paradise. At the sixth beach from the north, a narrow channel leads to a Gilligan's Island–style lagoon.

Koh Kong Island Resort (☑035-936371; www.kohkongisland.net; Koh Kong Island; bungalows d US$25-50, f US$70) offers daily transport on its boat for US$15 per person, departing Koh Kong City at 8.30am and returning at 3pm. Book in advance.

hire six-passenger (40-horsepower) and three-passenger (15-horsepower) outboards (speedboats). Destinations include Koh Kong Island's western beaches (big/small boats US$80/50), around Koh Kong Island (US$120/90) and Peam Krasaop Mangrove Sanctuary (US$40/30).

Ritthy's Koh Kong
Eco Adventure Tours   ADVENTURE TOUR
(☑012 707719; www.kohkongecoadventure.com; St 1; ⊙8am-9pm) A one-stop shop for all your tour needs in Koh Kong, this is the longest-running ecotourism operator in town. Ritthy's excursions include excellent Koh Kong Island boat tours, birdwatching, and jungle treks in the Koh Kong Conservation Corridor. The overnight jungle trekking and camping excursions (per person one night US$35, two nights US$70) get great reviews from travellers.

🛏 Sleeping

Some places pay *moto* drivers a commission, leading to a whole lot of shenanigans.

★Koh Kong City Hotel   HOTEL $
(☑035-936777; http://kkcthotel.netkhmer.com; St 1; r US$15-20; ❄@🛜) Ludicrous value for what you get: squeaky-clean rooms include a huge bathroom, two double beds, 50 TV channels, full complement of toiletries, free water and – in the US$20 rooms – glorious river views. Friendly staff top off the experience.

Oasis Bungalow Resort   BUNGALOW $$
(☑092 228342; http://oasisresort.netkhmer.com; d/tr US$30/35; ❄🛜≋) Surrounded by lush forest 2km north of Koh Kong centre, Oasis

really lives up to its name. Five large, airy bungalows set around a gorgeous infinity pool with views of the Cardamoms provide a tranquil base in which to chill out and reset your travel batteries. To get here, follow the blue signs from Acleda Bank.

🍴 Eating & Drinking

Baan Peakmai   ASIAN $
(St 1; mains 7000-15,000r; ⊙11am-2pm & 5-10pm; 🍴) Sure, you'd find more ambience in a paper bag but don't be put off by the plain-Jane decor. Baan Peakmai does a fine line in pan-Asian dishes with large portions and on-the-ball service. The menu romps through Thai, Chinese and Khmer favourites and there are plenty of vegetarian options.

★Café Laurent   INTERNATIONAL $$
(St 1; mains US$4-15; ⊙10.30am-11pm Wed-Mon; 🛜) This chic waterfront cafe and restaurant offers atmospheric dining in over-water pavilions where you can sit back and watch the sunset while feasting on refined Western and Khmer cuisine. As well as French-accented steaks and a decent pasta menu, there's a huge range of fresh seafood and Asian classics, all served with fine-dining panache.

Fat Sam's   BAR
(off St 3; ⊙9am-10pm Mon-Sat, 4-10pm Sun; 🛜) This informal, Welsh-run bar-restaurant has a decent selection of beers, spirits and wines and an impressive food menu that runs the full gamut from fish-and-chips and chilli con carne to authentic Khmer and Thai favourites. Useful travel information is dished out for free, plus there are motorbikes available for rent.

ℹ Information

Guesthouses, hotels and pubs are the best places to get the local low-down. You can also look for the free *Koh Kong Visitors Guide* (www. koh-kong.com), which is mostly advertisements.
Canadia Bank (St 1; ⊙8am-3.30pm Mon-Fri, to 11.30am Sat, ATM 24hr)
Sen Sok Clinic (☑012 555060; kkpao@ camintel.com; St 3; ⊙24hr) Has doctors who speak English and French.

ℹ Getting There & Away

Most buses drop passengers at Koh Kong's unpaved **bus station** (St 12), on the northeast edge of town, where *motos* and *remorks* await, eager to overcharge tourists. Don't pay more than US$1/2 for the three-minute *moto/remork* ride into the centre.

Rith Mony (☎ 012 640344; St 3), **Phnom Penh Sorya** (☎ 077 563447; St 3), **Olympic Transport** (☎ 011 363678; St 3) and **Virak Buntham** (☎ 089 998760; St 3) each runs two or three buses to Phnom Penh (US$7, six hours, last departure at 11.30am) and one or two trips to Sihanoukville (US$8 to US$10, five hours).

Virak Buntham and Rith Mony offer midday trips to Bangkok with a bus change at the border (US$20, eight hours). There are also trips to Koh Chang (US$14, including ferry) with a change of bus at the border, plus a local ferry to the island.

From the taxi lot next to the bus station, share taxis head to Phnom Penh (US$11, five hours) and occasionally to Sihanoukville (US$10, four hours).

❶ Getting Around

Ritthy's Koh Kong Eco Adventure Tours (p114) rents out bicycles for half-/full day US$1/2, as well as motorbikes.

Koh Kong Conservation Corridor របៀងអភិរក្សខេត្តកោះកុង

Stretching along both sides of NH48 from Koh Kong to the Gulf of Kompong Som, the Koh Kong Conservation Corridor encompasses many of Cambodia's most outstanding natural sites, including the most extensive mangrove forests on mainland Southeast Asia and the southern reaches of the fabled **Cardamom Mountains**, an area of breathtaking beauty and astonishing biodiversity.

The next few years will be critical in determining the future of the Cardamom Mountains. NGOs such as Conservation International (www.conservation.org), Fauna & Flora International (www.fauna-flora.org) and Wildlife Alliance (www.wildlifealliance.org) are working to help protect the region's 16 distinct ecosystems from loggers and poachers. Ecotourism is playing a huge role in their plans – Wildlife Alliance is promoting several enticing projects in the **Southern Cardamoms Protected Forest** (1443 sq km).

Tatai Waterfall ទឹកធ្លាក់តាតៃ

About 18km east of Koh Kong on the NH48, the Phun Daung (Tatai) Bridge spans the Tatai River. Nestled in a lushly forested gorge upstream from the bridge is the **Tatai Waterfall**, a thundering set of rapids in the wet season, plunging over a 4m rock shelf. Water levels drop in the dry season but you can swim year-round in refreshing pools around the waterfall.

The turn-off to Tatai is about 15km southeast of Koh Kong, or 2.8km northwest of the Tatai Bridge. From the highway it's about 2km to the falls along a rough access road. From Koh Kong, a half-day *moto/remork* excursion to Tatai Waterfall costs US$10/15 return.

CHI PHAT

Once notorious for its loggers and poachers, Chi Phat (សហគមន៍ទេសចរណ៍ជីផាត់) is now home to a pioneering **community-based ecotourism project**, established by WIldlife Alliance (www.wildlifealliance.org), which offers adventurous travellers a unique opportunity to explore the Cardamoms ecosystem while contributing to its protection. Visitors can take day treks through the jungle, go sunrise birdwatching by boat, mountain bike to several sets of rapids, and look for monkeys and hornbills with a former poacher as a guide. Also possible are one- to four-night mountain-bike safaris and jungle treks deep into the Cardamoms. In the village, visitors can relax by playing volleyball, badminton or pool with the locals.

Basic accommodation options in Chi Phat include 18 CBET-member guesthouses (US$5 to US$6) and 13 homestays (US$4). Reserve through the **CBET Community Visitor Centre** (☎ 092 720925, 035-6756444; www.chi-phat.org; Chi Phat; ☺7am-7pm) in Chi Phat. Meals are available at the visitor centre, costing US$2.50 for breakfast or US$3.50 for lunch and dinner. On busy nights, the centre doubles as a bar of sorts.

Chi Phat is on the Preak Piphot River 17km upriver from Andoung Tuek, which is 98km east of Koh Kong on the NH48. Any Koh Kong–bound bus can drop you in Andoung Tuek. From Andoung Tuek to Chi Phat it's a two-hour boat ride (US$10 per person, 1pm) or a 45-minute motorbike ride (US$7) on an unpaved but smooth road. Call the CBET office to arrange a boat or *moto* in advance.

Sihanoukville ក្រុងព្រះសីហនុ

☎ 034 / POP 91,000

Surrounded by white-sand beaches and relatively undeveloped tropical islands, Sihanoukville (aka Kompong Som) is Cambodia's premier seaside resort. While backpackers flock to the party zone of Serendipity Beach, the gorgeous Otres Beach, south of town, has made an incredible comeback and is now equally popular for a more relaxed stay. It's also the jumping-off point for Cambodia's southern islands, where castaway-cool beckons.

◉ Sights & Activities

Coastal **Ream National Park**, 15km east of Sihanoukville, offers invigorating boat trips through coastal mangroves and long stretches of unspoiled beach, not to mention trekking in primary forest.

Beaches

Sihanoukville's beaches all have wildly different characters, offering something for just about everyone. Most central is **Occheuteal Beach**, lined with ramshackle restaurants, whose northwestern end – a tiny, rocky strip – has emerged as a happy, easy-going travellers' hang-out known as **Serendipity Beach**.

South of Occheuteal Beach, beyond a small headland, lies **Otres Beach**, lined by dozens of bungalow-style restaurants and resorts. Otres has cleaner water and is more relaxed than anything in Sihanoukville proper, and is lengthy enough that finding your own patch of private sand is not a challenge...just walk south. Otres Beach is about 5km south of the Serendipity area. It's a US$2/5 *moto/remork* ride to get here (more at night).

One beach north of Serendipity lies Sihanoukville's prettiest beach, 1.5km-long

Sihanoukville

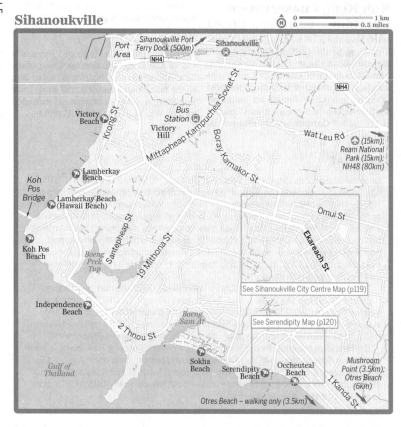

Sokha Beach. Its fine, silicon-like sand squeaks loudly underfoot. The tiny eastern end of Sokha Beach is open to the public and rarely crowded. The rest is part of the exclusive Sokha Beach Resort.

Moving north from Sokha Beach, you'll hit Independence Beach near the classic Independence Hotel, most of which has been taken over by a huge new development, and the original backpacker beach, Victory Beach, now under Russian management. The latter is clean, orderly and devoid of buzz.

Diving

The diving near Sihanoukville isn't Southeast Asia's finest. It gets better the further out you go, although you still shouldn't expect anything on a par with the western Gulf of Thailand or the Andaman Sea. Most serious trips will hit Koh Rong Sanloem, while overnight trips target the distant islands of Koh Tang and Koh Prins. Overnight trips cost about US$100 per day including two daily dives, food, accommodation on an island, and equipment. Two-tank dives out of Sihanoukville average US$80 including equipment. PADI open-water courses average about US$400 to US$450, pretty competitive by world standards.

Scuba Nation   DIVING
(Map p120; ☑012 604680; www.divecambodia. com; Serendipity Beach Rd; 2-dive package US$85, PADI Open Water US$445; ☺8am-6.30pm) The longest-running dive operator in Sihanoukville, Scuba Nation is a PADI five-star centre with a comfortable boat for day and liveaboard trips.

Dive Shop   DIVING
(Map p120; ☑034-933664; www.diveshopcam bodia.com; Serendipity Beach Rd; PADI Discover Scuba US$95, 1-/2-dive package US$65/80; ☺9am-7pm) PADI five-star dive centre offering full gamut of PADI courses, as well as fun-dives and liveaboards. Also has a dive shop on Koh Rong Sanloem.

Massage

NGO-trained blind and disabled masseurs deftly ease away the tension at Seeing Hands Massage 3 (Map p119; 95 Ekareach St; per hr US$6; ☺8am-9pm) and Starfish Bakery & Café (Map p119; off 7 Makara St; per hr US$6-10; ☺7am-6pm) .

Courses

Don Bosco Hotel Khmer Cooking Course   COOKING COURSE
(☑034-934478; www.donboscohotelschool.com/ cooking; Don Bosco Hotel School, Ou Phram St; per person US$30) ⏺ The cooking classes here provide a great opportunity to support the worthy Don Bosco Hotel School plus learn some Khmer culinary skills. They include a trip to the market and a slap-up three-course lunch (which you've helped create), as well as a tour of the hotel school. Classes usually run from 10am to 12.30pm on Tuesdays, Thursdays and Saturdays.

☞ Tours

Popular day tours go to some of the closer islands and to Ream National Park. Booze cruises are popular.

Eco-Trek Tours   ADVENTURE TOUR
(Map p120; ☑012 987073; www.ecotourscambo dia.com; ☺8am-10pm) This travel agency runs highly recommended boat tours and trekking trips to Ream National Park as well as boat trips around the islands.

Party Boat   BOAT TOUR
(Map p120; www.thepartyboat.asia; Serendipity Beach Pier; per person US$25) The daily cruise (9.30am to 5pm) to Koh Rong Sanloem includes snacks, lunch, snorkelling and a free drink. It also runs return transport to Koh Rong island's full-moon parties, leaving Sihanoukville at 5pm and returning around 8am.

🛏 Sleeping

Most backpackers shoot for the Serendipity area if they want to party, Otres Beach if they want to chill. Other decent options exist in the town centre (for those who want to escape tourists) and on long-running Victory Hill, a former backpacker ghetto that is now one of Sihanoukville's sleazier strips. There are popular bungalow resorts popping up all over the islands off Sihanoukville.

Serendipity & Occheuteal

The road to Serendipity is the main backpacker hang-out, while down the hill tiny Serendipity Beach offers a string of mellow midrange resorts perched over the rocky shoreline.

Monkey Republic   HOSTEL $
(Map p120; ☑012 490290; http://monkey
republic.info; Serendipity Beach Rd; dm US$6, r with
fan US$15-22, r with air-con/US$18-30; ❀@⧈)
Self-proclaimed 'backpacker central', Monkey Republic rose from the ashes in 2013
following a dramatic fire (no casualties). It
offers decent dorms and plain, affordable
rooms in a building fronted by a yellow
French colonial facade. The bar-restaurant
constantly heaves with young travellers.

Big Easy   HOSTEL $
(Map p120; ☑081 943930; Serendipity Beach Rd;
dm US$3, r US$6-10; ⧈) This classic backpacker joint is accommodation, comfort food and
a lively rock bar all rolled into one. Rooms
are basic but you'll most likely spend your
time in the bar, which has a great vibe with
occasional live music and live EPL games.

One Stop Hostel   HOSTEL $
(Map p120; ☑096 3390005; onestophostelshv@
gmail.com; Golden Lions Roundabout; dm US$7;
❀⧈❀) Dorm beds just got a makeover. The
eight-bed dorms here, decked out in lashings
of white-on-white, boast beds with individual reading lamps and luggage lock-boxes.
Rooms are centred around a wall-to-ceiling
glassed courtyard with a small pool, proving
slick styling doesn't have to cost the earth.

Chochi Garden   GUESTHOUSE $
(Map p120; ☑070 865640; www.chochigarden.
com; Serendipity Beach Rd; r with fan/air-con
US$15/25; ⊜❀⧈) Finally! Serendipity gets
its first boutique backpacker pad. Italian-
Japanese couple Francesca and Taka have
created the nearest Serendipity gets to a
tranquil oasis right in the heart of the action. Out front is a cool bar-restaurant while
simple rooms, some with palm-thatch roofs
and pretty painted window-grills, are in a

plant-filled garden strewn with comfy seating areas.

🛏 Otres Beach   ឆ្នេរអូរត្រេះ

Most guesthouses are in a cluster about 1km
south of Queen Hill Resort, an area known
as Otres 1. About 2.5km of empty beach
separates this cluster from a smaller, more
isolated colony of resorts at the far southern
end of the beach, known as Otres 2.

★ Wish You Were Here   HOSTEL $
(☑097 241 5884; http://wishotres.com; Otres 1;
dm US$6, r US$14-16, bungalows US$18; ⊜⧈)
This rickety wooden building is one of the
hippest hang-outs in Otres. The rooms are
simple but the balcony upstairs encourages serious sloth-time and the bar-restaurant downstairs has a great vibe thanks to
chilled-out tunes and friendly staff.

SeaGarden   BUNGALOW $
(☑096 2538131; www.seagardenotres.com; Otres
1; dm US$5, r US$15-20; ⧈) Look no further
for a cheap bungalow right on the sand.
SeaGarden offers basic beach huts, and
rooms in a stilted building, both on the
beach. The new owner keeps everything
neat as a pin and was building a spacious
dorm when we last pulled into town.

Hacienda   HOSTEL $
(☑070 814643; Otres Village; dm US$4, r US$8-15;
⧈) Hacienda is a laid-back backpacker zone
on Otres' estuary with cheap dorm beds
and basic bungalows. There's also a popular
bar-restaurant that often breaks into a party.

Mushroom Point   BUNGALOW $$
(☑078 509079; www.mushroompoint.com; Otres
1; dm US$8, bungalow US$25-30; ⧈) The open-
air dorm in the shape of a mushroom wins
the award for most creative in Cambodia.
Even those averse to communal living will
be content in their mosquito-net–draped
pods, good for two. Quirky 'shroom-shaped
bungalows are beautifully conceived with
hammocks outside for lounging. The beach
annex has more bungalows and a bar.

🍴 Eating

Sihanoukville's centre of culinary gravity is
the Serendipity area.

🍴 Serendipity Area

For romance, nothing beats dining on the
water, either at one of the resorts at Seren-

Sihanoukville City Centre

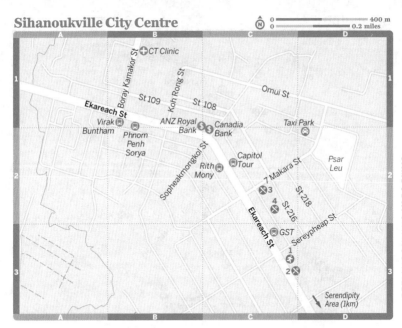

dipity Beach or – more cheaply – in one of the shacks along adjacent Occheuteal Beach.

Nyam
CAMBODIAN $
(Map p120; www.nyamsihanoukville.com; 23 Tola St; mains US$2-4.25; ⏱5-10pm; 📶) Translating as 'Eat' in Khmer, this is a great spot for a contemporary Cambodian dinner experience. All the favourites are here such as *amok* (baked fish dish), but there are also some healthy seafood offerings reflecting the coastal location.

Cafe Mango
ITALIAN $
(Map p120; Serendipity St; mains US$3-6; ⏱7am-10pm; 📶) A cracking little Italian cafe turning out wood-fired pizzas, homemade pasta and delicate gnocchi. Dine at lunchtime or before 6.30pm for a main course accompanied by garlic bread or bruschetta and a drink for just US$5.

★Sandan
CAMBODIAN $$
(Map p120; 2 Thnou St; mains US$4-10; ⏱7am-9pm Mon-Sat; 📶🍴) 🖉 Loosely modelled on the beloved Phnom Penh restaurant Romdeng (p81), this superb restaurant is an extension of the vocational-training programs for at-risk Cambodians run by local NGO M'lop Tapang. The menu features creative Cambodian cuisine targeted at a slightly up-

---

Sihanoukville City Centre

🟢 Activities, Courses & Tours
1 Seeing Hands Massage 3 ....C3
   Starfish Bakery & Café...............(see 4)

✖ Eating
2 Holy Cow C3
3 Samudera Supermarket.....................C2
4 Starfish Bakery & Café........................C2

---

scale clientele. There's a kids' play area and occasional cultural shows.

So
INTERNATIONAL $$
(Map p120; Serendipity Beach Rd; mains US$4-10; ⏱8am-10pm; 📶) So is renowned for serving up some of Serendipity's tastiest cuisine. Come for dinner when the candles come out, the menu changes and the top chef is in action. Specialities include wasabi prawns and baked scallops in wine sauce. Early diners benefit from two courses for US$5 between 5pm and 6.30pm.

🍴 Around the City

Starfish Bakery & Café
CAFE $
(Map p119; www.starfishcambodia.org; off 7 Makara St; sandwiches US$2.50-4.50; ⏱7am-6pm; 📶📝) 🖉 This relaxing, NGO-run garden

Serendipity

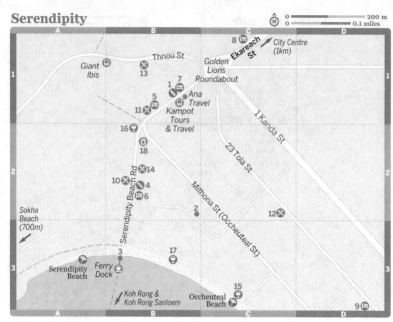

Serendipity

⚙ Activities, Courses & Tours
1	Dive Shop	B1
2	Eco-Trek Tours	B2
3	Party Boat	B3
4	Scuba Nation	B2

🛏 Sleeping
5	Big Easy	B1
6	Chochi Garden	B2
7	Monkey Republic	B1
8	One Stop Hostel	C1
9	Ropanha Boutique Hotel	D3

🍴 Eating
10	Cafe Mango	B2
11	Dao of Life	B1
12	Nyam	C2
13	Sandan	B1
14	So	B2

🍷 Drinking & Nightlife
15	JJ's Playground	C3
16	Led Zephyr	B2
17	Sessions	B3

🛍 Shopping
18	Tapang	B2

cafe specialises in filling Western breakfasts, baked cakes and tarts, and healthy, innovative sandwiches heavy on Mexican and Middle Eastern flavours. Sitting down for coffee here on the shady terrace is a peaceful reprieve from Sihanoukville's hustle. Income goes to sustainable development projects.

Dao of Life　　　　　　　　　　VEGAN $
(Map p120; Serendipity Beach Rd; mains US$3.50-6; ⊙8am-3pm & 6pm-10pm Tue-Sun; 🛜🎤) 🍴 This rooftop cafe, full of hammocks and recycled furniture, dishes up creative and tasty vegan meals. The veggie burger (made from sweet potato and black beans) is particularly good, or tuck into healthy options such as spiralized zucchini linguine. It has movie nights every Wednesday and regularly hosts social projects with local community involvement.

Samudera Supermarket　　SUPERMARKET $
(Map p119; 64 7 Makara St; ⊙6am-10pm) Good selection of fruit, veggies and imported food brands, including European cheeses and wine.

Holy Cow　　　　　　　INTERNATIONAL $$
(Map p119; 83 Ekareach St; mains US$2.50-7; ⊙8.30am-11pm; 🛜🎤) As well as solid com-

fort food such as pasta, burgers and shepherd's pie, this funky cafe-restaurant dishes up bagels with cream cheese, sandwiches on homemade bread and a good selection of veggie options. The menu includes two vegan desserts, both involving chocolate.

Drinking & Nightlife

The party tends to start up on the road to Serendipity before heading downhill (literally and figuratively) to the all-night beach discos along Occheuteal Beach. A few long-standing regular bars remain amid the hostess bars of Victory Hill, but the overall impression is Sinville rather than the more relaxed beach vibe of Sihanoukville.

Some of the guesthouses have lively bars, including Monkey Republic (happy hour 6pm to 9pm), the Big Easy and Wish You Were Here.

Sessions BAR
(Map p120; Occheuteal Beach; ⊙5pm-1am) The music selection makes Sessions the top sundowner bar on Occheuteal Beach. The crowd of expats and backpackers assembled usually lingers well into the evening before the hard-core partiers move on to the late-night venues.

Led Zephyr BAR
(Map p120; Serendipity Beach Rd; ⊙7am-midnight) Sihanoukville's premier live-music venue; the house band (and friends from time to time) are rockin' here most nights. Covers include many of the big anthems from the '60s to '80s, with a bit of Chili Peppers thrown in for good measure.

JJ's Playground BAR
(Map p120; Occheuteal Beach; ⊙6pm-6am) For a while now JJ's has been the go-to spot for those seeking late-night debauchery. The scene here is pretty much summed up by their tag line 'let's get wasted'. Expect shots, loud techno, a fire show or two, and a lot of chaos. And don't say we didn't warn you about the toilets.

Shopping

Tapang HANDICRAFTS
(Map p120; www.mloptapang.org; Serendipity Beach Rd; ⊙10am-8pm) Run by a local NGO that works with at-risk children, this shop sells good-quality bags, scarves and T-shirts made by street kids (and their families) so that they can attend school instead of peddling on the beach.

ℹ Information

Internet cafes (per hour 4000r) are sprinkled along the road to Serendipity and, in the city centre, along Ekareach St near Sopheakmongkol St.

Theft is a problem, especially on Occheuteal Beach, so leave your valuables in your room. As in Phnom Penh, drive-by bag-snatchings occasionally happen and are especially dangerous when you're riding a *moto*. Hold your shoulder bags tightly in front of you. At night, both men and women should avoid walking alone along dark, isolated beaches and roads.

Ana Travel (Map p120; ☑034-933929; Serendipity Beach Rd; ⊙8am-10pm) Handles Cambodia visa extensions and arranges Vietnam visas the same day.

ANZ Royal Bank (Map p119; 215 Ekareach St; ⊙8am-3.30pm Mon-Fri, to 11.30am Sat, ATM 24hr)

Canadia Bank (Map p119; 197 Ekareach St; ⊙8am-3.30pm Mon-Fri, to 11.30am Sat, ATM 24hr)

CT Clinic (Map p119; ☑081 886666, 034-936666; 47 Boray Kamakor St; ⊙emergencies 24hr) The best medical clinic in town. Can administer rabies shots, and antivenin in the event of a snakebite.

ℹ Getting There & Away

AIR

Cambodia Angkor Airlines (☑023-6660330; www.cambodiaangkorair.com) has direct flights from Sihanoukville to Phnom Penh and Siem Reap daily. The airport is 15km east of town, just off the NH4. Figure on US$5/10 for a one-way *moto/remork*.

BUS

All of the major bus companies have frequent connections with Phnom Penh (US$5 to US$11, four to five hours) from early morning until at least 2pm, after which trips are sporadic.

Kampot Tours & Travel runs minibuses to Kampot (US$6, 1½ hours), which continue to Kep (US$8, 2½ hours). Travel agents can arrange hotel pickups.

Virak Buntham and Rith Mony have morning buses to Bangkok (US$28, change buses on the Thai side) via Koh Kong (US$8, four hours). GST and Virak Buntham have night buses to Siem Reap (US$13 to US$17).

Most bus departures originate at the company terminals on Ekareach St and stop at the **bus station** (Map p116; Mittapheap Kampuchea Soviet St) on the way out of town.

The main bus companies are:

Capitol Tour (Map p119; ☑034-934042; 169 Ekareach St)

Giant Ibis (Map p120; ☑ 089 999818; www. giantibis.com; Thnou St)

GST (Map p119; ☑ 015 995950; Ekareach St)

Kampot Tours & Travel (Map p120; ☑ in Kampot 092 125556; Ana Travel, Serendipity Beach Rd)

Phnom Penh Sorya (Map p119; ☑ 034-933888; 236 Ekareach St)

Rith Mony (Map p119; ☑ 093 465858; Ekareach St)

Virak Buntham (Map p119; ☑ 016 754358; Ekareach St)

SHARE TAXI

Cramped share taxis (US$6 per person, US$45 per car) to Phnom Penh depart from the new bus station until about 8pm. Share taxis to Kampot (US$5, 1½ hours) leave mornings only from an open lot on 7 Makara St, across from Psar Leu. This lot and the new bus station are good places to look for rides to Koh Kong or the Thai border (US$45 to US$60 to charter).

❶ Getting Around

Arriving in Sihanoukville, most buses terminate at the bus station and do not continue to their central terminals. Prices to the Serendipity Beach area from the bus station are fixed at a pricey US$2/6 for a *moto/remork*. You can do better by walking out to the street.

A *moto/remork* should cost about US$1/2 from the city centre to Serendipity, but overcharging is rife.

Motorbikes can be rented from many guesthouses for US$5 to US$7 a day. For fundraising purposes, the police sometimes 'crack down' on foreign drivers. Common violations: no driving licence, no helmet, or driving with the lights on during the day.

Bicycles can be hired from many guesthouses for about US$2 a day, or try Eco-Trek Tours (p117) for mountain bikes.

Southern Islands

They may lack the cachet of Southern Thailand, but the two-dozen or so islands that dot the Cambodian coast offer the chance to see what places like Koh Samui and Koh Pha-Ngan were like back in the early days of Southeast Asia overland travel. This is paradise the way you dreamt it: endless crescents of powdered sugary-soft sand, hammocks swaying in the breeze, photogenic fishing villages on stilts, technicolour sunsets and the patter of raindrops on thatch as you slumber. It seems too good to last and pockets of Koh Rong are already getting a tad rowdy. Enjoy it while you can.

❶ Getting There & Away

The logical jumping-off point for the most popular islands is Sihanoukville. Scheduled boat services link Sihanoukville with Koh Rong and Koh Rong Sanloem. Other islands are reached by private boats, usually owned by the resort you're visiting.

Koh Rong & Koh Rong Sanloem
កោះរ៉ុង និងកោះរ៉ុងសន្លឹម

These deceptively large neighbouring islands are the rapidly emerging pearls of the South Coast. They boast isolated white-sand beaches and heavily forested interiors populated by an incredible variety of wildlife.

Plans to turn Koh Rong into a Cambodian version of Thailand's Koh Samui, complete with ring road and airport, have stalled, allowing DIY developers to move in with rustic resorts targeting backpackers. The epicentre of the action is rapidly developing **Koh Tuch Beach** on Koh Rong's southeastern corner, which hosts a fabled full-moon party once a month.

If you want to hang out with fellow travellers, hit an all-night rave and crash out on the sand during the day, Koh Rong's the spot. Those looking for a more relaxed vibe would be wise to pick a bungalow-resort well away from Koh Tuch village (on lovely **Long Beach** or the even-less-imaginatively named **4km Beach**) or head to Koh Rong Sanloem.

However, be aware that security can be an issue on Koh Rong, with incidents of theft and occasional attacks on female tourists in remote parts of the island, so do not go walking in the jungle interior alone.

Koh Rong Sanloem is also taking off. Several colonies of bungalows have sprung up on **Saracen Bay** on the east coast, and more isolated options exist elsewhere on the island. Those looking for an alternative island experience can head to the village of **M'Pai Bay** at the island's northern tip, which has an authentic local vibe that will suit the more intrepid.

❄ Activities

High Point Rope Adventure   ADVENTURE SPORTS
(☑ 016 839993; www.high-point.asia; Koh Tuch village; per person US$35; ⊙ 9am-6pm) A collection of ziplines, swing bridges and walking cables take thrill-seekers on an adrenalin-packed, 400m-long journey through the for-

est canopy, not far from Koh Tuch. Your ticket gets you unlimited access to the course for the entire day. From April to October, tickets are US$10 cheaper.

Koh Rong Dive Center
DIVING

(☑ 034-934744; kohrong-divecenter.com; Koh Rong Pier) Koh Rong's main dive centre organises trips in the waters around both Koh Rong and Koh Rong Sanloem.

🛏 Sleeping & Eating

Most island resorts run their generators from about 6pm to 10.30pm.

KOH RONG

Natural Lounge
GUESTHOUSE $

(☑ 069 541177; hengseksa@gmail.com; Koh Tuch; dm US$8, r with/without bathroom from US$30/20; 🛜) A family-run calm oasis amid the Koh Tuch hubbub with small, spotless, wood-floored rooms set around a leafy courtyard. Downstairs there's a couple of bijou ensuite rooms with two double beds that you could fit four people in if you don't mind a squeeze.

Green Ocean Guesthouse
HOSTEL $

(☑ 096 9169267; mengly007@gmail.com; Koh Tuch; dm US$8-10, d US$25; 🛜) The recently renovated rooms with tiled floors here are some of the nicest, and most spacious, in Koh Tuch village. There's a great communal balcony out front and the 12-bed dorm has sea views.

Vagabonds
HOSTEL $

(www.vagabondskohrong.com; Koh Tuch; dm US$5, r with shared bathroom US$10) Firstly, you don't come here for the facilities. Bare-bones rooms and four-bed dorms (with lockers) are made cheery by colourful murals. Vagabonds' following is instead due to friendly staff and the fun vibe of the cafe downstairs, which dishes up huge portions of comfort food (US$3 to US$5). Walk-ins only.

Loops Bar
INTERNATIONAL $

(Koh Tuch; mains US$2.50-5.50; ⊙ 8am-11pm; 🛜) Downstairs from Dreamcatch Inn is this cafe-bar decorated with recycled water bottles, strung from the ceiling as pot plants. Breakfast options are stellar and include fruity French toast with a tropical twist, and coconut muesli. Lunch and dinner feature decent Khmer options along with comfort-food classics such as bangers and mash. Manager Te puts on a fire-poi show every Saturday night.

KOH RONG SANLOEM

The Beach Resort
RESORT $$

(☑ 034-666 6106; www.thebeachresort.asia; Saracen Bay; dm US$7.50, bungalow with/without bathroom US$35/25, deluxe US$50-85; 🛜) This lively resort caters for the full gamut of budgets with an open-air dorm, bijou seafront bungalows and deluxe stone-walled options. It's also the stop-off point for Sihanoukville's Party Boat, whose day-trippers fill up the bar area most afternoons, which – depending on your outlook – will either be a major plus or minus to staying here.

Easy Tiger
GUESTHOUSE $

(☑ 096 9153370; www.easytigerbungalows.com; M'Pai Bay; dm US$7.50, r/bungalow US$15/30) This friendly guesthouse in M'Pai Bay village has plenty of homespun appeal, thanks to its helpful owners. There are simple dorms and small private rooms in the main building. Out back are sturdy basic bungalows with large verandas for those seeking more privacy.

The Drift
GUESTHOUSE $

(☑ 015 865388; www.thedriftcambodia.com; M'Pai Bay; dm/r US$8/15) A new player on the M'Pai Bay scene, The Drift has spic-and-span dorms and a couple of private rooms in a cute wooden house on the sand. There's a good social vibe with home-cooked meals (US$3) often eaten communally.

Fishing Hook
INTERNATIONAL $

(M'Pai Bay; mains US$2.50-5.50; ⊙ 6-10.30pm) Some of the finest food on Koh Rong Sanloem is served up at this place perched on M'Pai Bay pier. The menu waltzes from Khmer-influenced seafood (such as grilled fish in tamarind sauce) to more global offerings, while the cushion-strewn dining terrace over the water is the epitome of beach-casual ambiance.

ⓘ Getting There & Away

From Koh Tuch on Koh Rong, **Speed Ferry Cambodia** (www.speedferrycambodia.com; one way/return US$13/26) departs for Sihanoukville at 10am, noon and 4pm daily; and the **TBC Speed Boat** (☑ 088 7811711; www.tbckohrong speedboat.com; one way/return US$12.50/$20) to Sihanoukville leaves at 10.30am, 1.30am and 4pm. Both journeys take between 45 minutes and one hour.

Both companies also connect Saracen Bay on Koh Rong Sanloem with Sihanoukville. Speed Ferry Cambodia has departures from Saracen Bay Pier at 9.30am and 3.30pm, which then continue on to drop off/pick up passengers at M'Pai Bay (about 15 minutes later), and Koh Rong Island (US$5 to hop between the islands) before heading for Sihanoukville. TBC Speed Boat departs Saracen Bay Pier for Sihanoukville at 10.30am, 1.30pm and 4pm.

If you have a return ticket, go to the relevant ferry office the day before you want to travel to make sure of a seat. During high season extra ferry times are usually added. When sea conditions are bad (particularly from June to October) ferries are sometimes cancelled. Ticket prices drop from June to October.

Other Islands

Closer to Sihanoukville, Koh Ta Kiev and Koh Russei appear on most island-hopping itineraries out of Sihanoukville, with day trips running from US$12 to US$15 depending whether you launch from Otres Beach or Serendipity Beach. Both islands have accommodation, although both are slated for development.

Kampot កំពត

📞 033 / POP 39,500

There is something about this little charmer that encourages visitors to linger. It might be the lovely riverside setting or the ageing French buildings, or it could be the great little guesthouses and burgeoning bar scene. Whatever the magic ingredient, this is the perfect base from which to explore nearby caves and tackle Bokor Hill Station.

◉ Sights & Activities

This is not a town where you come and do, but a place to come and be. Sit on the riverbank and watch the sun set beneath the mountains, or stroll among the town's fine French shophouses (in the triangle delineated by 7 Makara St, the central roundabout and the post office).

Kampot Traditional Music School CULTURAL CENTRE
(www.kcdi-cambodia.com; St 724; ⊙ 2-5pm Mon-Tue & 5-7pm Fri) ✏️ FREE During visitor hours you are welcome to observe traditional music and dance training sessions and/or performances at this school that trains children who are orphaned or have disabilities. Donations are very welcome.

Seeing Hands Massage 5 MASSAGE
(River Rd; per hr US$5; ⊙ 7am-11pm) Blind masseurs offer soothing bliss.

☞ Tours

The big tour is to Bokor Hill Station, which everybody and their grandmother offers. Excursions also hit the pepper farms and other sights in the countryside around Kampot and nearby Kep.

Some of the riverside places send boats out on evening firefly-watching tours. Many a sceptic has returned from these trips in awe.

Bart the Boatman BOAT TOUR
(📞 092 174280; 2 people US$40) Known simply as Bart the Boatman, this Belgian expat runs original private boat tours along the small tributaries of the Kampong Bay River. His backwater tour is highly recommended by travellers.

Captain Chim's BOAT TOUR
(📞 012 321043; Captain Chim's Guesthouse, St 724; sunset boat trip per person US$5) Sunset cruises and firefly-watching trips on a traditional boat include a cold beer and are a real bargain. Also on offer are fishing trips for US$11 including lunch, and bicycle hire (US$2 per day).

Climbodia ROCK CLIMBING
(📞 095 581951; www.climbodia.com; Phnom Kbal Romeas, off NH33; half-day US$35-40, full-day US$70) Cambodia's first outdoor rock-climbing outfit offers highly recommended half-day and full-day programs of climbing, abseiling and caving amid the limestone formations of Phnom Kbal Romeas, 5km south of Kampot. *Via ferratas* (cabled routes) have been established across some of the cliffs and the variety of programs caters for both complete novices and the more experienced.

SUP Asia WATER SPORTS
(📞 093 980550; www.supasia.org; Kompong Bay River east bank; daily 2½hr tour US$25; ⊙ mid-Oct–Jul) SUP (stand-up paddleboarding) has come to Kampot in a big way with this company offering an alternative form of touring the river. Daily tours depart at 8.30am and 3.30pm, taking in the riverbank sights of the local area (with a SUP lesson beforehand). There's also a two-day (18km) trip that traverses the Kampong Bay River to the sea.

Sok Lim Tours TOUR
(📞 012 796919; www.soklimtours.com; St 730; ⊙ 8am-7pm) Kampot's longest-running outfit is well regarded and organises all the usual day tours and river cruises. For private coun-

Kampot

larly cranks into the wee hours. Those after some semblance of sleep would be wise not to opt for the US$5 dorm.

Naga House   BUNGALOW $
(📞012 289916; www.facebook.com/nagahouse kampot; Tuk Chhou Rd; bungalow US$7-12; 🛜) This classic backpacker hang-out offers basic ground-level and stilted thatched bungalows (all with shared bathroom) amid lush foliage. There's an extremely social bar-restaurant on the riverfront that often rocks into the night and regularly hosts live music and DJ sets.

Captain Chim's
Guesthouse   GUESTHOUSE $
(📞012 321043; www.facebook.com/captainchims guesthousekampot; St 724; dm US$3, r with/without air-con US$13/8; ❄🛜) This family-run guesthouse offers simple, spick-and-span rooms and a spacious dorm with its own balcony. Bathrooms only have cold water. Guests get free laundry and free bicycle hire.

🍴 Eating & Drinking

Cafe Espresso   CAFE $
(St 731; mains US$4-6; ⊙8.30am-4pm Tue-Fri, 9am-4.30pm Sat & Sun; 🛜🌿) A blink-and-you'll-miss-it cafe; we advise you don't blink. The Aussie owners are real foodies and offer a global menu that traipses from vegetarian quesadillas to Brazilian-style pork sandwiches with some especially tempting breakfast options. But it is caffeine-cravers who will be really buzzing, thanks to their

tryside tours it has good English-speaking *remork* driver-guides who understand the process and history behind Kampot pepper. If there's no one in the actual office, they'll be in the neighbouring Jack's Place restaurant.

🛏 Sleeping

You can stay in the centre of the old town, or stay a little out of town in one of several places strung out along the riverbank.

Magic Sponge   GUESTHOUSE $
(📞017 946428; www.magicspongekampot.com; St 730; dm US$4, r with air-con US$10-15, without air-con US$15-20; 😊❄🛜) This popular backpacker place has a rooftop dorm with impressive through-breezes, personalised fans and reading lights. Good-value private rooms are exceptionally well cared for and bright. Downstairs is a movie lounge and a lively bar-restaurant with happy hours from noon to 8pm and well-regarded Indian food.

Arcadia Backpackers   HOSTEL $
(📞077 219756; www.arcadiabackpackers.com; Tuk Chhou Rd; dm US$5-8, r with bathroom US$17-20, without bathroom US$10, bungalow US$25; 🛜) Kampot's biggest backpacker party scene, Arcadia is about sunbathing on the river pontoon during the day and later, joining in the revelry at the bar-restaurant that regu-

KAMPOT PEPPER

In the years before the Cambodian civil war took its toll, no self-respecting French restaurant in Paris would be without Kampot pepper on the table. Pepper plantations are once again a common sight in the Kampot region and come in a variety of colours, including white, black, green and red.

regionally grown coffee blends, roasted daily in-house.

Epic Arts Café CAFE $
(www.epicarts.org.uk; St 724; mains US$2-4; ☺7am-4pm; 🛜) 🍴 A great place for breakfast, homemade cakes, infused tea and light lunches, this mellow eatery is staffed by young people who are deaf or have a disability. Profits fund arts workshops for Cambodians with a disability and it's possible to learn some sign language at 3pm every Friday.

Rusty Keyhole INTERNATIONAL $$
(River Rd; small/large/extra-large ribs US$5/7.50/10; ☺8am-11pm Nov-May, 11am-11pm Jun-Oct; 🛜) This popular riverfront bar-restaurant turns out a global menu of comfort food and Khmer home-cooking. Most people are here for their famous ribs; order in advance, but beware the enormous extra-large portions.

KAMA BAR
(Kampot Arts and Music Association; St 726; ☺6pm-midnight Wed-Sun; 🛜) Owned by Julien Poulson, a founding member of the acclaimed band Cambodian Space Project, KAMA is part boho bar, part art space. It spins tunes from an eclectic vinyl collection, plays movies nightly and regularly hosts creative events. Pop in for a beer, or the dish of the day, and check out what's happening while you're in town.

Oh Neils BAR
(River Rd; ☺5pm-late; 🛜) The liveliest of the little bars that dot the riverfront in Kampot, Oh Neils has walls plastered with rock 'n' roll memorabilia and a who's-who soundtrack of classic tunes from down the decades.

ℹ️ Information

The free and often hilarious *Kampot Survival Guide* takes a tongue-in-cheek look at local expat life, and there's also the free guide *Coastal* (www.coastal-cambodia.com).

Canadia Bank (Durian Roundabout; ☺8am-3.30pm Mon-Fri, to 11.30am Sat, ATM 24hr)

Tourist Information Centre (☏033-655 5541; lonelyguide@gmail.com; River Rd; ☺7am-7pm) Led by the knowledgeable Mr Pov, Kampot's tourist office doles out free advice, sells tours and can arrange transport to area attractions such as caves, falls and Kompong Trach.

ℹ️ Getting There & Away

Kampot is 105km from Sihanoukville and 148km from Phnom Penh.

Capitol Tours and Phnom Penh Sorya sell bus tickets from offices opposite the Total petrol station near the Four Nagas Roundabout. Both have daily trips to Phnom Penh (US$5 to US$6, 2½ hours) until lunchtime. Giant Ibis and Kampot Express run comfortable express vans to Phnom Penh (US$8 to US$9, two hours).

For Sihanoukville, ask your guesthouse to set you up with a minibus service (US$5).

A *moto/remork* to Kep should cost about US$6/12.

ℹ️ Getting Around

Bicycles (US$2) and motorbikes (from US$5) can be rented from guesthouses in town.

Around Kampot

The limestone hills east towards Kep are honeycombed with fantastic caves, some of which can be explored with the help of local kids and a reliable torch (flashlight).

👁️ Sights

Phnom Chhnork CAVE
(ភ្នំឆ្នក; admission US$1; ☺7am-6pm) Phnom Chhnork is a short walk through a quilt of rice paddies from Wat Ang Sdok, where a monk collects the entry fee and a gaggle of friendly local kids offer their services as guides.

From the bottom, a 203-step staircase leads up the hillside and down into a cavern as graceful as a Gothic cathedral.

The view from up top, and the walk to and from the wat, is especially magical in the late afternoon.

Phnom Sorsia CAVE
(ភ្នំសរសៀរ, Phnom Sia; ☺7am-6pm) FREE
Phnom Sorsia is home to several natural caves. From the parking area, a stairway leads up the hillside to a gaudy modern

temple. From there, steps lead left up to **Rung Damrey Saa** (White Elephant Cave). A slippery, sloping staircase where one false step will send you into the abyss leads down and then up and then out through a hole in the other side. Exit the cave and follow the right-hand path, which leads back to the temple.

Bokor Hill Station

កស្ដានីយភ្នំបូកគោ

The 1581-sq-km **Bokor National Park** (ឧទ្យានជាតិបូកគោ, Preah Monivong National Park; admission motorbike/car 2000/4000r) has impressive wildlife, lush primary forests and a refreshingly cool climate, but is most famous for its once-abandoned **Bokor Hill Station** (កស្ដានីយភ្នំបូកគោ) FREE, established atop Phnom Bokor (1080m) in the 1920s.

Unfortunately it is now becoming more famous for the ugly casino that blights the summit, part of a massive development project that has sadly destroyed the atmosphere of bygone Bokor. Until recently the main attraction here was the old French hill station and its grand, four-storey hotel, the Bokor Palace, opened in 1925. The hill station was abandoned to the howling winds in the 1970s when Khmer Rouge forces infiltrated the area. The once-grand buildings became eerie, windowless shells.

To visit the park you can rent a motorbike or join an organised tour (US$10 to US$15 per person).

Kep

កែប

☎ 036 / POP 35,000

Kep was founded as a seaside retreat for the French elite in 1908 and was a favoured haunt of Cambodian high-rollers during the 1960s. Today tourists are being drawn back to Kep (Krong Kep, also spelled Kaeb) thanks to its spectacular sunsets and splendid seafood. Some travellers find Kep a tad soulless because it lacks a centre. Others are oddly charmed by its torpid pace.

Most of Kep's beaches are too shallow and rocky to make for good swimming. The best is centrally located Kep Beach, but it's still somewhat pebbly and tends to fill up with locals on weekends. The best place for sunset viewing is the long wooden pier in front of Knai Bang Chat's Sailing Club.

◉ Sights & Activities

Kep National Park
PARK

(ឧទ្យានជាតិកែប; admission 4000r) The interior of Kep peninsula is occupied by Kep National Park, where an 8km circuit, navigable by foot and mountain bike, winds through thick forest passing by wats and viewpoints. Quirky yellow signs point the way and show trailheads to off-shooting walking paths which lead into the park's interior. The 'Stairway to Heaven' trail is particularly worthwhile, leading up the hill to a pagoda, a nunnery and the Sunset Rock viewpoint.

The main park entrance is behind Veranda Natural Resort.

Koh Tonsay (Rabbit Island)
ISLAND

(កោះទន្សាយ) If you like the rustic beachcomber lifestyle, Koh Tonsay's 250m-long main beach is for you, but come now as the island is tagged for development. The beach is one of the nicest of any of the Kep-area islands but don't expect sparkling white sand. This one has shorefront flotsam, chickens and wandering cows.

Restaurant-shacks and rudimentary bungalows (from US$7 per night) rim the sand.

Boats to Rabbit Island (30 minutes) leave from **Rabbit Island pier** at 9am, returning to Kep at 4pm (US$10 return).

Wat Kiri Sela
BUDDHIST TEMPLE

(វត្តគិរីសីលា; ⊙7am-6pm) This Buddhist temple sits at the foot of Phnom Kompong Trach, a dramatic karst formation riddled with more than 100 caverns and passageways. From the wat, an underground passage leads to a fishbowl-like formation, surrounded by vine-draped cliffs and open to the sky. Various stalactite-laden caves shelter reclining Buddhas and miniature Buddhist shrines.

The closest town is Kompong Trach. From here, take the dirt road opposite the Acleda Bank, on NH33 in the town centre, for 2km.

⌂ Sleeping

★ Botanica Guesthouse
BUNGALOW $

(☎097 8998614; www.kep-botanica.com; NH33A; r with fan US$19, with air-con US$29; ❀🛜❀) A little way from the action (if Kep can be said to have any action), Botanica offers exceptional value for money with attractive bungalows boasting contemporary bathrooms. There is a small swimming pool and guests can use free bicycles to hit the beach.

GETTING TO VIETNAM: KEP TO HA TIEN

The Prek Chak/Xa Xia border crossing (open 6am to 5.30pm) has become a popular option for linking Kampot and Kep with Ha Tien and the popular Vietnamese island of Phu Quoc.

Getting to the border The easiest way to get to Prek Chak and on to Ha Tien, Vietnam, is on a bus or van from Sihanoukville (US$16, five hours), Kampot (US$8, 1½ hours) or Kep (US$5, one hour). Several companies ply the Sihanoukville–Kampot–Kep–Ha Tien route.

A more flexible alternative from Phnom Penh or Kampot is to take any bus to Kompong Trach, then a *moto* (about US$3) for 15km to the border. In Kep, tour agencies and guesthouses can arrange a direct *remork* (US$13, one hour) or taxi (US$20, 30 minutes). Rates are almost double from Kampot.

At the border Pick up *motos* on the Vietnamese side of the border to Ha Tien (7km). You'll save money walking across no-man's land and picking up a *moto* on the other side for about US$3.

Moving on Travellers bound for Phu Quoc should arrive in Ha Tien no later than 12.30pm to secure a ticket on the 1pm ferry (230,000d or about US$11, 1½ hours). Extreme early risers may be able to make it to Ha Tien in time to catch the 8am ferry.

For information on making this crossing in reverse, see p898.

Tree Top Bungalows   BUNGALOW $
(☑ 012 515191; www.keptreetop.com; bungalow with/without bathroom US$25/5, treehouse bungalow from US$10; @ 🛜) Chilled out to the max, the bamboo 'treehouse' bungalows here are as quirky as it gets (each pair shares a bathroom). Back down on the ground are solid, roomy bungalows with private bathrooms, and Kep's cheapest rooms – shacks separated by flimsy partitions.

Kep Guest House   HOSTEL $
(☑ 097 3748080; www.kepguesthouse.com; NH33A; dm US$5-7, r US$9-17; ❄ 🛜) This modest hostel is Kep's nicest backpacker pad with bright, airy and clean rooms, and a dorm with double beds. There's great sea views from the rooftop restaurant. The US$17 room has air-con.

🍴 Eating

Eating fresh crab fried with Kampot pepper at the **Crab Market** – a row of wooden waterfront shacks next to a wet fish market – is a quintessential Kep experience. There are lots of great places to choose from. **Kimly** (☑ 036-904077; Crab Market; mains US$2.50-8; ☉ 10am-10pm) has a good reputation with crab prepared 27 different ways. The crab shacks also serve prawns, squid, fish and terrestrial offerings.

Sailing Club   FUSION $$
(mains US$7-12.50; ☉ 10am-10pm; 🛜) With a small beach, breezy wooden bar and a wooden jetty poking out into the sea, this is one of Cambodia's top sundowner spots. The Asian fusion food is excellent and you can get your crab fix here too. Try the Kep Special Fish (served in a Kampot pepper and coconut sauce) for a local taste sensation.

❶ Getting There & Away

Kep is 25km from Kampot and 41km from the Prek Chak/Xa Xia border crossing to Vietnam.

Phnom Penh Sorya and Hua Lian buses link the town with Kampot (US$2, 45 minutes) and Phnom Penh (US$5, four hours). A private taxi to Phnom Penh (three hours) costs US$40 to US$45.

A *moto/remork* to Kampot costs about US$6/12. Guesthouses can arrange minibus/bus combos to Sihanoukville and Koh Kong.

Motorbike rental is US$5 to US$7 per day and can be organised through guesthouses.

EASTERN CAMBODIA

If it's a walk on the wild side that fires your imagination, then the northeast is calling. It's home to forest elephants, freshwater dolphins and funky gibbons. Peppering the area are thundering waterfalls, crater lakes and meandering rivers. Trekking, biking, kayaking and ziplining are all beginning to take off. The rolling hills and lush forests provide a home to many ethnic minority groups. Do the maths: it all adds up to an amazing experience.

Kompong Cham កំពង់ចាម

🚌 042 / POP 73,000

This quiet Mekong city, an important trading post during the French period, serves as the gateway to Cambodia's northeast. Most of the action is on the riverfront.

💿 Sights & Activities

Koh Paen ISLAND
(កោះប៉ែន) For a supremely relaxing bicycle ride, it's hard to beat Koh Paen, a rural island in the Mekong River, connected to the southern reaches of Kompong Cham town by an elaborate **bamboo bridge** (toll 500r to 1000r) in the dry season or a local ferry (with/without bicycle 1500/1000r) in the wet season. The bamboo bridge is an attraction in itself; it's built entirely by hand each year and, from a distance, looks as if it were made of matchsticks.

Wat Nokor Bachey BUDDHIST TEMPLE
(វត្តនគរបាជ័យ; admission US$2) The original fusion temple, Wat Nokor is a modern Theravada Buddhist pagoda squeezed into the walls of a 12th-century Mahayana Buddhist shrine of sandstone and laterite. It's a kitschy kind of place; many of the older building's archways have been incorporated into the new building as shrines for worship. On weekdays there are only a few monks in the complex and it's peaceful to wander among the alcoves and their hidden shrines.

🛏️ Sleeping & Eating

⭐**Moon River Guesthouse** GUESTHOUSE $
(🚌 016 788973; moonrivermekong@gmail.com; Sihanouk St; r with fan US$7-11, with air-con US$13-19; ❄️🛜) One of the newer riverfront guesthouses, Moon River is a great all-rounder with smart, spacious rooms, including some triples. Downstairs is a popular restaurant-bar that serves hearty breakfasts and draws a crowd by night.

Mekong Sunrise GUESTHOUSE $
(🚌 011 449720; bong_thol@yahoo.com; Sihanouk St; dm US$3, r with fan US$5-7, with air-con US$12; ❄️🛜) A backpacker crashpad over a popular riverfront bar-restaurant, Mekong Sunrise has spacious upper-floor rooms with access to a sprawling rooftop. Furnishings are sparse, but it's cheap enough and there's a pool table.

⭐**Smile Restaurant** CAMBODIAN $
(www.bdsa-cambodia.org; Sihanouk St; mains US$3-5; ⏱️6.30am-9pm; 🛜) 🍴 Run by the Buddhism and Society Development Association, this handsome nonprofit restaurant is a huge hit with the NGO crowd for its big breakfasts and authentic Khmer cuisine, such as *char k'dau* (stir-fry with lemongrass, hot basil and peanuts) and moreish black-pepper squid. Western dishes are on the menu as well, and it sells BSDA-made *kramas* and trinkets.

Lazy Mekong Daze INTERNATIONAL $
(Sihanouk St; mains US$3-5.50; ⏱️7.30am-last customer; 🛜) One of the go-to places to gather after dark thanks to a mellow atmosphere, a pool table and a big screen for sports and movies. The menu includes a range of Khmer, Thai and Western food, plus the best wood-fired pizzas in town, chilli con carne and tempting ice creams.

ℹ️ Information

Lazy Mekong Daze hands out a decent map that highlights the major sights in and around Kompong Cham.
Canadia Bank (Preah Monivong Blvd; ⏱️8am-3.30pm Mon-Fri, 8-11.30am Sat, ATM 24hr) Free ATM withdrawals for some cards, plus free cash advances on credit cards.

BUSES FROM KOMPONG CHAM

DESTINATION	FARE	DURATION (HR)	FREQUENCY
Ban Lung	32,000r	7	10am
Kratie via Chhlong	20,000r	2	9.30am
Kratie via Snuol	21,000r	4	10.30am, 2pm
Pakse (Laos)	US$22	12	10am
Phnom Penh	20,000r	3	hourly to 3.45pm
Sen Monorom	28,000r	5	11.45am
Siem Reap	24,000r	5	7.30am, 9.30am, noon

❶ Getting There & Around

Phnom Penh is 120km southwest. If you are heading north to Kratie or beyond, secure transport via the sealed road to Chhlong rather than taking a huge detour east to Snuol on NH7.

Phnom Penh Sorya (Preah Monivong Blvd) is the most reliable bus company operating and serves all of the locales listed in the Buses from Kompong Cham table (p129).

Share taxis (15,000r, 2½ hours) and overcrowded local minibuses (10,000r) also make the run to Phnom Penh, departing from the **taxi park** near the New Market (Psar Thmei).

Morning share taxis and minibuses to Kratie (US$5, 1½ hours) depart when full from the **Caltex station** at the main roundabout, and there are morning minibuses from the taxi park as well.

Kratie

ក្រចេះ

✒ 072 / POP 44,000

The most popular place in Cambodia to glimpse Southeast Asia's remaining freshwater Irrawaddy dolphins, Kratie (pronounced 'kra-cheh') is a lively riverside town with a rich legacy of French-era architecture and some of the best Mekong sunsets in Cambodia.

Lying just across the water from Kratie is the island of **Koh Trong**, an almighty sandbar in the middle of the river. Cross here by boat and enjoy a slice of rural island life. Catch the little ferry from the port or charter a local boat (around US$2) to get here. Bicycle rental is available on the island near the ferry landing for US$1, or do the loop around the island on a *moto* (US$2.50) steered by a female *motodup* (*moto* driver) – a rarity for Cambodia.

MEKONG DISCOVERY TRAIL

It's well worth spending a couple of days exploring the various bike rides and activities on offer along the **Mekong Discovery Trail** (www.mekongdiscoverytrail. com), an initiative designed to open up stretches of the Mekong River around Stung Treng and Kratie to community-based tourism. Once managed by the government with foreign development assistance, the project is now being kept alive by private tour companies, such as **Xplore-Asia** (✒ 011 433836, 074-973456; www.xplore-cambodia.com) in Stung Treng and **CRDTours** (p130) in Kratie.

☞ Tours

CRDTours TOUR
(✒ 099 834353; www.crdtours.org; St 3; ☺ 8am-noon & 2-5.30pm; 🐾) ☞ Run by the Cambodian Rural Development Team, this company focuses on sustainable tours along the Mekong Discovery Trail. Homestays, volunteer opportunities and various excursions are available on the Mekong island of **Koh Pdao**, 20km north of Kampi. The typical price is US$38 to US$60 per day, including all meals and tours. Tours and homestays on **Koh Preah** (near Stung Treng) and **Koh Trong** are also possible. Mountain-bike tours from Kratie to Koh Pdao are another option.

Sorya Kayaking Adventures KAYAKING
(✒ 090 241148; www.soryakayaking.com; Rue Preah Suramarit) Sorya has a fleet of eight kayaks and runs half-day and multi-day trips (with homestay accommodation) on the Mekong north of Kratie, or on the Te River to the south. This is a great way to get close to the dolphins. Other highlights include a small flooded forest north of Kampi, Vietnamese floating villages, and a sunset trip around Koh Trong. There's a small cafe onsite and it sells handicrafts woven by disadvantaged widows.

🛏 Sleeping

There are homestays available on the island of Koh Trong opposite Kratie town.

Silver Dolphin Guesthouse HOSTEL $
(✒ 012 999810; silver.dolphinbooking@yahoo. com; 48 Rue Preah Suramarit; dm US$4, r US$4-14; ❄ @ 🐾) This backpacker hostel is a great deal. The dorm is spacious, with a soaring ceiling, and even the cheapest doubles have a TV, bathroom and some furniture. There is a popular upstairs bar-restaurant with a riverfront balcony. Owner Pech speaks great English and French.

U-Hong II Guesthouse GUESTHOUSE $
(✒ 085 885168; 119 St 10; r US$4-13; ❄ @ 🐾) A lively little shoes-off guesthouse between the market and the riverfront. There are eight rooms here, plus 11 more in a nearby annex, some with air-con. There is a buzzing bar-restaurant that boasts the most extensive cocktail list in town.

Kratie

0 ─────── 100 m
0 ─────── 0.05 miles

Ⓝ

Kampi (15km);
Sambor (35km)

Canadia
Bank St 4

St 5

Rue Preah Suramarit (Riverside St)

St 6

St 7

Boat
Dock

St 8

St 9

Psar

St 10

Preah Mohaksat Iranie Kosomak

Koh Trong
(1km)

St 11

Rue Preah Sihanouk

Mekong
River

St 12

St 13

Tourist
Office

Tokae Restaurant CAMBODIAN $
(St 10; mains US$2-4; ☺6am-11pm; 🛜) Look out for Cambodia's largest *tokae* (gecko) on the wall and you've found this excellent little eatery. The menu offers a good mix of cheap Cambodian food like curries and *amok* (a baked fish dish), plus equally affordable Western breakfasts and comfort food.

ⓘ Information

All of the recommended guesthouses are pretty switched-on to travellers' needs. Silver Dolphin Guesthouse has public internet access (per hour 3000r).

Canadia Bank (Rue Preah Suramarit; ☺8.30am-3.30pm Mon-Fri, ATM 24hr) ATM offering cash withdrawals, plus currency exchange.

ⓘ Getting There & Away

Kratie is 348km northeast of Phnom Penh (250km via Chhlong) and 141km south of Stung Treng.

Phnom Penh Sorya runs three buses per day to Phnom Penh (US$8, five to seven hours). Sorya buses to Siem Reap involve a change in Suong.

Going the other way, Sorya's bus from Phnom Penh to Pakse, Laos (US$20, eight hours), hits Kratie around 11.30am. Sorya also has a 1pm bus to Ban Lung (US$8, five hours), and a 3pm bus to Stung Treng (US$5, three hours).

Express vans, which pick you up from your guesthouse, are a faster way to Phnom Penh (US$7, four hours, about six per day). There's also an express van to Siem Reap (US$13, six hours, 7.30am).

For Sen Monorom, take a local minibus from the taxi park (30,000r, four hours, two or three early morning departures). Local minibuses also serve Ban Lung, with most departures between 11am and 2pm.

Most guesthouses can arrange bicycle (from US$1) and motorbike hire (from US$5). An

**Le Tonlé Tourism Training
Center** GUESTHOUSE $
(☎072-210505; www.letonle.org; St 3; r US$10-20; ❄🛜) 🅿 Following on from the success of its long-running Le Tonlé project in Stung Treng (p132), CRDT has opened a slightly smarter operation in Kratie. The expanded property has nine rustic but attractive rooms in a beautiful wooden house, and delicious food prepared by at-risk program trainees. Some rooms have bathrooms, some rooms share.

✗ Eating

Red Sun Falling INTERNATIONAL $
(Rue Preah Suramarit; mains US$2-4; ☺7am-9pm; 🛜) One of the liveliest spots in town, the long-running Red Sun has a relaxed cafe ambience, a supreme riverfront location, used books for sale and a good selection of Asian and Western meals.

CAMBODIA KRATIE

DOLPHIN WATCHING AROUND KRATIE

The freshwater Irrawaddy dolphin (trey pisaut) is an endangered species throughout Asia, with shrinking numbers inhabiting stretches of the Mekong in Cambodia and Laos, and isolated pockets in Bangladesh and Myanmar.

The dark blue to grey cetaceans grow to 2.75m long and are recognisable by their bulging foreheads and small dorsal fins. They can live in fresh or saltwater, although they are seldom seen in the sea. For more on this rare creature, see www.worldwildlife.org/species/irrawaddy-dolphin.

Before the civil war, locals say, Cambodia was home to as many as 1000 dolphins. However, during the Pol Pot regime, many were hunted for their oils, and their numbers continue to plummet even as drastic protection measures have been put in place, including a ban on fishing and commercial motorised boat traffic on much of the Mekong between Kratie and Stung Treng. The dolphins continue to die off at an alarming rate, and experts now estimate that there are fewer than 85 Irrawaddy dolphins left in the Mekong between Kratie and the Lao border.

The best place to see them is at Kampi, about 15km north of Kratie, on the road to Sambor. A moto/remork should be around US$7/10 return depending on how long the driver has to wait. Motorboats shuttle visitors out to the middle of the river to view the dolphins at close quarters. It costs US$9 per person for one to two persons and US$7 per person for groups of three to four. Encourage the boat driver to use the engine as little as possible once near the dolphins, as the noise is sure to disturb them. It is also possible to see the dolphins near the Lao border in Stung Treng province.

English-speaking motodup will set you back US$10 to US$15 per day, a remork about US$25.

Stung Treng ស្ទឹងត្រែង

☑ 074 / POP 35,000

Located on the Tonlé San near its confluence with the Mekong, Stung Treng is a quiet town with limited appeal, but sees a lot of transit traffic passing through between Laos and Cambodia.

🛏 Sleeping & Eating

Le Tonlé Tourism Training Center   GUESTHOUSE $
(☑ 074-973 638; www.letonle.org; s US$6-10, d US$8-12; 🖘) In a shady spot on the riverfront about 500m west of the port, this small guesthouse doubles as a training centre to help underprivileged locals get a start in the tourism industry. Rooms are simple but tastefully furnished. The four rooms share an immaculate bathroom and a comfy balcony, where delicious meals can be ordered in advance.

Riverside Guesthouse   GUESTHOUSE $
(☑ 012 257257; kimtysou@gmail.com; r US$5-8; @) Overlooking the riverfront area, the Riverside has long been a popular travellers' hub. Rooms are basic, but then so are the prices. It's a good spot for travel information and there's a popular bar-restaurant downstairs.

ℹ Information

Canadia Bank (◴ 8.30am-3.30pm Mon-Fri, ATM 24hr) Has an international ATM.

ℹ Getting There & Away

Phnom Penh Sorya (☑ 092 181805) has a 6.30am bus to Phnom Penh (40,000r, nine hours) via Kratie (20,000r, three hours). Sorya's bus from Laos to Phnom Penh comes through Stung Treng around 11.30am. There is a comfortable tourist van to Ban Lung (US$6, two hours, 8am).

The new highway west from Thala Boravit to Preah Vihear via Chhep is in great shape. **Asia Van Transfer** (☑ in Siem Reap 063-963853; www.asiavantransfer.com) has an express minibus to Siem Reap at 2pm daily (US$23, five hours), with a stop in Preah Vihear City (US$12, three hours).

Riverside Guesthouse rents out motorbikes (from US$8) and bicycles (US$1 to US$2).

Ratanakiri Province

ខេត្តរតនគិរី

Popular Ratanakiri Province is a diverse region of natural beauty that provides a remote home for a mosaic of minority peoples – Jarai, Tompuon, Brau and Kreung – with their own languages, traditions and customs. Adrenaline-pumping activities abound. Swim in clear volcanic lakes, shower under waterfalls, or trek in the vast Virachey National Park, it's all here.

Ban Lung ⟨ ⟩ បានលុង

📞 075 / POP 40,000

Affectionately known as *'dey krahorm'* (red earth) after its rust colour, Ban Lung provides a popular base for a range of Ratanakiri romps. It is one of the easiest places in Cambodia to arrange a jungle trek and has several beautiful lakes and waterfalls nearby.

◉ Sights & Activities

Boeng Yeak Lom   LAKE

(បឹងយក្សឡោម; admission US$1) At the heart of the protected area of Yeak Lom is a beautiful, emerald-hued crater lake set amid the vivid greens of the towering jungle. It is one of the most peaceful, beautiful locations Cambodia has to offer and the water is extremely clear. Several wooden piers are dotted around the perimeter, making it perfect for swimming. A small Cultural & Environmental Centre has a modest display on ethnic minorities in the province and hires out life jackets for children.

Waterfalls   WATERFALL

(per waterfall 2000r) Tucked amid the sprawling cashew and rubber plantations just west of Ban Lung are three waterfalls worth visiting: Chaa Ong, Ka Tieng and Kinchaan. All are within a 20-minute *moto* ride of town, and visits to all three are usually included in tour companies' half- and full-day excursions. The turn-offs to all three are 200m west of the new bus station, just beyond a Lina petrol station. There's signage but it's barely visible.

Virachey National Park   PARK

(admission US$5) This park is one of the largest protected areas in Cambodia, stretching for 3325 sq km east to Vietnam, north to Laos and west to Stung Treng Province. Virachey has one of the most organised ecotourism programs in Cambodia, focusing on small-scale culture, nature and adventure trekking. The program aims to involve and benefit local minority communities. All treks into the park must be arranged through the **Virachey National Park Eco-Tourism Information Centre** (📞075-974013, 097 896 4995; virachey@camintel.com; ☺8am-noon & 2-5pm) in Ban Lung.

☞ Tours

Overnight treks with nights spent camping or staying in minority villages north of Veun Sai or Ta Veng are popular. Figure on US$50 per person per day for a couple (less for larger groups).

Backpacker Pad, Tree Top Ecolodge and Yaklom Hill Lodge are good at arranging tours, but we recommend using one of the following dedicated tour companies.

Highland Tours   TOUR

(📞097 658 3841; highland.tour@yahoo.com) Kimi and Horng are husband-and-wife graduates of the Le Tonlé Tourism Training Center (p132) in Stung Treng, who have moved to the highlands to run a range of tours, including fun day trips and a multi-day tour

---

GETTING TO LAOS: STUNG TRENG TO SI PHAN DON

The remote Trapeang Kriel/Nong Nok Khiene border (open 6am to 6pm) is 60km north of Stung Treng.

Getting to the border Phnom Penh Sorya, in partnership with Pakse-based Lao operator Sengchalean, has buses from Phnom Penh straight through to Pakse's 2km (VIP) bus station (US$27, 12 to 14 hours). This bus leaves Phnom Penh at 6.45am, with pick-ups possible in Kompong Cham (around 9.30am), Kratie (around 11.30am) and Stung Treng (around 3pm). The only other option to the border from Stung Treng is a private taxi (US$35 to US$40) or *moto* (around US$15).

At the border Both Lao and Cambodian visas are available on arrival. Entering Laos, you'll pay US$30 to US$42 for a visa, depending on nationality, plus a US$2 fee.

Moving on Aside from the Sorya bus, there's virtually zero traffic on either side of the border. If you're dropped at the border, expect to pay 150,000r/50,000K (US$12/4) for a taxi/*săhmlór* heading north to Ban Nakasang (for Don Det).

For information on making this crossing in reverse, see p370.

Ban Lung

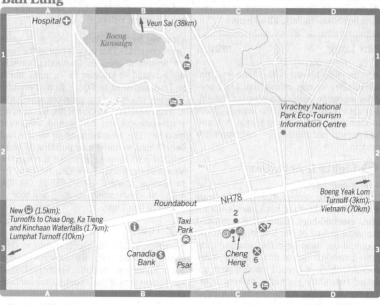

Ban Lung

Activities, Courses & Tours

Sleeping

Eating

from I Tub village (northwest of Veun Sai) to Siem Pang by bike, then on to Stung Treng by boat. Horng is the only female guide in Ratanakiri.

DutchCo
Trekking Cambodia TOUR
(☑097 679 2714; www.trekkingcambodia.com) One of the most experienced trekking operators in the province, run by – wait for it – a friendly Dutchman. Runs four- to five-day treks north of Veun Sai through Kavet villages and community forests, and one- to two-day trips around Kalai (south of Veun Sai), among many other tours.

🛏 Sleeping

⭐ **Tree Top Ecolodge** BUNGALOWS $
(☑012 490333; www.treetop-ecolodge.com; d US$7, cottage with cold/hot water US$12/15; 🐱)
This is one of the best places to stay in Cambodia's 'wild east', with oodles of atmosphere. 'Mr T's' place boasts rough-hewn walkways leading to huge bungalows with mosquito nets, thatch roofs and hammock-strewn verandas with verdant valley vistas. Like the bungalows, the restaurant is fashioned from hardwood and dangles over a lush ravine.

Backpacker Pad HOSTEL $
(☑088 944 1616; banlungbackpackerpad@yahoo. com; dm US$2, d without/with bathroom US$4/5; 🐱) Popular Backpacker Pad is the cheapest deal in town, with small rooms or communal dorms at rock-bottom prices. The cosy common area out front is a good place to meet other travellers. Owner Sophat is a great source of info and runs an eponymous tour company.

Banlung Balcony GUESTHOUSE $
(☑097 809 7036; www.balconyguesthouse.net; Boeng Kansaign; d US$4-7; @🐱) This is one of Ban Lung's best deals at the budget end of the market. The rooms are basic but have high ceilings and wooden floors, and there's

a huge public balcony. The restaurant-bar has decent food and a snooker table.

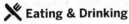

Eating & Drinking

★ **Green Carrot** INTERNATIONAL $
(US$2-6; ⊙7am-10pm; 🛜) A great little hole-in-the-wall restaurant that turns out surprisingly sophisticated food, including healthy salads, sandwiches and wraps, plus a good range of Khmer favourites. It even does a decent burger and some very affordable pizzas. Happy hour has two-for-one on cocktails from 6pm to 8pm.

Cafe Alee INTERNATIONAL $
(mains US$1.50-5.50; ⊙7am–last customer; 🛜) Cafe Alee has one of the more interesting menus in town, including a generous smattering of vegetarian options, a hearty lasagne and the full gamut of Khmer food (minus the MSG that sometimes shows up in local restaurants). It also serves hearty breakfasts for trekkers.

ℹ Information

Canadia Bank (⊙8.30am-3.30pm Mon-Fri, ATM 24hr) Full-service bank with an international ATM.
Srey Mom Internet (per hr 4000r; ⊙6.30am-10pm) Fan-cooled internet access.

ℹ Getting There & Away

There is a vast bus station on the western outskirts of town, 2.5km west of Ban Lung's main roundabout, but guesthouses and tour companies can arrange pickups in town.

Phnom Penh Sorya, Rith Mony and Thong Ly run early-morning buses to Phnom Penh (US$9 to US$10, 11 hours) via Kratie and Kompong Cham.

GETTING TO VIETNAM: EASTERN BORDERS

Kompong Cham to Tay Ninh

The Trapeang Plong/Xa Mat crossing (open 7am to 5pm) is convenient for those using private transport to travel between northeast Cambodia or Siem Reap and Ho Chi Minh City.

Getting to the border From Kompong Cham take anything heading east on NH7 toward Snuol, and get off at the roundabout in Krek (Kraek) on NH7. From there, it's 13km south by *moto* (US$3) along NH72 to snoozy Trapeang Plong.

At the border This border is a breeze; just have your Vietnamese visa ready.

Moving on On the Vietnamese side, motorbikes and taxis go to Tay Ninh, 45km to the south.

Snuol to Binh Long

The Trapeang Sre/Loc Ninh crossing (open 7am to 5pm) is useful for those trying to get straight to Vietnam from Kratie or points north.

Getting to the border First get to Snuol by bus, share taxi or minibus from Sen Monorom, Kratie or Kompong Cham. In Snuol catch a *moto* (US$5) for the 18km trip southeastward along smooth NH74.

At the border Some nationalities need a prearranged visa to enter Vietnam.

Moving on On the Vietnamese side, the nearest town is Binh Long, 40km to the south. Motorbikes wait at the border.

Ban Lung to Pleiku

The O Yadaw/Le Thanh crossing (open 7am to 5pm) is 70km east of Ban Lung along smooth NH19.

Getting to the border From Ban Lung, guesthouses advertise a 6.30am van to Pleiku (US$12, 3½ hours) involving a change of vehicle at the border. This picks you up at your guesthouse.

At the border Formalities are straightforward and lines nonexistent; just make sure you have a Vietnamese visa if you need one.

Moving on On the Vietnamese side of the frontier, the road is nicely paved. *Motos* await to take you to Duc Co (20km), where there are buses to Pleiku, Quy Nhon and Hoi An.

For information on making this crossing in reverse, see p879.

ℹ WARNING

The Ho Chi Minh Trail once passed through the hills of Ratanakiri, where it was nicknamed the Sihanouk Trail in reference to Cambodia's then head of state. This region was heavily bombed by the Americans and there is still some unexploded ordnance (UXO; see p937) around. Never touch anything that looks vaguely like UXO.

Speedy express-van services pick you up at your guesthouse and head to Phnom Penh (US$15, eight hours, 6am and 1pm) and Stung Treng (US$7, two hours, around 8am). Organise these through your guesthouse. Call Backpacker Pad or Tree Top Ecolodge to arrange an express-van pickup if coming from Phnom Penh.

There is also a daily minivan south to Sen Monorom (US$8, two hours, 8am) in Mondulkiri. Various local slow minibuses also depart in the morning to Phnom Penh (50,000r), Stung Treng (20,000r) and O'Yadaw (12,000r), and throughout the day to Lumphat (10,000r, one hour) and Kratie (25,000r, four hours).

ℹ Getting Around

Bicycles (US$1 to US$3), motorbikes (US$5 to US$7), cars (from US$30) and 4WDs (from US$50) are available for hire from most guesthouses in town.

Motodups hang out around the market and some double as guides. Figure on US$15 to US$20 per day for a good English-speaking driver-guide. A *moto* to Yeak Lom costs about US$5 return; to Veun Sai is US$15 return; to any waterfall is about US$6 return.

Cheng Heng (☑ 088 851 6104; ⊗ 6am-8pm) has some 250cc trail bikes for rent (US$25) in addition to a stable of well-maintained smaller motorbikes (US$6 to US$8).

Mondulkiri Province
ខេត្តមណ្ឌលគិរី

Mondulkiri (Meeting of the Hills), the original 'wild east' of the country, is a world apart from the lowlands with not a rice paddy or palm tree in sight. Home to the hardy Bunong people and their noble elephants, this upland area is a seductive mix of grassy hills, pine groves and jade-green rainforests. Activities are taking off in a big way with a new zipline and quad-biking adventures on tap.

Conservationists have grand plans for the sparsely populated province, with wildlife encounters such as walking with the herd at Elephant Valley Project and spotting doucs and gibbons in the Seima Protected Forest, but are facing off against loggers, poachers and speculators.

Sen Monorom
សែនមនោរម្យ

📔 073 / POP 10,000 / ELEV 800M

The provincial capital of Mondulkiri, Sen Monorom is really an overgrown village, a charming community set in the spot where the legendary hills meet. The area around Sen Monorom is peppered with minority villages and picturesque waterfalls, making it the ideal base to spend some time. It's set at 800m; when the winds blow it's notably cooler than the rest of Cambodia, so bring warm clothing.

⊙ Sights & Activities

As in Ratanakiri, multiday forest treks taking in minority villages are the big draw. We recommend securing indigenous Bunong guides for these trips. They know the forests intimately and can break the ice with the locals in any Bunong villages you visit.

Monorom Falls WATERFALL
(ទឹកជ្រោះកំមនោរម្យ) **FREE** A 10m drop into a popular swimming hole, Monorom Falls is lovely if you can beat the crowds. From the west side of the air strip, head northwest for 2.3km, turn left and proceed 1.5km. There's no legible sign at the turn-off.

Bou Sraa Waterfall WATERFALL
(ទឹកជ្រោះប៊ូស្រា; admission 5000r) Plunging into the dense jungle below, this is one of Cambodia's most impressive falls. Famous throughout the country, this double-drop waterfall has an upper tier of 10m and a spectacular lower tier with a thundering 25m drop. Getting here is a 33km, one-hour journey east of Sen Monorom on a mostly sealed road.

Elephant Valley Project WILDLIFE RESERVE
(EVP; ☑ 099 696041; www.elephantvalleyproject.org; ⊗ Mon-Fri) For an original elephant experience, visit the Elephant Valley Project. The project entices local mahouts to bring their overworked or injured elephants to this 1600-hectare sanctuary. It's very popular, so make sure you book well ahead. You can visit for a whole day (US$85) or half-day (US$55). It does not take overnight visitors on Friday and Saturday nights and is not open to day visitors on Saturday and Sunday.

Mayura Zipline ZIPLINE
(🗷 088 888 8629; Bou Sraa Waterfall; US$69) The new Mayura Zipline is an adrenaline rush in the extreme, as the longest 300m-line passes right over the top of Bou Sraa Waterfall. The zipline course starts on the far bank of the river; there are a total of six lines to navigate, plus a suspension bridge. The first four zips are warm-ups for the high-speed flight over the waterfall; the course finishes with a short tandem line for couples or new friends.

👉 Tours

Green House TOUR
(🗷 017 905659; www.greenhouse-tour.blogspot.com; NH76) 🖉 Owner Sam Nang is a good source of information about Mondulkiri. Green House operates the **Elephant Community Program**, which offers affordable elephant encounters for US$35 per person, plus some longer overnight tours. As well as treks, Green House offers full-day mountain-bike tours (from US$20), plus Trek and Giant mountain bikes (per day US$8) and motorbikes (US$7) for hire.

Hefalump Cafe TOURIST INFORMATION
(⏲ 7am-6pm Mon-Fri, 9am-4pm Sun) This NGO-run cafe doubles as a 'drop-in centre' for Bunong people and is the best source of information on sustainable tourism in Mondulkiri Province, including the Elephant Valley Project, the Seima Protected Forest and responsible tours to Bunong communities.

Kouprey ATV Tours ADVENTURE TOUR
(🗷 088 888 8629; Mayura Hill Resort; US$29) Quad-biking has come to the hills of Mondulkiri – and it's a whole lot of fun. Organised by Mayura Hill Resort, the trip takes in some of Sen Monorom's main sights, including the Monorom Falls, Samot Cheur ('Ocean of Trees') and the Wat Phnom Doh Kromom viewpoint. It's great value and a fun way to get a bit of ATV experience under your belt in a low-traffic environment.

🛏 Sleeping

⭐ **Nature Lodge** GUESTHOUSE $
(🗷 012 230272; www.naturelodgecambodia.com; r US$10-30; 🛜) Sprawling across a windswept hilltop near town are 30 solid wood bungalows with private porches, hot showers and mosquito nets. Among them are incredible Swiss Family Robinson–style chalets with sunken beds and ante-rooms. The magnificent restaurant has comfy nooks, a pool table and an enviable bar where guests chill out and swap travel tales.

RESPONSIBLE TREKKING AROUND NORTHEAST CAMBODIA

Treks taking in the remote forests and minority villages of Ratanakiri and Mondulkiri are very popular these days. Where possible, we recommend using indigenous guides for organised treks and other excursions around the provinces. They speak the local dialects, understand tribal taboos and can secure permission to visit cemeteries that are off-limits to Khmer guides. Their intimate knowledge of the forests is another major asset.

More tips on visiting indigenous communities responsibly:

➡ Try to spend some real time in minority villages – at least several hours if not overnight. If you don't have a few hours to invest, don't go.

➡ Travel in small, less disruptive groups.

➡ Do not photograph without asking permission first – this includes children. Some hill tribes believe the camera will capture their spirit.

➡ Dress modestly.

➡ Taste traditional wine if you are offered it, especially during a ceremony. Refusal will cause offence.

➡ Individual gifts create jealousy and expectations. Instead, consider making donations to the local school, medical centre or community fund.

➡ Honour signs discouraging outsiders from entering a village, for instance during a spiritual ceremony. A good local guide will be able to detect these signs.

➡ Never give children sweets or money.

➡ Don't buy village treasures, such as altarpieces or totems, or the clothes or jewellery locals are wearing.

Indigenous Peoples Lodge
BUNGALOW **$**

(📱012 317368; indigenouspeopleslodge@gmail.com; r US$7-20; @🛜) Run by a Bunong family, this is a great place to stay with a whole range of accommodation set in minority houses, including a traditional thatched Bunong house with an upgrade or two. The cheapest rooms involve a shared bathroom, but are good value. Perks include free internet and free drop-offs in town.

Tree Lodge
BUNGALOWS **$**

(📱097 723 4177; www.treelodgecambodia.com; r US$5-15; 🛜) Basic A-frame huts made from native materials extend in perfect linear formation down a hill at the back; there are also some smarter new bungalows. Hang out at the restaurant, where hammocks and tasty Khmer food await. The young family in charge is very welcoming and can help with tour arrangements.

Eating & Drinking

Khmer Kitchen
CAMBODIAN **$**

(mains US$2-4; ☺6am-10pm; 🛜) This unassuming street-side eatery whips up some of the most flavoursome Khmer food in the hills. The *kari saik trey* (fish coconut curry) and other curries are particularly noteworthy, plus it also offers a smattering of international dishes.

Hefalump Cafe
CAFE **$**

(cakes US$1-3; ☺7am-6pm Mon-Fri, 9am-4pm Sun; 🛜) 🍴 A collaboration of various NGOs and conservation groups in town, this cafe doubles as a training centre for Bunong people in hospitality. Local coffee or Lavazza, a range of teas, and some delicious homemade cakes make this a great spot to plan your adventures over a cuppa.

Chilli on the Rocks
BAR

Sleepy Sen Monorom has a real bar at long last. Run by a friendly Swedish couple, it has cheap beer, strong cocktails and a menu of international bites, including a tasty tapas platter to go with the drinks. Closing hours are flexible, depending on the crowd.

ⓘ Information

The recommended guesthouses are all very good sources of information and run the full gamut of tours.

Acleda Bank (NH76; ☺8.30am-3.30pm, ATM 24hr) Changes major currencies and has a Visa-only ATM.

ⓘ Getting There & Away

Phnom Penh Sorya runs a 7.30am bus to Phnom Penh (35,000r, eight hours). Kim Seng Express runs comfortable minivans (US$11) that do the trip in five hours and has six departures daily between 7am and 2pm. Virak-Buntham also operates a minibus to Phnom Penh (US$12), with departures at 7.15am and 1.30pm.

Local minibuses are the way to get to Kratie (30,000r, four hours). Count on at least one early-morning departure and two or three departures around lunchtime.

There are now minibuses plying the new road to Ban Lung in Ratanakiri, which cost US$8 and take about two hours.

THE REAL GIBBON EXPERIENCE

The Mekong region is awash with tours that have gibbon in their name, but you don't always get to see gibbons. Here it is possible to see rare yellow-cheeked crested gibbons in the Veun Sai-Siem Pang Conservation Area (VSSPCA), just outside the border of Virachey National Park north of Veun Sai.

Gibbon Spotting Cambodia (📱in Siem Reap 063-966355; www.gibbonspottingcambodia.com) is a recent initiative from Conservation International (CI; www.conservationinternational.org) to allow visitors to observe a colony that was only discovered in 2010 and is believed to be one of the world's largest at about 500 groups. Hearing their haunting dawn call echo through the jungle and seeing them swing through the canopy is memorable.

Stay at least one night in the jungle, sleeping in hammocks or in a community-based homestay, rising well before dawn to spend time with the gibbons. CI has an exclusive arrangement with the village near the gibbon site to run these tours. The gibbon-viewing season runs from November to mid-June – it's too wet at other times – and the maximum group size is six. The tour price varies based on the exact group size. Most companies in Ban Lung can arrange these trips on behalf of CI.

The VSSPCA is highly susceptible to the types of illegal and legal logging that have ravaged most of the forests around Ban Lung.

MONKEY BUSINESS IN MONDULKIRI

A recent Wildlife Conservation Society study estimated populations of 20,600 black-shanked doucs and more than 1000 yellow-cheeked crested gibbons in Seima Protected Forest, the world's largest known populations of both species. **Jahoo Gibbon Camp** offers the chance to trek into the wild near the Bunong village of Andong Kraloeng and try to spot these primates, along with other elusive animals.

The Jahoo Gibbon Camp provides local villagers with an incentive to conserve the endangered primates and their habitat through providing a sustainable income. Treks wind their way through mixed evergreen forest and waterfalls with an excellent chance of spotting the doucs and macaques along the way.

Guides accompany visitors together with local Bunong guides to identify the trails, and a conservation contribution is included in the cost of the trip. This is a new project and the prices of tours are dependent on transport and group size: sample prices are US$80 per person for a one-day tour, or US$150 for an overnight tour at the Jahoo Gibbon Camp, a rustic tented camp; both prices include guides and food.

For information and booking contact the Sam Veasna Center team at the Hefalump Cafe in Sen Monorom. The Jahoo Gibbon Camp lies within the protected forest near the highway, just 25km southwest of Sen Monorom.

ℹ️ Getting Around

English-speaking *moto* drivers cost about US$15 to US$20 per day. Most guesthouses rent out motorbikes for US$6 to US$8 and a few have bicycles for US$2. **Adventure Rider Asia** (📱 078 250350; www.adventureriderasia.com; NH76; tours per day from US$75) has well-maintained 250cc dirt bikes (US$25) for rent.

UNDERSTAND CAMBODIA

Cambodia Today

The Cambodian People's Party (CPP) has dominated the politics of Cambodia since 1979 when it was installed in power by the Vietnamese. Party and state are intertwined and the CPP leadership has been making plans for the future with dynastic alliances between its offspring.

However, this control was shaken in the last election when the opposition was able to make significant gains. Long-standing opposition leader Sam Rainsy joined with Human Rights Party leader Kem Sokha to launch the Cambodia National Rescue Party (CNRP). While official results confirmed a CPP victory, opposition counts suggested the CNRP may have actually won the popular vote by a slight majority.

Following months of demonstrations, the opposition entered the national assembly, but heated topics remain, including the

shared border with Vietnam and land reform. Huge geopolitical forces are at play in the region with China's push into the South China Sea. Cambodia finds itself caught in the middle of a simmering conflict between its two closest allies, China and Vietnam, and cannot please both.

Badly traumatised by decades of conflict, Cambodia's economy was long a gecko amid the neighbouring dragons. The government, perenially shunned by international big business, is keen to benefit from newfound opportunities. China has come to the table to play for big stakes and is investing some serious money.

Aid was long the mainstay of the Cambodian economy, and NGOs have done a lot to force important sociopolitical issues onto the agenda. However, Cambodia remains one of Asia's poorest countries and the minimum wage is only US$140 per month.

History

The good, the bad and the ugly is a simple way to sum up Cambodian history. Things were good in the early years, culminating in the vast Khmer empire, unrivalled in the region during four centuries of dominance. Then the bad set in, from the 13th century, as ascendant neighbours steadily chipped away at Cambodian territory. In the 20th century it turned downright ugly, as a brutal civil war culminated in the genocidal rule of the Khmer Rouge (1975–79), from which Cambodia is still recovering.

Funan & Chenla

The Indianisation of Cambodia began in the 1st century AD as traders plying the sea route from the Bay of Bengal to southern China brought Indian ideas and technologies to what is now southern Vietnam. The largest of the era's nascent kingdoms, known to the Chinese as Funan, embraced the worship of the Hindu deities Shiva and Vishnu and, at the same time, Buddhism.

From the 6th to 8th centuries Cambodia seems to have been ruled by a collection of competing kingdoms. Chinese annals refer to 'Water Chenla', apparently the area around the modern-day town of Takeo, and 'Land Chenla', further north along the Mekong and around Sambor Prei Kuk.

The Rise & Fall of Angkor

The Angkorian era lasted from AD 802 to 1432, encompassing periods of conquest, turmoil and retreat, revival and decline, and fits of remarkable productivity.

In 802 Jayavarman II (reigned c 802–50) proclaimed himself a *devaraja* (god-king). He instigated an uprising against Javanese domination of southern Cambodia and, through alliances and conquests, brought the country under his control, becoming the first monarch to rule most of what we now call Cambodia.

In the 9th century Yasovarman I (r 889–910) moved the capital to Angkor, creating a new centre for worship, scholarship and the arts. After a period of turmoil and conflict, Suryavarman II (r 1113–52) unified the kingdom and embarked on another phase of territorial expansion, waging successful but costly wars against both Vietnam and Champa (an Indianised kingdom that occupied what is now southern and central Vietnam). His devotion to the Hindu deity Vishnu inspired him to commission Angkor Wat.

The tables soon turned. Champa struck back in 1177 with a naval expedition up the Mekong, taking Angkor by surprise and putting the king to death. But the following year a cousin of Suryavarman II – soon crowned Jayavarman VII (r 1181–1219) – rallied the Khmers and defeated the Chams in another epic naval battle. A devout follower of Mahayana Buddhism, it was he who built the city of Angkor Thom.

During the twilight years of the empire, religious conflict and internecine rivalries were rife. The Thais made repeated incursions into Angkor, sacking the city in 1351 and again in 1431, and from the royal court making off with thousands of intellectuals, artisans and dancers, whose profound impact on Thai culture can be seen to this day.

From 1600 until the arrival of the French, Cambodia was ruled by a series of weak kings whose intrigues often involved seeking the protection of either Thailand or Vietnam – granted, of course, at a price.

French Colonialism

The era of yo-yoing between Thai and Vietnamese masters came to a close in 1864, when French gunboats intimidated King Norodom I (r 1860–1904) into signing a treaty of protectorate. An exception in the annals of colonialism, the French presence really did protect the country at a time when it was in danger of being swallowed by its more powerful neighbours. In 1907 the French pressured Thailand into returning the northwest provinces of Battambang, Siem Reap and Sisophon, bringing Angkor under Cambodian control for the first time in more than a century.

Led by King Norodom Sihanouk (r 1941–55 and 1993–2004), Cambodia declared independence on 9 November 1953.

Independence & Civil War

The period after 1953 was one of peace and prosperity, and a time of creativity and optimism. Dark clouds were circling, however, as the war in Vietnam began sucking in neighbouring countries. As the 1960s drew to a close, the North Vietnamese and the Viet Cong were using Cambodian territory in their battle against South Vietnam and US forces, prompting devastating American bombing and a land invasion into eastern Cambodia.

In March 1970 Sihanouk, now serving as prime minister, was overthrown by General Lon Nol, and took up residence in Beijing. Here he set up a government-in-exile that allied itself with an indigenous Cambodian revolutionary movement that Sihanouk had dubbed the Khmer Rouge. Violence engulfed large parts of the country.

Khmer Rouge Rule

Upon taking Phnom Penh on 17 April 1975, two weeks before the fall of Saigon, the

Khmer Rouge implemented one of the most radical and brutal restructurings of a society ever attempted. Its goal was to transform Cambodia, renamed Democratic Kampuchea, into a giant peasant-dominated agrarian cooperative, untainted by anything that had come before. Within days, the entire populations of Phnom Penh and provincial towns, including the sick, elderly and infirm, were forced to march into the countryside and work as slaves for 12 to 15 hours a day. Intellectuals were systematically wiped out – wearing glasses or speaking a foreign language was reason enough to be killed. The advent of Khmer Rouge rule was proclaimed Year Zero.

Leading the Khmer Rouge was Saloth Sar, better known as Pol Pot. Under his rule, Cambodia became a vast slave labour camp. Meals consisted of little more than watery rice porridge twice a day, meant to sustain men, women and children through a back-breaking day in the fields. Disease stalked the work camps, malaria and dysentery striking down whole families.

Khmer Rouge rule was brought to an end by the Vietnamese, who liberated the almost-empty city of Phnom Penh on 7 January 1979. It is estimated that around two million people perished at the hands of Pol Pot and his followers. The Documentation Center of Cambodia (www.dccam.org) records the horrific events of the period.

A Sort of Peace

The Vietnamese installed a new government led by several former Khmer Rouge officers, including current Prime Minister Hun Sen, who had defected to Vietnam in 1977. In the dislocation that followed liberation, little rice was planted or harvested, leading to a massive famine.

The Khmer Rouge continued to wage civil war from remote mountain bases near the Thai border throughout the 1980s. In February 1991 all parties, including the Khmer Rouge, signed the Paris Peace Accords, according to which the UN Transitional Authority in Cambodia (UNTAC) would rule the country for two years before elections

THE KHMER ROUGE TRIAL

The Vietnamese ousted the Khmer Rouge on 7 January 1979, but it wasn't until 1999 – after two decades of civil war – that serious discussions began about a trial to bring to justice those responsible for the deaths of about two million Cambodians. After lengthy negotiations, agreement was finally reached on establishing a war crimes tribunal to try the surviving leaders of the Khmer Rouge.

It took another decade for the first verdict in the Extraordinary Chambers in the Courts of Cambodia (ECCC) trial. In that time one of the key suspects, the one-legged general Ta Mok ('The Butcher'), died in custody. Case 001, the trial of Kaing Guek Eav, aka Comrade Duch, finally began in 2009. Duch was seen as a key figure as he provided the link between the regime and its crimes in his role as head of S-21 prison. Duch was sentenced to 35 years in 2010, a verdict that was later extended on appeal to life imprisonment.

Case 002 began in November 2011, involving the most senior surviving leaders of the Democratic Kampuchea (DK) era: Brother Number 2 Nuon Chea (age 84), Brother Number 3 and former foreign minister of DK Ieng Sary (age 83), and former DK head of state Khieu Samphan (age 79). Justice may prove elusive, however, due to the slow progress of court proceedings and the advancing age of the defendants. Ieng Sary died in 2013, and his wife and former DK Minister of Social Affairs Ieng Thirith (age 78) was ruled unfit to stand trial because of dementia. Both Nuon Chea and Khieu Samphan received life sentences for crimes against humanity in August 2014, but are currently facing additional charges of genocide.

Case 003 against head of the DK navy, Meas Muth, and head of the DK air force, Sou Met, is meant to follow Case 002. However, investigations into this case stalled back in 2009 under intense pressure from the Cambodian government. Although Prime Minister Hun Sen is opposed to Case 003, the international judges went ahead and charged Meas Muth with genocide, crimes against humanity and war crimes in 2015.

To keep abreast of developments in the trial, visit the official ECCC website at www. eccc.gov.kh or the Cambodian Tribunal Monitor at www.cambodiatribunal.org.

were held in 1993. But the Khmer Rouge boycotted the elections and re-established a guerrilla network throughout Cambodia.

The last Khmer Rouge hold-outs, including Ta Mok, were not defeated until the capture of Anlong Veng and Prasat Preah Vihear by government forces in the spring of 1998. Pol Pot cheated justice by dying a sorry death near Anlong Veng during that year; he was cremated on a pile of old tyres.

People & Culture

Population

Around 16 million people live in Cambodia. With a rapid growth rate of about 2% a year, the population is predicted to reach 20 million by 2025. More than 40% of the population is under the age of 16. According to official statistics, around 96% of the people are ethnic Khmers, making the country the most homogeneous in Southeast Asia, but in reality anywhere between 10% and 20% of the population is of Cham, Chinese or Vietnamese origin. Cambodia's diverse Khmer Leu (Upper Khmer) or Chunchiet (minorities), who live in the country's mountainous regions, probably number between 75,000 and 100,000.

The official language is Khmer, spoken by 95% of the population. English has taken over from French as the second language of choice, although Chinese is also growing in popularity. Life expectancy is currently 64 years.

Lifestyle

For many older Cambodians, life is centred on faith, family and food, an existence that has stayed the same for centuries. Faith is a rock in the lives of many older Cambodians, and Buddhism helped them to survive the terrible years and then rebuild their lives after the Khmer Rouge. Family is more than the nuclear family we now know in the West; it's the extended family of third cousins and obscure aunts – as long as there is a bloodline, there is a bond. Families stick together, solve problems collectively, listen to the wisdom of the elders, and pool resources. The extended family comes together during times of trouble and times of joy, celebrating festivals and successes, mourning deaths and disappointments. Whether the Cambodian house is big or small, there will be a lot of people living inside.

However, the Cambodian lifestyle is changing as the population gets younger and more urbanised. Cambodia is experiencing its very own '60s swing, as the younger generation stands ready for a different lifestyle to the one their parents had to swallow. This creates plenty of friction in the cities, as rebellious teens dress as they like, date whoever they wish and hit the town until all hours. More recently this generational conflict spilled over into politics as the Facebook generation helped deliver a shock result that saw the Cambodian People's Party majority slashed in half in the 2013 general elections.

Corruption remains a way of life in Cambodia. It is a major element of the Cambodian economy and exists to some extent at all levels of government. Sometimes it is overt, but increasingly it is covert, with private companies often securing very favourable business deals on the basis of their connections. It seems everything has a price, including ancient temples, national parks and even genocide sites.

Religion

The majority of Khmers follow the Theravada branch of Buddhism. Buddhism in Cambodia draws heavily on its predecessors, incorporating many cultural traditions from Hinduism for ceremonies such as birth, marriage and death, as well as genies and spirits, such as Neak Ta, which link back to a pre-Indian animist past.

Under the Khmer Rouge, the majority of Cambodia's Buddhist monks were murdered and nearly all of the country's wat (more than 3000) were damaged or destroyed. In the late 1980s Buddhism once again became the state religion.

Other religions found in Cambodia include: Islam, practised by the Cham community; animism, among the hill tribes; and Christianity, which is making inroads via missionaries and Christian NGOs.

MUST SEE
....

The Killing Fields (1984) is a poignant film about American journalist Sydney Schanberg and Cambodian photographer Dith Pran during and after the Khmer Rouge takeover.

Arts

The Khmer Rouge regime not only killed the living bearers of Khmer culture, it also destroyed cultural artefacts, statues, musical instruments, books and anything else that served as a reminder of a past it was trying to efface. The temples of Angkor were spared as a symbol of Khmer glory and empire, but little else survived. Despite this, Cambodia is witnessing a resurgence of traditional arts and a growing interest in cross-cultural fusion.

Cambodia's royal ballet is a tangible link with the glory of Angkor and includes a unique *apsara* (heavenly nymphs) dance. Cambodian music, too, goes back at least as far as Angkor. To get some sense of the music that Jayavarman VII used to like, check out the bas-reliefs at Angkor.

In the mid-20th century a vibrant Cambodian pop-music scene developed, but it was killed off by the Khmer Rouge. After the war, overseas Khmers established a pop industry in the USA and some Cambodian-Americans, raised on a diet of rap, are now returning to their homeland. The Los Angeles–based sextet Dengue Fever, inspired by 1960s Cambodian pop and psychedelic rock, is the ultimate fusion band.

The people of Cambodia were producing masterfully sensuous sculptures – much more than mere copies of Indian forms – in the age of Funan and Chenla. The Banteay Srei style of the late 10th century is regarded as a high point in the evolution of Southeast Asian art.

Food & Drink

Some traditional Cambodian dishes are similar to those of neighbouring Laos and Thailand (though not as spicy), others closer to Chinese and Vietnamese cooking. The French left their mark, too.

Thanks to the Tonlé Sap, freshwater fish – often *ahng* (grilled) – are a huge part of the Cambodian diet. The legendary national dish, *amok,* is fish baked with coconut and lemongrass in banana leaves. *Prahoc* (fermented fish paste) is used to flavour foods, with coconut and lemongrass making regular cameos.

A proper Cambodian meal almost always includes *samlor* (soup), served at the same time as other courses. *Kyteow* is a rice-noodle soup that will keep you going all day.

Bobor (rice porridge), eaten for breakfast, lunch or dinner, is best sampled with some fresh fish and a dash of ginger.

Tap water *must* be avoided, especially in rural areas. Bottled water is widely available but coconut milk, sold by machete-wielding street vendors, is more ecological and may be more sterile.

Beer is immensely popular in the cities, while rural folk drink palm wine, tapped from the sugar palms that dot the landscape. *Tukaloks* (fruit shakes) are mixed with milk, sugar and sometimes a raw egg.

Environment

The Land

Cambodia's two dominant geographical features are the mighty Mekong River and a vast lake, the Tonlé Sap. The rich sediment deposited during the Mekong's annual wet-season flooding has made central Cambodia incredibly fertile. This low-lying alluvial plain is where the vast majority of Cambodians live, fishing and farming in harmony with the rhythms of the monsoon.

In Cambodia's southwest quadrant, much of the land mass is covered by the Cardamom Mountains and, near Kampot, the Elephant Mountains. Along Cambodia's northern border with Thailand, the plains collide with the Dangkrek Mountains, a striking sandstone escarpment more than 300km long and up to 550m high. One of the best places to get a sense of this area is Prasat Preah Vihear.

In the northeastern corner of the country, in the provinces of Ratanakiri and Mondulkiri, the plains give way to the Eastern

TONLÉ SAP: THE HEARTBEAT OF CAMBODIA

During the wet season (June to October) the Mekong River rises dramatically, forcing the Tonlé Sap river to flow northwest into Tonlé Sap (Great Lake). During this period the lake swells from around 3000 sq km to almost 13,000 sq km, and from the air Cambodia looks like one almighty puddle. As the Mekong falls during the dry season, the Tonlé Sap river reverses its flow, and the lake's floodwaters drain back into the Mekong. This unique process makes Tonlé Sap one of the world's richest sources of freshwater fish.

Highlands, a remote region of densely forested mountains and high plateaus.

Wildlife

Cambodia's forest ecosystems were in excellent shape until the 1990s and, compared with its neighbours, its habitats are still relatively healthy. The years of war took their toll on some species, but others thrived in the remote jungles of the southwest and northeast. Ironically, peace brought increased threats as loggers felled huge areas of primary forest and the illicit trade in wildlife targeted endangered species.

Still, with more than 200 species of mammal, Cambodia has some of Southeast Asia's best wildlife-watching opportunities. Highlights include spotting gibbons and black-shanked doucs in Ratanakiri and Mondulkiri provinces, and viewing some of the last remaining freshwater Irrawaddy dolphins in Kratie and Stung Treng provinces. The country is a birdwatcher's paradise – feathered friends found almost exclusively in Cambodia include the giant ibis, Bengal florican, sarus crane and three species of vulture. The marshes around Tonlé Sap are particularly rich in birdlife. The Siem Reap-based Sam Veasna Center runs birding trips.

Globally threatened species that you stand a slight chance of seeing include the Asian elephant, banteng (a wild ox), gaur, clouded leopard, fishing cat, marbled cat, sun bear, Siamese crocodile and pangolin. Asian tigers were once commonplace but are now exceedingly rare – the last sighting was in about 2007.

Environmental Issues

Cambodia's pristine environment is a big draw for adventurous ecotourists, but much of it is currently under threat. Ancient forests are being razed to make way for plantations, rivers are being sized up for major hydroelectric power plants, and the south coast is being explored by leading oil companies. Places like the Cardamom Mountains are in the front line and it remains to be seen whether the environmentalists or the economists will win the debate.

The greatest threat is illegal logging, carried out to provide charcoal and timber, and also to clear land for cash-crop plantations. The environmental watchdog Global Witness (www.globalwitness.org) publishes meticulously documented exposés on corrupt military and civilian officials and their well-connected business partners.

In the short term, deforestation is contributing to worsening floods along the Mekong, but the long-term implications of deforestation are mind-boggling. Siltation, combined with overfishing and pollution, may lead to the eventual death of Tonlé Sap lake, a catastrophe for future generations of Cambodians.

Throughout the country, pollution is a problem, and detritus of all sorts, especially plastic bags and bottles, can be seen in distressing quantities everywhere.

The latest environmental threats to emerge are dams on the Mekong River. Environmentalists fear that damming the mainstream Mekong may disrupt the flow patterns of the river and the migratory patterns of fish, as well as the critically endangered freshwater Irrawaddy dolphin. Work on the Don Sahong (Siphandone) Dam just north of the Cambodia–Laos border has begun, and plans under consideration include the Sambor Dam, a massive 3300MW project 35km north of Kratie.

SURVIVAL GUIDE

 Directory A–Z

ACCOMMODATION

Accommodation in Cambodia is terrific value. In popular tourist destinations, budget guesthouses generally charge US$5 to US$10 for a room with a cold-water bathroom. Dorm beds usually cost US$3 to US$10, but you can get a whole room for these prices at locally run guesthouses. Rooms with air-con start at US$10. Spend US$15 or US$20 and you'll be living in style. Spend US$30 and up and we're talking boutique standards with a swimming pool.

Accommodation is busiest from mid-November to March. There are substantial low-season rates available at major hotels in Phnom Penh, Siem Reap and Sihanoukville, although this tends to affect midrange and top-end places more than budget digs.

Homestays are popular in more rural areas and on Mekong islands. These are a good way to meet the local people and learn about Cambodian life.

Price Ranges

The following price ranges refer to the cheapest double room on offer, with or without a bathroom, in the high season.

$ less than US$25
$$ US$25 to US$80
$$$ US$80

ACTIVITIES

Cambodia is steadily emerging as an ecotourism destination. Activities on offer include the following:

➡ Jungle trekking in Ratanakiri, Mondulkiri and the Cardamom Mountains of the south coast

➡ Walking with elephants in Mondulkiri

➡ Scuba diving and snorkelling near Sihanoukville

➡ Cycling around Battambang, in Mondulkiri, along the Mekong Discovery Trail between Kratie and Stung Treng, and around the temples of Angkor

➡ Adventurous dirt biking all over the country (for those with some experience)

BOOKS

A whole bookcase-worth of volumes examine Cambodia's recent history, including the French colonial period, the spillover of the war in Vietnam into Cambodia, the Khmer Rouge years and the wild 1990s. The best include the following:

➡ *Cambodia's Curse*, by Joel Brinkley (2011). Pulitzer Prize–winning journalist pulls no punches in his criticism of the government and donors alike.

➡ *Hun Sen's Cambodia*, by Sebastian Strangio (2015). A no-holds-barred look at contemporary Cambodia and the rule of Prime Minister Hun Sen.

➡ *River of Time* by John Swain (1995). Takes readers back to an old Indochina, lost to the madness of war.

➡ *The Gate* by François Bizot (2003). Bizot was kidnapped by the Khmer Rouge, and later held by them in the French embassy.

➡ *First They Killed My Father* by Loung Ung (2001). Covers the destruction of an urban Cambodian family through execution and disease during the Khmer Rouge period.

CUSTOMS REGULATIONS

A 'reasonable amount' of duty-free items is allowed into the country. Alcohol and cigarettes are on sale at well below duty-free prices on the streets of Phnom Penh.

It is illegal to take antiquities out of the country.

ELECTRICITY

The usual voltage is 220V, 50 cycles, but power surges and power cuts are common, particularly in the provinces. Electrical sockets are usually two-prong, mostly flat but sometimes round pin.

EMBASSIES & CONSULATES

Australian Embassy (Map p78; ☎ 023-213470; 16 National Assembly St, Phnom Penh)

French Embassy (Map p109; ☎ 023-430020; 1 Monivong Blvd, Phnom Penh)

German Embassy (Map p78; ☎ 023-216381; 76-78 St 214, Phnom Penh)

Lao Embassy (Map p109; ☎ 023-982632; 15-17 Mao Tse Toung Blvd, Phnom Penh)

Myanmar Embassy (Map p109; ☎ 023-223761; 181 Norodom Blvd, Phnom Penh)

Thai Embassy (Map p109; ☎ 023-726306; 196 Norodom Blvd, Phnom Penh)

UK Embassy (Map p109; ☎ 023-427124; 27-29 St 75, Phnom Penh)

US Embassy (Map p76; ☎ 023-728000; 1 St 96, Phnom Penh)

Vietnamese Embassy (Map p109; ☎ 023-726274; 436 Monivong Blvd, Phnom Penh)

FOOD

The following price ranges refer to the average price of a main course.

$ US$5
$$ US$5 to US$10
$$$ US$10

INSURANCE

Make sure your medical insurance policy covers emergency evacuation: limited medical facilities mean that you may have to be airlifted to Bangkok for problems such as a traffic accident or dengue fever.

INTERNET ACCESS

Free wi-fi is pretty much ubiquitous at hotels, guesthouses and cafes in tourist hubs like Phnom Penh, Siem Reap and the South Coast and is usually easy to find in all but the most remote locales.

Internet access is widespread and there are internet shops in all provincial capitals. Charges range from 1500r to US$2.50 per hour.

RESPONSIBLE TRAVEL IN CAMBODIA

Cambodia has been to hell and back and there are many ways that you can put a little back into the country. Staying longer, travelling further and avoiding package tours is obvious advice. For those on shorter stays, consider spending money in local markets and in restaurants and shops that assist disadvantaged locals. If visiting minority villages, pay attention to a few basic rules such as those in the Responsible Trekking box (p137).

The looting of stone carvings from Cambodia's ancient temples has devastated many temples. Don't contribute to this cultural plunder by buying antiquities of any sort. Classy reproductions are available in Phnom Penh and Siem Reap, complete with export certificates.

Cambodians dress very modestly and may be offended by skimpily dressed foreigners. Just look at the Cambodians frolicking in the sea – most are fully dressed. Wearing bikinis on the beach is fine but cover up elsewhere. Topless or nude bathing is a definite no-no.

The sexual exploitation of children is now taken very seriously in Cambodia. Report anything that looks like child-sex tourism to the ChildSafe hotlines listed here. Tourism establishments that sport the ChildSafe logo have staff trained to protect vulnerable children and, where necessary, intervene.

Phnom Penh ☑ 012 311112

Siem Reap ☑ 017 358758

Sihanoukville ☑ 012 478100

Police Hotline ☑ 023-997919

Friends International (www.friends-international.org) has lots of practical ideas for responsible travel.

LEGAL MATTERS

All narcotics, including marijuana, are illegal in Cambodia. However, marijuana is traditionally used in food preparation, so you may find it sprinkled across some pizzas.

Many Western countries have laws that make sex offences committed overseas punishable at home.

LGBT TRAVELLERS

Cambodia is a very tolerant country when it comes to sexual orientation and the scene is slowly coming alive in the major cities. But as with heterosexual couples, displays of public affection are a basic no-no. Handy websites:

Cambodia Gay (cambodia-gay.com) Promoting the GLBT community in Cambodia.

Sticky Rice (www.stickyrice.ws) Gay travel guide covering Cambodia and Asia.

MAPS

The best all-round map is Gecko's *Cambodia Road Map* at a 1:750,000 scale.

MONEY

➜ Cambodia's currency is the riel (r).

➜ The US dollar is accepted everywhere and by everyone, though change may arrive in riel (handy when paying for things such as *moto* rides and drinks).

➜ When calculating change, the US dollar is usually rounded off to 4000r.

➜ Near the Thai border, many transactions are in Thai baht.

➜ Avoid ripped banknotes, which Cambodians often refuse.

ATMs

ATMs that accept debit cards and credit cards are found in all major cities and a growing number of provincial towns, and at border crossings. Machines dispense US dollars or riel. Most banks charge a withdrawal fee of US$4 to US$5 per transaction. Acleda Bank has the largest network of ATMs countrywide, closely followed by ANZ Royal Bank and Canadia Bank.

Bargaining

Bargaining is expected in local markets, when travelling by share taxi or *moto* and, sometimes, when taking a cheap room. The Khmers are not ruthless hagglers, so a persuasive smile and a little friendly quibbling is usually enough to get a good price.

Tipping

Tipping is not traditionally expected here, but in a country as poor as Cambodia, a dollar tip (or 5% to 10% on bigger bills) can go a long way.

OPENING HOURS

Most Cambodians get up very early and it's not unusual to see people out exercising at 5.30am if you're heading home – ahem, sorry, getting up – at that time.

Banks Most keep core hours of 8am to 3.30pm Monday to Friday, plus Saturday morning.

Government offices Open from Monday to Friday and on Saturday mornings. They theoretically begin the working day at 7.30am, break for a siesta from 11.30am to 2pm, and end the day at 5pm.

Local markets Operate seven days a week and usually open and close with the sun, running from 6.30am to 5.30pm. They close for a few days during major holidays.

Shops Tend to open from about 8am until 6pm, sometimes later.

POST

➤ The postal service is hit-and-miss. Letters and parcels sent further afield than Asia can take up to two or three weeks to reach their destination.

➤ Send anything valuable by courier service, such as **EMS** (☑ 023-723511; www.ems.com.kh; Main Post Office, St 13, Phnom Penh), or from another country.

➤ Ensure postcards and letters are franked before they vanish from your sight.

➤ Phnom Penh's main post office has the most reliable poste restante service.

PUBLIC HOLIDAYS

It is widely believed that Cambodia has more public holidays than any other country on earth.

In addition to the following, the whole country basically shuts down for an entire week for Chaul Chnam Khmer (Khmer New Year, usually in April) and P'chum Ben (Festival of the Dead, in September or October).

Chinese New Year (January or February) and Bon Om Tuk (Water Festival, October or November) usually mean several days off for the masses as well.

International New Year's Day 1 January
Victory over Genocide Day 7 January
International Women's Day 8 March
International Labour Day 1 May
King's Birthday 13–15 May
International Children's Day 1 June
King Mother's Birthday 18 June
Constitution Day 24 September
Anniversay of Paris Peace Accords 23 October
Coronation Day 29 October
King Father's Birthday 31 October
Independence Day 9 November
International Human Rights Day 10 December

SAFE TRAVEL

Mines & Mortars

Cambodia is one of the most heavily mined countries in the world, especially in the north-west of the country near the Thai border. Many mined areas are unmarked, so *do not* stray from well-worn paths and *never, ever* touch any unexploded ordnance (UXO) you come across, including mortars and artillery shells. If you find yourself in a mined area, retrace your steps only if you can clearly see your footprints. If not, stay where you are and call for help. If someone is injured in a minefield, do not rush in to help even if they are crying out in pain – find someone who knows how to enter a mined area safely.

Crime

Given the number of guns in Cambodia, there is less armed theft than one might expect. Still, hold-ups and motorcycle theft are a potential danger in Phnom Penh and Sihanoukville. There is no need to be paranoid, just cautious. Walking or riding alone late at night is not ideal, certainly not in rural areas.

Bag-snatching has become an increasing problem in Phnom Penh in recent years and the motorbike thieves don't let go, dragging passengers off *motos* and endangering lives. If riding a *moto* carry your shoulder bag in front of you and be careful when riding on *remorks* as well.

Should anyone be unlucky enough to be robbed, it is important to note that the Cambodian police are the best that money can buy! Any help, such as a police report, is going to cost you. The going rate depends on the size of the claim, but anywhere from US$5 to US$50 is a common charge.

Scams

Most scams are fairly harmless, involving a bit of commission here and there for taxi or *moto* drivers, particularly in Siem Reap.

There have been one or two reports of police set-ups in Phnom Penh involving planted drugs.

DANGEROUS DRUGS 101

Watch out for *yama* (known as *yaba* in Thailand), which ominously shares its name with the Hindu god of death. Known as ice or crystal meth elsewhere, it is homemade methamphetamines often laced with toxic substances, such as mercury and lithium. It is more addictive than many users would like to admit, provoking reactions such as powerful hallucinations, sleep deprivation and psychosis.

Also be wary of buying 'cocaine'. Most of what is sold as coke, particularly in Phnom Penh, is actually pure heroin and far stronger than what may be found elsewhere.

This seems to be very rare, but if you fall victim to the ploy, it may be best to pay them off before more police get involved at the local station, as the price will only rise when there are more officials to pay off.

Beggars in places such as Phnom Penh and Siem Reap are asking for milk powder for an infant in arms. Some foreigners succumb to the urge to help, but the beggars usually request the most expensive milk formula available and return it to the shop to split the proceeds after the handover.

Moto and *remork* drivers will always try to get an extra buck or two out of you. Some price inflation for foreigners is natural, but you are being gouged if they charge three times the prices we quote. Fares are pretty cheap and don't tend to rise much year on year.

TELEPHONE

In many areas landline service is spotty. Mobile phones, whose numbers start with 01, 06, 07, 08 or 09, are hugely popular with both individuals and commercial enterprises. Buying a local SIM card is highly recommended to avoid expensive roaming charges. SIM cards are widely available and cost almost nothing. Mobile-phone calls and 3G internet access are also quite cheap. Foreigners usually need to present a valid passport to purchase a local SIM card.

If you don't have a phone, the easiest way to make a local call in most urban areas is to head to one of the many small private booths on the kerbside, with prices around 300r.

For listings of businesses and government offices, check out www.yp.com.kh.

TIME

Cambodia, like Laos, Vietnam and Thailand, is seven hours ahead of Greenwich Mean Time or Universal Time Coordinated (GMT/UTC).

TRAVELLERS WITH DISABILITIES

Although Cambodia has one of the world's highest rates of limb loss (due to mines), the country is not designed for people with impaired mobility. Few buildings have lifts/elevators, footpaths and roads are riddled with potholes, and the staircases and rock jumbles of many Angkorian temples are daunting even for the able-bodied. Transport-wise, chartering is the way to go and is a fairly affordable option. Also affordable is hired help if you require it, and Khmers are generally very helpful should you need assistance.

VISAS

Visas on Arrival

➡ For most nationalities, one-month tourist visas (US$30) are available on arrival at Phnom Penh and Siem Reap airports and all land border crossings. If you are carrying an African, Asian or Middle Eastern passport, there are some exceptions.

➡ One passport-sized photo is required and you'll be 'fined' US$2 if you don't have one. Citizens of ASEAN member countries do not require a visa.

➡ Visas are issued extremely quickly at the airports and lines are usually minimal, so it's not really worth paying US$5 extra for an e-visa. However, you might consider the e-visa option if you plan to cross at the Poipet or Koh Kong land borders. Overcharging for visas is rampant at these crossings, and with an e-visa you'll avoid these potential charges.

E-Visas

➡ One-month tourist e-visas cost US$30 plus a US$5 processing fee.

➡ E-visas are available from www.mfaic.gov.kh and take three business days to process.

➡ E-visas can be used at all airports and at the Bavet, Koh Kong and Poipet land border crossings. They cannot be used at the more remote land crossings, so you are on your own dealing with corrupt border officials at remote Thai and Lao land borders (corruption is less of a problem at Vietnamese borders).

Visa Extensions

➡ Tourist visas can be extended once for one month only. If you're planning a longer stay, upon arrival request a one-month business visa (US$35), which can be extended for up to a year through any travel agent in Phnom Penh. Bring a passport photo.

➡ Extensions for one/three/six/12 months cost about US$45/75/155/285 and take three working days.

➡ For one-month extensions, it may be cheaper to do a 'visa run' to Thailand, getting a fresh visa when you cross back into Cambodia.

➡ Overstayers are charged US$5 per day at the point of exit.

Visa Regulations for Neighbouring Countries

Vietnam One-month single-entry visas cost US$60/70 for one-day/one-hour processing in Phnom Penh, Sihanoukville or Battambang. Many visitors no longer need visas following a 2015 change in regulations.

Laos Most visitors can obtain a visa on arrival, costing US$3 to US$42 depending on nationality.

Thailand Most visitors do not need a visa.

VOLUNTEERING

Cambodia hosts a huge number of NGOs, some of whom do require volunteers from time to time. The best way to find out who is represented in the country is to drop in on the **Cooperation Committee for Cambodia** (CCC; Map p109; ☑ 023-214152; www.ccc-cambodia.org; 9-11 St 476) in Phnom Penh.

Professional Siem Reap–based organisations helping to place volunteers include **ConCERT** (p93) and **Globalteer** (☑ 063-761802; www.globalteer.org); the latter program involves a weekly charge.

WORK

Jobs are available throughout Cambodia, but apart from teaching English or helping out in guesthouses, bars or restaurants, most are for professionals and are arranged in advance. There is a lot of teaching work available for English-language speakers; those with an English-language teaching certificate can earn considerably more than those with no qualifications.

Places to look for work include the classifieds sections of the *Phnom Penh Post* and the *Cambodia Daily*, and noticeboards at guesthouses. For information about work opportunities with NGOs, call into the CCC, which posts vacant positions.

ⓘ Getting There & Away

AIR

Cambodia's two major international airports, Phnom Penh International Airport and Siem Reap International Airport, have frequent flights to destinations all over eastern Asia.

Airlines

Air Asia (www.airasia.com) Daily budget flights connecting Phnom Penh and Siem Reap to Kuala Lumpur and Bangkok.

Asiana Airlines (www.asiana.co.kr) Regular connections between Phnom Penh and Seoul.

Bangkok Airways (www.bangkokair.com) Daily connections from Phnom Penh and Siem Reap to Bangkok.

Cambodia Angkor Air (www.cambodiaangkorair.com) Daily connections from Phnom Penh and Siem Reap to Bangkok and Ho Chi Minh City (Saigon).

Cebu Pacific (www.cebupacificair.com) Budget flights between Siem Reap and Manila three times a week.

China Eastern Airlines (www.ce-air.com) Regular flights from Siem Reap to Kunming.

China Southern Airlines (www.cs-air.com) Daily flights from Phnom Penh to Guangzhou.

Dragon Air (www.dragonair.com) Daily flights between Phnom Penh and Hong Kong.

Eva Air (www.evaair.com) Daily flights between Phnom Penh and Taipei.

Jetstar (www.jetstar.com) Daily budget flights from Phnom Penh and Siem Reap to Singapore.

Korean Air (www.koreanair.com) Regular flights connecting Phnom Penh and Siem Reap with Seoul and Incheon.

Lao Airlines (www.laoairlines.com) Regular flights from Phnom Penh and Siem Reap to Pakse, Vientiane and Luang Prabang.

Malaysia Airlines (www.malaysiaairlines.com) Daily connections from Phnom Penh and Siem Reap to Kuala Lumpur.

Qatar Airways (www.qatarairways.com) Regular flights from Phnom Penh to Ho Chi Minh City and Doha.

Silk Air (www.silkair.com) Daily flights linking Phnom Penh and Bangkok.

Thai Airways (www.thaiair.com) Daily flights connecting Phnom Penh and Bangkok.

Vietnam Airlines (www.vietnamair.com.vn) Daily flights linking both Phnom Penh and Siem Reap with both Hanoi and Ho Chi Minh City, as well as Phnom Penh with Vientiane, and Siem Reap with Luang Prabang.

LAND
Border Crossings

There are land border crossings shared with Laos, Thailand and Vietnam. These are covered throughout this chapter.

ⓘ Getting Around

AIR

There are three domestic airlines in Cambodia operating flights between Phnom Penh and Siem Reap (seven flights a day) and Siem Reap and Sihanoukville (three flights a day).

Bassaka Air (☑ 023-217613; www.bassakaair.com)

Cambodia Angkor Air (☑ 023-212564; www.cambodiaangkorair.com)

Cambodia Bayon Airlines (☑ 023-231555; www.bayonairlines.com)

BICYCLE

Some guesthouses and hotels rent out bicycles for US$1 to US$2 per day. If you'll be doing lots of cycling, bring along a bike helmet, which can also provide some protection on a *moto*.

Cambodia is a great country for cycle touring as travelling at gentle speeds allows for lots of interaction with locals. Much of Cambodia is pancake flat or only moderately hilly. Safety, however, is a considerable concern on paved roads as trucks, buses and cars barrel along at high speed. Usually flat unpaved trails run roughly parallel to the highways, allowing for a more relaxed journey and much more interaction with the locals.

AIRPORT TAXES

There's a tax of US$25 on all international flights out of Cambodia. The airport tax for domestic flights is US$6. Both are now included in the ticket price, so you do not need cash at the airport.

Cycling around Angkor is an incredible experience, as it really gives you a sense of the size and scale of the temple complex. Adventure mountain biking is likely to take off in the Cardamom Mountains and in Mondulkiri and Ratanakiri provinces over the coming years.

BOAT

Long-distance public boats are increasingly rare as the roads improve, but fast boats still ply the Tonlé Sap from Phnom Penh to Siem Reap, while smaller boats take on the sublime stretch between Siem Reap and Battambang.

BUS & MINIBUS

About a dozen bus companies serve all corners of the country. Comfort levels and prices vary wildly, so shop around. Booking bus tickets through guesthouses and travel agents is convenient, but often incurs a commission. Also note that travel agents tend to work with only a handful of preferred companies, so won't always offer your preferred company and/or departure time.

Express vans (usually modern Ford Transits or Toyota Hiaces) are an option between most major cities. They operate a one seat/one passenger policy. They cost about the same as the big buses, but are much faster, often too fast for many people's taste. Also, they don't have much legroom; big buses are considerably more comfortable.

Older local minibuses serve most provincial routes but are not widely used by Western visitors. They are very cheap but often uncomfortably overcrowded (you are almost guaranteed to be vomited on) and sometimes driven by maniacs. Only really consider them if there is no alternative.

CAR & MOTORCYCLE

Renting a (self-drive) motorbike is a great way to get around provincial cities and their surrounding sights (although tourists are forbidden from renting motorbikes in Siem Reap). Basic 100cc to 125cc motorbikes are widely available and cheap (about US$5 per day). No one will ask you for a driving licence except, occasionally, the police. Make sure you have a strong lock and always leave the bike in guarded parking where possible.

For longer-distance travel, motorcycles and cars offer travellers flexibility to visit out-of-the-way places and to stop when they choose. Cambodia's main national highways (NH) are generally in good shape but can be quite dangerous due to the prevalence of high-speed overtaking/passing.

While major national highways are too heavily trafficked for happy motorcycling, many of Cambodia's less-travelled tracks are perfect for two-wheeled exploration. However, forays on motorcycles into the remote and diabolical roads of the northwest and northeast should only be attempted by experienced riders. In all cases, proceed cautiously, as outside Phnom Penh and Siem Reap medical facilities are rudimentary and ambulances are rare.

CYCLO

A few *cyclos* (pedicabs) can still be seen on the streets of Phnom Penh and Battambang. They are a charming and environmentally friendly, if slow, way to get around, and cost about the same as a *moto*.

MOTO, REMORK & TAXI

Motos, also known as *motodups* (meaning *moto* driver), are small motorcycle taxis. They are a quick way of making short hops around towns and cities. Prices range from 2000r to US$1.50 or more, depending on the distance and the town. Chartering a *moto* for the day costs around US$10, but can cost more if a greater distance is involved or the driver speaks good English.

The vehicle known in Cambodia as a *remork-moto (tuk tuk)* is a canopied two-wheeled trailer hitched to the back of a motorbike. These generally cost a bit more than double what a *moto* costs. Still, for two or more people a *remork* can be cheaper than a *moto*, not to mention safer and much more comfortable if you've got luggage or it's raining.

Although locals rarely agree on a price in advance for a *moto* or *remork*, it's best for tourists to agree to a price beforehand. Many optimistic drivers have gotten into the habit of overcharging foreigners, or trying to charge per passenger (you should never let them do this, although paying an extra dollar or two is fair if you are stuffing four to six people into a *remork*).

Taxis can be ordered via guesthouses and hotels to get around Phnom Penh, Siem Reap and Sihanoukville, and usually cost a bit more than a *remork*. Expect to pay around US$30 per day and up depending on the itinerary.

SHARE TAXIS

Share taxis (usually Toyota Camrys) are faster, more flexible in terms of departure times, and a bit more expensive than buses. They leave when full, which is usually rather quickly on popular routes. For less-travelled routes, you may have to wait a while (possibly until the next day if you arrive in the afternoon) before your vehicle fills up, or pay for the vacant seats yourself.

Share taxis can be pretty cramped. In addition to the driver, each one carries four to seven passengers, with the price fluctuating according to how many people are in the car. It's not uncommon to see two in the front seat, four in the back, and a seventh passenger squished between the driver and his door! Pay double the regular fare and you get the front seat all to yourself; pay six fares and you've got yourself a private taxi. Haggle patiently, with a smile, to ensure fair prices.

Indonesia

♪ 62 / POP 255 MILLION

Best Beaches

➡ Kuta Beach, Lombok (p195)

➡ Gili Air (p231)

➡ Komodo National Park (p239)

➡ Pulau Ai (p294)

Best Places for Culture

➡ Museum Nasional, Jakarta (p157)

➡ Dance, Ubud (p214)

➡ Funeral rites, Tana Toraja (p283)

➡ Banda Islands (p292)

Why Go?

Indonesia defines adventure: the only limitation is how many of its 17,000-odd islands you can reach before your visa expires. Following the equator, Indonesia stretches between Malaysia and Australia in one long, intoxicating sweep. The nation's natural diversity is staggering: snow-capped peaks in Papua, sandalwood forests in Sumba, dense jungle in Borneo and impossibly green rice paddies in Bali and Java. Indonesian reefs are a diver's fantasy, while the surf breaks above are the best anywhere.

But even as the diversity on land and sea run like a traveller's dream playlist, it's the mash-up of people and cultures that's the most appealing. Bali justifiably leads off, but there are also Papua's stone-age folk, the many cultures of Flores and West Timor, the artisans of Java, mall-rats of Jakarta, orangutans of Sumatra and much more. Whether it's an idyllic remote beach, a glorious discovery underwater or a Bali all-nighter, Indonesia scores.

When to Go
Jakarta

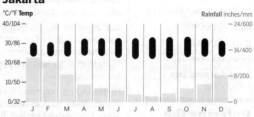

Sep–Mar Rainy season; starts later in the south-east. Rain everywhere in January and February.	**Apr–Jun** Dry days and high temps that aren't withering. Hill towns like Bali's Ubud can be chilly at night.	**Aug** High season. Prices peak on Bali and the Gilis; book ahead. Remote spots may also fill up.

AT A GLANCE

Currency Rupiah (Rp); 100,000Rp notes can be hard to break

Language Bahasa Indonesia; English in tourist areas

Money ATMs in major centres; carry rupiah for remote islands

Visas 30 days on arrival for most

Mobile phones SIMs (from 5000Rp) sold everywhere; cheap voice/data rates

Fast Facts

Area 1.9 million sq km

Capital Jakarta

Emergency Ask the nearest local for advice

Exchange Rates

Australia	A$1	9,780Rp
Euro Zone	€1	14,500Rp
Malaysia	RM1	3,170Rp
Singapore	S$1	9,480Rp
UK	£1	18,680Rp
US	US$1	13,060Rp

Daily Costs

Budget room 200,000Rp

Meal 30,000Rp

Beer 20,000Rp

Two-tank dive US$90

Long-distance bus 100,000Rp

Entering the Country

Fly into Jakarta or Bali; flights to Sulawesi, Lombok etc also available. Ferries to Sumatra from Malaysia and Singapore are popular.

Don't Miss

With so many islands, it would be a shame not to get a sense of this vast archipelago by limiting your visit to only one or two – try to see as many as possible. Ferries – never luxurious, often a bit squalid – provide myriad links and truly adventurous island-hopping. Shorten distances with flights on any of the many discount airlines and connect overland dots with buses bombing down the middle of the road at breakneck speeds.

ITINERARIES

One Week

This is a tough one, but Bali is the obvious choice. Spend a couple of days in the south, possibly partying in Seminyak and/or surfing and chilling on the Bukit Peninsula. Head up to Ubud for rice-field walks and intoxicating culture. Catch a fast boat to/from the nearby Gili Islands for a heaving travellers' scene.

One Month

Include your week on Bali and the Gilis, but start on Java and cross through the cultural city of Yogyakarta and the Unesco treasure of Borobudur. From Lombok catch ferries and buses across Sumbawa to Flores, with stops at beaches and dragon-filled Komodo. Finish your time either following the spine of Sulawesi, or head further east for Maluku's idyllic Banda Islands, or track down orangutans on Kalimantan or Sumatra.

Essential Activities

Diving & Snorkelling Diving highlights include western Flores and Komodo, the Gili Islands, Pulau Menjangan in Bali, Pulau Bunaken and the Togean Islands in Sulawesi, Pulau Weh in Sumatra, the Banda Islands in Maluku and the incredible Raja Ampat Islands in Papua.

Spas & Treatments Bali leads the way, with a multitude of affordable salons and spas in all the main traveller centres.

Surfing All the islands on the Indonesian archipelago's southern side, from Sumatra to Timor, get reliable – often exceptional – and sometimes downright frightening surf. Many start at the legendary breaks of Bali's Bukit Peninsula, such as Ulu Watu.

Hiking In Java, organised hiking centres on some spectacular volcano hikes, such as Gunung Bromo and the Ijen Plateau. There's more variety in Bali: the wonderful Gunung Batur region and the hills around Munduk, which offer walks amid cool hillside forests, spice plantations and waterfalls. Gunung Rinjani on Lombok is a dramatic and rewarding hike. On Sumatra, try the jungles of Bukit Lawang. The Baliem Valley in Papua is popular; Tana Toraja has fabulous trekking opportunities through Sulawesi's spectacular traditional villages.

Indonesia Highlights

1 Surfing by day, partying at night and absorbing amazing culture in **Bali** (p192).

2 Ascending the ancient Buddhist stupa of **Borobudur** (p181) before trawling the batik markets of nearby **Yogyakarta** (p178).

3 Gazing at the iconic dragons at **Komodo National Park** (p240),

then rocking on in hopping **Labuanbajo** (p242) in Nusa Tenggara.

4 Paying primate-to-primate respects to the **orangutans** (p276) native to Sumatra and Kalimantan.

5 Diving the pristine walls and coral canyons beneath seas of dimpled glass at **Pulau Bunaken** (p290) in Sulawesi.

6 Exploring the lovely time capsule that is Maluku's **Banda Islands** (p292).

7 Hiking along raging rivers and scaling exposed ridges to reach interior Papua's remote tribal villages in the **Baliem Valley** (p297).

8 Diving and lazing following fun-filled nights on Nusa Tenggara's **Gili Islands** (p230).

JAVA

The heart of the nation, Java is an island of megacities, mesmerising natural beauty, magical archaeological sites and profound traditions in art, music and dance.

Boasting a dazzling array of bewitching landscapes – iridescent rice paddies, smoking volcanoes, verdant rainforest and savannah, not to mention virgin beaches – most journeys here are defined by scenic wonders. The island is at its most excessive in the cities: crowded, polluted, concrete labyrinths that buzz and roar. Dive into Jakarta's addictive mayhem, soak up Yogyakarta's soul and stroll though Solo's batik laneways en route to the island's all-natural wonders.

Home to 140 million people, Java travel can be slow-going, particularly in the west. However, the rail network is generally reliable and efficient, and flights are inexpensive.

Your endurance will be rewarded with fascinating insights into Indonesia's most complex and culturally compelling island.

ℹ️ Getting There & Around

AIR

Jakarta has numerous international and domestic connections; useful international gateway cities include Surabaya, Solo (Surakarta), Bandung, Yogyakarta and Semarang. Domestic fights can be very convenient and affordable: Jakarta–Yogyakarta is a popular route. If you're short on time, it's worth booking a few internal flights to cut down on those hours on the road.

BOAT

Very few travellers now use Pelni passenger ships, but there are connections between Jakarta and most ports in the nation.

There are very frequent ferries between Java and Bali, and from Java to Sumatra.

Java

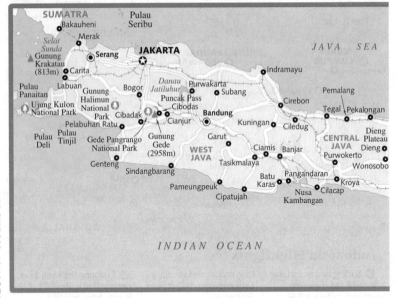

BUS

Buses connect virtually anywhere and everywhere in Java, and also run to Sumatra, Bali and even Nusa Tenggara. Unfortunately Java's road network is woefully inadequate, so journeys tend to be very slow and tiring, particularly in the west of the island.

TRAIN

Java has a fairly punctual and efficient rail service running right across the island. Overall, train travel certainly beats long bus journeys, so try to take as many as you can. You can check timetables and make online bookings at www. kereta-api.co.id, though it's not very user-friendly. Book ahead when possible.

Jakarta

📱 021 / POP 10.2 MILLION

One of the world's greatest megalopolises, Jakarta is a dynamic city of daunting extremes – one that's developing at a pace that offers challenges and surreal juxtapositions on every street corner. An organism unto itself, this is a town in the midst of a very public metamorphosis, and despite the maddening traffic, life here is lived at an all-out rush, driven by an industriousness and optimism that's palpable. Dysfunction be damned.

Translation: it's no oil painting, yet beneath the unappealing facade of newly built high-rises, relentless concrete and gridlocked streets, fringed with rickety slums and shrouded in a persistent blanket of smog, Jakarta has many faces and plenty of surprises.

⊙ Sights & Activities

⊙ Kota

Jakarta's crumbling historic heart is Kota, home to the remnants of the Dutch capital of Batavia. **Taman Fatahillah**, the old town square, features cracked cobblestones, postcard vendors, fine colonial buildings, a flurry of museums and, on weekends, masses of locals enjoying a carnival-like atmosphere. Trains from Gondangdia, near Jl Jaksa, run here. A taxi will cost around 50,000Rp from Jl Thamrin.

In and around Taman Fatahillah are a number of interesting buildings and monuments, including the **Gereja Sion** (Map p159; Jl Pangeran Jayakarta) **FREE**, the oldest remaining church in Jakarta. It was built in 1695 for the 'black Portuguese', who were brought to Batavia as slaves and given their freedom if they joined the Dutch Reformed Church.

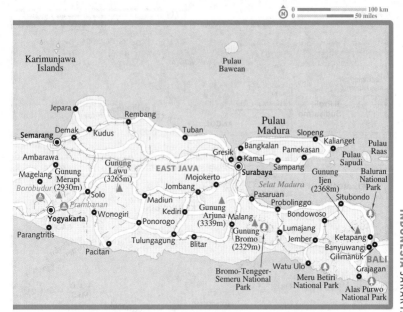

Some fine Dutch architecture lines the grotty Kali Besar canal, including the **Toko Merah** (Map p159; Jl Kali Besar Barat, Red Shop), formerly the home of Governor General van Imhoff. Further north, the **Chicken Market Bridge** – the last remaining Dutch drawbridge – spans the canal.

Also don't miss a drink at the Café Batavia (p163), which drips with colonial nostalgia.

Museum Bank Indonesia   MUSEUM

(Map p159; Pintu Besar Utara III; audio guides 50,000Rp; ◎8am-3.30pm Tue-Thu, 8-11.30am & 1-3.30pm Fri, 8am-4pm Sat & Sun) `FREE` One of the nation's best, this museum is dedicated to the history of Indonesia from a loosely financial perspective, in a grand, expertly restored, neoclassical former bank headquarters that dates from the early 20th century. All the displays (including lots of zany audiovisuals) are slickly presented on flat screens and engaging, with exhibits about the spice trade and the financial meltdown of 1997 (and subsequent riots) as well as a gallery dedicated to currency, with notes from virtually every country in the world.

Museum Sejarah Jakarta   MUSEUM

(Map p159; Taman Fatahillah; admission 5000Rp; ◎9am-3pm Tue-Sun) Also known as Museum Kesejarahan Jakarta, the Jakarta History Museum is housed in the old town hall of Batavia, a stately Dutch colonial structure that was once the epicentre of an empire. This bell-towered building, built in 1627, served the administration of the city and was also used by the city law courts. Today it's a poorly presented museum of peeling plasterwork and lots of heavy, carved ebony and teak furniture from the Dutch period.

Museum Wayang   MUSEUM

(Map p159; ☑021-692 9560; Taman Fatahillah; admission 5000Rp; ◎9am-3pm Tue-Sun) This puppet museum has one of the best collections of *wayang* puppets in Java and its dusty cabinets are full of a multitude of characters from across Indonesia, as well as China, Vietnam, India, Cambodia and Europe. The building itself dates from 1912. There are free *wayang* performances here on Sunday at 10am. Be warned: we have received reports of a scam involving freelance guides who pressure people into making exorbitant purchases after a tour of the exhibits.

Museum Bank Mandiri   MUSEUM

(Map p159; Jl Pintu Besar Utara; ◎9am-3pm Tue-Sun) `FREE` In complete contrast to the polish and modernity at the Museum Bank Indonesia next door, this banking museum is all but empty, with echoing corridors and deserted

Jakarta

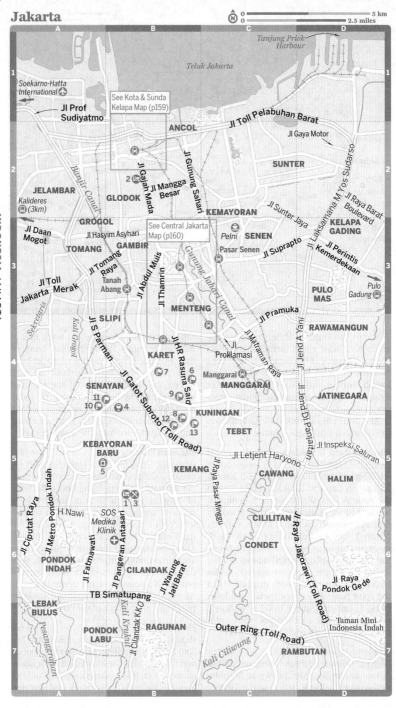

Jakarta

tills. Nevertheless, it's fascinating to explore the interior of this fine art deco structure, marvelling at the marble counters and vintage counting machines, abacuses and colossal cast-iron safes.

Balai Seni Rupa   MUSEUM
(Map p159; Taman Fatahillah; admission 5000Rp; ⊙9am-3pm Tue-Sun) Built between 1866 and 1870, the former Palace of Justice building is now a fine arts museum. It houses contemporary paintings with works by prominent artists, including Affandi, Raden Saleh and Ida Bagus Made. Part of the building is also a ceramics museum, with Chinese ceramics and Majapahit terracottas.

◉ Sunda Kelapa

Among the hubbub, floating debris and oil slicks, the old Dutch port of **Sunda Kelapa** (admission 2000Rp) is full of magnificent *pinisi* (Makassar schooners). The dock scene here has barely changed for centuries, with porters still unloading cargo from sailing ships by hand and trolley, though it's far less busy today. The port is a 1km walk from Taman Fatahillah.

Museum Bahari   MUSEUM
(Map p159; www.museumbahari.org; admission 5000Rp; ⊙9am-3pm Tue-Sun) Near the entrance to Sunda Kelapa, several old VOC warehouses (dating back to 1652) have been converted into the Museum Bahari. This is a

good place to learn about the city's maritime history, and though the wonderful old buildings (some renovated) are echoingly empty, there are some good information panels (in English and Bahasa Indonesia).

◉ Central Jakarta

If you had to choose a centre for this sprawling city, then Merdeka Square (Lapangan Merdeka) would be it. This huge grassy expanse, home to Sukarno's monument to the nation, is surrounded by a couple of museums and some fine colonial buildings.

★ Museum Nasional   MUSEUM
(Map p160; ☎021-381 1551; www.museumnasional. or.id; Jl Merdeka Barat 12; admission 10,000Rp; ⊙8am-4pm Tue-Fri, 8am-5pm Sat-Sun) The National Museum, built in 1862, is the best of its kind in Indonesia and an essential visit. The enormous collection begins in an open courtyard stacked with magnificent millennia old statuary including a colossal 4.5m stone image of a Bhairawa king from Rambahan in Sumatra, who is shown trampling on human skulls. The ethnology section is superb, with Dayak puppets and wooden statues from Nias sporting beards (a sign of wisdom) plus some fascinating textiles.

Lapangan Banteng   AREA
(Map p160; Banteng Sq) Just east of Merdeka Sq, Lapangan Banteng has some of Jakarta's best colonial architecture. The **twin spired Catholic cathedral** (Jl Katedral 7B) was built in 1901. Directly opposite is Jakarta's principal place of Muslim worship. The striking, modernist **Mesjid Istiqlal** (Jl Veteran I), highlighted by geometrically grated windows, was designed by Catholic architect Frederich Silaban and completed in 1978. The mosque has five levels, representing the five pillars of Islam; its dome is 45m across and its minaret tops 90m.

Monas   MONUMENT
(Monumen Nasional; Map p160; Merdeka Sq; museum entry 5,000Rp, to reach the top 10,000Rp; ⊙8.30am-5pm, closed last Mon of month) Ingloriously dubbed 'Sukarno's final erection', this 132m-high National Monument, which rises into the shroud of smog and towers over Merdeka Sq, is both Jakarta's principal landmark and the most famous architectural extravagance of the former president. Begun in 1961, Monas was not completed until 1975, when it was officially opened by Suharto. The monument is constructed

from Italian marble, and is topped with a sculpted flame, gilded with 35kg of gold leaf.

◉ Glodok

The neighbourhood of Glodok, the traditional enclave of the Chinese community, is an archetypal downtown district full of bustling lanes, street markets, a shabby mall or two and some of the world's most decadent nightlife.

Most of the fun here is simply experiencing the local vibe, eating some dumplings and browsing the myriad stalls and shops.

Jin De Yuan   BUDDHIST TEMPLE
(Dharma Bhakti Temple; Map p159; www.jinde yuan.org; Jl Kemenangan III 13) FREE This large Chinese Buddhist temple compound dates from 1755 and is one of the most important in the city. The main structure has an unusual roof crowned by two dragons eating pearls, while the interior is richly atmospheric: dense incense and candle smoke waft over Buddhist statues, ancient bells and drums, and some wonderful calligraphy. Unfortunately, recent Chinese New Year celebrations – including fireworks – set fire to half of the original structure. It was undergoing reconstruction when we visited.

Petak Sembilan Street Market   MARKET
(Map p159) Be sure to wander down the impossibly narrow Petak Sembilan street market off Jl Pancoran, lined with crooked houses with red-tiled roofs. It's a total assault on the senses, with skinned frogs and live bugs for sale next to an open sewer.

☞ Tours

Jakarta Hidden Tours   GUIDED TOUR
(☑ 0812 803 5297; www.realjakarta.blogspot.com; per person US$50) Want to see the other Jakarta, away from air-conditioned malls? Jakarta Hidden offers tours of the city's traditional *kampung*, the urban villages of the poor. These warts-and-all tours take you along trash-choked riverways, into cottage industry factories and allow you to take tea in residents' homes.

★★ Festivals & Events

Java Jazz Festival   MUSIC
(www.javajazzfestival.com) Held at the Jakarta Convention Center in Senayan in early March. Attracts acclaimed international art-

ists, including jazz heavyweights like Ramsey Lewis and Brad Mehldau. Crossover pop stars such as Bobby McFerrin and Michelle Ndegeocello played in 2015.

Jakarta Anniversary   FAIR
The 22nd of June marks the establishment of the city in 1527. Celebrated with fireworks and the Jakarta Fair.

Independence Day   CULTURAL
Indonesia's independence is celebrated on 17 August; the parades in Jakarta are the biggest in the country.

JiFFest   FILM
(Jakarta International Film Festival; ☑ 021-3005 6090; www.muvila.com/jiffest) Internationally sponsored and lauded, Indonesia's premier film festival is held in November and December.

🛏 Sleeping

Backpackers be prepared: Jakarta lacks good budget options, so book ahead or consider a midrange option (which are plentiful). Jalan Jaska was once Jakarta's backpacking hub, but travellers are thin on the ground these days, probably because most hotels on Jl Jaksa are grungy (if not outright sleazy). That said, you'll find a selection of restaurants and bars and some terrific midrange accommodations on nearby Jl Wayid Hasim and Jl Sabang. The location, near Jl Thamrin (for the busway) and Gambir train station, is excellent.

★ Hostel 35   GUESTHOUSE $
(Map p163; ☑ 021-392 0331; Jl Kebon Sirih Barat I 35; r incl breakfast with fan/air-con 150,000/ 250,000Rp; ❄❂) A good option for the price. The clean, if aged, tiled rooms have high ceilings, and the lobby/lounge area with rattan sofas is inviting and decorated with fine textiles and tasteful photography.

Packer Lodge   HOSTEL $
(Map p156; ☑ 021-629 0162; www.thepacker lodge.com; Jl Kermunian IV 20-22; dm 145,000-155,000Rp, s 205,000-215,000Rp, d 310,000Rp; ❄❂) The new cute hostel on the block, this self-annointed, owner-operated boutique hostel set in Glodok offers hip, Ikea-chic environs and plenty of amenities close to the Kota. Choose among the four- or eight-bed dorms where the bunks are curtained pods with electrical outlets, lights and USB chargers. Earplugs included.

Kota & Sunda Kelapa

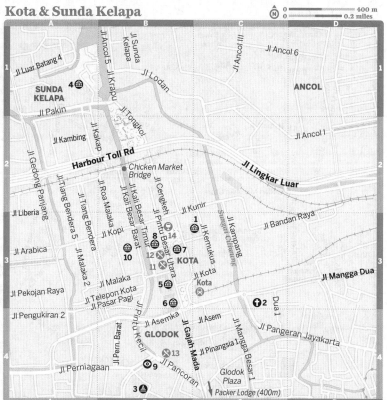

Kota & Sunda Kelapa

Six Degrees HOSTEL **$**
(Map p160; ☑021-314 1657; www.jakarta-backpackers-hostel.com; Jl Cikini Raya 60B-C, Cikini; dm 125,000-160,000Rp; d 280,000Rp; ❄@⏰) Set in a mini-mall, this hostel – run by a helpful and friendly Irish/English/Sumatran team – remains popular with travellers. There's a relaxed, sociable atmosphere, a pool table and large-screen TV room, a guests' kitchen and roof garden. Dorms are tight but clean; breakfast is included. It's tricky to find, but located right opposite the Ibis Budget hotel.

Gondia International Guesthouse GUESTHOUSE **$**
(Map p160; ☑021-390 9221; www.gondia-guesthouse.com; Jl Gondangdia Kecil 22; r incl breakfast

Central Jakarta

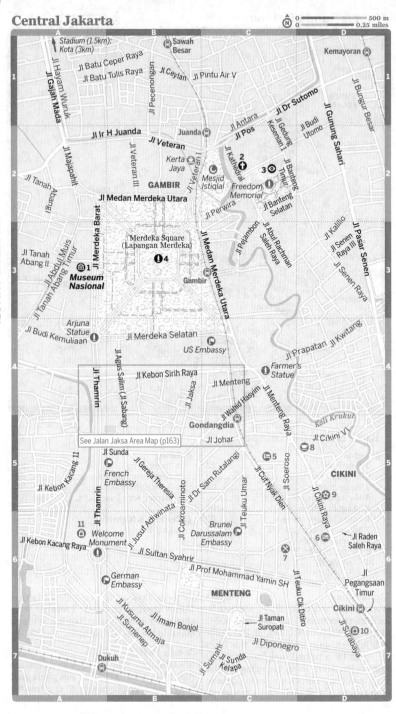

Central Jakarta

400,000-500,000Rp; ❄) This modest looking guesthouse, with hostel-esque signage, occupies a leafy garden plot on a quiet suburban street and has spacious tiled rooms.

★**Kosenda Hotel**   BOUTIQUE HOTEL $$
(Map p163; ☑021-3193 6868; www.kosendahotel. com; Jl KH Wahid Hasyim 127; r from 750,000Rp; ▣❄🛜) Hip but not overbearing, minimalist and modern but comfortable, rooms aren't huge but they are very clean and tastefully designed with wall-length built-in desks, floating beds and glass-box baths. Prices are a steal when offered on booking websites. There is a lovely breakfast buffet, excellent coffee, a good 24-hour restaurant in the lobby and a superb rooftop bar (p163).

Max One   HOTEL $$
(Map p163; ☑021-316 6888; www.maxonehotels. com; Jl Agus Salim 24; r from 550,000Rp; ❄@🛜) Max One is a moderately priced and hip hotel. The rooms here are smallish but nicely styled, with a pleasing pastel colour scheme. We love the steep weekend discounts on offer, the in-house minimart and the excellent location.

Fave Hotel   HOTEL $$
(Map p156; ☑021-718 1320; www.favehotels.com; Jl Kemang 16, Kemang; r from 421,200Rp) Modern and creative, this edition of the Indonesian three-star micro-hotel offers small but livable quarters with room service, pre-fab furnishings, plush linens and not much else. Still a solid value.

🍴 Eating

Jakarta is a world-class eating destination. You'll find amazing options, including oh-so-refined Javanese Imperial cuisine, hit-the-spot street grub and, if you're pining for something familiar, even Western faves.

Two excellent street-food hot spots are Jl Pecenongan (about 500m north of Monas) for *sate babi* (pork sate) and fresh seafood, and Jl Sabang (just west of Jl Jaksa) for *sate ayam* (chicken sate) with *lontong* (sticky rice) and other delicacies.

Shopping malls are also good tucker terrain – many have inexpensive food courts.

🍴 Jalan Jaksa Area

Jalan Jaksa has a crop of backpacker-geared cafes and many authentic places on nearby streets.

Daoen Sirih   INDONESIAN $
(Map p163; Jl Kebon Sirih 41-43; meals 12,000-25,000Rp; ⊙11am-10pm) Non-touristy and a short stroll northwest of Jl Jaksa, this large bamboo-roofed, open-sided food court has a wide selection of cook-shacks offering dishes such as *nasi goreng kambing* (spicy rice with goat) and *sate madura* (skewered meat with sweet soy sauce), as well as noodles and espresso.

KL Village   MALAY, INDONESIAN $
(Map p163; ☑021-3192 5219; Jl Jaksa 21-23; mains from 23,000Rp; ⊙7am-11pm Sun-Wed, 24hr Thu-Sat; 🛜) Ever-popular Malaysian-style place that serves up inexpensive grub such as black-pepper chicken, *canai* (Malay-Indian bread) and *martabak* (stuffed pancake). If you're suffering after a long flight (or a long night), try one of the health-kick juices: 'heart and the brain' or 'sugar balance'.

Sate Khas Senayan   INDONESIAN $
(Map p163; ☑021-3192 6238; Jl Kebon Sirih Raya 31A; mains 30,000-50,000Rp; ⊙11.30am-10pm; 🛜) Upmarket air-conditioned restaurant at the northern end of Jl Jaksa. It is renowned for its superb *sate* – skewers of chicken, beef and lamb – plus Indonesian favourites such as *ayam goreng kremes* (fried chicken in batter) and *gurame bakar* (grilled fish).

★ Garuda

INDONESIAN $$

(Map p163; ☑ 021-6262 9440; Jl Hayam Wuruk 100; meals from 100,000Rp; ⊘ 24hr; 🔊) A smoky, fluorescent-lit, all-day, all-night depot of locally loved Padang food goodness, throbbing with Bollywood tunes and Indo-pop, and packed with locals. Little dishes of tempting flavours are piled on your table with lightning speed: jackfruit curry, chilli prawns, *tempe penyet* (fried tempe with spicy sauce), *rendang* (beef coconut curry), potato and corn fritters. All of it made fresh.

If you touch one part, you buy it all, so prices add up. But it's so worth it.

✖ Other Areas

The upmarket suburb of Kemang is popular with expats for its stylish bars, clubs and restaurants, but backpackers are a rare species here. It does have a couple of food courts where you can chow down on the cheap before clubbing till dawn.

The Kota neighbourhood has a few options. Most are aimed at the tourist market (both domestic and international) but they're generally very pleasant places for a slow lunch in between bouts of sightseeing.

D'Fest

FOOD COURT $

(Map p156; Jl Kemang Raya 19C; mains 20,000-60,000Rp; ⊘ 5pm-midnight) Very sociable and popular open-air food court complete with

---

SPLURGE

If a never-ending diet of nasi goreng is leaving you a little jaded, you'll find that Jakarta is a great place to splash out on something that'll make your taste buds love you again. **Lara Djonggrang** (Map p160; ☑ 021-315 3252; www.tuguhotels.com/laradjonggrang; Jl Teuku Cik Ditiro 4; mains 48,000-108,000Rp; ⊘ 12.30pm-11pm; 🔊), where you dine surrounded by museum-worthy statues, antiques and temple treasures, is a very civilised setting for sublime Imperial Javanese cuisine. For tasty dishes from around the archipelago, **Historia** (Map p159; ☑ 021-3176 0555; Jl Pintu Besar Utara 11; mains 35,000-73,000Rp; ⊘ 10am-10pm Sun-Thu, to 2am Fri & Sat) serves excellent Indonesian fare in hip, tiled warehouse environs with soaring ceilings and an attached bar where DJs spin and bands rock out.

---

stylish sofa seating and an array of international and local food stalls. It has Middle Eastern kebab joints, lots of Japanese options, *soto* (soup) places, *roti canai* (Malay-Indian flaky flatbread), plus a beerhouse. There's often live music here on weekend nights.

Santong Kuo Tieh 68

CHINESE $

(Map p159; ☑ 021-692 4716; Jl Pancoran; 10 dumplings 20,000Rp; ⊘ 10am-9pm) You'll see cooks preparing fried and steamed Chinese pork dumplings out front of this humble but highly popular little place. The *bakso ikan isi* (fish balls) are also good.

Warung Kota Tua

INDONESIAN $

(Map p159; Jl Pintu Besar Utara 11; meals 20,000-25,000Rp; ⊘ 8am-8pm) On the west side of Taman Fatahillah square, this partly renovated old warehouse (an open-sided space with exposed brick walls and artwork) is a relaxed location for a reasonably priced meal, coffee, tea or juice. Try the *ayam bakar* (grilled chicken), *mie medan* (Sumatran noodles) or *nasi cap cai* (rice with mixed vegetables).

Kedai Seni Djakarté

INDONESIAN $

(Map p159; Jl Pintu Besar Utara 17; mains 21,000-45,000Rp; ⊘ 9am-9pm Sun-Thu, to 10pm Fri & Sat) One of several similar places around Taman Fatahillah square, this is installed in the basement of an old Dutch building. You can eat inside under the ceiling fans or sweat it out on the outdoor tables. The cheap and tasty dishes are classic Indonesian comfort food (think nasi goreng).

🍷 Drinking & Nightlife

If you're expecting the capital of the world's largest Muslim country to be a sober city with little in the way of drinking culture, think again. Bars are spread throughout the city, with casual places grouped around Jl Jaksa, fancy-pants rooftop lounge bars and beer gardens in central and south Jakarta and many more places in between. Cafe culture has really taken off in the last few years.

Jakarta has been one of Southeast Asia's biggest clubbing hot spots for decades, thanks to great venues (mostly dark 'n' sleazy in the north of the city and polished 'n' pricey in the south), internationally renowned DJs and bombastic sound systems. Entrance typically costs 50,000Rp to 100,000Rp, but includes a free drink.

The recent national crackdown on selling beer and alcohol has cost some restaurants

Jalan Jaksa Area

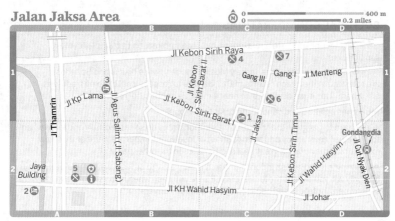

their liquor license; the ban on selling beer from minimarts was still in effect in Jakarta in 2015, even while the law was reversed in Bali. In addition, the so-called 'no-fun initiative' capped closing time of all bars and clubs at midnight, though enforcement has been lax thus far.

Listings websites such as www.indo-clubbing.com, www.jakarta100bars.com and (especially) www.whatsnewjakarta.com can be helpful for planning your night out.

★ Awan Lounge   BAR
(Map p163; www.awanlounge.com; Jl Wahid Hasyim 127; ⊙ 5pm-1am Sun-Thu, to 2am Fri & Sat) Set on the top floor of Kosenda Hotel, here is a lovely rooftop garden bar that manages to be both understated and dramatic. There's a vertical garden, ample tree cover, plenty of private nooks flickering with candlelight, and a vertigo-inducing glass skylight that plummets nine floors down.

Potato Head Garage   CLUB
(Map p156; ☑ 021-5797 3330; www.pttgarage.com; Jl Sudirman 52-53; cover charge varies; ⊙ 11am-1am) Leave it to the Potato Heads to convert an abandoned stadium into a massive thumping dance club, swirling with style. They serve food, and the decor is typically tasteful with a lean toward vintage, but this is first and foremost a dance spot where you and 1000 friends can get loose and rejoice in the night.

Café Batavia   BAR
(Map p159; www.cafebatavia.com; Jl Pintu Besar Utara 14) This classy restaurant doubles as an

Jalan Jaksa Area

🛏 Sleeping
1 Hostel 35	C1
2 Kosenda Hotel	A2
3 Max One	B1

🍴 Eating
4 Daoen Sirih	C1
5 Garuda	A2
6 KL Village	C1
7 Sate Khas Senayan	C1

🍸 Drinking & Nightlife
Awan Lounge	(see 2)

evocative place for a cocktail, a cool Bintang or a coffee.

Dua Nyonya   CAFE
(Map p160; www.duanyonyacafe.com; Jl Cikini Raya 27; ⊙ 11am-10pm) Primarily a cafe, Dua Nyonya is an intimate place on two levels that serves fine Indonesian coffee (from Bali, Toraja and Aceh) and traditional food including rice dishes such as *nasi bebek goreng keramat* (fried rice with duck). Classical music and art add to the ambience.

★ Entertainment

Taman Ismail Marzuki   PERFORMING ARTS
(TIM; Map p160; ☑ 021-3193 7325; www.tamanismailmarzuki.com; Jl Cikini Raya 73) Jakarta's premier cultural centre has a great selection of cinemas, theatres and exhibition spaces. Performances (such as Sundanese dance and gamelan music events) are always high quality and the complex has a couple of good casual restaurants, too.

CULTURAL CONSIDERATIONS

Generally Indonesians are a relaxed lot, but that's no reason to trample on their sensibilities.

➡ Indonesia is a conservative, largely Muslim country; while bikinis and Speedos are tolerated in the beach resorts of Bali, be sure to respect local clothing traditions elsewhere. This is particularly true near a mosque or other holy place.

➡ Couples should avoid canoodling or kissing in public.

➡ You have to haggle in Indonesia, but it's important to do so respectfully and learn when to draw the line. It's very bad form to shout or lose your temper. Remember that a few extra rupiah may make a great deal of difference to the other party.

➡ Learning a little Bahasa Indonesia, which is very easy to pick up, will get you a long way. Not only will you delight the locals, but it'll save you cash when it comes to dealing with stall owners, hoteliers and becak (bicycle rickshaw) drivers.

🔒 Shopping

Jakartans love their air-conditioned malls – there are over 100 in the metropolitan area. Cikini and Menteng are the destinations for glitzy malls, all manner of electronics and one hell of a flea market.

Flea Market MARKET
(Map p160; Jl Surabaya; ⊘8am-4pm) Jakarta's famous flea market is in Menteng. It has woodcarvings, furniture, textiles, jewellery, old vinyl records and many (dubious) antiques. Bargain like crazy.

Plaza Indonesia MALL
(Map p160; www.plazaindonesia.com; Jl Thamrin 28-30; 🔊) This mall is centrally located and very classy, with a wide selection of stores that includes leading Indonesian design boutiques and the likes of Cartier and Lacroix. Check out Toko Ampuh for local medicines and remedies and Batik Karis for high-quality Indonesian batik. In the basement there's an excellent, inexpensive food mall.

Pasaraya DEPARTMENT STORE
(Map p156; www.pasaraya.co.id; Jl Iskandarsyah II/2) Opposite Blok M Mall, this department store has two huge floors that seem to go on forever and are devoted to batik and handicrafts from throughout the archipelago.

ℹ Information

DANGERS & ANNOYANCES

For such a huge city with obvious social problems, Jakarta is surprisingly safe. Violent crime is rare and tourists are seldom targeted. You should exercise more caution after dark, however, particularly late at night in Glodok and Kota, where there are some seedy clubs and bars. Robberies by taxi drivers have been known to take place, so always opt for reputable firms, such as the citywide Bluebird group.

Jakarta's buses and trains can be hopelessly crowded, particularly during rush hours – this is when pickpockets ply their trade.

EMERGENCY
Tourist Police (Map p163; ☑021-566000; Jl KH Wahid Hasyim) On the 2nd floor of the Jakarta Theatre.

INTERNET ACCESS
Free wi-fi is common in cafes, restaurants, hotels and malls. Internet cafes are not easily found in the central area.

MEDICAL SERVICES
SOS Medika Klinik (Map p156; ☑021-750 6001; Jl Puri Sakti 10, Cipete; ⊘7am-10pm) Offers English-speaking GP appointments, dental care, and emergency and specialist healthcare services.

MONEY
There are banks all over the city – you're never far from an ATM in Jakarta.

TOURIST INFORMATION
Jakarta Visitor Information Office (Map p163; ☑021-316 1293, 021-314 2067; www.jakarta tourism.go.id; Jl KH Wahid Hasyim 9; ⊘9am-7pm Mon-Fri, to 4pm Sat) Inside the Jakarta Theatre building. A helpful office; the staff here can answer many queries and set you up with tours of West Java. Practical information can be lacking but there is a good stock of leaflets and publications and a colour map. There's also a desk at the airport.

ℹ Getting There & Away

Jakarta is the main travel hub for Indonesia, with flights and ships to destinations all over the archipelago. Buses depart for cities across Java, and for Bali and Sumatra; trains are also an excellent way to get across Java.

AIR

All international flights and most domestic flights operate from **Soekarno-Hatta International Airport** (CGK; www.jakartaairportonline. com). Check the website for information and schedules.

BOAT

Pelni shipping services operate on regular schedules to ports all over the archipelago. The **Pelni ticketing office** (Map p156; ☑ 021-6385 0960, 021-439 3106; www.pelni.co.id; Jl Angkasa 18) is in Kemayoran, northeast of the city centre. Tickets (plus commission) can also be bought from the agent **Kerta Jaya** (Map p160; ☑ 021-345 1518; Jl Veteran I 27), opposite Mesjid Istiqlal.

Pelni ships all arrive at and depart from Pelabuhan Satu (dock No 1) at Tanjung Priok, 13km northeast of the city centre. Busway Koridor 12 provides a direct bus link; a taxi from Jl Jaksa is around 120,000Rp.

BUS

Jakarta's four major bus terminals are all a long way from the city centre. Take the TransJakarta busway to these terminals as the journey can take hours otherwise. Trains are generally a better alternative for travelling to/from Jakarta. Tickets (some including travel to the terminals) for the better buses can be bought from agencies.

Kalideres Serves points west of Jakarta. Buses run to Merak (35,000Rp, 2½ hours) and Labuan (50,000Rp, 3½ hours). A few buses go to Sumatra from Kalideres, but most depart from Pulo Gadung terminal. Take Busway Koridor 3 to get there.

Kampung Rambutan Mainly handles buses to points south and southwest of Jakarta such as Bogor (normal/air-con 12,000/20,000Rp, 45 minutes), Cianjur (air-con 35,000Rp, 2½ hours), Bandung (normal/air-con 50,000/60,000Rp, three hours), Pangandaran (85,000Rp to 90,000Rp, eight to nine hours) and Pelabuhan Ratu (55,000Rp, four hours). Take Busway Koridor 7 to get there.

Lebak Bulus Long-distance deluxe buses to Yogyakarta, Surabaya and Bali; take Koridor 8 to get there.

Pulo Gadung Buses to Bandung, Central and East Java, Sumatra, Bali and even Nusa Tenggara. Bandung buses travel the toll road (47,000Rp to 60,000Rp, three hours), as do the long-haul Yogyakarta coaches (200,000Rp to 260,000Rp, 12 hours). Sumatra is another long haul from Jakarta by bus, but destinations include Bengkulu (from 300,000Rp) and Palembang (from 350,000Rp). Take Busway 2 or 4 to get to the terminal.

MINIBUS

Door-to-door *travel* minibuses are not a good option in Jakarta: it can take hours to pick up or drop off passengers in the traffic jams. Some travel agencies book them, but you may have to go to a depot on the city outskirts.

TRAIN

Jakarta's four main train stations are quite central, making trains the easiest way out of the city. The most convenient and important is Gambir station, on the eastern side of Merdeka Sq, a 15-minute walk from Jl Jaksa. Gambir handles express trains to Bogor, Bandung, Yogyakarta, Solo (Surakarta), Semarang and Surabaya. Pasar Senen station is to the east and mostly has economy-class trains, while Tanah Abang station has economy trains to the west. Jakarta Kota station is in the north; some trains from Gambir stop here.

Check timetables online at www.kereta-api. co.id, or consult the helpful staff at the station's **information office** (☑ 021-692 9194). There's a slightly pricey taxi booking desk inside Gambir station; the fare to Jl Jaksa is roughly 45,000Rp. Popular destinations include the following:

Bandung There are frequent trains to Bandung along a scenic hilly track, but be sure to book in advance (especially on weekends and public holidays). Comfortable *Argo Parahyangan* services depart from Gambir station six times daily (business 60,000Rp, executive 80,000Rp to 95,000Rp, 3¼ hours) between 5.55am and 8.25pm.

Bogor Trains leave from Gambir and Jakarta Kota stations. Air-conditioned trains (one hour, 15,000Rp) leave hourly or so; there are also much slower (and dirtier) *ekonomi* trains (two hours, 8000Rp). All trains are horribly crowded during rush hours.

Surabaya There are four daily exclusive-class trains between Gambir station and Surabaya (395,000Rp to 520,000Rp, 10½ to 11 hours).

Yogyakarta & Solo From Gambir there are six daily exclusive-class trains (300,000Rp to 450,000Rp, 7¼ to nine hours) to Yogyakarta, leaving between 8am and 8.45pm; four of these continue to Solo, 45 minutes further on.

ℹ Getting Around

Taxis and the TransJakarta busway network are most travellers' normal way of getting about the city. Other buses are not very useful for visitors, as they are much slower, hotter (no air-con) and crowded (pickpockets can be a problem).

TO/FROM THE AIRPORT

Jakarta's Soekarno-Hatta International Airport is 35km west of the city centre. A toll road links the airport to the city; the journey takes about an hour (longer during rush hour).

Damri (☑ 021-550 1290, 021-460 3708; www. busbandara.com; tickets 40,000Rp) airport buses run every 15 to 30 minutes between 4am and 8pm to Gambir train station (near Jl Jaksa) and several other points in the city, including Blok M, Tanjung Priok and Kampung Rambutan bus station. From Gambir train station to Jl Jaksa or Cikini, a taxi is around 45,000Rp, or you could walk (it's just under 1km). Damri buses also run regularly to Bogor (55,000Rp to 75,000Rp, every 15 to 30 minutes). Taxis from the airport to Jl Thamrin/Jl Jaksa cost about 170,000Rp to 200,000Rp including tolls. Be sure to book via the official taxi desks, rather than using the unlicensed drivers outside.

Halim Perdana Kusuma Airport (HLP), 11km south of the Cikini district, is not served by pubic transport. A taxi from central Jakarta costs around 100,000Rp.

BUS

Jakarta has the good TransJakarta express busway system, which has really sped up city travel in recent years. One of the most useful routes is Koridor 1, which runs north to Kota, past Monas and along Jl Sudirman. The tourist office can provide a map that plots the busway routes.

LOCAL TRANSPORT

Bajaj (bah-*jai*; motorised three-wheeler taxis) are similar to Indonesian túk-túks, though they're not that common these days. If you hire one keep in mind that they're not allowed on many major thoroughfares.

Ojek are motorcycle taxis. Drivers wait on busy street corners and usually wear a fluores-cent-coloured vest. Getting about Jakarta on two wheels is a lot quicker than in a car, though it's obviously less safe and you're directly exposed to the city's air pollution. Negotiate a price first; a short ride will be about 20,000Rp. A new city-wide *ojek* network called **Go-Jek** (☑ 021-725 1110; www.go-jek.com) has recently been introduced, using registered drivers and an app so you can book and pay directly from your smart phone (much like Uber).

In Kota you'll find becak – bicycle-rickshaws with an additional padded seat on the back. These contraptions are ideal for shuttling to and from Sunda Kelapa; expect to pay 10,000Rp to 20,000Rp for a short ride.

TAXI

Taxis are inexpensive in Jakarta. All are metered and cost 5000Rp to 8000Rp for the first kilo-metre and around 300Rp for each subsequent 100m. Tipping is expected, if not demanded.

Many taxi drivers provide a good service, but Jakarta has enough rogues to give its taxis a variable reputation. Stick to reputable compa-nies such as **Bluebird** (☑ 021-794 1234; www. bluebirdgroup.com); a minimum of 30,000Rp is charged for ordered taxis. Uber is also in Jakarta these days, and can frequently be the same price and more comfortable than a taxi. Any tolls and parking fees – there are lots of them – are extra and paid by the passenger.

Bogor

☑ 0251 / POP 1.02 MILLION

'A romantic little village' is how Sir Stam-ford Raffles described Bogor when he made it his country home during the British in-terregnum. As an oasis of unpredictable weather – it's credited with 322 thunder-storms a year – cool, quiet Bogor was the chosen retreat of colonials escaping the stifling, crowded capital.

Today, the long arm of Jakarta reaches the whole way to Bogor, infecting this second city with the overspill of the capital's perennial traffic and air-quality problems. The city itself isn't charmless, however. The local people are quite warm and friendly and the world-class botanical gardens are still beautiful; both are certainly worthy of a visit.

◉ Sights

Jalan Suryakencana, steps from the garden gates, is a whirlwind of activity as shoppers spill en masse from within the byzantine concrete halls of **Pasar Baru** (cnr Jl Otto Iskandardinata & Suryakencana; ◷ 6am-1pm) onto the street. Inside, the morning market is awash with all manner of produce and flow-ers, meat and fish, secondhand clothes and more. Hot, sweltering and loud, it's a hell of a browse. Dive into the barter and trade to really experience Bogor.

Kebun Raya   GARDENS
(Great Garden; www.bogor.indo.net.id/kri; admis-sion 26,000Rp; ◷ 8am-5pm) At the heart of Bogor are the fabulous botanical gardens, known as the Kebun Raya, the city's green lung of around 87 hectares. Governor Gen-eral Raffles first developed a garden here, but the spacious grounds of the Istana Bo-gor (Presidential Palace) were expanded by Dutch botanist Professor Reinwardt, with assistance from London's Kew Gardens, and officially opened in 1817. Colonial cash crops, such as tea, cassava, tobacco and cinchona, were first developed here by Dutch botanists.

Bogor & Kebun Raya

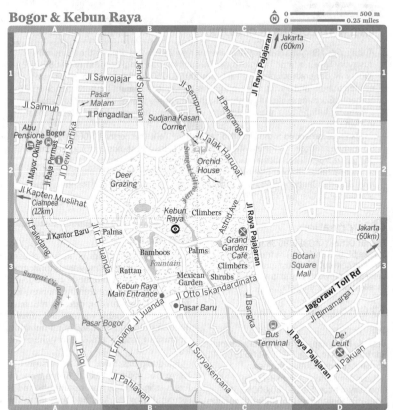

🛏 Sleeping

Most people visit Bogor on a day trip from Jakarta.

Abu Pensione   GUESTHOUSE **$**
(☏0251-832 2893; Jl Mayor Oking 15; r with fan/air-con from 175,000/275,000Rp; ☀) Safe, secure and set back from the road, rooms around the garden are spacious and well maintained; others facing the river at the rear are a bit dark. All are fine for a night or two. It's across the street from the train station and well-located for ramblers.

🍴 Eating

For street food check out the **night market** along Jl Dewi Sartika and Jl Jenderal Sudirman. If it's raining, the food court inside the Botani Square shopping mall is another good bet.

★ De' Leuit   INDONESIAN **$$**
(☏0251-839 0011; Jl Pakuan III; meals 10,000-99,000Rp; ☺11am-9pm; 🕾🖉) The most happening eatery in Bogor. There's seating on three floors beneath a soaring, pyramid-shaped thatched roof, though the best tables are on the first two levels. It does *sate*, mixed rice dishes, fried fish and chicken, and a variety of local vegie dishes. Come with a group and eat Sundanese family style.

Grand Garden Café   INTERNATIONAL **$$**
(☏0251-835 0023; Kebun Raya; mains 30,000-80,000Rp; ☺10am-8pm Mon-Thu, 10am-10pm Fri-Sun) The cafe-restaurant in the botanical gardens is a wonderfully civilised place for a bite or a drink, with sweeping views down to the water-lily ponds. It's a little pricey, but the tasty international and Indonesian food and sublime setting make it an essential stop.

WORTH A TRIP

LIVE WITH LOCALS IN CIANJUR

Author Yudhi Suryana (who for years lived in New Zealand) is building the tourism industry in Cianjur, a famed market town. Through his wonderful **homestay** (☑ 0813 2172 9004; www.cianjuradventure.com; all-inclusive 200,000-250,000Rp), and through his rare agenda of treks and driving tours, his goal is to offer independent travellers a slice of authentic Sundanese life. All guests at his homestay are offered a free tour to Cangling, a **floating village** on a nearby lake with a fish-farming economy, and to a local school in town.

Also recommended is the **Traditional Village Tour** (per person 175,000Rp). The 90-minute hike goes past elegantly terraced rice fields and stands of clove, cardamom and guava trees. It includes a delicious homestyle lunch.

Yudhi arranges airport pick-ups and drop-offs, as well as bus and train tickets to or from Jakarta, Bandung or Yogyakarta. Buses leave Jakarta's Kampung Rambutan every 30 minutes to Cianjur (35,000Rp, 2½ hours).

ⓘ Information

Tourist Office (☑ 081 6195 3838; Jl Dewi Sartika 51; ⊙ 8am-6pm) The friendly team here can help out with most queries about the region, provide a city map and also offer excellent, well-priced tours.

ⓘ Getting There & Away

BUS

Buses to Bogor depart from Jakarta's Kampung Rambutan bus terminal (10,000Rp to 15,000Rp, 45 minutes) every 15 minutes or so.

Buses depart frequently to Bandung (economy/air-con, 50,000/60,000Rp, 3½ hours), Pelabuhan Ratu (55,000Rp, three hours) and Labuan (55,000Rp, four hours). For Cianjur (30,000Rp, two hours), white minibuses (called *colt*) depart regularly from Jl Raya Pajajaran. Door-to-door *travel* minibuses go to Bandung for 100,000Rp.

Damri buses head direct to Jakarta's Soekarno-Hatta International Airport (55,000Rp, two to three hours) every 20 minutes (from 4am to 11pm) from Jl Raya Pajajaran.

TRAIN

Express trains (15,000Rp, one hour) connect Bogor with the capital roughly every hour, though try to avoid travelling during rush hour. Economy trains are more frequent, but they are packed with people – some clinging to the roof.

ⓘ Getting Around

Green *angkot* minibuses (3000Rp) shuttle around town, particularly between the bus terminal and train station. Angkot 03 does a counterclockwise loop of the botanical gardens on its way to Jl Kapten Muslihat, near the train station. Angkot 06 gets you to the bus terminal from the train station.

Bandung

A city of punks and prayer, serious religion and serious coffee – almost everything great and terrible about Indonesia can be found in Bandung. Here are teeming markets and good shopping, thriving cafes in reclaimed Dutch relics, palpable warmth and camaraderie on street corners...and mind-numbing, air-trashing traffic almost everywhere you look.

Bandung has three distinct districts of interest to visitors. The **Jl Braga** area offers a strip of cafes and restaurants and is surrounded by markets and museums. The **Jl Cihampelas** district, or so-called Jeans Street area, offers discount retail and plenty of nibbles and hotels too, but the leafier, northern part of town is the most upmarket, with the city's newest and trendiest restaurants dotting **Jl Tirtayasa** and **Jl Trunojoyo**.

The main drag, Jl Asia Afrika, runs through the heart of the city centre, past the *alun-alun* (main public square). Two places to consider for sleeping: **Chez Bon** (☑ 022-426 0600; Jl Braga 45; per person 150,000Rp; ❀ 🛜) is a newish and well-run hostel, while **Hotel Kenangan** (☑ 022-421 3244; www.kenanganhotel.com; Jl Kebon Sirih 4; r incl breakfast with fan/air-con from 265,000/395,000Rp; ❀ 🛜) is breezy, comfy and popular with travellers.

Five kilometres south of the city centre, **Leuwi Panjang bus terminal** (Jl Sukarno Hatta) has buses heading west to places such as Bogor (50,000Rp to 60,000Rp, 3½ hours) and to Jakarta's Kampung Rambutan bus terminal (37,000Rp to 47,000Rp, three hours).

Pangandaran

☎ 0265 / POP 52,200

Situated on a narrow isthmus, with a broad sweep of sand to either side and a thickly forested national park on the nearby headland, Pangandaran is West Java's premier beach resort. Most of the year it's quiet, but the town fills up on holidays (and weekends). Swimming is dodgy, with heavy dumping surf and strong currents, but it's not a bad place to get out on a board, or to learn how, on small swells. When the waves are maxed out (which is often), head an hour up the coast to sheltered Batu Karas (p171).

⊙ Sights & Activities

Pangandaran National Park   NATIONAL PARK
(Taman Nasional Pangandaran; admission 210,000Rp; ⊙ 7am-5pm) The Pangandaran National Park, which takes up the entire southern end of Pangandaran, is a wild expanse of dense forest. Within its boundaries live porcupines, *kijang* (barking deer), hornbills, monitor lizards and monkeys (including Javan gibbons). Small bays within the park enclose pretty tree-fringed beaches. The park is divided into two sections: the recreation park and the jungle.

Due to environmental degradation, the jungle is usually off limits. Well-maintained paths allow the recreation park to be explored, passing small caves (including Gua Jerang, which was used by the Japanese in the war), the remains of a Hindu temple, Batu Kalde, and a nice beach on the eastern side. English-speaking guides hang around both entrances and charge around 100,000Rp (per group of four) for a two-hour walk or up to 200,000Rp for a five-hour trip.

Pangandaran's best swimming beach, white-sand Pasir Putih, lies on the western side of the national park. It's a thin stretch of soft sand fronted by a reef that's pretty well thrashed though plenty of fish still live, eat and love there. You can swim over here from the southern end of the main resort beach if the surf is not too rough, but take care of rip currents and that steady stream of boats that shuttle people back and forth (50,000Rp return). They will not be looking for you. The beach stretches to a point that gets a break when the swell is big. On calm days, the swim out to the point is peaceful and devoid of boat traffic. If you hop a boat from the main Pangandaran beach you won't have to pay the steep national park entry fee.

At sunset, huge fruit bats emerge from the forest. They fly down the length of Pangandaran's beach but have to evade local boys who patrol with barbed-wire kites. Few are trapped this way, but every now and then a bat's wing will get caught on a kite string and the creature will be brought crashing to the ground in a fit of squeals, before being dispatched to the cooking pot.

Surfing Lessons   SURFING
(half-day lessons incl board hire 200,000-250,000Rp) Surfing lessons are offered at the northern end of the beach. Pangandaran is a good place to learn, and local instructors have 'soft' boards ideal for beginners. The friendly staff from **Pangandaran Surf** (www. pangandaransurf.com; beachside, Steak House) all lifesavers, speak English and understand local conditions. Board hire runs about 70,000Rp per day.

☞ Tours

Local boatmen offer tours to Paradise Island, an uninhabited nearby island with good beaches (including a 5km white-sand beach) and waves. Factor on around 400,000Rp per person (minimum six people). Before you leave, make an early-morning visit to Pangandaran's *pasar ikan* (p170) and fire up a fish barbecue when you get to the island for lunch.

Mas Rudin   ADVENTURE TOUR
(☎ 0813 8005 6724; www.pangandaran-guide.com) Mas Rudin is a tremendous local guide who operates out of MM Books and offers fair prices on a range of tours. His website is a wealth of information.

🛏 Sleeping

Many places have flexible prices that are dependent on demand, so you might get a good deal on weekdays outside the main holiday periods. The main area for budget or independent travellers is off the northern section of the main beach, where guesthouses are dotted along a grid of quiet lanes just inland from the beach.

Rinjani Homestay   GUESTHOUSE $
(☎ 0265-639757; r with fan/air-con 140,000/ 180,000Rp; ※ 🛜) A welcoming family-run place with 10 pleasant, tiled rooms with wood furnishings and private porches. Sweet, quiet and good value. Holiday periods see price increases of up to 100,000Rp.

INDONESIA PANGANDARAN

Pangandaran

0 — 400 m
0 — 0.2 miles

INDONESIA PANGANDARAN

✖ Eating

Pangandaran is famous for its excellent seafood. The best place by far for sampling it is the *pasar ikan* (fish market).

Rumah Makan Christi INDONESIAN **$**
(Jl Pamugaran; meals 15,000-40,000Rp; ⊙7am-11pm) This clean, orderly *rumah makan* (restaurant), with a large interior and bench seating outside, is a good bet for local food. Staff fry, grill and stew tofu, chicken and fish, and offer a range of vegetarian dishes too. All authentic Javanese. Pick and mix to your pleasure, then sit at the common table and dine with your new friends.

★Pasar Ikan SEAFOOD **$$**
(Fish Market; Jl Raya Timor; large fish 40,000-70,000Rp; ⊙11am-10pm) Pangandaran's terrific fish market consists of more than a dozen large, open-sided restaurants just off the east beach. **Karya Bahari** is considered the best – which is why it's so crowded – but all operate on exactly the same basis.

ⓘ Information

A 3500Rp admission charge is levied at the gates on entering Pangandaran.

ⓘ Getting There & Away

Set roughly halfway between Bandung and Yogyakarta, Pangandaran can be a frustratingly slow and complicated place to get to.

BUS

Many *patas* (express) buses to Jakarta and Bandung leave from the Sari Bakti Utama depot, just north of town, and Budiman bus depot, about 2km west of Pangandaran along Jl Merdeka. Other services also leave from the main bus terminal.

Mini Tiga Homestay GUESTHOUSE **$**
(✆0265-639436; www.minitigahomestay.weebly.com; s/d/tr incl breakfast 100,000/150,000/250,000Rp; @🔊) Great brick and wood chalets with reasonable rates. The nine rooms are clean, spacious and have nice decorative touches – including bamboo walls and batik wall hangings. All have en suite bathrooms and Western toilets. Good tours and transport tickets are also offered, including a popular tour of the nearby Green Canyon (250,000Rp).

★Adam's Homestay HOTEL **$$**
(✆0265-639396; www.adamshomestay.com; Jl Pamugaran; r 250,000-550,000Rp; ❄🔊🏊) Panangdaran's only real gem is a wonderfully relaxed, enjoyable place to stay with artistically presented rooms (many with balconies and outdoor bathrooms) spread around a verdant tropical garden bursting with exotic plants, lotus ponds and bird life. There's good international and local food available too.

Buses run to Bandung roughly every hour (40,000Rp to 63,000Rp, six hours) and to Jakarta's Kampung Rambutan terminal (85,000Rp to 90,000Rp, eight to nine hours).

TRAIN

The nearest train station, Sidareja, is 41km away. Speak to Mas Rudin (p169) about organising train tickets. From Sidareja there are two daily trains (3½ to four hours) to Yogyakarta. Agents in Pangandaran organise combined minibus to Sidareja station and economy/business/exclusive class train tickets for 140,000/230,000/350,000Rp.

Batu Karas

🎵 0265 / POP 3000

The idyllic fishing village and surfing hot spot of Batu Karas, 32km west of Pangandaran, is one of the most enjoyable places to kick back in West Java. It's as pretty as a picture – a tiny one-lane fishing settlement, with two beaches separated by a wooded promontory.

The main surfing beach is the smaller one: it's a sweet bay tucked between two rocky headlands. The other is a long, arcing black-sand number parked with pontoon fishing boats that shove off each night looking for fresh catch in the tides. There's good swimming, with sheltered sections calm enough for a dip, but many visitors are here for the breaks, and there's a lot of surf talk.

🏃 Activities

This is one of the best places in Java to learn to surf. The Point (offshore from Java Cove) is perfect for beginners, with paddle-in access from the beach and slow, peeling waves over a sandy bottom.

The locally run **surf co-op**, just off the beach, charges 200,000Rp for a two-hour lesson (including board hire). Longboards and shortboards (from 70,000Rp per day) are available from locals or the co-op.

🛏 Sleeping & Eating

Nayla Homestay HOMESTAY $
(📱 0852 1755 3017; d 150,000Rp) No wi-fi and no frills, just two small concrete rooms, clean and simple, on the main road and steps from the beach.

Wooden House GUESTHOUSE $
(📱 0813 6919 4405; woodenhouse@yahoo.com; r 200,000Rp) Going for the log cabin look, these three lovely rooms with high ceilings are

kept tidy and access a shared balcony with sea views. Downstairs there's a good warung for local food, jaffles, salads and pancakes.

BK Homestay HOMESTAY $
(📱 0822 6023 7802; r incl breakfast 200,000Rp; 🅿🛜) Four terrific-value, fan-cooled rooms, all with floor-to-ceiling glass on one side, high ceilings, wood floors and wi-fi in the restaurant below. No hot water, but that won't matter much here. It's set off the main beach parking lot, right in the centre of the action.

Pondok Cowet GUESTHOUSE $$
(📱 0815 7316 2286; www.facebook.com/pondok cowet; r 450,000-600,000Rp; ❄🛜) Tucked down a dirt road 50m from the main fishing beach, this new addition offers cool brickhouse bunkers and rather creative modern rooms with a mosaic of floor-to-ceiling glass, exposed brick walls, pebbled bathroom floors and cow-print blankets.

❶ Getting There & Away

You have to pay a toll of 3000Rp to enter the village. There's no public transport to Batu Karas but it can be reached from Pangandaran by taking a bus to Cijulang (10,000Rp), then an *ojek* (30,000Rp). Or else you can hire a motorcycle in Pangandaran (per day 50,000Rp) and drive yourself.

Around Batu Karas

About 6km inland from Batu Karas, pleasure boats run upriver to **Green Canyon** (Cujang Taneuh; per boat 150,000Rp; ⏰ 7.30am-4pm Sat-Thu, 1-4pm Fri), a lush river valley where you can swim in surging emerald currents and take a natural power shower under the streams that tumble into the gorge (don't look up!). Day trips can be organised from Pangandaran for 300,000Rp, but it's easy enough to get here on a hired motorcycle, as the route to the canyon is very well signposted.

Wonosobo

🎵 0286 / POP 113,000

Wonosobo, a typical country town with a busy market, is the main gateway to the Dieng Plateau. Its location 900m above sea level in the central mountain range gives it a comfortable climate.

Wisma Duta Homestay (📱 0286-321674; dutahomestay@yahoo.com; Jl Rumah Sakit III; r incl breakfast 300,000Rp; 🅿❄🛜) has been hosting travellers for years. The attractive rooms have exposed stonework and are decorated with antiques – in fact, the entire house is decorated with the owner's marvellous collection. Book ahead.

Shanti Rahayu (Jl A Yani 122; meals 12,000-25,000Rp; ⊙7am-9pm) is considered by locals to be among the best cheap eateries in the town centre; its chicken curry is great. **Dieng** (☑0286-321266; Jl Sindoro 12; meals 25,000-40,000Rp; ⊙10am-8pm) is a well-presented pick-and-mix restaurant set in an old Dutch colonial.

Wonosobo's bus terminal is 4km out of town on the Magelang road.

From Yogyakarta take a bus to Magelang (25,000Rp, 1½ hours) and then another to Wonosobo (10,000Rp, 2½ hours). Regular buses also connect Borobudur and Magelang (10,000Rp, 40 minutes) until about 4pm. **Rahayu Travel** (☑0286-321217; Jl A Yani 95) has door-to-door minibuses to Yogyakarta (55,000Rp, 3½ hours).

Frequent buses to Dieng (12,000Rp, one hour) leave throughout the day from Jl Rumah Sakit.

Dieng Plateau

☑0286 / ELEV 2000M

A startling contrast from the heat and fecundity of the lowlands, the plateau of Dieng (Abode of Gods) is another world: a windswept volcanic landscape of swirling clouds, green hills, mist and damp punctuated with ancient ruins.

You can see all the main sights, including dozens of ancient Hindu temples, on foot in a morning or afternoon, though to really explore the plateau and its crater lakes, allow a couple of days.

◎ Sights & Activities

The plateau's natural attractions and remote allure are as much a reason to visit as the temples. From the village you can do a two-hour loop walk that takes in the turquoise lake of **Telaga Warna** (admission weekdays/weekends 100,000/150,000Rp; ⊙8am-4.30pm) and the steaming vents and frantically bubbling mud pools of the **Kawah Sikidang** (admission included in ticket for Arjuna temples) volcanic crater.

The walk to **Sembungan village** (2300m) to see the sunrise is heavily touted by the guesthouses, though having to pay to get up at 4.30am is a dubious privilege (particularly on cloudy mornings).

Arjuna Complex   HINDU TEMPLE
(admission incl Candi Gatutkaca & Kawah Sikidang 25,000Rp) The five main temples that form the Arjuna Complex are clustered together on the central plain. They are Shiva temples, but like the other Dieng temples they have been named after the heroes of the *wayang* stories of the Mahabharata epic: Arjuna, Puntadewa, Srikandi, Sembadra and Semar. All have mouth-shaped doorways and strange bell-shaped windows and some locals leave offerings, burn incense and meditate here.

🛏 Sleeping & Eating

Dieng's dozen or more guesthouses are notoriously poor value. Spartan conditions, semiclean rooms and cool or lukewarm water are the norm. The village is tiny and most accommodation is on the main road.

Bu Djono   GUESTHOUSE $
(☑0852 2664 5669, 0286-642046; Jl Raya Dieng, Km26; r without bathroom 100,000Rp; 🛜) This simple, friendly place has been hosting backpackers for years and has a certain ramshackle charm with basic, clean, economy rooms. The pleasant, orderly restaurant downstairs (mains 15,000Rp to 25,000Rp) has tablecloths and lace curtains. Good tours to **Gunung Prau** (2565m) are offered. It's close to the turn-off for Wonosobo.

Hotel Gunung Mas   HOTEL $
(☑0286-334 2017; Jl Raya Dieng 42; d 180,000-275,000Rp) This solidly built hotel has a wide choice of reasonably clean rooms, with good light. Upstairs rooms have a little deck and keyhole views to the farmland. It's almost opposite the access road to the Arjuna Complex.

Homestay Flamboyan   HOMESTAY $
(☑0852 2744 3029, 0813 2760 5040; www.flamboyandieng.com; Jl Raya Dieng; r 200,000Rp; 🛜) One of three homestays on this corner, and all are decent value. The carpets may be stained, but the cubist paint jobs are creative. All rooms have private bathrooms, high ceilings and good vibes.

ℹ Getting There & Away

Dieng is 26km from Wonosobo, which is the usual access point. Buses run frequently (12,000Rp, one hour).

Yogyakarta

☑ 0274 / POP 636,700

If Jakarta is Java's financial and industrial powerhouse, Yogyakarta is its soul. Central to the island's artistic and intellectual heritage, Yogyakarta (jog-ja-*kar*-ta; called Yogya or Jogja for short) is where the Javanese language is at its purest, the arts at their brightest and traditions at their most visible.

Fiercely independent and protective of its customs – the city is still headed by its sultan, whose *kraton* (walled city palace) remains the hub of traditional life – contemporary Yogya is nevertheless a huge urban centre (the entire metropolitan area is home to over 3.3 million), complete with cybercafes, malls and traffic jams, even as it remains a stronghold of batik, gamelan and ritual.

Put it all together and you have Indonesia's most liveable and loveable city, with countless hotels offering the best value in Java across all price ranges. Its restaurants offer tasty food and there are cultural attractions everywhere you look, both within the city and on the outskirts, where you'll find Borobudur and Prambanan, Indonesia's most important archaeological sites.

◎ Sights

Most of Yogya's sights are in a small central area of the city, centred on the *kraton* complex, and just to the north.

Kraton   PALACE
(Map p174; ☑ 0274-373321; admission 12,000Rp, camera 1000Rp, guided tour by donation; ☺ 8.30am-2pm Sat-Thu, to 1pm Fri) The cultural and political heart of this fascinating city is the huge palace of the sultans of Yogya, the *kraton*.

Effectively a walled city, this unique compound is home to around 25,000 people, and has its own market, shops, batik and silver cottage industries, schools and mosques. Around 1000 of its residents are employed by the sultan. Alas, the treasures here are poorly displayed, so don't expect much information to put the palace, its buildings or contents in context.

Taman Sari   PALACE
(Map p174; Jl Taman; admission 7000Rp; ☺ 9am-3pm) Just southwest of the *kraton* is this complex, which once served as a splendid pleasure park of palaces, pools and waterways for the sultan and his entourage. It's

said that the sultan had the Portuguese architect of this elaborate retreat executed, to keep his hidden pleasure rooms secret. Built between 1758 and 1765, the complex was damaged first by Diponegoro's Java War, and an earthquake in 1865 helped finish the job.

Sono-Budoyo Museum   MUSEUM
(Map p174; ☑ 0274-376775; admission 5000Rp; ☺ 8am-1.30pm Tue-Thu & Sun, to noon Fri & Sat) This dusty, dimly lit treasure chest is the pick of Yogya's museums, with a first-class collection of Javanese art, including *wayang kulit* puppets, *topeng* (wooden masks), kris and batik. It also has a courtyard packed with Hindu statuary and artefacts from further afield, including superb Balinese carvings. *Wayang kulit* performances are held here.

Pasar Beringharjo   MARKET
(Map p174; Jl A Yani; ☺ 8am-4pm) Yogya's main market, 800m north of the *kraton*, is a lively and fascinating place. The front section has a wide range of batik – mostly inexpensive *batik cap* (stamped batik). More interesting is the old section towards the back. Crammed with warungs and stalls selling a huge variety of fruit and vegetables, this is still very much a traditional market. The range of *rempah rempah* (spices) on the 1st floor is quite something. Come early in the morning for maximum atmosphere.

☞ Tours

Tour agents on Jl Prawirotaman and in the Sosrowijayan area offer a host of tour options at similar prices. Typical day tours (per-person rates exclude entrance fees) include Borobudur (from 90,000Rp to 100,000Rp), Dieng (275,000Rp), Prambanan (75,000Rp), Borobudur (250,000Rp), and Solo and Candi Sukuh (300,000Rp).

Operators also arrange cars with a driver, with rates starting at 500,000Rp per day.

Via Via Tours   TOUR
(Map p174; www.viaviajogja.com; Jl Prawirotaman I 30) This famous cafe-restaurant offers a dozen different tours, including some really creative options. There are numerous bike and motorbike tours, including a backroad trip to Prambanan (190,000Rp to 210,000Rp), city walks (120,000Rp to 135,000Rp) and even a *jamu* (herbal medicine) and massage tour (235,000Rp to 265,000Rp) that takes in a visit to a specialist market. Tours to East Java are also offered.

Yogyakarta

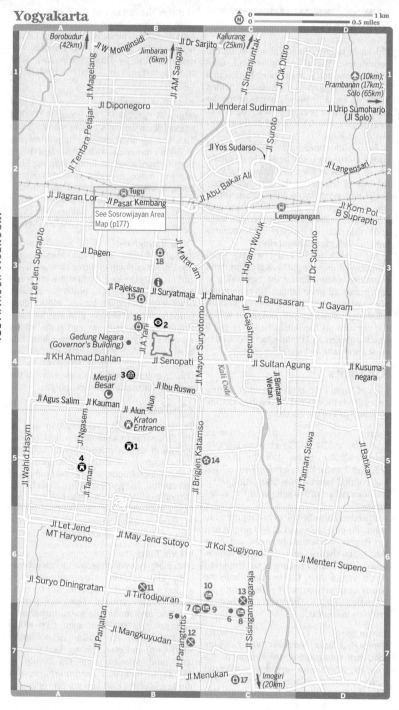

0 ____ 1 km
0 ____ 0.5 miles

Borobudur (42km)
Jl W. Monginsidi
Jimbaran (6km)
Jl Dr Sarjito
Kaliurang (25km)
Jl Simanjuntak
Jl Cik Ditiro

(10km);
Prambanan (17km);
Solo (65km)

Jl Magelang
Jl AM Sangaji
Jl Diponegoro
Jl Jenderal Sudirman
Jl Urip Sumoharjo (Jl Solo)

Jl Tentara Pelajar
Jl Yos Sudarso
Jl Suroto
Jl Langensari

Jl Jlagran Lor
Tugu
Jl Pasar Kembang
Jl Abu Bakar Ali
Lempuyangan
Jl Kom Pol B Suprapto

See Sosrowijayan Area
Map (p177)

Jl Let Jen Suprapto
Jl Dagen
18
Jl Mataram
Jl Hayam Wuruk
Jl Dr Sutomo

Jl Pajeksan
15
Jl Suryatmaja
Jl Jeminahan
Jl Bausasran
Jl Gayam

16
2
Jl Gajahmada

Gedung Negara
(Governor's Building)
Jl A Yani
Jl Senopati
Jl Sultan Agung
Jl Kusuma-negara

Jl KH Ahmad Dahlan
Jl Mayor Suryotomo
Kali Code

Mesjid Besar
3
Jl Ibu Ruswo
Jl Bintaran Wetan

Jl Agus Salim
Jl Kauman
Jl Alun
Jl Ngasem
Alun
Kraton Entrance
Jl Brigjen Katanso
Jl Taman Siswa
Jl Batikan

1

Jl Wahid Hasym
4
Jl Taman
14

Jl Let Jend MT Haryono
Jl May Jend Sutoyo
Jl Kol Sugiyono
Jl Menteri Supeno

Jl Suryo Diningratan
11
10
13
Jl Tirtodipuran
Jl Sisingamangaraja

Jl Panjaitan
7
9
5
6
8
Jl Mangkuyudan
12
Jl Parangtritis

Jl Menukan
17
Imogiri (20km)

Yogyakarta

Kaleidoscope of Java   TOUR
(Map p174; ☑0812 2711 7439; www.kaleido
scopeofjavatour.com; Gang Sartono 823, Rumah
Eyang) Fascinating tours of the Borobudur
region. The day trip (300,000Rp) from
Yogya involves sunrise from Menoreh hill;
visits to Borobudur, Pawon and Mendut
temples and a monastery, cottage industries
and Javanese dance practices; and all meals.

✹ Festivals & Events

The three Gerebeg festivals – held each year
at the end of January and April and the beginning of November – are Java's most colourful and grand processions.

🛏 Sleeping

Yogya has Java's best range of guesthouses
and hotels, many offering excellent value
for money. During the high season – July,
August and Christmas and New Year – you
should book ahead.

🛏 Sosrowijayan Area

This area is very popular with backpackers
as most of Yogya's cheap hotels are in the
souk-like maze of *gang* (alleys) within this
traditional neighbourhood. But the best
part about staying in what feels like a *bule*
(foreigner) ghetto is that those little lanes
spill out onto Jl Sosrowijayan and are within a short stroll of the more authentic Jl
Malioboro.

Dewi Homestay   HOMESTAY $
(Map p177; ☑0274-516014; dewihomestay@hot
mail.com; Jl Sosrowijayan Gt I 115; r 125,000Rp)
An attractive, long-running place that has
character with a leafy, shady garden and

spacious, charming rooms – many have
four-poster beds draped with mosquito nets.

Losmen Lucy   GUESTHOUSE $
(Map p177; ☑0274-513429; r with fan/air-con
125,000/200,000Rp; ❉) One of the best losmen in the area, this place is run by a houseproud lady and has 12 tidy, tiled rooms with
good beds; all have en-suite *mandi*.

Tiffa   GUESTHOUSE $
(Map p177; ☑0274-512841; tiffaartshop@yahoo.
com; Jl Sosrowijayan Wetan Gt II 12; s/d incl breakfast 125,000/150,000Rp) A tidy little losmen
owned by a hospitable family, with a handful of smallish, quirky and charming rooms,
each with private *mandi*. There's a communal balcony where you can tuck into your
free breakfast and slurp tea or coffee. It's
above an art shop.

105 Homestay   GUESTHOUSE $
(Map p177; ☑0274-582896; homestay_105@
yahoo.co.id; r with fan/air-con 120,000/200,000Rp;
❉☏) A lobby complete with Gaudí-esque
tiles and a welcoming owner sets a nice
introduction at this guesthouse, which has
seven classes of neat rooms in the heart of
Sosrowijayan's souk-like backstreets.

Bladok Losmen & Restaurant   HOTEL $
(Map p177; ☑0274-560452; www.bladok.web.id;
Jl Sosrowijayan 76; s with fan 100,000Rp, d with
fan 150,000-240,000Rp, d with air-con 320,000Rp;
❉☏☀) A dependable, well-run place that
looks vaguely like an apline Austrian chalet.
Bladok's rooms won't disappoint with lovely chunky wooden beds and furniture, high
cleanliness standards and crisp, fresh linen;
some have balconies. The (small) pool is a

real bonus and the cafe-restaurant serves European food and homemade bread.

1001 Malam
HOTEL **$$**

(Map p177; www.1001malamhotel.com; Sosrowijayan Wetan Gt I/57; d from 550,000Rp; ❋ 🛜) A beautifully built Moroccan-style structure complete with hand-carved wooden doorways and a lovely Moorish courtyard decked out with artisan tile. It's certainly an inspirational setting, though arguably a bit overpriced given the competition.

🏠 Jalan Prawirotaman Area

This area has a few cheap places mixed in with lots of midrange choices. Plenty have pools and the choice of restaurants is excellent. But it does feel like a tourist ghetto within an Indonesian city.

Kampoeng Djawa Hotel
GUESTHOUSE **$**

(Map p174; ✎0274-378318; www.kampoengdjawahotel.com; Jl Prawirotaman I 40; r with fan 111,000-190,000Rp, with air-con 230,000Rp; ❋ 🛜) Occupying a long, thin house, this place has character to spare. The rooms (in five price categories) have artistic touches including exposed brick walls, mosaic tiling and pebble-walled bathrooms. There's a peaceful rear garden for your complimentary tea or coffee (available all day) and afternoon snack. Staff are eager to help.

Delta Homestay
GUESTHOUSE **$**

(Map p174; ✎0274-327051; www.dutagardenhotel.com; Jl Prawirotaman II 597A; r with shared mandi 115,000-135,000Rp, r 230,000-250,000Rp; ❋ 🛜) A sunny backstreet guesthouse with a selection of small but perfectly formed rooms built from natural materials, each with a porch, grouped around a pool. It's peaceful here, staff are welcoming and breakfast is included.

Via Via
GUESTHOUSE **$**

(Map p174; ✎0274-386557; www.viaviajogja.com; Jl Prawirotaman 3/514A; r incl breakfast 150,000-200,000Rp; ❋ 🛜) Part of the expanding Via Via empire, this fine guesthouse enjoys a quiet side-street location not far from the mothership cafe-restaurant (Map p174; ✎0274-386557; Jl Prawirotaman I 30; mains 27,000-115,000Rp; 🛜). It has seven stylish rooms with high ceilings, good-quality beds and semi-open bathrooms.

There is also a garden at the rear for socialising.

Rumah Eyang
GUESTHOUSE **$**

(Map p174; ✎0812 2711 7439; Jl Parangtritis, Gang Sartono 823; r incl breakfast from 220,000Rp; ❋ @ 🛜) A stylish suburban house that's been converted into an inviting guesthouse and art space. Rooms are simple and comfortable, but the real benefit here is that Atik, the Javanese writer-owner, is a font of knowledge about the region and offers great tours.

Prambanan Guesthouse
HOTEL **$$**

(Map p174; ✎0274-376167; www.prambananghbe; Jl Prawirotaman I 14; s/d with fan & cold shower 245,000/285,000Rp, with air-con & hot shower 380,000/400,000Rp; ❋ 🛜 🏊) It's looking a bit tired these days, but it remains a peaceful place to stay with a small pool and attractive gardens. Cheaper rooms are quite plain, but the better options are plenty comfortable and have *ikat*-style textiles draped on good-quality beds.

🍴 Eating & Drinking

In the evening, street-food vendors line the northern end of Jl Malioboro; here you can try Yogya's famous *ayam goreng* (deep-fried chicken soaked in coconut milk) and dishes such as *sambal welut* (spicy eel) and *nasi langgi* (coconut rice with tempe).

🍴 Sosrowijayan Area

There are loads of inexpensive noshing options in this area, including a row of good warungs on Jl Pasar Kembang, beside the train line.

Bedhot Resto
INTERNATIONAL **$**

(Map p177; Gang II; mains 18,000-42,000Rp; ⊙8am-11pm; 🛜🍴) Bedhot means 'creative' in old Javanese and this place is one of the more stylish eateries in Sosrowijayan. There's tasty Indonesian and international food – a cut above usual tourist fare – good juices and wi-fi.

Hanis Restaurant & Bakery
INTERNATIONAL **$**

(Map p177; Jl Sosrowijayan, Gang II; mains 24,000-49,000Rp; ⊙8am-11pm) If you are in dire need of international fare like, say, a breakfast of muesli and yoghurt, some decent brown bread or chicken fajitas, this cute bakery and cafe could be your salvation. The cakes and pies look serious too.

Oxen Free
PUB **$$**

(Map p177; www.oxenfree.net; Jl Sosrowijayan 2; mains 30,000-60,000Rp; ⊙11am-2am Sun-Thu,

Sosrowijayan Area

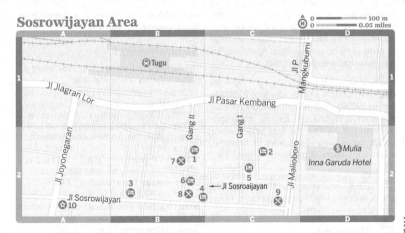

to 3am Fri & Sat; 🛜) The coolest new spot in the area is set in an old colonial, dotted with reclaimed booths and lit by raw bulbs and old camping lanterns. Most descend on the beer garden in the back for all-day Western breakfasts and roast chicken and lamb dinners. Attention veg-heads: there's a mean tempe steak, too.

It gets a fun bar crowd most nights.

✕ Jalan Prawirotaman Area

Bu Ageng　　　　　　　　　　INDONESIAN $
(Map p174; 📞 0274-387191; Jl Tirtodipuran 13; mains 14,000-30,000Rp; ⊗ 11am-11pm Tue-Sun) Traditional Javanese dishes such as *eyem penggeng* (chicken simmered in spiced coconut cream then broiled) are served in Bu Ageng's tasteful interior space, with wood columns and a bamboo-mat ceiling with twirling fans. Its adventurous array of

mixed rice platters includes dishes such as beef tongue, smoked fish or beef stewed in coconut milk. It even does a durian bread pudding.

Milas　　　　　　　　　　　　INDONESIAN $
(Map p174; 📞 0274-742 3399; Jl Prawirotaman IV 127; dishes 15,000-45,000Rp; ⊗ 3-9pm Tue-Fri, noon-9pm Sat & Sun; 🖋) A great retreat from the streets, this secret garden restaurant is part of a project centre for street youth. It offers tasty vegetarian cooking including healthy snacks, sandwiches, salads and organic coffee.

Tempo del Gelato　　　　　　GELATERIA $
(Map p174; Jl Prawirotaman I; small/medium/large 20,000/40,000/65,000Rp; ⊗ 11am-11pm) A stone-and-glass chapel to Italian ice cream. Flavours on rotation include ginger, guava, dragon fruit, chocolate, green tea, praline, lemon grass, rum raisin and coconut. Four months old at research time and already extremely popular.

☆ Entertainment

Dance, *wayang* or gamelan are performed most mornings at the *kraton* (admission free). Most dance performances in and around town are based on the Ramayana – or at least billed as 'Ramayana ballet' because of the famed performances at Prambanan. *Wayang kulit* performances can be seen at several places around Yogya every night of the week.

Jl Sosrowijayan is something of a live-music hub, with casual venues often rocking with local bands.

INDONESIA YOGYAKARTA

Purawisata DANCE
(Map p174; ☑0274-375705; Jl Brigjen Katamso; 300,000Rp) This amusement park stages Ramayana performances daily at 8pm. You can dine here and watch the show.

Sono-Budoyo Museum PUPPETRY
(Map p174; ☑0274-376775; admission 20,000Rp, camera 3000Rp; ☺8pm-10pm Mon-Sat) Popular two-hour performances nightly from 8pm to 10pm (20,000Rp); the first half-hour involves the reading of the story in Javanese, so most travellers skip this and arrive later.

Lucifer LIVE MUSIC
(Map p177; Jl Sosrowijayan) An intimate bar and one of the city's key live-music venues. There are bands most nights.

🛍 Shopping

Yogyakarta is a shopper's paradise for crafts and antiques. Jl Malioboro is one great, throbbing bazaar of souvenir shops and stalls selling cheap clothes, leatherwork, batik bags, *topeng* masks and *wayang golek* puppets. Look in some of the fixed-price shops on Jl Malioboro or nearby streets to get an idea of prices. **Hamzah Batik** (Map p174; ☑0274-588524; Jl A Yani 9; ☺9am-9pm) is an excellent place to start looking; when you're done shopping here try the traditional Javanese food on the roof terrace.

For regular shopping in the heart of town, head to **Mal Malioboro** (Map p174; Jl Malioboro; ☺10am-9pm Mon-Sat, to 8pm Sun).

Batik Keris CLOTHING
(Map p174; www.batikkeris.co.id; Jl A Yani 71; ☺9am-8pm) Excellent-quality batik at fixed prices. Best for traditional styles – men's shirts start at about 200,000Rp.

Lana Gallery ART
(Map p174; ☑0877 3929 3119, 0818 0412 8277; rlhwildan@yahoo.com; Jl Menukan; ☺Tue-Sun) A great range of contemporary art from new and emerging artists from across the archipelago, many graduates of Yogya's fine arts

school. It's run by Wildan, one of the friendliest people you'll ever meet.

ℹ Information

The website www.yogyes.com is an excellent portal to the city and central Java.

Hassles from smooth-talking batik salesmen are a constant issue for every traveller in town: their goal is to get you into a shop (such as the 'sultan's batik workshop') where they will earn a huge commission. A time-honoured scam is to pressure you to visit a 'fine-art student exhibition' or a 'government store' – there are no official shops or galleries in the city.

Ludira Husada Tama Hospital (☑0274-620333; Jl Wiratama 4; ☺24hr)

Mulia (Map p177; Inna Garuda Hotel, Jl Malioboro 60) The best exchange rates in Yogya.

Tourist Information Office (Map p174; ☑0274-562000; Jl Malioboro 16; ☺8am-8pm Mon-Thu, to 7pm Fri & Sat) Perhaps the most well-organised office of its kind in the country. Here is delightful, helpful staff, free maps and good transport information. It produces a number of publications (including a calendar of events and a great map), and it can book any and all transport, as well as local attractions and performances. Also has counters at the airport and on the eastern side of the Tugu train station.

ℹ Getting There & Away

AIR

Yogyakarta's airport (JOG) has international connections to Singapore and Kuala Lumpur, plus many domestic links.

BUS

Yogya's main bus terminal, Giwangan, is 5km southeast of the city centre; bus 3B connects it with Tugu train station and Jl Malioboro. Buses run from Giwangan to points all over Java, and also to Bali. For long trips make sure you take a luxury bus. It's cheaper to buy tickets at the bus terminal, but it's less hassle to simply check fares and departures with the ticket agents along Jl Mangkubumi, Jl Sosrowijayan or Jl Prawirotaman. These agents can also arrange pick-up from your hotel.

BUSES FROM YOGYAKARTA

DESTINATION	FARE (RP)	DURATION (HR)	FREQUENCY
Bandung	air-con 120,000	10	3 daily
Borobudur	normal 20,000 (bring small bills)	1½	every 30min
Denpasar	air-con 325,000	19	3 daily
Jakarta	normal/air-con 200,000/260,000	12	10-12 daily between 3pm & 5pm

To go to Prambanan (3600Rp) take a 1A city bus from Jl Malioboro. Buses to/from Borobudur use the Jombor terminal. To get there take a TransJogja bus 3A from Jl Malioboro to Jl Ahmad Dahlan, and change to a 2B for Jombor.

MINIBUS
Door-to-door *travel* minibuses run to all major cities from Yogya. Sosrowijayan and Prawirotaman agents sell tickets. Destinations served include Semarang (80,000Rp, four hours), Surabaya (90,000Rp) and Malang (110,000Rp). For Pangandaran (110,000Rp, eight hours), **Estu Travel** (☑ 0274-668 4567; Jl Gampingan) has minibuses daily at 8am and 6.30pm.

TRAIN
Centrally located, Yogya's Tugu train station handles all business- and executive-class trains. Economy-class trains also depart from and arrive at Lempuyangan station, 1km to the east.

ⓘ Getting Around

TO/FROM THE AIRPORT
Yogya's Adi Sucipto airport, 10km east of the centre, is very well connected to the city by public transport. Bus 1A (3600Rp) runs there from Jl Malioboro.

BICYCLE
Bikes cost about 30,000Rp a day from hotels. Always lock your bike.

BUS
Yogya's reliable bus system, TransJogja consists of modern air-conditioned buses running from 6am to 10pm on six routes around the city to as far away as Prambanan. Tickets cost 3600Rp per journey. TransJogja buses stop only at the designated bus shelters. Bus 1A is a very useful service, running from Jl Malioboro past the airport to Prambanan. TransJogja route maps are available at the tourist information office.

LOCAL TRANSPORT
Yogyakarta has an oversupply of becak (bicycle-rickshaws); most drivers are quite pushy, but it can be a fun way to get around. Watch out for drivers who offer cheap hourly rates, unless you want to do the rounds of all the batik galleries

that offer commissions. A short trip is about 10,000Rp to 15,000Rp. To go from Jl Prawirotaman to Jl Malioboro costs around 25,000Rp.

TAXI
Metered taxis are cheap, costing 10,000Rp to 30,000Rp for short trips.

Prambanan

Jaw-dropping and mystical, the spectacular temples of Prambanan, set in the plains, are the best remaining examples of Java's extended period of Hindu culture and are an absolute must-visit.

All the temples in the Prambanan area were built between the 8th and 10th centuries AD, when Java was ruled by the Buddhist Sailendras in the south and the Hindu Sanjayas of Old Mataram in the north.

Following this creative burst, the Prambanan Plain was abandoned when the Hindu-Javanese kings moved to East Java. In the middle of the 16th century there is said to have been a great earthquake that toppled many of the temples. Their destruction was accelerated by treasure hunters and locals searching for building materials. Most temples have now been restored to some extent; like Borobudur, Prambanan made the Unesco World Heritage list in 1991.

Prambanan suffered extensive damage in the 2006 earthquake. Today, the main structures have been restored, though there remains a lot of work to be done, so expect some temples to be fenced off.

⊙ Sights

Prambanan Temples   TEMPLE
(www.borobudurpark.co.id; admission 225,000Rp; ⊙6am-6pm) The huge Prambanan complex was erected in the middle of the 9th century – around 50 years later than Borobudur – but little is known about its early history. Today, it's a hugely popular site – come late in the day for some respite from the crowds. The main temple's spire soars 47m over hundreds

TRAINS FROM YOGYAKARTA

DESTINATION	FARE (RP)	DURATION (HR)	FREQUENCY
Bandung	200,000-300,000	7-8¾	6 daily
Jakarta	300,000-450,000	7-9	6 daily
Malang	250,000-300,000	7	3 daily
Sidareja (for Pangandaran)	150,000	3½-4	2 daily
Solo (Surakarta)	6000-20,000	1	14 daily

GUNUNG MERAPI & KALIURANG

Few of Southeast Asia's volcanoes are as evocative, or as destructive, as Gunung Merapi (Fire Mountain). Towering 2930m over Yogyakarta, Borobudur and Prambanan, this immense, Fuji-esque peak is a threatening, disturbingly close presence for thousands of people. Merapi has erupted dozens of times over the past century; the massive 2010 eruption killed 353 and forced the evacuation of 360,000 more.

Officially Indonesia's most active volcano – quite an accolade in a nation with 127 active cones – it's thought by some to have been responsible for the mysterious evacuation of Borobudur and the collapse of the old Mataram kingdom during the 11th century.

The hill resort of Kaliurang, 25km north of Yogyakarta, is the main access point for views of Merapi. It has two good museums: **Ullen Sentalu** (☑0274-895161; www.ullensentalu.com; admission 50,000Rp; ☺8.30am-4pm Tue-Fri, to 5pm Sat & Sun), with a rich collection of Javanese fine art, and **Merapi Museum** (Jl Kaliurang Km25.7; admission 5000Rp, film 5000Rp; ☺8am-3.30pm Tue-Sun), which has exhibits on all things volcanic.

Merapi is frequently declared off-limits to visitors. But if conditions permit, climbing the cone is possible in the dry season (April to September). Access is via the small village of Selo, on the northern side of the mountain. Extreme caution is advised. Guides (250,000Rp) should warn against climbing if it looks dangerous; while they don't want to endanger lives, they may be prepared to take risks in order to get paid. Entry into the national park costs 150,000Rp.

It has not been possible to climb the peak from Kaliurang since 1994 due to volcanic activity. However, there is still excellent **hiking** around the lower reaches of Merapi, with superb views of lava flows. Christian Awuy, owner of the legendary **Vogels Hostel** (☑0274-895208; www.vogelshostel.blogspot.com; Jl Astamulya 76, Kaliurang; dm 25,000Rp, d with shared bathroom 100,000Rp, bungalows with bathroom & hot water 150,000Rp, mains 13,000-35,000Rp; @🛜), has organised climbs for years and is an excellent reference point. Six-hour sunrise hikes (US$25, minimum two people) from his hostel usually start at 4am.

Kaliurang is 26km north of Yogya. *Angkot* minibuses from Yogyakarta's Jl Kaliurang street cost 15,000Rp to 20,000Rp; the last leaves at 3pm. A taxi from Malioboro will cost around 150,000Rp each way.

of smaller temples in varying states of repair. Its restored interior features a chamber with a four-armed statue of Shiva the Destroyer.

Plaosan Temples
TEMPLE

FREE Built around the same time as the Prambanan temple group, the Plaosan temples also combine both Hindu and Buddhist religious symbols and carvings. Plaosan Lor (Plaosan North) comprises two restored, identical main temples, surrounded by some 126 small shrines and solid stupas, most of which are now just a jumble of stone. Two giant *dwarapala* (temple guardian statues) stand at the front of each main temple, which are notable for their unusual three-part design.

Southern Group
TEMPLE

(admission 110,000Rp) Kraton Ratu Boko (Palace of King Boko) is a partly ruined Hindu palace complex dating from the 9th century. Perched on a hilltop overlooking Prambanan, it is believed to have been the central court of the mighty Mataram dynasty. You can see the large gateway and the platform of the Candi Pembakaran (Royal Crematorium), as well as a series of bathing places staggered on different levels leading down to the village. The sunset view over the Prambanan Plain is magnificent.

Western Group
TEMPLE

(admission per temple 2000Rp) There are three temples in this group between Yogyakarta and Prambanan, two of them close to Kalasan village on the main Yogyakarta road. Kalasan and Prambanan villages are 3km apart, so it is easiest to take an *angkot* or bus to cover this stretch. Candi Kalasan, near Kalasan village, is one of the oldest Buddhist temples on the Prambanan Plain. A Sanskrit inscription of AD 778 refers to a temple dedicated to the female Bodhisattva Tara.

☆ Entertainment

Ramayana Ballet
DANCE

(☑021-496408; www.borobudurpark.com) Held at the outdoor theatre just west of the main temple complex, the famous *Ramayana Ballet* is Java's most spectacular dance-drama. The story of Rama and Shinta unfolds over four successive nights, two or three times each month from May to October (the dry season), leading up to the full moon.

ⓘ Getting There & Away

Prambanan is 17km northeast of Yogyakarta.

You can visit all the temples by bicycle from Yogyakarta. The most pleasant route is to take Jl Senopati to the eastern ring road, where you turn left. Follow this to Jl Solo and Jl Babarsari. Go past the Sahid Garden Hotel to the Selokan Mataram. This canal runs parallel to the Solo road, about 1.5km to the north, for around 6km to Kalasan, about 2km before Prambanan.

From Yogyakarta, take TransYogya bus 1A (3600Rp, 40 minutes) from Jl Malioboro.

Borobudur

📞0293

Along with Angkor Wat in Cambodia and Bagan in Myanmar, Java's Borobudur makes the rest of Southeast Asia's spectacular sites seem almost incidental. Looming out of a patchwork of bottle-green paddies and swaying palms, this colossal Buddhist monument has survived Gunung Merapi's eruptions, terrorist bombs and the 2006 earthquake to remain as enigmatic and as beautiful as it must have been 1200 years ago.

◉ Sights

Borobudur Temple   BUDDHIST TEMPLE
(admission 250,000Rp, sunrise & sunset 380,000Rp, 90min guided tour 1-5 people 100,000-150,000Rp; ⊙6am-5.15pm) Indonesia's signature Buddhist monument, Borobudur is built from two million stone blocks in the form of a massive symmetrical stupa that's wrapped around a small hill. Standing on a 118m by 118m base, its six square terraces are topped by three circular ones, with four stairways leading up through carved gateways to the top. Viewed from the air, the structure resembles a colossal three-dimensional tantric mandala (symbolic circular figure).

It has been suggested that the people of the Buddhist community that once supported Borobudur were early Vajrayana or Tantric Buddhists who used it as a walk-through mandala. Though the paintwork is long gone, it's thought that the grey stone of Borobudur was once coloured to catch the sun.

The monument was conceived as a Buddhist vision of the cosmos in stone, starting in the everyday world and spiralling up to nirvana, or enlightenment. At the base of the monument is a series of reliefs representing a world dominated by passion and desire, where the good are rewarded by reincarnation as a higher form of life, while the evil are punished with a lower reincarnation. These carvings and their carnal scenes are covered by stone to hide them from view, but they are partly visible on the southern side.

Starting at the main eastern gateway, go clockwise (as one should around all Buddhist monuments) around the galleries of the stupa. Although Borobudur is impressive for its sheer bulk, the delicate sculptural work when viewed up close is exquisite. The pilgrim's walk is about 5km long and takes you along narrow corridors past nearly 1460 richly decorated narrative panels and 1212 decorative panels in which the sculptors have carved a virtual textbook of Buddhist doctrines as well as many aspects of Javanese life 1000 years ago – a continual procession of ships and elephants, musicians and dancing girls, warriors and kings.

On the third level there's a lengthy panel sequence about a dream of Queen Maya, which involved a vision of white elephants with six tusks. Monks and courtiers interpret this as a premonition that her son would become a Buddha, and the sequence continues until the birth of Prince Siddhartha and his journey to enlightenment. Many other panels are related to Buddhist concepts of cause and effect or karma.

Some 432 serene-faced Buddha images stare out from open chambers above the galleries, while 72 more Buddha images (many now headless) sit only partly visible in latticed stupas on the top three terraces – one is considered the lucky Buddha. The top

---

BOROBUDUR GUIDES

Jaker (📞0293-788845; jackpriyana@yahoo.com.sg; Jl Balaputradewa) is a group of guides and local activists based in the small settlement of Borobudur.

Affordable rates are charged for trips to Selogriyo (towering rice terraces and a small Hindu temple), Tuksongo (a centre of glass-noodle production), tofu and pottery villages, a large batik workshop and to Setumbu Hill for sunrise over the Borobudur monument.

platform is circular, signifying never-ending nirvana.

Admission to the temple includes entrance to Karmawibhangga archaeological museum, which is just east of the monument and contains 4000 original stones and carvings from Borobudur and some interesting photographs. You can also glimpse the so-called Elephant House, where two small elephants suffer, with their front feet chained together, moaning and crying to no avail. Elephant House indeed. More like an elephant prison. This is the black eye of Borobudur, folks.

Mendut Temple & Monastery
BUDDHIST TEMPLE, MONASTERY

(admission 3500Rp; ☺8am-4pm) This exquisite temple, set within a cute neighbourhood around 3.5km east of Borobudur, may look insignificant compared with its mighty neighbour, but it houses the most outstanding statue in its original setting of any temple in Java. The magnificent 3m-high figure of Buddha is flanked by bodhisattvas: Lokesvara on the left and Vairapana on the right. The Buddha is also notable for his posture: he sits Western-style with both feet on the ground.

🛏 Sleeping & Eating

Most places to stay also rustle up meals, Cheap warungs are found at the temple entrance.

Rajasa Hotel & Restoran
GUESTHOUSE $

(✓0293-788276; Jl Badrawati II; r incl breakfast with fan & cold water/air-con & hot water 200,000/400,000Rp, meals 20,000-25,000Rp; ❄🏠) A deservedly popular, welcoming guesthouse with rooms that face rice fields (through railings) about 1.5km south of the bus terminal. The fan-cooled rooms are the best value, as you pay a lot more for air-conditioning and slightly smarter furniture. Meals are well priced.

Lotus II
GUESTHOUSE $$

(✓0293-788845; jackpriyana@yahoo.com.sg; Jl Balaputradewa 54; r incl breakfast 250,000-275,000Rp; ❄@🏠) This popular, friendly place is owned by one of the founders of Jaker, so there's great local information and everyone speaks English. Rooms are clean and simple with wooden beds and high ceilings. The long rear balcony, overlooking rice fields, is perfect for your breakfast or an afternoon tea or beer. Book well ahead.

❶ Getting There & Away

From Yogyakarta, buses leave Jombor terminal (20,000Rp, every 30 minutes, 1¼ hours) to Borobudur, 42km northwest. The last bus to/from Borobudur is at 4.30pm.

Solo (Surakarta)
📋 0271 / POP 520,000

Arguably the epicentre of Javanese identity and tradition, Solo is one of the least Westernised cities on the island. An eternal rival to Yogyakarta, this conservative town often plays second fiddle to its more conspicuous neighbour. But with backstreet *kampung* and elegant *kraton*, traditional markets and gleaming malls, Solo has more than enough to warrant at least an overnight visit; two nights is better. As there are some fascinating temples close by, it also makes a great base for forays into the lush hills of Central Java.

In many ways, Solo is also Java writ small, incorporating its vices and virtues and embodying much of its heritage. On the downside, the island's notoriously fickle temper tends to flare in Solo first – the city has been the backdrop for some of the worst riots in Java's recent history. On the upside, the city's long and distinguished past as a seat of the great Mataram empire means that it competes with Yogyakarta as the hub of Javanese culture.

◉ Sights & Activities

Kraton Surakarta
PALACE, MUSEUM

(Kraton Kasunanan; ✓0271-656432; admission 15,000Rp, guide 25,000-30,000Rp; ☺9am-2pm) Once the hub of an empire, today the Kraton Surakarta is a faded memorial of a bygone era. It's worth a visit, but much of the *kraton* was destroyed by fire in 1985. Many of the inner buildings were rebuilt, but today the allure of this once-majestic palace has largely vanished and its structures are left bare and unloved. The main sight for visitors is the Sasono Sewoko museum.

Istana Mangkunegaran
PALACE, MUSEUM

(admission 20,000Rp; ☺8.30am-2pm Mon-Sat, 8.30am-1pm Sun) Dating to 1757, the Istana Mangkunegaran is in better condition than the *kraton* and is the home of the second house of Solo. The centre of the compound is the *pendopo*, a pavilion built in a mix of Javanese and European architectural styles. Its high, rounded ceiling was painted

Solo (Surakarta)

INDONESIA SOLO (SURAKARTA)

in 1937 and is intricately decorated with a central flame surrounded by figures of the Javanese zodiac, each painted in its own mystical colour.

House of Danar Hadi MUSEUM
(☏ 0271-714326; www.houseofdanarhadi.com; Jl Slamet Riyadi 261; admission 35,000Rp; ⊙ 9am-4pm, showroom to 9pm) Danar Hadi is one of the world's best batik museums, with a terrific collection of antique and royal textiles from Java, China and beyond. It occupies a stunning whitewashed colonial building. Entry includes an excellent guided tour (around 1½ hours, in English), which explains the history of the many pieces (10,000 in the collection).

There's also a workshop where you can watch craftswomen at work creating new masterpieces, an upmarket storeroom and a souvenir shop.

★ Festivals & Events

Kirab Pusaka CULTURAL
(Heirloom Procession) Since 1633, these colourful processions have been held on the first day of the Javanese month of Suro (between March and May). They start at Istana Mangkunegaran in the early evening and continue late into the night.

🛏 Sleeping

Solo has plenty of great-value budget hotels.

Warung Baru Homestay GUESTHOUSE $
(☏ 0271-656369; Jl Banda; r incl breakfast with fan/air-con from 100,000/150,000Rp; ❄) This new guesthouse offers four great-value rooms set around a courtyard garden in a lovely home set down a small *gang*. The more expensive rooms have hot water and bathtubs. Check in at its restaurant.

Cakra Homestay HOMESTAY $
(☏ 0271-634743; Jl Cakra II 15; r with shared bath 150,000Rp, with private bath 200,000-250,000; ❄ 🛜 ⛱) This atmospheric place scores highly for those interested in Javanese culture (and the welcoming staff are keen to promote it). There's an amazing gamelan room with free performances on Tuesday and Thursday evenings. It also has a gorgeous pool area. However, the rooms are pretty simple. Breakfast included. Shared baths are Western and *mandi* style.

Red Planet HOTEL $
(☏ 0271-788 9333; www.redplanethotels.com; Jl Dr Supomo 49; r from 220,000Rp; ❄ @ 🛜) Another competitively priced, dressed-up three-star chain with branches in a handful of Indonesian cities. Rooms have wood floors, high ceilings, wall-mounted flat screens, rain showers and security boxes, but they aren't huge and can feel slightly soulless despite the good value.

Istana Griya 2 GUESTHOUSE $$
(☏ 0271-661118; Jl Imam Bonjol 35; r incl breakfast 225,000-350,000Rp; ❄ 🛜) In a good central location, this renovated place is a sister hotel to the original around the corner. It's more upmarket, with large modern rooms and hot-water showers.

✕ Eating

Solo has a superb street-food tradition and a traffic-free area called **Galabo** (Jl Slamet Riyadi; ⏰ 5pm-11pm), a kind of open-air food court with dozens of stalls. Local specialities such as *nasi gudeg* (unripe jackfruit served with rice, chicken and spices), *nasi liwet* (rice cooked in coconut milk and eaten with a host of side dishes) or *timlo solo* (beef noodle soup) can be found here.

There is no bar scene in Solo.

Warung Baru INTERNATIONAL $
(☏ 0271-656369; Jl Ahmad Dahlan 23; mains 10,000-18,000Rp; ⏰ 7.30am-10pm Mon-Sat, 5-10pm Sun; 🍴) An old-school backpackers' hang-out, the Baru bakes great bread and caters quite well to vegetarians but the rest of the enormous menu is a bit forgettable. Still, the friendly owners arrange tours and batik classes.

Nasi Liwet Wongso Lemu INDONESIAN $
(Jl Teuku Umar; meals 12,000-18,000Rp; ⏰ 4pm-1am) Solo street dining at its best, this evening-only stall, run by an *ibu* in traditional batik, specialises in *nasi liwet*: coconut-flavoured rice served on a banana leaf topped with shredded chicken, chicken liver (optional), egg, turmeric-cooked tofu and special seasonings. Tables are set up with pickled vegetables, tofu fried in turmeric and chicken feet. This is cultural dining deluxe!

Adem Ayem INDONESIAN $
(☏ 0271-716992; Jl Slamet Riyadi 342; mains 14,000-60,000Rp; ⏰ 7am-10pm) A huge canteen-like place with swirling fans and photos of ye olde Surakarta. Grab one of the plastic-fantastic chairs and order the chicken – souped, fried or served up *gudeg*-style.

Omah Sinten INDONESIAN $$
(www.omahsinten.com; Jl Diponegoro 34-54; mains 25,000-55,000Rp; ⏰ 8am-10pm) At this restaurant you can dine on quality Javanese fare including lots of local Solonese specialities, like beef sliced and stewed in herbs and green chillies, or duck stewed in coconut milk. Why not enjoy both while listening to the tinkle of fountains and the calming waft of classical Javanese music? It's opposite the entrance to the Istana Mangkunegaran (p182).

TRAINS FROM SOLO

DESTINATION	FARE (RP)	DURATION (HR)	FREQUENCY
Jakarta	90,000-535,000	8¼-9	4 daily
Surabaya	115,000–285,000	3½-4	6 daily

⭐ Entertainment

Solo is an excellent place to see traditional Javanese performing arts; both Istana Mangkunegaran and Kraton Surakarta have traditional Javanese dance practice. Contact the tourist office for the latest schedules.

RRI Auditorium   PERFORMING ARTS
(☑ 0271-641178; Jl Abdul Rahman Saleh 51) RRI holds an eclectic program of cultural performances, including *wayang orang* and *ketoprak* (folk theatre). There's a free *wayang orang* event on the second Tuesday of each month at 8pm.

ℹ️ Information

BCA Bank (cnr Jl Dr Rajiman & Jl Gatot Subroto; ⊙ 8am-4pm Mon-Sat) Has currency-exchange facilities.

Tourist Office (☑ 0271-716501; Jl Slamet Riyadi 275; ⊙ 8am-4pm Mon-Sat) Staff are only moderately helpful here. They have maps, brochures and information on cultural events. They also peddle (slightly pricey) tours.

ℹ️ Getting There & Away

AIR

Solo's Adi Sumarmo airport (SOC) offers regular flights to Jakarta.

BUS

The Tirtonadi bus terminal is 3km from the centre of the city. Only economy buses leave from here, to destinations such as Prambanan (14,000Rp, 1½ hours) and Semarang (30,000Rp, 3¼ hours), plus Surabaya and Malang. Near the bus terminal, the Gilingan minibus terminal has express air-con *travel* minibuses to Semarang (55,000Rp), Surabaya and Malang (both 80,000Rp). It's easiest to reach Yogyakarta by train.

TRAIN

Solo is located on the main Jakarta–Yogyakarta–Surabaya train line and most trains stop at **Balapan** (☑ 0271-714039), the principal train station. Jebres train station, in the northeast of Solo, has a few very slow economy-class services to Surabaya and Jakarta. Trains to Yogyakarta cost from 6000Rp to 20,000Rp.

ℹ️ Getting Around

Air-conditioned Batik Solo Trans buses connect Adi Sumarmo airport, 10km northwest of the centre, with Jl Slamet Riyadi. A taxi costs around 70,000Rp; **Kosti Solo taxis** (☑ 0271-856300) are reliable. Becak cost about 10,000Rp from the train station or bus terminal into the centre.

Around Solo

The fascinating and remote temple complex **Candi Sukuh** (admission 10,000Rp; ⊙ 8am-5pm), on the slopes of Gunung Lawu (3265m), some 36km east of Solo, is well worth a visit. Dating from the 15th century, Sukuh was one of the last temples to be built in Java by Hindus, who were on the run from Muslims and forced to isolated mountain regions (and Bali).

The main pyramid resembles an Incan or Mayan monument, with steep sides and a central staircase; at its base are flat-backed turtles that may have been sacrificial altars. It's clear that a fertility cult was practised here: several explicit carvings have led it to be dubbed the 'erotic' temple. It's a quiet, isolated place with a potent atmosphere. Restorations are due for completion in 2017.

There are a number of homestay options around Candi Sukuh and Nglorok, a nearby village. This area is a lovely place to relax for a few days and enjoy the slow and quiet village pace, the cool climate and the lush greenery.

Virtually all travellers reach the temples on a tour from Solo or Yogyakarta. Public transport is very tricky: take a bus bound for Tawangmangu from Solo as far as Karangpandan (6000Rp), then a Kemuning minibus (2000Rp) to the turn-off to Candi Sukuh; from here it's a steep 2km walk uphill to the site, or a 40,000Rp *ojek* ride. For around 70,000Rp, *ojeks* will take you to both Sukuh and Cetho, a 14th-century temple on the southern face of Gunung Lawi.

Malang & Around

☑ 0341 / POP 820,000

With leafy, colonial-era boulevards and a breezy climate, Malang moves at a far more leisurely pace than the regional capital, Surabaya. It's a cultured city with several important universities, home to a large student population. The central area is not too large and quite walkable.

Established by the Dutch in the closing decades of the 18th century, Malang earned its first fortunes from coffee, which flourished on the surrounding hillsides. With a number of Hindu temples and sights outside the city, Malang makes an ideal base for exploring this intriguing corner of East Java.

◉ Sights

The interior of the busy *alun-alun* in front of Hotel Tugu Malang is a lovely and lively park. Gorgeous spreading trees surround a pond floating with hundreds of lotus blossoms, at the centre of which is a monument to Indonesia's independence struggle.

Hotel Tugu Malang MUSEUM
(www.tuguhotels.com; Jl Tugu III; ☏) Malang's most impressive museum isn't actually a museum at all, but a hotel: the boutique, four-star **Hotel Tugu Malang** (✆0341-363891; r from 900,000Rp; ❋@☏❋). A showcase for its owner, arguably Indonesia's foremost collector of Asian art and antiquities, the exhibit includes 10th-century ceramics, jade carvings from the 13th century, Ming dynasty porcelain, Qing dynasty wood carvings and even the complete facade of a Chinese temple. Visitors are welcome to browse the collection, which is spread throughout the hotel premises (though you might consider it polite to buy a drink while you're here).

Jalan Besar Ijen STREET
Malang has some wonderful colonial architecture. Just northwest of the centre, Jl Besar Ijen is Malang's millionaires' row, a boulevard lined with elegant whitewashed mansions from the Dutch era. Many have been substantially renovated, but there's still much to admire.

In late May, the area is closed to traffic and becomes the setting for the city's huge Malang Kembali festival.

🛏 Sleeping

There's some superb budget accommodation in Malang.

★Kampong Tourist HOSTEL **$**
(✆0341-345797; www.kampongtourist.com; Hotel Helios, Jl Patimura 37; dm/r 120,000/160,000Rp; ☏) 𝄂 The owners of this superb backpacking place have fashioned an excellent hostel on the rooftop of Hotel Helios. Most of the buildings have been beautifully constructed from bamboo and timber, which sprout like village huts from the concrete rooftop. Dorm beds are comfy, as are the gazebo-style private rooms, and there's a great shared shower block and guests' kitchen too.

Jona's Homestay HOMESTAY **$**
(✆0341-324678; Jl Sutomo 4; s/d with fan 115,000/130,000Rp, d with air-con from 230,000Rp; ❋☏) This long-running homestay in a colossal colonial villa, with a digital ticker out front, is run by a sweet family who look after guests well and also offer tours. The location is convenient and quiet, although the rooms have aged somewhat. Some of the air-con options are huge and offer great value for money.

Hotel Emma HOTEL **$**
(✆0341-363198; Jl Trunijoyo 21; r with fan & cold water 150,000-175,000Rp, with air-con & hot water 215,000-250,000Rp; ❋) Almost opposite the train station, this is a tidy, friendly hotel. Rooms are clean and spacious – the deluxe rooms are enormous – and good value. Many rooms have windows that open onto the interior of the building; those can feel claustrophobic. Breakfast is included.

✖ Eating & Drinking

For cheap eats head for Jl Agus Salim, which comes alive at night to the sights and smells of Malang's **night market** (mains 10,000-25,000Rp).

Mie Tomcat NOODLES **$**
(Jl Trunijoyo; dishes 6000-9000Rp; ⏱9am-11pm) A cool new designer warung popular with locals, with a Jenga-like exterior and cherrywood furnishings inside and out. The staff speak no English but they do know how to make some tasty noodle soup, ramen and *mie goreng* (fried noodles). Use the helpful chalkboard spice-meter to stretch your personal heat index.

Goreng Kremes INDONESIAN **$**
(Jl Cokroaminoto 2d; dishes 5000-20,000Rp; ⏱10am-10pm) A dressed-up warung dangling with lovely rattan lanterns and lined with bamboo wallpaper, serving fried chicken and duck meals to the Malang masses. Platters come with raw cabbage and long beans on the side. Rice costs extra.

MALANG KEMBALI

Held in late May, Malang Kembali celebrates *ludruk*, an old-time music hall tradition that was very popular in Java in the last century. Jalan Besar Ijen, home to many wonderful old Dutch villas, is closed to traffic for five days to host street theatre, live music, shows, and actors in period costumes. You can also sample traditional food and drinks.

ℹ Information

Gunung Bromo National Park Head Office
(☑ 0341-490885; tn-bromo@malang.
wasantara.net.id; Jl Raden Intan 6; ⊗8am-3pm
Mon-Thu, to 11am Fri) For Bromo info.
Tourist Information Office (☑ 0341-558919;
Jl Gede 6; ⊗8am-4pm Mon-Fri) Helpful, but
3km northwest of the *alun-alun*.

ℹ Getting There & Away

BUS & ANGKOT

Malang has three bus terminals:
Arjosari, 5km north of town, is the main terminal, with regular buses to Surabaya, Probolinggo and Banyuwangi. Long-distance buses to
Solo, Yogyakarta, Denpasar and Jakarta leave
mostly in the early evening. Minibuses (called
angkot or *mikrolet* locally) run from Arjosari to
nearby villages such as Singosari and Tumpang.
Gadang bus terminal, 5km south of the city
centre, sends buses along the southern routes
to destinations such as Blitar (33,000Rp to
54,000Rp, two hours).
Landungsari bus terminal, 5km northwest of
the city, sends buses to destinations west of
the city, such as Batu (10,000Rp, 40 minutes).

MINIBUS

Plenty of door-to-door *travel* companies operate
from Malang, and hotels and travel agencies
can book them. **Helios Tours** (☑ 0341-362741;
www.heliostour.net; Jl Pattimura 37) and **Wijaya
Travel** (☑ 0341-327072) are two reliable agencies. Minibuses travel to Solo (150,000Rp),
Yogyakarta (150,000Rp) and Probolinggo
(60,000Rp).

TRAIN

Malang train station (☑ 0341-362208) is
centrally located but not well connected to
the main network. There are three daily trains
to Yogyakarta (250,000Rp, eight hours) via
Solo. Surabaya is served only by very slow and
crowded economy trains. There is also a daily
service to Banyuwangi (65,000Rp, 7½ hours),
where you can hop a ferry to Bali.

ℹ Getting Around

Mikrolet run all over town. Most buzz between
the bus terminals via the town centre. These are
marked A–G (Arjosari to Gadung and return),
A–L (Arjosari to Landungsari) or G–L (Gadang to
Landungsari). Trips cost 3000Rp.

Gunung Bromo

☑ 0335
A lunaresque landscape of epic proportions
and surreal beauty, Gunung Bromo (2329m)
is one of Indonesia's most breathtaking
sights. Bromo is the Javanese translation of
Brahma, the Hindu God of creation. It's an
apt name – each of the volcano's eruptions
reshapes the surrounding landscape.

The exploding cone of Bromo is just one
of three peaks to emerge from a vast caldera,
the Tengger Massif (which stretches 10km
across), its steep walls plunging down to a
vast, flat sea of lava and sand. This desolate
landscape has a distinctly end-of-the-world
feeling, particularly at sunrise.

An even larger cone, Java's largest mountain, the fume-belching Gunung Semeru
(3676m), oversees Bromo's beauty, and
the entire volcanic wonderland forms the
Bromo-Tengger-Semeru National Park.

The usual jumping-off point for Bromo is
the town of Probolinggo, which is served by
trains and buses from Surabaya and Banyuwangi; it's also easily reached via Malang.

◉ Sights & Activities

The classic Bromo tour peddled by all hotels
and guides in Cemoro Lawang (and other
villages) involves a pick-up around 3.30am
and a 4WD drive up to the neighbouring
peak of **Gunung Penanjakan** (2770m). This
viewpoint offers the best vistas (and photographs) of the entire Bromo landscape, with
Gunung Semeru puffing away on the horizon. After sunrise, 4WDs head back down
the steep lip of the crater and then over

INDONESIA GUNUNG BROMO

BUSES FROM ARJOSARI TERMINAL (MALANG)

DESTINATION	FARE (RP)	DURATION (HR)	FREQUENCY
Banyuwangi	39,500-71,000	7	7am & 1pm
Denpasar	150,000	12	5pm
Probolinggo	22,000-36,000	2½	hourly 5am-5pm
Solo (Surakarta)	100,000	10	6.30pm
Surabaya	25,000	2½-3	hourly
Yogyakarta	105,000	11	7am, 1pm & 6.30pm

TEMPLES AROUND MALANG

The beautiful countryside around Malang is littered with the debris of times past. It's worth getting a group together and hiring a car for a half-day temple exploration (you can also arrange a drop-off in the Bromo area afterwards). **Helios Tours** (☑ 0341-362741; www.heliostour.net; Jl Pattimura 37) are the best people to talk to about doing this. The Singosari temples are mostly funerary temples dedicated to the kings of the Singosari dynasty (AD 1222–92), the precursors of the Majapahit kingdom.

Candi Singosari (◎ 7am-5pm) Situated right in the village of Singosari, 12km north of Malang, this temple stands 500m off the main Malang–Surabaya road. One of the last monuments erected to the Singosari dynasty, it was built in 1304 in honour of King Kertanegara, the fifth and last Singosari king, who died in 1292 in a palace uprising.

Candi Sumberawan (◎ 7am-5pm) This small, squat Buddhist stupa lies in the terraced, cultivated foothills of Gunung Arjuna, about 5km northwest of Singosari. It was built to commemorate the 1359 visit of Hayam Wuruk, the great Majapahit king. Within the temple grounds are a lingam stone and the crumbling origins of additional stupa along with the remains of recent offerings. But what makes it special is the approach.

Candi Jago (Jajaghu; admission 25,000Rp; ◎ 7am-5pm) Along a small road near the market in Tumpang, 22km from Malang, Candi Jago was built between 1268 and 1280 and is thought to be a memorial to the fourth Singosari king, Vishnuvardhana. The temple has some interesting decorative carving from the Jataka and the Mahabharata, carved in the three-dimensional, *wayang kulit*–style typical of East Java.

Candi Kidal (admission 5000Rp; ◎ 7am-4pm) Set in the village of Kidal, with houses rising all around – along with one conspicuously clucking chicken farm – this graceful temple was built around 1260 as the burial shrine of King Anusapati (the second Singosari king, who died in 1248). Now 12m high, it originally topped 17m and is an example of East Javanese architecture. Its slender form has pictures of the garuda (Indonesia's mythical bird and national symbol) on three sides, plus bold, glowering *kala* heads and medallions of the *haruna*.

the Laotian Pasir (Sea of Sand) to the base of Bromo. It's usually easy to hook up with others for this tour to share costs. Private jeeps cost 500,000Rp. If you pay for a single seat, expect to be crammed in with four or five others, though the price (150,000Rp) is right. In busy times, expect crowds.

Alternatively, it's a two-hour hike to the top of Gunung Penanjakan, the so-called second viewpoint, from Cemoro Lawang. But King Kong Hill – perched just 20 minutes beyond the first viewpoint on Penanjakan, set on a ledge jutting out from the main trail – has even better views than the top. From here looking toward the west you'll see Bromo, along with Gunung Batok, bathed in that dawn light, with Gunung Semeru photobombing from behind. It can take up to an hour to reach it, but it's a stunning walk. Just up from the village, the slopes are planted with scallions, potatoes and cauliflower. You won't see them in the dark, but they make a lovely vista on the easy downhill stroll.

🛏 Sleeping & Eating

🛏 Cemoro Lawang

At the lip of the Tengger crater and right at the start of the walk to Bromo, Cemoro Lawang is the most popular place to stay and has plenty of cheap accommodation, although all of it's overpriced.

Tengger Indah HOMESTAY $
(r from 150,000Rp) An east-facing homestay in town, a stone's throw from the rim at the junction. It's prim and painted with murals on the exterior; the interiors are simple, tiled and affordable. Nothing fancy.

Cafe Lava Hostel HOTEL $$
(☑ 0335-541020; r without bathroom from 175,000Rp, with bathroom & breakfast from 425,000Rp; 🛜) With a sociable vibe thanks to its streetside cafe and attractive layout (rooms are scattered down the side of a valley), this is first choice for most travellers, despite the steep prices. Economy rooms are very small

but neat, and have access to a shared veran-dah and clean communual bathrooms (fitted with all-important hot showers).

Ngadisari

Another 3km back towards Probolinggo is the tiny village of Ngadisari.

Yoschi's Hotel   GUESTHOUSE $
(☎ 0335-541018; www.hotelyoschi.com; r without shower 240,000Rp, with shower from 540,000Rp, cottages from 900,000Rp; @ 🛜) This rustic place has lots of character, with bungalows and small rooms dotted around a large, leafy garden compound. However, many lack hot water and cleanliness standards could be better. There's a huge restaurant that serves up pricey Western and Indonesian food (subject to a stiff 20% service charge).

Probolinggo

On the highway between Surabaya and Banyuwangi, this is the jumping-off point for Gunung Bromo. Most travellers only see the bus or train station, but the town has hotels if you get stuck.

Sinar Harapan   HOTEL $
(☎ 0335-701 0335; Jl Bengawan Solo 100; r 120,000-200,000Rp; ❄🛜) This new hotel has a contemporary feel, but its shine is fading. It rents out motorbikes for 60,000Rp per day.

ⓘ Information

However you approach Bromo, a 75,000Rp park fee is payable at one of the many PHKA (National Parks Office) checkpoints.
PHKA Post (☎ 0335-541038; ⊙8am-3pm Tue-Sun) The PHKA post in Cemoro Lawang is opposite Hotel Bromo Permai, and has infor-mation about Bromo. Note that the Gunung Penanjakan viewpoint is outside the park and these fees are not applicable. The Sea of Sand, though, is within the national park and you'll need to pay your fee at the park office on the edge of Cemoro Lawang. Tickets are valid for the duration of your stay.

ⓘ Getting There & Away

Probolinggo is the main gateway to Bromo. Hotels in the Bromo area can book minivans to Probolinggo (35,000Rp, two hours) where you can catch long-distance buses to Yogyakarta (90,000Rp to 150,000Rp, 10 to 11 hours) and Denpasar (125,000Rp to 150,000Rp, 11 hours). Note that the bus station has a bad rep for touts.

Many people arrive on tours from Yogyakarta, which involves a punishing overland journey, usually in a cramped minibus. Alternatively, if you don't mind changing transport, the most comfortable (and fastest) way to cover this route is Yogyakarta to Surabaya by train, then a train or bus to Probolinggo and a minibus up to Cemoro Lawang.

Bondowoso

☎ 0332 / POP 71,000
Bondowoso is the gateway to Bromo and Ijen and home to some of the island's best *tape*, a tasty, sweet-and-sour snack made from boiled and fermented vegetable roots. It's mainly a transit and market town; tours to Ijen can be organised here.

Sleeping

Palm Hotel   HOTEL $$
(☎ 0332-421201; www.palm-hotel.net; Jl A Yani 32; r incl breakfast with fan & mandi 190,000Rp, with air-con 320,000-610,000Rp; ❄🛜❄) Just south of the huge, grassy *alun-alun*, this good-value hotel's huge, heat-busting pool makes it a great escape from Java's punishing humid-ity. Take your pick from simple fan-only options with cold-water *mandi* or smart, spacious air-conditioned rooms that show a minimalist design influence.

ⓘ Getting There & Away

There are many (cramped) minibuses to Ijen (35,000Rp), all leaving before noon for the 2½-hour trip.

Ijen Plateau

The Ijen Plateau is a vast volcanic re-gion dominated by the three cones of Ijen (2368m), Merapi (2800m) and Raung (3332m). A beautiful and thickly forested al-pine area, these thinly populated highlands harbour coffee plantations and a few isolat-ed settlements.

Virtually everyone who does come is here for the hike up to the spectacular crater lake of Kawah Ijen. You can see the mountain's dramatic, gaping mouth loom-ing above the highland rim. Those kinds of sweeping vistas, combined with a temper-ate climate, make the plateau a great base for a few days up in the clouds and away from the crowds.

SURABAYA

Surabaya's airport is the third-busiest in the country and many travellers transit through its scattered terminals. This may be your only reason to visit the city, which is polluted, congested and lacking in tourist appeal. Just crossing the eight-lane highways that rampage through the centre is a challenge in itself.

The centre does have a fascinating **Arab Quarter** – usually called Ampel or Kampung Arab – with the atmosphere and appearance of a North African medina. It's a warren of narrow lanes, marked by arched gateways crowned with Arabic script, and crowded with stalls. All alleys lead to the **Mesjid Ampel** (Jl Ampel Suci) `FREE`, where Sunan Ampel (one of the *wali songo*, the 'nine holy men' who brought Islam to Java) was buried in 1481.

If for some reason you need to spend the night, note that good budget options are few. The basic **Hotel Paviljoen** (☑031-534 3449; Jl Genteng Besar 94-98; r with fan/air-con from 150,000/198,000-220,000Rp; ✳) is a colonial villa that still has a twinkle of charm and grandeur. **Citihub** (☑031-535 7066, 031-502 9292; www.citihubhotels.com; Jl Gub Suryo IJ; r 375,000Rp; ✳@⊛) is a worthwhile step up for clean and comfortable rooms.

◉ Sights & Activities

The magnificent turquoise sulphur lake of **Kawah Ijen** lies at 2148m above sea level and is surrounded by the volcano's sheer crater walls. At the edge of the lake, sulphurous smoke billows from the volcano's vent and the lake bubbles when activity increases. Ijen's last major eruption was in 1936.

Ijen is a major sulphur-gathering centre and you'll pass the collectors as you hike up the trail. Most now ask for a fee for photographs, though a cigarette will usually be accepted as payment.

The ideal time to make the Kawah Ijen hike is in the dry season between April and October. However, while the path is steep, it's usually not too slippery, so the hike is certainly worth a try in the rainy season if you have a clear day. Make it for sunrise if you can.

The starting point for the trek to the crater is the **PHKA post** (admission weekdays/weekends 100,000/150,000Rp; ☉7am-5pm) at Pos Paltuding, which can be reached from Bondowoso or Banyuwangi. Sign in and pay your entry fee here. The steep 3km path up to the observation post (where there's a teahouse) takes just over an hour; keep an eye out for gibbons. From the post it's a further 30-minute walk to the lip of the wind-blasted crater and its stunning views.

From the crater, a steep, gravelly path leads down to the lake and the sulphur deposits. Due to the extreme conditions, many people choose not to descend down into the crater and content themselves with a peek over the crater rim. If you do continue down to the lake, make sure you are suitably equipped: the sulphur gases are highly noxious and it's absolutely essential that you have some kind of face mask. People with any kind of respiratory problems, or those travelling with children, should not descend into the base of the crater.

🛏 Sleeping & Eating

★**Catimor**   LODGE **$**
(☑0813 3619 9110, 0813 5799 9800; catimor_n12@yahoo.com; r 125,000-325,000Rp; ⊛⊛) This budget lodge boasts an excellent location in the Kebun Balawan coffee plantation, close to hot springs. Unfortunately, there has been little or no maintenance for some time and the whole place is pretty creaky (especially inside the original wooden Dutch lodge, which dates back to 1894). There's also a separate block of cheap, reasonably clean, if featureless rooms.

Arabika   LODGE **$**
(☑081 1350 5881, 082 8330 1347; arabica.homestay@gmail.com; r incl breakfast 175,000-325,000Rp; ⊛) This dated, usually chilly mountain lodge is managed by the Kebun Kalisat coffee plantation, which is a short walk away. Sadly, it's not in great shape these days, and cleanliness could be better – the more you pay the cleaner the rooms seem to get – but all rooms have hot water and a bathtub in which to enjoy it.

ℹ Getting There & Away

It is possible to travel nearly all the way to Kawah Ijen by public transport, but most visitors charter transport.

FROM BONDOWOSO

From Wonosari, 8km from Bondowoso towards Situbondo, a rough, potholed road runs via Suko-sari and Sempol to Pos Paltuding. It's normally passable in any high-clearance vehicle, but sometimes a 4WD is necessary. Sign in at the coffee-plantation checkpoints (around 5000Rp) on the way.

By public transport, several *angkot* run from Bondowoso to Sempol (25,000Rp, 2½ hours), most in the late morning, but there's a final one at 3pm. If passengers want to continue on to Pos Paltuding drivers will sometimes do so. Otherwise, *ojek* in Sempol charge around 30,000Rp one-way.

FROM BANYUWANGI

The Banyuwangi–Ijen road was in good condition at research time, though it has been known to be impossibly rutted in the past. Check locally for current conditions before setting off. There's no public transport all the way from Banyuwangi to Pos Paltuding, which is a sparsely populated region.

Jeep-style cars (650,000Rp per vehicle) can be arranged through the Banyuwangi Tourist Office. Chartering an *ojek* from Banyuwangi to Ijen is possible for around 200,000Rp (including a wait of four hours). *Ojek* drivers hang around the ferry terminal in Ketapang and Banyuwangi bus station.

Heading back down the mountain, *ojek* charge 75,000Rp to 100,000Rp for a one-way ride to Banyuwangi from Pos Paltuding.

Banyuwangi
☑ 0333 / POP 115,000

The end of the line, Java's land's end is a pleasant-enough town, and is a good base for the region. Confusingly, the ferry terminus for Bali, bus terminal and train station are all some 8km north of town in the port of Ketapang, even though all transport uses 'Banyuwangi' as a destination.

🛏 Sleeping & Eating

For cheap eats, there are warungs on the corner of Jl MT Haryono and Jl Wahid Haysim.

Hotel Ketapang Indah   HOTEL $$
(☑ 0333-422280; www.ketapangindahhotel.com; Jl Gatot Subroto; d from 600,000Rp; ❈ 🛜 🌊) This lovely hotel makes a peaceful place to stay. Its huge, well-kept rooms and traditional-style cottages are dotted around a sprawling garden, shaded with coconut palms and extending to the sea. The 18m pool is big enough for laps, though the restaurant is fair at best. It's 2km south of the ferry terminal.

ℹ Information

Banyuwangi Tourist Office (☑ 0333-424172; Jl Ahmad Yani 78; ⏰ 7am-4pm Mon-Thu, to 11am Fri) Staff are helpful at this office. They speak Dutch and some English, and can organise tours.

ℹ Getting There & Away

BOAT
Ferries depart around the clock for Gilimanuk in Bali (every 45 minutes, one hour). The ferry costs 7500Rp for passengers, 25,000Rp for a motorcycle and 148,000Rp for a car (including four passengers). Through-buses between Bali and Java include the fare in the bus ticket.

BUS
Banyuwangi has two bus terminals. The Sri Tanjung terminal is 3km north of Ketapang ferry terminal, 11km from the centre. Buses from here head along the north coast road to Probolinggo (normal/*patas* 40,000/50,000Rp, five hours) and Surabaya (46,000/66,000Rp, seven hours). Buses also go right through to Yogyakarta (*pa-tas* 150,000Rp, 15 hours) and Denpasar (from 70,000Rp, five hours including the ferry trip).

TRAIN
The main Banyuwangi train station is just a few hundred metres north of the ferry terminal. The express Mutiara Timur leaves at 8am and 9.45pm for Probolinggo (economy/business/executive from 60,000/105,000/140,000Rp, five hours) and Surabaya (130,000Rp, seven hours).

SURFING G-LAND

The huge surf at Plengkung, on the isolated southeastern tip of the remote Blambangan Peninsula on the south-eastern tip of Java, forms one of the best left-handed waves in the world, breaking over a shallow reef in perfect barrels. Surfers have dubbed it **G-Land**. It's best between April and September and is mostly experts-only surf territory, though there are also some beginner waves over a sand-bar bottom.

There are three seasonal, all-inclusive surf camps here, including **G-Land Joyo's Surf Camp** (☑ bookings in Bali 036-176 3166; www.g-land.com; three-night packages from US$625; ❈ 🛜) which has nice thatched wooden bungalows and good food. The surf camps arrange transport (including from Bali); other-wise, the best way here is to hire a motorcycle or car in Banyuwangi – the access roads are poor but usually do-able. Much of the area remains rugged and is part of Alas Purwo National Park.

BALI

Impossibly green rice terraces, pulse-pounding surf, enchanting Hindu temple ceremonies, mesmerising dance performances, ribbons of beaches, truly charming people: there are as many images of Bali as there are flowers on the ubiquitous frangipani trees.

This small island looms large for any visit to Indonesia. No place is more visitor-friendly. Hotels range from surfer dives to lavish retreats in the lush mountains. You can dine on local foods bursting with flavours fresh from the markets or let world-class chefs take you on a culinary journey around the globe. From a cold Bintang beer at sunset to an epic night out clubbing, your social whirl is limited only by your fortitude.

And small obviously doesn't mean homogeneous. Manic Kuta segues into glitzy Seminyak. The artistic swirl of Ubud is a counterpoint to misty treks amid the volcanoes. Mellow beach towns such as Bingin, Amed and Pemuteran are found right round the coast.

History

Bali's first prehistoric tourists strolled out of the spume and onto the island's western beaches around 3000 BC. Perhaps distracted by primitive beach life, however, they got off to a relaxed start and it was only in the 9th century that an organised society began to develop around the cultivation of rice.

Hinduism followed hot on the heels of wider cultural development, and as Islam swept through neighbouring Java in the following centuries, the kings and courtiers of the embattled Hindu Majapahit kingdom began crossing the straits into Bali, making their final exodus in 1478. The priest Nirartha brought many of the complexities of the Balinese Hindu religion to the island.

In the 19th century the Dutch began to form alliances with local princes in northern Bali. A dispute over the ransacking of wrecked ships was the pretext for the 1906 Dutch invasion of the south, which climaxed in a suicidal *puputan* (fight to the death). The Denpasar nobility burnt their own palaces, dressed in their finest jewellery and, waving golden kris (traditional daggers), marched straight into the Dutch guns.

In later years, Bali's rich and complex culture was actually encouraged by many Dutch officials. International interest was aroused and the first Western tourists arrived in the 1930s.

The tourism boom, which started in the early 1970s, has brought many changes, and has helped pay for improvements in roads, telecommunications, education and health. Though tourism and Bali's sizzling economic development has had marked adverse environmental and social effects, Bali's unique culture has proved to be remarkably resilient, even as visitor numbers approach four million per year.

ⓘ Dangers & Annoyances

Persistent hawkers are the bane of most visitors to Bali. The best way to deal with them is to ignore them from the first instance. 'Temporary' tattoos in any colour may cause permanent damage due to the use of toxic chemicals, and *arak* (alcohol typically distilled from the sap of the coconut palm or from rice) should always be viewed with suspicion. There's also an ongoing rabies problem.

The beaches on the west side of the island, including Kuta and Seminyak, are subject to heavy surf and strong currents. The sea water near touristed areas is commonly contaminated by run-off from both built-up areas and surrounding farmland, especially after heavy rains. You can smell it.

Bali's economic and tourism boom means that traffic is now a huge problem across South Bali. It's also a menace: someone dies on Bali's choked roads every day, reason enough to wear a helmet while riding your motorcycle.

ⓘ Getting There & Away

AIR

The only airport in Bali, Ngurah Rai International Airport (DPS) is just south of Kuta; however, it is sometimes referred to on flight-booking sites as Denpasar or simply as Bali. A vast new terminal opened in 2014.

Bali is a hub for international flights and is Indonesia's second busiest. Domestic services in Bali seem to be in a constant state of flux. However, competition is fierce and you can usually find flights to a range of destinations for under US$100.

BOAT

Ferries operate between Gilimanuk in western Bali and Ketapang, Java.

Lombok is accessible by regular public ferries from Padangbai. Fast boats for tourists serve the Gili Islands.

Pelni ships sporadically link Bali to several other islands. You can inquire and book at the **Pelni office** (☑ 0361-763963; www.pelni.co.id;

Bali

Scale:
20 km
10 miles

Betekan
Selogiri
Gunung
Prapat Agung (310m)
Pulau Menjangan
Labuhan
Ketapang
JAVA
Cekik
Gilimanuk
Banyuwangi
Melaya
Banyuwedang
Pemuteran
Celukanbawang
Gunung Musi (1224m)
Taman Nasional Bali Barat
Gungung Kelatakan (698m)
Gunung Sanglang (1004m)
Gunung Merbuk (13388m)
Negara
Mendoyo
Perancak
Pura Gede Perancak
Pura Rambut Siwi
Medewi
Balian Beach

Bali Sea

Singaraja
Kubutambahan
Sangsit
Sawan
Sukasade
Sangket
Jagaraga
Yeh
Sanih
Pacung
Tejakula
Sembirenteng
Tembok

Lovina
Seririt
Gitgit
Gunung Catur (2096m)
Danau Buyan
Danau Tamblingan
Pupuan
Munduk
Candikuning
Pura Ulun Danu
Bratan (Candikuning)
Pura Luhur Batukau
Gunung Batukau (2276m)
Wongayagede
Pujungan
Penebel

Pengastulen
Rangdu
Mayong

Pacung
Gunung Penulisan (1745m)
Catur
Penulisan
Kintamani
Danau Batur
Gunung Batur (1717m)
Toya Bungkah
Songan
Tianyar
Kubu
Tulamben
Culik
Tirta Gangga
Amed
Aas
Gunung Seraya (1175m)
Ujung
Amlapura
Tenganan
Candidasa
Padangbai
Pampatan
Muncan
Duda
Iseh
Sidemen
Besakih
Gunung Agung (3142m)
Pelaga
Penelokan
Bedugul
Pelaga
Jatiluwih
Petang
Kayubihi
Kayuanbua
Tampaksiring
Pujung
Sangeh
Marga
Pura Taman Ayun
Payangan
Kediri
Antosari

Sembiranteng

Tabanan
Kerobokan
Legian
Kuta
Seminyak
Canggu
Pura Tanah Lot
Ubud
Mas
Mengwi
Celuk
Batubulan
Sempidi
Batuan
Sidan
Sukawati
Ketewel
Bedulu
Pejeng
Bangli
Bukit Jambul
Lebih
Gianyar
Semarapura (Klungkung)
Kusamba
Pura Masceti
Nusa Lembongan
Padangbai

Denpasar
Sanur
Serangan
Pulau Serangan
Benoa Harbour
Ngurah Rai International Airport
Jimbaran
Tanjung Benoa
Nusa Dua
Bukit Peninsula
Bingin
Pecatu
Ulu Watu
Pura Luhur Ulu Watu

Badung Strait

Jungutbatu
Lembongan
Toyapakeh
Nusa Lembongan
Nusa Ceningan
Ped
Sampalan
Karangsari
Semaya
Nusa Penida
529m

Lombok Strait

INDIAN OCEAN

Bali Strait
Tanjung Sembulungan

JAWA TIMUR
322m
375m
Taman Nasional Alas Purwo
Blambangan Peninsula
Plengkung
Rogodjampi

Gili Trawangan (30km); Lombok (35km)
Lombok (25km)
Lombok (30km)

Jl Raya Kuta 299; ⊙ 8am-noon & 1-4pm Mon-Fri, 8am-1pm Sat) in Tuban.

BUS

The Mengwi bus terminal is 12km northwest of Denpasar, just off the main road to West Bali. Many long-distance buses to/from Denpasar's Ubung bus terminal stop here. When travelling to/from South Bali, you can save time (compared to Denpasar) by using this terminal. Metered taxis are available and fares should be 150,000Rp to 200,000Rp.

Ferry crossings to Java and Lombok from Bali are included in the services offered by numerous bus companies, many of which travel overnight to Java. It's advisable to buy your ticket at least one day in advance from a travel agent or at the terminals in Denpasar (Ubang) or Mengwi. Note that flying can be as cheap as the bus.

Fares vary between operators; it's worth paying extra for a decent seat (all have air-con). Typical fares and travel times include Surabaya (150,000Rp, 12 hours), Yogyakarta (350,000Rp, 16 hours) and Jakarta (470,000Rp, 24 hours). You can also get buses from Singaraja in North Bali and minibuses from Kuta.

TRAIN

The **state railway company** (🗷 0361-227131; Jl Diponegoro 150/B4; ⊙ 8am-3pm Mon-Fri, 9am-2pm Sat & Sun) has an office in Denpasar that sells combined tickets for buses that link to train services on Java. Fares and times are comparable to bus-only travel but the air-conditioned trains are more comfortable even in economy class. Note: on the website *'Jadwal'* means schedule.

ⓘ Getting Around

Bali is a small island with good but traffic-clogged roads and myriad transport options.

TO/FROM THE AIRPORT

Fixed-price taxis are found at the airport. The rather high fees range from 110,000Rp for Seminyak to 300,000Rp for Ubud. Save money by walking 300m northeast from the terminal, across the parking lot and busy access road, to catch a metered Bluebird taxi just outside the airport exit.

BEMO & BUS

The main bemo (minibus) hub is in Denpasar, but the proliferation of motorcycles and taxis means that the network is in decline. Bemos don't serve popular spots like Seminyak, and getting from Kuta to Ubud can be an all-day ordeal. Rides cost a minimum of 4000Rp.

Perama (🗷 0361-751170; www.peramatour. com) Along with a slew of other companies, Perama runs tourist shuttle-bus services in Bali. Book at least one day before you want

to travel and note that popular areas like Seminyak and the Bukit Peninsula are poorly served. Rates are about one-third of a taxi's.

Trans-Sarbagita (Jl Imam Bonjol; fare 3500Rp; ⊙ 5am-9pm) Runs large, air-con commuter buses like you find in major cities worldwide. Routes include Batubulan and along the bypass linking Sanur to Nusa Dua, and another running from Denpasar to Jimbaran. The highly visible roadside bus stops have maps. The routes converge at a stop just east of Kuta in the large parking lot south of the Istana Kuta Galleria shopping centre.

BICYCLE

Ask at your accommodation about where you can rent a good bike; hotels often have their own. Prices generally range from 30,000Rp per day.

BOAT

Boats of various sizes and speeds serve Nusa Lembongan and Nusa Penida from Serangan, Sanur and Padangbai.

CAR & MOTORCYCLE

A small jeep is the usual rental vehicle in Bali. Typical costs are 200,000Rp per day, including insurance and unlimited kilometres.

Motorcycles are a popular way to get around Bali, but can be dangerous. Typically you can expect to pay from around 50,000Rp a day. This includes a flimsy helmet, which is compulsory, and sometimes a surfboard rack.

If you don't have an International Driving Permit, ask the renter to take you to the relevant police station in Denpasar, where you can buy a temporary licence (200,000Rp).

Hiring a car with driver will cost from 600,000Rp for an eight- to 10-hour day (includes fuel). You can arrange rentals from your accommodation or in tourist areas just by walking down the street. Offers will pour forth. This is the most common way for transferring from one part of the island to another.

A speedy toll road links the Sanur bypass at Benoa with the airport and Nusa Dua.

TAXI

Metered taxis are common in South Bali. They are essential for getting around Kuta and Seminyak, where you can easily flag one down. But avoid any driver who claims there's a problem with the meter or who won't use it.

The most reputable taxi agency is **Bluebird Taxi** (🗷 0361-701111; www.bluebirdgroup.com), which uses blue vehicles with the words 'Bluebird Group' over the windshield (watch out for myriad fakes). Drivers speak reasonable English, won't offer you illicit opportunities and use the meter at all times. There's also a useful app for summoning a Bluebird taxi.

Uber is now operating in South Bali.

Kuta & Seminyak

☏ 0361

The **Kuta** region is overwhelmingly Bali's largest tourist beach resort. Many budget visitors come here because it's close to the airport and has the greatest range of cheap hotels, restaurants, bars and tourist facilities. It is fashionable to disparage Kuta and its immediate neighbour to the north, **Legian**, for their tawdry vibe and crass commercialism, but the cosmopolitan mixture of beach-party hedonism (magic mushrooms are now sold everywhere) and glitzy diversions like **Beachwalk** (Map p196; www.beachwalkbali.com; Jl Pantai Kuta; ⊙10am-midnight) give it a buzz. At its worst, Legian is the vulgar Oz ghetto not actually found in Australia.

Seminyak is immediately north of Kuta and Legian and in many respects it feels like another island. It's flash, brash and filled with hipsters and expats. Its beach is as wide and sandy as Kuta's, but less crowded. **Kerobokan**, immediately north, is more of the same. You'll find the trendiest restaurants and bars up here.

Busy Jl Legian runs roughly parallel to the beach through Legian and Kuta. Jl Raya Seminyak is the continuation of Jl Legian and is lined with hip shops. Jl Laksmana and Jl Petitenget are the heart of trendy Bali.

Between Jl Legian and the beach is a tangle of narrow side streets, with an amazing hodgepodge of tiny hotels, souvenir stalls, warungs, bars, construction sites and even a few remaining stands of coconut palms. A small lane or alley is known as a *gang*.

◉ Sights

Kuta Beach BEACH

(Map p196) Tourism in Bali began here and is there any question why? Low-key hawkers will sell you soft drinks and beer, snacks and other treats, and you can rent surfboards, lounge chairs and umbrellas (negotiable at 10,000Rp to 20,000Rp) or just crash on the sand. The sunsets here are legendary.

Legian Beach BEACH

(Map p196) An extension of Kuta Beach to the south, Legian Beach is quieter thanks to the lack of a raucous road next to the sand and fewer people.

Seminyak Beach BEACH

(Map p198) Seminyak continues the long sweep of beach past Kuta and Legian. A sunset lounger and an ice-cold Bintang on the beach at sunset is simply magical. A good stretch can be found near Pura Petitenget, and it tends to be less crowded than further south in Kuta.

Smaller crowds also means that the beach is less patrolled and the water conditions less monitored. The odds of encountering dangerous rip currents and other hazards are ever-present, especially as you head north.

🏃 Activities

Kuta's famed beach is a mighty fine place to catch a wave, or learn to catch one. Stalls on the side streets hire out surfboards (for a negotiable 30,000Rp per day) and boogie boards, repair dings and sell new and used boards.

Pro Surf School SURFING

(Map p196; ☏ 0361-751200; www.prosurfschool.com; Jl Pantai Kuta; lessons from €45) Right along Kuta Beach, this well-regarded school has been getting beginners standing for years. It offers all levels of lessons, and also has a hostel (dorms from €15).

Rip Curl School of Surf SURFING

(Map p196; ☏ 0361-735858; www.ripcurlschoolofsurf.com; Jl Arjuna; lessons from 700,000Rp) Usually universities sell shirts with their logos; here it's the other way round: the beachwear company sponsors a school. Lessons at all levels are given across the south; there are special courses for kids. It has a location for kitesurfing, windsurfing and SUP in Sanur.

Sundari Day Spa SPA

(Map p198; ☏ 0361-735073; www.sundari-dayspa.com; Jl Petitenget 7; massages from 200,000Rp; ⊙10am-10pm) This lovely spa strives to offer the services of a five-star resort without the high prices. The massage oils and other potions are organic, and there's a full menu of therapies and treatments on offer.

🛏 Sleeping

The popularity of South Bali means that you'll need to look hard for a place to stay for under 200,000Rp a night.

🛏 Kuta & Legian

Wandering the *gangs* looking for a cheap room is a rite of passage for many. Small and family-run options are still numerous even as chains and five-star resorts crowd in.

Kuta & Legian

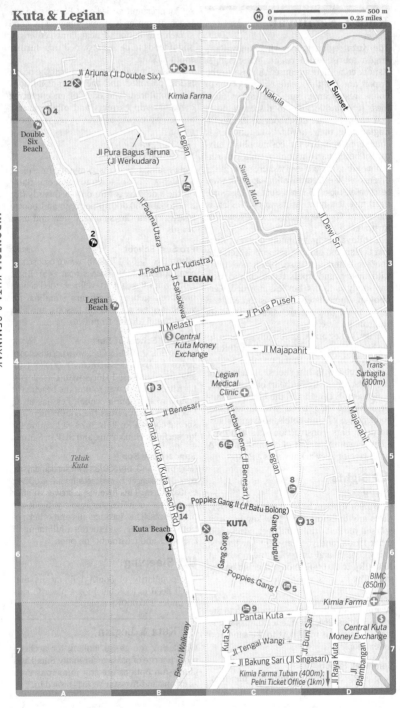

N

0   500 m
0   0.25 miles

Jl Arjuna (Jl Double Six)
12

4
Double Six Beach

Kimia Farma

Jl Nakula

Jl Sunset

Jl Legian

Jl Pura Bagus Taruna
(Jl Werkudara)

Jl Padma Utara

7

Sungai Mati

Jl Dewi Sri

2

Jl Padma (Jl Yudistra)

LEGIAN

Jl Sahadewa

Legian Beach

Jl Pura Puseh

Jl Melasti

Central Kuta Money Exchange

Jl Majapahit

Trans-Sarbagita
(300m)

Legian Medical Clinic

3

Jl Benesari

Jl Lebak Bene (Jl Benesari)

Jl Legian

Jl Majapahit

Teluk Kuta

6

8

Poppies Gang II (Jl Batu Bolong)

14

KUTA

13

Kuta Beach
1

10

Gang Sorga

Gang Bedugul

BIMC
(850m)

Poppies Gang I

5

Kimia Farma

9

Jl Pantai Kuta

Central Kuta Money Exchange

Kuta Sq

Jl Tengal Wangi

Jl Buni Sari

Jl Bakung Sari (Jl Singasari)

Jl Blambangan

Jl Raya Kuta

Beach Walkway

Kimia Farma Tuban (400m);
Pelni Ticket Office (1km)

Kuta & Legian

★ **Hotel Ayu Lili Garden** HOTEL **$**
(Map p196; ☏ 0361-750557; ayuliligardenhotel@
yahoo.com; off Jl Lebak Bene; r with fan/air-con
from 175,000/226,000Rp; ❄ ⚟) In a *relatively*
quiet area near the beach, this vintage
family-run hotel has 22 bungalow-style
rooms. Standards are high and for more
dosh you can add amenities such as a fridge.

Funky Monkey Hostel HOSTEL **$**
(Map p196; ☏ 0812 4636 4386; www.funkymonkey-
bali.com; Poppies Lane 1; dm 60,000-120,000Rp, r
300,000Rp; ❄ ⚟ ⚟) In a lovely location in the
back alleys of Kuta, close to Poppies Restaurant, this homely and intimate Dutch-run
hostel is a top place to meet fellow travellers. There's a small pool, free pancakes and
cheap beer. The cheaper dorms are outdoor
bunks.

**Kayun Hostel
Downtown** HOSTEL **$**
(Map p196; ☏ 0361-758442; www.kayun-downtown.
com; Jl Legian; dm incl breakfast from 190,000Rp;
❄ ⚟ ⚟) In the heart of Kuta, close to all
the nightlife, this hostel is the place to be if
you're here to party. Set in an elegant colonial building, the place has a sense of style
and there's a small plunge pool. Dorm rooms
have between four and 20 beds, with curtains for privacy.

**Kuta Bed &
Breakfast** GUESTHOUSE **$**
(Map p196; ☏ 0821 4538 9646, 0818 568 364;
hanafi@consultant.com; Jl Pantai Kuta 1 E; r from
250,000Rp; ❄ ⚟) There are nine comfortable rooms in this spanking-new guesthouse
right across from Bemo Corner – it's got all
the basics. It's a 10-minute walk from the
beach and a 10-minute ride from the airport.

Island GUESTHOUSE **$$**
(Map p196; ☏ 0361-762722; www.theislandhotel
bali.com; Gang Abdi; dm/r incl breakfast from
250,000/500,000Rp; ❄ @ ⚟ ⚟) One of Bali's
few flashpacker options, Island is a real find –
literally. Hidden in the attractive maze of
tiny lanes west of Jl Legian, this stylish place
with a sparkling pool lies at the confluence
of Gang 19, 21 and Abdi. It has a deluxe
dorm room with eight beds.

🛏 Seminyak & Kerobokan

The stylish surrounds can make it hard to
find a cheap sleep in these rarefied climes,
but persistence can pay off.

★ **Ned's Hide-Away** GUESTHOUSE **$**
(Map p198; ☏ 0361-731270; nedshide@dps.
centrin.net.id; Gang Bima 3; r with fan/air-con from
180,000/300,000Rp; ❄ ⚟) While its stand-
ards have slipped in recent times, Ned's
remains a good budget choice with its mix
of basic and more plush rooms. Wi-fi is only
available in the reception area.

M Boutique Hostel HOSTEL **$**
(Map p198; ☏ 0361-473 4142; www.mboutique
hostel.com; Jl Petitenget 8; dm 150,000Rp;
❄ @ ⚟ ⚟) A tasteful and contemporary
choice for backpackers, M Boutique's beds
are capsule dorms, which come with the
benefit of privacy. Each has shutter blinds,
a small table, a reading light and a power
point. The neatly trimmed lawn and small
plunge pool add charm. Rates go up slightly
on weekends.

Raja Gardens GUESTHOUSE **$**
(Map p198; ☏ 0361-730494; jdw@eksadata.com;
off Jl Camplung Tanduk; r with fan/air-con from
400,000/600,000Rp; ❄ ⚟ ⚟) Here since 1980,

Seminyak & Kerobokan

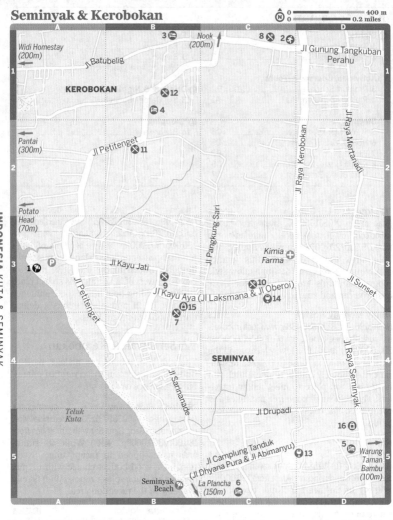

Seminyak & Kerobokan

this old-school guesthouse has spacious, grassy grounds with fruit trees and a quiet spot located almost on the beach. The eight rooms are fairly basic but there are open-air bathrooms and plenty of potted plants. The pool is a nice spot to lounge by, and it's generally a mellow place popular with youngish couples.

Brown Feather B&B $$
(Map p198; ☑ 0361-473 2165; www.brownfeather. com; Jl Batu Belig 100; r incl breakfast 700,000-900,000Rp; ❋ 🛜 🏊) On the main road, but backing on to rice paddies, this B&B exudes a Dutch-Javanese colonial charm. Rooms mix simplicity with old-world character, such as wooden writing desks and wash basins made from old Singer sewing machines. For rice-field views, go for room 205 or 206. There's a small, attractive pool and free bicycle rental, too.

✗ Eating

There's an incredible selection of restaurants in South Bali, from no-nonsense noodle bars to seriously swanky eateries in Seminyak. For excellent local fare, head north towards Kerobokan.

✗ Kuta & Legian

Busy Jl Pantai Kuta keeps beachside businesses to a minimum in Kuta. Beach vendors are pretty much limited to drinks. A clutch of cafes front popular Double Six beach at the end of Jl Arjuna.

Saleko INDONESIAN $
(Map p196; Jl Nakula 4; meals from 11,000Rp; ☉ 8am-11pm) If you haven't tried Masakan Padang food yet, you haven't eaten proper Indonesian. Saleko is a great place to sample this simple, delicious and cheap Sumatran street food. Spicy grilled chicken and fish dare you to ladle on the volcanic sambal – not de-spiced for timid tourist palates. All dishes are halal; there's no alcohol.

Warung Asia Thai Food ASIAN $
(Map p196; ☑ 0361-742 0202; Jl Werkudara; meals from 32,000Rp; ☉ 11am-late; 🛜) Staffed by exceptionally friendly waiters, this popular upstairs warung serves both Indo classics and Thai fare. It gets boozy and raucous at night.

★**Fat Chow** ASIAN $$
(Map p196; ☑ 0361-753516; www.fatchowbali.com; Poppies Gang II; mains from 60,000Rp; ☉ 10am-11pm; 🛜) A stylish, modern take on the traditional open-fronted cafe, Fat Chow serves up Asian-accented fare at long picnic tables, small tables and lounges. The food is creative, with lots of options for sharing. Among the favourites: crunchy Asian salad, pork buns, Tokyo prawns and authentic *pàt tai*.

✗ Seminyak & Kerobokan

Seminyak and Kerobokan have a great choice of inexpensive places, alongside some of Asia's most remarkable restaurants.

★**Warung Sulawesi** INDONESIAN $
(Map p198; Jl Petitenget; meals from 30,000Rp; ☉ 10am-6pm) Find a table in this quiet family compound and enjoy fresh Balinese and Indonesian food served in classic warung style. Choose a rice, then pick from a captivating array of dishes that are always at their peak at noon. The long beans are yum!

★**Nook** ASIAN $
(☑ 0813 3806 0060; Jl Umalas I; mains from 35,000Rp; ☉ 8am-11pm; 🛜) Sublimely positioned among the rice fields, this casual, open-air cafe is popular for its creative takes on Asian fare. It's got a modern vibe mixed with tropical flavours. Good breakfasts and lunchtime sandwiches.

Warung Aneka Rasa INDONESIAN $
(Map p198; Jl Kayu Aya; meals from 20,000Rp; ☉ 7am-8pm) Keeping things real in the heart of Seminyak's upmarket retail ghetto, this humble warung cooks up all the Indo classics in an inviting open-front cafe.

Revolver CAFE $
(Map p198; off Jl Kayu Aya; breakfast from 40,000Rp; ☉ 7am-6pm; 🛜) Wander down a tiny *gang* and push through narrow wooden doors to reach this matchbox of a coffee bar that does an

---

SPLURGE

Seafood fresh from the famous Jimbaran market is the star at elegant yet intimate, casual yet stylish **Sardine** (Map p198; ☑ 0811 397 8111; www.sardine-bali.com; Jl Petitenget 21; meals US$20-50; ☉ 11.30am-4pm & 6-11pm; 🛜), set in a beautiful bamboo pavilion. Open-air tables overlook a private rice field patrolled by Sardine's own flock of ducks. The inventive bar is a must and open to 1am. Fallen in love on your journey? Propose here! Booking is vital.

excellent selection of brews. There are just a few tables in the creatively retro room that's styled like a Wild West saloon; nab one and enjoy tasty fresh bites for breakfast and lunch. The juices are also worth a try.

Warung Taman Bambu　　　BALINESE $
(☑ 0361-888 1567; JI Plawa 10; mains from 25,000Rp; ☺ 9am-10pm; 🛜) This classic warung may look simple from the street but the comfy tables are – like the many fresh and spicy dishes on offer – a cut above the norm. There's a small stand for *babi guling* (suckling pig) right next door.

Warung Eny　　　BALINESE $
(Map p198; ☑ 0361-473 6892; JI Petitenget; mains from 35,000Rp; ☺ 8am-11pm) The eponymous Eny cooks everything herself at this tiny open-front warung nearly hidden behind various potted plants. Look for the roadside sign that captures the vibe: 'The love cooking'. The seafood, such as large prawns smothered in garlic, is delicious and most ingredients are organic. Ask about Eny's fun cooking classes.

Sisterfields　　　CAFE $$
(Map p198; ☑ 0811 386 0507; www.sisterfieldsbali. com; JI Kayu Cendana 7; mains from 60,000Rp; ☺ 7am-5pm; 🛜) Trendy Sisterfields does classic brekkies such as smashed avocado, and more inventive dishes such as truffled oyster mushrooms with duck eggs and crispy pig ears. There are also hipster faves like pulled-pork rolls and lobster sliders. Grab a seat at a booth, the counter or in the rear courtyard.

Drinking & Nightlife

Sunset on the beach at around 6pm is the big attraction, perhaps while enjoying a drink at a cafe with a sea view or with a beer vendor on the beach. Later on, the legendary nightlife action heats up.

Bali's rowdiest clubs cluster in about a 300m radius of **Sky Garden Lounge** (Map p196; www.skygardenbali.com; JI Legian 61; ☺ 24hr). You'll find many low-key boozers amid their flashier brethren along JI Legian. In Seminyak numerous scenester spots line JI Pantai Kaya Aya.

★**La Favela**　　　BAR
(Map p198; ☑ 0361-730603; www.lafavela.com; JI Kayu Aya 177X; ☺ noon-late; 🛜) Full of bohemian flair, La Favela is one of Bali's coolest and most original night spots. Themed rooms lead you on a confounding tour from dimly lit speakeasy cocktail lounges and antique dining rooms to graffiti-splashed bars. Tables are cleared after 11pm to make way for DJs and a dance floor.

It's equally popular for its garden restaurant, which has a Mediterranean-inspired menu.

La Plancha　　　BAR
(☑ 0361-730603; off JI Camplung Tanduk; ☺ 8am-midnight) The most substantial of the beach bars along the beach walk south of JI Camplung Tanduk, La Plancha has its share of ubiquitous brightly coloured umbrellas and beanbags on the sand, plus a menu of Spanish-accented bites. After sunset, expect DJs and beach parties.

SUNSET BEERS ON A BUDGET

Bali sunsets regularly explode in stunning displays of reds, oranges and purples. Sipping a cold one while watching this free show to the beat of the surf is the top activity at 6pm. Try these spots:

Legian The best place is the strip of beach that starts north of JI Padma. Along this car-free stretch of sand you'll find genial young local guys with simple chairs and cheap, cold beer (20,000Rp).

Seminyak At the beach end of JI Abimanyu turn left for a purely Balinese experience: all manner of simple bars line the path along the sand. You'll discover mock-Moorish affairs with oodles of huge pillows for lounging and more. A bit north, skip over-hyped Ku De Ta and grab a cheap beach beer (25,000Rp) from a vendor. Slouch in a lounger and enjoy the same views as the swells above you.

Kerobokan On Batubelig Beach, just north along the sand from the W Hotel, are a couple of open-air bamboo beach bars that have cheap drinks and fab views. The authorities regularly bulldoze **Pantai** (☺ 9am-9pm) but the plucky owners always return.

Potato Head BEACH CLUB

(☑0361-473 7979; www.ptthead.com; Jl Petitenget; ☺11am-2am; ☏) Bali's original beach club is still one of the best. Wander up off the sand or follow a long drive off Jl Petitenget and you'll find much to amuse, from an enticing pool to a swanky restaurant, plus lots of lounges and patches of lawn for chillin' the night away under the stars.

Bali Jo LGBT

(Map p198; ☑0361-847 5771; www.balijoebar.com; Jl Camplung Tanduk; ☺3pm-3am; ☏) One of several lively LGBT venues along this strip. Drag queens and go-go dancers rock the house nightly.

🛍 Shopping

Kuta has a vast concentration of cheap places, as well as huge, flashy surf-gear emporiums on Kuta Sq and Jl Legian.

Seminyak shops could occupy days of your holiday. Designer boutiques (Bali has a thriving fashion industry), retro chic stores, slick galleries, wholesale emporiums and family-run workshops are just some of the choices.

In Kerobokan look for boutiques interspersed with the trendy restaurants on Jl Petitenget.

★ Drifter CLOTHING, ACCESSORIES

(Map p198; ☑0361-733274; www.driftersurf.com; Jl Kayu Aya 50; ☺7.30am-11pm) High-end surf fashion, surfboards, gear, cool books and brands such as Obey and Wegener. Started by two savvy surfer dudes, the shop stocks goods noted for their individuality and high quality. There's also a small cafe-bar and a patio.

Duzty CLOTHING

(Map p198; Jl Raya Seminyak 67; ☺9am-10pm) In an industry dominated by foreigners, it's refreshing to see a local label. T-shirts here are designed by a young Balinese lad, Rahsun. They feature edgy rock-and-roll and counter-culture themes. There are also a few women's tank tops.

ℹ Information

You'll find tour-booking agencies every few metres along the main tourist streets of Kuta.

ATMs abound and can be found everywhere, including in the ubiquitous Circle K convenience stores (which have the best prices). Be very careful with 'authorised' money changers. Extra fees may apply, or they may be adeptly short-changing customers.

Kimia Farma is a good chain of local pharmacies.

BIMC (☑0361-761263; www.bimcbali.com; Jl Ngurah Rai 100X; ☺24hr) On the bypass road just east of Kuta near the Bali Galleria shopping mall. It's a modern Australian-run clinic that can do tests, hotel visits and arrange medical evacuation. Visits can cost US$100 or more. It has a branch in Nusa Dua.

Central Kuta Money Exchange (Map p196; ☑0361-762970; Jl Raya Kuta; ☺8am-6pm) Trustworthy and deals in numerous currencies. Has many locations, including a branch in **Legian** (Map p196; Jl Melasti; ☺8am-10pm) and counters inside some Circle K convenience stores.

ℹ Getting There & Away

Bemos regularly travel between Kuta and the Tegal terminal in Denpasar – the fare should be 8000Rp. The route goes from Jl Raya Kuta near Jl Pantai Kuta, loops past the beach, and then on Jl Melasti and back past Bemo Corner for the trip back to Denpasar.

Tourist buses serve Sanur, Ubud, Padangbai and Lovina.

ℹ Getting Around

Metered cabs from Bluebird (p194) are easily hailed. A taxi to the heart of Kuta from Seminyak will be about 40,000Rp. You can beat the horrific traffic, save the ozone and have a good stroll by walking there along the beach instead.

Canggu & Around

Canggu adjoins Kerobokan to the north, and with its neighbour Umalas, is the next fast-developing area of the south. Look for great beaches, epic surf and cool businesses – often run by trendy and entrepreneurial expats.

Just up the coast from Batubelig Beach, **Batu Bolong Beach** is a few kilometres along the sand northwest of Seminyak (but a long drive around). Just 500m northwest of Batu Bolong Beach (walk up the sand), **Echo Beach** (Batu Mejan) has condos, trendy shops and beachside cafes. Both are popular with expats living in nearby villas.

🛏 Sleeping

Serenity Eco Guesthouse & Yoga GUESTHOUSE $

(☑0361-846 9257; www.serenityecoguesthouse.com; Jl Nelayan; dm/s/d with fan 165,000/203,000/440,000Rp, d with air-con 495,000Rp; ❋☏✿) ✔ This hotel is an oasis among the sterility of walled villas. Rooms range from shared-bathroom singles to quite nice doubles with bathrooms. The grounds are appealingly eccentric; Nelayan Beach is a five-minute walk. There are yoga classes (from 100,000Rp) and you can rent surfboards, bikes, cars and more.

Widi Homestay HOMESTAY $
(☑ 0819 3303 2322; widihomestay@yahoo.co.id; Jl Pantai Berawa; r from 250,000Rp; ❋ ⟨) There's no faux hipster vibe here, just a spotless, friendly, family-run homestay. The four rooms have hot water and air-con; the beach is barely 100m away.

Ketapang Guest House GUESTHOUSE $
(☑ 0815 5843 4626; barbequw@yahoo.com; Jl Pantai Batu Mejan; s/d incl breakfast 250,000/350,000Rp; ❋) Given its proximity to Echo Beach, Ketapang offers exceptional value, with huge modern tile-floor rooms, free breakfast, air-con, hot-water showers and free drinking-water refills.

✗ Eating & Drinking

Betelnut Cafe CAFE $
(☑ 0821 4680 7233; Jl Pantai Batu Bolong; mains from 45,000Rp; ⟨ 7am-10pm; ⟨) There's a hippie-chic vibe at this thatched cafe with a mellow open-air dining room upstairs. The menu leans towards healthy, but not too healthy – you can get fries. There are juices and lots of mains featuring vegies. Good baked goods, nice shakes.

Mandira Cafe CAFE $
(Jl Pura Batu Mejan; meals 25,000-50,000Rp; ⟨ 8am-10pm; ⟨) Although Echo Beach is

---

BUKIT PARTY CIRCUIT

Though it's the beaches and waves that bring travellers to Bukit, it's also got a reputation as a place to party. On Sunday nights beautiful people descend en masse upon **Single Fin** (☑ 0361-769941; www.singlefinbali.com; Jl Mamo; ⟨ 8am-11pm; ⟨) for DJs and sunset sounds (Wednesdays are also popular). On Saturdays it's Padang Padang's turn, with its famed evening beach parties. On Thursdays things get lively at Bingin's **Cashew Tree** with live bands, while on Fridays it's back to Ulu Watu for the roof-top bash at **Mamo Hotel** (☑ 0361-769882; www.mamohoteluluwatu.com; Jl Labuan Sait; ⟨).

---

rapidly going upscale, this classic surfers' dive has battered picnic tables with front-row seats for surfing action. Quaff a cheap Bintang while you Instagram the best action out on the breaks. The timeless menu includes jaffles, banana pancakes, club sandwiches and smoothies.

★**Old Man's** BEER GARDEN
(☑ 0361-846 9158; www.facebook.com/oldmans bali; Jl Pantai Batu Bolong; mains from 50,000Rp; ⟨ 8am-midnight) You'll have a tough time deciding where to sit to enjoy your drink at this popular coastal beer garden overlooking Batu Bolong Beach. The menu is aimed at surfers and surfer-wannabes: burgers, pizza, fish and chips, and, for New Agers, salads. Wednesday nights are an institution, while Fridays (live rock and roll) and Sundays (DJs) are also big.

❶ Getting There & Around

You can reach the Canggu area by road from the south by taking Jl Batubelig west in Kerobokan almost to the beach and then veering north. It's much longer to go up and around via the traffic-clogged Jl Raya Kerobokan.

Getting to the Canggu area can cost 80,000Rp or more by taxi from Kuta or Seminyak. Don't expect to find taxis cruising anywhere, although any business can call you one.

Bukit Peninsula

☑ 0361

Hot and arid, the southern peninsula is known as Bukit (meaning 'hill' in Bahasa Indonesia). The booming west coast (often generically called Pecatu) is a real hot spot for its string-of-pearls beaches. Accommodation sits precariously on the sand at Balangan Beach, while the cliffs are dotted with idiosyncratic lodges at Bingin and elsewhere. New places sprout daily and most have views of the turbulent waters here, which have world-famous surf breaks all the way south to the important temple of Ulu Watu.

❶ Getting There & Away

Public transport is unheard of around here. Ride your rented motorcycle or arrange for transport with your accommodation. Bluebird taxis from Kuta to Jimbaran cost about 100,000Rp; to the Bukit beaches and surf breaks will average 300,000Rp. Hire a car or scoot down on a (surfboard-rack-equipped) motorcycle.

Jimbaran

Just south of Kuta and the airport, Teluk Jimbaran (Jimbaran Bay) is an alluring crescent of white sand and blue sea, fronted by a long string of popular seafood warungs. These open-sided affairs are right on the beach and perfect for enjoying sea breezes and sunsets. The usual deal is to select your seafood fresh from iced displays or tanks and to pay according to weight.

Balangan Beach

Balangan Beach is a long and low strand at the base of the cliffs, covered with palm trees and fronted by a ribbon of near-white sand, picturesquely dotted with sun umbrellas. Surfer bars (some with bare-bones sleeping rooms), cafes in shacks and even slightly more permanent guesthouses precariously line the shore where buffed first-world bods soak up rays amid third-world sanitation.

Balangan Beach is 6.5km off the main Ulu Watu road via Cenggiling.

🛏 Sleeping

Santai Bali Homestay　　　BUNGALOW **$**
(📞 0338-695942; balanganbrothers@yahoo.com; r from 200,000Rp) Right on the sands of Balangan Beach, the bare-bones rooms at this shack bungalow are perfect for surfers and beach bums wanting easy access to the water. Its restaurant has tables and chairs plonked on the beach.

Bingin

An ever-evolving scene, Bingin comprises scores of unconventionally stylish lodgings scattered across cliffs and on the strip of white-sand **Bingin Beach** below. The scenery here is simply superb, with sylvan cliffs dropping down to surfer cafes and the foaming edge of the azure sea. The beach is a five-minute walk down steep steps.

🛏 Sleeping & Eating

Dozens of places to stay are scattered amid the trees, right up to – and down – the cliffs.

Chocky's Place　　　GUESTHOUSE **$**
(📞 0818 0530 7105; www.chockysplace.com; Bingin Beach; s/d from 100,000/200,000Rp; 🛜) Down the bottom of the stairs on Bingin

Beach, this classic surfer hang-out has cosy rooms varying from charming with awesome views to rudimentary with shared bathrooms. Its bamboo restaurant looks out to the beach; it's a great place to meet fellow travellers over a few cold ones.

Bingin Garden　　　GUESTHOUSE **$**
(📞 0816 472 2002; tommybarrell76@yahoo.com; off Jl Pantai Bingin; r with fan/air-con 300,000/400,000Rp; 🌀 🛜 🏊) There's a relaxed hacienda feel to Bingin Gardens, where six bungalow-style rooms are set among an arid garden and a large pool. It's back off the cliffs and about 300m from the path down to the beach. It's run by gun local surfer Tommy Barrell and his lovely wife.

★Cashew Tree　　　CAFE **$**
(📞 0353-218157; www.facebook.com/the-cashew-tree; Jl Pantai Bingan; meals from 40,000Rp; ⏰ 8am-10pm; 🛜) The Cashew Tree is *the* place to hang out in Bingin. Surfers and beach-goers gather for tasty vegan and vegetarian meals. Expect the likes of tempe rice-paper rolls with tahini dipping sauce, and smoothies with banana, raw cacao and cashews. It's also a good spot for a drink; Thursday nights especially go off, attracting folk from up and down the coast.

Padang Padang

Small in size but not in perfection, **Padang Padang Beach** is a cute little cove. Its Saturday night beach parties are legendary. It's a short walk through a temple and down a well-paved trail. Experienced surfers seeking tubes flock here.

🛌 Sleeping & Eating

Bali Rocks GUESTHOUSE $
(📞 0817 344788; www.facebook.com/balirocks padang; r 200,000Rp) Down the cliff face, this thatched bit of wonder has dead simple rooms with stunning views of the surf breaks and the ocean. Showers and toilets are down a couple flights of stairs from the rooms. At high tide you can jump directly into the water.

Om Burger BURGERS $$
(📞 0812-391 3617; JI Labuan Sait; burgers from 65,000Rp; ⏰ 7am-10pm; 📶) 'Superfood burgers' – that's the come-on at this joint with nice 2nd-floor views. The burgers are indeed super and supersized. The wagyu burger is the speciality, but the nasi goreng vegie burger is unique. There are intimations of health across the menu: baked sweet potato fries, vitamin-filled juices and more. It's very popular; expect to wait for a table at night.

Ulu Watu & Around

Ulu Watu has become the generic name for the southwestern tip of the Bukit Peninsula. It includes the much-revered temple and the nearby fabled surf breaks.

About 2km north of the temple is a dramatic cliff with steps that lead to the legendary Ulu Watu surf breaks. All manner of cafes and surf shops spill down the nearly sheer face to the water below. Views are stellar and it's quite the scene.

◉ Sights & Activities

★ Pura Luhur Ulu Watu HINDU TEMPLE
(JI Ulu Watu; admission incl sarong & sash rental adult/child 10,000/10,000Rp; ⏰ 8am-7pm) This important temple is perched precipitously on the southwestern tip of the peninsula, atop sheer cliffs that drop straight into the ceaseless surf. You enter through an unusual arched gateway flanked by statues of Ganesha. Inside, the walls of coral bricks are covered with intricate carvings of Bali's mythological menagerie.

Ulu Watu SURFING
On its day Ulu Watu is Bali's biggest and most powerful wave. It's the stuff of dreams and nightmares, and definitely not one for beginners! Since the early 1970s when it featured in the legendary surf flick *Morning of the Earth*, Ulu Watu has drawn surfers from around the world for left breaks that seem to go on forever. The area boasts numerous small inns and warungs that sell and rent

Ulu Watu & Around

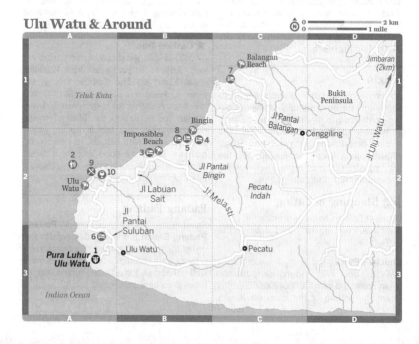

out surfboards, and provide food and drink, ding repairs or a massage – whatever you need most.

🛏 Sleeping & Eating

The cliffs above the main Ulu Watu surf break are lined with a hodgepodge of cafes and guesthouses. Some cling to rocks over the waves. You can enter from the east (crowded) or from the south (a pretty walk).

Gong GUESTHOUSE $
(📱0361-769976; www.thegonguluwatubali.com; Jl Pantai Suluban; r from 220,000Rp; @🖥) The 12 tidy rooms here have good ventilation and hot water, and face a small compound with a lovely pool. Some 2nd-floor units have distant ocean views. It's about 1km south of the Ulu Watu cliffside cafes; the host family is lovely.

Delpi CAFE $
(meals 40,000-60,000Rp; ☺7am-7pm; 🛜) A relaxed cafe-bar sitting on a cliff away from other cafe spots, with stunning views. There are also simple rooms for rent (with fan/aircon US$35/40).

Nusa Dua & Tanjung Benoa

The peninsula of Tanjung Benoa extends about 4km north from the gated resort area of Nusa Dua to the fishing village of Benoa. The area caters to top-end travellers and those on package holidays.

Ulu Watu & Around

Denpasar
📱 0361 / POP 820,000

Sprawling, hectic and ever-growing, Bali's capital is home to most Balinese and you can sense here the island's growing wealth. Mostly untrodden by tourists, Denpasar can seem a little daunting and chaotic, but spend some time on the tree-lined streets in the relatively affluent government and business district of Renon and you will discover a more genteel side to the city.

👁 Sights

★ **Museum Negeri Propinsi Bali** MUSEUM
(📱0361-222680; adult/child 20,000/10,000Rp; ☺8am-4pm Sat-Thu, 8.30am-12.30pm Fri) Think of this as the British Museum or the Smithsonian of Balinese culture. It's all here, but unlike those world-class institutions, you have to work at sorting it out; the museum could use a dose of curatorial energy. Most displays are labelled in English. The museum comprises several buildings and pavilions, including many examples of Balinese architecture, housing prehistoric pieces, traditional artefacts, Barong (mythical lion-dog creature), ceremonial objects and rich displays of textiles.

🛏 Sleeping & Eating

Beaches, smeaches. Stay in Denpasar and savour contemporary urban Balinese life. It has the island's best range of Indonesian and Balinese food: savvy locals and expats have their own favourite warungs and restaurants.

Nakula Familiar Inn GUESTHOUSE $
(📱0361-226446; www.nakulafamiliarinn.com; Jl Nakula 4; s with fan/air-con 175,000/225,000Rp, d with fan/air-con 200,000/250,000Rp; ❄🛜) The eight rooms at this sprightly urban family compound, a longtime traveller favourite, are clean and have small balconies. There is a nice courtyard and cafe in the middle. Tegal–Kereneng bemos go along Jl Nakula.

★ **Café Teduh** INDONESIAN $
(📱0361-221631; off Jl Diponegoro; mains 12,000-23,000Rp; ☺10am-10pm; 🛜) A little oasis hidden down a tiny lane, with hanging orchids, trees, flowers and ponds with fountains. Try *ayam dabu-dabu* (grilled chicken with chilli paste, tomatoes, shallots, lemongrass and spices) or *nasi bakar cumi hitam* (rice and marinated squid wrapped in banana leaf and grilled).

Denpasar

Denpasar

◎ Top Sights
1 Museum Negeri Propinsi Bali..............B2

🛏 Sleeping
2 Nakula Familiar Inn...............................B1

🍽 Eating
3 Café Teduh B3
4 Cak Asmo..C4

🛍 Shopping
5 Pasar Badung A2

Cak Asmo

INDONESIAN $

(Jl Tukad Gangga; meals from 15,000Rp; ⊙ 9.30am-10.30pm) Join the government workers and students from the nearby university for superb dishes cooked to order in the bustling kitchen. Order the buttery and crispy *cumi cumi* (calamari) battered in *telor asin* (a heavenly mixture of eggs and gar-

lic). Fruity ice drinks are a cooling treat. An English-language menu makes ordering a breeze. It's halal, so there's no alcohol.

🛍 Shopping

A must-see destination: shoppers browse and bargain at the sprawling **Pasar Badung** (Jl Gajah Mada; ⊙ 6am-5pm) from morning to night. It's a retail adventure where you can find produce and food from all over the island. Sadly, a fire ripped through the market in early 2016 as this guidebook was going to press and it was unclear if/when it would be rebuilt.

The shops lining Jl Sulawesi by the market site are famous for textiles.

ℹ Getting There & Around

Denpasar is *the* hub for the creaky bemo network around Bali. The city has several terminals – you'll often have to go via Denpasar and transfer from one terminal to another. Each terminal has regular bemo connections to the other terminals in Denpasar for 7000Rp. Key terminals for buses and bemos include Batubalan and Ubung, and Tegal for bemos.

Sanur

📞 0361

Sanur is a genteel alternative to Kuta. The white-sand beach is sheltered by a reef, and the resulting low-key surf contributes to Sanur's nickname 'Snore' (although this is also attributable to the area's status as a haven for expat retirees).

Sanur's **beachfront walk** was the first in Bali and from day one has been delighting locals and visitors alike. Over 4km long, it follows the sand as it curves to the southwest. Oodles of cafes with tables in the sand give plenty of reason to pause.

🛏 Sleeping

Usually the best places to stay are right on the beach; however, beware of properties that have been coasting for decades.

Yulia 1 Homestay   GUESTHOUSE $

(📞 0361-288089; yulia1homestay@gmail.com; Jl Danau Tamblingan 38; r incl breakfast with fan & cold water 170,000-220,000Rp, with air-con 300,000-350,000Rp; ❋ 🛜 🏊) Run by a friendly family, this mellow guesthouse is set in a lovely bird-filled garden full of palms and flowers. Rooms vary in standards (some cold water, fan only), but all come with minibars. The plunge pool is a nice area for relaxing.

Pollok & Le Mayeur Inn   HOMESTAY $

(📞 0361-289847; pollokinn@yahoo.com; Jl Hang Tuah, Museum Le Mayeur; r with fan/air-con from 250,000/350,000Rp; ❋ 🛜) The grandchildren of the late artist Le Mayeur de Merpes and his wife Ni Polok run this small homestay. It's within the **Le Mayeur museum compound** (📞 0361-286201; Jl Hang Tuah; adult/child 20,000/10,000Rp; ⊙ 8am-3.30pm Sat-Thu, 8.30am-12.30pm Fri), and offers a good budget option on the beachfront. The 17 rooms vary in size; ask to see a few.

🍴 Eating & Drinking

The beach path offers restaurants, warungs and bars where you can catch a meal, a drink or a sea breeze.

Warung Little Bird   INDONESIAN $

(📞 0361-745 4968; Jl Danau Tamblingan 34; mains from 25,000Rp; ⊙ 10am-10pm) The charming Little Bird does tasty Indonesian dishes

including beef rendang, and Balinese specialities such as *ayam betutu* (slow-cooked chicken stuffed with Balinese spices), which you will need to reserve in advance. Its inviting little bar makes it a good spot for a drink, too.

⭐ **Manik Organik**   HEALTH FOOD $$

(📞 0821 4416 8228; www.manikorganikbali.com; Jl Danau Tamblingan 85; meals from 55,000Rp; ⊙ 9am-11pm; 🍴) 🌿 Trees shade the serene terrace at this creative and healthful cafe that smells of lemongrass. Vegetarians and raw-food enthusiasts are well cared for, but there are also meaty dishes made with free-range chicken and the like. Smoothies include the fortifying 'immune tonic'.

Warung Pantai Indah   CAFE $$

(Beachfront Walk; mains 30,000-110,000Rp; ⊙ 9am-9pm) Sit at battered tables and chairs with your toes in the sand at this timeless beach cafe. It specialises in fresh barbecue-grilled seafood and cheap local dishes.

ℹ Getting There & Around

Tourist bus destinations include Kuta (35,000Rp, 30 minutes), Ubud (50,000Rp, one hour) and Padangbai (75,000Rp, two hours). There's a **Perama** (📞 0361-285592; www.peramatour.com; Jl Hang Tuah 39; ⊙ 7am-10pm) office.

Bemos go up and down Jl Danau Tamblingan and Jl Danau Poso for 5000Rp.

Nusa Lembongan

📞 0366

Laid-back Nusa Lembongan is one of three islands (along with Nusa Penida and Nusa Ceningan) that together comprise the Nusa Penida archipelago. It's the Bali many imagine but never find: rooms on the beach, cheap beers with incredible sunsets, days spent surfing and diving, and nights spent enjoying a favourite book or hanging with new friends.

⊙ Sights

The main beach, **Pantai Jungutbatu**, a mostly lovely arc of white sand with clear blue water, has views across to Gunung Agung in Bali. The pleasant seawall walkway is ideal for strolling, especially – as you'd guess – at sunset. Floating boats and seaweed being farmed and dried save the scene from being clichéd idyllic.

Pantai Tanjung Sanghyang   BEACH
This beautiful bay, unofficially named Mushroom Bay after the mushroom corals offshore, has a crescent of bright white beach. By day, the tranquillity can be disturbed by banana-boat riders or parasailers. At other hours, this is a beach of dreams.

The most interesting way to get here from Jungutbatu is to walk along the trail that starts from the southern end of the main beach and follows the coastline for a kilometre or so. Alternatively, get a boat from Jungutbatu.

🏃 Activities

Most places will rent bicycles for 30,000Rp per day, surfboards for 50,000Rp per day and motorcycles for 30,000Rp per hour. Good **snorkelling** can be had just off Mushroom Bay, as well as in areas off the north coast of the island. The **diving** at Nusa Penida is legendary and challenging. **Surfing** off Jungutbatu is a major draw.

★ **World Diving**   DIVING
(🖉 0812 390 0686; www.world-diving.com; Jungubatu Beach; 2 dives excl equipment from 1,200,000Rp, open-water course 5,500,000Rp) World Diving, based at Pondok Baruna, is very well regarded. It offers a complete range of courses, plus diving trips to dive sites all around the three islands. Equipment is first-rate.

🛏 Sleeping & Eating

Rooms and amenities generally become increasingly posh as you head south and west along the water to Mushroom Bay. Walk the beachfront in Jungutbatu and look for deals.

★ **Pondok Baruna**   GUESTHOUSE $
(🖉 0812 394 0992; www.pondokbaruna.com; Jungutbatu Beach; r 250,000-650,000Rp; 🏵 🛜 🏊) Associated with World Diving, a local dive operator, this place offers fantastic rooms with terraces facing the ocean. Plusher rooms surround a dive pool behind the beach. There are another eight rooms at sister site **Pondok Baruna Frangipani** (🖉 0812 394 0992; www.pondokbaruna.com; s/d incl breakfast 600,000/650,000Rp; 🏵 🛜 🏊), set back in the palm trees around a large pool. Staff members, led by Putu, are charmers.

Alam Nusa Huts   GUESTHOUSE $
(🖉 0819 1662 6336; www.alamnusahuts.com; Tanjung Sanghyang; r from US$40; 🏵 🛜) This small property is less than 100m from the beach.

Four bungalows sit in a small, lush garden; each has an open-air bathroom and a secluded terrace. The interiors feature a lot of rich wood and bamboo. The staff is especially welcoming.

ℹ Information

It's vital that you bring sufficient cash for your stay, as the ATM can fail and doesn't accept most foreign cards; there are few other services.

ℹ Getting There & Around

Boats anchor offshore, so be prepared to get your feet wet. And travel light – wheeled bags are comically inappropriate in the water and on the beach and dirt tracks. There are numerous ways of travelling between Nusa Lembongan and Sanur.

Regular public boats run to Nusa Lembongan from the north end of Sanur beach: a slow boat (100,000Rp, 1½ hours) at 10.30am or fast boat (175,000Rp, 30 minutes, four daily). Boats to Nusa Penida (175,000Rp, 35 minutes, six daily) start running at 7am.

Fast boats to Sanur (30 minutes) run several times daily, operated by **Rocky Fast Cruises** (🖉 0361-283624; www.rockyfastcruise.com; Jungubatu Beach; one way/return US$30/50, 30 minutes, four daily) and **Scoot** (🖉 0361-285522; www.scootcruise.com; one way/return 400,000/600,000Rp, 30 minutes, four daily).

There are also useful fast-boat links between Nusa Lembongan and the Gilis.

The island is fairly small and you can easily walk most places. There are no cars. One-way rides on motorcycles or trucks cost 20,000Rp and up.

Ubud

🖉 0361

Perched on the gentle slopes leading up towards the central mountains, Ubud is the other half of Bali's tourism duopoly. Unlike South Bali, however, Ubud's focus remains on the remarkable Balinese culture in its myriad forms.

It's not surprising that many people come to Ubud for a day or two and end up staying longer, drawn in by the rich culture and many activities. Besides the popular dance-and-music shows, there are numerous courses that allow you to become fully immersed in Balinese culture.

Ubud is home to chilled-out restaurants and cafes, numerous yoga studios and artful and serene places to stay. Around Ubud are temples, ancient sites and whole villages producing handicrafts (albeit mostly for visitors). Although the growth of Ubud has engulfed several neighbouring villages, leading to an urban sprawl and awful traffic, parts of the surrounding countryside remain unspoiled, with lush rice paddies and towering coconut trees.

◉ Sights

Spend time in the museums and walking the beautiful countryside. If you visit only for a brief time on a day trip you may wonder what the fuss is all about.

★ Agung Rai Museum of Art   GALLERY
(ARMA; Map p210; ☑0361-976659; www.arma bali.com; Jl Raya Pengosekan; adult/child incl drink 60,000Rp/free; ☺9am-6pm, Balinese dancing 3-5pm Mon-Fri, classes 10am Sun) Founded by art patron Agung Rai as an art museum, cultural centre, botanical gardens and hotel, the impressive ARMA features a world-class collection of Balinese, Indonesian and European artists. The collection is well labelled in English. Exhibits include classical Kamasan paintings, Batuan-style work from the 1930s and '40s, and works by Lempad, Affandi, Sadali, Hofker, Bonnet and Le Mayeur. The museum is housed in several traditional buildings set in gardens with water coursing through channels.

Sacred Monkey Forest Sanctuary   PARK
(Mandala Wisata Wanara Wana; Map p212; ☑0361-971304; www.monkeyforestubud.com; Monkey Forest Rd; adult/child 30,000/20,000Rp; ☺8.30am-6pm) This cool and dense swathe of jungle, officially called Mandala Wisata Wanara Wana, houses three holy temples. The sanctuary is inhabited by a band of grey-haired and greedy long-tailed Balinese macaques who are nothing like the innocent-looking doe-eyed monkeys on the brochures. Nestled in the forest, the interesting **Pura Dalem Agung** (Map p210) FREE has a real *Indiana Jones* feel to it; the entrance to the inner temple features Rangda figures devouring children.

Museum Puri Lukisan   MUSEUM
(Museum of Fine Arts; Map p212; ☑0361-975136; www.museumpurilukisan.com; off Jl Raya Ubud; adult/child incl drink 85,000Rp/free; ☺9am-5pm) It was in Ubud that the modern Balinese art movement started, when artists first began to abandon purely religious themes and court subjects for scenes of everyday life. This museum displays fine examples of all schools of Balinese art, all well-labelled in English. It was set up by Rudolf Bonnet, with Cokorda Gede Agung Sukawati (a prince of Ubud's royal family) and Walter Spies.

Neka Art Museum   GALLERY
(Map p210; ☑0361-975074; www.museumneka. com; Jl Raya Sanggingan; adult/child 50,000Rp/ free; ☺9am-5pm Mon-Sat, noon-5pm Sun) The creation of Suteja Neka, a private collector and dealer in Balinese art, Neka Art Museum has an excellent and diverse collection. It's a good place to learn about the development of painting in Bali. You can get an overview of the myriad local painting styles in the **Balinese Painting Hall**. Look for the *wayang* works.

🏃 Activities

As well as visiting the museums and galleries, it is well worth exploring the natural beauty that inspires so much of it. There are wonderful walks around Ubud: east to Pejeng; south across picturesque ravines to Bedulu; north along the Campuan ridge; and west to Penestanan and Sayan, with views over the Sungai Ayung (Ayung River) gorge.

Ubud is a nexus of pampering: spas, yoga and plentiful New Age activities are on offer. Check the bulletin board outside Bali Buda (p213), a health-food cafe and shop, for listings. You can also find myriad courses in Balinese arts.

Yoga Barn   YOGA
(Map p212; ☑0361-971236; www.theyogabarn. com; off Jl Raya Pengosekan; classes from 120,000Rp; ☺7am-8pm) The chakra for the yoga revolution in Ubud, the Yoga Barn sits in its own lotus position amid trees back near a river valley. The name exactly describes what you'll find: a huge range of classes in yoga, Pilates, dance and life-affirming offshoots, held throughout the week.

Bali Botanica Day Spa   SPA
(Map p210; ☑0361-976739; www.balibotanica. com; Jl Raya Sanggingan; massage from 155,000Rp; ☺9am-9pm) Set beautifully on a lush hillside past little fields of rice and ducks, this spa offers a range of treatments, including Ayurvedic. The herbal massage is popular. Transport is provided if needed.

Bali Nature Herbal Walks   WALKING TOUR
(☑0812 381 6024; www.baliherbalwalk.com; walks 200,000Rp per person; ☺8.30am) Conducts

Ubud Area

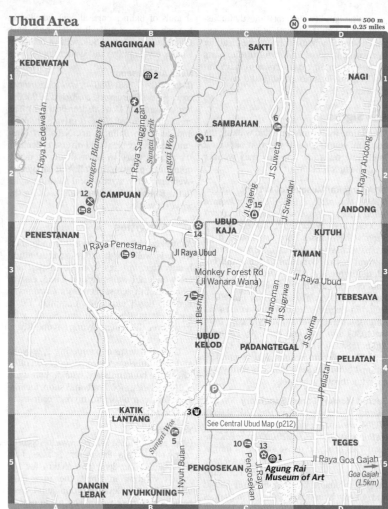

three-hour walks through lush Bali land-scape. Medicinal and cooking herbs and plants are identified and explained in their natural environment. Includes herbal drinks.

🛏 Sleeping

There are hundreds of places to stay in Ubud. Choices range from simple little losmen to world-class luxurious retreats. Inexpensive family lodgings are very small and tend to operate in clusters, so you can easily look at a few before choosing. There's no

need to pay for air-con, as it's cool at night here.

🛏 Central Ubud

Small streets east of Monkey Forest Rd, including Jl Karna and Jl Maruti, have numerous, family-style homestays, as does Jl Goutama. Don't settle for a room with road noise along Ubud's main drags.

In Tebesaya, Jl Sukma and the *gang* that runs parallel just to the east are excellent hunting grounds for budget stays. Going

Ubud Area

north from Jl Raya Ubud, you are soon in rolling terraces of rice fields.

★ **Nirvana Pension** GUESTHOUSE **$**
(Map p212; ☑ 0361-975415; www.nirvanaku. com; Jl Goutama 10; s/d/tr with fan 250,000/ 350,000/500,000Rp, s/d with air-con 350,000/ 450,000Rp; ✳ 🛜) Nirvana has *alang-alang* (thatched roofs), a plethora of paintings, ornate doorways and six rooms with modern bathrooms, all set in a shady, secluded locale next to a large family temple. Batik courses are also held here. It's a great location, back off trendy Goutama.

Happy Mango Tree HOSTEL **$**
(Map p210; ☑ 0812 3844 5498; www.thehappy mangotree.com; Jl Bisma 27; dm/d from 100,000/250,000Rp; 🛜) This bright and bubbly hostel revels in its hippie vibe. Bright colours abound inside the rooms and out on the various terraces, some of which have rice-field views. Mixed dorms have four or five beds; doubles come with names (and matching decor) such as Love Shack and Ceiling Museum. There's a social bar and a restaurant, too.

Han Snel Siti Bungalows GUESTHOUSE **$**
(Map p212; ☑ 0361-975699; www.sitibungalow. com; Jl Kajeng 3; r incl breakfast with fan/air-con from 250,000/350,000Rp; ✳ 🛜 ☒) Owned by the family of the late Han Snel, a well-known Dutch painter, Siti Bungalows is one of Ubud's original guesthouses. While its standards have slipped, it remains excellent value and a wonderful choice for those seeking somewhere with character, a delightful garden and spacious bungalows – some of which overlook the river gorge.

d'Rompok House GUESTHOUSE **$**
(Map p212; ☑ 0353-344837; drompokhouse@ yahoo.com; Jl Hanoman 39; r incl breakfast 250,000Rp; ✳ 🛜) Tucked down a tight *gang*, the well-priced d'Rompok is more suave than your usual homestay, with large modern rooms decorated with contemporary art. Go for one of the top-floor rooms with views of the rice fields.

Biangs HOMESTAY **$**
(Map p212; ☑ 0361-976520; wah_oeboed@yahoo. com; Jl Sukma 28; s/d with fan 100,000/200,000Rp, r with air-con 300,000Rp; ✳ 🛜) In a little garden, Biangs (meaning 'mama') homestay has six well-maintained rooms, with hot water. The friendly family makes it feel like a genuine homestay, and its residential street has a local feel.

Bali Asli Lodge HOMESTAY **$**
(Map p210; ☑ 0361-970537; www.baliaslilodge. com; Jl Suweta; r incl breakfast 300,000Rp; 🛜) Escape the central Ubud hubbub here. Made is your friendly host, and her four rooms are in traditional Balinese stone-and-brick houses set in verdant gardens. There are terraces where you can let the hours pass; interiors are clean and comfy. Town is a 15-minute walk.

Shift DESIGN HOTEL **$$**
(Map p210; www.theshifthotelbali.com; Jl Raya Penestanan Kelod; r incl breakfast US$49-79; ✳ 🛜) Set in an old renovated apartment, this hipster, vegan hotel has your classic motel configuration but with plenty of rock-and-roll panache. The modern rooms are comfortable and include minibars and fibre optic wi-fi. The rooftop deck has sunloungers, a restaurant, a single-origin speciality cafe, a raw vegan sushi bar and a yoga space that's also used for movies and dance parties.

Central Ubud

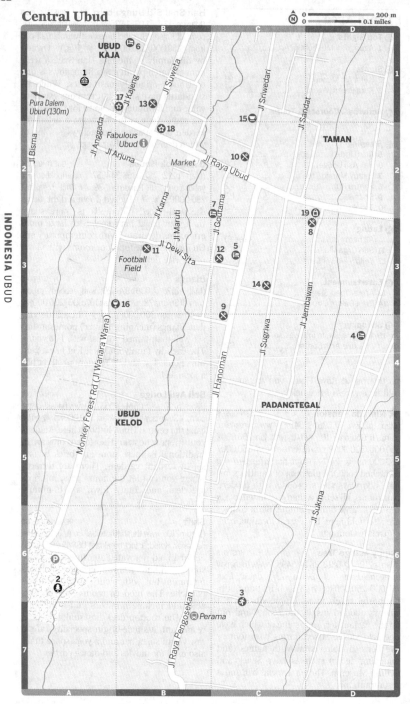

Central Ubud

Tegal Sari HOTEL $$
(Map p210; ☑0361-973318; www.tegalsari-ubud.com; r 330,000-990,000Rp; ✱@☎☀) Though written literally a stone's throw from the hectic main road, here rice fields (along with ducks) miraculously materialise. Go for a superdeluxe cottage (770,000Rp) with bathtub looking out to wonderful bucolic views. Units in the new brick buildings, on the other hand, are stark. It has two pools, including one on the rooftop, and a yoga space.

Penestanan

Penestanan is west of Ubud but still within walking distance. Out here, you can hear water coursing through the surrounding rice fields.

★**Santra Putra** GUESTHOUSE $
(Map p210; ☑0361-977810; wayankarja@gmail.com; off Jl Raya Campuan; r incl breakfast 300,000-400,000Rp; ☎) Run by internationally exhibited abstract artist I Wayan Karja (whose studio-gallery is also on-site), this place has 11 big, open, airy rooms with hot water. Enjoy paddy-field views from all vantage points. Painting and drawing classes are offered by the artist.

✗ Eating

Ubud's cafes and restaurants are some of the best in Bali. Local and expat chefs produce a bounty of authentic Balinese dishes, as well as inventive Asian and other international cuisines. It's also known for its organic and vegetarian fare.

★**Warung Sopa** VEGETARIAN $
(Map p212; ☑0361-276 5897; Jl Sugriwa 36; mains 30,000-60,000Rp; ☺8am-9.30pm; ☎✏) This popular open-air place in a residential street captures the Ubud vibe with creative and tasty vegetarian fare with a Balinese twist. Look for specials of the day on display; the ever-changing *nasi campur* is a treat.

Sari Organik HEALTH FOOD $
(Warung Bodag Maliah; Map p210; ☑0361-972087; Subak Sok Wayah; meals from 38,000Rp; ☺8am-8pm) ✏ In a beautiful location on a plateau overlooking rice terraces and river valleys, this attractive cafe is in the middle of a big organic farm. The food's healthy and the drinks are refreshing. The walk through the rice fields means half the fun is getting here.

Bali Buda CAFE $
(Map p212; ☑0361-976324; www.balibuda.com; Jl Jembawan 1; meals from 30,000Rp; ☺7.30am-10pm; ✏) This breezy upper-floor place offers a full range of vegetarian *jamu* (health tonics), salads, sandwiches, savoury crêpes, pizzas and gelato. The bulletin board downstairs is packed with idiosyncratic Ubud notices.

Warung Ibu Oka BALINESE $
(Map p212; Jl Suweta; mains from 50,000Rp; ☺11am-7pm) Opposite Ubud Palace, lunchtime crowds are waiting for one thing: Balinese-style roast *babi guling* (suckling pig). Order a *spesial* to get the best cut.

Tutmak Cafe CAFE $
(Map p212; ☑0361-975754; www.tutmak.com; Jl Dewi Sita; mains 30,000-90,000Rp; ☺8am-11pm; ☎) This smart, breezy multilevel terrace restaurant is a popular place for a refreshing drink or something to munch on from

SPLURGE

Just south of the Monkey Forest in Nyuhkuning, **Alam Indah** (Map p210; ☑ 0361-974629; www.alamindahbali.com; Jl Nyuh Bulan; r incl breakfast US$65-135; ❊ ☎ ⌨) feels isolated but is a short walk from everything. The spacious resort has 16 rooms that are beautifully finished in traditional designs using natural materials. The Wos Valley views are entrancing, especially from the multi-level pool area. There's a free shuttle into central Ubud.

the menu of Indo classics. The *nasi campur* with fresh tuna is one of Ubud's finest.

Earth Cafe & Market
VEGETARIAN $

(Map p212; www.dtebali.com/earth-cafe-market-ubud; Jl Gotama Selatan; meals from 30,000Rp; ☎ ☑) 'Eliminate free radicals' is but one of many healthy drinks at this hard-core outpost for vegetarian organic dining and drinking. The seemingly endless menu has a plethora of soups, salads and platters that are heavy on Med flavours. There's a market on the main floor.

Yellow Flower Cafe
INDONESIAN $

(Map p210; ☑ 0361-889 9865; off Jl Raya Campuan; mains from 30,000Rp; ❊ 8am-9pm; ☎) New Age Indonesian right up in Penestanan along a little path through the rice fields. Organic mains such as *nasi campur* or rice pancakes are good; snackers will delight in the decent coffees, cakes and smoothies. From 5.30pm Sunday evenings there's an excellent Balinese buffet (99,000Rp).

★ Waroeng Bernadette
INDONESIAN $$

(Map p212; ☑ 0821-4742 4779; Jl Goutama; mains from 60,000Rp; ❊ 11am-11pm; ☎) It's not called the 'Home of Rendang' for nothing. The west Sumatran classic dish of long-marinated meats (beef is the true classic, but here there's also a vegie jackfruit variety) is pulled off with colour and flair. Other dishes have a zesty zing missing from lacklustre versions served elsewhere. The elevated dining room is a vision of kitsch.

Hujon Locale
INDONESIAN $$

(Map p212; ☑ 0361-849 3092; www.hujanlocale.com; Jl Sriwedari 5; mains 110,000-200,000Rp; ❊ noon-10pm; ☎) From the team of the critically acclaimed Mama San in Sem-inyak, Hujon Locale is one of Ubud's finest restaurants. The menu mixes traditional Indonesian dishes with modern, creative flair, from Sulawesi salt-baked barramundi and Achenese prawn curry to slow-braised Sumatran lamb curry. The setting within a chic colonial-style two-storey bungalow is made for a balmy evening.

Alchemy
VEGAN $$

(Map p210; ☑ 0361-971981; www.alchemybali.com; Jl Raya Penestanan 75; mains from 50,000Rp; ❊ 7am-9pm; ☎ ☑) A prototypical 100% vegan Ubud restaurant, Alchemy features a vast customised salad menu as well as cashew-milk drinks, durian smoothies, ice cream, fennel juice and a lot more. The raw-chocolate desserts are addictive.

🍷 Drinking & Nightlife

No one comes to Ubud for wild nightlife. A few bars get lively around sunset and later in the night, but the venues certainly don't aspire to the club partying found in Kuta and Seminyak.

★ Coffee Studio Seniman
CAFE

(Map p212; ☑ 0361-972085; www.senimancoffee.com; Jl Sriwedari; coffee 30,000Rp; ❊ 8am-10pm; ☎) That 'coffee studio' moniker isn't for show; all the equipment is on display at this temple of single-origin coffee. Take a seat on the designer rocker chairs and choose from an array of pourovers, siphon, Aeropress or espresso using a range of quality Indonesian beans. It's also popular for food (mains from 40,000Rp) and drinks in the evening.

CP Lounge
BAR, CLUB

(Map p212; www.cp-lounge.com; Monkey Forest Rd; ❊ 11am-4am) Open till late morning, CP is the place to kick on once everything else has closed. It has garden seating, live bands and a club with DJ and sound system.

☆ Entertainment

Few travel experiences can be more magical than experiencing a Balinese dance performance, especially in Ubud. Cultural entertainment keeps people returning and sets Bali apart from other tropical destinations. Get there a little early and buy a beer from the old women selling them out of ice-filled buckets.

Tourist office Fabulous Ubud has performance information and sells tickets (usually about 80,000Rp). For performances outside Ubud, transport is often included in the price. Tickets are also sold at the venues.

In a week in Ubud, you can see *kecak*, *legong* and *barong* dances, *wayang kulit* puppets, gamelan and more.

Arma Open Stage — DANCE
(Map p210; ☑ 0361-976659; Jl Raya Pengosekan) Has among the best troupes performing Kecak and Legong dance.

Pura Dalem Ubud — DANCE
(Map p210; Jl Raya Ubud) At the west end of Jl Raya Ubud, this open-air venue has a flame-lit carved-stone backdrop and is one of the most evocative places to see a dance performance.

Pura Taman Saraswati — DANCE
(Ubud Water Palace; Map p212; Jl Raya Ubud) The beauty of the setting may distract you from the dancers, although at night you can't see the lily pads and lotus flowers that are such an attraction by day.

Ubud Palace — DANCE
(Map p212; Jl Raya Ubud) Performances are held here almost nightly against a beautiful backdrop.

Shopping

In Ubud, Jl Hanoman and Jl Dewi Sita should be your starting points. Surrounding villages are hotbeds for arts and crafts, as you'll have probably noticed on your drive to Ubud.

★ Threads of Life Indonesian Textile Arts Center — TEXTILES
(Map p210; ☑ 0361-972187; www.threadsoflife.com; Jl Kajeng 24; ☺ 10am-7pm) This small, professional textile gallery and shop sponsors the production of naturally dyed, handmade ritual textiles from around Indonesia. It exists to help recover skills in danger of being lost to modern dyeing and weaving methods. Commissioned pieces are displayed in the gallery, which has good explanatory material. Also runs regular textile appreciation courses.

Ganesha Bookshop — BOOKS
(Map p212; www.ganeshabooksbali.com; Jl Raya Ubud; ☺ 9am-8pm) A quality bookshop with an excellent selection of titles on Indonesian studies, travel, arts, music, fiction (including used books) and maps. Staff can offer good recommendations.

ⓘ Information

Along the main roads, you'll find most services you need, including lots of ATMs.

Fabulous Ubud (Yayasan Bina Wisata; Map p212; ☑ 0361-973285; www.fabulousubud.com; Jl Raya Ubud; ☺ 8am-8pm) Set up by the Ubud

---

BALINESE DANCE & MUSIC

Enjoying a Balinese dance performance is for many a highlight of a visit to Bali: you can choose among many quality dance performances virtually every night in Ubud. The haunting sounds, elaborate costumes, careful choreography and even light-hearted comic routines add up to great entertainment. Swept up in the spectacle, you'll soon understand why Balinese culture is among the world's most developed.

Balinese music is based around an ensemble known as a gamelan, also called a *gong*. This melodic, sometimes upbeat and sometimes haunting percussion that often accompanies traditional dance is one of the most lasting impressions for tourists to Bali.

There are more than a dozen different basic dances in Bali and myriad variations. The most important:

Kecak Probably the best-known dance for its spell-binding, hair-raising atmosphere, the *kecak* features a 'choir' of men and boys who sit in concentric circles and slip into a trance as they chant and sing 'chak-a-chak-a-chak', imitating a troupe of monkeys.

Barong & Rangda Features the good – a mischievous and fun-loving shaggy dog-lion called a *barong* – battling the bad, an evil widow-witch called Rangda. One or more monkeys attend the *barong* and these characters often steal the show.

Legong Characterised by flashing eyes and quivering hands, this most graceful of Balinese dances is performed by young girls. Their talent is so revered that in old age, a classic dancer will be remembered as a 'great *legong*'.

Kekak Fire Dances These dances were developed to drive out evil spirits from a village. Two young girls dance a dream-like *legong* in perfect symmetry and a boy in a trance dances around and through a fire of coconut husks.

royal family, this is the one really useful tourist office in Bali. It has a good range of information and a noticeboard listing current happenings and activities. The staff can answer most regional questions and has up-to-date information on ceremonies and traditional dances held in the area; dance tickets are sold here.

ℹ Getting There & Around

Transport between South Bali and Ubud costs about 250,000Rp whether you take a metered taxi or arrange it with a guy on the street. There are no local metered taxis, but the ubiquitous drivers and motorcycle owners will take you around town for a negotiable 20,000Rp to 50,000Rp, depending on distance.

Ubud is on two bemo routes; they travel to Gianyar (10,000Rp) and Batubulan terminal in Denpasar (13,000Rp). Ubud doesn't have a bemo terminal; there are bemo stops on Jl Suweta, near the market in the centre of town.

Tourist shuttles include **Perama** (Map p212; ☑ 0361-973316; www.peramatours.com; Jl Raya Pengosekan; ◔ 9am-9pm). Services include Kuta (60,000Rp, two hours), Sanur (50,000Rp, one hour), Padangbai (75,000Rp, two hours), Lovina (125,000Rp, three hours) and Amed (175,000Rp, 3½ hours).

Shops renting bikes have their cycles on display along the main roads; your accommodation can always arrange bike rental.

Around Ubud

Two kilometres east of central Ubud, the cavern of **Goa Gajah** (Elephant Cave; Jl Raya Goa Gajah; adult/child 15,000/7500Rp, parking motorcycle/car 2000/5000Rp; ◔ 8am-5.30pm) was discovered in the 1920s; the fountains and bathing pool were not unearthed until 1954. It is believed to have been a Buddhist hermitage.

In Tampaksiring, 18km northeast of Ubud, you'll find the most impressive ancient site in Bali, **Gunung Kawi** (adult/child incl sarong 15,000/7500Rp, parking 2000Rp; ◔ 7am-6pm). This astonishing group of stone *candi* (shrines) cut into cliffs on either side of the plunging Sungai Pakrisan (Pakrisan River) valley is being considered for Unesco Heritage status. They stand in awe-inspiring, 8m-high sheltered niches cut into the sheer cliff face. From the end of the access road, a steep, stone stairway leads down to the river, at one point making a cutting through an embankment of solid rock.

East Coast Beaches

The main road that runs east from Sanur passes many black-sand beaches. One good stop is **Pura Masceti Beach**, 15km east of Sanur. Pura Masceti, one of Bali's nine directional temples, is right on the beach. It's architecturally significant and enlivened with gaudy statuary. Nearby **Pantai Keramas** is great for surfing.

Semarapura (Klungkung)

Once the centre of an important Balinese kingdom, Semarapura (also known as Klungkung) is the capital of Klungkung regency (a historical and present-day administrative area) and a great artistic and cultural focal point. Formerly the seat of the Dewa Agung dynasty, **Klunkkung Palace** (Klungkung Palace; Jl Puputan; adult/child 12,000/6000Rp; ◔ 6am-6pm) has now largely crumbled away, but history and architecture buffs will enjoy a wander past the **Kertha Gosa** (Hall of Justice) and **Bale Kambang** (Floating Pavilion).

The nearby **market**, which teems with goods, is also worth a visit.

Sidemen Road

Winding through one of Bali's most beautiful river valleys, the Sidemen road offers marvellous paddy-field scenery, a delightful rural character and extraordinary views of Gunung Agung (when the clouds permit). The region is getting more popular every year as a verdant escape, where a walk in any direction is a communion with nature.

Among the many mellow places scattered about the impossibly green rice fields, **Pondok Wisata Lihat Sawah** (☑ 0852 0511 0916; www.lihatsawah.com; r incl breakfast 300,000-500,000Rp; ☎ ☒) has 12 rooms with views of the valley and mountain; all have hot water – nice after a morning hike – and the best have lovely wooden verandahs.

Padangbai

☑ 0363

There's a real backpacker vibe about this little beach town, which is also the port for the main public ferry connecting Bali with Lombok, as well as fast boats to the Gilis.

Padangbai sits on a small bay and has a nice little curve of beach. It has a whole, compact seaside travellers' scene with cheap places to stay and some fun cafes. The pace is slow, but should ambition strike there's good snorkelling and diving, plus some easy walks and a couple of great beaches.

🛏 Sleeping & Eating

Accommodation in Padangbai – like the town itself – is pretty laid-back. Prices are fairly cheap; simple cafes and warungs are common.

Bamboo Paradise GUESTHOUSE $
(☑ 0822 6630 4330; www.bambooparadisebali.com; Jl Penataran Agung; dm incl breakfast with air-con 95,000Rp; r incl breakfast with fan/air-con from 200,000/300,000Rp; ❄🛜) Away from the main strip, 200m up a gentle hill from the ferry port, this popular backpacker has the cheapest crash in town (in four-bed dorms). Regular rooms are comfortable and it has a nice large lounging area with hammocks and bean bags. The owners have recently opened **Fat Barracuda** (Jl Segara; dm/r 95,000/300,000Rp; 🛜) overlooking the water, which is also popular.

Topi Inn GUESTHOUSE $
(☑ 0363-41424; www.topiinn.nl; Jl Silayukti; dm/r from 60,000/150,000Rp; @🛜) Sitting at the east end of the strip in a serene location, Topi has six charming but rudimentary cold-water rooms. Some share bathrooms, others are literally a mattress on the outdoor deck. There's a popular restaurant downstairs, plus various workshops on offer; find details on the website.

WORTH A TRIP

AMED & THE FAR EAST COAST

Stretching from Amed to Bali's far eastern tip, this once-remote stretch of semiarid coast draws visitors to a succession of small, scalloped, black-sand beaches and a relaxed atmosphere. The coast here is often called simply 'Amed', but this is a misnomer, as the coast is a series of seaside *dusun* (small villages) that start with the actual Amed in the north and then run southeast to Aas via Jemeluk and Lipah.

In nearby Tulamben (a 20-minute drive from Amed), the big attraction sank over 60 years ago. The WWII wreck of the US cargo ship *Liberty* is among the best and most popular dive sites in Bali, and has given rise to an entire town based on scuba diving.

Snorkelling is excellent along the coast (in addition to the *Liberty*) and scuba diving is good. There are scores of dive operators in the area. Several, such as **Eco-Dive** (☑ 0363-23482; www.ecodivebali.com; Jemeluk Beach; 🛜) 🍃, have shown a commitment to the communities by organising regular beach clean-ups. All have similar prices for a long list of offerings (eg local dives from about US$80 and open-water dive courses at about US$400).

Every place to stay has a cafe, if not a restaurant. Driving the long road along the Amed coast you will find many eating options.

At chilled-out hideaway **Meditasi** (☑ 0828 372 2738; www.meditasibungalows.blogspot.com; Aas; r 300,000-500,000Rp) you can take a break from the pressures of life. Meditation and yoga help you relax, and the four rooms are close to good swimming and snorkelling. Open-air baths allow you to count the colours of the bougainvillea and frangipani that grow in profusion.

The **Hoky Home Stay & Cafe** (☑ 0819 1646 3701; madejoro@yahoo.com; Jemeluk; r incl breakfast 200,000Rp; 🛜) has great, cheap rooms (with fan and hot water) near the beach. The owner, Made, is tuned in to budget-traveller needs. The cafe (mains 25,000Rp; ⊙ 8am to 10pm) has fresh and creative local foods, especially seafood.

Set on the hill-side of the road amid a nice garden, **Galang Kangin Bungalows** (☑ 0363-23480; bali_amed_gk@yahoo.co.jp; Jemeluk; r incl breakfast with fan/air-con from 300,000/500,000Rp; ❄🛜) has a mix of rooms. The modern air-con rooms open to the beach, while the fan rooms across the road have a more traditional, ornate Balinese style.

Most people drive to the Amed area via the main road from Tirta Gangga to Culik (a car ride from South Bali will cost 500,000Rp). Public-transport options are limited. Many hotels rent bicycles for about 35,000Rp per day. There are fast boats to/from the Gilis, which are just east on the horizon.

ℹ️ Getting There & Away

Padangbai is 2km south of the main Semarapura–Amlapura road.

Among the tourist buses, **Perama** (📞 0363-41419; Jl Pelabuhan; ⏰ 7am-8pm) has a stop here for its services around the east coast; trips include Kuta (75,000Rp, three hours) and Ubud (75,000Rp, two hours).

Ferries run hourly, day and night, to Lembar on Lombok (adult/motorcycle/car 44,000/123,000/879,000Rp, five to seven hours). There are also fast boats to the Gili Islands and Lombok (see p231).

Candidasa

Candidasa is slouching into middle age, no longer the tourism darling it once was. The main drawback is the lack of a beach, which, except for the far eastern stretch, has eroded away as fast as hotels were built. It's a favourite place for sedate travellers to be, well, sedate.

Tirta Gangga

📞 0363

Tirta Gangga (Water of the Ganges) is the site of a holy temple, some great water features and some of the best views of rice fields and the sea beyond in East Bali. High on a ridge, it's a relaxing place to stop for an hour – or even a bit longer to allow for some treks through the surrounding terraced countryside, which ripples with coursing water.

⊙ Sights & Activities

Hiking in the surrounding hills is recommended. The rice terraces around Tirta Gangga are some of the most beautiful in Bali. Back roads and walking paths take you to many picturesque traditional villages. You can also ascend the side of Gunung Agung. Hiring a guide is a good idea; ask at either of the accommodation we've listed (especially Homestay Rijasa).

★ **Taman Tirta Gangga**   PALACE

(admission 20,000Rp, parking 2000Rp; ⊙ site 24hr, ticket office 7am-6pm) Amlapura's water-loving rajah, after completing his lost masterpiece at Ujung, had another go at building the water palace of his dreams in 1948. He succeeded at Taman Tirta Gangga, which has a stunning crescent of rice-terrace-lined hills for a backdrop.

🛏️ Sleeping & Eating

Most places to stay have cafes with mains under 20,000Rp.

Pondok Lembah Dukah   GUESTHOUSE $

(📞 0813 3829 5142; dukuhstay@gmail.com; s/d/f 150,000/200,000/350,000Rp) Atop a hill with divine views over the rice fields, this guesthouse has charming bungalows. Rooms are basic but a stay here is a good chance to get close to local life. It's a 10-minute walk from the palace, down the path to the right of Good Karma guesthouse; follow the signs for 300m along the rice field and then up a steep set of steps.

Homestay Rijasa   HOMESTAY $

(📞 0363-21873; Jl Tirta Gangga; s/d incl breakfast from 100,000/150,000Rp; 🛜) With elaborately planted grounds, this well-run homestay is located opposite the water palace entrance. Expect to pay around double the price for rooms with hot water, which is good for the large soaking tubs. It has a fantastic little warung at the front.

ℹ️ Getting There & Around

It's easiest to visit this region with your own transport.

Gunung Batur Area

📞 0366

Volcanic Gunung Batur (1717m) is a major tourist magnet, offering treks to its summit and spectacular views of Danau Batur (Lake Batur), set at the bottom of a huge caldera. Annoying touts and tourist buses detract from the experience around the rim of the vast crater, but the crater lake and cone of Batur are well worth exploring. Entry to the area costs 30,000Rp per person.

On a clear day, the village of **Penelokan** has superb views across to Gunung Batur and down to the lake at the bottom of the crater. It has numerous huge tourist restaurants catering to busloads of day trippers – avoid these.

The villages of **Batur** and **Kintamani** now virtually run together. Kintamani is famed for its large and colourful **market**, which is held every three days. If you don't want to go on a trek, the sunrise view from the road here is pretty good.

ℹ️ Getting There & Around

From Batubulan terminal in Denpasar, bemos make regular trips to Kintamani (18,000Rp); you can also get a bus there on the busy Denpasar–Singaraja route, which makes stops in both Penelokan and Kintamani (about 18,000Rp). Alternatively, you can just hire a car or use a driver. From South Bali expect to pay around 500,000Rp. Bemos shuttle between Penelokan and Kintamani (about 10,000Rp to Toya Bungkah). Later in the day, you may have to charter transport (50,000Rp or more).

Toya Bungkah

The main tourist centre is Toya Bungkah, which is scruffy but has a cute charm and a serene lakeside setting in the ancient caldera below the peaks.

The most popular local trek is from Toya Bungkah to the top of Gunung Batur for sunrise – a magnificent sight requiring a 4am start from the village. The **PPPGB** (Mt Batur Tour Guides Association; ☑0366-52362; Toya Bungkah; ⏰3am-6pm) has a monopoly on guided climbs up Gunung Batur and charges about 450,000Rp for one to four people to hike Batur. Those attempting to trek Batur alone can expect hassle from the PPPGB.

With a lovely, quiet lakeside location opposite vegetable plots, **Under the Volcano III** (☑0813 3860 0081; Toya Bungkah; s/d incl breakfast 150,000/200,000Rp; 🛜) has six clean and pretty rooms. Other nearby inns are run by the same clan.

Danau Bratan Area

Approaching from the south, you gradually leave the rice terraces behind and ascend into the cool, often misty mountain country around Danau Bratan. The name **Bedugul** is sometimes used to refer to the whole lakeside area, but strictly speaking, Bedugul is just the first place you reach at the top of the hill when coming up from South Bali. Candikuning and Munduk hold the star attractions in this area.

The big sight is **Pura Ulun Danau Bratan** (off Jl Raya Denpasar-Singaraja; adult/child 30,000/15,000Rp, parking 5000Rp; ⏰6am-6pm), a graceful, very important Hindu-Buddhist lakeside temple. It dates to the 17th century.

ℹ️ Getting There & Away

Danau Bratan is beside the main north–south road, so it's easy to reach from South Bali or

WORTH A TRIP

PULAU MENJANGAN

Bali's most rewarding dive area, Pulau Menjangan has a dozen superb dive sites. The diving is excellent – iconic tropical fish, soft corals, great visibility (usually), caves and a spectacular drop-off. Most of the sites are close to shore and suitable for snorkellers or diving novices. Some decent snorkelling spots are not far from the jetty – ask the boatman where to go.

The most convenient place to stay for diving Menjangan is Pemuteran (p222) where every hotel runs snorkelling trips and there are good dive shops. Day trips from other parts of Bali entail long, early-morning drives.

Lovina using your own transport. Most minibuses running from Denpasar's Ubung terminal to Singaraja (for Lovina) will stop along the road near the temple.

Munduk

West from Danau Bratan, Munduk is a pretty, spread-out village perched high on a ridge. It's popular for its good trekking and hiking to oodles of waterfalls, coffee plantations, rice paddies and villages. Arrange a guide through your lodgings.

🛏️ Sleeping & Eating

Meme Surung   GUESTHOUSE **$**
(☑0851 0001 2887; www.memesurung.com; r incl breakfast from 200,000Rp; 🛜) Two atmospheric old Dutch houses adjoin each to form a compound of 11 rooms, immersed among an English-style garden. The decor is traditional and simple; the view from the long wooden verandah is both the focus and joy here. It's located along the main strip of Munduk's township.

Don Biyu   CAFE **$**
(☑0812 3709 3949; www.donbiyu.com; mains 26,000-80,000Rp; ⏰7.30am-10pm; 🛜) Catch up on your blog; enjoy good coffee; zone out before the sublime views; and choose from a mix of Western and interesting Asian fare. Dishes are served in mellow open-air pavilions. It also has six double rooms (600,000Rp), all with balconies and views. It's on the main road leading into Munduk.

WORTH A TRIP

GUNUNG BATUKAU AREA

Often overlooked, Gunung Batukau is Bali's second-highest mountain (2276m), the third of Bali's three major mountains and the holy peak of the island's western end. Enjoy a magical visit to one of the island's holiest and most underrated temples, **Pura Luhur Batukau** (donation 20,000Rp; ⊗8am-6pm). It has a seven-roofed *meru* (multi-roofed shrine) dedicated to Maha Dewa, the mountain's guardian spirit. Mountain streams tumble down around the site.

At **Jatiluwih**, which means 'Truly Marvellous', you will be rewarded with vistas of centuries-old rice terraces that exhaust your ability to describe green. The locals will also be rewarded with your 'green', as there's a road toll for visitors (20,000Rp per person, plus 5000Rp per car). The terraces have acheived Unesco status. You'll understand why just viewing the panorama from the narrow, twisting 18km road, but get out for a **ricefield walk**.

All this serenity can be intoxicating and you can ponder your own karma at one of Bali's most unusual places to stay, the **Bali Silent Retreat** (✉0813 5348 6517; www.balisilentretreat.com; Penatahan; dm $15, r $40-120). Set amid gorgeous scenery, it's just what the name says: a place to meditate, practice yoga, go on nature walks and more – all in total silence. The minimalist ethos stops at the food, however, which is organic and fabulous (US$30 per day, including programs).

The only realistic way to explore the Gunung Batukau area is with your own transport.

Lovina & the North

✆ 0362

'Relaxed' is how people most often describe Lovina, and they are correct. This low-key, low-rise beach resort is the polar opposite of Kuta. Days are slow and so are the nights.

Almost merging into Singaraja, the regional capital to the west, the town is really a string of coastal villages – Pemaron, Tukad Mungga, Anturan, Kalibukbuk (the main area), Kaliasem and Temukus – that have taken on this collective name.

Lovina is a convenient base for trips around the north coast or the central mountains. The beaches are made up of washed-out grey and black volcanic sand, and they are mostly clean near the hotel areas, but generally unspectacular. Reefs protect the shore, so the water is usually calm and clear.

◉ Sights & Activities

In Lovina you'll find yourself walking the modest beach path and not doing much of anything; the sights are in the hills to the south, where waterfalls pour down into dense forest.

★**Komang Dodik**   HIKING
(✆0877 6291 5128; lovina.tracking@gmail.com; hikes from 400,000Rp) Komang Dodik leads hikes in the hills along the north coast. Trips can last from three to seven hours. The highlight of most trips is a series of waterfalls,

more than 20m high, in a jungle grotto. Routes can include coffee, clove and vanilla plantations.

🛏 Sleeping

Hotels are spread out along the many side roads running off Jl Raya Lovina to the beach. There are decent places to stay in every price range.

A bit over 10km from Singaraja, Kalibukbuk is the 'centre' of Lovina, with the biggest concentration of hotels. Anturan has a narrow beach and charming fishing village vibe.

★**Harris Homestay**   HOMESTAY $
(✆0362-41152; Gang Binaria, Kalibukbuk; s/d incl breakfast 130,000/150,000Rp; 🛜) Sprightly, tidy and white, Harris avoids the weary look of some neighbouring cheapies. The charming family lives in the back; guests enjoy four bright, modern rooms up the front.

Sea Breeze Cabins   GUESTHOUSE $
(✆0362-41138; off Jl Bina Ria, Kalibukbuk; r incl breakfast 350,000-400,000Rp; ❋🛜🏊) One of the best choices in the heart of Kalibukbuk, the Sea Breeze has five bungalows and two rooms by the pool and the beach, some with sensational views from their verandahs. The only downside is that it can get noisy from nearby bars at night.

Padang Lovina   GUESTHOUSE $
(✆0362-41302; padanglovina@yahoo.com; Gang Binaria, Kalibukbuk; r with fan/air-con

250,000/300,000Rp; ❀ 🛜 🖼) Down a narrow lane in the very heart of Kalibukbuk, 12 comfortable, unpretentious bungalow-style rooms are set around spacious grounds teeming with flowers. The nicest rooms have air-con and bathtubs. There's wi-fi by the pool.

✕ Eating & Drinking

Lovina's modest social scene centres on Kalibukbuk. Cafes by the beach are popular at sunset.

Global Village Kafe   CAFE $
(📞 0362-41928; Jl Raya Lovina, Kalibukbuk; mains from 19,000Rp; ⊙ 8am-10pm; 🛜) Che Guevara, Mikhail Gorbachev and Nelson Mandela are just some of the figures depicted in the paintings lining the walls of this artsy cafe. The baked goods, fruit drinks, pizzas, breakfasts and much more are excellent. There are free book and DVD exchanges, plus a selection of local handicrafts. Watch for art-house movie nights.

Akar   VEGETARIAN $
(📞 0817 972 4717; Jl Bina Ria, Kalibukbuk; mains 40,000-65,000Rp; ⊙ 7am-10pm; 🛜🍴) 🌿 The many shades of green at this vegetarian cafe aren't just for show. They reflect the earth-friendly ethics of the owners. Enjoy organic smoothies, house-made gelato, and fresh and tasty international dishes, such as chargrilled aubergine filled with feta and chilli.

ⓘ Getting There & Around

From South Bali by public transport, take a minibus from Denpasar (Ubung terminal, 40,000Rp) via Bedugul to Singaraja, where you connect to a blue bemo to Kalibukbuk (about 10,000Rp).

Perama (📞 0362-41161; www.peramatour. com; Jl Raya Lovina) links Lovina with Kuta (125,000Rp, four hours), Ubud (125,000Rp, three hours) and other destinations.

The Lovina strip is *very* spread out, but you can easily travel back and forth on bemos (5000Rp). Bikes cost about 30,000Rp per day.

Southwest Bali

From the busy western road along the south coast, turn north to **Mengwi**, where there's the impressive **Pura Taman Ayun** (adult/child 15,000/7500Rp; ⊙ 8am-6pm) water palace and temple.

A bit further west, and south of the main road, is **Pura Tanah Lot** (adult/child

30,000/15,000Rp, parking cars/motorcycles 5000/2000Rp; ⊙ 7am-7pm), a reconstructed temple and major tourist trap, especially at sunset.

West Bali

Balian Beach

Wild waves pounding an almost empty shore are driving the newfound popularity of this beach, which has a cool surfer's vibe and some laid-back guesthouses. It's 800m off the main road west at Lalang-Linggah.

🛏 Sleeping

★**Surya Homestay**   GUESTHOUSE $
(📞 0813 3868 5643; wayan.suratni@gmail.com; r incl breakfast 150,000-200,000Rp) There are five rooms in bungalow-style units at this sweet little family-run place (Wayan and Putu are charmers) that is about 200m along a small lane. It's spotless, and rooms have cold water and fans. Ask about long-term rates.

Ayu Balian   HOMESTAY $
(📞 0812 399 353; Jl Pantai Balian; r incl breakfast 100,000-150,000Rp) The 15 rooms in this slightly shambolic two-storey cold-water block look down the road to the surf. The small cafe serves crowd-pleasing fare. The friendly owner Ayu is a genuine character.

Gilimanuk

Charm-challenged Gilimanuk is the terminus for the ferries to/from Banyuwangi just across the turbulent channel on Java.

Ferries from Gilimanuk (one hour) depart every 45 minutes. The ferry costs 7500Rp for

INDONESIA SOUTHWEST BALI

SPLURGE

Recalling an older, more refined Bali, **Taman Selini Beach Bungalows** (📞 0362-94746; www.tamanselini.com; Jl Singaraja-Gilimanuk; r incl breakfast US$90-160; ❀ 🛜 🖼) offers quaint thatched roofs, antique carved doors and detailed stonework. The 11 rooms, which open onto a large garden running to the beach, have four-poster beds and large outdoor bathrooms. The outdoor day-beds can be addictive. It's immediately east of Pondok Sari, on the beach and off the main road.

passengers, 25,000Rp for a motorcycle and 148,000Rp for a car (including four passengers). Through-buses between Bali and Java include the fare in the bus ticket.

Taman Nasional Bali Barat

Visitors to Bali's only national park, Taman Nasional Bali Barat (West Bali National Park), can hike through bird-filled forests, enjoy the island's best diving at Pulau Menjangan (p219) and explore coastal mangroves.

The **park headquarters** (☎0365-61060; Jl Raya Cekik; ⊙24hr) at Cekik displays a topographic model of the park and has some information about plants and wildlife. The **Labuhan Lalang visitors centre** (Jl Singaraja-Gilimanuk; ⊙7am-7pm) is in a hut located on the northern coast; snorkellers and dive boats launch here. At both places you can arrange for trekking guides (from 350,000Rp).

Pemuteran

This oasis on a little bay in the far northwest corner of Bali is the place to come for a real beach getaway. Most people dive or snorkel the underwater wonders at nearby Pulau Menjangan while here.

The bay and beach are great for swimming and strolling.

🏃 Activities

★ Reef Seen Divers' Resort DIVING
(☎0362-93001; www.reefseenbali.com; shore/boat dives from 315,000/555,000Rp) Right on the beach in a laid-back resort, Reef Seen is a PADI dive centre and has a full complement of classes. It also offers **pony rides** on the beach for kids (from 200,000Rp for 30 minutes). Some dive packages include accommodation at the resort. The company is active in local preservation efforts.

🛏 Sleeping & Eating

Pemuteran has many midrange resorts on the bay. Just behind them is a growing collection of budget guesthouses and cafes along both sides of the main road.

★ Kubuku Ecolodge GUESTHOUSE $
(☎0362-343 7302; www.kubukuhotel.com; Jl Singaraja-Gilimanuk; r incl breakfast with fan/air-con from 350,000/450,000Rp; ❋🗐) A slice of Seminyak style in Pemuteran, Kubuku has a chic pool and bar with an inviting patch of lawn. Comfortable rooms are excellent value, and the restaurant serves tasty organic meals. It also offers yoga and cooking classes, and bike hire.

Jubawa Homestay GUESTHOUSE $
(☎0362-94745; www.jubawa-pemuteran.com; r 300,000-600,000Rp; ❋🗐🏊) One of Pemuteran's originals, Jubawa is a rather plush budget choice. The 24 rooms are set in expansive gardens around a pool. The popular cafe-bar serves Balinese and Thai food.

❶ Getting There & Away

Pemuteran is served by any of the buses and bemos on the Gilimanuk–Lovina run. Labuhan Lalang and Taman Nasional Bali Barat are 12km west. It's at least a four-hour drive from South Bali, either over the hills or around the west coast.

Nusa Tenggara

NUSA TENGGARA

If you're seeking white sand, azure bays, frothing hot springs and hidden traditional villages, Nusa Tenggara (NTT) is your wonderland. Here's an arc of islands that is lush and jungle-green in the north, and more arid savannah in the south. In between are some of the world's best diving spots, limitless surf breaks and technicolour volcanic lakes. It's a land of pink-sand beaches, schooling sharks and rays, and swaggering dragons.

You'll also find a cultural diversity that is unmatched elsewhere in Indonesia. Animist rituals and tribal traditions still thrive alongside the countless minarets, temples, convents and chapels, and though Bahasa Indonesia is a unifying tongue, each main island has at least one native language, which is often subdivided into dialects. Drop into the easy, tourist-ready life of a car-free Gili island, or venture somewhere less comfortable, more challenging and a shade deeper.

❶ Getting There & Away

Most visitors use Bali as the gateway to Nusa Tenggara. However, you can reach Lombok from Kuala Lumpur and Singapore and the main cities have flights to Jakarta.

❶ Getting Around

The easiest and most popular way to explore Nusa Tenggara is to fly from Bali to Labuanbajo (Flores) or Kupang (West Timor) and island-hop from there.

AIR
Airports dot NTT. Major airports include Lombok, Labuanbajo and Kupang.

BOAT
Regular vehicle/passenger ferries include Bali–Lombok, Lombok–Sumbawa, Sumbawa–Flores and Flores–Sumba. Tourist boats link Lombok with Flores. Fast boats link Bali to Lombok and the Gilis.

In the wet season, when seas get rough, your ship's service may be cancelled for days on end.

BUS
Air-con coaches run across Lombok and Sumbawa, and from Kupang to Dili in Timor, but elsewhere small, slow minibuses are the norm.

CAR & MOTORCYCLE
Overland travel is slow in mountainous Nusa Tenggara. Busy Lombok, Sumbawa, Flores and Timor have fairly decent, surfaced main roads. Get off the highways, and things slow down considerably.

Lombok

Lombok is an easy hop from Bali. It has a spectacular, mostly deserted coastline with palm coves, Balinese Hindu temples, looming cliffs and epic surf. The majestic and sacred Gunung Rinjani rises from its centre – a challenging and rewarding climb.

The Gilis, a car-free collection of islands infused with a sun-drenched party vibe, are Lombok's biggest draw, although the beautiful surf breaks and beaches of Kuta are fast gaining popularity.

❶ Getting There & Away

AIR
Lombok International Airport (LOP; www. lombok-airport.co.id), near Praya, is getting ever more busy. There's good service to Bali

INDONESIA LOMBOK

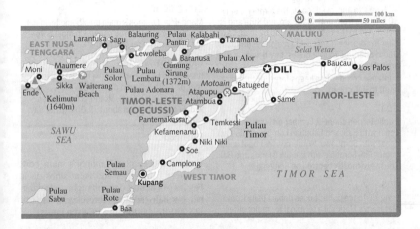

Lombok

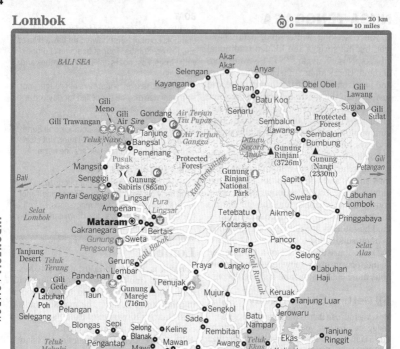

0   20 km
0   10 miles

INDONESIA LOMBOK

and Java, with fewer services going east into Nusa Tenggara. Flights also serve the international hubs of Singapore and Kuala Lumpur. You'll find travel agents for airline tickets in Kuta, Mataram and Senggigi.

Thanks to improved roads, the airport is only 30 minutes from both Mataram and Kuta and is well linked to the rest of the island by road. Taxis offer fixed-price transport to major destinations. Damri operates tourist buses; buy tickets in the arrivals area.

Intense competition keeps fares for the quick jaunt to Bali cheap.

BOAT

Public ferries connect Lembar on Lombok's west coast with Bali, and Labuhan Lombok on its east coast with Sumbawa. Numerous fast boat companies link Lombok with the Gili Islands and Bali. These are mostly centred on Senggigi.

BUS

Long-distance public buses depart daily from Mataram's Mandalika terminal for major cities

in Bali and Java in the west, and to Sumbawa in the east.

ⓘ Getting Around

BUS & BEMO

Mandalika, Lombok's main bus/bemo terminal, is a hub for service. You can reach most corners of Lombok in under two hours.

CAR & MOTORCYCLE

It's easy to hire a car in all the tourist areas (per day with/without driver from 600,000/300,000rp). Motorcycles are also widely available from about 70,000Rp per day.

Lembar

☑ 0370

Hassle-filled Lembar, Lombok's main port, is where Bali ferries and Pelni ships dock. Ferries run hourly, day and night, to Padangbai on Bali (adult/motorcycle/car 44,000/123,000/879,000Rp, five to seven hours).

Bus connections are abundant and bemos run regularly to the Mandalika bus/bemo terminal (25,000Rp), so there's no reason to linger. Taxis cost 80,000Rp to Mataram and 150,000Rp to Senggigi.

Mataram

☑ 0370 / POP 420,000

Lombok's sprawling capital, actually a cluster of four towns – Ampenan (port), Mataram (administrative centre), Cakranegara (commercial centre) and Sweta (bus terminal) – has some allure. There are large malls, decent restaurants and some cultural sights, but few travellers spend any time here.

⊙ Sights

Pura Meru   HINDU TEMPLE
(Jl Selaparang; admission 10,000Rp; ⊙8am-5pm) Pura Meru is the largest and second most important Hindu temple on Lombok. Built in 1720, it's dedicated to the Hindu trinity of Brahma, Vishnu and Shiva. The inner court has 33 small shrines and three thatched, teak-wood *meru* (multi-tiered shrines). The central *meru*, with 11 tiers, is Shiva's house; the *meru* to the north, with nine tiers, is Vishnu's; and the seven-tiered *meru* to the south is Brahma's.

Pura Lingsar   HINDU TEMPLE
(off Jl Gora II; grounds free, temple admission by donation; ⊙7am-6pm) This large temple compound is the holiest in Lombok. Built in 1714 by King Anak Agung Ngurah, and nestled beautifully in lush rice fields, it's multi-denominational, with a temple for Balinese Hindus (Pura Gaduh), and one for followers of Lombok's mystical take on Islam, the Wektu Telu religion.

It's just 6km northeast of Mataram in the village of Lingsar. Take a bemo (minibus) from the Mandalika terminal to Narmada, then another to Lingsar. Ask to be dropped off near the entrance to the temple complex.

🛏 Sleeping & Eating

Staying in central Mataram is a good way to fully engage with nontourist local life. **Mataram Mall** (Jl Selaparang; ⊙7am-9pm), and the streets around it, are lined with Western-style fast-food outlets, Indonesian noodle bars and warungs (food stalls). The mall is sprawling and offers a fascinating look at modern, consumer-driven Indonesia; it also has good cafes and a superb supermarket.

Hotel Melati Viktor   GUESTHOUSE $
(☑ 0370-633830; Jl Abimanyu 1; r 150,000-250,000Rp; ❀ 🛜) The high ceilings, 37 clean rooms and Balinese-style courtyard, complete with Hindu statues, make this one of the best-value places in town. The cheapest rooms have fans.

★ Ikan Bakar 99   SEAFOOD $
(☑ 0370-664 2819, 0370-643335; Jl Subak III 10; mains 20,000-55,000Rp; ⊙11am-10pm) Think squid, prawns, fish and crab, brushed with chilli sauce, perfectly grilled or fried, and drenched in spicy Padang or sticky sweet-and-sour sauce. You will dine among the Mataram families who fill the long tables in the arched, tiled dining room.

ℹ Information

Banks on wide Jl Selaparang and Jl Pejanggik have ATMs. Most change foreign cash.
Rumah Sakit Harapan Keluarga (☑ 0370-670000; www.harapankeluarga.co.id; Jl Ahmad Yani 9; ⊙24hr) The best private hospital on Lombok is just east of downtown Mataram and has English-speaking doctors.

ℹ Getting There & Around

The chaotic Mandalika terminal is 3km from the centre and is a bus and bemo hub. It's surrounded by the city's chaotic main market. Use the official ticket office to avoid touts. Yellow bemos shuttle to the centre (4000Rp).

Buses and bemos departing hourly from the Mandalika terminal include the following:

TO	DISTANCE	FARE (RP)	DURATION
Airport	27km	15,000	45min
Kuta (via Praya & Sengkol)	54km	15,000	90min
Labuhan Lombok	69km	15,000	2hr
Lembar	22km	15,000	30min

Senggigi

☑ 0370

The beaches around the 10km of Senggigi's coast are hard to beat. Think: a series of sweeping bays with white-sand beaches, coconut palms, cliff and mountain backdrops, and blood-red sunset views of Bali's Gunung Agung. Lombok's original tourist area, it's tatty along the main road and the 'karaoke bars' to the south are loud and illicit.

Senggigi

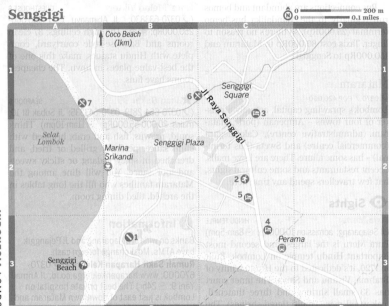

With the Gilis stealing all the cool, Senggigi is best used as a jumping-off point to the rest of Lombok.

☉ Sights & Activities

There's decent **snorkelling** off the rocky point that bisects Senggigi's sheltered bay in front of Windy Cottages; many hotels and restaurants in central Senggigi hire out mask/snorkel/fin sets for 50,000Rp per day. Diving trips from Senggigi normally visit the Gili Islands, so consider basing yourself there.

Stroll the beaches and/or make plans for an ascent of Gunung Rinjani.

Blue Marlin
DIVING

(☑ 0370-613 2424, 0370-693719; www.bluemarlin dive.com; Holiday Resort Lombok, Jl Raya Senggigi; single dive trips 490,000Rp) The local branch of a well-regarded Gili Trawangan dive shop; offers dive courses and trips.

Rinjani Trekking Club
ADVENTURE SPORTS

(☑ 0817 573 0415, 0370-693202; www.info2lom bok.com; Jl Raya Senggigi; ⊙ 9am-8pm) Well informed about routes and trail conditions on Gunung Rinjani, and offers a wide choice of guided hikes. It's the best of the many places hawking Rinjani treks along the strip.

🛏 Sleeping

Senggigi has a lot of budget rooms, but beware of those south of the centre, which may be rattled by the all-night blare of 'karaoke' joints.

★ Wira
GUESTHOUSE $

(☑ 0370-692153; www.thewira.com; Jl Raya Senggigi; dm from 100,000Rp, r 250,000-450,000Rp; ❄🔊) This boutique losmen (a type of budget accommodation) is on the beach side of the main Senggigi strip. It has 11 simple, tasteful, sizeable rooms with bamboo furnishings and private porches out back. There is also a 10-bed fan-cooled dorm room. Use the quiet entrance on the side street, away from Jl Raya Senggigi.

Hotel Elen
HOTEL $

(☑ 0370-693077; Jl Raya Senggigi; r with fan/air-con from 120,000/200,000Rp; ❄🔊) Elen is the long-time backpackers' choice. Rooms are very basic, but those facing the waterfall fountain and koi pond come with spacious tiled patios that catch the ocean breeze.

Sendok Hotel
INN $

(☑ 0370-693176; www.sendokhotellombok. com; Jl Raya Senggigi; r with fan/air-con from 250,000/400,000Rp; ❄🔊🏊) This guesthouse is more attractive than the (friendly) pub

Senggigi

behind which it sits. The 28 rooms pair love-ly Javanese antiques with garish tiles, and have high ceilings and decent bathrooms; all are bright and airy with their own private front porch. Some rooms have hot water.

✖ Eating & Drinking

Senggigi's dining scene ranges from tourist-friendly dining to simple warungs. Many places offer free transport for evening din-ers; phone for a ride. Few miss the chance to enjoy a sunset beverage at one of the many low-key places along the beach.

Cafe Tenda Cak Poer   INDONESIAN $
(Jl Raya Senggigi; mains 12,000-20,000Rp; ☺6pm-late) Barely enclosed, this roadside warung (food stall) wows the stool-sitting masses with hot-outta-the-wok Indo classics. Get the nasi goreng (fried rice) made extra hot (ekstra pedas) and with extra garlic (bawang putih ekstra) and you'll be smiling through tears and sweating.

Office   INTERNATIONAL $
(☏0370-693162; Jl Raya Senggigi, Pasar Seni; mains 25,000-70,000Rp; ☺9am-10pm) This pub near the euphemistic 'art market' offers typ-ical Indonesian and Western choices along with pool tables, ball games and barflies. It also has a Thai menu, which is the choice of those in the know. Tables on the sand near fishing boats are among Senggigi's best places for a relaxed sunset drink.

★**Coco Beach**   INDONESIAN $$
(☏0817 578 0055; Pantai Kerandangan; mains from 60,000Rp; ☺noon-10pm; ✐) This won-derful beachside restaurant has a blissfully secluded setting off the main road. It's pretty and stylish, with many choices for vegetar-ians. The nasi goreng is locally renowned and the seafood is the best in the area. It has a full bar and blends its own authentic jamu

tonics (herbal medicines). It's about 2km north of central Senggigi.

ⓘ Information

The main drag groans with ATMs.

ⓘ Getting There & Around

Fast boats to Bali leave from the large pier right in the centre of the beach. A ticket office is out on the pier.

Marina Srikandi (☏0361 729818; www.marinasrikandi.com; Senggigi Pier; one-way from 375,000Rp) has daily fast boats to Padangbai.

Perama (☏0370-693008; www.peramatour.com; Jl Raya Senggigi; ☺8am-8pm) has an economical shuttle-bus service that connects with the public ferry from Lembar to Padangba, Balii (125,000Rp), from where there are onward shuttle-bus connections to Sanur, Kuta and Ubud (all 175,000Rp). These trips can take eight or more hours. It also offers a bus and boat con-nection to the Gilis for a reasonable 150,000Rp (two hours). It saves some hassle at Bangsal Harbour.

Regular bemos travel between Senggigi and Ampenan's Kebon Roek terminal (3000Rp), where you can connect to Mataram; wave them down on the main drag. There's no public bemo service north to Bangsal Harbour. A metered taxi costs about 90,000Rp.

Damri runs buses to/from the airport (30,000Rp, 90 minutes). Metered taxis to the airport in Praya cost about 150,000Rp and take an hour.

A taxi to Lembar is 150,000Rp.

Gunung Rinjani

Lombok's highest peak, and the second-highest volcano in Indonesia, Gunung Rinjani (3726m) supports a smattering of villages and is of great climatic importance to Lombok. The Balinese call it 'the seat of the Gods' and place it alongside Gunung Agung in spiritual lore. Lombok's Sasaks also revere it and make biannual pilgrim-ages to honour the mountain spirit.

It is a legendary climb. Reach the sum-mit and look down upon a 6km-wide cal-dera with a crescent-shaped cobalt lake, hot springs and smaller volcanic cones. The stunning sunrise view from the rim takes in north Lombok, Bali's Gunung Agung and the Indian Ocean, drenched in an unforget-table blue hue.

Note that eruptions in 2015 closed the peak to trekkers at various times.

TREKKING GUNUNG RINJANI

Treks to the rim, lake and peak should not be taken lightly, and guides are mandatory. June to August is the best trekking season. During the wet season (November to April), tracks can be slippery and dangerous.

Good Senaru outfitters include **John's Adventures** (☑0817 578 8018; www.rinjani master.com; Senaru) and **Rudy Trekker** (☑0818 0365 2874; www.rudytrekker.com; Senaru). You can also make arrangements in Sengiggi. The official website for **Rinjani National Park** (Taman Nasional Gunung Rinjani; ☑0370-660 8874; www.rinjaninationalpark.com) has good maps, plus info and a useful section on reported scams by dodgy hiking operators.

The most common trek is to climb from Senaru to Pos III (2300m) on the first day (about five hours of steep walking), camp there and climb to Pelawangan I, on the crater rim (2600m), for sunrise the next morning (about two hours). From the rim, you can descend into the crater and walk around to the hot springs (two hours) on a very exposed track. The hot springs, revered by locals for their healing properties, are a good place to relax and camp for the second night.

Or continue east from the hot springs and camp at Pelawangan II (about 2900m). From there a track branches off to the summit. It's a heroic climb (three or four hours) over loose footing to the top (3726m). Start at 3am so that you can glimpse the sunrise on the summit.

The most popular package is the three-day, two-night trek from Senaru to Sembalun Lawang via the summit. It includes food, equipment, guide, porters, park fee and transport back to Senaru, and costs about US$300 per person.

Bring several layers of clothing, solid footwear, rain gear, extra water (do not depend on your guide for your water supply) and a torch (flashlight). Buy food and supplies in Mataram or Senggigi. People die every year on the mountain – it shouldn't be approached lightly.

Senaru

☑0370

With sweeping views and an eternal spring climate, the mountain village of Senaru is the best base for Rinjani climbs. Be sure to make the 20-minute walk to the spectacular waterfall, **Air Terjun Sindang Gila** (admission 10,000Rp).

🛏 Sleeping & Eating

All of Senaru's places to stay and eat are strung along the 6.5km-long road that starts in Bayan and runs uphill via Batu Koq to the main Gunung Rinjani park office.

★**Rinjani Lighthouse**   GUESTHOUSE $
(☑0818 0548 5480; www.rinjanilighthouse.mm.st; r 350,000-800,000Rp; 🛜) Set on a wide plateau just 200m from the Rinjani park office, this impressive guesthouse (with hot water) has thatched-roof bungalows in sizes ranging from double to family. The owners are founts of Rinjani info.

Pondok Senaru & Restaurant   LODGE $
(☑0818 0362 4129; pondoksenaru@yahoo.com; r 250,000-700,000Rp; ❋🛜) This place has

14 lovely little cottages (most are fan-only) with terracotta-tiled roofs, and some well-equipped superior rooms with such niceties as hot water. The restaurant, with tables perched on the edge of a rice-terraced valley, is a sublime place for a meal (mains 20,000Rp to 50,000Rp; open 7am to 9pm). It's at the waterfall entrance.

❶ Getting There & Away

From Mandalika terminal in Mataram, catch a bus to Anyar (25,000Rp to 30,000Rp, 2½ hours). Bemos no longer run from Anyar to Senaru, so you'll have to charter an *ojek* (from 20,000Rp per person, depending on your luggage).

Kuta

☑0370

What could be a better gateway to the wonderful beaches of South Lombok? Imagine a crescent bay, turquoise in the shallows and deep blue further out, where rollers crash on a reef 300m from shore. The water licks a huge, white-sand beach, as wide as a football pitch and framed by headlands. Now imagine a coastline of nearly a dozen such bays, all backed by a rugged range of coastal hills spotted with lush patches of banana trees and tobacco fields, and you'll have a notion of Kuta's immediate appeal.

Among the area's beaches seek out **Tanjung An** (or variously Aan or Ann), an empty horseshoe bay with looming headlands. **Pantai Segar** is likewise gorgeous. Note that construction of a long-rumoured huge international resort here has finally begun.

🏃 Activities

For surfing, stellar lefts and rights break on the reefs off Kuta Bay (Telek Kuta) and east of Tanjung An. Boatmen will take you out for around 150,000Rp. Seven kilometres east of Kuta is the fishing village of **Gerupuk**, where there's a series of reef breaks, both close to the shore and further out, but they require a boat, at a negotiable 300,000Rp per day. However savvy surfers buzz past Gerupuk and take the road to **Ekas**, where crowds are thin and surf is plentiful.

West of Kuta you'll find **Mawan**, a stunning swimming beach, and **Mawi**, a popular surf paradise with world-class swells and a strong rip current.

Kimen Surf SURFING
(📞0370-655064; www.kuta-lombok.net; Jl ke Mawan; board rental per day 100,000Rp, lessons per person from 500,000Rp; ⊙9am-8pm) Swell forecasts, tips, kite-surfing, board rental, repairs and lessons. It runs guided excursions to breaks such as Gerupuk (400,000Rp).

Scuba Froggy DIVING
(📞0877 6510 6945; www.scubafroggy.com; Jl ke Mawan; open-water course US$360; ⊙9am-8pm) Runs local trips to a dozen sites, most no deeper than 18m. From June to November it also runs trips to the spectacular and challenging ocean pinnacles in Blongas Bay, famous for schooling hammerheads and mobula rays. Snorkelling trips are 150,000Rp.

🛏 Sleeping

Most accommodation is on or within walking distance of the beach. Simple guesthouses and cafes dominate. A dearth of street names makes navigation an adventure.

⭐**Bombara Bungalows** GUESTHOUSE $
(📞0370-615 8056; bomborabungalows@yahoo.com; Jl Raya Kuta; r 350,000-450,000Rp; ❄️🛜🏊) One of the best places for a low-cost stay in Kuta, these eight (some fan-cooled) bunga-

lows are built around a lovely pool area. Coconut palms shade loungers and the entire place feels like an escape from the hubbub of town. The staff understands the needs of surfers, and everyone else for that matter.

Bule Homestay GUESTHOUSE $
(📞0819 1799 6256; www.bulehomestay.com; Jl Raya Bypass; r 250,000-300,000Rp; ❄️🛜) Although it's about 2km back from the beach near the junction of Jl Raya Kuta and Jl Raya Bypass, this eight-bungalow complex is worth consideration simply for the snappy way it's run. Dirt doesn't dare enter the small compound, where rooms gleam with a hospital white. It is surrounded by a wall that could have been in *The Flintstones*.

Sekar Kuning INN $
(📞0370-615 4856; Jl Raya Pantai Kuta; r from 200,000Rp; ❄️🛜) A charming beach-road inn. Tiled rooms have high ceilings, pastel paint jobs, ceiling fans, and bamboo furniture on the patio. Top-floor rooms have ocean views and are more expensive.

Mimpi Manis B&B $
(📞0818 369 950; www.mimpimanis.com; off Jl Raya Kuta; r 150,000-350,000Rp; ❄️🛜) An inviting English–Balinese-owned B&B in a two-storey house with three spotless rooms (one with air-con), with en-suite showers, TVs and DVD players. There are plenty of good books to browse and DVDs to borrow. It's 1km inland from the beach; the owners offer a free drop-off service to the beach and town, and arrange bike and motorbike rental.

🍴 Eating & Drinking

Full Moon Cafe CAFE $
(Jl Raya Pantai Kuta; mains from 30,000Rp; ⊙8am-late; 🛜) Right across from the beach, the 2nd-floor cafe here is like a tree house with killer ocean views. The menu has all the standards, from banana pancakes to various Indo rice creations. Come for the view and sunset, then hang out.

Warung Bule SEAFOOD $$
(📞0819 1799 6256; Jl Raya Pantai Kuta; mains 40,000-250,000Rp; ⊙8am-10pm; 🛜) Arguably the best restaurant in Kuta, founded by the long-time executive chef at the Novotel, who delivers tropical seafood tastes at an affordable price. We like the tempura starter. His trio of lobster, prawns and mahi mahi might have you cooing. It gets very busy in high season, so be prepared for a wait.

Warung Rasta BAR
(☎0882 1907 1744; Jl Raya Pantai Kuta; ⊙8am-late)
The local owners of this barely there shack of a bar have created a laid-back party vibe that draws in crowds each night. Guitars get strummed and surfers compete in 'strawpedo' contests that involve beer-chugging with the strategic aid of straws. Hungry? Enjoy cheap Indo standards.

❶ Information

Wi-fi is common and there are ATMs.

Reports of deals gone bad make it worthwhile to rent a vehicle or motorcycle only from your accommodation.

As you venture up the coastal road west and east of Kuta, watch your back – especially after dark. There have been reports of muggings in the area.

❶ Getting There & Away

You'll need at least three bemos to get here just from Mataram. Take one from Mataram's Mandalika terminal to Praya (15,000Rp), another to Sengkol (5000Rp) and a third to Kuta (5000Rp).

Simpler are the daily tourist buses serving Mataram (125,000Rp) plus Senggigi and Lembar (both 150,000Rp).

Ride-share cars are widely advertised around town. Destinations include Bangsal for Gili Islands public boats (160,000Rp), Seminyak (Bali) via the public ferry (200,000Rp), and Senaru (400,000Rp).

A taxi to the airport costs 60,000Rp.

Labuhan Lombok

You're here to catch a Sumbawa-bound ferry. Frequent buses and bemos travel between Labuhan Lombok and Mandalika terminal (35,000Rp, 2½ hours) in Mataram. Some buses drop you at the port entrance road. If they do, catch another bemo to the ferry terminal: it's too far to walk.

Ferries run hourly, 24 hours a day, to Poto Tano (19,000Rp, 1½ hours).

Gili Islands

☑ 0370
Picture three minuscule desert islands, fringed by white-sand beaches and coconut palms, sitting in a turquoise sea: the Gilis are a vision of paradise. These islets have exploded in popularity, and are booming like nowhere else in Indonesia – speedboats zip visitors direct from Bali and a hip new hotel opens practically every month.

It's not hard to understand the Gilis' unique appeal, for a serenity endures (no motorcycles or dogs!) and a green consciousness is growing. Development has been more tasteful than rapacious and there are few concrete eyesores.

Each of the three islands has its own special character. Trawangan (which is universally known as Gili T) is by far the most cosmopolitan, its bar and party scene vibrant, its accommodation and restaurants close to definitive tropical chic. Gili Air has the strongest local character, but also a perfect mix of bustle and languor. Meno is simply a desert-island getaway, albeit one with growing buzz.

🏃 Activities

Diving around the Gilis is great. Marine life is plentiful and varied. Turtles and black-and white-tip reef sharks are common, and the macro life (small stuff) is excellent, with seahorses, pipefish and lots of crustaceans. Around full moon, large schools of bumphead parrot fish appear to feast on coral spawns, while at other times of year, mantas soar.

Safety standards are generally high in the Gilis. Rates are fixed (no matter who you dive with) at about 500,000Rp a dive, with discounts for packages of five dives or more. A PADI open-water course costs 5,500,000Rp.

Snorkelling is fun and the fish are plentiful on all the beach reefs. Gear can be rented for 50,000Rp per day. You can get to good sites right off the beaches; no boat is needed.

Walking and cycling are the best land activities. Bikes can be hired from 50,000Rp per day (although island paths sometimes have soft sand that bogs down bikes). On Trawangan, time your circumnavigation (2½ hours on foot) with the sunset, and watch it from the hill on the southwest corner, where you'll have a tremendous view of Bali's Gunung Agung.

Beaches are deceiving as each island seems ringed by perfect white sand – although you'll soon discover that many of the beaches have coral and rocks right up to the water's edge, making just getting in and out (not to mention swimming) a literal pain. However, each island has stretches of sand bordering open water where conditions are idyllic.

ⓘ Information

Wi-fi is widespread. Gili T and Air have ATMs.

DANGERS & ANNOYANCES

➡ There are seldom police on any of the Gilis (though this is changing). Report thefts to the island *kepala desa* (village head) immediately, who will deal with the issue; staff at the dive schools will direct you to him.

➡ Although it's rare, some women have experienced sexual harassment and even assault while on the Gilis – walk home in pairs to the quieter parts of the islands.

➡ As tranquil as these seas do appear, currents are strong in the channels between the islands. Do not try to swim between Gilis – it can be deadly.

➡ The drug trade remains endemic to Gili Trawangan.

➡ Tourists have been injured and killed by adulterated *arak* on the Gilis; skip it.

ⓘ Getting There & Away

PRIVATE BOATS

Fast boats advertise swift connections (about two hours) between Bali and Gili Trawangan. They leave from several departure points in Bali, including Serangan, Sanur, Padangbai and Amed. Some go via Nusa Lembongan. Many dock at Teluk Nare on Lombok north of Senggigi before continuing onto Air and Trawangan (you'll have to transfer for Meno). Note that with land connections and various stops, your travel time may be much greater than advertised.

The website **Gili Bookings** (www.gilibookings. com) presents a range of fast-boat operations. Book well ahead in July and August. One-way fares (with transport to/from tourist areas of Bali) average about US$60 but are negotiable at slow times.

Be warned that the sea between Bali and Lombok can get very rough (particularly during rainy season). For more on safety, see p312.

Long-running operators include:

Amed Sea Express (☑ 0878 6306 4799; www.gili-sea-express.com; per person from 600,000Rp) Makes 75-minute crossings to Amed on a large speedboat; this makes many interesting itineraries possible. Also serves Sanur.

Blue Water Express (☑ 0361-895 1111; www.bluewater-express.com; one-way from 750,000Rp) From Serangan and Padangbai (Bali), to Teluk Kade, Gili T and Gili Air.

Gili Getaway (☑ 0813 3707 4147; www.gili getaway.com; one-way from 675,000Rp; ☺ Gili T office 9am-8pm) Very professional; links Serangan on Bali with Gili T and Gili Air.

Perama (☑ 0361-750808; www.peramatour. com; per person 225,000Rp; ☺ Gili T office 9am-8pm) Links Padangbai, the Gilis and Senggigi by a not-so-fast boat.

PUBLIC BOATS

Coming from other parts of Lombok, most people use the public boats that leave from Bangsal Harbour. (Beware of touts.)

Coming by public transport via Mataram and Senggigi, catch a bus or bemo to Pemenang, from where it's a 1.2km walk (5000Rp by *ojek*) to Bangsal Harbour. A metered taxi to the port will take you to the harbour.

Public boats run to all three islands before 11am; after that you may only find one to Gili T or Gili Air. Public boats in both directions leave when the boat is full (about 30 people). When no public boat is running to your Gili, you may have to charter a boat (400,000Rp to 500,000Rp, carries up to 25 people).

One-way fares are 10,000Rp to Gili Air, 12,000Rp to Gili Meno and 15,000Rp to Gili Trawangan. Boats often pull up on the beaches; be prepared to wade ashore. Public fast boats also link Gili T, Gili Air and Bangsal; they run several times a day and cost 100,000Rp. Buy tickets at the large office.

Arriving in Bangsal, you'll be offered rides in shared vehicles at the port. To Senggigi, 100,000Rp is a fair price. Otherwise, walk 500m down the access road past the huge new tsunami shelter to the Bluebird Lombok Taksi stand (always the best taxi choice) for metered rides to Senggigi (90,000Rp), the airport (200,000Rp) and Kuta (300,000Rp).

ⓘ Getting Around

There's a twice-daily island-hopping boat service that loops between all three islands (35,000Rp to 40,000Rp), so you can sample another Gili's pleasures for the day – although you can't hit all three in one day by public boat. Check the latest timetable at the islands' docks.

Cidomos (horse-drawn carts) operate as taxis. Prices have soared in recent years; even a short ride can cost 50,000Rp. For an hourlong clip-clop around an island expect to pay at least 100,000Rp. We cannot recommend using *cidomos* due to significant questions about the treatment of the horses.

Gili Air

Closest to Lombok, for many people Air is 'just right'. It has great eating and drinking options to rival Gili T, but lacks the frenetic crowds. The southern and eastern coasts have the best swimming beaches. Walking around the island takes about 90 minutes

Gili Air

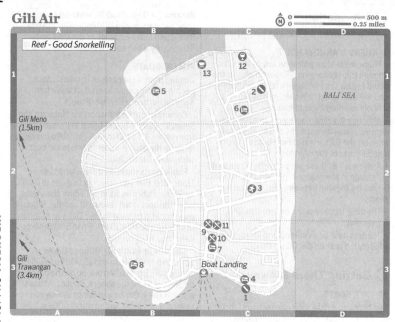

Reef - Good Snorkelling

BALI SEA

Gili Meno
(1.5km)

Gili
Trawangan
(3.4km)

Boat Landing

and you'll find minimal development along most of the north and west coasts.

🏃 Activities

Blue Marine Dive Centre   DIVING
(☑ 0812 377 0288; www.bluemarinedive.com; night dives 570,000Rp) 🏊 Has a nice location on the beautiful northeast corner of the island. Offers free-diving courses. The owner is very active in reef preservation efforts.

7 Seas   DIVING
(☑ 0370-663 2150; www.7seasdivegili.com; 4-day TEC diving packages 6,400,000Rp) 🏊 A vast dive shop with a range of accommodation and a good pool for training or just playing. A local leader in recycling.

H2O Yoga   YOGA
(☑ 0877 6103 8836; www.h2oyogaandmeditation.com; classes 100,000Rp, 3hr workshops 300,000Rp) This wonderful yoga and meditation retreat centre is set back from the beach on a well-signed path in the village. Top-quality classes are held in a lovely circular *beruga* (open-sided pavilion). Massage is also available, and there's candlelight yoga at 5pm.

🛏 Sleeping

Gili Air's 50 or so places to stay are located mostly on the east coast. You'll find more isolation in the west.

⭐ **Gili Air Hostel**   HOSTEL $
(www.giliairhostel.com; dm/r from 125,000/ 350,000Rp; ⊙ reception 7.30am-7pm; ❄ 🛜) A great addition to the island. Beds here are in two- to seven-bed rooms, all of which share bathrooms. The decor defines cheery, and there's a cool bar, a huge frangipani tree and even a climbing wall.

⭐ **Bintang Beach 2**   BUNGALOW $
(☑ 0877 6522 2554; r from 350,000Rp; ❄) On Gili Air's quiet northwest coast, this sandy but tidy compound has basic rooms and bungalows that range from budget-friendly and fan-cooled to mildly snazzy. The bar area is a delight. This enterprising clan has a few other guesthouses nearby.

⭐ **Villa Casa Mio**   BUNGALOW $$
(☑ 0370-646160; www.villacasamio.com; cottages from 900,000Rp; ❄ 🛜 ≋) Casa Mio has fine cottages with pretty garden bathrooms, as well as a riot of knick-knacks (from the artistic to the kitsch). Rooms have fridges, stereos and nice sun decks with loungers. The

Gili Air

casa also boasts a lovely beach area, and good access via a paved portion of the beach lane from the boat landing. Several competitors have sprung up nearby.

7 Seas HOTEL $$
(☎0819 0700 3240; www.7seas-cottages.com; dm from 80,000Rp; r 450,000-800,000Rp; ❄🐾❄) Part of the 7 Seas dive empire, this is an attractive bungalow compound in a great location. Rooms are tidy and comfy; cottages have soaring ceilings and thatch. There are also fan-cooled, bamboo, loftlike hostel rooms.

Damai GUESTHOUSE $$
(☎0878 6142 0416; www.facebook.com/damai-homestay.giliair; r 450,000-650,000Rp; ❄🐾) It's worth seeking out this thatched enclave. The 11 rooms range from basic bungalows to deluxe crash pads, which are tasteful and open onto a garden. The cosy dining patio has cushioned seating, and is elegantly lit with paper lanterns.

🍴 Eating & Drinking

Most places on Gili Air offer an unbeatable setting for a meal, with tables right over the water facing Lombok's Gunung Rinjani. Almost every place closes by 10pm.

⭐ Eazy Gili Waroeng INDONESIAN $
(mains 25,000-40,000Rp; ⊗8am-10pm) In the buzzy main village, this spotless corner cafe serves up local fare aimed at visitors. It's the slightly Westernised face of the beloved

Warung Muslim, immediately to the east. It also does breakfasts, sandwiches and a superb *pisang goreng* (fried banana).

Warung Sasak II INDONESIAN $
(mains from 15,000Rp; ⊗8am-10pm) A fine find in the village, this dead simple warung has excellent versions of all the standards such as chicken satay and fish curry. It also has many variations on *parapek,* a Sasak speciality where foods are cooked in a spicy sauce.

Pasar Malam MARKET $
(Night Market; mains from 15,000Rp; ⊗6-11pm) Inspired by the wild success of the night market on Gili T, Air's has the requisite stalls with fresh Indo fare arrayed around open-air tables. It gets lively after 8pm. Half the fun is just browsing.

⭐ Legend Bar BAR
(⊗7am-late) Painted the requisite Rasta colours of red, green and gold, this raffish reggae bar has a large dance party every full moon.

Little Bar CAFE
(⊗9am-late) Set on a sublime stretch of beach with technicolour sunsets, there is no better place for a sundowner than Little Bar. The menu includes snacks and vegie options.

Gili Meno

Gili Meno is the smallest of the three islands and a good setting for your desert-island fantasy. Meno has a certain Robinson Crusoe charm, although new resorts under construction mean Crusoe will have to upgrade to some fancier digs.

Most accommodation is strung out along the east coast, near the most picturesque beach. Inland you'll find scattered homesteads, coconut plantations and a salty lake. However the once-lonely west coast is seeing some high-profile development, including an enormous beachside condo project set to open in 2017.

🏊 Activities

Gili Meno Divers DIVING
(☎0878 6536 7551; www.giliairdivers.com; Kontiki Cottages; introductory dives from 900,000Rp; ⊗9am-5pm) French and Indonesian owned; offers a range of courses including some good ones in underwater photography.

Gili Meno

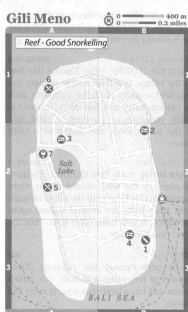

N 0 —————— 400 m
0 —————— 0.2 miles

Reef - Good Snorkelling

Salt Lake

BALI SEA

---

our their heritage by serving excellent food (the crème brûlée is particularly good).

✗ Eating & Drinking

Almost all of Meno's restaurants have absorbing sea views. Here 'dressing for dinner' means putting on clothes.

★ Sasak Cafe INDONESIAN $
(mains 25,000–80,000Rp; ⊗ kitchen 7am-9pm, bar till late) Considering its out-of-the-way location, this bamboo-and-thatch, island-casual hang-out has tasty Indo standards, which literally take on a rosy glow when the sun sets. The tunes and the drinks flow late into the night.

Webe Café INDONESIAN $
(☑ 0821 4776 3187; mains from 25,000Rp; ⊗ 8am-10pm; ☏) A wonderful location for a meal, Webe Café has low tables sunk in the sand, with the turquoise water just a metre away. It scores well for Sasak and Indonesian food such as *kelak kuning* (snapper in yellow spice); staff fire up a seafood barbecue most nights too. There are also basic bungalows for rent (from 400,000Rp).

Diana Café BAR
(⊗ 8am-9pm) If you find the pace of life on Meno too busy, head to this intoxicating little tiki bar par excellence. Diana couldn't be simpler: a wobbly looking bamboo-and-thatch bar, a few tables on the sand, a shack offering tattoos, a hammock or two, reggae on the stereo and a chill-out zone.

Gili Trawangan

Gili Trawangan is a paradise of global repute, ranking alongside Bali and Borobudur as one of Indonesia's top destinations.

⊨ Sleeping

★ Gili Meno Eco Hostel HOSTEL $
(☑ 0878 6249 2062; www.gilimenoecohostel.com; dm/r from 90,000/200,000Rp; ☏) ✦ A fantasy in driftwood, this is the place you dream about staying when you're stuck in the snow waiting for a train. A volleyball court, groovy lounge, tree house, beach bar and much more open right onto the sand. Recycling and other ecofriendly practices, such as using sustainable construction materials, are a feature.

Tao Kombo BUNGALOW $
(☑ 0878 6033 1373; www.tao-kombo.com; r 200,000-400,000Rp; ☏) ✦ This innovatively designed place has seven *lumbung* cottages with thatched roofs, stone floors and outdoor bathrooms. It's home to the popular Jungle Bar, and is 200m inland from the main strip. The owners are heavily involved in community projects; the whole place is run with an eye to sustainability.

★ Kebun Kupu Kupu GUESTHOUSE $$
(☑ 0819 0742 8165; www.kupumenoresort.com; r from 800,000Rp; ❄ ☏ ☲) Situated 300m from the beach, this collection of bungalows (the ones made from wood are lovely) has a great pool, palm trees overhead and a quiet spot near the salt lake. The French owners honour

Trawangan's heaving main drag, busy with bikes, horse carts and mobs of scantily clad visitors, can surprise those expecting some languid tropical retreat. Instead, a wall-to-wall roster of lounge bars, hip guesthouses, ambitious restaurants, minimarts and dive schools clamour for attention.

And yet behind this glitzy facade, a bohemian character endures, with rickety warungs and reggae joints surviving between the cocktail tables, and quiet retreats dotting the much less busy north coast. Even as massive 200-plus-room hotels begin to colonise the still mostly wild and ragged west coast, you can head just inland to a village laced with sandy lanes roamed by free-range roosters, kibbutzing *ibu* (mothers) and wild-haired kids playing hopscotch. Here the call of the muezzin, not happy hour, defines the time of day.

🏃 Activities

Gili T is ringed by the sort of powdery white sand people expect to find on Bali (but don't). It can be crowded along the bar-lined main part of the strip, but walk just a bit north or south and east and you'll find some of Gili T's nicest beaches for swimming and snorkelling. You can find even more solitude along the west and north coasts, where it will be just you and your towel on the sand – although water- and Bintang-vendors are never far away.

Note that at low tide large portions of the west and north coasts have rocks and coral near the surface, which makes trying to get off the shore deeply unpleasant. The reef is in good shape off the northwest coast but rocks and coral make access difficult.

★**Lutwala Dive**   DIVING
(📞 0877 65492615; www.lutwala.com; divemaster courses 14,000,000Rp) 🤿 A nitrox and five-star PADI centre owned by Fern Perry, who held the women's world record for deepest open-circuit dive (190m). A GIDA member, it also rents top-quality snorkelling gear.

Big Bubble   DIVING
(📞 0370-612 5020; www.bigbubblediving.com; fun dives day/night 490,000/600,000Rp) 🤿 The original engine behind the Gili Eco Trust, and a long-running dive school. It's a GIDA member.

Freedive Gili   DIVING
(📞 0370-614 0503; www.freedivegili.com; beginner/advanced courses US$275/375) Free-diving is an advanced breath-hold technique that allows you to explore much deeper depths than snorkelling (to 30m and beyond). Trawangan's professional school is owned by an expert diver who has touched 90m on a single breath, and offers two-day beginner and three-day advanced courses. After a two-day course many students are able to get down to 20m on a single breath of air.

Gili Yoga   YOGA
(📞 0370-614 0503; www.giliyoga.com; per person from 100,000Rp) Runs daily vinyasa classes, and is part of Freedive Gili.

🛌 Sleeping

Cheap places are inland from the main strip and are actually some of the most serene choices on Gili T, as the lanes back here are quiet and flower-lined. Book ahead in July and August.

★**Gili Hostel**   HOSTEL $
(📞 0877 6526 7037; www.gilihostel.com; dm from 175,000Rp; ❄🤳🏊) This co-ed dorm complex has a shaggy Torajan-style roof. The seven rooms each sleep seven, and have concrete floors, high ceilings and a sleeping loft. There's a rooftop bar with beanbags, sun loungers and hammocks, plus views of the treetops, the hills and the big party pool.

Sama Sama Bungalows   BUNGALOW $
(📞 0370-612 1106; r 300,000-550,000Rp; ❄🤳) Just a few metres from where the fast boats drop you on the beach, the eight *lumbung*-style units here are perfect if you want to be right in the very heart of the action.

Pondok Gili Gecko   GUESTHOUSE $
(📞 0818 0573 2814; r from 250,000Rp; 🤳) An inviting guesthouse with a charming gecko motif. The four rooms are super clean, and have ceiling fans and private tiled patios overlooking the garden.

ℹ CULTURAL RESPECT

As you get offered your 100th magic mushroom it may be hard to remember that Gili T is a devout Muslim island, but it is. Strolling the lanes barely clad in your bathing suit, going topless and snogging in general are best done in private. The entire island dials it down a notch during Ramadan.

Gili Trawangan

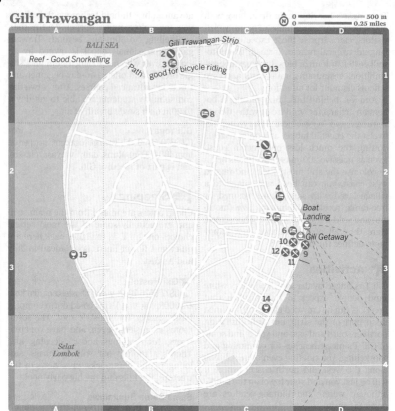

Gili Trawangan

★ **Eden Cottages**   COTTAGE **$$**
(☎ 0819 1799 6151; www.edencottages.com; cottages 550,000-850,000Rp; ❉ ❈) Six clean, thatched concrete bungalows wrapped around a pool, fringed by a garden and shaded by a coconut grove. Rooms have tasteful furnishings, stone baths, TV-DVD and fresh-cold-water showers. The owner avoids wi-fi, which only increases the serenity.

Soundwaves   BUNGALOW **$$**
(☎ 0819 3673 2404; www.soundwavesresort.com; r 400,000-700,000Rp; ❉ ☎) The 13 rooms here are simple and clean with tiled floors. Some are set in wooden A-frames, others in a two-storey concrete building with staggered and recessed patios offering beach views from each room. Some rooms are fan-only.

Woodstock   BUNGALOW **$$**
(☎ 0821 4765 5877; www.woodstockgili.com; r with fan/air-con from 540,000-600,000Rp; ❉ ☎ ❈) The hippest spot on Trawangan. Commune

with the spirit of the Dead, Baez and Hendrix in 12 pristine rooms with tribal accents, private porches and outdoor baths, which surround a laid-back pool area.

Eating

With more than a hundred places for a meal, you'll be spoilt for choice. There's few interesting options in the west, so picnic as you perambulate.

★ Pasar Malam   MARKET $
(mains   15,000-30,000Rp;   ☺6pm-midnight) Blooming every evening in front of Gili T's market, this night market is the place to indulge in ample local eats, including tangy noodle soup, savoury fried treats, scrumptious *ayam goreng* (fried chicken) and grilled fresh catch. Just wandering around the stalls (we like Green Cafe) looking at all the dishes vying for your attention will get you drooling. Seating is at long tables.

La Dolce Vita   ITALIAN $
(mains 20,000-40,000Rp; ☺7.30am-5pm Tue-Sun) There comes that moment when another nasi goreng will just make you turn nasty. Don't delay, hop right on over to this little cafe that's not much bigger than one of its excellent espressos. Slices of authentic pizza and a whole range of pastries are joined by daily specials to sate the ravenous.

Warung Kiki Novi   INDONESIAN $
(mains from 15,000Rp; ☺8am-10pm) Long-time islanders will tell you that this is the best place for *nasi campur* (rice with a choice of side dishes) in the Gilis, and they are right; this cheery dining room is the scene of budget-dining nirvana. Besides fine Indo mains there's a smattering of Western sandwiches and salads.

★ Kayu Café   CAFE $$
(☏0878 6239 1308; mains 40,000-80,000Rp; ☺8am-10pm; 🐾) There are two options here: the main cafe on the inland side of the strip has a lovely array of healthy baked goods, salads, sandwiches and the island's best juices, all served in air-con comfort. Across the road the beach cafe is all open air and exposed wood. Service on the sand can be slow – head inside to order.

🍸 Drinking & Nightlife

The island has oodles of beachside drinking dens, ranging from sleek lounge bars to simple shacks. Parties are held several nights a week, shifting between mainstay bars (such as Tir na Nog and Rudy's Pub) and various upstarts.

★ La Moomba   BAR
(☺10am-midnight) If you wish to chill on a luscious white beach, with bamboo lounges and reggae pumping from the tiki bar, head to La Moomba, Trawangan's best beach bar.

Vintage Sunset Beach   BAR
(☺11am-10pm) The kind of sunset bar that you won't want to leave after the sun has set. While strains of Billie Holiday add mellifluous accents to the lapping surf, enjoy excellent Jamaican food (the spicy chicken, yum!; mains from 60,000Rp). Or just let the sand caress your toes as you hang low in a hammock.

Tir na Nog   PUB
(☏0370-613 9463; ☺7am-2am Thu-Tue, to 4am Wed; 🐾) Known simply as 'The Irish', this hanger of hangovers has a sports-bar interior with big screens. Enjoy tasty chow such as kebabs (mains 35,000Rp to 80,000Rp). Its shoreside open-air bar is probably the busiest meeting spot on the island. Jovial mayhem reigns on Wednesday nights when the DJ takes over.

Sumbawa

Elaborately contorted and sprawling into the sea, Sumbawa is all volcanic ridges, terraced rice fields, dry expanses and sheltered bays. Two main areas draw visitors: the southwest coast from Maluk is essentially a layered series of headlands and wide, white beaches with renowned surf, while in the southeast near Hu'u, Lakey Peak has become Sumbawa's premier year-round surf magnet.

Though well connected to Lombok, Sumbawa is a very different sort of place. It's far less developed, much poorer and conservatively Islamic. Transport connections off the cross-island road are infrequent and uncomfortable, and most overland travellers don't even get off the bus as they roll from Lombok to Flores. For now, it's the domain of surfers, miners and mullahs.

ⓘ Dangers & Annoyances

Most Sumbawans are hospitable, albeit taciturn, but you may encounter some tension. In the past, protests against foreign-owned mining operations have turned violent. Note that the island is much more religiously conservative

INDONESIA SUMBAWA

than neighbouring Lombok or Flores; behave modestly at all times.

ℹ️ Getting There & Around

Ferries link Labuhan Lombok and Poto Tano. In the east, Sape has ferries to Labuanbajo, Flores.

Sumbawa's main highway is in good condition and runs from Taliwang (near the west coast) through Sumbawa Besar, Dompu and Bima to Sape (the ferry port on the east coast). It's relatively traffic-free – a relief if you've made the trek through Java, Bali and Lombok. Fleets of long-distance buses, most of them air-conditioned, run between the west coast ferry port of Porto Tano and Sape, serving all the major towns between.

Car hire is possible through hotels: prices are about 600,000Rp to 800,000Rp per day, including a driver. Motorcycles cost 50,000Rp to 80,000Rp a day.

Poto Tano

Poto Tano is the Lombok-bound ferry port; there's no reason to hang around. Most travellers pass straight through to the beaches around Maluk or continue east towards Flores.

ℹ️ Getting There & Around

Ferries run hourly, 24 hours a day, between Labuhan Lombok and Poto Tano (passengers 19,000Rp, 1½ hours). Cars cost 466,000Rp, motorcycles 54,000Rp. Buses travelling through from Lombok, Bali and Java include the ferry fare.

Buses meet the ferry and go to Taliwang (20,000Rp, one hour) and Sumbawa Besar (30,000Rp, two hours).

Maluk & Rantung

South of Taliwang, the beaches and bays try to outdo one another. Your first stop is the working-class commercial district of **Maluk**, 30km south of Taliwang. Yes, the town is ugly, but the beach is superb.

Directly south of Maluk, within walking distance of the beach (though it is a long walk), is **Supersuck**, consistently rated by surfers as the best left in the world. It really pumps in the dry season (May to October).

About a 12km serpentine drive further south, **Pantai Rantung** (commonly called Rantung Beach), spills onto a secluded and majestic bay framed by 100m-high headlands. The water is crystal-clear and waves roll in year-round at **Yo Yo's**, a right break at the north end of the bay.

Among the simple beachside places on Rantung Beach, **Santai Beach Bungalows** (☑️0878 6393 5758; r 100,000-200,000Rp; @) offers a collection of 12 spacious, well-tended tiled rooms.

Bemos travel between Taliwang and Maluk (20,000Rp, two hours) almost hourly from 7am to 6pm. Three daily buses leave Terminal Maluk, north of town across from the entrance to the Newmont mine (look for the big gates and massive parking area), for Sumbawa Besar (40,000Rp, four hours).

Sumbawa Besar

☑️0371 / POP 54,000

Sumbawa Besar, nestled in a lush, sun-kissed breadbasket, is the main town on the western half of the island. There's no reason to linger here. If you miss a bus connection, the aptly named **Sumbawa Transit Hotel** (☑️0371-21754; Jl Garuda 41; r 250,000-600,000Rp; ❄️🛜) is conveniently located across the main road and to the left as you emerge from the airport.

ℹ️ Getting There & Away

The airport (SWQ) is very close to the centre. Transnusa has flights to Bali; Garuda Indonesia has flights to Lombok.

Sumbawa Besar's main long-distance bus station is Terminal Sumur Payung, 5.5km northwest of town on the highway. You can book tickets at the station and at **Tiara Mas** (☑️0371-21241; Jl Yos Sudarso; ⊙9am-6pm). Destinations served include the following:

Bima 80,000Rp, seven hours, several daily

Mataram 80,000Rp (including ferry ticket), six hours, several daily

Poto Tano 30,000Rp, three hours, hourly from 8am to midnight

Pantai Lakey & Hu'u

Pantai Lakey, a gentle crescent of golden sand 3km south of Hu'u, is where Sumbawa's tourist pulse beats year-round, thanks to seven world-class surf breaks that curl and crash in one massive bay. From August to October the wind gusts, which turns Pantai Lakey into Indonesia's best kitesurfing destination.

🛏️ Sleeping & Eating

Puma Bungalows & Restaurant   BUNGALOW $

(☑️0373-623061; Jl Raya Hu'u; r 90,000-350,000Rp; ❄️) Expect 23 colourful concrete bungalows with tiled roofs and shady front porches, plus sprawling, palm-shaded grounds with fabulous views. Cheaper rooms are fan-only. The two-storey cafe (mains 30,000Rp to 50,000Rp) has sweeping views and a rickety, bamboo vibe; the ginger prawns are popular. On some days yoga classes are held.

Lakey Beach Inn GUESTHOUSE $
(☏0373-623576; www.lakey-beach-inn.com; Jl Raya Hu'u; r 90,000-250,000Rp; ❄️🛜) Enjoy tasty homestyle fish dinners, pizza and Indo classics at the large and driftwoody waterfront cafe (mains 25,000Rp to 60,000Rp). Rooms are basic – the cheapest have fans and cold water. French owner Rachel is a legendary local character.

★**Vivian's Lakey Peak Homestay** HOMESTAY $$
(☏0878 6698 1277; www.lakeypeakhomestay.com; off Jl Raya Hu'u; r 250,000-300,000Rp; ❄️🛜) Set along a little lane between the beach and the main road, this five-room family compound offers the area's warmest welcome. Rooms are newish and large with nice furnishings. The yard is shaded by banana trees and there's a genial cafe-cum-day room.

ℹ️ Information

There is community wi-fi, although some places offer their own (faster) service.

The nearest ATMs are in Dompu, 37km to the north.

ℹ️ Getting There & Away

From Dompu there are two daily (slow) buses as far as Hu'u (25,000Rp, 1½ hours), where you can hire an *ojek* (15,000Rp) to Pantai Lakey. *Ojeks* to/from Dompu on the Trans-Sumba highway cost 150,000Rp.

Try doing this with a surfboard and you'll see why so many people take a taxi from Bima airport (around 800,000Rp, four people). Buses to/from Bima cost from 50,000Rp (one to two daily).

The *ojek* cartel is omnipresent in Lakey; rates to the breaks range from 30,000Rp to 80,000Rp.

Bima & Raba
☏0374 / POP 149,000
These twin cities – grubby but lively Bima and orderly but dull Raba – form Sumbawa's main port and commercial hot spot, but there's no good reason to nest here.

However, should flight or bus connections demand it, **Hotel Lila Graha** (☏0374-42740;

Jl Lombok 20; r 200,000-350,000Rp; ❄️🛜) has a wide range of rooms; ground-floor suite rooms are the newest and nicest.

ℹ️ Getting There & Away

Bima's airport (BMU) is 17km west of the city and is the main airport for travellers to Pantai Lakey. Services include the following:

Bali Garuda Indonesia, Lion Air (1¼ hours, daily)

Makassar Garuda Indonesia (1½ hours, daily)

Buses heading west leave from the Bima bus terminal, a 10-minute walk south along Jl Sultan Kaharuddin from the centre of town. You can buy a ticket in advance from bus company offices on Jl Sultan Kaharuddin. Buses for Sape depart from the Kumbe terminal in Raba (a 3000Rp bemo ride away). Routes include the following:

Dompu 25,000Rp, two hours, almost hourly from 6am to 5pm

Mataram 250,000Rp, 11 to 14 hours, two daily

Sape 35,000Rp, two hours, almost hourly from 6am to 5pm

Sumbawa Besar 80,000Rp, seven hours, several daily

Sape
☏0374
This tumbledown port town is not a place to linger. The docks, perfumed with the conspicuous scent of drying cuttlefish, are 3km from town.

ℹ️ Getting There & Away

Express buses with service to Lombok and Bali meet arriving ferries.

Regular breakdowns and big water disrupt ferry services – always double-check the latest schedules in Bima and Sape. Ferries from Sape include the following:

Labuanbajo 60,000Rp, six to seven hours, one to two daily

Waikelo (Sumba) 65,000Rp, eight hours, two weekly

Komodo & Rinca

Parched, desolate and beautiful Komodo and Rinca rise from waters that churn with rips and whirlpools and are patrolled by lizard royalty, the **komodo dragon**. Drawing ever-more visitors each year, the park is driving the booming popularity of Flores.

Komodo National Park (www.komodopark.com) established in 1980, encompasses Komodo, Rinca, several neighbouring

KOMODO DRAGONS

The Komodo dragon (*ora*) is a monitor lizard, albeit one on steroids. Growing up to 3m in length and weighing up to 100kg, they are an awesome sight and make a visit to Komodo National Park well worth the effort. Lounging about lethargically in the sun, they actually are as fearsome as their looks imply. Park rangers keep them from attacking tourists; random encounters are a bad idea. Some dragon details:

➡ They are omnivorous, and enjoy eating their young. Juvenile dragons live in trees to avoid becoming a meal for adults.

➡ *Ora* often rise up on their hind legs just before attacking, and the tail can deliver well-aimed blows that knock down their prey.

➡ Bacteria in the dragons' mouth are their secret weapon. One bite from a dragon leads to septic infections that inevitably kill the victim. The huge lizard lopes along after its victim waiting for it to die, which can take up to two weeks.

➡ Komodos will feed on mammals weighing up to 100kg. They do this at one sitting and then retire for up to a month to digest the massive meal.

➡ On Komodo, *ora* have been seen chasing deer into the ocean and then waiting on shore while the hapless deer tries to come back ashore. Eventually the exhausted animal staggers onto the beach, where the dragon inflicts its ultimately deadly bite.

➡ There is no accepted reason why the dragons are only found in this small area of Indonesia, although it's thought that their ancestors came from Australia four million years ago. There are about 4000 in the wild today.

➡ A recent discovery has biologists baffled: female dragons kept isolated from other dragons their entire lives have recently been observed in zoos giving birth to fertilised eggs.

➡ Your odds of seeing a dragon at either Rinca or Komodo are good.

islands, and the rich marine ecosystem within its 1817 sq km.

Fees for visitors add up quickly:

➡ Landing fee for Komodo and Rinca islands: 50,000Rp per person

➡ Basic guided walk fee: 80,000Rp per person

➡ Diving fee (per person per day): Monday to Saturday 175,000Rp, Sunday 250,000Rp

➡ Snorkelling fee (per person per day): Monday to Saturday 165,000Rp, Sunday 240,000Rp

Tour operators (including dive shops) usually collect the fees in advance. If not, you pay them in the park offices on Komodo or Rinca, or in Labuanbajo.

At both Komodo and Rinca you have a choice of **walks**, from short to long, which you arrange with a ranger when you arrive at the relevant island's park office.

The islands are easily reached from Labuanbajo on day trips, which usually include stops for **snorkelling** and **swimming** at various idyllic little beaches on tiny islets in the beautiful waters west of Labuanbajo.

🏃 Activities

On **Rinca**, you have a choice of guided hikes from the pleasant ranger station close to the docks. The 90-minute 'medium' hike is really 'just right', as it includes the shady lowlands plus a trip up the hillside where the views across the arid landscape to palm-dotted ridges, achingly turquoise waters and pearly white specks of beach are spectacular. Besides dragons, you may see deer, snakes, monkeys, wild pigs and myriad birds. For many, Rinca, which can be reached from Labuanbajo in under an hour, is the best option for park visits since it packs a lot into a compact area.

Spectacular **Komodo** – its steep hillsides jade in the short wet season, frazzled by the sun and winds to a deep rusty red for most of the year – is the largest island in the national park. A succession of eastern peninsulas spread out like so many fingers, fringed in pink sand, thanks to the abundance of red coral offshore. The main camp of Loh Liang and the PHKA office, where boats dock and guided walks and treks start, is on the east coast.

Of the various walks, the medium walk (2.5km, 90 minutes) is a winner and includes a hill with sweeping views and a chance to see colourful cockatoos.

Komodo Island is at the centre of myriad **diving** and **snorkelling** sites. Most people visit as part of day trips to the island, on dive-shop excursions from Labuanbajo while on a liveaboard.

ⓘ Getting There & Away

Organise your visit to Komodo and Rinca from Labuanbajo (Flores), where there are dozens of dive shops and agencies offering tours.

A typical day trip on a fast boat (under one hour one-way to Rinca, about 80 minutes to Flores) costs about 300,000Rp per person and includes beach and snorkelling stops. A simple lunch is usually included, as well as snacks plus the use of snorkelling gear (but confirm beforehand).Chartering a boat for the day costs at least 950,000Rp but will allow you to fully customise your trip. Note that regular (slow) boats take double the times above to reach the islands. Shop around to compare the many offers.

Flores

Flores, the island named 'flowers' by 16th-century Portuguese colonists, has become Indonesia's 'Next Big Thing'. In the far west, Labuanbajo is a booming tourist town that combines tropical beauty with nearby attractions such as Komodo National Park, myriad superb dive spots and beach-dappled little islands.

The often lush interior is attracting an ever-greater river of travellers who, in just a few days' journey overland, encounter smoking volcanoes, spectacular rice fields and lakes, exotic cultures and hidden beaches. You'll even see plenty of steeples, as away from the port towns most people are nominally Catholic. Many more people are part of cultures and groups that date back centuries, and live in traditional villages seemingly unchanged in millennia.

The 670km, serpentine – yet rapidly improving – Trans-Flores Hwy skirts knife-edge ridges that sheer into spectacular river canyons, brushes by dozens of traditional villages, and always seems to have a perfectly conical volcano in view. Roads of varying quality branch off into areas few tourists have explored.

ⓘ Information

Foreign aid money has funded an excellent string of tourist offices in key towns across Flores. Their enthusiastic information is backed by an excellent website (www.florestourism.com), free town maps and several publications well worth their modest price, including a huge, detailed island map, and books covering activities and culture.

ⓘ Getting There & Away

Air You can easily get flights connecting Flores to Bali, Lombok and Kupang (West Timor), among other destinations. Labuanbajo is the main gateway, while Maumere and Ende are also serviced by daily flights. It's easy to fly into, say Labuanbajo, tour the island, and fly out of Maumere. However, note that the booming popularity of Flores means that flights are booked solid at peak times.

Boat Daily ferries connect Labuanbajo with Sape (Sumbawa). From Larantuka, infrequent ferries go to Kupang (West Timor). From Ende and Aimere, boats will take you to Waingapu (Sumba).

ⓘ Getting Around

Regular buses ply the Trans-Flores Hwy. They're cheap and cramped. Much more comfortable and only somewhat more expensive are public

SEVEN DAYS ON FLORES

You can take as long as you like exploring Flores, but a common trip for the visa-expiry-date-conscious, using a hired car and driver, goes like this:

➡ Three days in Labuanbajo and the surrounding park and waters

➡ One day driving to the hill town of Bajawa

➡ One day driving to the sweet mountain village of Moni, via the Ngada village of Bena and the steamy port town of Ende

➡ One day exploring the area around Moni, including Kelimutu National Park

➡ One day driving to Maumere, with a stop at the beach in Paga

You can fly out of Maumere and you can do this trip in either direction, although it's easiest to find a driver you'll like in Labuanbajo. Add a couple of extra days to the schedule above if you're sticking to buses.

BOAT TOURS BETWEEN LOMBOK & FLORES

Travelling by sea between Lombok and Labuanbajo is a popular way to get to Flores, as you'll glimpse more of the region's spectacular coastline and dodge the slog by bus across Sumbawa. Typical three- and four-day itineraries take in snorkelling at Pulau Satonda or Pulau Moyo off the coast of Sumbawa, and a dragon-spotting hike on Komodo or Rinca.

But note: this is usually no luxury cruise – a lot depends on the boat, the crew and your fellow travellers. Some operators have reneged on 'all-inclusive' deals en route, and others operate decrepit old tugs without life jackets or radio. And this crossing can be hazardous during the rainy season (October to January), when the seas are rough.

Most travellers enjoy the journey though, whether it involves bedding down on a mattress on deck or in a tiny cabin. The cost for a three- to- four-day itinerary ranges from about US$170 to US$400 per person and includes all meals, basic beverages and use of snorkelling gear.

Other considerations:

➡ Carefully vet your boat for safety (see p312).

➡ Find out just what's included in the price, and what's not. For instance, if drinking water is included, how much is provided? If you need more, can you buy it on the boat or do you need to bring your own?

➡ If you're flexible, you can often save money by travelling west from Flores, as travelling eastwards to Flores is more popular. Look for deals with agents once you're in Labuanbajo.

We recommend the following two long-running and reliable operators:

Kencana Adventure (☑ 0370-693432; www.kencanaadventure.com; Jl Raya Senggigi, Senggigi, Lombok; one-way deck/cabin from 1,750,000/4,500,000Rp) Offers basic boat trips between Lombok and Labuanbajo with deck accommodation as well as cabins that sleep two. Also has a branch in **Labuanbajo** (Jl Soekarno Hatta, front of Gardena Hotel).

Perama Tour (☑ 0361-750808; www.peramatour.com; Jl Raya Legian 39; one-way deck/cabin from 1,300,000/2,000,000Rp) Runs basic boat trips between Lombok and Labuanbajo with deck accommodation as well as small two-person cabins. Also has a branch in **Labuanbajo** (Jl Soekarno Hatta).

---

minibuses (often a Toyota Kijang) that link major towns in air-con comfort. Many visitors hire a car and driver, which costs from 600,000Rp to 800,000Rp per day. If you have a group of six, this is a fair deal. Motorcycles (from 50,000Rp per day) are also popular but aren't for the faint of heart.

Your accommodation will usually have details on all the above options.

Labuanbajo

☑ 0385

Ever more travellers are descending on this gorgeous, slightly ramshackle harbour town, freckled with offshore islands and blessed with idyllic views that offer surrealist sunsets.

Labuanbajo's main drag, Jl Soekarno Hatta, is lined with cool cafes, guesthouses, travel agents and a few hopping bars. The waterfront is spiffed up and the connections to other parts of Indonesia are excellent. With the many beguiling islands just offshore, you may find Labuanbajo (or Bajo as

it's commonly called) hard to leave, even as the draw of Flores proper lures you east.

Activities

The pristine reefs and preponderance of underwater life in Komodo National Park and the surrounding waters is one of the big draws to Labuanbajo. Prices tend to be uniform.

★ **Wicked Diving**   DIVING
(☑ 0812 3964 1143; www.wickeddiving.com/komodo; Jl Soekarno Hatta; floating dm per night from US$100; ⊗ 8am-8pm) 🌿 Offers popular multi-day liveaboards on a classic Bugis schooner and has a 'floating hostel' set among the northern islands of Komodo National Park. Its day trips are justifiably popular and the company wins plaudits for nurturing local divers, promoting strong green practices and giving back to the community. Accommodation rates include dives and transport.

CNDive
DIVING

(📞 0823 3908 0808; www.cndivekomodo.com; Jl Soekarno Hatta; per person per day from US$150; ☺8am-8pm) 🏊 Condo Subagyo, the proprietor of CNDive, is the area's original Indonesian dive operator and a former Komodo National Park ranger. The staff are all locals who have been thoroughly trained and have intimate knowledge of over 100 dive sites.

Uber Scuba
DIVING

(📞 0812 3653 6749; www.uberscubakomodo.com; Jl Soekarno Hatta; three-dive fun dive 1,400,000Rp; ☺8am-8pm) This new dive shop is riding the wave of ever-increasing visitor numbers to the Komodo area. Besides extensive courses, it offers a full range of free-diving excursions and instruction.

🛏 Sleeping

July to August is peak season: be sure to book. Booming popularity means that deals are scant; skip the over-priced beach resorts south of the centre. New guesthouses are opening regularly and many of the dive shops offer a few simple rooms.

★ Bajo Sunset Hostel
HOSTEL $

(📞 0812 3799 3814; Jl Reklamasi Pantai; dm/r from 150,000/250,000Rp; ❄️🛜) A great addition to the Bajo scene, this newly built guesthouse sits on reclaimed land on the waterfront. There is a modest cafe and a large open-air common area with great views out to sea. Accommodation is in a 14-bed dorm and four-bed rooms. Smaller private rooms are planned.

Palulu Garden Homestay
HOMESTAY $

(📞 0822 3658 4279; www.palulugarden.wordpress. com; off Jl Ande Bole; r economy/budget/air-con from 140,000/200,000/350,000Rp; ❄️) Long-time local guide Kornelis Gega and his family run this four-room homestay just a short walk above the centre. The cheapest room shares a bathroom, while the top room has air-con. It's pure Flores throughout, and utterly spic and span. Kornelis can help with your trip planning and arrange transport.

Bajo Beach Hotel
GUESTHOUSE $

(📞 0385-41008; Jl Soekarno Hatta; r 150,000-250,000Rp; ❄️🛜) A fine cheapie in the city centre with 16 basic but spacious tiled older rooms that are clean and well tended. Each has a private seating area out front. You'll get the same room either way, but pay a bit more for air-con.

Green Hill Hotel
GUESTHOUSE $$

(📞 0385-41289; www.greenhillboutiquehotel.com; Jl Soekarno Hatta; r from 500,000Rp; ❄️🛜) The communal terrace bar with its view of the town, bay and sunsets makes this an excellent choice. The 11 rooms are a brief climb from the very centre of town and range from scruffy and older to sprightly and newer. Breakfasts are excellent.

🍴 Eating & Drinking

Labuanbajo punches way above its weight in the food department. Look for market fare and cheap stalls at the north end of the waterfront.

★ Pasar Malam
INDONESIAN $

(Night Market; Jl Soekarno Hatta; mains from 20,000Rp; ☺6pm-midnight) At sunset, grab a tarp-shaded table at Bajo's waterfront night market, as a dozen stalls come alive with all manner of Indo classics, fried delights and grilled seafood. Get cold beer from the market across the road.

Cafe in Hit
CAFE $

(📞 0813 5367 3884; Jl Soekarno Hatta; mains from 40,000Rp; ☺7am-10pm; 🛜) You may forget you're in Bajo, let alone Flores, at this semi-slick coffee house. Let the air-con cool you down while you choose a drink from the blackboards, which could be in any upscale hipster cafe worldwide. The food is well executed and includes sandwiches, baked goods, brownies and more. Breakfasts are heavy on whole grains and fruit.

Warung Mama
INDONESIAN $

(📞 0822 3926 4747; Jl Soekarno Hatta; mains from 30,000Rp; ☺8am-10pm) Set slightly above Bajo's main drag, this bamboo haven offers

---

SPLURGE

Set on its own 15-hectare island and linked to Labuanbajo by private boat, the **Angel Island Resort** (📞 0385-41443; www.angelisleflores.com; Pulau Bidadari; d per person from €145; ❄️🛜) has 10 sweet villas scattered about the trees behind one of three white-sand beaches. All meals are included; the food and service is casual and superb. You can easily while away your days here relaxing on the deserted beaches, or go out snorkelling, diving and visiting the park.

cheap and cheerful local fare to discerning budget eaters. There's no MSG, the vegies aren't cooked to death, the juices are fresh, and standards such as the *rendang* (beef coconut curry) are very well done.

★ **Made In Italy** ITALIAN $$
(☑ 0385-41366; www.miirestaurants.com; Jl Soekarno Hatta; mains 50,000-90,000Rp; ⊙ 11am-11pm; 🕿) A fun and stylish indoor-outdoor dining room known the island over for its fantastic pizza and pasta. In fact we'll just say it: it's some of the best pizza we've ever had anywhere – wafer thin and crunchy with perfectly delectable toppings. You'll dig the rattan lighting, custom wood furnishings, ceiling fans and long drinks menu.

Paradise Bar BAR
(☑ 0823 3935 4854; off Jl Binongko; ⊙ 11am-2am) Set on a hilltop, Paradise satisfies all the requirements of a definitive tropical watering hole. There's ample deck space, a mesmerising sea view, a natural wooden bar serving ice-cold beer, and live music. There's food too – main meals are priced between 22,000Rp and 60,000Rp. This is as wild as it gets for Bajo nightlife – divers get up early. The bar is a 10-minute walk up hill from the centre.

🛈 Information

Banks, ATMs and shops line Jl Soekarno Hatta.
Tourist Office (www.florestourism.com; Jl Soekarno Pelabuhan; ⊙ 8.30am-4.30pm Mon-Sat) This excellent office has details on local activities, updated maps and books plus all the transport info – and tickets – you'll need. The porch has comfy chairs you can use while you plot out your visit.

🛈 Getting There & Away

AIR
Labuanbajo's Komodo Airport (LBJ) has a huge new airport terminal and a newly lengthened runway, which gives some idea of the expected tourism growth.

Garuda Indonesia (www.garuda-indonesia. com), **Transnusa** (www.transnusa.co.id) and **Wings Air** (www.lionair.co.id) serve the airport and have counters in the terminal. There are several daily flights to/from Bali but these are booked solid at busy times. Don't just expect to turn up and go. Garuda also flies to Kupang five times weekly.

BOAT
The ASDP ferry from Labuanbajo to Sape (60,000Rp, six to seven hours) has a morning run and often another in the afternoon. Confirm all times carefully. Buy your tickets the day of departure at the **ferry port office** (Jl Soekarno Hatta; ⊙ 7am-5pm).

Agents for the boats running between Labuanbajo and Lombok (p242) line Jl Soekarno Hatta.

BUS
With no bus terminal in Labuanbajo, most people book their tickets through a hotel or agency. If you get an advance ticket, the bus will pick you up from your hotel. All buses run via Ruteng, so no matter where you're headed just take the first available east-bound bus.

Ticket sellers for long-distance buses to Lombok and Bali work the ferry port office. The fares include all ferries (three to Bali!) and air-con buses in between.

Ruteng
☑ 0385
The greatest site locally is actually 20km west of town, just off the Trans-Flores Hwy near the village of Cancar. The legendary **Spiderweb Rice Fields** are vast creations that are shaped exactly as their name implies. The surrounding region is beautifully lush with paddies.

Ruteng makes a fine lunch stop thanks to **Agape** (☑ 0385-22561; Jl Bhayangkara; dishes 8000-30,000Rp; ⊙ 8am-10pm; 🕿), a great cafe that's popular with both locals and seemingly every traveller who drives past.

There are regular buses to Bajawa (60,000Rp, five hours).

TRANSPORT FROM LABUANBAJO

DESTINATION	TYPE	FARE (RP)	DURATION (HR)	FREQUENCY
Denpasar (Bali)	bus & ferry	500,000	38	1 daily
Bajawa	bus	120,000	10	several daily
Mataram (Lombok)	bus & ferry	350,000	24	1 daily
Ruteng	bus	60,000	4	every 2hr, 6am-6pm

THE NGADA

Over 60,000 Ngada people inhabit the upland Bajawa plateau and the slopes around Gunung Inerie. Older animistic beliefs remain strong, and most Ngada practise a fusion of animism and Christianity. They worship Gae Dewa, a god who unites Dewa Zeta (the heavens) and Nitu Sale (the earth).

The most evident symbols of continuing Ngada tradition are pairs of *ngadhu* and *bhaga*. The *ngadhu* is a parasol-like structure about 3m high, consisting of a carved wooden pole and thatched 'roof', and the *bhaga* is a miniature thatched-roof house.

The *ngadhu* is 'male' and the *bhaga* is 'female', and each pair is associated with a particular family group within a village. Some were built over 100 years ago to commemorate ancestors killed in long-past battles.

Bajawa

☑ 0384

With a pleasant climate and surrounded by forested volcanoes, Bajawa is a great base from which to explore dozens of traditional villages that are home to the Ngada people. Their fascinating architecture features *ngadhu* (carved poles supporting a conical thatched roof).

☉ Sights & Activities

Bajawa's top attractions are the traditional villages. Guides linger around hotels and arrange day trips for 250,000Rp per person with motorcycle transport, village entry fees and lunch. Alternatively, the villages are easily reached if you're driving across Flores. **Bena**, 19km south of Bajawa on the flank of picture-perfect Gunung Inerie (2245m), is the best village in the area, with several megalithic tombs and soaring thatched roofs. Women with betel-nut-stained grins sell elaborate ikat fabrics and macadamia nuts. Nearby **Luba** is also fascinating.

🛏 Sleeping & Eating

★**Hotel Happy Happy**   GUESTHOUSE **$$**
(☑ 0384-421763, 0853 3370 4455; www.hotelhappy happy.com; Jl Sudirman; r 300,000-350,000Rp; 🛜)
A simple yet classy guesthouse with seven immaculate tiled rooms, brushed with lavender walls and dressed with high-quality linen – a scarcity in Bajawa. There's an amiable sitting area on the patio, free water-bottle refills and an excellent included breakfast. It's a short walk from the main cluster of tourist businesses.

Hotel Bintang Wisata   HOTEL **$$**
(☑ 0384-21744; Jl Palapa 4; r 200,000-350,000Rp; 🛜) In a central two-storey block, 24 basic tiled rooms are set in an arc around a parking lot where drivers lounge about awaiting their charges. Upstairs VIP rooms have terraces, hot water and great views of the surrounding hills. The cheapest rooms are cold-water only – a bracing prospect as nights can get chilly.

Dito's   INDONESIAN **$**
(☑ 0384-21162; Jl Ahmad Yani; mains 25,000-50,000Rp; ⊙8am-10pm) Dito's does a brisk business serving pork and chicken *sate* and fresh tuna *bakar,* which is sourced from nearby Aimere and grilled to perfection. The tamarillo juice is *delish.*

ℹ Information

Tourist Office (www.florestourism.com; Jl Ahmad Yani; ⊙8.30am-4.30pm Mon-Sat) Small but highly useful; good for Ngada info. Various trekking and travel agencies have shops nearby.

ℹ Getting There & Away

Hotels arrange bus tickets and pick-ups. Buses to Ende (60,000Rp, five hours) depart several times a day.

Ende

☑ 0381 / POP 65,000

The most obvious merit of this muggy port town is its spectacular setting. The eye-catching cones of Gunung Meja (661m) and Gunung Iya (637m) loom over the city and the nearby black-sand and blue-cobblestone coastline. Ende is worth more than a pause at its traffic circles. It has a compact and atmospheric centre, and an intriguing grittiness.

☉ Sights

Pasar   MARKET
(Jl Pasar; ⊙7am-6pm) Meander through the aromatic waterfront market with the

requisite fruit pyramids and an astonishing fish section. The adjacent **ikat market** (cnr Jls Pabean & Pasar; ⊙9am-5pm) sells hand-woven tapestries from across Flores and Sumba.

🛏 Sleeping & Eating

Accommodation is spread all over town, but frequent bemos make it easy to get around.

Guesthouse Alhidayah
GUESTHOUSE $

(☑0381-23707; Jl Yos Sudarso; r 150,000-250,000Rp; ❇) This spot offers seven sparkling, but otherwise basic, tiled rooms with high ceilings and a private porch area. Priciest rooms have air-con and hot water, and are decent value. It's a solid budget choice.

★ Dasi Guest House
GUESTHOUSE $$

(☑0381-262 7049; yosdam@yahoo.co.id; Jl Durian Atas 2; s/d from 200,000/225,000Rp; ❇🛜) This excellent family-run guesthouse has 15 rooms in a new building. Some are dark, some are bright, but all have air-con and TV. There's a pleasant common room with views south. It's located about 3km east of the centre in a residential neighbourhood.

★ Sari Rasa
INDONESIAN $

(Jl Ahmad Yani; mains 13,000-26,000Rp; ⊙6pm-midnight) One of the best restaurants not just in Ende, but in all of Nusa Tenggara. Looks are deceiving: just a few plastic stools at fluorescent-lit metal tables. But once the food arrives, you'll understand. The menu is short but shows the incredible care of the family in the kitchen.

❶ Information

ATMs and banks dot the centre.

❶ Getting There & Away

Air and ferry schedules in East Nusa Tenggara are historically fluid, so it's best to confirm all times and carriers prior to planning your trip. Wings Air and Transnusa serve **Ende Airport** (ENE; Jl Ahmad Yani), which is right in the centre.

There's a ferry to Kupang (149,000Rp, 19 hours, twice weekly) and Waingapu (115,000Rp, 13 hours, weekly).

East-bound buses (Maumere, 80,000Rp, five hours) leave from the Wolowana terminal, 5km from town. Buses heading west (Bajawa, 60,000Rp, five hours) leave from the Ndao terminal, 2km north of town on the beach road.

Kelimutu

Kelimutu National Park (☑0381-23405; Jl El Tari 16; admission per person Mon-Sat/Sun 150,000/225,000Rp, per ojek/car 5000/10,000Rp; ⊙ticket office 5am-5pm) remains a Nusa Tenggara must: there aren't many better ways to wake up than to witness the sun cresting Mt Kelimutu's western rim, filtering through mist and revealing three deep volcanic lakes, each one a different and striking primary colour that seems the thickness of paint.

Most visitors glimpse them at dawn, leaving nearby Moni at 4am, but afternoons are usually empty and peaceful at the top of Mt Kelimutu, and when the sun is high the colours sparkle. The main viewing spot is a mere 20-minute walk from the car park.

To get there from Moni, hire an *ojek* (50,000Rp one-way) or car (300,000Rp return, maximum five people). You can walk the 13.5km down through the forest and back to Moni in about three hours. A *jalan potong* (shortcut) leaves the road back to Moni 3km south of the ticket office and goes through Manukako village, then meanders back to the main road 750m uphill from Moni.

Moni

Moni, the gateway to Kelimutu, is a picturesque hillside village sprinkled with rice fields, ringed by soaring volcanic peaks, and with distant sea views. The cool, comfortable climate invites long walks and a few extra days. Ask about routes to waterfalls and hot springs.

🛏 Sleeping & Eating

Moni has a cluster of budget guesthouses along the main – and only – road. Prices peak in July and August, when it's wise to book ahead.

Watugana Bungalows
BUNGALOW $

(☑0813 3916 7408; Jl Trans Flores; r 150,000-350,000Rp) Downstairs rooms are older and kept reasonably clean, though they are dark and the bathrooms are a bit moist. The newish rooms upstairs are bright and have hot water.

Daniel Lodge
GUESTHOUSE $$

(☑0812 4602 8875; wanggeyanto@yahoo.co.id; r from 250,000Rp) A sprightly new guesthouse with three bungalow-style rooms, where you can bed down to the whoosh of a running stream. The yard is scented with myriad flowers. Relax on comfy bamboo chairs on the porches.

Bintang Lodge GUESTHOUSE $$
(☑0852 3790 6259, 0812 3761 6940; Jl Trans Flores km 54; r 350,000-400,000Rp; ❋@) Easily the best of the old guesthouse standbys; the four rooms here are the cleanest and largest in the town centre. They also have hot water, which is nice on chilly mornings and evenings. The cafe (mains from 25,000Rp) has a great open terrace with views over the green surrounds. Real travellers order the garlic sandwich for breakfast.

❶ Getting There & Away

Maumere is four hours to the east (bus/minibus 50,000/80,000Rp).

Paga

Halfway between Moni and Maumere, the village of Paga has a long, white-sand beach that's the stuff of fantasy.

Don't miss **Pantai Koka** (admission per car 20,000Rp), a gorgeous twin beach about 5km west of Pantai Naga; look for a small, partially paved road.

Right off the road and on the sand, **Restaurant Laryss** (☑0852 5334 2802; www.floresgids.com; Jl Raya Maumere-Ende; mains from 50,000Rp; ⊘kitchen 8am-8pm), a bamboo fish joint, serves ultra-fresh seafood with superbly prepared sides. The owner, Agustus Naban, is also a talented guide.

Maumere

☑0382 / POP 54,000
Maumere has the second-busiest airport on the island, and you'll likely need to spend a night here if you're doing the one-way, cross-Flores drive. Unfortunately, the drab city centre holds little interest.

🛏 Sleeping & Eating

Hotel Wini Rai II HOTEL $
(☑0382-21362; Jl Soetomo; s/d with fan only 100,000/150,000Rp; s/d with air-con 150,000/200,000Rp; ❋) Maumere's best budget option (and the competition is *not* fierce) is bare-bones but very friendly. Small rooms face a covered courtyard. The cheapest are fan-only and can get steamy. It's close to various eating options.

★**Wailiti Hotel** HOTEL $$
(☑0382-23416; Jl Raya Don Silva; r 400,000-500,000Rp; ❋@🛜🏊) Rooms at Maumere's most pleasant accommodation are in one-storey blocks and bungalows. The flash-free vibe here extends to the spacious grounds, large pool and narrow black-sand beach with views of off-shore islands. The simple cafe serves superb seafood and some amazingly good aubergine fritters. It's 6.5km west of the centre; airport transport costs 100,000Rp and is reliable.

❶ Information

The non-compact centre has banks and ATMs.

❶ Getting There & Around

Maumere's Frans Seda Airport (MOF) is 3km east of town. Destinations serviced by Kalstar and Wings Air include Bali and Kupang. Hop on an *ojek* to/from the airport for 10,000Rp, avoiding the high fixed taxi fare.

Buses to Larantuka (60,000Rp, minibus 80,000Rp, four hours) leave from the Lokaria (or Timur) terminal, 3km east of town. Buses west to Moni leave from the Ende terminal 1km southwest of town.

Around Maumere

A small army of expert artisans lies in wait in the weaving village of **Sikka**, 26km south of Maumere. Along the north coast, east of Maumere, is where you'll find the best beaches and healthiest reefs.

The beaches of **Ahuwair**, **Wodong** and **Waiterang**, about 26km east of Maumere, ooze tranquillity. **Lena House** (☑0813 3940 7733; www.lenahouseflores.com; Wodong; r from 150,000Rp) offers eight clean bamboo bungalows set on a spectacular beach.

Ankermi (☑0812 466 9667; www.ankermihappydive.com; r 300,000-400,000Rp; ❋), located 29km east of Maumere, has cute, tiled, thatched bungalows with private porches and stunning sea views. The dive shop is the best in the Maumere area. They also grow their own organic rice and vegetables on-site, and the meals are delicious.

Larantuka

☑0383
A bustling little port of rusted tin roofs at the easternmost end of Flores, Larantuka rests against the base of Gunung Ili Mandiri (1510m), separated by a narrow strait from

ALOR

Alor, the final link in an island chain that extends east of Java, is as remote, rugged and beautiful as it gets. Thanks to impenetrable terrain, the nearly 200,000 inhabitants of the Alor Archipelago are fractured into over 100 tribes with 52 dialects, and they were still taking heads into the 1950s. Alor is also famous for its strange, bronze *moko* drums.

Superb diving can be arranged through **La Petite Kepa** (☑ SMS only 0813 3910 2403; www.la-petite-kepa.com; bungalows incl meals per person 225,000-450,000Rp, dives from €32) ☑ on Pulau Kepa. **Alor Dive** (☑ 0386-222 2663, 0813 3964 8148; www.alor-dive.com; Jl Suharto; 2-tank dives from €80; ☉ 8am-4pm) also arranges trips.

Kalabahi, located on a sweeping, palm-fringed bay, is the main port; it has banks and ATMs. **Cantik Homestay** (☑ 0813 3229 9336, 0386-21030; Jl Dahlia 12; r 150,000-200,000Rp; ❄) has seven simple rooms. The owner rents out motorcycles, and the home cooking here is sensational.

Transnusa and Wings Air make the one-hour flight to Kupang. The tiny airport (ARD) is comically disorganised, but offers one of the most dramatic approaches in the country. It's 9km from Kalabahi. Check in early to avoid the mad scrum that often develops.

There are two weekly ferries to Kupang (116,000Rp to 170,000Rp, 18 hours), and one to Larantuka (115,000Rp to 170,000Rp, 24 hours).

Pulau Solor and Pulau Adonara. It has a fun, street-market vibe at dusk, but most visitors stay just one night on their way to Kupang or Alor.

🛏 Sleeping & Eating

⭐ **Asa Hotel & Restaurant**　　HOTEL **$$**
(☑ 0383-232 5018; www.asahotel-larantuka.com; Jl Soekarno Hatta; r from 360,000Rp; ❄) The best place to stay has an impressive complex overlooking the harbour, 5km east of the centre. The 27 modern and well-designed rooms are in one- and two-storey blocks, and have fridges and balconies. There is a good restaurant (mains from 25,000Rp), and a bar with views.

❶ Getting There & Away

All boats depart from the main pier in the southern part of town. Double-check departure times.

Ferries run to Kupang (105,000Rp to 154,000Rp, 15 hours, two per week) and Kalabahi (economy/VIP 115,000/170,000Rp, 24 hours, one per week).

The main bus terminal is 5km west of town. Buses (60,000Rp, four hours) and cars (80,000Rp, three hours) to Maumere run frequently between 7am and 5pm.

West Timor

With amazing traditional villages, rugged countryside and empty beaches, West Timor is an undiscovered gem. Deep within its mountainous, *lontar* palm–studded interior, animist traditions persist alongside tribal dialects, and ikat-clad, betel-nut-chewing chiefs govern beehive-hut villages. Meanwhile Kupang, the coastal capital and East Nusa Tenggara's top metropolis, buzzes to a frenetic Indonesian beat.

❶ Getting There & Around

A good way to explore East Nusa Tenggara (also known as Nusa Tenggara Timur, NTT) is to fly directly from Bali to Kupang and island-hop from there.

The good main highway is surfaced all the way from Kupang to East Timor. Away from the highway, roads are improving but can be impassable in the wet season.

Kupang
☑ 0380 / POP 350,000

Kupang, the capital of East Nusa Tenggara is noisy, energetic, scruffy, bustling with commerce and a fun place to hang around for a few days. (Captain Bligh did, after his mutiny problems in 1789.)

🛏 Sleeping & Eating

Near the airport and the new commercial district are several large and bland chain hotels. Any of the properties on the waterfront will be much more pleasant, and will enjoy ocean breezes and views.

⭐ **Lavalon Bar & Hostel**　　HOSTEL **$**
(☑ 0812 377 0533, 0380-832256; www.lavalon-touristinfo.com; Jl Sumatera 44; dm 50,000Rp, r

150,000-250,000Rp; ❄🗺) The best value in town with clean rooms and Western-style bathrooms. Excellent meals and cold beer are served in the open-air common area, which has fine views. It's run by the much-loved living NTT encyclopedia and former Indonesian film star Edwin Lerrick. Expansion plans will bring more private rooms to this prime waterfront location.

⭐**Hotel Maliana** GUESTHOUSE **$**
(📞0380-821879; Jl Sumatera 35; r with fan/air-con 175,000/250,000Rp; ❄🗺) These 14 basic yet comfy motel rooms are a popular budget choice. Rooms are clean and have ocean glimpses from the front porch, which dangles with vines. Breakfast is included.

⭐**Pasar Malam** MARKET **$**
(Night Market; Jl Garuda; mains from 12,000Rp; ⊙6-11pm) Kupang was never considered a good eating town until this wonderful, lamp-lit market launched and turned a lane off Jl Garuda over to street-side grill and wok chefs, who expertly prepare inexpensive dishes. The seafood selection is vast, the grilling superb.

ℹ Information

Kupang has scores of banks, ATMs and services, as befitting a regional capital.

Lavalon (📞0380-832256, 0812 377 0533; www.lavalontouristinfo.com; Jl Sumatera 44; ⊙8am-late) Edwin Lerrick, the proprietor, is a vital source for the latest transport information, as well as cultural attractions throughout NTT. His website is must-read for information.

ℹ Getting There & Around

AIR
Kupang's El Tari airport (KOE) is 15km east of town. The most important hub in East Nusa Tenggara, it offers regular services to Bali and throughout the region. Taxi fare into town is fixed at 60,000Rp.

BOAT
Bolok Harbour, where you get regular ferries to Kalabahi, Larantuka and Waingapu, is 11km west of the centre.

LOCAL TRANSPORT
Long-distance buses depart from Oebobo terminal on the eastern side of town – catch bemo 10. Kupang is spread out, so use the bemo system (2000Rp).

It's possible to rent a car with a driver from 400,000Rp to 750,000Rp per day, depending upon the destination. Motorcycles cost around 60,000Rp per day. You can arrange one at your hotel or through **Lavalon** (📞0380-832256, 0812 377 0533; www.lavalontouristinfo.com; Jl Sumatera 44; mains from 30,000Rp; ⊙7am-late; 🗺).

Soe

About 110km east from Kupang, the cool, leafy market town of Soe (800m) makes a decent base from which to explore West Timor's interior. Arrange tours of traditional villages here or in Kupang.

Air-con isn't needed here. **Hotel Bahagia I** (📞0853 3830 3809; Jl Diponogoro; r 120,000-275,000Rp; ❄) and **Timor Megah Hotel** (📞0388-22280; Jl Gajah Mada; r 250,000-400,000Rp; ❄🗺) are fine choices.

INDONESIA WEST TIMOR

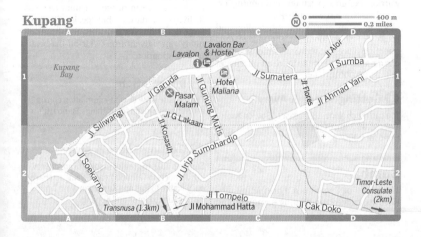

Kupang

GETTING TO TIMOR-LESTE: KUPANG TO DILI

Besides pure tourism, many head to Timor-Leste from West Timor to renew their Indonesian visa. If you decide to go, be aware that Timor-Leste is considerably more expensive than Indonesia, and the return trip normally takes more than a week by the time you get to Dili, wait for your Indonesian visa and return to West Timor.

Getting to the border Direct minibuses (10 to 11 hours) to Dili from Kupang are operated by **Timor Tour & Travel** (☑0380-881543; one-way 230,000Rp) and **Paradise** (☑0380-830414, 0813 3944 7183; one-way 230,000Rp). Call for a hotel pickup. Departures can be as early as 5am, so brace yourself.

At the border Apply for your visa to Timor-Leste at the **Timor-Leste Consulate** (☑0813-3936 7558; Jl Eltari II; ☺8am-4pm Mon-Thu, to 2pm Fri) in Kupang with a valid passport, a photocopy and passport photos. It costs US$30 and takes one to three working days to process. There are no buses waiting on either side of the border if you arrive independently; you'll have a long wait hoping for one to show up. The through minibus is by far the best option.

Moving on The through minibuses take you direct to Dili, where most people start their Timor-Leste visit. They do drop-offs at guesthouses and hotels.

For information on doing this crossing in the other direction, see p797.

The Haumeni bus terminal is 4km west of town (3000Rp by bemo). Regular buses go to Kupang (30,000Rp, three hours).

None

None is Kefamananu's last head-hunting village and one of the area's best attractions. A trail runs for 900m from where the bemo drops you off on the main road. Stroll past corn and bean fields and hop over a meandering stream (often dry) and you'll reach scattered *ume bubu* (traditional beehive huts), home to 56 families that have lived here for nine generations. At the cliff's edge you'll find a **totem pole**, where shamans once met with warriors before they left on head-hunting expeditions (the last was in 1945).

Villagers are warm and welcoming, and break out their looms at the village *lopo* (meeting place) for weaving demonstrations upon request. Be sure to leave an offering of at least 20,000Rp each.

❶ Getting There & Away

You can reach None, 18km east of Soe, on an *ojek* (30,000Rp). Or hop on a Soe–Niki Niki bemo for 5000Rp.

Sumba

The island of Sumba is a dynamic mystery. With its rugged, undulating savannah and low limestone hills knitted together with more maize and cassava than rice, it physically looks nothing like Indonesia's volcanic islands to the north. Sprinkled throughout the countryside are hilltop villages with thatched clan houses clustered around megalithic tombs, where villagers claim to be Protestant but still pay homage to their indigenous *marapu* (gods) with bloody sacrificial rites.

Sumba is one of the poorest islands in Indonesia, but an influx of welcome government investment has brought recent improvements in infrastructure, best seen in Tambolaka, the island's newest city. And change has trickled down to traditional villages in the form of modest improvements in living standards – but locals still expect large donations from visitors. Sumba is definitely an adventurous, far-off-the-beaten path destination.

❶ Information

The website www.sumba-information.com is a vast compendium for all things Sumba. It's a must for any visitor.

❶ Getting There & Away

Sumba's links to greater Indonesia are improving. Airports in Tambolaka and Waingapu have daily flights to Bali and Kupang in West Timor. Ferries run to Flores and Kupang.

Waingapu

📞 0387 / POP 55,000

Waingapu is a leafy, laid-back town that is plenty walkable and makes a decent base from which to explore the surrounding villages. It became an administrative centre after the Dutch military 'pacified' the island in 1906 and has long been Sumba's main trading post for textiles, prized Sumbanese horses, dyewoods and lumber. The town has an appealing harbourfront dining scene and a few ikat shops and workshops. Traders with bundles of textiles and carvings hang around hotels or walk the streets touting for rupiah.

🛏 Sleeping & Eating

Most hotels are in the new part of Waingapu, near the bus station. The best dinner option is the *pasar malam* (night market) at the old wharf.

★**Tanto Hotel**   GUESTHOUSE $
(📞 0387-61048, 0387-62500; Jl Prof Dr WZ Yohanes; r 200,000-450,000Rp; ❄ 🐾) The newest hotel in town is also the best. Bright, fresh rooms and good service set the Tanto apart from most of its competition. The decor is primarily white, with natural wood and vivid-red accents. Many rooms have fridges; the breakfast is good.

ⓘ Getting There & Around

The airport (WGP) is 6km south on the Melolo road.

Pelni (📞 0387-61665; www.pelni.co.id; Jl Hasanuddin; ⊙9am-4pm) ships leave from the newer Darmaga dock to the west of town, but the ticket office is at the old port. Ferry schedules are subject to change: check the **ASDP** (📞 0214-288 2233) hotline or see the schedules at the port.

The terminal for eastbound buses is in the southern part of town, close to the market. The West Sumba terminal (aka Terminal Kota) is about 5km west of town.

Around Waingapu

Several traditional villages in the southeast can be visited from Waingapu by bus and bemo. The stone tombs are impressive and the area produces some of Sumba's best ikat. Donations are expected.

Praiyawang, the ceremonial centre of Rende, has a traditional Sumbanese compound and stone-slab tombs. The massive one belongs to a former raja. There are several daily buses to Rende from Waingapu (20,000Rp, 1½ hours).

There's epic surf at **Tarimbang**, a palm-draped cove south of Lewa. There's also some nearby snorkelling, and rustic accommodation at **Marthen's Homestay** (📞 0852 8116 5137; r from 150,000Rp). Daily trucks to Tarimbang leave Waingapu in the morning (40,000Rp, five hours).

Waikabubak

📞 0387 / POP 22,000

A conglomeration of thatched clan houses, ancient tombs, concrete office buildings and

(Side margin) INDONESIA SUMBA

ⓘ GUIDES

Sumba is such a mystery that the services of a guide can make all the difference in fully appreciating the island and its multitude of cultures and practices, such as the Pasola. Two to consider:

Sumba Adventure Tours & Travel (📞 0813 3710 7845; sumbaadventure@yahoo.com; Desa Kalena Wanno, Tambolaka; guiding services per day 250,000Rp, per day with car & driver 850,000Rp) With an office close to the airport, experienced guide Philip Renggi is one of the best in West Sumba. He and his team of guides lead trips into seldom-explored villages, including his native Manuakalada and Wawarungu, where there are several sacred *marapu* houses that only shaman can enter. He can arrange itineraries, set you up for Pasola, rent cars etc.

Yuliana Ledatara (📞 0852 3918 1410; yuli.sumba@gmail.com; Kampung Tarung, Waikabubak; per day from 450,000Rp) A wonderful local English- and French-speaking guide who lives in Tarung – Waikabubak's hilltop traditional village – Yuliana can organise tours of traditional villages throughout West Sumba, where she sniffs out funerals and sacrifices, takes horse tours through rice fields, and can arrange village homestays too. She's one of Indonesia's very few female guides, and she's a good one.

WORTH A TRIP

PASOLA – SUMBA AT WAR

The thrilling, often gruesome mock battles between spear-hurling horsemen during Sumba's Pasola festival are a must for travellers passing through Nusa Tenggara in February or March. The high-energy pageant aims to placate the spirits and restore harmony through the spilling of blood. Happily, blunt spears have been used in recent decades to make the affair less lethal. The ritualistic war kicks off when a sea worm called *nyale* washes up on shore, a phenomenon that also starts the planting season.

In February, Pasola is celebrated in the Kodi area (centred on Kampung Tosi) and the Lemboya area (Kampung Sodan); in March it's in the Wanokaka area (Kampung Waigalli) and the remote Gaura area, west of Lamboya (Kampung Ubu Olehka). Exact dates are known two weeks before Pasola. Check with the guides and hotels in Waikabubak and Tambolaka, as well as East NTT expert Edwin Lerrick at Lavalon (p249) in Kupang.

satellite dishes, Waikabubak is strange but appealing. Interesting traditional villages such as **Kampung Tarung**, up a path next to Tarung Wisata Hotel, are right within town.

Right beside the main road to Waingapu, 22km east of Waikabubak, **Kampung Pasunga** boasts one of Sumba's most impressive tombs.

Gorgeous beaches abound. Typical are the idyllic white sands of **Pantai Marosi**, 32km south of Waikabubak.

🛏 Sleeping & Eating

Warungs congregate opposite the mosque on the main strip.

Karanu Hotel   GUESTHOUSE $
(☑ 0387-21645; Jl Sudirman 43; r 150,000-250,000Rp) A bright garden hotel east of the downtown swirl and within view of nearby rice fields. Rooms are clean if worn. It doesn't have air-con, but it does have a fading *Last Supper* rug tacked to the lobby wall.

★ **D' Sumba Ate**   INTERNATIONAL $$
(☑ 0857 3775 6606; Jl Ahmad Yani 148; mains 20,000-70,000Rp; ⊙ 10am-10pm) A very welcome addition to the West Sumba food scene, this excellent restaurant cooks up wood-fired pizzas, pasta, burgers and the usual Indo suspects. There's a cool open-air bamboo vibe and a competent bar, plus Sumba's cleanest toilets!

❶ Getting There & Away

Tambolaka, 42km northwest of Waikabubak, has the closest airport.

Bemos, trucks and minibuses service most other towns and villages in West Sumba. Generally, it's best to leave early in the day, when they tend to fill up and depart quickest. There are several daily buses to Waingapu (50,000Rp, five hours).

Around Waikabubak

Set in a lush valley 22km east of Waikabubak, **Anakalang** sports some of Sumba's most captivating megalithic tombs. Additional interesting villages are south of town past the market. **Kabonduk** has Sumba's heaviest tomb; it took 2000 workers more than three years to carve it.

Located south of Waikabubak is Wanokaka district, which is a centre for the Pasola festival. **Praigoli**, a somewhat isolated village, is deeply traditional.

Our favourite place in West Sumba, Oro Beach Houses & Restaurant (p253), is not far from Tambolaka along a mostly rutted dirt road. Think three wild beachfront acres featuring a simple, artful house. There are excellent seafood meals, local village tours and snorkelling just off shore.

Tambolaka

Located 42km northwest of Waikabubak, this once sleepy market town has become West Sumba's main transport hub – it's booming and it's got a whole new name, at least in tourism brochures and other government literature. (We've followed suit, even if many locals of a certain age still refer to it as Waitabula.) While still in the early stages of growth, Tambolaka is easily accessible from Bali, and is the gateway to the island's sensational western half.

This is a good base for West Sumba explorations. While not as nice as the southern beaches, the ones here have some nice hotels.

🛏 Sleeping & Eating

Penginapan Melati
GUESTHOUSE $

(☑ 0813 5396 6066, 0387-24055; Jl Waitabula; r with fan/air-con 150,000/250,000Rp; ❄🤖) Shaded by a huge tree, the 15 rooms here are simple but immaculate with fresh paint and tile throughout. They even have rain shower heads in the *mandi*. There's a simple Padang-style restaurant right next door.

★ Oro Beach Houses & Restaurant
BUNGALOW $$

(☑ 0813 3911 0068, 0813 5378 9946; www. oro-beachbungalows.com; r US$45-60) Think: three wild beachfront acres owned by a special family (she used to run an NGO, he's an architect with a disaster relief background), where you can nest in a circular thatched bungalow blessed with a canopied driftwood bed and outdoor bath. They offer excellent meals, mountain biking and snorkelling just off their stunning 200m long beach.

★ Warung Gula Garam
INTERNATIONAL $

(☑ 0387-252 4019; Bandara Udara; mains 12,000-100,000Rp; ⊙ 10am-11pm; 🤖) 'They have a wood-burning pizza oven!' exclaimed more than one expat as they enthused about this stylish new cafe in an open-air pavilion near the airport. Elsewhere a full coffee and juice bar, plus a menu of organic salads, pastas and burgers, would raise nary an eyebrow, but here it's revolutionary.

ℹ Getting There & Away

Tambolaka's airport (TMC) terminal is shiny and modern. There are daily flights to Bali and Kupang (West Timor) by Garuda Indonesia and Wings Air. Note that on some websites it is listed as 'Waikabubak'.

Waikelo, a small and predominantly Muslim town north of Tambolaka, has a small picturesque harbour that is the main port for West Sumba and offers ferry service to Sape (Sumbawa) twice a week (65,000Rp, eight hours).

Buses leave throughout the day for Waikabubak (10,000Rp to 15,000Rp, one hour), departing from the centre of town.

SUMATRA

Few isles tempt the imagination with the lure of adventure quite like the fierce land of Sumatra. An island of extraordinary beauty, it bubbles with life and vibrates under the power of nature. Eruptions, earthquakes and tsunamis are Sumatran headline grabbers. Steaming volcanoes brew and bluster while standing guard over lakes that sleepily lap the edges of craters. Orangutan-filled jungles also host tigers, rhinos and elephants. And down at sea level, idyllic deserted beaches are bombarded by clear barrels of surf.

As varied as the land, the people of Sumatra are a spicy broth of mixed cultures, from the devout Muslims in Aceh to the hedonistic Batak Christians around Danau Toba and the matrilineal Minangkabau people of Padang. All are unified by a fear, respect and love of the wild and wondrous land of Sumatra.

ℹ Getting There & Away

These days, most travellers reach Sumatra via budget airline flight or ferry from Java. The old sea routes are largely redundant.

When making travel plans, keep in mind that Sumatra is one hour behind Singapore and Malaysia.

The international airports at Medan, Padang, Banda Aceh and Pekanbaru are visa-free, as are the seaports of Sekupang (Pulau Batam), Dumai, Padang and Sibolga.

AIR

Medan is Sumatra's primary international airport, with frequent flights to mainland Southeast Asian cities such as Singapore, Kuala Lumpur and Penang. In West Sumatra, Padang receives flights from Singapore and Kuala Lumpur.

You can also hop on a plane from Jakarta to every major Sumatran city aboard a range of airlines. Flights from Sumatra to other parts of Indonesia often connect through Jakarta.

GETTING TO SINGAPORE: THE RIAU ARCHIPELAGO TO SINGAPORE

Getting to the border Although backpackers seldom visit Sumatra's Riau Archipelago, some do transit through Pulau Batam on their way to Singapore. Ferry operators on this route include BatamFast (www.batamfast.com). You can get to Pulau Batam by boat and bus connections from Dumai, Palembang and Pekanbaru.

At the border Citizens of most countries will be granted a 30-day visa when they arrive in Singapore.

Moving on Ferry services from the Riau Islands serve several terminals in Singapore, where it's easy to get onward public transport connections.

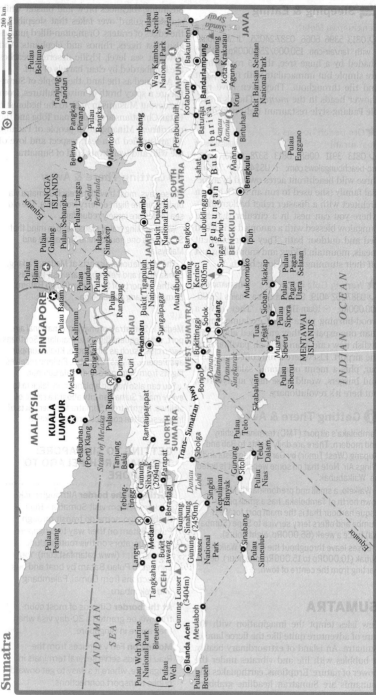

Sumatra

SUMATRA

BOAT

Ferries run between Dumai (on Sumatra's east coast) and Melaka and Klang (for Kuala Lumpur) in Malaysia; Singapore; and Pulau Batam, but Dumai is only useful if you have your heart set on an international boat journey or if you're transporting a motorcycle between Sumatra and Malaysia.

From Singapore, ferries make the quick hop to Pulau Batam and Pulau Bintan, the primary islands in the Riau Archipelago. From Batam, boats set sail for Dumai, Palembang and Pekanbaru, but few travellers use these routes.

Ferries cross the narrow Sunda Strait, which links the southeastern tip of Sumatra at Bakauheni to Java's westernmost point of Merak. The sea crossing is a brief dip in a day-long voyage that requires several hours' worth of bus transport from both ports to Jakarta and, on the Sumatra side, Bandarlampung.

⊙ Getting Around

Most travellers bus around northern Sumatra and then hop on a plane to Java, largely avoiding Sumatra's highway system. Most of the island is mountainous jungle and the poorly maintained roads form a twisted pile of spaghetti on the undulating landscape. Don't count on getting anywhere very quickly on Sumatra.

AIR

Short plane journeys can be an attractive alternative to spending an eternity on packed buses. Competition between domestic carriers means internal flights are inexpensive and largely reliable, with the exception of Susi Air and their small planes, which are particularly susceptible to bad weather. Dry-season smog affects planes along the east coast.

BOAT

Most boat travel within Sumatra connects the main island with the many satellite islands lining the coast.

BUS & MINIBUS

If you stick to the Trans-Sumatran Hwy and other major roads, the big air-con buses can make travel fairly comfortable – which is fortunate since you'll spend a lot of time on the road in Sumatra. The best ones have reclining seats, toilets and video but run at night to avoid the traffic, so you miss out on the scenery. The non-air-con buses are sweaty and cramped, but unforgettable. Numerous bus companies cover the main routes and prices vary greatly, depending on the comfort level. Buy tickets directly from the bus company. Agents usually charge 10% more.

Travel on the back roads is a different story. Progress can be grindingly slow and utterly exhausting.

For midrange and shorter journeys, many locals and travellers prefer to use minibus and shared car services, which can be more convenient than hustling out to the bus terminal as they run intercity and door-to-door. They are not necessarily faster, but more comfortable and convenient.

TRAIN

The only three useful train services in Sumatra run from Medan's new airport to the centre of Medan, and from Bandarlampung to Palembang and Lahat (for the Pasemah Highlands).

Padang

📋 0751 / POP 877,000

Most backpackers fly into Padang only to catch the first bus to Bukittinggi. Big mistake. Sumatra's largest west-coast city has a gorgeous waterfront setting, with Minangkabau roofs soaring from modern public buildings and a leafy old quarter dominated by a narrow, brackish river harbour crowded with colourful fishing boats, yachts and luxe Bugis schooners. The coastline south of town is also magnificent, and the city beach is edged by a popular promenade – where you'll want to be when the sun drops.

⊙ Sights & Activities

Locals converge on the beach promenade at sunset for snacks, cool drinks and football games on the sand.

Colonial Quarter　　　　　　NEIGHBOURHOOD
Although damaged in the 2009 earthquake, Padang's colonial-era quarter around Jl Batang Arau is still worth a lazy stroll. Old Dutch and Chinese warehouses back onto a river brimming with fishing boats. The beach along Jl Samudera is the best place to watch the sunset.

**Adityawarman
Museum**　　　　　　　　　MUSEUM
(Jl Diponegoro; admission 2500Rp; ⊙8am-4pm Tue-Sun) Adityawarman Museum, built in the Minangkabau tradition, has pleasant grounds and the exhibits are a thorough introduction to everyday Minangkabau life. A healthy imagination helps, since the exhibits are in Bahasa Indonesia. The entrance is on Jl Gereja.

INDONESIA PADANG

Padang

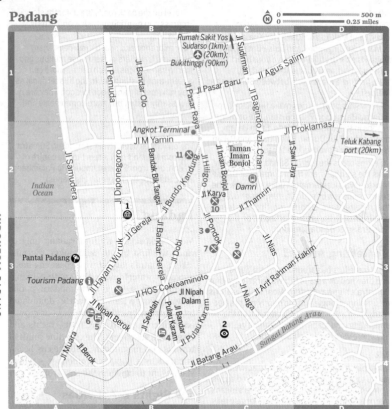

★ **Regina Adventures** TOUR, SURFING
(☑ 0751-781 0835, 0812 6774 5464; www.regina adventures.com; 10-day surf packages per person from US$450) Reliable local operator Elvis offers trekking on the Mentawai Islands, trips to Danau Maninjau and Bukittinggi, and ascents of Gunung Merapi and Gunung Kerinci. Check the website for good-value surf trips to Mentawai and Krui further south.

Nando Sumatra Tours
CULTURAL TOUR
(☑ 0812 6672 8800, 0852 6335 7645; www.nando sumatratour.com; Jl Tanjung Indah I blok E; 10-day Mentawai treks from per person US$700) A young, up-and-coming company with friendly owner Nando at the helm. Arranges 10-day Mentawai cultural immersion tours, as well as tours of North and West Sumatra and trekking around Danau Maninjau.

🛏 Sleeping

Brigitte's House
HOMESTAY $
(☑ 0813 7425 7162; www.brigittehouse.blogspot. com; Jl Kampung Sebalah 1/14; dm/s/d from 95,000/100,000/230,000Rp; ❄ 🛜) Brigitte's has a relaxed and homely ambience, with backpackers chilling in the common area or mingling on the porch. This residential neighbourhood is quiet and leafy, and Brigitte is a treasure trove of information on buses, ferries and Mentawai adventures (and can help you with bookings). A short walk away is the separate building with air-con rooms.

Yani's Homestay
HOMESTAY $
(☑ 0852 6380 1686; yuliuz.caesar@gmail.com; dm 80,000Rp, r 120,000-175,000Rp, all incl breakfast; ❄ 🛜) Run by friendly young owner Yuliuz, this central homestay provides bona fide backpacker digs in the form of an air-con dorm with lockers and rooms with colourful

Padang

bedspreads. If you don't want to share your bathroom, splurge on the standard double. Motorbikes are available for guest use (60,000Rp per day).

Golden Homestay   HOMESTAY $
(☏0751-32616; Jl Nipah Berok 1B; r 200,000-375,000Rp; ✲☏) Spotless private rooms named after Sydney's classic surfing beaches. Grab a bed in the cheaper Bronte room, or splash out on the Bondi or Manly rooms with private bathrooms.

✗ Eating

Padang is the mother of the cuisine that migrated across Indonesia. You can pay homage to the native cooks with a visit to one of these famous franchises: **Pagi Sore** (Jl Pondok 143; dishes 9000Rp; ☺lunch & dinner), **Sari Raso** (Jl Karya 3; dishes 10,000Rp; ☺lunch & dinner) and **Simpang Raya** (Jl Bundo Kandung; dishes 8000Rp; ☺lunch & dinner).

Jl Batang Arau is full of cheap warungs that spring to life at night, while discerning foodies head for Jl Pondok and Jl HOS Cokroaminoto. Juice wagons loiter near the end of Jl Hayam Wuruk. For cheap *sate*, grilled seafood and a few cold Bintangs, head to the beachfront shacks lining Jl Sumadera at sunset.

Pondok Indah Jaya   INDONESIAN $
(Jl Niaga 138; meals around 40,000Rp; ☺lunch & dinner) This warung is an excellent intro to Padang cuisine, your feast of dishes including spicy tofu, beef *rendang, ayam* sambal and tempe. Cool the fire in your mouth with *sirsak* (soursop), cucumber or mango juice.

★ **Pak Tri's**   SEAFOOD $$
(Jl HOS Cokroaminoto 91; meals from 50,000Rp; ☺5pm-late) The fish and squid are flame-grilled to perfection with a sweet, spicy sambal sauce here. The fresh-every-afternoon marine selection includes shoals of different fish and squid, with a supporting cast of *kangkung* (water spinach) and aubergine dishes. Grab a spot at the shared tables and tuck in for a quintessential Padang experience, occasionally accompanied by the serenading of street minstrels.

ⓘ Information

Imigrasi Office (☏0751-444511; Jl Khatib Sulaiman; ☺8am-4pm Mon-Fri) Thirty-day visa extensions can be made for US$35 at the Padang Imigrasi office. It's about 5km out of town by *ojek* or taxi.
Rumah Sakit Yos Sudarso (☏0751-33230; Jl Situjuh 1) Privately owned hospital.
Tourism Padang (☏0751-34186; Dinas Kebudayaan Dan Pariwisata, Jl Samudera 1; ☺7.30am-4pm Mon-Fri, 8am-4pm Sat & Sun) Maps of town and a few English-language regional brochures.

ⓘ Getting There & Away

AIR
Padang's airport, **Bandara Internasional Minangkabau** (BIM; www.minangkabau-airport.co.id; Jl Adinegoro), is 20km north of town.

BUS
Tranex (☏0751-705 8577) buses depart for Bukittinggi (20,000Rp, three hours) from the city's northern fringes, outside the Wisma Indah building. It's half the price of a door-to-door minibus but it means you have to catch any white *angkot* (3000Rp) heading north on Jl Permuda (ask for 'Tranex' or 'Wisma Indah'), and then find transport from Bukittinggi bus terminal, which is miles from the centre. In reality you save very little money.

The minibuses most relevant to travellers depart from Jl Jhoni Anwar. **Putra Mandau** (☏0751-782 2218; Jl Jhoni Anwar) links Padang to Dumai if you're travelling to/from Sumatra by sea from Malaysia or Singapore.

ⓘ Getting Around

Airport taxis charge around 150,000Rp from the airport, but 300,000Rp to the airport. If you're travelling light, step outside the airport boundaries and hail an *ojek* to get to central Padang. White **Damri** (☏0751-780 6335) buses are a cheaper alternative (35,000Rp) that loop through Padang, though there are no clearly designated stops and they run to an erratic schedule.

MENTAWAI ISLANDS

It was surfing that put the Mentawais on the tourism radar: nowhere else on earth has such a dense concentration of world-class surf spots in such a small area. Today, dozens of wave-hunting liveaboards run from Padang harbour year-round and a growing number of dedicated surf camps populate the banner spots. Surfing is big business here year-round, but the season peaks between April and October. Like many Indonesian surf areas, the Mentawais are not suitable for learners. The waves, which break over shallow reefs, tend to be fast, hollow, heavy and unforgiving.

The most consistent cluster of waves is in the **Playground** area, but things can get rather crowded during peak season. **Bintang Surf Camp** (☑ 0812 6617 4454; Pulau Masokut; per person 400,000Rp) is the best of the local budget lot, with basic thatched huts and shared rooms.

It's not just surfers who come out here; more and more ecotourists are also braving the rugged ocean crossing and muddy jungle of this remote archipelago to trek, glimpse traditional tribal culture and spot endemic primates.

The economic, and culturally responsible, choice for touring is to take a public boat to Siberut and seek out a Mentawai guide. You pay less and directly benefit the community you've come to experience.

As far as surfing tours go, the vast majority of surfers pre-arrange boat charters or surf camp accommodation with a surf travel company in their home country. These are ideal if all you want to do is get off a plane and surf your guts out. However, it's a real bubble-like existence and the only Indonesians you're actually likely to meet will be your boat crew. If you've got lots of time then it's perfectly possible, and much closer to the true spirit of old-school surf travel, to take the public ferry out to the islands and once there arrange local boat transport and accommodation in one of the cheap and simple losmen that can be found close to many of the breaks.

Getting There & Away

The Mentawai Islands have become considerably easier to reach with the introduction of a 200-seater speedboat, **Mentawai Fast** (☑ 0751-893 489; mentawaifast@gmail.com; one way 295,000Rp, surfboard 230,000Rp). There are also ferries that make the overnight journey from the Sumatran mainland to the islands; they leave from the Teluk Kabang port at Bungus, around 20km south of Padang, and take around 10 to 12 hours, depending on sea conditions.

In Padang, ferry operators to the Mentawais include **Ambu Ambu** and **Gambolo**. Fares range from 50,000Rp to 180,000Rp, depending upon route and travel class. Tickets can be booked through most surfer-friendly homestays, as well as tour agencies (see p255) such as **Sumatran Surfariis** (☑ 0751-34878; www.sumatransurfariis.com; Komplek Pondok Indah B 12, Parak Gadang).

Bukittinggi

☑ 0752 / POP 112,000

The market town of Bukittinggi sits high above the valley mists as three sentinels – fire-breathing Merapi, benign Singgalang and distant Sago – all look on impassively. Sun-ripened crops grow large in the rich volcanic soil, as frogs call in the paddies, *bendis* (two-person horse-drawn carts) haul goods to the *pasa* (market), and the muezzin's call is heard through the town. Modern life seems far removed...until 9am. Then the traffic starts up, and soon there's a mile-long jam around the bus terminal. The air turns the colour of diesel and the mosques counter the traffic by cranking their amps. Such is the incongruity of modern Bukittinggi – blessed by nature, choked by mortals. Lush. Fertile. Busy. And at 930m above sea level, deliciously temperate all year round.

The town (alternatively named Tri Arga, which refers to the triumvirate of peaks) has had a chequered history, playing host at various times to Islamic reformists, Dutch colonials, Japanese invaders and Sumatran separatists. It's a good base for setting out to the Harau Valley and Danau Maninjau.

⊙ Sights & Activities

A vast array of local tours can be arranged in Bukittinggi. Generally these fall into two categories: culture and nature. They can range from a half-day meander through neighbouring villages, a scour of the nearby jungles for the world's largest (and smelliest) flowers, *Rafflesia arnoldii* and *Amorphophallus titanium*, or, for something more demanding, a three-day jungle trek to Danau Maninjau, or an overnight assault on Gunung Merapi.

Guides hang out in all the cafes. Be clear about what you want and what is and isn't included. If going solo, make sure somebody knows who's guiding you. Full-day tours start around 250,000Rp. **Roni's Tour & Travel** (☑ 0812 675 0688; www.ronistours.com; Orchid Hotel, Jl Teuku Umar) is a good operator.

Taman Panorama   VIEWPOINT
(Panorama Park; Jl Panorama; admission 10,000Rp) Taman Panorama, on the southern edge of town, overlooks the deep **Ngarai Sianok** (Sianok Canyon), where fruit bats swoop at sunset. Friendly guides will approach visitors to lead you through **Gua Jepang** (Japanese Caves), wartime defensive tunnels built by Japanese slave labour; settle on a price (around 30,000Rp) before continuing. Another path (and extra admission) gives you access to the **Koto Gadang** (Great Wall), a cheesy scaled-down Great Wall of China.

🛏 Sleeping

Most hotels include a simple breakfast. On holidays, rooms fill quickly with Indonesian visitors. In Bukittinggi's temperate climate, hot water is more desirable than air-con.

★ **Hello Guesthouse**   GUESTHOUSE $
(☑ 0752-21542; helloguesthouse12@gmail.com; Jl Teuku Umar 6b; dm/s/d from 75,000/120,000/150,000Rp; 🛜) This excellent new guesthouse with bright and modern rooms is run by thoughtful owner Ling, who understands the needs of budget travellers. She is happy to provide maps of town, has displays on town attractions, and

has thoughtfully kitted out her digs with comfy mattresses and earplugs to counter the guesthouse's proximity to a mosque. Spacious deluxe rooms come with balconies.

★ **Rajawali Homestay**   HOMESTAY $
(☑ 0752-31905; ulrich.rudolph@web.de; Jl Ahmad Yani 152; r 80,000Rp) The eight rooms at this friendly, central homestay are basic and come with Indonesian bathrooms. The irrepressible Ulrich is the best source of local (and regional) knowledge in town, with advice on detailed walks and motorcycle rides around Bukittinggi and excellent GPS maps. The roof terrace is perfect for sunset beers as you watch the twilight squadrons of bats flying past.

Orchid Hotel   HOTEL $
(☑ 0752-32634; roni_orchid@hotmail.com; Jl Teuku Umar 11; r 120,000-150,000Rp; 🛜) This popular backpacker inn is ground zero for arranging tours and activities with Roni's Tour & Travel (p260), which is highly praised by travellers. The rooms here could do with sprucing up though.

🍴 Eating & Drinking

Bukittinggi has long been the one place in Sumatra where weary road bums can give their poor chilli-nuked organs a chance to recover with lashings of lovingly bland Western food.

In the evenings, *sate* stalls spring up on the western side of the square, while the tents lining Jl Ahmad Yani cook up *mie* (noodles) and nasi goreng (fried rice), *murtabak mesir* (filled pancake) and *roti cane* (flatbread).

★ **Waroeng Jalal**
Spesifik Sambal   INDONESIAN $
(Jl Kesehatan; mains 6000-20,000Rp; ⊙ lunch & dinner; 🛜☑) Fans of spicy dishes will love this shady garden warung specialising mostly in sambal dishes. Squid, prawns, chicken, tofu, tempe and aubergine are all cooked in a rich, fiery chilli sauce, with *kangkung* (water spinach) providing a mild accompaniment. The beer may well be Bukittinggi's

INDONESIA BUKITTINGGI

BUSES FROM BUKITTINGGI

DESTINATION	FARE (RP)	DURATION (HR)
Medan	160,000-200,000	20
Parapat	180,000-200,000	16
Sibolga	110,000-150,000	12

Bukittinggi

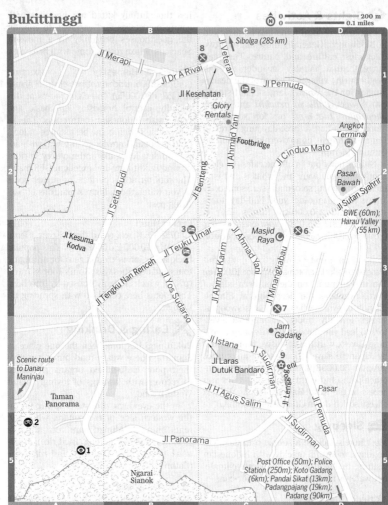

coldest. Get here early lest they run out of the most popular dishes.

Simpang Raya INDONESIAN $
(Jl Minangkabau; meals around 50,000Rp; ⏲lunch & dinner) The best place in town to sample the fabled Padang cuisine – spicy, flavourful dishes, with a particularly savoury *rendang* (beef coconut curry). Just ask for the assortment of what's on offer.

Ramadan Market MARKET $
(Jl Cinduo Mato; dishes from 10,000Rp; ⏲8am-6pm) During the month of Ramadan, this car park turns into a whirlwind of culinary activity as dozens of stalls press sugar-cane juice, cook up *rendang,* concoct elaborate desserts and deep-fry all sorts of artery-clogging goodies. Locals shop here during the day in preparation for the breaking of the fast and it's a terrific place to try local dishes.

☆ Entertainment

Gedung Medan Nan Balinduang DANCE
(Jl Lenggogeni; tickets 50,000Rp; ⏲8.30pm) Medan Nan Balinduang presents Minangkabau dance performances. Check with your lodgings for the latest schedule.

Bukittinggi

⊙ Sights

1 Gua Jepang	A5
2 Taman Panorama	A5

⊕ Activities, Courses & Tours

Roni's Tour & Travel	(see 4)

⊜ Sleeping

3 Hello Guesthouse	B3
4 Orchid Hotel	B3
5 Rajawali Homestay	C1

⊗ Eating

6 Ramadan Market	D3
7 Simpang Raya	C3
8 Waroeng Jalal Spesifik Sambal	C1

⊕ Entertainment

9 Gedung Medan Nan Balinduang	C4

ⓘ Information

Banks with ATMs and money changers are clustered along Jl Ahmad Yani, home also to dozens of travel agents and many more services.

ⓘ Getting There & Away

The chaos of the main bus terminal, Aur Kuning, 3km south of town is easily reached by *angkot* (3000Rp); ask for 'terminal'. Heading to central Bukittinggi on arrival ask for 'Kampung China'.

The main bus terminal is useful for some bus departures but not all. Minibuses to Sibolga depart from offices on Jl Veteran, as do minibuses to Parapat; scheduled door-to-door transfers to Padang are more convenient than waiting for a bus at the terminal. Most lodgings can point you in the right direction and assist with booking passage.

The best way to get to Dumai – for ferries to Melaka and Kuala Lumpur in Malaysia – is with **BWE Travel** (☑ 0752 625 140, 0752 625 139; Jl Pemuda 81). Minibuses leave Bukittinggi nightly at 8pm, and departures are timed to link with the ferry from Dumai to Melaka. Prebooking is required.

ⓘ Getting Around

Angkot around town cost 3000Rp. *Bendi* start from 20,000Rp; bargain hard. An *ojek* from the bus terminal to the hotels costs 15,000Rp; a taxi costs 30,000Rp. Transfers to Padang airport can be arranged from any travel agent for around 55,000Rp.

For motorcycle rental, visit **Glory Rentals** (Tilal Bookshop, Jl Ahmad Yani; per day 60,000Rp) or enquire at your lodgings.

Danau Maninjau

☑ 0752

The first glimpse of this perfectly formed volcanic lake sucks your breath away as you lurch over the caldera lip and hurtle towards the first of the 44 hairpin bends (yep, they're numbered) down to the lakeshore.

Ground zero is the intersection where the Bukittinggi highway meets the lake road in the middle of Maninjau village. Turn left or right and drive 60km and you'll end up back here. The lake is 17km long, 8km wide and 460m above sea level. Most places of interest spread out north along the road to Bayur and beyond. If coming by bus, tell the conductor where you're staying and you'll be dropped off at the right spot.

⚡ Activities

Swimming and **canoeing** in the lake (warmed by subterranean springs) are the main drawcards here but there are plenty of other options.

The caldera, covered in rainforest that hides waterfalls and traditional villages, is a hiker's dream. **Hike** to the rim from Bayur, or cheat by catching the bus up the hill to Matur, then walking back down via the lookout at **Puncak Lawang**. Check out the map at Beach Guest House for more good trekking information.

Zipping around the lake on a motorcycle will take roughly three hours.

🛏 Sleeping & Eating

The majority of Maninjau options front onto aquaculture. There's a sprinkling of hotels, cheap losmen and restaurants between Maninjau and Bayur. Outside Maninjau village, most losmen are reached by walking along rice-paddy paths, so look for the sign by the roadside.

★ **Beach Guest House**   GUESTHOUSE **$**
(☑ 0752-861799, 0813 6379 7005; www.beach guesthousemaninjau.com; Jl Raya Maninjau; dm 40,000Rp, r 75,000-150,000Rp; 🛜) Run by a friendly, energetic local couple, this is Danau Maninjau's bona fide traveller central. Owners organise excursions, from round-the-lake bicycle or motorbike jaunts to hiking the caldera (seven hours). As for the digs, choose between bunking in the dorm or a range of rooms, the plushest lined up on the lakefront and boasting hot showers.

Muaro Beach Bungalows BUNGALOW **$**
(🖉0813 3924 0042, 0752-61189; neni967@yahoo.
com; Jl Muaro Pisang 53; r 80,000-120,000Rp;
🛜) Down a maze of footpaths (about 300m
northwest of the main intersection), these
beachfront bungalows are the best value in
Maninjau. The beach is (almost) free of aquaculture and fish farming, and there's a good
restaurant that's also open to nonguests. Local tours and activities are on offer.

Arlen Nova's Paradise BUNGALOW **$**
(🖉0853 7475 9288; www.nova-maninjau.id.or.id;
Sungai-Rangeh; r 175,000Rp) Walk through rice
paddies (5.5km north of Maninjau) to these
five simple bungalows, draped in passionfruit vines on a private beach, with nary a
fish pond in sight. The setting is gorgeous
and a plethora of friendly cats hang out
at the on-site restaurant, but the lodgings
could use some TLC.

ℹ️ Getting There & Around

Buses run hourly between Maninjau and Bukittinggi (20,000Rp, 1¾ hours). Taxis from Bukittinggi start at 160,000Rp.

Rent mountain bikes (45,000Rp per day),
motorcycles (100,000Rp per day) and canoes
(40,000Rp per day) from **PT Kesuma Tour &
Travel** (🖉0752-61422, 0812 669 9661; www.
sumatratravelling.com; Jl Panurunan Air Hangat)
or **Waterfront Zalino** (🖉0815 3541 1074).

Minibuses (3000Rp) travel the lake road during daylight hours. An *ojek* from the intersection
to Bayur will cost around 10,000Rp.

Danau Toba

🖉0625
There's no denying the beauty of Danau
Toba (Lake Toba), home of the fun-loving
Christian Batak people. This 1707-sq-km,
450m-deep lake, set in the collapsed caldera of an extinct volcano, is surrounded
by mountains ribboned with waterfalls and
terraced with rice fields. Its pale-blue mag-
nificence hits you on the bus ride into Parapat, when you'll also spot, in the middle of
the lake, Pulau Samosir – a Singapore-sized
island of blissful greenery and chilled-out
vibes. When there's a touch of mist in the
air and the horizon is obscured, the water
seems to blend perfectly with the sky. Combine the climate, scenery, sights and friendly
locals with some great food and an impressive array of cheap accommodation and
you'll see why Lake Toba is Sumatra's backpacker hang-out par excellence.

Parapat

The mainland departure point for Danau
Toba, Parapat has everything a transiting
tourist needs: transport, lodging and supplies. But unless you get here too late to
catch a boat to Tuk Tuk, there's no reason to
overnight here.

The commercial sector of the town is
clumped along the Trans-Sumatran Hwy (Jl
SM Raja) and has banks, ATMs and plenty
of eateries. Most buses pick up and drop off
passengers at ticket agents along the highway or at the pier.

ℹ️ Getting There & Away

PT Bagus Holiday (🖉0812 8083 8222, 0625-
41747) is one of several operators next to the
ferry pier that arranges tourist minibuses and
car transfers to the most popular destinations.
Tourist minibuses go to Berastagi (150,000Rp,
four hours), Bukittinggi (180,000Rp, 16 hours),
Bukit Lawang (230,000Rp, six hours), Medan
(80,000Rp to 100,000Rp, four hours), Padang
(285,000, 18 hours) and Sibolga (100,000Rp,
six hours).

Pulau Samosir

Trek, swim, explore traditional Batak villages, soak in hot springs, party or just chill
with cool local people on Pulau Samosir.
Your bus-beaten body will begin to unwind
on the slow, 8km ferry cruise over to this
volcanic isle. (It's actually connected to the
mainland by a narrow isthmus, but why
quibble?) **Tuk Tuk**, the island's resort town,
has low prices, high value and heaps of
tranquillity.

⊙ Sights

King Sidabutar Grave HISTORIC SITE
(admission by donation; ⊙dawn-dusk) The Batak
king who adopted Christianity is buried in
Tomok village, 5km southeast of Tuk Tuk.
The king's image is carved on his tombstone,
along with those of his bodyguard and An-
teng Melila Senega, the woman the king
is said to have loved for many years without fulfilment. The tomb is also decorated
with carvings of *singa* (mythical creatures
with grotesque three-horned heads and
bulging eyes). To get here, look out for the
small brown signpost shortly after you pass
through Tomok.

INDONESIA DANAU TOBA

Danau Toba

Stone Chairs
HISTORIC SITE

(admission by donation, guide 20,000Rp; ⊙8am-6pm) Ambarita, 5km north of Tuk Tuk, features a group of 300-year-old stone chairs where important matters were discussed among village elders. Here wrongdoers were tried and led to a further group of stone furnishings where they were bound, blindfolded, sliced, rubbed with garlic and chilli, and then beheaded.

Rumours abound that the story is the product of an overactive imagination and that the chairs are just 60 years old. On the premises you can peek into a traditional Batak kitchen.

Museum Huta Bolon Simanindo
MUSEUM

(admission 50,000Rp; ⊙10am-5pm) At Samosir's northern tip, in the village of Simanindo, 15km north of Tuk Tuk, there's a beautifully restored traditional house that now functions as a museum. It was formerly the home of Rajah Simalungun, a Batak king,

Danau Toba

⊜ Sleeping

1	Bagus Bay Homestay	C2
2	Harriara Guesthouse	D1
3	Liberta Homestay	C2
4	Merlyn Guesthouse	D1
	Romlan Guesthouse	(see 4)
5	Samosir Cottages	C1
6	Tabo Cottages	C2

⊗ Eating

7	Jenny's Restaurant	C1
8	Juwita Cafe	D2
	Today's Cafe	(see 8)

⊙ Drinking & Nightlife

| 9 | Brando's Blues Bar | C1 |

and his 14 wives. The roof was originally decorated with 10 buffalo horns, representing the 10 generations of the dynasty. The museum has a small, interesting collection of brass cooking utensils, weapons, Mula Jadi sculptures and Batak carvings.

Lacklustre displays of traditional Batak dancing are performed at 10.30am from Monday to Saturday if enough people show up; audience participation tends to be required.

Sleeping

The best sleeping options are along the north and south coasts. Little guesthouses are surrounded by hallmarks of village life, such as laundry drying on rocks and news being spread by neighbours.

Liberta Homestay
GUESTHOUSE $

(☑ 0625-451035; liberta_homestay@yahoo.com.co.id; r without bathroom 50,000Rp, with bathroom 70,000-90,000Rp; 🖀) This backpacker fave may have only limited lake views, but a chill universe is created here by a lush garden and arty versions of traditional Batak houses. Crawling around the balconies and shortened doors of the rooms makes you feel like being a deckhand on a Chinese junk (or a Hobbit). The popular Mr Moon is a great source of travel information.

Merlyn Guesthouse
GUESTHOUSE $

(☑ 0625-451057, 0813 6116 9130; Rio@merlynguesthouse.com; r 80,000-90,000Rp; 🖀) Situated right on the lake shore, this German-Indonesian-run place has traditional, characterful wooden Batak houses with dwarf-sized doors and shared bathrooms, as well as modern rooms in sunny colours with hot-water bathrooms.

Harriara Guesthouse
GUESTHOUSE $

(☑ 0625-451183; http://hariara-guesthouse.webs.com; Tuk Tuk; r 150,000Rp; 🖀) This guesthouse has a top-notch lakeside setting, riotous tropical flower gardens and sparkling rooms with mozzie nets and porches overlooking the water. There's good swimming from that spot, too. If there's nobody at reception, enquire at the nearby restaurants.

SPLURGE

German-run, lakeside **Tabo Cottages** (☑ 0625-451318; www.tabocottages.com; r 350,000-390,000Rp, cottage 500,000-950,000Rp; 🖀 @ 🖀) has beautiful, traditional-style Batak houses, which come with huge bathrooms and hammocks swinging lazily on the terrace. The house-made cakes are worthy of mention as well.

Romlan Guesthouse
GUESTHOUSE $

(☑ 0625-451386; www.romlantuktuk.com; Tuk Tuk; r 80,000-150,000; 🖀🖀) Run by a German-Indonesian family, this waterfront guesthouse is one of the original places to stay in Tuk Tuk and it's still going strong. Choose between a Western-style room with hot shower and verandah, one of two traditional Batak houses, or save your pennies in the budget room.

Eating

The guesthouses tend to mix eating and entertainment in the evening. Most restaurants serve the Batak speciality of barbecued carp (most from fish farms). Magic or 'special' omelettes are commonly seen on restaurant menus. We probably don't need to warn you that the mushrooms contained in these are not the sort that you can buy at your local supermarket.

★ Jenny's Restaurant
INTERNATIONAL $

(Tuk Tuk; mains 26,000-55,000Rp; ☉5-10pm) There are lots of different options on the menu at Jenny's, but one dish really shines – lake fish grilled right in front of you and served with chips and salad. Follow it up with the generously portioned fruit pancake. We enjoyed few meals in Sumatra more than this one.

Juwita Cafe
INDONESIAN $

(mains 25,000-46,000Rp; ☉lunch & dinner) This cosy family restaurant does Batak and other Indonesian dishes extremely well. We're particularly big fans of the aubergine sambal. Friendly matriarch Heddy also hosts cooking courses; a three-hour course includes a chicken, fish and vegetable dish, as well as dessert. Book a day in advance.

Today's Cafe
INTERNATIONAL $

(Tuk Tuk; mains 30,000-50,000Rp; ☉breakfast, lunch & dinner; 🖉) This little wooden shack has a laid-back vibe in keeping with Tuk Tuk life. It's run by a couple of friendly ladies who whip up some fabulous and eclectic dishes such as *sak sang* (chopped pork with brown coconut sauce, cream and a wealth of spices), aubergine curry and chapatis with guacamole.

Drinking & Entertainment

On most nights, music and spirits fill the night air with the kind of camaraderie that only grows in small villages. The Toba Bataks are extremely musical, and passionate

SOUTHERN SUMATRA

Aside from Krakatau and the ferry crossing to Java, southern Sumatra is something of a blank on the backpacker map, but the region hides plenty of enticing little secrets. Chief among these are the wild forests and swamps of the **Way Kambas National Park** to the northeast of Bandarlampung. It's home to very endangered elephants, rhinos and tigers.

If sun, sand and surf is more your thing, the laid-back village of **Krui** has your name all over it. Five hours' drive from Bandarlampung, Krui has recently gained a serious name for itself among travelling surfers thanks to a coastline littered with world-class spots (many of them *not* beginner-friendly).

The main city in these parts, and a place you're certain to transit, is **Bandarlam-pung**. There's nothing much to see here but if you need to stay try the **Grand Citihub Hotel @Kartini** (☑0721-240420; www.citihubhotels.com; Jl Kartini 41; r from 275,000Rp; ⊜❄🛜). You've got several bus options for getting from here to Java. The most convenient option is the **Damri** (☑0751-780 6335) bus-boat-bus combination ticket to Jakarta (184,000Rp, eight to 10 hours). Buses leave from Bandarlampung's train station at 9am, 10am, 8pm and 9pm. Damri's office is in front of Bandarlampung's train station. Heading north through Sumatra there are a number of buses to Padang, Medan or elsewhere, but needless to say this is one very long bus ride.

choruses erupt from invisible corners. The parties are all local – celebrating a wedding, a new addition on a house or the return of a Toba expat. Invitations are gladly given and should be cordially accepted.

Bagus Bay Homestay (☑0625-451287; www.bagusbay.com; Tuk Tuk; s/d without bathroom 30,000/40,000Rp, d 100,000-175,000Rp; @🛜) and **Samosir Cottages** (☑0625-451170; www.samosircottages.com; Tuk Tuk; r 100,000-425,000Rp; @🛜🏊) both have traditional Batak music and dance performances on Wednesday and Saturday evenings at 8.15pm.

Brando's Blues Bar BAR
(☑0625-451084; Tuk Tuk; ⊙6pm-late) One of a handful of foreigner-oriented bars that gets particularly lively on weekends. Happy hour is a civilised 6pm to 10pm and you can take to the small dance floor during the reggae and house sets.

❶ Getting There & Away

BOAT
Ferries between Parapat and Tuk Tuk (15,000Rp, 11 daily) operate about every hour from 8.30am to 7pm. Ferries stop at Bagus Bay (35 minutes); other stops are by request. The first and last ferries from Tuk Tuk leave at 7am and 5.30pm respectively; check exact times with your lodgings. When leaving for Parapat, stand on your hotel jetty and wave a ferry down. Fourteen ferries a day shuttle motorcycles and people between Parapat and Tomok (10,000Rp), from 7am to 7pm.

BUS
To get to Berastagi from Samosir by public bus, catch a bus from Tomok to Pangururan (16,000Rp, 45 minutes), then take another bus to Berastagi (48,000Rp, three hours). This bus goes via Sidikalang. Most guesthouses and travel agencies can pre-book the pricier, direct shared minibus tickets from Parapat for you.

❶ Getting Around

Local buses serve the whole of Samosir except Tuk Tuk. The peaceful, generally well-maintained (yet narrow) island roads are good for travelling by motorcycle (80,000Rp to 100,000Rp per day) or bicycle (30,000Rp per day); both are easily rented in Tuk Tuk. Minibuses run between Tomok and Ambarita (5000Rp), continuing to Simanindo (10,000Rp) and Pangururan (15,000Rp); flag them down on the main road. Services dry up after 5pm.

Berastagi

☑0628 / POP 43,000

Escaping from the infernal heat of sea-level Medan, the colonial Dutch traders climbed high into the lush, cool volcanic hills, took one look at the stunningly verdant, undulating landscape and decided to build a rural retreat where Berastagi (also called Brastagi) now stands.

Beyond the town are the green fields of the Karo Highlands, dominated by two volcanoes: Gunung Sinabung (2450m) to the west and the smoking Gunung Sibayak

Berastagi

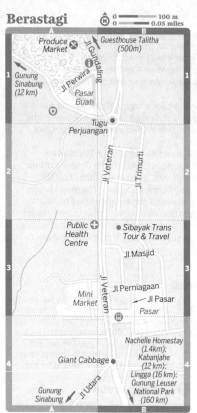

N 0 ——— 100 m
0 ——— 0.05 miles

Produce Market ✕
Guesthouse Talitha
(500m)

Jl Gundaling

Gunung
Sinabung
(12 km)

Jl Perwira

Pasar
Buah

Tugu
Perjuangan

Jl Veteran

Jl Trimurti

Public
Health
Centre ✚

● Sibayak Trans
Tour & Travel

Jl Masjid

Jl Perniagaan

Mini
Market

Jl Pasar

Pasar

Jl Veteran

Nachelle Homestay
(1.4km);

Giant Cabbage ●
Kabanjahe
(12 km);

Lingga (16 km);
Gunung Leuser
National Park
(160 km)

Gunung
Sinabung

Jl Udara

(2094m) to the north. Each is a day hike, making them two of Sumatra's most accessible volcanoes and the primary reason why tourists get off the bus in the first place.

☉ Sights & Activities

★ Gunung Sibayak   VOLCANO
(guide along the road 400,000Rp, through the jungle 650,000Rp) At 2094m, Gunung Sibayak is one of Indonesia's most accessible volcanoes. There are three ways to tackle the climb, depending on your energy level; a guide is only essential if taking the route through the jungle, but if you're trekking alone it's a good idea. The hike can be done in five hours return, and you should set out as early as possible.

Lingga   VILLAGE
(admission 4000Rp) The best-known and most visited of the villages around Berast-

agi is Lingga, a few kilometres northwest of Kabanjahe. There are about half-a-dozen traditional houses here with characteristic soaring thatched roofs topped with cattle horns. To get here, take a yellow KT minibus from Berastagi (7000Rp, 45 minutes). Some only go as far as Kabanjahe, so check first if you'll have to change.

🛏 Sleeping & Eating

Jalan Veteran sees heavy traffic and many rooms along the main road can be very noisy. With one notable exception, the quality of accommodation in Berastagi leaves much to be desired.

The rich volcanic soils of the surrounding countryside supply much of North Sumatra's produce, which passes through Berastagi's colourful **produce markets**. Passionfruit is a local speciality, as is *marquisa Bandung* (a large, sweet, yellow-skinned fruit). The *marquisa asam manis* (a purple-skinned fruit) makes delicious drinks.

Guesthouse Talitha   HOMESTAY $
(☑ 0813 7066 4252; Jl Kolam Renang 60B; r incl breakfast 100,000-150,000Rp; 🛜) A 15-minute walk north of the centre is this tranquil family-run guesthouse. The rooms could use a facelift, but there are hot-water showers in the pricier rooms and the friendly owners will perk you up with good home-brewed coffee.

★ Nachelle Homestay   HOMESTAY $$
(☑ 0821 6275 7658, 0813 6242 9977; nachelle homestay@gmail.com; r without bathroom 225,000Rp, with bathroom 275,000-400,000Rp; 🛜) The friendliest of Berastagi's lodgings is run by Mery and Abdy, who speak excellent English and will issue you with a map of the area; Abdy guides guests up Gunung Sibayak. Rooms are new and plush; the loveliest have king-sized beds and volcano views. Nachelle is 1.5km south of the giant cabbage on Jl Veteran; email for directions.

ℹ Information

Sibayak Trans Tour & Travel (☑ 0628-91122; dicksonpelawi@yahoo.com; Jl Veteran 119; ☺8am-5pm) A solid port of call for almost any onward travel advice as well as local tours.

Tourist Information Centre (☑ 0628-91084; Jl Gundaling 1; ☺8am-5pm Mon-Sat) Has maps and can arrange trekking guides, as well as private transport to Medan, Danau Toba and Kutacane. Opening hours are rather flexible.

ℹ Getting There & Away

The **bus terminal** (Jl Veteran) is conveniently located near the centre of town. Long-distance buses pass through Berastagi en route to Kabanjahe, the local hub. You can catch buses to Medan's Padang Bulan (15,000Rp, three to four hours) anywhere along the main street between 6am and 8pm.

The cheapest way to reach Danau Toba is to catch an *angkot* to Kabanjahe (5000Rp, 20 minutes), change to a bus for Pematangsiantar (28,000Rp, three hours), then connect with a Parapat-bound bus (15,000Rp, 1½ hours). For Bukit Lawang, take a bus to Pinangbari (13,000Rp, two hours) and change for Bukit Lawang (25,000Rp, three hours).

A couple of private companies run a shared minibus or car services, connecting Berastagi to Bukit Lawang (170,000Rp, three to four hours), Danau Toba (to Parapat; 150,000Rp, 3½ to four hours), Medan's Padang Bulan (100,000Rp, 2½ hours) and Medan airport (150,000Rp, three hours).

Medan

📝 061 / POP 2.2 MILLION

Sumatra's major metropolis, and Indonesia's third-largest city, Medan is seen as a necessary evil by many Sumatra-bound travellers. It's almost inevitably a place to pass through en route to more exciting destinations and also, for some, a welcome return to the trappings of 'civilisation' (ie modern malls and restaurants). It's a brash urban sprawl, chocked by streams of cars and becaks, but it's also filled with real Indonesian character. So get over the culture shock, give Medan some time and discover an amenity-filled, modern city with crumbling Dutch-colonial-era charm and a couple of worthwhile museums.

⊙ Sights

★ Museum of North Sumatra   MUSEUM

(Museum Negeri Privinci Sumatera Utara; Jl HM Joni 51; admission 10,000Rp; ⊙8am-4pm Tue-Thu, to 3.30pm Fri-Sun) Housed in a striking traditional building, this museum has a well-presented collection ranging from early North Sumatran civilisations to Hindu, Buddhist and Islamic periods to Dutch colonial-era and military history. There are also sections devoted to traditional occupations such as fishing and farming. Highlights include fine stone carvings and extravagantly carved wooden dragon coffins from Nias, Batak scrolls for fending off misfortune, fine textiles and a kris (ornamental dagger) collection. It's a short way east of the centre.

Tjong A Fie Mansion   HISTORIC BUILDING

(Jl Ahmad Yani 105; admission incl guide 35,000Rp; ⊙9am-5pm) The former house of a famous Chinese merchant who died in 1921 – formerly the wealthiest resident of Medan – mixes Victorian and Chinese style. The original hand-painted ceilings, Tjong's huge bedroom, imported dark-wood furniture inlaid with marble and mother-of-pearl, interesting art pieces, an upstairs ballroom and Taoist temples help to make it one of the most impressive historic buildings in town.

INDONESIA MEDAN

WORTH A TRIP

PULAU NIAS

Sitting off the west coast of Sumatra, the lonely island of Nias is home to one of the world's best surf spots – the legendary righthander of Lagundri Bay. For nonsurfers the island also has much to offer: the traditional hill villages, such as **Tundrumbaho** and **Bawomataluo**, will captivate even casual cultural tourists as well as ethno-architectural buffs.

The waves of **Teluk Lagundri** (or more correctly Pantai Sorake), on the southwest corner of the island, are best between April and October. On smaller days it's a fairly accessible wave for all but total beginners, but as soon as the swell starts to pick up, it becomes an experts-only barrel machine.

The point here is lined by a string of basic and almost identical losmen. The going rate is about 100,000Rp per night, but you're expected to eat at your losmen, too. And that'll cost you – a plate of chicken or fish can fetch 50,000Rp. The owner of **Lagundri Beach House** (📝0813 9656 7202; ian@lagundri.net; r 150,000-250,000Rp; ❄ 🗑) can arrange local tours.

To get to Nias you have the option of flying from Medan several times a day. The more romantic way of reaching the island is by ferry from the seedy mainland port of Sibolga. Ferries run daily from Sibolga to Gunung Sitoli, the 'capital' of Nias (80,000Rp), or three times weekly to Teluk Dalam (100,000Rp) in the south of Nias (which is much closer to the surf).

Medan

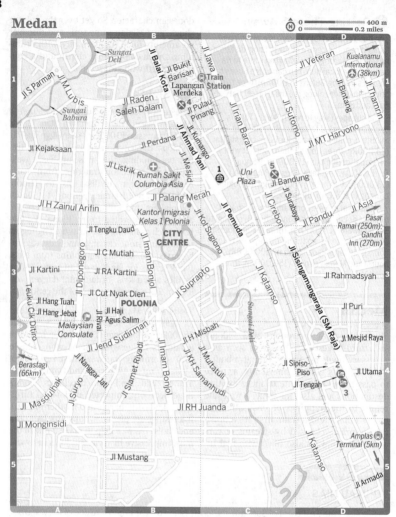

🛏 Sleeping

Pondok Wisata Angel GUESTHOUSE $
(☎061-732 0702; a_zelsy_travel@yahoo.com; Jl SM Raja 70; s with fan 70,000Rp, d with fan/air-con 100,000/130,000Rp; ❄🛜) The best backpacker option in town. Angel's clean rooms are a swirl of vivid blues and yellows, a colour scheme that almost succeeds in offsetting the noisy traffic. It has a sociable street-front cafe.

Residence Hotel HOTEL $
(☎061-732 1249; www.residencehotelmedan.com; Jl Tengah 1; r 70,000-150,000Rp; ❄🛜) The lime-green Residence has enough rooms, at a range of different prices, to mean that there's usually something to suit both your mood and your pockets. Warning: the cheaper rooms are top-floor, windowless cells with a Dickensian prison vibe and they get hot. The pricier rooms are pleasant.

K77 Guest House GUESTHOUSE $$
(☎061-736 7087, 0813 9653 8897; www.k77guesthousemedan.blogspot.com; Jl Seto 6B; r/f 250,000/300,000Rp; ❄🛜) This backpacker haven is not in the city centre. Instead, you get a typical residential neighbourhood

Medan

◉ **Sights**

  1 Tjong A Fie Mansion C2

◉ **Sleeping**

  2 Pondok Wisata Angel D4

  3 Residence Hotel...................................D4

◉ **Eating**

  4 Merdeka Walk.......................................B1

  5 Mie Tiong Sim Selat Panjang C2

experience, and the hosts, Johan and Lola, go out of their way to make it a good one. Rooms are clean, snug and cool, and Johan can organise pickup and all manner of tours.

Gandhi Inn   HOTEL **$$**

(☑ 061-733 2330; www.gandhiinn.com; Jl Gandhi 125 A-B; r 338,000-598,000Rp; ❋ ⊛) Decked out in sedate creams and browns, rooms at this budget (for Medan!) hotel are compact, comfortable and just a short walk from Thamsin Plaza Mall and the Pasar Ramai market. The owner and his team do their best to assist guests and recommend local culinary secrets. A place to chill out in between Sumatra adventures, do laundry and sleep.

✖ Eating

Medan has the most varied selection of cuisines in Sumatra, from basic Malay-style rice and noodle joints to top-class hotel restaurants.

★ **Merdeka Walk**   SOUTHEAST ASIAN **$**

(Lapangan Merdeka, Jl Balai Kota; dishes 10,000-35,000Rp; ⊙ 5pm-11pm; ⊛) Inspired by Singapore's alfresco dining, this collection of outdoor eateries in Lapangan Merdeka offers everything from doughnut stalls to breezy sit-down restaurants serving grilled seafood and Malaysian-style noodles. There is also what may possibly be the world's glitziest Pizza Hut.

Mie Tiong Sim Selat Panjang   NOODLES **$**

(Jl Selat Panjang 7; meals around 70,000Rp; ⊙ 10am-10pm) This stall, on a street of food stalls, is locally (and justifiably) famous for its *mie tiong sim* (soft, handmade noodles topped with sweet, flavourful char siu pork). The chicken noodle is almost equally as good, as are the wontons. It's behind the Hotel Swiss-Belinn.

Pasar Ramai   MARKET **$**

(Ramani Market; Jl Thamrin) The main fruit market is a profusion of colour and smells, and has an impressive selection of local and imported tropical fruit. It's next to Thamrin Plaza.

❶ Information

Kantor Imigrasi Kelas 1 Polonia (☑ 061-453 3117; 2nd fl, Jl Mangkubumi 2; ⊙ 8am-4pm Mon-Fri) For visa extensions. Technically the process takes three days, costs 350,000Rp and cannot be done until a few days before your current visa expires. Bring photocopies of your passport and Indonesian visa, as well as your onward ticket. The office you need is on the 2nd floor.

Rumah Sakit Columbia Asia (☑ 061-456 6730; www.columbiaasia.com; Jl Listrik 2A; ⊙ 24hr) The best hospital in the city, with a 24-hour walk-in clinic and pharmacy, as well as English-speaking doctors and specialists.

❶ Getting There & Away

AIR

You can fly from Medan to other Sumatran cities and major cities across Indonesia, as well as to Malaysia and Singapore.

Kualanamu International Airport (KNO; ☑ 061-8888 0300; www.kualanamu-airport. co.id) Opened in 2014, the international airport is 39km from the city centre and handily connected to central Medan by frequent trains and buses.

BUS

There are two main bus stations. Buses south leave from the **Amplas bus terminal** (Jl SM Raja), 6.5km south of downtown. Almost any *opelet* heading south on Jl SM Raja will get you to Amplas. A bemo from Amplas to the centre costs 5000Rp.

Buses to the north leave from **Pinang Baris bus terminal** (Jl Gatot Subroto), 10km west of the city centre. Get there by taxi (around 40,000Rp) or by *opelet* down Jl Gatot Subroto.

❶ Getting Around

The fastest and most comfortable way to reach central Medan from the airport is by air-conditioned train (100,000Rp, 45 minutes, 5am to 11.30pm). A taxi journey to the city centre is likely to set you back at least 150,000Rp.

Paradep (☑ 061-77123029; one-way 60,000Rp) and **Damri** (☑ 061-7865466; one-way 50,000Rp) shuttles pass through the city centre en route from the airport.

BUSES FROM MEDAN

DESTINATION	COST (RP)	DURATION (HR)	FREQUENCY
Banda Aceh	150,000-210,000	12-14	Several daily
Bukittinggi	200,000-320,000	22	Several daily
Bukit Lawang	30,000	4-5	Twice daily
Parapat	30,000	5-6	Several daily

Becak journeys across the city centre cost between 15,000Rp and 20,000Rp. *Angkots* cost 5000Rp.

Bukit Lawang

📋 061 / POP 30,000

This sweet little town, 96km northwest of Medan next to dense Sumatran jungle, is built around the popularity of its orangutan viewing centre. But Bukit Lawang has much more to offer beyond our red-haired cousins. It's very easy to while away a few days lounging in hammocks, splashing in the river and hiking in the jungle. The forests surrounding Bukit Lawang are part of the vast Gunung Leuser National Park, which is one of the richest tropical-forest ecosystems in the word – and home to eight species of primate, plus tigers, rhinos, elephants and leopards.

However, aside from orangutans, baboons, various macaque species and the elusive Thomas leaf monkey, you'd have to be very lucky to see any other large mammals here, as palm oil plantations extend right up to the edge of the village. At weekends, when foreign tourists are joined by masses of domestic visitors, Bukit Lawang can feel rather overrun, so try to arrive on a weekday.

◎ Sights

★ Orangutan Feeding Centre   WILDLIFE RESERVE

(feedings 8.30am-9.30am & 3pm-4pm) Bukit Lawang's famous orangutan centre was set up in 1973 to help primates readjust to the wild after captivity or displacement through land clearing. The twice-daily feedings, provided to semidependent orangutans, take place at a feeding platform, a 10-minute scramble up steep steps beyond the park office. The office is reached by an inflatable boat crossing upriver from the village. These feedings provide a wonderful close-up view of these magnificent creatures; no guide necessary.

🏃 Activities

Treks into the Gunung Leuser National Park require a guide and can last anywhere from three hours to several days. Most people opt for two days so they can spend the night in the jungle, which increases their likelihood of seeing orangutans and other wildlife. It's best to hike in the smallest group possible and to set off early.

Take your time in choosing a guide. Talk to returning hikers and decide how much jungle time you really need. Hiking in the jungle is no stroll in the park. You'll encounter steep, slippery ascents and precipitous drops amid intense humidity, so a good level of fitness is essential.

🛏 Sleeping & Eating

The further upriver you go, the more likely you are to spot the swinging monkeys and apes from your porch hammock. You won't find hot water, but all serve food.

Green Hill   GUESTHOUSE $

(📋 0813 7034 9124; www.greenhillbukitlawang. com; r incl breakfast 100,000-300,000Rp; 🛜) Run by an English conservation scientist and her Sumatran husband, Green Hill has three lovely stilt-high rooms ideal for couples, with ensuite bamboo-shoot showers that afford stunning jungle views while you wash, as well as a few-frills budget room. The restaurant serves some of the tastiest sambal in the village (among other dishes) and the service is friendly and prompt.

Back to Nature   GUESTHOUSE $

(📋 0821 7055 6999, 0813 7540 0921; www.backtonature.asia; r 150,000-200,000Rp; 🛜) 🍴 Preserving a giant patch of jungle otherwise destined to become a oil-palm plantation, the eco-minded owner has built this lodge on a gorgeous bend in the river. The comfortable wooden rooms, raised off the ground on stilts, are a half-hour walk upstream from the river crossing for the orangutan feeding centre. Jungle treks and pick ups from Bukit Lawang are offered.

Rainforest Guesthouse
GUESTHOUSE $

(Nora's; ☑ 0813 6207 0656; www.bukitlawang.com; d 50,000-150,000Rp) This cluster of wooden rooms set close to the gurgling river equals backpacker bliss. Cheaper rooms have a mattress on the floor and shared bathrooms, but pricier rooms come with bathrooms and fans. There's a friendly dining area (with Western meals like pasta, burgers and all the rest) and it's a super place to hook up with other travellers.

Garden Inn
GUESTHOUSE $

(☑ 0813 9600 0571; www.bukitlawang-garden-inn.com; r 100,000-250,000Rp; 🛜) A popular backpacker choice, the ever-growing Garden Inn empire spreads over several buildings, which house a variety of different rooms, from cosy, wooden jungle shacks to pristine, modern white rooms. There's a sweet little cafe for swapping ape-spotting tales.

ℹ Information

The nearby village of Gotong Royong, 2km southeast of Sungai Bohorok, is where most of the nontourist-related facilities can be found. If you arrive by public bus it's about a 1km walk north to where the Bukit Lawang accommodation begins. There are no banks, but you'll find moneychangers along the strip.

Bukit Lawang Visitors Centre (🕑7am-3pm) Park tickets are sold here. There's also displays of the flora and fauna found in Gunung Leuser National Park, plus a book of medicinal plants and their uses. Past visitors often record reviews of guides in the sign-in book. It's located down in the heart of the village.

ℹ Getting There & Away

Direct public buses go to Medan's Pinang Baris terminal (30,000Rp, four hours, half-hourly) between 5.30am and 5pm. There are also tourist minibuses (120,000Rp, three hours, daily at 8am).

GUNUNG LEUSER TREKKING FEES

Guide rates are fixed by the Sumatra Guide Association. Prices are based on a three-person minimum; singles and couples will still have to pay this amount.

TREK DURATION	PER PERSON (RP)
Half-day	395,000
1 day	550,000
2 days	945,000
3 days	1,340,000

For Berastagi, there's a daily public bus (38,000Rp, six to seven hours) and tourist bus (170,000Rp, four to five hours, daily 8.30am) Tourist minibuses also go to Medan Airport (190,000Rp, around four hours, daily 8am) and Parapat (for Danau Toba; 180,000Rp, six hours, daily 8.30am).

Tangkahan

The word is out: tiny Tangkahan has become synonymous with elephants, and visitors trickle in from nearby Bukit Lawang and Medan to get up close and personal with the mighty pachyderms.

Tangkahan is not so much a village as a bus stop, a park entrance and a handful of basic riverside bungalows on the wild banks of the Kualsa Buluh River. A small community of amiable loggers-turned-guides lives on the edge of untamed jungle.

🏃 Activities

Elephant Interaction
ELEPHANT INTERACTION

(elephant bathing 250,000Rp; 🕑elephant bathing 8.30am & 3.30pm Tue, Wed & Fri-Sun) For many, the elephants are the main draw in Tangkahan. While elephant rides are available here, consider opting for the more sustainable (and pachyderm-friendly) option of giving them their daily bath. On Mondays, Thursdays and public holidays there are no elephant-based activities. Elephant activities are booked directly through the CTO visitor centre (p272).

🛏 Sleeping & Eating

Mega Inn
GUESTHOUSE $

(☑ 0813 7021 1009; www.mega-inn-tangkahan.op-het-web.be; r 200,000Rp) The first place you come to after the river crossing has pretty bungalows made of twisted wood. Some of the bathrooms contain such a mass of foliage they could almost be classed as jungles themselves. The restaurant is a good spot for gobbling down fried noodles.

Dreamland Resort
BUNGALOW $

(☑ 0812 6963 1400; bungalow 150,000-170,000Rp; ❄) Run by two friendly, young brothers who speak good English, Dreamland has three appealing A-frame cottages with private bathroom sitting partially hidden amid lush greenery. The cafe gives you a bird's-eye view of the river.

GETTING TO MALAYSIA: DUMAI TO MELAKA

Getting to the border Dumai is a busy and charmless port on Sumatra's north coast. Bus services to Dumai include those from Bukittinggi (160,000Rp, 10 hours, 7pm daily) and Padang (150,000Rp, 12 hours, frequent). High-speed ferries make the trip from Dumai to Melaka daily (one-way about 350,000Rp, 1¾ hours).

At the border Nationals of most countries are given a 30- or 60-day visa on arrival, depending on the expected length of stay.

Moving on Melaka is a large and popular city with connections to the rest of Malaysia.

ⓘ Information

CTO Visitor Centre (☏ 0852 7560 5865, 0813 6142 3245; www.tangkahanecotourism.com; ◷ 8am-4pm) Across the river from the lodges and near the bus terminal, this visitor centre organises everything from elephant bathing to jungle treks and caving; pay your fees here.

ⓘ Getting There & Away

Two direct, daily buses go to Medan's Pinang Baris terminal (20,000Rp, four hours) at 5.30am and 7.30am.

To get to Tangkahan from Bukit Lawang, you have two options. The slow, cheap, roundabout way: take one of the many buses to Binjai (12,000Rp to 15,000Rp, 2½ hours), then connect to one of the twice-daily buses directly to Tangkahan (30,000Rp, 2½ hours) if you time it well, or take a bus to Tittamangga (26,000Rp, two hours) and from there hop on the back of a motorcycle to Tangkahan (70,000Rp). The fast, pricier way: get a guide to take you directly from Bukit Lawang on a motorcycle (one-way/return 200,000/300,000Rp, two hours) – but be warned that the road is unpaved. Alternatively, team up with other travellers to hire a 4WD (550,000Rp to 650,00Rp, 2½ hours).

Banda Aceh

☏ 0651 / POP 223,000

Indonesian cities are rarely coupled with pleasant descriptions, but Banda Aceh breaks the mould. The laid-back provincial capital is a pleasant enough spot to spend a couple of days. (Pedestrians will notice with delight that the city has actual pavements.) Given that Banda Aceh bore the brunt of the 2004 tsunami, with 61,000 killed here (of 170,000 across the province), and that much of the city had to be rebuilt, it's little wonder that it looks well maintained and affluent.

Banda Aceh is a fiercely religious city and the ornate mosques are at the centre of daily life. Respectfully dressed visitors shouldn't face any hassles and most travellers find the Acehnese to be friendly and extremely hospitable.

◉ Sights

★**Tsunami Museum** MUSEUM
(Jl Iskandar Muda; ◷ 9am-4.15pm Sat-Thu, noon-2pm Fri) **FREE** A visit to this hard-hitting museum commences with a walk through a dark, dripping tunnel that symbolises the tsunami waves, with plaintive, terrified voices and the sound of rushing water all around you. This is followed by a powerful set of images of the devastation projected from tombstone-like receptacles, and a circular chamber engraved with the names of the lost. Upstairs a very graphic short film is aired, along with photographs of rebuilding, loss, hopefulness, displacement and reunited families.

Mesjid Raya Baiturrahman MOSQUE
(admission by donation; ◷ 7-11am & 1.30pm-4pm) With its brilliant-white walls, ebony-black domes and towering minaret, the 19th-century Mesjid Raya Baiturrahman is a dazzling sight. The best time to visit the mosque is during Friday afternoon prayers, when the entire building and yard is filled with people. A headscarf is required for women.

🛏 Sleeping & Eating

There is very little in the way of budget accommodation here; the cheapies on Jl Khairil Anwar don't seem to accept foreign guests. Shoestringers may find themselves racing straight through Banda Aceh and out to the mellower prices of Pulau Weh.

★**Hotel Sei** HOTEL $$
(☏ 0651-21866; www.seihotelaceh.com; Jl Tanoh Abe 71, Kampung Mulia; d 550,000Rp; 🅿 ❄ 🛜) This new lemon-yellow hotel down a quiet side street is one of Banda Aceh's swankiest options. Expect compact rooms with reliable wi-fi, the Arctic chill of air-con, a pleasant respite from the outdoors, as well as friendly but erratic service and a seemingly deserted but actually decent restaurant.

Linda's Homestay
HOMESTAY $$

(☑ 0823 6436 4130, 0811 680 305; www.lindas-homestay.blogspot.com; Jl Mata Lorong Rahmat 3, Lambneu Barat; r 350,000-400,000Rp; ❀ 🛜)
Staying in the home of hospitable Linda, 4km out of town, is a good way of experiencing local life and many travellers rave about her. Linda cooks up a storm of Acehnese food and her sons are on hand to give you a tour of the city. However, some travellers report misunderstandings about prices and ensuing bad feelings.

Rumah Makan
Spesifik Aceh
INDONESIAN $

(Jl T Hasan Dek; mains from 30,000Rp; ☺ 11am-10pm) An excellent introduction to Acehnese cuisine, with such delights as *asam keeng* (hot and sour soup), *mie aceh* (spicy noodle dish), *udang goreng kunyit* (turmeric shrimp), and curried fish.

ⓘ Information

Note that women will need to fully cover up in Aceh. Also, religious police have arrested publicly affectionate gay couples (and sent them for 're-education').
Regional Tourist Office (Dinas Parawisata; ☑ 0651-852020; www.bandaacehtourism.com; Jl Chik Kuta Karang 3) The staff are exceptionally friendly and sometimes have free copies of an excellent guidebook to the province. The tourist office is on the 1st floor of a government building.

ⓘ Getting There & Away

There are several flights a day from Banda Aceh to Medan with Garuda, Sriwiyaya and Lion Air. **Air Asia** (www.airasia.com) flies daily to Kuala Lumpur, and **Firefly** (www.fireflyz.com.my) to Penang in Malaysia.

South of the city centre you'll find the **Terminal Bus Bathoh** (Jl Mohammed Hasan), which has numerous buses to Medan. *Ekonomi* buses (175,000Rp, 14 hours) depart at 4pm, while *eksekutif* buses leave all day (230,000Rp, 12 hours).

AIR

Banda Aceh's Sultan Iskandar Muda International Airport (BTJ) is 16km southeast of the centre. Destinations include Jakarta, Kuala Lumpur, Medan and Penang.

BOAT

Boats serving Pulau Weh depart from the port at Uleh-leh, 5km northwest of Banda Aceh's city centre.

BUS

Terminal Bus Bathoh is located 2km south of the city centre. Large buses to Medan aside, most accommodation can arrange for the relevant minibus to pick you up.

TO	FARE (RP)	DURA-TION (HR)	FREQUENCY
Ketambe/ Kutacane	220,000	15-18	daily
Medan	210,000	12	hourly until 10pm
Singkil	230,000	15	daily

ⓘ Getting Around

Taxis from the airport to the city centre charge around 100,000Rp. A taxi from the airport to the Uleh-leh port will cost around 130,000Rp.

Labi-labi (small minibuses) are the main form of transport around town and cost 2500Rp. The **labi-labi terminal** (Jl Diponegoro) is that special breed of Indonesian mayhem.

From the bus terminal, a becak into town will cost around 25,000Rp. A becak around town should cost between 10,000Rp and 20,000Rp, depending on your destination.

Pulau Weh

☑ 0652 / POP 25,000

A tiny tropical rock off the tip of Sumatra, Weh is a little slice of peaceful living that rewards travellers who've journeyed up through the turbulent greater mainland below.

After hiking around the jungles, volcanoes and lakes of the mainland, it's time to jump into the languid waters of the Indian Ocean. Snorkellers and divers bubble through walls of swaying sea fans, deep canyons and rock pinnacles, while marvelling at the prehistorically gargantuan fish.

Both figuratively and geographically, Pulah Weh is the cherry on top for many visitors' trip to Sumatra.

🏃 Activities

Most travellers come to Weh for the **diving** and **snorkelling**. On an average day, you're likely to spot morays, lionfish and stingrays. During plankton blooms, whale sharks come to graze. Unlike at other dive sites, the coral fields take a back seat to the sea life and landscapes. There are close to 20 dive sites around the island. Dive operators are based in Gapang and Iboih.

Snorkelling gear can be hired almost anywhere for around 30,000Rp per day.

About a 2km walk from Sabang town is **Pantai Kasih** (Lover's Beach), a palm-fringed crescent of white sand. Popular with a mixture of domestic and international tourists, **Gapang Beach** offers terrific swimming, with frequent turtle sightings.

★ Lumba Lumba Diving Centre
DIVING

(☑ 0811 682 787; www.lumbalumba.com; discover dive/Open Water Diver course €45/300) The established and professional Dutch-run Lumba Lumba Diving Centre has been introducing divers to Pulau Weh's underwater world for two decades now and is the only PADI-certified diving centre on the island. The owners Ton and Marjan Egbers maintain a helpful website with detailed descriptions of dives and need-to-know information. Highly recommended.

Rubiah Tirta Divers
DIVING

(☑ 0652-332 4555; www.rubiahdivers.com; discover dive/Open Water Diver course €40/270) Local-run Rubiah Tirta Divers is the oldest dive operation on the island and gets consistently good feedback from travellers.

🛏 Sleeping & Eating

Iboih, with its simple palm-thatch bungalows, many built on stilts and overhanging crystal-clear water, is Pulau Weh's backpacker hangout par excellence. There are dozens of different places to stay with almost nothing whatsoever to differentiate them from each other. Whichever you choose, if you stay for several days, you can usually negotiate a discount on the normal daily rates.

Rates and visitors double on weekends.

Yulia's
HUT $

(☑ 0821 6856 4383; r with/without bathroom 280,000/120,000Rp; 🛜) A 500m trudge past the rest of the guesthouses rewards you with cheerful green huts, some excellent front-door snorkelling and a pink restaurant serving a mix of Indonesian and Western dishes.

Olala
HUT $

(☑ 0852 6060 7311; r 70,000-150,000Rp; 🛜) Offering cheap and cheerful huts on stilts, Olala caters both to shoestringers (basic digs with shared bathrooms) and splurgers who want their own bathroom and fan. Its restaurant (open to all) is a popular traveller hang out and receives an equal amount of praise.

ⓘ Information

There are ATMs in Sabang.

ⓘ Getting There & Away

Slow car ferries (economy/air-con 25,000/50,000Rp, two hours) ply the route between Uleh-leh, 5km northwest of Banda Aceh on the mainland, and Balohan port, around 8km south of Sabang on Pulau Weh.

The **Express Ferry** (☑ 0651-43791, 0652-332 4800; business/executive/VIP 125,000/150,000/165,000Rp) departs Banda Aceh for Pulau Weh at 9.30am and 4pm daily (45 minutes to one hour). Services from Pulau Weh to Banda Aceh depart at 8am and 2.30pm daily.

ⓘ Getting Around

From the Balohan port, there are regular minibuses to Sabang (25,000Rp, 15 minutes), and Gapang and Iboih (60,000Rp, 40 minutes).

KALIMANTAN

Skewered by the equator and roasting under a tropical sun, the steamy forests of Kalimantan serve up endless opportunities for epic rainforest exploration. The island has no volcanoes and is protected from tsunamis, which has allowed its ancient forests to grow towering trees that house some of the world's most memorable species. The noble orangutan shares the canopy with acrobatic gibbons, while prehistoric hornbills patrol the air above.

The indigenous people, collectively known as Dayak, have long lived in concert with this rich, challenging landscape. Their longhouses dot the banks of Kalimantan's many waterways, creating a sense of community unmatched elsewhere in a country already well known for its hospitable people. Given Kalimantan's ongoing environmental struggles, particularly with palm oil plantations, there has never been a more vital time to visit.

History & Culture

Kalimantan's riches drew Chinese and Indian traders as far back as AD 400. Dutch and English imperialists began sparring over Kalimantan in the early 17th century; Holland won and England took Sarawak and Sabah. Global industrialisation and expanding wealth spurred demand for traditional commodities and new ones: coal and oil. Petroleum drew Japan's attention during

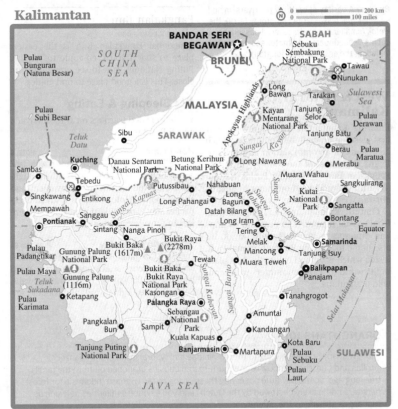

WWII. It also spelled the end of European rule, for the war's end brought independence to Indonesia. Over the past six decades, Kalimantan has struggled to find its place in Indonesia. Economic opportunity increasingly attracts outsiders: with a cast of crusading missionaries and imams, loggers, palm oil planters and conservationists, government administrators and traditional leaders, the struggle for Kalimantan's soul continues.

🛈 Getting There & Away

The only entry points to Kalimantan that issue visas on arrival are Balikpapan's Sepinggan Airport, Pontianak's Supadio Airport and the Tebedu–Entikong land crossing between Kuching (Sarawak) and Pontianak. All other entry points require a visa issued in advance.

AIR

Most major cities can be reached from Jakarta or Surabaya. Pontianak connects with Kuching

(Malaysia), while Balikpapan has direct flights to Kuala Lumpur, Malaysia and Singapore.

BOAT

Major ferry ports in Kalimantan include Balikpapan, Samarinda, Banjarmasin and Pontianak. **Pelni** (www.pelni.co.id) and other carriers connect to Jakarta, Semarang and Surabaya on Java, as well as Makassar and Pare Pare on Sulawesi.

🛈 Getting Around

Kalimantan is both immense and undeveloped. River travel is as common as road travel, and transport options can form a complex picture.

By Road Highways between major cities are improving daily, and range from excellent to pockmarked. Buses are fairly ubiquitous, except in East and North Kalimantan. Most major routes offer air-con for a bit extra. Intra-city travel usually involves a minibus known as an *angkot* or *opelet*.

By River A variety of craft ply the rivers, including the *kapal biasa* (large two-storey ferry), the *klotok* (smaller boat with covered passenger cabins), speedboats, and motorised canoes, including the *ces* (the local longtail).

West & Central Kalimantan

Entering Kalimantan from Sarawak, your first destination will be Pontianak, which has plenty of accommodation and forward flights to the rest of the country (including Pangkalan Bun for Tanjung Puting National Park). We've focused on major highlights *outside* West Kalimantan.

Central Kalimantan (KalTeng) segues from coastal mangrove to peatland swamps and dipterocarp forest. Heavily Dayak, it's also home to Tanjung Puting National Park, inside which is Camp Leakey, the best place in the world for close encounters with semi-wild orangutans.

Pangkalan Bun

☑ 0532 / POP 43,000

Functional Pangkalan Bun is the easiest place to stay if you're en route to Tanjung Puting National Park to see orangutans up close. This is a good place to find guides.

🛏 Sleeping & Eating

You'll find good warungs on Jl Kasumayuda and Jl P Antasari.

Hotel Tiara HOTEL $
(☑ 0532-22717; Jl P Antasari 16; r with fan/air-con 120,000/170,000Rp; ❄) With its high-ceilinged, well-maintained, convenient and cheap rooms, Hotel Tiara is a great backpacker stay. A new addition next door promises to provide even more options.

★ **Yayorin Homestay** HOMESTAY $$
(Yayasan Orangutan Indonesia; ☑ 0532-29057; info@yayorin.com; Jl Bhayangkara Km1; r incl breakfast 300,000Rp) 🍃 Woven rattan walls. Solar-powered lights. Verdant woodland set-

---

ORANGUTANS 101

Four great ape species belong to the Hominidae family: orangutans, chimpanzees, gorillas and humans. Although our auburn-haired cousins branched off from the family tree long ago, spend any time observing these *orang hutan* (Bahasa Indonesia for forest person, a name likely bestowed by the Dutch) and you'll notice similarities between us that are as striking as the differences.

The bond between a mother and her young is among the strongest in the animal kingdom. For the first two years infants are entirely dependant and carried everywhere. For up to seven years mothers continue to teach them how to thrive in the rainforest.

The territorial males are entirely absent from child-rearing, living mostly solitary lives punctuated by sometimes violent battles for alpha status. Once a young male secures a territory, he rapidly undergoes physical changes, growing impressive cheek pads and throat pouches. He advertises his dominion by issuing booming long calls that echo through the forest for kilometres.

Both species of orangutan, Sumatran and Bornean, are endangered. Much of their habitat is being converted to palm oil plantations. Mothers are frequently shot, their infants sold as pets. Currently, all of the orangutan rescue and rehabilitation centres in Indonesia are operating at or above capacity.

For more information on orangutan conservation efforts and volunteer opportunities in Kalimantan, check out the following:

Friends of the National Parks Foundation (www.fnpf.org) Funds forest restoration at Pasalat.

Orangutan Foundation International (www.orangutan.org) Founded by Biruté Galdikas; runs the park's feeding stations.

Orangutan Foundation UK (www.orangutan.org.uk) UK organisation focused on saving orangutan habitats.

Orangutan Land Trust (www.forests4orangutans.org) Influences policy and supports a wide range of organisations dedicated to the long-term survival of orangutans.

ting. Check, check and check. These peaceful cottages are a fundraising effort by Yayorin, a local NGO working to preserve Kalimantan's forests through education and community engagement. About 7km south of town; take Jl HM Rafi'i at the paratrooper roundabout.

ℹ Getting There & Away

Air service includes Jakarta, Pontianak and Surabaya.

DAMRI's (☑ 0812 5186 3651; Nantai Suka Terminal) bus service to Pontianak (350,000Rp, 13 hours, daily at 7am) and all **Logos** (☑ 0532-24954; Jl Pangeran Antasari) buses depart from **Terminal Nantai Suka** (Jl Jend A Yani), while **Yessoe Travel** (☑ 0532-21276; Jl Kawitan 68) services depart from its own office. Destinations aboard Logos and Yessoe include Sampit (85,000Rp, six hours), Palangka Raya (125,000Rp, 12 hours) and Banjarmasin (175,000Rp to 290,000Rp, 16 hours).

ℹ Getting Around

Taxis to/from the airport (8km) cost 70,000Rp *Opelet* around town cost 10,000Rp. Minibuses to Kumai (20,000Rp, 20 minutes) leave across from Hotel Abadi. Taxis to Kumai start at 100,000Rp.

Kumai

☑ 0532 / POP 25,000

The port of departure for Tanjung Puting National Park, Kumai is also known for its bird's-nest business, which fills the town with screeching warehouses. A handful of guesthouses and warungs line the main street, Jl HM Idris. Backpackers sometimes meet here to share the price of a *klotok*. There is an ATM downriver near the port, and the national park dock is upriver on the edge of town.

ℹ Getting There & Away

Reach Kumai by minibus from Pangkalan Bun (20,00Rp, 20 minutes). Taxis from Pangkalan Bun airport to Kumai cost 150,000Rp, including all stops for visiting Tanjung Puting National Park.

Tanjung Puting National Park

Possibly *the* highlight of Borneo, this unforgettable adventure takes you on a boat puttering up Sungai Sekonyer (Sekonyer River) to Camp Leakey, established in 1971 by eminent primatologist Dr Biruté Galdikas.

GETTING TO MALAYSIA: PONTIANAK TO KUCHING

Getting to the border A number of bus companies ply the route between Pontianak's Ambawang terminal, 9km east of the city, and Kuching Sentral bus terminal (and other cities along the Sarawak coast). Buses pass through the Tebedu–Entikong crossing, 80km south of Kuching.

At the border Nationals of most countries are given a 30- or 60-day visa on arrival, depending on the expected length of stay.

Moving on Kuching is well linked to the rest of Malaysia by bus and plane.

A visit here almost guarantees you intimate encounters with orangutans. En route you'll see macaques, pot-bellied proboscis monkeys, kingfishers, majestic hornbills and – if you're lucky – false gharial crocodiles. Around the camp you may also spot sun bears, porcupines, gibbons and Sambar deer.

◉ Sights & Activities

Part of the rehabilitation process here is the daily feeding of orangutans at jungle platforms, where you'll go and view them. Rangers armed with panniers of bananas whoop to empty trees and gradually orangutans appear.

Feedings take place at three camps: **Tanjung Harapan** at 3pm, **Pondok Tangui** at 9am and **Camp Leakey** at 2pm (check for schedule changes). Reaching feeding stations requires a short, sometimes slippery walk (about 15 minutes) from the dock. Bring rain protection and vats of insect repellent!

Two-tiered *klotoks* are the most romantic way to visit Tanjung Puting and serve as your restaurant, watchtower and home, accommodating up to four guests. Come twilight, moor up beside the jungle, your *klotok* aflicker with candlelight. You usually bed down early – the upper deck transformed with mattress and mozzie net – then wake at dawn to the gibbon's mellow call and myriad animal sounds.

The cost of hiring a *klotok* varies with its size. They range from small (two to four passengers, 450,000Rp to 550,000Rp per day) to large (eight to 10 passengers, 650,000Rp to 1,000,000Rp per day), including captain, mate and fuel. Cooks are an additional 100,000Rp per day, with food on top of that. When you factor in a guide (150,000Rp to 250,000Rp per day), permits (150,000Rp per person per day) and boat parking fees (100,000Rp per boat per day) the total cost for a three-day, two-night guided trip for two people easily tops 4,000,000Rp, even if you painstakingly haggle every step of the way.

When you consider these prices, the hassle, transport to and from the airport, and all the other details, the additional cost you may pay going through a reasonably priced company suddenly feels more affordable.

★ **Jenie Subaru**   ADVENTURE TOUR
(☑ 0857 6422 0991; jeniesubaru@gmail.com) 🛶
It is a shame that the passionate and charismatic Jenie does few trips these days, instead (admirably) devoting much of his time to training the next batch of local guides in sustainable tourism. Proceeds from his trips go toward buying land along the park's border to protect orangutan habitat.

Orangutan House
Boat Tours   ADVENTURE TOUR
(☑ 0857 5134 9756; www.orangutanhouseboattour.com) Local resident Fardi may be young, but he's hard-working and passionate about both his homeland and orangutans.

Borneo Orangutan
Adventure Tour   ADVENTURE TOUR
(☑ 0852 4930 9250; www.orangutantravel.com) Run by the excellent Ahmad Yani, the first official guide in the area.

🛏 Sleeping

If you're looking to stay outside the park (typically before or after your cruise), try Kumai or Pangkalan Bun.

★ **Flora Homestay**   HOMESTAY **$$**
(☑ 0812 516 4727; r 500,000Rp, set meals 75,000Rp) Located directly on the river at the end of Sekonyer village, these rough-hewn wood cabins provide everything you need for a truly immersive Borneo experience. Pak Bana is eager to please, even offering to boil up water if you require a hot shower. Tours to a feeding station, canoe trips and jungle trekking are all available.

ℹ Information

Independent travellers must register at Pangkalan Bun police station upon arrival. Bring photocopies of your passport and visa (airport taxi drivers know the steps). This can also be organised by your guide.

ℹ Getting There & Around

Tanjung Puting is typically reached via a flight to nearby Pangkalan Bun, then a taxi to Kumai (150,000Rp, 20 minutes).

Speedboats from Kumai cost 700,000Rp per day, and take about two hours to reach Camp Leakey (it's just transport, not wildlife-spotting).

For the cheapest route to Sekonyer village, take a ferry from Kumai across the bay (5000Rp), then an *ojek* (25,000Rp, 30 minutes) to the village.

Canoes are a quiet alternative for exploring the river's shallow tributaries, and can be rented at Sekonyer village store for 50,000Rp per day.

East Kalimantan

East Kalimantan (KalTim) may have been long exposed to logging and oil extraction, but it can still boast vast unpenetrated jungle, the mighty Mahakam River and some of the best off-coast diving in Borneo.

Balikpapan

☑ 0542 / POP 560,000

As Kalimantan's only cosmopolitan city, Balikpapan is almost worthy of being considered a destination unto itself. A long history of oil money and foreign workers has had a tremendous impact, bringing Western aesthetics to this eastern port town. The city is clean and vibrant, with several enormous shopping areas and some decent beaches like Kemala.

Most of the action takes place in the centre off Jl Sudirman, which comes alive at night. **Wisma Kemala Bhayangkari** (☑ 0812 5490 2392, 0542-421260; Jl Sudirman 6; r 250,000-385,000Rp; ✵) is a great budget find near Kemala Beach. **Soto Queen** (Warung Kuin Abduh, SQ; Jl Ahmad Yani; soto Banjar 15,000Rp; ⊙ 2-11pm) serves addictive *soto Banjar* (chicken soup seasoned with a delicate blend of spices).

There are flights to major Indonesian cities, plus Kuala Lumpur and Singapore. Taxis to the city centre from the airport (BPN) cost 70,000Rp; or you can walk 150m to the road and hail a green-and-white *angkot* 7 heading west (5000Rp).

Berau
☎ 0554 / POP 63,000

Riverbound Berau lacks charm, but is an important waypoint to Pulau Derawan.

🛏 Sleeping

Hotel Mitra HOTEL $
(☎ 0812 5315 0715; Jl Gajah Mada 531A; r incl breakfast 220,000-240,000Rp; ❄ 🖥) Immaculate with friendly staff, Mitra feels less like a hotel and more like a giant homestay. As a long-standing favourite with local NGOs, Mitra has a staff well-used to dealing with foreigners. All rooms have air-con and cold water only.

ℹ Getting There & Away

AIR
Service at the airport (BEJ) 9km from town includes Balikpapan.

BUS & KIJANG
Kijang gather in the morning across from the former bus terminal and will wait for a minimum of three passengers; you can buy multiple seats to leave faster. Destinations include Tanjung Batu (100,000Rp, 2½ hours) and Balikpapan (400,000Rp, over 20 hours).

Pulau Derawan
☎ 0551

The tiny, offbeat backpacker's magnet of Derawan is the best known of the archipelago, and the closest to the mainland. It is also increasingly crowded. However, despite the near constant presence of tourists, the locals still maintain a friendly attitude and kids are eager to steal high-fives. You'll compete for solitude with local tourists on banana boats during weekends and holidays. For more idyllic surroundings, consider the truly remote Maratua Island.

🏃 Activities

The **diving** and **snorkelling** rank among the best in Indonesia, offering an assortment of reef and pelagic species including barracuda, sharks, mantas and turtles, all the way down.

A full-day snorkelling trip in the area runs from 1,500,000Rp to 2,000,000Rp, depending on how far you go. It is four hours of spine-compressing travel from Derawan to the popular snorkelling areas around Kakaban and Sangalaki, return. Organise diving at upmarket Derawan Dive Lodge.

🛏 Sleeping & Eating

Stilted losmen here are cosy and offer the sea as your back garden. Cafes along Main St serve up fresh seafood.

★ Miranda Homestay HOMESTAY $
(☎ 0813 4662 3550; r 200,000Rp) Tucked back toward shore with not much of a view, these two spotless rooms are still great value. Pak Marudi's spacious and relaxing *klotok* is at your disposal for slow coffee-filled snorkelling excursions (700,000Rp per day), or transport to Tanjung Batu (100,000Rp per person).

Sari Cottages GUESTHOUSE $$
(☎ 0813 4653 8448; r 350,000Rp; ❄) Centrally located Sari has 22 freshly painted rooms, strung along two parallel piers connected by a footbridge. The large, private back porches all have (as yet) unobstructed views, and the restaurant has the best location in town. Turn off the street at the sign for 'Pinades', and keep walking the plank.

Derawan Dive Lodge LODGE $$$
(☎ 0431-824445; www.derawandivelodge.com; s/d incl breakfast US$80/95) A small enclave of 10 comfortable, individually designed rooms, with a cosy outdoor cafe and private beach, at the west end of the island. If you want to combine a dive holiday with some island life, this is your top choice on Derawan.

ℹ Getting There & Away

Most trips to the islands leave from the coastal town of Tanjung Batu, accessible from Berau by road (500,000Rp charter, 100,000Rp regular seat, 2½ hours). From there, a regular morning boat takes passengers to Pulau Derawan (100,000Rp per person, 30 minutes); otherwise you must charter a speedboat (300,000Rp, seats four).

A charter to Maratua is 1,300,000Rp for the 1½-hour journey from Tanjung Batu, or 1,100,000Rp for the one-hour trip from Derawan. Prices are sometimes negotiable.

SULAWESI

Sulawesi is as wild in reality as it appears on a map. The massive island's many-limbed coastline is drawn with sandy beaches, fringing coral reefs and a mind-boggling variety of fish. Meanwhile, the interior is shaded, with impenetrable mountains and jungles thick with wildlife such as rare nocturnal

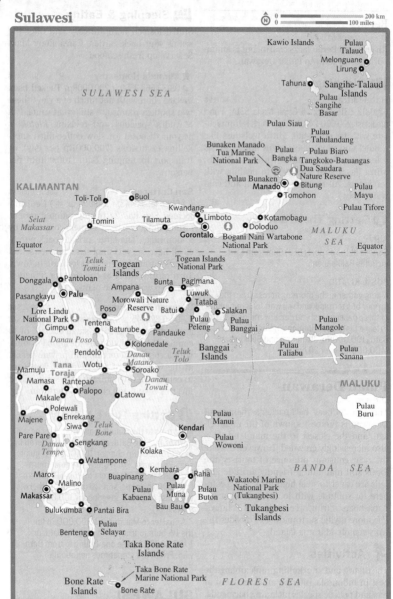

0   200 km
0   100 miles

SULAWESI SEA

Kawio Islands

Pulau Talaud
Melonguane
Lirung

Tahuna

Sangihe-Talaud Islands

Pulau Sangihe Basar

Pulau Siau

Pulau Tahulandang

Bunaken Manado Tua Marine National Park

Pulau Bangka

Pulau Biaro

Tangkoko-Batuangas

Dua Saudara Nature Reserve

Pulau Bunaken

Manado

Bitung

Pulau Mayu

Tomohon

Pulau Tifore

KALIMANTAN

Toli-Toli

Buol

Kwandang

Kotamobagu

MALUKU SEA

Selat Makassar

Tomini

Tilamuta

Limboto

Gorontalo

Doloduo

Bogani Nani Wartabone National Park

Equator   Equator

Teluk Tomini

Togean Islands

Togean Islands National Park

Donggala

Pantoloan

Ampana

Bunta

Pagimana

Pasangkayu

Palu

Morowali Nature Reserve

Luwuk

Tataba

Lore Lindu National Park

Poso

Batui

Salakan

Gimpu

Tentena

Baturube

Pandauke

Pulau Peleng

Pulau Banggai

Pulau Mangole

Karosa

Danau Poso

Kolonedale

Teluk Tolo

Banggai Islands

Pulau Taliabu

Pulau Sanana

Pendolo

Danau Matano

Tana Toraja

Wotu

Soroako

Danau Towuti

MALUKU

Mamuju

Mamasa

Rantepao

Latowu

Palopo

Pulau Buru

Makale

Polewali

Pulau Manui

Majene

Enrekang

Kendari

Siwa

Teluk Bone

Pulau Wowoni

Pare Pare

Danau Tempe

Sengkang

Kolaka

BANDA SEA

Watampone

Maros

Buapinang

Kembara

Raha

Wakatobi Marine National Park (Tukangbesi)

Malino

Pulau Kabaena

Pulau Muna

Pulau Buton

Makassar

Bulukumba

Pantai Bira

Bau Bau

Tukangbesi Islands

Benteng

Pulau Selayar

Taka Bone Rate Islands

Bone Rate Islands

Taka Bone Rate Marine National Park

Bone Rate

FLORES SEA

tarsiers and flamboyantly colourful maleo birds.

Just exploring this ink blot of an island can gobble up a 30-day visa before you know it. Be sure to leave time for the diving around Pulau Bunaken. It's reached by the legendary travellers' trail along Sulawesi's spine: from bustling Makassar to Tana Toraja and its famous funeral ceremonies, on to the chilled Togean Islands and finally Manado and Bunaken.

❶ Getting There & Around

AIR

The three transport hubs are Makassar and Manado, which are well connected with the rest of Indonesia, and Palu, which offers connections to Balikpapan in Kalimantan. **SilkAir** (www.silkair.com) flies to Manado from Singapore; **Air Asia** (www.airasia.com) flies to Makassar from Kuala Lumpur.

BOAT

Sulawesi is on several boat routes, with more than half of Pelni's fleet calling at Makassar and Bitung (the seaport for Manado), as well as a few other towns.

BUS

Excellent air-conditioned buses connect Rantepao with Makassar. Elsewhere you're looking at pretty clapped-out local buses that stop every few minutes. There are some decent long-distance minibus services.

Makassar (Ujung Padang)

🗘 0411 / POP 1.71 MILLION

Makassar – the long-time gateway to eastern Indonesia, and Sulawesi's most important city – can be unnerving, so most travellers immediately head for Tana Toraja. However, you're likely to spend at least one night here, so check out the busy harbour and the newly gentrified waterfront in the centre, where you can join the strolling and snacking masses. Shopping is good, as are the seafood restaurants.

Makassar played a key role in Indonesian history. The 16th-century Gowa empire was based here until the Dutch weighed in. Three centuries later, in the 1950s, the Makassarese and Bugis revolted unsuccessfully against the central government.

⊙ Sights

Most of the action takes place in the west, near the sea. The port is in the northwest; Fort Rotterdam is in the centre of the older – and walkable – commercial hub. Look for remnants of the old Kingdom of Gowa 7km southeast of the centre.

★ Fort Rotterdam   HISTORIC SITE

(Jl Pasar Ikan; ⊙8am-6pm) FREE One of the best-preserved examples of Dutch architecture in Indonesia, Fort Rotterdam continues to guard the harbour of Makassar. A Gowanese fort dating back to 1545 once stood here, but failed to keep out the Dutch.

The original fort was rebuilt in Dutch style, and includes many fine, well-restored colonial structures. You can walk the enclave's ramparts and see sections of the original walls.

Inside you'll find the **Museum Negeri La Galigo** (admission Rp10,000; ⊙8am-6pm Tue-Sun), the collection of which is divided between two buildings.

Masjid Amirul Mukminin   MOSQUE

(Jl Pasar Ikan) FREE Rising above the sea at the southern end of Pantai Losari, this elegant twin-domed structure (built using concrete piles driven into the seabed) is known as the 'floating mosque'. Visitors of all faiths are welcome. Built in 2009, it enjoys fine coastal views, and the landscaped area around the mosque is *the* place to break the daily fast during Ramadan.

🛏 Sleeping

★ Dodo's Homestay   HOMESTAY $

(🗘0812 412 9913; www.dodopenman.blogspot.co.uk; Jl Abdul Kadir Komplek Hartaco Indah Blok 1Y/25; s/d incl breakfast 75,000/100,000Rp; ❋ ❐) An excellent homestay owned by Dodo, a superfriendly local who's been assisting travellers for more than 20 years. His home is a spacious, air-conditioned house in a quiet neighbourhood 4km south of the centre; one of the rooms has an en-suite bathroom. There's free tea and coffee, and Dodo arranges transport (including motorbike and car rental) and tours around Sulawesi.

New Legend Hotel   HOTEL $

(🗘0411-363-2123; www.newlegendhotel.com; Jl Jampea 1; dm/r/ste incl breakfast from 123,000/242,000/440,000Rp; ❋ ❐) In a convenient Chinatown location, this new place is owned by the same helpful people who used to run Makassar's only hostel. Their new venture is primarily a modern hotel, with clean, well-presented rooms, all with TV/DVD, air-con and en suite bathrooms (with hot water), though the cheapest lack windows. The city's only dorms are fan cooled and have shared bathrooms.

★ Ge Jac Mart   HOMESTAY $$

(🗘0411-859-421; www.ge-jacmart-homestay.blogspot.co.uk; Jl Rambutan 3; r incl breakfast 290,000Rp; ❋ ❐) This is a wonderful place to stay, just off the seafront. It's run by the Pongrekun family (originally from Tana Toraja), who are hospitable, speak good English and enjoy looking after guests. The modern,

Makassar (Ujung Padang)

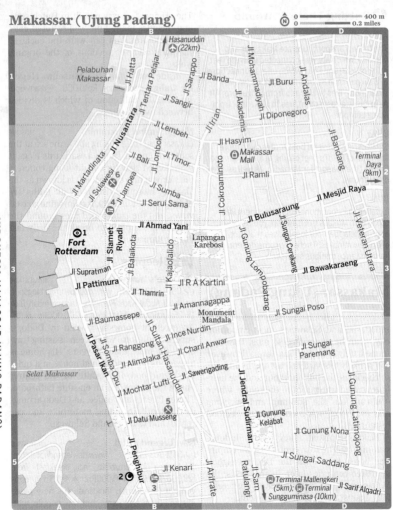

immaculately clean family home has white-washed walls and a splashes of art, and the seven very comfortable rooms each include a private bathroom with hot water.

✖ Eating

For many it's the food that makes Makassar a great destination. There's an abundance of seafood, Chinese dishes and local specialities such as *coto Makassar* (a spicy beef soup).

Hundreds of night warungs line Jl Penghibur and the surrounds. Savour the delicious *piseng epe* (grilled bananas with palm syrup).

★ **Lae Lae** SEAFOOD $
(☎ 0411-334-326; Jl Datu Musseng 8; meals from 30,000Rp; ☺ noon-10pm) A famous seafood restaurant, Lae Lae is a crowded, unadulterated food frenzy: expect no-nonsense surrounds, discarded crab shells around your feet and great food. You enter via a smoking street-side barbecue area sizzling with grilled fish and seafood, and eat at long tables, where you'll rub shoulders with locals. Three accompanying sambal sauces are offered and there are tasty vegetable side dishes.

Makassar (Ujung Padang)

◎ Top Sights
 1 Fort Rotterdam A3

◎ Sights
 2 Masjid Amirul Mukminin B5
   Museum Negeri La Galigo ....(see 1)

🛏 Sleeping
 3 Ge Jac Mart...B5
 4 New Legend Hotel B2

🍴 Eating
 5 Lae Lae...B4
 6 Rumah Makan Pate'ne........................B2

Rumah Makan Pate'ne   INDONESIAN $
(Jl Sulawesi 48; mains 11,000-34,000Rp; ⊗8am-9pm) Serving up delicious, inexpensive Javanese dishes and Indonesian classics, Pate'ne offers fine value and authentic flavours. Enjoy *soto ayam* (chicken soup) for just 11,000Rp, or feast on a filling *nasi campur* (rice with a choice of side dishes) for 27,500Rp. Fresh juices including melon, mango, apple and avocado are available.

ⓘ Information

Countless banks with ATMs are found on the main streets along the waterfront.

ⓘ Getting There & Away

AIR
Makassar's slick and modern Sultan Hasanuddin airport (UPG) is well connected to the rest of Indonesia. (Note that many airline websites still use 'Ujung Padang' for bookings.)

BUS
Buses heading north leave from Terminal Panai-kang, aka Terminal Daya, in the eastern suburbs. There are numerous services to Rantepao (from 80,000Rp, eight hours) in Tana Toraja. Get to the terminal with a *pete-pete* (minibus) from Makassar Mall (3000Rp, 30 minutes).

ⓘ Getting Around

The airport is 22km east of the city centre; it's 125,000Rp by taxi or 27,000Rp by Damri bus. The main *pete-pete* station is at Makassar Mall; the base fare is 5000Rp. Becak drivers/hawkers can be charming and exhausting all at once. Their shortest fare is a negotiable 10,000Rp. Bluebird taxis are metered.

Tana Toraja

Get ready for a dizzying cocktail of stunningly serene beauty; elaborate, brutal and disturbing funeral rites; exquisite traditional architecture; and a profoundly peculiar fascination with the dead. It comes garnished with a pinch of Indiana Jones intrigue and is served by some of the warmest and toughest people you'll ever meet: the Torajans. Life for the Torajans revolves around death and their days are spent earning the money to send away their dead properly. During funeral season, in July and August, the tourist numbers swell and prices soar, but the rest of the year it's nearly empty, which means grateful hosts, good deals and a frontier-like appeal.

The main centres are Makale, the capital, and Rantepao, the largest town and tourist magnet. Bemos link them to surrounding villages, where you'll find cultural hot spots tucked into spectacular countryside.

Rantepao

🖉 0423 / POP 49,000
With a variety of lodgings, Rantepao is the best base for exploring Tana Toraja. There is one unforgettable sight: **Pasar Bolu**, the market 2km northeast of town. It peaks every six days, overflowing with livestock. The main market is a very big, social occasion that draws crowds from all over Tana Toraja.

🏃 Activities

Plan on spending your days exploring this captivating region. Guides charge 350,000Rp to 400,000Rp per day. In addition, motorcycles cost about 70,000Rp per day; a guide with a car for up to four people costs 600,000Rp per day. You'll get to some of the most interesting places by foot or motorcycle, although improving roads have made much accessible by car.

Be sure to hire a Torajan guide, as interlopers from elsewhere won't have the same access and sensitivity to funerals and other cultural events. Guides will also inevitably find you.

To fully immerse yourself in Toraja land, trek off the main roads. Good footwear is vital, as is ample food, water, a torch (flashlight; some villages lack electricity) and rain gear. If you desire a professional trekking outfitter, contact **Indosella** (🖉0813 4250

Tana Toraja

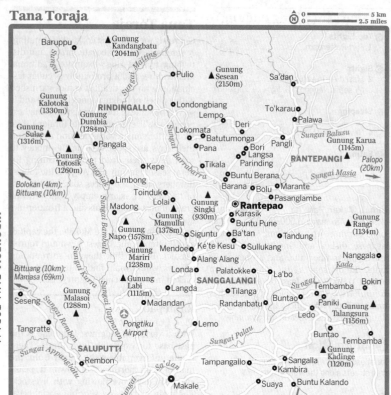

5301, 0423-25210; www.sellatours.com; Jl Andi Mappanyukki 111), which also organises complex tours and white-water rafting trips (from 800,000Rp per person, minimum two).

For a brilliant day trek, take a morning bemo to Deri, then veer off-road and traverse the incredible cascading rice fields all the way to Tikala. Farmers and villagers will help point the way, but a guide would be a wise decision for this trek.

Another good day trek starts in the hills at Batutumonga and follows rice fields back to Rantepao. Popular multiday treks include the following:

Batumonga–Lokomata–Pangala–Baruppu–Pulu Pulu–Sapan Three days.

Bittuang–Mamasa Three days.

Pangala–Bolokan–Bittuang Two days on a well-marked trail.

🛏 Sleeping

★ Pia's Poppies Hotel   GUESTHOUSE $
(☎ 0423-21121, 0813 4202 6768; poppiestoraja@yahoo.co.id; s/d 135,000/175,000Rp; ☞) Resembling an Alpine mountain lodge, this excellent place in a tranquil location 10 minutes' walk from the centre has very helpful staff and a welcoming ambience. Rooms face a verdant garden and have quirky details such as stone bathrooms (en-suites have hot water). Be sure to eat in the charming cafe which serves excellent local food. Breakfast not included.

Rosalina Homestay   HOMESTAY $
(☎ 0423-25530; www.rosalinahomestayrantepao.blogspot.co.uk; Jl Pongitiku Karassik; d incl breakfast 200,000Rp; ☞) Opened in 2015, this fine place is owned by Enos, a highly experienced Torajan guide, and his family. They take really good care of their guests, including by preparing filling breakfasts. The spacious

rooms are on the upper floor of the family's home, and overlook an ocean of ride paddies from a large shared balcony.

Wisma Monika GUESTHOUSE $$
(☑ 0423-21216; 36 Jl Sam Ratulangi; r incl breakfast 250,000-400,000Rp; ✳ 🛜) A grandiose-looking cream villa in a central spot with a choice of plain but well-maintained and clean rooms, all with bedside reading lights. Staff prepare a good breakfast.

🍴 Eating

The best-known dish is *pa'piong* (meat stuffed into bamboo tubes along with vegetables and coconut). Order in advance and enjoy it with black rice.

Pia's INDONESIAN, INTERNATIONAL $
(☑ 0423-21121; meals 30,000-60,000Rp; ⊙ 7-10am & 6-10pm; 🛜) The dining room at Pia's Poppies Hotel is a fine place to try local food including *pa'piong*, plus decent pizza. All food is cooked to order, so it's essential to order well ahead (at least two hours) or be prepared to wait. Bintangs cost just 30,000Rp. It's a 10-minute walk south of the centre. Note it's closed for lunch.

Rumah Makan Saruran INDONESIAN, CHINESE $
(Jl Diponegoro 19; mains from 15,000Rp; ⊙ 8am-10pm; 🛜) Reliable, freshly prepared Indonesian-style Chinese food is served at this hopping restaurant that's popular with young Indonesians. It looks a bit scruffy from the street, but once you're past the kitchen's smoking woks you'll find the comfortable interior has plush banquette seating. There's a full bar and good juices for 12,000Rp.

Rimiko Restoran INDONESIAN $
(☑ 0423-23366; Jl Andi Mappanyukki 115; dishes 20,000-50,000Rp; ⊙ 8am-10pm; 🛜) A long-running, very friendly place that serves authentic local food. It offers good Torajan specialities including buffalo, pork and eel in black sauce (50,000Rp), as well as Indo staples such as gado gado.

ℹ Information

Jl Diponegoro has banks and ATMs. Bring sunscreen, as none is sold locally.

Government Tourist Office (☑ 0423-21277; Jl Ahmad Yani 62A; ⊙ 9am-2pm Mon-Sat) The friendly staff here can provide accurate, independent information about local ceremonies and festivals, and recommend guides.

ℹ Getting There & Away

BUS

Most long-distance buses leave from the bus company offices along Jl Andi Mappanyukki. Buses often run at night. Prices vary according to speed and the level of comfort and space.

Several bus companies offer comfortable buses to/from Makassar, including Charisma (which has wi-fi).

CAR

A car and driver between Makassar and Rantepao costs from 600,000Rp and takes six hours. Make arrangements with your accommodation at either end. Cars seat up to five, so this can be a good bus alternative.

ℹ Getting Around

Kijangs leave for Makale (6000Rp, 30 minutes) constantly, and will drop you at the signs for Londa, Tilanga or Lemo to walk to the villages. From Terminal Bolu, 2km northeast of Rantepao, frequent vehicles go east to Palopo, and regular bemos and Kijangs go to all the major villages, such as Lempo (near Batutumonga).

Motorcycles can be rented from hotels and tour agencies for 60,000Rp per day.

Around Rantepao

On day trips from Rantepao there's the beautiful – stunning panoramas, magical bamboo forests and rice terraces, shaped by natural boulders and fed by waterfalls, that drop for 2000m; there's the strange – *tau tau* (wooden effigies) of long-lost relatives guarding graves carved out of vertical limestone rock faces or hung from the roofs of deep caves; and there's the intermingling of the two – incredibly festive and colourful four-day funerals where buffalo are slaughtered and

BUSES FROM RANTEPAO

DESTINATION	COST (RP)	DURATION (HR)
Makassar (Terminal Daya)	110,000-220,000	8-9
Poso	150,000	12
Tentena	130,000	10

stewed, palm wine is swilled from bamboo carafes and a spirit soars to the afterlife.

SOUTH OF RANTEPAO

Karasik (1km from Rantepao) is on the outskirts of town, just off the road leading to Makale. The traditional houses were erected years ago for a funeral.

Just off the main road, southeast of Rantepao, **Londa** (6km) is famed for its woodcarving. On the cliff face behind the village are cave graves and some very old hanging graves – the rotting coffins are suspended from an overhang.

Located about 2km off the Rantepao–Makale road, **Ke'te Kesu** (6km) is an extensive burial cave, one of the most interesting in the area. Above the cave is a line-up of *tau tau* that peer down, in fresh clothes, from their cliffside perch. Inside the dank darkness, coffins hang above dripping stalagmites. Others lie rotting on the stone floor, exposing skulls and bones.

Lemo (11km) is among the largest burial areas in Tana Toraja. The sheer rock face has dozens of balconies for *tau tau*; there would be even more *tau tau* if they weren't in such demand by unscrupulous antique dealers who deal in bad karma. A bemo from Rantepao will drop you off at the road leading up to the burial site, from where it's a 15-minute walk.

TORAJA CULTURE

The local culture in Tana Toraja is among the world's most unique and distinctive. That the people are genuinely welcoming of visitors makes it unmissable.

Architecture

Traditional *tongkonan* houses – shaped like boats or buffalo horns, with the roof rearing up at the front and back – are the enduring image of Tana Toraja. They are similar to the Batak houses of Sumatra's Danau Toba and are always aligned north–south, with small rice barns facing them.

A number of villages are still composed entirely of these traditional houses, but most now have corrugated-iron roofs. The houses are painted and carved with animal motifs, and buffalo skulls often decorate the front, symbolising wealth and prestige.

Burial Customs

The Toraja generally have two funerals, one immediately after the death and a second, more elaborate, four-day ceremony held after enough cash has been raised. Between the two ceremonies, the embalmed dead are kept at home in the best room of the house – visitors will be obliged to sit, chat and have coffee with them. Regularly. This all ends once buffalo are sacrificed (one for a commoner, as many as 24 for a high-ranking figure) and the spirit soars to the afterlife.

The expenses associated with funerals are *the* major expense for locals. People keep careful track of who brings what to ceremonies (gifts are often announced to the funeral throngs over a loudspeaker) and an offering considered 'cheap' is cause for great shame. A run-of-the-mill buffalo costs 25 million rupiah, while the most prized animals (with white heads and perfect hides) cost 80 million rupiah – about the same as a new house.

To deter the plundering of generous burial offerings, the Toraja started to hide their dead in caves or on rocky cliff faces. You can often see *tau tau* – life-sized, carved wooden effigies of the dead – sitting in balconies on rock faces, guarding the coffins. Descendents are obliged to change and update their fake deceased relatives' clothing regularly.

Funeral ceremonies are the region's main tourist attraction. Visitors are welcomed to the multiday affairs and are shown great hospitality, including tea and snacks. In return your guide will advise you on what modest gifts to bring (cigarettes and snacks in lieu of, say, a buffalo). The ritual slaughter of buffalo, pigs and other animals is grisly, often inhumane, and disturbing to many.

Ceremonies & Festivals

The end of the rice harvest, from around May onwards, is ceremony time in Tana Toraja. These festivities involve feasting and dancing, buffalo fights and *sisemba* kick-boxing. Guides will also take you to these ceremonies.

EAST OF RANTEPAO

Marante (6km) is a traditional village right by the road east to Palopo, near rice fields and stone and hanging graves guarded by *tau tau*. Further off the Palopo road, Nanggala (16km) has a grandiose traditional house with 14 rice barns. Charter a bemo from Rantepao and you can be taken straight here, or take a public one and walk 7km from the Palopo road.

NORTH & WEST OF RANTEPAO

This is where you'll find the finest scenery in Tana Toraja. Batutumonga (20km) has an ideal panoramic perch, sensational sunrise views and a few homestays. The best is Mentirotiku (☑0813 4257 9588; r 125,000-350,000Rp). The views are even more stunning from the summit of Gunung Sesean, a 2150m peak towering above the village. Most bemos stop at Lempo, an easy walk from Batutumonga.

There are more cave graves and beautiful scenery at Lokomata (26km), just a few kilometres west past Batutumonga.

The return to Rantepao is an interesting and easy trek down the slopes through tiny villages to Pana, with its ancient hanging graves, and baby graves in the trees. The path ends at Tikala, where regular bemos go to Rantepao.

The three-day, 59km trek from Mamasa in the west to Bittuang is popular, and there are plenty of villages en route with food and accommodation (remember to bring gifts). Morning buses link Rantepao and Mamasa (150,000Rp), taking 12 hours because the roads are appalling. SUVs tackle the legs from Mamasa to Ponding (where you overnight) and then on to Bittuang. Each segment costs 150,000Rp and takes three hours.

MAKALE & AROUND

The Makale Market, held every six days, is one of the region's best.

One of the most stunning sights in Tana Toraja is the *tau tau* at Tampangallo, between Sangalla and Suaya, which is 6km east of Makale. The graves belong to the chiefs of Sangalla, descendants of the mythical divine being Tamborolangiq, who is believed to have introduced the caste system, death rituals and agricultural techniques into Torajan society. Take a Kijang from Makale to Sangalla, get off about 1km after the turn-off to Suaya, and walk a short distance (less than a kilometre) through the rice fields to Tampangallo.

Tentena

☑0458

This lakeside town of white picket fences and churches is a good place to break your bus journey north from Rantepao. Surrounded by clove-covered hills, it's a peaceful and very easy to manage town.

The price is right, service is good and the 18 rooms are clean at the popular Hotel Victory (☑0458-21392; victorytentena@yahoo.com; Jl Diponegoro 18; r incl breakfast 175,000-375,000Rp; ❄ 🛜). Only the higher-end rooms have air-con. This is a good spot to meet guides.

Buses make the run to Poso (40,000Rp, two hours) throughout the day.

Poso

☑0452 / POP 48,000

Poso is the main town, port and terminal for road transport on the northern coast of Central Sulawesi. It's a spread out, noisy place and there's little reason to stay besides to hit up an ATM, change money, shop or catch a bus. Services are few until Manado.

New Armada (☑0452-23070; Jl Sumatera 117; r with shared bathroom 90,000Rp, r with private bathroom 165,000-200,000Rp) is a reliably decent yet simple place that's centrally located.

Buses leave the terminal, 800m north of the post office, for Tentena and Ampana (minibus 75,000Rp, five hours).

Ampana

☑0464

Ampana is the gateway to the Togeans. Given bus and ferry schedules, you will likely spend a night here.

Oasis Hotel (☑0464-21058; Jl Kartini; r incl breakfast with fan/air-con from 120,000/200,000Rp; ❄ 🛜) has 17 clean rooms and dorms, but don't expect to sleep till the karaoke shuts down at 11pm. The most expensive rooms include air-con and hot water. It's near the Togean Islands boat dock.

Minibuses travel each day to Luwuk (120,000Rp, seven hours) and Poso (minibus 75,000Rp, five hours).

Togean Islands

Yes, it does take some determination to get to the Togean Islands, but believe us, it takes much more determination to leave. Island-hop from one forested golden-beach beauty to the next, where hammocks are plentiful, the fish is fresh and the welcome is homely. There are lost lagoons and forgotten coves, and arguably the best diving in Sulawesi (which ranks it near the top worldwide). Plunge into crystal-clear, bottomless seas to explore all three major reef systems – atoll, barrier and fringing. Colours absolutely pop. Fish are everywhere.

❶ Getting There & Away

Getting boat information in advance of a trip to the Togeans can be a challenge. Your best option is to contact the place you intend to stay at and let them advise you. If you are travelling the length of Sulawesi, try to go from Ampana to the Togeans to Gorontolo (or the reverse), which will save you the endless land journey via Palu.

FROM THE SOUTH

Boats depart Saturday to Thursday from Ampana to Wakai, the Togeans' hub (about 52,000Rp, three hours) and usually make other stops in the islands.

FROM THE NORTH

Overnight boats from Gorontalo to Wakai cost 64,000Rp (cabins 500,000Rp), take 13 hours and run a couple of times per week.

❶ Getting Around

Charters around the Togeans are easily arranged in Wakai, Bomba, Kadidiri and through your accommodation (about 450,000Rp).

Pulau Kadidiri

This is definitely the island to go to if you're feeling social, but in low season you could potentially wind up on your own here. Just a short boat trip from Wakai, the three lodging options (all right next to each other) are on a perfect strip of sand with OK snorkelling and swimming, and superb **diving** beyond.

🛏 Sleeping & Eating

Hotels usually provide transport from Wakai. Rates usually include all meals.

Kadidiri Paradise Resort   RESORT **$$**
(📞0464-21058; www.kadidiriparadise.com; r per person incl all meals 200,000-325,000Rp) This

resort enjoys a stunning location on a lovely beach and has extensive grounds that hug the coastline. Wooden bungalows are spacious and have generous front decks, though maintenance and attention to detail could be better. The dive centre is particularly well run.

Togean Island & Around

The main settlement on Togean Island is the very relaxed Katupat village, which has a small market and a couple of shops.

Around the island there are magical **beaches**, and some decent **hikes** for anyone sick of swimming, snorkelling and diving.

🛏 Sleeping

Fadhila Cottages   BUNGALOW **$$**
(📞0852 4100 3685; www.fadhilacottages.com; Pulau Katupat; bungalows per person incl all meals 250,000-350,000Rp) Clean wooden bungalows with terraces and hammocks line a palm-shaded beach facing either Katupat village or the ocean. There's a good PADI dive centre here and a breezy, classy restaurant area. Take a free canoe to find snorkelling spots around the island or enjoy one of Fadhila's excursions. Rates drop by 50,000Rp in the low season.

Pulau Batu Daka

BOMBA

This tiny outpost at the southeastern end of Pulau Batu Daka has nearby reefs and exquisite beaches.

Pitate Resort (📞0813 4107 7371; www.pitate-resort.weebly.com; r per person incl all meals 175,000Rp) is a newly opened place on a slim, sandy beach with simple, attractive wood-and-bamboo bungalows. Snorkelling tours can be arranged.

WAKAI

The Togeans' largest settlement is a departure point for ferries to Ampana and Gorontalo and for charters to Pulau Kadidiri and beyond. There are a few stores, if you need supplies, but there's no reason to stay the night.

Gorontalo

📞0435 / POP 186,000

The port of Gorontalo has the feel of an overgrown country town, where all the locals seem to know each other. The town features some of the best-preserved Dutch houses in Sulawesi; it offers the best services north of Poso.

New Melati Hotel (☎0435-822934; yfvelberg@yahoo.com; Jl Wolter Monginsidi 1; r incl breakfast 130,000-300,000Rp; ❀@☎) is a long-time traveller favourite. It's based around a lovely home, built in the early 1900s. Rooms in the original house are basic but atmospheric; the newer rooms are set around a pretty garden.

❶ Getting There & Away

Wings Air has daily flights from Manado (40 minutes). Several carriers fly from Makassar (90 minutes).

The main bus terminal is 3km north of town. There are direct buses to Manado (from 100,000Rp, nine hours); minibuses/minivans are more comfortable and cost about 150,000Rp.

Manado

☎0431 / POP 458,000

With an overabundance of shopping malls and cavernous holes in the sidewalk, Manado doesn't usually register as one of North Sulawesi's highlights. It's a well-serviced and friendly place, however, with more than its share of comfortable hotels and some good places to eat. Nearby adventures include Pulau Bunaken and Tomohon.

Along Jl Sam Ratulangi, the main north–south artery, you'll find restaurants, hotels and supermarkets. The flash shopping-mall blitz dominates parallel Jl Piere Tendean (aka 'The Boulevard') and continues right to the waterfront.

⌂ Sleeping

Manado Grace Inn HOTEL $
(☎0431-888 0288; www.manadograceinn.com; Jl Samratulangi Manado 113-H; r incl breakfast 175,000Rp; ❀☎) Good-value, newish hotel where the no-frills cream-and-white rooms are small but have air-con, private shower rooms (with hot water) and in-room wi-fi. Breakfast is very basic – just a bread roll and tea or coffee.

Celebes Hotel HOTEL $
(☎0431-870425; www.hotelcelebesmdo.com; Jl Rumambi 8A; r with fan/air-con from 145,000/250,000Rp; ❀☎) This big block looms over the market and port, so is very handy for boats to Pulau Bunaken. Rooms are functional and kept pretty clean. Angle for one on an upper floor with a view of the sea.

★**Libra Homestay** HOMESTAY $$
(☎0821 9268 6320; www.librahomestaymanado.com; Jl Pramuka XI 16; r incl breakfast 300,000-325,000Rp; ❀☎) An excellent place in a smart, spacious villa on a quiet street, where the kindly Chinese owner (who studied in London) looks after guests well. There are five rooms, all with air-con, cable TVs, desks and private bathrooms with hot water. It's in the south of the city, a five-minute walk from restaurants.

✗ Eating

Adventurous Minahasan cuisine can be found around Manado. Get a taste of *rica-rica,* a spicy stir-fry made with *ayam* (chicken) or *babi* (pork). *Bubur tinotuan* (corn porridge) and fresh seafood are local specialities worth looking out for.

Along Jl Sam Ratulangi are upmarket restaurants and supermarkets. Most of the city's malls have extensive food courts, including Bahu Mall.

Rumah Makan
Green Garden CHINESE, INDONESIAN $
(Jl Sam Ratulangi 170; meals 20,000-50,000Rp; ◷8am-midnight) Popular Indo-Chinese restaurant with excellent pork dishes (try it barbecued or go for the pork belly), as well as good seafood, fresh juices and Bintang beer.

❶ Getting There & Around

AIR
Manado is well connected by air to major cities across Indonesia.

Mikrolet from Sam Ratulangi International Airport (MDC) go to Terminal Paal 2 (6000Rp), where you can change to a *mikrolet* for elsewhere. There are also four daily air-conditioned buses (30,000Rp) to/from Jl Piere Tendean. Fixed-price taxis cost around 75,000Rp from the airport to the city (13km).

BOAT
Boats to Pulau Bunaken leave from a harbour near Pasar Jengki fish market.

BUS
Terminal Malalayang (far south of the city) has service to Gorontalo.

PUBLIC TRANSPORT
There's no *mikrolet* shortage in Manado. Destinations are shown on a card in the front windscreen. There are various bus stations around town for destinations outside Manado; get to any of them from Pasar 45, the main traffic circle near the harbour. Bluebird taxis use their meters.

Pulau Bunaken

Pulau Bunaken is Sulawesi's top destination: 300 varieties of pristine coral and 3000 species of fish in **Bunaken Manado Tua Marine National Park** draw accolades from around the globe. Tourist accommodation is spread out along two beaches and there is a delightful island vibe, thanks especially to the lovely locals. When not on the water, you can wander the lush paths alongside the mangroves.

🏃 Activities

Bunaken is uniquely surrounded by deep water with strong, nutrient-laden currents, while having a mangrove ecosystem that protects much of the beaches and corals from erosion – making it one of the best diving and snorkelling spots in the world.

Snorkellers are rewarded with rich reefs close to the surface; divers have a menu of choices, from muck to drop-offs. Trips around Bunaken and nearby islands all cost from US$80 for two dives. Whole schools of dive operators are at the resorts and most people usually go with the outfit native to where they're staying.

🛏 Sleeping & Eating

Pantai Liang, to the west, is remote from the rest of the island and has a beautiful stretch of sand. **Pantai Pangalisang**, near Bunaken village, is the eco-choice. There's no beach to lie on, but it overlooks an armada of stately mangrove trees closer to Bunaken village, and the nearby reef is ideal for snorkelling. Most hotels quote rates per person for full board. Stroll around for simple places under 200,000Rp per night.

🛏 Pantai Liang

Froggies   DIVE RESORT **$$**
(☏0812 430 1356; www.divefroggies.com; cottage per person incl all meals €27-42; ❋ 🛜) One of the first dive centres and still going strong, with a fine beachfront location and 16 cottages (some with two bedrooms) all with terraces.

🛏 Pantai Pangalisang

Lorenso's Beach Garden   GUESTHOUSE **$$**
(☏0852 5697 3345; www.lorensobunaken.com; r per person incl all meals from €32; 🛜) Lorenso's is an excellent choice for travellers; it has a good selection of accommodation on a pret-ty mangrove-lined bay, and there's world-class snorkelling offshore. The staff is very helpful; there's a good communal vibe; and when the tin-can band rocks up, great live music. Walk-in rates (from 250,000Rp per person) are well below the official prices quoted here.

Cakalang Bunaken   GUESTHOUSE **$$**
(☏0811 431 0208; www.cakalang-bunaken.com; s/d incl all meals 425,000/650,000Rp; ❋ 🛜) Intimate new Dutch-owned place on a small cove with four attractive, spacious rooms and perhaps the fastest wi-fi on Bunaken. There's a good dive school and meals are excellent.

Novita Homestay   GUESTHOUSE **$$**
(r per person incl all meals 150,000Rp) An authentic local experience right in Bunaken village (at the northern end of the island). Owned and operated by Vita, a terrific cook, who prepares filling, delicious local food.

ℹ Getting There & Away

Every day between 2pm and 3pm (except Sunday), a public boat leaves Manado harbour, near Pasar Jengki fish market, for Bunaken village and Pulau Siladen (30,000Rp, one hour). A charter speedboat costs at least 250,000Rp to 400,000Rp one-way (bargain hard). Many places to stay will also arrange transport.

Tomohon

Pleasantly cool and lush, this popular weekend escape from Manado rests at the foot of the regularly erupting Gunung Lokon in the Minahasa Highlands. It is renowned for its beauty and its **market**, which reaches its lurid peak on Saturdays, when all manner of species are sold for food.

Mikrolets travel frequently to Tomohon (9000Rp, 40 minutes) from Manado's Karombasan terminal.

MALUKU

Welcome to the original 'spice islands'. Back in the 16th century when nutmeg, cloves and mace were global commodities that grew nowhere else, Maluku was a place where money really did grow on trees. Today the spices have minimal economic clout and Maluku (formerly known as 'the Moluccas') has dropped out of global consciousness. The region is protected from mass tourism by distance.

Maluku

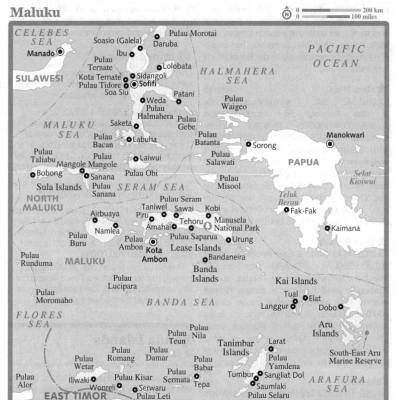

Recent improvements in transport have opened up the amazing Bandas and their beaches, as well as nutmeg forests and ruined Dutch fortresses.

ℹ Getting There & Around

Ambon is the region's air hub. There are flights daily to Jakarta and Makassar, which is a good place to transfer for other points on Sulawesi and Bali. There are also connections to Papua.

Pulau Ambon

Pulau Ambon is ribboned with villages, dressed in shimmering foliage and defined by two great bays. This is your launch pad to the Bandas, but it is also a charming retreat and diving base in its own right. Although at times a source of friction, the close proximity of Christian churches – often filled with hymn-singing parishioners – and

mosques is an interesting study of Indonesian multiculturalism.

Kota Ambon

☑ 0911 / POP 331,000

By the region's dreamy tropical standards, Maluku's capital, commercial centre and transport hub is a busy, bustling hub. Sights are minimal (although look for the odd mouldering colonial pile) but it does retain a languid charm. And its waterfront location can't be beaten.

🛏 Sleeping & Eating

Browse Jl Diponegoro and Jl Said Perintah for good eats. Accommodation clusters in the compact centre.

Penginapan the Royal　　GUESTHOUSE **$**
(☑ 0911-348 077; Jl Anthony Rhebok 1D; r 165,000-248,000Rp; P ❋ 🛜) A decent budget option,

with Ikea-chic wardrobes and desks, new air-con units, hot water, small flat-screens and wi-fi. The walls are a touch grubby and some rooms smell of stale smoke, but unadvertised discounts can make the Royal excellent value.

★ **Hero Hotel**   HOTEL $$

(☑ 0911-342 898; www.cityhubhotels.com; Jl Wim Reawaru 7B; standard/deluxe r 385,000/480,000Rp; P ❄ ☎) Deluxe rooms are a steal at this new Indo chain, with floating desks, queen beds and 32in wall-mounted LCD flat screens. Standard rooms are slightly smaller and have twin beds, but share the same slick, modern styling. There's a 200,000Rp cash security deposit upon check-in, and wi-fi throughout the hotel. Breakfast is 25,000Rp extra.

★ **Beta Rumah**   INDONESIAN $

(☑ 0822 4840 5481; Jl Said Perintah 1; mains 20,000-50,000Rp; ⊙ 9am-9pm Mon-Sat; ☎) The Beta is the Alpha and Omega of real Ambonese food. Laid out in simple *rumah makan* style beneath a glass sneeze shield, you'll find local delicacies such as *kohu kohu*, made with smoked skipjack tuna, green beans and shaved coconut, or squid with papaya leaves, steamed in a banana leaf with *kenari* nuts and *colo colo* (citrus dip).

Sibu-Sibu   CAFE

(☑ 0911-312 525; Jl Said Perintah 47A; snacks from 3000Rp, breakfasts from 20,000Rp; ⊙ 7am-10pm; ☎) Ambonese stars of screen and song deck the walls of this sweet little coffee shop, which plays Malukan and Hawaiian music to accompany local snacks such as the wonderful *koyabu* (cassava cake, 3000Rp), and *lopis pulut* (sticky rice with palm jaggery).

LEIHITU

The portion of land across the bay from Ambon, Leihitu is much more than just the location of the airport. It has beaches and historic places of genuine interest, especially if you're having transport challenges and need to kill time. Chartering a car and driver will cost about 400,000Rp for a half-day's touring of Ambon's most picturesque and archetypal coastal villages. In Hila the 1649 Benteng Amsterdam (admission 20,000Rp; ⊙ 8am-6pm) retains hefty ramparts and a three-storey keep.

It also has free wi-fi, good full breakfasts, fried breadfruit that you'll dip into melted palm sugar, and rocket-fuelled ginger coffee.

ℹ Information

Change or withdraw enough money in Kota Ambon for trips to outlying islands where there are no exchange facilities whatsoever.

Michael Erenst (☑ 0813 4302 8872; erenst_michael@yahoo.co.id) Highly helpful fixer; usually found working the info desk at the airport. Works with Banda guesthouses on transport logistics for guests. Can arrange very basic homestays (100,000Rp) near the airport.

ℹ Getting There & Around

Pattimura airport (AMQ) is 37km round the bay from central Kota Ambon. By road it can take an hour (although a new bridge will drastically cut this when complete). An ojek costs about 80,000Rp, a taxi 200,000Rp.

There is also an airport bus (35,000Rp per person) that leaves from the Peace Gong in the city centre daily at 5am, 10am and 1pm. It runs to Ambon when the main jet flights arrive.

Banda Islands

☑ 0910 / POP 22,000

Combining raw natural beauty, a warm local heart and a palpable and fascinating history, this remote cluster of 10 picturesque islands isn't just Maluku's choice travel destination, it's one of the very best in all of Indonesia.

The Dutch and the English wrestled for control of these islands for several centuries (beginning in the 1600s) all because of nutmeg, which is native to the islands and once commanded extravagant prices in Europe. The legacy of this era is everywhere, with ruined forts, evocative colonial buildings and still-thriving plantations.

Crystal-clear seas, shallow-water dropoffs and coral gardens teeming with multicoloured reef life offer magnificently pristine snorkelling off Hatta, Banda Besar and Ai. **Dive Bluemotion** (☑ 0812 4714 3922; www.dive-bluemotion.com; Laguna Inn, Jl Pelabuhan; dives from 350,000Rp, equipment per day from 100,000Rp; ⊙ Feb-May & Aug-Dec) is a well-run dive shop.

ℹ Getting There & Around

New transport options are opening the Bandas up to visitors. Guesthouses can advise on options and help with bookings.

PULAU TERNATE & TIDORE

The perfect volcanic cone of Ternate is an unforgettable sight. Pulau Tidore, Ternate's age-old, next-door rival, is a laid-back island of charming villages and empty beaches.

The dramatic volcanic cone of 1721m Gamalama *is* Pulau Ternate. Settlements are sprinkled around its lower coastal slopes, with villages on the east coast coalescing into North Maluku's biggest town, Kota Ternate. The city makes a useful transport gateway for the region, and neighbouring volcano islands look particularly photogenic viewed from the few remaining stilt-house neighbourhoods, colourful boats in the harbour or hillside restaurant terraces. It has three 17th-century Dutch forts that have been over-restored.

Gently charming Tidore makes a refreshing day-trip escape from the bustle of Ternate, its neighbour and implacable historical enemy. An independent Islamic sultanate from 1109, Tidore's sultanate was abolished in the Sukarno era, but the 36th sultan was reinstated in 1999. The island's proud volcanic profile looks especially magnificent viewed from Bastiong on Ternate.

Ternate has places to stay for all budgets strung out along its encircling, volcano-hugging ring road. It can be reached by air from Manado and Ambon.

AIR

Susi Air (☎ 62 265-631 220; www.fly.susiair. com; Jl Merdeka 312, Pangandaran, West Java) airlines is the latest to win the Ambon–Bandaneira route. Its small, twin-prop plane makes the trip on Wednesday, Thursday and some Friday mornings (300,000Rp, 40 minutes). It's wise to organise your (return) ticket at least 10 days in advance, and cancellations (for weather and lack of passengers) are common. However, if it lands in Bandaneira on any given morning, it will fly back to Ambon for sure.

BOAT

Banda is expecting a visitor surge, with a new, fast ferry greatly simplifying connections to Ambon. The Express Bahari 2B leaves Tulehu for Bandaneira at 9am on Monday and Friday, returning at the same time on Tuesday and Saturday. The trip takes six hours, and the VIP tickets (400,000Rp) aren't really necessary (the 300,000Rp seats are comfortable enough).

Pelni (☎ 0910-21196; www.pelni.co.id; Jl Kujali; ticket from 100,000Rp; ⏱ 8.30am-1pm & 4-6pm Mon-Sat) has various ships that pass through sporadically. The run to/from Ambon takes seven to 12 hours. Ships are usually overcrowded (try to reserve a cabin) and, in the case of the *Kelimutu*, quite dirty.

Passenger longboats buzz between Bandaneira and Pulau Banda Besar (5000Rp) and Pulau Ai (25,000Rp). Guesthouses can arrange tours and boat charters (from 600,000Rp for a journey with stops to/from Pulau Ai).

Bandaneira

Situated on Pulau Neira, the main port of the Banda Islands is a friendly, pleasantly sleepy town. Its streets are lined with a stunning array of colonial buildings.

Stop by the impressive **Benteng Belgica**, built on the hill above Bandaneira in 1611. The fort's upper reaches have incredible views of **Gunung Api**. Several historic Dutch houses have been restored. Down in the flats, **Benteng Nassau** is a moody ruin.

🛏 Sleeping & Eating

Most accommodation is here in the Banda's main town, along with a couple of cafes. Three guesthouses stand out.

⭐**Mutiara Guesthouse**   GUESTHOUSE $
(☎ 0910-21344, 0813 3034 3377; www.bandamutiara.com; r with fan/air-con from 150,000/200,000Rp; ❄ 🛜) A special boutique hotel disguised as a homestay, Mutiara is the first venture of Abba, the tirelessly helpful and well-connected owner of Cilu Bintang Eastate (p294). The front garden is a wonderful spot for an afternoon snooze, or to catch the resident cuscus raiding the cinnamon tree at night.

Delfika   GUESTHOUSE $
(☎ 0910-21027; delfika1@yahoo.com; Jl Gereja Tua; r with fan 100,000-150,000Rp, with air-con 175,000-250,000Rp; ❄) Built around a shady courtyard, the charming Delfika has a range of mostly well renovated rooms on the main village drag. There's also a bric-a-brac-stuffed sitting room and an attached **cafe** (Jl Gereja Tua; mains 15,000-50,000Rp; ⏱ 10am-9pm), one of Banda's best.

Vita Guesthouse   GUESTHOUSE **$**
(Fita; ☑0910-21332, 0812 4706 7099); allandar
man@gmail.com; Jl Pasar; d with fan/air-con from
140,000/175,000Rp; ❄) Popular with Euro
backpackers, Vita offers a great bayside location with seven comfortable rooms set in
a colonnaded L-shape around a waterfront
palm garden (ideal for an evening beer, con-
templating Gunung Api). The beds are adequate, there's some decent wooden furniture
in the rooms and it has Western-style toilets.

★**Cilu Bintang Estate**   BOUTIQUE HOTEL **$$**
(☑0813 3034 3377, 0910-21604; www.cilubintang.
com; Jl Benteng Belgica; d 300,000-400,000Rp,
VIP 750,000Rp; ❄🛜ⓦ) After storming the
charts with his first guesthouse, the still-
excellent Mutiara (p293), Abba (Rizal, the
owner) has outdone himself with the diffi-
cult sophomore release. Cilu Bintang is head
and shoulders above any other accommoda-
tion in all the Banda Islands – an immac-
ulate, breezy Dutch-colonial reproduction
with superb rooms, beds, food and company.

Other Islands

Pulau Banda Besar is the largest of the
Banda Islands, and the most important his-
torical source of nutmeg. You can explore
nutmeg groves or the ruins of fort **Benteng
Hollandia** (c 1624). Arrange a spice tour
with your Bandaneira lodging.

Pulau Hatta has crystal waters and a
mind-expanding, coral-encrusted vertical
drop-off near Lama village.

Pulau Ai is also blessed with rich coral
walls and postcard beaches. It has a few very
simple homestays, from which you can ex-
plore the empty white-sand beaches. Simple
guesthouses near the dock have fine views.
Enjoy pure tropical fantasy at **CDS Bunga-
low** (per person incl meals r 250,000-300,000Rp),
which has two secluded rooms perched over
a nearly deserted beach; book through Cilu
Bintang Estate).

Furthest west, **Pulau Run** is mostly
notable as the island the Dutch received
from the English in return for Manhattan –
guess who got the better deal?

PAPUA (IRIAN JAYA)

Even a country as full of adventure travel
as Indonesia has to have its final frontier,
and here it is – Papua, half of the world's
second-biggest island, New Guinea. A land

where numberless rivers rush down from
5km-high mountains to snake across sweat-
ing jungles populated by rainbow-hued birds
of paradise and kangaroos that climb trees.
Peaks are frosted with glaciers and snow-
fields, and slopes and valleys are home to an
array of exotic cultures (250 and counting),
like the gourd-wearing Dani, wood-carving
Asmat warriors and tree-house-dwelling Ko-
rowai. The coast is more modern, and more
'Indonesian'-feeling, unless you venture
to the Raja Ampats, a remote archipelago
where you can find empty beaches and, ac-
cording to experts, the world's richest reefs.

Papua's history is no slouch either. The
battle for the Pacific was decided here – with
memorials and WWII wrecks to prove it.
Indonesia didn't inherit Papua until 1963,
when they named it Irian Jaya and imme-
diately began capitalising on its abundant
resources. This did not sit well with the
Papuans, whose Free Papua Organisation
(OPM) remains active. Many Papuans want
independence, but the chances of that seem
slim now that Papua is home to over one
million non-Papuans.

❶ Getting There & Around

Papua is well connected by air with the rest
of Indonesia; with so few viable roads, flying
is the only way to travel once you're here. The
transport centres are Sorong (the biggest city
on the bird's-head-shaped west coast), Biak and
Jayapura.

Jayapura
☑0967 / POP 316,000

Most residents are Indonesian and street life
pulses to their rhythm, but the environment
is all Papua. Dramatic jade hills cradle the
city on three sides, while the gorgeous bay
of Teluk Yos Sudarso kisses the north coast.
Unless you're headed to PNG, it's not neces-
sary to stay here, as the airport is in nearby
Sentani, which has all the services.

◎ Sights

Museum Loka Budaya   MUSEUM
(Jl Abepura, Abepura; admission 25,000Rp;
⊙7.30am-4pm Mon-Fri) Cenderawasih Uni-
versity's cultural museum contains a fasci-
nating range of Papuan artefacts including
the best collection of Asmat carvings and
'devil-dance' costumes outside Agats, plus
fine crafts from several other areas, histori-
cal photos and musical instruments. There's

Papua

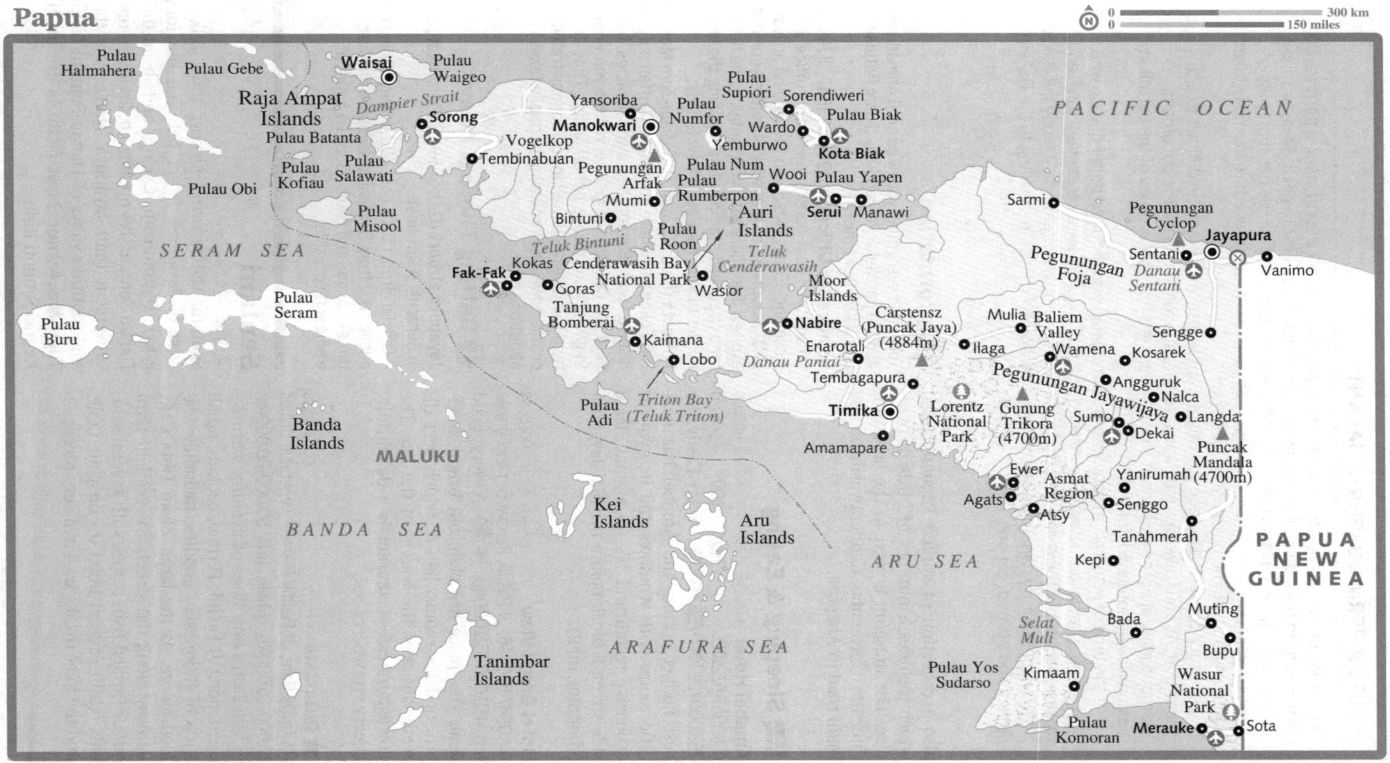
0 300 km
0 150 miles
PACIFIC OCEAN
SERAM SEA
BANDA SEA
ARAFURA SEA
ARU SEA
MALUKU
PAPUA NEW GUINEA
Pulau Halmahera
Pulau Gebe
Pulau Obi
Pulau Buru
Pulau Seram
Banda Islands
Kei Islands
Aru Islands
Tanimbar Islands
Raja Ampat Islands
Pulau Batanta
Pulau Kofiau
Pulau Salawati
Pulau Misool
Waisai
Pulau Waigeo
Dampier Strait
Sorong
Tembinabuan
Vogelkop
Yansoriba
Manokwari
Pegunungan Arfak
Mumi
Bintuni
Teluk Bintuni
Fak-Fak
Kokas
Goras
Cenderawasih Bay National Park
Tanjung Bomberai
Kaimana
Lobo
Pulau Adi
Triton Bay (Teluk Triton)
Pulau Roon
Wasior
Pulau Numfor
Pulau Num
Pulau Rumberpon
Auri Islands
Teluk Cenderawasih
Pulau Supiori
Sorendiweri
Wardo
Yemburwo
Pulau Biak
Kota Biak
Wooi
Pulau Yapen
Serui
Manawi
Moor Islands
Nabire
Enarotali
Danau Paniai
Carstensz (Puncak Jaya) (4884m)
Tembagapura
Timika
Amamapare
Lorentz National Park
Ilaga
Mulia
Baliem Valley
Wamena
Kosarek
Gunung Trikora (4700m)
Pegunungan Jayawijaya
Angguruk
Nalca
Langda
Sumo
Dekai
Puncak Mandala (4700m)
Sarmi
Pegunungan Foja
Pegunungan Cyclop
Sentani
Danau Sentani
Jayapura
Vanimo
Sengge
Ewer
Agats
Asmat Region
Atsy
Yanirumah
Senggo
Tanahmerah
Kepi
Bada
Muting
Bupu
Selat Muli
Pulau Yos Sudarso
Kimaam
Wasur National Park
Pulau Komoran
Merauke
Sota

VISITOR PERMITS (SURAT JALAN)

If you plan on venturing into remote Papua, you must obtain a *surat jalan*, a permission to travel, from the local police station (*polres*). They are easiest to get in Jayapura. Take your passport, two passport photos, and one photocopy each of the passport pages showing your personal details and your Indonesian visa. The procedure normally takes about an hour with no payment requested.

List every conceivable place you might want to visit, as it might be difficult to add them later. As you travel around Papua, you are supposed to have the document stamped in local police stations. It's worth keeping a few photocopies of the permit in case police or hotels ask for them.

At the time of research, exactly where a *surat jalan* was required depended on who you asked. The police in Jayapura insisted one was required for almost every town and area in Papua, but the reality was that in all but the remotest areas you'll rarely get asked to produce a *surat jalan*. To be on the safe side, however, if you're heading to the Baliem Valley and beyond, get one.

also a collection of stuffed Papuan fauna, which includes a number of birds of paradise. The museum is next to the large Auditorium Universitas Cenderawasih on the main road in Abepura.

🛏 Sleeping & Eating

Amabel Hotel HOTEL **$**
(☑0967-522102; Jl Tugu 100; s/tw/d 253,000/297,000/363,000Rp; ❉🛜) Easily the best budget option, the Amabel has neat little rooms with windows and its own inexpensive restaurant. It's up a small, leafy side street, a block before the Mal Jayapura (shopping mall).

Hotel Grand View HOTEL **$$**
(☑0967-550646; Jl Pasifik Permai 5; r incl breakfast 450,000-750,000Rp; ❉🛜) A very good deal. This place has plain but bright, modern, no-frills rooms, half of which peer directly out over the waters of the bay. The downstairs cafe-restaurant is a delightfully cheery strawberry red.

★ Duta Cafe SEAFOOD **$$**
(Duta Dji Cafe; Jl Pasifik Permai; vegetable dishes 15,000-25,000Rp, whole fish 50,000-80,000Rp; ⊙5pm-2am) Long lines of evening warungs open along Jl Pasifik Permai, cooking up all sorts of Indonesian goodies, including seafood galore. At the large, clean Duta Cafe, halfway along the street, an excellent *ikan bakar* (grilled fish) comes with several sambals (chilli sauces) lined up on your table, and the juice drinks go down very nicely.

ℹ Information

You'll find everything you need on Jl Ahmad Yani and the parallel Jl Percetakan. Jl Sam Ratulangi and Jl Koti front the bay.

Immigration Office (☑0967-533647; Jl Percetakan 15; ⊙8am-4pm Mon-Fri) This office will issue one 30-day extension to a visa on arrival (VOA): apply at least one week before your visa expires. Travellers with VOAs must come here for a (free) exit stamp before crossing the land border to Vanimo, Papua New Guinea.

Polresta (Polda; Jl Yani 11; ⊙9am-3pm Mon-Fri) Police elsewhere in Papua will often only issue a *surat jalan* for their own regencies, but here you can get one for everywhere you want to go in Papua (that's not off limits). They do tend to request a donation for 'administrative costs', however. Processing normally takes about one hour.

ℹ Getting There & Away

Jayapura airport (DJJ; ☑591 809) is located in Sentani, 36km west.

Official airport taxis cost 450,000Rp. Going by public *taksi* from Sentani to Jayapura involves three changes and takes about 1½ hours (if traffic is favourable).

Sentani

☑0967 / POP 48,000

Sentani, the growing airport town 36km west of Jayapura, is set between the forested Pegunungan Cyclop and beautiful Danau Sentani. It's quieter, cooler and more convenient than Jayapura. Don't miss the soul-soothing views of Danau Sentani from **Tugu MacArthur**. Most facilities are on Jl Kemiri Sentani Kota.

🛏 Sleeping & Eating

Rasen Hotel HOTEL **$$**
(📞 0967-594455; rasenhotel_papua@yahoo.com; Jl Penerangan; s 250,000, d 350,000-400,000Rp; ❄️🛜) The best choice near the airport, the Rasen has small, clean rooms with hot showers and TVs, plus a decent restaurant, free airport drop-offs and even a small fish pond. Unsurprisingly, it fills up so try to call ahead. Some staff speak English. Breakfast included.

★ Yougwa Restaurant INDONESIAN **$$**
(📞 0967-571570; Jl Raya Kemiri; mains 25,000-60,000Rp; ⊙ 10am-8.30pm Mon-Sat, to 4pm Sun & holidays) Sentani's most charming dining is on the Yougwa's breezy wooden terraces over the lake, 13km east of town. Try *ikan gabus* (snakehead), a tasty lake fish that doesn't fill your mouth with little bones.

❶ Getting There & Away

The airport is well-connected to major cities to the west.

Baliem Valley

The Baliem Valley is the most accessible gateway to tribal Papua. It's a place where *koteka* (penis gourds) are not yet out of fashion; pigs can buy love, sex or both; and the hills bloom with flowers and deep-purple sweet-potato fields. The main valley is about 60km long and 16km wide and bounded by high mountains on all sides.

Unless you land here during the August high season, when Wamena and nearby villages host a festival with pig feasts, mock wars and traditional dancing to attract the tourism buck, you'll be outnumbered by Christian missionaries (a constant presence since the valley's 'discovery' in 1938) and Javanese *transmigrasi* (migrants through a resettlement program). You may also be startled by evidence of Indonesia's neocolonisation of Papua, but mostly you will marvel at the mountain views, roaring rivers and tribal villages – and at the tough but sweet spirit of the warm Dani people.

Wamena
📞 0969 / POP 31,000

Wamena is a sprawling Indonesian creation with nothing traditional about it, but it's the obligatory base for any travels around the valley. The population is a mix of Papuans and non-Papuans – the latter run all the businesses. Purple mountains peek through billowy white clouds and local markets are enthralling.

🛏 Sleeping & Eating

★ Hotel Rainbow Wamena HOTEL **$$**
(Hotel Pelangi; 📞 0969-31999; Jl Irian 28; r incl breakfast 450,000-750,000Rp; 🛜) A great option. Rooms are excellent, clean and of a good size with aprés-trek soothing hot-water bathrooms and nice touches such as shampoo, tissues, coffee and tea. The real highlight, though, is the staff who bend over backwards to charm and help. Hit and miss wi-fi in the pop-art-decorated reception.

Baliem Pilamo Hotel HOTEL **$$**
(📞 0969-31043; baliempilamohotel@yahoo.co.id; Jl Trikora 114; r incl breakfast 456,000-726,000Rp; 🛜) The hotel of choice for most visitors. The more expensive rooms are tasteful, contemporary, brown-and-white affairs in the newer section at the rear. Of the cheaper ones, the standards are smallish and plain but acceptable, and the superiors have a semi-luxury feel along with quirky garden-style bathrooms.

GETTING TO PAPUA NEW GUINEA: JAYAPURA TO VANIMO

Getting to the border There are no flights between Papua and Papua New Guinea (PNG). The only route across the border that is open to foreigners is between Jayapura (northeast Papua) and Vanimo (northwest PNG, about 65km from Jayapura).

At the border Most visitors to PNG need a visa; the standard 60-day tourist visa can be obtained (after a three-day wait) at the **Papua New Guinea Consulate** (📞 0967-531250; congenpng_id@yahoo.com; Jl Raya Argapura; ⊙ 9am-noon & 1-3pm Mon-Thu, variable hours Fri), 3km south of downtown Jayapura. You can charter a *taksi* from the market at Abepura (called Pasar Abepura or Pasar Yotefa), 13km south of downtown Jayapura, to the border at Wutung (1½ hours) for 250,000Rp to 400,000Rp.

Moving on Cross the border itself on foot, then hire a car to Vanimo from a driver there.

ⓘ Information

No banks exchange foreign cash but there are ATMs.

Papua.com (☑ 0969-34488; fuj0627@yahoo.co.jp; Jl Ahmad Yani 49; per hour 12,000Rp;

⊘ 9am-8.30pm Mon-Sat, 1-8.30pm Sun) This efficient internet cafe has fax and scanning services, and also functions as an informal tourist information centre. Its owner is a highly experienced Papua traveller and a willing mine of information.

DON'T MISS

HIKING & TREKKING IN THE BALIEM VALLEY

Beyond the reach of roads you come closer to traditional Dani life. In one day you may climb narrow rainforest trails, stroll well-graded paths past terraces of purple-leafed sweet-potato plants, wend through villages of grass-roofed *honai* (circular thatched huts), cross rivers on wobbly hanging footbridges and traverse hillsides where the only sounds are birds, wind and water far below.

The classic trekking area, offering up to a week of walking, is in the south of the valley (beyond Kali Yetni), along with branch valleys to the east and west. Dani life here is still relatively traditional, the scenery gorgeous and the walking varied.

Accommodation is available in nearly all villages. Some have dedicated guesthouses (sometimes in *honai*-style huts); elsewhere you can often stay in a teacher's house, the school or other houses. Either way you'll usually be asked for 120,000Rp per person. You sleep on the floor, but it may be softened with dried grass and you may get a mat. Make sure you've been invited before entering any compound or hut.

Larger villages have kiosks selling basics such as biscuits, noodles and rice (the final reliable supplies are at Manda and Kimbim in the north and Kurima in the south) and you can obtain sweet potatoes, other vegetables and fruit here and there. But you need to take at least some food with you from Wamena. Villages can normally supply firewood for cooking, for 20,000Rp a load.

Guides & Porters

Finding a good, reliable guide can be a challenge. You should allow at least one day to find a guide you're happy with and make trek preparations. It's worth seeking out one of the Baliem Valley's 20 or so officially licensed guides. These are not the only good guides around, but they usually speak reasonable English and have a professional reputation to look after.

There are no fixed prices in the Baliem trekking world. Hard bargaining is the norm. Don't be put off by glum faces and do insist on clarifying any grey areas. No decent guide will agree to anything he's unhappy about. Official guides request 700,000Rp per day (and more for harder treks to, for example, the Yali or Korowai areas), but some decent, English-speaking guides will work for less. Dependable Wamena-based agencies and individual guides include the following:

Jonas Wenda (☑ 0852 4422 0825; jonas.wenda@yahoo.com; Wamena) Highly experienced and notably knowledgeable on flora and fauna.

Kosman Kogoya (☑ 0852 4472 7810; kogoyakosmam@gmail.com; Wamena) A popular, reliable guide who will quote reasonable prices from the outset and won't waste your time bargaining.

Trek-Papua Tours & Travel (☑ 0812 4762 8708; www.papuatravels.com; Jl Airport, Sentani) A young but energetic, internet-wise agency, which also offers tours to other parts of Papua.

In addition to a guide, porters are a good idea and cost 200,000Rp each per day, depending partly on the toughness of the trek. A cook costs 250,000Rp per day, but guides or porters can cook if you're looking to cut costs. You'll have to provide enough food for the whole team (for two trekkers, a guide and two porters doing a one-week trek this is likely to cost around 2,500,000Rp to 3,000,000Rp in total) and probably cigarettes for them and your village hosts. A 10% tip at the end is also expected for each member of the team.

Police Station (☑ 0969-31972; Jl Safri Darwin; ⊙7am-2pm) Come here to obtain a *surat jalan*.

ⓘ Getting There & Around

A number of carriers run several flights a day between Jayapura (Sentani) and Wamena's airport (WMX). Book ahead in peak season.

Sorong

☑ 0951 / POP 190,000

Papua's second-biggest city, Sorong, sits at the northwest tip of the Vogelkop. It's a busy port and a base for oil and logging operations in the region. Few travellers stay longer than it takes to book passage to the epic Raja Ampat Islands.

🛏 Sleeping & Eating

Sorong restaurants are generally better stocked with alcohol (beer, at least) than those elsewhere in Papua. For cheaper eats, dozens of seafood warungs set up in the evenings along waterfront Tembok Berlin (Jl Yos Sudarso).

JE Meridien Hotel HOTEL $$
(☑ 0951 327 999; www.hoteljemeridiensorong. blogspot.com; Jl Basuki Rahmat Km7.5; r 534,000-836,500Rp, ste from 1,009,000Rp, all incl breakfast; ❋ 🛜) Handily located opposite the airport, the Meridien offers nicely aged, slightly old-fashioned rooms of generous proportions. Rooms come with TVs and tea and coffee makers, plus you can get a free ride to the airport or the Raja Ampat ferry. The buzzing lobby has a good coffee shop and the Raja Ampat Tourism Management Office (though at the time of research this was scheduled to move).

Hotel Waigo HOTEL $$
(☑ 0951 333 500; Jl Yos Sudarso; r 489,000-705,600Rp, ste from 1,029,000Rp, all incl breakfast; ❋ 🛜) This hotel, facing the Tembok Berlin waterfront, offers fair value, large and bright (sometimes a bit *too* bright and pink!) rooms, which have a few nice touches like art and masks on the walls. The ocean-view 'suites' are massive. The in-house restaurant (mains 25,000Rp to 65,000Rp) is good value.

ⓘ Information

Raja Ampat Tourism Management Office
(☑ 0811 485 2033; JE Meridien Hotel, Jl Basuki Rahmat Km7.5; ⊙9am-4pm Mon-Fri, to 1pm Sat) This incredibly helpful office can tell you almost anything you need to know about the Raja Ampat Islands, and it's the best place to buy the tag permitting you to visit the islands. It may have moved to a new office next to the airport by the time you read this.

ⓘ Getting There & Around

Flights serve Ambon, Jakarta, Makassar and regional destinations.

Official airport taxis charge 100,000Rp to hotels at the western end of town; on the street outside you can charter a public *taksi* for half that or less. Using the yellow public *taksi* (minibuses; 5000Rp), first get one going west outside the airport to Terminal Remu (600m), then change there to another for Jl Yos Sudarso. Short *ojek* (motorcycle) rides of 2km to 3km are 5000Rp; between the western end of town and the airport is 20,000Rp.

Raja Ampat Islands

POP 43,000

The sparsely populated Raja Ampat islands comprise around 1000 islands just off Sorong. With their sublime scenery of steep, jungle-covered islands, scorching white-sand beaches, hidden lagoons, spooky caves, mushroom-shaped islets and luminous turquoise waters, Raja Ampat has to be one of the most beautiful island chains in Southeast Asia.

The diversity of marine life and the huge, largely pristine coral-reef systems are a diver's dream come true – and fantastic for snorkellers too. It's like swimming in a tropical aquarium.

The four biggest islands are Waigeo in the north, with the fast-growing new regional capital, Waisai; Salawati, just southwest of Sorong; Batanta, off northern Salawati; and Misool to the southwest. The Dampier Strait between Waigeo and Batanta has many of the best dive sites.

Visitors to the islands must pay an entry fee (Indonesians/others 500,000/1,000,000Rp) at the Raja Ampat Tourism Management Office in Sorong or Waisai's Tourism Information Centre (p300).

🛏 Sleeping & Eating

There are several dive resorts and dozens of village homestays scattered among the islands.

⭐**Lumba Lumba** GUESTHOUSE $$
(☑ 081 281 009244, 082 198 294400; www. lulumba.com; r incl full board 500,000Rp) On the blissfully quiet southern shore of Pulau Kri,

Lumba Lumba is one of the most professionally run guesthouses on Kri and all of Raja Ampat. The five comfortable over-water huts are well maintained and have attractive seashell decorations. Looking over the eye-searing white sands and sheer jungle tinged cliffs, you'll probably decide this is the perfect spot to drop out of life for a while.

Kordiris Homestay GUESTHOUSE $$
(☑085 399 040888, 081 248 569412; www.kordiris.com; Pulau Gam; per person incl full board 300,000-350,000Rp) This well-organised homestay, which sits in a secluded, dreamy bay dotted with tiny coral islands, is one of the best around. The rooms are made of palm thatch, and while some are in the cool shade of trees, others are exposed to the breezes on the salty white sand.

Mangkur Kodon Homestay HOMESTAY $$
(☑0852 4335 9154; enzomo@libero.it; s/d incl full board 400,000/600,000Rp) This guesthouse is set where two perfect beaches meet in one tight triangle – a sight known to induce tears of joy. Combine that with friendly staff, top-class snorkelling out front and inviting palm-thatch huts hung over the water and you've all the ingredients for happiness.

It's on the far southwestern edge of the island, and a short walk (or wade at high tide) from the other accommodation options.

ℹ Information

Tourism Information Centre (☑0852 4202 0251, 0852 5455 0411; Acropora Cottage, Jl Badar Dimara, Waisai; ☉10am-2pm Mon-Fri) Tourist tags, which are required by all visitors to Raja Ampat, are available here.

ℹ Getting There & Around

Waisai has a new and impressive airport. There are Susi Air flights on Sunday and Friday between Sorong and Waisai.

Fast Marina Express passenger boats (economy/VIP 130,000/220,000Rp, two hours) and a larger, slower, boat (100,000Rp, three hours) depart for Waisai from Sorong's **Pelabuhan Feri** (Pelabuhan Rakyat; Jl Feri, off Jl Sudirman). The slower boats have great open-air deck space. To arrange transport around the islands once there, your best bet is to ask at your accommodation or Waisai's Tourism Information Centre. Prices depend on boat, distance and petrol price, and are usually negotiable.

UNDERSTAND INDONESIA

Indonesia Today

Nothing ever seems settled in Indonesia, whether it's the land, the sea or society itself. Yet there was justifiable cause for celebration after the 2014 national elections continued the almost entirely peaceful traditions set during the previous vote five years earlier – an achievement for a country with a violent political past, including a 1965 political genocide chronicled by two widely praised documentaries. Still, economic and environmental challenges remain hugely significant as the nation feels its way to the future.

Joko Widodo was called the Indonesian Obama after he won the landmark 2014 presidential election. The first democratically elected Indonesian president with no obvious ties to the old Suharto dictatorship or the military, Jokowi, as he's commonly known (or simply Joko), soon struggled to make his own imprint on an entrenched bureaucracy and the sprawling archipelago's sputtering economy. Whether he will be the visionary and forceful leader many hope for remains to be seen. Meanwhile, religious conservatives made themselves felt by the passage of laws restricting the sale of beer and alcoholic beverages (although enforcement was sporadic). And in 2015, Jokowi did nothing to stop the executions of people convicted of drug offences, including two Australians in the notorious 'Bali Nine' case.

Indonesia's environmental woes are also more pressing than ever; for evidence one needs only to look at the vast haze over Sumatra (and its neighbours) from forest burning.

History

Beginnings

Until the last few years it was widely believed that the first humanoids *(Homo erectus)* lived in Central Java around 500,000 years ago – having reached Indonesia across land bridges from Africa – before either dying off or being wiped out by the arrival of *Homo sapiens.*

But the discovery in 2003 of the remains of a tiny islander, dubbed the 'hobbit', seems to indicate that *Homo erectus* survived much longer than was previously thought, and that previously accepted timelines of Indonesia's evolutionary history need to be re-examined (though many scientists continue to challenge the 'hobbit theory').

Most Indonesians are descendents of Malay people who began migrating around 4000 BC from Cambodia, Vietnam and southern China. They steadily developed small kingdoms and by 700 BC these settlers had developed skilful rice-farming techniques.

Hinduism & Buddhism

The growing prosperity of these early kingdoms soon caught the attention of Indian and Chinese merchants, and along with silks and spices came the dawn of Hinduism and Buddhism in Indonesia.

These religions quickly gained a foothold in the archipelago and soon became central to the great kingdoms of the 1st millennium AD. The Buddhist Srivijaya empire held sway over the Malay Peninsula and southern Sumatra, extracting wealth from its dominion over the strategic Straits of Melaka. The Hindu Mataram and Buddhist Sailendra kingdoms dominated Central Java, raising their grandiose monuments, Borobudur and Prambanan, over the fertile farmland that brought them their prosperity.

When Mataram slipped into mysterious decline around the 10th century AD, it was fast replaced with an even more powerful Hindu kingdom. Founded in 1294, the Majapahit empire made extensive territorial gains under its ruler, Hayam Wuruk, and prime minister, Gajah Mada, and while claims that they controlled much of Sulawesi, Sumatra and Borneo now seem fanciful, most of Java, Madura and Bali certainly fell within their realm.

But things would soon change. Despite the Majapahit empire's massive power and influence, greater fault lines were opening up across Indonesia, and Hinduism's golden age was swiftly drawing to a close.

Rise of Islam

With the arrival of Islam came the power, the reason and the will to oppose the hegemony of the Majapahits, and satellite kingdoms soon took up arms against the Hindu kings. In the 15th century the Majapahits fled to Bali, where Hindu culture continues to flourish, leaving Java to the increasingly powerful Islamic sultanates. Meanwhile, the influential trading kingdoms of Melaka (on the Malay Peninsula) and Makassar (in southern Sulawesi) were also embracing Islam, sowing the seeds that would later make modern Indonesia the most populous Muslim nation on earth.

European Expansion

Melaka fell to the Portuguese in 1511 and European eyes were soon settling on the archipelago's riches, prompting two centuries of unrest as the Portuguese, Spanish, Dutch and British wrestled for control. By 1700 the Dutch held most of the trump cards, with the Dutch East India Company (Vereenigde Oost-Indische Compagnie; VOC) controlling the region's lucrative spice trade and becoming the world's first multinational company. Following the VOC's bankruptcy, however, the British governed Java under Sir Stamford Raffles between 1811 and 1816, only to relinquish control again to the Dutch after the end of the Napoleonic wars; they then held control of Indonesia until its independence 129 years later.

It was not, however, a trouble-free tenancy: the Dutch had to face numerous rebellions. Javan prince Diponegoro's five-year guerrilla war was finally put down in 1830, costing the lives of 8000 Dutch troops.

Road to Independence

By the beginning of the 20th century, the Dutch had brought most of the archipelago under their control, but the revolutionary

TOP READS

A Brief History of Indonesia (2015) Indonesian expert Tim Hannigan's highly readable and entertaining narrative.

Indonesia Etc (2014) Elizabeth Pisani's brilliant travelogue and exploration of the nation.

This Earth of Mankind (1980) A canvas of Indonesia under Dutch rule by Pramoedya Ananta Toer (1925–2006), one of Indonesia's top writers.

Stranger in the Forest (1988) Eric Hansen was possibly the first nonlocal to walk across Borneo.

Krakatoa: The Day the World Exploded (2003) Simon Winchester melds history, geology and politics, all centred on the 1883 eruption.

TOP FILMS

The Act of Killing (directed by Joshua Oppenheimer, 2012) A searing Oscar-nominated documentary about the 1965 slaughter of accused Communist sympathisers in Indonesia, which resulted in over 500,000 deaths and remains a taboo subject today.

The Look of Silence (directed by Joshua Oppenheimer, 2014) The follow-up to *The Act of Killing* follows an optician as he confronts men accused of killing his brother during the 1965 slaughters.

Shackled (directed by Upi Avianto, 2012) A man driving in Jakarta finds a character in a rabbit suit and an abused woman in his car, with horrifying consequences. Avianto is one of Indonesia's most popular directors; her films are usually commercial successes.

Sang Penari (The Dancer; directed by Ifa Isfansyah, 2011) Based on a trilogy of novels by Ahmad Tohari, this critically acclaimed film focuses on a young man and a Javanese village's new poetic dancer.

Eat Pray Love (directed by Ryan Murphy, 2010) A critical and box-office flop, the film is Bali's glossiest appearance on screen. Look for Ubud and Padang Padang beach.

tradition of Diponegoro was never truly quashed, bubbling beneath the surface of Dutch rule and finding a voice in the young Sukarno. The debate was sidelined as the Japanese swept through Indonesia during WWII, but with their departure came the opportunity for Sukarno to declare Indonesian independence, which he did from his Jakarta home on 17 August 1945.

The Dutch, however, were unwilling to relinquish their hold over Indonesia and – supported by the British, who had entered Indonesia to accept the Japanese surrender – moved quickly to reassert their authority over the country. Resistance was stiff and for four bitter years the Indonesian resistance fought a guerrilla war. But American and UN opposition to the reimposition of colonialism and the mounting casualty toll eventually forced the Dutch to pack it in, and the Indonesian flag – the *sang merah putih* (red and white) – was finally hoisted over Jakarta's Istana Merdeka (Freedom Palace) on 27 December 1949.

Depression, Disunity & Dictatorship

Unity in war quickly became division in peace, as religious fundamentalists and nationalist separatists challenged the fledgling central government. After almost a decade of political impasse and economic depression, Sukarno made his move in 1957, declaring Guided Democracy (a euphemism for dictatorship) with army backing and leading Indonesia into nearly four decades of authoritarian rule.

Despite moves towards the one-party state, Indonesia's three-million-strong Communist Party (Partai Komunis Indonesia; PKI) was the biggest in the world by 1965 and Sukarno had long realised the importance of winning its backing. But as the PKI's influence in government grew, so did tensions with the armed forces. Things came to a head on the night of 30 September 1965, when elements of the palace guard launched an attempted coup. Quickly put down by General Suharto, the coup was blamed – perhaps unfairly – on the PKI and became the pretext for an army-led purge that left as many as 500,000 communist sympathisers dead. Strong evidence later emerged from declassified documents that both the US (opposed to communism) and the UK (seeking to protect its interests in Malaysia) aided and abetted Suharto's purge by drawing up hit lists of communist agitators. By 1968 Suharto had ousted Sukarno and was installed as president.

Suharto brought unity through repression, annexing Papua in 1969, and reacting to insurgency with an iron fist. In 1975 Portuguese Timor was invaded, leading to tens of thousands of deaths; separatist ambitions in Aceh and Papua were also met with a ferocious military response. But despite endemic corruption, the 1980s and 1990s were Indonesia's boom years, with meteoric economic growth and a starburst of opulent building ventures transforming the face of the capital.

Suharto's Fall

As Asia's economy went into freefall during the closing years of the 1990s, Suharto's house of cards began to tumble. Indonesia went bankrupt overnight and the country found an obvious scapegoat in the cronyism and corruption endemic in the dictator's regime. Protests erupted across Indonesia in 1998, and the May riots in Jakarta left thousands, many of them Chinese, dead. After three decades of dictatorial rule, Suharto resigned on 21 May 1998.

Passions cooled when Vice President BJ Habibie took power on a reform ticket, but ambitious promises were slow to materialise, and in November of the same year riots again rocked many Indonesian cities. Promises of forthcoming elections succeeded in closing the floodgates, but separatist groups took advantage of the weakened central government and violence erupted in Maluku, Papua, East Timor and Aceh. East Timor won its independence after a referendum in August 1999, but only after Indonesian-backed militias had destroyed its infrastructure and left thousands dead.

Democracy & Reform

Against this unsettled backdrop, the June 1999 legislative elections passed surprisingly smoothly, leaving Megawati Sukarnoputri (Sukarno's daughter) and her reformist Indonesian Democratic Party for Struggle (PDI-P) as the largest party, with 33% of the vote. But months later the separate presidential election was narrowly won by Abdurrahman Wahid (Gus Dur), whose efforts to undo corruption met with stiff resistance. Megawati was eventually sworn in as president in 2001, but her term proved a disappointment for many Indonesians, as corrupt infrastructures were left in place, the military's power remained intact, poverty levels remained high and there were high-profile terrorism attacks such as the 2002 Bali bombings.

Megawati lost the 2004 presidential elections to Susilo Bambang Yudhoyono (aka 'SBY'), an ex-army officer who served in East Timor. His successes included cracking down on Islamic militants and pumping more money into education and health.

SBY's term was also marked by a series of disasters, beginning with the 2004 Boxing Day tsunami that ravaged Aceh in northern Sumatra. In 2006, a quake shook Yogyakarta, killing 6800 people, and in 2009 a quake devastated Padang in Sumatra.

Elections in 2009 were largely peaceful. SBY cruised to an easy re-election on a platform of continuing moderate policies. Extremist Islamic parties have fared poorly against more moderate parties. In the years following, the nation enjoyed a good run of peace and prosperity.

People & Culture

The old Javanese saying '*bhinneka tunggal ika*' (they are many; they are one) is said to be Indonesia's national dictum, but with a population of over 255 million, 300-plus languages and more than 17,000 islands it's not surprising that many from the outer islands resent Java, where power is centralised. Indonesia is loosely bound together by a single flag (which is increasingly flown with pride during national holidays) and a single language (Bahasa Indonesia), but in some ways can be compared to the EU – a richly diverse confederacy of peoples.

The world's most populous Muslim nation is no hardline Islamic state. Indonesians have traditionally practised a relaxed form of Islam, and though there's no desire to imitate the West, most see no conflict in catching a Hollywood movie in a Western-style shopping mall after prayers at the mosque. The country is becoming more cosmopolitan; Facebook usage is epic. Millions of Indonesians now work overseas – mainly in the Gulf, Hong Kong and Malaysia – bringing back external influences to their villages when they return. A boom in low-cost air travel has enabled a generation of Indonesians to travel internally and overseas conveniently and cheaply for the first time, while personal mobility is much easier today – it's possible to buy a motorcycle on hire purchase with as little as a 500,000Rp deposit.

But not everyone has the cash or time for overseas jaunts and there remains a yawning gulf between the haves and the have-nots. Indonesia is much poorer than many of its Asian neighbours, with over 40% surviving on US$2 a day, and in many rural areas opportunities are few and far between.

Population

Indonesia's population is the fourth-biggest in the world, with over 255 million people. Over half this number live on the island of Java, one of the most crowded places on earth, with a population density of over 1100 people per square kilometre. But while Java (and Bali and Lombok) teem with people, large parts of the archipelago are sparsely populated, particularly Papua (under 10 people per square kilometre) and Kalimantan.

Religion

If Indonesia has a soundtrack, it is the muezzin's call to prayer. Wake up to it once and it won't come as a surprise that Indonesia is the largest Islamic nation on earth, with over 224 million Muslims (88% of the total population).

But while Islam has a near monopoly on religious life, many of the country's most impressive historical monuments, such as the temples of Borobudur and Prambanan, hark back to when Hindu and Buddhist kingdoms dominated Java. These religions maintain important communities, with Hinduism (1.5% of the population) continuing to flourish in Bali, while Buddhists (1%) are scattered throughout the country. Christians make up about 10% of the nation, forming the majority in Papua, on several islands of Nusa Tenggara and Maluku, and in parts of Sumatra. Animist traditions also survive below the surface in many rural areas.

Arts

DANCE

Indonesia has a rich heritage of traditional dances. In Yogyakarta there's the *Ramayana Ballet*, a spectacular dance drama; Lombok has a mask dance called the *kayak sando*

and war dances; Malaku's *lenso* is a hand-kerchief dance; while Bali has a multitude of elaborate dances, a major reason to visit the island.

MUSIC

Indonesia has a massive contemporary music scene that spans all genres. The popular *dangdut* is a melange of traditional and modern, Indonesian and foreign musical styles that features instruments such as electric guitars and Indian *tablas* (a type of drum), and rhythms ranging from Middle Eastern pop to reggae or salsa. Among the best performers and bands of late are Neonomora, Frau, Glovves and Banda Neira.

Gamelan is the best-known traditional Indonesian music: besides Bali, Java has orchestras composed mainly of percussion instruments, including drums, gongs and *angklung* (bamboo tubes shaken to produce a note), along with flutes and xylophones.

Environment

Indonesia has lost more tropical forest than anywhere else in the world, bar Brazil, in the last few decades. That said, some incredible national parks and landscapes remain virtually untouched, mainly in remote areas away from the main centres of population.

The Land

At 1.9 million sq km, Indonesia is an island colossus, incorporating 10% of the world's forest cover and 11,508 uninhabited islands (6000 more have human populations). From

---

BE THE SOLUTION: ANIMAL EXPLOITATION

You will still see plenty of animal exploitation in Indonesia, including performing monkeys on street corners in big cities and endangered birds in markets. Taking photos or paying the handlers money only encourages this behaviour.

Shops sell turtle-shell products, rare seashells, snakeskin, stuffed birds and framed butterflies. Avoid these. Not only are they illegal, but importing them into most countries is banned and items will probably be confiscated by customs. See the **Convention on International Trade in Endangered Species** (CITES; www.cites.org) for more information.

Some animal exploitation is more subtle. Consider the life of a cute civet locked in a warehouse cage and force-fed coffee to 'naturally' process the beans, for example. It's a far cry from the happy story plantations sell to justify charging outrageous prices for *kopi luwak* (civet coffee).

Finally, rubbish is an obvious problem. And while packing out your biscuit wrapper from some already rubbish-strewn waterfall may feel futile, your guides and other trekkers will notice, and might even join you. It's a small but important step in the right direction.

the low-lying coastal areas, the country rises through no fewer than 129 active volcanoes – more than any country in the world – to the snow-covered summit of Puncak Jaya (4884m) in Papua. Despite the incredible diversity of its landscapes, it is worth remembering that Indonesia is predominantly water; Indonesians refer to the country as Tanah Air Kita (literally 'Our Earth and Water').

Wildlife

In his classic study, *The Malay Archipelago*, British naturalist Alfred Russel Wallace divided Indonesia into two zones. To the west of the so-called Wallace Line (which runs between Kalimantan and Sulawesi and south through the straits between Bali and Lombok) the flora and fauna resemble that of the rest of Asia, while the species and environments to the east become increasingly like those of Australia. Scientists have since fine-tuned Wallace's findings, but while western Indonesia is known for its orangutan, rhinos and tigers, as well as spectacular *Rafflesia* flowers, eastern Indonesia boasts fauna such as the komodo dragon and marsupials, including Papuan tree kangaroos.

National Parks

There are officially 50 *taman nasional* (national parks) in Indonesia. Most are in remote areas and have basic visitor facilities, but they are remarkable in their ecological diversity and wildlife. Some of the finest include Tanjung Puting (in Kalimantan) for its orangutans and wetland birds, and Komodo and Rinca for their dragons and official coral reefs.

Environmental Issues

Resource exploitation threatens virtually every corner of Indonesia.

The side effects of deforestation and mining are felt across the nation and beyond: floods and landslides wash away valuable topsoil, rivers become sluggish and fetid, and haze from forest-clearing fires blankets Malaysia and Singapore every dry season, increasing international tensions (2015 was an especially bad year). The carbon released from deforestation and fires is a significant contributor to global climate change, which – in a vicious cycle – creates a longer dry season, allowing for more fires.

The problems flow right through to Indonesia's coastline and seas, where more than 80% of reef habitat is considered to be at risk. A long history of cyanide and bomb fishing has left much of Indonesia's coral lifeless or crumbled. Shark finning and manta hunting have taken their toll on populations, while overfishing threatens to disrupt the marine ecosystem.

Meanwhile, the burgeoning middle class is straining the nation's infrastructure. Private vehicles clog urban streets, creating choking air pollution; waste-removal services have difficulty coping with household and industrial refuse; and a lack of sewage disposal makes water from most sources undrinkable without boiling, putting further pressure on kerosene and firewood supplies.

Food & Drink

By eating in Indonesia you savour the essence of the country, as few nations are so well represented by their cuisine. The abundance of rice reflects Indonesia's fertile landscape, the spices are reminiscent of a time of trade and invasion, and the fiery chilli echoes the passion of the people. Indonesian cuisine is really one big food swap: Chinese, Portuguese, colonists and traders have all influenced the ingredients that appear at the Indonesian table, and the cuisine has been shaped over time by the archipelago's diverse landscape, people and culture.

Coriander, cumin, chilli, lemongrass, coconut, soy sauce and palm sugar are all important flavourings; sambal is a crucial condiment. Fish is a favourite and seafood restaurants are common in this island nation. Indonesians traditionally eat with their fingers, hence the stickiness of the rice. Satay (skewered meat), nasi goreng (fried rice) and *gado gado* (vegetables with peanut sauce) are some of Indonesia's most famous dishes. *Nasi campur* (mixed rice) is the national dish and includes a sampling of dishes served in myriad variations.

Regional Variations

Popular dishes are, not surprisingly, diverse in this land of over 300 languages.

JAVA

The cuisine of the Betawi (original inhabitants of the Jakarta region) is known for its richness. *Gado gado* is a Betawi original,

WHERE TO SURF

New surf spots are being enjoyed all the time – in Indonesia, the choices simply never end.

Java

Batu Karas Fine breaks, and an enjoyable place to kick back (p171).

Pangandaran West Java's premier beach resort (p169).

G-Land Locally known as Plengkung, an isolated haven of East Java surf camps (p191).

Bali

It really is a surfer's paradise in Bali. Breaks are found right around the south side of the island and there's a large infrastructure of schools, board-rental places, cheap surfer dives and more that cater to the crowds.

Six famous spots you won't want to miss:

Kuta Beach Where surfing came to Asia. This is a good place for beginners, with long, steady breaks (p195).

Bingin A white-sand beach backed by laid-back accommodation makes this a natural (p203).

Ulu Watu Some of the largest sets in Bali (p204).

Nusa Lembongan The island is a mellow scene for surfers and nonsurfers. You can watch the breaks from your lodging (p207).

Pantai Keramas One of the rapidly developing East Bali surf beaches (p216).

Nusa Tenggara

Lombok Excellent breaks are found along the south beaches centering on Kuta (p228).

Sumbawa Maluk features Supersuck, one of the world's best lefts, while Pantai Lakey has a bevy of breaks (p237).

Sumatra

Pulau Nias An isolated island with the legendary righthander of Lagundri Bay (p267).

Mentawai Islands An offshore playground of surf camps and liveaboards (p258).

---

as *zis ketoprak* (noodles, bean sprouts and tofu with soy and peanut sauce). *Soto Betawi* (beef soup) is made creamy with coconut milk. There's also *nasi uduk* (rice cooked in coconut milk, served with meat, tofu and/or vegetables).

Central Javan food is sweet – even the curries, such as *gudeg* (jackfruit curry). Yogyakarta specialities include *ayam goreng* (fried chicken) and *kelepon* (green rice-flour balls with a palm-sugar filling).

BALI

High-quality warungs (food stalls) popular with visitors can be found across Bali. *Babi guling* (spit-roast pig stuffed with chilli, turmeric, garlic and ginger) is widely sold, as is *bebek betutu* (duck stuffed with spices, wrapped in banana leaves and coconut husks and cooked in embers). The local sa-

tay, *sate lilit*, is made with minced, spiced meat pressed onto skewers.

NUSA TENGGARA

In dry East Nusa Tenggara you'll eat less rice and more sago, corn, cassava and taro. Fish remains popular: one local dish is Sumbawa's *sepat* (shredded fish in coconut and mango sauce).

The Sasak people of Lombok like spicy *ayam Taliwang* (roasted chicken served with a peanut, tomato, chilli and lime dip) and *pelecing* (sauce made with chilli, shrimp paste and tomato). In fact, Lombok-style chicken is popular across the nation.

SUMATRA

In West Sumatra, beef is used in *rendang* (beef coconut curry). Padang food is famed for its rich, chilli-heavy sauces and is popular throughout Indonesia. It's usually delicious, though not cooked fresh – dishes are displayed for hours (days even) in the restaurant window. Padang restaurant *(masakan Padang)* food is served one of two ways: usually a bowl of rice is plonked in front of you, followed by a whole collection of small bowls of vegetables, meat and fish; or you approach the window display and pick a few dishes yourself.

KALIMANTAN

Dayak food varies, but you may sample *rembang,* a sour fruit that's made into *sayur asem rembang* (sour vegetable soup). The regional soup, *soto banjar,* is a chicken broth made creamy by mashing boiled eggs into the stock. Chicken also goes into *ayam masak habang,* cooked with large red chillies.

SULAWESI

South Sulawesi locals love seafood, especially *ikan bakar* (grilled fish). For sugar cravers, there's *es pallubutun* (coconut custard and banana in coconut milk and syrup). The Toraja people have their own distinct cuisine: the best-known dish is *pa'piong* (meat stuffed into bamboo tubes along with vegetables and coconut).

MALUKU

A typical Maluku meal is tuna and *dabu-dabu* (raw vegetables with a chilli and fish-paste sauce). Sometimes fish is made into *kohu-kohu* (fish salad with citrus fruit and chilli).

PAPUA (IRIAN JAYA)

In the highlands of Papua the sweet potato is king. Other plants, such as sago palms, are also cultivated. The locals eat the pith of the sago palm and also leave the plant to rot so that they can collect and eat beetle grubs. On special occasions, chickens and pigs are cooked in earth ovens.

Drinks

Bottled water and soft drinks are available everywhere, and many hotels and restaurants provide *air putih* (boiled water) for guests. Iced juice drinks can be good, but take care that the water/ice has been purified or is bottled. (Ice in Jakarta and Bali is usually fine.)

Indonesian tea is fine and coffee can be excellent; for a strong local brew ask for *kopi java* or *kopi flores,* depending on where you are.

Beer is quite good: Bintang is one of Asia's finest lagers. Efforts to restrict sales of beer and alcohol in 2015 were loosely enforced or ignored in some areas (like Bali) and embraced in other, more conservative areas.

Bali Brem rice wine is really potent, and the more you drink the nicer it tastes. *Es buah,* or *es campur,* is a strange concoction of fruit salad, jelly cubes, syrup, crushed rice and condensed milk – and it tastes absolutely *enak* (delicious).

SURVIVAL GUIDE

ℹ Directory A–Z

ACCOMMODATION

Places to stay in tourist areas can be excellent at any price range. But elsewhere in Indonesia, standards quickly fall: slack maintenance and uneven service are common, although staff are usually cheery.

Hostels are appearing in top tourist destinations like Bali, the Gilis and Flores, although often a private room in a family-run place can be found for similar rates. Other options include liveaboard boats, bamboo-and-thatch surf camps and much more. Camping is very uncommon.

Shop online and contact hotels directly and bargain to find the best rates. There's no one formula that works across Indonesia. Accommodation attracts a combined tax and service charge (called 'plus plus') of 21%. In budget places, this is generally included in the price, but check first.

At various price ranges, expect the following:

Budget The cheapest accommodation is in small places that are simple but clean and comfortable. Names usually include the word 'losmen,' 'homestay,' 'inn' or *'pondok'*. Standards vary widely. Features:

➨ Maybe air-con

➨ Maybe hot water

➨ Sometimes no window

➨ Private bathroom with shower and sometimes a Western-style toilet

➨ Often a pool (on Bali)

➨ Simple breakfast

Midrange Many hotels have a range of rooms, from budget to midrange. The best may be called VIP or some other moniker. In addition to what you'll get at a budget hotel, expect:

➨ Balcony/porch/patio

➨ Satellite TV

➨ Small fridge

➨ Usually wi-fi

Top-End Indonesia has some of the world's best hotels, including beach resorts and isolated luxury retreats. If you're looking to splurge, you may find something fabulous for less than you'd expect.

Price Ranges

Average prices are higher in Bali and Lombok's Gili Islands; in this chapter, our price indicators are separated into two price bands.

Note that the Indonesian government may redenominate the rupiah in the next year or two, meaning the last three zeroes will be lopped off each denomination (eg a 20,000Rp note will become a 20Rp note). Expect confusion if this long-promised change occurs.

Bali & Lombok

$ less than 450,000Rp
$$ 450,000Rp to 1,400,000Rp
$$$ more than 1,400,000Rp

Rest of Indonesia

$ less than 250,000Rp
$$ 250,000R to 800,000Rp
$$$ more than 800,000Rp

CUSTOMS REGULATIONS

Indonesia has the usual list of prohibited imports, including drugs, weapons, fresh fruit and anything remotely pornographic.

Items allowed include the following:
➡ 200 cigarettes (or 50 cigars or 100g of tobacco)
➡ a 'reasonable amount' of perfume
➡ 1L of alcohol

ELECTRICITY

Indonesia uses 220/230V 50Hz electricity; plugs usually have two round pins, like those found in much of the EU.

EMBASSIES & CONSULATES

Bali

Australian Consulate (☏ 0361-241 118; www.bali.indonesia.embassy.gov.au; Jl Tantular 32, Denpasar; ⊘ 8am-4pm Mon-Fri) The Australian consulate has a consular sharing agreement with Canada.

US Consulate (☏ 0361-233 605; BaliConsularAgency@state.gov; Jl Hayam Wuruk 310, Renon, Denpasar; ⊘ 9am-noon & 1-3.30pm Mon-Fri)

Jakarta

Australian Embassy (Map p156; ☏ 021-2550 5555; www.indonesia.embassy.gov.au; Jl HR Rasuna Said Kav C 15-16, Jakarta Selatan)

Brunei Darussalam Embassy (Map p160; ☏ 021-3190 6080; www.mofat.gov.bn; Jl Teuku Umar No 51, Menteng)

Canadian Embassy (Map p156; ☏ 021-2550 7800; www.jakarta.gc.ca; 6th fl, World Trade Centre, Jl Jenderal Sudirman Kav 29-31)

Dutch Embassy (Map p156; ☏ 021-524 8200; http://indonesia.nlembassy.org; Jln HR Rasuna Said Kav S-3)

French Embassy (Map p160; ☏ 021-2355 7600; www.ambafrance-id.org; Jl MH Thamrin No 20)

German Embassy (Map p160; ☏ 021-3985 5000; www.jakarta.diplo.de; Jl MH Thamrin No 1)

Malaysian Embassy (Map p156; ☏ 021-522 4974; www.kln.gov.my/web/idn_jakarta/home; Jl HR Rasuna Said Kav X/6, No 1-3, Kuningan)

New Zealand Embassy (Map p156; ☏ 021-2995 5800; www.nzembassy.com; 10th fl, Sentral Senayan 2, Jl Asia Afrika No 8)

Papua New Guinea Embassy (Map p156; ☏ 021-725 1218; www.kundu-jakarta.com; 6th fl, Panin Bank Centre, Jl Jenderal Sudirman 1)

Singaporean Embassy (Map p156; ☏ 021-2995 0400; www.mfa.gov.sg/jkt; Block X/4 Kav 2, Jl HR Rasuna Said)

UK Embassy (Map p156; ☏ 021-2356 5200; www.ukinindonesia.fco.gov.uk; Jl Patra Kuningan Raya Blok L5-6)

US Embassy (Map p160; ☏ 021-3435 9000; http://jakarta.usembassy.gov; Jl Medan Merdeka Selatan, No 3-5)

Medan

Malaysian Consulate (☏ 061-453 1342; www.kln.gov.my/web/idn_medan; Jl Diponegoro 43)

FESTIVALS & EVENTS

Religious events and official holidays are a vital part of Indonesian life. There are many through the year and they're often cause for celebrations and festivals. With such a diversity of people in the archipelago, there are many local holidays, festivals and cultural events. This is especially true on Bali, where religious events can easily occupy a third of the typical person's calendar.

The Muslim fasting month of Ramadan requires that Muslims abstain from food, drink, cigarettes and sex between sunrise and sunset. Many bars and restaurants close and it is important to avoid eating or drinking publicly in Muslim areas during this time. For the week before and after Lebaran (Idul Fitri), the festival to mark the end of the fast, transport is often fully booked and travelling becomes a nightmare – plan to stay put at this time. Ramadan, Idul Fitri and Idul Adha (Muslim day of sacrifice) move back 10 days or so every year, according to the Muslim calendar.

Although some public holidays have a fixed date, the dates for many events vary each year depending on Muslim, Buddhist or Hindu calendars.

January/February
New Year's Day Celebrated on 1 January.

Imlek (Chinese New Year) Special food is prepared, decorations adorn stores and homes, and *barongasai* (lion dances) are performed; held in January/February.

Muharram (Islamic New Year) The date varies each year; it's usually in late January.

Maulid Nabi Muhammad (Mohammed's Birthday) Celebrated in December in 2016 and 2017 and November in 2018; prayers are held in mosques throughout the country, and there are street parades in Solo and Yogyakarta.

March/April
Hindu New Year (Nyepi) Held in March/April; in Bali and other Hindu communities, villagers make as much noise as possible to scare away devils. Virtually all of Bali shuts down.

Good Friday Occurs in March or April.

April/May
Waisak (Buddha's Birthday) Mass prayers are said at the main Buddhist temples, including Borobudur.

May/June
Ascension of Christ Occurs in May/June.

Ascension of Mohammed Special prayers are held in mosques.

August
Independence Day Celebrated on 17 August with plenty of pomp and circumstance; government buildings are draped in huge red-and-white flags and banners, and there are endless marches.

Lebaran (Idul Fitri) Everyone returns to their home village for special prayers and gift giving; it's also a time for charity donations.

October
Idul Adha The end of the Haj is celebrated with animal sacrifices, the meat of which is given to the poor.

November/December
Christmas Day Marked by gift giving and special church services in Christian areas; celebrated on 25 December.

FOOD
Food is cheaper outside the main tourist hubs of Bali and Lombok's Gili Islands. As such, our price indicators for a main course or meal are separated into two price bands.

Bali & Lombok
$ less than 60,000Rp
$$ 60,000Rp to 250,000Rp
$$$ more than 250,000Rp

Rest of Indonesia
$ less than 50,000Rp
$$ 50,000Rp to 200,000Rp
$$$ more than 200,000Rp

INTERNET ACCESS
Indonesia is getting wired, though speed varies from fast to painfully slow.

➤ Wi-fi (pronounced 'wee-fee' in Indonesia) is commonly available in hotels except in rural areas. It's often free but watch out for hotels that may charge ridiculous rates by the hour or by data use.

➤ Data through your smartphone is often the fastest way to connect to the internet. 3G service is widespread.

LEGAL MATTERS
Drugs, gambling and pornography are illegal; the executions of two Australian nationals of the so-called 'Bali Nine' in 2015 for drug offences serve as a grim reminder.

Generally, you are unlikely to have any encounters with the police unless you are driving a rented car or motorcycle, in which case you may be stopped for a dubious reason and asked to pay an impromptu 'fine' of about 50,000Rp.

LGBT TRAVELLERS
Gay travellers in Indonesia should follow the same precautions as straight travellers: avoid public displays of affection. This is especially important in conservative areas such as Aceh, where two women hugging were sent for 're-education' by religious police in 2015.

➤ Gay men in Indonesia are referred to as *homo* or *gay;* lesbians are *lesbi*.

➤ Indonesia's community of transvestite/transsexual *waria* – from the words *wanita* (woman) and *pria* (man) – has always had a very public profile; also known by the less polite term *banci*.

➤ Islamic groups proscribe homosexuality, but queer-bashing is rare.

➤ Bali is especially LGBT-friendly, with a large community of expats and people from elsewhere in Indonesia.

MONEY
➤ ATMs are common across Indonesia except in rural areas; most now accept cards affiliated with international networks. Bank BNI is reliable.

➤ Always carry a sizeable amount of rupiah when you are travelling outside of cities and tourist areas as ATM networks go down and/or you can be on an island where the only ATM is broken or non-existent.

➤ In cities and touristed areas (eg Bali), credit cards will be accepted at midrange and better hotels and resorts. More expensive shops as

RELIABLE TRANSPORT INFO

In a country where accurate information for ferries, airlines and buses can be elusive at best, guesthouses, hotels and resorts are good sources of information, especially for more obscure destinations. They need you to reach them to stay in business and often can give you all the up-to-date details needed.

well as travel agents will also accept them, but often with a surcharge of around 3%.

➡ Stick to banks, exchange counters in airports or large and reputable storefront operations as scams are common. It can be hard to exchange currencies other than the US dollar outside of major cities.

OPENING HOURS

The following are typical opening hours found across Indonesia.

Banks 8am to 2pm Monday to Thursday, 8am to noon Friday, 8am to 11am Saturday.

Government offices Generally 8am to 3pm Monday to Thursday, 8am to noon Friday.

Restaurants 8am to 10pm.

Shopping 9am or 10am to 5pm; larger shops and tourist areas to 8pm. Many closed Sunday.

PUBLIC HOLIDAYS

Official holidays and religious events are intertwined in the Indonesian calendar, with the result being a plethora of days when much of the nation shuts down or has the day off.

SAFE TRAVEL

If you've never been before, Indonesia might seem like one of the world's most dodgy nations: accident-prone and cursed by natural disasters and terrorist outrages.

But even though transport safety standards are dodgy, earthquakes are frequent and there has been a number of highly publicised incidents of terrorism and sectarian violence, Indonesia is actually a very safe nation for travellers.

Personal safety, even in the big cities, is not usually a major concern. Keep your wits about you, yes, but violent crime is rare in Indonesia. Be mindful of your valuables and take the usual precautions and the chances of getting into trouble are small.

It *is* important to keep abreast of current political developments, however. At the time of writing, the country was peaceful.

Drug penalties can be severe. Be very wary of *arak*, the potent rice or palm alcohol that figures in many drinks aimed at tourists and locals alike;

deaths and serious injuries occur constantly due to unscrupulous vendors using dangerous chemicals. And on Bali, beware of dogs, as there is an ongoing rabies problem.

Tap water is never safe to drink.

TELEPHONE

Cheap SIM cards (which should never cost more than 5000Rp more than any included calling credit) and internet calling make it easy to stay in touch with home at reasonable prices.

TIME

Indonesia has three time zones. Western Indonesia time (Sumatra, Java, West and Central Kalimantan) is seven hours ahead of GMT, Central Indonesia time (Bali, South and East Kalimantan, Sulawesi and Nusa Tenggara) is eight hours ahead, and East Indonesia time (Maluku and Papua) is nine hours ahead.

TOILETS

Public toilets are rare except in bus and train stations. Expect to use restaurants and hotels.

Indonesian toilets are holes in the ground with footrests on either side (although Western toilets are common in tourist areas). To flush, scoop water from the nearby tank.

VISAS

The visa situation is constantly in flux. Your passport must be valid for at least six months from the date of your arrival.

At the time of research, the main visa options for visitors to Indonesia were:

Visa in Advance Visitors can apply for a visa before they arrive in Indonesia. Typically this is a visitor's visa, which comes in two flavours: 30 or 60 days. Details vary by country; contact your nearest Indonesian embassy or consulate to determine processing fees and times.

Visa on Arrival Citizens of over 65 countries may apply for a 30-day visa when they arrive at major airports and harbours (but not most land borders). The cost is US$35; be sure to have the exact amount in US currency. Eligible countries include Australia, Canada, much – but not all – of the EU plus New Zealand and the USA. VOA renewals for 30 days are possible. If you don't qualify for VOA, you must get a visa in advance.

Visa Free Citizens of dozens of countries can receive a 30-day visa for free upon arrival. But note that this visa cannot be extended and you may be limited to which airports and ports you can use to exit the country (eg it may not work for Timor-Leste).

Fines for overstaying your visa expiration date are 300,000Rp per day and include additional hassles.

VOLUNTEERING

There are excellent opportunities for aspiring volunteers in Indonesia, but Lonely Planet does not endorse any organisations that we do not work with directly, so it's essential that you do your own thorough research before agreeing to volunteer with or donate to any organisation. A three-month commitment is recommended for working with children.

Borneo Orangutan Survival Foundation (www.orangutan.or.id) Accepts volunteers for its orangutan and sun bear rehabilitation and reforestation programs.

East Bali Poverty Project (☑ 0361-410 071; www.eastbalipovertyproject.org) Works to help children in the impoverished mountain villages of East Bali. Uses English teachers.

IDEP (Indonesian Development of Education & Permaculture; ☑ 0361-294993; www.idep-foundation.org) Has projects across Indonesia; works on environmental projects, disaster planning and community improvement.

ProFauna (www.profauna.net) A large non-profit animal-protection organisation operating across Indonesia; has been active in protecting sea turtles.

Sea Sanctuaries Trust (www.seasanctuaries.org) Diving-based marine conservation volunteering in Raja Ampat.

Yayasan Bumi Sehat (☑ 0361-970002; www.bumisehatfoundation.org) Operates an internationally recognised clinic and gives reproductive services to disadvantaged women in Ubud; accepts donated time from medical professionals.

ⓘ Getting There & Away

The main bureaucratic consideration for entering Indonesia involves visas.

AIR

Jakarta and Bali are the main hubs, but other useful international connections include Balikpapan (Kalimantan), Mataram (Lombok), Manado (Sulawesi), Medan (Sumatra), Palembang (Sumatra), Padang (Sumatra), Solo (Java) and Surabaya (Java).

LAND

There are three land links between Indonesia and neighbouring countries. Buses link Pontianak and Kuching on Borneo and West Timor with Timor-Leste, and you can cross from Jayapura to Vanimo in Papua New Guinea.

SEA

Malaysia and Singapore are linked to Sumatra by boats and ferries, although the links are inconvenient and most travellers fly. Boats make the Melaka (Malaysia) to Dumai (Indonesia) crossing. From Singapore, ferries make the quick hop to Pulau Batam and Bintan, the primary islands in the Riau Archipelago.

There is a link on Borneo from Nunukan in East Kalimantan to Tawau in Malaysian Sabah. There is currently no sea travel between the Philippines and Indonesia.

ⓘ Getting Around

AIR

Getting reliable information on Indonesian domestic flights is a challenge – many airlines don't show up on travel websites, although www.traveloka.com is fairly complete. You can also check with local airline offices and travel agents; local hotel and tour operators are often the best sources.

➡ The domestic network continues to grow; schedules and rates are in a constant state of flux.

➡ Small carriers servicing remote routes often operate cramped and dated aircraft.

➡ With tiny regional airlines, reconfirm your ticket and hang around the check-in desk if the flight is full. Sometimes reservations are 'lost' when another passenger with more clout shows up.

Almost a dozen major airlines fly domestically. Air disasters are an ongoing problem for Indonesian airlines, especially fast-growing budget carriers.

Tickets

The larger Indonesian carriers have websites listing fares. However it may be hard, if not impossible, to purchase tickets over the internet using non-Indonesian credit cards. It's also usually difficult to purchase tickets at airports.

Travel agents are a good way to buy domestic tickets once in Indonesia, and often the best way to get the lowest fares. Airline city offices are another option.

Large international booking websites (such as Expedia) may only show **Garuda Indonesia** (www.garuda-indonesia.com) flights and then only offer very expensive airfares. Try the following to purchase tickets online:

Airline Websites Some carriers, notably Garuda Indonesia and Indonesia AirAsia, have websites that accept foreign accept cards. Lion Air is a notable exception.

skyscanner.com Accepts foreign cards but doesn't show all airlines.

ⓘ DEPARTURE TAX

Beginning in 2015, the departure tax is usually included in the cost of international and domestic airline tickets.

tiket.com Not all foreign cards work but it shows most domestic airlines.

traveloka.com Lists many domestic airlines although foreign cards don't always work. A good source for schedule info.

BICYCLE

Bicycles can be hired in all major centres from hotels, travel agents and shops for 20,000Rp to 50,000Rp per day. The tropical heat, heavy traffic and poor road conditions make long-distance travel a challenge, but some hardy souls manage it.

BOAT

Sumatra, Java, Bali and Nusa Tenggara are connected by ferries. Pelni, the national passenger line, covers the archipelago, albeit infrequently.

Pelni Ships

Pelni (www.pelni.co.id) has a fleet of large vessels linking Indonesia's major ports and the majority of the archipelago's outlying areas. Pelni's website is a good resource, showing arrivals and departures about a month in advance, although times can change right until the vessel leaves port. (Note that service frequency can be sporadic, making Pelni a tough option for those with schedule and visa constraints.)

Pelni ships have four cabin classes, plus *kelas ekonomi*. Class I has two beds per cabin (and is often more expensive than using a low-cost airline); Class IV has eight beds to a cabin. *Ekonomi* is extremely basic, with mattresses that can be rented. However, these designations are often meaningless on the many boats that are both filthy and overcrowded. Book the best class of service you can afford, noting that the bathroom may be unworkable, the decks impassable with throngs of passengers and the food unpalatable.

You can book tickets up to two weeks ahead; it's best to book at least a few days in advance.

Other Boats

Sumatra, Java, Bali, Nusa Tenggara and Sulawesi are all connected by regular ferries, and you can use them to island-hop all the way from Sumatra to Timor. These ferries run either daily or several times a week. Check with shipping companies, the harbour office or travel agents for current schedules and fares.

However, schedules are often vague, so be prepared to hang around until something turns up. Be warned that because vessels may be ancient and routinely overcrowded, safety standards are at times poor.

It's also possible to make some more unusual sea trips. Tourist boats travelling between Lombok and Flores are popular (see p242).

BUS

Most Indonesians use buses to get around, so there is a huge variety of services, with everything from air-con deluxe buses with blaring TVs, toilets and karaoke to *trek* (trucks) with wooden seats that rumble along remote dirt roads. Local buses are the cheapest; they leave when full and stop on request – on the outer islands this is often your only choice.

TRAVELLING SAFELY BY BOAT

Boat safety is an important consideration across Indonesia, where boats that barely seem seaworthy may be your only option to travel between islands. In many cases these services are accidents waiting to happen, as safety regulation is lax at best.

This is especially true on the busy routes linking Bali, Nusa Lembongan, Lombok and the Gilis, where both the fast tourist boats and the public car ferries have had accidents. Given Indonesia's poor record, it is essential that you take responsibility for your own safety, as no one else will.

Consider the following points for any boat travel in Indonesia:

Bigger is better It may take you 30 minutes or more longer, but a larger boat will simply deal with the open ocean better than the over-powered small speedboats.

Check for safety equipment Make certain your boat has life preservers and that you know how to locate and use them. In an emergency, don't expect a panicked crew to hand them out. Also, check for life rafts.

Avoid over-crowding Travellers report boats leaving with more people than seats and with aisles jammed with stacked luggage.

Look for exits Cabins may only have one narrow entrance, making them death traps in an accident.

Avoid fly-by-nighters Taking a fishing boat and jamming too many engines on the rear in order to cash in on booming tourism is a recipe for disaster.

Look for 'public cars' or other permutations, which are minivans with air-con offering greater comfort and speed for about twice the rate of regular buses.

CAR & MOTORCYCLE

Self-drive small SUVs can be hired for as little as 80,000Rp to 150,000Rp a day with limited insurance in Bali, but become increasingly expensive and hard to come by the further you get from tourist areas. If you're not happy negotiating Indonesia's chaotic roads, a vehicle with driver can usually be hired for between 500,000Rp and 800,000Rp per day; the more remote areas tend to be the most expensive.

Motorcycles and scooters can be hired across Indonesia for 30,000Rp to 70,000Rp per day. Be sure to get a helmet, as wearing one is supposed to be compulsory.

LOCAL TRANSPORT

Public minibuses (most commonly called be-mos, but also known as *colt, opelet, mikrolet,* *angkot, angkudes* and *pete-pete*) are everywhere. Bemos run standard routes (fares average 3000Rp to 5000Rp), but can also be chartered like a taxi.

Cycle rickshaws are called becak, while *bajaj* are Indonesian túk-túk: three-wheelers that carry two passengers (three at a squeeze) and are powered by rasping two-stroke engines. In quieter towns, you may find horse-drawn carts, variously called *dokar, cidomo, andong* and *ben hur.*

An extremely handy form of transport is the *ojek* (motorcycle taxi); expect to pay about 2500Rp to 10,000Rp for a short ride. Most towns have taxis, which require careful negotiations. In major cities (Jakarta, South Bali etc) look for Bluebird taxis (which are reliable and use their meters) and Uber.

TRAIN

Java has a good railway service running the length of the island. There is also an extremely limited rail service in Sumatra.

Laos

♩ 856 / POP 6.9 MILLION

Why Go?

It's no accident that Laos appears as a favourite in many Southeast Asian odysseys, for this landlocked country lays claim to incredibly genuine people and the chance for your inner adventurer to let rip. The 'Land of a Million Elephants' oozes magic from the moment you spot a Hmong tribeswoman looming through the mist; trek through a glimmering rice paddy; or hear the dawn call of the endangered gibbon. But it's also a place to pamper yourself in a spa like a French colonial, or chill under a wood-blade fan in a delicious Gallic restaurant. 'Old World' affordable refinement is found in pockets across the country, especially in languid Vientiane and Unesco superstar Luang Prabang.

The country offers green tourism with excellent forest treks and tribal homestays operated by eco-responsible outfits. Be it flying along forest ziplines, exploring creepy subterranean river caves or tackling the jungle on motocross adventures, Laos will burn herself into your memory.

Best for Regional Specialities

➡ Makphet Restaurant (p324)

➡ Tamarind (p339)

➡ Lao Kitchen (p323)

Best Places for Culture

➡ Handicraft Night Market (p340)

➡ Minority villages (p337)

➡ Luang Prabang's temples (p333)

When to Go
Vientiane

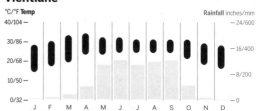

Jan Cool-season breezes; even the normally sweltering south is pleasantly bearable.

Oct Cooling weather; locals celebrate the full moon and boat-racing festivals.

Nov & Dec Celebrations for Bun Pha That in November. Cool weather but peak prices in December.

Don't Miss

There's no better way to discover the real Laos than by trying a homestay. Beyond the cities, 80% of the population lives in rural villages and, with minimal impact on the community and the environment, you can experience an evening with them. Given Laos' rich ethnicity and varied geography no two homestays will be the same, but you can rely on a few commonalities: you'll be woken by children and the local rooster, communally bathe and eat by the fire, and be guaranteed one of your most memorable nights in this country.

ITINERARIES

One Week

After spending a few days in riverside Vientiane sampling its Soviet-Franco architecture, sophisticated bars and Asian-fusion cuisine, travel north three hours to the beautiful karst country of Vang Vieng, a former party town turned outdoor activity haven for cycling, climbing, trekking and ziplining. From here catch a bus to unforgettable Luang Prabang to experience its temples, crumbling villas, pampering spas, bike rides and Gallic cuisine.

Two Weeks

Follow the one-week itinerary, then take a two-day slow boat up the Mekong River to Huay Xai, having already booked yourself in for the memorable Gibbon Experience and its overnight stays in jungle treehouses. If you've got time head up to Luang Namtha for a trek in the wild Nam Ha National Protected Area, where you can also kayak and take a homestay with a number of great tour providers. From here you can fly back to Vientiane to catch your flight out.

Essential Outdoor Activities

National Protected Areas Trek the dense forests of 20 national protected areas spread across Laos.

Vang Vieng Go ape with the latest craze of ziplines.

The Loop This two-day adventure by motorbike through jungle and karst, frontier town and dam country, gets under Laos' skin.

Tha Khaek One of the most beautiful places in the country to climb limestone karsts.

Gibbon Experience Zipline through the jungle canopy with the Gibbon Experience.

AT A GLANCE

Currency Kip (K)

Language Lao

Money ATMs in major centres. Credit cards accepted in Luang Prabang and Vientiane.

Visas On arrival (valid for 30 days; US$30 to US$42 depending on which passport you hold).

Mobile phones Prepaid SIMs available for as little as 10,000K. Decent connections.

Fast Facts

LAOS

Area 236,000 sq km

Capital Vientiane

Emergency Police ☎191

Exchange Rates

Australia	A$1	5730K
Cambodia	1000r	1192K
Euro	€1	8600K
Thailand	10B	2240K
UK	UK£1	12,250K
USA	US$1	8025K

Daily Costs

Budget hotel room US$10

Evening meal US$5

Beer US$1

Museum entrance US$2

Entering the Country

There are more than a dozen border crossings into Laos from Cambodia, China, Thailand and Vietnam. Frequent flights also connect Laos with neighbouring countries.

Laos Highlights

1 Experiencing **Luang Prabang** (p333), the ancient city of temples that has it all: royal history, Indochinese chic, colourful monks, waterfalls, stunning river views and world-class French cuisine.

2 Taking a boat ride through exhilaratingly spooky **Tham Kong Lo** (p356), a 7.5km cave home to fist-sized spiders and stalactite woods.

3 Trekking and zipping across the forest by day at the Gibbon Experience in **Huay Xai** (p355), guided by ex-poachers turned forest rangers, and sleeping in cosy treehouses at night.

4 Trekking through **Nam Ha National Protected Area** (p350) to some of the wildest, densest jungle in the country, home to a rich variety of ethnic tribes.

5 Relaxing at **Si Phan Don** (Four Thousand Islands; p367), hammock capital of Laos; a steamy traveller's idyll where the Mekong turns turquoise.

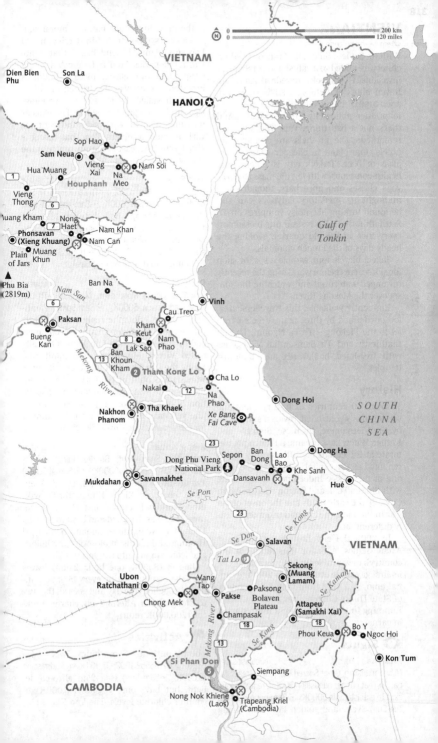

VIENTIANE

♪ 021 / POP 506,000

With its Soviet-, Sino- and Franco-styled architecture added to a raffish past of Siamese invasions, CIA spooks, daredevil American Raven pilots and Russian advisers, Vientiane (ວງຈັນ) has a very different charm to its prettier sibling city, Luang Prabang. And that's not a bad thing. Paul Theroux once remarked: 'The brothels are cleaner than hotels, marijuana is cheaper than a cold glass of beer.' Today's city is much more health-conscious, with terrific massage spas, yoga classes and juice bars, though come midnight its predatory ladyboys can still be found lurking like noisy vampires on Th Setthathirath. Gallic restaurants blossom at every turn in the old quarter, evoking the heady days of the French colonials.

Take a bicycle tour, sample a spa, or shop for silk scarves before wandering the recently revamped waterfront and watching the sunset over the Mekong River.

Eminently walkable, this travellers' area, loosely defined by three main streets parallel to the Mekong – Th Fa Ngoum, Th Setthathirath and Th Samsenthai – beguiles with tree-lined boulevards and Buddhist temples.

History

Through 10 centuries of history Vientiane was variously controlled, ravaged and looted by the Vietnamese, Burmese, Siamese and Khmer. When Laos became a French protectorate at the end of the 19th century it was renamed as the capital, rebuilt and became one of the classic Indochinese cities, along with Phnom Penh and Saigon (Ho Chi Minh City). By the early 1960s and the onset of the war in Vietnam, the city had taken on a vastly different face.

In 2009 the city hosted the Southeast Asian Games, a major illustration of the country's new profile. In 2012 Vientiane saw its first gay pride event, and in 2013 the capital enjoyed a visit from then US Secretary of State Hilary Clinton. And in 2015 China's Kunming to Vientiane express route started in earnest.

◉ Sights

Pha That Luang
BUDDHIST STUPA

(ພະທາດຫລວງ, Great Sacred Reliquary, Great Stupa; Th That Luang; admission 5000K, rental of long skirt to enter temple 5000K; ◷8am-noon & 1-4pm Tue-Sun) Svelte and golden Pha That Luang is the most important national monument in Laos; a symbol of Buddhist religion and Lao sovereignty. Legend has it that Ashokan missionaries from India erected a *tâht* (stupa) here to enclose a piece of Buddha's breastbone as early as the 3rd century BC.

A high-walled cloister with tiny windows surrounds the 45m-high stupa. The cloister measures 85m on each side and contains various buddha images. Pha That Luang is about 4km northeast of the city centre at the end of Th That Luang.

Wat Si Saket
BUDDHIST TEMPLE

(ວັດສີສະເກດ; Map p320; cnr Th Lan Xang & Th Setthathirath; admission 5000K; ◷8am-noon & 1-4pm, closed public holidays) Built between 1819 and 1824 by Chao Anou, Wat Si Saket is believed to be Vientiane's oldest surviving temple. And it shows: this beautiful temple turned national museum is in dire need of a facelift.

Patuxai
MONUMENT

(ປະຕູໄຊ, Victory Monument; Map p319; Th Lan Xang; admission 5000K; ◷8am-5pm) Vientiane's Arc de Triomphe replica is a slightly incongruous sight, dominating the commercial district around Th Lan Xang. Officially called 'Victory Monument' *and* commemorating the Lao who died in prerevolutionary wars, it was built in 1969 with cement donated by the USA intended for the construction of a new airport; expats refer to it as 'the vertical runway'. Climb to the summit for panoramic views over Vientiane.

Xieng Khuan
MUSEUM

(ຊຽງຄວນ, Suan Phut, Buddha Park; admission 5000K, camera 3000K; ◷8am-4.30pm) Twenty-five kilometres southeast of Vientiane, eccentric Xieng Khuan thrills with other-worldly Buddhist and Hindu sculptures, and was designed and built in 1958 by Luang Pu, a yogi-priest-shaman who merged Hindu and Buddhist philosophy, mythology and iconography into a cryptic whole.

Bus 14 (8000K, one hour, 24km) leaves the Talat Sao Bus Station every 15 or 20 minutes throughout the day and goes all the way to Xieng Khuan. Alternatively, charter a tuk-tuk (200,000K return).

🏃 Activities

The **Vientiane Swimming Pool** (Map p320; ♪020-5552 1002; Th Ki Huang; admission 15,000K; ◷8am-7pm) is a 25m alfresco delight, but buy some goggles (15,000K) to counter chlorine levels. The **Lao Plaza Ho-**

Vientiane

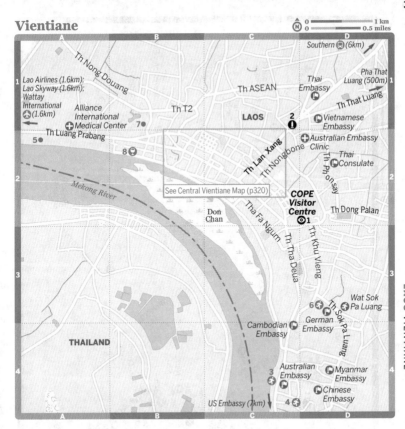

tel (Map p320; ☎021-218800; Samsenthai Rd; admission 120,000K; ⊗7am-7pm) has a rooftop pool and plenty of loungers but will set you back a few Kip, and for Hollywood glamour sample the kidney-shaped pool at the **Settha Palace Hotel** (Map p320; ☎021-217581; 6 Th Pangkham; admission 160,000K; ⊗7am-7pm).

Ultimate Frisbee   OUTDOORS
(Map p319; American soccer pitch; 12,000K; ⊗6.30pm Mon) Every Monday at 6.30pm aerial wizards meet at the American soccer pitch to play Ultimate Frisbee (two teams of seven players). Check out the Facebook page (Vientiane Ultimate Frisbee) for more info. Mixed boys and girls, Lao and expats.

Lao Bowling Centre   BOWLING
(Map p320; ☎021-218661; Th Khun Bulom; per game with shoe hire 16,000K; ⊗9am-midnight) Bright lights, Beerlao and boisterous bowlers are what you'll find here.

Bee Bee Fitness   HEALTH & FITNESS
(Map p319; ☎021-315877; opposite the Australian Embassy; 1-day membership 40,000K; ⊗6am-9pm Mon-Fri, 7am-9pm Sat & Sun) This terrific gym

Central Vientiane

LAOS VIENTIANE

0 — 400 m
0 — 0.2 miles

Th Lan Xang

Post, Telephone & Telegraph
Th Saylom

Tourist Police
Tourist Information Centre

Th Nongbone

Thai-Lao International Bus
Talat Sao Bus Station

Th Sakkarine
Th Galleni

Bank of Ayudhya
Joint Development Bank
32

Th Hatsady
Talat Sao

ANZ Bank

Th Khu Vieng
Th Mahasot

French Embassy

Talat Sao Taxi Stand

Th Bartholomie

Siam Commercial Bank

Th Phai Nam

Th Pangkham

Th Chanthakoummane

1
Th Setthathirath

5
2
6
3

Th Khun Bulom
Th Ky Huong

National Stadium

Th Phnom Penh

Th Samsénethai

14

Th Saigon

17

Nam Phu

Colonial Villas

Th Don Chan
Th Don Chan

Internet Cafes
True Coffee Internet

31
28
38
25
19

20
26
33

3715
40
34

16
12
9
11

Wat Xieng Nyean

Th Manthatourath

Th Nokeokoummane

Banque pour le Commerce Extérieur Lao

Th Sihom
Th Hengboun

Poppy's Pharmacy & Beauty

Th Setthathirath

8
30
10
13

35

Th François Ngm

22

Night Market

Mekong River

Th Chao Anou

Wat Chanthabuli
18
4
41

Joint Development Bank ATM

Th Luang Prabang
Th Khun Buong

36
23

Th In Paeng

29

Th Sithane

Don Chan

Central Vientiane

LAOS VIENTIANE

overlooks the Mekong so you can run on the treadmill and watch passing boats. Loads of room to enjoy its decent equipment: rowing machines, spinning bikes, weightlifting apparatus. There was a pool being built when we visited, and regular Zumba and Pilates classes too.

Wat Sok Pa Luang   MASSAGE, SPA
(Map p319; www.facebook.com/laosauna; Th Sok Pa Luang; ☺1-7pm) Healthy herbal sauna Lao-style, in the leafy grounds of Wat Sok Pa Luang. A witch's broth of eucalyptus, lemongrass, basil and lime is stirred in a giant cauldron, the fumes of which are then fed into the sauna (20,000K). Traditional massage (40,000K) and meditation class (free) are also available at 3pm on Saturday.

★Oasis   MASSAGE
(Map p320; Th François Ngin; ☺9am-9pm) Cool, clean and professional, this is an excellent central place to enjoy a foot massage (50,000K), a Lao-style body massage (60,000K) or a peppermint body scrub (200,000K), to name a few. The best-value spa in the city.

🎓 Courses

Lao-language courses are held at the Centre Culturel et de Coopération Linguistique (p325).

Cooking

Villa Lao   COOKING COURSE
(Map p319; ☎021-242292, 021-242291; www.villalaos.com; off Th Nong Douang; half-day class per person US$25) Courses at beautiful Thongbay Guesthouse are organised on demand (maximum 10 people) and start at 9am, finishing at 4pm. The price includes a trip to the market for ingredients.

Meditation & Yoga

Foreigners are welcome at a regular Saturday afternoon meditation sitting at Wat Sok Pa Luang. The session runs from 3pm until 4.30pm with an opportunity to ask questions afterwards.

Vientiane Yoga Studio   YOGA
(Map p319; ☎020 58872027; www.vientianeyoga. weebly.com; 90min class 80,000K; ☺9am & 6pm Mon-Fri, 8.30am, 1.30pm, 3.30pm & 5.30pm Sat) Hatha, Vinyasa, Yin and advanced (upside down)

COPE VISITOR CENTRE

Since the end of the Secret War in Laos (1964–73; Laos' clandestine conflict running parallel to the Vietnam War) over 20,000 people have fallen victim to unexploded ordnance (UXO) – many of them children. A 10-minute bike ride from the city centre, the excellent **COPE Visitor Centre** (ສູນພື້ນຟູຄົນພິການແຫ່ງຊາດ; Map p319; ☑ 021 218427, 021 88427; www.copelaos.org; Th Khu Vieng; donations more than welcome; ⊙9am-6pm) **FREE** is an inspiring not-for-profit organisation dedicated to supporting victims, and providing clinical mentoring and training programs for local staff in the manufacture of artificial limbs and related rehabilitation activities. COPE makes high-tech but low-cost artificial limbs, transforming the lives of people who've had to make do with their own improvised limbs. In addition to UXO victims, COPE helps children with leprosy, polio and club foot.

The UXO exhibition is fascinating, with photographs portraying the salvaged lives of victims, as well as the 'Cave' cinema, a bunker-style screening room showing a number of documentaries. Take a free tour around the centre accompanied by an English-speaking guide.

yoga, as well as Pilates at a new premises in a quiet garden down a secluded street. Nanci the instructor has 10 years' experience. To get here follow the first sidestreet off Th Sokpaluang after Th Khouvieng.

☞ Tours

★ Tuk Tuk Safari
CULTURAL TOUR

(☑+856 20 5433 3089; www.tuktuksafari.com; adult/child under 12yr US$70/40; ⊙8am-5pm) This community-conscious tour company gets under the skin of Vientiane in a tuk-tuk. Tour guide Ere spirits you to a Lao market; a silversmith's workshop; behind the scenes at a restaurant helping street kids learn to become chefs (before sampling their delicious food!); and finally, the inspiring COPE Visitor Centre for UXO victims.

Beyond this sample tour there are many other options and, given fair warning, the husband-and-wife team can devise tailored tours for people with disabilities.

Vientiane By Cycle
BICYCLE TOUR

(Map p319; ☑020 5581 2337; www.vientianeby cycle.com; full/half day 500,000/450,000K) Meander by bike along Vientiane's riverfront, through affluent and poor suburbs, and past schools and temples as you experience another side of the city. Run by Aline. Starts 8am at Kong View on the Mekong.

⚜ Festivals & Events

Pi Mai
FESTIVAL

(⊙Apr) Lao New Year is celebrated once more in mid-April for this mass water fight. Be warned – drunk driving and theft go through the roof at these times so remain vigilant of your driver and wallet!

Bun Nam
SPORTS

(Bun Suang Héua; ⊙Oct) A huge annual event at the end of *pansăh* (the Buddhist rains retreat) in October, during which boat races are held on the Mekong River. Rowing teams from all over the country, as well as from Thailand, China and Myanmar, compete. The riverbank is lined with food stalls, temporary discos, carnival games and beer gardens for three days and nights.

Bun Pha That Luang
CULTURAL

(That Luang Festival; ⊙Nov) Bun Pha That Luang, usually held in early November, is the largest temple fair in Laos. Festivities begin with a *wéean téean* (circumambulation) around Wat Si Muang, followed by a procession to Pha That Luang, which is illuminated all night for a week. The festival climaxes on the morning of the full moon with the *đák bàht* ceremony, in which thousands of monks from across Laos receive alms.

🛏 Sleeping

Expect clean, basic guesthouses, great midrange hotels and decent cool dorms.

★ Mixay Paradise Guesthouse
GUESTHOUSE $

(Map p320; ☑021-254223; laomixayparadise@ yahoo.com; Th François Ngin; s/d with fan & shared bathroom 100,000/130,000K, r with air-con & bathroom 150,000K; ❄🤍🛜) There are 50 rooms with pastel-coloured walls, some of which have balconies, bathrooms and air-con. Spotless floors, a lovely lobby cafe with lime-green walls, and a lift. Safety deposit lockers cost 50,000K. One of your best, most hygienic budget options in the city.

 LAOS VIENTIANE

Mixok Inn Guesthouse GUESTHOUSE **$**
(Map p320; ☑021-254781; cnr Th Setthathirath & Th Nokéokoummane; r incl breakfast 150,000K; ☺❋⏁) Mixok Inn excels with fresh tiled floors, white walls, simple furniture, flat-screen TVs, bathrooms and a great downstairs cafe. Friendly staff too. Don't confuse it with below-par Mixok Guest House a few yards west of it.

Syri 1 Guest House GUESTHOUSE **$**
(Map p320; ☑021-212682; Th Saigon; r 30,000-150,000K; ❋@⏁) Syri sits on a quiet street and has been a traveller fave for many years, and with good reason: generously sized rooms (air-con and fan, en suite and shared bathroom), recesses to chill, a DVD lounge, bikes for rent, and tailored bike tours of the city. And 100% friendly.

Lucky Backpacker HOSTEL **$**
(Map p320; ☑021-255636; Th Manthatourath; dm/d 40,000/140,000K; ❋) A new, clean and friendly joint, with spacious dorms, decent showers, and a private double room with air-con but no window. Beds have lockers underneath but no locks. Friendly management.

Niny Backpacker HOSTEL **$**
(Map p320; ☑020 96663333; ninybackpack@hotmail.com; Th Nokèokoummane; dm 50,000K; ⏁) A new hostel with cheerful orange walls, and fresh dorms accommodating four or 20 berths. Safety deposit lockers, free breakfast (toast and eggs) and clean facilities. There's no self-catering.

Vientiane Backpackers Hostel HOSTEL **$**
(Map p320; ☑020 97484277; www.vientiane backpackershostel.com; Th Nokèokoummane; dm 40,000K; @⏁) This fresh hostel has three mixed dorms for 12, 16 and 20 people. There's a cafe selling burgers and shakes; laundry services; free wi-fi; and bike (10,000K) and scooter (70,000K) rental. Bathrooms and showers are modern and clean; there's no self-catering. Free breakfast, ticketing and visa services, plus friendly management.

Sport Guesthouse GUESTHOUSE **$**
(Map p320; ☑021-241352; sportguesthouse.sg@hotmail.com; Th François Ngin; with fan/air-con r 80,000/100,000K, tr 120,000/150,000K; ❋⏁) Rooms here are a little boxy but fragrant, with spotless bathrooms and polished tiled floors, and what the place lacks in refinement it makes up for in amenities, including a decent cafe and juice bar, ticketing servic-es, bike (10,000K) and scooter (60,000K) rental, and friendly staff.

★Lani's House GUESTHOUSE **$$**
(Map p320; ☑021-215639; www.lanishouse.com; Th Setthathirath; s/d US$45/65; ℗❋⏁) Down a narrow sidestreet leading to a temple, this white art-deco-accented villa evokes Indochina with its authentic Parisien chandeliers, antique furniture, lobby peppered with stunning images of old Laos, and coy carp turning orange arabesques in an ornamental pool. Hard to believe you're in the city centre! Huge rooms with shabby-chic armoire, cable TV and fridge. Pure taste.

★Auberge Sala Inpeng GUESTHOUSE **$$**
(Map p320; ☑021-242021; www.salalao.com; Th In Paeng; r incl breakfast US$30-50; ❋⏁⊞) Unlike anything else in the city, this vernal oasis of wood cabanas and a handsome traditional Laotian house is set in gardens spilling with tamarind and champa flowers. The grander rooms whiff of rustic chic with bathroom and air-con. And although the cheaper cabanas are small, they're bursting with atmosphere. Meanwhile staff are as welcoming as a slice of home.

Vayakorn House HOTEL **$$**
(Map p320; ☑021-241911; www.vayakorn.biz; 91 Th Nokèokoummane; s/d/tr US$17/22/23; ☺❋⏁) Vayakorn has 21 clean, simple rooms, with doubles and twins, and cramped single rooms, with TV, air-con and city views. There's a welcoming lobby and very helpful staff. Accepts credit cards. Wi-fi up to the 2nd floor.

✖ Eating

Vientiane is celebrated for its global spectrum of cuisine, as well as its bakeries.

★Lao Kitchen LAOTIAN **$**
(Map p320; ☑021-254332; www.lao-kitchen.com; Th Hengboun; mains 40,000-50,000K; ⏱11am-10pm; ☺🍴) This superb contemporary Lao restaurant is unfailingly creative in its execution of trad-Lao dishes. Colourful walls, indie tunes and decent service complement a menu spanning stews to Luang Prabang sausage and *laap* variations, stir-fried Morning Glory, spring rolls, Mekong fish soup and palate-friendly sorbets. Choose the level of your piquant sauce with a one to three grading.

TOP BAKERIES

Le Banneton (Map p320; Th Nokèok-oummane; breakfast 45,000K; ☺7am-9pm; ☻) Get here early before the country's best croissants run out. The simple interior makes for a nice place to read a newspaper over a tart, salad, panini or tasty omelette, or you can sit outside on the small terrace. Tasty breakfasts and homemade marmalade and jam.

JoMa Bakery Café (Map p320; Th Setthathirath; mains 29,000K; ☺7am-9pm Mon-Sat; ☻☎❖) Vientiane's most contemporary bakery has a friendly, air-con chilled atmosphere and cornucopia of lush salads (30,000K) and bespoke subs and bagels – choose from salami, ham, salmon, chicken, cheese and salad fillings. It also serves brownies, cake and delicious yoghurt. Comfy couches, free wi-fi, unfailing cleanliness, and superb staff.

Pho Dung   LAOTIAN $
(Map p320; ☑021-213775; 158 Th Hengboun; noodle soup 12,000-15,000K; ☺6am-2pm) This excellent *főe* (rice noodle soup) diner is packed with a melting pot of locals and travellers. Choose from pork, beef or chicken noodle soup. Run by a friendly Vietnamese family, the gargantuan bowls here are served Lao-style, ie with heaps of optional seasonings and immense plates of fresh veggies and herbs.

Ban Anou Night Market   LAOTIAN $
(Map p320; meals 10,000-15,000K; ☺5-10pm) Setting up on a small street off the northern end of Th Chao Anou every evening, this atmospheric open-air market dishes up Lao cuisine, from grilled meats to chilli-based dips with vegetables and sticky rice.

Phimphone Market   SELF-CATERING $
(Map p320; 94/6 Th Setthathirath; ☺7am-9pm Mon-Sat; ☎) This self-catering oasis stocks everything from gleaming fresh veg, Western magazines, ice cream, imported salami, bread, biscuits and chocolate, as well as Western toiletries. It also stocks Hobo maps of the city.

Little Hanoi   VIETNAMESE $
(Map p320; Th Fa Ngum; 40,000K; ☺9am-11.30pm; ☎) This mercifully chilled restaurant on the waterfront is peaceful and shadowy, with wall-mounted antique drums and soft lighting that transports you to the artist quarter of its eponymous city. The menu is varied and ranges from Hanoi soup with beef, spring rolls, papaya salad and fried Morning Glory to Hanoi duck with rice, and fried squid in celery.

★**Makphet Restaurant**   LAOTIAN $$
(Map p320; ☑021-260587; contact@makphet-restaurant.org; Th In Paeng; mains 60,000K; ☺11am-10.30pm; ☎✐❖) ✐ Makphet, managed by Friends International (www.friends-international.org), helps disadvantaged kids build a future as chefs and waiters. The stunning villa sits in lush gardens lit at night with fairy lights. The interior is no less inviting, the service a cut above average, and the cuisine superb with Lao fare like *lahp*. Try the red hibiscus sorbet and coconut ice cream. Romantic.

Istanbul   TURKISH $$
(Map p320; ☑020 77978190; Th François Ngin; mains 70,000-100,000K; ☺9.30am-10.30pm; ☎) An authentic slice of Istanbul, this welcoming place has doner and shish kebabs, meatballs, hummus and falafel. Try the Iskender kebab – grilled beef with pepper sauce, yoghurt and green chilli. All meats are fully marinated and the super-charged Turkish coffee will put a spring in your step.

Sputnik Burger   AMERICAN $$
(Map p320; ☑030-9376504; www.facebook.com/SputnikBurger; Th Setthathirath; mains 45,000-75,000K; ☺11am-10pm; ☎) Cool new burger joint featuring great beef burgers with Swiss cheese, bacon, eggplant and many other additions and sauces. Salads and milkshakes too. Exposed brick walls, low lighting and a bisected VW bug outside – which serves as two little booths – make this a fun spot.

Osaka   JAPANESE $$
(Map p320; ☑021-213352; Th Nokèokoummane; mains 30,000-80,000K; ☺8am-10pm) A lively hole-in-the-wall, with slatted chairs on a plant-filled verandah, cosy Osaka tempts you inside with its lipstick-red booths. There are oodles of noodle variations, sashimi, veggie dishes, sushi and tempura.

★**Pimentón**   SPANISH $$$
(Map p320; ☑021-215506; www.pimentonrestaurant-vte.com; Th Nokeokoummane; mains 80,000-170,000K; ☺11am-2.30pm & 5-10pm Mon-Sat; ☻☎) With its high ceilings and sleek bar

this is widely considered the best steak restaurant in the capital. Only the choicest cuts of sirloin, chateaubriand and ribeye make it to its fiery open grill. At lunch there's tapas – think imported *jamón ibérico, calamares* and charcuterie of cured meats. Run by a lovely husband-and-wife team.

Drinking & Nightlife

Khop Chai Deu
BAR

(Map p320; ☑ 021-223022; www.inthira.com; Th Setthathirath) KCD boasts low-lit interiors and a sophisticated drinks list, plus activities like speed dating and women's arm wrestling. Upstairs on the 3rd floor there's a super-slick bar with great views.

iBeam
BAR

(Map p320; ☑ 021-254528; Th Setthathirath; ⊙11am-11pm; 🛜) iBeam balances old-world service with contemporary style. Bar eats like croquettes, nachos con carne and marinated vegetables, plus an excellent wine list. Wednesday is ladies night and nets you 50% off. Thursday evenings there's live jazz.

Spirit House
COCKTAIL BAR

(Map p319; ☑ 021-262530; Th Fa Ngoum; cocktails 40,000K; ⊙7am-11pm; 🛜) This traditional Lao house facing the Mekong has a well-stocked bar with enough cocktails on the menu to keep a roué smiling. Chillsome tunes complement the dark woods and comfy couches of its stylish interior.

Bor Pennyang
BAR

(Map p320; ☑ 020 7873965; Th Fa Ngoum; ⊙10am-midnight) Overlooking mother Mekong, a cast of locals, expats, bar girls and travellers assemble at this tin-roofed, wood-raftered watering hole to gaze at the sunset over nearby Thailand. Western tunes, pool tables and a huge bar to drape yourself over, as well as international football and rugby on large flat-screen TVs.

☆ Entertainment

By law, entertainment venues close at 11.30pm.

Centre Culturel et de Coopération Linguistique
CINEMA

(French Cultural Centre; Map p320; ☑ 021-215764; www.ambafrance-laos.org; Th Lan Xang; admission free, cinema 10,000K; ⊙9.30am-6.30pm Mon-Fri, to noon Sat) Dance, art exhibitions, literary discussions and live music all take place in this Gallic hive of cultural activity. As well as cult French films – shown weekends at 3pm

(kids) and 6.30pm (adults) – the centre also offers French and Lao language lessons.

Shopping

Numerous handicraft and souvenir boutiques are dotted around streets radiating from Nam Phu, particularly Th Pangkham and Th Setthathirath.

★ T'Shop Lai Gallery
BEAUTY, HOMEWARES

(Map p320; www.laococo.com/tshoplai.htm; off Th In Paeng; ⊙8am-8pm Mon-Sat, 10am-6pm Sun) Vientiane's finest shop. Imagine a melange of aromas: coconut, aloe vera, honey, frangipani and magnolia, all of them body oils, soaps, sprays, perfumes and lip balms; bangles, prints, fountain pens... These wonderful products are made with sustainable, locally sourced products by disadvantaged women who make up the Les Artisans Lao cooperative.

Indochina Handicrafts
HANDICRAFTS

(Map p320; ☑ 021-223528; Th Setthathirath; ⊙10am-7pm) Laos' version of the Old Curiosity Shop, this enchanting den of Buddha statuary, antique Ho Chi Minh and Mao busts, Russian wristwatches and communist memorabilia, Matchbox cars, medals, snuff boxes and vintage serving trays is a visit that shouldn't be missed. Next to Carterie Du Laos; look for the plant-crowded exterior.

Dee Traditional Antique Textiles
HANDICRAFTS

(Map p320; ☑ 020 55519908; khamtanh44@hotmail.com; Th Setthathirath; ⊙8am-9pm) It might not look much from outside but within this chilled shop, stuffed from floor to ceiling with fine silk scarves and Akha tapestries, there are great bargains to be found. Has the best-value quality scarves on the block.

LAOS VIENTIANE

DOS & DON'TS IN LAOS

➡ Always ask permission before taking photos.

➡ Don't prop your feet on chairs or tables while sitting.

➡ Refrain from touching people on the head, or having any physical contact with monks.

➡ Remove your shoes before entering homes or temple buildings.

➡ Don't hold hands or kiss in a Buddhist temple.

Book Café BOOKS
(Map p320; Th Hengboun; ☉8am-8pm Mon-Fri)
Vientiane's best-stocked secondhand book-shop sells travel guides, thrillers and inform-ative books on Laos' culture and history.

ⓘ Information

EMERGENCY
Ambulance (☎1195)
Fire (☎1190)
Police (☎1191)
Tourist Police (Map p320; ☎021 251 128; Th Lan Xang)

INTERNET ACCESS
Wi-fi is free at many of Vientiane's cafes.
True Coffee Internet (Map p320; Th Set-thathirath; per hour 8000K; ☉9am-9pm) The coolest spot to catch up on your emails, this roomy cafe also has brownies, yoghurt and fresh juices. Skype on its terminals. Free wi-fi.

MEDIA
Laos' only English-language newspaper is the hopelessly state-censored *Vientiane Times*, while *Sabaidee* is a free monthly glossy with lush photos and quality articles on Lao life, plus help-ful listings of upcoming events.

MEDICAL SERVICES
Vientiane's medical facilities will do for broken bones and the diagnosis of dengue fever and malaria, but for anything more serious cross to Thailand for the nearby **Aek Udon Interna-tional Hospital** (☎042 342555; Th Phosri) which can dispatch an ambulance, or in critical situations an airlift, to take you to Udon Thani. The Friendship Bridge is closed between 10pm and 6am, but Thai/Lao immigration will open for ambulances.
Alliance International Medical Center (Map p319; ☎021-513095; www.aimclao.com; Th Luang Prabang) This hospital is fresh and clean and treats basic ailments like broken bones and dispenses antibiotics.
Australian Embassy Clinic (Map p319; ☎021-353840; Th Thadeua; ☉8.30am-5pm Mon-Fri) For nationals of Australia, Britain, Canada, Papua New Guinea and New Zealand only. This clinic's Australian doctor treats minor problems by appointment; it doesn't have emergency facilities. Accepts cash or credit cards.
Poppy's Pharmacy & Beauty (Map p320; ☎030-9810108; Th Hengboun; ☉8am-10pm) Bright and clean, this modern, well-stocked pharmacy is great for toiletries, cosmetics, sun cream, malaria pills (not Larium), and sleeping tablets for long bus journeys.

MONEY
Licensed money-changing booths can be found along Th Setthathirath. Banks change cash and travellers cheques and issue cash advances (mostly in kip, but occasionally in US dollars and Thai baht) against Visa and/or MasterCard. Most ATMs work with foreign cards.
Bank of Ayudhya (Map p320; ☎021-214575; 79/6 Th Lan Xang) Cash advances on Visa cards here carry a 1.5% commission.
Banque pour le Commerce Extérieur Lao (BCEL; Map p320; cnr Th Pangkham & Th Fa Ngoum; ☉8.30am-7pm Mon-Fri, to 3pm Sat & Sun) Best rates; longest hours. Exchange booth on Th Fa Ngum and three ATMs attached to the main building.
Joint Development Bank (Map p320; 75/1-5 Th Lan Xang) Usually charges the lowest com-mission on cash advances. Also has an ATM.

POST
Post, Telephone & Telegraph (PTT; Map p320; ☎020 22206362; Th Saylom; ☉8am-5pm Mon-Fri, to noon Sat & Sun) Come here for post restante, stamps, wiring money and courier service.

TELEPHONE
International calls can be made from most inter-net cafes for about 5000K per minute, though it's better if you can Skype.

TOURIST INFORMATION
Tourist Information Centre (NTAL; Map p320; ☎021-212248; www.ecotourismlaos.com; Th Lan Xang; ☉8.30am-noon & 1.30-4pm) A worthwhile tourist information centre with easy-to-use descriptions of each province, helpful staff who speak decent English, as well as brochures and regional maps. At the time of writing there were plans to move the office to Nam Phu fountain in the centre of the traveller area.

TRAVEL AGENCIES
Green Discovery (Map p320; ☎021-264528; www.greendiscoverylaos.com; Th Setthathi-rath) Deservedly the country's most respected adventure tours specialist. As well as kayaking, cycling, ziplining and trekking trips, it can also help with travel arrangements.
Lin Travel Service (Map p320; ☎021-218707, 021-28190166; 239 Th Hanoi/Phnom Penh; ☉8.30am-9pm) Excellent travel agent run by Mrs Lin; international and domestic flights, bus tickets and hotel bookings.
Chantha Guesthouse Ticketing (Map p320; ☎021-243204; Th Setthathirath; ☉8.30am-9pm) Mrs Phanthnavong has a desk in the lobby of Chantha Guest House, and organises bus and plane tickets

ⓘ Getting There & Away

AIR

Wattay International Airport is the main transport hub for the rest of the country. Beside it is the rickety domestic terminal. The newly established **Lao Skyway** (p378) flies from Vientiane to domestic destinations, while **Lao Airlines** (☑ 021-512028; Wattay Airport International Terminal; ⏰ 4am-8pm) covers domestic and international destinations.

BUS & SŎRNGTǍAOU

Buses use three different stations in Vientiane.

For buses to China, contact **Tong Li Bus Company** (☑ 021-242657) at the Northern Bus Station. For Vietnam, **SDT** (☑ 720175) has buses leaving daily from the Southern Bus Station: for Hanoi (230,000K, 24 hours) via Vinh (180,000K, 16 hours), and for Danang (230,000K) via Hué (180,000K, 19 hours). On Monday, Thursday and Sunday they leave at 6pm. For Ho Chi Minh City

change at Danang. Some buses to Vietnam also leave from the Northern Bus Station.

Northern Bus Station (Th Asiane) The Northern Bus Station is exactly 9km northwest of the centre, and serves all points north of Vang Vieng, including China and some buses to Vietnam. Destinations and the latest ticket prices are listed in English.

Southern Bus Station (Rte 13 South) The Southern Bus Station is commonly known as Dong Dok Bus Station or just *khíw lot lák káo* (Km 9 Bus Station). It is 9km out of town and serves everywhere south. Buses to Vietnam will usually stop here.

Talat Sao Bus Station (Map p320; ☑ 216507; Th Khu Vieng) International VIP buses to Thailand's Udon Thani (100,000K) leave here at 10.30am and 11.30am. A VIP bus for Bangkok also leaves from here.

ⓘ Getting Around

Central Vientiane is all accessible on foot.

BUSES FROM VIENTIANE

Northern Bus Station

DESTINATION	FARE (K)	DURATION (HR)	DISTANCE (KM)
Huay Xai	230,000	30-35	869
Kunming	635,000	30	781
Luang Namtha	200,000	18	676
Luang Prabang	110,000	11	384
Phonsavan	110,000-150,000	9-11	394
Sam Neua	170,000-210,000	15-17	612
Udomxai	170,000-190,000	13-17	578
Vang Vieng	65,000	4	161

Southern Bus Station

DESTINATION	FARE (K)	DURATION (HR)	DISTANCE (KM)
Attapeu	220,000	22-24	812
Lak Sao	85,000	7-9	334
Pakse	110,000-170,000	14-16	677
Phonsavan	sleeper 110,000-150,000	6-7	394
Savannakhet	75,000-120,000	8-11	457
Tha Khaek	65,000-85,000	7	332

Talat Sao Bus Station

DESTINATION	FARE (K)	DURATION (HR)	DISTANCE (KM)
Nong Khai	17,000	1½	95
Udon Thani	22,000	2	76

GETTING TO THAILAND: VIENTIANE TO NONG KHAI

Getting to the border The Thai–Lao Friendship Bridge at the Tha Na Long/Nong Khai border is 22km southeast of Vientiane. The easiest way to cross is on the comfortable Thai–Lao International bus (22,000K, 1½ hours), which leaves Vientiane's Talat Sao Bus Station for the border roughly every hour from 7.30am till 6pm. The VIP bus, which continues on to Bangkok (248,000K), leaves Talat Sao daily at 6pm. Alternatively, catch a taxi (300B) or jumbo (four-wheeled tuk-tuk, seating 12; 250B), or public bus 14 from Talat Sao (15,000K) between 6am and 6.30pm.

It's also possible to cross the bridge by train, as tracks have been extended from Nong Khai's train station 3.5km into Laos, terminating at Dongphasy Station, about 13km from central Vientiane. From Nong Khai there are two daily departures (9.30am and 4pm, fan/air-con 20/50B, 15 minutes) and border formalities are taken care of at the respective train stations.

At the border Travellers from most countries can travel visa-free to Thailand.

Moving on From the Thai border catch a tuk-tuk (20B) to Nong Khai train station where a sleeper train leaves for Bangkok at 6.20pm and costs US$23/37 for a 2nd-class/sleeper ticket.

For information on doing this crossing in reverse, see p727.

TO/FROM THE AIRPORT

Wattay International Airport is about 4km northwest of the city centre. Fixed-fare airport taxis cost US$8 into town. Alternatively, walk 500m to the airport gate where you can get a shared tuk-tuk for about 20,000K. Official tuk-tuk tariffs from the city centre list the airport as a 60,000K ride. Finally, there's a new metered service which gives you a chance to keep any eye on your fare; call **Tourist Taxi** (☑ 1420; ☉ 24hr). A taxi to the airport costs around 50,000K.

BICYCLE, MOTORCYCLE & CAR

Bicycles can be rented for 10,000K per day, and scooters for 70,000K.

Avis (Map p320; ☑ 021-223867, 020 22864488; www.avis.la; Th Setthathirath; ☉ 8.30am-6.30pm Mon-Fri, 8.30am-1pm Sat & Sun) Hires quality cars from small sedans (US$55) to sturdy 4WDs (US$77) per day. If you want to drive outside Vientiane it will incur a surcharge to cover the driver's keep. You can even leave the car at your destination for a charge. Third-party insurance as standard.

First-One Motorbike Rental (Map p320; ☑ 020 55528299; Th François Ngin; scooters per day 70,000K; ☉ 8.30am-6pm) Loads of decent scooters for tootling around the city. Enquire within to see the heavy-duty dirtbikes for rental.

TUK-TUK

Many tuk-tuk have a laminated list of vastly inflated tourist prices, and won't budge for less than the price already agreed upon with the other drivers. You can also flag down shared, fixed-route tuk-tuk (with passengers already in them), which cost around 20,000K, depending on your destination. Avoid buying hash from these drivers: they're often in collusion with local police.

NORTHERN LAOS

Whether you're here to trek, zipline, learn to cook, kayak, cycle or try a homestay, a visit to Laos' mountainous north is unforgettable. Bordered by China, Vietnam and Myanmar, there's a fascinating cast of ethnic peoples here. Hidden amid this rugged simplicity is Southeast Asia's premier Shangri La, Luang Prabang.

Vang Vieng ວັງວຽງ

☑ 023 / POP 33,612

Your first glimpse of Vang Vieng (VV) is like looking at an oriental silk painting, for the town, crouched low on the banks of the Nam Song (Song River), is backdropped by magnificent karsts like the sawtoothed back of some sleeping titan. Imagine rice paddies, caves, river tubing and endless coffee houses to chill in. This is one of the most beautiful places in the country and its outdoor offerings, from climbing and cycling to kayaking and ziplining, will keep you busy.

☉ Sights & Activities

Laos' HQ of outdoor pursuits has ziplining, tubing, cycling, trekking, caving, kayaking and climbing.

Kayaking is popular, with day trips (120,000K per person) typically taking you down a few rapids and stopping at caves and villages. Before using an operator, check guides' credentials and that they issue life jackets and have medical kits.

Floating down the Nam Song in a tractor inner tube (55,000K rental, 60,000K deposit), beneath jungle and karst, is a traveller rite of passage. There are barely any bars to detain you now, so just soak up the ride. Return by 6pm or invite a penalty of 20,000K. A tuk-tuk to the start of your riverine adventure costs 10,000K each.

Caves

The stunning limestone karsts around Vang Vieng are honeycombed with tunnels and caverns, and after tubing, caving has to be the town's main draw. You can buy a map and do the caves yourself, or it's possible to go in an organised group.

The most famous cave, **Tham Jang** (ຖ້ຳຈັງ; admission 17,000K), 1km south of town, was used as a hideout from marauding Yunnanese Chinese in the early 19th century. A set of stairs leads up to the main cavern entrance. There's also a cool spring at the foot of the cave.

Another popular cave is **Tham Phu Kham** (Blue Lagoon, ຖ້ຳພູຄຳ; admission 10,000K), known for its sapphire water pool referred to as the blue lagoon, where, sadly, a tacky slide has been erected, but you can still jump into its cool midst from high up in an overhanging tree. To reach it, cross the bamboo footbridge then walk or pedal 7km along a scenic, unsealed road to Ban Na Thong, from where you have to walk 1km to a hill on the northern side of the village. It's a tough final 200m climb but worth it for a dip in the blue stream afterwards.

Tham Sang (Elephant Cave; admission 5000K), 13km north along Rte 13, is a small cavern containing a few Buddha images and a Buddha 'footprint', plus the elephant-shaped stalactite that gives the cave its name.

☞ Tours

Green Discovery   ADVENTURE TOUR
(☑ 023-511230; www.greendiscoverylaos.com; Th Luang Prabang; 1-day cycling tour per person US$25-34 (depending on group size), half-/full-day rock climbing US$27/36) Vang Vieng's most reliable operator offers trekking, rock climbing, caving and ziplining. Try the new Vang Vieng Challenge: climbing a waterfall attached by via ferrata, abseiling down, overnighting in a mountain hut, riding eight ziplines then trekking down the mountain. You need to be fit. It costs from US$100 per person.

★ **Adam's Rock Climbing School**   ADVENTURE TOUR
(☑ 020 55010832, 020 56564499; www.laosclimbing.com; opposite the hospital; half-/full-day climbing 180,000/260,000K, 2-day course US$100, private climbing guide (for advanced climbers) 320,000K) The only dedicated climbing outfit in town, with experienced, multilingual guides and sturdy kit. Adam is a great guy and can also take you kayaking.

🛏 Sleeping

Increasingly, midrangers and boutique hotels are moving in as VV ditches its dreads in favour of a stylish coiffure. Avoid the ugly town and head downriver or to the other side of the Song.

LAOS VANG VIENG

A FRESH START

Back in '99 Vang Vieng was a little-known affair where travellers came to float down the river on tractor inner tubes, smoke the odd spliff and explore its fantastical caves. Then the rumour was out – Vang Vieng was Southeast Asia's next hedonistic mecca. Lao locals were quick to erect more guesthouses, then the drugs got heavier, the party darker.

By 2009 makeshift rave platforms were spawning along the tubing route, with many ignoring the natural environment in favour of reefer, methamphetamine and opium cocktails. By 2011 a staggering 20-odd tourists were dying each year from heart attacks, drowning and broken necks, plus there were frequent drug busts. In August 2012 most of the river bar owners were ordered by the government to shut down, thus ending a dark chapter in the town's history.

The upshot? Vang Vieng is no longer party central: the 2012 government rout left just 12 bars remaining, which now operate in strict rotation with four open per day.

Vang Vieng

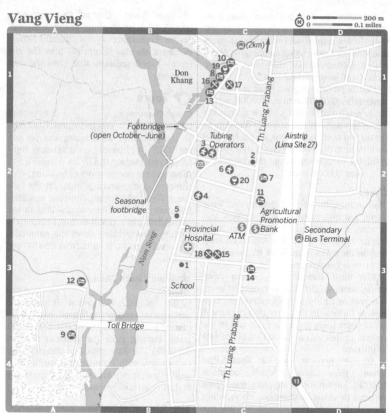

🛏 Over the River & Out Of Town

★ Vang Vieng Organic Farm
GUESTHOUSE **$**

(☑023-511220; www.laofarm.org; dm 30,000K, r 40,000-150,000K, deluxe cliff-facing bungalows 180,000K; 🅿@🛜👶) 🌿 Located by the Nam Song in an idyllically quiet spot a few kilometres out of town, this organic farm has sparklingly clean cabanas with mosquito nets, bedside lamps, en suites and verandahs looking out onto the soaring cliffs. Up the hill are also three eight-bed dorms in fan-cooled, tin-roofed, spotless buildings. There's also a great restaurant – try the mulberry pancakes or mulberry mojitos!

And if you have time, ask about volunteering for the permaculture program or teaching English to kids. Minimum two weeks. Cooking classes here cost US$30.

★ Maylyn Guest House
GUESTHOUSE **$**

(☑020 55604095; jophus_foley@hotmail. com; bungalow 60,000K, r 100,000-120,000K; 🅿✳🛜👶) Over the bridge and run by gregarious Jo, Maylyn's cosy, well-spaced cabanas afford dramatic views of the karsts. There's also a number of immaculate rooms including a brand new wing of en suite doubles overlooking the river and cliffs with tasteful decor and private balcony. The lush garden is a kids wonderland.

Chez Mango
GUESTHOUSE **$**

(☑020 54435747; www.chezmango.com; r with/ without bathroom 80,000/60,000K; ✳) Located over the bridge, Mango is friendly, scrupulously clean and has seven basic but colourful cabanas (some with bathrooms) in its flowery gardens with private balconies. Shaded by trees there's also a sala to read in. Run by Noé, who also runs the excellent **Vang Vieng Jeep Tours** (☑020 54435747;

Vang Vieng

noedouine@yahoo.fr; minimum group of 4, per person 180,000K) from here, this is a soporific and restful spot. Recommended.

In Town

★ **Champa Lao** GUESTHOUSE $
(☑ 020 58234612; www.facebook.com/champalao bungalows; r without bathroom 70,000K, tr with bathroom 150,000K, cabanas with/without bathroom 120,000/60,000K; @ 🛜) With new Thai owners, this stilted Lao house has basic fan rooms with mozzie nets. The garden, choking on plants, is a delight and you can swing on a hammock while taking in the sunset and karst from its aerial balcony. There are also bungalows down by the riverbank. Bliss.

Pan's Place GUESTHOUSE $
(☑ 023-511484; Th Luang Prabang; dm 30,000K, s/d without bathroom 50,000/64,000K, s/d with bathroom 70,000/88,000K; @ 🛜) Radiating a welcoming vibe, Pan's is a VV backpacking institution. Basic but cosy fan rooms with tiled floors and en suites. Outback are cabanas in a leafy garden, plus a communal chilling area. There's also a little cafe (crepes, fruit salads) and a cinema room upstairs with hundreds of DVDs to choose from.

Nam Song Garden GUESTHOUSE $
(☑ 023-511544; r 80,000K; 🛜) At the northern end of town this higgledy-piggledy hillside affair enjoys one of the best views in town from its leafy garden. Three rooms with private balcony and bathroom, mozzie net, tiled floor, and welcoming rustic interior.

Central Backpacker's Hostel HOSTEL $
(☑ 020 56770677; www.vangviengbackpackers. com; dm 40,000K, r with fan/air-con 100,000/ 150,000K, tr 200,000K; ❋ 🛜) This hostel, with wedding-cake-style architecture, boasts private rooms with fan or air-con and private balcony and TV; comfy, well-spaced dorms; and communal balconies to drink up the view of the cliffs. There's a huge lobby with a cafe and DVD bar, and safety lockers too (BYO lock). Not much atmosphere but lovely and cool and decent value.

Easy Go Hostel HOSTEL $
(☑ 020 55366679; www.easygohostel.com; next to Champa Lao guesthouse; dm 28,000K, r with/ without air-con 100,000/60,000K, tr with air-con 120,000K) Crafted from bamboo and rattan and run by a great team, Easy Go recently refined its accomodation with an eight- and four-berth dorm and eight private rooms. The ace card is its lovely chilling lounge with comfy cushions and flat-screen TV, with even wider-screen views of the cliffs. Friendly.

Inthira Hotel BOUTIQUE HOTEL $$
(☑ 023-511070; www.inthirahotel.com; Th Luang Prabang; standard/superior/deluxe r incl breakfast US$32/43/54; ⊜ ❋ @ 🛜 ⊞) Although on the main drag and not by the river, the Inthira is still a fine place to stay, with oxblood rooms (upstairs) enjoying views of the karsts and the old CIA runway (Lima Site 27). Expect hardwood floors, elegant furniture and spotless bathrooms. The restaurant is pleasant too. Avoid the downstairs rooms simply because they're dark.

Eating

Vang Vieng sees contemporary Lao food mixing it up with Western, and a few affordable French cuisine options. Come evening there are delicious pancakes cooked up opposite the hospital.

★ **Living Room** ASIAN, FUSION $
(☑ 020 54919169; next to Champa Lao guesthouse; mains 30,000K; ⊙ 3-11pm) Classy custard-coloured cafe with unbroken views of the cliffs from its hilltop eyrie, and a romantic place to eat with its low-lit and

LAOS VANG VIENG

exposed brick and bamboo interior. Gazpacho, homemade bread, NZ lamb, spicy beef goulash...this Lao-Austrian affair is in every sense a fusion cafe. The best spot in town for a sunset Bloody Mary.

Le Café De Paris
FRENCH $$

(mains 70,000K; ☺6pm-11pm) The best spot in town for Gallic grub like duck pâté, chicken and mushroom sauce, steak tartare, and boeuf bourguignon. Add to this a cosy interior of vintage film posters and low-lit atmosphere and you have a winner.

Pizza Luka
PIZZA $$

(☑020 98190831; mains 60,000K; ☺6pm-11pm) Based at a pretty wooden Lao house, eat inside Luka's mint-green interior or alfresco in the garden where homemade pizza is baked in a wood-fired oven. Flavoured with sausage, goat cheese, bacon and many more ingredients, the pizzas are decked in sauces made from locally grown vegetables.

Nam Song Garden
ASIAN, FUSION $$

(☑023-511544; mains 50,000K; ☺7am-11.30pm; 🐾) Blissful view of the karsts from this hilltop Franco-Belgian eatery, with a canvas sail

---

GREATEST ZIPS OF VV

It's all about air and cable these days, with the jungles around Vang Vieng criss-crossed with adrenalising ziplines. The following tour outfits combine a trek, kayak, abseil or tubing session with zipping:

Wonderful Tours (☑023-511566; www.wonderfultourslaos.la; Th Khann Muang) has 1200m of cable, the longest ride of which is 380m over the Nam Song.

Nam Thip Tours (☑023-511318, 020 23333616; ☺9am-7pm) has 1km-worth of ziplines across 12 platforms. The zipping follows a visit to Buddha Cave, followed by a swim in the sapphire water of nearby Blue Lagoon.

TCK (☑023-511691, 020 5533901; tck-amazingtour@gmail.com; ☺9am-8pm) boasts 14 ziplines, one abseil and three bridges to cross on its half-day tour.

AK Home Ziplining (☑020 55033665, 020 52349078; tour US$25; ☺9am-12.30pm) offers half-day tubing trips to Tham Nam, combined with 10 zips and a swim at the Blue Lagoon.

---

ceiling and fairy lights galore. The menu spans chicken and pepper sauce, steak, yellow curry, sandwiches, breakfasts, *lahp* variations and sweet and sour dishes.

🍷 Drinking & Nightlife

Vang Vieng has ditched all-night parties in favour of chilling. The last bar shuts at 11.30pm.

Gary's Irish Bar
IRISH PUB

(☑020 58255774; www.irishbar.weebly.com; mains 40,000K; ☺9am-11.30pm) Still the best bar in town thanks to its friendly, unpretentious atmosphere, excellent indie tunes, free pool and fantastic grub like homemade pies, burgers and Lao fare. When there's live international rugby or footy you'll find it on the flat-screen TV. It's also a good spot for breakfast (full Irish). And watch out for live music. If only all bars were like this!

Earth
BAR

(mains 20,000K; ☺5-11.30pm) Made from driftwood and clay, this hip new hillside bar pipes out fine tunes to match the ambience. Check out the sumptuous view of the cliffs from the candlelit garden, between snacking on toasties, waffles, sandwiches and curries. Look for the glowing green sign to find it.

Fluid Bar
BAR

(☑020 59295840; ☺varies; 🐾) Out of town opposite Tham Lom Cave, this river bar has trippy art, mosaics, a relaxing balcony bar, pool table, cool tunes, loungers and hammocks. There is also a menu with Thai dishes. Open in rotation with the other 11 river bars; its hours vary.

ℹ Information

Agricultural Promotion Bank (Th Luang Prabang) Exchanges cash only.

Banque pour le Commerce Extérieur Lao (☺8.30am-3.30pm) Just west of Xayoh Café, does exchanges and cash advances and has a 24-hour ATM.

Post Office (☑023-511009) Beside the old market.

Provincial Hospital (☑023-511604) This modest hospital has X-ray facilities and is fine for broken bones, cuts and malaria. When we visited, the doctor spoke reasonable English.

DANGERS & ANNOYANCES

The Nam Song is lethal when it runs high after the wet season: *never* hire a tube on your own, nor attempt to return after dark.

Since the 2012 clean up, hard drugs are not so widespread, but dope is still around and local police are adept at sniffing it out. If you're caught with a stash of marijuana (or anything else) the normal practice is for police to take your passport and fine you US$600.

ℹ Getting There & Away

From the bus station (Rte 13) 2km north of town, minibuses/VIP buses leave for Luang Prabang (90,000/100,000K, six to eight hours, 168km, several daily), Vientiane (fan/minibus/air-con 40,000/60,000/80,000K, three to 4½ hours, 156km, several daily) and a new quick(er!) route to Phonsavan (100,000K, minibus only, five hours, 219km, daily at about 9.30am).

Alternatively, *sŏrngtăaou* (pick-up trucks; 40,000K, 3½ to 4½ hours) leave for Vientiane about every 20 minutes from 5.30am until 4.30pm.

Tickets for minibuses and VIP buses are sold at guesthouses, tour agencies and internet cafes in town.

ℹ Getting Around

The township is small enough to walk around with ease. Bicycles/mountain bikes can be rented for around 10,000/30,000K per day, while scooters rent for 50,000K per day (automatics cost 70,000K). For cave sites out of town you can charter *sŏrngtăaou* near the old market site – expect to pay around US$10 per trip up to 20km north or south of town.

Luang Prabang

ຫລວງ ພະ ບາງ

☑ 071 / POP 70,000

Enjoying its 20th year of Unesco protection in 2015, this unique pearl of 33 glittering Buddhist temples is a traveller's dream, with affordable, top-class cuisine and French colonial-era buildings. There are few places in Southeast Asia that can compete with such a special mix of chic refinement and ancient charm as found on Luang Prabang's hallowed peninsula.

The good news is there are still bags of great-value digs and the best things are cheap or free: hiring a bike, chilling by the riverbank, temple-hopping, shopping in the night market, taking a spa or yoga class, and visiting the menthol-blue Kuang Si cascades. Spend a little more and you can eco-trek or take a cooking course – your choices are myriad.

The stamp of the French lives on as freshly baked croissants send out aromas from Gallic-style cafes, and old Indo-Chinese mansions have been reborn as boutique hotels. Prepare to relax and re-plot your itinerary. Luang Prabang will effortlessly seduce you with her fireflies and soporific pace.

◉ Sights

★ **Royal Palace Museum**　　MUSEUM
(ພະຮາຊະວັງຫຼວງພກາວ, Ho Kham; ☑ 071 212470; Th Sisavangvong; admission 30,000K; ⊙ 8-11.30am & 1.30-4pm Wed-Mon, last entry 3.30pm) Evoking traditional Lao and French beaux-arts styles, the former Royal Palace was built in 1904 and was home to King Sisavang Vong (r 1905–59), whose statue stands outside. Within are tasteful, decidedly sober residential quarters, with some rooms preserved much as they were when the king was captured in 1975.

Separate outbuildings display the **Floating Buddha collection** of meditation photographs and the five-piece **Royal Palace Car Collection**.

No single treasure in Laos is more historically resonant than the **Pha Bang**, an 83cm-tall gold-alloy buddha. To find it, walk east along the palace's exterior south terrace and peep in between the bars at the eastern end. In the southeastern corner of the palace gardens, **Wat Ho Pha Bang** was built to house the Pha Bang buddha.

Footwear cannot be worn inside the museum, no photography is permitted and you must leave bags in a locker room to the left-hand side of the main entrance.

★ **Wat Xieng Thong**　　BUDDHIST TEMPLE
(ວັດຊຽງທອງ; off Th Sakkarin; admission 20,000K; ⊙ 8am-5pm) Luang Prabang's best-known monastery is centred on a 1560 *sĭm*. Its roofs sweep low to the ground and there's a stunning 'tree of life' mosaic set on its

Central Luang Prabang

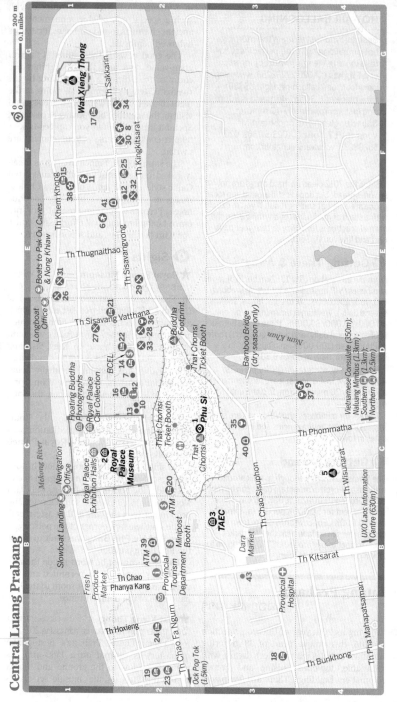

Central Luang Prabang

LAOS LUANG PRABANG

western exterior wall. Close by are several stupas and three compact little chapel halls called *hŏr*. **Hŏr Đại**, shaped like a tall tomb, now houses a standing buddha. The **Hŏr Đại Pha Sai-nyàat**, dubbed La Chapelle Rouge – Red Chapel – by the French, contains a rare reclining Buddha.

Fronted in lavish gilt work, the **Hóhng Kép Mîen** stores a ceremonial carriage, festooned with red-tongued *naga* (river serpents) designed to carry the golden funeral urns of the Lao royalty.

★**UXO Laos Information Centre**   MUSEUM
(☏ 071-252073; www.uxolao.gov.la; admission by donation; ☺ 8-11.45am & 2-4pm Mon-Fri) Behind a manicured new park lies the sobering UXO Laos Information Centre. Visiting here helps to get a grip on the devastation Laos suffered in the Second Indochina War and how nearly 40 years later death or injury from unexploded ordnance remains an everyday reality in several provinces. If you miss it here, there are similar centres in Phonsavan and Vientiane.

Wat Wisunarat   BUDDHIST TEMPLE
(ວັດວິຊຸນ, Wat Visoun; Th Wisunarat; admission 20,000K; ☺ 8am-5pm) Though touted as one of Luang Prabang's oldest operating temples, it's actually an 1898 reconstruction built following the Black Flag raids. As a rather meagre return for paying the entrance fee you can peruse a sizeable collection of old gilded 'Calling for Rain' buddhas with long sinuous arms held to each side. These were placed here, along with some medieval ordination stones, for their protection having been rescued from various abandoned or ravaged temples.

★**Phu Si**   HILL
(ພູສີ; admission 20,000K; ☺ 8am-6pm) Dominating the old city centre and a favourite with sunset junkies, the 100m-tall hill of Phu Si (prepare your legs for a steep 329-step ascent) is crowned by a 24m gilded stupa called **That Chomsi** (admission incl with Phu Si). Viewed from a distance, especially when floodlit at night, the structure seems to float in the hazy air like a chandelier. From the

summit, however, the main attraction is the series of city views.

Wat Xieng Mouane   BUDDHIST TEMPLE

(ວັດຊຽງມວນ; ◎8am-5pm) In the Old Quarter, the ceiling of Wat Xieng Mouane is painted with gold *naga* (mythical serpent-being) and the elaborate *háang thíen* (candle rail) has *naga* at either end. With backing from Unesco and New Zealand, the monks' quarters have been restored as a classroom for training young novices and monks in the artistic skills needed to maintain and preserve Luang Prabang's temples. Among these skills are woodcarving, painting and buddha-casting, all of which came to a virtual halt after 1975.

★TAEC   MUSEUM

(Traditional Arts & Ethnology Centre; ☑071-253364; www.taeclaos.org; admission 25,000K; ◎9am-6pm Tue-Sun) Visiting this professionally presented three-room museum is a must to learn about northern Laos' various hilltribe cultures, especially if planning a trek. There's just enough to inform without overloading a beginner. TAEC is within a former French judge's mansion that was among the city's most opulent buildings of the 1920s.

Pak Ou Caves   CAVE

(Tham Ting; admission to caves 80,000K, return boat tickets per person/boat 65,000/300,000K; ◎boats depart 8.30am-11am) Where rivers Ou and Mekong meet at Ban Pak Ou, two famous caves in the limestone cliff are crammed with myriad buddha images. In the lower cave a photogenic group of buddhas are silhouetted against the stunning riverine backdrop. The upper cave is five minutes' climb up steps (you'll need a torch), 50m into the rock face. Most visitors en route to Pak Ou stop at the 'Lao Lao Village' Ban Xang Hay, famous for its whiskey. Buy boat tickets from the Luang Prabang longboat office.

Tat Kuang Si   PARK

(admission 20,000K, tuk-tuk from Luang Prabang 1 person 250,000K, per person in group of three 85,000K; ◎7.30am-5.30pm) Thirty kilometres southwest of Luang Prabang, Tat Kuang Si is a many-tiered waterfall tumbling over limestone formations into a series of cool, swimmable turquoise pools; the term 'Edenic' doesn't do it justice. Between swinging off ropes into the water, there's a public park with shelters and picnic tables at which you can take lunch. Don't miss **Kuang Si**

Rescue Centre (www.freethebears.org.au/web/Projects/Laos; ◎8.30am-4.30pm) **FREE**, where Asiatic Wild Moon bears, confiscated from poachers who sell them for their precious bile, are given a new lease of life.

🏃 Activities

The best way to explore the city is by bike, taking time to meander through the peninsula past scenes of monastic life and children playing. Basic/mountain bikes cost 15,000/30,000K per day and can be hired along Th Sisavangvong. For easier journeys, automatic one-gear scooters cost around US$20 per day. Motorcycle rental typically costs US$15 a day or US$20 for 24 hours. **KPTD** (☑071-253447, 020 97100771; Th Kitsarat; 250cc dirtbikes per day US$70; ◎8am-5pm) has a wide range of scooters.

Massage & Yoga

Luang Prabang is all about easing your soul and pampering those trekked-out calves.

Hibiscus Massage   MASSAGE

(☑030-9235079; Th Sakkarin; traditional massage from 60,000K; ◎10am-10pm) Set in a former gallery in an old French building, Hibiscus wafts chilled tunes through its silk-draped walls while you get pummelled to perfection.

Spa Garden   MASSAGE, SPA

(☑071-212325; massage 60,000-350,000K, sauna/manicure 30,000/60,000K) Attractive property set amid a flourishing garden, with various relaxation and detox packages.

Luang Prabang Yoga   YOGA

(www.luangprabangyoga.org) Slow down, unwind and sync your spirit to the city's Buddhist vibe with yoga classes taught at serene locations, from lush riverside garden decks at sunrise, to rooftop sunset views. The city's yoga cooperative keeps up-to-date information on classes and venues on its website.

🗺 Courses

Tamarind   COOKING COURSE

(☑020 77770484; www.tamarindlaos.com; Ban Wat Nong; full-day course 285,000K; ◎9am-3pm Mon-Sat) Join Tamarind at its lakeside pavilion for a day's tuition in the art of Lao cuisine, meeting first at its restaurant before heading to the market for ingredients for classic dishes such as *mok pa* (steamed fish in banana leaves). Evening classes are available from 4.30pm for 215,000K, minus the market visit.

☞ Tours

If you have a few days, whimsical Kuang Si waterfalls and Pak Ou Caves are well worth a visit. There's a plethora of tour companies down Th Sisavangvong. We recommend **All Lao Travel** (☑071-253522, 020 55571572; www.alllaoservice.com; Th Sisavangvong; ⊙8am-10pm) as a one-stop shop for flights, boat and VIP bus tickets, and visa extensions.

★**Living Land**   CULTURAL TOUR
(☑020 55199208; www.livinglandlao.com; Ban Phong Van; tour per person 344,000K; ⊙8.30am-noon) Five clicks out of Luang Prabang is this brilliant rice farm where you spend half a day learning how to plant and grow sticky rice, the ubiquitous dish of Laos. This includes prepping the paddy with gregarious water buffalo Susan – expect to be knee deep in glorious mud! You'll never taste rice in the same way.

★**Motolao**   ADVENTURE TOUR
(☑020 54548449; www.motolao.com; Ban Phone Peang Rd, 06030 Luang Prabang; ⊙9am-6pm) This excellent outfit is the country's best motocross tour operator and has terrific two-wheel odysseys exploring authentic Lao life. Top kit, excellent well-maintained bikes.

Green Discovery   OUTDOORS
(☑071-212093; www.greendiscoverylaos.com; 44/3 Th Sisavangvong; ⊙8am-9pm) The daddy of ecotourism in Laos offers safety-conscious kayaking, trekking, mountain biking and multiday trips north.

Tiger Trail   HIKING
(☑071-252655; www.laos-adventures.com; Th Sisavangvong; ⊙8.30am-9pm) ✐ Focusing on socially responsible treks benefitting local people, Tiger Trail offers hikes through Hmong and Khamu villages, cultural bike tours, and off-road mountain biking. All tours can be tailored to include kayaking, rafting or mountain biking.

✦ Festivals & Events

The two most important annual events in Luang Prabang are **Pi Mai** in April, when Luang Prabang is packed to the gills with locals armed with water pistols (book accommodation well in advance), and boat races during **Bun Awk Phansa** in October.

⌂ Sleeping

The most memorable area to stay is on the historic peninsula. There are also decent

guesthouses near the Mekong, a few blocks southwest of the Hmong handicraft night market.

⌂ Old Quarter

Sackarinh Guest House   GUESTHOUSE $
(☑071-254412; Th Sisavangvong; r 160,000K; ❋☞) Easily missed down a side alley in the main street, this simple belle is something of a Tardis, with 14 scrupulously clean, spacious rooms with little interior decor but clean linen and comfy beds.

Bou Pha Guesthouse   GUESTHOUSE $
(☑071-252405; Th Sisavangvong; r 60,000-100,000K; ☞) This takes us back to 1990s Luang Prabang – an old house in the heart of the city with rooms for less than a tenner. It's run by a lovely older couple and the cheapest rooms have a shared bathroom. Upstairs rooms at 100,000K include a street view.

Paphai Guest House   GUESTHOUSE $
(☑071-212752; Th Sisavang Vatthana; r without bathroom 50,000K; ☞) Did the owners forget to put the prices up at this rickety old wooden traditional house near the heart of the peninsula? Rooms are fan-cooled, rattan-walled and have padlocks on the doors. There's a nice garden out front too.

★**Khong Kham Villa**   HOTEL $$
(☑071-212800; off Th Sisavangvong; r US$45; ❋☞) This hidden surprise sits close to the night market, and is bookended between the main street and a temple. Small but lovely rooms with dough-soft beds, tasteful interiors, cable flat-screen TVs, bathrooms, safety deposit boxes and balconies, plus a lush courtyard to read in. Recommended.

En Provence Guesthouse GUESTHOUSE $$
(☑071-212380, 071-212035; www.enprovencelaos.
com; Ban Phong Hua; r incl breakfast 414,000K;
❄🐾) At the peaceful end of the peninsula,
this handsome Lao villa is run by a pleas-
ant Frenchman and has lemon-hued rooms
with flat-screen TVs, darkwood floors and
furniture, and immaculate bathrooms with
roomy bath. Mekong River views, Hmong
bed-runners and a fine restaurant down-
stairs make this a favourite.

Nora Singh Guesthouse GUESTHOUSE $$
(☑071-212035; Th Sisavangvong; r 200,000K;
❄🐾) In the verdant skirts of Mt Phu Si,
this guesthouse has seven clean rooms with
lowered beds, and white and ochre walls
hung with tapestries and private bathroom.
Air-con, hot water and free wi-fi. Central but
peaceful.

**Khoum Xiengthong
Guesthouse** GUESTHOUSE $$
(☑071-212906; www.khoumxiengthong.com; Th
Sisalernsak; r US$65, tr US$80; ❄🐾) Bedecked
in tea lights by night, by day this delightful
guesthouse with a strong whiff of Indo-chic
nestles around a pretty garden. Stone-
floored, white-walled rooms enjoy golden
tapestries and chrome fans: rooms 2 (lower
floor) and 5 (upper floor) are vast and in-
clude four-poster beds.

Villa Senesouk HOTEL $$
(☑071-212074; senesouk@laohotel.com; Th Sakka-
rin; r US$30-40; ❄🐾) The morning monks'
procession passes right outside the cheaper rooms. The upper ones are brighter and
share a wat-view balcony. Wood-panelled
rooms have full mod-cons, with the US$40
options offering additional space.

BIG BROTHER MOUSE

If you want to get involved in improving
local literacy, seek out **Big Brother
Mouse** (BBM; ☑071-254937; www.bigbro-
thermouse.com; Th Sothikuman), a home-
grown initiative that brings the delights
of the written word to children in remote
villages who, for lack of materials, rarely
get the chance to read. If a bunch of you
sponsor a book party (US$350), you
can go with the BBM staff and distribute
books. Alternatively, hang out at the
BBM office for a couple of hours and
read to, or with, the kids who attend
(9am to 11am and 5pm to 7pm).

🛏 Around Luang Prabang

Lemon Laos Backpackers HOSTEL $
(☑071-212500; www.spicylaosbackpacker.com; Th
Noradet; dm with/without air-con 40,000/30,000K;
❄🐾) We like this place for its shabby old-
school backpacker soul; think jamming
guitar, Hendrix mural and cramped dorms.
BBQs and cheap shots add up to a carnival
atmosphere.

LPQ Backpackers Hostel HOSTEL $
(☑020 91138686; lpqbackpackershostel@gmail.
com; Th Wat That; dm 40,000K, r with/without air-
con incl breakfast 120,000/90,000K; ❄) These
are basic digs with plenty of four-berth
dorms, as well as private doubles with bathroom. While they're clean, the place lacks atmosphere and the staff could work on their
interpersonal skills. There's a pool table,
loads of DVDs, noisy safety lockers and the
place is close to the night market.

★ **Sayo Naga Guesthouse** GUESTHOUSE $$
(☑071-212484, 071-252614; www.sayoguesthouse.
com; Th Wat That; r US$5-55) Guarded by *naga*,
this serene white, green-shuttered house
boasts atmospheric rooms with polished
wood floors, bathroom, mozzie nets, fine
furniture and balcony. Add to this bedside
lamps and Hmong throws and it seems a
fair steal. Romantic and well located near
the night market.

Souksavath Guesthouse GUESTHOUSE $$
(☑071-212043; Th Hoxieng; r 200,000K; ❄🐾)
These houseproud wood-walled rooms are
intimate (a bit small) with TV, armoire, air-
con and private bathroom. There's also a
balcony to sit and read on.

🍴 Eating

The city's bakeries and French restaurants
could give Paris' Left Bank a run for its money. Quick, cheap eats are found at baguette
stalls opposite the tourist office from early
morning till sunset. After this the adjacent
night market is packed with exotic barbecued food.

Saffron CAFE $
(Th Khem Khong; mains 25,000-40,000K; ⊙7am-
9pm; 🐾) Parked by the river this is a great
alfresco spot under the shade of palms and
mango trees, or within its inviting interior
hung with black-and-white photography of
Lao tribes. Well-executed pasta dishes, excellent coffee and warm service.

★**Le Banneton** BAKERY $
(Th Sakkarin; meals 20,000-40,000K; ☺6.30am-6pm; 🔊) The city's best bakery, located on the peaceful end of the peninsula, serves up melt-in-your mouth croissants, pain au chocolat, fruit shakes, quiches and homemade sorbets, as well as pizza and sandwiches. Fair-trade coffee too. Get here early morning for the freshest pastries.

Xieng Thong Noodle-Shop LAOTIAN $
(Th Sakkarin; noodle soup 15,000K; ☺7am-2pm) The best *kòw běeak sèn* (round rice noodles served in a broth with pieces of chicken or deep-fried crispy pork belly) in town is served from an entirely unexotic shopfront well up the peninsula. Stocks are usually finished by 2pm.

JoMa Bakery Cafe BAKERY $
(www.joma.biz; Th Kingkitsarat; mains 40,000K; ☺7am-9pm) The newest addition to JoMa in Luang Prabang has the usual tempting offering of sorbets, fruit salads, cookies, bespoke subs and fair-trade coffee. Eat in the cosy wood-accented interior, or on the fan-cooled terrace with sumptuous views of the Nam Khan. Perfection.

★**Tamarind** LAOTIAN $
(☑071-213128; www.tamarindlaos.com; Th Kingkitsarat; mains 40,000K, set dinners 100,000-150,000K; ☺11am-10pm; 🔊) On the banks of the Nam Khan, mint-green Tamarind has created its very own strain of 'Mod Lao' cuisine. The à la carte menu boasts delicious sampling platters with bamboo dip, stuffed lemongrass and *meuyang* (DIY parcels of noodles, herbs, fish and chilli pastes, and vegetables). There's also buffalo *lahp* and Luang Prabang sausage.

Café Toui FUSION $$
(Th Sisavang Vatthana; mains 45,000-80,000K; ☺7am-10pm; 🔊☑) Elegant and bijou, candlelit Café Toui is a delight of Lao cuisine. Gold-stencilled oxblood walls, great service and an Asian fusion menu with standout dishes such as *mok pa* (steamed fish wrapped in banana leaves) and zingy *lahp*, plus an inviting sampler menu.

Big Tree Café KOREAN, INTERNATIONAL $$
(www.bigtreecafe.com; Th Khem Khong; mains 35,000-50,000K; ☺9am-9pm; 🔊) Located in a quirky wooden house, the Korean food is the best in the city and is always packed with, not surprisingly, Koreans. You can also buy celebrated photographer Adri Berger's work here in the upstairs gallery. Eat inside or out on the terrace in the leafy garden. There's also a choice of Western and Japanese dishes. Restful.

Dao Fa Bistro INTERNATIONAL $$
(Th Sisavangvong; mains 50,000K; ☺11am-11pm; 🔊) Dao Fa has long been a stalwart of the gastro scene while so many others have come and gone on Main St. Its well-executed pasta dishes are perfect, with possibly our favourite carbonara in town, while salads are fresh and desserts full of taste.

Tangor FUSION $$
(☑071-260761; www.letangor.com; Th Sisavangvong; mains 40,000-80,000K; ☺11am-10pm; 🔊) Tangor serves beautifully crafted fusion food, blending the best of seasonal Lao produce with French flair. Dishes like beef tenderloin, pork medallions, delicious tomato soup and a simple dessert menu are proving very popular with travellers. Add to this a very cosy interior and you can see why it's usually full.

Chez Marius FRENCH $$
(☑071-212380; www.enprovencelaos.com; Th Khem Khong; 3-course lunch 70,000K; ☺noon-3pm) French people in-the-know gather here for the fabulous southern French menu that changes daily. Expect regular appearances from cucumber salad with Greek sauce, roast pork and potato gratin, and chicken breast and pepper sauce, with flavoursome crème caramel. On Friday the friendly chef dishes up Marseillian specialities.

🍸 Drinking & Entertainment

★**Icon Klub** BAR
(Th Sisavang Vatthana; ☺5pm-late; 🔊) Imagine a place in the afterlife where writers meet and conversation is as free-flowing as the mixology cocktails; you pull up a pew next to Jack Kerouac, Anaïs Nin is reading in a cosy chair nearby... Icon may just be this place. A sculpted angel rises out of the wall, and there are poetry slams and jam sessions.

A night here can lead you somewhere magical and may well be your highlight of the city. Run by a Hungarian poet, this is Laos' most atmospheric bar, bar none.

Utopia BAR
(☺8am-11pm; 🔊) Lush riverside bar with peaceful views of the Nam Khan: think recliner cushions, low-slung tables and hookah pipes. Chill over a fruit shake, play a

board game or volleyball, or lose yourself in a sea of candles come sunset.

Hive Bar
BAR

(Th Kingkitsarat; ⏱10am-11.30pm; 📶) Low-lit stylish den of hidden coves. Out back in the garden there's a dance floor, a projector wall and more tables. Check out the excellent ethnic fashion show every night at 7pm, which also features a hip-hop crew. Tapas, happy hour and cocktails.

Garavek Storytelling
THEATRE

(📞020 96777300; www.garavek.com; Th K, just off Th Khem Khong; tickets 50,000K; ⏱6.30pm) Garavek means 'magical bird' and this enchanting hour-long show – comprising an old man dressed in tribalwear playing a haunting *khene* (Lao-style lyre) alongside an animated storyteller (in English) recalling local Lao folk tales and legends – is just this; taking your imagination on a flight of fancy. In an intimate 30-seat theatre. Book ahead.

🛍 Shopping

★Big Tree Gallery
ARTS

(📞071-212262; Th Khem Khong; ⏱9am-10pm) Photographer and filmmaker Adri Berger's compositions of rural Lao are exquisite and capture that honeyed afternoon light like no-one else. His relocated gallery-cum-restaurant is in a lovely wooden house and prints can be safely sent to your house so you have a little piece of Laos waiting for you when you get home. Prices start at US$150.

Handicraft Night Market
MARKET

(Th Sisavangvong; ⏱5.30-10pm) Every evening this market assembles along Th Sisavangvong and is one of Luang Prabang's biggest tourist lures. Low-lit and quiet, it's devoid of hard selling with myriad traders hawking silk scarves and wall hangings, plus Hmong appliqué blankets, T-shirts, clothing, shoes, paper, silver, bags, ceramics, bamboo lamps and more.

Ock Pop Tok
CLOTHING, HANDICRAFTS

(📞071-254406; Th Sakkarin; ⏱8am-9pm) Ock Pop Tok works with a wide range of different tribes to preserve their handicraft traditions. Fine silk and cotton scarves, chemises, dresses, wall hangings and cushion covers make perfect presents.

L'Etranger Books & Tea
BOOKS

(Th Kingkitsarat; ⏱8am-10pm Mon-Sat, 10am-10pm Sun) Although it has barely a hundred novels and guidebooks for sale now, this great little cafe sells choice silk shawls, paintings and Lao art. There's a gallery-cum-cinema upstairs and a shaded terrace outside. Great range of films shown at 7pm, and if it's quiet you usually get to choose which.

ℹ Information

INTERNET ACCESS & TELEPHONE
Free wi-fi is avaliable at cafes all over the city.

MEDICAL SERVICES
Luang Prabang's **Provincial Hospital** (📞071-254025; Ban Naxang; doctor's consultation 100,000K) is OK for minor problems but for any serious illnesses consider flying to Bangkok or returning to Vientiane for Aek Udon International Hospital (p326) just over the Thai border. Note the Provincial Hospital charges double for consultations on weekends or anytime after 4pm.

MONEY
BCEL (Th Sisavangvong; ⏱8.30am-3.30pm Mon-Sat) Changes major currencies in cash or travellers cheques, has a 24-hour ATM and offers cash advances against Visa and MasterCard.

Minipost Booth (Th Sisavangvong; ⏱7.45am-8.30pm, cash advances 9am-3pm) Changes most major currencies at fair rates and is open daily.

POST
Post Office (Th Chao Fa Ngum; ⏱8.30am-3.30pm Mon-Fri, to noon Sat) Phone calls and Western Union facilities.

TOURIST INFORMATION
Provincial Tourism Department (www.tourismlaos.com; Th Sisavangvong; ⏱8am-4pm Mon-Fri) General information on festivals and ethnic groups. Also offers some maps and leaflets, plus information on buses and boats. Unfortunately staff speak limited English.

ℹ Getting There & Away

AIR
Around 4km from the city centre, **Luang Prabang International Airport** (📞071-212173) services Bangkok (from US$120, 100 minutes); Bangkok Airways (www.bangkokair.com) and Lao Airlines (www.laoairlines.com) both fly twice daily.

Lao Airlines also serves Vientiane (US$103, several daily), Pakse (US$184, daily), Chiang Mai (US$155, daily), Hanoi (US$175, daily), Siem Reap (US$190, daily), Jinghong (US$225, twice weekly) and Seoul (US$390, four weekly).

Vietnam Airlines flies to both Siem Reap and Hanoi daily.

BOAT

Slow boats motor northwest daily to Huay Xai (220,000K), departing at 8am by the **Navigation Office** (☺8-11am & 2-4pm) located behind the Royal Palace. You can buy tickets direct from there or from a travel agent. The trip takes two days with an overnight stop in Pak Beng (130,000K, nine hours). From Pak Beng it's also possible to take the bus northeast to Udomxai.

White-knuckle speedboats up the Mekong leave from around 8.30am daily (when boats are full) from Ban Don pier, 7km north of the town centre (turn west off Rte 13 beside the Km 390 post, then head 300m down an unpaved road). Compared to the slow boat, they rocket to Pak Beng (190,000K, three hours) and Huay Xai (320,000K, six hours) in a fraction of the time but with 10 times the danger. After the wet season when the river is high is the better time to catch it – if you must! Bring a cushion for your back, earplugs and an extra layer. Tall people should get there early and bag a seat at the front so you can stretch your legs out over the luggage.

BUS & SŎRNGTĂAOU

Most interprovincial buses and *sŏrngtăaou* heading north depart from the northern bus station, while southbound vehicles use the southern bus station, 3km south of town. On all these routes the durations can vary wildly during monsoonal weather.

A better option is the **Naluang minibus station** (☑071-212979; souknasing@hotmail.com; Rte 13, 800m past Km 382) – opposite the southern bus station – that runs minibuses to Nong Khiang, Vang Vieng, Phonsavan, Luang Namtha, Hanoi and Kunming. Although you can travel as one or two people and just turn up in the morning, for less than double the bus fare, a great option is to gather your own group and rent a comfortable six-seater minivan. Directly booked through the minibus station, prices are about 1,000,000K to Phonsavan or Vang Vieng and 600,000K to Nong Khiaw, including pick-up from your guesthouse.

Nong Khiaw & Sam Neua

For Nong Khiaw (55,000K, four hours), 9am minibuses start from Naluang minibus station. Alternatively, from the northern bus station board the *sŏrngtăaou* (55,000K) at 9am, 11am and 1pm or the 8.30am bus that continues to Sam Neua (140,000K, 17 hours) via Vieng Thong (120,000K, 10 hours). Another Sam Neua–bound bus (from Vientiane) should pull in sometime around 5.30pm.

Vientiane & Vang Vieng

From the southern bus station there are up to 10 daily Vientiane services (express/VIP/sleeper 110,000/130,000/150,000K, nine to 12 hours) via Vang Vieng between 6.30am and 7.30pm. Sleepers leave at 8pm and 8.30pm, while VIP buses leave at 9am. A plethora of morning minibuses to Vang Vieng (95,000K, seven hours) depart from the Naluang minibus station.

China, Udomxai, Luang Namtha & Phonsavan

The sleeper bus to Kunming, China (450,000K, 24 hours), departs from the southern bus station at 7am, sometimes earlier. From the northern bus station buses run to Udomxai (60,000K, five hours) at 9am, noon and 4pm; Luang Namtha (100,000K, nine hours) at 9am; and Huay Xai (Borkeo; 150,000K, 15 hours) at 5.30pm and a VIP service at 7pm (170,000K).

For Phonsavan there's an 8.30am minibus (95,000K, 10 hours) from Naluang minibus station and an 8am bus (ordinary/express 85,000/105,000K, 10 hours) from the southern bus station.

ⓘ Getting Around

From the airport into town, 4km away, jumbos (motorised three-wheeled taxis) or minitrucks charge a uniform 50,000K per vehicle, and up to six can share the ride. In the reverse direction you can usually pay less.

Most of the town is accessible on foot. Jumbos usually ask foreigners for 25,000K a ride. Scooters cost US$15 per day, mountain/ordinary bikes cost 50,000/20,000K per day.

Nong Khiaw ຫນອງຂຽວ

☑071

Nestled along the cherry blossom banks of the Nam Ou, bookended by gothic karsts and stitched together by a French colonial-era bridge, pretty Nong Khiaw is a haven of cafes and guesthouses and is increasingly the place to reset your equilibrium with a dose of massage or yoga. And, thanks to the presence of Green Discovery, Tiger Trail and a few local adventure outfits, it now has plenty of activities to keep you busy. Where once folk headed upriver straight to soporific Muang Ngoi Neua, most now find this a more rewarding option.

Note: the opposite side of the river where most guesthouses are based is called Ban Sop Houn. There's now a BCEL ATM on the Nong Khiaw side.

⊙ Sights & Activities

Head to the bridge at dusk when fabulous star shows turn the deep indigo sky into a pointillist canvas that subtly outlines the riverside massifs.

You can walk to **Tham Pha Tok**, an enormous cave of many levels where villagers hid out during the Second Indochina War. Head 2.5km east of the bridge then look for a clearly visible cave mouth in the limestone cliff on the right. It costs 5000K, and is open from 7.30am until 6.30pm.

Viewpoint
VIEWPOINT

(Ban Sop Houn, Nong Khiaw; admission 20,000K) An hour-and-a-half walk up a sinuous path cut through the jungle, directly above the town, is a viewpoint with an unforgettable panorama. Drink up the sunset view (but bring a strong torch for your descent) or head here at 6am to witness the valley below veiled in mist, the mountain peaks painted gold.

Pay the admission to the guy in the kiosk at the bottom.

Tiger Trail
HIKING, CYCLING

(☑ 071-252655; www.laos-adventures.com; Delilah's Place; ⏰ 7.30am-11pm) ✐ This eco-conscious outfit has treks and homestays around the local area, including memorable one-day trips to the '100 waterfalls' (US$62 per person, group of four) and one-day trek and boat rides (US$86). The emphasis at this particular Tiger Trail office is on trekking, though kayaking is also available.

Green Discovery
HIKING, CYCLING

(☑ 071-810018; www.greendiscoverylaos.com; ⏰ 7.30am-10pm) Reliable Green Discovery has a range of trips including a three-day kayaking adventure with homestays from Muang Khua downriver to Nong Khiaw through fabulous karst country (US$118); a new two-day trek to a Hmong village involving a homestay and five hours trekking per day (US$87); and challenging one-day cycling trips on forest dirt tracks covering 56km (US$39).

NK Adventure
ADVENTURE TOUR

(☑ 020 58686068, 020 28633010; ⏰ 7.30am-9pm) Run by a local, this outfit has a great one-day combo trip to a Khmu village, then on to a waterfall where you can swim, followed by a trek and kayak downriver. Starting 9am and finishing 2pm, it's good value at 220,000K per person for a group of six (includes lunch and guide).

Sabai Sabai
MASSAGE

(☑ 020 58686068; Ban Sop Houn; body massage 40,000K, steam bath 15,000K; ⏰ 9am-8pm) Set in a peaceful Zen-style garden this wooden house is the perfect spot to restore the spirit and aching limbs with treatments like traditional Lao massage (one hour, 50,000K) and herbal steam bath (one hour, 40,000K).

🛏 Sleeping & Eating

Guesthouses in Nong Khiaw are near the bridge on the western side of the river, and in the more popular village of Ban Sop Houn, on the eastern side.

Sunrise Guesthouse
GUESTHOUSE $

(☑ 020 22478799; Ban Sop Houn; bungalows 60,000-150,000K; ❇ 🛜) Friendly and family-run, the tightly packed older bungalows are a little rough around the edges, but have views to the river and bridge. There are four newer bungalows that include swish bathrooms, and one of these has air-con. There's also a decent cafe here with Western breakfasts and Lao fare.

Sengdao Chittavong Guesthouse
GUESTHOUSE $

(☑ 030-9237089; r 90,000K; 🅿 🛜) This family-run spot on the western bank has wooden bungalows located in gardens of cherry blossom. En suite rooms are rattan-walled, with simple decorations, mozzie nets, clean linen and balconies. There's also a convivial fairy-lit restaurant with river-garden views.

Delilah's Place
HOSTEL $

(☑ 030-19758048, 020 54396686; www.delilahs cafenongkhiaw.wordpress.com; Main St; dm 35,000K, d/tr 55,000/75,000K; 🛜) Delilah's rooms are clean and vibrantly coloured with oxblood quilts, while the dorms are cosy with mozzie nets, super-thick mattresses and safety lockers. Shared bathroom all round. Tiger Trail is based here so it's a handy spot to stay if you're headed into the boonies early the next day. There's also a great cafe to 'carb-up' beforehand.

★ Mandala Ou Resort
BOUTIQUE HOTEL $$

(☑ 030-5377332; www.mandala-ou.com; opposite bus station; r US$65; ❇ 🛜 🏊) This sparkling boutique addition to Nong Khiaw has beautiful vanilla-coloured villas, some with river views; fine interiors with inlaid bottles in the walls allowing more light; contemporary bathrooms; and swallow-you-up beds. There's a terrific Thai menu, the town's only swimming pool, and also a yoga deck used by Luang Prabang Yoga, which runs retreats here monthly. The owners are lovely.

★**Coco Home Bar &
Restaurant**   LAOTIAN, INTERNATIONAL $
(☏ 020 58491741; Main St; mains 40,000-60,000K;
☺ 7.30am-10pm; 🛜) This riverside oasis, spilling with plants, has a billowing orange
canvas arbour and a great menu. It charms
with dishes like papaya salad, coconut soup,
fried Morning Glory, beef *lahp,* red curry,
and sweet and sour duck breast, as well as
Western staples such as spaghetti carbonara
or beef steak with pepper sauce. Eat in the
garden or upstairs.

Vongmany Restaurant   LAOTIAN $
(Ban Sop Houn; mains 30,000K) This large open
rattan-and-wood restaurant serves very tasty
locally sourced Lao food – the *lahp* here will
put a bounce in your taste buds, while the
buffalo steak is delicious, and the steamed
fish and river shrimp are full of flavour.

Delilah's Place   INTERNATIONAL, LAOTIAN $
(mains 15,000-35,000K; ☺ 7am-10pm; 🛜) With
Bach floating across the wood floors and a
herd of African elephants thundering silently toward you on the mural, Delilah's, run by
the excellent Harp, is fast becoming an NK
institution. Eggs, smoky bacon, fruit salad,
chocolate cake, homemade ice cream. Spoil
yourself.

**CT Restaurant &
Bakery**   INTERNATIONAL, LAOTIAN $
(Ban Sop Houn; mains 30,000K; ☺ 7am-10pm) At
the end of the bridge, this is the best view
in town. CT has a Western-friendly menu of
pasta, pancakes, breakfasts, sandwiches and
tasty staple Lao dishes. It also offers takeaway sandwiches for trekking.

❶ Getting There & Away

BOAT

In the high season, boats heading up the Nam
Ou to Muang Ngoi Neua (one way 25,000K,
1¼ hours) leave at 11am and 2pm. Tickets are
bought at an office at the bus station. The 11am
boat continues to Muang Khua (120,000K, sev-
en hours) for connections to Phongsali and Dien
Bien Phu in Vietnam.

Public boats used to make the five- to eight-
hour trip through striking karst scenery to Luang
Prabang; however, in late 2015 the river was
dammed.

BUS & SŎRNGTǍAOU

The journey to Luang Prabang takes three
to four hours. Minibuses (55,000K) head to
Luang Prabang's Southern Bus Station, while
sŏrngtǎaou (40,000K) go to Luang Prabnang's

Northern Bus Station. Both start around 9am
till 1pm. Tickets are sold at the bus stand, but
the 11am service starts at the boat office, filling
up with folks arriving off the boat(s) from Muang
Ngoi.

For Udomxai a direct minibus (45,000K, three
hours) leaves at 11am. Alternatively take any
westbound transport and change at Pak Mong
(25,000K, 50 minutes).

The daily minibus to Sam Neua (170,000K,
12 hours) makes a quick lunch stop in Nong Khiaw around noon, with another passing through
at 7pm.

Muang Ngoi Neua
ເມືອງງອຍເໜືອ

Muang Ngoi Neua abounds in authentic rural life, as street stalls fry up pancakes in the
morning, mist hangs on the pyramid-shaped
karsts and river life in Muang Ngoi Neua
slowly crackles to life. Chill in your hammock and take in the jaw-dropping views
of the karsts, or ready yourself for trekking,
caving and kayaking.

☞ Tours

Lao Youth Travel   KAYAKING
(☏ 030   514   0046;   www.laoyouthtravel.com;
☺ 7.30-10.30am & 1.30-6pm) This local outfit
provides trekking and kayaking in the surrounding area.

🛏 Sleeping

Muang Ngoi Neua has 'budget' tattooed
over its dip-and-pour, hammock-slung cabanas. Restaurants are generally tagged on to
guesthouses.

Bungalows Ecolodge   GUESTHOUSE $
(d/tr 120,000/150,000K) These inviting rattan-walled, spacious cabanas have milk-
white sheets, mozzie nets, fans and bathrooms, private balconies and hammocks,
and most importantly, widescreen views of
the karsts that can be seen while lying in
bed. Prepare to chill!

Rainbow Guest House   GUESTHOUSE $
(☏ 020 22957880; r 150,000K) Close to the
boat ramp, this large house has clean, basic
rooms with fresh linen and bathrooms, and
a lovely restaurant out front called the Bamboo Bar with tasty Lao food.

★**Ning Ning Guest House**   GUESTHOUSE $$
(☏ 020 33863306, 020 23880122; r incl breakfast
200,000K; 🛜) Nestled around a peaceful

garden, Ning Ning is the smartest place in the village, offering immaculate wooden bungalows. The trim includes mosquito nets, verandahs, en suite bathrooms and bed linen, plus the walls are draped with ethnic tapestries. There's a nice restaurant with riverfront views.

✖ Eating

The best food is served by street-side vendors.

★ **Riverside Restaurant**　　LAOTIAN $
(meals 40,000K; ☺ 7.30am-10pm) Shaded by a mature mango tree festooned with lanterns and scatter cushions, Riverside has gorgeous views of the Nam Ou. Its menu encompasses noodles, fried dishes, *lahp* and Indian fare.

★ **Pakphon Sabai**　　LAOTIAN $
(Main St; mains 20,000K; ☺ 8am-9pm) Serving up waffles, decent coffee, French toast, Muang Ngoi sausage and more, this cafe-cum-bookshop is an unexpected boho treat with secondhand novels, scatter cushions, massage (one hour 60,000K) and original art. Halfway down Main St.

Meem Restaurant　　LAOTIAN $
(Main St; mains 20,000K; ☺ 7am-9.30pm) Halfway down Main St, this cosy den serves up very flavoursome Lao and Indian fare, such as tomato curry, paneer butter massala, prawn massala, spring rolls and barbecued chicken and duck.

Phetdavanh Street Buffet　　LAOTIAN $
(per person 20,000K; ☺ buffet 6.30pm-9pm, restaurant 6am-10.30pm) Phetdavanh runs a nightly buffet serving barbecued pork, chicken, fish, sticky rice and vegetables.

ⓘ Information

There is now electricity in the village and wi-fi too, but no bank so bring plenty of cash.

ⓘ Getting There & Away

Boats to Nong Khiaw leave at 9am (or when full) and cost 30,000K. Heading north, a 9.30am boat goes most days to Muang Khua (minimum 10 persons, 150,000K, seven hours) for those headed for the Sop Hun/Tay Trang border crossing. Buy tickets at the boat office, halfway up the boat landing stairs next to Ning Ning Guesthouse. There's a boat to Nong Khiaw from Muang Khua that stops in Muang Ngoi Neua at 1.30pm.

Phonsavan　　ໂພນສະຫວັນ

☑ 061 / POP 60,000

Phonsavan bears its cratered war wounds like an acne-scarred pensioner, as stoic locals make the most of decommissioned unexploded ordnance (UXO), using it to decorate houses and hotel foyers. Touchingly, while other areas of Laos erupt in pockets of sophistication, Phonsavan, like some retro-leaning Muscovite, barely changes. Often mist-shrouded, this dusty old town (latterly known as Xieng Khuang) has a rugged charm if you look past its nondescript, Soviet facade – blame that on its hasty rebuild after it was decimated.

The town is inhabited by an intriguing cast of Chinese, Vietnamese, Lao and Hmong, and is well serviced by an airport, and a handful of guesthouses and restaurants.

⊙ Sights

★ **Xieng Khouang UXO-Survivors' Information Centre**　　INFORMATION CENTRE
(www.laos.worlded.org; ☺ 8am-8pm) The insightful Xieng Khouang UXO-Survivors' Information Centre displays prosthetic limbs, wheelchairs and bomb parts and gives harrowing insight into the UXO problem.

Mulberries　　FARM
(ປ່ສາ; ☑ 061-561271; www.mulberries.org; ☺ 8am-4pm Mon-Sat) This is a fair-trade silk farm that offers interesting free visits that include a complete introduction to the silk-weaving process, from cocoon to colourful scarves. It's off Rte 7 just west of the main bus station.

ⓖ Tours

Amazing Lao Travel　　HIKING
(☑ 020 22340005; www.amazinglao.com; Rte 7) Runs treks to the Plain of Jars and two-day treks in the mountains, including a homestay in a Hmong village. As ever, the more the merrier, with prices falling for larger groups.

Sousath Travel　　TOUR
(☑ 061 312 031) Run by a pair of well-informed brothers, Sousath offers reliable tours to the Plain of Jars and the Ho Chi Minh Trail as well as homestays in Hmong villages. It's based at Maly Hotel.

🛏 Sleeping

★ Kong Keo Guesthouse   GUESTHOUSE $

(📞 061-211354; www.kongkeojar.com; r 60,000-90,000K; 🖥🚲) Atmosphere is hard to come by in Phonsavan but the alfresco UXO-decorated restaurant-bar here with its nightly barbecue can still bring a little cheer to a chilly night. Cabins with en suites have unforgivably hard mattresses, while there's also another block of more comfortable rooms. Charismatic owner Mr Keo runs excellent tours to the Plain of Jars, as well as specialised trips, a highlight of many a trip to Laos.

Nice Guesthouse   GUESTHOUSE $

(📞 061-312454; vuemany@hotmail.com; r 90,000-130,000K; 🖥) With fresh rooms with tiled floors, private bathrooms and firm beds, Nice shows no signs of ageing. Chinese lanterns cast a ruby glow into the chilled night and upstairs rooms include a bathtub. Central, friendly and clean.

White Orchid Guesthouse   GUESTHOUSE $

(📞 061-312403; r incl breakfast US$10; 🌬🖥) The menthol-green walls include en suite bathrooms and welcome blankets. The price includes a pick-up from the airport or bus station and there's also a little tour office that can arrange trips to see the Plain of Jars. Basic and clean.

Anoulack Khen Lao Hotel   HOTEL $$

(📞 061-213599; www.anoulackkhenlaohotel.com; Main St; r incl breakfast 200,000K; 🌬🖥) This modern tower-style hotel boasts a great restaurant on the 5th floor where you take breakfast, wi-fi and cable TV, and clean, comfy rooms with white linens, kettles, fridges and welcome hot showers. There's also a lift. A cut above the average digs and worth the extra spend.

🍴 Eating & Drinking

Wild matsutake mushrooms *(hét wâi)* and fermented swallows *(nok qen dąwng)* are local specialities. Try the **fresh food market** (🕑 6am-5pm) behind Rte 7. Several Vietnamese restaurants serve *thit chó* (dog).

★ Bamboozle

Restaurant & Bar   INTERNATIONAL $

(Rte 7; meals 25,000-52,000K; 🕑 7-10.30am & 3.30-11pm; 🖥) 🍴 Bamboozle enjoys a well-earned rep as serving the best Western grub in town, with good-sized cheeseburgers, tasty pizza and terrific Lao cuisine. Add to this chilled beers and a rock-and-roll soundtrack and it's a winner. A percentage of profits go towards the Lone Buffalo Foundation (www.facebook.com/lonebuffalo), which supports the town's youth.

Nisha Restaurant   INDIAN $

(Rte 7; meals 20,000-30,000K; 🕑 7am-10pm; 🖊) It doesn't look like much from the outside, but inside Nisha turns out to be one of the best Indian restaurants in northern Laos. The menu includes a wide range of vegetarian options. There's also delicious dosa (flat bread), tikka masala and rogan josh, as well as great lassi.

Simmaly Restaurant   LAOTIAN $

(Rte 7; meals 20,000-30,000K; 🕑 6am-9pm) Dishes up a tasty line of rice dishes, noodles and spicy meats, including steaming *fér*. The pork with ginger is lovely.

LAOS PHONSAVAN

LAOS' UNEXPLODED ORDNANCE

Between 1964 and 1973, the USA conducted one of the largest sustained aerial bombardments in history, flying 580,344 missions over Laos and dropping two million tonnes of bombs, costing US$2.2 million a day. Around 30% of the bombs dropped on Laos failed to detonate, leaving the country littered with unexploded ordnance (UXO).

For people all over eastern Laos (the most contaminated provinces being Xieng Khuang, Salavan and Savannakhet), living with this appalling legacy has become an intrinsic part of daily life. Since the British **Mines Advisory Group** (MAG; www.mag.org.uk; Rte 7, Phonsavan; 🕑 4-8pm) began clearance work in 1994, only a tiny percentage of the quarter of a million pieces in Xieng Khuang and Salavan has been removed. At the current rate of clearance it will take more than 100 years to make the country safe. Visit its **UXO Information Centre** (📞 61-211010; www.maginternational.org/laos; Phonsavan; 🕑 8am-8pm Mon-Fri, 4pm-8pm Sat & Sun) **FREE** to watch a number of late-afternoon documentaries including *Bomb Harvest* (4.30pm), *Surviving the Peace* (5.50pm) and *Bombies* (6.30pm).

★ **Cranky-T Café & Bar** FUSION $$

(☑ 030-5388003; www.facebook.com/CrankyT Laos; Main St; mains 35,000-50,000K; ⊙ 7am-11pm; ⊜ 🛜) Enjoying an immediate following thanks to its stylish red wine and exposed brick interior, and beautifully executed food, the new kid on the block boasts bar snacks like sirloin steak and mash, chicken teriyaki, and sweet-toothed, freshly cooked butterscotch almond bar, Japanese cheesecake, chocolate cake, brownies... Not forgetting Tokyo iced tea, mojitos, lattes to go, and high-speed wi-fi. Enjoy!

ℹ️ Information

Currency exchange is available at **Lao Development Bank** (☑ 061-312188), at **BCEL** (☑ 061-213291; Rte 7), and from several travel agents. There are two ATMs along Rte 7. Don't underestimate the dangers of UXO (unexploded ordnance); keep to established paths.

Lao-Mongolian Friendship Hospital (☑ 061-312166) Might be able to assist with minor health concerns.

Post Office (⊙ 8am-4pm Mon-Fri, to noon Sat) Domestic phone service.

Xieng Khuang Tourist Office (☑ 061-312217, 020 22340201; www.xiengkhouangtourism.com; Hwy 1E; ⊙ 8am-4pm) This helpful office has English-speaking staff, brochures and souvenirs recycled from war junk. Free maps for Phonsavan and Xieng Khuang district are available. Also, keep an eye out for its free photocopied sheet entitled 'What Do I Do Around Phonesavanh Town' for alternative ideas on things to do aside from the jar sites.

GETTING TO VIETNAM: NORTHERN BORDERS

Muang Khua to Dien Bien Phu

Getting to the border The Sop Hun/Tay Trang border in Phongsali Province has now opened as an international entry point to Tay Trang in Vietnam. There are daily buses bound for Dien Bien Phu leaving from the Lao village of Muang Khua (50,000K, 6.30am).

At the border This remote crossing sees a handful of travellers. Organise a Vietnamese visa in advance.

Moving on There are no facilities or waiting vehicles at either border posts, which are separated by about 4km of no man's land. From the Tay Trang side of the border, it is about 31km to Dien Bien Phu.

For information on doing this crossing in reverse, see p842.

Phonsavan to Vinh

Getting to the border Direct buses to Vinh (on the Vietnamese side) leave Phonsavan four times per week, crossing at the lonely Nong Haet/Nam Can border (open 8am to noon and 1.30pm to 5pm).

At the border If entering Vietnam, you'll need to have organised a Vietnamese visa in advance.

Moving on The first town en route to Vinh, 403 km away, is Mu'òng Xén, where there's a basic hotel. From here there's a 4pm bus to Vinh.

For information on doing this crossing in reverse, see p848.

Sam Neua to Thanh Hoa

Getting to the border If you're crossing the Nam Soi/Na Meo border (open 7.30am to 11.30am and 1.30pm to 4.30pm), take the daily bus from Sam Neua's Pkoutanou bus station bound for Thanh Hoa (180,000K, 11 hours, 8am). Buy your ticket at the bus station to avoid being overcharged on the bus.

At the border Heading into Vietnam you'll need to have prearranged a visa. There are no ATM facilities at this remote border crossing. On the Lao side there are a couple of restaurants.

Moving on There's a night train from Thanh Hoa to Hanoi departing at 11.30pm and arriving at 4am. Departing for Laos from Thanh Hoa is an 8am bus which should cost 200,000d, but you may be asked to pay more.

ℹ️ Getting There & Away

AIR

Lao Airlines (✆ 061-212027; www.laoairlines.com) has daily flights to/from Vientiane (US$103).

BUS

Longer-distance bus tickets presold by travel agencies typically cost around 40,000K more than standard fares but include a transfer to the **Northern Bus Station** (✆ 030-5170148), around 3km northwest of the centre. From here daily Vietnam-bound buses depart to Vinh (150,000K, 10 hours) at 6am. For Vientiane (110,000K, 11 hours) there are air-con buses at 7.30am, 8.30am, 6.30pm and a VIP bus (130,000K) at 8.30pm. These all pass through Vang Vieng, to where there's an additional 7.30am departure (95,000K). For Luang Prabang (10 hours), air-con buses (110,000K, eight hours) depart at 8.30am and 7.30pm on Monday, Wednesday and Friday. There's an 8am and a 4pm bus to Sam Neua (100,000K, eight to 10 hours) plus two Vientiane–Sam Neua buses passing through.

The minivan station has recently relocated to **Phoukham Minivan Station** (Th Xaysana) on the main drag through town and has daily buses to Vientiane (110,000K) at 6.30am, 7.30am, 8am and 5.30pm. A daily 8.30am minibus leaves for Vang Vieng (100,000K), and an 8.30pm bus for Luang Prabang (110,00K).

Plain of Jars ທົ່ງໄຫຫິນ

The Plain of Jars represents a huge area of Xieng Khuang Province, scattered with thousands of limestone jars of undetermined age. Thought to be funerary urns after bones were discovered within them, the jars have been divided into 160 sites, three of which represent the greatest concentration. These are the designated UXO-cleared tourist areas you should visit.

Site 1 (Thong Hai Hin; admission 15,000K), the biggest and most accessible site, is 15km southwest of Phonsavan and features over 300 jars, most of which weigh from 600kg to 1 tonne each. The largest jar weighs as much as 6 tonnes; it is said to have been the victory cup of mythical King Jeuam, and so is called **Hai Jeuam**.

Two other jar sites are readily accessible by road from Phonsavan. **Site 2** (Hai Hin Phu Salato; admission 10,000K), about 25km south of town, features 90 jars spread across two adjacent hillsides. Vehicles can reach the base of the hills, then it's a short, steep walk to the jars.

More impressive is **Site 3** (Hai Hin Lat Khai; admission 10,000K), with 150 jars. It's about 10km south of Site 2 (or 35km from Phonsavan) on a scenic hilltop near the charming village of **Ban Xieng Di**, where there's a small monastery containing the remains of Buddha images damaged in the war. The site is a 2km hike through rice paddies and up a hill.

ℹ️ Getting Around

Tuk-tuk cost from 10,000K for a short hop to about 20,000K to the airport. **Lao-Falang Restaurant** (✆ 020 22212456; Rte 7; ⏰ 8am-6pm) rents bicycles (40,000K per day) and 100cc motorbikes (100,000K), ideal for reaching a selection of jar sites. It also has some Chinese quad bikes (160,000K) if you're feeling brave.

Chauffeured six-seater vans or 4WDs can be chartered through most guesthouses and hotels, but you're looking at US$150 to Sam Neua or US$120 to Luang Prabang.

It's possible to charter a jumbo to the jar sites for about 100,000K.

Sam Neua ຊຳເໜືອ

✆ 064 / POP 16,000

Sam Neua roughly translates as 'wrapped head'; locals have an idiosyncratic style of combatting the cold by wrapping their heads up in scarves. Check out the eye-widening produce markets (think dissected rats and a panoply of not-so-mouthwatering insects) plus a colourful ethnic diversity, and use Sam Neua as a base for visiting nearby Vieng Xai or catching the daily bus to Vietnam. There's not many travellers here, and that's half its charm. At an altitude of roughly 1200m, pack a jumper and expect thick morning fog, chilled further by Soviet monuments.

🛏️ Sleeping & Eating

Sam Neua's digs are found beside the Nam Sam (Sam River). For cheap *fĕr*, samosas, spring rolls and fried sweet potato, the nearby **market** is the place to go.

Phonchalern Hotel HOTEL $
(✆ 064-312192; www.phonechalernhotel.com; r 100,000-120,000K; ❄️🌐) The first place in Sam Neua to install a lift, this hotel is a real deal for such a clean and comfortable place to stay, with rooms including a TV and fridge. Try to bag a front-facing room with a balcony overlooking the river.

Bounhome Guest House GUESTHOUSE $
(☑ 064-312223; r 80,000K; 🛜) Plenty of sunlight fills the fine little rooms upstairs in this guesthouse. Their neat interiors have firm, low-set beds, wardrobes and clean linen and are fan-cooled and include hot-water showers.

★ **Xayphasouk Hotel** HOTEL $$
(☑ 064-312033; xayphasoukhotel@gmail.com; r 170,000-200,000K; 🆒🛜) Currently the smartest hotel in Sam Neua. The huge lobby-restaurant is woefully underused, but the rooms are very comfortable for such a remote region of Laos. All include piping hot showers, flat-screen TVs, tasteful furnishings and crisp linen. And there's free wi-fi.

Dan Nao Muang Xam Restaurant LAOTIAN $
(mains 15,000-50,000K; ⊙ 7am-9.30pm) This hole-in-the-wall spot is hardly brimming with atmosphere, but it has the most foreigner-friendly menu in town in concise English. Breakfast includes cornflakes and a delicious *fĕr*. Dinner includes some excellent rice and soup combinations, plus a steak with al dente vegetables arranged star-like around the plate. It also serves decent portions of *lahp*, fried rice variations and omelettes.

ℹ Information

Agricultural Promotion Bank (⊙ 8am-noon & 1.30-4pm Mon-Fri) Exchanges Thai baht and US dollars at fair rates.

Lao Development Bank (☑ 064 312 171; ⊙ 8am-4pm Mon-Fri) On the main road 400m north of the bus station on the left; exchanges cash and travellers cheques.

Post Office (⊙ 8am-4pm Mon-Fri) In a large building directly opposite the bus station. A telephone office at its rear offers international calls.

Provincial Tourist Office (☑ 064 312 567; ⊙ 8am-noon & 1.30-4pm Mon-Fri) An excellent tourist office with English-speaking staff eager to help.

ℹ Getting There & Away

Lao Air flies to Vientiane on Monday, Wednesday and Friday (915,000K, 1½ hours). The airport is 3km from town.

Set on a hilltop, Sam Neua's main bus station is roughly 1.2km away from town (tuk-tuk 8500K). There are four buses a day to Vientiane (170,000K, 22 hours) via Phonsavan (80,000K, eight to 10 hours), at 10am, 1pm, 3pm and 5pm. It's a sinuous but beautiful hike through the

mountains. An additional 8am bus to Vientiane goes via Nong Khiaw (140,000K, 12 hours) and continues to Luang Prabang (150,000K, 17 hours) and Vang Vieng. If you're heading for Udomxai, take this bus and change at Pak Mong (140,000K). A bus to Than Hoa (180,000K) leaves at 8am.

Nathong bus station is 1km to the east of town, heading for Vieng Xai. *Sŏrngtăaou* run from here to Vieng Xai (20,000K, 50 minutes, 29km) at 8am, 10am, 11am, 2.30pm and 4pm; the scenery is among the most stunning in Laos. The 'Nameo' (actually the Nam Soi border post) bus leaves at 8am (40,000K, three hours), and the Sam Tai (Xamtay) bus at 9.30am (60,000K, five hours).

Vieng Xai ວຽງໄຊ

☑ 064 / POP 10,000

Set amid valleys glistening with rice paddies and towered over by dramatic karsts, Vieng Xai seems an unlikely place to have suffered a decade's worth of American air assaults. Its 450 limestone caves provided sanctuary for more than 23,000 people during the Secret War, playing host to bakeries, a hospital, a school, a metalwork factory and, more importantly, the political headquarters of the communist Pathet Lao party.

Six kilometres from Vieng Xai bus station heading towards Sam Neua, keep an eye out for **Tham Nok Ann** (ຖ້ຳນົກແອນ; Nok Ann Cave; admission 10,000K, twin kayak 30,000K; ⊙ 8am-5pm), a newly opened cave complex you can kayak through.

⊙ Sights & Activities

Joining a truly fascinating 18-point tour is the only way to see Vieng Xai's seven most important war-shelter cave complexes, along with several 1970s postwar buildings associated with major liberation heroes. All of the **Vieng Xai Caves** (ຖ້ຳວຽງໄຊ; ☑ 064-314321; admission incl audioguide 60,000K; ⊙ 8am-noon & 1.30-4.30pm) are set in beautiful gardens backed by fabulous karst scenery. A local guide unlocks each site, while an audioguide gives a wealth of first-hand background information and historical context, offering a moving, uniquely fascinating glimpse of how people struggled on through the war years.

Most caves have minor elements of original furnishings. Some have 'emergency rooms' – air-locked concrete caves-within-caves designed to protect top politburo members from possible chemical or gas attacks. No such attacks occurred but the emergency room of the **Kaysone Phomvihane Cave** still has its air-circulation pump in working order. Enjoy bamboo-framed views of town from the ledge of the **Nouhak Phoumsavan Cave** and look for two rocket-impact holes in the karst outcrop above the **Souphanouvong Cave**, once the hideout of Laos' famous 'Red Prince'. Almost all the main cave sites are well illuminated but bring a torch (flashlight) if you want to traverse the unadorned hospital cave (occasionally flooded).

Steps lead down from the hand-dug **Khamtay Siphandone Cave** to the **Barracks Caves**, extensive natural caverns that would have housed hundreds of conscripted liberation soldiers. Above is the Artillery Cave from whose open ledge spotters would watch for incoming American planes. The tour culminates in the **Xanglot Cave**, a wide double-ended cavern that was used as a wedding hall, a cinema and even as a theatre.

Tours start at 9am and 1pm from the caves office. By arrangement private visits are also possible at other times (costing an extra 50,000K per group), depending on guide availability. Seeing all 18 sites in the three hours available is possible without feeling unduly rushed, assuming you rent a bicycle – available for 15,000/30,000K per tour/day from the **Vieng Xai Cave Tourist Office** (☑064-314321; www.visit-viengxay.com; ◷8-11.30am & 1-4.30pm) – and that you listen to the longer audiotracks while travelling between the sites rather than waiting to arrive before pressing play.

🛏 Sleeping & Eating

By 9pm the town is in hibernation. Several *fĕr* shops in the market serve rice and cheap noodle dishes until around 5pm.

Naxay Guesthouse　　GUESTHOUSE $
(☑064-314330; r 60,000-80,000K) Opposite the cave office, Vieng Xai's most comfortable option offers bamboo-lined bungalows or concrete cubicles set around a patch of greenery backed by an impressive split-toothed crag. Beds are comfy, hot water flows and the attached beach-style cafe pavilion occasionally serves up food.

Thongnaxay Guesthouse　　GUESTHOUSE $
(☑030-99907206; r 60,000K) Close to the caves this new guesthouse has six OK rooms with private bathroom, fan, clean linen and double bed.

ⓘ Getting There & Around

Sŏrngtăaou to Sam Neua (20,000K, 50 minutes) leave at 7am, 10am, 1pm, 2.30pm and 4pm from the market. Buses between Sam Neua and Sam Tai, Nam Soi or Thanh Hoa bypass Vieng Xai 1km to the north but will usually stop on request.

Bicycles can be rented from the visitor centre for 30,000K per day.

Udomxai　　ອຸດົມໄຊ
☑081 / POP 25,000
Increasingly untypical of Laos with a bolshy cast of Chinese truck drivers, hookers and ugly Soviet-style buildings, Udomxai has been relegated to a dusty waypoint for trade en route south. That said, it takes minimal effort to find the 'real' Laos nearby; Udomxai Province is home to some of Laos' thickest forests and is a great place to visit Khmu and Hmong villages. The well-organised tourist office can connect you with paper-making and cooking courses (both from 100,000K per person), and some great treks and homestays. Meanwhile **Samlaan Cycling** (☑020 55609790, 030-5130184; www.

DEADWOOD: LAOS' ILLEGAL LOGGING TRADE

Laos has some of the largest remnant tracts of primary rainforest in mainland Southeast Asia and represents a vulnerable target for foreign companies. The Environmental Investigation Agency (EIA) claims that the furniture industry in Vietnam has grown tenfold since 2000, with Laos facilitating the flow of its timber to enable this. An estimated 500,000 cu metres of logs find their way over the border every year. While an outwardly hard-line approach has been taken against mass logging by the government, it's the self-funded military and local officials in remote areas who can fall prey to bribes.

Though unconfirmed, locals have reported a Chinese-built road is currently being proposed to cut straight to the Nam Han National Protected Area, allegedly for the benefit of the villagers.

Forest cover fell from 70% in the 1940s to less than 40% in the early 2000s. An estimated 30% of forest cover will remain in Laos by 2020.

samlaancycling.com; Ban NaLao Village) ✐ runs recommended one-day/multiday cycling tours.

🛏 Sleeping & Eating

Most places are along – or just off – Rte 1.

Saylomen Guesthouse   GUESTHOUSE $
(☑ 081-211377; r with fan/air-con 60,000/80,000K; P ❄ 🛜) Off the main drag this old guesthouse has charmless, basic rooms somewhat redeemed by mint-fresh floors and fragrant linen. Private bathroom. You'll have to wake up the lady at reception. Air-con is a good investment in the hot season.

★ Villa Keoseumsack   HOTEL $$
(☑ 081-312170; Rte 1; r 160,000K; P ❄ 🛜) Udomxai's best guesthouse is in a handsome Lao house with inviting rooms. Crisp linen, decent fittings, varnished floors, TV, Hmong bedrunners, free wi-fi and a communal reading balcony finish it off.

Meuang Neua Restaurant   LAOTIAN $
(mains 20,000-40,000K; ⊙ 7am-9pm) Festooned with lanterns and Che Guevara graffiti, you'll find this hole-in-the-wall a 10-minute walk off the main drag. It's worth the seat for the fresh spring rolls, pancakes, juices, pad thai and noodle soup.

★ Cafe Sinouk   LAOTIAN, INTERNATIONAL $$
(www.sinoukcafe.com; Charming Lao Hotel; mains 45,000-60,000K; ⊙ 7am-9pm; 🛜) Cafe Sinouk provides a much-needed respite from gastro mediocrity. With it comes great coffee and well-executed cuisine like barbecued pork, steamed fish, papaya salad and decent breakfasts, all laid out on fresh blue check-cloth tables in a warm custard-yellow interior. The garden courtyard features live music at weekends.

❶ Information

BCEL (☑ 211260; Rte 1) Has an ATM, changes several major currencies and accepts some travellers cheques (2% commission).

Tourist Office (Provincial Tourism Department of Oudomxay; ☑ 081-211797; www.oudomxay. info; ⊙ 7.30-11.30am & 1.30-6pm Mon-Fri Apr-Sep, 8am-noon & 1.30-4pm Mon-Fri Oct-Mar) The tourist office has masses of information about onward travel, accommodation and local sights, free town maps and sells GT-Rider Laos maps. There are 11 different tours on offer, including the two-day, one-night tour to an impressive local cave, and three-day, two-night treks and homestays to local ethnic villages.

❶ Getting There & Away

Lao Airlines flies to Vientiane (one way 695,000K) every Tuesday, Thursday and Saturday.

The **bus terminal** (☑ 081-212218) is at the southwestern edge of town. Buses head to Luang Prabang (ordinary 60,000K, five hours, three daily; VIP 100,000K, three hours, two daily), Nong Khiaw (45,000K, three to five hours, four daily), Pak Beng (40,000K, five hours, two daily), Luang Nam Tha (40,000K, four hours, three daily), Muang Khua (40,000K, four hours, three daily), Boten (ordinary/VIP 50,000/70,000K, four hours, two daily), Phongsali (80,000K, eight to 12 hours, one daily) and Vientiane (ordinary 150,000K, 16 hours, two daily; VIP 190,000K, 16 hours, one daily at noon).

A new bus station has opened 4km south of town on the same road as the old bus station. A regular bus to Vientiane (150,000K) leaves at 11am and an express (190,000K) at 2pm. Buses for Luang Prabang (60,000K) depart at 9am, noon and 3.30pm. A bus for Nong Khiaw (45,000K) leaves at 9am, and one at 1pm for Pakmong (30,000K).

Luang Namtha   ຫລວງນ້ຳທາ

☑ 086 / POP 21,000

Amiable Luang Namtha sits amid rice paddies ringed by mountains with the looming presence of Nam Ha National Protected Area (NPA) close by. With the demise of Muang Sing as a competitive base for treks to this great wilderness, Luang Namtha has excelled with a range of decent, eco-minded tour companies – this is after all the place where Laos' globally recognised green trekking policies were minted – and *falang*-oriented cafes and restaurants.

There's a lively night market packed with locals selling witchy-looking broths and chickens turning on spits, as well as a couple of banks and cycle-hire and scooter shops. Take a day to explore the valley's local waterfalls and temples before setting out into the wilds of Nam Ha.

◎ Sights & Activities

The dense jungle of the Nam Ha National Protected Area is home to clouded leopards, gaur and elephants (plus, perhaps, the odd tiger – we know, we met one a number of years ago!). Visiting the NPA involves going on a tour with an experienced guide. Guides also offer rafting, canoeing and mountain biking along the Nam Tha River, as well as homestays.

Places of interest within easy cycling or motorbiking distance include Wat Ban Vieng Tai and Wat Ban Luang Khon, near the airfield; a hilltop stupa, That Phum Phuk, about 4km west of the airfield; a small waterfall about 6km northeast of town past Ban Nam Dee; plus a host of Khamu, Lanten, Thai Dam and Thai Lü villages dotted along dirt roads through rice fields. Pick up a map and brochures at the provincial tourism office before setting off.

Luang Nam Tha Museum
MUSEUM

(ພິພິດຫະພັນຫຼວງນໍ້າທາ; admission 5000K; ⊙8.30-11.30am & 1.30-3.30pm Mon-Thu, 8.30-11.30am Fri) The Luang Nam Tha Museum contains a collection of local anthropological artefacts, such as ethnic clothing, Khamu bronze drums and ceramics. There are also a number of buddha images and the usual display chronicling the Revolution.

👉 Tours

★ Green Discovery
ECOTOUR

(✍086-211484; www.greendiscoverylaos.com; Main St; ⊙8am-9pm) 🌿 The granddaddy of ecotourism in Laos offers a combo of boat trips, mountain biking, kayaking, homestays and one- to three-day treks in Nam Ha NPA. Safety is a given and staff are helpful. At the time of writing they had plans to move to a new office.

Forest Retreat Laos
ECOTOUR

(✍020 55680031, 020 55560007; www.forestretreatlaos.com; ⊙7am-11.30pm) 🌿 Based at the Minority Restaurant, this ecotourism outfit offers kayaking, trekking, homestays and mountain biking. It also offers one- to six-day multi-activity adventures and recruits staff and guides from ethnic minority backgrounds where possible.

Discovering Laos
KAYAKING, RAFTING

(✍086-212047, 086-212025, 020 22990344; www.discoveringlaos.com; ⊙8am-9pm) 🌿 Specialises in kayaking and rafting trips through Khamu and Lenten villages as well as specialised cycling trips around Muang Sing. Also facilitates homestays.

🛏 Sleeping

In the high season (November to February) the town gets busy, so it's worth calling ahead to book a room.

Zuela Guesthouse
GUESTHOUSE $

(✍020 55886694; www.zuela-laos.com; r 80,000-120,000K; 🅿🌀📶) Located in a leafy courtyard, Zuela is a cut above the competition given its location off the main drag down a quiet lane, verdant grounds, swing-chair, scooter rental and large wood-floored rooms with exposed brick walls and spotless bathroom. Not forgetting its great restaurant serving up everything from pancakes to salads. It also operates an air-con minivan to Huay Xai.

Adounsiri Guest House
GUESTHOUSE $

(✍020 22991898, 055-445532; adounsiri@yahoo.com; r 70,000-130,000K; 📶) Located down a quiet street, in the house of a friendly Lao family, rooms here have white walls draped in handicrafts, fresh tiled floors, private bathrooms and a few sticks of furniture. The front room is fresh and welcoming with places to sit and chill. Outside is a little breakfast area. TVs in every room, plus free wi-fi, tea and coffee.

LAOS LUANG NAMTHA

GETTING TO CHINA: LUANG NAMTHA TO MENGLA

Getting to the border The Lao immigration post at the Boten/Mohan border crossing is a few minutes' walk north of Boten market. Tuk-tuk shuttle across no man's land to the Chinese immigration post in Mohan (Bohan) or it's an easy 10-minute walk. The border is open from 7.30am to 4.30pm Laos time, or 8.30am to 5.30pm Chinese time.

Alternatively, take one of the handy Laos–China through-bus connections such as Udomxai–Mengla, Luang Namtha–Jinghong or Luang Prabang–Kunming.

At the border It is necessary to have a Chinese visa in advance before attempting to enter the country.

Moving on From the Chinese immigration post it's a 15-minute walk up Mohan's main street to the stand where little buses depart for Mengla (RMB16, one hour) every 20 minutes or so till mid-afternoon. These arrive at Mengla's bus station No 2. Nip across that city to the northern bus station for Jinghong (RMB42, two hours, frequent till 6pm) or Kunming (mornings only).

GETTING TO THAILAND: NORTHERN BORDERS

Huay Xai to Chiang Rai

Since the completion of the Thai–Lao Friendship Bridge 4 at the Huay Xai/Chiang Khong border in late 2013, the former boat crossing across the Mekong is only for locals.

Getting to the border Tuk-tuk cost about 80B per person to the immigration post.

At the border A bus (20B to 30B) crosses the bridge. A 15-day Thai visa waiver is automatically granted when entering Thailand. Arriving in Chiang Khong, pay the 30B port fee and catch a 30B tuk-tuk to take you to the bus station. The nearest ATM on the Thai side is 2km south.

Moving on Many travellers leave Huay Xai bound for Chiang Rai (365B, 2½ hours), with buses typically departing from Chiang Khong's bus station every hour from 6am till 5pm. Greenbus (☑ in Thailand 66 5365 5732; www.greenbusthailand.com) has services to Chiang Mai at 6am, 9am and 11.40am. Several overnight buses for Bangkok (500 to 750B, 10 hours) leave at 3pm and 3.30pm.

For information on doing this crossing in reverse, see p703.

Hongsa to Phrae

Getting to the border The Muang Ngeun/Ban Huay Kon border crossing (8am to 5pm) is around 2.5km west of Muang Ngeun junction. Several *sŏrngtăaou* make the run from Hongsa (50,000K, 1½ hours) to Muang Ngeun. Once the new bridge north of Pak Beng is open, there will also be a bus service.

At the border Lao visas are available on arrival here, payable in US dollars or Thai baht. Most nationalities entering Thailand don't need a visa.

Moving on From the Thai side, if you don't want to walk your bags across the 1km of no man's land you can pay 100B for a motorbike with luggage-carrying sidecar. The Thai border post, Ban Huay Kon, is not quite a village but does have simple noodle shops. The only public transport is a luxurious minibus (☑ 083-024 3675) to Phrae (160B, five hours) via Nan (100B, three hours) departing from the border post at 11.45am. Northbound it leaves the bus stations in Phrae at 6am, and Nan at 8am.

For information on doing this crossing in reverse, see p703.

Pak Lai to Loei

Getting to the border The quiet rural Kaen Thao/Tha Li border crossing (8am to 6pm) is the home of yet another (small) Friendship Bridge, this time over the Nam Heuang. From Pak Lai, there are *sŏrngtăaou* to the border post at Kaen Thao at around 10am and noon (50,000K, 1¾ hours).

At the border Lao visas are available on arrival here, payable in US dollars or Thai baht. You'll need a passport-sized photo. Most nationalities entering Thailand don't need a visa.

Moving on After walking across the bridge you'll have to take a short *sŏrngtăaou* ride (30B) 8km to Tha Li before transferring to another *sŏrngtăaou* (40B) for the remaining 46km to Loei, from where there are regular connections to Bangkok and elsewhere.

For information on doing this crossing in reverse, see p724.

★ **Phou Iu III Guesthouse**   GUESTHOUSE **$$**
(☑ 030-5710422; www.luangnamtha-oasis-resort.com; r US$25) Part of the same family as the Phou Iu II in Muang Sing, this place is cracking value. Bungalows are spacious and nicely fitted out with lumber-wood beds, fireplaces and inviting terraces. It's well-signposted from the centre of town.

Thoulasith Guesthouse   GUESTHOUSE **$$**
(☑ 086-212166; www.thoulasith-guesthouse.com; r 80,000-120,000K, newer r 200,000K; P❋🛜) This traveller-friendly spot on the main strip offers spotless rooms with bedside lamps, art on the walls and comfortable wi-fi-enabled balconies. It's set back from the road and is a peaceful spot to wind down before or after

a trek. New is a block of swish rooms with baths and slightly kitsch decor.

Eating

★ Bamboo Lounge   INTERNATIONAL $
(☑ 020 22392931; mains 50,000K, pizzas 75,000K; ◷ 7am-11.30pm) This moss-green facade is alluring by night with winking fairy lights, and an outdoor terrace piping delicious aromas from its wood-fired oven. Myriad pizza choices. And unusually for Laos, completely nonsmoking.

Minority Restaurant   LAOTIAN $
(mains 35,000K; ◷ 7am-10.30pm; 🛜) This inviting, wood-beamed restaurant hidden down a little side alley offers the chance to sample typically ethnic dishes from the Khamu, Tai Dam and Akha tribes, as well as *lahp*, stir-fries, chicken curry and fried fish.

Boat Landing Restaurant   LAOTIAN $$
(meals 350,000-160,000K; ◷ 7am-8.30pm) The relaxing riverside setting complements some of the most authentic northern Lao cuisine on offer. From five-dish menus for two or three people to one-plate meals, the flavour combinations are divine. If you're baffled by the choice try snacking on a selection of *jqaou* used as dipping sauces for balls of sticky rice. Located 7km out of town.

ℹ Information

BCEL (◷ 8.30am-3.30pm Mon-Fri) Changes major currencies (commission-free), travellers cheques (2% commission, minimum US$3) and has a 24-hour ATM.

Provincial Tourism Office (☑ 086-211534; ◷ 8am-noon & 2-5pm) Helpful resource for local information, including trekking advice.

ℹ Getting There & Away

AIR
Lao Airlines flies to Vientiane (US$129) daily, while **Lao Skyway** (p378; US$70) flies three times per week.

BOAT
You can reach Huay Xai on a two-day longboat odyssey down the Namtha, sleeping en route at a roadless village. Luang Namtha agencies charge around US$170 to US$400 per person depending on exact numbers, including accommodation, meals and a tour guide throughout. You might get a better deal from the boat station beside the Boat Landing Restaurant. When river levels are low (January to June), departures are from Na Lae, with agencies providing tuk-tuk transfers and prearranging a boat.

BUS
There are two bus stations. The district bus station is walking distance from the traveller strip, while the main long-distance bus station is 10km south of town. For Nong Khiaw take a Vientiane or Luang Prabang bus and change at Pak Mong.

ℹ Getting Around
Chartered tuk-tuk charge 15,000K per person (minimum 40,000K) between the bus station or airport and the town centre. Most agencies and guesthouses sell ticket packages for long-distance buses, which include a transfer from the guesthouse and cost around 20,000K above the usual fare.

Cycling is the ideal way to explore the wat, waterfalls, villages and landscape surrounding Luang Namtha. There are a couple of **bicycle shops** (bicycle per day 10,000-25,000K; motorcycle per day 30,000-50,000K; ◷ 9am-6.30pm) in front of the Zuela Guesthouse that also rent scooters.

BUSES FROM LUANG NAMTHA

DESTINATION	FARE (K)	DURATION (HR)	STATION	FREQUENCY
Boten	35,000	2	district	6 daily 8am-3.30pm
Huay Xai ('Borkeo')	60,000	4	long distance	9am, 12.30pm & 4pm
Jinghong (China)	90,000	6	long distance	8am
Luang Prabang	100,000	8	long distance	9am bus, 8am minibus
Luang Sing	30,000	2	district	6 daily 8am-3.30pm
Mengla (China)	50,000	3½	long distance	8am
Muang Long	60,000	4	district	8.30am
Na Lae	40,000	3	district	9.30am, noon
Udomxai	40,000	4	long distance	8.30am, noon, 2.30pm
Vieng Phukha	35,000	1½	long distance	9.30am, noon
Vientiane	200,000	21-24	long distance	8.30am, 2.30pm

Huay Xai

ຫ້ວຍຊາຍ

✎ 084 / POP 20,000

It's unlikely you'll be sending a postcard home from this dustblown low-slung border town, with Thailand just a few hundred metres across the coffee-brown Mekong. A clandestine US heroin processing plant was allegedly based here during the Secret War, but these days the only things spirited through Huay Xai are travellers en route to Luang Prabang and those headed here for a visit to the fabled Gibbon Experience (p355), *still* Laos' most talked-about and eco-conscious jungle adventure.

By night Huay Xai's central drag dons fairy lights and roadside food vendors fire up their wares. There are some welcoming guesthouses and a couple of choice bars to tide you over.

🛏 Sleeping & Eating

Budget sleeping and eating haunts are mainly clustered on the main drag.

★ Daauw Homestay
HOMESTAY $

(✎ 030-9041296; www.projectkajsiablaos.org; r 60,000-80,000K) Run by lovely Hmong folk, your stay in a cosy bungalow near the heart of town enables you to contribute something to women's empowerment and minority rights, for this place is a grassroots initiative run by Project Kajsiab. Lovely alluring rooms with sunset views, hammock, balcony and private bathroom; these little bungalows may be the cosiest choice in town.

There's a small handicrafts shop, and you can also volunteer here. It's located just off the stairs to Wat Jom Khao Manilat, half way up on the right-hand side.

Phonetip Guesthouse
GUESTHOUSE $

(✎ 084-211084; Th Saykhong; r 40,000-90,000K; ✳ ⧉) Central and friendly. Although it's basic, the owners ensure the place smells fragrant, the sheets and floors are clean, the wi-fi works and the staff are friendly. The cheapest options are just beds in boxes but there's a pleasant road-facing communal area to sit upstairs if you can grab a seat.

Oudomphone Guesthouse 2
GUESTHOUSE $

(✎ 084-211308, 020 55683134; Main St; r with fan/air-con 80,000/120,000K; ✳ ⧉) Clean and central, these digs have a pleasant breakfast cafe and spacious nondescript rooms with bathroom. Nothing spectacular but one of the slightly better options.

BAP Guesthouse
GUESTHOUSE $

(Th Saykhong; r 60,000-130,000K; mains 15,000-35,000K; ⧉) Run by English-speaking Mrs Changpeng, trusty old BAP has 16 rooms of varying appeal, some with fan or air-con and private bathroom. There are four newish ones which merit a mention for their colourful quilts, wood accents, TV and sunset views over the Mekong, particularly rooms 108 and 109. The restaurant is also popular for its fried rice dishes, pasta and hearty breakfasts.

Riverview Cafe
LAOTIAN, INTERNATIONAL $

(Gecko Bar; Th Saykhong; meals 40,000K; ⊙ 6.30am-11pm) With its rattan ceiling dramatically on the verge of collapse and the thirsty walls peeling, it might not look much, but notice it's always full and stand and catch the aromas from the kitchen, and in no time you'll be tucking into wood-fired pizzas, burgers, stir-fries, soup noodles and very zestful *lahp*.

It's next door to the Gibbon Experience; stock up on a sandwich to take with you to the jungle.

Daauw
LAOTIAN $

(mains 30,000-50,000K; ⧉) The friendliest vibe in town: soak up the sunset view on its chill-out terrace decked in low cushions and an open pit fire, and choose from freshly prepared organic Hmong food, wood-fired pizza, plenty of vegetarian options, or whole barbecued Mekong fish or chicken. Linger for *laojitos* if there's a crowd, a mojito made with *lòw-lów* (rice wine).

🍷 Drinking & Nightlife

Bar How
BAR

(Th Saykhong; mains 25,000-40,000K; ⊙ 6.30am-11pm; ⧉) Decked in old muskets and rice paddy hats, Bar How is dark and atmospheric. By night it's even more inviting, a row of sinister-looking homemade *lòw-lów* (rice wine) infused with everything from blueberry to tamarind, honey to lychee, catching the low light like something out of a Victorian apothecary. Pasta, steak, juices and breakfast too.

ⓘ Information

BCEL (Th Saykhong; ⊙ 8.30am-4.30pm Mon-Fri) Twenty-four-hour ATM, exchange facility and Western Union.

Lao Development Bank Exchange Booth (⊙ 8am-5pm) Handy booth right beside the pedestrian immigration window. Most major currencies exchanged into kip. US-dollar bills must be dated 2006 or later.

Tourist Information Office (📞 084-211162; Th Saykhong; ⏰ 8am-4.30pm Mon-Fri) Has free tourist maps of the town and some suggestions for excursions around the province.

❶ Getting There & Away

AIR

Huay Xai's airport is perched on a hillside 1.5km northwest of the bus station. Lao Airlines flies daily to/from Vientiane for 895,000K.

BOAT

Slow boats headed down the Mekong River to Luang Prabang (220,000K per person, two days, not including overnight accommodation) hold about 70 people. Boats leave from the boat landing at the northern end of town at 11am and stop for one night in Pak Beng (110,000K, six to eight hours). Tickets are available from the boat landing the afternoon before you travel, or from guesthouses.

Speedboats to Pak Beng (190,000K, three hours) and Luang Prabang (320,000K, six hours) leave when they are full, from a landing

about 2km south of town, from 8am daily. Buy your ticket at any one of the guesthouses or on arrival at the kiosk above the boat landing. Deaths are not uncommon given the recklessness of the drivers.

Slow boats also run to Luang Namtha (1,530,000K to 1,700,000K per boat split between passengers, plus 40,000K each for food and accommodation) via Ban Na Lae. Ask at BAP Guesthouse for more information.

For any journey take plenty of water, food supplies and padding for your back (earplugs are useful for the speedboat).

BUS

The bus station is 5km east of town. Buses to Luang Prabang (120,000K, 14 to 17 hours) depart at 10am and 4pm, Udomxai (85,000K, nine hours) at 9.30am, and one for Vientiane (230,000K, 25 hours) at 11.30am. There is also a bus to Muengla (120,000K) at 8.30am and Xieng Khong (160,000K) at 8am. For Luang Namtha (60,000K, four hours) an additional bus departs at 9am.

Travel-agency minibuses to Luang Namtha (100,000K) leave from central Huay Xai at around 9am.

THE GIBBON EXPERIENCE

Back in 1996 poaching was threatening the extinction of the black-crested gibbon in Laos until the **Gibbon Experience** (📞 084-212021; www.gibbonexperience.org; express 2-day US$190, 3-day classic or waterfall US$310) came to their rescue with a brilliantly inventive eco-meets-adrenalin concept: a series of navigable 'ziplines' criss-crossing the canopy of some of Laos' most pristine forest, and, more crucially, poachers re-employed as Gibbon Experience guides. Local wildlife including tigers, clouded leopards, black bears and the eponymous black-crested gibbon have as a direct result been given the chance to replenish, while you have the satisfaction that your money goes directly into conserving their habitat. This is one of the most successful illustrations of ecotourism in Laos today.

And the zipping? Given the lush territory, one of the wildest spots in Laos, and the fact that this is where zipping started, this is *still* the best place to lose your breath in Laos. You'll stay in one of the world's tallest tree houses complete with cooking facilities and running rainwater showers, while in between scouting for wildlife, you'll be zipping. It's a heart-stopping, superhero experience.

Your day will also involve a serious amount of trekking. Bring a pair of hiking boots and long socks to deter the ever-persistent leeches, plus a torch and earplugs. The guides are helpful, though be vigilant with the knots in your harness.

There are three options to choose from: the three-day 'Classic' (less trekking), and 'Waterfall' (increased slog balanced by a dip in a cascade pool); and the two-day 'Express' maximising zipping time. Fees include transport to and from the park, plus all food and refreshments.

Payments can be made well in advance via PayPal. Turn up in Huay Xai the day before your trek and report to the **Gibbon Experience office** (📞 084-212021; www.gibbonexperience.org; Th Saykhong; ⏰ 8am-7pm). Next door you can buy gloves, torches and stock up on treats.

CENTRAL & SOUTHERN LAOS

Steamy rice plains and protected forests await travellers heading south to tackle other-worldy Tham Kong Lo, a vast 7.5km subterranea in Khammuane Province, also celebrated for its ragged charcoal-black karsts and the legendary Loop, a terrific three-day motorbike adventure. Nearby colonial Tha Khaek and further south Savannakhet merit a visit for their old French buildings, while close to the rural charms of turquoise-watered Si Phan Don (Four Thousand Islands), you'll find sleepy Champasak with its beautiful Khmer ruins.

Route 8 to Lak Sao

Wind your way through a lost world of jungle and dreamlike rock formations in some of the country's trippiest landscape. The first major stop is **Ban Khoun Kham** (also known as Ban Na Hin), 41km east of Rte 13, in the lush Hin Bun valley. The village makes a base from which to explore Phu Hin Bun National Protected Area. You can also catch your onward bus to Ban Kong Lo, the base for extraordinary Tham Kong Lo. Community-based treks gear up at the **tourist information centre** (☑020 55598412; Rte 8; ◷8am-4pm) just south of the Tat Namsanam entrance.

◉ Sights

Tham Kong Lo   CAVE

(close to Ban Kong Lo; per boat 130,000K) Situated in the 1580-sq-km wilderness of **Phu Hin Bun National Protected Area**, this 7.5km river tunnel, running beneath an immense limestone mountain, ratchets up the fear dial like some natural gothic ghost ride. Puttering into its 100m church-high darkness by longtail is the only way to travel, your stomach turning as the cave entrance becomes a pinpoint of light. Halfway, you'll moor up and stroll through a dramatically lit stalactite wood, like an abandoned old *Star Trek* set.

Remember to bring a decent torch, plus rubber sandals. Kong Lo village (about 1km downstream of the cave mouth) is your base for this unforgettable trip. Takes around two hours for the return trip with a 20-minute drinks break at a sala on the other side of the cave. Lifejackets are handed out at the ticket office.

⌸ Sleeping & Eating

⌸ Ban Khoun Kham

Digs in Ban Khoun Kham are basic, with warm showers and private bathrooms.

Xok Xai Guesthouse   GUESTHOUSE $

(☑051-233629; Rte 8; r 80,000K; P❋≋) Lovely rooms in a traditional house set back off Rte 8 (400m north from the market). Details include spotless varnished floors, thick duvets, TV, air-con, powder-blue curtains and hot-water en suites.

Sainamhai Resort   RESORT $$

(☑020 2331683; www.sainamhairesort.com; s/d US$20/25; P❋≋) By far the dreamiest, most cosy accommodation in town – except it's not in town. Thankfully Sainamhai sits by the Nam Hai (Hai River) a little out of the village. There's a handsome longhouse restaurant (mains 25,000K), a fertile garden and 12 well-maintained rattan-walled cabanas with private balconies, en suites and clean linen. Add to this warm service, air-con...convinced?

It's 3km east of Rte 8 via a turn-off a few kilometres down the road that leads to Tham Kong Lo. Staff will pick you up for free at the *sŏrngtǎaou* station if you call ahead.

⌸ Kong Lo Village

Not as comfortable as Chantha Guest House perhaps, but definitely more memorable are the **homestay** options in Kong Lo village (per person including breakfast and dinner 50,000K). Ask around and a family will take you in.

Chantha Guest House   GUESTHOUSE $

(☑020 2100002; www.chanthahouse.com; Ban Kong Lo; r US$15-20; P❋@≋) This Swiss-style accommodation on the main road to Kong Lo and at the beginning of the village has 15 cool and well-kept rooms, plus a dorm. There's a DVD lounge and a small cafe and the owners are friendly. There's a bike for rent and, best of all, magnificent views of the cliffs.

Mithuna Restaurant   LAOTIAN $

(Ban Kong Lo; mains 30,000K; ◷7am-8pm) Close to the entrance to Tham Kong Lo, this semi-alfresco, fan-cooled restaurant serves up noodles, fried rice and pork *lahp*, as well as Western breakfasts.

ℹ Getting There & Away

From Tha Khaek there's daily 8am and 9am departures for Ban Khoun Kham (60,000K). Alternatively, there's a direct daily bus to Kong Lo (80,000K) from Tha Khaek's Talat Phetmany at 7am. All transport along Rte 8 stops at Ban Khoun Kham. If you're coming from Vientiane hop off at Vieng Kham and continue by *sŏrngtǎaou* (30,000K, 7am to 7pm) to Ban Khoun Kham.

A bus for Vientiane (80,000K, six hours) leaves at 10am. For Tha Khaek (80,000K, three hours, 143km), there are a couple of buses in the morning; for Lak Sao take any passing bus or *sŏrngtǎaou* (30,000K).

From Ban Khoun Kham to Ban Kong Lo, it's a 20-minute journey by *sŏrngtǎaou* (30,000K), which depart at 10am, 12.30pm and 3pm. Headed the other way from Ban Kong Lo to Ban Khoun Kham, *sŏrngtǎaou* depart at 6.30am, 8am and 11am.

Tha Khaek   ທ່າແຂກ

☑ 051 / POP 81,000

This ex Indochinese trading post is a pleasing melange of crumbling French villas and wilting Chinese merchant shopfronts, and, despite the new bridge over to nearby Thailand, it shows little signs of radical change.

Catch a riverside sundowner or wander along its atmospheric streets as dusk's amber light kicks in and douses the old buildings in charm. With its dusty centrepiece fountain and tree-shaded boulevards glowing with braziers, Tha Khaek is reminiscent of Vientiane 15 years ago.

Tha Khaek is also a comfy base from which to do the Loop, the legendary three-day motorbike odyssey. For a proper dirtbike rental – a little more expensive than cheap Chinese scooters but far more adhesive to gravelly roads – head to Mad Monkey Motorbike (p359).

☞ Tours

The Tourist Information Centre run by reliable Mr Somkiad runs various adventures, such as two-day treks in the Phu Hin Bun National Protected Area, typically involving a homestay. Ask him too about the 3km-long newly discovered river cave, Tham Pa Seuam (Fish Cave), 15km away.

Green Climbers Home ROCK CLIMBING
(☑ 020 59667532, 020 59667539; www.green climbershome.com; Ban Kouanphavang, Xiangliab; ½- to 2-day courses from 200,000-100,000K, depending on numbers of group) This efficiently run training school set in a valley in soaring

---

GETTING TO THAILAND: CENTRAL BORDERS

Tha Khaek to Nakhon Phanom

Getting to the border A Friendship Bridge has opened here (the ferry boat that used to run is now closed to foreigners). The bridge is some 7km from Tha Khaek and a tuk-tuk carrying two people over the bridge will cost 25,000K per person from Tha Khaek's bus station (departing every half-hour). The immigration office on the bridge opens at 7am and closes at 4pm.

At the border A free 15-day visa is granted on entry to Thailand. There's an exchange booth and 24-hour ATM.

Moving on From the bridge it's a 30B tuk-tuk ride to Thailand's Nakhon Phanom bus station, from where buses leave regularly for Udon Thani and also Bangkok (at 7.30am and from 7pm to 8pm).

For information on doing this crossing in reverse, see p724.

Paksan to Bueng Kan

Getting to the border In Paksan follow a sign to the port and Lao border post (open 8am to noon and 1.30pm to 4.30pm). The boat across the Mekong to Bueng Kan takes a few minutes and costs 60B per person or charter for 480B.

At the border Fifteen-day Thai visas are granted on arrival but check in advance with the Thai Embassy in Vientiane as this is a remote spot seldom used by travellers.

Moving on Buses leave Bueng Kan in Thailand for Udon Thani and Bangkok.

For information on doing this crossing in reverse, see p724.

karst country is hugely popular and often booked up thanks to its cosy cabanas, great food and excellent courses. It also boasts one of the easiest overhangs in the world to learn on and has beginner, intermediate and expert level climbs; 170 routes, class 4 to 8B.

Located 12km from Tha Khaek, a tuk-tuk by day costs 100,000K.

Green Discovery ADVENTURE TOUR
(☑ 051-251390; Inthira Hotel, Th Chao Annou; ☉ 8am-9pm) A range of treks and kayaking excursions in the lush Phu Hin Bun NPA, including Tham Kong Lo (US$141). Also offers cycling, climbing and kayaking.

🛏 Sleeping

★ Thakhek Travel Lodge GUESTHOUSE $
(☑ 051-251390, 030-5300145; travell@laotel.com; Rte 13; dm 30,000K, r with bathroom & fan 60,000-90,000K, r with bathroom & air-con 90,000K; P ✱ @ 🛜) It's an inconvenient five minutes

out of town by tuk-tuk, but this place has a great vibe thanks to its nightly garden fire-pit, drawing travellers together; a cafe serving *lahp*, salads, pork chops and juices; and rooms varying from basic to romantic, and overpriced. Check out the log book for news of the Loop.

Mekong Hotel HOTEL $
(☑ 051-250777; Th Setthathirat; r with fan/air-con 100,000/140,000K; P ✱ 🛜) Thanks to a recent repaint this blue, Soviet-inspired monolith is much improved, with houseproud, decent rooms enjoying cable TV, air-con and fresh en suites. There's also a restaurant facing the Mekong.

Thipphachanh Guesthouse GUESTHOUSE $
(☑ 051-212762; Rte 13; r with fan/air-con 60,000/80,000K; P ✱) Based around a courtyard, fragrant rooms have white walls, tiled floors, TV and en suite.

GETTING TO VIETNAM: CENTRAL BORDERS

Tha Khaek to Dong Hoi

Getting to the border The Na Phao/Cha Lo border (open 7am to 4pm) is so out of the way it might be better to opt for an easier crossing elsewhere. Transport on either side is slow and scarce, though there are two daily *sŏrngtăaou* from Tha Khaek (50,000K, 3½ hours, 142km) at 8am and noon bound for Lang Khang, 18km short of the border. Catch the early *sŏrngtăaou* as you'll need to organise your own onward transport to the border.

At the border This is a small, sleepy border post. On the Vietnamese side the nearest sizeable city is Dong Hoi. Remember to organise your Vietnamese visa in advance.

Moving on A direct bus from Tha Khaek to Dong Hoi (90,000K, 10 to 14 hours) leaves four times a week at 7pm, making this the easiest way to cross this border.

For information on doing this crossing in reverse, see p848.

Lak Sao to Vinh

Getting to the border The Nam Phao/Cau Treo border crossing (open 7am to 4.30pm) is at the Kaew Neua Pass, 36km from Lak Sao. *Sŏrngtăaou* (25,000K, 45 minutes) leave every hour or so from Lak Sao market and drop passengers at the border. Alternatively, direct buses from Lak Sao to Vinh, Vietnam (120,000K, five hours), leave several times a day between noon and 2pm (you may have to change buses at the border).

At the border You'll need to prearrange a visa if heading into Vietnam. There's an exchange booth on the Laos side with ungenerous rates and, inconveniently, the Vietnam border post is another 1km up the road.

Moving on On the Vietnamese side beware of people who'll offer to take you to Vinh by minibus for US$30 – it *should* cost US$5 per person. A metered taxi costs around US$40 while a motorbike fare is 200,000d. Hook up with other travellers to improve bargaining power. These woes can be avoided by taking the direct bus from Lak Sao to Vinh. Once in Vinh take the sleeper train, the Reunification Express (www.vr.com.vn), direct to Hanoi.

For information on doing this crossing in reverse, see p848.

✗ Eating

Several *khào jìi* (baguette) vendors can be found on or near Fountain Sq in the morning, and the adjacent riverfront is good for a cheap meal any time.

Duc Restaurant   LAOTIAN $
(Th Setthathirat; mains 20,000K; ⊗6am-10pm; 🖋) On the riverfront just off Fountain Sq, this fan-cooled, family-run joint has the most delicious *fěr hàang* (dry rice noodles served in a bowl with various herbs and seasonings but no broth) in town.

★ Kitchen   FUSION $$
(Inthira Hotel, Th Chao Anou; mains 45,000K; ⊗7am-10pm; 🖙🖋) Classy and low-lit, this fine restaurant is as sophisticated as sleepy Tha Khaek gets. Based in a pretty French colonial-era building, the open range kitchen, visible but behind glass, dishes up tasty Lao salads, burgers, substantial tenderised steak and decent cocktails from the sleek glass bar. You can eat on the street if it's cool out.

ℹ Information

There are three ATMs in town (including one in Fountain Sq) plus one at the bus station.

BCEL (Th Vientiane) Changes major currencies and travellers cheques, and makes cash advances on Visa.

Lao Development Bank (Th Vientiane) Cash only.

Tha Khaek Hospital (cnr Th Chao Anou & Th Champasak) Fine for minor ailments. Seek out English-speaking Dr Bounthavi.

Tourist Information Centre (📞030-5300503, 020 55711797; www.khammuane tourism.com; Th Vientiane; ⊗8.30am-5pm) This excellent tourist office offers exciting one- and two-day treks in Phou Hin Boun NPA (where you have a 50% chance of spotting the red-footed Douc lemurs), including a homestay in a local village. There are also treks to the waterfall by Ban Khoun Kham and Kong Lo Cave (800,000K).

Tourist Police (📞250610; Fountain Sq) The police here know how to write insurance reports – if you can track down an officer.

ℹ Getting There & Away

Tha Khaek's bus station is on Rte 13, about 3.5km from the centre of town. For Vientiane (70,000K, six hours, 353km), buses leave every hour or so between 5.30am and 9am; there's also a VIP departure at 9.15am (85,000K, six hours) and a sleeper VIP at 1am (85,000K). Any buses going north stop at Vieng Kham (Thang Beng; 35,000K, 1½ hours, 102km) and Paksan (50,000K, three to four hours, 193km). There are daily services to Attapeu (90,000K, 10 hours, 3.30pm and 11pm), Salavan (85,000K, 11pm) and Sekong (80,000K, 10am and 3.30pm).

Southward buses to Savannakhet (30,000K) depart every half-hour, plus there's a VIP bus (70,000K, six hours) to Pakse that leaves at 9am, plus hourly local buses (70,000K). For travellers heading to Vietnam, buses for Hué (120,000K) leave Monday, Tuesday, Wednesday and Saturday at 8am; every Monday and Friday at 8pm for Danang (120,000K); 8pm on Tuesday and Saturday for Hanoi (160,000K, 17 hours); and every Monday and Friday for Dong Hoi (90,000K, 10 hours).

If you're headed direct to Don Khong (150,000K, 15 hours, 452km) in the Four Thousand Islands, a bus from Vientiane stops around 5.30pm.

Sŏrngtăaou depart every hour or so from Talat Phetmany to Mahaxai Mai (35,000K, 1½ hours, 50km). One also goes direct to Ban Kong Lo (80,000K, four hours) at 7.30am.

Sook Som Boon Bus Terminal has buses that serve the Khammuane Province interior with *sŏrngtăaou* leaving every hour between 7.30am and 9.30am for Gnommalath (45,000K, two to three hours, 63km), Nakai (45,000K, 2½ to 3½ hours, 80km) and an 8pm departure for Na Phao (for the Vietnam border; 80,000K, 3½ hours, 142km).

ℹ Getting Around

It should cost about 20,000K to hire a jumbo to the bus terminal. Rides around town cost around 20,000K per person.

The one and only place to hire a tough, reliable motocross bike to tackle the Loop is **Mad Monkey Motorbike** (📞020 59939909, 020 23477799; www.madmonkey-thakek.com; Fountain Sq; 250cc dirt bikes/scooters per day 350,000/160,000; ⊗9am-8pm). If you break down you can phone the owner and for a price he'll come and get you. He can also take you to Tham Kong Lo and back, leaving at 8am and returning at 8pm.

Mr Ku's Motorbike Rental (📞020 2206070; per day 100,000K; ⊗7.30am-4.30pm), located at Thakhek Travel Lodge, has 110cc Korean bikes for getting around town or to the closer caves.

Phavilai Restaurant (Fountain Sq; per day 60,000K; ⊗6am-9pm) has a few scooters for hire, as does the **Wangwang** (📞020 56978535; Fountain Sq; per day 50,000-60,000K; ⊗8am-9pm) internet shop.

Around Tha Khaek

Travellers rave about the **Loop**, a brilliant three-day motorbike trip through dense jungle and karst country passing via Nakai, Lak Sao, Khoun Kham (Na Hin) and Tham Kong Lo; for details look at the travellers' log book at Thakhek Travel Lodge (p358).

Meanwhile, buzz continues in anticipation of trips to the fantastical 9.5km subterranea of **Xe Bang Fai cave**, located at the edge of Hin Namno NPA.

Also don't miss the myriad caves that can be swum and explored right on Tha Khaek's doorstep. Talk to English-speaking Mr Somkiad at Tha Khaek's Tourist Information Centre.

Savannakhet ສະຫວັນນະເຂດ

☑ 041 / POP 139,000

Modern Savannakhet is a restless engine of activity, too busy for aesthetics as it conducts trade with neighbours Thailand and Vietnam. Fortunately for you the prettiest section of the city is within its historic quarter; it's enchantingly quiet and seems to be trapped in time. You almost feel as if you've walked into an old film as you wander along its bougainvillea-blown streets, strolling past decaying early-20th-century villas from Indochina's heyday. While most of these buildings are crying out for a makeover, a few faded belles have finally begun restoration programs.

There's little to do but amble along the riverfront and plonk yourself down in a clutch of stylish restaurants and bijou cafes. That said, there's loads to do *nearby*; Savannakhet has a dedicated tourist information centre and ecoguide unit, which has myriad trips to tempt you into the nearby national protected areas (NPAs).

◉ Sights

Hire a bicycle and pedal the parched streets along the riverfront, or take a trek in the neighbouring protected areas with Savannakhet's Eco Guide Unit (p362).

Savannakhet
Provincial Museum   MUSEUM
(ພິພິດທະພັນແຂວງຊະຫວັນນະເຂດ; Th Khanthabuli; admission 10,000K; ☺ 8-11.30am & 1-4pm Mon-Sat) The Savannakhet Provincial Museum is a good place to see war relics, artillery pieces and inactive examples of the deadly UXO (unexploded ordnance) that has claimed the lives of more than 20,000 Lao since the end of the Secret War.

Musée Des
Dinosaures   MUSEUM
(ຫໍພິພິດທະພັນໄດໂນເສົ້າ, Dinosaur Museum; ☑ 041-212597; Th Khanthabuli; admission 10,000K; ☺ 8am-noon & 1-4pm) In 1930 a major dig in a nearby village unearthed 200-million-year-old dinosaur fossils. The enthusiastically run Dinosaur Museum is an interesting place to see three different dinosaurs. Savannakhet Province is home to five dinosaur sites.

GETTING TO VIETNAM: SAVANNAKHET TO DONG HA

Getting to the border Crossing the Dansavanh/Lao Bao border is a relatively easy exercise. From Savannakhet buses leave for Dansavanh (60,000K, four to six hours, 236km) at 7am, 8.30am and 11am. Alternatively, if you're passing this way it's worth breaking the trip for a night in Sepon (50,000K, four hours) as a base for seeing the Ho Chi Minh Trail. The bus station in Dansavanh is about 1km short of the border: Vietnamese teenagers on motorbikes can take you the remainder of the journey for about 20,000K.

At the border Vietnam visas must be arranged in advance, which can be done at the Vietnam consulate in Savannakhet. The border is open from 7am to 6pm.

Moving on Once through take a motorbike (15,000d) 2km to the Lao Bao bus terminal and transport to Dong Ha (50,000d, two hours, 80km) on Vietnam's main north–south highway and railway. Simple accommodation is available on both sides of the border. If you're in a hurry just grab a bus from Savannakhet bound for the Vietnamese cities of Dong Ha, Hue and Danang.

For information on doing this crossing in reverse, see p849.

kitsch decor in comfortable, peach-coloured rooms. The clean rooms have tiled floors, hot-water showers and TVs, and there's a pleasant breakfast area where you can pick up wi-fi. An oldie but a goodie, the air-con rooms are larger and fresher looking. There's also a cafe.

🍴 Eating

Choose between sidewalk cafes, French restaurants and **riverside snack and drink vendors** (◷ 5-10pm) for cheap quick eats.

★ Lin's Café   INTERNATIONAL $
(Th Latsaphanith; mains 40,000K; ◷ 8am-8pm; 🛜🍴) Savannakhet's number one traveller fave, this delightful cafe sits in a former 1930s Chinese merchant's house and is loved for its easy vibe, soporific water feature, friendly staff, reservoir of local information, retro eclectic interior and gallery upstairs. But most of all, its repeat visitors love the nutty smooth cappuccinos, Thai green curry, tasty beef burgers, fruit salad, fresh pastry... We could go on!

Chai Dee   JAPANESE, INTERNATIONAL $
(☏ 030-5003336; www.cafechaidee.com; Th Ratsavongsouk; mains 30,000K; ◷ 9am-9.30pm Mon-Sat; 🛜🍴) This spotless cafe has rattan mats to lounge on, a book exchange and a wide menu of samosas, homemade yoghurt, Thai food and tofu, plus healthy shakes. Great breakfasts too. Expect super-fresh, well-presented food, quick wi-fi and warm service.

Xokxay Restaurant   LAOTIAN $
(Th Si Muang; mains 20,000K; ◷ 9am-9pm; 🍴) This cheap-as-chips hole-in-the-wall near the Catholic church dishes up authentic tasty Laotian food, including noodle dishes, fried rice, salads and crispy fried shrimp.

LAOS SAVANNAKHET

🛏 Sleeping

Souannavong Guest House   GUESTHOUSE $
(☏ 041-212600; Th Saenna; r with/without air-con 100,000/80,000K; 🅿❄🛜🐾) Unfailingly fresh with clean en suite rooms, this little guesthouse is down a quiet street that's abloom with bougainvillea. It has wi-fi and bikes to rent and is a welcoming place to stay.

Leena Guesthouse   GUESTHOUSE $
(☏ 041-212404; leenaguesthouse@hotmail.com; Th Chaokeen; r 60,000-100,000K; 🅿❄@🛜) Fairy-lit Leena is something of a motel with

ⓘ Information

Eco Guide Unit (☏ 041-214203; Th Latsa-phanith; ⊘ 8am-noon & 1-4.30pm Mon-Fri) The industrious eco-guide unit provides helpful information ranging from bookings for treks to Dong Natad PPA and Dong Phu Vieng NPA, to bus times and accommodation. Staff can also suggest where to get a decent massage or hire a motorbike (although obviously not both at the same time!).

Provincial Hospital (☏ 020 2601993, 041-212717; Th Khanthabuli; ⊘ 8am-noon & 1-4pm) Ask for English-speaking Dr Outhon.

Provincial Tourism Office (☏ 041-212755; Th Muang Sing; ⊘ 8-11.30am & 1.30-4.30pm) Has helpful city maps and English-speaking staff with suggestions of things to do, from dining recommendations to local sights.

ⓘ Getting There & Away

Savannakhet's airport fields daily flights to and from Vientiane (US$128), Pakse (US$75) and Bangkok (US$155). Buy tickets at the **Lao Airlines** (☏ 041-212140; Savannakhet Airport; ⊘ 6.30am-4.30pm) office.

Savannakhet's **bus terminal** (☏ 041-212143) is 2km north of town on Th Makkasavan. Buses leave for Vientiane (75,000K, nine hours, 470km) hourly from 6am to 11.30am. Thereafter you'll have to catch buses headed to Pakse that pass through Tha Khaek (30,000K, 2½ to four hours, 125km) until 10pm. A sleeper VIP bus to Vientiane (120,000K, six to seven hours) leaves at 9.30pm.

Heading south, at least 10 buses start here or pass through from Vientiane for Pakse (45,000K, five to six hours, 230km) and a daily bus to Don Khong (80,000K, six to eight hours) leaves at 7pm.

Buses for Dansavanh (60,000K, five to seven hours) on the Lao/Vietnamese border leave at 7am, 8.30am and 11am, stopping at Sepon (50,000K, four to six hours). A daily local bus heads to Hué (90,000K), while a VIP bus (110,000K) runs Monday to Friday at 10.30am. A bus to Danang (110,000K) leaves Tuesday, Thursday and Saturday at 10pm, continuing to Hanoi (200,000K, 24 hours, 650km).

ⓘ Getting Around

A tuk-tuk to Savannakhet's bus terminal will cost about 20,000K; note that prices double after dark. The town is fairly sprawled out so it might be a good idea to rent a scooter (70,000K) from Souannavong Guest House (p361). Or you can hire bikes (10,000K) along Th Ratsavongseuk.

Pakse ປາກເຊ

☏ 031 / POP 75,000

Wilting under the force of the unrelenting southern sun, this sprawling riverside city is showing signs of gentrification with new bakeries and upscale restaurants constantly opening, and acquits itself well to travellers with an efficiently run tourist office, a couple of tour companies and myriad guesthouses.

Those destined for the Four Thousand Islands and to Cambodia beyond will unavoidably stay here. Thanks to Green Discovery's Tree Top Explorer ziplining adventure, the city's proximity to beguiling Khmer ruins, Wat Phu, and also the Bolaven Plateau coffee-growing region with its Edenic waterfalls, Pakse makes for a useful springboard.

◉ Sights & Activities

Champasak Historical Heritage Museum   MUSEUM
(ພິພິດທະພັນມໍລະດົກປະຫວັດສາດຈຳປາສັກ; Rte 13; admission 10,000K; ⊘ 8-11.30am & 1-4pm Mon-Fri) This museum features ancient Dong Son bronze drums, a 7th-century Siam-style sandstone buddha head, and a textile and jewellery collection from the Nyaheun, Suay and Laven groups, interesting for its large iron ankle bracelets and ivory ear plugs. Also on display are musical instruments, stelae in Tham script dating from the 15th to 18th centuries, a small lingam (Shiva phallus), a scale model of Wat Phu Champasak, and some American unexploded ordnances (UXO).

Dok Champa Massage   MASSAGE
(Th 5; massages from 40,000K, body scrub 200,000K; ⊘ 9am-10pm) Again and again Dok Champa comes out on top as the favourite Pakse spa, thanks to its friendly staff, oils, and bespoke service offering you exactly the level of robust or soft pampering your weary muscles require.

☞ Tours

Most hotels and guesthouses can arrange day trips to the Bolaven Plateau, Wat Phu Champasak and Si Phan Don (Four Thousand Islands). The provincial tourism office (p365) also arranges community-based two- or three-day treks in Se Pian NPA and Phou Xieng Thong NPA, involving kayaking and camping combos, as well as homestays on Don Kho and Don Daeng.

Pakse

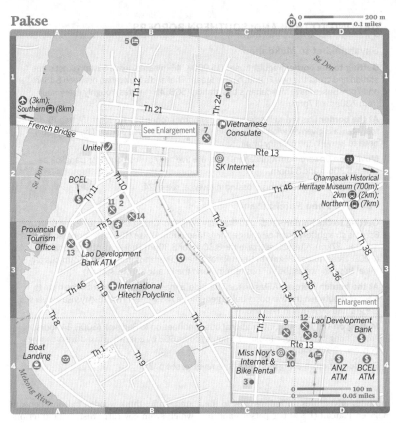

Pakse

Activities, Courses & Tours
1 Dok Champa Massage B3
2 Green Discovery B2
3 Xplore-Asia C4

Sleeping
4 Alisa Guesthouse D4
5 Kaesme Guest House B1
6 Sabaidy 2 Guesthouse C1

Eating
7 Daolin Restaurant C2

8 Friendship Minimart D4
9 Jasmine Restaurant C4
10 Lankham Noodle Shop C4
11 Le Panorama B2
12 Mengky Noodle Shop D4
13 Parisien Café A3
14 Xuan Mai Restaurant B2

Information
Lankham Hotel Currency
  Exchange Counter .... (see 10)

Green Discovery   ADVENTURE TOUR
(☑ 031-252908; www.greendiscoverylaos.com; Th
10; 2-day Tree Top Explorer tour 2-/4-person group
per person US$280/217) Green Discovery's
signature tour is the Tree Top Explorer adventure in Dong Hua Sao NPA near Paksong on the Bolaven Plateau. It consists of
two or three days of ziplining, canopy walks

and jungle trekking. Accommodation is in
eco-friendly huts set high up above the forest floor. There's lots more on offer in the
region – check the website.

Xplore-Asia   ADVENTURE TOUR
(☑ 031-251983; www.xplore-laos.com; Th 14;
⏰9am-7pm) This outfit specialises in

GETTING TO THAILAND: SOUTHERN BORDERS

Savannakhet to Mukdahan

Getting to the border Regular buses (15,000K, 45 minutes) leave Savannakhet's bus station and cross the new Friendship Bridge for Thailand's Mukdahan between 8.15am and 7pm. Buses leave Mukdahan's bus station (50B, 45 minutes) roughly every hour from 7.30am till 7pm.

At the border This is a well-organised, busy border (open 6am to 10pm). A free 15-day tourist visa is given on entering Thailand. Note that to obtain a 30-day Thai visa, you'll need to arrive in the country by air.

Moving on Onward from Mukdahan, there are five daily buses bound for Bangkok between 5.30pm and 8.15pm.

For information on doing this crossing in reverse, see p724.

Pakse to Ubon Ratchathani

Getting to the border Heading to the busy Vang Tao/Chong Mek border (open 6am to 8pm) is straightforward if catching a *sŏrngtăaou* from Pakse (10,000K per person, 75 minutes, 37km). Alternatively, take the 8.30am or 3.30pm Thai–Lao international bus (200B, three hours, 126km) to Ubon Ratchathani (Thailand) from Pakse's 2km bus terminal (also known as the VIP bus terminal and the Kriang Kai bus station).

At the border There are ATMs on the Thai side, a market and restaurants. You have to walk a bit between the two posts but in general it's hassle free. Free 15-day visa waivers are granted on arrival in Thailand.

Moving on The Thai–Lao international bus continues on to Bangkok (800B, 14 hours). From Chong Mek to Ubon (80km, 1½ hours) costs 60B by bus, while taxi drivers charge between 1000B and 1200B.

For information on doing this crossing in reverse, see p724.

---

multiday adventures, including trips to the Bolaven Plateau (U$20 per person) and to Wat Phu (US$45). English-speaking guides are US$35 to US$50 per day. It also sells some interesting books and guidebooks to the region.

🛏 Sleeping

★ Alisa Guesthouse   HOTEL $
(📞 031-251555; www.alisa-guesthouse.com; Rte 13; s/d/tr 110,000/120,000/150,000K; ❀@⊚) Well located in the heart of the tourist zone, Alisa has sparkling rooms, tiled floors (clean enough to eat your lunch off!), fresh linen, solid wood beds, armoires and flat-screen TVs as well as private bathrooms. Add working sat TV and a fridge.

★ Sabaidy 2 Guesthouse   GUESTHOUSE $
(📞 031-212992; www.sabaidy2tour.com; Th 24; dm 35,000K, s/d without bathroom 45,000/70,000K, d with bathroom & air-con 138,000K; @⊚) Exuding an easy, relaxed vibe, Sabaidy is based in a wood house and has clean dorms and doubles. The new private rooms out back are terrific; think wooden balcony, beneath which swim coy carp, rustic chic interiors, private bathroom, desk and air-con. There's a communal area to swap tales in the garden, free breakfast, and helpful staff can organise onward travel.

Kaesme Guest House   GUESTHOUSE $
(📞 020 99481616; Se Don riverfront; r with fan/air-con 70,000/100,000K; ❀⊚) With its riverside position and rickety reading sun deck shipwrecked over the bank, this friendly house at the end of a lane has clean and simple rooms with fan or air-con. Towels and soap are a nice bonus at these prices. Friendly owner.

🍴 Eating

Chow down with locals at the **Lankham Noodle Shop** (under the Lankham Hotel, Rte 13; noodles 15,000-25,000K; ⊙7am-10pm; ⊚) and at the **Mengky Noodle Shop** (Rte 13; meals 8000-15,000K; ⊙7am-10pm). Self-caterers can head to the **Friendship Minimart** (Rte 13; ⊙8am-8pm).

Daolin Restaurant
LAOTIAN, INTERNATIONAL $
(Rte 13; mains 20,000-30,000K; ☺6.30am-10pm)
Catching any whisper of a breeze (you'll be lucky!), open-air Daolin is run by lovely people attentive to your preferred levels of spiciness. Breakfast, lunch and dinner expect a spectrum of nicely executed Vietnamese, Thai, Lao and Western dishes, among them: sandwiches, steak, salad, spicy chicken with lemongrass, sundaes...and many more.

Jasmine Restaurant
INDIAN $
(Rte 13; mains 20,000-30,000K; ☺8am-10pm; 🖉) In all the years we've sampled Jasmine, it's never been less than bulging with happy customers. Veggies delight over dishes like green peas masala and *aloo bhaiga* (eggplant and potatoes), while the sizzling chicken tikka masala is so tasty you'll be wiping the bowl with the pillow-soft naan. Eat in or out.

Parisien Café
CAFE $
(Th 9; juices 40,000K; ☺7am-10pm) This bright new cafe-cum-bakery is infused with sunlight and puts a calorific sugar-coated spring in your step with its fresh cakes, doughnuts, pastries and juices. Cement rendered walls, exposed brick and comfy modern seating.

Xuan Mai Restaurant
LAOTIAN, VIETNAMESE $
(Th 5; mains 18,000-30,000K; ☺6am-11.30pm) Super-fresh Vietnamese-run Xuan Mai serves freshly prepared *fěr* (rice noodles), *năam néuang* (pork balls), *kòw bûn* (white flour noodles with sweet-spicy sauce), mekong fish, spring rolls, fruit shakes and even garlic bread. The house *lahp* (meat salad) is full of zing too. Eat in or out, and if you have time take one of its cooking classes.

Drinking & Nightlife
Wander down the Mekong riverfront and stop at a terrace bar for a beer. Alternatively, nurse a Bloody Mary on the Parisien-style rooftop Panorama Bar (Th 5; mains 30,000-70,000K; ☺4.30-10pm; 🛜) at the Pakse Hotel.

Information
ATMs are strung out along Rte 13, including an ANZ machine outside the Lankham Hotel on Rte 13. The Lankham also has a useful currency exchange counter (☺7am-7pm) that offers decent rates and does cash advances on Visa cards.
International Hitech Polyclinic (VIP Clinic; ☎031-214712; ihpc_lao@yahoo.com; Th 46; ☺24hr) Adjacent to the public hospital, with English-speaking staff and much higher standards of care, service and facilities, plus a pharmacy.

Lao Development Bank (Rte 13; ☺8am-4pm Mon-Fri, to 3pm Sat & Sun) Changes cash and travellers cheques. Also houses a Western Union (money transfers only available weekdays).
Miss Noy's Internet & Bike Rental (Rte 13; per day bikes/scooters 15,000/60,000K; ☺7am-8pm) Witty Miss Noy and her husband rent reliable, well-maintained scooters and bikes.
Provincial Tourism Office (☎031-212021; Th 11; ☺8am-noon & 1.30-9pm) The well-organised English-speaking staff can book you onto community-based two- or three-day treks in Se Pian NPA and Phou Xieng Thong NPA, involving kayaking and camping combos, as well as homestays on Don Kho and Don Daeng. They dole out maps of Pakse and southern Laos and are also armed with all the latest schedules for buses heading anywhere from Pakse.
Unitel (Rte 13; ☺8am-5pm Mon-Fri, to noon Sat) A convenient stop for a local SIM card if you are just arriving in Laos. Staff can set your smart phone up with 3G internet.

❶ Getting There & Away

AIR
Lao Airlines flies twice daily between Pakse and Vientiane (one way US$125, 70 minutes), and thrice weekly to Luang Prabang (US$172, one hour 40 minutes), as well as Savannakhet (US$65, 30 minutes) four times per week. Internationally there are four weekly flights to Ho Chi Minh City (US$175), and Bangkok (US$170) and daily flights to Siem Reap (US$160). A tuk-tuk to the airport from Pakse costs 30,000K, a taxi US$18.

Purchase your ticket online or at the **Lao Airlines** (☎031-212252; www.laoairlines.com; ☺7am-noon & 1-5pm Mon-Fri, 7am-noon Sat) office at Pakse Airport.

BOAT
A tourist **boat to Champasak** (☎020 22705955; per boat US$80, per person for 10 people US$8) leaves Pakse at 8.30am, provided there are enough punters; it takes two hours. The return trip from Champasak is at 1.30pm. Skipper Mr Khamlao can also take you to Four Thousand Islands. Book ahead.

BUS & SÖRNGTÄAOU
Confusingly, Pakse has several bus and *sörngtäaou* terminals. 'Sleeper' VIP buses leave from the **2km bus station** (VIP Bus Station; ☎031-212428; Rte 13, Km2) off Rte 13, for Vientiane (170,000K, eight to 10 hours, 677km) every evening. The same bus passes through Tha Khaek (140,000K, 4½ hours). The handy Thai–Lao International Bus, which heads to Bangkok (800B, 3pm) and Ubon (200B) also departs from here. It's also possible to buy a

combo bus/sleeper train ticket to Bangkok (280,000K) from Pakse travel agents.

From the northern bus terminal (Rte 13), sometimes referred to as 'Km7 bus terminal', agonisingly sweltering local buses crawl north every 40 minutes or so between 6.30am and 4pm for Savannakhet (40,000K, four to five hours, 277km), Tha Khaek (70,000K, eight to nine hours) and, for those with a masochistic streak, Vientiane (110,000K, 16 to 18 hours). Fancier air-con buses also leave for Vientiane (140,000K, 10 to 12 hours) throughout the day from the southern bus terminal (Rte 13). Daily buses for Vietnam's Danang (220,000K, 18 hours) leave here daily at 7am, and Hué at 6.30pm (180,000K, 15½ hours).

For buses or *sŏrngtăaou* anywhere south or east, head to the southern bus terminal, also known as 'Km8 bus terminal'. It costs 40,000K per tuk-tuk to get there. For Si Phan Don, transport departs for Muang Khong on Don Khong island (including ferry 50,000K, three hours, 120km) between 8.30am and 3pm, and for Ban Nakasang (for Don Det and Don Khon; 50,000K, three to four hours) hourly between 7.30am and 4pm. A *sŏrngtăaou* runs to Kiet Ngong (Xe Pian NPA) and Ban Phapho (40,000K, two to three hours) at 1pm.

To the Bolaven Plateau, transport leaves the southern bus terminal for Paksong (25,000K, 1½ hours) hourly between 7am and 4pm, stopping at Tat Fan if you ask. For Tat Lo take the Salavan bus (40,000K, three to four hours, five daily).

Regular buses and *sŏrngtăaou* leave Talat Dao Heung (New Market) for Champasak (25,000K, one to two hours).

❶ Getting Around

A jumbo to the airport, 3km northwest of town, should cost about 30,000K. Pakse's main attractions are accessible by foot. Bicycles/scooters (around 15,000/60,000K per day) can be hired from Miss Noy's Internet & Bike Rental (p365).

Champasak   ຈຳປາສັກ

☑ 031 / POP 14,000

Languid, riverine Champasak hums with the chirrup of schoolkids on bicycles, the slow turn of the Mekong, and a handful of restaurants in faded old French villas leading up to the main course of whimsical Wat Phu. Backed by a mountain flanked in leprechaun-green rice paddies, Champasak is currently redefining 'rustic escape', for here you can enjoy chillsome digs, a quality massage and spa, yoga, meditation and shadow

puppet theatre, all at a price that will slow your pulse without straining your wallet.

◉ Sights & Activities

Wat Phu Champasak   BUDDHIST TEMPLE
(admission 50,000K; ⏰ site 8am-6pm, museum 8am-4.30pm) Bucolic Wat Phu sits in graceful decrepitude, and while it lacks the arresting enormity of Angkor in Cambodia, given its few visitors and more dramatic natural setting, these small Khmer ruins evoke a more soulful response. While some buildings are more than 1000 years old, most date from the 11th to 13th centuries. The site is divided into six terraces on three levels joined by a frangipani-bordered stairway that's flanked by stone lions and *naga*, flowing down from the mountain to the barays.

Visit early morning for cooler temperatures and capturing the ruins in the best light.

★**Shadow Puppet Theatre & Cinéma Tuktuk**   THEATRE
(www.cinema-tuktuk.org; Main St, beside Tourist Office; 50,000K; ⏰ 8.30pm-10pm) Run by Frenchman Yves Bernard, this magical theatre tells the story of the epic *Ramayana* using the ancient art of shadow puppets. On alternate nights it screens the enchanting silent film *Chang* (1924), made here in Laos by the director of Hollywood's original *King Kong*. What makes it so perfect is the presence of live musicians providing the soundtrack. At time of writing there was talk of the 8.30pm slot changing to an earlier time.

Champasak Spa   SPA
(☑ 020 56499739; www.champasak-spa.com; massages 90,000-150,000K; ⏰ 10am-noon & 1-7pm) 🏃 Run by Natalie, this is a fragrant oasis of free tea and sensitively executed treatments using locally grown and sourced organic bio products. Creating jobs for local women, the spa offers yoga and free dawn meditation sessions (but you must book ahead). A full-day spa package comprising facial, body scrub, hair spa and massage costs 550,000K.

🛏 Sleeping & Eating

Anouxa Guesthouse   GUESTHOUSE $
(☑ 031-511006; Main St; r with fan 60,000K, with air-con 100,000K, tr with air-con 150,000K; 🅿 ❄ 🛜) Set in a garden thick with mango trees and trilling birdsong, Anouxa has mint-green cool rooms with private bathroom, mozzie nets, Hmong tapestries, balcony and lush river views. There's also a

tempting riverside restaurant. It rents bikes for 10,000K to 20,000K.

Thavisab Guesthouse
GUESTHOUSE $

(📞020 55354972; r with/without air-con 100,000/50,000K; ❄) Salmon-pink Thavisab has a motel courtyard set up with freshly painted rooms with private bathroom, clean linen and a river-facing verandah. There's also bags of rooms in the old house.

★Inthira Hotel Champanakone
BOUTIQUE HOTEL $$

(📞031-511011; r standard/duplex 334,000/ 383,000K; ❄🛜) The belle of the river, Inthira's sumptuous rooms and low-lit Asian fusion restaurant give us yet another reason to stay another day in Champasak. It's based in an old Chinese shophouse, with a second complex over the road and even newer two-storey duplex rooms. Expect Inthira signatures of luxury – brick floors, ambient lighting, flat-screen TVs, safes, rain shower-heads and marble baths.

★Nakorn Restaurant
THAI $

(Main St; mains: 30,000K; ⊘7am-9pm) This stylish new cafe and restaurant by the river promises to be stunning when finished, with a chic, open library room, handsome bar and salas dotted around a landscaped garden flickering with burning tapers. Its Asian fusion menu is already winning plaudits for its tasty *lahp*, pad thai, and steak and chips. Lovely owners, lovely food.

Champasak with Love
FUSION $

(Main St; mains 20,000-40,000K, r with fan/air-con 60,000/100,000K; ⊘8am-10pm; 📶) This banana-yellow eatery has a marvellous riverfront patio made of solid wood where Thai and Western food is served with a smile. Brownies, fruit salad, sandwiches, plenty of veggie options and breakfast. Bicycle rental is available and it now has a couple of basic, wood-accented rooms in the creaky old house.

Frice and Lujane Restaurant
ITALIAN $$

(Main St; mains 45,000-65,000K; ⊘5-9pm) Enjoy cuisine inspired by Italy's Friulian Alpine region, at the most recent incarnation of this swish restaurant, in a lovely villa by the Mekong. Gnocchi, marinated pork ribs, goulash and homemade sausage grace the menu.

ℹ Getting There & Around

Regular buses and *sŏrngtǎaou* run between Champasak and Pakse (20,000K, one hour) from about 7am until 9am. A boat for Pakse leaves at 8.30am (on demand). Book it through your guesthouse (50,000K).

If you're heading south to Ban Nakasang (for Don Det) or Muang Khong (on Don Khong), a minivan leaves at 8.30am (70,000K).

Bicycles (per day 15,000K) and scooters (per half-/full day 50,000/80,000K) can be hired from guesthouses.

Si Phan Don (Four Thousand Islands)
ສີ່ພັນດອນ

📞031

This beguiling archipelago of islets is the emerald jewel near the end of the Mekong's 4350km journey. The river passes around thousands of sandbars sprouting with sugar palms, and provided you're here from December through to July, after the rain season when Mother Mekong is churned chocolate-brown, expect to be dazzled by soul-affirming turquoise-green water. Between tubing, kayaking and cycling around the three main islands – Don Khong, and sister islands Don Det and Don Khon – spotting the rare Irrawaddy dolphin or visiting waterfalls, there's little to do but hammock-dwell.

Don Khong
ດອນໂຂງ

POP 13,000

Life moves slowly on Don Khong, an 18km-long, 8km-wide sleepy idyll where fishing nets dry in the sun, the turquoise Mekong slips by and locals barely look up from their Beerlao to register your arrival. Its main settlement is Muang Khong, a one-street affair with a couple of guesthouses and restaurants.

🛏 Sleeping & Eating

There are a few great-value oases at which to rest your bones; all of them are located in Muang Khong.

★Ratana Riverside Guesthouse
GUESTHOUSE $

(📞020 22201618, 031-213673; vongdonekhong@ hotmail.com; r 100,000K❄🛜) The four comfortable river-facing rooms here enjoy a desk, marble floor, balcony, Siberian air-con and handsome furnishings. Ground-floor rooms have enormous windows close to the road so get one upstairs. The river-deck

Si Phan Don

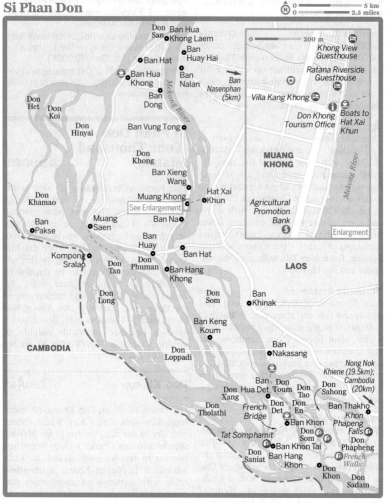

Don Hua San — Ban Hua Khong Laem
Ban Huay Hai
Ban Hat
Ban Hua Khong
Ban Nalan
Ban Nasenphan (5km)
Ban Dong
Don Het
Don Koi
Don Hinyai
Ban Vung Tong
Don Khong
Ban Xieng Wang
Muang Khong
See Enlargement
Hat Xai Khun
Don Khamao
Muang Saen
Ban Na
Ban Pakse
Ban Huay
Kompong Sralao
Don Tan
Don Phuman
Ban Hat
Ban Hang Khong
Don Long
Don Som
Ban Khinak
Ban Keng Koum
CAMBODIA
Don Loppadi
LAOS
Ban Nakasang
Nong Nok Khiene (19.5km); Cambodia (20km)
Ban Toum
Don Hua Det
Don Tao
Don Sahong
Don Xang
Don Tholathi
French Bridge
Don Det
Don En
Don Som
Ban Thakho Khon
Tat Somphamit
Ban Khon
Don Som
Phapeng Falls
Ban Khon Tai
Don Phapeng
French Walls
Don Saniat
Ban Hang Khon
Don Khon
Don Sadam

Enlargement

Khong View Guesthouse
Ratana Riverside Guesthouse
Villa Kang Khong
Don Khong Tourism Office
Boats to Hat Xai Khun
MUANG KHONG
Agricultural Promotion Bank
Mekong River

0 — 5 km
0 — 2.5 miles
0 — 200 m

restaurant (mains 25,000-40,000K) has a selection of Western food.

Khong View Guesthouse GUESTHOUSE $
(☑020 22446449; r with fan/air-con 80,000/ 100,000K; ❄🛜) It's hard to beat the location of this place, where the rooms are set around a breezy wood deck overlooking a big bend in the Mekong. Choose between dark woody riverfront rooms or bright tiled rooms at the back, facing the road. The small rooms have disproportionally large king-sized beds. No restaurant.

Villa Kang Khong GUESTHOUSE $
(☑020 22403315, 020 29252811; r 70,000K) This creaky old teak house is an atmospheric old-timer with wicker chairs in its shady lounge to chill on, and lovely rooms with polished floors, mahogany beds, colourful linen and private bathrooms and air-con. The most romantic budget digs in town.

ℹ Information

One road back from the river, 400m south of Wat Phuang Kaew, the **Agricultural Promotion Bank** (⊙8.30am-3.30pm Mon-Fri) exchanges travellers cheques and cash and has an ATM that works with Visa and MasterCard. There's also a BCEL ATM next to the post office. For medical complaints, the hospital is a little further south of the bank; ask for English- and French-speaking Dr Bounthavi.

The **Don Khong Tourism Office** (☑ 020 97846464, 029-250303; panhjuki@yahoo.com; ☻ 8.30am-4pm Mon-Fri) can organise boats to Don Khon and Don Det (250,000K).

❶ Getting There & Away

From Don Khong to Pakse, buses (60,000K including ferry, 2½ to three hours, 128km) and *sŏrngtǎaou* leave from Hat Xai Khun over the river on the mainland. Be there by 11am.

For those heading to Cambodia, there's usually a 9am connection to Stung Treng, Kratie, Ban Lung, Siem Reap and Phnom Penh.

There are regular boats between Hat Xai Khun and Don Khong's Muang Khong town – 15,000K per person.

Boats for Don Det and Don Khon (250,000K per boat, 1½ hours, up to six passengers) leave when you stump up the cash – boatmen are under the tree near the bridge.

❶ Getting Around

Bicycles/scooters (10,000/40,000K per day) can be hired from guesthouses and elsewhere along the main street.

Don Det & Don Khon
ດອນເດດ/ດອນຄອນ

While many choose to hammock-flop here, there are loads of inexpensive activities to busy yourself with, be it cycling, tubing and kayaking by day, or relaxing in the river bars come sunset. Expect to see fishermen in pirogues, doe-eyed buffalo in the shallows and villagers taking morning ablutions. By night, campfires burn on the beach and conversation flows.

A tropical yin and yang, Don Det is overcrowded with *falang* – particularly by the ferry point of **Ban Hua Det** (known as 'Sunrise Boulevard') – while sultry Don Khon is quieter, teems with rapids, and rare Irrawaddy dolphins swim off its southern tip.

◉ Sights

Most sights are on Don Khon and are accessed on a bicycle hired from just about any guesthouse for 10,000K per day. When you cross the French bridge to Don Khon, you will be asked to pay 35,000K. This covers the entrance fee to Li Phi Falls.

Tat Somphamit　　　　　　WATERFALL
(ຕາດສົມພະມິດ, Li Phi Falls; admission 35,000K; ☻ ticket booth 8am-5pm) Located 1.5km downriver from the French bridge on Don Khon, Tat Somphamit – aka Li Phi Falls – is a raging set of rapids. Li Phi means 'spirit trap' and locals believe the falls act as just that – a trap for bad spirits as they wash down the river. Local fishermen risk their skin edging out onto rocks in the violent flow of the cascades to empty bamboo traps, each of which can catch half a tonne of fish a day.

There are plenty of restaurants and concession stands at the falls entrance.

✦ Activities

A pod of rare Irrawaddy dolphins hangs out beneath the rapids in a wide pool known as Boong Pa Gooang, off the southern tip of Don Khon. Boats are chartered (60,000K, maximum three people) for one-hour trips from the old French landing pier in Ban Hang Khon. Sightings are regular year-round, but the best viewing is from January to May. Try to go early evening or first thing in the morning, when sightings are more regular.

Full-day kayaking tours (180,000K per person) combined with taking in the dolphin pool and **Khon Phapeng Falls** (ຕາດຄອນພະເພັງ; admission 35,000K) are the norm; starting at 9.30am you first kayak, then are picked up before the falls off Don Khon, and you and your kayaks are transported overland to Ban Hang Khon. **Wonderful Tours** (☑ 020 55705173; combo kayak, waterfall & dolphin 1-day trip per person 180,000K) is useful.

HOW'S YOUR FOOTPRINT?

Are there slightly less smiles from locals these days? If that's the case it's probably the hangover from the island offering itself as a stoner haven before realising the price to pay. Thankfully, things have turned around in the last five years, with the island cultivating a range of activities such as cycling and kayaking, and eschewing 'happifying' menus. Remember that the impact you make on the islanders – hopefully a good one – will radiate directly to those travellers who follow in your footsteps.

Note also that the locals find the revealing of flesh culturally offensive, so it's best to wear more than a bikini around the island.

GETTING TO CAMBODIA: SI PHAN DON TO STUNG TRENG

Getting to the border Many travellers from the Four Thousand Islands take a minibus and pass through the Nong Nok Khiene/Trapeang Kriel border for Cambodia. From Pakse catch the Sorya Penh Transport bus which leaves at 7.30am from the VIP (Km2) bus terminal (also known as the Kriang Kai bus station) and goes to Phnom Penh (US$27, 12 to 14 hours) via Stung Treng (US$15, 4½ hours) and Kratie (US$20, seven hours) in Cambodia.

At the border Thirty-day tourist visas for Cambodia are available at the border and cost around US$25. You'll also pay US$2 for a cursory medical inspection.

Moving on If you're not on a direct bus, head to Stung Treng to catch a bus to Phnom Penh, Siem Reap and Ban Lung. Taxis from the border cost US$40.

For information on doing this crossing in reverse, see p133.

Renting a kayak to paddle around on your own costs around 50,000K per day, but don't go past the French bridge or you'll hit the fast currents that feed into the lethal falls. The same rule applies to inner tubes, which cost 10,000K (avoid these during the monsoon when the river runs dangerously fast).

Guesthouses offer sunset boat cruises and full-day island hops. Prices vary, but figure on 50,000K to 75,000K per person provided you have a few people.

Finally there's a stylish 18m-long swimming pool at **Little Eden Guesthouse** (Sunset side, Ban Hua Det; admission 50,000K) to take laps, float or enjoy a drink at its poolside bar.

On Don Khon, **Lao Garden Massage** (☑ 020 9367136; halfway up Don Khon; 30 mins/1hr 50,000/70,000K; ☺9am-11pm) offers treatments in an ice-cool room.

🛏 Sleeping

Don Det's 'Sunrise Boulevard' on the northern tip is claustrophobic and noisy, but if you want to keep the party going (at least till the 11pm curfew) head here. More upscale digs are further south and over on sedate Don Khon.

In low season prices drop by around 25%.

🛏 Don Det

River Garden   GUESTHOUSE $
(☑020 77701860; Sunrise, 300m short of French bridge; r with shared/private bathroom 30,000/50,000, large cabana 100,000K; ☎) Gay-friendly River Garden brings a whiff of budget style to Don Det. Think carved-wood doors and windows, tidy bathrooms, Lao textiles, bamboo lamps, seductive maroon-stained walls and twin hammocks outside each bungalow. Opposite them is a

shaded riverfront terrace restaurant with a Western and Asian fusion menu.

Easy Go Hostel   GUESTHOUSE $
(☑020 578228309; Sunset side, last house on left; dm 35,000K, bungalow with fan/air-con 60,000/70,000K) Way down south on the Sunset side, this lovely guesthouse is based around a courtyard garden with dorms for five and three, and shared bathroom cabanas with hammock. Over by the river there's a chillsome deck facing Cambodia, and a beach for shallow dips. Look out for the tree studded with global direction signs.

Sengthavan Guesthouse & Restaurant   GUESTHOUSE $
(☑020 56132696; Sunset Blvd; r 100,000K; ☎) Probably the best the Sunset side has to offer in the budget range, Sengthavan's powder-blue en suite rooms are fastidiously clean and enjoy uncluttered balcony views of Cambodia. Its low-key cafe has recliner cushions, checked tablecloths and a Lao and Western menu.

Last Resort   RESORT $
(mrwatkinsonlives@googlemail.com; d/tr 50,000/60,000K) This teepee 'resort' in a field about a 15-minute walk south of the main Sunset Blvd strip embraces the natural life, with the owner growing veggies and baking bread. Made with natural materials, the teepees are in the shade of mature trees, and there's a barbecue and shared bathroom. Alfresco movies are screened come evening

Green Guesthouse   GUESTHOUSE $
(☑020 91803519; road btwn Sunset & Sunrise, Ban Hua Det; r with fan/air-con 100,000/130,000K; ✳@☎) Very much the new face of Don Det accommodation, these unapologetically fresh, plush rooms are in a white house with

bathroom, fan, wi-fi and communal balcony fronting a betel-studded rice paddy.

★ **Ba Ba Guesthouse** GUESTHOUSE $$
(☑ 020 98893943; www.dondet.net; Sunrise central, Ban Hua Det; r 200,000-300,000K; ✹ 🐱) This beautiful new guesthouse looks out on the Mekong on one side, and emerald paddy fields on the other. Rooms are sleekly white and luxurious, with private balcony, tasteful decor and spotless bathroom. There's also a cafe serving spring rolls, pasta and tasty breakfast. A new terraced restaurant is being built over the river. Owner Basil and wife are the perfect hosts. Blissful.

★ **Little Eden Guesthouse** GUESTHOUSE $$
(☑ 030-5346020; www.littleedenguesthouse-dondet.com; Ban Hua Det; r 320,000K; ✹ @ 🐱 ✹ ♨) Don Det's most luxurious complex is set in lush sugar palm gardens on the northern tip. Fragrant rooms tempt with contemporary darkwood furniture, polished wood floors, TV, fridge, desk and stunning granite bathroom. Better still, the hotel has a beautiful free 18m-long swimming pool, a bar, and a brand new restaurant.

🏯 Don Khon

Pa Ka Guesthouse GUESTHOUSE $
(☑ 055-847522; Don Khon riverfront; r with fan/air-con 80,000/100,000K; ✹ 🐱) Great-value new digs with welcoming, clean rooms with bathroom and balcony. There's also a natty cafe in the garden courtyard. Wi-fi in rooms.

★ **Auberge Sala
Done Khone** BOUTIQUE HOTEL $$
(☑ 031-260940; www.saladonekhone.salalao.com; r incl breakfast US$15-35; ✹ @ 🐱 ✹) In a handsomely renovated French-era hospital in large gardens, this belle delights with four-poster beds, mozzie nets, and art-deco-signatured rooms. Outside are spotless A-frame bungalows built in the classic Lao style with ambient-lit, minimalist interiors, while out on the river the Sala Phae wing (r US$60) features equally stylish floating cottages with bio-safe toilets.

Pan's Guesthouse GUESTHOUSE $$
(☑ 020 23655151; www.donkhone.com; d garden/riverfront 150,000/180,000K; tr 220,000K; ✹ @ 🐱) Enticing riverside bungalows flickering with butterflies finished in solid stained wood with creamy white rattan interiors, immaculate bathrooms and balconies slung with hammocks. Spring for a river-front room. Wi-fi is in the restaurant only. There's also a travel office here to book tours and forward travel. Dependable.

🍴 Eating & Drinking

★ **Four Thousand Sunsets** FUSION $
(Don Khon; mains 35,000K; ⏰ 8am-11pm; 🐱 ✒) Aptly named, this floating restaurant lowers your pulse with the metronomic flow of the river and is effortlessly chic with its old-world style. Steamed and grilled fresh river fish, Thai fish cakes, Lao smoking sausage and pork stir-fry are just a few of the options. Treat yourself to a vodka martini as you drink up the amber sunset.

Street View Restaurant PIZZA $
(Sunrise Blvd, halfway down, Don Det; mains 30,000K; ⏰ 8am-11pm) This attractive wooden riverside haunt has chilling decks and a long, well-stocked bar. Tuck into fresh-cut barbecued Australian steak, mouthwatering wood-fired pizza, barbecued chicken, Mekong fish, beef chops, burgers, salads and healthy breakfasts. Seven minutes' walk from Ban Hua Det.

Crazy Gecko LAOTIAN $
(www.crazygecko.ch; Sunrise Blvd, halfway down; mains 25,000K; ⏰ 7am-10pm) Lit by ropes of fairy lights by night, this riverside restaurant has tables and decks with scatter cushions to chill in. There's board games, pool table and hammocks for rainy days, and delicious Asian and Western food including pasta and *lahp*. Deservedly one of the most popular spots on the island.

Jasmine Restaurant INDIAN $
(Sunrise Blvd, Ban Hua Det; mains 20,000-35,000K) With tables next to the river, this Indian restaurant (and sibling of the excellent Jasmine in Pakse) packs them in with its consistently tasty Malay and Indian fare, and melt-in-your-mouth naan. Friendly service, run by warm people.

★ **Little Eden
Restaurant** LAOTIAN, INTERNATIONAL $$
(Ban Hua Det, Don Det; mains 40,000-60,000K; 🐱) Catching the breeze from the tip of the island, Little Eden's stunning new restaurant is one of the best places to eat upmarket Laotian and Western cuisine. Think tender New Zealand beef steak, spaghetti Bolognese and fish *lahp*, to name a few. It's also the only place to sell Mekong catfish (not the endangered giant catfish!).

4000 Island Bar   BAR

(Sunrise Blvd, Don Det) Near the boat landing with a pool table and desert island decor – think *Swiss Family Robinson* meets *The Beach* – this is the thumping heart of Ban Hua Det. While it officially closes before midnight, it's likely to stay open unofficially until 1am.

ⓘ Information

There is no bank, so take the ferry over to Ban Nakasang, which has a BCEL with an ATM. Little Eden Guesthouse on Don Det will do cash advances on your card for a 5% commission.

Ban Nakasang is also the place to go for medical and postal services.

ⓘ Getting There & Around

Boats regularly leave Don Det for Ban Nakasang (per person/boat 15,000/30,000K). You can charter a private boat to Don Khong from Paradise Bungalows for 75,000K per person with a minimum of two people.

For Pakse (70,000K, 2½ to three hours, 148km), VIP minibuses leave Ban Nakasang at around 11am, while *sŏrngtăaou* (40,000K, 3½ hours) leave early morning up until 9am. Wonderful Tours (p369) organises daily VIP buses to Stung Treng (US$24), Ban Lung (US$24), Kratie (US$23), Phnom Penh (US$30) and Siem Reap (US$35) in Cambodia (which leave Ban Nakasang at about 9.30am).

UNDERSTAND LAOS

Laos Today

In 2011, despite widespread global gloom, Laos' economy reported a growth of 8%, one of the strongest in Asia, thanks to its ambitious hydroelectric power sector. Around 85 dams, many of which are already built, are to be constructed around the country. By 2020 Laos hopes to produce 12,500 megawatts of power annually.

China is now Laos' best mate: ever the opportunist, it has moved in to grab what it can in return for improving Laos' transport infrastructure, while many Lao children are eagerly encouraged by middle-class parents to learn Chinese. Beijing's Southeast Asian rail network, connecting the red giant with countries as far afield as Pakistan, India and Singapore, has finally been ratified and construction began in November 2015 on the route that will pass directly through Laos,

bisecting the country. Meanwhile, despite UN pressure, the Lao government fails to answer human rights critics lobbying for an answer to the disappearance of social progressive figures.

As US relations begin to improve and the first rumblings of gay expression make themselves heard in the capital, Laos is on one hand embracing the 21st century, while holding fast to its old-guard hegemony.

History

The Kingdom of Lan Xang

Before the French, British, Chinese and Siamese drew a line around it, Laos was a collection of disparate principalities subject to an ever-revolving cycle of war, invasion, prosperity and decay. Laos' earliest brush with nationhood was in the 14th century, when Khmer-backed Lao warlord Fa Ngum conquered Wieng Chan (Vientiane). It was Fa Ngum who gave his kingdom the title still favoured by travel romantics and businesses – Lan Xang, or (Land of a) Million Elephants. He also made Theravada Buddhism the state religion and adopted the symbol of Lao sovereignty that remains in use today, the Pha Bang Buddha image, after which Luang Prabang is named. Lan Xang reached its peak in the 17th century, when it was the dominant force in Southeast Asia.

French Rule

By the 18th century the nation had crumbled, falling under the control of the Siamese, who coveted much of modern-day Laos as a buffer zone against the expansionist French. It was to no effect. Soon after taking over Annam and Tonkin (modern-day Vietnam), the French negotiated with Siam to relinquish its territory east of the Mekong, and Laos was born.

The first nationalist movement, the Lao Issara (Free Lao), was created to prevent the country's return to French rule after the invading Japanese left at the end of WWII. In 1953, without any regard for the Lao Issara, sovereignty was granted to Laos by the French. Internecine struggles followed with the Pathet Lao (Country of the Lao) Army forming an alliance with the Vietnamese Viet Minh (which opposed French rule in their own country). Laos was set to become a chessboard on which the clash of communist ambition and US anxiety over the perceived Southeast Asian 'domino effect' played itself out.

The Secret War

In 1954 at the Geneva Conference, Laos was declared a neutral nation – as such neither Vietnamese nor US forces could cross its borders. Thus began a game of cat and mouse as a multitude of CIA operatives secretly entered the country to train anticommunist Hmong fighters in the jungle. From 1964 to 1973 the US, in response to the Viet Minh funnelling massive amounts of war munitions down the Ho Chi Minh Trail, devastated eastern and northeastern Laos with nonstop carpet-bombing (reportedly a planeload of ordnance dropped every eight minutes). The intensive campaign exacerbated the war between the Pathet Lao and the Royal Lao armies and, if anything, increased domestic support for the communists.

The US withdrawal in 1973 saw Laos divided up between Pathet Lao and non-Pathet Lao, but within two years the communists had taken over and the Lao People's Democratic Republic (PDR) was created under the leadership of Kaysone Phomvihane. Around 10% of Laos' population fled, mostly to Thailand. The remaining opponents of the government – notably tribes of Hmong (highland dwellers) who had fought with and been funded by the CIA – were suppressed, often brutally, or sent to re-education camps for indeterminate periods.

A New Beginning

Laos entered the political family of Southeast Asian countries known as Asean in 1997, two years after Vietnam. Politically, the Party remains firmly in control. And with neighbours like one-party China and Vietnam, there seems little incentive for Laos to move towards any meaningful form of democracy. While still heavily reliant on foreign aid (some 8.5% of its GDP), Laos has committed to income-generating projects in recent years in a bid to increase its prosperity.

The year 2012 saw the international press starting to ask questions over the disappearance of Sombath Somphone, an award-winning civil-society activist and land-rights campaigner, with fingers directly pointed at the Lao government as the main culprit. In 2015, in an effort to counterbalance China's growing influence over the region, President Obama met with the Laos premier in New York.

People & Culture

National Psyche

Laos is a patchwork of different beliefs, ranging from animism to the prevailing presence of Thervada Bhuddism – and often both combined. But, certainly, there's a commonality in the laid-back attitude you'll encounter. Some of this can be ascribed to Buddhism, with its emphasis on controlling extreme emotions by keeping *jai yen* (cool heart), making merit and doing good in order to receive good. You'll rarely hear a heated argument, and can expect a level of kindness seldom experienced in neighbouring countries.

Etiquette

Touching another person's head is taboo, as is pointing your feet at another person or at a buddha image. Strong displays of emotion are also discouraged. The traditional greeting gesture is the *nop* or *wâi*, a prayerlike placing together of the palms in front of the face or chest, although in urban areas the handshake is becoming more commonplace.

For all temple visits, dress conservatively.

SPIRITS, ARE YOU THERE?

The *pěe héuan* (good spirits) represent both the guardian spirits of the house and ancestral spirits. In the backyard or garden, you'll often see what look like miniature ornamental temples, the *pha phum* (spirits of the land). Their task is to protect the grounds from any malignant spirits – for in Laos the air is thick with them. Before anything is built within their grounds, offerings must be made and permission granted. The same goes for a tree that must be knocked down to make way for a bridge, a field before a harvest… and so on. It's an endless animistic communion between the seen and unseen, the prosaic and the spiritual.

Population

One hundred and 32 ethnic groups make up the population of Laos. Around 60% of these are Lao Loum (lowland Lao), who have the most in common with their Thai neighbours, and it's their cultural beliefs and way of life that are known as 'Lao culture'. The remainder is labelled according to the altitude at which the groups live: Lao Theung (midlevel mountain group including Khamu, Lamet and Alak), Lao Thai (upland valleys), Lao Thoung (upland Lao) and Lao Soung (1000m or more above sea level, including Hmong, Mien and Akha).

Laos' strongest cultural and linguistic links are with Thailand; Thai music and TV are an almost ubiquitous presence in the country.

Religion

Most lowland Lao are Theravada Buddhists and many Lao males choose to be ordained temporarily as monks, typically spending anywhere from a month to three years at a wat (temple). After the 1975 communist victory, Buddhism was suppressed, but by 1992 the government had relented and it was back in full swing, with a few alterations. Monks are still forbidden to promote *phǐ* (spirit) worship, which has been officially banned in Laos along with *sǎiyasàht* (folk magic).

Despite the ban, *phǐ* worship remains the dominant non-Buddhist belief system. Even in Vientiane, Lao citizens openly perform the ceremony called *sukhwǎn* or *bąsǐ*, in which the 32 *kwǎn* (guardian spirits of the body) are bound to the guest of honour by white strings tied around the wrists (you'll see many Lao people wearing these).

Outside the Mekong River valley, the *phǐ* cult is particularly strong among tribal Thai, especially among the Thai Dam. The Khamu and Hmong-Mien tribes also practise animism.

Arts

The true expression of Lao art is found in its religious sculpture, temples, handicrafts and architecture. Distinctively Lao is the Calling for Rain Buddha, a standing image with hands held rigidly at his sides.

Wat in Luang Prabang feature *sǐm* (chapels), with steep, low roofs. The typical Lao *tâht* (stupa) is a four-sided, curvilinear, spirelike structure.

Upland crafts include gold- and silversmithing among the Hmong and Mien tribes, and tribal Thai weaving (especially among the Thai Dam and Thai Lü). Classical music and dance have all but evaporated, partly due to the vapid tentacles of Thai pop and the itinerant nature of Laos' young workforce.

Food & Drink

Food

The standard Lao breakfast is *fěr* (rice noodles), usually served in a broth with vegetables and meat of your choice. *Lahp* is the most distinctively Lao dish, a delicious spicy salad made from minced beef, pork, duck, fish or chicken, mixed with fish sauce, small shallots, mint leaves, lime juice, roasted ground rice and lots and lots of chillies.

In lowland Laos almost every dish is eaten with *khào nǐaw* (sticky rice), which is served in a small basket. Take a small amount of rice and, using one hand, work it into a walnut-sized ball before dipping it into the food.

Drink

Beerlao remains a firm favourite with 90% of the nation, and, although officially illegal, *lào-láo* (Lao liquor, or rice whisky) is a popular drink among lowland Lao. It's usually taken neat and offered in villages as a welcoming gesture. Water purified for drinking purposes is simply called *nâm deum* (drinking water), whether it's boiled or filtered. All water offered to customers in restaurants or hotels will be purified, and purified water is sold everywhere. Juice bars and cafes proliferate in cities. Lao coffee is usually served strong and sweet.

Environment

The Land

With a landmass of 236,800 sq km, Laos is a little larger than the UK and, thanks to its relatively small population and mountainous terrain, is one of the least altered environments in Southeast Asia. Unmanaged vegetation covers an estimated 85% of the country, and a dwindling 10% of Laos is original-growth forest. A hundred years ago this last statistic was nearer 75%, which provides a clear idea of the detrimental effects of relentless logging and slash-and-burn farming.

In 1993 the government set up 18 National Protected Areas (NPAs) comprising a total of 24,600 sq km, just over 10% of the land. An additional two were added in 1995 (taking the total coverage to 14% of Laos). Despite these conservation efforts, illegal timber felling and the smuggling of exotic wildlife are still significant threats to Laos' natural resources. The WWF claims that in 2014 China imported US$1 billion worth of timber from Laos, up from US$45 million in 2008.

Wildlife

Laos is home to Asian elephants, jackals, Asiatic black bears, black-crested gibbons, langurs, clouded leopards, pythons, king cobras, 437 kinds of bird and the rare Irrawaddy dolphin. Tigers are all but extinct. The illegal wildlife trade is flourishing, driven by neighbours – particularly China – who seek body parts of endangered animals for traditional medicine and aphrodisiac purposes.

Almost two-thirds of Lao people live in rural areas and rely on wildlife as a source of protein to supplement their diet.

SURVIVAL GUIDE

❶ Directory A–Z

ACCOMMODATION

Budget digs – usually a room with a fan and sometimes private bathroom – are getting better every year. Even though guesthouse prices are rising, particularly in the cities, they're still unbeatable value when compared with the West. At less than US$10 (80,000K) a night, who can argue?

Homestays

For more than 75% of Laotians, the 'real Laos' is life in a village. Minority people in villages across the country now welcome travellers into their homes to experience life Lao-style. This means sleeping, eating and washing as they do. It's not luxury – the mattress will be on the floor and you'll 'shower' by pouring water over yourself. But it's exactly this level of immersion that makes a homestay so worthwhile. It's also good

to know that the 50,000K you'll pay for bed, dinner and breakfast is going directly to those who need it most.

Price Ranges

The following price ranges refer to the price of a double room in high season.

$ less than 160,000K (US$20)

$$ 160,000K to 640,000K (US$20 to US$80)

$$$ more than 640,000K (US$80)

ACTIVITIES

Cycling

Laos' uncluttered roads are a haven for cyclists. Many roads are now sealed, though if you're visiting straight after the monsoon you'll find them potholed or, in the case of the Bolaven Plateau, mired in mud. In Vientiane be careful about leaving bags in the front basket, as passing motorcyclists have been known to lift them. Laos' main towns all have bicycle-rental shops. Several companies offer mountain-bike tours, particularly from Luang Namtha, Nong Khiaw and Luang Prabang.

Kayaking & Rafting

Laos has several world-class rapids, as well as lots of beautiful, less challenging waterways. The industry remains dangerously unregulated, however, and you should not go out on rapids during the wet season unless you are completely confident about your guides and equipment. Vang Vieng and Nong Khiaw are great for kayaking. Green Discovery (www.greendiscoverylaos.com) has a good reputation.

Rock Climbing

Organised rock-climbing operations are run by Green Discovery and Adam's Rock Climbing School (p329) in the karst cliffs around Vang Vieng, and recently the excellent Green Climbers Home near Tha Khaek. Vang Vieng has the most established scene, with dozens of climbs ranging from beginner to expert.

Trekking

Where else can you wander past ethnic hill tribe villages, the triple canopy of the ancient forest towering above you? Several environmentally and culturally sustainable tours allow you to enter these pristine areas and experience the lives of the indigenous people without exploiting them. These treks are available in several provinces and are detailed on www.ecotourismlaos.com. You can trek from Luang Nam Tha, Muang Sing, Udomxai, Luang Prabang, Nong Khiaw, Tha Khaek, Savannakhet and Pakse. Treks organised through the provincial tourism offices are the cheapest, while companies such as Tiger Trail (p342) and Green Discovery offer more expensive and professional operations.

Tubing

Tubing involves floating down a river in an enormous tractor inner tube, and Vang Vieng, Muang Ngoi Neua and Si Phan Don are all hot spots to do this. Just keep an eye on reefer intake and how much you drink; the two combined can be lethal, especially in the dark if you take a tumble in a rogue current.

BOOKS

Lonely Planet's *Laos* has all the information you'll need for extended travel in Laos, with more detailed descriptions of sights and wider coverage to help get you off the beaten track. The following offer further insights:

➺ *A Dragon Apparent* (1951) Follows Norman Lewis' travels through the twilight of French Indochina.

➺ *The Lao* (2008) Robert Cooper's locally published book (available in Vientiane) offers a penetrating insight into Lao culture and its psyche.

➺ *The Ravens: Pilots of the Secret War of Laos* (1987) Christopher Robbins' page-turning account of the Secret War and the role of American pilots and the Hmong is an excellent read.

COURSES

Short courses in cooking are available in the capital and Luang Prabang, and informal Lao-language lessons are advertised in Vientiane.

CUSTOMS REGULATIONS

You can expect borders to be fairly sleepy affairs, and customs officers are equally chilled – so long as you're not carrying more than 500 cigarettes and 1L of spirits, or any drugs, knives or guns on your person.

ELECTRICITY

Electricity is 230V, 50Hz, and plugs have either two or three flat pins or two round pins.

EMBASSIES & CONSULATES

Australian Embassy (Map p319; ☑ 021-353800; www.laos.embassy.gov.au; Th Tha Deua, Ban Wat Nak, Vientiane; ⊙8.30am-5pm Mon-Fri) Also represents nationals of Canada and New Zealand.

Cambodian Embassy (Map p319; ☑ 021-314952; Th Tha Deua, Km3, Ban That Khao, Vientiane) Issues visas for US$20.

Chinese Embassy (Map p319; ☑ 021-315105; http://la.china-embassy.org/eng; Th Wat Nak Nyai, Ban Wat Nak, Vientiane; ⊙8-11.30am Mon-Fri) Issues visas in four working days.

French Embassy (Map p320; ☑ 021-215258; www.ambafrance-laos.org; Th Setthathirath, Ban Si Saket, Vientiane; ⊙9am-12.30pm & 2-5.30pm Mon-Fri)

German Embassy (Map p319; ☑ 021-312110; www.vientiane.diplo.de; Th Sok Pa Luang, Vientiane; ⊙9am-noon Mon-Fri)

Myanmar Embassy (Map p319; ☑ 021-314910; Th Sok Pa Luang, Vientiane) Issues tourist visas in three days for US$20.

Thai Embassy (Map p319; ☑ 021-214581; www.thaiembassy.org/vientiane; Th Kaysone Phomvihane, Vientiane; ⊙8.30am-noon & 1-3.30pm Mon-Fri) Head to the Vientiane consulate for visa renewals and extensions. Thailand also has a consulate in Savannakhet, which issues same-day tourist and non-immigrant visas (1000B).

Thai Consulate (Map p319; ☑ 021-214581; 15 Th Bourichane, Vientiane; ⊙8am-noon & 1-4.30pm) Visa renewals and extensions.

Thai Consulate (☑ 041-212373; cnr Th Tha He & Th Chaimeuang, Savannakhet) Tourist and non-immigrant visas issued the same day.

US Embassy (☑ 021-487000, weekend emergency line 020 55502016; http://laos.us embassy.gov; Th Thadeua, Ban Somvang Thai, Km 9, Hatsayfong district; ⊙8.30am-5pm Mon-Fri) Based in a new building to the south of the city.

Vietnamese Embassy (Map p319; ☑ 021-413400; www.mofa.gov.vn/vnemb.la; Th That Luang, Vientiane; ⊙8.30am-5.30pm Mon-Fri) Issues tourist visas in three working days for US$45, or in one day for US$60. The Luang Prabang consulate issues tourist visas for US$60 in a few minutes or US$45 if you wait a few days. At the consulates in Pakse and Savannakhet, visas cost US$60.

Vietnamese Consulate (Th Naviengkham, Luang Prabang)

Vietnamese Consulate (☑ 031-214199; www.vietnamconsulate-pakse.org; Th 21, Pakse; ⊙7.30-11.30am & 2-4.30pm Mon-Fri) Issues same-day visas for US$60.

Vietnamese Consulate (☑ 041-212418; Th Sisavangvong, Savannakhet) One-month tourist visas cost US$60; bring one photo and allow three working days.

FOOD

The following price ranges refer to the cost of a main course.

$ less than 40,000K (US$5)

$$ 40,000K to 80,000K (US$5 to US$10)

$$$ more than 80,000K (US$10)

LEGAL MATTERS

There is virtually nothing in the way of legal services in Laos. If you get yourself in legal strife, contact your embassy in Vientiane, though the assistance it can provide may be limited.

It's against the law for foreigners and Lao to have sexual relations unless they're married.

Be aware that a holiday romance could result in being arrested and deported.

LGBT TRAVELLERS

Laos has a liberal attitude towards homosexuality, but a very conservative attitude towards public displays of affection. Gay couples are unlikely to be given frosty treatment anywhere. Laos doesn't have an obvious gay scene, though Luang Prabang has Laos' first openly gay bar, Khob Chai (opposite Hive Bar, p340), and has the rainbow-coloured gay pride flag flying in a few places around town.

Lesbians won't be bothered, but do expect some strange looks from Lao men.

MAPS

The best all-purpose country map available is *Laos* by GT-Rider (http://gt-rider.com), a sturdy laminated affair with several city maps. Look for editions dated from 2005 onwards.

Hobo Maps has produced a series of decent maps for Vientiane, Luang Prabang, Vang Vieng and other Northern Laos towns. These maps are widely available in the relevant destinations.

MEDIA

Sabaidee (www.sabaidee-magazine.com) is a monthly glossy covering lifestyle and travel in Laos as well as upcoming events. The *Bangkok Post, Economist, Newsweek* and *Time* can be found in minimarts and bookshops. BBC and CNN are widely available on satellite TV.

MONEY

The official national currency in Laos is the Lao kip (K). Although only kip is legally negotiable in everyday transactions, in reality three currencies are used for commerce: kip, Thai baht (B) and US dollars (US$).

Bargaining

With the exception of tuk-tuk drivers in Vientiane (who are a law unto themselves), most Lao are not looking to rip you off. When haggling, keep in perspective that you're a comparatively rich person in a very poor country.

Exchanging Money & Travellers Cheques

US dollars and Thai baht can be exchanged all over the country. Banks in Vientiane and Luang Prabang change UK pounds, euro, Thai baht, Japanese yen, and Canadian, US and Australian dollars. The best exchange rate is usually offered by BCL.

Banks in all provincial centres will exchange US-dollar travellers cheques. If you are changing cheques into kip, there is usually no commission, but changing into dollars attracts a minimum 2% charge.

OPENING HOURS

Government offices are typically open from 8am to noon and 1pm to 4pm Monday to Friday. Banking hours are generally 8.30am to 4pm Monday to Friday. Shops have longer hours and are often open on weekends. Restaurants typically close by 10pm and bars stay open until around 11.30pm, sometimes later.

POST

Postal services from Vientiane are painfully slow but generally reliable; the provinces less so. If you have valuable items or presents to post home, there is a FedEx office inside the new main post office compound in Vientiane.

PUBLIC HOLIDAYS

Aside from government offices, banks and post offices, many Lao businesses do not trouble themselves with weekends and public holidays. Most Chinese- and Vietnamese-run businesses close for three days during Vietnamese Tet and Chinese New Year in January/February. International Women's Day is a holiday for women only.

International New Year 1 January

Army Day 20 January

International Women's Day 8 March

Lao New Year 14 to 16 April

International Labour Day 1 May

International Children's Day 1 June

Lao National Day 2 December

SAFE TRAVEL

Urban Laos is generally very safe thanks to the gentle, nonconfrontational nature of its people. You should still exercise vigilance at night in Vientiane (due to more widespread drug taking and bag-snatching scooter thieves), while Vang Vieng occasionally suffers from theft in budget accommodation.

In the eastern provinces, particularly Xieng Khuang, Salavan and Savannakhet, UXO (unexploded ordnance) is a hazard. *Never* walk off well-used paths.

TELEPHONE

Laos' country code is ☑ 856. To dial out of the country press ☑ 00 first. As a guide, all mobile phone numbers have the prefix ☑ 020, while the newer WIN phones (fixed phones without a landline) begin with ☑ 030.

DRESS ETIQUETTE

To avoid offence, women visiting Buddhist temples should cover their arms and legs with a sarong or dress, while men should ensure they are not bare-chested, and cover their legs with a sarong or trousers.

TOILETS

Unlike in Thailand, the hole-in-the-floor toilet is not common in Laos. The exception is if you're visiting destinations such as hill-tribe villages.

TOURIST INFORMATION

The Lao National Tourism Administration (NTAL) and provincial tourism authorities have offices throughout Laos. The offices in Tha Khaek, Savannakhet, Pakse, Luang Nam Tha, Sainyabouli, Phongsali and Sam Neua are excellent, with well-trained staff and plenty of brochures.

NTAL also has three good websites:

Central Laos Trekking www.trekkingcentrallaos.com

Ecotourism Laos www.ecotourismlaos.com

Lao National Tourism Administration www.tourismlaos.org

For the latest listings try www.thisisvientiane.com, www.sabaidee-magazine.com and www.visit-laos.com.

TRAVELLERS WITH DISABILITIES

Given Laos' surprisingly short-sighted view of its own people with disabilites (who are often hidden from view), it is hardly surprising that they've poorly acquitted themselves to visitors with special physical needs. Vientiane's international-style hotels have ramps, lifts and toilets for people with mobility limitations; though if you're in a wheelchair, trying to navigate the sometimes broken pavements and scooters parked on the sidewalk is going to be tough. Luang Prabang, with less vehicles and a more navigable historic quarter, is fine. Sadly, transport is a no-no, with cramped conditions on public buses. Contact hotels in advance to see what transport facilities they have.

VOLUNTEERING

It's not easy to find short-term volunteer work in Laos. The Organic Mulberry Farm (p330) in Vang Vieng needs volunteers occasionally, as does Big Brother Mouse (p338). If you're an orthopaedic surgeon, physio or an IT and graphic designer, you may be able to work at the COPE Visitor Centre.

WOMEN TRAVELLERS

Stories of women being hassled are few. Much of the time any attention will be no more than curiosity, as non-Asian women are generally so physically different to Lao women.

WORK

English teaching is the most common first job for foreigners working in Laos, and schools in Vientiane are often hiring. There are also an inordinate number of development organisations – see www.directoryofngos.org for a full list – where foreigners with technical skills and volunteer experience can look for employment. Ask around.

ℹ Getting There & Away

AIR

With well over a dozen border crossings into Laos, visiting the country has never been easier. Also, the newly improved Lao Airlines, with a fleet of 10 new planes, is servicing most corners of the country and neighbouring countries with frequent flights.

Bangkok Airways (www.bangkokair.com) Connects Luang Prabang, Vientiane and Pakse to Bangkok, plus Luang Prabang to Chiang Mai.

China Eastern Airlines (www.ce-air.com) Flies daily to Kunming and Nanning from Vientiane.

Lao Airlines (www.laoairlines.com) National carrier. The extensive international flight network includes Vientiane to Bangkok, Chiang Mai, Danan, Guangzhou, Hanoi, Ho Chi Minh City, Kunming, Phnom Penh, Siem Reap and Singapore; Luang Prabang to Bangkok, Chiang Mai, Hanoi and Siem Reap; Pakse to Bangkok, Danang, Ho Chi Minh City and Siem Reap; and Savannakhet to Bangkok and Danang.

Thai Airways International (www.thaiairways.com) Vientiane to Bangkok connections twice daily.

Vietnam Airlines (www.vietnamairlines.com) Connects Vientiane with Ho Chi Minh City, Hanoi and Phnom Penh, plus Luang Prabang with Hanoi and Siem Reap.

LAND

Laos has open land borders with Cambodia, China, Thailand and Vietnam, but not Myanmar. Under current rules, 30-day tourist visas are available on arrival at several (but not all) international checkpoints. We also recommend checking the Thorn Tree (www.lonelyplanet.com/thorntree) for other travellers' accounts, as things change frequently.

ℹ Getting Around

AIR

Lao Airlines handles all domestic flights in Laos, including between Vientiane and Luang Prabang (US$103, 40 minutes, three daily), Luang Nam Tha (US$128, six times weekly), Pakse (US$147, four times weekly), Phonsavan (Xieng Khuang; US$103, daily), Savannakhet (US$128, four times weekly) and Udomxai (US$128, four times weekly).

Lao Skyway (☏ 021-513022; www.laoskyway.com; Domestic Terminal, Wattay International Airport; ⊗ 8am-8pm) is a new domestic airline with flights from Vientiane to Udomxai

(499,000K), Luang Prabang (649,000K), Huay Xai (599,000K) and Luang Namtha (499,000K). Flights are subject to change, see the website.

BICYCLE

The light and relatively slow traffic in most Lao towns makes for favourable cycling conditions. Bicycles are available for rent in major tourist destinations, costing around 10,000K per day for a cheap Thai or Chinese model.

BOAT

The most popular river trip in Laos – the slow boat between Huay Xai and Luang Prabang – remains a daily event. Other popular journeys – between Pakse and Si Phan Don, and Pakse and Champasak – are recommended if you have time. Sadly the route up the Nam Ou from Luang Prabang is no longer possible due to the damming of the Nam Ou.

River ferries are basic affairs and passengers usually sit, eat and sleep on the wooden decks; it's definitely worth bringing some padding. The toilet is an enclosed hole in the deck at the back of the boat. For shorter river trips, such as Luang Prabang to the Pak Ou Caves, you can easily hire a river taxi.

Between Luang Prabang and Huay Xai deafeningly loud and painfully uncomfortable speedboats operate, covering the same distance in six hours as that of a river ferry in two days. Be warned that passengers are killed and injured every year when the boats disintegrate on contact with floating debris, or flip when they hit a standing wave.

BUS & SŎRNGTĂAOU

Long-distance public transport in Laos is either by bus or sŏrngtăaou (literally 'two rows'), which are converted trucks or pick-ups with benches down either side. Buses are more frequent and go further than ever. Privately run VIP buses operate on some busier routes, but slow, simple standard buses (occasionally with air-con) remain the norm.

Sŏrngtăaou usually service shorter routes within a given province. Most decent-sized villages have at least one sŏrngtăaou, which will run to the provincial capital daily except Sunday, stopping wherever you want.

CAR & MOTORCYCLE

Scooters can be rented for 50,000K to 90,000K a day in Vientiane, Tha Khaek, Savannakhet, Pakse and Luang Nam Tha. In Vientiane, Luang Prabang, Tha Khaek and Pakse it's also possible to rent dirt bikes for around US$35 per day. First-One Motorbike Rental (p328) and Mad Monkey Motorbike (p359) have a range of performance dirt bikes, and the former offers the option to rent in Vientiane and drop off in Luang Prabang or Pakse for an additional charge. Motolao (p337) are a forward-thinking new company catering to keen riders who want to experience seldom seen parts of Laos on top notch dirtbikes.

Car rental in Laos is a great if relatively costly way of reaching remote places. Avis (p328) offers vehicles from US$55 per day, charging US$20 extra for an optional driver.

HITCHING

Hitching is possible in Laos, if not common. It's never entirely safe and not recommended, especially for women, as the act of standing beside a road and waving at cars might be misinterpreted.

Malaysia

Best for Regional Specialities

➡ Laksa, Penang (p404)

➡ Satay celup, Melaka (p399)

➡ Sarawak laksa, Kuching (p451)

➡ Tea, Cameron Highlands (p401)

Best Beaches

➡ Pulau Perhentian (p424)

➡ Pulau Langkawi (p414)

➡ Pulau Tioman (p418)

➡ Pulau Kapas (p420)

Why Go?

The catchy slogan 'Malaysia, Truly Asia' continues to ring true. The multicultural peninsula flaunts Malay, Chinese and Indian influences, beautiful beaches and islands. The landscapes only improve across the South China Sea in Malaysian Borneo with its rainforests that are home to orangutans, granite peaks and remote tribes. Human habitats range from the soaring skyscrapers and stupendous shopping malls of Kuala Lumpur (KL) to the jungle-surrounded longhouse villages of Sarawak. The supreme expression of the national diversity is its amazing range of delicious culinary offerings. Start with Chinese-Malay 'Nonya' fare, then move on to Indian curries, Chinese buffets, Malay food stalls and even impressive Western food. The icing on the cake is that Malaysia is one of the safest, most stable and manageable countries in Southeast Asia.

When to Go
Kuala Lumpur

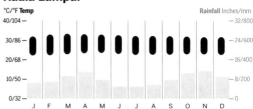

Dec–Feb High season: school holidays and Chinese New Year. Prices rise; bookings essential.

Nov–Mar Monsoon season sees many east-coast peninsular islands shut; Cherating fills with surfers.

Jun–Aug Ramadan food bazaars open at night. End of Ramandan (Hari Raya) is also a time for feasting.

Don't Miss

You'll find excellent food markets and hawkers all around the country but the west coast, and in particular Kuala Lumpur and Penang, has a thriving street-food scene that offers up some of the best eats in Southeast Asia. Hit up Jln Alor or the Imbi Market in KL or try one of the hawker centres in Penang. Every place has a speciality but follow your nose, appetite and instincts to choose your favourite noodles, rice dishes, salads, grilled meats and icy desserts. Go for busy stalls, where the wok is kept hot, and you'll avoid tummy troubles too.

ITINERARIES

One Week

Spend a day in Kuala Lumpur then fly to Penang to gorge on endless street food. Next cool off in the Cameron Highlands by exploring mossy forests and tea plantations. Hop over to the Perhentian Islands for snorkelling, diving and beachside revelry.

Two Weeks

Follow the one-week itinerary backwards then catch a flight to Kota Kinabalu and spend the next week trekking the wild jungles of Borneo, perhaps ascending Mt Kinabalu, one of the highest mountains in Southeast Asia.

Essential Food & Drink

→ **Breakfast** *Nasi lemak* (coconut rice served with a variety of accompaniments), *roti canai* (Indian flat bread), *won ton mee* (egg noodles and wontons), dim sum or rice congee (savoury rice porridge).

→ **Barbecue** Fish, lobster, prawns, squid, cockles and stingray. Point to it then watch it get slathered in sambal and grilled in a banana leaf.

→ **Noodles** Fried or in soup. The best include *char kway teow* (fried noodles with egg, soy sauce, chilli and a variety of additions), laksa, *curry mee* (curry noodles), Hokkien mee (fried noodles with chicken, pork and other additions) and *won ton mee*.

→ **Rice** *Nasi campur* is a lunch favourite of rice and a buffet of toppings.

→ **Dessert** Malaysians drink their sweets via sugared fruit juices, sweetened condensed milk in hot beverages and scary looking icy concoctions such as *cendol* and *ais kacang* (also known as ABC; shaved ice covered in coconut cream, jellies, beans and other crazy stuff).

AT A GLANCE

→ **Currency** Malaysian ringitt (RM)

→ **Languages** Bahasa Malaysia (official), Chinese (Hakka and Hokkien), Tamil, English

→ **Money** ATMs in large towns

→ **Visas** Most nationalities get a 30- to 90-day visa on arrival

→ **Mobile phones** SIMs start at RM5, calls are 15 sen per minute, data 4G plans are RM10 per week

Fast Facts

→ **Area** 329,874 sq km
→ **Capital** Kuala Lumpur
→ **Emergency** ☑ 999

Exchange Rates

Australia	A$1	RM3.07
Euro	€1	RM4.68
Singapore	S$1	RM3.06
Thailand	10B	RM1.21
UK	UK£1	RM6.63
US	US$1	RM4.30

Daily Costs

Dorm bed RM15–50

Hawker stall meal RM5–7

Beer RM8

Snorkel gear hire RM15

Entering the Country

Kuala Lumpur is the main flight hub on the peninsula; Kota Kinabalu receives most Sabah flights and Kuching Sarawak flights.

MALAYSIA

Malaysia Highlights

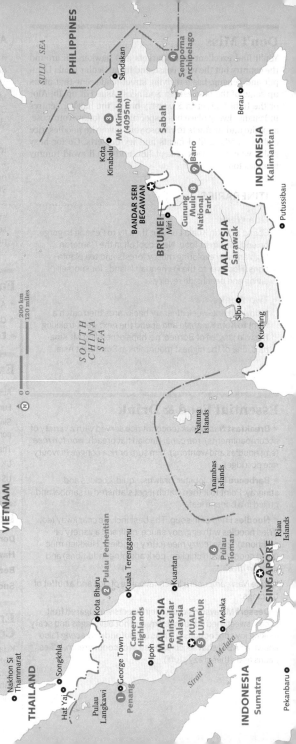

1 Exploring George Town's heritage district and grazing on street food on **Penang** (p404).

2 Swimming, lying on the beach, snorkelling and eating on **Pulau Perhentian** (p424).

3 Hiking past pitcher plants and moonscapes for sunrise atop **Mt Kinabalu** (p440).

4 Passing turtles, sharks and coral as you scuba dive in the **Semporna Archipelago** (p448).

5 Admiring the view of **Kuala Lumpur** (p383) from the KL Tower or the rooftop Heli Lounge Bar.

6 Hopping between idyllic beach villages, diving reefs and wrecks, and spotting monkeys on **Pulau Tioman** (p418).

7 Admiring the verdant, rolling tea plantations then enjoying a cuppa in the **Cameron Highlands** (p401).

8 Climbing the crags of the Pinnacles at **Gunung Mulu National Park** (p466).

9 Sipping wild teas at a wobbly longhouse in **Bario** (p468).

KUALA LUMPUR

☑03 / POP 1.5 MILLION

In the 150 years since tin miners hacked a base out of the jungle, Kuala Lumpur (KL) has evolved into an affluent 21st-century metropolis remarkable for its cultural diversity. Ethnic Malays, Chinese prospectors, Indian immigrants and British colonials all helped shape the city, and each group has left its indelible physical mark as well as a fascinating assortment of cultural traditions. Historic temples and mosques rub shoulders with space-age towers and shopping malls; traders' stalls are piled high with pungent durians and counterfeit handbags; monorail cars zip by lush jungle foliage; and locals sip cappuccinos in wi-fi-enabled cafes or feast on delicious streetside hawker food.

KL's city centre is surprisingly compact – from Chinatown to Masjid India takes little more than 10 minutes on foot; it's often quicker to walk than take public transport or grab a cab. Merdeka Sq is the focus of colonial-era KL. Southeast across the river, Chinatown is popular with travellers for its budget accommodation and lively night market. East of Pudu Sentral bus station are the Golden Triangle and Kuala Lumpur City Centre (KLCC) areas around the Petronas Towers – this is where contemporary KL thrives.

◉ Sights

◉ Chinatown, Merdeka Square & Bukit Nanas

★ **KL Forest Eco Park**   NATURE RESERVE
(Taman Eko Rimba KL; Map p390; www.forestry. gov.my; ⊙7am-7pm; ⏚KL Tower) Don't miss traversing the lofty, newly constructed **canopy walkway** set in this thick lowland dipterocarp forest covering 9.37 hectares in the heart of the city. The oldest protected jungle in Malaysia (gazetted in 1906), the park is commonly known as Bukit Nanas (Pineapple Hill), and is also threaded through with short trails up from either Jln Ampang or Jln Raja Chulan. Pick up a basic map to the trails from the **Forest Information Centre** (Map p384; ☑03-2026 4741; www.forestry.gov.my; Jln Raja Chulan; ⊙9am-5pm; ⏚KL Tower) FREE.

Menara Kuala Lumpur   TOWER
(KL Tower; Map p390; ☑03-2020 5444; www. menarakl.com.my; 2 Jln Punchak; observation deck adult/child RM52/31, open deck adults only RM105; ⊙observation deck 9am-10pm, last tickets 9.30pm;

⏚KL Tower) Although the Petronas Towers are taller, the 421m Menara KL, rising from the crest of Bukit Nanas, offers the best city views. Surrounded by a pocket of primary rainforest, this lofty spire is the world's fourth-highest telecommunications tower. The bulb at the top (its shape inspired by a Malaysian spinning toy) contains a revolving restaurant, an interior **observation deck** at 276m and, most thrilling of all, an **open deck** at 300m, access to which is weather dependent.

Sri Mahamariamman Temple   HINDU TEMPLE
(Map p386; 163 Jln Tun HS Lee; ⊙6am-8.30pm, to 9.30pm Fri; ⏆Pasar Seni) FREE This lively Hindu temple – the oldest in Malaysia and rumoured to be the richest – was founded in 1873. Mariamman is the South Indian mother goddess, also known as Parvati. Her shrine is at the back of the complex. On the left sits a shrine to the elephant-headed Ganesh, and on the right one to Lord Murugan. During the Thaipusam festival, Lord Murugan is transported to Batu Caves from the temple on a silver chariot.

Merdeka Square   SQUARE
(Dataran Merdeka; Map p386; ⏆Masjid Jamek) The huge open square where Malaysian independence was declared in 1957 is ringed by heritage buildings, such as the magnificent **Sultan Abdul Samad Building** (Map p386; Jln Raja; ⏆Masjid Jamek) and **St Mary's Anglican Cathedral** (Map p386; ☑03-2692 8672; www.stmaryscathedral.org.my; Jln Raja;

━━━━━━━━━━━━━━━━━
WORTH A TRIP

BATU CAVES

Hindu deities rule over the Batu Caves, a system of three caves 13km northwest of the capital. The main focus is **Temple Cave** (⊙8am-8.30pm; ⏚Batu Caves) FREE, which contains a Hindu shrine reached by a straight flight of 272 steps, guarded by a 42.7m golden statue of Murugan, said to be the largest in the world. The caves are busy every day, but hundreds of thousands of pilgrims converge on the caves every year during Thaipusam (January/February) to engage in or watch the spectacularly masochistic feats of the devotees.

Take KTM Komuter Trains to Batu Caves (RM2.60, 30 minutes) every 15 to 30 minutes. A taxi costs RM20 to RM30.

MALAYSIA KUALA LUMPUR

Kuala Lumpur

0 — 1 km
0 — 0.5 miles

Batu Caves (7km)

Sentul Park

Sentul LRT

Jln Sentul

Jln Ipoh

Sungai Gombak

Sungai Batu

Jalan Kuching

Titiwangsa LRT

Titiwangsa Monorail

Jln Tun Razak

Lake Titiwangsa

Titiwangsa Lake Gardens

National Visual Arts Gallery

TITIWANGSA

Sungai Batu

Hospital Kuala Lumpur

Jln Ipoh

PWTC LRT

Jln Putra

Putra KTM

Chow Kit Monorail

CHOW KIT

Jln Raja Muda Abdul Aziz

KAMPUNG BARU

Ampang Elevated Hwy

Sultan Ismail LRT

Jln Raja Laut

Kampung Baru Walking Tour

Kampung Baru LRT

Jln Yap Kwan Seng

KLCC LRT

Medan Tuanku Monorail

Jln Raja Abdullah

Bandaraya LRT

Bank Negara KTM

Jln Dang Wangi

Dang Wangi LRT

Bukit Nanas Monorail

Kuala Lumpur City Centre (KLCC) Park

Jln Sultan Salahuddin

Capital Café

Masjid India Pasar Malam

MASJID INDIA

Jln Ampang

KL Forest Eco Park

Jln Raja Chulan

Raja Chulan Monorail

Container Hotel (300m); Zouk (900m)

National Monument

Jln Parlimen

Immigration Office (7km)

Masjid Jamek LRT

MERDEKA SQUARE

Forest Information Centre

GOLDEN TRIANGLE

Perdana Botanical Garden

COLONIAL DISTRICT

Jln Cheng Lock

AirAsia Bukit Bintang Monorail

KL Bird Park

CHINATOWN

Jln Pudu

Jln Imbi

Tasik Perdana

Pasar Seni LRT

Plaza Rakyat LRT

Imbi Monorail

Kuala Lumpur

Maharajalela Monorail

Hang Tuah Monorail
Hang Tuah LRT

See Golden Triangle & KLCC Map (p390)

National Museum

See Chinatown, Merdeka Square & Masjid India Map (p386)

PUDU

BRICKFIELDS

Jln Istana

Pudu LRT

Jln Pasar

Jln Travers

KL Sentral

Jln San Peng

Jln Tun Sambanthan

Tun Sambanthan Monorail

Jln Syed Putra

Jln Lapangan Terbang

Jln Loke Yew

RAIL SYSTEMS
KTM
LRT
MRT

Jln Sungai Besi

Chan Sow Lin LRT

Sungai Klang

Terminal Bersepadu Selatan (TSB) (10km)

Ⓜ Masjid Jamek), both designed by AC Norman. There's also an enormous flagpole and fluttering Malaysian flag. In the British era, the square was used as a cricket pitch and called the Padang ('field').

Masjid Jamek MOSQUE
(Friday Mosque; Map p386; off Jln Tun Perak; ⊗ 9am-12.30pm & 2.30-4pm Sat-Thu; Ⓜ Masjid Jamek) FREE Gracefully designed in Mughal style by British architect AB Hubback, this onion-domed mosque is situated at the confluence of the Gombak and Klang rivers. At the time of research the surroundings were being relandscaped as part of the River of Life project and the original steps down to the river reinstated. You can visit the inside, outside of prayer times, but dress conservatively and remember to remove your shoes before entering the prayer halls.

Sin Sze Si Ya Temple CHINESE TEMPLE
(Map p386; Jln Tun HS Lee; ⊗ 7am-5pm; Ⓜ Pasar Seni) FREE Kuala Lumpur's oldest Chinese temple was built on the instructions of Kapitan Yap Ah Loy and is dedicated to Sin Sze Ya and Si Sze Ya, two Chinese immigrants instrumental in Yap's ascension to Kapitan status. Several beautiful objects decorate the temple, including two hanging carved panels, but the best feature is the almost frontier-like atmosphere. This is still an important temple for the community, much as it was in 1864 when 10,000 people turned out for opening day.

◉ KLCC & Around

★ **Petronas Towers** TOWER
(Map p390; ☎ 03-2331 8080; www.petronas twintowers.com.my; Jln Ampang; adult/child RM84.80/31.80; ⊗ 9am-9pm Tue-Sun, closed 1-2.30pm Fri; ♿; Ⓜ KLCC) Resembling twin silver rockets plucked from an episode of *Flash Gordon*, the Petronas Towers are the perfect allegory for the meteoric rise of the city from tin-miners' hovel to 21st-century metropolis. Half of the 1440 tickets for 45-minute guided tours – which take in the Skybridge connection on the 41st floor and the observation deck on the 86th floor at 370m – are sold in advance online. Otherwise turn up early to be sure of scoring a ticket to go up.

★ **ILHAM** GALLERY
(Map p390; www.ilhamgallery.com; 3rd & 5th fl, Ilham Tower, 8 Jln Binjai; ⊗ 11am-7pm Tue-Sat, 11am-5pm Sun; Ⓜ Ampang Park) FREE KL's latest public art gallery provides an excellent reason to admire close up the slick 60-storey ILHAM Tower designed by Foster + Partners. With a mission to showcase modern and contemporary Malaysian art, ILHAM kicked off in style in August 2015 with a blockbuster show of works by Hoessein Enas (1924–95). There's no permanent collection, with exhibitions changing every three to four months.

KLCC Park PARK
(Map p390; KLCC, Jln Ampang; ⊗ 7am-10pm; Ⓜ KLCC) The park is the best vantage point for eyeballing the Petronas Towers. In the early evening, it can seem like everyone in town has come down here to watch the glowing towers punching up into the night sky. Every night at 8pm, 9pm and 10pm the Lake Symphony fountains play in front of the Suria KLCC.

◉ Tun Abdul Razak Heritage Park & Around

★ **Islamic Arts Museum** MUSEUM
(Muzium Kesenian Islam Malaysia; Map p386; ☎ 03-2274 2020; www.iamm.org.my; Jln Lembah Perdana; adult/child RM14.85/7.40; ⊗ 10am-6pm; ℝ Kuala Lumpur) This outstanding museum is home to one of best collections of Islamic decorative arts in the world. Aside from the quality of the exhibits, which include fabulous textiles, carpets, jewellery and calligraphy-inscribed pottery, the building itself is a stunner, with beautifully decorated domes and glazed tile work. There's a good Middle

> ❶ **GETTING TO THE TUN ABDUL RAZAK HERITAGE PARK**
>
> The Tun Abdul Razaka Heritage Park, an area still best known by its colonial moniker of the Lake Gardens, can seem like an island of greenery cut off from the city by railway lines and highways. However, it is possible to walk here: take the pedestrian bridge across from the Central Market to Kompleks Dayabumi, then head south around the back of the post office to the underpass leading to the Masjid Negara. Another set of overhead pedestrian bridges leads into KL Station, from where you can also walk up to the gardens. Once in the park, you can use the hop-on, hop-off **electric tram** (adult/child RM2/1, 9am to 6pm) to get between the major attractions.

MALAYSIA KUALA LUMPUR

Chinatown, Merdeka Square & Masjid India

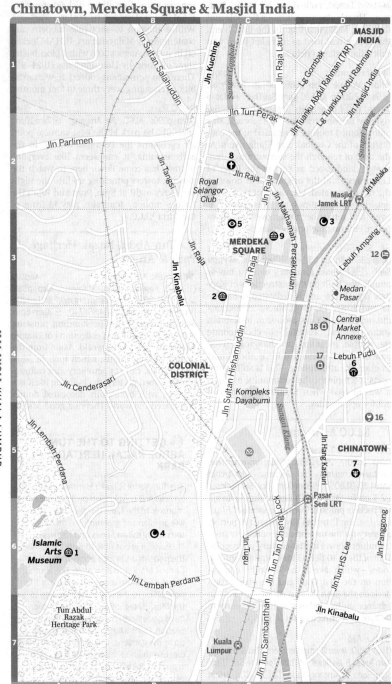

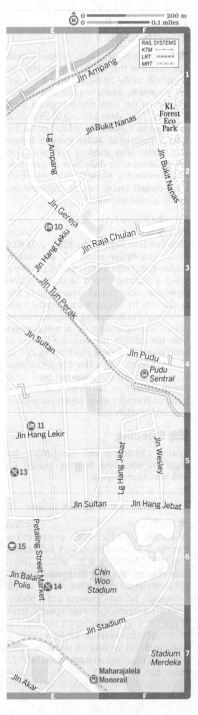

MALAYSIA KUALA LUMPUR

Eastern restaurant and one of KL's best museum gift shops stocking beautiful products from around the Islamic world.

KL Bird Park AVIARY
(Map p384; ☎03-2272 1010; www.klbirdpark. com; Jln Cenderawasih; adult/child RM50/41; ☺9am-6pm; 🐾; 🚉Kuala Lumpur) This fabulous 21-hectare aviary houses some 3000 birds comprising 200 species of (mostly) Asian birds. The park is divided into four sections: in the first two, birds fly freely beneath an enormous canopy. Section three features the native hornbills (so-called because of their enormous beaks), while section four offers the less-edifying spectacle of caged species.

Perdana Botanical Garden PARK
(Map p384; ☎03-2617 6404; www.klbotanical garden.gov.my; ☺7am-8pm; 🐾; 🚉Kuala Lumpur) ✔FREE KL's oldest public park (hailing back to the 1880s) showcases a wide variety of native and overseas plants with sections

dedicated to ferns, rare trees, trees that have lent their names to places in Malaysia, medicinal herbs, aquatic plants and so on. The gardens are well laid out with boardwalks and gazebos, but there is almost no signage. If you want to know more, book one of the free guided walks on Sundays at 8am and 10am.

National Monument MONUMENT
(Map p384; Plaza Tugu Negara, Jln Parlimen; ⊙7am-6pm; MMasjid Jamek, then taxi) FREE
This impressive monument commemorates the defeat of the communists in 1950 and provides fine views across the park and city. The giant militaristic bronze sculpture was created in 1966 by Felix de Weldon, the artist behind the Iwo Jima monument in Washington, DC, and is framed beautifully by an azure reflecting pool and graceful curved pavilion.

National Museum MUSEUM
(Muzium Negara; Map p384; ✐03-2282 6255; www.muziumnegara.gov.my; Jln Damansara; adult/child RM5/2; ⊙9am-6pm; 🚌Hop-On-Hop-Off Bus Tour, 🚇KL Sentral, then taxi) Exhibit quality varies, but overall this museum offers a rich look at Malaysian history. The best exhibits are Early History, with artefacts from neolithic and Bronze Age cultures; and the Malay Kingdoms, which highlights the rise of Islamic kingdoms in the Malay Archipelago.

Outside, look for a gorgeous traditional raised house; ancient burial poles from Sarawak; a regularly changing exhibition (extra charge); and two excellent small free side galleries, the **Orang Asli Craft Museum** and **Malay World Ethnology Museum**.

Masjid Negara MOSQUE
(National Mosque; Map p386; www.masjidnegara. gov.my/v2; Jln Lembah Perdana; ⊙9am-noon, 3-4pm & 5.30-6.30pm, closed Fri morning; 🚇Kuala Lumpur) FREE The main place of worship for KL's Malay Muslim population is this gigantic 1960s mosque, inspired by Mecca's Grand Mosque. Able to accommodate 15,000 worshippers, its umbrella-like blue-tile roof has 18 points symbolising the 13 states of Malaysia and the five pillars of Islam. Rising above the mosque, a 74m-high minaret issues the call to prayer, which can be heard across Chinatown. Non-Muslims are welcome to visit outside prayer times; robes are available for those who are not dressed appropriately.

◉ Kampung Baru & Northern KL

★**Kampung Baru** NEIGHBOURHOOD
The charm of this Malay area, gazetted by the British in the 1890s, lies in just wandering the streets, which you can also do with a guide on the city's free **Kampung Baru Walking Tour** (Map p384; ✐03-2698 0332; www.visitkl.gov.my/visitklv2; ⊙4.30-7pm Tue, Thu & Sun). Traditional Malay wooden houses stand amid leafy gardens and people go quietly about their daily lives as they have done for decades. Along the way enjoy tasty home-cooked Malay food at unpretentious roadside cafes and stalls.

National Visual Arts Gallery GALLERY
(Balai Seni Lukis Negara; Map p384; ✐03-4026 7000; www.artgallery.gov.my; 2 Jln Temerloh; ⊙10am-6pm; monorail Titiwangsa) FREE Occupying a pyramid-shaped block, the NVAG showcases modern and contemporary Malaysian art. It's always worth turning up to see a variety of interesting temporary shows of local and regional artists, as well as pieces from the gallery's permanent collection of 4000 pieces, including paintings by Zulkifli Moh'd Dahalan, Wong Hoy Cheong, Ahmad Fuad Osman and the renowned batik artist Chuah Thean Teng. On the ground floor, the National Portrait Gallery also hosts regularly changing exhibitions.

🛏 Sleeping

Vibrant Chinatown and the Golden Triangle are your best hunting ground for rock-bottom crash pads.

🛌 Chinatown & Little India

★**BackHome** HOSTEL $
(Map p386; ✐03-2022 0788; www.backhome. com.my; 30 Jln Tun HS Lee; dm/d/tr incl breakfast from RM53/134/192; ✳@🛜; MMasjid Jamek) This chic pit stop for flashpackers offers polished-concrete finishes, Zen simple decoration, fab rain showers and a blissful central courtyard sprouting spindly trees. It can be noisy on the street outside, but the hostel offers earplugs for light sleepers. Also check out its cool on-site cafe, **LOKL** (Map p386; http://loklcoffee.com; mains RM15-22; ⊙8am-8pm Tue-Sun; 🛜).

★ **Reggae Mansion** HOSTEL $
(Map p386; ☑03-2072 6877; www.reggaehos
telsmalaysia.com/mansion; 49-59 Jln Tun HS Lee;
dm/d from RM50/150; ❄@☎; ⓜMasjid Jamek)
Grooving to a beat that's superior to most
backpacker places, including its own guesthouses in the heart of Chinatown, this is one
cool operation. The decor is whitewashed
faux colonial with contemporary touches
including a flash cafe-bar, rooftop bar and
mini cinema.

Lantern Hotel HOTEL $
(Map p386; ☑03-2020 1648; www.lanternhotel.
com; 38 Jln Petaling; r incl breakfast from RM98;
❄☎; ⓜPasar Seni) You can't get more central
to Chinatown than this slickly designed new
hotel. The simple, whitewashed rooms with
lime or tangerine feature walls all have their
own bathrooms (the cheapest ones with no
windows (but spared some of the noise from
the market outside). A huge plus is the cool
terrace with a bird's-eye view of Petaling
Street Market.

🛏 Golden Triangle

Classic Inn HOSTEL $
(Map p390; ☑03-2148 8648; www.classicinn.com.
my; 36 & 52 Lg 1/77a; dm/s/d incl breakfast from
RM40/98/128; ❄@☎; monorail Imbi) Check-
in is at the newer, more upmarket branch
of Classic Inn at No 36 where there's spotless rooms all with private bathrooms and
a pleasant verandah cafe. The original yel-
low-painted shophouse at No 52 continues
to be a retro-charming choice with dorms
and private rooms, a small grassy garden
and welcoming staff.

Paloma Inn HOTEL $
(Map p390; ☑03-2110 6677; www.hotelpaloma
inn.com.my; 12-14 Jln Sin Chew Kee; dm/s/d incl
breakfast from RM42/95/128; ❄@☎; monorail
Hang Tuah) Set on a backstreet of painted pre-
war shophouses, Paloma is a great hangout
that's well run, quiet but also super central.
VCR cafe (Map p390; ☑03-2110 2330; www.vcr.
my; 2 Jln Galloway; ☺8.30am-10pm; ☎; monorail
Hang Tuah) is just around the corner for superb espresso, while the nightlife of Chankit
Bukit Bintang is a 10-minute walk away.
Rates are slightly higher Friday to Sunday.

Container Hotel DESIGN HOTEL $
(☑03-2116 4388; www.containerhotel.com; 1 Jln
Delima; dm/s with shared bathroom/d incl breakfast RM39/110/139; ❄☎; monorail AirAsia-Bukit

Bintang) Stacked shipping containers turned
into en suite rooms (sadly, not too well maintained) are the basis of this inventive place.
We preferred the singles in giant concrete
cylinders. There's also a roof terrace and free
bike rental. It's close by the excellent bakery
cafe Levain and megaclub Zouk (p391).

Rainforest Bed & Breakfast GUESTHOUSE $
(Map p390; ☑03-2145 3525; www.rainforest
bnbhotel.com; 27 Jln Mesui; dm/d/tw incl breakfast RM37/115/130; ❄@☎; monorail Raja Chulan) The lush foliage sprouting around and
tumbling off the tiered balconies of this
high-quality guesthouse is eye-catching and
apt for its name. Inside, bright-red walls
and timber-lined rooms (some without windows) are visually distinctive, along with the
collection of Chinese pottery figurines. The
location for nightlife, cafes and restaurants
couldn't be better.

✖ Eating

Inexpensive and delicious street food is
readily available but when it's too hot outside, head to central KL's air-con shopping
malls for international and local food.

✖ Chinatown & Masjid India

★ **Madras Lane Hawkers** HAWKER $
(Map p386; Madras Lane; noodles RM5-6; ☺8am-
4pm Tue-Sun; ⓜPasar Seni) Enter beside the
Guandi Temple to find this alley of hawker
stalls. It's best visited for breakfast or lunch,
with standout operators including the one
offering 10 types of *yong tau fu* (vegetables
stuffed with tofu and a fish and pork paste).
The *bah kuh teh* (pork and medicinal herbs
stew) and curry laksa stalls are also good.

Golden Triangle & KLCC

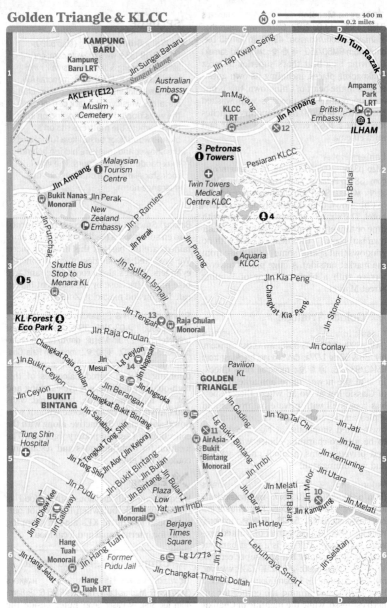

★ **Masjid India Pasar Malam**　　　HAWKER **$**

(Night Market; Map p384; Lg Tuanku Abdul Rahman; street food RM5-10; ☺3pm-midnight Sat; ⓂMasjid Jamek) From around 3pm until late every Saturday, stalls pack out the length of Lg Tuanku Abdul Rahman, the alley between the Jln TAR and Masjid India. Amid the headscarf and T-shirt sellers are plenty of stalls serving excellent Malay, Indian and Chinese snacks and colourful soya- and fruit-based drinks.

Golden Triangle & KLCC

◉ Top Sights
1 ILHAM..D1
2 KL Forest Eco Park A4
3 Petronas Towers.............................C2

◉ Sights
4 KLCC Park......................................C2
5 Menara Kuala Lumpur A3

⬢ Sleeping
6 Classic Inn.....................................B6
7 Paloma Inn.....................................A5

8 Rainforest Bed & Breakfast B4
9 Wolo Bukit Bintang.........................B5

⬢ Eating
10 Imbi Market...................................D5
11 Lot 10 Hutong C5
12 Nasi Kandar Pelita.........................C2

⬢ Drinking & Nightlife
13 Heli Lounge Bar B4
14 Taps Beer Bar B4
15 VCR A6

Capital Café　　　　　　　　MALAYSIAN $
(Map p384; 213 Jln TAR; dishes RM4-6; ⏰10am-8pm Mon-Sat; Ⓜ Bandaraya) Since it opened in 1956, this truly Malaysian cafe has had Chinese, Malays and Indians all working together, cooking up excellent renditions of Malay classics such as mee goreng, *rojak* (salad doused in a peanut-sauce dressing) and satay (only available in the evenings).

★**Merchant's Lane**　　　　　　FUSION $$
(Map p386; ✆03-2022 1736; level 1, 150 Jln Petaling; mains RM20-30; ⏰10.30am-6pm Thu & Sun-Tue, to 10pm Fri & Sat; 🛜; monorail Maharajalela) Look for the narrow doorway at the end of the block for the stairs leading up to this high-ceilinged charmer of a cafe. The vibe is relaxed, the staff young, hip and friendly and the food a very tasty mash up of Eastern and Western dishes, such as Italian chow mein and their take on a Japanese savoury pancake *okonomiyaki*.

✕ Golden Triangle & KLCC

★**Imbi Market**　　　　　　　　HAWKER $
(Pasar Baru Bukit Bintang; Map p390; Jln Kampung; dishes RM5-10; ⏰6am-1pm Tue-Sun;) Breakfast is a cheerful affair in the courtyard of this walled traditional market. Time-tested stalls include Sisters Crispy Popiah for wraps; Teluk Intan Chee Cheung Fun for oyster-and-peanut congee and egg pudding, and Ah Weng Koh Hainan Tea for coffee or tea.

The market is slated to move in 2017 as the area's developed into the Tun Razak Exchange financial district.

Nasi Kandar Pelita　　　　　　MAMAK $
(Map p390; www.pelita.com.my; 149 Jln Ampang; dishes RM3-9; ⏰24hr; Ⓜ KLCC) There's round-the-clock eating at the Jln Ampang branch of this chain of excellent *mamak* (Muslim

Indian-Malay) food courts. Among the scores of dishes available from the various stalls are magnificent *roti canai* (flat, flaky bread) and *hariyali tikka* (spiced chicken with mint, cooked in the tandoor).

Lot 10 Hutong　　　　　　　　HAWKER $
(Map p390; Basement, lot 10, 50 Jln Sultan Ismail; dishes RM9-18; ⏰10am-10pm; monorail AirAsia-Bukit Bintang) Lot 10 Hutong was the first mall to encourage top hawkers to open branches in a basement food court. In its well-designed space it pulled in names such as Soong Kee, which has served beef noodles since 1945. Look also for Kong Tai's oyster omelettes, Hon Kee's Cantonese porridge, and Kim Lian Kee's Hokkien mee.

🍷 Drinking & Nightlife

★**Aku Cafe & Gallery**　　　　　　CAFE
(Map p386; ✆03-2857 6887; www.oldchina.com.my/aku.html; 1st fl, 8 Jln Panggong; ⏰11am-8pm Tue-Sun; 🛜; Ⓜ Pasir Seni) This relaxed coffee haunt serves good hand-drip brews starting at RM10. There are also flavoured drinks such as mint and lemon iced coffee, cakes, and light *kopitiam*-style meals. Exhibitions change on a monthly basis and there are some nice local craft souvenirs for sale.

★**Reggae Bar**　　　　　　　　　BAR
(Map p386; www.facebook.com/reggaechinatown; 158 Jln Tun HS Lee; ⏰11.30am-3am; Ⓜ Pasir Seni) Travellers gather in droves at this pumping bar in the thick of Chinatown, which has outdoor seats if you'd like to catch the passing parade. There are beer promos, pool tables and pub grub served until late.

★**Zouk**　　　　　　　　　　　　CLUB
(www.zoukclub.com.my; 436 Jln Tun Razak; admission from RM50; ⏰9pm-3am Tue-Sun; monorail Bukit Bintang, then taxi) If you're going to visit

MALAYSIA KUALA LUMPUR

one club in KL, make it this one. Not only does Zouk's new location at the emerging TREC entertainment complex offer no fewer than around nine DJ spaces, bars and a cafe, if you bring your passport as a tourist you gain free entry to some of the enormous complex. Cover charges vary between venues.

Heli Lounge Bar
COCKTAIL BAR

(Map p390; ☑ 03-2110 5034; www.facebook.com/Heliloungebar; level 34, Menara KH, Jln Sultan Ishmail; ☉ 5pm-midnight Mon-Wed, 5pm-3am Thu-Sat; 🛜; monorailRaja Chulan) If the weather's behaving, this is easily the best place for sundowners in KL. Nothing besides your lychee martini and the cocktail waiter stands between you, the edge of the helipad and amazing 360-degree views. Steady your hands as you have to buy your first drink at the somewhat cheesy bar below and carry it up yourself. Weekend entry often requires your group to stump for a bottle.

Taps Beer Bar
MICROBREWERY

(Map p390; www.tapsbeerbar.my; One Residency, 1 Jln Nagasari; ☉ 5pm-1am Mon-Sat, noon-1am Sun; 🛜; monorail Raja Chulan) Taps specialises in ale from around the world with some 80 different microbrews on rotation, 14 of them on tap. There's live music Thursday to Saturday at 9.30pm and an all-day happy hour on Sunday. Taps also serves pub grub (with a few Malaysian dishes) and a Sunday roast.

DON'T MISS

JALAN ALOR

The collection of roadside restaurants and stalls lining Jln Alor (Map p390, B5) is the great common denominator of KL's food scene, hauling in everyone from sequined society babes to penny-strapped backpackers. From around 5pm till late every evening, the street transforms into a continuous open-air dining space with hundreds of plastic tables and chairs and rival caterers shouting out to passers-by to drum up business. Most places serve alcohol and you can sample pretty much every Malay Chinese dish imaginable, from grilled fish and satay to *kai-lan* (Chinese greens) in oyster sauce and fried noodles with frogs' legs.

🛍 Shopping

Central Market Shops
ARTS, CRAFTS

(Map p386; www.centralmarket.com.my; Jln Hang Kasturi; ☉ 10am-10pm; Ⓜ Pasar Seni) This 1930s art-deco building houses dozens of shops selling Malaysian arts and crafts including batik clothing and hangings, *songket* (fine cloth woven with silver and gold thread), *wau bulan* (moon kites), baskets, Royal Selangor pewter, as well as vintage items from daily life. Don't miss the fascinating private museum (Map p386; ☑ 03-2301 1468; 2nd fl, The Annexe, 10 Jln Hang Kasturi; ☉ 11am-7pm; Ⓜ Pasar Seni) FREE of ethnic art in the Annexe where most items are for sale.

Petaling Street Market
MARKET

(Map p386; Jln Petaling; ☉ noon-11pm; Ⓜ Pasar Seni) Malaysia's relaxed attitude towards counterfeit goods is well illustrated at this heavily hyped night market bracketed by fake Chinese gateways. Traders start to fill Jln Petaling from mid-morning until it is jam-packed with market stalls selling everything from fake Gucci handbags to bunches of lychees. Visit in the afternoon if you want to take pictures or see the market without the crowds.

ℹ Information

IMMIGRATION OFFICES

Immigration Office (☑ 03-6205 7400; 69 Jln Sri Hartamas 1, off Jln Duta; ☉ 7.30am-1pm & 2pm-5.30pm Mon-Fri) Handles visa extensions; offices are opposite Publika mall.

INTERNET ACCESS

Internet cafes are everywhere; the going rate per hour is RM3. Wi-fi is free at hundreds of restaurants, bars and more around the city.

MEDICAL SERVICES

Hospital Kuala Lumpur (Map p384; ☑ 03-2615 5555; www.hkl.gov.my; Jln Pahang; Ⓜ Titiwangsa, monorail Titiwangsa) City's main hospital, north of the centre.

Twin Towers Medical Centre KLCC (Map p390; ☑ 03-2382 3500; http://ttmcklcc.com.my; level 4, Suria KLCC, Jln Ampang; ☉ 8.30am-6pm Mon-Sat; Ⓜ KLCC) Handily located in the mall attached to the Petronas Towers.

MONEY

You'll seldom be far from a bank or ATM. Moneychangers offer better rates than banks for changing cash and (at times) travellers cheques; they are usually open later hours and on weekends and are found in shopping malls.

POST

Main Post Office (Map p386; www.pos.com.my; Jln Raja Laut; ⊙6am-11.30pm; Ⓜ Pasar Seni) Across the river from the Central Market. Packaging is available for reasonable rates at the post-office store.

TOURIST INFORMATION

Visit KL (Map p386; ☑03-2698 0332; www.visitkl.gov.my; KL City Gallery, 27 Jln Raja, Merdeka Sq; ⊙9am-6.30pm; Ⓜ Masjid Jamek) Official city tourism office. In addition to tons of useful brochures and maps, it runs free walking tours of Merdeka Sq and Kampung Baru.

Malaysian Tourism Centre (Map p390; ☑03-9235 4800; www.matic.gov.my/en; 109 Jln Ampang; ⊙8am-10pm; monorail Bukit Nanas) Information on KL and tourism across Malaysia. There's also a free traditional dance and music show staged at the theatre here (3pm to 3.45pm Monday to Saturday), plus a branch of the chocolate emporium Cocoa Boutique. The main office is housed in a handsome bungalow built in 1935 for rubber and tin tycoon Eu Tong Sen.

ⓘ Getting There & Away

Kuala Lumpur is Malaysia's principal international arrival gateway and it forms the crossroads for domestic bus, train and taxi travel.

AIR

Kuala Lumpur International Airport (KLIA; ☑03-8777 7000; www.klia.com.my; Ⓡ KLIA) Kuala Lumpur's main airport has two terminals and is about 55km south of the city.

SkyPark Subang Terminal (Sultan Abdul Aziz Shah Airport; ☑03-7842 2773; www.subangskypark.com; M17, Subang) Firefly, Berjaya Air and some Air Asia and Malindo Air flights go from SkyPark Subang Terminal, around 23km west of the city centre.

BUS

KL's main bus stations are **Pudu Sentral** (Map p386; Jln Pudu; Ⓜ Plaza Rakyat), just east of Chinatown, and **Terminal Bersepadu Selatan** (TBS; ☑03-9051 2000; www.tbsbts.com.my; Bandar Tasik Selatan; Ⓜ Bandar Tasik Selatan; Ⓡ Bandar Tasik Selatan), connected to the Bandar Tasik Selatan rail hub, about 15 minutes south of KL Sentral and serving destinations south of KL and the northeastern states of Kelantan and Terengganu. For Jerantut (for access to Taman Negara) go to Pekeliling bus station next to Titiwangsa LRT and monorail stations.

Buses from KL:

DESTINATION	FARE (RM)	DURATION (HR)
Alor Setar	43	5
Butterworth	35	4½
Cameron Highlands	35	4
Ipoh	28	2½
Johor Bahru	34.30	4
Kuantan	24.30	4
Melaka	10-12.50	2
Penang	30-40	5
Singapore	45-50	6

TAXI

Shared-taxi fares for chartering the whole taxi, seating four, from the depot on the 2nd floor of Pudu Sentral bus station include Melaka (RM200), Penang (RM550) and Johor Bahru (RM480). Toll charges are normally included.

TRAIN

KL Sentral is the hub of the **KTM** (Keretapi Tanah Melayu Berhad; ☑1300 88 5862; www.ktmb.com.my; ⊙info office 9am-9pm, ticket office 6.30am-9.30pm) railway system. There are daily departures for Butterworth, Johor Bahru and Thailand; fares are cheap, especially if you opt for a seat rather than a berth (for which there are extra charges), but journey times are slow.

KTM Komuter trains also run from KL Sentral, linking the city with the Klang Valley, Seremban and Ipoh.

ⓘ Getting Around

TO/FROM THE AIRPORT

Kuala Lumpur International Airport (KLIA)

The fastest way to the city is on the comfortable **KLIA Ekspres** (www.kliaekspres.com; adult/child one way RM35/15), with departures every 15 to 20 minutes from 5am to 1am. From KL Sentral you can transfer to your final destination by monorail, LRT, KTM Komuter train or by taxi.

The **Airport Coach** (www.airportcoach.com.my; one way/return RM10/18) takes an hour to KL Sentral; for RM18 it will take you to any central KL hotel from KLIA, for RM25 it will also pick you up for the return journey. The bus stand is clearly signposted inside the terminal.

Taxis from KLIA operate on a fixed-fare coupon system. Purchase a coupon from a counter at the arrival hall and use it to pay the driver. Standard taxis cost RM75.

SkyPark Subang Airport

Taxis from the city centre to Subang take between 30 minutes and one hour depending on traffic and cost RM40 to RM50.

Trans MVS Express (☑ 019-276 8315; http://klia2airporttransfer.com) runs buses on the hour from KL Sentral to Subang (RM10, one hour) between 9am and 9pm; and from Subang to KLIA 1 & 2 (RM10, one hour) roughly every two hours between 5am and 11pm.

BUS

Most buses in KL are provided by either **Rapid KL** (☑ 03-7885 2585; www.rapidkl.com.my) or **Metrobus** (☑ 03-5635 3070). The fare is RM2 to RM3; have the correct change ready when you board.

There's an information booth (7am to 9pm) near Pasir Seni station in Chinatown, where you can also board the free Go KL City Bus (www.gokl.com.my) services to the Golden Triangle and KLCC.

TAXI

KL's taxis are cheap, starting at RM3 for the first three minutes, with an additional 25 sen for each additional 36 seconds. From midnight to 6am there's a surcharge of 50% on the metered fare.

Although required to use the meter by law, some taxi drivers will refuse to do this and try to overcharge you. It should cost no more than RM10 to go right across the central city area, even in moderate traffic.

TRAIN

The user-friendly **Light Rail Transit** (LRT; ☑ 03-7885 2585; www.myrapid.com.my; ticket RM1.10; ⊘ every 6-10min, 6am-11.45pm, to 11.30pm Sun & holidays) system is composed of the Ampang/Sentul Timur, Sri Petaling/Sentul Timur and Kelana Jaya/Terminal Putra lines.

KL's handy **monorail** (www.myrapid.com.my; ticket RM1.20-4.10; ⊘ 6am-midnight) runs between KL Sentral in the south to Titiwangsa in the north, linking many of the city's sightseeing areas.

KTM Komuter (www.ktmb.com.my; ticket from RM1; ⊘ 6.45am-11.45pm) links Kuala Lumpur with outlying suburbs and the historic railway station.

KL Sentral is the central transit station for all train travel in KL.

PENINSULAR MALAYSIA – WEST COAST

Malaysia's multiculturalism is best viewed along the west coast. Nestled against the Strait of Melaka, the convenient shipping route has, over the centuries, created a cosmopolitan populace, well schooled in English. Besides Pulau Langkawi, the islands of this coast don't compare to those in the east or in Thailand, but they are always host to great seafood and an array of cultural adventures.

Melaka

☑ 06 / POP 860,000

Bright, loud, and practically preening with its wealth of homegrown galleries, crimson colonial-era buildings and showy trishaws, Melaka is the peacock of Malaysian cities.

Founded in the 14th century by Parameswara, a Sumatran prince/pirate (take your pick), the city has witnessed a flourishing of Malay civilisation as well as Portuguese, Dutch and finally British colonisation in 1795. Its historic centre was awarded Unesco World Heritage status in 2008. Old shophouses and mansions have been transformed into galleries and hotels, helping to preserve the city's kaleidoscope of architectural styles – spanning Peranakan (Straits Chinese), Portuguese, Dutch and British elements. Meanwhile, restaurants have found a booming audience of weekend visitors, all eager to sample the varied cuisines that have spawned from Melaka's cultural mosaic of residents.

Inevitably, a strong whiff of commercialism has accompanied this success. But Chinatown's charm still lingers. Town Sq, also known as Dutch Sq, is the centre of a well-preserved museum district. Further northeast is Melaka's tiny Little India. Backpacker guesthouses are found in Chinatown and around the nearby, less scenic Jln Taman Melaka Raya.

◉ Sights

◉ Town Square & Bukit St Paul

Stadthuys HISTORIC BUILDING

(☑ 06-282 6526; Dutch Sq; foreign/local visitor RM10/5; ⊘ 9am-5.30pm Sat-Thu, 9am-12.15pm & 2.45-5.30pm Fri) Melaka's most unmistakable landmark and favourite trishaw pick-up spot is the Stadthuys. This cerise town hall and governor's residence dates to 1650 and is believed to be the oldest Dutch building in the East. The building was erected after Melaka was captured by the Dutch in 1641, and is a reproduction of the former Stadhu-

Peninsular Malaysia

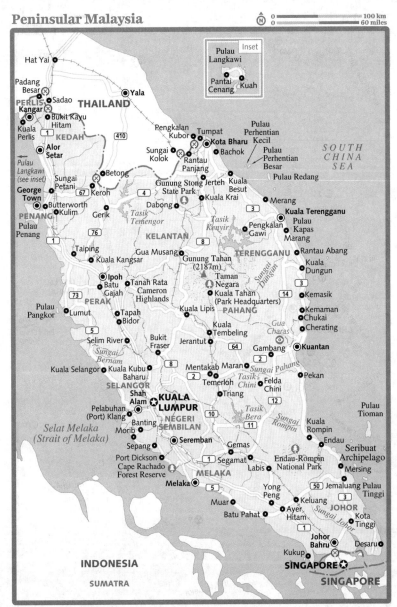

is (town hall) of the Frisian town of Hoorn in the Netherlands. Today it's a museum complex, with the **History & Ethnography Museum** as the highlight. Admission covers all the museums. There is no fee for guided tours.

St Paul's Church   RUIN
(Jln Kota; ☺24hr) **FREE** The evocative ruin of St Paul's Church crowns the summit of Bukit St Paul, the hill overlooking central Melaka. A steep flight of stairs, signposted from Jln Kota, leads to this faded sanctuary,

Melaka

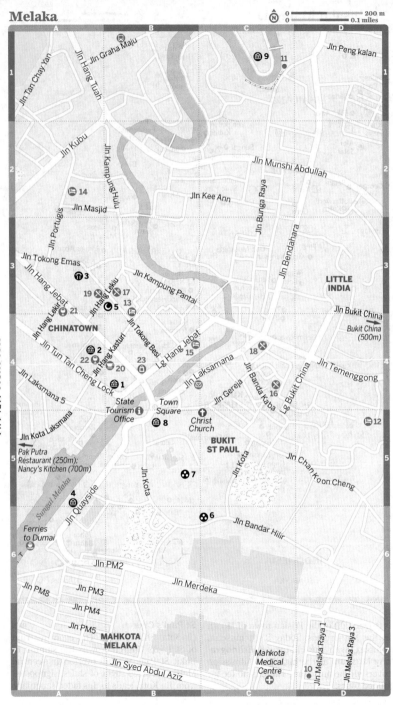

0 —————— 200 m
0 —————— 0.1 miles

Jln Peng kalan

Jln Tan Chay Yan

Jln Hang Tuah

Jln Graha Maju

9

11

Jln Kubu

Jln Munshi Abdullah

Jln Kampung Hulu

Jln Kee Ann

14

Jln Masjid

Jln Portugis

Jln Bunga Raya

Jln Bendahara

LITTLE
INDIA

Jln Tokong Emas

Jln Hang Jebat

3

Jln Kampung Pantai

19

Jln Hang Lekiu

17

Jln Hang Lekir

5

13

Jln Bukit China

Bukit China
(500m)

21

CHINATOWN

Jln Tokong Besi

Lg Hang Jebat

15

18

Jln Temenggong

2

Jln Tun Tan Cheng Lock

22

Jln Hang Kasturi

20

23

1

Jln Laksmana

16

Lg Bukit China

Jln Laksmana 5

Jln Gereja

Jln Banda Kaba

12

Jln Kota Laksmana

State
Tourism
Office

Town
Square

8

Christ
Church

Pak Putra
Restaurant (250m);
Nancy's Kitchen (700m)

BUKIT
ST PAUL

Jln Chan Koon Cheng

Sungai Melaka

Jln Kota

7

Jln Kota

4

Jln Quayside

6

Jln Bandar Hilir

Ferries
to Dumai

Jln PM2

Jln Merdeka

Jln PM8

Jln PM3

Jln PM4

Jln PM5

MAHKOTA
MELAKA

Mahkota
Medical
Centre

10

Jln Melaka Raya 1

Jln Melaka Raya 3

Jln Syed Abdul Aziz

MALAYSIA MELAKA

Melaka

originally built by a Portuguese captain in 1521. The church was regularly visited by St Francis Xavier, and following his death in China, the saint's body was temporarily interred here for nine months before being transferred to Goa.

Porta de Santiago
RUIN
(A'Famosa; Jln Bandar Hilir; ⊘24hr) **FREE** A quick photo stop at Porta de Santiago is a must. Built by the Portuguese as a fortress in 1511, the British took over in 1641, and set about destroying it at the turn of the 19th century to prevent it falling into the hands of Napoleon. Fortunately Sir Stamford Raffles happened by in 1810 and saved what remains today.

Maritime Museum & Naval Museum
MUSEUM
(☏06-283 0926; Jln Quayside; adult/child RM6/2; ⊘9am-5pm Mon-Thu, 9am-8.30pm Fri-Sun) Embark on a voyage through Melaka's maritime history at these linked museums. The most enjoyable of the three (one ticket covers them all) is housed in a huge recreation of the *Flor de la Mar,* a Portuguese ship that sank off the coast of Melaka. The fun of posing on the deck and clambering between floors rather eclipses the displays and dioramas, though the audioguide (RM3) adds engaging detail and a soundtrack of seagulls.

Chinatown

Chinatown is the heart of Melaka. Stroll along Jln Tun Tan Cheng Lock, formerly called Heeren St, which was the preferred address for wealthy Baba (Straits-born Chinese) traders who were most active during the early 20th century. The centre street of Chinatown is Jln Hang Jebat, formerly known as Jonker St (or Junk St), which was once famed for its antique shops but is now more of a collection of clothing and craft outlets and restaurants. On Friday, Saturday and Sunday nights the street is transformed into the Jonker Walk Night Market (p400). The northern section of quiet Jln Tokong (also known as Harmony St) has a handful of authentic Chinese shops.

Baba & Nyonya Heritage Museum
MUSEUM
(☏06-283 1273; http://babanyonyamuseum.com; 48-50 Jln Tun Tan Cheng Lock; adult/child RM16/11; ⊘10am-1pm & 2-5pm Wed-Mon) Touring this traditional Baba-Nonya (Peranakan) townhouse transports you to a time when women peered at guests through elaborate partitions, and every social situation had its specific location within the house. The captivating museum is arranged to look like a typical 19th-century Baba-Nonya residence. Tour guides enliven the setting with their arch sense of humour. Book ahead or arrive just before the strike of the hour. Last tour of the day is an hour before closing time.

8 Heeren Street
HISTORIC BUILDING
(8 Jln Tun Tan Cheng Lock; ⊘11am-4pm Tue-Sat) **FREE** This 18th-century Dutch-period residential house was restored as a model conservation project. The project was partially chronicled in the beautifully designed coffee-table book *Voices from the Street,* which is for sale at the house, along with other titles. You can also pick up an *Endangered*

Trades: A Walking Tour of Malacca's Living Heritage (RM5) booklet and map for an excellent self-guided tour of the city centre. Entry is free but donations are appreciated.

Cheng Hoon Teng Temple   CHINESE TEMPLE
(Qing Yun Ting or Green Clouds Temple; 25 Jln Tokong Emas; ◷7am-7pm) **FREE** Malaysia's oldest traditional Chinese temple, constructed in 1673, remains a central place of worship for the Buddhist community in Melaka. Notable for its carved woodwork, the temple is dedicated to Kuan Yin, the goddess of mercy.

Masjid Kampung Kling   MOSQUE
(Jln Hang Lekiu) **FREE** This Chinatown mosque dates to 1748. The 19th-century rebuild you see today mingles a number of styles. Its multi-tiered meru roof (a stacked form similar to that seen in Balinese Hindu architecture) owes its inspiration to Hindu temples, the Moorish watchtower minaret is typical of early mosques in Sumatra, while English and Dutch tiles bedeck its interior. Admission times to go inside vary; dress modestly and if you're female bring a scarf.

◉ Elsewhere

Villa Sentosa   HISTORIC BUILDING
(Peaceful Villa; ☏06-282 3988; Jln Kampung Morten; entry by donation; ◷hours vary, usually 9am-1pm & 2pm-5pm) Malay village Kampung Morten is nestled right within central Melaka. The highlight of exploring the area, with its merry bridge and homes shaded by palm trees, is a visit to this living museum within a 1920s *kampung* house. Visitors (or rather, guests) are welcomed by a member of the household who points out period objects including photographs, Ming dynasty ceramics and a century-old Quran. You're unlikely to leave without a photo-op on plush velvet furniture or a few strikes of the lucky gong.

Bukit China   CEMETERY
(Jln Puteri Hang Li Poh) More than 12,500 graves, including about 20 Muslim tombs, cover the 25 grassy hectares of serene 'Chinese Hill'. Since the times of British rule, there have been several attempts to acquire Bukit China for road widening, land reclamation or development purposes. Fortunately, Cheng Hoon Teng Temple, with strong community support, has thwarted these attempts.

✦ Activities

Melaka River Cruise   BOAT TOUR
(☏06-281 4322, 06-286 5468; www.melakarivercruise.com; adult/child RM15/7; ◷9am-11.30pm) Forty-minute riverboat cruises along Sungai Melaka (Melaka River) leave from two locations: one from the 'Spice Garden' on the corner of Jln Tun Mutahii and Jln Tun Sri Lanang in the north of town, and one at the quay near the Maritime Museum. Cruises go 9km upriver past Kampung Morten and old *godown* (river warehouses) with a recorded narration explaining the riverfront's history.

Eco Bike Tour   BICYCLE TOUR
(☏019-652 5029; www.melakaonbike.com; 117 Jln Tiang Dua; per person RM100) Explore the fascinating landscape around Melaka with Alias on his three-hour bike tour (minimum two people) through 20km of oil-palm and rubber-tree plantations and delightful *kampung* communities surrounding town. Flag your level of fitness when you book.

⊨ Sleeping

Ringo's Foyer   GUESTHOUSE $
(☏06-281 6393, 016-668 8898; www.ringosfoyer.com; 46A Jln Portugis; dm/s/d/tr incl breakfast from RM15/18/30/60; ✳☎) This convivial hostel offers bike rental, laundry (RM8), guitars and the occasional rooftop barbecue: in short, this place has everything a weary backpacker could want. Slightly removed from central Chinatown's clamour, digs are as plain as the price suggests but they are clean and adorned with hilariously blunt etiquette signs. Rates for double rooms increase by RM5 at weekends.

Apa Kaba Home & Stay   GUESTHOUSE $
(☏012-798 1232, 06-283 8196; www.apa-kaba.com; 28 Kg Banda Kaba; d RM45-90, tr RM60-129; ✳☎) This tranquil homestay has rooms as low-key and relaxing as its *kampung* (village) setting, despite being close to the roaring maelstrom of central Melaka. Rooms are simple (some have air-con) and there's a large garden to lounge in, complete with dangling mango trees and the occasional speeding chicken. The 1912 building is a mish-mash of Malay and Chinese styles.

Jalan Jalan Guesthouse   GUESTHOUSE $
(☏06-283 3937; 8 Jln Tokong Emas; dm/s/d RM16/30/40; @☎) This agreeable hostel is based within a restored old blacksmith's shop painted periwinkle blue. Fan-cooled

rooms with one shared bathroom are spread around a tranquil inner garden-courtyard. As with some other older places, noise from your neighbours might keep you awake at night. Bike rental and laundry are available.

Tidur Tidur GUESTHOUSE $
(☑014-928 3817; tidurtidurgh@yahoo.com; 92 Lg Hang Jebat; weekday/weekend per person RM15/20; ☜) The name promises sweet dreams (*tidur* means 'sleep') but really you're here for the local feel and the hip riverside location of this simple guesthouse behind a T-shirt shop. The two- and four-bed dorm rooms aren't too airy but they are exceptional value.

✖️ Eating

Peranakan cuisine is the most famous type of cooking here; it's also known as 'Nonya', an affectionate term for a Peranakan woman (often the family chef). There's also Portuguese Eurasian food, Indian, Chinese and more.

★**Nancy's Kitchen** PERANAKAN $
(☑06-283 6099; eat@nancyskit.com; 13 Jln KL 3/8, Taman Kota Laksamana; mains RM10; ☺11am-5pm Wed-Mon) The mouth-watering meals stirred up in this Peranakan (Nonya) restaurant are revered in Melaka, and Nancy's Kitchen lives up to the hype. Local diners crowd this small restaurant, especially at weekends, their bellies rumbling for a taste of signature dishes like candlenut chicken (succulent meat simmered in a nutty sauce, fragrant with lemongrass). The restaurant stays open until 9pm on public holidays.

★**Pak Putra Restaurant** PAKISTANI $
(☑012-601 5876; Jln Kota Laksamana 4; mains RM8-10; ☺6pm-1am, closed alternate Mondays; ✐) Scarlet tikka chickens rotate hypnotically on skewers, luring locals and travellers to this excellent Pakistani restaurant. With aromatic vegetarian dishes, seafood and piquant curries, there's no shortage of choice (try the masala fish). The unchallenged highlights are oven-puffed naan bread and chicken fresh from the clay tandoor. Portions are generous and service is speedy.

★**Selvam** INDIAN $
(☑06-281 9223; 3 Jln Temenggong; mains RM6-9; ☺7am-10pm; ☜✐) This classic banana-leaf restaurant is excellent value, with efficient

---

DON'T LEAVE MELAKA WITHOUT TRYING...

Cendol Shaved-ice treat with jellies, coconut milk and Melaka's famous cane syrup.

Laksa The regional version is distinguished by its coconut milk and lemongrass-infused broth.

Nonya pineapple tarts Buttery pastries with a chewy pineapple-jam filling.

Popiah An uber spring roll stuffed with shredded carrots, prawns, chilli, garlic, palm sugar and much, much more.

Satay celup Like fondue but better; dunk tofu, prawns and more into bubbling soup to cook it to your liking.

---

and amiable staff. Generous servings of aromatic chicken biryani are eclipsed by the vegetarian offerings, in particular the Friday afternoon veggie special.

Capitol Satay MALAYSIAN $
(☑06-283 5508; 41 Lg Bukit China; mains from RM8; ☺5pm-midnight; ✐) Famous for its *satay celup* (a Melaka adaptation of satay steamboat), this place is usually packed and is one of the cheapest outfits in town. Stainless-steel tables have bubbling vats of soup in the middle where you dunk skewers of okra stuffed with tofu, sausages, chicken, prawns and bok choy.

Low Yong Mow CHINESE $
(☑06-282 1235; Jln Tokong Emas; dim sum RM1-8; ☺5.30am-noon Wed-Mon) Famous across Melaka for its large and delectably well-stuffed *pao* (steamed pork buns), this place is Chinatown's biggest breakfast treat. With high ceilings, plenty of fans running and a view of Masjid Kampung Kling, the atmosphere oozes all the charms of Chinatown. It's usually packed with talkative, newspaper-reading locals by around 7am. Food offerings thin out by 11am, so arrive early.

Shui Xian Vegetarian CHINESE $
(43 Jln Hang Lekiu; mains RM5; ☺7.30am-2.30pm Mon-Sat; ✐) In a city where vegetable dishes so often arrive strewn with shrimp or pork, vegetarians can breathe a sigh of relief here. This no-frills canteen whips up meat-free versions of *nasi lemak*, laksa and even 'chicken' rice ball.

MALAYSIA MELAKA

GETTING TO INDONESIA: MELAKA TO DUMAI

Getting to the border High-speed ferries (one way/return RM110/170, 1¾ hours) make the trip from Melaka to Dumai in Sumatra, Indonesia, daily at 10am. The quay is walking distance or a short taxi ride from most hotels and guesthouses. Tickets are available at **Indomal Express** (☑06-281 6766, 019-665 7055) and other ticket offices near the wharf.

At the border Citizens of most countries can obtain a 30-day visa on arrival (VOA) in Indonesia (US$35; see p310).

Moving on Dumai is on Sumatra's east coast and is a 10-hour bus ride from Bukittinggi.

For information on making this crossing in the opposite direction, see p272.

🍷 Drinking & Nightlife

During the weekend night market on Jonker St, the happening bar strip on Jln Hang Lekir turns into a street party closed off to traffic.

Geographér Cafe BAR
(☑06-281 6813; www.geographer.com.my; 83 Jln Hang Jebat; ⊙10am-1am Wed-Sun; 🛜) Some come to socialise, others are drawn by the free wi-fi. Either way, a swinging soundtrack of Eurotrash, jazz and classic pop keeps the beers flowing at traveller magnet Geographér. This well-ventilated cafe-bar, strewn with greenery, feels like a haven despite bordering busy Jonker St. Monday nights have live jazz while Friday and Saturday bring a father-daughter vocal-keyboard duet (both 8.30pm).

Calanthe Art Cafe COFFEE
(13 States Coffee; ☑06-292 2960; 11 Jln Hang Kasturi; ⊙10am-11pm; 🛜) Full-bodied Johor or classic Perak white? Choose a Malaysian state's favourite coffee and this perky place, also known as '13 States', will have it blended with ice and jelly cubes for a refreshing caffeine kick. Breakfasts are served here too (10am to 11.45am).

Me & Mrs Jones PUB
(☑016-234 4292; 3 Jln Hang Kasturi; ⊙7pm-midnight Tue-Sun) This cosy pub is staunchly un-hip and all the more enjoyable for it. At weekends there is live blues and rock, often with retired co-owner Mr Tan leading a jam session. Relax and grab a beer or juice (long menus are not the Jones' style).

🛍 Shopping

★ **Jonker Walk Night Market** MARKET
(Jln Hang Jebat; ⊙6-11pm Fri-Sun) Melaka's weekly shopping extravaganza keeps the shops along Jln Hang Jebat open late while trinket sellers, food hawkers and the occasional fortune teller close the street to traffic. It has become far more commercial, attracting scores of tourists, but it is an undeniably colourful way to spend an evening shopping and grazing.

ℹ Information

Moneychangers are scattered about town, especially near the guesthouses off Jln TMR and Chinatown.

Mahkota Medical Centre (☑06-281 3333, emergency 06-285 2991; www.mahkota medical.com; Jln Merdeka) A private hospital offering a full range of services including accident and emergency.

Post Office (Jln Laksamana; ⊙8.30am-5pm Mon-Sat) The post office is just north of Dutch Sq.

State Tourism Office (☑06-281 4803; www.melaka.gov.my; Jln Kota; ⊙9am-2pm & 3-6pm) Tourism office diagonally across Dutch Sq from Christ Church.

ℹ Getting There & Away

Melaka is 144km southeast of KL.

Melaka's local bus station, express bus station and taxi station are all combined into the massive Melaka Sentral, roughly 5km north of Town Sq. Because Melaka is a popular weekend destination, make advance bus reservations for Singapore and Kuala Lumpur.

Buses run to Kuala Lumpur International Airport (RM24 to RM28, two hours, hourly) and most destinations on the peninsula.

Buses from Melaka:

DESTINATION	FARE (RM)	DURATION (HR)
Cameron Highlands	37.50	5
Johor Bahru	20-24	3½
Kota Bharu	51	10
Kuala Lumpur	10-17	2
Mersing	28	4½
Singapore	24-27	4½

❶ Getting Around

A taxi into town from Melaka Sentral should cost RM20 to RM25, or you can take bus 17 (RM1.40).

Melaka is a walking city. Bicycles can be hired at some guesthouses and hotels for around RM3 per hour.

Taking to Melaka's streets by trishaw is a must – by the hour they should cost RM40, or RM15 for any one-way trip within the town, but you'll have to bargain.

Taxis should cost around RM15 for a trip anywhere around town.

Cameron Highlands

📋05

In Malaysia's largest hill station area, the breeze is freshened by eucalyptus, fuzzy tea plantations roll into the distance, and strawberry farms snooze under huge awnings. Temperatures in these 1300m to 1829m heights rarely top 30°C.

Tourism is big business so expect quiet contemplation to be interrupted by the din of building sites, and hilltop views occasionally obscured by megaresorts. But the highlands' combination of genteel tea culture, hiking trails and mild temperatures remains irresistible. With eco-conscious hiking, unexplored forests and some interesting temples, there is serenity to be found amid the hubbub.

The Cameron Highlands stretches along the road from the town of Ringlet, through to the main highland towns of Tanah Rata, Brinchang and beyond to smaller villages in the northeast. There are a handful of ATMs in the tourist centre at Tanah Rata.

◉ Sights & Activities

There are over a dozen numbered hiking trails in the area and maps are available at most guesthouses and tour offices. Ask about trail conditions before you set out as not all routes are maintained, and people occasionally get lost. At the highest elevations on Gunung Brinchang (take the main road or the steep and challenging trail 1 uphill), you'll be in the unique mossy forest environment that's like a *Lord of The Rings* world of orchids and green fuzz. There are also strawberry, honey and butterfly farms to visit and produce markets to peruse.

Boh Sungei Palas Tea Estate   TEA PLANTATION
(📞05-496 2096; www.boh.com.my; ☺9am-4.30pm Tue-Sun) FREE The Cameron Highlands' most famous tea plantation has a modern visitors centre, where you can watch a video on the estate's history. There's also a giftshop selling every version of Boh tea you can imagine and a pleasant cafe where you can sip tea while looking out over the lush plantations below. Free 15-minute tours showing the tea-making process are conducted during opening hours; wait for a staff member to collect you from the visitor centre.

Sam Poh Temple   BUDDHIST TEMPLE
(Brinchang) FREE As unexpected sites in the hills go, a temple dedicated to a Chinese eunuch and naval officer just about tops the list. This temple, just below Brinchang about 1km off the main road, is a brilliant pastiche of imperial Chinese regalia, statuary dedicated to medieval admiral and eunuch Zheng Ho and, allegedly, the fourth-largest Buddha in Malaysia.

☞ Tours

★Eco Cameron   TOUR
(📞05-491 5388; www.ecocameron.com; 72-A Psn Camellia 4, Tanah Rata; tours RM50-120; ☺8am-9.30pm) This outfit specialises in nature tours of the Cameron Highlands: hiking, orchid walks, birdwatching and insect-spotting. Most enthralling are guided hikes through the Mossy Forest – Eco Cameron has exclusive access to a protected trail.

Jason Marcus Chin   TOUR
(📞010-380 8558; jason.marcus.chin@gmail.com; half-/full-day tour from RM50/90) Exceptional nature guide Jason Marcus Chin leads guided hikes on request, sharing superlative knowledge of flora and fauna along the way.

CS Travel & Tours   TOUR
(📞05-491 1200; www.cstravel.com.my; 47 Jln Besar, Tanah Rata; ☺7.30am-7.30pm) This agency leads popular half-day countryside tours (adult/child RM25/20) of the Highlands, departing at 8.45am and 1.45pm. Longer tours, such as the full-day adventure tour (adult/child RM80/70), take in Gunung Brinchang and an Orang Asli village.

🛏 Sleeping

The Highlands are at their busiest during the school holidays in April, August and December. During these times, book well in advance. Prices go up by around 25% at weekends and during holidays.

★Father's Guest House   GUESTHOUSE $
(📞016-566 1111; www.fathersguesthouse. net; 4 Jln Mentigi, Tanah Rata; dm/d/tr/q from

MALAYSIA CAMERON HIGHLANDS

Cameron Highlands

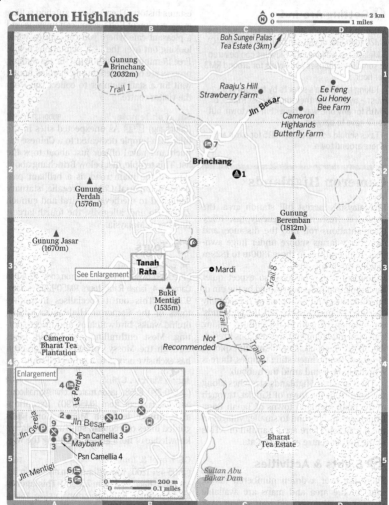

RM210/74/95/127; P@🛜) Pleasant double rooms and clean 10-person dorms elicit sighs of relief from travellers checking in at Father's. Friendly staff ooze local knowledge, while hairdryers, good wi-fi, free tea and coffee, and a cafe are fine perks.

Snooze GUESTHOUSE $
(📞014-669 0108, 016-666 2102; chsnooze@gmail.com; 4 Jln Besar, Brinchang; d/tr/q from RM88/120/145; 🛜🚿) The bright and cheery rooms at Snooze are excellent value. The cupcake wallpaper and buttercup bedsheets might be a little kitsch for some, but this

clean guesthouse with friendly service is one of Brinchang's better places to stay. There are colourful sitting areas to chill or play, a fridge and laundry facilities, plus there are family rooms. Find more digs down the road at Snooze Too.

Eight Mentigi GUESTHOUSE $
(📞05-491 5988; www.eightmentigi.com; 8A Jln Mentigi, Tanah Rata; s/d/q from RM50/70/150; P@🛜) The digs, from six-bed dorms to spacious family rooms, are simple. But your host Smith gives a welcoming ambience to this fuss-free hostel. The main drawback is

the unsightly location, near a building site, though it's only a stone's throw from Tanah Rata's main drag. The better doubles cost around RM90.

Daniel's Lodge　　　　　　　　　HOSTEL $
(☏ 05-491 5823; www.daniels.cameronhighlands. com; 9 Lg Perdah, Tanah Rata; dm RM15, r with bathroom RM40-100, without bathroom RM20-60; @☎) The backpacker force remains strong at this longstanding hostel, also known as Kang's. The accommodation won't win prizes for comfort but despite the grungy feel it's a functional place with perks like wi-fi, laundry service and a jungle-themed bar.

🍴 Eating

Restaurant Bunga Suria　　　　　　INDIAN $
(66A Persiaran Camellia 3, Tanah Rata; set meals RM6-10; ⊗ 7am-10pm; 🖉) The most crowd-pleasing (yet least manic) of Tanah Rata's Indian canteens has great value banana leaf meal specials and a good selection of curries. But where it really excels is at breakfast, when fresh *idli* (savoury, soft, fermented-rice-and-lentil cakes) pop out of the steamer, ready to surrender to a dunking in coconut chutney.

Restoran Sri Brinchang　　　　　　INDIAN $
(25 Jln Besar, Tanah Rata; mains RM4-20; ⊗ 7am-10pm; 🖉) This busy place heaps spiced aubergine, pappadams and rice onto banana leaves for its filling lunches; it prides itself on spring chicken served straight from the tandoor.

Lord's Cafe　　　　　　　　　　　　CAFE $
(Jln Besar, Tanah Rata; mains RM2.50-4.90; ⊗ 10am-9pm Wed-Fri & Mon, 10am-6pm Sat) Despite the neon threat from Tanah Rata's

controversial new Starbucks, Lord's Cafe, reassuringly decorated like your grandma's living room, lives on. Specialities include thick mango and banana lassis and apple pie, the standout star on a menu of cakes and ice cream sundaes. Find the cafe by following the Christian signage to the floor above Marrybrown fast food.

❶ Getting There & Around

Book tickets at the Tanah Rata bus station (also known as Terminal Freesia).

Local buses run from Tanah Rata to Brinchang (RM2, every two hours from 6.30am to 6.30pm).

Taxi services from Tanah Rata include Ringlet (RM25) and Brinchang (RM9).

Buses from Tanah Rata:

DESTINATION	FARE (RM)	DURATION (HR)
Ipoh	18	2
Kuala Lumpur	35	4
Melaka	65	6
Penang	32	5
Singapore	135-140	10

Ipoh

🖉 05 / POP 757,892

Ipoh (ee-po) is undergoing a renaissance. Its faded tropical mansions and shophouses are being restored, with new cafes and craft shops springing up within historic buildings. The mellow Old Town showcases elegant colonial-era architecture, including the magnificent train station (known locally as the 'Taj Mahal').

A self-led **walking tour** of the Old Town is the best way to cover all of the colonial-era architecture; pick up the Ipoh Heritage Trail maps 1 and 2 at **Tourism Malaysia Perak** (☏ 05-255 9962, 05-255 2772; www.tourism.gov.my; 12 Medan Istana 2 Bandar; ⊗ 8am-5pm Mon-Fri).

🛏 Sleeping

The majority of lodgings are east of the Sungai Kinta, over in the new town.

Eloft　　　　　　　　　　　　　　HOSTEL $
(☏ 017-336 5592; 115 Jln Sultan Iskandar; dm incl breakfast RM30; ❄☎) Ipoh's friendliest backpacker accommodation opened its doors in July 2015. Partly run by volunteers, Eloft has one air-conditioned 14-bed mixed dorm, a pleasant common area and a

balcony overlooking busy Jln Sultan Iskandar. Bike rental is available (six/24 hours RM8/20). Ring the bell for access (the doorway is easy to miss).

Abby By The River HOSTEL $
([phone] 05-241 4500; www.abbyhotel.my; cnr Jln Laxamana & Jln Sultan Iskandar; dm/d/tr from RM35/100/125; [P][air][wifi]) Nestled right by Sultan Iskandar bridge, the Ipoh branch of this Perak chain is well positioned for exploration of the old or new towns. Choose from three-bed single sex dorms, doubles or family rooms that sleep three. Rooms are comfy enough but the bland interior rather unfortunately evokes a hospital.

✕ Eating

Ipoh's culinary specialities include *ayam tauge* (chicken with beansprouts and rice cooked in broth) – look for it at restaurants on Jln Dato Onn Jaafar around the Tengkar Pasar intersection – and Ipoh white coffee, made with palm-oil margarine and served with condensed milk, and found all around town.

★ Lim Ko Pi CHINESE $
([phone] 05-253 2898; 10 Jln Sultan Iskandar; mains RM12; [clock] 8.30am-6pm) From its colourful tiles to the pretty inner courtyard, this relaxing cafe has a strong whiff of Ipoh's old glory days. Meals include generous portions of prawn fried rice, curry noodles and smoky-but-sweet stewed pork, best accompanied by a perfectly prepared white coffee. Service is wonderfully unrushed compared to many of Ipoh's eateries.

★ Restaurant Lou Wong MALAYSIAN $
([phone] 05-254 4190; 49 Jln Yau Tet Shin; mains RM12; [clock] noon-10pm) This is the place to try Ipoh's esteemed signature dish, *ayam tauge* (chicken with beansprouts). You'll have to fight for space on the plastic stools that spill out from Lou Wong onto the road, but it's worth it for a taste of smooth poached chicken served with generous mounds of rice and plump beansprouts.

Sri Ananda Bahwan Banana Leaf INDIAN $
([phone] 05-253 9798; 7 Persiaran Bandar Timah; mains RM5; [clock] breakfast, lunch & dinner; [veg]) Some of Ipoh's best Indian food is cooked up in this simple cafeteria in Little India. Mop up chutney and dhal with a fluffy dosa or order the generous banana leaf special, with mountains of rice and spiced okra. Leave space to take away a box of the excellent

barfi, fudge-like confectionery in flavours from cashew to chocolate.

ℹ Getting There & Away

The long-distance bus station, **Terminal Amanjaya** ([phone] 05-526 7818, 05-526 7718; www.peraktransit.com.my; Persiaran Meru Raya 5), is approximately 8km north of Ipoh. Bus 116 (RM2) connects Amanjaya and the more central Medan Kidd station, which handles services around Perak, while taxis cost roughly RM20 to RM25.

Ipoh's **train station** (Jln Panglima Bukit Gantang Wahab) has frequent services to both KL (RM12, 4½ hours) and Butterworth (RM17, five hours), the latter continuing to Hat Yai in Thailand (RM30, 10 hours).

Buses from Ipoh:

DESTINATION	FARE (RM)	DURATION (HR)
Cameron Highlands	18.50-20	2
Butterworth/George Town (Penang)	20	2
Kuala Lumpur	from 20	2½-3
Alor Setar	29	4
Melaka	36-40	5
Kota Bharu	40	6
Hat Yai (Thailand)	55	6-7
Johor Bahru	60	7
Singapore	56-75	8

Penang

Located at the intersection of Asia's great kingdoms and Europe's powerful colonial empires, the island of Penang has long served as the link between Asia's two halves. This history has resulted in a culture that is one of Malaysia's most diverse, cosmopolitan and exciting.

The culmination of this is undoubtedly George Town, Penang's main city, and an urban centre that delivers the old-world Asia in spades: think trishaws pedalling past watermarked Chinese shophouses, blue joss smoke perfuming the air. In 2008 the historic centre of George Town was designated a Unesco World Heritage Site. Penang also offers abundant tropicalness, palm-fringed beaches and fishing villages and mountainous jungle. If there's a more compact, convenient and exciting microcosm of the exotic East than Penang, we've yet to find it.

Penang Island

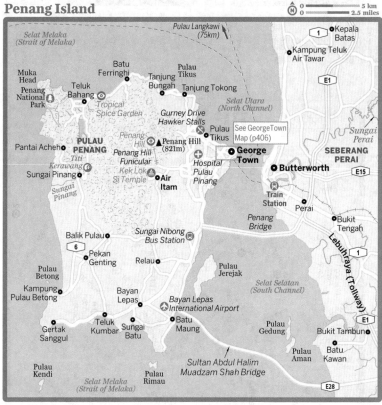

George Town

📷 04 / POP 510,996

George Town is able to woo even the most acute cityphobe with its explosive cultural mishmash. Dodge traffic while strolling past Chinese shophouses where people might be roasting coffee over a fire or sculpting giant incense sticks for a ceremony. The maze of chaotic streets and narrow lanes are lined with British Raj–era architecture, temples, mosques, strings of paper lanterns and trendy cafes and bars. Outside the historic centre, soaring skyscrapers and massive shopping complexes gleam high above.

This is also Malaysia's, if not Southeast Asia's, food capital. Home to five distinct cuisines, cheap and delicious open-air hawker centres, lauded seafood and legendary fruit, it's the kind of place that can boast both quality *and* quantity.

⊙ Sights

Khoo Kongsi   HISTORIC BUILDING

(Map p406; www.khookongsi.com.my; 18 Cannon Sq; adult/child RM10/1; ⊙9am-5pm) The Khoo are a successful clan, and their eponymous clanhouse is the most impressive one in George Town.

Guided tours begin at the stone carvings that dance across the entrance hall and pavilions, many of which symbolise or are meant to attract good luck and wealth. The interior is dominated by incredible murals depicting birthdays, weddings and, most impressively, the 36 celestial guardians. Gorgeous ceramic sculptures of immortals, carp, dragons, and carp becoming dragons dance across the roof ridges.

Blue Mansion   HISTORIC BUILDING

(Map p406; www.thebluemansion.com.my; 14 Lebuh Leith; adult/child RM16/8; ⊙tours 11am, 2pm & 3.30pm) The magnificent 38-room,

George Town

MALAYSIA PENANG

N

0 ————— 200 m
0 ————— 0.1 miles

Selat Utara
(North Channel)

Selat Selatan
(South Channel)

Ferry to Butterworth

Tourism Malaysia

Langkawi Ferry Service

Jetty Swettenham

Immigration Office

Standard Chartered Bank

Penang Global Tourism

Heritage Trust

HSBC Bank

Pesara King Edward

Weld Quay Bus Terminal

Gat Lebuh Gereja

Gat Lebuh China

Padang

Lebuh Light

COLONIAL DISTRICT

Jln Tun Syed Sheh Barakbah

Lebuh Duke

Green Hall

Unesco World Heritage Zone

Lebuh Bishop

Lebuh Gereja

Lebuh China

Lebuh Pantai

Lebuh Victoria

Lebuh Farquhar

Gat Lebuh Leith

Lebuh Farquhar

Lebuh Penang

Lebuh Pasar

Lebuh King

Lebuh Queen

Jln Masjid Kapitan Keling

LITTLE INDIA

Lebuh An Quee

Lebuh Armenian

Cannon Square

Lebuh Acheh

Pengkalan Weld

Lebuh Victoria

Lebuh Leith

Jln Penang

Lebuh Muntri

CHINATOWN

Lebuh Chulia

Lebuh Stewart

LoveBike

Lg Stewart

Lg Chulia

Lg Pasar

Love La

Lg Seckchuan

Lebuh Carnarvon

Lebuh Buckingham

Lebuh Carnarvon

Lg Carnarvon

Unesco World Heritage Zone

Lebuh Melayu

Lebuh Pantai

Jln Sri Bahari

Jln Transfer

Jln Argyll

Jln A.S. Mansor

Jln Hutton

Jln Kedah

Jln Datok Koya

Lg Hutton

Lebuh Dickens

Jln Kampung Malabar

Lebuh Campbell

Lebuh Cintra

Kuala Kangsar

Jln Pintal Tali

Lebuh Pesara Clalmant

Rope Walk

Lebuh Kimberley

Jln Sg Ujong

Jln Dr Lim Chwee Leong

Lebuh Chulia

Jln Penang

Lebuh Phee Choon

Komtar Bus Station

Lebuh Tek Soon

Lebuh Gladstone

Jln Magazine

Pulau Tikus Hawker Stalls (1.9km);
Gurney Drive Hawker Stalls (2.2km)

Jln Burma

Lg Kinta

Lg Macalister

Lg Madras

Jln Macalister

Jln Datok Keramat

Jln Gurdwara

Lebuh Noordin

Lebun Gurdwara

George Town

220-window 'Blue Mansion' was built in the 1880s and rescued from ruin in the 1990s. It blends Eastern and Western designs with louvred windows, art nouveau stained glass and beautiful floor tiles, and is a rare surviving example of the eclectic architectural style preferred by wealthy Straits Chinese. Its distinctive (and once-common in George Town) blue hue is the result of an indigo-based lime wash.

Hour-long guided tours (included in the admission fee) provide a glimpse of the interior as well as an insight into traditional Chinese architecture.

Pinang Peranakan Mansion   MUSEUM
(Map p406; www.pinangperanakanmansion.com. my; 29 Lebuh Gereja; adult/child RM21.20/10.60; ⊙9.30am-5.30pm) This ostentatious, mint green structure is among the most stunning restored residences in George Town. A self-guided tour reveals that every door, wall and archway is carved and often painted in gold leaf; the grand rooms are furnished with majestic wood furniture with intricate mother-of-pearl inlay; there are displays of charming antiques; and bright-coloured paintings and fascinating black-and-white photos of the family in regal Chinese dress grace the walls.

Chew Jetty   HISTORIC NEIGHBOURHOOD
(Map p406; Pengkalan Weld) During the late 18th and early 19th centuries, George Town's Pengkalan Weld was the centre of one of the world's most thriving ports and provided plentiful work for the never-ending influx of immigrants. Soon a community of Chinese grew up around the quay, with floating and stilt houses built along rickety docks; these docking and home areas became known as the clan jetties. The largest and most intact of these remaining today is Chew Jetty.

Penang Museum   MUSEUM
(Map p406; www.penangmuseum.gov.my; Lebuh Farquhar; admission RM1; ⊙9am-5pm Sat-Thu) Penang's state-run museum includes exhibits on the history, customs and traditions of the island's various ethnic groups, with photos, videos, documents, costumes, furniture and other well-labelled, engaging displays. Upstairs is the history gallery, with a collection of early 19th-century watercolours by Captain Robert Smith, an engineer with the East India Company, and prints showing landscapes of old Penang.

Kuan Yin Teng   BUDDHIST TEMPLE
(Temple of the Goddess of Mercy; Map p406; Jln Masjid Kapital Keling; ⊙24hr) **FREE** This temple is dedicated to Kuan Yin – the goddess of mercy, good fortune, peace and fertility. Built in the early 19th century by the first Hokkien and Cantonese settlers in Penang, the temple isn't so impressive architecturally, but it's very central and popular with the Chinese community, and seems to be forever swathed in smoke from the outside furnaces where worshippers burn paper money, and from the incense sticks waved around inside.

☞ Tours

There's a huge variety of self-guided tours of George Town, from food walks to those focussing on traditional trades or architecture – pick up a pamphlet of the routes at the state tourist office or at the **Penang**

Heritage Trust (PHT; Map p406; ☑04-264 2631; www.pht.org.my; Lebuh Gereja; ⊙9am-5pm Mon-Fri, 9am-1pm Sat). Likewise, the Penang Global Ethic Project (www.globalethicpenang.net) has put together a World Religion Walk that takes you past the iconography and houses of worship of Christians, Muslims, Hindus, Sikhs, Buddhists and Chinese traditional religion.

🛏 Sleeping

Ryokan   HOSTEL $
(Map p406; ☑04-250 0287; www.myryokan.com; 62 Jln Muntri; incl breakfast dm RM34-50, r RM158; ✳@🛜) This flashpacker hostel boasts a minimalist – if not particularly Japanese – feel. The dorms, which range from four to six beds (and two women-only rooms), are almost entirely white, and the communal 'Chillax', TV and reading rooms are similarly chic, and come equipped with iPads. Private rooms with en suite bathrooms have the same vibe, yet lacking windows and space, feel slightly overpriced.

80s Guesthouse   HOSTEL $
(Map p406; ☑04-263 8806; www.the80sguesthouse.com; 46 Love Lane; incl breakfast dm RM36-39, r RM63-99; ✳@🛜) The 1980s theme here rather confusingly includes film posters from the early 1950s, but that has no impact on the minimalist but comfortable dorms (which range from four to six beds) and rooms, all of which share central bathrooms.

Siok Hostel   HOSTEL $
(Map p406; ☑04-263 2663; 48 Lebuh Chulia; incl breakfast dm RM42-47, r RM120) Taking full advantage of its huge, colonial-era structure is this spacious, airy-feeling hostel. Being renovated when we stopped by, dorms are set

---

SPLURGE

....

A lengthy and careful restoration has transformed **Ren i Tang** (Map p406; ☑04-250 8383; www.renitang.com; 82A Lebuh Penang; r incl breakfast RM218-455; ✳🛜) from a Chinese medicine wholesaler's into a warm, inviting small hotel. The rooms, which carry charming reminders of the building's former life, span several types, sizes and layouts; we particularly like corner Tub Room, equipped with a wooden soaking tub and fragrant bath salts.

---

to range from six to eight beds, and there's a rooftop communal area.

Time Capsule Hotel   HOSTEL $
(Map p406; ☑04-263 0888; www.timecapsule.my; 418 Lebuh Chulia; dm incl breakfast RM55; ✳@🛜) If you aspire to feel like a Japanese salaryman in the '80s – or just want to save some ringgit – consider a stay at this new and unique hostel. Upon checking in, you'll receive a bag of toiletries, slippers and, if needed, pyjamas, before being led to your bed: a futuristic pod equipped with TV, wi-fi, lights and a safe.

Reggae Penang   HOSTEL $
(Map p406; ☑04-262 6772; www.reggaehostels malaysia.com; 57 Love Lane; dm incl breakfast RM30-40; ✳@🛜) Perfect for the social traveller, this expansive heritage building holds several four- to 12-bed dorm rooms. Beds are double-decker pod style, and have individual lights, power point and free wi-fi. The lobby, outfitted with pool table and coffee shop, feels more like a bar than a hostel. There's another branch nearby on Lebuh Chulia.

🍴 Eating

Penang cuisine is legendary: Indian, Chinese and Malay purveyors jostle with one another for affection from a constantly snacking populace. Along with Melaka, Penang boasts the indigenous fusion of Peranakan (Nonya) cuisine.

Veloo Villas   INDIAN $
(Map p406; 22 Lebuh Penang; mains from RM2, set meals RM5-9.50; ⊙7am-10pm; 🖋) For one meal, set aside notions of service – and ambience – and instead focus on the vibrant, fun southern Indian cuisine. Come from approximately 11am to 4pm for hearty and diverse rice-based set meals, or outside of these hours for *dosa* (paper-thin rice-and-lentil crêpes) and other snacks.

Sup Hameed   MALAYSIAN $
(Map p406; 48 Jln Penang; mains from RM3; ⊙24hr) On the surface, this is very much your typical *nasi kandar* (South Asian Muslim-influenced) shop found all over Malaysia, and we don't particularly recommend eating here during the day. But come night, Hameed sets out tables on the street and serves his incredibly rich and meaty soups (try *sup kambing* – goat soup), served with slices of white bread.

HAWKER-STALL HEAVEN

Not eating at a stall in Penang is like missing the Louvre in Paris – you simply can't do it. Prices are cheap and most serve beer as well.

Lg Baru (New Lane) Hawker Stalls (Map p406; cnr Jln Macalister & Lg Baru; mains from RM3; ⊘dinner) Ask locals what their favourite hawker stalls are, and they'll always mention this night-time street extravaganza. Just about everything's available here, but we like the *char koay kak* stall, which in addition to spicy fried rice cakes with seafood, also does great *otak otak* (a steamed fish curry). Lg Baru intersects with Jln Macalister about 250m northwest of the intersection with Jln Penang.

Pulau Tikus Hawker Stalls (cnr Solok Moulmein & Jln Burma; ⊘6am-2pm) Before yet another bland guesthouse breakfast gets you down, consider a visit to this busy morning market area. A cluster of cafes sell Hokkien *mee*, curry *mee*, *mee goreng* and other dishes that have earned die-hard fans.

The market is located across from Pulau Tikus's police station, about 2.5km north of Jln Penang; a taxi here will set you back about RM20.

Gurney Drive Hawker Stalls (Map p405; Persiaran Gurney; mains from RM3; ⊘5pm-midnight) Penang's most famous food area sits amid modern high-rise buildings bordered by the sea. It's particularly known for its laksa stalls (try stall 11) and the delicious *rojak* (a 'salad' of crispy fruits and vegetables in a thick, slightly sweet dressing) at Ah Chye. Persiaran Gurney is located about 3km west of George Town, near Gurney Plaza. A taxi here will set you back at least RM20.

Joo Hooi Cafe (Map p406; cnr Jln Penang & Lebuh Keng Kwee; mains from RM3; ⊘11am-5pm) The hawker centre equivalent of one-stop shopping, this tiny shophouse has all of Penang's best dishes in one location: laksa, *rojak*, *char kway teow* and the city's most famous vendor of *cendol* (a sweet snack of squiggly noodles in shaved ice with palm sugar and coconut milk).

Kafe Kheng Pin (Map p406; 80 Jln Penang; mains from RM4; ⊘7am-3pm Tue-Sun) The must-eats at this old-school-feeling hawker joint include a legendary *lor bak* and an exquisite Hainanese chicken rice (steamed chicken with broth and rice).

Sky Cafe CHINESE $
(Map p406; Lebuh Chulia; mains RM1-6; ⊘11am-2pm) This gem sits in the middle of the greatest concentration of travellers in George Town, yet is somehow almost exclusively patronised (in enthusiastic numbers) by locals. Come on the early side of the three-hour open window for *char siew* (barbecued pork) and *siew yoke* (pork belly) that are considered among the best in town.

Hameediyah MALAYSIAN $
(Map p406; 164 Lebuh Campbell; mains RM5-35; ⊘10am-11pm Sat-Thu, 10am-12.30pm & 2-11pm Fri) Dating back to 1907 and allegedly the oldest *nasi kandar* in Malaysia, Hameediyah looked it until a recent and much-needed face-lift. In addition to rich curries served over rice, try the *murtabak*, a *roti prata* (flaky, flat bread) stuffed with minced mutton, chicken or vegetables, egg and spices.

Yin's Sourdough Bakery BAKERY $
(Map p406; 11 Pesara Claimant; mains RM4.50-25; ⊘7am-6pm Mon-Fri, to 2pm Sat; 🖉) Tired of rice? Weary of noodles? Head here for some of the city's best bread, served in the form of creative sandwiches, pastries and breakfasts.

Tho Yuen Restaurant CHINESE $
(Map p406; 92 Lebuh Campbell; dim sum RM1-5; ⊘6am-3pm Wed-Mon) Our favourite place for dim sum. It's packed with newspaper-reading loners and chattering groups of locals all morning long, but you can usually squeeze in somewhere. Servers speak minimal English but do their best to explain the contents of their carts.

🍷 Drinking & Nightlife

★**Canteen** BAR
(Map p406; www.chinahouse.com.my; China House, 183B Lebuh Victoria; dishes RM10.60-61.50; ⊘9am-11pm) This is about as close as George

Town comes to a hipster bar – minus the pretension. Canteen has an artsy/warehouse vibe, there's live music from 9.30pm, and there are great bar snacks. Canteen is also accessible via China House's entrance on Lebuh Pantai.

★ **Alabama Shake** BAR

(Map p406; www.facebook.com/cjalabamashake; 92 Lebuh Gereja; ⊙4pm-late) Just your average American boozer – if your average American bar was located in Malaysia and was run by a gregarious Serbian and a local. Come to think of it, there's little ordinary about this bar, previously known as B@92, but it gets it right, from tasty American-themed cocktails to slow-cooked pulled-pork sandwiches.

Mish Mash BAR

(Map p406; www.mishmashpg.com; 24 Jln Muntri; ⊙2pm-midnight Tue-Sun) Mish Mash has brought some unique booze – not to mention some much needed panache – to George Town's drinking scene. Come for the city's most well-stocked bar, clever cocktails and some great non-alcoholic drinks (try the 'traditional ginger soda'), as well as a full tobacco counter. There's also food, although we hesitate to endorse Mish Mash as a dinner locale.

Micke's Place BAR

(Map p406; 94 Love Lane; ⊙noon-late) This eclectic bar/restaurant is both the longest-standing and most fun of the area's backpacker bars. Pull up a grafittied chair, bump

to the vintage soundtrack, suck on a shisha and make a new friend.

Behind 50 Love Lane BAR

(Map p406; Lebuh Muntri; ⊙6pm-1am Wed-Mon) Pocket-sized, retro-themed bar/restaurant that draws a largely local following, despite being close to the backpacker strip. There's a classic rock soundtrack and a short menu of Western-style comfort dishes (RM14.90 to RM18.90).

ⓘ Information

Branches of major banks are on Lebuh Pantai and Lebuh Downing, near the main post office. Most have 24-hour ATMs. At the northwestern end of Lebuh Chulia there are a few moneychangers.

Almost every guesthouse has internet access, and it's easy to pick up on a wi-fi signal around town.

Hospital Pulau Pinang (Map p405; ☑04-222 5333; http://hpp.moh.gov.my/v2; Jln Hospital) The island's largest public hospital, with general health care and emergency services.

Immigration Office (Map p406; ☑04-250 3410; 29A Lebuh Pantai; ⊙7.30am-1pm & 2-5.30pm Mon-Thu, 7.30am-12.15pm & 2.45-5.30pm Fri)

Penang Global Tourism (Map p406; ☑04-264 3456; www.mypenang.gov.my; Whiteways Arcade, Lebuh Pantai; ⊙9am-5pm Mon-Fri, to 3pm Sat, to 1pm Sun) This, the visitor centre of the state tourism agency, is the best all-around place to go for maps, brochures and local information.

ⓘ Getting There & Away

AIR

Penang's **Bayan Lepas International Airport** (Map p405; ☑04-643 4411; www.penangair port.com) is served by more than a dozen airlines with international destinations that include several cities in China, Indonesia and Thailand, as well as Hong Kong, Singapore and Taiwan, and numerous domestic destinations.

BOAT

Several providers, including **Langkawi Ferry Service** (LFS; Map p406; ☑04-264 2088; www.langkawi-ferry.com; PPC Bldg, Lebuh King Edward; ⊙7am-5.30pm Mon-Sat, 7am-3pm Sun), operate a shared ferry service to Langkawi (adult/child one way RM68.10/49.20, return RM136.20/98.40, 1¾ to 2½ hours). Boats leave at 8.15am, 8.30am and 2pm.

Boats return from Langkawi at 10.30am, 2.30pm and 5.15pm.

Book a few days in advance to ensure a seat.

STREET ART

You won't fail to notice that George Town has gone all out for street art. The trend goes back to 2010, when Penang's state government commissioned the studio Sculpture At Work (www.sculptureatwork.com) to do a series of cartoon steel art pieces across town. Affixed to George Town street walls, these 3D artworks detail local customs and heritage with humour, while also providing a quirky counterpoint to the natural urban beauty of the historic core.

The star of George Town's street art scene is undoubtedly Lithuanian artist Ernest Zacharevic (www.facebook.com/Ernestzachas). For the 2012 George Town Festival, Zacharevic was commissioned to do a series of public paintings in central George Town, some of which he chose to combine with objects such as bicycles, motorcycles and architectural features. The art has been a smash hit, with the piece on Lebuh Armenian having become a legitimate tourist destination, complete with long lines and souvenir stalls.

Based in a former bus terminal, **Hin Bus Depot Art Centre** (Map p406; www.facebook.com/hinbusdepot; 31A Jln Gurdwara; ⊙noon-7pm) `FREE` has become a hub for the city's art scene. The open-air areas are bedecked with street art, and the covered area spans exhibitions that change every couple months, and a cafe.

BUS

All long-distance buses to George Town arrive at the **Sungai Nibong Bus Station** (Map p405; ☑04-659 2099; www.rapidpg.com.my; Jln Sultan Azlan Shah, Kampung Dua Bukit), just to the south of Penang Bridge, while buses bound for Butterworth arrive at the Butterworth Bus Station. A taxi from Sungei Nibong to George Town costs around RM25; a taxi from Butterworth can cost as much as RM50.

Buses to destinations in Malaysia can be boarded at Sungai Nibong and, more conveniently, at the **Komtar Bus Station** (Map p406; www.rapidpg.com.my; Jln Penang); international destinations only at the latter. Note that transport to Thailand (except to Hat Yai) is via minivan. Transport can also be arranged to Ko Samui and Ko Phi Phi via a transfer in Surat Thani and Hat Yai respectively.

Buses from Penang:

DESTINATION	FARE (RM)	DURATION (HR)
Tanah Rata (for Cameron Highlands)	40	5
Ipoh	25	2½
Johor Bahru	60	9
Kuala Lumpur	38	5
Melaka	50	7

ℹ Getting Around

TO/FROM THE AIRPORT

Penang's Bayan Lepas International Airport is 18km south of George Town. The fixed taxi fare to most places in central George Town is RM44.70; taxis take about 30 minutes to the centre of town. Bus 401 runs to and from the airport (RM4) every half-hour between 6am and 11pm daily, and stops at Komtar and Weld Quay, taking at least an hour.

BUS

Buses around Penang are run by the government-owned **Rapid Penang** (☑04-238 1313; www.rapidpg.com.my). Fares range from RM1.40 to RM4. Most routes originate at **Weld Quay Bus Terminal** (Map p406; 19-24 Pengkalan Weld) and most also stop at Komtar and along Jln Chulia.

BICYCLE

There are several places near the intersection of Gat Lebuh Armenian and Lebuh Victoria offering one-day hire of city bikes for around RM12. Alternatively, for something more specific, consider the more specialised bicycles at **LoveBike** (Map p406; ☑012-476 9918; 31 Love Lane; per 6hr RM10-25; ⊙9.30am-9.30pm).

MOTORCYCLE

You can hire motorcycles from many places, including guesthouses and shops along Lebuh Chulia. Manual bikes start at about RM30 and automatic about RM40, for 24 hours.

TAXI

Penang's taxis all have meters, which nearly all drivers flatly refuse to use, so negotiate the fare before you set off. Typical fares to places just outside of the city centre start at around RM15.

TRISHAW

Bicycle rickshaws are a fun, if touristy, way to negotiate George Town's backstreets and cost around RM40 per hour – agree on the fare before departure. Drivers can be found waiting at the northernend of Jln Penang.

ⓘ GETTING TO/FROM BUTTERWORTH

Butterworth, the city on the mainland bit of Penang, is home to Penang's main train station and is the departure point for ferries to Penang Island. Unless you're taking the train or your bus has pulled into Butterworth's busy bus station from elsewhere, you'll probably not need to spend any time here.

The **ferry** (Map p406; per adult/car RM1.20/7.70; ☺5.30am-1am) takes 10 minutes and fares are charged only for the journey from Butterworth to Penang; returning to the mainland is free. If you choose to take a taxi to/from Butterworth (approximately RM50), you'll cross the 13.5km Penang Bridge. There's a RM7 toll payable at the toll plaza on the mainland, but no charge to return.

There are four daily trains to Kuala Lumpur (six hours, RM19 to RM138) and two in the opposite direction to Hat Yai in Thailand (four hours, RM24 to RM156).

Greater Penang

There's much more to Penang than George Town. You can cool down on Penang Hill and go beach-hopping around Batu Ferringhi and Teluk Bahang at the north of the island (although note the beaches can't compare to Malaysia's best).

◉ Sights

★ Penang Hill   HILL
(Map p405; www.penanghill.gov.my; funicular adult/child RM30/15; ☺6.30am-11pm) The top of Penang Hill, 821m above George Town, provides a spectacular view over the island and across to the mainland.

The top is reached by a funicular, and on weekends and public holidays lines can be horrendously long, with waits of up to 30 minutes. From Weld Quay, Komtar or Lebuh Chulia, you can catch the frequent bus 204 (RM2.70) to Air Itam. A taxi here from the centre of George Town will set you back about RM25.

★ Penang National Park   NATIONAL PARK
(Taman Negara Pulau Pinang; Map p405; ☑04-881 2016; ☺8am-5pm) **FREE** At just 2300 hectares, Penang National Park is the smallest in Malaysia; it's also one of the newest, having attained national park status in 2003. A Penang highlight, it has some interesting and challenging trails through the jungle, as well as some of the island's finest and quietest beaches.

The park can be reached on Teluk Bahang–bound bus 101 (RM4) from George Town.

Tropical Spice Garden   GARDENS
(Map p405; ☑04-881 1797; www.tropicalspice garden.com; Jl Teluk Bahang; adult/child RM26/15, incl tour RM35/20; ☺9am-6pm) Between Teluk Bahang and Batu Ferringhi is the Tropical Spice Garden, an oasis of tropical, fragrant fecundity of more than 500 species of flora, with an emphasis on edible herbs and spices.

You can explore the grounds on your own, or join one of four daily guided tours at 9am, 11.30am, 1.30pm and 3.30pm.

The garden also offers **cooking courses** (☑04-881 1797; www.tropicalspicegarden.com; Jl Teluk Bahang; adult/child RM233.20/116.60; ☺lessons 9am-1pm Mon-Sat), there's a good shop, the restaurant is worth a visit and just across from the gardens there's a beautiful roadside white-sand beach.

To get here by bus, take any Teluk Bahang-bound bus (RM4) and let the driver know that you want to get off here.

Kek Lok Si Temple   BUDDHIST TEMPLE
(Map p405; www.keklok sitemple.com; ☺7am-9pm) **FREE** The 'Temple of Supreme Bliss' is also the largest Buddhist temple in Malaysia and one of the most recognisable buildings in the country. Built by an immigrant Chinese Buddhist in 1890, Kek Lok Si is a cornerstone of the Malay-Chinese community, who provided the funding for its two-decade-long building (and ongoing additions).

The temple is in Air Itam, 8km from the centre of George Town. A taxi starts at about RM25, or you can hop on bus 204 (RM2.70).

To reach the entrance, walk through a maze of souvenir stalls, past a tightly packed turtle pond and murky fish ponds, until you reach Ban Po Thar (Ten Thousand Buddhas Pagoda; admission RM2), a seven-tier, 30m-high tower. The design is said to be Burmese at the top, Chinese at the bottom and Thai in between. A **cable car** (one way/return RM3/6; ☺8.30am-5.30pm) whisks you to the highest level, which is presided over by an awesome 36.5m-high bronze statue of Kuan Yin, goddess of mercy.

There are several other temples in this complex, as well as shops and a **vegetarian restaurant** (mains from RM5; ☻10am-7pm Tue-Sun; ☑).

Alor Setar

☑ 04

The capital of Kedah, also known as Alor Star, is a jumping-off point to Langkawi or southern Malaysia with enough around to keep you exploring for a day. This is a very Malay city, culturally rooted in a conservative Islamic mindset. Thai temples are scattered around town, while its small Chinese population lives in an atmospheric, compact Chinatown.

🛏 Sleeping & Eating

Comfort Motel   HOTEL $

(☑04-734 4866; 2C Jln Kampung Perak; r RM28-40; ☒) This is a good-value, Chinese-style budget hotel, located in a renovated wooden house across from a mosque. The rooms are tidy and come equipped with TV and air-con, but are otherwise bare and share bathrooms.

Muda Coffee Shop   CHINESE $

(Jln Pekan China; mains RM3-20; ☻2.30-11pm) We should start by saying that this place is for adventurous eaters only: the staff don't speak much English, and the highlight is a dish of steamed fish head. But, oh, what a fish head. Accompanied with *lor mee* (noodles fried with dark soy sauce) and a beer, it was one of the tastiest meals we had in Malaysia. Located near the corner with Jln Sultan Muhammad Jiwa.

ℹ Getting There & Away

The main bus terminal, Shahab Perdana, is 4km north of the town centre. The bus to Shahab Perdana from the city centre costs RM1.30 and a taxi there costs RM10.

A local bus links Shahab Perdana and Kuala Kedah (RM3, one hour, frequent departures from 7am to 10pm), passing through central Alor Setar on the way. Ferries (adult/child RM23/17) from Kuala Kedah leave for Langkawi approximately every hour from 7am to 7pm.

The train station (Jln Stesyen) is 850m southeast of the town centre. There is one daily northbound train to Hat Yai (RM9 to RM48, 3½hours, 7.56am) in Thailand and one to Bangkok (about RM110, 18½ hours, 2pm); there is also one daily southbound train to Butterworth

---

GETTING TO THAILAND

Alor Setar to Hat Yai

Getting to the border The Bukit Kayu Hitam/Sadao border, 48km north of Alor Setar, is the main road crossing between Malaysia. As there are no taxis or local buses at this border, the only practical way to cross here is on a through bus from points elsewhere in Malaysia.

At the border The Malaysian border post is open every day from 6am to midnight. All passengers must disembark to clear customs and immigration (both Thai and Malaysian) before reboarding.

Moving on The lack of local transport means that you'll most likely pass this border on a bus already bound for Hat Yai.

Kangar to Hat Yai

Getting to the border There are four buses a day from Kangar to Padang Besar (RM4.20), stopping at an unmarked bus stop by a roundabout about 500m from the border.

At the border The Malaysian borderpost is open every day from 6am to 10pm. Few people walk the more than 2km of no-man's land between the Thai and Malaysian sides of the border. Motorcyclists shuttle pedestrian travellers back and forth for about RM2 each way. For train passengers, customs and immigration are dealt with at Padang Besar station.

Moving on Once in Thailand there are frequent buses to Hat Yai, 60km away. There are trains at 10.30am and 6.40pm connecting Padang Besar and Hat Yai (RM6 to RM13, 50 minutes).

(RM8 to RM26, two hours, 11.09am) and one to Kuala Lumpur (9½ hours, RM39 to RM51, 7.55pm).

Kangar

🍴 04

Kangar, 45km northwest of Alor Setar, is the state capital of Perlis and has a small-town vibe. There's not a whole lot to do here besides relax or chat, which are fine options for those awaiting an onward bus to Kuala Perlis, about 10km to the southwest, from where there are ferries to Pulau Langkawi.

Should you end up here for the night, the basic Chinese-style **Hotel Ban Cheong** (☑ 04-976 1184; 79 Jln Kangar; r RM40-65; ❄ ☎) is your best budget option.

Ferries (RM17) depart from the port in Kuala Perlis for Kuah, on Pulau Langkawi, roughly every hour between 7am and 7pm.

To get from Kangar to the pier take a frequent bus (RM3) from the local bus station on Jln Tun Abdul Razak or a taxi for RM16. Buses also run to/from Kuala Perlis to destinations such as Butterworth (RM15.10, three hours) and KL (from RM47.10, eight hours).

Pulau Langkawi

🍴 04

The Langkawi archipelago sits 30km off the coast from Kuala Perlis and 45km from the border town of Satun. The main island of a string of 99 tropical dots is dominated by knife-edged peaks floating in dark vegetation. Surrounded by ocean blues, this island is an undisputed tropical paradise, despite the resort build-up. Get just a little way off the main beaches and this is idyllic rural Malaysia, with traditional *kampung* (villages) and a laid-back vibe. Plus Langkawi's been duty-free since 1987, so is one of the few places in Malaysia you can drink relatively cheaply.

ℹ FERRY WARNING

During the wet season, from July to September, you may want to shelve any notions of taking the ferry to Langkawi, particularly from Penang. At this time of year the seas are typically very rough and the ferry ride can be a terrifying and quite literally vomit-inducing experience. Consider yourself warned.

◉ Sights

Move on briskly from **Kuah**, the major town and the arrival point for ferries, to **Pantai Cenang** (cha-nang). This gorgeous 2km-long strip of sand on Langkawi's west coast has the biggest concentration of hotels and tourist facilities. The water is good for swimming, but jellyfish are common. If you're looking for somewhere a bit quieter try adjacent **Pantai Tengah**.

In Pantai Kok, northwest of Pantai Cenang, it's also worth riding the **Panorama Langkawi** (☑ 04-959 4225; www.panorama langkawi.com; Oriental Village, Burau Bay; SkyCab ticket adult/child RM35/25; ⊙ 9.30am-7pm) cable car to the top of Gunung Machinchang to enjoy spectacular views.

🛏 Sleeping

During peak tourist times (November to February) Langkawi's rooms fill quickly but at other times of the year supply far outstrips demand.

🛏 Pantai Cenang

Lots of backpacker places are found along the small roads running inland away from the beach, so it's easy to shop around.

Sweet Inn   HOTEL $
(☑ 04-955 8864; www.sweetinns.net; r RM80-100; 🅿 ❄ ☎) One of the cleaner, brighter budget options in Pantai Cenang, with plain rooms that manage to keep cool in the heat. The wi-fi doesn't reach beyond reception and the place lacks a bit of atmosphere, but it does gain points for easy beach access.

Izz Room   GUESTHOUSE $
(☑ 04-955 1397; www.izzroom.blogspot.com; r RM50-80; ❄ ☎) Basic, sparsely furnished accommodation is spread around a pleasant gravel courtyard with shady palm trees. The best rooms are in the brightly coloured block opposite reception, while cheaper doubles have fans and shared bathrooms. Laundry service is available (RM4 per kilo).

Rainbow Lodge   HOTEL $
(☑ 04-955 8103; www.rainbowlangkawi.com; dm RM22, r RM50-90; ❄ @ ☎) Set a little way back from the beach, this friendly place has a sociable cafe area with views over neighbouring fields. Partitions and curtains give dorm beds some privacy. Popular with backpackers seeking a cheap place to rest between beers.

🛏 Pantai Tengah

Pantai Tengah is less built-up and is popular with Malay families. Its main drag is stuffed with upscale eateries and bars.

Zackry Guest House   GUESTHOUSE $
(zackryghouse@gmail.com; r RM60-110; ❀@🛜)
This ramshackle, family-run guesthouse has a homely, sociable atmosphere. Rooms are basic, yet clean and cosy, and the recently spruced-up communal areas include a small kitchen with a fridge but no cooking facilities. Note that there's a two-night minimum, no phone bookings, and only about half of the rooms have an attached bathroom.

🍴 Eating

There's a roving *pasar malam* (6pm to 10pm), which is held north of Pantai Cenang Thursdays, in Kuah on Wednesdays and Saturdays, and other locations the rest of the week; it's a good place to get authentic Malay food on the cheap.

Padang Pasir   INDIAN $
(☏04-966 6786; Jln Pantai Cenang; mains RM11-16; ⊙7am-1am) This well-positioned food stall with open-air seating on the main Cenang strip sells tempting chicken, lamb and naan bread fresh from the tandoor oven, as well as *nasi kandar* (rice with curry sauces) and rotis. It's open from 7am for breakfast to 1am at night, making it a good place to stop and refuel at any time of day.

Melayu   MALAYSIAN $
(☏04-955 4075; Jln Teluk Baru; mains RM5-10; ⊙3-10.30pm) The comfortable dining room, pleasant outdoor seating area and efficient service here belie the reasonable prices. A good place to go for cheap, authentic Malaysian food in the evening, since most of the island's local restaurants are lunchtime buffets. Alcohol isn't served but you can bring your own for no charge.

🍸 Drinking & Nightlife

Langkawi is arguably the best (and cheapest) spot for a drink in Malaysia. Most bars open around 5pm and close late.

Little Lylia's Chill Out Cafe   BAR
(Pantai Cenang; ⊙noon-1am) This longstanding, chummy bar spills out onto Pantai Cenang until the late hours. The chairs and tables may be practically falling apart, but friendly service and a chilled-out vibe hold the place together.

GETTING TO THAILAND: PULAU LANGKAWI TO SATUN & KO LIPE

Getting to the border There are three daily ferries from Kuah on Pulau Langkawi to Satun (one way RM30, 1¼ hours) on the Thai mainland. **Tropical Charters** (☏012-588 3274; www.tropicalcharters.com.my; Pantai Tengah; cruises from RM260) also runs two ferries daily between Langkawi and Ko Lipe (one way RM118, 1½ hours) in Thailand.

At the border You'll get stamped out of Malaysia at immigration at the ferry terminal then get stamped into Thailand when you arrive at the ferry terminal in Satun. Most visitors will get a 30-day Thai visa on arrival.

Moving on From Satun there are more bus and boat connections. From Ko Lipe there are onward services available to as far as Ko Lanta.

For information on doing this crossing in reverse, see p774.

Yellow Café   BAR
(Pantai Cenang; ⊙noon-1am Wed-Mon; 🛜) A fun, breezy place with beanbags on the beach and a few imported beers. Come between 4pm and 6pm when beers are buy one get one free.

Cliff   BAR
(www.theclifflangkawi.com; Pantai Cenang; ⊙noon-11pm) Perched on the rocky outcrop that divides Pantai Cenang and Pantai Tengah, the Cliff is well located for a sunset cocktail. Expect a full bar, a good wine selection, and an eclectic menu that spans from Europe to Malaysia (mains RM23 to RM72).

ℹ Information

The only banks are at Kuah, although there are ATMs at the airport and Underwater World in Pantai Cenng where you'll also find money-changers.

Tourism Malaysia (☏04-966 7789; Jln Persiaran Putra, Kuah; ⊙9am-5pm) With three offices in Langkawi – located opposite the ferry terminal entrance at Kuah jetty, on Jalan Persiaran Putra (next to the mosque) in Kuah Town, and in the airport arrivals hall (open until 10pm) – Tourism Malaysia offers comprehensive information on the whole island.

❶ Getting There & Away

AIR

Langkawi International Airport (☏04-955 1311; www.langkawiairport.com) is located in the west of the island, about a 10-minute taxi ride from Pantai Cenang.

BOAT

All passenger ferries to/from Langkawi operate out of Kuah. From about 8am to 6.30pm, ferries operate roughly every hour to/from the mainland port of Kuala Perlis (RM18, 1¼ hours) and to/from Kuala Kedah (RM23, 1½ hours).

Langkawi Ferry Services (LFS; ☏04-966 9439; www.langkawi-ferry.com) operates daily ferries between Kuah and George Town on Penang (RM60, two hours 45 minutes).

❶ Getting Around

There is no public transport. Car hire is excellent value starting at RM70 per day, or RM35 for a motorbike. A few places also rent mountain bikes for RM15 per day.

Otherwise, taxis are the main way of getting around. Fixed taxi fares from the airport include Kuah jetty (RM30), Pantai Cenang or Pantai Kok (RM20). Buy a coupon at the desk before leaving the airport terminal and use it to pay the driver. The fare from Kuah jetty to Pantai Cenang is RM30.

PENINSULAR MALAYSIA – SOUTH & EAST COAST

As you travel around the south of Peninsular Malaysia and up the east coast, the communities you encounter become more laid-back, more Malay and more Islamic. Headscarves, skullcaps and the hauntingly melodious call to prayer are as ubiquitous here as the white-sand beaches that fringe the sunrise-drenched coasts and jewel-like islands.

Johor Bahru

☏07

The frenetic border town of Johor Bahru (known as JB) is connected to Singapore by the 1038m-long Causeway bridge. Over the last few years the city has been cleaned up and has quietly broken out of its old mould as a dodgy, lacklustre border town to become a really decent place to hang out. Indian women hawk gold bracelets on the sidewalk as incense wafts from Chinese

shops, giving the walkable heritage downtown area an exotic vibe.

◉ Sights

Arulmigu Sri Raja Kalliamman   HINDU TEMPLE

(Glass Temple; 22 Lorong 1; RM10; ⊙7am-noon, 6-10pm Mon-Fri, 7am-10pm Sat & Sun) FREE Step through the looking glass into this wonderland temple built from mirrors, glass and metal. Not a single inch of the vaulted roof or wall goes unadorned. The temple is dedicated to Kali, known as the goddess of time, change, power and destruction.

Heritage District   ARCHITECTURE, AREA

Wandering around the heritage area between Jln Ibrahim and Jln Ungku Puan is a real highlight of Johor Bahru. Walk past old colourful shophouses filled with sari shops, barbers, Ayurvedic salons, gorgeous temples, a few modern-art galleries and old-style eateries.

Royal Abu Bakar Museum   MUSEUM

(☏07-223 0555; Jln Ibrahim; adult/child RM21/9; ⊙9am-5pm Sat-Thu) The marvellous Istana Besar, once the Johor royal family's principal palace, was built in Victorian style by Anglophile sultan Abu Bakar in 1866. It was opened as a museum to the public in 1990 and displays the incredible wealth of the sultans. It's now the finest museum of its kind in Malaysia, and the 53-hectare palace grounds (free entry) are beautifully manicured.

🛏 Sleeping & Eating

Meldrum Hotel   HOTEL **$$**

(☏07-227 8988; www.meldrumhotel.com; 1 Jln Siu Nam; d RM131-189, q RM225-260; ❄🛜) All options here are air-conditioned, clean, spacious and freshly painted, and the rooms have TVs, free drinking water and kettles. It's worth upgrading to a superior room with free wi-fi and requesting a non-smoking room if you don't puff. Back rooms will save on street noise.

Reaz Corner   INDIAN **$**

(Jln Duke; meals RM8-12.50) You can't go wrong with the yellow rice topped with a spicy chicken curry at this clean, open-air curry joint. The ginger tea is a not-to-be-missed-nor-soon-forgotten accompaniment.

Medan Selera Meldrum Walk   HAWKER **$**

(Medan Selera Meldrum; meals from RM3; ⊙dinner) Every late afternoon, the little food stalls crammed along this alley (parallel to Jln Meldrum) start frying up everything from

GETTING TO INDONESIA: JOHOR BAHRU TO RIAU ISLANDS

Getting to the border There are several daily departures to Batam (one way RM69, 1½ hours) and Bintan (one way RM86, 2½ hours), both part of Indonesia's Riau Islands. Ferries depart from the **Berjaya Ferry Terminal** (Zon Ferry; www.berjayawaterfront.com. my; 88 Jln Ibrahim Sultan) that's serviced by several buses from downtown Johor Bahru.

Additional boats on **Tuah Ferry Services** (www.ferrytuah.comoj.com; Terminal Antarabangsa Kukup) depart from Kukup, southwest of JB, to Tanjung Balai on Karimun (three times daily, RM130) and to Sekupang, Batam (twice daily, RM165). Buses travel to Kukup from JB (RM7, 1½ hours) and KL (RM26, 3½ hours). A taxi from JB to Kukup is RM80.

At the border From JB there's a RM10 seaport tax as you're stamped out of Malaysia; port fees at Kukup are RM25 per person.

Moving on From Batam, boats connect to the Sumatran ports of Dumai, Palembang and Pekanbaru, which are served by buses. Thirty-day visas on arrival are available at all these ports (see p310).

---

ikan bakar to the local curry laksa. Wash down your meal with fresh sugar-cane juice or a Chinese herbal jelly drink. Nothing here is excellent, but it's all good.

ℹ Information

Tourism Malaysia & Johor Tourist Information Centre (☑07-223 4935; www.johortourism.com.my; 3rd fl, Jotic Bldg, 2 Jln Air Molek; ⌚9am-5pm Mon-Sat) One of two Tourism Malaysia offices in JB; the other is at the CIQ complex, right after you pass through immigration from Singapore.

ℹ Getting There & Away

AIR

Senai International Airport (☑07-599 4500; www.senaiairport.com) is 32km northwest of JB, and linked to the city centre by regular shuttle buses (RM8, 45 minutes) that run from the bus station at Kotaraya 2 Terminal.

BOAT

Ferries leave Johor Bahru for Batam and Bintan islands in Indonesia.

BUS

Larkin Bus Terminal is about 5km north of town.
 Buses from Johr Bahur:

DESTINATION	FARE (RM)	DURATION (HR)
Butterworth	62.60	9
Kuala Lumpur	31	4
Kuala Terengganu	33	8
Kuantan	20	5
Melaka	21	2½
Mersing	13	2

TAXI

JB's main long-distance taxi station is at the Larkin bus station; there's a handier terminal on Jln Wong Ah Fook. Regular taxi destinations and costs (shared taxi with four passengers) include Kukup (RM80), Senai Airport (RM50), Melaka (RM280), KL (RM460) and Mersing (RM160).

TRAIN

Express trains leave from JB Sentral train station in the CIQ complex, running to KL (6.30am, 2.56pm and 8.25pm daily). The line passes through Tampin (for Melaka), Seremban, KL Sentral, Ipoh, Tapah Rd (for Cameron Highlands) and Butterworth. The line splits at Gemas so you can board the 'jungle train' for Jerantut (for Taman Negara) and Kota Bharu (portions of this line were closed at research due to flooding).

Mersing

☑07

You may end up spending a night or two at this busy, compact port waiting for ferries (due to weather or the tides) to Pulau Tioman. The town has everything that travellers might need but is short on sights.

🛏 Sleeping & Eating

Seafood stalls open up nightly along Jln Endau by the river.

Zeeadam Backpacker House HOSTEL $
(☑07-799 1280; ahmadzamani_77@yahoo.com; 10-1 Atas Jln Abu Bakar; dm RM20; @ 🛜) The only true dorm-bed backpacker place in town, the Zeeadam has just two dorm rooms, sleeping six to eight people on ultra-firm beds. There's a little TV and a hangout chill area at this second-storey spot that is short on charms but long on value.

GETTING TO SINGAPORE: JOHOR BAHRU TO SINGAPORE

Getting to the border There are frequent buses between JB's Larkin Bus Terminal, 5km north of the city, and Singapore's Queen St bus station. Most convenient is **Causeway Link** (www.causewaylink.com.my; 6.30am-midnight, every 10min; from JB/Singapore RM3.40/S$3.30). **Trans Star Cross Border Coaches** (www.regentstar.travel/crossborder; 5am-11pm, every hour; from JB/Singapore RM10/S$9) run between JB's Larkin Bus Terminal and Singapore's Changi International Airport (embarking in the Terminal 2 coach area).

Registered taxis to Singapore depart from the Plaza Seni Taxi Terminal in the centre of JB, with taxis to Orchard Rd or Queen St bus station costing around RM60. Local city taxis cannot cross the Causeway.

KTM Intercity (☑ 300-885862; www.ktmintercity.com.my) trains (RM3) run from JB Sentral to Woodlands in Singapore, leaving JB at 5:50am, 6:55am, 2:20pm and 9pm. You go through passport checks and switch to the Singapore metro system at Woodlands.

At the border All buses stop at Malaysian immigration. Disembark from the bus with your luggage and go through immigration then reboard your bus (keep your ticket). The bus then brings you to Singapore immigration where you get off the bus with your luggage once more, clear Singapore customs then get back on your bus (again keep your ticket), which will take you to Singapore's Queen St bus station.

Moving on At Queen St there are buses, taxis and an MRT (light rail) system that can take you almost anywhere you need to go in the city. There are ATMs at Singapore immigration and at the Queen St bus station if you need Singapore dollars.

For information on making this crossing in the opposite direction, see p640.

Hotel Embassy HOTEL $
(☑ 07-799 3545; 2 Jln Ismail; r RM55; ❀ ☎) This is a fabulous choice compared with the other cheapies in town, and is a great place to clean up and get back to reality after bumming it on island beaches. All rooms are huge and bright, and have cable TV, turbocharged air-con and attached bathrooms.

Loke Tien Yuen Restaurant CHINESE $
(55 Jln Abu Bakar; mains RM3.50-15; ☺ lunch & dinner) Mersing's oldest Chinese restaurant is one of the friendliest and busiest places in town. You may have to wait for a marble table to enjoy the deliciously prepared prawn and pork dishes. The speciality – whole steamed fish that you'll see all the locals eating – isn't on the English menu, so ask your server.

ⓘ Information

Mersing Tourist Information Centre (Jln Abu Bakar; ☺ 8am-5pm Mon-Sat) On the road to the pier. Stop in for helpful info, bus schedules and pamphlets.

ⓘ Getting There & Away

Most buses depart from the station near the bridge on the river, although a few leave from bus company offices near the pier. Some buses will also drop you at the pier – it pays to ask.

There are ferries to/from Pulau Tioman. Buses from Mersing:

DESTINATION	FARE (RM)	DURATION (HR)
Johor Bahru	13	2½
Kuala Lumpur	40	5½
Kuala Terengganu	34	9
Kuantan	17	5
Melaka	25	4
Singapore	16	3

Pulau Tioman

☑ 09

From late nights at Salang bars to days of trekking through the wild jungles, surfing the beaches at Juara or diving the reefs and wrecks off the coast, Tioman has as much action or nonaction as anyone could hope for. The proximity to Singapore and the availability of upscale digs has made Tioman particularly popular with Singaporean and domestic tourists but the 20km long and 11km wide island is so big and the locals are so mellow that the weekend crowds are absorbed without affecting the laid-back vibe.

⊙ Sights & Activities

Beaches

Most budget accommodation is clustered in Air Batang (ABC) and Salang on the northern end of the west coast. Salang has wider stretches of sand and is most backpacker-esque of Tioman's *kampung*, while ABC is slightly more upscale. On Tioman's east coast Juara has a stunning beach, surfing during the monsoon and affordable accommodation. Other small beaches reachable only by boat run south along the west coast.

Juara Turtle Project · · · · · VOLUNTEERING

(☑ 09-419 3244; www.juaraturtleproject.com; Juara; tour RM10, volunteering with breakfast, lunch & dm (min 4 nights) RM120; ⊙ 10am-5pm) ✆ On the southern end of Juara, this voluntourism operation works to protect declining sea turtle populations by collecting eggs and moving them to a hatchery, and patrolling the beaches for poachers and predators. Volunteers get basic dorm accommodation. They also work patrols and give information seminars. Daily activities including sea kayaking, treks and cooking classes are also offered.

Diving

Most places rent snorkelling gear (RM115 per day) and you can join day trips to Pulau Tulai (Coral Island), where you can swim with tropical fish and sometime sharks.

Open Water Diver courses cost from RM1100 and fun dives from RM115. There are plenty of dive operations, so shop around for the best deal.

Hiking

There's a fantastic 7km hike that crosses the island's waist from near the jetty at Tekek to Juara (carry plenty of water). It takes around two and a half hours and is steep in parts.

There are also several other trails on the island connecting beaches and climbing to waterfalls.

🛏 Sleeping & Eating

In late July through August, accommodation becomes tight on weekends. Either side of these months it's a buyer's market. Budget digs around the island are nearly identical and are of low standard – think old mattresses and saggy floors – but most do have private bathrooms, fans and mosquito nets.

Restaurants, with similar menus, are usually attached to chalet operations. ABC, Tekek and Salang all have small convenience stores.

🛏 Air Batang (ABC)

Mokhtar's Place · · · · · · · · · · BUNGALOW $

(☑ 019-704 8299; www.mohktarplace.blogspot.com; ABC; s/d with fan RM50/60, q with air-con RM220; ✴ �🛜) Great budget value, this cluster of 16 bungalows along the beach south of town features little patios and mozzie nets. If the wind's just right, you can catch a cooling ocean breeze at night.

Johan's Resort · · · · · · · · · · · BUNGALOW $

(☑ 09-419 1359; dm/chalet/f RM20/40/100) A friendly, welcoming place offering tons of information. The two four-bed dorms up the hillside are decent value; the chalets are pretty much the same as other cheapies on the beach.

🛏 Salang

Ella's Place · · · · · · · · · · · · · · BUNGALOW $

(☑ 09-419 5004; Salang; bungalows RM60-120; ✴) There's usually a loungeable patch of sand at this cute-as-a-button family-run place at the quiet northern end of the beach.

Pulau Tioman ⓝ ⎸0————4 km / ⎸0————2 miles

Pulau Tulai (Coral Island) · Kampung Salang Beach · Bukit Kerayung Kecil (390m) · ▲ Bukit Kerayung Besar (409m) · Kampung Salang · *Monkey Bay* Monkey Beach · SOUTH CHINA SEA · Kampung Panuba · Kampung Air · Kampung Batang (ABC) · *Air Batang Bay* · Tanjung Gemok (55km) · Kampung Tekek · Kampung Dungung · Pulau Rengis · *Airstrip* · Bukit Parang Panjang (488m) · *Barok* · Kampung Paya · Bunut · Gua Teh Angin (945m) · Kampung Juara · *Mentawak* · ▲ Gunung Kajang (1038m) · Kampung Genting · Bukit Seperok (958m) · Kampung Nipah · Nenek Semukut (690m) · Mersing (51km) · Batu Sirau (753m) · Kampung Asah · Kampung Mukut

WORTH A TRIP

PULAU KAPAS

Pretty Kapas is a worthy place to chill out for a few days, but do try to visit during the week, as the island becomes overrun with day-trippers on holidays and long weekends. All accommodation on Kapas is concentrated on three small beaches on the west coast, but you can walk or kayak to quieter beaches. During the east-coast monsoon season (November to March), the seas are too rough and the island largely shuts down.

Six kilometres offshore from Marang, Kapas is reached by boats in 15 minutes from Marang's main jetty. Tickets (RM40 return) can be purchased from any of the agents nearby and boats depart when four or more people show up. Be sure to arrange a pick-up time when you purchase your ticket. You can usually count on morning departures from 8am.

In Marang there are regular local buses to/from Kuala Terengganu (RM4). If you're around on Sunday, check out the excellent **Sunday Market**, which starts at 3pm near the town's jetties.

Captain's Longhouse (☑012-3770214; dm/r RM40/80) Formerly known as the Light-house, this superhip longhouse sits on the southernmost tip of the bay. Guests can enjoy art-covered walls, dorm beds bedecked in colourful batik blankets, and a sociable front porch with hammocks, chairs and even an out-of-tune piano. Surrounded by trees, it's pretty rustic but very comfortable.

Kapas Beach Chalet (dm RM20, r RM50-80; 🛜) The most laid-back spot on Kapas offers accommodation ranging from basic 'backpacker' rooms with outside (but private) toilets to comfortable A-frame huts. There's a great social vibe, courtesy of the hip shared spaces including 'The Big Chill,' a breezy beachfront pavilion equipped with hammocks and loads of cushions. Chilled beats bubble away, and most nights someone brings out a guitar. Walk-in guests only.

There are 10 clean bungalows (some with air-con) and a small cafe.

Khalid's Place   BUNGALOW $
(☑09-419 5317; salangpusaka@yahoo.com; Salang; d bungalow with air-con RM80; ❄) South of the jetty, behind the Salang Complex and across a festering section of Sungai Salang. It has 47 cleanish bungalows set in a large grassy area, back from the beach; air-con chalets come with fridge and hot shower.

🛏 Juara

★Rainbow Chalets   BUNGALOW $
(☑012-989 8572; rainbow.chalets@gmail.com; Juara; r with fan/air-con RM60/100; ❄🛜) Eight colourful bungalows – three air-con and five fan-cooled – await you. All come with wooden porches and are decorated with shells and coral. The beach and views onto the South China Sea are frickin' glorious.

Bushman   BUNGALOW $
(☑09-419 3109; matbushman@hotmail.com; r with fan/air-con RM60/100; ❄🛜) Nabbing one of Bushman's five varnished wood bungalows, with their inviting wicker-furnished terraces, is like winning the Juara lottery – reserve in advance! The location is right up against the boulder outcrop and a small river that marks the end of the northern beach.

❶ Information

Don't rely on Tioman's sole cash machine in Tekek across from the airport – it's been known to run dry, so also bring cash from the mainland. There's a moneychanger at the airport. There's a small post office not far north of the Babura Seaview Resort in Tekek.

❶ Getting There & Away

Mersing is the ferry port for Tioman (RM70 return, two to three hours). There are usually two to six ferry departures throughout the day between 7am and 5pm, but specific departure times vary with the tides. Ferries drop off passengers in south-to-north order on the island.

Boat departures during the monsoon season (November to February) can be erratic, with sailings becoming more regular during the low monsoon months (January and February).

Ferries also depart for Tioman from the Tanjung Gemok ferry terminal (return RM70), 35km north of Mersing.

🛈 Getting Around

You can walk from ABC to Tekek in about five minutes. But you'll need to charter a boat through a guesthouse or restaurant to travel between ABC and Salang (RM30).

To get to Juara hire a 4WD taxi (RM25 to RM40 for up to four people) in Tekek – better is to book your room in advance so your host can pick you up at the Tekek pier. Alternatively, you can walk through the jungle to Juara from Tekek (7km).

Kuantan

Most travellers only stop in busy Kuantan, Pahang's capital, to break up long bus trips. While the city isn't geared towards tourism, it is definitely interesting enough to warrant a day or two's exploration, offering some of the coast's best eating opportunities. Kuantan's star attraction is **Masjid Negeri** (State Mosque; Jln Mahkota). This impressive mosque, with its spires and lit turrets, is particularly impressive when illuminated at night.

🍴 Eating

The **food stalls** near the long-distance bus terminal are particularly good.

Akob Patin House   MALAYSIAN $
(Jln Besar; mains RM7-15; ☺lunch) Fancy trying *patin*, the local delicacy? This riverfront place serves both wild-caught (RM20) and farmed (RM8) *patin* in a *tempoyak* (fermented durian sambal) sauce served as part of a buffet with other Malay-style meat and vegetable dishes – the price is per fish. The friendly staff can help explain what's what.

🛈 Information

Lots of banks (many with 24-hour ATMs) are on or near the aptly named Jln Bank.
Tourist Information Centre (☎09-516 1007; Jln Mahkota; ☺8am-5pm Mon-Fri) Has particularly helpful staff and a range of useful leaflets.

🛈 Getting There & Away

AIR
Sultan Ahmad Shah Airport (☎09-531 2123) is 15km from the city centre and has flights to

Kuantan

KLIA, SkyPark Subang Terminal and Penang; a taxi should cost (RM15).

BUS & TAXI
Long-distance buses arrive and depart from Terminal Sentral Kuantan, about 20 minutes from the city centre (taxi RM20). Buses for Cherating depart from near the Central Market.

Ask your hotel to order you a long-distance taxi, or grab one from in front of the Terminal Sentral Kuantan. Destinations and approximate cost (per car): Mersing (RM200), Johor Bahru (RM350), Cherating (RM50 to RM70), Kuala Terengganu (RM200), Jerantut (RM200) and KL (RM280).

Buses from Kuantan:

DESTINATION	FARE (RM)	DURATION (HR)
Butterworth	51	8½
Cherating	5	1½
Jerantut	18	3½
Kota Bharu	31	6
Kuala Lumpur	24	4
Kuala Terengganu	17	4
Melaka	35	6
Singapore	30	6

Cherating

☑ 09

A sweeping white beach bordered by coconut palms and a small village of guesthouses and shops with more monkeys, monitor lizards and cats walking around than humans, Cherating is a popular spot for surfing and general beachfront slacking. With plenty of beach bars, Cherating has the best nightlife on the coast.

🏃 Activities

Cherating's bay has a long sandy shelf, making this a peaceful spot for swimming most of the year. Watch out for jellyfish in June and July.

Some of Malaysia's best surfing waves kick up here during monsoon season from late October to the end of March.

Several places around town run nature tours and walks, including turtle-watching (April to September).

Turtle Sanctuary　　　ANIMAL SANCTUARY
(admission RM30; ◷ 9am-5pm Tue-Sun) The turtle sanctuary next to Club Med has a few basins with baby and rehabilitating green turtles, and can offer information about the laying and hatching periods.

🛏 Sleeping & Eating

Cherating has a 'strip' where most of the restaurants and guesthouses congregate. Book in advance during the monsoon surf season from November through January.

Payung Guesthouse　　　BUNGALOW $
(☑09-581 9658; d/q RM60/120, d with air-con RM80; ❋☏) This friendly main-drag choice backs onto the river with a neat row of bungalows and well-manicured gardens. The bungalows all have mozzie nets, and this is an excellent spot to get information on local happenings.

Lilo's Travelers Home　　　GUESTHOUSE $
(☑019-996 1723; r RM50) Located on a little dusty backroad, this broad-smiling spot is just getting going. But you'll get super-clean basic white rooms, a shared kitchen and cool central hangout. Plans are in place to build a community garden.

Don't Tell Mama　　　BURGERS $
(Cherating Beach; burger RM5-10; ◷ till late) 🌶
Don't Tell Mama was relaunching when we passed through, relocating next to Eco Bar. It's bound to be a hit with a full menu and its legendary burgers still on offer. Ask to see the cool hydroponic garden set-up.

🍷 Drinking & Nightlife

★ Eco Bar　　　BAR
(Rhana Pippin; Cherating Beach; ◷noon-4am) 🌶
Grab a low-slung table at this super-friendly beach bar and feel the sand between your toes as you check out the quirky local characters who spice up Cherating's nightlife scene.

❶ Information

There are no banks or ATMs in Cherating.

❶ Getting There & Away

From Kuantan's local bus station catch a bus marked 'Kemaman' and ask to be dropped at Cherating Lama. Buses leave every 30 minutes (RM5, one hour). When coming from the north, any bus heading for Kuantan will drop you on the main road. A taxi from Kuantan should cost about RM80.

For Kuala Terengganu book long-distance bus tickets (RM17, three hours, frequent) through Payung Guesthouse.

Kuala Terengganu

☑ 09

A microcosm of Malaysia's economic boom: fishing village finds oil, money flows in, modernity ensues. Kuala Terengganu (KT) is surprisingly attractive: there's a boardwalk, a couple of decent beaches, a few old *kampung*-style houses hidden among the high rises, and one of Eastern Peninsular Malaysia's prettiest and most interesting Chinatowns. With seafood-heavy local cuisine and good transport links, KT is worth a day or two of exploration.

◉ Sights

Chinatown　　　NEIGHBOURHOOD
Centred on Jln Kampung Cina (also known as Jln Bandar), KT's picturesque and interesting Chinatown area features watermarked buildings and faded alleyways. Contemporary and quirky street art is slowly being added to the laneways of this compact neighbourhood, and other attractions include heritage buildings and temples. Pick up the Chinatown Heritage Trail brochure at the tourist information office.

Central Market　　　MARKET
(cnr Jln Kampung Cina & Jln Banggol; adult/child RM1/0.50) The central market is a lively

Kuala Terengganu

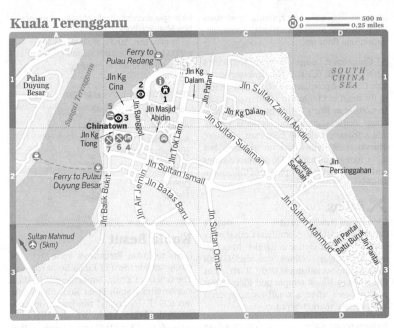

place to graze on exotic snacks, and the floor above the fish section has a wide collection of batik and *kain songket* (traditional hand-woven fabric). Dubbed the Pasar Payang by locals.

Kompleks Muzium Negeri Terengganu   MUSEUM
(Terengganu State Museum; ☑ 09-622 1433; http:// museum.terengganu.gov.my; adult/child RM15/10; ☺ 9am-5pm Sat-Thu, 9am-noon & 3-6pm Fri) Comprised of interconnected buildings on 26 hectares of land, around 6km west of Kuala Terengganu, exhibits range from the historically interesting (a Jawi – traditional Malay text – inscription that essentially dates the arrival of Islam to the nation) to the mildly bizarre (a wildlife exhibit featuring somewhat threadbare taxidermy).

The complex of traditional houses that fronts the grounds is worth the price of admission. English signage is sparse, however. To get here, catch Heritage Bus C-02 from the main bus station. A taxi will cost around RM10.

Bukit Puteri   FORT
(Princess Hill; adult/child RM1/0.50; ☺ 9am-5pm Sat-Thu, to 3pm Fri) Across the road from the central market, look for a steep flight of steps leading up to Bukit Puteri, a 200m-high hill with good views of the city. On top are the scant remains of a mid-19th-century fort, some cannons and a bell.

🛏 Sleeping

Jen's Homestay   APARTMENT $
(☑ 019-957 8368; www.jenhomestay.weebly.com; Jln Kampung Tiong, 8-12 Pangsapuri Kampung Tiong; s/d from RM60/80; ☻✳🖥) Comprising two stylish bedrooms – choose between 'Paris' or 'Pisa' – and a shared lounge, the highlight of this rental apartment is the stunning view across the river and on to the ocean. The entire apartment can be rented, or just by the bedroom. When we

dropped by, the enterprising operators were looking to add additional accommodation one floor up.

KT Chinatown Lodge GUESTHOUSE **$**
(☎09-6221 938, 013-9316 194; lawlorenz@gmail.com; 113 Jln Kampung Cina; r RM90-110; ❋ ☎) Right in the heart of Chinatown – and in proximity to nesting swiftlets – this two-storey guesthouse features simple but spotless rooms, and a friendly welcome from owner Lorenz. The cheapest rooms have no windows, but all include multichannel TV, private en suites and air-con. Retro B&W photos of Chinatown reinforce a heritage ambience.

🍴 Eating

Chinatown Hawker Centre HAWKER **$**
(off Jln Kampung Cina; ⊙7am-11pm) Chinatown's outdoor hawker centre is divided into Chinese and Malay sections, and sizzles with cooking and socialising at night. Turn left at the Ho Ann Kiang temple and follow your nose. There's often a small morning craft and produce market here too.

T Homemade Cafe CHINESE, MALAY **$**
(Jln Kampung Cina; mains from RM5; ⊙10am-5pm) Located right next to Chinatown's Dragon Arch, this place is a cooperative of a few food stalls. You can try Chinese and Malay dishes here, as well as clay pots and homemade juices. Take a seat under the faded Milo-branded bamboo shades and revive yourself before more Chinatown exploration.

ⓘ Information

Jln Sultan Ismail is the commercial hub and home to most banks, which are open 9.15am to 4.30pm, except Friday.
Tourist Information Office (☎09-622 1553; www.tourism.terengganu.gov.my; Jln Sultan Zainal Abidin; ⊙9am-5pm Sat-Thu) Helpful staff and good brochures and maps.

ⓘ Getting There & Away

AIR
Sultan Mahmud Airport (☎09-667 3666; www.malaysiaairports.com.my; Jln Lapangan Terbang), 15km north from KT, has flights to KL.

BUS & TAXI
At the time of writing, the bus station on Jln Masjid Abidin was the terminus for both local buses and long-distance express buses. A new express bus station near Shahbandar Jetty may

be in operation, so check your departure location when you book.

The main taxi stand is at Jln Masjid Abidin across from the main bus station.

Buses from Kuala Terengganu:

DESTINATION	FARE (RM)	DURATION (HR)
Johor Bahru	48	8
Kota Bahru	17	3
Kuala Besut (Perhentian Islands)	13	2
Kuala Lumpur	43	8
Kuantan	20	6
Melaka	48	8

Kuala Besut

Boats to Pulau Perhentian leave from the lovely seaside town of Kuala Besut (bee-su). The bus from Kuala Terengganu is RM13, a taxi around RM80. From Kota Bharu take bus 639 (RM6, around two hours) or a taxi (around RM45). There are also two daily buses from KL (RM50, nine hours). Many travel agents run minibus services to Kuala Besut from other tourist hot spots around Malaysia.

Pulau Perhentian

☑ 09

Not only one of Malaysia's most popular backpacker spots, the Perhentians are one of the cheapest places on the planet to get your Open Water Diver (OWD) certification – and the diving is spectacular. The traffic-free pair of islands – Kecil ('Small'), popular with the younger backpacker crowd, and Besar ('Large'), with higher standards of accommodation and a more relaxed ambience – both offer near-perfect crescents of white sand, jungle backdrops, a hypnotically fun vibe and turquoise water. It's all utterly sublime.

While you can usually find a beach party, the Perhentians are a long way from having a Thai-style party atmosphere. Alcohol is available at a few restaurants and bars.

The best time to visit is from March to mid-November. The Perhentians close for the monsoon season – some places don't bother opening till April or later – although some hotels remain open for hardier tourists. Some diving outfits stay open year-round but in the low season there's often poor visibility and the sea is rough.

🏃 Activities

With relatively shallow, calm waters and great visibility, the Perhentians are the ideal place to snorkel or learn to dive. Competition between the many dive shops keeps prices for a four-day OWD course at between RM800 to RM1100. For the surface skimmers, guesthouses can arrange snorkelling trips for around RM40.

There's plenty of hiking on both islands. On Kecil, the jungle track between Long Beach and Coral Bay is an easy, signposted 15-minute walk (around 1km) through scrubby forest. On Besar try the hilly track (around one hour, 2.5km) cutting from north to south from close to Perhentian Island Resort to Teluk Dalam.

🛏 Sleeping & Eating

On Kecil, Long Beach has the biggest range of budget chalets and 'nightlife'. In the high season (usually from late May to early September), finding accommodation here can be tough, so book ahead or arrive early. Accommodation on Besar usually includes aircon and a private bathroom.

🛏 Pulau Kecil: Long Beach

The surf can get big on Long Beach and several places along the beach rent boogie boards and old clunky surfboards. Take care when swimming here as there have been several drownings.

Lemon Grass　　BUNGALOW $

(✆ 019-981 8393; bungalow from RM50) At the southern tip of Long Beach, Lemon Grass has friendly management and 16 no-frills fan huts with shared bathrooms. There are great views from the verandah at reception and nice secluded spots to sit and gaze out to sea. All huts are the same price; try to get one with a sea view.

🛏 Pulau Kecil: Coral Bay

More rocky than sandy, Coral Bay faces the west for brilliant sunsets and calm swimming. Seafood barbecue on the beach offers a nightly feast and many people head over here from Long Beach for better deals on meals.

RainForest Camping　　CAMPGROUND $

(www.facebook.com/rainforestcamping.perhentian island.malaysia; Sandy Coral Bay; camping RM20)

Simple tents equipped with compact bamboo decks sit in a sylvan rainforest glade. Shared toilets and bathrooms are rudimentary, but the real attractions here are the perfect arc of the private beach and the chilled vibe in the attached cafe. The semi-bright lights of Coral Bay are an easy 15-minute walk away north along the coast.

Ewan's Place　　BUNGALOW $

(✆ 014-817 8303; d RM80) Cookie-cutter prefab huts on the path leading from Coral Bay to Long Beach. Rooms inside are clean and colourful, with comfortable double beds, mosquito netting and cold-water showers. The attached cafe serves the usual variety of Asian and international cuisine.

🛏 Pulau Kecil: Petani Beach & Teluk Kerama

★ D'Lagoon Chalets　　BUNGALOW $

(✆ 019-985 7089; www.dlagoon.my; Teluk Kerma; camp site RM15, dm RM25, r RM70-210) Teluk Kerma is a pretty, isolated bay with fine coral and a wonderfully tranquil location. Accommodation ranges from a longhouse with dorm beds to simple stilt bungalows and a honeymoon treehouse. Activities include snorkelling, shark- and turtle-watching trips, and jungle hikes to remote beaches. Management will also arrange local music at night on request.

Mari Mari Beach Bar & Resort　　BUNGALOW $

(✆ 017-998 5462; Petani Beach; r RM50-150) Look no further if you're after a more remote Perhentians stay. Mari Mari is constructed solely of recycled and salvaged material, and there's a real Robinson Crusoe vibe to the simple beach huts with shared bathrooms and the more private treehouses with rustic en suites. The attached beach bar and restaurant is also the real deal in laid-back island life.

🛏 Pulau Besar: Main Beach

Besar has a busy main beach facing Pulau Kecil that offers skinny but shady stretches of white sand.

Reef Chalets　　BUNGALOW $$

(✆ 09-690 3669; www.facebook.com/The.Reef. Chalets; bungalow RM120-350; ❄🛜) This family-owned resort offers 12 beautiful bungalows set along the beach, and surrounding a beautifully maintained jungle garden featuring trees filled with occasional lemurs, monkeys, birds and bats. The friendly owners rent out canoes and snorkelling equipment and can help you plan your stay. All bungalows have sea views; some are fan-cooled, while the more expensive ones have air-conditioning.

🛏 Pulau Besar: Teluk Dalam

Teluk Dalam (also called Flora Bay), over the hill, is a silken secluded bay with good snorkelling and more peace and quiet.

Samudra Beach Chalet BUNGALOW $

(☑ 09-691 1677; www.samudrabeachchalet.com; Teluk Dalam; r RM60-160; ❄ 🛜) Samudra has traditional Malaysian A-frame bungalows. They are slightly dark on the inside, but cheaper ones have fans. The air-conditioned family room with two double beds is a decent deal.

Mandalica Beach Resort CAMPGROUND $

(☑ 019-983 7690; Teluk Dalam; camping per person RM25, beach hut RM40) The lovely Halim family lives along sandy Teluk Dalam and offers covered camp sites and simple beach huts. Shared bathroom facilities are basic but clean. Pick ups from all over the Perhentians are available and fishing trips can be arranged; aquatic gear is also available for hire. There's a cafe serving juices, evening barbecues and amazing roti – Ida's banana chocolate roti is worth the walk across the island.

❶ Information

There is a RM5 conservation fee for everyone entering the marine park around the Perhentians. This is usually payable at a booth at the jetty in Kuala Besut.

There are no banks or ATMs on the Perhentians so bring plenty of cash. There are no public phones but mobile phones work and most accommodation has wi-fi.

❶ Getting There & Around

Speedboats (RM70 return, 30 to 40 minutes) run several times a day from Kuala Besut to the Perhentians from 8.30am to 5.30pm. The boats will drop you off at any of the beaches. In the other direction, speedboats depart from the islands daily at around 8am, noon and 4pm.

When the waves are high on Long Beach, you'll be dropped off or picked up on the other side of the island at Coral Bay.

The easiest way to beach-hop is by boat (around RM15). From island to island, the trip costs RM20 per boat.

Kota Bharu

☑ 09

Very Islamic but supremely mellow Kota Bharu has the energy of a midsized city, the compact feel and friendly vibe of a small town, superb food and a good spread of accommodation. It's the logical overnight stop between Thailand and the Perhentians, but you'd be wise to give Kota Bharu more time than a pit stop.

◉ Sights

Istana Jahar MUSEUM

(Royal Ceremonies Museum; Jln Istana; adult/child RM3/1.50; ⊙8.30am-4.45pm Sat-Wed, to 3.30pm Thu) Kota Bharu's best museum, both in terms of exhibits and structure. It's housed in a beautiful chocolate-brown building that dates back to 1887, easily one of the most attractive traditional buildings in the city. The interior displays focus on Kelantanese ritual and crafts, from detailed descriptions of batik-weaving to the elaborate ceremonies of coming-of-age circumcision, wedding nights and funerary rights.

Istana Batu MUSEUM

(Royal Museum, Muzium Diraja; Jln Istana; adult/child RM4/2; ⊙8.30am-4.45pm Sat-Wed, to 3.30pm Thu) The pale yellow Istana Batu, constructed in 1939, was the crown prince's palace until donated to the state. The richly furnished rooms give a surprisingly intimate insight into royal life, with family photos and personal belongings scattered among the fine china, chintzy sofas, and the late sultan's collection of hats.

Central Market MARKET

(Pasar Besar Siti Khadijah; Jln Hulu; ⊙6am-6pm) One of the most colourful and active markets in Malaysia, KB's central market is at its busiest first thing in the morning, and has usually packed up by early afternoon. Downstairs is the produce section, while upstairs stalls selling spices, brassware, batik and other goods stay open longer. On the 1st floor, there's a tasty array of food stalls and it's a top spot for breakfast or lunch.

🛏 Sleeping

★ Zeck's Traveller's Inn HOMESTAY $

(☑ 019-946 6655; zecktravelers@gmail.com; 7088-G Jln Sri Cemerlang; dm/s/d from RM12/15/25, r with air-con RM45-70; ❄ @ 🛜) Zeck and Miriam Zaki's home is located in a peaceful nook north of the city centre, with an attractive

Kota Bharu

little garden to lounge about in and light meals and drinks always at hand. This family-owned place is a great way to get a feel for genuine Malaysian *kampung* (village) life in the heart of Kota Bharu.

Room @ Zishi GUESTHOUSE **$**
(☑012-921 8103; theroom.zishi@hotmail.com; 67 Jln Pintu Pong; r/f from RM90/165; ❋ 🛜) Stylish decor features at this well-run guesthouse located opposite Kota Bharu's central market. Rooms are furnished with an Asian Zen simplicity, and the shared downstairs area, complete with a full kitchen, has a cool relaxation space with lots of throw cushions and shag pile carpet. A key-card system guarantees security. Note that cheaper rooms don't have windows.

KB Backpackers Lodge HOSTEL **$**
(☑019-944 5222, 09-748 8841; backpackers lodge2@yahoo.co.uk; 1872-D Jln Padang Garong; dm/r from RM15/35; ❋ @) Owner Pawi is a wealth of information, dorms and rooms are simple but clean, there's a rooftop terrace, and local city tours can be arranged. Pawi is also a mad bicycling enthusiast and organises bike trips (on and off road) and rents out high-quality bicycles to guests. Make sure you've got the right place – a somewhat dingy hostel calling itself KB Backpackers Inn operates across the street.

Kota Bharu

◎ Sights
1 Central Market B1
2 Gelanggang Seni C3
3 Istana Batu B1
4 Istana Jahar B1

🛏 Sleeping
5 KB Backpackers Lodge B2
6 Room @ Zishi B1
7 Zeck's Traveller's Inn C1

⊗ Eating
8 Night Market B1
9 Sri Devi Restaurant C2

ℹ Transport
10 Central Bus Station B2
 Taxi Stand .... (see 10)

✘ Eating

★ Night Market MARKET **$**
(Jln Parit Dalam; mains from RM4; ☺5-9pm) The most popular spot for the best and cheapest Malay food in town is KB's night market, where stalls are set up in the evening. Specialties include *ayam percik* (marinated chicken on bamboo skewers) and *nasi kerabu* (blue rice with coconut, fish and spices), squid-on-a-stick and *murtabak*

(pan-fried flat bread filled with everything from minced meat to bananas). Say '*Suka pedas*' ('I like it hot') to eat as the locals do.

Sri Devi Restaurant
INDIAN **$**

(4213-F Jln Kebun Sultan; mains from RM5; ⊘ 7am-9pm; 🍴) As popular with locals as it is with tourists, this is a great place for an authentic banana-leaf curry and a mango lassi. They also serve a great *ayam percik* (marinated chicken on bamboo skewers), and terrific *roti canai* (flaky flat bread served with curry) in the morning and evening.

ℹ Information

ATMs are scattered around town. Banks are open from 10am to 3pm Saturday to Wednesday and 9.30am to 11.30am Thursday.

Tourist Information Centre (☑ 09-748 5534; www.tic-kelantan.gov.my; Jln Sultan Ibrahim; ⊘ 8am-5pm Sun-Wed, to 3.30pm Thu, to 1.30pm Fri & Sat) Information on homestays, tours and transport.

ℹ Getting There & Away

AIR

Sultan Ismail Petra Airport (☑ 09-773 7400; www.malaysiaairports.com.my; Sultan Ismail Petra Airport Darul Naim) is 10km northeast of the city centre.

BUS

Transnasional express buses operate from the **central bus station** (☑ 09-747 5971, 09-747 4330; Jln Padang Garong). Other express and long-distance buses leave from Lembah Sireh Bus Station near the Kota Bharu Tesco. A taxi

from this bus station to the centre of town is around RM15.

Most regional buses leave from the central bus station including those to Rantau Panjang (bus 29, RM5) and Kuala Besut (bus 639, RM6, around two hours), for the Perhentian Islands.

DESTINATION	FARE (RM)	DURATION (HR)
Alor Setar	43	7
Butterworth	42	7
Ipoh	40	6
Kuala Lumpur	49	8
Kuala Terengganu	19	3
Kuantan	31	6
Melaka	64	10
Singapore	98	12

TAXI

The taxi stand is on the southern side of the central bus station. Avoid the unlicensed cab drivers who will pester you around town, and take an official taxi as these are cheaper and safer.

TRAIN

The nearest railway station is **Wakaf Baharu** (☑ 09-719 6986), reached by local buses 19 or 17. At the time of writing, trains to the south were suspended following severe floods. The service was scheduled to recommence in late 2016. Check with the tourist information centre in Kota Bharu, or see www.ktmb.com.my, the website for Malaysian Railways.

PENINSULAR INTERIOR

A thick band of jungle buffers the two peninsular coasts from one another. Within the middle is Taman Negara, the peninsula's most famous national park, and the Jungle Railway, an engineering feat.

Jerantut
☑ 09

This small town is the gateway to Taman Negara, and most travellers do little more than spend a night here before heading into the jungle. However, the town is pleasant enough to spend an afternoon.

Several banks in town can change cash and travellers cheques (change money before heading into Taman Negara). The ATMs do dry up sometimes so it's best to get money before reaching Jerantut.

MALAYSIA JERANTUT

DON'T MISS

GET CULTURED

If you want to see *gasing uri* (top-spinning), *silat* (a Malay form of martial arts), kite-making, drumming, shadow-puppet shows and the like, the **Gelanggang Seni** (Cultural Centre; ☑ 03-744 3124; Jln Mahmud) **FREE** is the place to go. Check with the tourist information centre, or your hotel's owners, who should have a full timetable of events.

A note on *wayang kulit* (shadow puppetry): performances are interesting, but can be difficult to appreciate without any prior context. You may want to check out http://discover-indo.tierranet.com/wayang for a primer before catching a shadow-puppet show.

GETTING TO THAILAND: KOTA BHARU TO SUNGAI KOLOK

Getting to the border The Thailand border is at Rantau Panjang; bus 29 departs on the hour from Kota Bharu's central bus station (RM4, 1½ hours). Shared taxis from Kota Bharu to Rantau Panjang cost around RM40 per car and take 45 minutes.

There's another border crossing at Pengkalan Kubor, on the coast, but transport links aren't as good and crossing here can be dodgy during periods of sectarian violence in southern Thailand. Inquire at the Tourist Information Centre before using this crossing. During the day a large car ferry (RM1 for pedestrians) crosses the river to busy Tak Bai in Thailand. From Kota Bharu, take bus 27 or 43 (RM2.40) from the central bus station.

At the border From Rantau Panjang you can walk across the border to Sungai Kolok, where you can arrange onward transport to Bangkok.

Moving on Trains to Bangkok depart at 11.30am and 2pm, buses at 8am, 11.30am and 3.30pm, and there are hourly minibuses from Sungai Kolok to Hat Yai.

See p754 for information on making this crossing in the opposite direction.

🛏 Sleeping & Eating

On Jln Pasar Besar there are excellent food stalls, while cheap *kedai kopi* (coffee shops) serving Chinese food and Malay favourites are scattered around town.

Sakura Castle Inn   HOTEL $
(☑ 09-266 5200; http://sakuracastleinn.blogspot. com; 51-52 Jln Bomba; r RM55-75; 🕸🛜) This is the classiest place in town, and has clean, comfortable rooms – all with TV, hot water and air-con. The people who work here are as friendly and helpful as it gets.

ⓘ Getting There & Away

BUS

NKS Hostel (21-22 Jln Besar) arranges minibuses and buses to a variety of destinations, including Tembeling jetty for boats to Taman Negara (RM15), KL (RM40), Kuala Besut (RM90) and the Cameron Highlands (RM80). Buses leave from the hostel's on-site NKS Café. NKS can also help you to arrange your onward river trip to the national park from the jetty in Kuala Tembeling.

If you want to skip the riverboat, its minibuses go directly from Kuala Tahan for Taman Negara (RM15) at 8am and sometimes 1pm. Note many travellers cite the voyage upriver from Kuala Tembeling as a highlight of visiting Taman Negara.

Public buses from the central bus station go to the jetty at Kuala Tembeling (RM2, 45 minutes), for the boat to Taman Negara every hour from 7.45am to 5pm, although schedules are unreliable and don't necessarily coincide with boat departures.

There are also several daily buses to/from KL's Pekeliling bus station (RM55, four hours) and to/ from Kuantan (RM18, 3½ hours).

TAXI

The taxi stand is next to the bus station. Taxi fares are as follows: Kuala Tembeling (RM20), Kampung Kuala Tahan (RM65), Temerloh (RM50), Cherating (RM240), KL (RM200) and Kuantan (RM180). A surcharge of RM30 is enforced after 3pm.

TRAIN

Jerantut train station (☑ 09-266 2219) is on the Tumpat–Gemas railway line (also known as the Jungle Railway) – which, at the time of writing, was closed for repairs. When service resumes, trains should run daily to Singapore (2am, 12.30pm), via Johor Bahru. For KL Sentral, take the 12.30am express. For an up-to-date timetable and list of fares, consult KTM (www.ktmb.com.my).

Taman Negara
☑ 09

Taman Negara blankets 4343 sq km in shadowy, damp, impenetrable jungle. Inside this tangle, trees with gargantuan buttressed root systems dwarf luminescent fungi and orchids. Trudge along muggy trails in search of elusive wildlife (elephants can hide much better than you'd think), balance on the creaky canopy walk or spend the night in a 'hide' where jungle sounds make you feel like you've gone back to the caveman days.

Kuala Tahan is the budget base camp for Taman Negara. Across Sungai Tembeling is the entrance to the national park, the upmarket Mutiara Taman Negara Resort and the park headquarters located at the Wildlife Department.

Most people purchase permits when they buy their bus and/or boat tickets to Kuala Tahan in Jerantut. Otherwise you'll need to get your permits at the **Tourist Information Counter** (north of the river behind Mutiara Resort; park entrance/camera/fishing/canopy/blinds RM1/5/10/5/5; ☺8am-10pm Sun-Thu, 8am-noon & 3-10pm Fri).

🏃 Activities

Hikes & Treks

There are hikes and treks to suit all levels of motivation, from a half-hour jaunt to a steep nine-day tussle up and down Gunung Tahan (2187m).

Canopy Walkway & Around   HIKING

(adult/child RM5/3; ☺10am-3.30pm Sat-Thu, 9am-noon Fri) This is easily the area's most popular hike. It begins east of park headquarters and leads along the Sungai Tembeling to the Canopy Walkway, 30 minutes away. The walkway is suspended between huge trees and the entire circuit takes around 40 minutes. Get here early for the best birding and wildlife watching.

Kuala Trenggan   HIKING

The well-marked main trail along the bank of Sungai Tembeling leads 9km to Kuala Trenggan, a popular trail for those heading to the Bumbun Kumbang hide. Allow five hours. From here, boats go back to **Nusa Holiday Village** (☎09-266 2369; www.taman negara-nusaholiday.com.my; dm RM15, r with fan RM55-90, r with air-con RM110; ❄) and Kam-

pung Kuala Tahan, or it's a further 2km walk to Bumbun Kumbang.

Lata Berkoh   HIKING

North from park headquarters, this day hike leads to Gunung Tahan, but you can do an easy day walk to Lata Berkoh, the cascading rapids on Sungai Tahan. The trail passes the Lubok Simpon swimming hole and Bumbun Tabing, 1¼ hours from Kuala Tahan.

River Bus & Boat Trips

The Mutiara Taman Negara resort has daily boats that go upriver to Kuala Trenggan at 10am and 2.30pm. In the reverse direction, boats leave Kuala Trenggan at 11.15am and 3.15pm. These services are intended for guests only, but the following trips into the park are open to the public.

DESTINATION	PRICE (RM)	FREQUENCY (PER DAY)
Bunbun Yong	5	3
Canopy Walkway	15	2
Gua Telinga	15	4
Kuala Tembeling	301	1

Tours

Trekking

You really don't need a guide or tour for day trips – or even overnight trips – to the hides if you're prepared to organise your own gear, food and water. You'll need one for longer treks, however, and the going rate is RM180 per day (one guide can lead up to 12 people), plus a RM100 fee for each night spent out on the trail. Guides who are licensed by

HIDES & SALT LICKS

Animal-observation hides (*bumbun*) are built overlooking salt licks and grassy clearings, which attract feeding nocturnal animals. You'll need to spend the night in order to see any real action but staying in the heart of the jungle is what the Taman Negara experience is all about. There are several hides close to Kuala Tahan and Kuala Trenggan that are too close to human habitation to attract the shy animals, but even if you don't see any wildlife, the jungle sounds are well worth it – the 'symphony' is best at dusk and dawn.

Hides (per person per night RM5) need to be reserved at the Tourist Information Counter; they are very rustic with pit toilets. Some travellers hike independently in the day to the hides, then camp overnight and return the next day, while others go to more far-flung hides that require some form of transport and a guide. For overnight trips you'll need food, water and a sleeping bag. Rats on the hunt for tucker are problematic, so hang food high out of reach.

Popular hides include Bumbun Blau and Bumbun Yong on Sungai Yong, 3.1km from park headquarters; Bumbun Kumbang, roughly five hours' walk from headquarters or a 45-minute walk from Kuala Trenggan; and Tabing Hide, about 1½ hours' walk (3.1km) from park headquarters, or accessible by boat (it's near the river).

the Wildlife Department have completed coursework in forest flora, fauna and safety and are registered with the department. Often the Kuala Tahan tour operators offer cheaper prices than the Wildlife Department, although there is no guarantee that the guide is licensed.

Wildlife & Rapids

Everyone in Kuala Tahan wants to take you on a wildlife or boat tour (from RM40) where you motor down the rapids. There are popular night tours (from RM25) on foot or by 4WD. You're more likely to see animals (such as slow loris, snakes, civets and flying squirrels) on the drives, which go through oil palm plantations outside the park, but even these don't guarantee sightings.

Orang Asli

Many travellers sign up for tours to an Orang Asli settlement (RM45 to RM80), where you'll be shown how to use a long blowpipe and start a fire. While local guides insist that these tours provide essential income for the Orang Asli, most of your tour money will go to the tour company. A small handicraft purchase in the village will help spread the wealth.

🛏 Sleeping & Eating

Kampung Kuala Tahan is where most of Taman Negara's lodging, restaurants and shops are found. There are a handful of secluded places just 10 minutes' walk south and north of Kampung Kuala Tahan that are

worth checking out if you are looking for a little more tranquility.

Arrive early in the day or book in advance since the better places fill up quickly and there's invariably a nightly collection of lost souls searching for rooms in the rain.

Kuala Tahan is no culinary centre. Floating barge restaurants line the rocky shore, all selling the same ol' cheap basic noodle and rice meals plus bland Western fare. The village is also dry.

Mahseer Chalet BUNGALOW $
(☑019-383 2633; mahseerchalet@gmail.com; dm with fan/air-con RM15/20, r RM70-100; 🌬🛜) The best part of this clutch of jungle bungalows is its location just by the river. The rooms and bungalows have spankin' new sheets; the hostel rooms are hot and buggy (yes, the extra RM5 for air-con is well worth it). Cats patrol the grounds and there's a cool vibe that's wide-grinning friendly.

Tembeling Riverview Lodge LODGE $
(☑09-266 6766; www.trvtamannegara.blogspot.com; dm/d/tr RM10/50/60) Straddling the thoroughfare footpath, this place has fan-cooled rooms with cold showers and mosquito netting and pleasant communal areas overlooking the river. Staff are friendly, and there's a lovely restaurant serving *roti john* (a Malaysian sandwich made with local bread, meat, cheese and vegetables; RM6).

Teresek View Motel MOTEL $
(☑09-266 9744; teresekviewmotel@gmail.com; r with fan/air-con RM70/90; 🌬🛜) You can't miss this eyesore of a cement building in

the 'centre' of Kuala Tahan. The rooms have leather headboards and playful cartoon-sheep sheets, and are spic 'n' span with clean pink tiles throughout. Ask for one of the few rooms with a view; number 19 is our favourite.

❶ Information

There are no banks in Taman Negara.

❶ Getting There & Away

Most people reach Taman Negara by taking a bus from Jerantut to the jetty at Kuala Tembeling then a river boat from there to the park, but there are also popular private minibus services that go directly to/from Jerantut and several tourist destinations around Malaysia directly to/from Kampung Kuala Tahan.

BOAT

The river jetty for Taman Negara–bound boats is in Kuala Tembeling, 18km north of Jerantut.

Boats (one way RM35) depart Kuala Tembeling daily at 9am and 2pm (9am and 2.30pm on Friday). On the return journey, boats leave Kuala Tahan at 9am and 2pm (and 2.30pm on Friday). The journey takes three hours upstream and two hours downstream. Note that the boat service is irregular during the November-to-February wet season.

BUS & TAXI

There are buses and taxis from Jerantut to Kuala Tembeling. Han Travel (www.taman-negara.com), **NKS** (☑03-2072 0336; www.tamannegara.nks.com) and **Banana Travel & Tours** (☑04-261 2171; www.bananapenang.com; Information Centre, Kampung Kuala Tahan) run several useful private services, including daily buses to KL (RM35), a bus/boat combination (RM70) and minibuses to Penang (RM120), the Perhentian Islands (RM165 including boat) and the Cameron Highlands (RM95). These minibuses can also drop you off en route anywhere in between.

❶ Getting Around

There is a frequent cross-river ferry (RM1) that shuttles passengers across the river from Kuala Tahan to the park entrance and Mutiara Taman Negara Resort.

MALAYSIAN BORNEO – SABAH

Most visitors come to Sabah to experience nature in all its riotous glory: the spectacular reefs of Sipadan; climbers' paradise Mt Kinabalu, reaching 4095m into the clouds;

the jungle-clad banks of Sungai Kinabatangan teeming with monkeys, hornbills and other exotic creatures; and Sepilok, one of the only places in the world where you can see semi-wild ginger orangutans in their native habitat. And while Sabah's cities are not as pretty as their Sarawakian counterparts, cosmopolitan Kota Kinabalu (known as KK) will soon win you over.

Kota Kinabalu

☑088 / POP 457,000

Kota Kinabalu won't immediately overwhelm you with its beauty, but the centre is compact and walkable, there's a colourful waterfront packed with atmospheric markets, and you'll find some damn fine food. Few travellers come to Sabah for the urban scene, but if you need to book permits, hang out and recover from Mt Kinabalu or connect to onward travel, KK is a good (and sometimes the only) place to do it.

⊙ Sights

Sabah Museum   MUSEUM
(Kompleks Muzium Sabah; ☑088-253 199; www.museum.sabah.gov.my; Jln Muzium; admission RM15; ⊙9am-5pm Sat-Thu; ℗) About 2km south of the city centre, this refurbished museum is the best place to go in KK for an introduction to Sabah's ethnicities and environments, with new signage and clear explanations. Expect tribal and historical artefacts including ceramics and a centrepiece whale skeleton, and replica limestone cave. The Heritage Village has traditional tribal dwellings, including Kadazan bamboo houses and a Chinese farmhouse, all nicely set on a lily-pad lake.

Sunday Market   MARKET
(Jln Gaya; ⊙6am to about noon Sun) On Sunday, a lively Chinese street fair takes over the entire length of Jln Gaya. It's vividly chaotic, with stalls cheek-by-jowl hawking batik sarongs, umbrellas, fruit and antiques.

**Kota Kinabalu
Wetland Centre**   BIRD SANCTUARY
(☑088-246 955; www.sabahwetlands.org; Jln Bukit Bendera Upper, Likas District; admission RM15; ⊙8.30am-6pm Tue-Sun; ℗) Featuring 1.4km of wooden walkways passing through a 24-hectare mangrove swamp, expect to see scuttling fiddler and mangrove crabs, mud lobsters, mudskippers, skinks, turtles, water monitors and mangrove slugs (sadly, there

are also plastic bottles.). For many, the big attraction is a stunning variety of migratory birds. To get here, take the bus towards Likas from the bus stations in front of City Hall or Wawasan Plaza in the city, to Likas Sq. A taxi from KK costs around RM15.

**Tunku Abdul Rahman
National Park** PARK

(adult/child RM10/6) Just west of Kota Kinabalu, the five islands of Manukan, Gaya, Sapi, Mamutik and Sulug and the reefs in between make up the Tunku Abdul Rahman National Park, covering a total area of just over 49 sq km. Only a short boat ride from the Kota Kinabalu city centre, they have some nice beaches and the water in the outer areas is usually clear, offering ideal day-trip material for anyone wanting to escape the city and unwind.

Atkinson Clock Tower LANDMARK

The modest timepiece at the foot of Signal hill is one of the only structures to survive the Allied bombing of Jesselton in 1945. It's a square, 15.7m-high wooden structure that was completed in 1905 and named after the first district officer of the town, FG Atkinson, who died of malaria aged 28.

Tours

KK has a huge number of tour companies, enough to suit every taste and budget. Head to Wisma Sabah – this office building on Jln Haji Saman is full of agents and operators.

Sticky Rice Travel ADVENTURE TOUR

(☑088-251 654; www.stickyricetravel.com; 3rd fl, 58 Jln Pantai; ⊙9am-6pm) ✈ National Geographic prefers this outfit for a reason; they're organised, original in their choice of tours and have excellent knowledgeable guides. Responsible community-based tourism; expect adventure, culture and something very different. Sticky Rice will sit down with you and tailor your experience around your interests, fitness and budget; your trip may last four days or a few weeks.

**Adventure
Alternative Borneo** ADVENTURE TOUR

(☑019-802 0549; www.aaborneo.com; 1st fl, 97 Jln Gaya; ⊙9am-6pm) ✈ Sustainable and ethical travel are key to this British-owned company, which works closely with Sabah Tourist Board, and run tours to Lupa Masa rainforest camp, close to Mt Kinabalu. If you're looking for remote natural immersion, they also operate trips to Orou Sapulot.

Borneo Divers DIVING

(☑088-222 226; www.borneodivers.net; 9th fl, Menara Jubili, 53 Jln Gaya) The original and still one of the best dive outfits thanks to their high safety standards, quality equipment, excellent PADI teachers and divemasters. The office is located in Kota Kinabalu, plus a lovely resort on Mabul. Recommended.

Sleeping

Check out the Sabah Backpacker Operators Association (www.sabahbackpackers.com), which was set up in an effort to help shoestring travellers in the region.

★**Pod's Backpackers** HOSTEL **$**

(☑088-287 113; admin-kk@podsbackpacker.com; 1st fl, Api-Api Centre, Jln Centre Point; dm/s/d RM35/60/80; ✴☎) Everyone's rightly talking about Pod's. This uber-friendly hostel is clean, helps you with onward travel and organising trips, and has six fresh avocado-green rooms with a zen-like simplicity (three doubles, three dorms), free wi-fi and free safety lockers. But most of all, we love the easy vibe they've created here; they want you to feel like you're at home.

★**Borneo Backpackers** HOSTEL **$**

(☑088-234 009; www.borneobackpackers.com; 24 Lg Dewan; dm/s/d incl breakfast from RM37/60/80; ✴☎) Turquoise and chic with Hoi An lanterns, choice art, wood floors, and an excellent cafe down below firing up Asian fusion cuisine, this is one of KK's best backpacker haunts. Dorms and rooms are immaculate with art-stencilled walls, a balcony and reading room to chill in, and constantly whirring fans. Better still, it's Sticky Rice Travel's HQ.

> **SPLURGE**
>
> If after climbing Mt Kinabalu you feel you deserve some four-star indulgence, look no further than the ultra-stylish **Grandis Hotel** (☑088-522 888; www.hotelgrandis.com; Suria Sabah Shopping Mall 1, Jln Tun Fuad Stephens; r from RM370-500; ✴✴@☎✴✴). The huge, modern rooms have soaring views of the waterfront, while the hotel's rooftop pool and bar is the perfect place to relax.

Borneo Gaya Lodge
HOSTEL **$**

(☏088-242 477; www.borneogayalodge.com; 1st fl, 78 Jln Gaya; dm incl breakfast from RM25, d/q with bathroom RM85/119; ✳@❧) This friendly hostel pipes air-con through its entirety – phew! With a cosy communal lounge, the place is quiet and clean, while the friendly staff are happy to help you book tours and give you general advice.

Lucy's Homestay
HOSTEL **$**

(Backpacker's Lodge; ☏088-261 495; http://borneohostel.wix.com/lucyshomestay; lot 25, Lg Dewan, Australia Pl; dm/s/d incl breakfast RM28/58/68; ❧) Lucy's welcomes with brightly muralled walls, a book exchange (lots of travel tomes) and a plant-filled balcony to flop on. There's a house-proud kitchen and basic wood floor, fan-only rooms and dorms, all with shared bathroom. It's calm, quiet and without a hint of laddish noise. Check out the 100-year-old banyan tree towering above you out the back.

Seasons Street Lodge
HOSTEL **$**

(☏088-253 867; seasonsstreet123@gmail.com; 123 Jln Gaya; dm/s/d/f incl breakfast RM40/50/75/130; ✳@❧) This popular new digs has a busy, happening vibe and thumping soundtrack in reception. There's a TV room, plenty of places

Malaysian Borneo

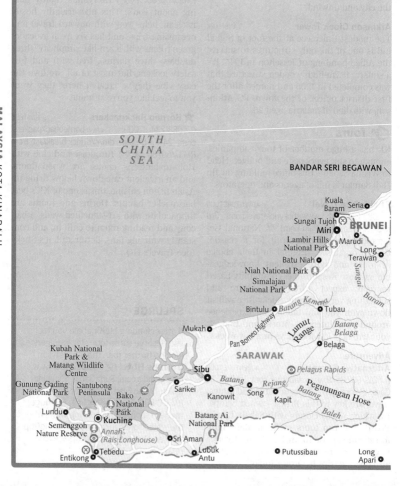

SOUTH CHINA SEA

BANDAR SERI BEGAWAN

Kuala Baram
Seria
Sungai Tujoh
Miri
BRUNEI
Lambir Hills National Park
Marudi
Long Terawan
Batu Niah
Niah National Park
Simalajau National Park
Bintulu
Batang Kemena
Tubau
Baram
Mukah
Pan Borneo Highway
Lumut Range
Batang Belaga
Belaga
Kubah National Park & Matang Wildlife Centre
SARAWAK
Pelagus Rapids
Gunung Gading National Park
Santubong Peninsula
Bako National Park
Sibu
Batang
Rejang
Sarikei
Kanowit
Song
Kapit
Batang
Pegunungan Hose
Lundu
Kuching
Baleh
Semenggoh Nature Reserve
Annah Rais Longhouse
Batang Ai National Park
Entikong
Tebedu
Sri Aman
Lubuk Antu
Putussibau
Long Apari

to sit in the breezy lobby, fresh basic dorms and rooms with stencilled artwork, colourful walls, free lockers, and clean bathrooms.

Hotel Sixty3 $\quad$ HOTEL $$

(☎088-212 663; www.hotelsixty3.com; Jln Gaya 63; r/f from RM276/452; ❄@☎) This fabulous hotel has an international feel in its 100 rooms, with glossy floors, evocative black-and-white photos on the walls, dark-wood fittings, subtle down-lighting, olive colour schemes, flatscreen TVs and safety deposit boxes. Stylish.

Hotel Eden 54 $\quad$ BOUTIQUE HOTEL $$

(☎088-266 054; www.eden54.com; 54 Jln Gaya; d/f RM139/239; ❄☎) In the shadow of Signal Hill, this dinky hotel boasts plenty of boutique flair with stylish rooms decked in chocolate drapes, glass-topped desks, contemporary bedsteads and burgundy or peacock-green walls. Eden is fragrant, like walking into a perfume factory, and there's a communal kitchen area behind the lounge. A fine choice for flashpackers, couples, even families. Avoid the windowless rooms.

Kota Kinabalu

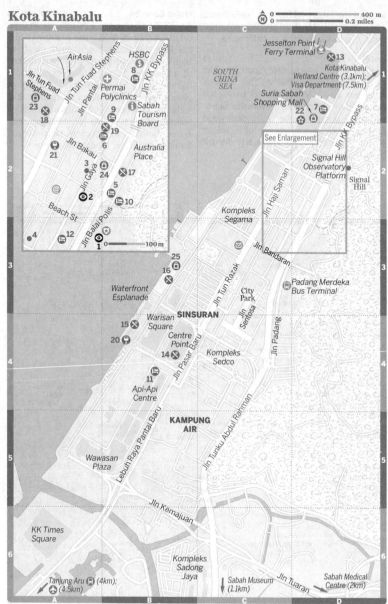

🍴 Eating

KK has an eating scene diverse enough to refresh the noodle-jaded palate. Besides the ubiquitous Chinese *kedai kopi* (coffee shops) and Malay halal restaurants, you'll find plenty of interesting options around the city centre.

Local specialities include *sayur manis* (a jungle fern) and *hinava* (raw fish pickled with fresh lime juice, chilli, sliced shallots and grated ginger).

Kota Kinabalu

★ Print Cafe
CAFE $
(☏ 013-880 2486; 12 Lg Dewan; mains RM12; ☺ 8.30am-10.30pm) In the backpacker street of Lg Dewan, this brilliant cafe is a cool (in both senses of the word) place to catch your breath, read a book or play Jenga at one of its tables. Excellent coffee, papaya and orange shakes, a selection of cakes and waffles, pizza and lovely service. Keep an eye out for ingeniously foamed cappuccinos.

Night Market
HAWKER $
(Jln Tun Fuad Stephens; fish/prawn per 100g from RM4/15, satay RM1; ☺ 5-11pm) The night market is the best, cheapest and most interesting place in KK for barbecued squid, ray and a vast selection of delicious seafood cooked up right before your eyes. Vegetarian options available.

Centre Point Food Court
FOOD COURT $
(basement, Centre Point Shopping Mall, Jln Raya Pantai Baru; mains from RM3; ☺ 9am-9.30pm; ☏) Your ringgit will go a long way at this popular and varied basement food-court in the Centre Point shopping mall. There are Malay, Chinese and Indian options, as well as drink and dessert specialists.

Biru Biru
FUSION $
(24 Lg Dewan; mains RM9-13; ☺ 9am-late) Based at Borneo Backpackers, this blue joint is Asian fusion galore, with dishes like fish cooked in lime and ginger, huge tacos, and an ever evolving menu. Try the Lihing rice wine (aka, rocket fuel). With its parasols and

bikes on the wall, and lovely manager Jules, it's easy to fall in love with this place.

Ya Kee Bah Kut Teh
CHINESE $
(☏ 088-221 192; 74 Jln Gaya; mains from RM8; ☺ 4-11pm) Expect brisk service at this rammed plastic-chair joint spilling noisily onto the pavement in the centre of old town. The buffet counter bubbles with noodles and glistens with sauce-laden pork. That's right, Cantonese-style pork, in herbal soup, fatty pork ribs... Every which way you can. It's hot, crowded and delicious.

Wisma Merdeka Food Court
FOOD COURT $
(Wisma Merdeka, Jln Haji Saman; mains from RM5; ☺ 9am-5pm) For cheap, excellent eats, head to the top floor of the Wisma Merdeka mall and get stuck into stalls serving mainly Asian street food; the Chinese dumpling stand is particularly delicious. In general this is a breakfast and lunch food court.

★ Alu-Alu Cafe
SEAFOOD $$
(Jessleton Point; mains from RM15-30; ☺ 10.30am-2.30pm & 6.30-10pm; ☺) ⌘ Drab on the outside, perhaps, but this restaurant wears its stripes in the tastiness of its food, and the fact it gets its seafood from sustainable sources – no shark-fin soup here. Alu-Alu excels in taking the Chinese seafood concept to new levels, with dishes such as lightly breaded fish chunks doused in a mouth-watering buttermilk sauce, or simmered amid diced chillies.

MALAYSIA KOTA KINABALU

SPLURGE

Located on a hidden beach near Kota Belud (a two-hour bus trip from KK), **Mañana** (☏ 014-679 3679, 014-679 2679; www.manana-borneo.com; chalet/villa/family villa from RM120/180/350) has cabanas with soulful views over an aquamarine bay. You can do yoga, paddle-board, surf or just relax and enjoy the vibe. To get here you'll need to catch a boat from Kampung Pituru Laut. Book ahead!

Kohinoor   INDIAN $$
(☏ 088-235 160; lot 4, Waterfront Esplanade; mains RM17-30; ☺ 11.30am-2.30pm & 5.30-11pm; ☏) Come to this silk-festooned waterfront restaurant, for northern Indian cuisine and classic dishes ranging from chicken tikka masala to prawn biryani and lamb rogan josh. The aromas from its tandoori oven are mouthwatering, the naan bread pillowy-soft, and the service pure old-world charm. You'll be back more than once.

🍸 Drinking & Nightlife

In the early evening, head to Tanjung Aru at the southern end of town near the airport for sunset cocktails and light snacks along the ocean – to get here, take bus 16, 16A or city bus 2 (RM 2) from Wawasan Plaza.

★ El Centro   BAR
(32 Jln Haji Saman; ☺ 5pm-midnight Tue-Sun) El Centro is understandably popular with local expats and travellers alike; it's friendly, the food is good and it makes for a nice spot to meet other travellers. Cool tunes, non-smoky, and a laid-back vibe. El Centro also hosts impromptu quiz nights, costume parties and live-music shows.

Bed   CLUB
(☏ 088-251 901; Waterfront Esplanade; admission Fri & Sat incl drink RM20, beer from RM21; ☺ 8pm-2am, until 3am Fri & Sat) KK's largest club thunders with pop, gyrating Filipino musicians, shrill teenagers and boasts guest DJs nightly. It's overcrowded and cheesy, but if you're looking for a party, this is it. Bands play from 9pm.

☆ Entertainment

Suria Sabah   CINEMA
(Suria Sabah Mall, Jln Haji Saman) The Suria Sabah mall houses a huge multiplex that shows all the Hollywood hits, usually in the original English with subtitles.

Shopping

Cracko Art Gallery   ARTS
(www.facebook.com/crackoart; cnr Jln Bakau & Jln Gaya; ☺ noon-8pm) Made up of a group of brilliantly talented KK artists, high up on the 3rd floor (look for the Cracko sign outside on the street), you'll find a vivid working studio of abstract and figurative art, stunning jewellery, and sculpture from Manga-style figurines to mannequin art. Affordable and original work, a visit here makes for a great hour.

Handicraft Market   MARKET
(Filipino Market; Jln Tun Fuad Stephens; ☺ 8am-9pm) The Handicraft Market is a good place to shop for inexpensive souvenirs. Offerings include pearls, textiles, seashell crafts, jewellery and bamboo goods, some from the Philippines, some from Malaysia and some from other parts of Asia. Needless to say, bargaining is a must!

Borneo Shop   BOOKS
(☏ 088-241 050; shop 26, ground fl, Wisma Merdeka Phase 2, Jln Haji Saman; ☺ 10am-8pm Mon-Sun) Books, gifts, prints and postcards. There's a wealth of wildlife and flora books all focused on Borneo.

ℹ Information

EMERGENCY
Ambulance (☏ 088-218 166, 999)
Fire (☏ 994)
Police (☏ 088-253 555, 999; Jln Dewan, near Australia Pl)

INTERNET ACCESS
The majority of accommodation options have some form of wi-fi internet connection.
Net Access (lot 44, Jln Pantai; per hour RM5; ☺ 9am-midnight) Plenty of connections and less noise than other net places in KK. LAN connections are available for using your own laptop.

MEDICAL SERVICES
Permai Polyclinics (☏ 088-232 100; www.permaipolyclinics.com; 4 Jln Pantai; consultation weekday RM60, Sat & Sun RM80; ☺ doctors on duty 8am-6pm, emergency 24hr) Excellent private outpatient clinic.
Sabah Medical Centre (☏ 088-211 333; www.sabahmedicalcentre.com; Lg Bersatu, off Jln Damai) Good private hospital care, located about 6km southeast of the city centre.

MONEY

Central KK is chock-a-block with 24-hour ATMs.
HSBC (📞088-212 622; 56 Jln Gaya; ⏰9am-4.30pm Mon-Thu, to 4pm Fri)

POST

Main Post Office (Jln Tun Razak; ⏰8am-5pm Mon-Sat) Western Union cheques and money orders can be cashed here.

TOURIST INFORMATION

Immigration office (📞088-488 700; Kompleks Persekutuan Pentadbiran Kerajaan, Jln UMS; ⏰7am-1pm & 2-5.30pm Mon-Fri) In an office complex near the Universiti Malaysia Sabah (UMS), 9km north of town. Open on weekends, but only for Malaysian passport processing.

Sabah Tourism Board (📞088-212 121; www.sabahtourism.com; 51 Jln Gaya; ⏰8am-5pm Mon-Fri, 9am-4pm Sat, Sun & holidays) Housed in the historic post office building, KK's well-organised tourist office has plenty of brochures, maps and knowledgeable staff keen to help you with advice tailored around your needs – they won't just try to sell you a package tour! Its website, packed with helpful information from accommodation to sights, is equally worth a visit.

ⓘ Getting There & Away

AIR

AirAsia (www.airasia.com; ground fl, Wisma Sabah, Jln Haji Saman; ⏰8.30am-5.30pm Mon-Fri, to 3pm Sat) has nonstop flights to Singapore, Jakarta, Bali, Manila, Hong Kong, Taipei and China. Within Malaysia, it flies to Sandakan and Tawau (Sabah); Miri and Kuching (Sarawak); and KL, Penang and Kota Bharu (Peninsular Malaysia).

Destinations served by direct **Malaysia Airlines** (📞1300 883 000; www.malaysiaairlines.com) flights include Kuching, KL, Taipei, Shanghai and Tokyo.

MASwings (www.maswings.com.my) serves Bornean destinations such as Bandar Seri Begawan (Brunei), Sandakan, Tawau and Labuan; and, in Sarawak, Miri, Sibu, Kuching and Mulu National Park.

Other airlines have direct flights to Hong Kong and cities in China, Korea, Indonesia and the Philippines.

BOAT

Passenger ferries connect **Jesselton Point Ferry Terminal** (Jln Haji Saman, 500m northeast of Wisma Sabah) with Pulau Labuan (economy/business RM36/41, 3¼ hours, departures at 8am and 1.30pm), with onward services to Brunei.

Speedboats (RM30 return) link Jesselton Point with the five islands of **Tunku Abdul Rahman National Park** (p433). Most people head out in the morning (the first departures are at 8.30am or 9am); the last boats back leave the park about 5pm.

BUS & MINIVAN

KK has several terminals for inter-city travel. In general, land transport heading east departs from **Inanam** (Utara Terminal; 9km north of the city), while those heading north and south on the west coast leave from **Padang Merdeka (Merdeka Field) Bus Station** (also called Wawasan or 'old bus station') at the southern end of town.Reservations for many destinations can be made by phoning the bus company (your guesthouse can help) or online at www.busonlineticket.com. Same-day bookings are usually fine, although weekends can be busy and holidays even busier.

ⓘ Getting Around

TO/FROM THE AIPORT

The airport is 7km southwest of the city centre. Taxis to the city operate on a voucher system (RM30). Taxis heading from the city centre to the airport cost no more than RM40.

BUSES FROM KOTA KINABALU

DESTINATION	TERMINAL	FARE (RM)	DURATION (HR)
Bandar Seri Begawan (Brunei)	Jln Tugu	100	8
Kinabalu National Park	Inanam	30	2
Kinabalu National Park	Padang Merdeka	minibus 25, shared taxi 50	2
Miri (Sarawak)	Jln Tugu	90	12
Sandakan/Sepilok	Inanam	45	6
Semporna	Inanam	75	8-9
Tawau	Inanam	80	9

Airport shuttle buses (adult/child RM5/3) leave Padang Merdeka station hourly between 7.30am to 8.15pm daily, arriving first at Terminal 2 then Terminal 1.

BUS & MINIBUS
Minibuses serving destinations in greater KK use Padang Merdeka (also known as Terminal Wawasan). The vehicles, which run from about 7am to 9pm and depart when full, are colour-coded and have destinations painted on the side.

Local buses (RM1.80) from Wawasan can take tourists to Inanam if you don't want to splurge on the RM20 taxi.

TAXI
Expect to pay a minimum of RM15 for a ride in the city centre. Taxis can be found throughout the city and at all bus stations and shopping centres.

Mt Kinabalu & Kinabalu National Park

Climbing the great Mt Kinabalu (4095m) – the highest peak between the Himalayas and New Guinea and a Unesco World Heritage Site – is a heart-pounding adventure that will take you through gorgeous rainforest habitats to breath-taking panoramas.

After checking in at park headquarters (elevation 1563m) around 9am, hikers ride or walk the 4.5km to the Timpohon Gate trailhead (elevation 1866m) and then ascend for four to seven hours to Laban Rata (3270m), where they spend the night. Climbers usually hit the trail again at about 2.30am in order to reach the summit (one to two hours) in time for sunrise. This is the only time of day when the view from the summit is reliably clear. Note that certain parts of the trail are impassable in heavy rain.

The ascent of Kinabalu is unrelenting as almost every step you take will be uphill – or downhill. You'll have to negotiate a variety of obstacles along the way, including slippery rocks, blinding fog and frigid winds.

◉ Sights & Activities

Climbing Mt Kinabalu
Only a limited number of beds are available at Laban Rata (elevation 3272m), predawn launch point for the summit. As a result, the only way to get to the top is to book a package (it is no longer possible to do a one-day hike to the summit). If you're shooting for a specific date, especially one that falls in July or August or around Christmas, it's *highly*

recommended that you make reservations two or more months ahead.

Almost any tour operator in Sabah – including those with offices in the downtown KK office building known as Wisma Sabah – can organise a trip to the mountain. Solo travellers are usually charged around RM1400, but it's cheaper to book directly through Sutera Sanctuary Lodges, the private company that has a monopoly on accommodation within the national park. If you don't have your reservations squared away before arriving in KK, drop by its office to check last-minute options. The more lead time you allow and the more flexible your travel itinerary, the better the chance that a window will open up.

If you book through Sutera, additional fees have to be paid (cash only) at the Sabah Parks Visitor Centre:

➡ **Park entry fee** (adult/child RM15/10 per day)

➡ **Climbing permit** (RM230)

➡ **Guide fee** (RM230 for one to five people)

➡ **Insurance** (RM7)

All this does not include at least RM669 for dorm and board and RM1349 for private room and board on the mountain at Laban Rata. With said lodging, plus buses or taxis to the park, you're looking at spending around RM900 for the common two day, one-night trip to the mountain.

You can try your luck and just show up at the park to see if there's a last-minute cancellation – spaces at Laban Rata do open up. Do not attempt an 'unofficial' climb – permits are scrupulously checked at three points along the trail.

No special equipment is required to summit Mt Kinabalu. However, a headlamp is strongly advised for the predawn jaunt to the top – you'll need your hands free to negotiate the ropes on the summit massif. Expect freezing temperatures near the top, not to mention strong winds and the occasional rainstorm, so it's a good idea to bring along a quick-drying fleece jacket and a waterproof shell to go over it. Don't forget a water bottle, which can be refilled en route.

Via Ferrata
The *via ferrata* ('iron road' in Italian) is a permanent network of mountaineering cables, rungs and rails attached to Mt Kinabalu's dramatic granite walls. After ascending the mountain in the usual way, climbers can

use the *via ferrata*, managed by **Mountain Torq** (☑ 088-268126; www.mountaintorq.com; Low's Peak Circuit RM870, Walk the Torq RM650), to return from 3766m to the Laban Rata rest camp. The Low's Peak Circuit is a four- to five-hour scramble along Mt Kinabalu's sheer flanks.

The route's threadlike tightrope walks and swinging planks will have you convinced that the course designers are sadistic, but that's what makes it such fun – testing your limits without putting your safety in jeopardy.

Other Hiking Trails

If you're not up for an ascent to the summit, can't afford an expensive package and/or didn't reserve ahead for the dates you need, it's still well worth coming here to explore the nine interconnected nature trails that wend their way through the beautiful jungles around the base of Mt Kinabalu. A climbing permit and a guide are required if you go above Timpohon Gate.

🛏 Sleeping

Sleeping options at park HQ include two hostels, cabins (from RM650 per night) and two hotels (rooms from RM700 per night), all operated by **Sutera Sanctuary Lodges** (☑ 088-287 887; http://suterasanctuarylodges. com.my; lot G15, ground fl, Wisma Sabah; d/tw incl 3 meals & bedding RM669/1349, non-heated d incl 3 meals RM587). They're overpriced compared to sleeping spots just outside the park.

Grace Hostel   HOSTEL **$**
(dm incl breakfast RM250) Clean, comfortable 20-bed dorm with fireplace and drink-making area.

Rock Hostel   HOSTEL **$$**
(dm/d incl breakfast RM250/700) Small clean rooms with inviting colourful bedspreads, and decent dorms.

❶ Getting There & Away

Park headquarters is 88km by road northeast of KK. All buses from KK's Inanam Bus Terminal to east-coast destinations, including Sandakan, pass by the park (RM30, two hours), but if you're staying in central KK it's much more convenient to take a minibus from Padang Merdeka Bus Terminal (RM25, two hours). In order to check in by 9am, you'll need to leave KK by 7am – or consider spending the night somewhere near the mountain. A taxi from KK to the park costs RM200.

To get from the park to KK or Sadakan, you can flag down a bus from the park turn-off, 100m

---

THE DAY THE MOUNTAIN SHOOK

On 5 June 2015 an earthquake measuring 6.0 on the Richter scale struck Mt Kinabalu, tragically taking the lives of 18 climbers; a further 137 people were stranded on the mountain but later saved.

All trails, including the summit trail, have now reopened. The number of climbers per day allowed on the mountain has been reduced from 190 to 120.

---

uphill from the park entrance. Shared jeeps with room for five people park just outside of the park gates and leave when full for KK (RM200) and Sandakan (RM500).

Around Mt Kinabalu

Several places near Kinabalu National Park are well worth exploring.

⊙ Sights & Activities

Kundasang War Memorial   MEMORIAL
(Kota Kinabalu–Ranau Hwy; admission RM10; ⊘ 8.30am-5pm) The junction for the Mesilau Nature Resort on the KK–Ranau Hwy is the site of the Kundasang War Memorial, which commemorates the Australian and British prisoners who died on the infamous Sandakan Death Marches. While other memorials in Sabah often seem neglected and forgotten, the Kundasang gardens are remarkably touching. Four gardens, manicured in that bucolic yet tame fashion that is so very English, are separated by a series of marbled pavilions.

Mesilau Nature Resort   TREKKING
(☑ 088-871 519; Kudasang, Ranau; adult/child RM15/10, guided nature walk RM10; ⊘ 9am-4pm) Just 30 minutes' drive from Kinabalu Park, this peaceful resort, nestled amid lush jungle, sits at 6172m and is the highest point you can reach by car. The resort is terrific for walking trails, and is also an alternative starting point for ascending Mt Kinabalu, often favoured by trekkers as it's more challenging than the main route and much less crowded than park headquarters.

Poring Hot Springs   HOT SPRINGS
(Poring, Ranau; adult/child incl Kinabalu National Park RM15/10; ⊘ entrance gate 7am-5pm, park

until 8pm, Butterfly Garden & Canopy Walk closed Mon) One of the few positive contributions the Japanese made to Borneo during WWII, Poring Hot Springs has become a popular weekend retreat for locals. Located in a well-maintained forest park with nature paths that the elderly and children can enjoy, the springs steam with hot sulphurous water channelled into pools and tubs, some of which feel a little rundown. Remember your towel and swimming trunks.

🛏 Sleeping & Eating

There are privately owned sleeping options looping around Kinabalu's base. Most of these are located along the road between the park headquarters and Kundasang (east of the park's entrance).

Mountain Guest House GUESTHOUSE $
(☑016-837 4040, 088-888632; KM53, Jln Tinompok, off Kinabalu Park, Ranau; dm/s/d/q incl breakfast from RM30/60/70/80) This friendly but clean guesthouse is endearingly ramshackle and sits (or hangs?) on different levels up the side of the mountain. About a five-minute walk from the park entrance, houseproud basic rooms have a few sticks of furniture and spotless bathrooms. Breakfast included and vegetarian dinners (RM8) available. Run by lovely Anna.

★ Lupa Masa ECO-CAMP $$
(☑016-806 8194, 012-845 1987; http://lupamasa.com; Poring; per person incl meals tent/chalet RM90/250) 🌿 This incredible eco-camp is surrounded by forest and has two gin-clear rivers to bathe in, with waterfalls and natural jacuzzis. Lupa Masa isn't for everyone though... No electricity or wi-fi, but bugs and leeches at no extra cost. Accommodation is on mattresses in tents on raised platforms, or the delightful new chalets with striking river views.

Wind Paradise YURT $$
(☑088-714 563, 012-820 3360; http://windparadise2011.blogspot.com; Jln Mesilau, Cinta Mata, Kundasang; d/tr RM170/200, 4-person yurt RM300; 🅿) With staggeringly pretty views of the valley and town of Kundasang far below, these Mongolian yurts, and rooms in a central lodge – both set in pleasant lawns – are delightful. There's self-catering and a great lounge, and barbecue facilities to lap up the mountain view. Yurts have comfortable beds and make for a great sleep with natural ventilation.

ℹ Getting There & Around

KK round-trip buses stop in front of park headquarters and in Ranau (RM15 to RM20, two hours) from 7am to 8pm. Minivans operate from a blue-roofed shelter in Ranau servicing the nearby attractions (park HQ, Poring etc) for RM5. The national park operates a van service between the headquarters and Poring for RM25 – it leaves the park HQ at noon.

Sandakan

🗐 089 / POP 396,000

Sabah's second city has long been a major trading port, but these days the grubby city centre feels provincial compared to KK. Curiously, a completely new city centre is currently being built 2.5km west of the city.

The main draw here is not the city itself but the nature sites of nearby Sepilok.

◉ Sights

History buffs might be interested in the *Sandakan Heritage Trail* brochure available at the tourist office.

Agnes Keith House MUSEUM
(☑089-221 140; www.museum.sabah.gov.my; Jln Istana; admission RM15; ⊙9am-5pm) This atmospheric two-storey wooden villa, and former British colonial quarters, is now renovated as a museum. Living in Sandakan in the 1930s, Amercian Agnes Keith wrote several books about her experiences here, including the famous *Land Below the Wind*. The villa documents Sandakan in all its colonial splendour.

To reach the museum, head up the Tangga Seribu (100 Steps) to Jln Istana and turn left. Also on the grounds is the English Tea House & Restaurant.

Sandakan Memorial Park HISTORIC SITE
(⊙9am-5pm) A beautiful forest orchard and series of gardens marks the unlikely site of a Japanese POW camp and starting point for the infamous WWII 'death marches' to Ranau. Of the 1800 Australian and 600 British troops imprisoned here, the only survivors by July 1945 were six Australian escapees. Rusting machines testify to the camp's forced-labour program, and a pavilion includes accounts from survivors and photographs from personnel, inmates and liberators. See www.sandakan-deathmarch.com for more details of the death march route.

🛏 Sleeping

If you're only passing through Sandakan to see the orangutans, it's better to stay at Sepilok itself.

★ Borneo
Sandakan Backpackers   HOSTEL $
(☑089-215 754; www.borneosandakan.com; 1st fl, 54 Harbour Sq; dm/s/d RM30/55/70; 🌐❄🛜) These brilliant new digs are super-clean with warm orange walls, a welcoming lobby, air-con in every room with – get this – flatscreen TV and Xbox! Also, fresh sheets, safety lockers and a decent breakfast. Six rooms and two well-sized dorms. A great vibe and helpful staff who are also qualified guides and run a number of tours.

Sea View Sandakan   HOSTEL $
(☑089-221 221; www.seaviewsandakan.com; 1st fl, lot 126, Jln Dua, Harbour Sq 14; dm RM25, d with fan & shared bathroom RM66, d with bathroom & air-con RM84, breakfast incl; ❄🛜) You won't get any seaviews and the rooms are a bit airless and paint-thirsty. That said, it's a nice vibe here, and the Lemongrass cafe on the 3rd floor has a cool mural and misted glass, and dishes up pumpkin curry.

🍴 Eating

Sandakan Central Market   HAWKER $
(Jln Dua; mains RM1-8; ☀7am-3pm) Despite being located in what looks like a multistorey car park, this is the best spot in town for cheap eats and food stalls. Upstairs you'll find strictly halal food stalls, with a mix of Chinese, Malay, Indonesian and Filipino food. Hours given for the food stalls are a bit flexible, but by 3pm most are empty.

English Tea House & Restaurant   RESTAURANT $$
(☑089-222 544; www.englishteahouse.org; Jln Istana; mains RM15.50-55, cocktails RM16.80-20; ☀10am-11pm) More English than a Graham Greene novel, this beautiful stucco-pillared villa, with its manicured croquet lawn, wood-blade fans and wicker chairs parked under a giant mango tree, is great for lunch. The menu spans fish 'n' chips to Oxford stew, enjoyed with a serene view of the bay below and a pot of tea.

🍷 Drinking & Nightlife

Bandar Indah, commonly known as Mile 4 or Batu 4, is a buzzing grid of two-storey shophouses packed with restaurants, bars, karaoke lounges and nightclubs. A taxi here costs RM20.

★ Balin Roof Garden   BAR
(Balin; ☑089-272 988; www.nakhotel.com; 18th fl, Nak Hotel, Jln Pelabuhan Lama; mains RM20, cocktails RM20-25; ☀7.30am-1am, happy hour 2-8pm; 🛜) A hidden treat at the top of the Nak Hotel, this stylish restaurant/bar has retro bubble lights, a '70s wicker swing-chair, and swallow-you-up couches. Eat inside or out; on the shaded verandah or up on the rooftop. There's pizza, marinated NZ lamb, burgers and a wealth of juices and classy cocktails that any boutique 'mixologist' bar would be justifiably jealous of. Cool.

ℹ Information

Cyber Café (3rd fl, Wisma Sandakan, Lebuh Empat; per hour RM3; ☀9am-9pm)
Duchess of Kent Hospital (☑089-248 600; http://hdok.moh.gov.my; Batu 2 (Mile 2), Jln Utara; ☀8am-10pm) Best private care in the area.
Maybank (Lebuh Tiga) In addition to a full-service bank and ATM, a sidewalk currency-exchange window is open 9am to 5pm daily for changing cash and travellers cheques.

ℹ Getting There & Away

AIR
AirAsia and Malaysia Airlines both have flights to KK and KL, while MASwings flies to KK, Kudat and Tawau.

BUSES FROM SANKADAN

DESTINATION	FARE (RM)	DURATION (HR)	FREQUENCY
Kinabalu National Park	35	4-5	frequent 7am-2pm, then 8pm
Kota Kinabalu (Inanam Bus Terminal)	43	6-7	frequent 7am-2pm, then 8pm
Lahad Datu	22	2½	frequent 7am-8pm
Semporna	40	5½	7.30am, 2pm
Tawau	42	6	frequent 7am-8pm

ℹ️ BORDER CROSSING WARNING

Standard Marine (📞 089-216 996) links Sandakan with Zamboanga, on the Philippine island of Mindanao, but because of lawlessness (including kidnappings) and an Islamist insurgency, Western embassies warn against travel to or through Zamboanga. Check local conditions before considering making this risky border crossing.

BUS

Sandakan's long-distance bus station is at Batu 2.5 (Mile 2.5), 4km north of the city centre. To get here catch a local bus (RM1.50) from the stand at Sandakan waterfront; it takes about 20 minutes. The same bus leaves when full from the bus station for the city centre.

All buses to/from KK pass by Kinabalu National Park but won't stop to pick up passengers if they're full.

Minivans for Sukau (RM15) leave from a lot behind Centre Point Mall in town.

ℹ️ Getting Around

TO/FROM THE AIRPORT

The airport is 11km from the city centre. Batu 7 Airport bus (RM1.80) stops on the main road about 500m from the terminal. A coupon taxi to the town centre costs RM35; going the other way, around RM35.

BUS & MINIBUS

Terminal Bas Sandakan, in the city centre, is a chaotic parking lot behind the downmarket Centre Point Plaza shopping mall. Most buses head north out of the centre along Jln Utara. Each is marked with a sign indicating how far it goes – to Batu 2.5 (Mile 2.5, ie the long-distance bus station; RM1.50), for instance, or Batu 14 (the turn-off to Sepilok; RM3). The end of the line is Batu 32 (RM5), on the KK–Semporna highway.

Sepilok

📞 089

Sepilok's Orangutan Rehabilitation Centre is one of the only places in the world where you can see Asia's great ginger ape in its natural rainforest habitat. It's well worth sticking around to do some jungle hiking and mellow out in one of Sepilok's attractive, good-value guesthouses.

◉ Sights & Activities

Sepilok's newest attraction is the **Borneo Sun Bear Conservation Centre** (BSBCC; 📞 089-534 491; www.bsbcc.org.my; Jln Sepilok; kids under 12 free, adults RM30; ⊘ 9am-4pm) 🐾, home to some adorable rescued pint-sized yogis.

Sepilok Orangutan Rehabilitation Centre ANIMAL SANCTUARY (SORC; 📞 089-531 189, emergency 089-531 180; sorc64@gmail.com; Jln Sepilok; adult/child RM30/15, camera fee RM10; ⊘ ticket counter 9am-noon & 2-4pm Sat-Thu, 9-11am & 2-4pm Fri) 🐾 Around 25km north of Sandakan, and covering some 40 sq km of the Kabili-Sepilok Forest Reserve, this inspiring world-famous centre welcomes orphaned and injured orangutans for rehabilitation before returning them to forest life. There are currently between 60 to 80 living here. The new showstopper is the recently opened **outdoor nursery**, just two minutes' walk from the feeding platforms, where abandoned toddlers are taught the building blocks they'll need to keep them alive back in the wild.

Rainforest Discovery Centre NATURE RESERVE (RDC; 📞 089-533 780; www.forest.sabah.gov.my/rdc; adult/child RM15/7; ⊘ ticket counter 8am-5pm, park until 8pm) The RDC, about 1.5km from SORC, offers an engaging graduate-level education in tropical flora and fauna. Outside the exhibit hall filled with child-friendly displays, a botanical garden presents samples of tropical plants. There's a gentle 1km lakeside walking trail, and a series of eight canopy towers connected by walkways to give you a bird's-eye view of the rooftops of the trees; by far the most rewarding element of a trip here.

🛏️ Sleeping

The Sepilok area offers much more attractive and atmospheric accommodation options than Sandakan.

Sepilok B&B HOSTEL $ (📞 089-534 050, 019-833 0901; www.sepilokbednbreakfast.com.my; Jln Fabia; dm with fan/air-con RM35/45, d with fan only RM68, d with air-con RM108-188) Located opposite the Rainforest Discovery Centre, this place has an authentic hostel vibe with a cosmo cast of backpackers. Dorms are spartan but clean. Rooms are nice with white walls, colourful curtains and fresh linen. Pitta Lodge has self-catering facilities for families and fan-only rooms.

Camping here is better in March and April when there's less rain.

★ Paganakan Dii
Tropical Retreat BOUTIQUE HOTEL $$
(☑089-532 005; www.paganakandii.com; dm/s/d RM35/60/55, 2-/4-person bunaglow RM175/236; ❄❂) Popular with families wanting a taste of nature, there are hammocks at every turn, and brick-and-wood bungalows with balcony and nicely crafted furniture, wood floors and step-in showers. Make sure you ask for one with a view of the lake and mountains. There's also eight new box-standard rooms with shared bathroom. Transfers to Sepilok are included. Perfect.

Uncle Tan Guesthouse GUESTHOUSE $$
(☑016-824 4749; www.uncletan.com; Jln Batu 14; dm incl breakfast RM51, d without/with bathroom RM106/116; ❄@❂) The Uncle Tan empire is one of the oldest backpacker/adventure travel outfits in Sabah. Dorms are boxy, rooms with lino floors and bare walls, though both are clean. It's a summer camp vibe here, and the owners can hook you up with trips to places like the Sungai Kinabatangan (RM265).

Sepilok Forest Edge Resort RESORT $$
(☑089-533 190, 013-869 5069; www.sepilokforest edgeresort.com; Jln Rambutan; dm/d RM48/100, chalets RM265; ❄❂▨) Set within manicured lawns, this stunning accommodation is choking on plants and flowers and has chalets fit for a colonial explorer, with polished-wood floors, choice art, and private balcony with wrought-iron chairs. There's also a dorm and double rooms located in a pretty long house, plus a relaxing tropical pool-jacuzzi. About a 15-minute walk from the Orangutan Rehabilitation Centre.

❶ Getting There & Away
Sepilok is about 25km west of Sandakan. From Sandakan, bus 'Batu 14' (RM3) departs hourly from the city centre and stops at the SORC.

If coming from KK, board a Sandakan-bound bus and ask the driver to let you off at 'Batu 14' (Sepilok Junction), which is 2km or 3km north of the area's main sights. From there, catch a 'pirate' taxi (RM3 per person) – one is usually waiting.

A taxi from Sandakan or the airport costs RM45.

Sungai Kinabatangan

The 560km-long Kinabatangan River, Sabah's longest waterway, is one of the best places in Southeast Asia to see jungle wildlife in its native habitat. The reason, tragically, is that creatures such as orangutans, proboscis monkeys, macaques, hornbills (all eight species) and blue-eared kingfishers have been pushed to the banks of the Kinabatangan by encroaching oil palm plantations.

The cathedral-like **Gomantong Caves** (☑089-230 189; www.sabah.gov.my/jhl; Gomantong Hill, Lower Kinabatangan; adult/child RM30/15, camera/video RM30/50; ◷8am-noon & 2-4.30pm, closing periods apply), Sabah's most famous source of swiftlet nests, are about midway between Kampung Sukau and Sukau Junction.

To explore the Kinabatangan, you can book a tour with a KK- or Sandakan-based agency – but contrary to what you might hear, you can also come on your own and book boat trips à la carte. However, you do need to arrange accommodation in advance, if only to coordinate transport from Sandakan or Sukau Junction.

🏃 Activities
The best way to see wild rainforest creatures is to take guided river cruises run by local guesthouses (and tour agencies). Most take place early in the morning and around sunset, when the animals are most active, and cost from RM100 for a two-hour river cruise on a boat that can hold up to six people.

Night cruises, with their bright lights and camera flashes, can be intrusive – ask your guide how you and your group can avoid disturbing the animals.

🛏 Sleeping
★ Tungog Rainforest Eco Camp CABIN $
(☑089-551 070, 019-582 5214; www.mescot.org; per night incl 3 meals RM95, river cruises RM45) 🌿 This eco-camp faces a pretty oxbow lake by the Kinabatangan River. Luxurious it isn't – expect wooden shelters with mattress, sheets and pillows, plus a mozzie net and shared bathrooms – however, the immersion in nature and chance to put something back by planting trees is magical. Given there's no other camps for miles, you have the wildlife to yourself.

Sukau Greenview B&B B&B $
(☑089-565 266, 013-869 6922; www.sukaugreen view.net; dm/r RM45/60, 3-day, 2-night package incl breakfast & 3 x 2hr river trips per person RM499) Run by locals, this lime-green wooden affair has OK dorms and basic rooms. There's also a pleasant cafe looking out on the river. Greenview run special elephant-sighting trips, and

One of *National Geographic*'s 'Top 30 Lodges in the World', **Sukau Rainforest Lodge** (☑088-438 300; www.sukau. com; 3-day, 2-night package RM1688; ☻❋☎) ✐ is the most upscale digs on the river. Think beautifully appointed split-level rooms with wood and terrazo floors, rain showers, a lounge area and mozzie nets. There's a fine restaurant, an on-site naturalist who gives wildlife talks and night walks, plus a welcome plunge pool to cool off in. Romantic.

also crocodile trips in the early morning and at night (both priced at RM250).

Myne Resort   RESORT $$
(☑089-216 093; www.myne.com.my; longhouse/ chalet RM250/280; ❋☎) Situated on the bend of the river, Myne has an open, breezy reception, games room and restaurant festooned with lifeguard rings, and is vaguely reminiscent of an old wooden ship. Chalets are beautiful with peach drapes, river-facing balcony, glossed wood floors, comfy beds, dresser, flatscreen and cable TV. Night cruises cost RM75, transfers RM100.

ℹ Getting There & Away

To get to Sukau, take any bus travelling from KK or Sandakan to Lahad Datu or Semporna (or vice versa) and get off at Sukau Junction (Simpang Sukau); minibuses to Sukau (RM25 per person) stop next to the tin-roofed rain shelter. Prearrange pick-up with your guesthouse.

Semporna

☑089
The mainland town of Semporna is ugly and chaotic, but it's the gateway to some of the world's most stunning scuba diving, off legendary Sipadan and around other islands of the storied Semporna Archipelago. There are no beaches on the mainland.

🏃 Activities

A variety of scuba operators have offices around the Semporna seafront complex and/or in KK.

★**Scuba Junkie**   DIVING
(☑089-785 372; www.scuba-junkie.com; lot 36, block B, Semporna seafront; 4-days & 3-nights

on Mabul incl 3 dives per day at Kapilai, Mabul & 4 dives at Sipadan per person RM2385, snorkelling day trips incl lunch RM120; ☺9am-6pm) ✐ The most proactive conservationists on Pulau Mabul, Scuba Junkie employ two full-time environmentalists and recycle much of their profits into their turtle hatchery and rehab centre and 'shark week' initiative. They're also a favourite with Westerners thanks to their excellent divemasters and comfortable, non-package type digs at Mabul Beach Resort (p449).

Sipadan Scuba   DIVING
(☑089-784 788, 089-781 788, 012-813 1688, 089-919 128; www.sipadanscuba.com; lot 28, block E, Semporna seafront; 3-day, 2-night package incl dives, accommodation, transfer & equipment RM919) Twenty years' experience and an international staff makes Sipadan Scuba a reliable, recommended choice. You can take your PADI Open Water course here for RM760.

Seaventures   DIVING
(☑017-811 6023, 088-251 669; www.seaventures dive.com; lot 28, block E, Semporna seafront; 4-day, 3-night package incl 10 dives in total, with 3 dives on Sipadan, incl meals & transfers to island & airport RM2730) Based out of their funky blue/orange ocean platform close to Mabul island, this is a well-regarded outfit. Offices in Semporna and in KK's Wisma Sabah building.

Seahorse Sipadan   DIVING
(☑089-782 289, 012-279 7657; www.seahorse-sipadanscuba.org; 1st fl, lot 1, Semporna seafront; 3-day, 2-night package incl 3 dives per day, accommodation, equipment & boat transfer RM690) Backpacker-oriented outfit with a new 1st-floor office on Semporna seafront, and accommodation on Mabul. Seahorse has been around for five years now.

🛏 Sleeping

Scuba Junkie Dive Lodge   HOSTEL $
(☑089-785 372; www.scuba-junkie.com/accom modations; block B 36, 458 Semporna seafront; dm diver/non-diver RM25/50, r without bathroom diver/non-diver RM75/150, r with bathroom diver/ non-diver RM95/190; ❋☎) Fresh yellow walls peppered with underwater shots of marine life, clean bathrooms and a variety of air-con rooms to choose from, make this a sure bet. Also it's directly opposite Scuba Junkie's office, and next to the Diver's Bar, a good spot for breakfast before you head of to the Semporna Archipelago.

Borneo Global Sipadan
BackPackers HOSTEL **$**
(☑089-785 088; www.bgbsipadan.com; Jln Causeway; dm/tr/f incl breakfast RM27/99/130; ❀@☎)
There are nine rooms comprising dorm, triples and family options with bathroom. The walls are fresh, the air is cool and there's a friendly lobby area to chill in. They also run three-day PADI Open Water courses for RM920. Run by energetic Max.

Sipadan Inn HOTEL **$$**
(☑089-781 766; www.sipadaninn-hotel.com; lot 19-24, block D, Semporna seafront; d/f from RM110/170; ❀@☎) A slice of refrigerated comfort, the Inn has simple but tidy rooms with wood walls, fresh linen, bed runners, coffee-making facilities, spotless bathrooms and very friendly staff.

Holiday Dive Inn HOTEL **$$**
(☑089-919 128; www.holidaydiveinn.com; lot A5-A7, Semporna seafront; r RM86-96, f RM168; ❀☎)
This recent addition has spotless rooms with cheerful colours, fresh bathrooms, TVs and some rooms with balcony. Good value, it's affiliated with Sipadan Scuba nearby. There's also a nice sundowner roof lounge.

✖ Eating

Fat Mother CHINESE **$**
(Semporna seafront; mains RM15; ⊙5-10pm)
Mother's has terrific reviews for its warm service and wide-ranging seafood menu – your dinner will be glowering at you from the glass tanks. They'll even prepare your own fish if you've caught it. Grouper and mango sauce, fish porridge, salted egg and squid, Malay curries and noodle dishes, plus free Chinese tea and melon dessert.

ℹ Information

If you're arriving in Semporna under your own steam, leave the bus and minivan drop-off area and head towards the mosque's minaret. This is the way to the waterfront. Follow the grid of concrete streets to the right until you reach 'Semporna Seafront' – home to the diving outfitters, each stacked one next to the other in a competitive clump.

Semporna has several ATMs.

ℹ Getting There & Away

AIR
From Tawau Airport (situated 70km from Semporna, 30km from Tawau and about 2.5km off the main highway), Malaysia Airlines has flights to KL and AirAsia has flights to KK, KL and Johor Bahru. MASwings links Tawau with Sandakan, KK and the North Kalimantan (Indonesia) island of Tarakan.

From Semporna's bus station, a minibus to Tawau Airport costs RM20. A taxi costs RM100.

Remember that flying less than 24 hours after scuba diving can be dangerous.

BUS
The 'terminal' hovers around the Milimewa supermarket, 200m northwest of the big, light green mosque (past the mosque if you're coming from the Semporna seafront). All buses run from early morning until 4pm (except Kota Kinabalu) and leave when full.

Destinations include Kota Kinabalu (RM75, nine hours, leaves at around 7am or 7pm), Sandakan (RM45 to RM40, 5½ hours) and Tawau (RM25, 1½ hours).

GETTING TO INDONESIA: TAWAU TO TARAKAN & NUNUKAN

Getting to the border The port of Tawau, 100km southwest of Semporna, has an Indonesian consulate (☑089-772 052, 089-752 969; Jln Sinn Onn, Wisma Fuji; ⊙8am-noon & 1pm or 2-4pm Mon-Fri, closed Indonesian and Malaysian public holidays) known for being fast and efficient – many travellers are in and out in an hour. A 60-day tourist visa costs RM170 and requires two passport photos (see p310).

Visa applications are processed between 9.30am and 2pm Monday to Friday. You technically need to either provide proof of onward travel or a credit card. Bank on spending at least one night in town given the ferry departure schedule, and bring extra cash to the consulate as there are no ATMs nearby.

At the border Ferries link Tawau with two islands in North Kalimantan: Tarakan (RM140, three to four hours, late-morning departures daily except Sunday); and Nunukan (RM65, one hour, 10am and 3pm daily except Sunday). MASwings flies from Tawau to Tarakan.

Moving on From Nunukan and Tarakan, Pelni has ferries to Balikpapan (East Kalimantan) and the Sulawesi ports of Toli-Toli, Pare-Pare and Makassar (one to three days).

Semporna Archipelago

The stunning sapphires and emeralds of the Semporna Archipelago, accented with brightly painted boats, swaying palms and the white sand of desert islands plucked from your deepest fantasies, are a sight for cynical souls. But no one comes this way just for the island beaches – it's the ocean and everything in it that has brought fame to these islands as one of the most spectacular diving destinations in the world.

🏃 Activities

Sipadan, 40km from Semporna, is the shining star in the archipelago's constellation of shimmering islands. Volcanic in origin, it rises 600m from the seabed. Roughly a dozen delineated dive sites orbit the island – the most famous being Barracuda Point, where chevron and blacktail barracuda collide to form impenetrable walls of undulating fish.

The macro-diving around Mabul (Pulau Mabul) is world-famous. Dive sites around Kapalai (a large sandbar) and the islands of Mataking (fantastic for snorkelling; onshore there's an ultra-luxury resort) and Sibuan are also exceptional. The northern islands of the archipelago, which has many of the area's nicest beaches, are protected as Tun Sakaran Marine Park (101 sq km).

If Sipadan is your dream dive, make reservations at least two months ahead (and even further ahead for July and August and from mid-December to mid-January) – only 120 diving permits, divided among a dozen operators, are issued each day. These can be arranged through companies based in Semporna or KK.

To dive elsewhere in the archipelago (as 80% of visitors do – and have a great time!) or take a course (three-day Open Water Diver certification costs about RM975), advance reservations are a very good idea. Weather rarely, if ever, affects diving here.

The cheapest way to dive is to stay in the town of Semporna and take day trips (diving RM280 to RM350, snorkelling RM150 to RM170), but you'll miss out on post-dive chill sessions on the sand and some impossibly romantic equatorial sunsets.

🛏 Sleeping

The archipelago's only relatively inexpensive accommodation is on Mabul, 26km southeast of Semporna and 14km north of Sipadan (where sleepovers are completely banned). Prices rise and places fill fast in July and August. All the following places are affiliated with dive operators.

Mabul is endowed with a nice white-sand beach, fantastically blue waters, a marine police base and two small, impoverished settlements: on the northeast coast, a hamlet of Bajau sea gypsies, known for their colourful, pointy-prowed boats called *jonkong;* on the southwest coast, a Suluk and Malay stilt village is home to several guesthouses.

Sipadan Dive Centre (SDC) HOMESTAY **$**
(✆ 088-240 584, 012-821 8288; www.sdclodges. com; Mabul; dm/r RM150/190, 3 dives RM280; ❄) Simple rainbow-coloured huts with attached bathroom, air-con, Caribbean-blue walls, fresh linen, wood floors, and a dive outfit – and less cramped quarters compared to other budget digs thanks to its spacious compound – make this a winner. Friendly management too; they cook up barbecue feasts by night.

Uncle Chang's GUESTHOUSE **$**
(✆ 089-781 002, 089-786 988, 017-895 002; www. ucsipadan.com; Mabul; dm RM75, d with/without air-con & bathroom RM150/110; ❄) Shipwrecked amid the stilted weaveworld of the Malay

MALAYSIA SEMPORNA ARCHIPELAGO

MEN IN BLACK: THE ONGOING SECURITY SITUATION

If staying in Mabul, you'll notice the presence of black-clad armed police patrolling the beach and the fact there's a 6pm curfew to be back in your resort. Try not to be alarmed, they're here for your safety and as a powerful deterrent. Their presence is a response to a number of incidents involving kidnap-for-ransom groups from southern Philippines, including the kidnap of two Taiwanese tourists in 2013 and a Chinese tourist in 2014.

But is it safe to visit the archipelago? As of late 2015, Western embassies recommend you reconsider your need to travel here but for more than a year 120 divers per day have been enjoying one of the best dive sites in the world without incident. With the beefed-up police numbers on the islands, the kidnappers are having to look elsewhere for their ransoms.

village, if Chang's was an avuncular connection, he'd be a rough old seadog; think banana-yellow basic rattan-walled rooms in small chalets, a lively threadbare communal deck with occasional jam sessions and a happy, sociable vibe. There's also a well-known dive school here with seven daily dive permits to Sipadan.

Seahorse Sipadan
Scuba Lodge
GUESTHOUSE $

(☑Semporna 089-782 289; www.seahorse-sipadanscuba.com; Mabul; dm/d from RM70/100) Seahorse has a few rooms showing their age with patchy lino floors, yellow walls and an open deck to catch the breeze. With nice little touches like conch shells on tables, there's also a dependable dive outfit here.

★Scuba Junkie
Mabul Beach Resort
RESORT $$

(☑089-785 372; www.scuba-junkie.com; Mabul; dm RM175, d with fan RM245-310, d with air-con RM320-380; ❄️📶) ✈ Run by a lovely American couple, this place attracts a younger international crowd with a little cash to splash on semi-luxe digs. Super-fresh rooms come with porches and bathrooms, polished wood floors and choice decor. Dorms are airy and of a good size, plus there's a welcoming central gazebo which houses the lively restaurant/bar. Prices above include generous buffet meals.

ⓘ Getting There & Around

Transport from Semporna to the archipelago is handled by dive operators and guesthouse owners – ask for details when you book.

Pulau Labuan

☑087 / POP 87,000

The Federal Territory of Labuan (www.labuantourism.my) has been a duty-free port since the late 1840s, when it became a British crown colony. These days, Malaysians, Bruneians and expat oil workers flock to the island in search of duty-free shopping and cheap alcohol. The main town, Bandar Labuan – much cleaner and better organised than its counterparts in Sabah – is linked by ferry with both Kota Kinabalu and Brunei. WWII buffs will find several sights of interest, including the Australian and British Labuan War Cemetery, 2km northwest of the city centre.

GETTING TO BRUNEI: PULAU LABUAN TO BANDAR SERI BEGAWAN

Getting to the border Ferries from Bandar Labuan to the Bruneian port of Muara (RM35, 1¼ hours) generally depart at 9am, 1.30pm, 3.30pm and 4pm.

At the border Most travellers to Brunei are issued on-arrival visas (free for most nationalities but not Australians) valid for 14, 30 or 90 days.

Moving on Ferries from Bandar Labuan dock at Terminal Feri Serasa in Muara, 20km northeast of Bandar Seri Begawan. To get to the city centre, take bus 38 (B$1, one hour) from Muara town. A taxi should cost R$40.

For information on making this crossing in the opposite direction, see p63.

🛌 Sleeping

Labuan Homestay Programme HOMESTAY $

(☑013-854 0217, 016-824 6193, 087-422 622; 1/2 days incl full board RM70/150) This excellent service matches visitors with a friendly local in one of three villages around the island: Patau Patau 2, Kampong Sungai Labu and Kampong Bukit Kuda. If you want to be near Bandar Labuan, ask for accommodation at Patau Patau 2 – it's a charming stilt village out on the bay. If you want to enrol in the program, book at least a few days in advance.

Tiara Labuan HOTEL $$

(☑087-414 300; www.tiaralabuan.com; Jln Tanjung Batu; r incl breakfast from RM250; ❄️📶) Pulau Labuan's favourite hotel is a cut above the rest with its cobalt-blue outdoor pool nestled in manicured gardens at Tanjung Batu. There's an excellent Asian fusion restaurant and open-range kitchen, plus large and very alluring wood-signatured rooms with bed runners, snow-white linen, spotless bathrooms and recessed lighting.

ⓘ Getting There & Away

Daily passenger ferries link KK's Jesselton Point Ferry Terminal with Bandar Labuan (economy/business RM35/48, 3¼ hours, departures at 8am and 1.30pm Monday to Saturday, 3pm Sunday). In the other direction, boats depart from Bandar Labuan at 8am and 1pm Monday to Saturday, and 10.30am and 3pm Sunday.

Passenger ferries to the Bruneian port of Muara (RM35, 1¼ hours), 20km northeast of Bandar Seri Begawan, generally leave Bandar Labuan at 9am, 1.30pm and 3.30pm. A car ferry departs at 4pm (RM35, 1½ hours). Be at the terminal at least a half-hour before departure.

MALAYSIAN BORNEO – SARAWAK

Sarawak makes access to Borneo's natural wonders and cultural riches a breeze. From Kuching, the island's most sophisticated city, pristine rainforests – where you can spot orangutans, proboscis monkeys and the world's largest flower, the rafflesia – can be visited on day trips, with plenty of time in the evening for a delicious meal and a drink in a chic bar. More adventurous travellers can take a 'flying coffin' riverboat up the Batang Rejang, 'the Amazon of Borneo', on your way to visit the spectacular caves and extraordinary rock formations of Gunung Mulu National Park, a Unesco World Heritage Site. Everywhere you go, you'll encounter the warmth, unforced friendliness and sense of humour that make the people of Sarawak such delightful hosts.

Kuching

✍ 082 / POP 600,000

The capital of Sarawak brings together a kaleidoscope of cultures, cuisines and crafts. The bustling streets – some very modern, others with a colonial-era vibe – amply reward visitors with a penchant for aimless ambling. Chinese temples decorated with dragons abut shophouses from the time of the white rajahs, a South Indian mosque is a five-minute walk from stalls selling a range of Asian cuisines, and a landscaped riverfront park attracts families out for a stroll and a quick bite.

⊙ Sights

Leave plenty of time to wander aimlessly and soak up the relaxed vibe of areas such as Jln Carpenter (Old Chinatown), Jln India, Jln Padungan (New Chinatown) and the Waterfront Promenade.

★**Ethnology Museum**   MUSEUM
(www.museum.sarawak.gov.my; Jln Tun Abang Haji Openg; ⊙9am-4.45pm Mon-Fri, 10am-4pm Sat, Sun & holidays) **FREE** At the top of the hill, on the eastern side of Jln Tun Abang Haji Openg, the Ethnology Museum (the Old Building) – guarded by two colonial-era cannons – spotlights Borneo's incredibly rich indigenous cultures. Upstairs the superb exhibits include a full-sized Iban longhouse, masks and spears; downstairs is an old-fashioned natural-history museum.

At research time, there were plans to renovate the more than 100-year-old building, starting early 2016. During the renovations sections of the museum may be closed.

Chinese History Museum   MUSEUM
(cnr Main Bazaar & Jln Wayang; ⊙9am-4.45pm Mon-Fri, 10am-4pm Sat, Sun & holidays) **FREE** Housed in the century-old Chinese Court building, the Chinese History Museum provides an excellent introduction to the nine Chinese communities – each with its own dialect, cuisine and temples – who began settling in Sarawak around 1830. Highlights of the evocative exhibits include ceramics, musical instruments, historic photographs and some fearsome dragon- and lion-dance costumes. The entrance is on the river side of the building.

Indian Mosque   MOSQUE
(Indian Mosque Lane; ⊙6am-8.30pm except during prayers) **FREE** Turn off Jln India (between Nos 37 and 39A) or waterfront Jln Gambier (between Nos 24 and 25A – shops selling spices with a heady aroma) onto tiny Indian Mosque Lane (Lg Sempit) and you enter another world. About halfway up, entirely surrounded by houses and shops, stands Kuching's oldest mosque, a modest structure built of *belian* (ironwood) in 1863 by Muslim traders from Tamil Nadu.

Fort Margherita   FORT
(Kampung Boyan; ⊙9am-4.30pm) Built by Charles Brooke in 1879 and named after his wife, Ranee Margaret, this hilltop fortress long protected Kuching against surprise attack by pirates. It did so exclusively as a remarkably successful deterrent: troops stationed here never fired a shot in anger. To get there from Kampung Boyan, follow the signs up the hill for 500m.

☞ Tours

Lots of Kuching-based tour companies offer trips to places you can't easily visit on your own. Guesthouses are a good source of recommendations for itineraries and operators.

Adventure

Alternative Borneo
ADVENTURE TOUR

(☑082-248000, 019-892 9627; www.aaborneo.com; lot 37, Jln Tabuan) ✎ Offers ethical and sustainable trips that combine 'culture, nature and adventure'. Can help you design and coordinate an itinerary for independent travel to remote areas, including the Penan villages of the Upper Baram.

🛌 Sleeping

Most guesthouse rooms have shared bathrooms; prices almost always include a toast-and-jam breakfast. Rates at some places rise in July during the Rainforest World Music Festival.

★ Threehouse B&B
GUESTHOUSE $

(☑082-423499; www.threehousebnb.com; 51 Jln China; incl breakfast dm RM20, d without bathroom RM60-65; �) A spotless, family-friendly guesthouse in a great Old Chinatown location that is warm and welcoming – everything a guesthouse should be. All nine rooms are spaced over three, creaky wooden floors and share a bright-red colour scheme. Amenities include a common room with TV, DVDs and books, a laundry service and a kitchen.

★ Singgahsana Lodge
GUESTHOUSE $

(☑082-429277; www.singgahsana.com; 1 Jln Temple; incl breakfast dm RM31, d RM112–132; ❄@☎) Setting the Kuching standard for backpacker digs, this hugely popular guesthouse, decked out with stylish Sarawakian crafts, has an unbeatable location, a great chill-out lobby and a sociable rooftop bar. Dorms have 10 beds and lockers.

Radioman
HOSTEL $

(☑082 248816; 1 Jln Wayang; incl breakfast dm RM25, d without bathroom RM70; ❄☎) This centrally located, self-styled 'heritage hostel' occupies a century-old shophouse that was once used for radio repairs. The building still has the original ceilings, floors and fiendishly steep stairs and it has been thoughtfully designed with nice touches like records on the walls, jungly plants and a courtyard garden.

Marco Polo Guesthouse
GUESTHOUSE $

(☑082-246679, Samuel Tan 019-888 8505; www.marcopolo.net.tf; 1st fl, 236 Jln Padungan; incl breakfast dm RM27, d without bathroom RM56-60; ❄☎) A well-run, comfortable place with a breezy verandah and cosy indoor living room. The breakfast of fresh fruit, banana fritters and muffins is a popular bonus. Only some rooms have windows. Owner Sam is happy to give travel advice and sometimes takes guests to the market. Situated about 15 minutes' walk from the waterfront.

Nomad B&B
GUESTHOUSE $

(☑082-237831, 016 856 3855; www.borneobnb.com; 1st fl, 3 Jln Green Hill; incl breakfast dm RM20, s/d with fan & without bathroom RM50/60, d with air-con RM70-75; ❄@☎) There's a buzzing backpacker vibe at this relaxed, Iban-run place – guests often hang out in the lounge area with the friendly management. Breakfast times are flexible to suit late risers and there is a kitchen that guests can use. Of the 17 rooms, 10 have windows (the others make do with exhaust fans). Dorm rooms have eight beds.

Lodge 121
GUESTHOUSE $

(☑082-428121; www.lodge121.com; lot 121, 1st fl, Jln Tabuan; dm/s/d/tr without bathroom incl breakfast RM30/59/79/99; ❄☎) Polished concrete abounds in this former commercial space that has been transformed into a sleek, low-key guesthouse. The carpeted, 10-bed dorm room, with mattresses on the floor, is in the attic. All rooms share bathrooms that are on the small side.

Beds
GUESTHOUSE $

(☑082-424229; www.bedsguesthouse.com; 229 Jln Padungan; dm RM20, s/d without bathroom RM40/55; ❄@☎) This guesthouse has attracted a loyal following thanks to comfy couches in the lobby, a kitchen you can cook in and 12 spotless rooms, nine with windows. Dorm rooms have six metal bunks of generous proportions. Located in New Chinatown, about 15 minutes' walk from the Main Bazaar.

★ Batik Boutique Hotel
BOUTIQUE HOTEL $$

(☑082-422845; www.batikboutiquehotel.com; 38 Jln Padungan; d incl breakfast RM280; ❄☎) A superb location, classy design and super-friendly staff make this a top midrange

LAKSA LUCK

Borneo's luckiest visitors start the day with a breakfast of Sarawak laksa, noodle soup made with coconut milk, lemon grass, sour tamarind and fiery *sambal belacan* (shrimp paste sauce), with fresh calamansi lime juice squeezed on top.

Kuching

200 m
0.1 miles

KAMPUNG BOYAN

Jln Brooke

Sungai Sarawak

Astana (200m)

Square Tower

Main Bazaar

Jln China

Jln Carpenter

Jln Bishopsgate

National Park Booking Office

Jln Pearl

St Thomas's Cathedral

Jln Tun Abang Haji Openg

Padang Merdeka

Jln Barrack

Jln India

Jln Gambier

Indian Mosque Ln

Jln Mosque (Jln Masjid)

Gurdwara Sahib Kuching

Jln Khoo Hun Yeang

Saujana Bus Station

Jln P Ramlee

Jln Market

Kuching Mosque

Jln McDougall

Jln Reservoir

Reservoir Park

Visa Department (2.5km)

Jln Tabuan

Jln Wayang

Jln Temple

Klinik Chan

Tua Pek Kong Temple

Jln Green Hill

An Hui Motor

Jln Mathies

Bukit Mata

Jln Borneo

Jln Padungan

BUKIT MATA

Jln Bukit Mata Kuching

Jln Tunku Abdul Rahman

Cat Fountain

Sarawak Plaza

Mohamed Yahia & Sons

Tun Jugah Shopping Centre

Jln Chan Chin Ann

Jln Abell

Jln Padungan

Cat Column

PADUNGAN

Jln Song Thian Cheok

Persiaran Ban Hock

Jln Ban Hock

Beds (200m); Marco Polo Guesthouse (200m); Great Cat of Kuching (250m)

Museum Garden

1 Ethnology Museum

Jln Tun Haji Openg

Jln Satok

Sarawak General Hospital (1.2km)

Ethnology Museum 1
2
R 3
4
5
6
7
8
9
10
12
13
14
15
16
17
18
19
20
21
22
23
24
25
26

Kuching

choice. The swirling batik design used on the hotel's facade is continued in the lobby and the 15 spacious rooms, each with a distinct colour theme. Some rooms have balconies overlooking the courtyard.

Lime Tree Hotel HOTEL $$
(☑ 082-414600; www.limetreehotel.com.my; lot 317, Jln Abell; d incl breakfast RM170-250; ❀ @ ☎) Dashes of lime green – a pillow, a bar of soap, a staff member's tie, the lobby's Cafe Sublime – accent every room of this well-run semi-boutique hotel. The 55 rooms are sleek and minimalist and offer good value; promotional room rates are lower than those quoted here. The rooftop bar has river views and happy hour prices from 5pm to 8pm.

✗ Eating

Kuching is the best place in Malaysian Borneo to work your way through the entire range of Sarawak-style cooking. At hawker centres you can pick and choose from a variety of Chinese and Malay stalls, each specialising in a particular culinary tradition or dish.

★ Choon Hui MALAYSIAN $
(34 Jln Ban Hock; laksa RM5-7; ⊘ 7-11am Tue-Sun) This old-school *kopitiam* (coffee shop) gets our vote for the most delicious laksa in town, and we're not alone – the place can get crowded, especially at weekends. There is also a stall here selling excellent *popia*, a

kind of spring roll made with peanuts, radish and carrot (RM3).

Open-Air Market HAWKER $
(Tower Market; Jln Khoo Hun Yeang; mains RM3-6.50; ⊘ most stalls 6am-4pm, Chinese seafood 3pm-4am) Cheap, tasty dishes to look for include laksa, Chinese-style *mee sapi* (beef noodle soup), red *kolo mee* (noodles with pork and a sweet barbecue sauce), tomato *kueh tiaw* (a fried rice-noodle dish) and shaved ice desserts (ask for 'ABC' at stall 17). The Chinese seafood stalls that open in the afternoon are on the side facing the river.

Aroma Café DAYAK $
(☑ 082-417163; Jln Tabuan; mains RM10-16, buffet per plate RM5-6; ⊘ 7am-10.30pm Mon-Sat, buffet 10am-2pm) A great place to try local indigenous specialities such as *ayam pansuh* (chicken cooked in bamboo; RM10), fried tapioca leaves (RM6) and *umai* (a Sarawakian version of sushi; RM10). The lunchtime buffet is good value.

Yang Choon Tai Hawker Centre CHINESE $
(23 Jln Carpenter; mains RM3.50-8; ⊘ 4am-midnight) Six food stalls, run by members of the Teochew Chinese community, serve up an eclectic assortment of native bites, including rice porridge with pork (3am to 9am), *kolo mee* (flash-boiled egg noodles; available from 6am to 2pm), super fish soup (3pm to 10pm) and – the most popular stall – pork satay (from 2pm).

SPLURGE

Innovative and stylish, **Bla Bla Bla** (082-233944; 27 Jln Tabuan; mains RM22-90; 6-11.30pm Wed-Mon) serves excellent Chinese-inspired fusion dishes that – like the decor, the koi ponds and the Balinese Buddha – range from traditional to far-out. Specialities include *midin* (jungle fern) salad, mango duck (delicious), ostrich and deer, and pandan chicken. The generous portions are designed to be shared.

Zhun San Yen
Vegetarian Food Centre VEGETARIAN $
(Lot 165, Jln Chan Chin Ann; mains RM4.30-5.50; 8am-4.30pm Mon-Fri, 9am-4pm Sat;) A meat-free buffet lunch of Chinese-style curries, priced by weight, is served from 11am to 2pm (RM1.90 per 100g). When the buffet is over, you can order from a menu of dishes such as ginger 'chicken' (made with a soy-based meat substitute).

★**Dyak** DAYAK $$
(082-234068; Jln Mendu & Jln Simpang Tiga; mains RM25-35; noon-11pm, last order 8.30pm;) This elegant restaurant is the first to treat Dayak home cooking as true cuisine. The chef, classically trained in a Western style, uses traditional recipes, many of them Iban (a few are Kelabit, Kayan or Bidayuh), and fresh, organic jungle produce to create mouth-watering dishes unlike anything you've ever tasted. Situated 2km southeast of Old Chinatown.

Tribal Stove DAYAK $$
(082-234873; 10 Jln Borneo; mains RM15-20; 11.30am-10.30pm Mon-Sat;) This laid-back restaurant serving delicious Kelabit food has somehow managed to capture something of the atmosphere of Bario, the Highland 'capital', and transport it to downtown Kuching. Specialities include *labo senutuq* (shredded beef cooked with wild ginger and dried chilli), *ab'eng* (shredded river fish) and pineapple curry. Popular dishes sometimes sell-out by early evening. Food is prepared without MSG.

Top Spot Food Court SEAFOOD $$
(Jln Padungan; fish per kg RM30-70, vegetable dishes RM8-12; noon-11pm) A perennial favourite among local foodies, this neon-lit courtyard and its half-a-dozen humming seafooderies

sits, rather improbably, on the roof of a concrete parking garage – look for the giant backlit lobster sign. Grilled white pomfret is a particular delicacy. Ling Loong Seafood and the Bukit Mata Seafood Centre are especially good.

Self-Catering

Ting & Ting SUPERMARKET
(30A Jln Tabuan; 9am-9pm, closed Sun & holidays) A good selection of wine, snack food, chocolate, toiletries and nappies.

Drinking & Nightlife

Ruai BAR
(7F Jln Ban Hock; 6pm-2.30am) This Iban-owned bar has a laid-back, welcoming spirit all its own. Decorated with old photos and Orang Ulu art (and, inexplicably, several Mexican sombreros), it serves as an urban *ruai* (the covered verandah of an Iban longhouse) for aficionados of caving, hiking and running. Has a good selection of *tuak* (local rice wine). Starts to pick up after about 9pm.

Monkee Bar BAR
(www.monkeebars.com; Jln Song Thian Cheok; beer RM6.50-12, mixed drink RM13; 3pm-2am) At Monkee Bar, 50% of profits go to the Orangutan Project, a wildlife conservation NGO that works at Matang Wildlife Centre (p459). If the idea of 'drinking for conservation' doesn't entice you, the prices might; Monkee Bar has some of the cheapest drinks in town. It's a smoky joint with a young local crowd interspersed with volunteers enjoying downtime from cage-cleaning.

Black Bean Coffee & Tea Company CAFE
(Jln Carpenter; drinks RM3-4.80; 9am-6pm Mon-Sat;) The aroma of freshly ground coffee assaults the senses at this tiny shop, believed by many to purvey Kuching's finest brews. Specialities, roasted daily, include Arabica, Liberica and Robusta coffees grown in Java, Sumatra and, of course, Sarawak. Also serves oolong and green teas from Taiwan. Has just three tables. Decaf not available.

Shopping

If it's traditional arts and crafts you're after, then you've come to the right place – Kuching is the best shopping spot in Malaysian Borneo for traditional handwoven textiles and baskets, masks, drums, beaded headdresses and the like. Don't be afraid to negotiate – there's plenty to choose from, and the quality varies as much as the price.

Main Bazaar HANDICRAFTS

(Main Bazaar; ⊘some shops closed Sun) The row of old shophouses facing the Waterfront Promenade is chock-full of handicrafts shops, some outfitted like art galleries, others with more of a 'garage sale' appeal, and yet others (especially along the Main Bazaar's western section) stocking little more than kitschy-cute cat souvenirs.

Juliana Native Handwork HANDICRAFTS

(☑082-230144; ground fl, Sarawak Textile Museum, Jln Tun Abang Haji Openg; ⊘9am-4.30pm) As well as her own Bidayuh beadwork pieces – most of which have been displayed in an exhibition in Singapore – Juliana sells quality rattan mats (RM490) made made by Penan artists and *pua kumba* Iban woven cloths. The intricate, 50cm-long beaded table runners (RM680) she sells take her three months to complete.

ℹ Information

EMERGENCY
Police, Ambulance & Fire (☑999)

MEDICAL SERVICES
Klinik Chan (☑082-240307; 98 Main Bazaar; ⊘8am-noon & 2-5pm Mon-Fri, 9am-noon Sat, Sun & holidays) Conveniently central. A consultation for a minor ailment costs from RM35.

Normah Medical Specialist Centre (☑082-440055, emergency 082-311999; www. normah.com.my; 937 Jln Tun Abdul Rahman, Petra Jaya; ⊘emergency 24hr, clinics 8.30am-4.30pm Mon-Fri, to 1pm Sat) Widely considered to be Kuching's best private hospital. Has a 24-hour ambulance. Situated north of the river, about 6km by road from the centre. Served by bus 1 from **Saujana Bus Station** (p456), departures on the hour from 7am to 5pm.

Sarawak General Hospital (Hospital Umum Sarawak; ☑082-276666; http://hus.moh. gov.my/v3; Jln Hospital; ⊘24hr) Kuching's large public hospital has modern facilities and remarkably reasonable rates but is often overcrowded. Situated about 2km south of the centre along Jln Tun Abang Haji Openg. To get there, take bus K6, K8 or K18.

MONEY
Many of Kuching's banks and ATMs are clustered around the Cat Fountain on Jln Tunku Abdul Rahman.

Mohamed Yahia & Sons (basement, Sarawak Plaza, Jln Tunku Abdul Rahman; ⊘10am-9pm) No commission, good rates and accepts over 30 currencies (including US$100 bills), as well as traveller's cheques in US dollars, euros, Australian dollars and pounds sterling. Situated inside the bookshop.

TOURIST INFORMATION
National Park Booking Office (☑082-248088; www.sarawakforestry.com; Jln Tun Abang Haji Openg, Sarawak Tourism Complex; ⊘8am-5pm Mon-Fri, closed public holidays) Sells brochures on each of Sarawak's national parks and can supply the latest newsflash on Rafflesia sightings. Telephone enquiries are not only welcomed but patiently answered. Bookings for accommodation at Bako, Gunung Gading and Kubah National Parks and the Matang Wildlife Centre can be made in person, by phone or via http://ebooking. com.my.

Visitors Information Centre (☑082-410942, 082-410944; www.sarawaktourism.com; UTC Sarawak, Jln Padungan; ⊘8am-5pm Mon-Fri, closed public holidays) Usually located in the atmospheric old courthouse complex, at research time the Visitors Information Centre was about to move to a temporary new home in the UTC building on Jln Padungan while the Old Court House buildings were redeveloped.

The office has helpful and well-informed staff, lots of brochures and oodles of practical information (eg bus schedules).

GETTING TO INDONESIA: KUCHING TO PONTIANAK

Getting to the border A variety of bus companies ply the route between Kuching's Kuching Sentral bus terminal (and other cities along the Sarawak coast) and the West Kalimantan city of Pontianak (economy/1st class RM60/80, nine hours), crossing to the Tebedu/Entikong border.

At the border Travellers from 64 countries can get a one-month Indonesian 'visa on arrival' at the road crossing between Tebedu (Malaysia) and Entikong (Indonesia), 80km south of Kuching, the only official land border between Sarawak and Kalimantan (p310).

Moving on Pontianak is linked to other parts of Indonesia and to Singapore by air.

For information on making this crossing in the opposite direction, see p277.

VISA EXTENSIONS

Visa Department (Bahagian Visa; ☑ 082-245661; www.imi.gov.my; 2nd fl, Bangunan Sultan Iskandar, Kompleks Pejabat Persekutuan, cnr Jln Tun Razak & Jln Simpang Tiga; ⏰ 8am-5pm Mon-Thu, 8-11.45am & 2.15-5pm Fri) Situated in a 17-storey federal office building about 3km south of the centre (along Jln Tabuan). Served by City Public Link buses K8 or K11, which run every half-hour or so. A taxi from the centre costs RM15.

🛈 Getting There & Away

AIR

Kuching is linked by budget carrier AirAsia with Kuala Lumpur, Johor Bahru, Penang and Singapore; and, within Borneo, Bintulu, Sibu, Miri and Kota Kinabalu. Malaysia Airlines has direct flights to Singapore, Kota Kinabalu and Kuala Lumpur. MASwings flies to Bandar Seri Begawan, Pontianak and 22 destinations in Sarawak and Sabah.

BOAT

Ekspress Bahagia (☑ 016-800 5891, 016-889 3013, in Kuching 082-412 246, in Sibu 084-319228) runs a daily express ferry from Kuching's Express Wharf, 6km east of the centre, to Sibu (RM45, five hours, daily at 8.30am). A taxi from town to the wharf costs RM35.

BUS

Buses for many destinations can be booked online via www.busonlineticket.com. Kuching has two bus stations:

Kuching Sentral (cnr Jln Penrissen & Jln Airport)

Saujana Bus Station (Jln Masjid & Jln P Ramlee)

🛈 Getting Around

TO/FROM THE AIRPORT

Kuching International Airport is 12km south of the centre. The price of a red-and-yellow taxi into Kuching is fixed at RM30. Coupons are sold inside the terminal.

BOAT

Bow-steered wooden boats known as *tambang*, powered by an outboard motor, shuttle passengers back and forth across Sungai Sarawak, linking jetties along the Waterfront Promenade with Kampung Boyan and the Astana. Crossing the river costs RM1.

MOTORCYCLE

An Hui Motor (☑ 016-886 3328, 082-240508; 29 Jln Tabuan; ⏰ 8am-6pm Mon-Sat, 8am-10.30am Sun) A motorcycle repair shop that charges RM40 per day for a Vespa-like Suzuki RG (110cc) or RGV (120cc) and RM40 for a 125cc scooter (including helmet), plus a deposit of RM100. Insurance covers the bike but not the driver and may be valid only within an 80km radius of Kuching, so check before you head to Sematan, Lundu or Annah Rais.

TAXI

Kuching taxis are required to use meters; overcharging is rare. Fares are 50% higher from midnight to 6am. To order a cab, call **Kuching City Radio Taxi** (☑ 082-348898, 082-480000).

Around Kuching

Western Sarawak offers a dazzling array of natural sights and indigenous cultures, most within day-trip distance of Kuching.

BUSES FROM KUCHING

DESTINATION	STATION	FARE (RM)	DURATION (HR)	FREQUENCY
Batu Niah Junction (for Niah National Park)	Kuching Sentral	80	12-14	hourly
Bintulu	Kuching Sentral	70	11-13	hourly
Kubah National Park	Saujana	4	1	4 per day
Lambir Hills National Park	Kuching Sentral	80	13-15	hourly
Lundu (for Gunung Gading National Park)	Kuching Sentral	12	2-3	4 per day
Miri	Kuching Sentral	80	13-15	hourly
Semenggoh Wildlife Centre	Saujana	3	1	6 per day
Sibu	Kuching Sentral	50	7-8	hourly

Bako National Park

Occupying a jagged peninsula jutting out into the South China Sea, **Bako National Park** (✍ Bako terminal 082-370434; www.sarawakforestry.com; admission RM20; ☺ park office 8am-5pm) is just 37km northeast of downtown Kuching but feels worlds away. It's one of the best places in Sarawak to see rainforest animals in their natural habitats.

The coast of the 27-sq-km peninsula has lovely pocket beaches tucked into secret bays interspersed with wind-sculpted cliffs, forested bluffs and stretches of brilliant mangrove swamp. The interior of the park is home to streams, waterfalls and a range of distinct ecosystems, including classic lowland rainforest (mixed dipterocarp forest) and *kerangas* (heath forest).

Bako provides protected habitat for incredible natural diversity. Scientists estimate that the park is home to about 200 kinds of bird, 24 reptile species and 37 species of mammal. The area around park headquarters is one of the best places to spot wildlife, including reddish-brown proboscis monkeys, the males' pendulous noses flopping as they chew on tender young leaves.

◉ Sights & Activities

Bako's hiking trails – colour-coded and clearly marked with stripes of paint – are suitable for all levels of fitness and motivation, with routes ranging from short nature strolls to strenuous all-day hikes. The ranger-led **night walk** (per person RM10; ☺ 8pm) gets great reviews.

At park headquarters it's possible to hire a boat to one of the more distant beaches and then hike back, or to hike to one of the beaches and arrange for a boat to meet you there.

🛏 Sleeping & Eating

In-park accommodation (110 beds) often fills up, especially from June to August, so if you'd like to stay over it's a good idea to book ahead online via http://ebooking.com.my, in person at the National Park Booking Office (p455) in Kuching, or by phoning the park.

Accommodation includes Forest Lodges **Type 5** (✍ park booking office in Kuching 082-248088; ebooking.com.my; r RM100; ✳) and **Type 6** (✍ park booking office in Kuching 082 248 088; ebooking.com.my; d RM50, 2-room cabin RM75), and the **Forest Hostel** (✍ park booking office in Kuching 082-248088; ebooking.com.my;

dm RM15, q RM40). Space sometimes opens up at the last minute. **Camping** (per person RM5) is permitted.

Kerangas Café   CAFETERIA $
(Canteen; meals RM8-10; ☺ 7.30am-10.30pm) The cafeteria, designed to be macaque-proof, serves a varied and tasty selection of fried rice, chicken, fish, cakes, fresh fruit and packaged snacks. Buffet meals are available from 11.30am to 2pm and 6.30pm to 8pm.

ⓘ Getting There & Away

Getting from Kuching to Bako National Park is a cinch. Bus 1 starts its run to Bako Bazaar (RM3.50, 50 minutes) at 5 Jln Khoo Hun Yeang, in Kuching, across the street from the food stalls of the Open-Air Market. Departures from Kuching are every hour on the hour from 7am to 5pm, and from Bako Bazaar every hour on the half-hour from 6.30am to (usually) 5.30pm. If you miss the last bus, ask around the village for a minibus or private car (RM55) to Kuching.

Boat transfers to Bako Park HQ from Bako Terminal (at Bako Bazaar) are managed by **Koperasi Warisan Pelancongan Bako Berhad** (Bako boat transfers; ✍ 011-2513 2711, 011-2509 5070; ☺ 7.30am-4pm), who have a counter at the terminal and at the park. The 20-minute journey to the park costs RM20 per person. From May to September transfers are usually every hour from 8am to 4pm (ask at the counter for the day's schedule). The last boat back from Bako is at 4pm. From late November to February or March, the sea is often rough and scheduled boat trips may be less frequent.

Santubong Peninsula

The Santubong Peninsula (also known as Damai) is a 10km-long finger of land jutting out into the South China Sea. The main drawcards are the Sarawak Cultural Village, some of Malaysian Borneo's best beaches, and Gunung Santubong (880m), which can be climbed from a point about 1km south of Damai Central.

◉ Sights & Activities

Access to **Damai Central Beach**, across the parking lot from the Sarawak Cultural Village, is free. For a small fee, nonguests can hang out on the sand and in the waves at **Permai Rainforest Resort** (✍ 082-846490; www.permairainforest.com; Damai Beach; adult/child RM5/3; ☺ 7am-7pm).

Sarawak Cultural Village   MUSEUM
(SCV; ✍ 082-846411; www.scv.com.my; Damai Central; adult/child RM90/30; ☺ 9am-4.45pm)

This living museum is centred on seven traditional dwellings: three longhouses, a Penan hut, a Malay townhouse and a Chinese farmhouse. It may sound contrived but the SCV is held in high esteem by locals for its role in keeping their cultures and traditions alive.

Twice a day (at 11.30am and 4pm) a cultural show presents traditional music and dance. The lively Melanau entry involves whirling women and clacking bamboo poles, while the Orang Ulu dance includes balloons and a blowpipe hunter.

🛏 Sleeping & Eating

Damai Central has several inexpensive eateries.

BB Bunkers   HOSTEL $
(☑ 082-846835; www.bbbunkers.com; Damai Central; dm RM53; 🅷 🕸) Situated a few metres from Damai Central Beach, this sleek hostel has the peninsula's only dorm beds. The industrial, hangar-like space is subdivided by curtains, creating cosy spaces for one to three beds, either twins or queens. Secure storage is available.

Village House   GUESTHOUSE $$
(☑ 016-860 9389, 082-846166; www.villagehouse. com.my; lot 634, off Jalan Pantai Puteri, Kampung Santubong; incl breakfast dm RM102, d RM278-552) Tucked away in the quiet Malay village of Santubong, this place has an air of serenity and relaxation. Rooms with belian wood floors and four-poster beds are arranged around a gorgeous pool with frangipani trees at either end. A well-stocked bar and menu of local dishes (mains RM14 to RM60) means there is really no reason to leave.

ⓘ Getting There & Away

Damai Shuttle (☑ 082-846999; one-way adult/child RM12/6) Has departures from Kuching's Grand Margherita Hotel to Damai Beach and Sarawak Cultural Village six times a day between 9am and 6.15pm. The last run back to Kuching leaves the Sarawak Cultural Village at 5.15pm.

Semenggoh Nature Reserve

One of the best places in the world to see semi-wild orangutans in their natural habitat, the **Semenggoh Wildlife Centre** (☑ 082-618325; www.sarawakforestry.com; Jln Puncak Borneo; admission adult RM10; ⊗ 8-11am & 2-4pm, feeding 9am & 3pm) can be visited on

a half-day trip from Kuching or combined with a visit to Annah Rais Longhouse. The shaggy creatures often swing by (literally) park HQ to dine on bananas, coconuts and eggs at daily feeding sessions. There's no guarantee that any orangutans will show up, but even when there are plenty of fruits in the forest the chances are excellent. Sometimes they arrive a little late, so don't rush off straightaway even if everything seems quiet.

ⓘ Getting There & Away

Two bus companies provide reliable public transport from Kuching's Saujana Bus Station to the park gate, situated 1.3km down the hill from park headquarters (RM3, one hour):

City Public Link (☑ 082-239178) Bus K6 departs from Kuching at 7.15am, 10.15am, 1pm and from Semenggoh at approximately 8.45pm, 11.15am, 2.15pm and 4.15pm. Buses have been known to leave *before* their scheduled departure time, so get there early.

Sarawak Transport Company (STC; ☑ 082-233579) Bus 6 has Kuching departures at 6.45am and 12.15pm; buses back pass by Semenggoh at about 10am and 3.45pm.

Tours to Semenggoh are organised by Kuching guesthouses and tour agencies. A taxi from Kuching costs RM60 to RM70 one way or RM120 return, including one hour of wait time.

Annah Rais

Although the 97-door **Bidayuh longhouse** (adult/student RM8/4) here has been on the tourist circuit for decades, it's still an excellent place to get a sense of what a longhouse is and what longhouse life is like.

The 500 residents of Annah Rais are as keen as the rest of us to enjoy the comforts of modern life – they do love their mobile phones and 3G internet access – but they've made a conscious decision to preserve their traditional architecture and the social interactions it engenders. They've also decided that welcoming tourists is a good way to earn a living without moving to the city, something most young people end up doing.

Once you pay your entry fee (in a pavilion next to the parking lot), you're free to explore Annah Rais' three longhouses, either with a guide or on your own. The most important feature is the *awah*, a long, covered common verandah – with a springy bamboo floor – used for economic activities, socialising and celebrations.

🛏 Sleeping

Several families run homestays with shared bathrooms, either in one of the three longhouses or in an adjacent detached house. Standard rates, agreed upon by the community, are RM200 per person for accommodation and delicious Bidayuh board. It is also possible to arrange a package including activities such as hiking, rafting, fishing, (mock) blowgun hunting, soaking in a natural hot spring and a dance performance.

Akam Ganja HOMESTAY **$$**
(☑010-984 3821; winniejagig@gmail.com; per person incl meals RM200) Akam, a retired forestry official, and his wife Winnie, an English teacher, run a welcoming homestay at their comfortable detached house on the riverbank.

ℹ Getting There & Away

Annah Rais, 60km south of Kuching, is not served by public transport. A taxi from Kuching costs RM70 one way.

In Kuching, a variety of guesthouses and tour agencies offer half-day tours to Annah Rais.

Kubah National Park & Matang Wildlife Centre

Mixed dipterocarp forest, among the lushest and most threatened habitats in Borneo, is front and centre at 22-sq-km **Kubah National Park** (☑082-845033; www.sarawak forestry.com; admission incl Matang Wildlife Centre RM20; ☺8am-5pm), which makes an ideal day or overnight trip from Kuching.

When you pay your entry fee, you'll receive a hand-coloured schematic map of the park's interconnected trails. They're well marked, so a guide isn't necessary, and also offer a good degree of shade, making them ideal for the sun averse. And when you're hot and sweaty from walking you can cool off under a crystal-clear waterfall.

A 3.8km trail (or 3½ hours' walk) leads from Kubah National Park to the **Matang Wildlife Centre** (☑082-374869; www.sarawak forestry.com; admission incl Kubah National Park RM20; ☺8am-5pm, animal encloure trail 8.30am-3.30pm), which lies within the park boundaries. The centre has had remarkable success rehabilitating jungle animals rescued from captivity, especially orangutans and sun bears. The highly professional staff do their best to provide their abused charges with natural living conditions with limited funds, but there's no denying that the centre looks like a low-budget zoo plopped down in the

jungle. Because of the centre's unique role, there are endangered animals here that you cannot see anywhere else in Sarawak.

🛏 Sleeping & Eating

Accommodation, available at both Kubah and Matang, is of a better standard at Kubah, where attractive, inexpensive options include the **forest hostel** (☑082-248088; ebooking.com.my; dm RM15) and **forest lodges** (☑082-248088; ebooking.com.my; 6-bed cabin RM225; ✺). Cooking is allowed in the chalets, which have fully equipped kitchens, but there's nowhere to buy food, so bring everything you'll need.

ℹ Getting There & Away

Kubah National Park is 25km northwest of Kuching. A taxi from Kuching costs RM60.

From Kuching's Saujana Bus Station, bus K21 to 'Politeknik' stops on the main road 400m from park headquarters (RM3.50, one hour), next to the Kubah Family Park. Departures from Kuching are at 8am, 11am, 2pm and 5pm, and from the main road (opposite the turn-off for Kubah) at 6.30am, 9.30am, 12.30pm and 3.30pm (be there at 3pm, the bus sometimes leaves early).

Wind Cave & Fairy Cave

About 26km southwest of Kuching, the town of **Bau** is a good access point to two interesting cave systems. Situated 5km southwest of Bau, the **Wind Cave** (Gua Angin; ☑082-765472; adult/child RM5/2; ☺8.30am-4.30pm) is essentially a network of underground streams, while nearby **Fairy Cave** (Gua Pari Pari; adult/child RM5/2; ☺8.30am-4pm) – almost the size of a football pitch and as high as it is wide – is an extraordinary chamber whose entrance is 30m above the ground in the side of a cliff.

ℹ Getting There & Away

The caves are difficult to reach by public transport. Bau is linked to Kuching's Saujana Bus Station (RM5, 1½ hours) by bus 2. Bus 3A from Bau passes 1km from the Wind Cave and bus 3 from Bau passes 1.5km from the Fairy Cave.

A taxi from Kuching costs RM70 one way, or RM150 to RM200 return for a visit to both caves with three hours of wait time.

Gunung Gading National Park

The best place in Sarawak to see the world's largest flower, the renowned rafflesia, 41-sq-km **Gunung Gading National Park** (☑082-735144; www.sarawakforestry.com; admission adult

RM20; ⏰8am-5pm) makes a fine day trip from Kuching. Its old-growth rainforest covers the slopes of four *gunung* (mountains) – Gading, Lundu, Perigi and Sebuloh – traversed by well-marked walking trails that are great for day hikes.

To find out if a rafflesia is in bloom – something that happens here only about 25 times a year – and how long it will stay that way (never more than five days), call the park or the National Park Booking Office (p455) in Kuching.

🛏 Sleeping & Eating

The park has a **hostel** (📞Kuching booking office 082-248088, park HQ 082-735144; ebooking.com.my; Gunung Gading National Park HQ; dm/r without bathroom RM15/40) with four fan rooms and two three-bedroom **forest lodges** that can sleep up to six people. **Camping** is possible at park headquarters.

Cooking is permitted in park accommodation. There are restaurants, food stalls and a large market in the town of Lundu, a walkable 2.5km from the park.

❶ Getting There & Away

Gunung Gading National Park is 85km northwest of Kuching. Four public buses a day link Kuching Sentral long-distance bus station with Lundu, but from there you'll either have to walk 2.5km to the park, or hire an unofficial taxi (about RM5 per person).

Sibu

📞084 / POP 255,000

Gateway to the Batang Rejang, Sibu has grown rich from trade with Sarawak's interior since the time of James Brooke. These days, although the 'swan city' does not rival Kuching in terms of charm, it's not a bad place to spend a day or two before or after a boat trip to the wild interior.

◉ Sights

Sibu Heritage Centre   MUSEUM
(Jln Central; ⏰9am-5pm, closed Mon & public holidays) FREE Housed in a gorgeously airy municipal complex built in 1960, this excellent museum explores the captivating history of Sarawak and Sibu. Panels, rich in evocative photographs, take a look at the various Chinese dialect groups and other ethnic groups, Sarawak's communist insurgency (1965–90), Sibu's Christian (including Methodist) traditions, and even local opposition to Sarawak's incorporation into Malaysia in 1963.

Tua Pek Kong Temple   TAOIST TEMPLE
(Jln Temple; ⏰6.30am-8pm) FREE A modest wooden structure existed on the site of this colourful riverfront Taoist temple as far back as 1871; it was rebuilt in 1897 but badly damaged by Allied bombs in 1942.

For panoramic views over the town and the muddy Batang Rejang, climb the seven-storey Kuan Yin Pagoda, built in 1987; the best time is sunset, when a swirl of swiftlets buzzes around the tower at eye level. Ask for the key at the ground-floor desk.

🛏 Sleeping

★Li Hua Hotel   HOTEL $
(📞084-324000; www.lihua.com.my; cnr Jln Maju & Jln Teo Chong Loh; s/d/ste RM50/65/150; ✼@🛜) Sibu's best-value hotel has 68 spotless, tile-floor rooms spread out over nine storeys and staff that are professional and friendly. It's especially convenient if you're arriving or leaving by boat. Light sleepers should avoid the rooms above the karaoke bars on Jln Teo Chong Loh that blare out music late into the night.

River Park Hotel   HOTEL $
(fax 084-316688; 51-53 Jln Maju; d RM55-75; ✼🛜) A well-run, 30-room hotel in a convenient riverside location. The cheapest rooms don't have windows.

🍴 Eating

Sibu is a great spot for street food, especially Foochow-style Chinese. Try the city's signature dish, *kam pua mee* (thin round noodles soaked in pork fat and served with a side of roast pork).

★Sibu Central Market   HAWKER $
(Pasar Sentral Sibu; Jln Channel; mains RM3-5; ⏰food stalls 3am-midnight) Malaysia's largest fruit-and-veg market has more than 1000 stalls. Upstairs, Chinese-, Malay- and Iban-run food stalls serve up local specialities, including porridge (available early in the morning and at night), *kampua mee* and *kompia*. Most of the noodle stalls close around noon.

Night Market
MARKET, HAWKER **$**

(Pasar Malam; Jln Market; ☻5-11pm or midnight) Chinese stalls (selling pork and rice, steamed buns etc) are at the western end of the lot, while Malay stalls (with superb satay and barbecue chicken) are to the northeast. Also has a few Iban-run places.

★ Payung Café
MALAYSIAN **$$**

(☑016-890 6061; 20F Jln Lanang; mains RM8-19; ☻11am-3pm & 6-11pm Mon-Sun) An exquisitely decorated cafe where diners feast on healthy local food (no re-used oil, deep frying or MSG) such as spicy *otak-otak* barbecued fish (RM13), deliciously fresh herbs salad (RM8) and generous servings of the volcano-like Mulu icecream.

ⓘ Information

Rejang Medical Centre (☑084-323333; www.rejang.com.my; 29 Jln Pedada; ☻emergency 24hr) Has 24-hour emergency services, including an ambulance. Situated about 4km northeast of the city centre.

Visitors Information Centre (☑084-340980; www.sarawaktourism.com; Sublot 3a & 3b, Sibu Heritage Centre, Jln Central; ☻8am-5pm Mon-Fri, closed public holidays) Well worth a stop. Has friendly and informative staff (ask for Jessie), plenty of maps, bus and ferry schedules, and brochures on travel around Sarawak.

ⓘ Getting There & Around

BOAT

Unless you fly, the quickest way to get from Sibu to Kuching is by boat. **Ekspress Bahagia** (☑016-800 5891, in Kuching 082-429242, in Sibu 084-319228; ☻from Sibu 11.30am, from Kuching 8.30am) runs a daily express ferry from Sibu's **Express Ferry Terminal** (Terminal Penumpang Sibu; Jln Kho Peng Long) to Kuching's Express Wharf (RM55, five hours, departure at 11.30am).

'Flying coffin' express boats (named for their shape) run by half-a-dozen companies head up the Batang Rejang to Kapit (RM25 to RM35, 2½ to three hours, 140km) once or twice an hour from 5.45am to 2.30pm.

One boat a day, departing at 5.45am, goes all the way to Belaga (RM60, 11 hours, 295km) – unless water levels are too low to pass beyond Kapit.

For all ferries, be on board at least 15 minutes before departure.

BUS

Sibu's **long-distance bus station** (Jln Pahlawan), which has departures almost 24 hours a day, is about 3.5km northeast of the centre (along Jln Pedada).

ⓘ Getting Around

To get from the local bus station (in front of the Express Ferry Terminal) to the long-distance bus station, take Lanang Bus 21 (RM2, 15 minutes, once or twice an hour 6.30am to 5.15pm).

Batang Rejang

A trip up the tan, churning waters of the Batang Rejang (Rejang River) – the 'Amazon of Borneo' – is one of Southeast Asia's great river journeys. Though the area is no longer the jungle-lined wilderness it was in the days before Malaysian independence, it still retains a frontier, *ulu-ulu* (upriver, back-of-the-beyond) vibe, especially in towns and longhouses accessible only by boat.

Kapit

☑084 / POP 19,500

The main upriver settlement on the Batang Rejang, Kapit is a bustling trading and transport centre dating back to the days of the white rajahs. Its lively markets, including **Pasar Teresang** (☻5.30am-6pm), are important commercial hubs for nearby longhouse communities.

⊙ Sights & Activities

Fort Sylvia
MUSEUM

(Jln Kubu; ☻10am-noon & 2-5pm, closed Mon & public holidays) Built by Charle Brooke in 1880 to take control of the Upper Rejang, this wooden fort – built of *belian* – was

MALAYSIA BATANG REJANG

BUSES FROM SIBU

DESTINATION	FARE (RM)	DURATION (HR)	FREQUENCY
Bintulu	30	3¼	roughly hourly 6am-3.30am
Kuching	50	7-8	7am-4am
Miri	50	6½	roughly hourly 6am-3.30am

ⓘ UPRIVER TRAVEL PERMITS

An outdated permit system is in place for tourists travelling from Kapit to Belaga, or up the Batang Belah. Although the **Resident's Office** (☑ 084-796230; www.kapitro.sarawak.gov.my; 9th fl, Kompleks Kerajaan Negeri Bahagian Kapit, Jln Bleteh; ⊙ 8am-1pm & 2-5pm Mon-Thu, 8-11.45am & 2.15-5pm Fri), linked to Pasar Teresang by minibus (RM2), continues to issue permits (which are free), we've never heard of any authority actually checking if travellers have them. A permit is not required for travel to Belaga from Bintulu.

renamed in 1925 to honour Ranee Sylvia, wife of Charles Vyner Brooke.

The exhibits inside offer a pretty good introduction to the traditional lifestyles of the indigenous groups of the Batang Rejang and include evocative colonial-era photographs. Also on show is the peace jar presented during the historical 1924 peacemaking ceremony between previously warring Iban, Kayan and Kenyah groups.

🛌 Sleeping & Eating

New Rejang Inn　　　　　　　　HOTEL $
(☑ 084-796600, 084-796700; 104 Jln Teo Chow Beng; d RM78; 🏵 🛜) A welcoming and well-run hotel whose 15 spotless, good-sized rooms come with comfortable mattresses, hot water, TV, phone and mini-fridge. The best-value accommodation in town.

Hiap Chiong Hotel　　　　　　　HOTEL $
(☑ 084-796314; 33 Jln Temenggong Jugah; d RM50; 🛜) The 15 rooms have outdated furniture but are clean and have tiny flat-screen TVs.

Night Market　　　　　　　　　　MARKET $
(Taman Selera Empurau; mains RM2.50-5; ⊙ 5-11pm or midnight) Delicious satay and barbecue chicken are the highlight of this night market, which has tables to eat at. Situated a block up the slope from Kapit Town Sq.

ⓘ Information

Kapit has several banks with ATMs.

ⓘ Getting There & Away

Express boats to Sibu (RM25 to RM35, 2½ to three hours, once or twice an hour) depart between 6.40am and 3.15pm from the **Kapit Passenger Terminal** (Jln Panglima Balang).

Water levels permitting, an express boat heads upriver to Belaga (RM55, 4½ hours) from the Kapit Town Square jetty, two blocks downriver from the Kapit Passenger Terminal, once a day at about 9.30am. Be on board by 9.15am.

Belaga

☑ 086 / POP 2500

There's not much to do in Belaga except soak up the frontier outpost vibe, but nearby rivers are home to quite a few Kayan, Kenyah and Penan longhouses.

☞ Tours

The main reason travellers visit Belaga is to venture into the jungle in search of remote longhouses and hidden waterfalls. But you'll need to find a guide. Guesthouse owner **Daniel Levoh** (☑ 086-461198, 013-848 6351; daniellevoh@hotmail.com; Jln Teh Ah Kiong) can help out – he offers day trips (RM85 per person, including lunch) and three-day, two-night longhouse visits (RM750 for a group of three).

🛌 Sleeping

Daniel Levoh's Guesthouse　　GUESTHOUSE $
(☑ 013-848 6351, 086-461198; daniellevoh@hotmail.com; Jln Teh Ah Kiong; dm RM20, d without bathroom RM40; 🛜) The four simple rooms are on the 2nd floor, opening off a large open verandah decorated with a traditional Kayan mural. Owner Daniel Levoh is happy to share stories of longhouse life. Situated two blocks behind Main Bazaar.

Belaga B&B　　　　　　　　　　HOTEL $
(☑ 013-842 9760; freeland205@gmail.com; Main Bazaar; with fan dm/d RM25/15, with air-con d RM35; 🏵) Has seven basic rooms, some with air-con, and shared bathroom facilities. Don't let the name fool you: breakfast isn't included. Owned by Hasbee, a former longhouse guide who now runs the eponymous cafe downstairs. He is happy to help arrange longhouse visits.

ⓘ Information

Belaga's BSN bank branch has an unreliable ATM.

ⓘ Getting There & Away

If the water levels at the Pelagus Rapids (32km upriver from Kapit) are high enough, you can take an express boat to Kapit (RM55, 4½ hours) departing at about 7.30am. To find out if the boat is running, call tour guide Daniel Levoh (☑086-461198, 013-848 6351). When the river is too low, the only way to get out of Belaga is by 4WD to Bintulu.

There are 4WDs that link Belaga's Main Bazaar with Bintulu (RM50 per person, four hours) pretty much daily, with departures at about 7.30am. If you're heading towards Miri, ask to be dropped off at Bakun Junction (Simpang Bakun), 53km northeast of Bintulu and 159km southwest of Miri, where you can flag down a passing bus.

Bintulu

☑086 / POP 190,000

Roughly midway between Sibu and Miri (about 200km from each), the gritty port of Bintulu owes its existence to vast offshore natural gas fields. There's no reason to stay overnight here unless you're heading overland to Belaga.

🛏 Sleeping

Kintown Inn HOTEL $
(☑086-333666; 93 Jln Keppel; s/d RM80/87; ❉🌐) The carpeted rooms, though small and rather musty, are a reasonable option for those on a budget who aren't put off by a bit of peeling paint.

Riverfront Inn HOTEL $$
(☑086-333111; riverfrontinn@hotmail.com; 256 Taman Sri Dagang; s/d from RM81/104; ❉🌐) A long-standing favourite with business and leisure visitors alike, the Riverfront is low-key but has a touch of class. Try to get a deluxe room (RM120) overlooking the river – the view is pure Borneo.

🍴 Eating

Famous Mama MAMAK, HALAL $
(10 Jln Somerville; mains RM5-10; 🌐) Famous Mama does Mamak (halal Indian-Malay) cuisine and is a popular place for quick, cheap *nasi kandar* (rice served with side dishes of different curries) and *roti canai*.

Night Market MALAYSIAN $
(Pasar Malam; off Jln Abang Galau; mains RM2-5; ⊙4-10pm) A good place to pick up snacks, fresh fruit and Malay favourites such as satay and *nasi lemak*.

ℹ Getting There & Away

Bintulu's long-distance bus terminal is 5km northeast of the centre at Medan Jaya; a taxi to/from the city centre costs RM20. A dozen

companies run buses approximately hourly to Kuching (RM70, 11 hours, departures 6am to midnight) and Miri (RM25, four hours, departures from 6am to 9.30pm).

Buses to Kuching go via Sibu (RM25, four hours); buses to Miri stop at Niah Junction (RM15 to RM20, two hours).

To arrange a 4WD inland to Belaga (per person RM50, four hours), contact Daniel Levoh (☑086-461198, 013-848 6351). Departures are generally between noon and 2pm.

A taxi to/from Bintulu airport costs RM35. **AirAsia** (www.airasia.com) and **Malaysia Airlines** (☑086-331349; www.malaysiaairlines.com) have direct flights to Kuching and Kuala Lumpur. **MASwings** (☑086-331349; www.maswings.com.my; Bintulu airport; ⊙7am-7pm) flies to Kota Kinabalu, Miri, Sibu and Kuching.

Niah National Park

Near the coast about 115km south of Miri, 31-sq-km **Niah National Park** (☑085-737450, 085-737454; www.sarawakforestry.com; admission RM20; ⊙park office 8am-5pm) is home to one of Borneo's gems, the Niah Caves. In addition to lots of bats and swiftlets, they shelter some of the oldest evidence of human habitation in Southeast Asia. Across the river from park HQ, **Niah Archaeology Museum** (motor launch per person RM1, 5.30-7.30pm RM1.50; ⊙9am-4.45pm Tue-Fri, 10am-4pm Sat & Sun) has informative displays on Niah's geology, ecology and prehistoric archaeology, including an original burial canoe that's at least 1200 years old and a reproduction of the interior of the Painted Cave.

👁 Sights

★ Great Cave CAVE
A raised boardwalk leads 3.1km (3½ to four hours return) through swampy, old-growth rainforest to the mouth of the Great Cave, a vast cavern approximately 2km long, up to 250m across and up to 60m high. Inside, the trail splits to go around a massive central pillar, but both branches finish at the same point, so it's impossible to get lost if you stick to the boardwalk. The stairs and handrails are usually covered with guano, and can be slippery.

🛏 Sleeping

Bookings for the **hostel** (Niah National Park HQ; r RM40, towel rental RM6) and **forest lodges** (Niah National Park HQ; q with fan RM100, d/q with air-con RM250/150) can be made at park headquarters or through one of the **National Park Booking Offices** (☑in Kuching 082-248088, in Miri 085-434184). Camping (RM5 per person) is permitted near the park headquarters.

The Iban longhouse of Rumah Patrick Libau, near the Great Cave (3km on foot from park headquarters), has a **homestay** (☑Asan 014-596 2757; Niah National Park; per person incl meals RM70; ☎) program.

ℹ Getting There & Away

Park headquarters is 122km northeast of Bintulu and 115km southwest of Miri, not right on the main (inland) Miri–Bintulu highway but rather 15km north of the highway's Batu Niah Junction. The good news is that all the long-haul buses that link Miri with Bintulu, Sibu and Kuching pass by here. The bad news is that the only way to get from the junction to the park is to hire a private car (RM30, for four people RM40) – to find one, ask around outside Ngu's Garden Food Court. National park staff (or, after hours, park security personnel) can help arrange a car back to the junction.

Guesthouses in Miri offer day trips to Niah.

Lambir Hills National Park

The 69-sq-km **Lambir Hills National Park** (☑085-471609; www.sarawakforestry.com; Jln Miri-Bintulu; admission RM20; ☒8am-5pm, last entry 4pm) offers jungle waterfalls, cool pools where you can take a dip, and a bunch of great, colour-coded walking trails that branch off four primary routes and lead to 14 destinations. Rangers can supply you with a map and are happy to make suggestions. A guided night walk starts at 7pm.

🛌 Sleeping

Park accommodation is in reasonably comfortable **cabins** (☑085-471609; Jln Miri-Bintulu; 1/2 rooms with fan RM50/75, with air-con RM100/150). **Camping** (Niah National Park HQ; per person RM5) is permitted near the park headquarters. To book, call or email the park, or contact Miri's National Park Booking Office (p466). The park's **canteen** (Jln Miri-Bintulu; mains RM4-6; ☒8am-5pm or later) serves simple rice and noodle dishes. If you are staying in the park and would like to eat an evening meal at the canteen, inform staff in advance.

ℹ Getting There & Away

Park headquarters is 32km south of Miri on the Miri–Bintulu highway. All the buses linking Miri's Pujut Bus Terminal with Bintulu pass right by here (RM10 from Miri).

Miri

☑085 / POP 300,500

Miri, Sarawak's second city, is a thriving oil town that is busy and modern. There's plenty of money sloshing around, so the eating is good, the broad avenues are brightly lit and the city's friendly guesthouses are a great place to meet other travellers.

The city is a major transport hub, so if you're travelling to/from Brunei, Sabah, the Kelabit Highlands or the national parks of Gunung Mulu, Niah or Lambir Hills, chances are you'll pass this way.

◎ Sights

Miri City Fan PARK
(Jln Kipas; ☒24hr) An attractive open, landscaped park with Chinese- and Malay-style gardens and ponds that is a popular spot for walking and jogging. The complex also comprises a library, an indoor stadium and an Olympic-sized public swimming pool (RM1).

🛌 Sleeping

★ **Dillenia Guesthouse** GUESTHOUSE $
(☑085-434204; www.sites.google.com/site/dilleniaguesthouse; 1st fl, 846 Jln Sida; dm/s/d/f incl breakfast, without bathroom RM30/50/80/110; ❋@☎) This super-welcoming hostel, with 11 rooms and lots of nice little touches like plants in the bathroom, lives up to its motto, 'a home away from home'. Incredibly helpful Mrs Lee, whose beautiful embroidered quilts adorn the walls, is an artesian well of travel information and tips – and even sells leech socks (RM20).

Coco House GUESTHOUSE $
(☑085-417051; www.cocodive.com.my; lot 2117 Block 9, Jln Miri Pujut; dm/s/d incl breakfast RM35/55/80; ❋@☎) Coco House has bright, modern dorms with pod-like bunks and private rooms that are small but functional with splashes of colour. The spotless bathrooms have rainwater shower heads and there is a comfy common area with books, board games, DVDs and a microwave. There is talk of putting a barbecue on the roof terrace.

Next Room Guesthouse
GUESTHOUSE $

(☑085-411422, 085-322090; 1st & 2nd fl, lot 637, Jln North Yu Seng; incl breakfast dm per person RM28, d without bathroom RM55-85, with bathroom RM85-95; ❄@🕿) In the heart of Miri's dining and drinking district, this cosy establishment offers 13 rooms, a small kitchen, a DVD lounge and a great rooftop sun deck. Dorm rooms are pretty packed, with eight or 12 beds. Light sleepers be warned: the nightclub across the street pumps out music until 2am.

My Homestay
GUESTHOUSE $

(☑085-429091; staymyhomestay.blogspot.com; Lot 1091, Jln Merpati; dm incl breakfast RM35, d RM55-120; ❄@🕿) A friendly place in a good location with a spacious balcony overlooking the bustling street below. Most rooms, though clean and colourful, are windowless and a little stuffy. Prices are higher at weekends.

✖ Eating

Restaurants of all sorts line Jln North Yu Seng from the landmark Mega Hotel north to the Imperial Mall, with lots more cheap, popular places south of the Mega Hotel along pedestrians-only **Persiaran Kabor**. A number of informal but excellent seafooderies serve critters plucked live from tanks – but beware of the prices, which are per 100g.

★ Summit Café
DAYAK $

(☑019-885 3920; lot 1245, Centre Point Commercial Centre, Jln Melayu; meals RM8-15; ⊙7am-4pm Mon-Sat; ✍) If you've never tried Kelabit cuisine, this place will open up whole new worlds for your tastebuds. Queue up and choose from the colourful array of 'jungle food' laid out at the counter, including *dure* (fried jungle leaf), minced tapioca leaves, and *labo senutuk* (wild boar). The best selection is available before 11.30am – once the food runs out it closes.

Khan's Islamic Restaurant
INDIAN $

(☑012-878 9640; 229 Jln Maju; mains RM6-12; ⊙6.30am-9pm; ✍) This simple canteen is one of Miri's best North Indian eateries, serving up mouth-watering tandoori chicken (RM12), naan bread and mango lassi (RM4), as well as a variety of curries and vegetarian dishes.

Miri Central Market
HAWKER $

(Pasar Pusat Miri; Jln Brooke; mains RM2-6; ⊙24hr, most stalls 4am-noon) Of the Chinese food purveyors selling *kari ayam* (chicken curry), porridge and the usual rice and noodle dishes, stall 6 (open 3.30am to 10am) is particularly popular. Stall 20 serves up vegetarian fare.

Madli's Restaurant
MALAYSIAN $

(☑085-426615; www.madli.net; lot 1088, ground fl, Block 9, Jln Merpati; mains RM6-18.50; ⊙8am-midnight Sun-Thu, 8am-1am Fri & Sat) A long-running family business that started off as a satay stall in the 1970s; the first of three restaurants was opened in Miri 1995. As well as lip-smackingly good chicken and lamb satay (RM1 per stick), the menu includes Malaysian dishes like *nasi lemak* and kampung fried rice. Serves *roti canai* and Western breakfasts until noon.

ℹ Information

ATMs can be found at Miri airport and are sprinkled all over the city centre.

MALAYSIA MIRI

GETTING TO BRUNEI: MIRI TO BANDAR SERI BEGAWAN

Getting to the border The only company that's allowed to take passengers from Miri to destinations inside Brunei is **PHLS Express** (☑in Brunei +673 277 1668, in Miri 085-438301), which sends buses at 8.15am and 3.15pm daily from Miri's Pujut Bus Terminal to Bandar Seri Begawan (RM50).

Another option is a private transfer run by father-and-son team Mr Fu and Ah Pau (RM70 per person, three hours). Call Mr Fu on ☑013-833 2231; reservations can also be made through Dillenia Guesthouse.

At the border Border formalities (open 6am to 10pm) are usually quick, and for most nationalities (except Australians) Bruneian visas are free. If you'll be continuing on to Sabah, make sure you have enough pages in your passport for no fewer than 10 stamps.

Moving on The bus from Miri stops near the centre of BSB.

For information on making this crossing in the opposite direction, see p63.

EcoLaundry (☎ 085-414266; 638 Jln North Yu Seng; per kg RM6; ⊙7am-6pm Mon-Sat, to 5pm Sun) Free pick up and delivery within the town centre.

Miri City Medical Centre (☎ 085-426622; 916-920 Jln Hokkien; ⊙ emergency 24hr) Has an ambulance service, a 24-hour accident and emergency department and various private clinics. Located in the city centre.

National Park Booking Office (☎ 085-434184; www.sarawakforestry.com; 452 Jln Melayu; ⊙8am-5pm Mon-Fri) Inside the Visitors Information Centre. Has details on Sarawak's national parks and can book beds and rooms at Niah, Lambir Hills and Similajau (but not Gunung Mulu).

Visitors Information Centre (☎ 085-434181; www.sarawaktourism.com; 452 Jln Melayu; ⊙8am-5pm Mon-Fri, 9am-3pm Sat, Sun & public holidays) The helpful staff can provide city maps, information on accommodation and a list of licensed guides. Situated in a little park.

❶ Getting There & Away

Miri is 212km northeast of Bintulu and 36km southwest of the Brunei border.

AIR

Miri is the main hub of the Malaysia Airlines subsidiary **MASwings** (☎ 085-423500; www.maswings.com.my; ground fl, airport terminal; ⊙6am-9pm), whose destinations in Malaysian Borneo include Bario (Kelabit Highlands), Gunung Mulu National Park (Mulu), Kota Kinabalu, Kuching and Sibu.

AirAsia (☎ 600 85 8888; www.airasia.com; lot 946, Jln Parry; ⊙8.30am-5.30pm Mon-Fri, to 1pm Sat) can get you to Kuching, Kota Kinabalu, Kuala Lumpur, Johor Bahru, Singapore and Manila, while **Malaysia Airlines** (☎ 085-414155; www.malaysiaairlines.com; lot 10635, Airport Commercial Centre, Jln Airport) has direct flights to KL.

BUS

Long-distance buses use the Pujut Bus Terminal, about 4km northeast of the centre. It's linked to the city centre's local bus terminal (next to the tourist office) by buses 20 and 33A (RM1.60 or RM2.60), which run about every 1½hrs from 6.30am to 6.30pm. A taxi costs RM20.

A number of companies send frequent buses southwestward to destinations such as Bintulu, Sibu and Kuching from 6.30am to 10pm; all pass by Lambir Hills National Park. Taking a spacious 'VIP bus', with just three seats across, is like flying 1st class!

PHLS Express (p465) sends buses to Brunei, including Bandar Seri Begawan and Bangar, at 8.15am and 3.45pm. Tickets are sold at the

Bintang Jaya (☎ Kuching 082-531133, Miri 085-432178; www.bintangjayaexpress.com) counter.

Borneo Bus has a service to Kota Kinabalu (KK) every day at 7.45am, while Bintang Jaya's daily KK bus leaves at 8.30am.

Seats for many routes can be booked via www.busonlineticket.com.

Buses from Miri:

DESTINATION	FARE (RM)	DURATION (HR)
Bandar Seri Begawan (Brunei)	50	3½
Batu Niah Junction (for Niah NP)	10-12	1½
Bintulu	20-27	3½
Kota Kinabalu	90	10
Kuching	60-90	13-15
Sibu	40-50	7-8

Gunung Mulu National Park

Few national parks anywhere in the world pack so many natural marvels into such a small area. From caves of mind-boggling proportions to other-worldly geological phenomena such as the Pinnacles to brilliant old-growth rainforest, 529-sq-km **Gunung Mulu National Park** (Gunung Mulu World Heritage Area; ☎ 085-792300; www.mulupark.com; for five calendar days RM30) – declared a Unesco World Heritage Site in 2002 – is truly one of our planet's wonders.

⊙ Sights & Activities

When you register, helpful park staff will give you a schematic map of the park on which you can plan out your daily itineraries.

You can take several excellent jungle trails unaccompanied as long as you inform the park office (or, when it's closed, someone in the Park Security building) – options include the 8km Paku Valley Loop.

Mulu's 'show caves' (caves that can be visited without special training or equipment) are the park's most popular attractions and for good reason: they are truly awe-inspiring. Cave routes that require special equipment and a degree of caving experience are known as 'adventure caves'. For both, bring a torch.

All of the caves and some of the rainforest hikes require a certified guide. Advance reservations are a must, especially if you've got your heart set on adventure caving, or on hiking to the Pinnacles or up to the summit of Gunung Mulu. July, August and September are the park's busiest months, but even then spots do open up at the last minute if you're able to hang out at the park for a few days. Tour agencies charge more than the park itself but may be able to find a guide on short notice.

★ Deer Cave & Lang Cave CAVE
(per person RM30; ⊘ 2pm & 2.30pm) A 3km walk through the rainforest takes you to these adjacent caverns. The Deer Cave – over 2km in length and 174m high – is the world's largest cave passage open to the public, while the Lang Cave – more understated in its proportions – contains interesting stalactites and stalagmites. Be sure to stay on for the 'bat exodus' at dusk.

Wind Cave & Clearwater Cave CAVE
(per person incl boat ride RM65; ⊘ 8.45am & 9.15am) Zipping along a jungle river in a longboat on your way to the caves is not a bad way to start the day. The Wind Cave, named for the cool breezes blowing through it, has several chambers, including the cathedral-like King's Chamber, filled with dreamlike forests of stalagmites and columns. There is a sweaty 200-step climb up to Clearwater Cave and the subterranean river there. The cave itself is vast: more than 200km of passages have been surveyed so far.

Mulu Canopy Skywalk WALKING
(Gunung Mulu National Park; per person RM42.40; ⊘ 7am, 8.30am, 10am, 10.30am, 1pm & 2pm) Mulu's 480m-long skywalk, unforgettably anchored to a series of huge trees, has excellent signage and is one of the best in Southeast Asia. Often gets booked out early – for a specific time slot, reserve as soon as you've got your flight.

Pinnacles TREKKING
(per person RM400; ⊘ Tue-Thu & Fri-Sun) The Pinnacles are an incredible formation of 45m-high stone spires protruding from the forested flanks of Gunung Api. Getting there involves a boat ride and, in between two overnights at Camp 5 (per person incl boat ride RM190), an unrelentingly steep 2.4km ascent. Coming down is just as taxing, so by the time you stagger back to camp, the cool, clear river may look pretty enticing.

Gunung Mulu Summit TREKKING
(per person RM500, minimum 3 people) The climb to the summit of Gunung Mulu (2376m) – described by one satisfied ascendee as 'gruelling' and, near the top, 'treacherous' – is a classic Borneo adventure. If you're very fit and looking for a challenge, this 24km, three-day, four-night trek may be for you. The climb must be booked at least one month in advance.

Headhunters' Trail TREKKING
The physically undemanding Headhunters' Trail continues on from Camp 5 (at the Pinnacles) for 11km in the direction of Limbang and is an overland alternative to flying in or out of Mulu. The park does not offer guided trips along this trail, but several private tour operators do, and it is also (theoretically) possible to do it without a guide.

🛏 Sleeping

Options at park headquarters – a truly lovely spot – include a **hostel** (dm incl breakfast RM52) that has 20 beds in a clean, spacious dormitory-style room (lockers available), as well as **longhouse rooms** (s/d/tr/q incl breakfast RM209/247/277/313; ❄), **cabins** (q incl breakfast RM387; ❄) and **garden bungalows** (s/d/tr incl breakfast RM253/294/341; ❄). At the time of research, 12 new longhouse-style rooms were being constructed, which should go someway towards allieviating the accommodation shortage.

Several budget places, unaffiliated with the park, can be found across the bridge from park headquarters, along the banks of Sungai Melinau. There are plenty of beds, so if you don't mind very basic digs, you can fly up without worrying about room availability.

D'Cave Homestay HOMESTAY $
(✏ for Dina 012-872 9752; beckhamjunior40@ yahoo.com; incl breakfast dm RM30, d RM120, d without bathroom RM80) A friendly, rather ramshackle place with mismatched patterned lino, beds crammed into small rooms and basic, outdoor bathrooms. Owner Dina cooks buffet-style lunches (RM15) and dinners (RM18), has tea and coffee, and has boiled water for water-bottle refills. Situated between the airport and the turning for the park – about a 10-minute walk from each.

Mulu River Lodge HOSTEL $
(Edward Nyipa Homestay; ✏ 012-852 7471; dm/d/q incl breakfast RM35/70/140) Has 30 beds, most in a giant, non-bunk dorm room equipped

with clean showers and toilets at one end. Electricity flows from 5pm to 11.30pm. One of the few guesthouses outside the park, if not the only one, with a proper septic system. Located a five-minute walk from park HQ, just across the bridge from the entrance.

Mulu Backpackers GUESTHOUSE $
(☑ Helen 012-871 2947, Peter 013-846 7250; mulu backpackers@gmail.com; dm incl breakfast RM35) Mulu Backpackers, situated just past the airport, occupies a picturesque spot by the river but is a 15-minute walk from the park. There is a pleasant sheltered outdoor dining area with views of the water and electricity from 6pm to 6am. The 17 beds here are arranged in large, barn-like space with some randomly positioned partition walls.

✕ Eating

At park HQ, **Café Mulu** (mains RM12.50-16; ☻ 7.30am-8.30pm) serves up tasty meals for double what you'd pay on the coast. There are a number of slightly cheaper eateries just outside the park gates, including **Good Luck Cave'fe Mulu** (mains RM8-10; ☻ 11.30am-3pm & 5pm-midnight, kitchen closes at 9.15pm). Cooking is not allowed in park accommodation.

❶ Information

Park HQ accepts credit cards and can also do cash withdrawals of RM100 to RM300 (one transaction per day) for a 2% fee, but the machine is temperamental.The shop and cafe area at park HQ has an excruciatingly slow and unreliable wi-fi connection (RM5 per day).

❶ Getting There & Away

Unless you walk the Headhunters' Trail, pretty much the only way to get to Mulu is by air. MASwings flies to Miri, Kuching and KK. Park headquarters is a walkable 1km from the airport; taking a van costs RM5. Tickets can be bought at Mulu airport, though some discounts are only available online.

Kelabit Highlands

Nestled in Sarawak's northeastern corner, the upland rainforests of the Kelabit Highlands are sandwiched between Gunung Mulu National Park and the Indonesian frontier. The main activity here, other than enjoying the clean, cool air, is hiking from longhouse to longhouse on mountain trails.

Bario

The 'capital' of the highlands, Bario consists of about a dozen 'villages' spread over a beautiful valley, much of it given over to rice growing. Some of the appeal lies in the mountain climate (the valley is 1500m above sea level) and splendid isolation (the only access is by air and torturous 4WD track), but above all it's the unforced hospitality of the Kelabit people that will quickly win you over.

The highlands are famous for the delicious local cuisine; in July visitors flock to Bario for the annual three-day-long food festival.

◉ Sights & Activities

The temperate Kelabit Highlands offer some of the best jungle hiking in Borneo, taking in primary rainforest, rugged peaks and remote Kenyah, Penan and Kelabit settlements. Walks from Bario range from easy overnight trips to nearby longhouses to week-long slogs into the wilds of Kalimantan. Be prepared to encounter leeches – many trails are literally crawling with them.

Bario Asal Longhouse HOUSE
(admission RM5) This all-wood, 22-door longhouse has the traditional Kelabit layout. On the *dapur* (enclosed front verandah) each family has a hearth, while on the other side of the family units is the *tawa'*, a wide back verandah – essentially an enclosed hall over 100m long – used for weddings, funerals and celebrations and decorated with historic family photos.

Pa' Umor Megaliths HISTORIC SITE
From Bario it's a 1½-hour walk to Pa' Umor, and another 15 minutes to Arur Bilit Farm, home to Batu Narit, an impressive stone carving featuring a human in a spread-eagled position among its designs.

Take the log bridge across the small river to reach Batu Ipak. According to legend, this stone formation was created when an angry warrior named Upai Semering pulled out his *parang* (machete) and took a wrathful swing at the rock, cutting it in two.

Prayer Mountain HIKING
From the Bario Asal Longhouse, it's a steep, slippery ascent (two hours) up to the summit of Prayer Mountain, which has a cross that was erected in 1973, thickets of pitcher plants and amazing views of the Bario Valley

With very few exceptions, to explore the Kelabit Highlands you'll need to hire a local guide. Fortunately this could hardly be easier. Any of the guesthouses in Bario can organise a variety of short hikes and longer walks – such as a three- to four-day hike from Bario to Ba Kelalan – led by guides they know and rely on.

The going rate for guides is RM120 per day for either a Bario-based day trip or a longer hike. If your route requires that you camp in the forest, expect to pay approximately RM120 per night, and you may be asked to supply food. If you are connecting the dots between rural longhouses, expect to pay RM70 to RM80 for a night's sleep plus three meals. When hiking in one direction only you'll need to pay your guide for the time it takes him to walk home and also hire a porter (RM100 per day) for the whole trip so that the guide does not have to return alone.

and of the mixed Penan and Kelabit hamlet of Arur Dalan, with its three defunct wind turbines. Two-thirds of the way up is an extremely rustic church.

Sleeping & Eating

Bario's various component villages are home to over 20 guesthouses where you can dine on delicious Kelabit cuisine (accommodation prices almost always include board). See www.barioexperience.com for further options.

Libal Paradise GUESTHOUSE $
(019-807 1640; d RM60) Surrounded by a verdant fruit and vegetable garden where you can pick your own pineapples, this sustainably run farm offers accommodation in two neat wooden cabins, each occupying their own idyllic spot in the greenery. Run by Rose and her Canadian husband Stu. From the airport terminal, walk eastward along the road that parallels the runway. Meals cost RM45 per day.

Junglebluesdream GUESTHOUSE $$
(019-884 9892; www.junglebluesdream.weebly.com; Ulung Palang Longhouse, Bario; per person incl meals RM90) Owned by artist and one-time guide Stephen Baya, a Bario native, and his friendly Danish wife Tine, this super-welcoming lodge (and art gallery) has four mural-decorated rooms, good-quality beds and quilts, a library of books on local culture and wildlife and fantastic Kelabit food. Guests can consult Stephen's extraordinary hand-drawn town and trekking maps.

Bario Asal Longhouse HOMESTAY $$
(Julian 011-2508 1114; visitbario@gmail.com; per person incl meals RM80;) There are various homestays in this traditional longhouse, including a six-room guesthouse at Sinah Rang Lemulun. Staying at Bario Asal – which is home to 22 families – is a great way to experience longhouse living. Transport from the airport costs RM30.

Information

There are no banks, ATMs or credit-card facilities anywhere in the Kelabit Highlands, so bring plenty of small-denomination banknotes, plus extra cash in case you get stranded.

There's free wi-fi at the airport and solar-powered internet access at **Bario Telecentre** (www.unimas.my/ebario; Gatuman Bario; per hr RM4 ; 9.30-11.30am & 2-4pm, closed Sat afternoon & Sun). Several guesthouses offer wi-fi, at least in theory.

The best Malaysian cell phone service to have up here is Celcom.

Getting There & Away

Bario Airport is linked with Miri two or three times a day by 19-seat Twin Otters operated by **MASwings** (1300-88 3000; www.maswings.com.my); checked baggage is limited to 10kg. Weather sometimes causes delays and even cancellations.

The overland trip between Bario and Miri, on very rough logging roads, is possible only by 4WD (per person RM150, 12 to 15 hours or more).

UNDERSTAND MALAYSIA

Malaysia Today

National tragedies and political troubles have impacted Malaysia in recent years. Malaysian Airlines lost two of its passenger airplanes in tragic circumstances, with a combined death toll of 537. An earthquake

TRAVEL HINTS

➡ Malaysia is a Muslim country so dress appropriately by covering everything to the knees and over the shoulders.

➡ Airfares can be so cheap around Borneo that flying is sometimes cheaper than bussing.

struck Sabah on 5 June 2015 and claimed the lives of 18 people on Mt Kinabalu, shutting down the mountain to tourists for months.

In the meantime, Prime Minister Najib Razak – leader of the Barisan Nasional (BN) coaltion of political parties that has ruled Malaysia since the 1970s – has been battling allegations of corruption and a faltering economy. In recent years, Bersih (Coalition for Clean and Fair Elections), a group of nongovernment organisations, has staged several huge rallies in KL demanding electoral reform and investigations into alleged government corruption; in August 2015 tens of thousands peacefully protested on the streets of the capital.

The BN maintains that it has created a stable government that rightfully retains its popularity. But it has curtailed freedom of speech. Malaysia was ranked 147th out of 180 countries in the Reporters Without Borders 2015 World Press Freedom Index.

The BN is primarily supported by Malays and is veering with the Malay populace towards more conservative Islamic rule. Prime Minister Najib's three-pronged strategy has been a closer embrace of Islamic Sharia laws, a stronger *bumiputra* agenda that essentially acts as affirmative action for Malays while trying to mastermind how the BN can also woo the six million new, young voters eligible to vote in the next elections, which need to take place before August 2018.

History

Early Influences

The earliest evidence of human life in the region is a 40,000-year-old skull found in Sarawak's Niah Caves. But it was only around 10,000 years ago that the aboriginal Malays, the Orang Asli, began moving down the peninsula from a probable starting point in southwestern China.

By the 2nd century AD Europeans were familiar with Malaya, and Indian traders had made regular visits in their search for gold, tin and jungle woods. Within the next century Malaya was ruled by the Funan empire, centred in what's now Cambodia, but more significant was the domination of the Sumatra-based Srivijayan empire between the 7th and 13th centuries.

In 1405 Chinese admiral Cheng Ho arrived in Melaka with promises to the locals of protection from the Siamese encroaching from the north. With Chinese support, the power of Melaka extended to include most of the Malay Peninsula. Islam arrived in Melaka around this time and soon spread through Malaya.

European Influence

Melaka's wealth and prosperity attracted European interest and it was taken over by the Portuguese in 1511, then the Dutch in 1641 and the British in 1795.

In 1838 James Brooke, a British adventurer, arrived to find the Brunei sultanate fending off rebellion from inland tribes. Brooke quashed the rebellion and in reward was granted power over part of Sarawak. Appointing himself Raja Brooke, he founded a dynasty that lasted 100 years. By 1881 Sabah was controlled by the British government, which eventually acquired Sarawak after WWII when the third Raja Brooke realised he couldn't afford the area's upkeep. In the early 20th century the British brought in Chinese and Indians, which radically changed the country's racial make-up.

Independence to the Current Day

Malaya achieved *merdeka* (independence) in 1957, but it was followed by a period of instability due to an internal Communist uprising and an external confrontation with neighbouring Indonesia. In 1963 the north Borneo states of Sabah and Sarawak, along with Singapore, joined Malaya to create Malaysia.

In 1969 violent interracial riots broke out, particularly in Kuala Lumpur, and hundreds of people were killed. The government moved to dissipate the tensions, which existed mainly between the Malays and the Chinese. The New Economic Policy (NEP), a socioeconomic affirmative action plan, was introduced, with the aim of placing 30% of Malaysia's corporate wealth in the hands of indigenous

Malays and Orang Asli (known as *bumiputra* or princes of the land), within 20 years. This plan, which was partially successful, is still in force in various guises today.

Led from 1981 by outspoken, dictatorial Prime Minister Dr Mahathir Mohamad, Malaysia's economy grew at a rate of over 8% per year until mid-1997, when a currency crisis in neighbouring Thailand plunged the whole of Southeast Asia into recession. After 22 momentous years, Dr Mahathir Mohamad retired on 31 October 2003. He handed power to his anointed successor, Abdullah Badawi, who won the general election in March 2004.

However, in the next election in 2008, BN saw its parliamentary dominance slashed to less than the two-thirds majority it had previously held. The inroads were made by Pakatan Rakyat (PR), the opposition People's Alliance led by Anwar Ibrahim, a former deputy PM who had been jailed on corruption and sodomy charges that were widely regarded as politically motivated. Abdullah Badawi resigned in favour of Najib Razak, who would go on to win the 2013 election for BN, although it was the coalition's poorest showing in the polls since 1969.

People & Culture

The National Psyche

From the ashes of the interracial riots of 1969, the country has forged a more tolerant multicultural society, exemplified by the coexistence in many cities and towns of mosques, Christian churches and Chinese temples. Though ethnic loyalties remain strong and there are undeniable tensions, the concept of a single 'Malaysian' identity is national policy and for the most part everyone coexists harmoniously. The friendliness and hospitality of Malaysians is what most visitors see and experience.

Moving from the cities to the more rural parts of the country, the laid-back ethos becomes stronger and Islamic culture comes more to the fore, particularly on the peninsula's east coast. In Malaysian Borneo you'll be fascinated by the communal lifestyle of the tribes who still live in jungle longhouses (enormous wooden structures on stilts that house tribal communities under one roof). In longhouses, hospitality is a key part of the social framework.

Lifestyle

The *kampung* (village) is at the heart of the Malay world and operates according to a system of *adat* (customary law) that emphasises collective rather than individual responsibility. Devout worship of Islam and older spiritual beliefs go hand in hand with this. However, despite the mutually supportive nature of the *kampung* environment, and growing Westernisation across Malaysia, some very conservative interpretations of Islam continue in certain areas, particularly along the peninsula's east coast.

Malaysia's rapid modernisation has led to some incongruous scenes. In Sarawak, some ramshackle longhouses and huts sport satellite dishes and other mod cons. And almost everywhere you go people incessantly finger mobile phones as if they're simply unable to switch them off.

Population

Malaysians come from a number of different ethnic groups: Malays, Chinese, Indians, the indigenous Orang Asli (literally, 'Original People') of the peninsula, and the various

MALAYSIA PEOPLE & CULTURE

THE PERANAKANS

One of Malaysia's most celebrated cultures is that of the Peranakans, descendants of Chinese immigrants who, from the 16th century onwards, settled in Singapore, Melaka and Penang. While these arrivals often married Malay women, others imported their wives from China; all of them like to refer to themselves as Straits-born or Straits Chinese to distinguish themselves from later arrivals from China. Another name you may hear for these people is Baba-Nonyas, after the Peranakan words for males (*baba*) and females (*nonya*).

The Peranakans took the religion of the Chinese, but the customs, language and dress of the Malays. The Peranakans were often wealthy traders who could afford to indulge their passion for sumptuous furnishings, jewellery and brocades. Today they are most famous for their delicious fusion cooking that's best experienced in Melaka and Penang.

tribes of Sarawak and Sabah in Malaysian Borneo. The mixing of these groups has created the colourful cultures and delicious cuisine that makes Malaysia such a fabulous destination.

It's reasonable to generalise that the Malays control the government while the Chinese dominate the economy. Approximately 85% of the country's population of 29.72 million people lives in Peninsular Malaysia and the other 15% in Sabah and Sarawak on Borneo.

There are still small, scattered groups of Orang Asli in Peninsular Malaysia. Although most of these people have given up their nomadic or shifting-agriculture techniques and have been absorbed into modern Malay society, a few such groups still live in the forests.

Dayak is the term used for the non-Muslim people of Borneo. It is estimated there are more than 200 Dayak tribes in Borneo, including the Iban and Bidayuh in Sarawak and the Kadazan in Sabah. Smaller groups include the Kenyah, Kayan and Penan, whose way of life and traditional lands are rapidly disappearing.

Religion

The Malays are almost all Muslims. But despite Islam being the state religion, freedom of religion is guaranteed. The Chinese are predominantly followers of Taoism and Buddhism, though some are Christians. The majority of the region's Indian population comes from the south of India and are Hindu and Christian, although a sizeable percentage are Muslim.

While Christianity has made no great inroads into Peninsular Malaysia, it has had a much greater impact in Malaysian Borneo, where many indigenous people have been converted and carry Christian as well as traditional names. Others still follow animist traditions.

Arts

It's along the predominantly Malay east coast of Peninsular Malaysia that you'll find Malay arts and crafts, culture and games at their liveliest. Malaysian Borneo is replete with the arts and crafts of the country's indigenous peoples.

ARTS & CRAFTS

A famous Malaysian Bornean art is *pua kumbu,* a colourful weaving technique used to produce both everyday and ceremonial items.

The most skilled woodcarvers are generally held to be the Kenyah and Kayan peoples, who used to carve enormous, finely detailed *kelirieng* (burial columns) from tree trunks.

Originally an Indonesian craft, the production of batik cloth is popular in Malaysia and has its home in Kelantan. A speciality of Kelantan and Terengganu, *kain songket* is a handwoven fabric with gold and silver threads through the material. *Mengkuang* is a far more prosaic form of weaving using pandanus leaves and strips of bamboo to make baskets, bags and mats.

DANCE

Menora is a dance-drama of Thai origin performed by an all-male cast in grotesque masks; *mak yong* is the female version. The upbeat *joget* (better known around Melaka as *chakuncha*) is Malaysia's most popular traditional dance, often performed at Malay weddings by professional dancers.

Rebana kercing is a dance performed by young men to the accompaniment of tambourines. The *rodat* is a dance from Terengganu and is accompanied by the *tar* drum.

MUSIC

Traditional Malay music is based largely on the *gendang* (drum), of which there are more than a dozen types. Other percussion instruments include the gong, *cerucap* (made of shells), *raurau* (coconut shells), *kertuk* and *pertuang* (both made from bamboo), and the wooden *celampang.*

Wind instruments include a number of types of flute (such as the *seruling* and *serunai*) and the trumpetlike *nafiri,* while stringed instruments include the *biola, gambus* and *sundatang.*

The *gamelan,* a traditional Indonesian gong-orchestra, is also found in the state of Kelantan, where a typical ensemble will comprise four different gongs, two xylophones and a large drum.

Food & Drink

Food

The delicious food you'll enjoy in Malaysia strongly reflects the country's Malay, Chinese and Indian influences.

There are fewer culinary choices outside the cities, where staple meals of mee goreng (fried noodles) and nasi goreng (fried rice) predominate. Vegetarian dishes are usually available at both Malay and Indian cafes, but are hardly sighted at *kedai kopi* (coffee shops). You can also find an excellent selection of fruit and vegetables at markets.

Roti canai (flaky flat bread dipped in a small amount of dhal and potato curry) is probably the cheapest meal (around RM1.50). But really everything, from seafood laksa to the freshly caught and cooked wild cat or mouse deer you may be offered at a longhouse, is good and often cheap.

Halfway between a drink and a dessert is *ais kacang*, something similar to an old-fashioned snow-cone, except that the shaved ice is topped with syrups and condensed milk, and it's all piled on top of a foundation of beans and jellies (sometimes corn kernels). It tastes terrific.

Drink

Tap water is safe to drink in many big cities, but check with locals if you're unsure.

With the aid of a blender and crushed ice, simple and delicious juice concoctions are whipped up in seconds. Lurid soybean drinks are sold at street stalls and soybean milk is also available in soft-drink bottles. Medicinal teas are a big hit with the health-conscious Chinese.

Alcohol incurs incredibly high taxes. A mug of beer at a *kedai kopi* will cost around RM7, and around RM15 at bars and clubs. Anchor and Tiger beers are popular, as are locally brewed Carlsberg and Guinness. Indigenous people have a soft spot for *tuak* (rice wine), which tends to revolt first-timers but is apparently an acquired taste. Another rural favourite is the dark-coloured spirit *arak*, which is smooth and potent.

Environment

The Land

Malaysia covers 329,874 sq km and consists of two distinct regions. Peninsular Malaysia is the long finger of land extending south from Asia and through the mountainous northern half has some dense jungle coverage, though unprotected forests are getting cut down at an alarming rate, mostly to create oil palm plantations. The peninsula's western side has a large fertile plain running to the sea, while the eastern side is fringed with sandy beaches. Malaysian Borneo consists of Sarawak and Sabah; both

states are covered in thick jungle and have extensive river systems. Sabah is crowned by Mt Kinabalu (4095m), the highest mountain between the Himalaya and New Guinea.

Wildlife

Malaysia's ancient rainforests are endowed with a cornucopia of life forms. In Peninsular Malaysia alone there are over 8000 species of flowering plants, including the world's tallest tropical tree species, the *tualang*. In Malaysian Borneo, where hundreds of new species have been discovered since the 1990s, you'll find the world's largest flower, the rafflesia, measuring up to 1m across, as well as the world's biggest cockroach.

Mammals include elephants, tapirs, tigers, leopards, honey bears, *tempadau* (forest cattle), gibbons and monkeys (including, in Borneo, the proboscis monkey and orangutans) and pangolins (scaly anteaters). Colourful bird species include kingfishers, sunbirds, woodpeckers, barbets, spectacular pheasants and sacred hornbills. Snakes include cobras, vipers and pythons. Of the world's seven species of turtle, four are native to Malaysia: the hawksbill, green, olive ridley and giant leatherback.

National Parks

Malaysia's 23 national parks cover barely 5% of the country's landmass. The country's major national park is Taman Negara, on the peninsula, while Gunung Mulu and Kinabalu are the two main parks in Sarawak and Sabah, respectively. Especially on Borneo, the rarity and uniqueness of local flora and fauna is such that scientists – from dragonfly experts to palm-tree specialists – are regular visitors and vocal proponents of new parks and reserves both on land and in the surrounding waters. There are also 13 marine parks in Malaysia, notably around Pulau Perhentian, Tioman and Sipadan, although enforcement of protection measures is very loose.

Environmental Issues

There's a disparity between government figures and those of environmental groups, but it's probable that up to 80% of Malaysia's rainforests have been logged. There have also been huge environmental consequences as vast swathes of land have been razed and planted with trees that yield lucrative palm oil; Malaysia accounts for over 40% of global production of palm oil.

The crown of eco and social irresponsibility goes to Bakun Dam in Sarawak, which flooded some 690 sq km (the size of Singapore) of some of the world's most diverse rainforest in late 2010 and forced up to 10,000 indigenous peoples from their homes. The dam has been criticised as being corrupt, ill-planned and unnecessary, but the state already has plans to build more dams in the region.

Responsible ecotourism is the traveller's best antidote to these trends.

SURVIVAL GUIDE

❶ Directory A–Z

ACCOMMODATION
The following prices refer to a double room.

$ less than RM100 (US$23)
$$ RM100 to RM400 (US$23 to US$93)
$$$ more than RM400 (US$93)

CUSTOMS REGULATIONS
You are legally entitled to import 1L of alcohol and 200 cigarettes into Malaysia. Cameras, portable radios, perfume, cosmetics and watches do not incur duty. Trafficking of illegal substances can result in the death penalty – don't do it.

ELECTRICITY
Malaysia's electricity is 240V, 50Hz; power outlets have three flat pins.

EMBASSIES & CONSULATES
All the following foreign embassies are in Kuala Lumpur and are generally open 8am to 12.30pm and 1.30pm to 4.30pm Monday to Friday.

Australian Embassy (Map p390; ☑ 03-2146 5555; www.malaysia.highcommission.gov.au/klpr/home.html; 6 Jln Yap Kwan Seng; Ⓜ KLCC)

British Embassy (Map p390; ☑ 03-2170 2200; www.gov.uk/government/world/organisations/british-high-commission-kuala-lumpur; level 27 Menara Binjai, 2 Jln Binjai; Ⓜ Ampang Park)

Canadian Embassy (☑ 03-2718-3333; www.canadainternational.gc.ca; 17th fl, Menara Tan & Tan, 207 Jln Tun Razak; Ⓜ Ampang Park)

French Embassy (☑ 03-2053 5500; www.ambafrance-my.org; 196 Jln Ampang; Ⓜ Ampang Park)

German Embassy (☑ 03-2170 9666; www.kuala-lumpur.diplo.de; 26th fl, Menara Tan & Tan, 207 Jln Tun Razak; Ⓜ Ampang Park)

Irish Embassy (☑ 03-2161 2963; www.dfa.ie/irish-embassy/malaysia; 5th fl, South Block, The Amp Walk, 218 Jln Ampang; Ⓜ Ampang Park)

Netherlands Embassy (☑ 03-2235 3210; http://malaysia.nlembassy.org; 7th fl, South Block, The Amp Walk, 218 Jln Ampang; Ⓜ Ampang Park)

New Zealand Embassy (Map p390; ☑ 03-2078-2533; www.nzembassy.com/malaysia; Level 21, Menara IMC, 8 Jln Sultan Ismail; monorail Bukit Nanas)

US Embassy (☑ 03-2168 5000; http://malaysia.usembassy.gov; 376 Jln Tun Razak; Ⓜ Ampang Park)

FESTIVALS & EVENTS
There are many cultures and religions coexisting in Malaysia, which means there are many occasions for celebration throughout the year.

Ramadan is the major annual Muslim event – 30 days during which Muslims cannot eat, drink, smoke or have sex from sunrise to sunset. The dates of Ramadan change every year; in 2016 it starts on 6 June, in 2017 on 27 May and in 2018 on 16 May.

Chinese New Year (January/February) The most important celebration for the Chinese community is marked with lion and dragon dances and street parades.

Thaipusam (January/February) One of the most dramatic Hindu festivals, in which devotees honour Lord Subramaniam with acts of amazing physical resilience. Self-mutilating worshippers make the procession from Sri Mahamariamman Temple in KL to the Batu Caves.

Malaysian Grand Prix (March/April) Formula One's big outing in Southeast Asia is held at the Sepang International Circuit in Selangor either at the end of March or early April.

Gawai Dayak (late May/early June) Festival of the Dayaks in Sarawak, marking the end of the rice season. War dances, cock fights and blowpipe events take place.

Festa de San Pedro (June) Christian celebration on 29 June in honour of the patron saint of the fishing community; notably celebrated by the Eurasian-Portuguese community of Melaka.

Dragon Boat Festival (June to August) Celebrated in Penang.

Rainforest World Music Festival (July/August) Held for three days at the Sarawak Cultural Village, this music and arts festival features musicians from around the world and highlights indigenous music from Borneo.

National Day (Hari Kebangsaa; August) Malaysia celebrates its independence on 31 August with events all over the country, but particularly in KL where there are parades and a variety of performances in the Lake Gardens.

Moon Cake Festival (September) Chinese festival celebrating the overthrow of Mongol warlords in ancient China with the eating of moon cakes and the lighting of colourful paper lanterns.

Festival of the Nine Emperor Gods (October) Involves nine days of Chinese operas, processions and other events honouring the nine emperor gods.

Deepavali (November) The Festival of Lights, in which tiny oil lamps are lit outside Hindu homes; celebrates Rama's victory over the demon King Ravana.

FOOD

The following refers to the price of a main dish.

$ less than RM15 (US$3.50)

$$ RM15 to RM60 (US$3.50 to US$14)

$$$ more than RM60 (US$14)

LGBT TRAVELLERS

Conservative political parties and religious groups make a regular habit of denouncing gays and lesbians in Malaysia, a country where it is illegal for men of any age to have sex with other men. This said, outright persecution of gays and lesbians in the country is rare. Nonetheless, while in Malaysia, gay and lesbian travellers (particularly the former) should avoid any behaviour that attracts unwanted attention.

Visit www.utopia-asia.com which provides good coverage of gay and lesbian events and activities in the country.

INTERNET ACCESS

Malaysia is blanketed with hot spots for wi-fi connections (usually free). Internet cafes are less common these days, but do still exist if you're not travelling with a wi-fi-enabled device. Only in the most remote reaches of the peninsula and Malaysian Borneo are you likely to be without any internet access.

LEGAL MATTERS

In any of your dealings with the local police it pays to be deferential. Minor misdemeanours may be overlooked, but don't count on it and don't offer anyone a bribe.

It's simply not worth having anything to do with drugs in Malaysia: drug trafficking carries a mandatory death penalty, and even the possession of tiny amounts of drugs for personal use can bring about a lengthy jail sentence and a beating with the *rotan* (cane).

MONEY

Bargaining is not usually required for everyday goods in Malaysia, but feel free to bargain when purchasing souvenirs, antiques and other tourist items, even when the prices are displayed. Transport prices are generally fixed, but nego-

tiation is required for trishaws and taxis around town or for charter.

Tipping is not common in Malaysia.

OPENING HOURS

Banks 10am to 3pm Monday to Friday, 9.30am to 11.30am Saturday

Restaurants noon to 2.30pm and 6pm to 10.30pm

Shops 9.30am to 7pm, malls 10am to 10pm

In the more Islamic-minded states of Kedah, Perlis, Kelantan and Terengganu, government offices, banks and many shops close on Friday and on Saturday afternoon.

POST

Post offices are open from 8am to 5pm daily except Sunday and public holidays (also closed on Friday in Kedah, Kelantan and Terengganu districts).

Aerograms and postcards cost 50 sen to send to any destination, letters from RM1.20, parcels from RM20 for 1kg.

PUBLIC HOLIDAYS

Although some public holidays have a fixed annual date, Hindus, Muslims and Chinese follow either a lunar or lunisolar calendar, which means the dates for many events vary each year.

The major holiday of the Muslim calendar, Hari Raya Puasa marks the end of the month-long fast of Ramadan with three days of joyful celebration. During Hari Raya Puasa and Chinese New Year, accommodation may be difficult to obtain. At these times many businesses may also be closed and transport can be fully booked.

In addition to national public holidays, each state has its own holidays, usually associated with the sultan's birthday or a Muslim celebration.

Fixed annual holidays include the following:

New Year's Day 1 January

Federal Territory Day 1 February (in Kuala Lumpur and Putrajaya only)

Good Friday March or April (in Sarawak and Sabah only)

Labour Day 1 May

Yang di-Pertuan Agong's (King's) Birthday First Saturday in June

Governor of Penang's Birthday Second Saturday in July (in Penang only)

National Day (Hari Kebangsaan) 31 August

Malaysia Day 16 September

Christmas Day 25 December

SAFE TRAVEL

In general Malaysia is very safe, with violent attacks being uncommon. However, the usual travel precautions apply, such as restraining your urge to go wandering around seedy areas alone late at night. The snatching of bags by thieves on motorcycles is a recurring crime in KL, Johor Bahru, Melaka and Penang's George Town, so keep bags away from the roadside in these areas.

Credit-card fraud is a growing problem, so only use your cards at established businesses and guard your credit-card numbers.

Rabies is an ever-present problem in Malaysia – you should treat any animal bite very seriously. Leeches can be a nuisance after heavy rain on jungle walks.

TELEPHONE

If you have your mobile phone with you, once you've sorted out a local SIM (buy one for RM5) you should have no problem dialling overseas. If you're sticking to Peninsular Malaysia any of the major mobile phone service providers are fine, but if you're heading into the remoter parts of Malaysian Borneo then get Celcom (www.celcom.com.my), which has the largest coverage. Rates for a local call are around 36 sen per minute, an SMS is also 36 sen and 4G data service costs around RM7 per week. You can add credit to prepaid SIM cards at most convenience stores.

The access code for making international calls to most countries is ⬛ 00. For information on international calls, dial ⬛ 103.

To call Malaysia from outside the country, dial ⬛ 60, drop the 0 before the Malaysian area code, then dial the number you want.

TOILETS

Although there are still some places with Asian squat-style toilets in Malaysia, you'll most often find Western-style ones these days. At public facilities toilet paper is not usually provided. Instead, you will find a hose which you are supposed to use as a bidet or, in cheaper places, a bucket of water and a tap.

Public toilets in shopping malls and at transport depots are usually staffed by attendants and cost 10 sen to 30 sen to use; an extra 10 sen often gets you a dozen sheets of toilet paper.

TOURIST INFORMATION

Tourism Malaysia (www.tourismmalaysia.gov. my) has a network of overseas offices, which are useful for predeparture planning. Its domestic offices range from extremely helpful to hardly ever open, depending on the region. All stock some decent brochures and free maps.

TRAVELLERS WITH DISABILITIES

For the mobility impaired, Malaysia can be a nightmare. In most cities and towns there are often no footpaths, kerbs are very high and pedestrian crossings are few and far between. Budget hotels almost never have lifts. On the upside, KL's modern urban railway lines are reasonably wheelchair-accessible.

Malaysia Airlines and KTM (the national railway service) offer 50% discounts for travellers with disabilities.

VISAS

Visitors must have a passport valid for at least six months beyond the date of entry into Malaysia. Nationals of most countries are given a 30- to 60-day visa on arrival. As a general rule you'll be given 60 days if arriving by air; if you arrive overland you may be given 30 days unless you ask for a 60-day permit. Full details of visa regulations are available at www.kln.gov.my.

Citizens of Israel can only enter Malaysia under special circumstances.

Sarawak and Sabah are semi-autonomous. If you travel from Peninsular Malaysia or Sabah into Sarawak, your passport will be checked on arrival and a new stay-permit issued, usually for the period left on your original Malaysian visa. Travelling from either Sabah or Sarawak back to Peninsular Malaysia there are no formalities and you do not start a new entry period, so your permit from Sabah or Sarawak remains valid.

WOMEN TRAVELLERS

Foreign women travelling in Malaysia can expect some attention, though most of it will just involve stares from locals unfamiliar with (or curious about) Westerners. It helps, and is much more respectful of the culture, if you dress conservatively by wearing long pants or skirts and loose tops that cover the shoulders. Western women are not expected to cover their heads with scarves (outside mosques, that is). In resort areas you can wear shorts, sleeveless tops and swimwear, but it isn't appropriate anywhere in the country to sunbathe topless. On more remote beaches you're better off doing like the locals do and swimming fully clothed. Keep a watch out for sleazy local beach boys in Langkawi, Cherating and the Perhentians.

Tampons and pads are widely available, especially in big cities, and over-the-counter medications are also fairly easy to find.

ⓘ Getting There & Away

AIR

The bulk of international flights arrive at Kuala Lumpur International Airport (KLIA), 75km south of Kuala Lumpur (KL); it has two terminals, with KLIA2 being used mainly by budget airlines. There are also direct flights from Asia and Australia into Penang, Kuching, Kota Kinabalu and a few other cities.

LAND

Visas on arrival are available for land crossings into Brunei, Indonesia, Singapore and Thailand.

SEA
Indonesia

The following are the main ferry routes between Indonesia and Malaysia:
* Bengkalis (Sumatra) to Melaka
* Pulau Batam to Johor Bahru
* Dumai (Sumatra) to Melaka
* Medan (Sumatra) to Penang
* Pekanbaru (Sumatra) to Melaka
* Tanjung Pinang Bintan to Johor Bahru
* Tanjung Balai (Sumatra) to Pelabuhan Klang and Kukup
* Tarakan (Kalimantan) to Tawau

Philippines

Weekly ferries link Sandakan with Zamboanga, on the Philippine island of Mindanao.

Thailand

Ferries connect Kuah on Pulau Langkawi with Satun on the Thai coast and, from November to mid-May, with Ko Lipe; make sure you get your passport stamped going in either direction.

❶ Getting Around

AIR

The main domestic operators are **Malaysia Airlines** (MAS; ☑ 1300 883 000, international 03-7843 3000; www.malaysiaairlines.com); **Firefly** (☑ 03-7845 4543; www.fireflyz.com.my); **AirAsia** (☑ 600 85 8888; www.airasia.com); and **Malindo Air** (☑ 03-7841 5388; www.malindoair.com).

In Malaysian Borneo, **MASwings** (☑ 03-7843 3000, outside Malaysia 1300 883 000; www.maswings.com.my) offers domestic flights within and between Sarawak and Sabah. These services often book up during school holidays.

BICYCLE

The main road system in Malaysia has good surfaces, making the country good for bike touring, but the secondary road system is limited. Mountain bikes are recommended for forays off the beaten track.

KL Bike Hash (www.klmbh.org) has a whole load of useful information and links to other cycling-connected sites in Malaysia. Also see Bicycle Touring Malaysia (www.bicycletouringmalaysia.com)

BOAT

There are no ferry services between Malaysian Borneo and the peninsula. On a local level, there are boats and ferries between the peninsula and offshore islands, and along the rivers of Sabah and Sarawak. If a boat looks overloaded or otherwise unsafe, do not board it.

BUS

Peninsular Malaysia has an excellent bus system. In larger towns there may be several bus stations. Local and regional buses often operate from one station and long-distance buses from another; in other cases, KL for example, bus stations are differentiated by the destinations they serve.

On major runs you can usually just turn up and get on the next bus. On many routes there are air-conditioned buses – but take your arctic gear, the air-con is usually pumped up to the max! *Ekspres*, in the Malaysian context, often means indeterminate stops.

In Sabah, frequent buses, minivans and shared taxis follow the asphalt arc of the Pan Borneo Hwy from Beaufort to Kota Kinabalu to Tawau, passing by (or near) most of the state's tourism hot spots, including Mt Kinabalu, Sandakan and Semporna. For some destinations, such as the top of Mt Kinabalu and Sipadan, there's no real way to avoid booking a package.

In Sarawak, the Pan Borneo Hwy from Kuching to Sabah via Miri and Brunei is in great shape. Express buses ply the Kuching–Miri route many times a day. For travel between Kuching and Sibu, though, the ferry is faster, and boats (or aeroplanes) are the only way to get to some parts of the interior. Bus transport to/from Brunei, and from Miri through Brunei to KK, is limited to just a few buses a day.

CAR & MOTORCYCLE

Driving in Malaysia is fantastic compared with most Asian countries. The country's roads are generally of a high quality. New cars for hire are commonly available and fuel is inexpensive (RM1.95 per litre). There are tolls for driving along the North-South Expressway running along the west coast of Peninsular Malaysia; see http://www.plus.com.my for details.

Road rules are basically the same as in Britain and Australia. However, because of the one-way systems and traffic, driving in KL and some of the bigger cities can be a nightmare. Always keep an eye out for motorcyclists and, on country roads, animals. Cars are right-hand drive and you drive on the left side of the road. The speed limit is officially 110km per hour.

Unlimited-distance car-rental costs from around RM190/1320 per day/week, including insurance and collision-damage waiver. A valid overseas driving licence is required for vehicle rental. Be aware that insurance companies will most likely wash their hands of you if you injure yourself driving a motorcycle without a licence.

HITCHING

Hitching is never entirely safe and you do so at your own risk. That said, Malaysia has long had a reputation for being an excellent place to hitchhike but, with the ease of bus travel, most travellers

don't bother. On the west coast hitching is quite easy but it's not possible on the main *lebuhraya* (expressways). On the east coast traffic is lighter and there may be long waits between rides.

LOCAL TRANSPORT

Local transport varies but almost always includes local buses and taxis. In a few Peninsular Malaysia towns there are also bicycle rickshaws but in general these are dying out. The best towns for rickshaws are George Town and Melaka.

In the cities and larger towns of Malaysian Borneo you'll find taxis, buses and minibuses. Once you're out in the villages, though, you can either walk or find someone to give you a ride. If you're upriver or in the boondocks your alternatives are riverboats, aeroplanes or lengthy jungle treks.

TAXI

Drivers are legally required to use meters if they exist – you can try insisting that they do so, but more often than not you'll just have to negotiate the fare before you get in.

Compared to buses, long-distance (or shared) taxis are expensive. The taxis work on fixed fares for the entire car and between major towns you'll have a reasonable chance of finding other passengers without having to wait around too long; otherwise, you'll probably have to charter a whole taxi.

TRAIN

There are two main types of rail services: express and local trains. Express trains are air-conditioned and have 'premier' (1st class), 'superior' (2nd class) and sometimes 'economy' seats (3rd class). Similarly on overnight trains you'll find 'premier night deluxe' cabins, 'premier night standard' cabins and 'standard night' cabins. Local trains are usually economy-class only, but some have superior seats. Express trains stop only at main stations, while local services stop everywhere, including the middle of the jungle.

Peninsular Malaysia

Malaysia's privatised national railway company is **Keretapi Tanah Melayu** (KTM; ☑ 1300 885 862; www.ktmb.com.my). It runs a modern, comfortable and economical railway service, although for the most part services are slow.

One line runs up the west coast from Singapore, through KL, Butterworth and on into Thailand. The other branches off from this line at Gemas and runs through Kuala Lipis up to the northeastern corner of the country near Kota Bharu in Kelantan. Often referred to as the 'Jungle Railway', this line is properly known as the 'East Coast Railway'.

Malaysian Borneo

In Sabah the North Borneo Railway (www. suteraharbour.com/north-borneo-railway), a narrow-gauge line running through the Sungai Padas gorge from Tenom to Beaufort, offers tourist trips lasting four hours on Wednesday and Saturday.

Myanmar (Burma)

📱 95 / POP 51.4 MILLION

Best Places to Eat

➡ Aung Padamyar (p519)
➡ Cherry Mann (p486)
➡ Daw Yi (p500)
➡ Shan Ma Ma (p514)

Best Places for Culture

➡ Hsipaw (p520)
➡ Kyaingtong (p508)
➡ Mrauk U (p532)
➡ Mawlamyine (p499)

Why Go?

Now is the time to visit this extraordinary land, scattered with golden pagodas, where the traditional ways of Asia endure and previously off limits areas are seeing their first visitors in decades. As Myanmar takes tentative steps towards democracy, it is rapidly opening up to the outside world. But the pace of change is not overwhelming and the country remains a unique, magical place still unused to mass tourism.

Travelling in Myanmar offers the chance to suspend the demands of modern life and to immerse yourself in the spirituality of sacred temples and hushed monasteries. Enjoy slowly unfolding journeys through serene landscapes, including meandering rivers, lush jungles, ethnic minority villages and pristine, palm-fringed beaches. Best of all, you'll encounter locals who are gentle, humorous, engaging, considerate, inquisitive and passionate.

When to Go
Yangon

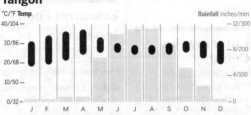

Jan Independence Day (4 January), celebrating the end of British rule, is marked by nationwide fairs.

Apr The Water Festival (Thingyan) is fun, but it's one of the hottest times of year.

Dec Peak season with many visitors heading here over the Christmas–New Year break.

AT A GLANCE

Currency Burmese kyat (K)

Language Burmese

Money Cash mainly

Visas 28 days

Mobile phones Local SIM cards are now widely available

Fast Facts

Area 676,578 sq km

Capital Nay Pyi Taw

Emergency Police (Yangon) ☏199

Exchange Rates

Australia	A$1	K912
Euro	€1	K1415
Laos	10,000K	K1571
Thailand	10B	K360
UK	UK£1	K1957
USA	US$1	K1279

Daily Costs

Guesthouse US$10–40

Street stall meal K3000

Large beer K2000

Short taxi ride in Yangon K2000

Entering the Country

The main land border crossings are from Mae Sai, Ranong and Mae Sot in Thailand, and Ruili in China.

Don't Miss

Myanmar is one of the most devout Buddhist countries in the world. Yangon's Shwedagon Paya, Mandalay's Mahamuni Paya and Bagan's plain of temples are all must-sees, but there are also many other Buddhist religious sites that will impress you with their beauty and spirituality. A 10-storey-tall seated buddha watches over Pyay's hill-top Shwesandaw Paya, providing sweeping views of the town. The old Rakhine capital of Mrauk U is dotted with ruined and functioning temples and monasteries, while at Mt Kyaiktiyo you can join the pilgrims who flock to see its golden boulder.

ITINERARIES

One Week

In Yangon, visit the Shwedagon Paya and shop for handicrafts at Bogyoke Aung San Market. Overnight on a bus to Mandalay, climb Mandalay Hill, see the famed Mahamuni Paya and beautiful teak monastery Shwe In Bin Kyaung. Take a morning boat to Mingun, home to a giant earthquake-cracked stupa, following up with a sunset boat ride past U Bein's Bridge at Amarapura. Connect by bus or boat to Bagan, allowing a couple of days to explore the temples there.

Three Weeks

After following the one-week itinerary, venture east to beautiful Inle Lake; consider trekking there from Kalaw (minimum two days). From Bago head to Mt Kyaiktiyo to view the amazing Golden Rock, then to Mawlamyine for a taste of tropical Myanmar. Head south to little-seen beaches, or use Hpa-an as a base for exploring lush countryside peppered with sacred caves and limestone mountains. Return to Yangon then fly to Sittwe, where you can take another boat to the amazing temple ruins of Mrauk U (minimum four days).

Essential Food & Drink

Ăthouq Light, tart and spicy salads made with raw vegetables or fruit tossed with lime juice, onions, peanuts, roasted chickpea powder and chillies. A common one is *leq-p'eq thouq*, which includes fermented tea leaves.

Mohinga ('moun-hinga') A popular breakfast dish of rice noodles served with fish soup and as many other ingredients as there are cooks.

Shan khauk-swe Shan-style noodle soup; thin wheat noodles in a light broth with meat or tofu, available across the country but most common in Mandalay and Shan State.

Htamin chin Literally 'sour rice', this turmeric-coloured rice salad also hails from Shan State.

Black tea Brewed in the Indian style: sweet with lots of milk.

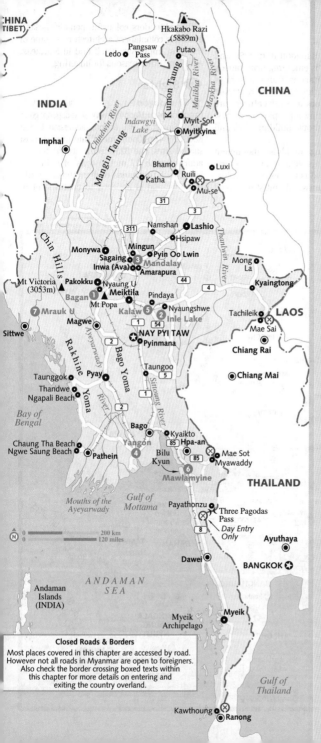

Myanmar (Burma) Highlights

1 Witnessing the beauty of a misty dawn breaking over 4000 Buddhist temples on the plains of **Bagan** (p521) from the upper terraces of one of the paya (temples).

2 Spending longer than you planned at gorgeous **Inle Lake** (p503), a magical landscape of floating villages, stilted monasteries and aquatic gardens.

3 Using **Mandalay** (p509) as the base for visiting the intriguing old cities of Amarapura, with its famed teak bridge, and some stupapendous views from Sagaing.

4 Being dazzled by Shwedagon Paya the country's most important Buddhist temple, and the buzz of a newly energised **Yangon** (p482).

5 Trekking through forested hills, fields and fascinating, friendly minority villages between Inle Lake and **Kalaw** (p506).

6 Heading to tranquil and tropical **Mawlamyine** (p499), home to colonial-era architecture, historic pagodas and nearby beaches.

7 Getting lost amid the hundreds of ruined temples and fortifications in timeless **Mrauk U** (p532), former grand capital of Rakhine.

Closed Roads & Borders

Most places covered in this chapter are accessed by road. However not all roads in Myanmar are open to foreigners. Also check the border crossing boxed texts within this chapter for more details on entering and exiting the country overland.

YANGON

📍 01 / POP 7.36 MILLION

Yangon, known as Rangoon until 1989 and the former capital, is emerging from bloody and neglectful military rule into an era of tantalising possibilities. Exiles are returning and foreign investors and adventurers are flooding in, triggering an explosion of new restaurants, bars, shops, building sites and traffic jams.

The awe-inspiring Buddhist monument Shwedagon Paya is visible from almost everywhere in Yangon and is the one sight in Myanmar you cannot miss. Vibrant streets lined with food vendors, colourful open-air markets, evocative colonial-era architecture – some of the most impressive you'll find in Southeast Asia – are other reasons for lingering.

⊙ Sights

★ **Shwedagon Paya**   BUDDHIST TEMPLE
(ရွှေတိဂုံဘုရား; Map p490; www.shwedagonpagoda. com; Singuttara Hill, Dagon; admission US$8/ K8000; ⊙ 4am-10pm) One of Buddhism's most sacred sites, the 325ft *zedi* (stupa) here is adorned with 27 metric tons of gold leaf, along with thousands of diamonds and other gems, and is believed to enshrine eight

Yangon

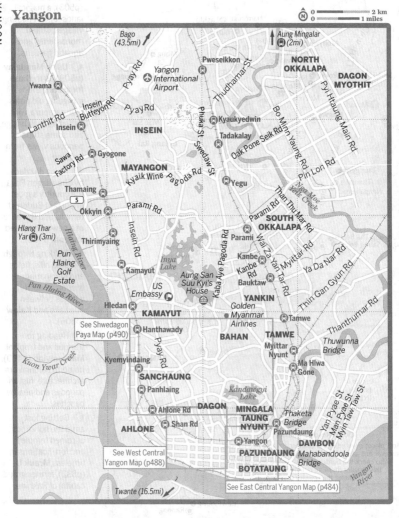

hairs of the Gautama Buddha as well as relics of three former buddhas.

Four entrance stairways lead to the main terrace. Visit in the cool of dawn if you want tranquility. Otherwise, pay your respects when the golden stupa flames crimson and burnt orange in the setting sun.

★**Botataung Paya**   BUDDHIST TEMPLE
(ဗိုလ်တထောင်ဘုရား; Map p484; Strand Rd, Botataung; admission US$3/K4000; ⊗6am-9.30pm)
Botataung's spacious riverfront location and lack of crowds give it a more down-to-earth spiritual feeling than Shwedagon or Sule Paya. Its most original feature is the dazzling zig-zag corridor, gilded from floor to ceiling, that snakes its way around the hollow interior of the 131ft golden *zedi* (stupa). Also look out for a bronze Buddha that once resided in the royal palace in Mandalay, and a large pond full of hundreds of terrapin turtles.

Sule Paya   BUDDHIST STUPA
(ဆူးလေဘုရား; Map p484; cnr Sule Paya Rd & Mahabandoola Rd, Pabedan; admission US$3/K3000; ⊗5am-9pm) It's not every city where the primary traffic circle is occupied by a 2000-year-old golden temple. This 46m *zedi*, said to be older than Shwedagon Paya, is an example of modern Asian business life melding with ancient Burmese tradition.

Just after the sun has gone down is the most atmospheric time to visit the temple.

National Museum   MUSEUM
(အမျိုးသားပြတိုက်; Map p488; 66/74 Pyay Rd, Dagon; admission US$5/K5000; ⊗9.30am-4.30pm Tue-Sun) Even though the museum's collection is appallingly labelled and lit, the treasures that lie within this cavernous building deserve a viewing.

The highlight is the spectacular 26ft-high, jewel-encrusted Sihasana (Lion Throne), which belonged to King Thibaw Min, the last king of Myanmar. It's actually more of an entrance doorway than a throne but let's not quibble – it's more impressive than your front door.

Mahabandoola Garden   PARK
(မဟာဗန္ဓုလပန်းခြံ; Map p484; Mahabandoola Garden St, Kyauktada; ⊗6am-6pm) This recently revamped park offers pleasant strolling in the heart of the downtown area and views of surrounding heritage buildings including the **City Hall**, the **High Court** and the old **Rowe & Co** department store.

The park's most notable feature is the **Independence Monument** (Map p484), a 165ft

white obelisk surrounded by two concentric circles of *chinthe* (half-lion, half-dragon deity). There's also a children's playground.

Musmeah Yeshua Synagogue   SYNAGOGUE
(Map p488; 85 26th St, Pabedan; ⊗9am-2pm, Shabbat service 4-5pm Fri) The lovingly maintained interior of this 1896 building contains a *bimah* (platform holding the reading table for the Torah) in the centre of the main sanctuary and a women's balcony upstairs. The wooden ceiling features the original blue-and-white Star of David motif. It's best to contact Sammy Samuels at info@myanmarshalom.com to be sure of gaining access to the synagogue.

★**Chaukhtatgyi Paya**   BUDDHIST TEMPLE
(ခြောက်ထပ်ကြီးဘုရား; Map p490; Shwegondine Rd, Tamwe; ⊗6am-8pm) Housed in a large metal-roofed shed, this beautiful 65m-long reclining Buddha is hardly publicised at all even though it's larger than a similar well-known image in Bago. The statue's placid face is topped by a crown encrusted with diamonds and other precious stones.

★**Ngahtatgyi Paya**   BUDDHIST TEMPLE
(ငါးထပ်ကြီးဘုရား; Map p490; Shwegondine Rd, Tamwe; admission US$2/K2000; ⊗6am-8pm) Virtually across the street from Chaukhtatgyi Paya is a gorgeous 46ft-tall seated Buddha image at the Ngahtatgyi Paya. Sitting in calm gold and white repose with a healthy splash of precious stones to boot, it's one of the most impressive sitting buddhas in southern Myanmar. In fact, it's worth going to see for its carved wooden backdrop alone.

Kandawgyi Lake   LAKE
(ကန်တော်ကြီး; Map p490; Kan Yeik Thar Rd, Dagon; admission K2000) Also known as Royal Lake, this artificial lake, built by the British as a reservoir, is most attractive at sunset, when the glittering Shwedagon is reflected in its calm waters. The boardwalk, which runs mainly along the southern and western sides of the lake, is also an ideal place for an early-morning jog or stroll.

🛏 Sleeping

Unless otherwise stated, the following accommodation listings include breakfast in the room price.

★**Pickled Tea Hostel**   HOSTEL $
(Map p490; ☏09 25090 3363; www.pickledteahostel.com; 11 Myaynigone Zay St; 4- 6-bed dm US$24/19, d US$38-52; ❀🖥) Tucked away

East Central Yangon

MYANMAR (BURMA) YANGON

See West Central Yangon Map (p488)

Gyo Phyu St

SST
● Tours

Aung San
Stadium

Upper Pansodan St

MINGALA
TAUNG NYUNT

Bo Min Yaung St

94th St

101st St

U Pho Kyar St

Thein Byu Rd

Kun Chan St
**Yangon
Train Station**

Yay Kyaw Rd

● Myanmar Railways
Booking Office

Bogyoke Aung San Rd

Sule Pagoda Rd

🏛 5

⊕ AA
Pharmacy

8 ▪ Mahabandoola Garden St

KYAUKTADA

35th St

36th St

Anawrahta Rd

Bo Aung Kyaw St

46th St

47th St

48th St

Bo Myat Tun St

49th St

⊗ 9

37th St

38th St

40th St

Myanmar
● Travels
& Tours

Mahabandoola Rd

50th St

Pansodan St

4 ⚓

2 ❶

12 ⊗

🔒
15

Thein Byu Rd

❶ 3

⊗
11

13 ⊗

● Indian
Embassy

Merchant St

41st St

42nd St

43rd St

44th St

BOTATAUNG

Seikkan Thar St

39th St

40th St

Bo Aung Kyaw St

Khiri ●
Travel

🔒
16

Bank St

14 🔒
🔒 🔒 UK Embassy
✉
Australian
Embassy

Bo Galay Zay St

Strand Rd

Yangon River

Pansodan Street Jetty
⚓

---

north of downtown – a 15-minute walk from
the Shwedagon – this secluded hostel has
large and posh dorms, with proper beds and
lockers. There's also an attractive outside
terrace and small communal area inside.

4 Rivers Youth Hostel   HOSTEL **$**
(Map p488; ☎ 09 79988 7215; info@fourrivers
hostels.com; 79 12th St; 3-/6-/8-/10-bed dm
US$18/15/15/13; ❋ 🛜) Dorms only at this
new hostel in the heart of downtown. Don't
expect windows, but the dorms themselves

are clean, if compact, with comfortable beds. There's a small communal area and kitchen, and the staff are eager to please.

MGM Hotel   HOTEL $

(Map p488; ☏01-212 455; www.hotel-mgm.com; 160 Wadan St; s/d/tr US$35/40/45; ✳🛜) Solid digs on the western edge of downtown. Rooms vary in size, from the very large to the less spacious, but all are well maintained and come with windows and reasonable bathrooms. The staff can book bus tickets and the wi-fi connection is reliable.

Mother Land Inn 2   HOTEL $

(Map p484; ☏01-291 343; www.myanmarmother landinn.com; 433 Lower Pazundaung Rd, Pazundaung; s/d US$30/35, with shared bathroom US$27/30; ✳@🛜) Rooms here are a little old-fashioned now, although clean and reasonably sized, and it's a long walk or a short taxi ride from the heart of downtown, but the staff remain helpful and pleasant and offer sound travel advice and services. Cheaper rooms are fan-only.

Three Seasons Hotel   GUESTHOUSE $

(Map p484; ☏01-901 0066; threeseasonshotel7 @gmail.com; 83-85 52nd St, Pazundaung; s/d/tr US$25/35/45; ✳@🛜) The eight rooms in this homey guesthouse are old-fashioned but spacious and spotless and come with big bathrooms. The outdoor terrace, with tree shade, is a decent place to sit and watch the world cruise by.

Beautyland Hotel II
HOTEL $

(Map p484; ☑ 01-240 054; www.goldenlandpages. com/beauty; 188-192 33rd St, Kyauktada; s US$26, d US$32-40; ❀☎) Tidy and decent-sized, if old-school, rooms, and efficient staff make this a reliable budget choice. The cheapest rooms don't have windows, while the more expensive ones boast heaps of natural light.

20th Street Hostel
HOSTEL $

(Map p488; ☑ 01-251 931; hostel.20street@gmail. com; 23 20th St; 10-bed dm US$9, r US$22; ❀☎) Cramped dorms and functional rooms, all with shared bathrooms. But they are clean, the price is right for downtown Yangon and the staff are keen.

🍴 Eating

Yangon has Myanmar's best range of restaurants. Central Yangon is packed with streetside stalls selling a dizzying array of cheap snacks, and many inexpensive Burmese, Chinese and Indian restaurants. Smarter Western places are found in the more affluent, expat-occupied north. Most restaurants are open from about 7am until 9pm daily; it can be hard to find a meal anywhere after 9pm.

SPLURGE

The **Rangoon Tea House** (Map p484; ☑ 01-122 4534; info@rangoonteahouse. com; 1/F 77-79 Pansodan Rd; mains from K4500; ☉ 8am-10pm; ☻ ☎ ☑) might be Yangon's future: a hipster teahouse that offers a twist on traditional Burmese cuisine and serves locally inspired cocktails. All the usual teahouse snacks (samosas, paratha and bao) are available, but in bigger portions than you'd get elsewhere and with better ingredients, as well as curries, biryanis and a few fusion dishes such as pork chops with a tea leaf marinade. The drinks are equally as good, with the Mandalay Rum Sour especially potent. Like the food, the cocktails don't come cheap, starting at K6500. But they are half-price during the daily happy hour from 4pm to 7pm. And if you just want a cup of tea, you can get that too, although it will set you back K1500. The teahouse is above a T-Land Mobile phone shop. The entrance is to the side of the shop.

Yangon's numerous teashops are not just places to have cups of milk tea and coffee or tiny pots of Chinese tea. They're also places to hang out with locals, grab a snack or a better breakfast than that provided at your guesthouse.

Along Anawrahta Rd, west of Sule Paya Rd, there are many super-cheap Indian biryani shops (*keyettha dan bauk* in Burmese). All-you-can-eat *thali* meals or biryani cost from about K1000.

★ Cherry Mann
BURMESE MUSLIM $

(Map p488; 80 Latha St; mains from K3000; ☉ 10.30am-11pm; ☑) Excellent and friendly Muslim restaurant; a fine spot for kebabs, curries and biryanis, with *paratha* (Indian-style bread) to accompany them. The kebabs are especially fine, but all the food is clean and tasty. You may have to wait for a table at busy times. No alcohol is served.

Lucky Seven
TEAHOUSE $

(Map p484; 49th St, Pazundaung; tea or snacks from K400; ☉ 6am-5.30pm Mon-Sat, to noon Sun; ☑) The most central of this small chain of high-class traditional teashops, Lucky Seven is much more than a pit stop for a cuppa. Its streetside tables are fringed by greenery and an ornamental pond. The *mohinga* (K600) is outstanding – order it with a side of crispy gourd or flaky-pastry savoury buns.

Nilar Biryani & Cold Drink
INDIAN $

(Map p488; 216 Anawrahta Rd, Pabedan; biryani from K1400; ☉ 4am-11pm; ☑) Giant cauldrons full of spices, broths and rice bubble away at the front of this Indian joint. It's never less than packed and with good reason: the biryanis are probably among the best your lips will meet. By the late afternoon there's not much left, so get here early.

Aung Thukha
BURMESE $

(Map p490; ☑ 01-525 194; 17A 1st St, Bahan; curries from K3000; ☉ 10am-9pm) This longstanding institution is a decent place to sample a wide range of Myanmar food – everything from rich, meaty curries to light, freshly made salads. It's almost constantly busy, but manages to maintain gentle, friendly service and a palpable old-school atmosphere, making the experience akin to eating at someone's home.

999 Shan Noodle Shop
SHAN $

(Map p484; 130/B 34th St, Kyauktada; noodle dishes from K1200; ☉ 6am-7pm; ☑) A handful of tables are crammed into this tiny, brightly

YANGON'S STREET EATS

Yangon's street-food options can be both overwhelming and challenging (pork offal on a skewer, anyone?). Some of our favourites and the best places to eat them:

Samusa thoke During the day a line of **vendors** (Map p484; Mahabandoola Garden St, Kyauktada; samosas K500) near Mahabandoola Garden sell this 'salad' of sliced samosas served with a thin lentil gravy.

Bein moun & moun pyar thalet These delicious 'Burmese pancakes' (K200), served sweet *(bein moun)* or savoury *(moun pyar thalet)*, can be found at most Yangon corners day and night.

Dosai At night along Anawratha St several streetside vendors sell this thin southern Indian crepe (from K500), known in Burmese as *to-shay*.

Mohinga This breakfast soup of thin rice noodles and fish broth is just about everywhere but our favourite is from **Myaung Mya Daw Cho** (Map p484; 149 51st St, Pazundaung; noodles from K600; ⏰4.30-9am). There's no English sign here; look for the green sign near some trees. There is a more formal **branch** (Map p490; ☑01-559 663; 118A Yay Tar Shay Old St, Bahan; noodles K600; ⏰5-11am) near Shwedagon Paya.

Grilled food Every night, the strip of 19th St between Mahabandoola and Anawrahta Rds hosts dozens of stalls and open-air restaurants serving **grilled snacks** (Map p488; 19th St, Latha; BBQ skewer from K400; ⏰5-11pm) and draught beer.

coloured eatery behind City Hall. The menu includes noodles such as *Shàn k'auq swèh* (thin rice noodles in a slightly spicy chicken broth) and *myi shay* (Mandalay-style noodle soup) and tasty non-noodle dishes such as Shan tofu (actually made from chickpea flour) and the delicious Shan yellow rice with tomato.

Cyclo
VIETNAMESE $
(Map p488; www.cycloresto-yangon.com; 133 Lanmadaw St; pho from K3200; ⏰7am-10pm; 🛜) This Burmese-Vietnamese-run place is the best in town for a bowl of pho. The many options have a rich broth and you can choose from a variety of different noodles. The menu also features spring rolls, salads and a number of more expensive grilled meat and hotpot dishes. This is also a fine spot for real Vietnamese coffee (K2000).

Feel Myanmar Food
BURMESE $
(Map p488; ☑01-511 6872; www.feelrestaurant. com; 124 Pyidaungsu Yeiktha St, Dagon; dishes from K1500, curries from K3800; ⏰6am-11pm; 🛜) This long-running operation is a fine place to start experimenting with Burmese cuisine. There's a big choice of curries on the picture menu, as well as soups, salads and rice and noodle dishes, and the food is fresh. It's popular at lunchtime with local business people and foreign embassy staff. There are food stalls offering ice cream and desserts next door.

Danuphyu Daw Saw Yee Myanma Restaurant
BURMESE $
(Map p488; 175-177 29th St, Pabedan; dishes K3000-6000; ⏰9am-9pm; 🍴) Ask locals where to eat Burmese food in downtown Yangon and they'll most likely point you in the direction of this traditional shophouse restaurant. It's a little more expensive than similar places, but the various curries are tasty and all dishes are served with sides of soup (the sour vegetable soup is particularly good) and *ngapi ye*, a pungent dip served with par-boiled veggies and fresh herbs.

Aung Mingalar Shan Noodle Restaurant
SHAN $
(Map p488; Bo Yar Nyunt St, Dagon; dishes K1500-3500; ⏰7am-9pm; 🍴) Aung Mingalar is an excellent spot to indulge simultaneously in people-watching and noodle-slurping. It's a simple and easy-going restaurant with a cafe-like feel.

★ Kaung Myat
BURMESE $$
(Map p488; 110 19th St; mains from K4000, barbecue from K400; ⏰noon-11.30pm; 🍴) The best of the many barbecue restaurants on busy 19th St: this is where Anthony Bourdain dined when he passed through Yangon. Pick from the skewers on display, which include meat, seafood and veggie options, or you can order dishes from the menu. You'll likely have to wait for a table, but it does K900 mojitos to keep you occupied.

West Central Yangon

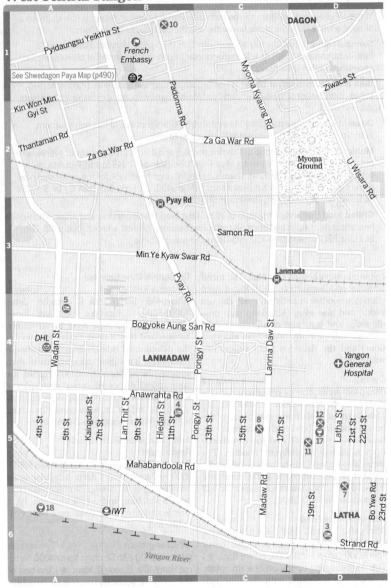

DAGON

Pyidaungsu Yeiktha St

French
Embassy

See Shwedagon Paya Map (p490)

2

Ziwaca St

Kin Won Min
Gyi St

Padonma Rd

Myoma Kyaung Rd

Thantaman Rd

Za Ga War Rd

Za Ga War Rd

Myoma
Ground

U Wisara Rd

Pyay Rd

Samon Rd

Min Ye Kyaw Swar Rd

Pyay Rd

Lanmada

5

Bogyoke Aung San Rd

Lanma Daw St

DHL

Wadan St

LANMADAW

Pongyi St

Yangon
General
Hospital

Anawrahta Rd

4th St

5th St

Kaingdan St

7th St

Lan Thit St

9th St

Hledan St

11th St

Pongyi St

13th St

15th St

17th St

12

Latha St

21st St

22nd St

17

8

11

Mahabandoola Rd

Madaw Rd

19th St

7

LATHA

Bo Ywe Rd

23rd St

18

IWT

3

Strand Rd

Yangon River

🍷 Drinking & Nightlife

Places that fit the Western concept of a bar or a club are becoming more common. But most locals prefer hanging out in a teahouse or air-conditioned cafe as much as one of the ubiquitous beer stations and beer gardens –

the last two being favourite places to catch soccer matches.

Myanmore (www.myanmore.com) is a useful online guide to Yangon's restaurant, bar and entertainment scene.

West Central Yangon

◉ Sights
1 Musmeah Yeshua Synagogue E6
2 National Museum B1

⬤ Sleeping
3 20th Street Hostel D6
4 4 Rivers Youth Hostel B5
5 MGM Hotel A4

⊗ Eating
6 Aung Mingalar Shan Noodle
   Restaurant F3
7 Cherry Mann D6
8 Cyclo C5
9 Danuphyu Daw Saw Yee
   Myanma Restaurant F4
10 Feel Myanmar Food B1
11 Grilled Snack Stalls D5
12 Kaung Myat D5
13 Nilar Biryani & Cold Drink F5

◉ Drinking & Nightlife
14 Bar Boon F4
15 Blind Tiger F3
16 Cafe Genius F4
17 Kosan D5
18 Wadan Jetty Beer Station A6

⬤ Shopping
19 Bogyoke Aung San Market E4
20 Theingyi Zei E5

expats out on the razzle. Beers cost K1700 and it does OK snacks too.

★ **Blind Tiger**   COCKTAIL BAR
(Map p488; ☎01-388 488; www.blindtiger-yangon. com; Unit 111 Condominium cnr Na Wa Day St & Ah Lan Paya Rd; ⊙noon-late Mon-Fri, 5pm-late Sat-Sun; 🛜) Speakeasy style comes to Myanmar, with this hidden-away cocktail bar that has paintings by local artists on the walls and old-school jazz as the soundtrack. It's a unique scene for Yangon, and correspondingly popular. Cocktails start at K6000, but all drinks are half-price during the daily happy hour from 5pm to 7pm. Great burgers and tapas too.

It is likely to move to a new location in 2016; check the website for details.

50th Street Bar & Grill   BAR
(Map p484; ☎01-397 060; www.50thstreetyan gon; 9-13 50th St, Botataung; ⊙11am-midnight; 🛜) One of Yangon's longest-established Western-style bars, in a handsomely restored colonial-era building, 50th Street continues to draw in the crowds with its mix of event nights, free pool table and sport on

★ **Kosan**   BAR
(Map p488; 108 19th St, Latha; ⊙1pm-11pm; 🛜) A reasonably decent mojito for K900? No wonder this relaxed, Japanese-owned bar with an upstairs area and seats spilling onto buzzing 19th St is popular with locals and

Shwedagon Paya

Shwedagon Paya

the TV. Happy hour is 8pm to 10pm Monday to Friday and all day on Sunday.

Cafe Genius
CAFE
(Map p488; www.cafe-genius.com; 220 31st St; ⊙10am-7pm; 🛜) Cute cubbyhole of a cafe that offers decent coffee, tea, smoothies and sandwiches and makes a good retreat from the surrounding chaos. Its coffee is sourced from the highlands of Shan State: beans can be bought by the bag.

Bar Boon
BAR
(Map p488; FMI Centre, 380 Bogyoke Aung San Rd, Pabedan; ⊙7.30am-9pm; 🛜) Recharge at this contemporary-styled cafe serving excellent coffee, iced tea and Dutch beer along with tasty but pricey snacks and pastries. The outdoor terrace offers decent people-watching near Bogyoke Aung San Market.

Strand Bar
BAR
(Map p484; Strand Hotel, 92 Strand Rd, Kyauktada; ⊙10am-11pm; 🛜) Primarily an expat scene, this classic bar inside the Strand Hotel has any foreign liquor you may be craving behind its polished wooden counter. Friday nights (5pm to 11pm) it gets busy as all drinks are half-price.

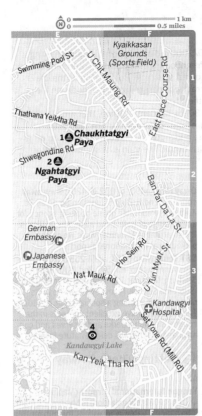

Wadan Jetty Beer Station
BAR

(Map p488; Wadan Jetty, Lanmadaw; ⊙6am-9pm) Entering the docks from the main road, turn right at the waterfront to find this small beer station with a cluster of outdoor seating. It's a great spot for sunset drinks when you can also watch (or join in) with locals playing football or the local sport of *chinlon*.

Shopping

★ Bogyoke Aung San Market
MARKET

(Map p488; Bogyoke Aung San Rd, Dagon; ⊙10am-5pm Tue-Sun) Half a day could easily be spent wandering around this sprawling covered market, sometimes called by its old British name, Scott Market. It has over 2000 shops and the largest selection of Myanmar handicrafts and souvenirs you'll find under several roofs, from lacquerware and Shan shoulder bags to puppets and jewellery.

★ Pomelo
HANDICRAFTS

(Map p484; www.pomeloyangon.com; 89 Thein Pyu Rd, Botataung; ⊙10am-10pm) The best selection of contemporary handicrafts in Yangon – and all produced by projects supporting disadvantaged groups in Myanmar. Fall in love with the colourful papier mâché dogs and bags featuring bold graphic images as well as the exquisite Chin weavings and jewellery made from recycled materials.

Theingyi Zei
MARKET

(Map p488; Shwedagon Pagoda Rd, Pabedan; ⊙9am-7pm) Most of the merchandise at downtown Yangon's largest market is ordinary housewares and textiles, but it's also renowned for its large selection of traditional herbs, cosmetics and medicines, which can be found on the ground floor of the easternmost building.

Bagan Book House
BOOKS

(Map p484; ☑01-377 227; 100 37th St, Kyauktada; ⊙8.30am-6.30pm) This Yangon institution has the most complete selection of English-language books on Myanmar and Southeast Asia, and genial owner U Htay Aung really knows his stock, which includes tomes dating back to the 19th century.

ⓘ Information

EMERGENCY

Your embassy may also be able to assist in an emergency.

Ambulance (☑192)
Fire (☑191)
Police (Map p484; ☑199)
Red Cross (☑01-383 680)

INTERNET ACCESS

All guesthouses, hostels and hotels and many restaurants, cafes and bars offer free wi-fi access; there's even free wi-fi at Shwedagon Paya. There are also a declining number of internet cafes scattered around town. Server speeds have improved, but still tend to be frustratingly slow in comparison to almost any other country.

MEDICAL SERVICES

AA Pharmacy (Map p484; 142-146 Sule Paya Rd, Kyauktada; ⊙9am-10pm) Just north of Sule Paya.

International SOS Clinic (☑01-657 922; www.internationalsos.com; Inya Lake Hotel, 37 Kaba Aye Pagoda Rd, Mayangone) Your best bet in Yangon for emergencies, this clinic claims to be able to work with just about any international health insurance and has a 24-hour emergency centre with an expat doctor.

RIDING THE CIRCLE LINE

The nearly 31-mile Yangon Circle Line (K1000/2000 ordinary/air-con) is a slow-moving, three-hour train trip around Yangon and the neighbouring countryside. The ancient carriages shake at times like washing machines on full spin cycle. But hopping on the line is a great way to experience commuter life, interact with passengers and vendors on the trains, and see off-the-beaten-track areas of the city.

Trains leave at 6.10am, 7.35am, 8.20am, 9.30am, 10.10am, 11.10am, 11.30am, 12.15pm, 1.05pm, 2.25pm, 3.25pm and 5.10pm from platform 6/7 at the Yangon train station, accessed off Pandsodan St; tickets are bought on the platform. Trains go in either direction and some don't always do the full circuit. The train is least crowded after 10am and before 4pm, and at weekends.

MONEY

You'll get the best rates for changing money at banks and official moneychangers. Bring your passport and crisp, new bills.

More and more ATMs in Yangon accept international Visa and Mastercards; there's a K5000 charge for using them.

POST

Central Post Office (Map p484; cnr Strand Rd & Bo Aung Kyaw St, Kyauktada; ⊙7.30am-6pm Mon-Fri) A short stroll east of the Strand Hotel. Stamps are for sale on the ground floor but go to the 1st floor to send mail.

DHL (Map p488; ☑01-215 516; www.dhl.com; 58 Wadan St, Lanmadaw; ⊙8am-6pm Mon-Fri, 8am-2pm Sat) Courier and logistics company that sends parcels and mail worldwide.

TOURIST INFORMATION

Myanmar Travels & Tours (MTT; Map p484; ☑01-374 281; 118 Mahabandoola Garden St; ⊙8.30am-5pm) This is the place to go to arrange the necessary paperwork and guides for areas of the country that still require travel permits. Staff can also arrange local sightseeing tours to a variety of locations.

TRAVEL AGENCIES

Yangon's privately run travel agencies are the best place in the country for hiring a car or guide, booking an air ticket and checking on the latest travel restrictions.

Good News Travels (☑09 5116 256; www. myanmargoodnewstravel.com; Room 18, 204 Yanshin Rd, Kyauktada) The owner, William Myatwunna, is extremely personable and knowledgeable, and can help arrange visits to remote parts of Myanmar. Highly recommended. Also has an office in Bagan.

Khiri Travel (Map p484; ☑01-375 577; http://khiri.com; 1st floor, 5/9 Bo Galay Zay St, Botataung) The friendly, professional team here offer biking and kayak trips in Shan and Kayin State, walking tours of markets and meetings with fortune-tellers, as well as many other options.

Oway (Map p490; ☑01-230 4201; www.oway. com.mm; 2nd fl, Bldg 6 Junction Sq, Pyay Rd, Kamayut) Reputable online booking agency for a wide range of hotels and all domestic flights. It also arranges Myanmar visas which can be picked up at international airports.

SST Tours (Map p484; ☑01-255 536; www.sstmyanmar.com; Rm 5-6, 2nd fl, Aung San Stadium, Mingalar Taung Nyunt) Standing for 'Supreme Service Team', SST lives up to its name as well as being a specialist for eco-tours. The managers have excellent contacts in the country's national parks and reserves and can arrange trips that will delight nature lovers.

❶ Getting There & Away

AIR

Yangon International Airport (Map p482; ☑01-533 031; Mingalardon) is Myanmar's main international gateway as well as the hub for domestic flights.

BOAT

IWT (Inland Water Transport; Map p488; ☑01-381 912, 01-380 764; Lan Thit jetty) Ferries to Pathein were not running at the time of research.

Pansodan Street Jetty (Map p484) The jumping-off base for daytime river-crossing boats to Dalah (one way US$2/K2700, return US$4/K5400, 10 minutes), which leave roughly every 20 minutes between 5am and 9pm.

BUS

Guesthouses can assist with purchasing tickets for a small additional fee. Several larger companies have convenient bus-ticket offices opposite Yangon train station.

Aung Mingalar Bus Station This is the only official bus terminal for all 150 bus lines leaving for the northern part of Myanmar, as well as for Kyaiktiyo (Golden Rock), Mawlamyine and destinations to the south. A taxi here costs K7000 and can take over an hour driving from downtown Yangon.

Hlaing Thar Yar Bus Station This terminal is for travel to the delta region (officially called Ayeyarwady Region) and to destinations west of Yangon. It's an hour west of the city centre by taxi (K8000).

TRAIN

Yangon's train station (☏ 01-202 178; ☺ 6am-4pm) is located a short walk north of Sule Paya, although advance tickets must be purchased at the adjacent **Myanmar Railways Booking Office** (Map p484; Bogyoke Aung San Rd; ☺ 7am-3pm).

Major destinations that can be reached by daily departures from Yangon include Bagan, Bago, Kyaikto, Mandalay, Mawlamyine, Nay Pyi Taw, Pyay, Taungoo and Thazi.

❶ Getting Around

TO/FROM THE AIRPORT

There is an official taxi counter as you exit the airport terminal, or drivers will approach you. The fare to downtown Yangon is K8000 and the journey will likely take an hour (more if traffic is heavy).

BUS

With taxis in Yangon being so cheap, you'd really have to be pinching pennies to rely on buses. They're impossibly crowded, the conductors rarely have change, the routes are confusing and there's virtually no English spoken or written.

If you're determined, the typical fare within central Yangon is K200 to K300; use small bills. Prices often double at night, but the buses are still crowded.

TAXI

Yangon taxis are one of the best deals in Asia, despite not using a meter. Most drivers speak at least some English (although it's advisable to have someone write out your destination in Burmese) and are mostly honest and courteous.

All licensed taxis have a visible taxi sign on the roof, but many other drivers will give you ride for a negotiated fare. If you'd prefer to book a taxi, a service we've had recommendations for

TRANSPORT FROM YANGON

DESTINATION	BUS	TRAIN	AIR
Bago	K2000, 1½hr	ordinary/upper class K600/1150, 2hr	
Chaung Tha Beach	K10,000, 7hr		
Dawei	K15,300, 15hr		US$96, 70min
Heho (for Inle Lake & Kalaw)			US$106, 1hr
Hpa-an	K6000, 7hr		
Hsipaw	K16,500, 15hr		
Kalaw	K17,500, 11hr		
Kyaikto	K8000, 4hr	ordinary/upper class K1200/2400, 4hr	
Mandalay	K10,800-18,300, 9hr	ordinary/upper class/sleeper K4650/9300/12,750, 10-16hr	US$112, 1hr
Mawlamyine	K6000, 7hr	ordinary/upper class K2150/4250, 9hr	
Myitkyina			US$195, 2hr
Ngwe Saung Beach	K10,000, 7hr		
Nyaung U (for Bagan)	K15,000-18,500, 10hr	upper class/sleeper K6000/16,500, 16hr	US$126, 70min
Pathein	K7000, 4½hr		
Pyay	K5500, 6hr	ordinary/upper class K1950/3900, 9hr	
Sittwe	K20,500, 24hr		US$117, 1¼hr
Taunggyi (for Inle Lake)	K17,500, 12hr		
Taungoo	K4500, 6hr	ordinary/upper class K2800/4000, 7hr	
Thandwe (for Ngapali)	K15,500, 14hr		

DALAH & TWANTE

One of the easiest and most enjoyable short trips out of Yangon is to board one of the double-decker ferries (return US$4/K5400, every 20 minutes) that shuttle between Pansodan St Jetty and Dalah (ဒလ႐ွိ.) across the Yangon River. Catch the ferry around 5.30pm and you get a cheap sunset cruise.

Dalah, which is one of Yangon's townships, is no great shakes; the main aim is to continue on to Twante, a pleasant town 30 to 45 minutes' drive west into the delta where you can visit **Shwesandaw Paya** (ေရႊဆံေတာ္ဘုရား; camera fee K200; ⊙6am-9pm), an ancient temple, and the **Oh-Bo Pottery Sheds** (အိုးဘို အိုးလုပ္ငန္း). Chances are you'll be approached on the ferry by someone offering their services as a motorbike taxi; the going rate is K10,000 to K15,000 return including stops at the various sights. Regular taxis charge around K30,000, while a squashed seat in a pick-up van to Twante is K1500.

is **Golden Harp** (☑ 09 4500 19186, 09 4281 17348), run by ex political prisoners.

The following should give you an idea of what to pay: a short hop (say from the Strand to Bogyoke Market) will be K1000; double this distance will be K2000; from downtown to Shwedagon Paya and the southern half of Bahan township will be K3000 depending on the state of traffic.

You can also hire a taxi for about K5000 an hour. For the entire day, you should expect to pay K75,000 to K100,000, depending on the quality of the vehicle and your negotiating skills.

TRISHAW

In Myanmar, trishaw passengers ride with the driver, but back-to-back (one facing forward, one backward). These contraptions are called *saiq-ka* (as in side-car) and to ride one costs K500 for short hops. Given the heaviness of downtown Yangon's traffic during the day, you may find trishaw pedallers reluctant to make a long journey across town at this time.

THE DELTA, WEST COAST BEACHES & NORTH OF YANGON

Unlike neighbouring Thailand, Myanmar's beaches are almost empty except on weekends. Ngapali Beach in the south of Rakhine State is the finest, but the long and/or expensive trip and lack of budget accommodation means most shoestringers skip it; for details see Lonely Planet's *Myanmar (Burma)* guide. Instead, head from Yangon through the Ayeyarwady Delta to sleepy Pathein and on to Ngwe Saung or Chaung Tha beaches.

North of Yangon the main roads pass through a few interesting towns that are worth a look or stopover en route to Bagan, Mandalay and Inle Lake.

Pathein   ပုသိမ္

☑ 042 / POP 169,773

An interesting staging post on the way to Chaung Tha or Ngwe Saung beaches, Pathein, 112 miles west of Yangon, is Myanmar's fourth-largest city. Despite being the commercial and administrative heart of the Ayeyarwady Delta, Pathein has a languid, easy-going feel. Still an important river port, it's better known now for its parasol industry and fragrant rice.

◉ Sights

Shwe Sar Umbrella Workshop   HANDICRAFTS
(☑ 042-25127; 653 Tawya Kyaung Rd; ⊙8am-5pm)
Sun shades are made in workshops scattered across the northern part of the city, particularly around the Twenty-Eight Paya, off Mahabandoola Rd. It's fun to wander the area, sticking your head into a workshop here and there to see how they're made. They're cheap, and the saffron-coloured ones, made for monks, actually are waterproof. This family-run workshop is particularly welcoming.

Shwemokhtaw Paya   BUDDHIST STUPA
(ေရႊမုဌောဘုရား; Shwezedi Rd; ⊙6am-8pm)
FREE Looming with grace over Pathein is the golden bell of the Shwemokhtaw Paya. The *hti* consists of a topmost layer made from 14lb of solid gold, a middle tier of pure silver and a bottom tier of bronze; all three tiers are gilded and reportedly embedded with a total of 829 diamond fragments, 843 rubies and 1588 semiprecious stones.

Settayaw Paya   BUDDHIST TEMPLE
(စက္ေတာ္ရာဘုရား) **FREE** This charming paya, spread across a hilly green setting, is dedicated to a mythical Buddha footprint

left by the Enlightened One during his legendary perambulations through Southeast Asia. The footprint symbol itself is an oblong, 3ft-long impression.

🛏 Sleeping & Eating

Day to Day Motel   HOTEL **$**
(✆042-23368; Jail St; s/d/tr K15,000/20,000/25,000; ❄️🛜) Reasonable rooms for the price, although the bathrooms are cramped and dark, in a quieter part of town, opposite the historic Sikh Temple. A big roof terrace provides a pleasant place to sit and take in the surrounding leafy view. Decent wi-fi connection. You can only pay in kyat here.

Taan Taan Ta Guest House   HOTEL **$**
(✆042-22290; taantaanta25@gmail.com; 7 Merchant St; s US$10-15, d US$15-30; ❄️🛜) This no-frills guesthouse is often full, even though the rooms are beaten-up and very basic. If you're not on a shoestring, check out the more expensive doubles on the top floor, which are bigger and come with air-con and TV.

Shwe Ayar   BURMESE MUSLIM **$**
(32-35 Mingalar Rd; mains from K1800; ⏰8am-9pm) It doesn't look like much but this place offers high-quality biryani, which you can

supplement with chicken or mutton. The lentil and bean soup is so delicious you'll want a second helping. Find it opposite Zaw Optical.

ℹ Getting There & Away

BOAT
At the time of writing, the boat service to/from Yangon was not running. If that changes, tickets can be bought with US dollars only at the **Inland Water Transport Office** (Mahabandoola Rd; ⏰10am-noon), located in a wooden colonial-era building near the jetty.

BUS
If you're bound for Yangon (four hours), head to the bus company offices located on Shwezedi Rd. The cheapest air-con service is offered five times a day by **Ayer Shwe Zin** (✆09 4974 5191) for K3600 but it's slow; other operators charge K7000.

Uncomfortable minibuses ply the route from Pathein to Chaung Tha Beach (K3000, 2½ hours) every two hours between 8am and 4pm, departing from an informal **bus station** (Yadayagone St) a couple of blocks northeast of the clock tower.

To Ngwe Saung Beach (K3500, two hours), buses leave from yet another bus station that's off Mingalar St at 8.30am, noon and 3pm.

WORTH A TRIP

CHAUNG THA & NGWE SAUNG BEACHES

If you're in search of a sea breeze and soft sand while visiting Myanmar, either Chaung Tha Beach (ချောင်းသာကမ်းခြေ) or Ngwe Saung Beach (ငွေဆောင်ကမ်းခြေ) do the trick.

A motorbike taxi trip between the two resort areas (K18,000 one way or return) is highly recommended. The route involves three river crossings on small wooden boats and passes deserted beaches and rustic villages amid palm groves.

Of the two resorts, Ngwe Saung, 28 miles west of Pathein, is the nicer with miles of white-sand beach, but it attracts upmarket Yangonites and so has limited budget accommodation; try **Shwe Hin Tha Hotel** (✆042-40340; bungalows US$25-50; ❄️) or **Silver Coast Beach Hotel** (✆042-254708; r US$55; ❄️🛜). For eats and drinks, **Royal Flower** (Myoma St; mains K4500; ⏰6-10pm; 📶) distinguishes itself from the other restaurants with nightly concerts by a mellow guitar-playing duo.

Chaung Tha, 25 miles west of Pathein, offers as much of a beach-party vibe as you're going to get in Myanmar and is popular with locals. The best places to crash here are **Hill Garden Hotel** (✆09 4957 6072; www.hillgardenhotel.com; r US$27-50; 🛜), a 20-minute walk north of the main resort area, or the centrally located **Shwe Ya Min Guesthouse & Restaurant** (✆042-42127; Main Rd; s/d US$40/60; ❄️🛜), which is also the best spot for a meal.

Connect between Chaung Tha and Pathein by minibus (K3000, 2½ hours, 8am, 10am, noon, 2pm and 4pm) or motorbike taxi (K12,000, two hours).

From Ngwe Saung there are also minibuses to Pathein (K3500, two hours, five daily) and buses to Yangon (K10,000, six hours, 6.30am and 8am).

Bago ပဲခူး

☑ 052 / POP 254,424

Founded in AD 573 by the Mon, this one-time capital probably contains a greater density of blissed-out buddhas and treasure-filled temples than any other similar-sized town in southern Myanmar. All this makes Bago a superb and simple day trip from Yangon, or the ideal first stop when you leave the city behind.

◉ Sights & Activities

Many of Bago's monuments are actually centuries old, but don't look it, due to extensive restorations. This is an excellent place to explore by bicycle, as most attractions are near each other. Bikes are available for rent at **Bago Star Hotel** (☑052-30066; bagostar@ myanmar.com.mm; 11-21 Kyaikpon Pagoda Rd; s/d US$35/40; ❈ ☎ ☎); it also has a basic map of the town you can follow.

To gain access to Bago's main sites, including Shwemawdaw Paya, foreigners must buy the **Bago Archaeological Zone ticket** (US$10/K10,000). Nearly all of the sights charge an additional K300 for cameras and K500 for videocameras.

Shwethalyaung Buddha   BUDDHIST TEMPLE

(ရွှေသာလျောင်းဘုရား; ⊙ 5am-8pm) **FREE** Legend has it that this gorgeous reclining buddha was built by the Mon king Mgadeikpa in the 10th century. Measuring 180ft long and 53ft high, the monument's little finger alone extends 10ft.

Following the destruction of Bago in 1757, the huge buddha was overgrown by jungle and not rediscovered until 1881, when a contractor unearthed it while building the Yangon–Bago railway line.

Shwemawdaw Paya   BUDDHIST STUPA

(ရွှေမော်တောဘုရား; Shwemawdaw Paya Rd; ⊙ 5am-8pm) A pyramid of washed-out gold in the midday haze and glittering perfection in the evening, the 376ft-high Shwemawdaw Paya stands tall and proud over the town. The stupa reaches 46ft higher than the Shwedagon in Yangon.

At the northeastern corner of the stupa is a huge section of the *hti* toppled by an earthquake in 1917. Shwemawdaw is a particularly good destination during Bago's annual pagoda festival, in March/April.

Hintha Gon Paya   BUDDHIST STUPA

(ဟင်္သာကုန်း) Located a short walk behind the Shwemawdaw, this shrine was once the one point in this whole vast area that rose above sea level and so was the natural place for the *hamsa* to land. Images of this mythical bird decorate the stupa built by U Khanti, the hermit monk who was the architect of Mandalay Hill.

Kyaik Pun Paya   MONUMENT

(ကျိုက်ပွန်ဘုရား; Kyikpon Pagoda Rd) Built in 1476 by King Dhammazedi, the Kyaik Pun Paya consists of four 100ft-high sitting buddhas (Gautama Buddha and his three predecessors) placed back to back around a huge, square pillar, about a mile south of Bago just off the Yangon road.

🛏 Sleeping & Eating

Few travellers spend the night in Bago and hotel choices are uninspired. Main Rd is deafeningly noisy – ask for a room at the back.

Mya Nanda Hotel   HOTEL $

(☑ 09 501 9799; 10 Main Rd; s/d US$10/18; ❈ ☎) Clean but basic rooms in a central location. The doubles offer more space and light.

San Francisco Guest House   HOTEL $

(☑052-22265; 14 Main Rd; s/d US$10/20; ❈ ☎) The six rooms here are rough and ready and there's a curfew from 10pm to 5am. Staff can arrange motorbike tours of Bago's sights (K8000).

Three Five Restaurant   CHINESE, BURMESE $

(10 Main Rd; mains K1300-4000; ⊙ 7am-10pm; ▣) This friendly but shabby place offers a menu

TRANSPORT FROM BAGO

DESTINATION	BUS	TRAIN (ORDINARY/UPPER CLASS)
Kyaikto	K3000-4000, 2hr	K650/1700, 3hr
Mandalay	K13,000-15,000, 9hr	K4150/8150, 14hr
Mawlamyine	K6000-7500, 6hr	K1600/4100, 7hr
Taungoo	K4500, 6hr	K1450/2900, 5hr
Yangon	K2000, 1½hr	K600/1150, 2hr

spanning Burmese and Chinese cuisine, with a few European dishes. At night, it's a popular spot for a beer.

Hanthawaddy CHINESE, BURMESE $$
(192 Hintha St; mains from K2000; ⊙10am-11pm; 🎐) The food here isn't amazing, but it's the only restaurant in central Bago with a bit of atmosphere. The open-air upper level is breezy and offers great views of Shwemawdaw Paya.

🕓 Getting There & Away

BUS

Buses to Yangon depart approximately every 30 minutes from 6.30am to 5.30pm.

Going south, buses to Kinpun, the starting point for Mt Kyaiktiyo (Golden Rock), leave hourly from 7am to 6pm. During the rainy season (May to October) most buses go only as far as Kyaikto, 10 miles from Kinpun.

Heading north, for Mandalay, Taungoo and Inle Lake, you can also try and hop on services coming from Yangon. Book ahead with a local agent, like the reliable **Sea Sar** (🕿 09 530 0987; seasar.tickets918@gmail.com), who has an office at the bus station.

TAXI

Some travellers make a day trip out of Bago with a hired car from Yangon. It costs around K100,000, but it does give you the advantage of having transport between sites once you get to Bago and saves traipsing all the way out to the bus station in Yangon.

One-way taxis from Bago straight to your hotel in Yangon cost about K45,000. A taxi from Bago to Mt Kyaikto will cost K40,000. Inquire at the town's **taxi stand** (Yangon-Mandalay Rd) or through any of the central Bago hotels.

TRAIN

Bago is connected by train with Yangon and Mawlamyine and stops north towards Mandalay.

🕓 Getting Around

Motorbike taxis and trishaws are the main forms of local transport. A one-way trip in the central area should cost no more than K500. Hiring a trishaw or motorcycle for the day costs about K7000.

Taungoo ⟨ေတာင်ငူ⟩

🕿 054 / POP 108,589

It's hard to imagine Taungoo, lying just under halfway from Yangon to Mandalay, was once the nerve centre of a powerful kingdom. Today it's a sleepy place that most people see from a bus or train window. However,

it gets the 'real-deal experience' thumbs up from those who do stop and is home to one of Myanmar's more memorable guesthouses.

On the town's west side Shwesandaw Paya (built 1597) is the main pilgrimage site. Nearby, pretty Kandawgyi Lake is pleasant to stroll or cycle around.

At the southern end of town **Myanmar Beauty Guest House II, III & IV** (🕿 054-23270; Pauk Hla Gyi St; s US$20-40, d US$25-50, tr US$40-60; 🅿🔌) consists of three teak houses with wide-open views of the rice paddies and hills that loom beyond. Rates include a gut-busting local breakfast.

Heading north or south on the air-con buses, you'll pay full Mandalay–Yangon fare. Most stop near the hospital, in the town centre. Local buses to Yangon (K4500, six hours) leave at 7am and 7pm. Mandalay buses (K7500 to K9000, nine hours) pass about 6.30pm.

Trains between Yangon (ordinary/upper K1950/3900, nine hours) and Mandalay (ordinary/upper class K1550/3500, eight hours) stop here too.

Pyay

🕿 053 / POP 134,861

With a breezy location on the Ayeyarwady, Pyay is the most interesting stop on the Yangon–Bagan Hwy. Soak up its lively atmosphere along the riverfront and the roundabout, at the centre of which is a gilded equestrian statue of Aung San.

⊙ Sights

The city's glory days date back to the ancient Pyu capital of **Thayekhittaya** (သရေခေတ္တရာ; admission US$5/K5000, incl museum US$10/K10,000; ⊙8am-5pm), the partially excavated remains of which lay 5 miles east of Pyay's main attraction: the dazzling Shwesandaw Paya. Perched atop a central hill, this temple is 3ft taller than Yangon's Shwedagon Paya and apparently dates from 589 BC. Facing the paya from the east is Sehtatgyi Paya (Big Ten Storey), a giant seated Buddha.

Follow Strand Rd north during the morning to catch all the action at the lively and colourful central market, which spreads over several blocks.

About 8.5 miles south of Pyay, Shwemyetman Paya is home to a large, white-faced, seated Buddha – sporting a pair of giant gold-plated glasses! Hop on a local

Yangon-bound bus or southbound pick-up, and get off in Shwedaung town.

Sleeping & Eating

The **night market** on Mya Zay Tann St between the Aung San statue and the river is well worth browsing for cheap eats.

Myat Lodging House   HOTEL $
(053-25695; 222 Bazaar St; s/d US$15/25;
⚙ 🛜) This small back-street guesthouse has simple rooms a block from the Pyay 'action'. Higher-priced rooms come with a private bathroom and are set at the back of the maze of buildings. Friendly English-speaking staff give out maps of Pyay and Thayekhittaya.

Getting There & Away

At the time of writing, there were no boats between Pyay and Yangon. If they are running, then tickets can be bought at the **IWT office** (053-24503; Strand Rd; ⊘ 9am-5pm Mon-Fri).

The highway bus station, 1 mile east of the town centre, sends frequent buses to Yangon (K5500, six hours). No direct buses go to Bagan; either jump on a Yangon–Bagan bus (for full fare) or take the 8.30am bus to Magwe (K5000, six hours), from where there are departures the next morning for Bagan.

A daily train leaves Pyay's central train station for Yangon (ordinary/upper class K1950/3900, nine hours). From Shwethekar station, 3 miles east of the city, you can also board the Bagan–Yangon train at 10pm.

SOUTHEASTERN MYANMAR

Teetering on a cliff edge, the Golden Rock of Kyaiktiyo draws a few visitors off the main trail for a tough but rewarding pilgrimage. Further south, Mawlamyine offers glimpses of old Burma while Hpa-an sits amid glorious countryside in off-the-beaten-track Kayin (Karen) State.

Mt Kyaiktiyo (Golden Rock) ကျိုက်ထီးရိုးတောင်
 057

The gravity-defying **Kyaiktiyo** (Golden Rock; K6000, ticket valid for 30 days) is one of Myanmar's most enigmatic and intriguing sights. Perched on the very edge of a cliff on Mt Kyaiktiyo, this giant, gold-leaf-covered boulder is topped by a stupa containing a Buddha hair donated by a hermit in the 11th century. Apparently, the hair was salvaged from the bottom of the sea and brought here by boat. The boat subsequently turned to stone and is visible a few hundred metres away.

Kyaiktiyo has a mystical aura; it's a place of miracles, not least of which is how the boulder has managed to hang on, withstanding several earthquakes, for all these years. Pilgrims come in their thousands and the experience is more interesting because of them. That said, on weekends especially the mountaintop can feel like a theme park.

Since the rock is especially beautiful illuminated in the evening, plan on spending a night in the 'base camp' of Kinpun, a collection of restaurants and guesthouses 7 miles from the summit of Mt Kyaiktiyo. Kyaikto, where trains and long-distance buses stop, has several guesthouses, none of them very appealing, and there really is no reason to stay here rather than in Kinpun.

There are two ways to the rock: hiking 7 miles uphill from Kinpun (four to six hours one way), or trucking (K2500 to K3000, 45 minutes, 6am to 6pm). Trucks depart from a station just off the main road. Walking down to Kinpun takes three to four hours and should not be attempted in the dark or if it is wet, it's too easy to stumble.

There is a K6000 government entrance fee, payable at the checkpoint near the top, just after the Mountain Top Hotel. Men shouldn't wear shorts at the shrine and women should wear long skirts only – no trousers, miniskirts or skimpy tops.

TRANSPORT FROM KYAIKTO

DESTINATION	BUS	TRAIN
Bago	K3000-4000, 2hr	ordinary/upper class K650/1700, 3hr
Hpa-an	K7000, 3hr	
Mawlamyine	K7000, 4hr	ordinary/upper class K1250/2500, 4hr
Yangon	K7000, 5hr	ordinary/upper class K1200/2400, 4hr

🛏 Sleeping & Eating

There are a number of simple restaurants at the summit. The few restaurants in Kinpun serve a mix of Burmese and Chinese dishes.

★ **Golden Sunrise Hotel** HOTEL $
(📞 01-500 351; www.goldensunrisehotel.com; Golden Rock Rd; s/d incl breakfast US$42/47; ❄ 🛜) A few minutes' walk outside the centre of Kinpun village in the direction of the highway, the Golden Sunrise is one of the best-value hotels in southern Myanmar. The low-slung, semi-detached rooms are undisturbed by noise, decked out with attractive wood furniture, and come with verandahs overlooking a secluded garden.

Sea Sar Hotel HOTEL $
(📞 09 872 3288; r incl breakfast US$8-35; ❄ 🛜) All the rooms here are overpriced; the cheapest are fan-only concrete boxes. The best are the various air-con bungalows out back, some of which are relatively new and attractive.

Bawga Theiddhi Hotel HOTEL $$
(no roman-script sign; 📞 09 4929 9899; www. bawgatheiddhihotel.com; r incl breakfast US$25-85; ❄ 🛜) Kinpun's flashiest hotel has rooms that are clean, spacious and equipped with TV, fridge and free wi-fi; a good deal if you can score one of the $25 ones.

Mountain Top Hotel HOTEL $$
(📞 09 871 8392, in Yangon 01-502 479; www.moun taintop.com; r incl breakfast US$100-120; ❄ 🛜) Yes, the rooms are grossly overpriced, but they're clean and well maintained, with good service, and the location at the summit of the mountain means stunning views. The attached restaurant is reliable.

ⓘ Getting There & Away

The major transport hub for Mt Kyaiktiyo is Kyaikto. This is where the train station is, and the town's main street is where you'll board (or disembark from) buses.

BUS & PICK-UPS

Tickets for Win Express buses can be purchased in Kinpun across from Sea Sar Hotel. The ticket price includes truck fare to Kyaikto. There are frequent buses to Yangon, Mawlamyine and Hpa-an between 8am and 4pm.

Pick-ups cruise between Kyaikto's train station and Kinpun from 7am to 4pm (K500, 20 minutes).

TRAIN

Two daily trains run to/from Yangon and Mawlamyine, stopping at Kyaikto at noon and 11.30pm.

Mawlamyine မော်လမြိုင်

📞 057 / POP 253,734

With a ridge of stupa-capped hills on one side, the Thanlwin River on the other and streets filled with crumbling colonial-era buildings, churches and mosques, Mawlamyine is a unique combination of landscape, beauty and melancholy. Indeed, the setting inspired two of history's finest English writers – George Orwell and Rudyard Kipling.

Formerly known as Moulmein, the city and its surrounds have enough attractions, ranging from beaches to caves, to keep a visitor happy for several days.

⊙ Sights & Activities

About 8.5 miles south of Mawlamyine is **Pa-Auk-Taw-Ya Monastery** (ဖားအောက်တောရသုန်းကြီးကျောင်း; 📞 057-22853; www.paaukforestmonastery.org) FREE, one of the largest meditation centres in Myanmar. Foreigners can stay the night or several days; sleeping and eating is free but you're up at 3am.

★ **Kyaikthanlan Paya** BUDDHIST TEMPLE
(ကျိုက်သံလန်ဘုရား; Kyaik Than Lan Phayar St; ⊙ daylight hours) FREE Rudyard Kipling's visit to Myanmar spanned just three days, but it resulted in a few lines that turned Burma into an Oriental fantasy: 'By the old Moulmein Pagoda, lookin' lazy at the sea...' The 'Moulmein Pagoda' cited in his poem 'Mandalay' was most likely **Kyaikthanlan Paya**, the city's tallest and most visible stupa.

It's a great spot for watching the sunset. To reach the temple complex, approach it via the long covered walkway that extends from Kyaik Than Lan Phayar St.

Mon Cultural Museum MUSEUM
(မွန်ယဉ်ကျေးမှုပြတိုက်; cnr Baho & Dawei Jetty Rds; admission K2000; ⊙ 10am-4.30pm Tue-Sun) Unlike most of Myanmar's regional museums, Mawlamyine's is actually worth a visit. It's dedicated to the Mon history of the region. The collection includes stelae with Mon inscriptions, 100-year-old wooden sculptures depicting old age and sickness (used as *dhamma*-teaching devices in monasteries), ceramics, silver betel boxes, royal funerary urns and Mon musical instruments, most of which are accompanied by English-language descriptions.

Gaungse Kyun (Shampoo Island)   ISLAND
(�‌ ‌ ‌ ‌; ⊘ daylight hours) FREE This picturesque little isle just off Mawlamyine's northern end is so named because, during the Ava period, the yearly royal hair-washing ceremony customarily used water taken from a spring on the island.

You can hire a boat out here from the pier at the northern end of town, not far from the former Mawlamyine Hotel, for K4000 return.

🛏 Sleeping & Eating

Most of Mawlamyine's accommodation is a K2000 motorcycle-taxi ride from the train station, bus station or boat pier.

Breeze Guest House   HOTEL $
(☑ 057-21450; breeze.guesthouse@gmail.com; 6 Strand Rd; r incl breakfast US$7-35; ❄ ☎) The rooms at this long-standing backpacker haunt in a colonial-style villa are functional at best, most with shared bathrooms, but the staff are an endless source of information, pleasant conversation and superb guiding skills. By the time you read this, a new annexe with more upmarket rooms may be open.

★ Cinderella Hotel   HOTEL $$
(☑ 057-24411; www.cinderellahotel.com; 21 Baho Rd; s/d/tr incl breakfast US$30/55/70; ❄ ☎) Ignore the shocking purple exterior because inside the rooms are spotless, the staff efficient and the breakfast one of the best in Myanmar. All rooms come with cable TV, fridges and decent wi-fi.

★ Daw Yi   BURMESE $
(off Strand Rd; curries from K2000; ⊘ 8am-10pm) Humble Daw Yi does some of the best Bur-

mese food we've come across. Highlights of our meal included an insanely fatty prawn curry and a deliciously tart soup of young tamarind leaves and tiny shrimp. The only downside is locating it; continue south along Strand Rd until you see Beer Garden 2 then start asking the locals for Daw Yi.

Mi Cho Restaurant   BURMESE MUSLIM $
(North Bogyoke Rd; meals from K2300; ⊘ 10am-9pm) This busy hole-in-the-wall place serves excellent Muslim-style Burmese cuisine, in particular, a rich biryani and a delicious dhal soup. Look for the tiny green English-language sign and get here early: the biryani goes quick.

ℹ Getting There & Away

AIR
During high season (November to March), **Myanma Airways** (☑ 21500, 09 871 8220; ⊘ 9am-3pm) operates a weekly flight to/from Yangon.

BUS & TRAIN
Frequent buses run to Bago, Hpa-an, Kyaikto and Yangon between 8am and 8.30pm. Two daily trains connect Mawlamyine with Yangon, Bago and Kyaikto. Foreigners can now travel south by train to Dawei. Frequent shared vans go to Myawaddy between 5am and 10am.

Bilu Kyun   ‌ ‌ ‌ ‌ ‌

Fascinating Bilu Kyun (Ogre Island), east of Mawlamyine, is peppered with villages involved in the production of coconut-fibre mats and even coconut-inspired and created cutlery and teapots.

There's public transportation to Bilu Kyun, but the boats run a confusing sched-

TRANSPORT FROM MAWLAMYINE

DESTINATION	BUS	TRAIN	VAN	AIR
Bago	K5500, 5hr	ordinary/upper class K2800/5500, 7hr		
Dawei	K12,000, 9hr	ordinary/upper class K2950/5950, 15hr		
Hpa-an	K1000, 2hr			
Kyaikto	K7000, 4hr	ordinary/upper class K950/1900, 5hr		
Mandalay	K15,500, 13hr			
Myawaddy			K11,000, 4hr	
Yangon	K6000-10,000, 7hr	ordinary/upper class K2950/4250, 10hr		US$120, 1hr

ule from a variety of piers. The local authorities also require notice to visit Bilu Kyun, so the best way to approach the island is via a day tour with Mr Antony or Mr Khaing at Breeze Guest House in Mawlamyine. They charge US$15 per person for the tour, which typically runs from 9am to 5pm, circling the island, stopping in at various craft workshops and even tacking on a swim stop. The fee covers transportation and lunch.

Hpa-An   ဘားအံ

📲 058 / POP 75,141

Scruffy Hpa-an feels more like an overgrown village than the capital of Kayin State. But it is the logical base from which to explore the Buddhist caves, sacred mountains and cloud-scraping islands of the surrounding countryside.

💿 Sights & Activities

Take a boat across the Thanlwin River from Hpa-an (K500, every half-hour from 7am to 5pm) to reach Hpan Pu Mountain, a craggy pagoda-topped peak that can be scaled in one sweaty morning.

Another demanding two-hour climb is up Mt Zwegabin (2372ft), 7 miles south of town, for gods'-eye views, an 11am monkey-feeding session and a free monastery lunch at noon.

Around 17 miles southeast of Hpa-an, vast Saddan Cave (သဒ္ဓန်ဂူ; ⊘ daylight hours) FREE, aka the Gates of Hell, is full of Buddhist iconography and stalagmites, but can only be traversed during the dry season (November to April).

🛏 Sleeping & Eating

⭐ **Galaxy Motel**   GUESTHOUSE $
(📲 09 566 1863, 058-21347; cnr Thisar & Thida Rds; s/d US$15/20; ❄🐱) A real step up from Hpa-an's other budget options, the Galaxy is the sort of guesthouse Myanmar needs more of: tidy and clean with spacious rooms that fea-

ture air-con, wi-fi and modern bathrooms. The owners speak good English and can organise tickets and trips, as well as bicycle (K2000 per day) and motorbike (K8000 per day) hire.

Soe Brothers Guesthouse   BACKPACKER HOTEL $
(📲09 497 71823, 058-21372; soebrothers 05821372@gmail.com; 2/146 Thitsar St; r US$6-25; ❄🐱) A classic backpackers' crash pad, the rooms here are basic but the family that runs the place is tuned in to travellers' needs and can arrange many hassle-free excursions. The cheapest rooms are fan only and share bathrooms; the more expensive ones offer some space. By the time you read this, their second guesthouse by the river should be open as well.

⭐ **San Ma Tau Myanmar Restaurant**   BURMESE $
(1/290 Bo Gyoke St; curries from K2000; ⊘11am-9pm; 🍴) This local institution is one of our favourite Burmese restaurants anywhere in the country. The friendly and popular place serves a vast selection of rich curries, hearty soups and tart salads, all accompanied by platters of fresh veggies and herbs and an overwhelming 10 types of local-style dips to eat them with.

Khit Thit Restaurant   CHINESE, BURMESE $
(2/247 Zaydan St; dishes from K1500; ⊘8am-10pm; 🍴) Chinese-inspired dishes at this friendly, clean place that also shows the soccer. The English-language menu has many options, or it's OK just for a beer.

ℹ Getting There & Away

It's possible to charter a private boat seating about 10 people from Hpa-an to Mawlamyine (K8000 per person, two to three hours). The guesthouses can organise a boat.

Hpa-an's bus station is inconveniently located about 4 miles east of town but tickets can be bought and buses boarded at a few centrally located ticket stalls (clock tower).

TRANSPORT FROM HPA-AN

DESTINATION	BUS	VAN
Bago	K5300, 6hr, 4 daily 7am-7pm	
Kyaikto	K5300, 4hr, 4 daily 7am-7pm	
Mawlamyine	K1000, 2hr, hourly 6am-4pm	
Myawaddy		K10,000, 4hr, 6am & 7am
Yangon	K5300, 7hr, 5 daily 6am-7pm	

'Vans' (shared taxis) to Myawaddy depart, on odd-numbered days only, from a stall near the clock-tower intersection.

Dawei ထားဝယ်

The doorway to Myanmar's little-visited deep south, known as Tanintharyi Region (တနင်္သာရီတိုင်း), is its administrative capital Dawei. This sleepy, tropical seaside town, with plenty of interesting architecture, can be used a base for visiting the 243ft-long, 69ft-high Shwethalyaung Daw Mu, the largest reclining buddha in Myanmar, located a few miles outside of Dawei.

Comfortable rooms are available at the **Golden Guest Hotel** (☑059-21351; www. goldenguesthoteldawei.com; 59 Myotedwin St; incl breakfast s US$30, d US$40-55; ❇☎). A good place to eat is **Hla Hla Hnan** (no roman-script sign, Neik Ban St; dishes from K400; ☉noon-9pm).

The coastline south of Dawei consists of bridal-white beaches fronting a vast archipelago of more than 800 largely un-inhabited islands, nearly all of which have only recently opened to general tourism. The most accessible beach is **Maungmagan**, where places to stay include the delightful Burmese-French-run **Coconut Guesthouse & Restaurant** (☑09 737 00052; Phaw Taw Oo St; s/d incl breakfast US$15/30; ❇@☎).

At the time of research foreigners were barred from travelling by bus south of Da-wei. To continue southward to Myeik and the bordertown of Kawthoung, you'll need to take a boat or fly.

GETTING TO THAILAND

The following information is liable to change, so be sure to check the situation locally before you travel.

Hpa-an to Mae Sot

The Myawaddy/Mae Sot border crossing is 93 miles southeast of Hpa-an.

Getting to the border Shared taxis and vans (K11,000) terminate a short walk from the Friendship Bridge.

At the border The **Myanmar immigration office** (☑058-50100; AH1, Myawaddy; ☉6am-6pm) is at the foot of the Friendship Bridge. After walking across the 460yd bridge, if you don't already have a visa, the **Thai immigration office** (☑055 56 3004; AH1, Mae Sot; ☉6.30am-6.30pm) will grant you permission to stay in Thailand up to 15 days.

Moving on Mae Sot's bus station is 2 miles east of the border and has good connections to destinations in northern Thailand and Bangkok. Mae Sot's airport is 2 miles east of the border, offering connections to Bangkok, Chiang Mai and Yangon. Both the bus station and airport can be reached by frequent *sŏrng·tăa·ou* (pick-ups) that run between the Friendship Bridge and Mae Sot from 6am to 6pm (20B).

For information on doing this crossing in reverse, see p717.

Kawthoung to Ranong

Kawthoung (also known as Victoria Point) is at the far southern end of Tanintharyi Region.

Getting to the border The bright green **Myanmar border post** (Strand Rd; ☉7am-4pm) is located a few steps from Kawthoung's jetty.

At the border If you've arrived in Kawthoung from elsewhere in Myanmar, you're free to exit the country here. After clearing Myanmar immigration, you'll be herded to a boat (per person from 50B) for the 20-minute ride to Ranong. On the Thai side, the author-ities will issue you permission to stay in Thailand up to 15 days, or you can enter with a Thai visa obtained overseas.

Moving on Ranong is a 60B motorcycle-taxi ride or 20B *sŏrng·tăa·ou* ride from Saphan Pla Pier. There are two daily flights between Ranong and Bangkok (from 1955B, 1½ to 1¾ hours), while major bus destinations include Bangkok (445B to 692B, 10 hours), Hat Yai (420B, five hours) and Phuket (250B, five to six hours).

For information on doing this crossing in reverse, see p756.

TRANSPORT FROM DAWEI

DESTINATION	BOAT	BUS	TRAIN	AIR
Kawthoung	US$80, 12hr, 4.30am			US$116, 80min
Mawlamyine		K12,000, 9hr, 5am	ordinary/upper class K2950/5900, 15hr	
Myeik	US$40, 4hr, 4.30am			US$72, 40min
Yangon		K14,000, 16hr, 4pm		US$96, 70min

INLE LAKE & SHAN STATE

Slicing through the placid waters of Inle Lake in a boat; trekking among Pa-O and Danu villages outside Kalaw; feeling like you've travelled back in time at a remote hill-tribe market. What do some of Myanmar's most emblematic experiences have in common? They can all be tackled in the country's east in Shan State.

Trekking is hugely popular around here and Kalaw is the affordable base for adventure. Homestays are possible and the Shan are some of the friendliest folk in the country.

Inle Lake & Nyaungshwe
အင်းလေးကန် နှင့် ညောင်ရွှေ

📞 081 / POP 10,000

A wonderful watery world of floating gardens, stilted villages and crumbling stupas, Inle Lake is one of those few places that are a tonic for the soul. While away the days canoeing, cycling and walking through the lush countryside.

In September and October the Phaung Daw U festival runs for nearly three weeks, and is followed by the Thadingyut festival. Always cooler than the rest of the country, Inle gets downright chilly at night in January and February – bring warm clothes.

The village of Nyaungshwe, at the lake's northern end, is home to all the budget accommodation and traveller services and is easily navigated by foot or bicycle.

There is a compulsory US$10/K13,000 fee to enter the Inle Lake area, which you must pay on arrival at the **permit booth** (☉6am-9pm) by the bridge at the entrance to Nyaungshwe. Permits are valid for a week.

🅞 Sights & Activities

Every hotel in town can arrange boat trips around the lake, and freelance boat drivers will approach you in the street. A whole-day trip around the lake starts at K15,000, or K20,000 if you include a stop at Inthein, where the weather-beaten pagodas on the hilltop are incredibly atmospheric despite the crowds.

Other popular stops include the monastery Nga Phe Kyaung, on the eastern side of the lake, which is famous for its cats trained to leap through hoops by the monks; floating gardens, where Intha farmers raise flowers, fruit and vegetables on long wooden trellises supported on floating mats of vegetation; and village markets and artisans' shops, where weaving, blacksmithing and jewellery-making go on. There's no obligation to buy anything. Cloth is one of the better buys around Inle Lake.

Yadana Man Aung Paya   BUDDHIST TEMPLE
(ရတနာမာန်အောင်ဘုရား; Phoung Taw Site St; ☉daylight hours) FREE The oldest and most important Buddhist shrine in Nyaungshwe, this handsome gilded stupa is hidden away inside a square compound south of the Mingala Market. The stepped stupa is unique in Myanmar, and the surrounding pavilion contains a museum of treasures amassed by the monks over the centuries, including carvings, lacquerware and dance costumes.

Cultural Museum   MUSEUM
(ဗုဒ္ဓပြတိုက်; Museum Rd (Haw St); admission K2000; ☉10am-4pm Wed-Sun) This equal parts imposing and crumbling structure is the former *haw* (palace) of the last *sao pha* (sky prince) of Nyaungshwe, Sao Shwe Thaike, who also served as the first president of independent Burma. Today, the mostly empty building holds a few dusty displays and is worth visiting more for the stately brick-and-teak structure itself than any educational summary of Shan culture or history.

Mingala Market   MARKET
(မင်္ဂလာဈေး; Yone Gyi Rd; ☉5am-2pm) At the entrance to town, this busy market is packed with locals every morning, when traders

Nyaungshwe

⊙ Sights
1 Cultural Museum	D1
2 Mingala Market	C1
3 Yadana Man Aung Paya	B2

🛏 Sleeping
4 Aquarius Inn	B3
5 Inle Inn	D2
6 Nawng Kham – Little Inn	B2
7 Zawgi Inn	D2

🍴 Eating
8 Lin Htett Myanmar Traditional Food	C2
9 Mingala Market Food Stalls	C1
10 Night Market	C2
11 Sin Yaw Bamboo Restaurant	C2
12 Thukha Caffee	B2

🍸 Drinking & Nightlife
13 One Owl Grill	C2

from the lake bring in fresh fish and produce from the floating gardens. The market doubles in size when it hosts the five-day rotating market.

🛏 Sleeping

Nyaungshwe is teeming with budget rooms, so if the following options are full there are plenty of alternatives. Some places are looking their age now, so shop around. All include breakfast and most rent out bicycles (K1500 per day).

Nawng Kham – Little Inn GUESTHOUSE **$**
(📞 081-209 195; noanhom@gmail.com; Phaung Daw Pyan Rd; r US$15-40; ❄🛜) The seven fan-only rooms here go quick, but the more expensive rooms with air-con are almost as

good a deal. All look out on a pleasant garden, there's a small communal area and the staff are helpful.

Aquarius Inn GUESTHOUSE **$**
(📞 081-209 352; aquarius352@gmail.com; 2 Phaung Daw Pyan Rd; r incl breakfast US$12-35; ❄@🛜) The cheapest rooms at this family-run place are fan only and share bathrooms. The more expensive ones are spacious, nicely decorated and come with decent bathrooms. All are set around an attractive communal garden.

Zawgi Inn GUESTHOUSE **$**
(📞 081-209 929; zawgiinn@gmail.com; 122 Nandawun St; s/d US$25/30; ❄🛜) Tucked away in a quiet residential area, the nine

sizeable rooms at this tranquil place come with verandahs and are more comfortable than many others in the same price range.

Inle Inn HOTEL $$
([☎] 081-209 016; inleinns@gmail.com; Yone Gyi Rd; r incl breakfast US$45-85; [✦] [🛜]) Newly upgraded, attractive rooms off a courtyard filled with potted plants and a fine breakfast are the drawcards here. The pricier rooms have air-con and the wi-fi connection is strong throughout.

✖ Eating & Drinking

For cheap eats, check out the food stalls (Yone Gyi Rd; meals K1000; ⊙6-9am) in Mingala Market. Local specialities include *shàn k'auq-swèh* (Shan-style noodle soup) and *to·p'ù thouq* (Shan tofu salad), prepared using yellow chickpea tofu, chilli, coriander and chilli oil.

Every evening a very basic night market (off Yone Gyi Rd; dishes from K800; ⊙5-9pm) unfolds just off Yone Gyi Rd.

★ Lin Htett Myanmar Traditional Food BURMESE $
(Yone Gyi Rd; meals from K2500; ⊙10am-9pm; [📷]) Hands-down our favourite place to eat in Nyaungshwe, service at Lin Htett is as friendly as the food is delicious. Choose from a range of curries and salads, all accompanied by soup, dips and rice. Staff can also arrange cooking classes.

Sin Yaw Bamboo Restaurant CHINESE, SHAN $
(Kyaung Daw A Shae St; mains from K3500; ⊙9am-10pm; [📷]) The closest thing to an authentic Shan restaurant you'll find in Nyaungshwe, run by a pleasant Shan-Chinese couple. The food is good and spicy – they'll tone it down for Western palates – and has a distinct hint of the cuisine of neighbouring Yunnan Province in China.

Thukha Caffee TEAHOUSE $
(cnr Lan Ma Taw St & Yone Gyi Rd; tea or snacks from K300; ⊙5am-4pm; [🖊]) Nyaungshwe's sole Muslim teashop, this relaxed place serves good tea and, in the mornings, tasty *pakoda* (fritters), deep-fried vegetable dumplings and Shan noodles.

★ One Owl Grill BAR
(1 Yone Gyi St; beer/cocktails from K1000/2000; ⊙9am-11pm; [🛜]) This French-owned newcomer has proved a hit for the quality of its drinks and food, as well as because it stays open later than anywhere else in sleepy Nyaungshwe. Good choice of wine and reasonably priced cocktails. Excellent barbecue skewers, sandwiches and salads are also on offer.

ⓘ Getting There & Away

AIR
The region's main airport is at Heho, 25 miles northwest of Nyaungshwe on the way to Kalaw.

Either take a taxi from the airport to Nyaungshwe (K20,000, one hour) or hike half a mile to the highway and wait for a pick-up or bus bound for Taunggyi (K2000, 1½ hours); ask to be let off at Shwenyaung, from where you can change for Nyaungshwe (K6000) 7 miles away. Bear in mind that you might face a long wait.

BUS & PICK-UP
Any bus travelling from Mandalay or Yangon to Taunggyi can drop you at Shwenyaung for the full Taunggyi fare.

Nyaunshwe-based travel agents such as the reliable and honest **Thu Thu** ([☎] 081-209 258; thuthua79@gmail.com; Yone Gyi Rd; ⊙6.30am-9pm) can sell tickets and arrange hotel pick-up.

TRAIN
The train rumbling through the hills from Shwenyaung to Thazi (on the main Yangon–Mandalay route) is slow but the scenery en route is stunning. From Shwenyaung's tiny station, trains depart at 8am and 9.40am, arriving in Kalaw after three hours (K500/1200 ordinary/upper class) and reaching Thazi at least another six hours later (K1500/3000 ordinary/upper class).

TRANSPORT FROM NYAUNGSHWE

DESTINATION	BUS	AIR
Kyaingtong		US$123, 55min-2hr
Mandalay	K11,000-16,500, 10hr, 3 daily at 7pm	US$72, 40min
Nyaung U	K12,000, 10hr, 2 daily 7am & 7pm	US$100, 75min
Tachileik		US$123, 45min-1¾hr
Yangon	K17,500, 13hr, frequent 6am-7pm	US$106, 1hr

BIKE RIDE TO HOT SPRINGS

Rent a bike and pedal through beautiful countryside to Kaung Daing, a quiet Intha village on Inle's northwestern shore, about 5 miles from Nyaungshwe. Here take a dip in the **hot springs** (Kaung Daing; swimming pool US$5, private bath US$13; ⊙6am-6pm), which are also the start or end point of several trekking routes between Kalaw and Inle Lake. If you don't feel like pedalling all the way back, load your bike onto a boat and motor across to Maing Thauk (K8000, 30 minutes) before cycling home.

❶ Getting Around

Several shops on Yone Gyi Rd and Phaung Daw Pyan Rd rent out clunky Chinese bicycles for K1500 per day.

Motorcycle taxis at the stand (Lan Ma Taw St) near the market go to Shwenyaung for around K6000.

Pindaya ပင်းတယ

The **Shwe Oo Min Natural Cave Pagoda** (ရွှေဥမင်သဘာဝလိုဏ်ဂူဘုရား; Shwe U Min Pagoda Rd; admission K3000, camera fee K300; ⊙6am-6pm) at Pindaya is a popular stop on the Shan State circuit. More than 8094 Buddha images form a labyrinth throughout the chambers of the caves.

Pleasant rooms, a great location on the steps of the cave, and helpful staff make **Golden Cave Hotel** (☑081-66166; www.golden cavehotel.com; Shwe U Min Pagoda Rd; s/d incl breakfast US$35/45; ❄@☎) worth the money.

From Kalaw, take a bus or pick-up to Aungban (K1500, 20 minutes). There, you'll find two daily pick-ups (K1000 to K2000, 1½ hours, 8am and 11am), as well as waiting motorcycles (K6000 one way, K10,000 round-trip) and taxis (K30,000 one way, K50,000 round-trip).

Kalaw ကလော

☑081 / POP 57,797

Welcome to Myanmar's trekking heartland, combining cool mountain climbs and a chilled vibe beloved by backpackers. Located at 4330ft on the rolling, pine-clad hills of the Shan Plateau, Kalaw is the beginning point for treks heading west to Inle Lake (about 28 miles), over mountains dotted with Palaung, Pa-O, Intha and Shan villages.

Kalaw is easy to navigate on foot, with **Aung Chan Tha Zedi** (အောင်ချမ်းသာစေတီ; Aung Chan Thar St; ⊙daylight hours) **FREE**, a glittery stupa covered in gold- and silver-coloured glass mosaics, in the centre of town.

🏃 Activities

During high season (November to February) it can get pretty busy on the more popular trekking routes, while in the wet season paths get miserably muddy and few tourists head this way.

The most popular trek is the two- to four-day trek to Inle Lake. A less common route is the multiday trek to Pindaya, via Taung Ni. It's worth requesting a route via the villages of several different ethnic groups. Have good shoes and warm clothing for the cool evenings. Guesthouses can transport your unneeded bags for a small charge.

Trekking without a guide is not recommended – the trails are confusing, the terrain challenging and few people in the hills speak English. The going rate for a day hike is around K11,000 per person, with overnight treks around K15,000 per person, per day, in groups of two or more.

Recommended guiding outfits include **Ever Smile** (☑09401 623 4795, 081-50683; thuthu.klw@gmail.com; Yuzana St; ⊙8am-8pm), **Rural Development Society** (RDS; ☑081-50747, 09 528 0974; sdr1992@gmail.com; Min St), **Sam's Trekking Guide** (☑081-50237; samtrekking@gmail.com; 21 Aung Chan Thar St; ⊙7am-7pm) and **JP Barua** (☑081-50549).

🛏 Sleeping

Electricity is temperamental here, but you won't need air-con (or even a fan) to sleep. All rates include breakfast.

⭐**Dream Villa Hotel Kalaw** HOTEL $
(☑081-50144; dreamvilla@myanmar.com.mm; 5 Zat Ti' La St; s/d incl breakfast US$45/50; ☎) A cut above your average Myanmar hotel, the Dream Villa is a spotless, three-storey home with 24 tasteful, wood-panelled rooms attractively decorated with a few local design touches. All rooms have TV and fridge, while the more expensive have a bit more leg room and bathtubs.

Eastern Paradise Motel HOTEL $
(☑081-50315; easternmotel@gmail.com; 5 Thiri Min Ga Lar St; s/d incl breakfast US$25/35; ☎)

A central location, large, homey and well-equipped rooms, and gracious service make this one of the best deals in town.

Pine Breeze Hotel   HOTEL **$**
(☎081-50459; pinebreezehotel@gmail.com; 174 Thittaw St; r incl breakfast US$35-45; ❄️🛜) Located just west of 'downtown' Kalaw, this baby-blue hilltop structure has four floors of neat rooms equipped with TV, fridge, balcony and great views over the town.

Winner Hotel Kalaw   HOTEL **$**
(☎081-50025; winnerhotel.kalaw@gmail.com; Union Hwy (NH4); incl breakfast s US$15, d US$20-30; ❄️🛜) A large, modern Chinese-style hotel on the main road, the Winner holds few surprises, but rooms are large, uncluttered and clean, and include TV and fridge.

✗️ Eating & Drinking

⭐**Thu Maung Restaurant**   BURMESE **$**
(Myanmar Restaurant; Union Hwy (NH4); meals from K3000; ⊙11am-9pm) One of our fave Burmese curry restaurants in this part of the country, Thu Maung serves rich, meaty chicken, pork, mutton and fish curries coupled with exceptionally delicious dips, sides, salads, pickles and trimmings. The tomato salad, made from crunchy green tomatoes, is a work of art. The English-language sign says 'Myanmar Restaurant'.

Kalaw

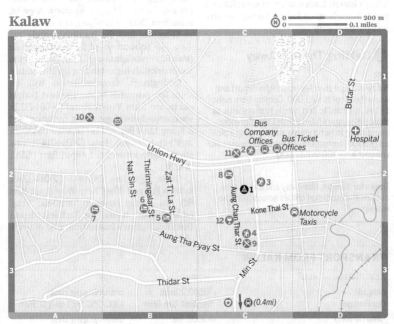

N | 0   200 m
0   0.1 miles

Everest Nepali Food Centre   NEPALI $

(Aung Chan Thar St; set meals from K3000; ⊙9.30am-10pm; ⊖🛜🖍) Relive memories of trekking in Nepal with a solid curry or plate of *dhal baht* (rice served with lentils and other side dishes) at this convivial eatery run by a Nepali family.

Pyae Pyae Shan Noodle   SHAN $

(Union Hwy (NH4); noodles from K500, mains from K1200; ⊙6.30am-9pm; 🖍) This cosy, friendly shop sells delicious bowls of its namesake noodles, and has an English-language menu of other one-plate dishes.

Hi Snack & Drink   BAR

(Kone Thai St; ⊙5-11pm) Hi is the size of a closet and boasts a fun, speakeasy feel; if you haven't had its trademark rum sour (K1000), you haven't been to Kalaw. No beer served; just the hard stuff.

❶ Getting There & Away

AIR

Kalaw is about 16 miles from Heho airport and a taxi there costs K20,000. Coming from Heho by taxi, it's hard to find people to share with, as most passengers head to Inle Lake. Consider negotiating to Heho village and boarding a pick-up (K3000) from there. A taxi direct to Inle Lake will cost K30,000 to K40,000.

BUS

Buses for Yangon, Mandalay and Bagan stop outside the bus ticket offices across from the market.

Buses and pick-ups bound for Taunggyi stop periodically outside the Winner Hotel and will drop you in Shwenyaung for Inle Lake.

TRAIN

Two daily trains depart from either end of the winding line that links Thazi and Shwenyaung.

Kyaingtong

Also known as Kengtung, or sometimes Chiang Tung, Kyaingtong is one of Myanmar's most attractive towns. The vast majority of its residents belong to one of several Tai ethnic groups. It's packed with Buddhist monasteries such as **Wat Jong Kham** (ဝတ်ကျင်ခန်း; off Mine Yen Rd; ⊙daylight hours) **FREE** and among other attractions are the **Central Market** (မြို့ မဈေး; Zeigyi Rd; mains from K500; ⊙5am-1pm), one of the best in Myanmar, and the Buddhist temple **Yat Taw Mu** (ရပ်တော်မူ; off Tachileik-Taunggyi Rd (Main Rd); ⊙daylight hours) **FREE**, home to the landmark 60ft-high standing buddha statue.

Kyaingtong's accommodation will inspire few postcards home; the best budget sleeps are **Sam Yweat Hotel** (☑084-21235; www.samyewhotel.blogspot.com; cnr Kyaing Lan 1 & Kyaing Lan 4 Rds; s/d incl breakfast US$30-35; ❄🛜) and **Private Hotel** (☑084-21438; www.privatehotelmyanmar.com; 5 Airport Rd; r US$42; ❄@🛜).

Shwe Myo Taw Express (☑084-23145; Tachileik Rd) and **Thet Nay Wun** (Kyain Nyan Rd) run air-con buses to Tachileik. 'Vans' (shared taxis) bound for Tachileik depart from Kyaingtong's bus station, west of town.

TRANSPORT FROM KALAW

DESTINATION	BUS	PICK-UP	TRAIN
Aungban (for Pindaya)		K1500, 20min, frequent 7am-6pm	ordinary/upper class K100/250, 1hr, 1 daily 11.35am
Heho (airport)		K3000, 1hr, frequent 7am-6pm	ordinary/upper class K200/400, 2hr, 1 daily 11.35am
Mandalay	K11,000-12,000, 7-8hr, 3 daily 9am, 10.30am & 9pm		
Nyaung U (for Bagan)	K11,000, 8hr, 2 daily 9am & 8pm		
Shwenyaung (for Inle Lake)		K4000, 2hr, frequent 7am-6pm	ordinary/upper class K500/1200, 3hr, 1 daily 11.35am
Thazi		K6000, 4hr, frequent 7am-6pm	ordinary/upper class K800/1850, 6hr, 2 daily 11.30am & 1.10pm
Yangon	K12,000-18,000, 10-12hr, frequent 7am-8pm		

GETTING TO THAILAND: TACHILEIK TO MAE SAI

The following information is liable to change, so be sure to check the situation locally before you travel.

Getting to the border The border is a short walk from 'downtown' Tachileik, or 1 mile and a 20B truck ride or a K1500/50B motorcycle-taxi ride from the town's bus station.

At the border If you've arrived in Kyaingtong or Tachileik via air from elsewhere in Myanmar, you can freely exit the country at Tachileik. The Myanmar border post is open from 6am to 6pm, and upon crossing to Thailand, the Thai authorities will issue you permission to stay in Thailand up to 15 days, or you can enter with a Thai visa obtained overseas.

Moving on Mae Sai's bus station is 1 mile from the border; pick-ups ply the route between the bus station and Soi 2, Th Phahonyothin (20B, five minutes, 6am to 9pm). Alternatively, it's a 50B motorcycle-taxi ride to the stand at the corner of Th Phahonyothin and Soi 4. From Mae Sai, major bus destinations include Bangkok, Chiang Mai and Chiang Rai.

For information on doing this crossing in reverse, see p704.

Several airlines connect Kyaingtong and other destinations in northern Myanmar via a confusing, web-like flight map. Note that most flights aren't direct, with many – including flights to Yangon – involving two stops. Taxis charge K5000 and *thoun bein* (tuk-tuk) K3000 for the 2-mile trip to/from Kyaingtong's airport.

MANDALAY & AROUND

Myanmar's second-biggest city – economically booming and culturally vibrant – is worth a stop if only to use it as a base for visiting the surrounding former royal capitals. Escape the sweltering flatlands in the surreal hill station of Pyin Oo Lwin, home to brilliant old colonial-era buildings, horse-drawn carriage taxis and good restaurants catering for an influx of Myanmar's nouveau riche. Further north, charming little Hsipaw makes a great alternative base for easy treks into fascinating minority villages.

Mandalay   မန္တလေး

02 / POP 1,225,546

For those who haven't been – and that includes *Mandalay* author Rudyard Kipling – the mention of 'Mandalay' typically conjures up images of Asia at its most traditional and timeless. The reality is instead a sprawling city where dusty streets teem with traffic and there's a construction site on every block. In spite of this, it's impossible not to be impressed by the golden buddha of Mahamuni Paya, or the sunset views across the flat landscape from stupa-studded Mandalay Hill. Mandalay is also the nation's cultural capital and a fine place to delve into many of Myanmar's arts.

Mandalay became the capital of the Burmese empire in 1861, an entity that by 1885 had been exiled into history by the British. Prior to Mandalay, several other places within a short distance also served as capitals, and it's these ancient cities that are the real attractions.

◉ Sights

Several of Mandalay's top attractions are covered by a K10,000 Archaeological Zone ('combo') ticket valid one week from first purchase. Currently the ticket is only checked (and sold) at Mandalay Palace and Shwenandaw Kyaung, two sites at Inwa (Ava) and one minor one in Amarapura.

★ Mandalay Hill   LANDMARK
(မန္တလေးတောင်; Map p510; camera fee K1000)
To get a sense of Mandalay's pancake-flat sprawl, climb the 760ft hill that breaks it. The barefooted walk up covered stairways on the hill's southern slope is a major part of the experience, passing through and around a colourful succession of prayer and shopping opportunities. The climb takes a good 30 minutes, but much longer if you allow for stops en route. The summit viewpoint is especially popular at sunset when young monks converge on foreigners for language practice.

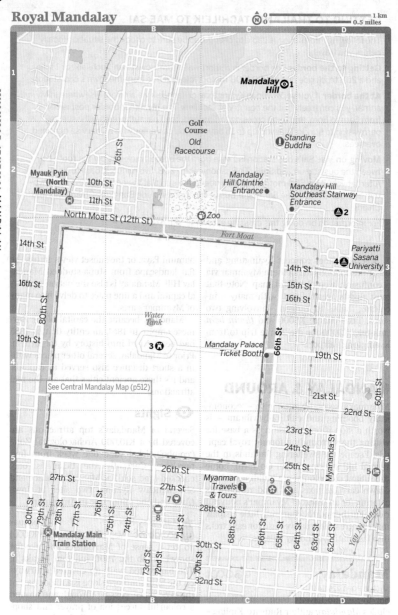

N
0   1 km
0   0.5 miles

Mandalay Hill ◉1

Golf Course
Old Racecourse

Standing Buddha

Myauk Pyin (North Mandalay)
10th St
11th St

Mandalay Hill Chinthe Entrance

Mandalay Hill Southeast Stairway Entrance

2

North Moat St (12th St)
Zoo

Fort Moat

14th St
16th St
19th St

80th St
76th St

Water Tank

3

Mandalay Palace Ticket Booth

Pariyatti Sasana University

14th St
15th St
16th St

4

66th St

14th St
15th St
16th St
19th St

See Central Mandalay Map (p512)

21st St
22nd St
23rd St
24th St
25th St

27th St
27th St
7
8

26th St
Myanmar Travels & Tours
9 6

28th St
30th St
32nd St

Mandalay Main Train Station

80th St
79th St
78th St
77th St
76th St
75th St
74th St
73rd St
72nd St
71st St
70th St
68th St
66th St
65th St
64th St
63rd St
62nd St

Myananda St
60th St

5

Yeu Ni Canal

★**Mahamuni Paya** BUDDHIST TEMPLE
(မဟာမုနိဘုရား; 83rd St; ⊙ complex 24hr, museum sections 8am-5pm) FREE Every day, thousands of colourfully dressed faithful venerate Mahamuni's 13ft-tall **seated Buddha**, a nationally celebrated image that's popularly believed to be some 2000 years old. Centuries of votary gold leaf applied by male devotees (women may only watch) has left the figure knobbly with a 6in layer of pure gold... except on his radiantly gleaming face, which is ceremonially polished daily at 4am.

Royal Mandalay

★ **Shwe In Bin Kyaung**   BUDDHIST MONASTERY
(ရွှေအင်ပင်ကျောင်း; Map p512; 89th St, 37/38)
If you want a place for quiet meditation in
Mandalay, you couldn't find a better spot
than this beautifully carved teak monastery.
Commissioned in 1895 by a pair of wealthy
Chinese jade merchants, the central building stands on tree-trunk poles and the interior has a soaring dark majesty. Balustrades
and roof cornices are covered in detailed
engravings, a few of them mildly humorous.

Shwenandaw Kyaung   BUDDHIST MONASTERY
(ရွှေနန်းတော်ကျောင်း; Golden Palace Monastery;
Map p510; combo ticket K10,000) Lavished in
carved panels, this fine teak monastery-tem-
ple is noted for its carvings, particularly the
interior gilded Jataka scenes (past-life stories of the Buddha). The building once stood
within the Mandalay Palace complex as the
royal apartment of King Mindon, who died
inside it in 1878.

Mandalay Palace   PALACE
(မန္တလေးနန်းတော်; Map p510; East Gate; combo
ticket K10,000; ⊙ 7.30am-4.30pm) The 1990s
reconstruction of Mandalay's royal palace
features over 40 timber buildings built to
resemble the 1850s originals. Climb the curious spiral, timber-walled watchtower for
a good general view. The palace's most striking structure is a soaring multi-layered pyramid of gilt filigree above the main throne
room. The westernmost building within
the palace oval contains a minor culture

museum where the most intriguing exhibit is King Thibaw's dainty, glass-pillared
four-poster bed.

Palace access for foreigners is only via the
east gate.

Kuthodaw Paya   BUDDHIST TEMPLE
(ကုသိုလ်တော်ဘုရား; Map p510; ⊙ 24hr) FREE
Kuthodaw Paya, aka the 'world's biggest
book', draws tour bus crowds to see its 729
slabs that retell the Tripitaka canon. It's
included in the K10,000 combo ticket, but
the ticket checkers tend to slope off after
4.40pm. Nearby, the Sandamuni Paya has
more such slabs and is free to enter.

🛏 Sleeping

The nearest thing to a 'backpacker zone' is
the three-block area around the Nylon Hotel. Many budget places fill up quickly in the
high season (October to March). Breakfast is
included at all listed places.

★ **Yoe Yoe Lay**   GUESTHOUSE $
(⌨ 09 331 05754, 09 444 041 944; nanbwe1@gmail.
com; 78 58th St, 35/36; 4- & 6-bed dm US$10, s & d
US$20-30; ✱ @ 🖥) Excellent new guesthouse
that has proper dorms with air-con, decent
beds and knowledgeable staff. Private rooms
are compact but comfortable; the cheapest
share bathrooms. There's an outside communal area and the only drawback is the
inconvenient location in eastern Mandalay;
a K1500 motorcycle taxi ride anywhere. But
bicycles (K2000 per day) and motorbikes
(K10,000 per day) can be rented.

ET Hotel   HOTEL $
(Map p512; ⌨ 02-65006, 02-66547; ethotelm-
dy@mandalay.net.mm; 83rd St, 23/24; s/d/tr
US$18/22/33, s/d with air-con US$20/25, with
shared bathroom US$15/18; ✱ 🖥) A good-value
backpacker favourite. Bare fluorescent bulbs
on pastel-blue corridor walls can feel a little
soulless but rooms are clean and mostly spacious with hot showers. The staff are helpful.

AD1 Hotel   HOTEL $
(Map p512; ⌨ 02-34505; ad.1hotel@gmail.com;
Eindawya St, 87/88; s/d US$15/25; ✱ 🖥) One of
the cheapest deals in town for solo travellers,
AD1 offers rooms that are simple and ageing,
but functional and clean. It's just off vibrant
'onion market street' in the eastern approach
lane to Eindawya Pagoda. Beware if asking
a taxi to take you here – to local ears 'AD1'
sounds very much like '81' (ie 81st St).

MYANMAR (BURMA) MANDALAY

Central Mandalay

Nylon Hotel HOTEL **$**

(Map p512; ☑02-69717; nylon33460@gmail.com; 25th St at 83rd St; s/d/tr US$18/22/35; ❄🗟) There are two annexes at the Nylon; go for the new one, which has reasonably sized and light rooms with modern bathrooms, even if some smell a little like a drain. Decent wi-fi connection.

Peacock Lodge GUESTHOUSE **$$**

(Map p510; ☑02-61429, 09 204 2059; www.pea cocklodge.com; 60th St, 25/26; r standard/deluxe

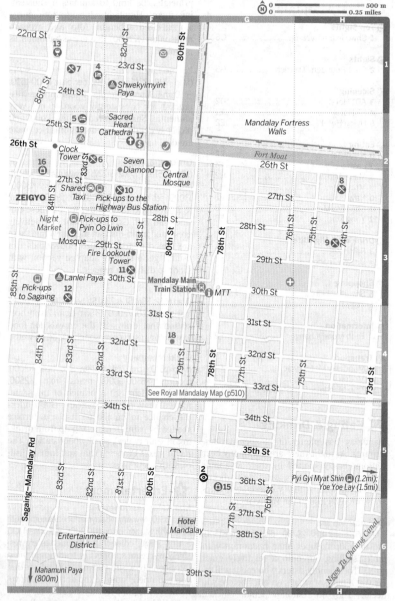

US$40/60; ✱ 🛜) One of Myanmar's great homestay-style inns; the Peacock's main 1960s house is set in a tree-shaded yard complete with fairy lights, parasol seating and an old horse cart. Dated if fair-sized standard rooms overlook a lotus-filled canal but far better are the boutique-style 'deluxe' rooms: choose the prized upper ones with balconies.

Central Mandalay

✗ Eating & Drinking

Mandalay has plenty of inexpensive restaurants. At night there are also many beer stations, easily spotted by their Myanmar or Dagon beer awnings. Most do barbecue skewers as well. A few Western-style cafes are scattered close to the Palace moat.

★ **Shan Ma Ma**　　　　　　SHAN $
(Map p512; 4-7 81st 29/30; dishes from K1500; ⊙11am-9.30pm) Super Shan restaurant with tables spilling out onto a relatively quiet street. The friendly sisters who run it will offer you a taste of what's on offer before you decide. They do a sublime lemon chicken here, as well as making their own spicy and tangy dips, but all the dishes are good and you can eat like a king very cheaply.

Marie-Min　　　　　　VEGETARIAN $
(Map p512; off 27th St, 74/75; mains K2000-3000; ⊙9am-10pm, closed Apr-Jun; ⚏🍴) An all-vegetarian menu fits the owners' stated

principle: 'Be kind to animals by not eating them.' Highlights include tofu curry, a meal-sized aubergine 'dip' and avocado milkshakes (K2000) that are as 'fabulous' as promised.

Lashio Lay　　　　　　SHAN $
(Map p512; 23rd St, 83/84; per plate K500-1500; ⊙10am-9.30pm) Simple long-running restaurant for consistently good, if not very authentic, Shan-inspired dishes. Point and pick, pay per dish. Two dishes plus rice make an ideal meal.

Green Elephant　　　　　　BURMESE $$
(Map p510; 📞02-61237; www.greenelephant-restaurants.com; 27th St, 64/65; mains K8000-13000, set menus K8500-15,000; ⊙10am-10pm; 📶🍴) It's hard to do better for Burmese cuisine than with Green Elephant's attractively presented multi-dish set menus. While these are aimed at tour groups, individuals can usually get a slightly adapted version with six or so dishes on request.

Rainbow　　　　　　BEER STATION
(Map p512; 83rd St at 23rd St; beer K700, barbecue/mains from K600/2000; ⊙9am-11pm) Lively beer station that draws in the crowds for footie-watching; serves reasonable food as well.

Ginki Mandalay　　　　　　BAR
(Map p510; cnr 71st & 28th Sts; beer K2000, cocktails K3500-6000, mains from K2500; ⊙10.30am-11pm; 📶) A branch of the same-named Yangon bar-restaurant, Ginki offers the chance to imbibe on its large terrace shaded by palm trees; a step up from drinking in your typical, scruffy beer station. The menu mixes Chinese, Thai and Indian dishes, with a few Western ones.

☆ Entertainment

Mandalay Marionettes　　　　　　PUPPET SHOW
(Map p510; www.mandalaymarionettes.com; 66th St at 27th St; admission K10,000; ⊙8.30pm) On a tiny stage, colourful marionettes expressively re-create snippets of traditional tales. Occasionally a sub-curtain is lifted so that you can briefly admire the deft hand movements of the puppeteers (one an octogenarian) who have performed internationally. You can also buy puppets here.

🛍 Shopping

Mandalay is a major crafts centre, and probably the best place in the country for traditional puppets and hand-woven embroidered tapestries. Virtually nothing you see will be 'antique'; items are often scuffed up or weathered to look much older than they are.

There are numerous **silk workshops** and a couple more handicraft emporia along the Sagaing road in Amarapura. There are also several interesting shops on 36th St beside the **gold-leaf-pounding workshops** (Map p512; 36th St, 77/79), where you can buy square gold-leaf sheets.

Shwe Pathein SOUVENIRS
(Map p512; 141 36th St, 77/78; parasols from US$15; ☉8am-5pm) Pathein-style parasols. Next door is a leather-workshop and a gold-leaf shop.

Zegyo MARKET
(Zaycho; Map p512; 84/86th, 26/28th) The 25-storey tower that brutally overpowers the Mandalay skyline balances atop one of three horrendous, neighbouring concrete 'malls', stiflingly crammed full of fabric sellers. However, the surrounding older market areas are fascinating places to wander amid piles of dried fish, sacks of chilli and giant hands of bananas.

ℹ️ Orientation

Mandalay city streets are laid out on a grid system and numbered from east to west (up to 49th) and from north to south (over 50th). A street address that reads 66th, 26/27 means the place is located on 66th St between 26th and 27th Sts. Corner addresses are given in the form 26th St at 82nd St.

ℹ️ Information

INTERNET ACCESS

Wi-fi is available in all guesthouses and hotels, as well as upmarket cafes. A dwindling number of internet cafes are located around town.

MONEY

Pristine banknotes can be changed at most banks in town, as well as at Mandalay airport and downtown moneychangers, such as **Faith** (Map p512; 26th St, 81/82; ☉9am-5pm). An ever-increasing number of ATMs take Western cards.

STREET DINING

Along with beer-station barbecues, the best-value dining is usually at street stalls. Certain corners or street sections have culinary specialities, but knowing which takes some insider knowledge.

Morning Only

➡ *Baosi* dumplings – **Yong Xing** (Map p512; 83rd St, 30/31; baozi K400; ☉5am-7.15am).

➡ Shan noodles with *dofubyo* (bean paste) – 29th St, 80/81 before 10am.

➡ *Mohinga* – Mandalay's best breakfast three-wheel street-trolley stall at 32nd St at 81st St, from 6.30am to 9.30am only.

Daytime

➡ Point-and-pick multi-curries are offered at several inexpensive family snack outlets dotted along an unnamed lane between 74th and 75th Sts. Our favourite is the furthest east – unsigned, super-cheap **Mtay Myint Thar** (Map p512; 74th-75th link-lane 28/29; dishes K100-200; ☉10am-7.30pm), a traditional wooden shophouse decked with contorted roots and plants.

➡ Burmese sweets to take away from near 85th St at 27th St in Zeigyo Market.

➡ Sweet tea and fresh *nanbya* (tandoor bread) from **Min Thiha** (Map p510; 28th St at 72nd St; tea/nanbya K350/300; ☉5am-5pm) or **Unison Teahouse** (Map p512; 38th St at 88th St; tea K300; ☉5am-1am).

Nighttime Only

➡ Indian chapatti and curry – 28th St at 82nd St or **Nay** (Map p512; 27th St at 82nd St; curry/chapatti K1500/200; ☉5pm-11pm).

➡ Indian/savoury 'pancakes' and biryanis – **Karaweik** (Map p512; 26th St at 83rd St; pancakes K500; ☉5.30pm-midnight).

➡ Chinese food stalls at 34th St – 76th St, with a night market (vegetables) stretching along 34th St.

POST

Main Post Office (Map p512; 22nd St, 80/81; ⊙10.30am-4pm Mon-Fri)

TELEPHONE

SIM cards are available from ever-multiplying phone shops from K1500.

TOURIST INFORMATION & TRAVEL AGENCIES

Myanmar Travels & Tours (MTT; Map p510; ☑02-60356; www.myanmartravelsandtours. com; 68th St at 27th St; ⊙9.30am-4.30pm) The government-run travel company doubles as a tourist office, giving away multi-city maps as well as selling transport tickets and permit-needing tours – notably to Mogok.

Seven Diamond (Map p512; ☑02-72868, 02-30128; www.sevendiamondtravels.com; 82nd St, 26/27; ⊙8.30am-6pm Mon-Sat) Helpful, major agency that can pre-book flights and hotels by email request and organise airport-bound shared taxis.

ⓘ Getting There & Away

AIR

Mandalay International Airport (www.man dalayairport.com), just over 20 miles south of the city, has both domestic and international connections.

BOAT

Taking a boat on the Ayeyarwady River is one of Mandalay's delights. Flits to Mingun or all-day rides to Bagan are most popular, though the new afternoon return service to Inwa is a great alternative. Pre-booking one day ahead is usually fine for Bagan or Bhamo – bring plenty of drinking water. For Mingun and Inwa just show up 30 minutes before departure. Passport required. Private boats to Bagan run October to March only.

IWT Ferries (Map p512; ☑02-36035; www. mot.gov.mm/iwt; Gawein Jetty) Slow boats to Katha, Bhamo and Bagan plus the more picturesque Hantharwaddy Bagan-bound cruiser depart from Gawein Jetty.

Malikha (Map p512; ☑02-72279; www.malikha-rivercruises.com) Three Malikha boats do the Bagan run; Malikha 3 is the most elegant. Buy tickets through hotels/agencies or online.

MGRG (Map p512; ☑011-202734; www.mgrg-express.com; Strand Rd) Bagan express ferries (October to March). Tickets from a booth at the jetty.

Nmai Hka (Map p512; ☑09 4027 00072; www. nmaihka.com; A-15, 2nd fl, train station) Shwei Keinnery ferries to Bagan (tourist season) and Bhamo (summer) plus seasonal Tharlarwaddy to Mingun and Inwa. Ticket office is 100yd east of IWT Ferries. Departures from Gawein Jetty.

Pan Lon (Map p512; Strand Rd; ⊙ticket office 5am-6pm) Express boats to Katha. Change there for Bhamo or Shwegu.

BUS & SHARED TAXI

Thiri Mandalar bus station (Map p512; 89th St, 21/22) is relatively central. Buses for Monywa, Shwebo and Bhamo leave from here (though foreigners currently may not take Bhamo services). Pyi Gyi Myat Shin bus station is 2 miles east of the centre and has buses for Hsipaw and Lashio. Kwe Se Kan Highway bus station is 6 miles south of centre and has buses for Bagan, Mrauk U and Yangon. It can take 45 minutes from the K3000/6000 motorbike/taxi ride from central Mandalay. Allow plenty of

TRANSPORT FROM MANDALAY

DESTINATION	BUS	BOAT	TRAIN	AIR
Bagan	K8000-9500, 6-7hr, 5 daily 8am-9.30pm	US$15-42, 10-12hr	ordinary/upper class K1100/1800, 8hr	US$62, 30min
Bhamo		deck/cabin US$12/54, 48hr, Mon, Thu & Sat		US$80-125, 1hr
Hsipaw	K6000, 7hr, 2 daily 6am & 12.30pm		ordinary/upper class K1700/3950, 11hr	
Inle Lake	K12,000-14,000, 9hr, 2 daily 7pm & 8.30pm			US$80 via Heho, 40min
Katha	K13,000, 12hr, 1 daily 5pm	deck/cabin US$9/45, 36hr, Mon, Thu & Sat	ordinary/upper class K2550/3150 to Naba and then 1hr bus, 13hr	
Yangon	K10,800-18,300, 9hr, 5 daily 9am-9.30pm		ordinary/upper class/sleeper K4650/9300/12,750 10-16hr	US$112, 1hr

time once you're there to find the right bus in the mayhem.

Pre-booking bus tickets for longer-distance routes is wise. Hotels charge a small commission, but that's rarely more than the motor-bike-taxi fare you'll pay when buying your own. Alternatively, use a city-centre ticket agency: they cluster on 32nd St.

Long-distance shared taxis, where available, are worth considering as most offer door-to-door service, saving potentially long trips to/from bus stations at either end of your journey.

TRAIN

Mandalay's gargantuan and ugly **train station** (30th St, 78/79) is in the city centre. The **MTT sub-office** (Myanmar Travel & Tours; Map p512; train station, near south door; ⊙ 9.30am-6pm) here can sell tickets (with commission) if the queues upstairs look too daunting.

ℹ Getting Around

GETTING TO/FROM THE AIRPORT

From Mandalay airport there are free shuttle buses for AirAsia customers (and leaving for the airport from 9am from 79th St, 26/28) and Golden Myanmar customers (5.30am from Sedona Hotel, picking up at Hotel Mandalay 5.45am). Otherwise there's no airport bus.

Several taxi companies with booths in the arrivals area offer shared taxis at K12,000/4000 per vehicle/seat. These include **Shwe Myanmar** (✓ 02-72325; 34th St, 79/80) and **Great Taxi** (✓ 02-32534). Even if you choose the K4000 'shared' option you'll still be collected/dropped at your hotel as long as it's reasonably central. Coming from town, book one day ahead if possible.

BICYCLE & MOTORCYCLE

Several rental agents in the central backpacker area charge K2000/10,000 per day for bicycles/motorbikes, including long-established **Mr Jerry** (Map p512; 83rd St, 25/26; ⊙ 8am-8pm). Several hotels rent bicycles too. Cyclists are advised to carry a head-torch at night.

To go further afield, expat-run **Mandalay Motorcycle** (Map p512; ✓ 09 4440 22182; www.mandalaymotorbike.com; 32nd St, 79/80; per day city bike K10,000-12,000, trail bike K40,000) has 125cc and 150cc trail bikes. The office is only manned by appointment and supply is limited so call ahead to book a bike.

TAXI

Motorcycle taxis lurk near hotels and on many a city corner. Expect to pay K1000 for a short hop, K1500 across the centre, and K10,000 for all-day hire within Mandalay (or K15,000 including Amarapura, Inwa and Sagaing). Guesthouses can help you find a reliable taxi or motorcycle driver.

TRISHAW

Traditionally the main form of city transport, pedal trishaws are now relatively rare except around the markets. Fares include city centre to the base of Mandalay Hill for K4000 return and all-day hire from around K10,000.

Around Mandalay

From Mandalay it's easy to day trip to four old cities nearby. Entry to Inwa's two main sites and Amarapura's Bagaya Kyaung are included in Mandalay's K10,000 'combo' ticket. A separate K3000 ticket for Mingun and Sagaing is patchily enforced. No one checks for tickets at the other sites.

A popular option is to combine Amarapura, Sagaing and Inwa into a full-day trip by motorcycle taxi (K15,000) or taxi (K35,000 to K40,000).

Motorbike taxis typically add around K2000 to drive around the Inwa ruins (if you insist). Add another K5000 more to include Mingun too. Beware that doing the whole lot in one very long day will feel very rushed. Ideally, make two or three more modest day trips.

Amarapura   အမရပူရ

The 'City of Immortality', a short-lived capital 7 miles south of Mandalay, is famed for U Bein's Bridge, the world's longest teak bridge at 1300yd. At 200 years old, the bridge sees lots of life along its 1086 teak posts, with monks and fishers commuting to and fro. It leads to Kyauktawgyi Paya and small Taungthaman village, with tea and toddy shops. A popular sunset activity is renting a **boat** (about K5000) to drift along as the skies turn orange, or watching life go by from a waterside beer station.

Just west is the monastery Maha Ganayon Kyaung, where hundreds of monks breakfast at 10.30am. Resist the temptation to thrust a camera in their faces, as some travellers do.

It's possible to cycle here from Mandalay in about 45 minutes.

Inwa   အင်းဝ

Cut off by rivers and canals, Inwa (called Ava by the British) served as the Burmese capital for nearly four centuries. **Horse carts** (one-/two-hour tours K6000/9000 for up to two people) make a loop around Inwa's beaten track; if you're lucky you may get them to stop at

WORTH A TRIP

ANISAKAN FALLS

About 1½ miles north of Anisakan village (5½ miles south of Pyin Oo Lwin), the plateau disappears into an impressively deep wooded amphitheatre, its sides ribboned with the Anisakan Falls (အန်းစခန်းရေတံခွန်).

To get here from Pyin Oo Lwin, take the main Mandalay highway. In Anisakan town, take the second asphalted turn right (signposted) and keep right past the first large pagoda. At the end of this road a pair of basic shack-restaurants mark the start of a forest trail along which the falls' base is reached by a 45-minute trek. Sales-kids act as guides (K1000) and can prove helpful, especially if taking the 'alternative' route back (very steep, almost a climb).

other crumbling sights sans vendors, or to allow you to rest your butt.

The finest sights are the atmospheric **Bagaya Kyaung** (ဘားကရာကျောင်း; combo ticket required), an 1834 teak monastery supported by 267 posts; the Maha Aungmye Bonzan (aka Ok Kyaung), which is a brick-and-stucco monastery dating from 1822; and the 88ft Nanmyin watchtower, which leans precariously.

Sagaing   စစ်ကိုင်း

Across the Ava Bridge from the Inwa junction and 11 miles from Mandalay, the stupa-studded hilltops of Sagaing are where Burmese Buddhists come to relax and meditate. Sagaing is also known for silver shops and guitars.

Sagaing Hill is the big attraction. Trees hang over stone steps leading past monasteries to the top. There are great views and pathways lead all the way to the water for the adventurer. The hill is half a mile north of the market.

Sagaing is spread out. Take a motorbike taxi (K7000) here from Mandalay, then rent a trishaw (K10,000) for the day.

Mingun   မင်းကွန်း

Home to a trio of unique pagodas, Mingun is a compact riverside village site that's a great half-day excursion from Mandalay. The journey is part of the attraction, whether puttering up the wide Ayeyarwady or roller-coasting from Sagaing along a rural lane through timeless hamlets of bamboo-weave homes.

The Mingun Paya is actually the remains of a planned 492ft stupa, surely a candidate for the world's largest pile of bricks. It is still possible to climb up. Just to the north is the Mingun Bell, which holds the record for the world's largest uncracked bell. Press on to the white, wavy-terraced Hsinbyume Paya nearby.

Mingun is a pleasant 35-minute drive from Sagaing, but it's more popular to go by boat (one hour out, 40 minutes back, passport required). From Mandalay's 26th St 'tourist jetty' (Mayan Chan), boats depart at 9am (foreigner/bicycle K5000/500 return), returning at 1pm. Alternatively, Nmai Hka's *Tharlarwaddy* (US$6 return, bicycles free) departs 8.30am from Gawein Jetty, returning 11.30am. For US$8 extra, the latter boat continues to Inwa.

Pyin Oo Lwin   ပြင်ဦးလွင်

Set in the foothills of northern Shan State, this colonial-era hill station was established by British Captain May as a retreat from the stifling heat of Mandalay, and was subsequently named Maymyo for him (*myo* means town). Under the British it served as a summer capital and domestic tourists still flock here during the hottest months (March to May).

The main activity is cycling through history, passing faded English-style country mansions and cute pony-led miniature wagons, straight out of the Wells Fargo stagecoach days of the American West (actually India, 1914, as one driver told us), that serve as local transport. You will also notice a lot of green uniforms around here as Pyin Oo Lwin is home to the Defence Services Academy.

Pyin Oo Lwin is very spread out. The Mandalay–Lashio Rd doubles as the main road. Bicycle is the best way to get around.

◉ Sights

Most of Pyin Oo Lwin's trademark colonial-era buildings are dotted amid the southeastern woodland suburbs on and off Circular Rd. Check out the splendid **former Croxton Hotel** (Gandamar Myaing Hotel; Circular Rd), as well as the **Number 4 High School** (Circular Rd) and the **Survey Training Centre** (Multi-Office Rd).

★National Kandawgyi
Gardens   PARK
(အမျိုးသားကန်တော်ကြီးဥယျာဉ်; Nandan Rd;
adult/child under 12yr US$5/3; ⊙8am-6pm, aviary 8am-5pm, orchid garden & butterfly museum 8.30am-5pm, Nan Myint Tower lift operates to 5pm)
Founded in 1915, this lovingly maintained 435-acre botanical garden features more than 480 species of flowers, shrubs and trees. For casual visitors, its most appealing aspect is the way flowers and overhanging branches frame views of Kandawgyi Lake's wooden bridges and small gilded pagoda. Admission includes the swimming pool, visits to the aviary, orchid garden and butterfly museum and the bizarre Nan Myint Tower.

Central Market   MARKET
(Zeigyo Rd; ⊙6.30am-5.30pm) Sample Pyin Oo Lwin's famous (if seasonal) strawberries and other fruit, fresh, dried or as jams and wine. Also has cheap Western clothes and *longyi*. There are tailors on the 1st floor if you need alterations or something knocked up.

Purcell Tower   LANDMARK
Marking the town centre, this 1936 clock tower thinks it's Big Ben, judging by its hourly chimes.

🛏 Sleeping & Eating

Many of Pin Oo Lwin's cheaper hotels aren't licensed to accommodate foreigners. The following are all in or within walking distance of the town centre and include breakfast. Decent Burmese, Chinese and Indian food is available on or just off the main road; eat early or miss out.

Bravo Hotel   HOTEL $
(☑085-21223; bravohotel.pol@gmail.com; Mandalay-Lashio Rd; s/d/tr $20/30/45; ❄🐾) Earthenware amphorae, ornate teak chests and carved gilded panel-work reveal that some thought has gone into the design here, although the rooms are a little musty for boutique status. A solid midrange option with helpful staff.

Grace Hotel 1   GUESTHOUSE $
(☑085-21230; 114A Nan Myaing Rd; s/d/tr incl breakfast US$15/25/35; 🐾) The high-ceilinged rooms are showing their age and the bathrooms are primitive, but the beds are OK, the staff obliging and there's a pleasant garden with sun-loungers. Bike hire is K2000 a day.

Grace Hotel 2   GUESTHOUSE $
(☑085-22081; 46/48 Mandalay-Lashio Rd; s/d incl breakfast US$8/16; 🐾) For the money, this place is the best deal in town. The rooms are compact and the cheapest are without windows and bathrooms, but the doubles with shower are acceptable.

★Aung Padamyar   INDIAN $
(44, Block 28 Thumingalar; curries K4000; ⊙11am-6.30pm) The finest Indian in Pyin Oo Lwin: a secluded, friendly, family-run joint with a range of curries, all of which come with side dishes to create a veritable feast. To find it, take the first right off Circular Rd after the Shan Market and then the first left down a small alley. Look for the red sign. Only kyat is accepted here.

Family Restaurant   BURMESE, THAI $
(off Mandalay-Lashio Rd; curries K3300-4500; ⊙9am-9.30pm) The decor is bland and there's no alcohol served, but the delicious curry spread comes with complimentary veggie side dishes, salad, rice, soup, pappadams and chutneys and dips.

TRANSPORT FROM PYIN OO LWIN

DESTINATION	BUS	SHARED TAXI	PICK-UP TRUCK	TRAIN
Mandalay		back/front seat K6000/7000, 2hr, frequent until 6pm	K1500, 2½hr, frequent until 6pm	ordinary/upper class K550/1200, 6hr, 1 daily 5.40pm
Hsipaw	K5000, 4hr, 2 daily 3.30pm & 4pm	back/front seat K7000/8000, 3hr, frequent until 4pm		ordinary/upper class K1200/2750, 7hr, 1 daily 8.22am
Yangon	K12,000-20,000, 11-12hr, frequent 8am-6pm			

❶ Getting There & Away

Yangon buses leave from the inconvenient main bus station Thiri Mandala, 2 miles east of the Shan Market.

All other buses leave from behind the San Pya Restaurant, a quarter of a mile south of the bus station, as do some shared taxis and pick-ups to Mandalay.

Pick-ups to Mandalay also leave from near the gas station at the roundabout at the entrance to town, as well as less frequently from outside the train station – north of the town centre.

Shared taxis to Mandalay leave from 4th St.

Trains to/from Mandalay are very slow and rarely run to schedule.

❶ Getting Around

BICYCLE

Crown Bicycle Rental (Mandalay-Lashio Rd; bicycles/motorbikes per day K2500/15,000; ⏰7.30am-6.30pm) rents bicycles and motorbikes.

MOTORCYCLE TAXI

Easy to find close to the Central Market and the Bravo Hotel. Expect to pay K1000/2000 one way/return to the National Kandawgyi Gardens. For longer hires, consider engaging English-speaking **Jeffrey** (☎09 4025 10483), who acts as a guide and motorcycle driver. Rates are US$20 for a full day.

THREE-WHEEL PICK-UPS

These congregate outside the market; it costs K2000/3000 one way/return to Kandawgyi Gardens.

WAGON

Pyin Oo Lwin's signature horse-drawn buggies can be found near the Central Market. Reckon on K7000 for the return trip to Kandawgyi Gardens, K20,000 for an all-day tour.

Hsipaw   သီပေါ

☎082 / POP 20,897

Travellers come to this laid-back highland town for a couple of days and before they know it a week has passed. Trekking is the main draw, but Hsipaw is not without charms, including a bustling riverside market, good food and, in season, lively guesthouses.

Guesthouses can arrange guides (K10,000 to K20,000 per day) to take you on fascinating treks into the hills above town visiting Shan, Palaung and Lisu villages. Mr Charles Guest House is especially well organised.

◉ Sights

Produce Market   MARKET

(⏰4.30am-1pm) Most interesting before dawn when the road outside is jammed with hill-villagers selling their wares: all will have cleared away by 7am, though the market continues until 1pm.

Mahamyatmuni Paya   BUDDHIST TEMPLE

(Namtu Rd) FREE South of the central area, Mahamyatmuni Paya is the biggest and grandest pagoda in the main town. The large brass-faced Buddha image here was inspired by the famous Mahamuni Buddha in Mandalay. He's now backed by an acid-trip halo of pulsating coloured lights that would seem better suited to a casino.

Myauk Myo   NEIGHBOURHOOD

At the northern edge of town, Hsipaw's oldest neighbourhood has a village-like atmosphere, two delightful old teak monasteries and a collection of ancient brick stupas known locally as Little Bagan. The multifaceted wooden Madahya Monastery looks especially impressive when viewed from across the palm-shaded pond of the Bamboo Buddha Monastery (Maha Nanda Kantha).

TRANSPORT FROM HSIPAW

DESTINATION	BUS	SHARED TAXI	TRAIN
Mandalay	K4500-6300, 7hr, 3 daily 5.30am, 9.30am & 7.50pm	back/front seat K13,000/15,000, 5hr, frequent until 4pm	ordinary/upper class K1700/3950, 13hr, 1 daily 9.25am
Pyin Oo Lwin	K4500-6300, 4hr, 3 daily 5.30am, 9.30am & 7.50pm	back/front seat K7000/8000, 3hr, frequent until 4pm	ordinary/upper class K1200/2750, 7hr, 1 daily 9.25am
Taunggyi (for Inle Lake)	K15,300, 12hr, 3 daily 3.30pm, 4.30pm & 5pm		
Yangon	K14,800-20,300, 15hr, 3 daily 4.15pm, 5.15pm & 6.15pm		

Sunset Hill   VIEWPOINT

For sweeping views across the river and Hsipaw, climb to **Thein Daung Pagoda**, also known as Nine Buddha Hill or, most popularly, Sunset Hill. It's part of a steep ridge that rises directly behind the Lashio road, around 1½ miles south of Hsipaw.

🛏 Sleeping & Eating

Market stalls offer Hsipaw's best cheap eats.

⭐ Mr Charles Guest House   HOTEL $

(☎082-80105; www.mrcharleshotel.com; 105 Auba St; dm US$7, r US$14-65; ❄🛜) Still the most efficient, comfortable and traveller-friendly guesthouse in town, the ever-expanding Mr Charles operation encompasses everything from simple mattresses on the floor in the dorms, to swish suites with heating and air-con. Expect to pay $16 and up for a room with its own bathroom. Book ahead in peak periods.

Lily Guesthouse   GUESTHOUSE $

(☎082-80318; namkhaemaoguesthouse@gmail. com; 108 Aung Tha Pyay Rd; dm US$10, r US$14-35; ❄@🛜) Tucked behind the pricier Lily Hotel, the new dorms here are bright, spacious and clean and the staff obliging. Private rooms are comfortable; the cheapest share bathrooms and are fan only. Treks can be organised and there's bike hire (K2000 per day).

San   SHAN, CHINESE $

(Namtu Rd; dishes K1500-4500; ⊙10am-midnight; 🗐) With its retro interior and small terrace, San is popular with travellers who come for the many barbecue options and the Chinese-style mains. Dali beer from China is K1000.

Law Chun   CHINESE $

(Mr Food; Namtu Rd; dishes K1500-3000; ⊙9am-8.30pm; 🗐) With Chinese dishes for Burmese and Western palates (so light on the spices), 'Mr Food' stands out from the pack thanks to its bright and breezy interior. There's Dagon beer on tap (K700).

ℹ Information

A remarkable source of local information is Ko Zaw Tun (aka Mr Book), who runs a small **bookstall** (Namtu Rd; ⊙9am-7pm) opposite the entrance to the Central Pagoda.

ℹ Getting There & Away

Buses and minibuses leave from a variety of locations: the bus stands on the Mandalay–Lashio road close to the Catholic and Baptist churches, and the Duhtawadi Cafe on Lammataw St opposite the market.

Hsipaw's tiny train station is across the tracks from the end of Thirimingalar St.

BAGAN & AROUND

Bagan   ပုဂံ

☎061

The Bagan Archaeological Zone stretches 26 sq miles across central Myanmar. Despite centuries of neglect, looting, erosion, regular earthquakes, including a massive one in 1975, not to mention dodgy restoration, this temple-studded plain remains a remarkably impressive and unforgettable vision.

In a 230-year building frenzy up until 1287 and the Mongol invasions, Bagan's kings commissioned over 4000 Buddhist temples. These brick-and-stucco religious structures are all that remain of their grand

Bagan

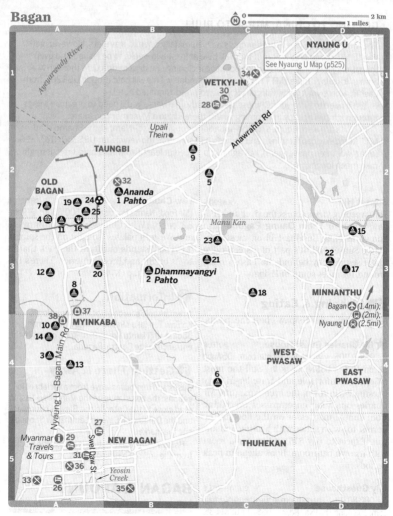

city, since the wooden 11th- to 13th-century buildings have long gone.

Many restoration projects have resulted in a compromised archaeological site that can barely be described as ruined. And yet, Bagan still remains a wonder. Working temples such as Ananda Pahto give a sense of what the place was like at its zenith, while others conceal colourful murals and hidden stairways that lead to exterior platforms and jaw-dropping views across the plain.

◉ Sights

Plan your daily temple viewing around a dawn or dusk visit, building in a leisurely lunch/siesta/poolside lounging period from around 12.30pm to 4pm. Temperatures at dawn and dusk will be more pleasant and the light is better for photographs.

All foreign visitors to the Bagan Archaeological Zone are required to pay a US$20 entrance fee. If you arrive by boat or air, the fee will be collected at the river jetty or airport. If you come by bus, the fee is collected at a booth as you head into town. The fee is valid

Bagan

for a five-day period, but it's unlikely you'll be asked to pay again if you stay longer.

◉ Old Bagan ပုဂံမြို့ဟောင်း

At just over 1 mile this circuit within the old city walls is manageable on foot or by bicycle.

North of the **Archaeological Museum** (ကျောက်စာသမိုင်းပြတိုက်; Map p522; Bagan-Nyaung U Rd; adult/child under 10yr K5000/free; ⏱9am-4.30pm Tue-Sun), the 197ft-high **Gawdawpalin Pahto** (ဂေါ်တော်ပလ္လင်ပုထိုး; Map p522) FREE is one of Bagan's most imposing temples. About 220yd south of here, a dirt road leads past **Mimalaung Kyaung** (မီးမလောင်ကျောင်း; Map p522) – note the *chinthe*, a half-lion, half-guardian deity – and the only remaining Hindu temple at Bagan, **Nathlaung Kyaung** (နတ်လှောင်ကျောင်း; Map p522), to the 207ft-tall **Thatbyinnyu Pahto** (သဗ္ဗညုပုထိုး; Map p522). Built in 1144, it has a square base, surrounded by diminishing terraces, rimmed with spires.

Another 220yd north of Thatbyinnyu is **Shwegugyi** (ရွှေဂူကြီး; Map p522), a temple dating from 1131 with lotus *sikhara* (Indian-style temple finial) atop and stucco carvings inside. Back on the main Nyaung U–Old Bagan Rd, continue to the 9th-century **Tharabar Gate** (သရပါတံခါး; Map p522), the former eastern entry to the walled city.

◉ North Plain

Roughly 490yd east of Thatbyinnyu, the 170ft-high **Ananda Pahto** (အာနန္ဒာပုထိုး; Map p522), with its golden *sikhara* top and gilded spires, is probably Bagan's top draw. Finished in 1105, the temple has giant teak Buddha images facing each of the four entranceways. On the full moon of the month of Pyatho (between mid-December and mid-January), a three-day paya festival attracts thousands of pilgrims.

Just northwest is **Ananda Ok Kyaung** (အာနန္ဒာအုတ်ကျောင်း; Map p522), with colourful murals detailing 18th-century life, some showing Portuguese traders. No photos allowed.

Midway between Old Bagan and Nyaung U, **Upali Thein** (ဥပါလိသိမ်; Map p522) features large, brightly painted murals from the early 18th century. Across the road, the location for the terraced 490ft-high **Htilominlo Pahto** (ထီးလိုမင်းလိုပုထိုး; Map p522) was picked in 1218 by King Nantaungmya, using a 'leaning umbrella'.

Just south of Anawrahta Rd, **Buledi** (ဘူးလယ်သီး; Map p522) is a good sunrise/sunset viewing spot and is also useful for getting your bearings.

Central Plain

South of Anawrahta Rd, the 11th-century, five-terraced **Shwesandaw Paya** (ရွှေဆံတော်ဘုရား; Map p522) is a graceful white pyramid-style pagoda with 360-degree views of Bagan's temples. It's packed for sunset, but pretty empty during the day. Note the original *hti* (decorated top of a stupa) lying to the south – it was toppled by a 1975 earthquake.

About 550yd east, monumental **Dhammayangyi Pahto** (ဓမ္မရံကြီးပုထိုး; Map p522) has two encircling passageways, the inner one of which has been intentionally filled. It's said that King Narathu, who commissioned the temple, was so cruel that the workers ruined it after his assassination in 1170.

About 880yd east, the broad two-storeyed 1181 **Sulamani Pahto** (စူဠာမဏိပုထိုး; Map p522) is one of the area's prettiest temples, with lush grounds and carved stucco. Just 165yd east, **Thabeik Hmauk** (သပိတ်မှောက်; Map p522) looks like a mini Sulamani, but without the hawkers – *and* you can climb to the top. And at sunset, don't miss the broad viewing platform at **Pyathada Paya** (ပြဿဒါးဘုရား; Map p522), about half a mile southeast.

Around Myinkaba

Just north of Myinkaba, the 1274 **Mingalazedi Paya** (မင်္ဂလာစေတီဘုရား; Map p522) has three receding terraces lined with 561 glazed tiles and tasty views of the nearby river and temples.

TOP BAGAN TEMPLES

Ananda Pahto One of the best-preserved and most revered of all the Bagan temples.

Dhammayangyi Pahto An absolute colossus, this red-brick temple is visible from all over Bagan.

Sulamani Pahto This late-period beauty is known as Crowning Jewel, and with good reason.

Pyathada Paya Super sunset (or sunrise) spot and typically less crowded.

Thatbyinnyu Pahto Named for omniscience, this is Bagan's highest temple.

On the northern edge of town, the 1113 **Gubyaukgyi** (ဂူပြောက်ကြီး; Map p522) sees a lot of visitors thanks to its richly coloured interior paintings. In the village, the modern-looking 1059 **Manuha Paya** (မနူဟာဘုရား; Map p522) was named for the Mon king who was held captive here. Note the four giant buddha images that are seemingly too large for the enclosure, symbolic of Manuha's discontent with his prison life. Stairs at the rear lead above the reclining Buddha.

Just south, **Nan Paya** (နန်းဘုရား; Map p522), from the same era, is a cave-style shrine; Nan Paya was possibly once Hindu, as suggested by the three-faced Brahma situated on the pillars.

About 550yd south of Myinkaba, the 11th-century **Abeyadana Pahto** (အပယ်ရတနာပုထိုး; Map p522) was likely to have been commissioned by King Kyanzittha's Bengali wife and features original frescoes. Across the road, **Nagayon** (နဂါးရုံ; Map p522) has some tight stairs leading up to the roof. Its corn-cob *sikhara* (finial) was possibly a prototype for Ananda.

South Plain

About 1¾ miles east of New Bagan, the 1196 **Dhammayazika Paya** (ဓမ္မရာဇိကဘုရား; Map p522) is unusual for its five-sided design. It's very well tended with lush grounds and lavish attention from worshippers. A dirt road leads a mile north to Dhammayangyi.

An excellent cluster of sites is about 2 miles east. North of the road, **Tayok Pye Paya** (တရုတ်ပြေးဘုရား; Map p522) has good westward views of Bagan. To the south, 13th-century **Payathonzu** (ဘုရားသုံးဆူ; Map p522), a small complex of three interconnected shrines, draws visitors to its murals.

About 220yd north, **Nandamannya Pahto** (နန္ဒပညာပုထိုး; Map p522), from the same period, features the 'temptation of Mura' murals – in the form of topless women reaping no response from a meditating buddha. It's often locked; ask at Payathonzu for the 'key master'. Just behind, **Kyat Kan Kyaung** (Map p522) has been a cave-style monastery for nearly 1000 years.

Nyaung U   ညောင်ဦး

The gilded bell of 1102 **Shwezigon Paya** (ရွှေစည်းခုံဘုရား; Map p525) is considered by many to be the prototype for many Burmese pagodas. A yellow compound on the eastern

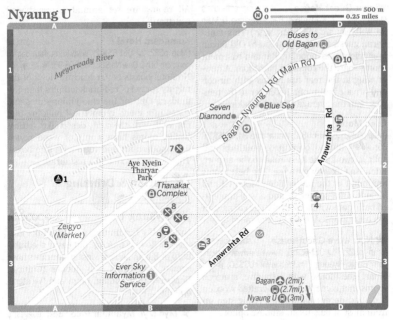

Nyaung U

side (called '37 Nats' in English) features figures of each of the animist spirits.

🛏 Sleeping

Bagan accommodation can be loosely categorised as: Nyaung U for budget travellers; New Bagan for good-value midrange rooms; and Old Bagan for top-end hotels. The following all include breakfast and some offer discounts in low season (April to September).

🛏 Nyaung U   ညောင်ဦး

New Park Hotel   HOTEL $
(Map p525; ☎ 061-60322; www.newparkmyanmar. com; 4 Thiripyitsaya; r US$35-55; ❄ 🛜) One of the best all-round budget hotels, the New Park

is tucked away in the leafy backstreets off Restaurant Row. The older rooms, with bungalow-style front decks, are comfortable, wood-floor set-ups, with reasonable bathrooms. The newer wing brings more space, a fridge, a TV and even a rain shower. Another annexe should be open by the time you read this.

Viewpoint Inn   GUESTHOUSE $
(Map p525; ☎ 061-61070; viewpointinn.vpi@gmail. com; Anawrahta Rd; r US$15-40; ❄ 🛜) There's a wide selection of digs at this solid budget choice. The cheapest rooms are fan only and share bathrooms, but all are clean and sizeable. The staff are helpful and there's a big outside communal area.

Winner Guest House
GUESTHOUSE **$**

(Map p522; ☑ 061-61069; Bagan-Nyaung U Main Rd, Wetkyi-in; s/d US$15/25; ❄ 🛜) This family-run guesthouse on the road to Old Bagan is efficient and popular. Bargain-basement rooms share the common bathroom. A newer wing at the rear has rooms with air-con and private bathroom. It's closer to the temples than the average Nyaung U address.

Eden Motel
GUESTHOUSE **$**

(Map p525; ☑ 061-60812; Anawrahta Rd; r US$15-35; ❄🛜) Spread over three buildings and split in two by the busy road to the airport, Eden isn't exactly paradise. The best rooms are found in the newer Eden Motel III and include a flat-screen TV and a well-appointed bathroom with a bathtub. The young staff are quite attuned to backpacker needs.

★ New Wave Guesthouse
GUESTHOUSE **$$**

(Map p522; ☑ 061-60731; www.newwavebagan. com; Bagan-Nyaung U Rd, Wetkyi-in; r US$60; ❄🛜) Smart guesthouse with attractive, spacious rooms that come with hand-crafted wooden beds and decent bathrooms. A big step up from most of Bagan's guesthouse options.

🛏 New Bagan
ပုဂံမြို့သစ်

★ Thurizza Hotel
HOTEL **$**

(Map p522; ☑ 061-65229; thirimarlarhotelbagan @gmail.com; Ingin St; r US$37-53; ❄@🛜) Formerly known as the Thiri Marlar Hotel, teak walkways lead to 15 lovely rooms wrapped around a small pagoda-style dining room, though most guests eat breakfast on the roof deck with temple views. Spotless standard rooms are rather compact but inviting, with shiny wood floors and small rugs. Superior rooms are much more spacious and worth the extra bucks.

Yun Myo Thu Motel
GUESTHOUSE **$**

(Map p522; ☑ 061-65276; 3 Khat Tar St; r US$45-50; ❄🛜) Translating rather romantically as 'the lady of lacquer city', this place sees fewer foreigners than other guesthouses. The well-tended rooms include flat-screen TV, air-con and hot water, but little English is spoken.

Bagan Central Hotel
HOTEL **$**

(Map p522; ☑ 061-65057; Khaye St (Main Rd); 4-bed dm US$15, r US$45-50; ❄🛜) There's one dorm here – really a room with four mattresses on the floor – but most of the accommodation is stone-clad chalets. The interiors are bamboo and the clean rooms include wooden floors and reasonable bathrooms.

All rooms are set around a tree-shaded courtyard.

Kumudara Hotel
HOTEL **$$**

(Map p522; ☑ 061-65142; www.kumudara-bagan. com; cnr 5th & Daw Na Sts; r US$56-95; ❄@🛜🏊) No hotel boasts better balcony views of the mighty sprawl of red-brick temples than Kumudara. Opt for the chic junior suites and suites in a green geometrical building that fits well with the arid, desert-like setting. Inside, rooms have a mix of wood panelling, modern art and retro-style safe boxes. There's also a pool and a restaurant.

🍴 Eating & Drinking

🍴 Nyaung U
ညောင်ဦး

Nyaung U's Yarkinnthar Hotel Rd (aka Restaurant Row) is touristy, but easily the hub(-bub) of Bagan action. Most restaurants have similar 'everything goes' menus (Chinese, Burmese, Thai, Indian, pizza and 'Western' options).

★ Myo Myo Myanmar Rice Food
BURMESE **$**

(Map p522; Bagan-Nyaung U Rd; meals K2000-4000; ⊙8am-8pm) Deservedly popular restaurant that specialises in the personalised tabletop buffets that characterise the national cuisine. But here they really go to town, with 25 dishes or more appearing at the table, including seasonal specials like asparagus. English is spoken. Bring a crowd to share.

★ Weather Spoon's Bagan
INTERNATIONAL **$**

(Map p525; Yarkinnthar Hotel Rd; mains K1900-4900; ⊙9am-11pm; 🛜📱) Brits abroad may be familiar with the name, borrowed from one of the UK's discount pub chains. Owner Winton studied balloon piloting in Bristol and spent some time in the local pubs. But Bagan benefits from his experience and he offers the best burger in town, as well as some Asian and international favourites. Lively drinking spot by night.

Aroma 2
INDIAN **$**

(Map p525; Yarkinnthar Hotel Rd; dishes K2500-6500; ⊙10.30am-9pm; 🛜📱) 'No good, no pay' is the mantra of this justifiably confident place serving delicious veggie and meat curries on banana leaves (or plates) with an endless stream of hot chapattis and five different condiments (including tamarind and mint sauces). With some advance notice, the chef can also whip up various biryani rice dishes.

San Kabar Restaurant & Pub   ITALIAN $
(Map p525; Bagan–Nyaung U Main Rd; pizza K4500-6000, mains K2500-6000; ⏲7.30am-10pm; 🛜📵)
The birthplace of Bagan pizza, San Kabar's streetside candlelit courtyard is all about its thin-crusted pies and well-prepared salads. The three menus the staff present here also include Thai and Chinese-style dishes.

Black Bamboo   EUROPEAN $$
(Map p525; ☑061-60782; off Yarkinnthar Hotel Rd; dishes K3000-9000; ⏲8.30am-10pm; 🛜)
Run by a French woman and her Burmese husband, this garden cafe and restaurant is something of an oasis. It's a pleasant place to relax over solid Burmese, Thai and Western dishes, a well-made espresso or a delicious homemade ice cream. Service is friendly but leisurely.

Shwe Ya Su   BEER STATION
(Map p525; Yarkinnthar Hotel Rd; dishes K1500-5000, BBQ from K400; ⏲10am-10.30pm) Thanks to endless draught Myanmar Beer (K700), this place with a large outside area and a menu of Chinese-inspired favourites has become quite the local hangout. A good spot for footie-watching, while the barbecue on offer is tasty too.

🍴 Old Bagan   ပုဂံမြို့ဟောင်း

Save yourself the schlep back to Nyaung U by having lunch in Old Bagan.

★ Starbeam Bistro   INTERNATIONAL $
(Map p522; mains K4000-7500; ⏲10am-10pm; 🛜) Located close to Ananda Pahto, this garden bistro was set up by Chef Tin Myint who spent several years working with the Orient-Express hotel group. Dishes include

---

CRUISING THE UPPER AYEYARWADY

Drifting down the Ayeyarwady, past friendly villagers for whom the river and its traffic are a lifeline to the outside world, is a memorable experience but one you will need to set aside a chunk of time for – the journey is quicker travelling downstream.

Since 2012 foreign travellers have been banned from arriving or leaving the Kachin State capital of Myitkyina by boat – you can fly there or take the train; for more details see Lonely Planet's Myanmar (Burma) guide.

An alternative start point is Bhamo, which has a bustling daily market, drawing Lisu, Kachin and Shan folk from surrounding villages. Worth searching out is the awesome **bamboo bridge** (return toll with bicycle K500), near the Shwe Kyina Pagoda, 3 miles north of Bhamo, that allows you to make your precarious way across the wide Tapin River. Bhamo's **Friendship Hotel** (☑074-50095, in China 0086-692 687 6670; Letwet Thondaya Rd; s/d/tr US$25/30/40, with shared bathroom US$10/20/30; ❄@🛜) is one of the better provincial pads, with good-value rooms and an English-speaking manager.

IWT ferries leave from a jetty 2½ miles south of Bhamo. Fast boats leave from a pier on the central riverfront, although foreigners aren't always allowed to use them. The airport is a 10-minute ride from the centre of town.

Between Bhamo and Shwegu, the scenery reaches a modest climax in the short second defile where the Ayeyarwady passes through a wooded valley with a rocky cliff face at one section (often described misleadingly as a gorge).

The next major stop is the sleepy town of Katha, where Eric Blair, better known by his pen name George Orwell, was stationed in 1926–27. Katha was the the setting for *Burmese Days* and several buildings that feature in the book are still standing but none are commercialised tourist attractions, so ask politely before barging in.

The best of Katha's accommodation options is **Eden Guesthouse** (☑074-25429; Shwe Phone Shein St; r US$25; ❄🛜), although the rooms are horribly overpriced for what you get.

IWT ferry tickets are only available an hour before departure and can be bought from opposite the main jetty.

Buy tickets for the Katha–Mandalay express boat a day before departure from the office on the riverfront.

At Naba, 16 miles west of Katha, there's a train station on the Mandalay–Myitkyina line. There are two afternoon buses to Naba (K1000, 2pm and 5pm). There is one daily bus from Katha to Mandalay (K13,000, 12 hours).

MT POPA

Spiritual HQ for Myanmar's infamous 37 'nat', Mt Popa (ပုပ္ပားတောင်) is the premier venue for worship of these pre-Buddhist, animist spirits and an easy day trip from Bagan.

A gilded Buddhist temple accessed by 777 steps teeters atop a towerlike 2418ft volcanic plug. The 20-minute climb up goes past devout pilgrims, cheeky monkeys and, occasionally, slow-stepping hermit monks called *yeti*. From the temple there are mammoth views back towards the Myingyan Plain and beyond.

At the foot of the complex, the Mother Spirit of Popa Nat Shrine features a display of the 37 nat. If you have more time, and a guide, there are tracks up the nearby 4980ft extinct volcano called Taung Ma-gyi (Mother Mountain), covered in lush forests protected within the Popa Mountain Park.

In high season (November to March), a pick-up (K3000, two hours) leaves Nyaung U bus station at 8.30am, and returns at 1pm. Far easier is a slot in a shared taxi (K40,000 for four passengers). Ask the driver to point out remnants of the petrified forest along the way and to pause at toddy palm plantations where you can sample the homemade alcohol and jaggery (palm sugar).

Rakhine fish curry, market fresh specials, traditional salads such as avocado or tea leaf, and classic baguettes and sandwiches. Best accompanied by a healthy blend or fresh juice.

Be Kind to Animals the Moon
BURMESE, VEGETARIAN $

(Map p522; off Bagan-Nyaung U Rd; mains K2000-4000; ⏰7am-10pm; 🖊) The original among the vegetarian restaurants clustered near Tharabar Gate, this place offers a friendly welcome and delicious food including pumpkin and ginger soup, aubergine curry and a lime and ginger tea that the owners claim is good for stomach upsets.

✖ New Bagan   ပုဂံမြို့သစ်

Naratheinkha Restaurant FRENCH $
(Map p522; 📱09 5242420; New Bagan; mains K2000-6000; ⏰11am-11pm) Blink and you'll miss it, this tiny little shopfront restaurant is well regarded thanks to the chef-owner's extensive experience at Le Planteur Restaurant in Yangon. The menu is predominantly French-accented or Asian fusion and includes a delicious pan-fried fish with lemon butter sauce.

Mother's House BURMESE $
(Map p522; Chauk Rd; dishes K350-4000; ⏰5am-10pm Mon-Sat) Big and busy teahouse with plenty of outdoor seating and an attached restaurant next door. Good for a traditional Burmese breakfast before exploring the temples, or after catching sunrise somewhere near New Bagan. Try Shan noodles or deep-fried doughnuts.

Silver House BURMESE, ASIAN $$
(Map p522; Khaye St (Main Rd); mains K3500-7500; ⏰7am-10pm; 🖼) A welcoming, family-run restaurant that offers large, tasty portions of dishes such as traditional Myanmar chicken curry and tomato salad.

🛍 Shopping

Bagan is the lacquerware capital of Myanmar. Head to Myinkaba, where several family-run workshops produce high-quality traditional pieces – look for earthy colours.

Golden Cuckoo CRAFTS
(Map p522; ⏰7.30am-7pm) Just behind the Manuha Paya, this family-run workshop spans four generations and focuses on high quality 'traditional' designs, which are applied to some unusual objects, including a motorbike helmet (US$1200). The really good stuff is in the room at the back.

Family Lacquerware Work Shop CRAFTS
(Map p522; ⏰7.30am-5.30pm) Smaller workshop off the eastern side of the road with some contemporary styles using alternative colours, such as blue and yellow with fewer layers of lacquer.

Mani-Sithu Market MARKET
(Map p525; ⏰6am-5pm Mon-Sat) Near the roundabout at the eastern end of the main road, this market offers a colourful display of fruit, vegetables, flowers, fish and textiles and is best visited early in the day to see it at its liveliest. There are plenty of traveller-oriented goods (woodcarvings, T-shirts, lacquerware) at its northern end.

ⓘ Orientation

Most independent travellers stay in Nyaung U. In Nyaung U, 'Main Rd' is used to refer to the main strip, which runs along the north–south Bagan–Nyaung U Rd, and along the Anawrahta Rd from the market to the Sapada Paya. Running off it is Yarkinnthar Hotel Rd, more popularly known as 'restaurant row', with lots of eating options.

ⓘ Information

Nyaung U is home to most traveller life-support systems, including banks and a post office.

Ever Sky Information Service (Map p525; ☏ 061-60895; everskynanda@gmail.com; 5 Thiripyitsaya St; ☺7.30am-9.30pm) Just off the restaurant strip, this friendly place can book tickets and has a secondhand bookshop. Staff can get shared taxis (to Mt Popa, Kalaw, Salay, around Bagan) for the best available rates.

ⓘ Getting There & Away

Most travel services operate from Nyaung U. Ask at Ever Sky Information Service or your guesthouse about air tickets or hiring a shared taxi.

AIR

Nyaung U airport is about 2 miles southeast of the market. Travel agencies often have cheaper tickets than the airline offices. Try **Seven Diamond** (Map p525; ☏ 061-61184; www.seven diamondtravels.com; ☺9am-8pm) on Nyaung U–Bagan Rd.

BOAT

Boats to Mandalay go from either Nyaung U or Old Bagan, depending on water levels. The Nyaung U jetty is about half a mile northeast of the market.

During low season (April to September) the government-run IWT ferry (aka 'slow boat') is the only boat that runs to Mandalay, a two-day journey with an overnight stop near Pakokku. Private boats include Malikha and Nmai Hka. They do the trip in 10 to 12 hours.

At the time of writing there were no south-bound passenger ferries operating to Magwe or Pyay.

If open (unlikely!), the IWT office, about 275yd inland from the jetty, sells tickets. Alternatively book a ticket through your hotel or a travel agency, who can also sell tickets for the private boats.

BUS

Bagan's new main bus station is around 3 miles south of Nyaung U, close to the train station. Pick-ups charge K3000 per person to/from Nyaung U. During peak season it's wise to book bus tickets for Mandalay, Taunggyi (for Inle Lake) and Yangon in advance.

TRAIN

The Bagan train station is about 2½ miles southeast of Nyaung U. The shop **Blue Sea** (Map p525; ☏ 061-60949; Bagan-Nyaung U Rd) sells tickets plus a K2000 commission.

ⓘ Getting Around

BICYCLE

Daily rental ranges from K1500 to K5000 depending on the condition of the bike. Carry water when you cycle as some temples don't have vendors.

TRANSPORT FROM BAGAN

TO YANGON	TIME	COST	DEPARTURES
Air	70min	US$126	frequent
Bus	9hr	K13,000-18,000	frequent
Car	9hr	K150,000	charter
Train	16hr	upper class/sleeper K6000/16,500	daily

TO MANDALAY	TIME	COST	DEPARTURES
Air	30min	US$60-65	frequent
Boat (slow)	2 days	US$15	2 weekly
Boat (fast)	10-12hr	US$42	daily Oct-Mar
Bus	6-7hr	K8000-9500	frequent
Car	4-5hr	K130,000	charter
Train	8hr	ordinary/upper class K1100/1800	daily

HORSE CART

Uncomfortable and slow but you get some shade from the canopy and the drivers do know the temples. Expect to pay K20,000 for the whole day, but there is only really enough space for two people.

PICK-UP

Between Nyaung U, Old Bagan and New Bagan, pick-ups (K500 to K1000, hourly 7am to 3pm) run along the main street, starting from the roundabout outside the Nyaung U market.

TAXI

Costs about K35,000 for the day. Taxis between Nyaung U and New Bagan cost about K6000, or K15,000 return. From the airport to Nyaung U/New Bagan is K5000/7000.

Monywa

📞 071 / POP 207,489

With a pleasant Chindwin riverside setting this engaging town is a sensible stopping point if you're looping between Mandalay and Bagan. The main sights are out of town.

About 6 miles south, **Thanboddhay Paya** (admission K3000; ⊙ 6am-5pm) bursts with carnival shades of pink, orange, yellow and blue. Inside are more than half a million buddhas filling nooks and crannies.

About 5 miles east of the paya is Bodhi Tataung, a buddha frenzy in the foothills, including Laykyun Setkyar, at 424ft the world's second-tallest standing Buddha. The easiest way to visit is by taxi.

Across the Chindwin River and 15 miles west, the 492 **Hpo Win Daung Caves** (admission K3000) were carved into a limestone

hillside between the 14th and 18th centuries. Many of the 'caves' are just big enough for a single buddha image but a few of the best (notably caves 478 and 480) have retained some colourfully well-executed murals. To get here, rent a motorbike taxi in Monywa for the day (around K15,000) and catch a boat from the Monywa jetty (one way K3000 for up to five people).

🛏 Sleeping & Eating

Monywa Hotel　　　　　　　　　HOTEL $

(📞 071-21581; monywahotel@goldenland.com.mm; Bogyoke Rd; s/d US$35/45; ❄ 🅿) Set well back from the busy street amid birdsong and creeper-draped trees, this collection of multiroom cabins is popular with small tour groups. Interiors are definitely dated and the colour schemes are hideous, but even the cheaper rooms are fair-sized with effective air-conditioning, desk, fridge, hot showers, satellite TV and reasonable beds.

❶ Getting There & Away

The bus station is just over a mile southeast of the clock tower down Bogyoke St.

Several companies operate hourly buses 5am to 4pm to Mandalay (K2500 to K3000, three hours). There are also regular buses to Pakokku (K3000, three hours) with onward connections to Bagan available there, taking an extra hour. Aung Gabar Express operates a direct service to Bagan (K3500) departing at 7.30am.

The train to Mandalay departs at 6am (K1100, six hours), but it takes twice as long as the bus in an uncomfortable box car.

WESTERN MYANMAR

Even as more of Myanmar's remote areas 'open' up and tourist numbers increase, Rakhine State remains staunchly untourested.

Adventurous travellers should aim for the scrappy, atmospheric capital Sittwe and the old capital of Mrauk U, an amazing archaeological site, studded with hundreds of temples.

Sittwe

📞 043 / POP 100,748

For most people, a trip to Mrauk U will include a stay in Sittwe, a port town with a dramatic setting where the wide Kaladan River meets the Bay of Bengal. The British moved the regional capital here from Mrauk U in the

1820s and called it Aykab. Sittwe is a scruffy place, but there are a few sights of note.

⊙ Sights

Central Market
MARKET

(မြို့ မဈ ေ ; Strand Rd; ⊘6am-6pm) Focused on the 1956 municipal market building, there's lots going on here from dawn up to noon and beyond – it's well worth popping by before your boat or plane leaves. Head straight past *longyi*, fishing-net and vegetable stands to the fish and meat area, where stingrays and gutted eels and drying sharks make quite a scene. In the bay, small boats jostle for space to unload their catch.

View Point
VIEWPOINT

(စစ်တွေ ျ ုး �)ိင်; Strand Rd) Strand Rd leads about 1.5 miles south to a location called the View Point, where you can watch the sun set over **Sittwe Beach**, a broad brown strip of sand, and the Bay of Bengal. It was being redeveloped at the time of writing, so there will likely be a restaurant or two here by the time you read this.

Auto rickshaws, known locally as *thoun bein,* will take you there and back for 5000K, taxis for 10,000K.

Lokananda Paya
BUDDHIST TEMPLE

(ေလာကနန္ဒာဘုရား; May Yu St; ⊘daylight hours) You can't miss this big golden pagoda between the airport and the centre. Its gilded, cavernous worship hall held aloft by decorated pillars is pretty spectacular.

On the western side of the compound is a small ordination hall, which houses the intriguing Sachamuni Image, a bronze buddha, the surface of which is entirely encrusted with mini-buddhas. Apparently the image dates from 24 BC and is said to have been found by Mrauk U fishermen.

Rakhine State Cultural Museum
MUSEUM

(ရခိုင်ပြည်နယ်ယဉ်ေက်းမ ု ပြတိုက်; Main Rd; admission K2000; ⊘9.30am-4.30pm Tue-Sat) This museum features two floors of Rakhine cultural goodies that benefit from just enough English subtitles. On the 1st floor are displays on local customs such as models showing off some of the 64 traditional Mrauk U royal hairstyles, and drawings illustrating key moves you may need for Rakhine wrestling. The 2nd floor features diagrams and artefacts that detail Rakhine's origins (around 3000 BC) and four key periods (Dhanyawadi, Vesali, Lemro and Mrauk U), complete with useful renderings and models.

🛌 Sleeping & Eating

There aren't many hotels in Sittwe and they fill up fast, so book ahead.

Mya Guest House
HOTEL $

(☑043-22358, 043-23315; 51/6 Bowdhi Rd; s/d US$30/45; ❀) Tucked just off Sittwe's busy main road, this basic cement building has simple, spacious rooms. The more expensive have air-con but none have hot water.

Noble Hotel
HOTEL $

(☑043-23558; anw.noble@gmail.com; 45 Main Rd; s/d incl breakfast $40/60; ❀ 🛜) The rooms here are small and a little musty. But they are clean and relatively modern and are equipped with desk, satellite TV, safe and fridge.

★Aung
BURMESE $

(off Thar Bar St; curries from K3000; ⊘10am-9pm; 🍴) Located on a small street directly behind the museum, this popular, friendly place does Burmese-style set meals with an emphasis on Rakhine-style spice and tartness. You could work from the English-language menu, but pointing to whatever looks tastiest is a better strategy. The fish curries are ace.

TRANSPORT FROM SITTWE

DESTINATION	BOAT	BUS	AIR
Mandalay		K25,000, 22hr, 2 daily 6am & 7am	
Mrauk U	IWT (slow boat) US$10, 4-7hr, 7.30am Tue & Fri; private boat US$15, 4-7hr, 7.30am Mon, Thu & Sat; speedboat K25,000, 2-3hr, 7.30am Wed & Sun	K5000, 4hr, 2 daily 6am & 7am	
Thandwe		K28,000, 20hr, 1 daily	US$80, 40min, daily Oct-Apr
Yangon		K20,500, 24hr, 1 daily 8am	US$116, 75min, daily

Móun·di Stand BURMESE **$**

(May Yu St; mains K300; ⊘6am-6pm) *Móun·di*, thin rice noodles in a peppery, fish-based broth, is Rakhine State's signature noodle dish. Sittwe's best – many claim – is served at this stall (look for the green awning) facing the city hall.

⊙ Getting There & Away

Overland routes between Sittwe, Yangon, Mandalay and Mrauk U are now open to foreigners. This was a new development at the time of research and some bus companies were still refusing to sell tickets on Sittwe and Mrauk U–bound buses to foreigners. That should have changed by the time you read this.

AIR

Flights connect Sittwe with Yangon daily and Thandwe in the high season (October to April).

The airport is about 1½ miles southwest of the centre. *Thoun bein* (K5000) and taxis (K8000) await flights.

BOAT

For Mrauk U, you have a choice of the slow IWT ferries and private boats, or the faster 'speed-boat' operated by **Shwe Pyi Tan** (☑ 09 4959 2709; no roman-script sign; cnr Main Rd & U Ottama St; ⊘7am-9pm). They depart on different days, meaning there's usually a boat of some sort sailing every day of the week.

Malikha (☑ 043-24037, 043-24248; Main Rd; ⊘9am-5pm) and Shwe Pyi Tan also have fast boats to Taunggok every day bar Saturday

---

OFF THE BEATEN TRACK

CHIN VILLAGES

Day-boat excursions along the Lemro River to traditional Chin villages can be arranged in Mrauk U. It's a long day, but we found the Chin villagers a hoot – let's just say that having a web pattern tattooed on their faces (a dying cultural practice) has done nothing to diminish the sense of humour of these old ducks.

Typical trips, which the Regional Guides Society – Mrauk U or your hotel can help arrange, include a half-hour car transfer to the jetty, an approximately two-hour boat trip upstream, and an hour or so at a couple of villages. Transport and a guide, which you'll need to communicate, will run to US$100. There's not much in the way of food or drink to buy in the Chin villages so bring your own.

(US$30 to US$35, 10 to 11 hours, 6am), from where you can connect by bus with Pyay.

The main boat jetty is about 1¾ miles north of the town centre. *Thoun bein* charge K2000 per person.

BUS

Buses to Yangon, Mandalay and Mrauk U depart from the highway, a K2000 ride in a *thoun bein* from the centre of town.

Mrauk U

☑ 043 / POP 36,139

'Little Bagan?' Not by a long shot. Mrauk U (pronounced 'mraw-oo') was the Rakhine capital from 1430 to 1826, during which time hundreds of temples were built. Unlike Bagan, goat shepherds and vegetable farmers live around the ruins and still functioning temples are sited amid gorgeous lush scenery of rounded hillocks. Think laid-back smiles, no hassle and few tourists.

Wi fi is sometimes available at the Mrauk U Princess Hotel (US$3 per hour or buy a drink at the bar).

⊙ Sights

The original site of Mrauk U is spread over 17.5 sq miles, although the town today and the bulk of the 700 or so temples to visit cover a 2.7-sq-mile area. With a bike, a packed lunch and the heart for exploration, you could take any path for DIY adventures.

The sights are not always marked so an experienced guide can come in handy. Not only do many of the guides in the **Regional Guides Society – Mrauk U** (☑ 09 4217 20296, 09 4217 20168; www.facebook.com/rgs.mrauku; per day US$20) speak English well and have a good grasp on local history and culture, but they're also locally based, work independently and are dedicated to the principles of community-based tourism.

For foreign visitors to Mrauk U there's an archaeological site 'entry fee' of K5000; this is usually collected at the Shittaung Paya or at the boat jetty; on the government ferry you'll be asked to show proof of payment before leaving.

★ Shittaung Paya HISTORIC SITE

(ရှစ်သောင်းဘုရား; admission K5000; ⊘7am-5pm) The usual starting point is at this, Mrauk U's most complex temple. Shittaung means 'Shrine of the 80,000 images', a reference to the number of holy images inside. King Minbin, the most powerful of Rakhine's

Mraukū U

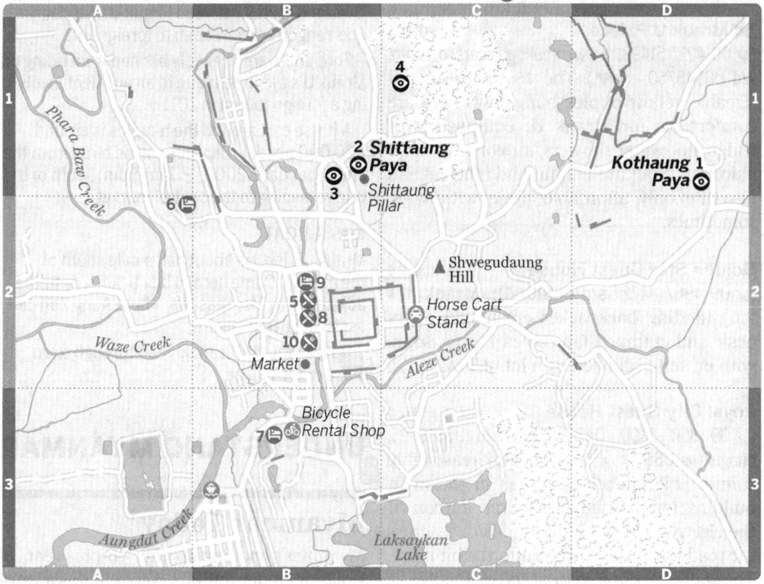

kings, built Shittaung in 1535. It's a frenzy of stupas of various sizes; some 26 surround a central stupa. Thick walls, with windows and nooks, surround the two-tiered structure, which has been highly reconstructed over the centuries – in some places, rather clumsily.

★Kothaung Paya HISTORIC SITE
(ကိုးသောင်းဘုရား; ⊙daylight hours) FREE One of Mrauk U's star attractions, Kothaung Paya is also the area's largest temple. It was built in 1553 by King Minbin's son, King Mintaikkha, to outdo his pop's Shittaung by 10,000 images ('Kothaung' means 'Shrine of 90,000 images').

Kothaung Paya is located a mile or so east of the palace; follow the road directly north of the market, veering left on the much smaller road before the bridge.

Dukkanthein Paya HISTORIC SITE
(ထုတ်ခံသိမ်ဘုရား; ⊙daylight hours) FREE Built by King Minphalaung in 1571, Dukkanthein Paya smacks of a bunker (with stupas). Wide stone steps lead up the southern and eastern sides of the building considered to be an ordination hall; take the eastern side steps to reach the entrance.

Mrauk U

Top Sights

1	Kothaung Paya	D1
2	Shittaung Paya	B1

Sights

3	Dukkanthein Paya	B1
4	Mahabodhi Shwegu	C1

Sleeping

5	Golden Star Guest House	B2
6	Mrauk U Palace	A2
7	Royal City Guest House	B3

Eating

8	For You	B2
9	Happy Garden	B2
10	Kaung Thant	B2

Mahabodhi Shwegu HISTORIC SITE
(မဟာဗောဓိရွှေဂူ; ⊙daylight hours) FREE The highlight of this squat, little-visited temple is its passageway with bas-relief illustrations of the tribumi – Buddhist visions of heaven, earth and hell – including acrobats, worshippers and animals. At the end there's a 6ft central buddha and four buddhas in niches; the throne of the former includes some erotic carvings.

🛏 Sleeping & Eating

★ Mrauk U Palace
HOTEL $

(☎09 4217 51498; www.mraukupalaceresort.com; s/d US$45/50; ❄🛜) The 18 identical and sizeable yellow duplex bungalows here are comfortable for Mrauk U: equipped with fridge, hot-water showers, air-con and small balconies. Staff are helpful and efficient. It's also the only affordable place with wi-fi, sometimes.

Golden Star Guest House
GUESTHOUSE $

(☎09 4967 4472; s/d US$10/20) Mrauk U's longstanding backpacker crash pad offers basic and cramped fan-cooled rooms, some with en suite, all needing a lot of TLC.

Royal City Guest House
HOTEL $

(☎09 850 2400, 043-24200; s/d US$10/25, bungalows US$40; ❄) Clean and reasonably comfortable fan-cooled rooms in the main building for the budget set, and air-con (if the electricity is working) bungalows across the road for those who can afford a bit more. The staff give out a map of the main sites.

Happy Garden
BURMESE, CHINESE $

(dishes from K2500; ⊗8am-11pm; 🍴) This beer-garden-style joint is the most lively spot in town come nightfall. The Chinese-sounding dishes are tasty enough, and there are a few Burmese options too. Fine for a beer as well. It rents five basic bungalows (K15,000) as well.

For You
BURMESE, CHINESE $

(mains from K1500; ⊗8am-10pm) Chinese-inspired dishes at this homely place. A good spot for morning noodles.

Kaung Thant
BURMESE $

(curries from K2500; ⊗9am-10pm) A bare-bones Burmese-style curry shop at the foot of the bridge just north of the market, 'Good and Clean' does Rakhine-style set meals served by a local family. Look for the partially hidden English sign.

ℹ Getting There & Around

Overland routes between Mrauk U, Mandalay and Yangon are now open to foreigners.

Foreigners are allegedly banned from riding on Mrauk U's *thoun bein* due to an accident involving a foreign tourist in 2011.

A horse cart around the temples is around K20,000 per day. Bicycles can be hired from the **shop** (per day K2000; ⊗7am-6pm) south of the bridge leading to the central market.

BUS & BOAT

Mrauk U's jetty is about half a mile south of the market. Come here to buy tickets, or to the adjacent Hay Mar teashop, where Aung Zan can assist in buying tickets.

Buses stop on the main road through town, close to the palace.

UNDERSTAND MYANMAR

Myanmar Today

Myanmar's opening up after 40-plus years of isolation under military rule remains a work in progress. For all the positive steps taken, Myanmar still has a constitution designed to exclude Aung San Suu Kyi, the country's most popular politician, from the presidency and which guarantees the army 25% of all seats in parliament.

But with the Aung San Suu Kyi–led National League for Democracy (NLD) winning a crushing victory in the November 2015 general election, there was cautious optimism that changes for the better are on their way.

Nevertheless, human rights abuses are still prevalent, as is corruption, while there is increasing animosity between Buddhists and Muslims. And there is no end in sight to the long-running conflicts between the government and some of the ethnic armies in the borderlands.

TRANSPORT FROM MRAUK U

DESTINATION	BUS	BOAT
Mandalay	K25,000, 22hr, 2 daily 9am & 10am	
Sittwe	K5000, 4hr, 2 daily 2pm & 4pm	IWT (slow boat) US$10, 4-7hr, 7am Wed & Sat; private boat US$15, 4-7hr, 7am Sun, Tue & Fri; speedboat K25,000, 2-3hr, 7am Mon & Thu
Yangon	K20,500, 24hr, 1 daily 9am	

So far, the major positives of Myanmar's opening up have been economic. Foreign investment and aid has jumped dramatically, especially from China, the EU and Japan. But many rural dwellers still subsist on as little as US$2 a day and it will likely be decades before they start to benefit from the political and economic reforms launched since 2011.

History

Long before the British took control of Burma in three successive wars in the 19th century, the area was ruled over by several major ethnic groups, with the Bamar only coming into prominence in the 11th century. Britain managed the mountainous border regions separately from the fertile plains and delta of central and lower Burma, building on a cultural rift between the lowland Bamar and highland ethnic groups that lingers today. Civil war erupted between minority groups after independence in 1948, and continues still in pockets of the country.

General Ne Win wrested control from the elected government in 1962 and began the world's longest-running military dictatorship, which pursued xenophobic policies, leading Burma to full isolation. State socialism ruined the economy, necessitating several major currency devaluations, the last of which sparked massive, yet peaceful, street protests in 1988.

The pro-democracy marches saw Aung San Suu Kyi, daughter of independence hero General Aung San, emerge as the leader of the National League for Democracy (NLD). The military allowed a national election in 1990 in which the NLD won 82% of the assembly seats, but refused to transfer power, placed Aung San Suu Kyi under house arrest and imprisoned many elected politicians and student leaders.

Despite Western sanctions, the generals continued to rule for the next two decades. But the junta's brutal reaction to the 2007 protests (the failed 'Saffron Revolution') and its shameful response to Cyclone Nargis in 2008, the worst natural disaster ever to befall the nation, caused it to become even more despised and feared.

An election in October 2010 brought in the quasi-civilian Union Solidarity and Development Party (USDP) to replace the junta. It was the first general election for 20 years but the UN described the poll as 'deep-

ly flawed'. Former general and prime minister Thein Sein was 'chosen' to be president.

The USDP guaranteed to undertake political and economic reforms in return for the West lifting sanctions. Most political prisoners have been released, but critics at home and abroad point to the reluctance of the military to step back from politics.

The NLD won a historic landslide victory in the November 2015 general election. At the time of writing, no decision had been taken on who will be Myanmar's next president. But while Aung San Suu Kyi remains barred from the presidency under a law that bans people with foreign spouses from taking power (her late husband was British), she has vowed to run Myanmar anyway, something that may put her and the NLD on a collision course with the still-powerful military.

People & Culture

Myanmar people are as proud of their country and culture as any nationality on earth. Locals gush over ancient kings, *pwe* (theatre), *mohinga* (noodles with chicken or fish) breakfasts, great temples and Buddhism. A typical Burmese Buddhist values meditation, gives alms freely and sees his or her lot as the consequence of sin or merit in a past life. The social ideal for most Burmese is a standard of behaviour commonly termed *bamahsan chin* (Burmese-ness). The hallmarks of *bamahsan chin* include showing respect for elders, acquaintance with Buddhist scriptures and discretion in behaviour towards the opposite sex. Most importantly, *bamahsan chin* values the quiet, subtle and indirect over the loud, obvious and direct.

DOS & DON'TS

➡ Don't touch anyone's head; it's considered the spiritual pinnacle of the body.

➡ Don't point feet at people if you can help it, and avoid stepping over people.

➡ Hand things – food, gifts, money – with your right hand, tucking your left under your right elbow.

➡ Dress modestly when visiting religious sites – avoid above-the-knee shorts, tight clothes or sleeveless shirts.

➡ Take off your shoes when entering temple precincts, usually including the long steps up to a hilltop pagoda.

Lifestyle

About three-quarters of Myanmar's population are rural-dwellers, where life revolves around villages and farming. Here, national politics pale in comparison to the season, the crop or the level of the river (used for bathing, washing and drinking water). People are known for helping each other when in need, and call each other 'brother' and 'sister' affectionately.

Families tend to be large; you might find three or four generations of one family living in a two- or three-room house. The birth of a child is a big occasion. Girls are as equally welcome as boys, if not more so, as they're expected to look after parents later in life. Some thatched huts in the countryside have generators, powering electric light and pumping life into the TV a couple of hours a night; many don't. Running water outside the cities and bigger towns is rare.

Life is much more 21st century in Yangon and Mandalay but even these big cities suffer power outages. The extremes of Myanmar's wealth and poverty are very apparent too in the urban centres.

Population

A 2014 census listed the population of Myanmar as 51,419,420. But this total included estimates for regions – parts of Kachin, Rakhine and Shan States – which were not surveyed. It is likely that the real figure is closer to 60 million.

There are 135 officially recognised ethnic groups in Myanmar. The most numerous of those groups are the Bamar, who make up around 68% of the population. Other major groups include the Shan, Kayin, Rakhine, Mon, Kayah and Kachin. There are also large numbers of Burmese Indians and Chinese, whose ancestors arrived mostly in the colonial era.

Under the 2008 constitution Myanmar is divided into seven regions (they used to be called divisions; these are where the Bamar are in the majority) and seven states (minority regions, namely Chin, Kachin, Kayah, Kayin, Mon, Rakhine and Shan States). In addition, there are six ethnic enclaves (Danu, Kokang, Naga, Palaung, Pa-O and Wa) with varying degrees of self-governance.

Religion

Freedom of religion is guaranteed under the country's constitution. But around 89% of Myanmar's citizens are Theravada Buddhists and the religion is given special status. The other major religions are Islam and Christianity. Many rural people believe also in *nat* spirits, a relic of the animist religions followed before Buddhism.

There has been an alarming upsurge in religious intolerance since Myanmar's opening up, driven by extreme Buddhist nationalists. Muslims have been the main target. In July 2015 a controversial new law was passed requiring Buddhist women to obtain official permission before marrying someone of a different faith.

BUDDHISM

For the average Burmese Buddhist much of life revolves around the merit (*kutho,* from the Pali *kusala,* meaning 'wholesome') that is accumulated through rituals and good deeds. One of the more common rituals performed by individuals visiting a stupa is to pour water over the buddha image at their astrological post (determined by the day of the week they were born) – one glassful for every year of their current age plus one extra to ensure a long life.

Every Burmese male is expected to take up temporary monastic residence twice in his life: once as a *samanera* (novice monk), between the ages of five and 15, and again

---

BURMA OR MYANMAR?

What to call the Republic of the Union of Myanmar (the country's official name as of 2011) has been a political flashpoint since 1989. That was the year in which the military junta dumped Burma, the name commonly used since the mid-19th century, along with a slew of other British colonial-era place names such as Rangoon, Pagan, Bassein and Arakan.

The UN recognises Myanmar as the nation's official name. But nearly all opposition groups (including the NLD), many ethnic groups and several key nations including the USA and UK continue to refer to it as Burma.

We go with Myanmar, with Burma used for periods before 1989. 'Burmese' refers to the Bamar people, the food and the language.

MYANMAR READING LIST

To grasp Myanmar's political and social complexities, doing some advance reading is highly recommended. Pick up Lonely Planet's *Myanmar (Burma)* for more comprehensive coverage of the country, and the helpful *Burmese Phrasebook*. Other recommended titles:

➡ *Burma/Myanmar: What Everyone Needs to Know* by David Steinberg has a series of concise and understandable Q&As on Myanmar's history and culture. Make sure you get the updated second edition.

➡ *River of Lost Footsteps: A Personal History of Burma* by Thant Myint U mixes his family history with that of Myanmar in this elegiac read.

➡ *Golden Parasol* by Wendy Law-Yone is a fascinating memoir that provides an insider's view on key events in modern Myanmar's history.

as a *pongyi* (fully ordained monk), some time after the age of 20. Almost all men or boys under 20 years of age participate in the *shinpyu* (initiation ceremony), through which their family earns great merit.

While there is little social expectation that they should do so, a number of women live monastic lives as *dasasila* ('ten-precept' nuns). Burmese nuns shave their heads, wear pink robes and take vows in an ordination procedure similar to that undertaken by monks.

NAT WORSHIP

Buddhism in Myanmar has overtaken, but never entirely replaced, the pre-Buddhist practice of *nat* worship. The 37 *nat* figures are often found side by side with Buddhist images. The Burmese *nat* are spirits that can inhabit natural features, trees or even people. They can be mischievous or beneficent.

The *nat* cult is strong. Mt Popa is an important centre. The Burmese divide their devotions and offerings according to the sphere of influence: Buddha for future lives, and the *nat* – both Hindu and Bamar – for problems in this life. A misdeed might be redressed with offerings to the *nat* Thagyamin, who annually records the names of those who perform good deeds in a book made of gold leaves. Those who commit evil are recorded in a book made of dog skin.

Arts

For centuries the arts in Myanmar were sponsored by the royal courts, mainly through the construction of major religious buildings that required the skills of architects, sculptors, painters and a variety of craftspeople. Such patronage was cut short during British colonial rule and has not been a priority since independence. This said, there are plenty of examples of traditional art to be viewed in Myanmar, mainly in the temples that are an ever-present feature of town and countryside. There's also a growing contemporary art scene, particularly in Yangon.

MARIONETTE THEATRE

Yok-thei pwe (Burmese marionette theatre) was the forerunner of Burmese classical dance. Marionette theatre declined following WWII and is now mostly confined to tourist venues in Yangon, Mandalay and Bagan.

MUSIC

Traditional Burmese music relies heavily on rhythm and is short on harmony, at least to the Western ear. Younger Burmese listen to Western-influenced sounds – you will often hear Burmese-language covers of classic oldies, as well as sappy love or pop tunes. A number of Burmese rock musicians, such as Lay Phyu of the band Iron Cross, produce serious songs of their own, while groups such as the Me N Ma Girls mimic the boy and girl bands of South Korea.

PWE

The *pwe* (show) is everyday Burmese theatre. A religious festival, wedding, funeral, celebration, fair, sporting event – almost any gathering – is a good excuse for a *pwe*. Once underway, a *pwe* traditionally goes on all night. If an audience member is flaking at some point during the performance, they simply fall asleep. To experience one, ask a trishaw driver if a *pwe* is on nearby.

Myanmar's truly indigenous dance forms are those that pay homage to the *nat*. In a special *nat pwe*, one or more *nat* are invited to possess the body and mind of a medium.

Sometimes members of the audience seem to be possessed instead, an event greatly feared by most Burmese.

Environment

Myanmar covers an area of 261,000 sq miles, which is roughly the size of Texas or France. From the snowcapped Himalaya in the north to the coral-fringed Myeik (Mergui) Archipelago in the south, Myanmar's length of 1250 miles crosses three distinct ecological regions, producing what is probably the richest biodiversity in Southeast Asia.

Unfortunately, that wildlife – which includes a third of the world's Asiatic elephants and the largest tiger reserve on the planet – is threatened by habitat loss. Rampant deforestation by the timber industry, which occurs in order to feed demand in China and Thailand, is a primary cause. Optimistically, about 7% of the country is protected in national parks and other protected areas, but most of these are just lines on maps. Wildlife laws in Myanmar are seldom enforced, due to a desperate lack of funding.

For travellers, seeing wildlife will be more a matter of luck than design. And without some serious cash, forget about visiting national parks.

Food & Drink

Food

Mainstream Burmese cuisine represents a blend of Bamar, Mon, Indian and Chinese influences. A typical meal has *htamin* (rice) as its core, eaten with a choice of *hin* (curry dishes), most commonly fish, chicken, pork, prawns or mutton. Soup is always served, along with a table full of condiments (including pickled veggies as spicy dipping sauces).

Most Burmese food is pretty mild on the chilli front, with cooks favouring a simple masala of turmeric, ginger, garlic, salt and onions, plus plenty (and we mean loads!) of peanut oil and shrimp paste. *Balachaung* (chillies, tamarind and dried shrimp pounded together) or the pungent *ngapi kyaw* (spicy shrimp paste with garlic) is always nearby to add some kick. Almost everything savoury in Burmese cooking is flavoured with *ngapi* (a salty paste concocted from dried and fermented shrimp or fish).

Noodle dishes are often eaten for breakfast or as light snacks between meals. The seafood served along the coasts is some of the best and cheapest you'll find in the entire region.

Drink
NON-ALCOHOLIC DRINKS
Teashops, a national institution, are good places to meet people over a drink and inexpensive snacks such as *nam-bya* and *palata* (flat breads) or Chinese fried pastries. Burmese tea (about K300 a cup), brewed Indian-style with lots of condensed milk and sugar, is the national drink. Ask for *lahpeq ye* (tea with a dollop of condensed milk); *cho bouk* is less sweet, and *kyauk padaung* is very sweet. Most restaurants will provide as much free Chinese tea as you can handle. Real coffee is limited to modern, Western-style cafes in Yangon and other large cities. Sugar cane juice is a very popular streetside drink.

MOUTH-WATERING SNACKS

Fancy yourself as an adventurous eater? Seek out *tha yei za* (mouth-watering snacks) at night markets in Yangon and street stalls around the country. Desserts are common, and come in the form of multicoloured sticky-rice sweets, poppy seed cakes, banana puddings and the like. Others test local claims that 'anything that walks on the ground can be eaten' – not to mention any claims you might have to 'hardcore traveller' status – and are definitely in the unidentified frying object category:

Wek thaa douk htoe (barbecue stands) Street stalls selling sliced-up pig.

Pa-yit kyaw (fried cricket) Sold on skewers or in a 10-pack for about K500.

Bi-laar (beetle) Prepared like crickets; locals suggest 'suck the stomach out, then chew the head part'.

Thin baun poe (larva) Insect larvae, culled from bamboo, are lightly grilled and served still wriggling.

ALCOHOL

Myanmar Beer is a little lighter in flavour and alcohol than other Southeast Asian beers. Mandalay Beer is weaker still.

There are a variety of stronger liquors, including the harsh local version of whisky. Then there's the rum produced in Mandalay, and the fermented palm juice known as toddy.

Popular in Shan State is a pleasant-tasting orange brandy called *shwe leinmaw* that packs quite a punch. There are a couple of vineyards making wine, and in Pyin Oo Lwin there are several sweet, fruit-based wines.

SURVIVAL GUIDE

ⓘ Directory A–Z

ACCOMMODATION

The cheapest places are very plain; think concrete floors, squashed mosquitoes on the walls, a fan and a shared bathroom down the hall, with a basic breakfast. For a few dollars more you get hot water, a private bathroom, air-con and sometimes TV. These, however, will be of limited value unless your lodging has a generator; electricity supplies are sketchy right across Myanmar.

Many hotels and guesthouses quote prices in US dollars. Almost all accept kyat and new regulations taking effect from the end of 2015 mean many hotels and guesthouses are likely to stop accepting payment in dollars in the near future. Prices listed in reviews are for peak season, roughly October to March. Discounts are normally available in the low season (April to September); haggle gently if planning a longer stay. Passport and visa details are required at check-in, but hotels don't need to hold your passport.

All accommodation supposedly must be licensed to accept foreign guests, meaning the cheapest places are usually off limits. In out-of-the-way towns, some unlicensed guesthouses will accept weary travellers.

Price Ranges

The following price ranges are for a double room. Note that most hotels charge one price for foreigners and another for locals.

$ less than K64,000/US$50

$$ K64,000 to K192,000/US$50 to US$150 (in Yangon K64,000 to K256,000/US$50 to US$200)

$$$ more than K192,000/US$150 (in Yangon more than K256,000/US$200)

CUSTOMS REGULATIONS

Any foreign currency of US$10,000 or more is supposed to be declared upon entry. Genuine antiques cannot be taken out of the country.

DRINKING WATER

Only drink purified water. Be wary of ice in remote areas, though it is usually factory-produced in towns and cities. Bottled water costs from K300 a litre and is widely available. Consider sterilising your water, and saving dozens of PET bottles, by using a UV sterilising wand.

ELECTRICITY

Connect (when it's working) to the electricity supply (230V, 50Hz AC). Many hotels have generators (some run at night only). Local power sources in many towns are scheduled for night hours only.

EMBASSIES & CONSULATES

Most foreign embassies and consulates are in Yangon. Check the government's Ministry of Foreign Affairs (www.mofa.gov.mm) for more information.

Australian Embassy (Map p484; ☑ 01-251 810; www.burma.embassy.gov.au; 88 Strand Rd, Kyauktada)

Bangladeshi Embassy (Map p490; ☑ 01-515 275; www.bdembassyyangon.org; 11B Than Lwin Rd, Kamayut)

Chinese Embassy (Map p490; ☑ 01-221 281; http://mm.china-embassy.org/eng; 1 Pyidaungsu Yeiktha Rd, Dagon)

French Embassy (Map p488; ☑ 01-212 520; www.ambafrance-mm.org; 102 Pyidaungsu Yeiktha Rd, Dagon)

German Embassy (Map p490; ☑ 01-548 952; www.rangun.diplo.de; 9 Bogyoke Aung San Museum Rd, Bahan)

Indian Embassy (Map p484; ☑ 01-391 219; www.indiaembassyyangon.net; 545-547 Merchant St, Kyauktada)

Japanese Embassy (Map p490; ☑ 01-549 644; http://www.mm.emb-japan.go.jp; 100 Nat Mauk Rd, Bahan)

New Zealand Embassy (☑ 01-230 5805; YangonOffice@mft.net.nz; 43 Inya Myiang Rd, Bahan)

Thai Embassy (Map p490; ☑ 01-226 721; www.thaiembassy.org/yangon/en; 94 Pyay Rd, Dagon)

UK Embassy (Map p484; ☑ 01-370 867, 01-370 865; www.gov.uk/government/world/burma; 80 Strand Rd, Kyauktada)

US Embassy (Map p482; ☑ 01-536 509; http://burma.usembassy.gov; 110 University Ave, Kamayut)

FESTIVAL & EVENTS

Myanmar follows a 12-month lunar calendar, and most festivals are on the full moon of the Burmese month in which they occur – hence shifting dates. The build-up to festivals can go on for days.

February/March

Shwedagon Festival Myanmar's largest *paya* festival takes place in Yangon.

March/April

Full-Moon Festival Biggest event of the year at Shwemawdaw Paya in Bago.

April/May

Buddha's Birthday The full moon also marks the day of Buddha's enlightenment and his entry to nirvana. One of the best places to observe this ceremony is at Yangon's Shwedagon Paya.

Thingyan (Water Festival) The Burmese New Year is the biggest holiday of the year, celebrated with a raucous nationwide water fight. It is impossible to go outside without getting drenched, so just join the fun. Businesses close and some transport – especially buses – stops running for around a week.

June/July

Buddhist Lent Start of the Buddhist Rains Retreat. Laypeople present monasteries with new robes, because during the three-month Lent period monks are restricted to their monasteries.

July/August

Wagaung Festival Nationwide exercise in alms-giving.

September/October

Thadingyut Celebrates Buddha's return from a period of preaching.

October/November

Tazaungdaing The biggest 'festival of lights' sees all Myanmar lit by oil lamps, fire balloons, candles and even mundane electric lamps.

Kathein A one-month period at the end of Buddhist Lent during which new monastic robes and requisites are offered to the monastic community.

December/January

Kayin New Year Karen communities throughout Myanmar celebrate by wearing their traditional dress and by hosting folk-dancing and singing performances. Big celebrations are held in the Karen suburb of Insein, just north of Yangon, and in Hpa-an.

Ananda Festival Held at the Ananda Pahto in Bagan at the full moon.

FOOD

The following price ranges refer to main dishes.

$ less than K6400/US$5
$$ K6400 to K19,200/US$5 to US$15
$$$ more than K19,200/US$15

INTERNET ACCESS

Online access has improved, with wi-fi becoming the norm – most hotels, guesthouses and cafes have it for free – and the internet is now spreading to more remote locations such as Mrauk U.

But with tightly squeezed bandwidth and power outages it can often be a frustrating exercise to send and receive emails or surf the internet, particularly in rural areas. Streaming and big downloads remain problematic.

LEGAL MATTERS

If you are arrested, you will most likely be permitted to contact your embassy in Myanmar for possible assistance.

If you purchase gems or jewellery from persons or shops that are not licensed by the government, you run the risk of having them confiscated if customs officials find them in your baggage when you're exiting the country.

Forming public assemblies of more than two people without the prior permission of the authorities is illegal. Drug-trafficking crimes are punishable by death.

LGBT TRAVELLERS

Gay and transgendered people in Myanmar are rarely 'out', except for 'third sex' spirit mediums who channel the energies of *nat* spirits. As elsewhere, it can be seen as a bit of a cultural taboo, though most of Myanmar's ethnic groups are known to be tolerant of homosexuality, both male and female. A local woman walking with a foreign man will raise more eyebrows than two same-sex travellers sharing a room. Public displays of affection, whether heterosexual or homosexual, are frowned upon. Utopia-Asia (www.utopia-asia.com) has some Yangon scene reports.

MAPS

Periplus Editions (scale 1:2,000,000), ITMB (1:1,350,000) and Nelles (1:1,500,000) all make dedicated maps of Myanmar.

Design Printing Services (www.dpsmap.com) prints useful tourist maps of Myanmar, Yangon, Mandalay and Bagan; sometimes these maps are sold locally for about K1000 or given away by tour agencies, at hotels and international gateway airports.

ℹ MEASUREMENTS

Petrol is sold by the gallon; distances are in miles, not kilometres; 1 Burmese viss or 100 tical = 3.5lb (1.6kg); 1 gaig = 36 inches (91cm).

MEDIA

Read the daily English-language newspaper *Myanmar Times* (www.mmtimes.com) and the online news sites Democratic Voice of Burma (www.dvb.no), Irrawaddy (www.irrawaddy.org) and Mizzima (www.mizzima.com).

MONEY

Prices listed alternate between kyat (K) and US dollars (US$), depending on the currency in which prices are quoted.

Banks & ATMs

The most useful of the local banks (which are open 9.30am to 3pm Monday to Friday) are CB and KBZ, both of which accept MasterCard and Visa cards and have ATMs in which you can use overseas cards for a K5000 charge per transaction. You'll find these ATMs all across Yangon and in other cities and tourist spots.

Credit Cards & Travellers Cheques

Credit cards and travellers cheques remain largely useless. However, the situation is rapidly changing and in Yangon and other major tourist spots you'll increasingly find credit cards accepted by top-end hotels, restaurants and some shops.

Moneychangers

Private, licensed exchange booths can be found at places such as Yangon and Mandalay airports, Bogyoke Aung San Market and Shwedagon Paya in Yangon.

Never hand over your money until you've received the kyat and counted them. Honest moneychangers will expect you to do this. Considering that K10,000 is the highest denomination, you'll get a lot of notes. Moneychangers give ready-made, rubber-banded stacks of a hundred K1000 bills. It's a good idea to check each note individually. Often you'll find one or two (or more) with a cut corner or taped tears, neither of which anyone will accept.

Tipping

Tipping is not customary, though little extra 'presents' are sometimes expected (even if they're not asked for) in exchange for a service (such as unlocking a locked temple at Bagan, helping move a bag at the airport or showing you around the 'sights' of a village).

Have some small notes (K50, K100, K200) handy when visiting temples or monasteries for donations.

OPENING HOURS

Government offices (including post offices and telephone centres) 9.30am to 4.30pm Monday to Friday

Shops 9.30am to 6pm or later Monday to Saturday

Restaurants 8am to 9pm

ⓘ BRING NEW BILLS!

We cannot stress enough the need to bring pristine 'new' US dollar bills to Myanmar – that means no folds, creases, tears and pen or other marks on the notes, and they should be post-2006, the ones with the larger full-frame heads. Anything else risks being rejected by moneychangers and banks.

PHOTOGRAPHY & VIDEO

Most internet cafes can burn digital photos onto a CD for about K1000. Certain sights, including some pagodas, charge small camera fees. Avoid taking photos of military facilities, uniformed individuals, and strategic locations such as bridges.

POST

Sending mail out of Myanmar is a hit-and-miss affair. But international postage rates are a bargain: a postcard is K500, a 1kg package to Australia/UK/US is K16,200/18,900/20,700.

Post offices are supposed to be open from 9.30am to 4.30pm Monday to Friday, but you may find some keep shorter hours.

In Yangon, DHL (p492) is a more reliable but expensive way of sending out bigger packages.

PUBLIC HOLIDAYS

Major public holidays:

Independence Day 4 January

Union Day 12 February

Peasants' Day 2 March

Armed Forces Day 27 March

Workers' Day 1 May

Martyrs' Day 19 July

National Day 27 November

Christmas Day 25 December

SAFE TRAVEL

Theft remains quite rare and usually the only time a local will be running with your money or belongings is if they're chasing you down the road with something you've dropped.

However, don't tempt fate in this poor country by flashing valuables or leaving them unguarded. The only real scams are dodgy moneychangers shortchanging you, and drivers or guides getting a commission for purchases at any shops you visit.

Areas around the Myanmar–Thai and Myanmar–China borders, home to the country's notorious drug trade, can be dangerous (and off limits) to explore.

Power outages are highly annoying and commonplace everywhere except the surreal capital, Nay Pyi Taw. Many businesses have their own generators, but check with your guesthouse whether the power will be on all night, especially in the hot season.

The poor state of road and rail infrastructure, plus lax safety standards and procedures for flights and boats, means that travelling can sometimes be dangerous.

TELEPHONE
Local Calls

Most business cards purposely list a couple of phone numbers, and often a mobile (cell) phone number, as lines frequently go dead and calls just don't go through.

Local call stands – as part of a shop, or sometimes just a table with a phone or two on a pavement – can be found all over Myanmar. A local call should be K100 per minute.

To dial long distance within Myanmar, dial the area code (including the '0') and the number.

International Calls

You can call abroad using a local SIM card or via international roaming. The mobile phone companies offer deals starting as low as K200 a minute, depending on where you're calling.

To call Myanmar from abroad, dial your country's international access code, then ✆ 95 (Myanmar's country code), the area code (minus the '0') and the five- or six-digit number.

Mobile Phones

Mobile-phone numbers begin with ✆ 09.

It's now easy and cheap to buy a SIM card in Yangon and Mandalay that will enable you to make calls and access the internet. Ooredoo, Telenor and the state-run MPT are the three mobile phone providers. SIM card prices start at K1500. Top-up cards can be bought at many street stalls or convenience stores in denominations of K1000, K3000 and K5000.

Make sure your phone is unlocked in your home country so you can use a local SIM.

A lack of infrastructure means that some rural areas can be mobile phone black spots.

TIME

Local Myanmar Standard Time (MST) is 6½ hours ahead of Greenwich Mean Time (GMT/UTC). When coming in from Thailand, turn your watch back half an hour; coming from India, put your watch forward an hour.

TOILETS

In most out-of-the-way places, Burmese toilets are often squat jobs, generally in a cobweb-filled outhouse that is reached by a dirt path behind a restaurant. In guesthouses and hotels you will usually find Western-style thrones. Toilet paper is widely available but consider carrying an emergency stash. Either way, don't flush it.

TOURIST INFORMATION

Myanmar Travels & Tours, part of the Ministry of Hotels & Tourism, is the main 'tourist information' service with offices in Yangon (p492), Mandalay (p516), New Bagan (MTT; Map p522; ✆ 061-65040; ⊙ 8.30am-4.30pm) and Inle Lake. Other than at Yangon, these offices are pretty quiet, and often the staff have sketchy knowledge on restricted areas.

Travellers who want to arrange a driver, or have hotel reservations awaiting them, would do well to arrange a trip with the help of private travel agents in Yangon and other major cities.

TRAVELLERS WITH DISABILITIES

Myanmar is a tricky country for mobility-impaired travellers. Pavements barely exist, wheelchair ramps are virtually unheard of and public transport is crowded and can be difficult, even for the fully ambulatory.

USEFUL WEBSITES

7 Days in Myanmar (http://7daysinmyanmar.com) Multimedia showcase for the country crafted by 30 internationally renowned photographers in April 2013.

Go Myanmar (http://go-myanmar.com) Up-to-date travel related information and advice.

Myanmar Image Gallery (http://myanmar-image.com) Pictures and text on many Myanmar topics.

Online Burma/Myanmar Library (http://burmalibrary.org) Database of books and articles on Myanmar.

VISAS

Everyone requires a visa to visit Myanmar. If you're applying for a tourist visa (valid 28 days) at home, you should start the process no later than three weeks before your trip, or a month before to be safe.

If you're already travelling, it's possible to get a tourist visa at short notice from the Myanmar embassy in Bangkok (p784); the cost is 1360B for same day processing, 1135B for the next day.

E Visa

Citizens of 100 countries can apply online for tourist visas via Myanmar's Ministry of Immigration and Population website (http://evisa.moip.gov.mm/index.aspx).

The cost is US$50. After your application is processed, you'll be emailed an approval letter. Print it out and give it to the passport official on arrival at the airport and you'll be stamped into the country.

Note that it is only possible to enter Myanmar on an e visa at Yangon, Mandalay and Nay Pyi Taw international airports, but you can exit the country at any overland border crossing (although you will need a permit and permission to exit to China).

RESPONSIBLE TRAVEL

➡ Travel independently or in small groups rather than in a big tour group.

➡ Support small independent businesses and those that have charitable and sustainable tourism programs in place.

➡ Spread your money around, ie hire different guides at each destination.

➡ Talk to locals but take their lead on the substance of the conversation.

➡ Contribute to local charitable causes.

➡ Be environmentally conscious in your travel choices, ie opt for buses, trains and river cruises over flights, avoid using air-conditioning.

➡ Be sensitive to, and respectful of, local customs and behaviour, ie dress and act appropriately when visiting religious sites and rural villages.

➡ Read up about Myanmar's history, culture and current situation.

➡ Check out Dos & Don'ts For Tourists (www.dosanddontsfortourists.com).

Citizens of 50 countries can also apply online for business visas, but you'll need a letter of invitation from a sponsoring company and proof of your company registration or business.

Applications

All visas are valid for up to three months from the date of issue and most embassies and consulates need at least a week to process an application.

Postal applications are usually OK, but it's best to check first with your nearest embassy about their specific application rules.

There is no need for you to conceal your profession on the visa application form, although journalists may want to put down a different job.

Visa Extensions & Overstaying

At the time of writing, it was not possible to extend a tourist visa.

Some travellers extend their trips by overstaying their visa. This is not normally a problem, as long as you don't overstay for weeks. You will be fined US$3 a day, plus a US$3 registration fee, at the airport or land border as you exit the country. The fine can be paid in kyat as well.

However, some hotels won't take guests who have overstayed their visas and domestic airlines may be unwilling to let you on planes. If you are overstaying, it's wise to stick with land routes and places within easy access of Yangon. There have been cases in the past of tourists being instructed to leave the country immediately if their visa has expired.

VOLUNTEERING

Official opportunities to volunteer are limited. A list of NGOs that may have volunteering opportunities can be found at www.ngo.mycitizen.net, although most postings require specific skills and experience. Also browse the links at Burma Volunteer Program (http://burmavolunteers.org).

Everyone in Myanmar wants to learn English, and few can afford to. Ask in towns or villages to sit in at an English class.

WOMEN TRAVELLERS

Women travelling alone are more likely to be helped than harassed. In some areas you'll be regarded with friendly curiosity – and asked, with sad-eyed sympathy, 'Are you only one?' – because Burmese women tend to travel in mobs.

At remote religious sites, a single foreign woman may be 'adopted' by a Burmese woman, who will take you and show you the highlights. At some sites, such as Mandalay's Mahamuni Paya and Golden Rock, 'ladies' are not permitted to the central shrine; signs will indicate if this is the case.

ⓘ Getting There & Away

AIR

International flights arrive at Yangon (Rangoon; RGN), Mandalay (MDL) and Nay Pyi Taw (NPT) airports. The most common route is via Bangkok, though there are regular direct flights with several other regional cities including Singapore and Kuala Lumpur. Good deals are often available on budget airlines such as AirAsia and Nok Air.

LAND

Exiting Myanmar by a land border to Thailand at the four regular crossings – Tachileik, Myawaddy, Kauthaung and Hteke – is now hassle-free. But if you want to exit to China, you will require a permit, a 'guide' and plenty of advance notice.

ⓘ Getting Around

Unless you fly, all travel in Myanmar takes time. Often lots of time. Large areas of the country are off limits, or accessible only with permission. Securing such permission:

➡ Takes time – a minimum of at least two weeks but more commonly around a month.

➡ Requires the help of an experienced travel agency.

➡ Always involves paying fees to the government, usually via the government-owned travel agency MTT, even if you're dealing with another agency.

➡ Usually means dancing to MTT's tune when it comes to how you visit the area in question and who you go with.

Sometimes areas that were possible to visit with or without a permit suddenly become off limits: that's how it is in Myanmar.

AIR

Travel agents sell flight tickets at a slightly discounted rate, so it usually makes little sense to buy directly from the airlines, whether online or at their offices.

It's sometimes difficult to buy a ticket that departs from a town other than the one you are in. There is no domestic departure tax.

Major domestic carriers:

Air Bagan (www.airbagan.com)
Air KBZ (www.airkbz.com)
Air Mandalay (www.airmandalay.com)
Asian Wings Airways (www.asianwingsair.com)
Golden Myanmar Airlines (www.gmairlines.com)
Myanmar National Airlines (www.flymna.com)
Yangon Airways (www.yangonair.com)

BOAT

There are 5000 miles of navigable river in Myanmar and, unlike elsewhere in Asia, slow boats remain a vital transport link here. Even in the dry season, boats can travel on the Ayeyarwady (Irrawaddy) from the delta to Bhamo, with small boats continuing to Myitkyina. Other important rivers include the Twante Canal, which links the Ayeyarwady to Yangon, and the Chindwin, which joins the Ayeyarwady a little north of Bagan. Most ferries are operated by the government's Inland Water Transport (IWT; www.iwt.gov.mm).

The Mandalay–Bagan service is popular among travellers. A government ferry runs at least twice a week, and during high season (October to April) there are also faster, more comfortable private boats; buy tickets from travel agencies.

BUS

Almost always faster than trains, Myanmar buses range from air-con express buses, less luxurious but OK buses (without air-con), local buses and mini 32-seaters.

Breakdowns are frequent and roads are bad. On the other hand, bus travel is cheap and reasonably frequent, and it's easy to meet local people during the regular food stops.

Buying tickets in advance is recommended, lest you get stuck sitting on a sack in the aisle. On minibuses, beware of the back seat – on Myanmar's rough roads you'll be bouncing around like popcorn. Keep some warm clothing handy for air-con buses or trips through mountains.

You can pay kyat for all bus fares. Note, foreigners will pay more than locals – and on occasion the price is 'set' on the spot.

CAR & MOTORCYCLE

There are no international car-rental agencies, but most travel agencies in Yangon, Mandalay and Bagan – as well as guesthouses and hotels elsewhere – can arrange cars and drivers. Rates range between US$80 and US$100 per day.

Some locals remain reluctant to rent motorcycles to foreigners, but it is possible in some places, including Mandalay and Myitkyina, for around K10,000 per day.

LOCAL TRANSPORT

In most places, horse carts (*myint hlei*), vintage taxis (*taxi*), tiny four-wheeled Mazdas (*lei bein*, meaning 'four wheels', or blue taxi) and bicycle rickshaws or trishaws (*saiq-ka* – that's pidgin for sidecar) double as public transport. We indicate sample rates, but prices are usually negotiable.

Larger cities – including Yangon, Mandalay, Pathein and Mawlamyine – have dirt-cheap public buses that ply the main streets.

Bicycles are widely available to hire from K1500 per day.

PICK-UP

You can get almost anywhere in Myanmar on the ubiquitous trucks with bench seats known variously as pick-ups (also called *kaa*), *lain-ka* (linecar) or *hi-lux*. They leave when full and stop pretty much everywhere. Sitting up the back is cheaper than a bus, while a seat at the front costs double for little more room. Journey times are wildly elastic.

TRAIN

Myanmar Railways is government owned and operated. Foreigners no longer have to buy tickets with US dollars, although you'll still pay more than the locals do. Trains are slow and dirty and services often run late, though as one local said: 'It's not as bad as some people say, not as good as you hope.'

Upper class offers reclining seats and (in theory) air-con, 1st class is hard-backed seats with some cushioning, and ordinary class involves stiff wooden seats. The Pyin Oo Lwin–Hsipaw line is the most scenic, particularly around the Gokteik Gorge.

Reservations and ticketing can be done at train stations.

Express trains are much more comfortable than the average Burmese train. Reserve sleepers (ie anything that contains sleeping berths, including some day trains) several days in advance.

Philippines

📱 63 / POP 106 MILLION

Why Go?

Just when you thought you had Asia figured out, you get to the Philippines. Instead of monks you have priests; instead of túk-túk you have tricycles; instead of *pho* you have *adobo*. At first glance the Philippines will disarm you more than charm you, but peel back the country's skin and there are treasures aplenty to be found. For starters, you can explore desert islands, scale volcanoes, gawk at ancient rice terraces, submerge at world-class dive sites, and venture deep into the mountains to visit remote tribes.

Beyond its obvious physical assets, the Philippines possesses a quirky streak that takes a bit longer to appreciate. There are secret potions and healing lotions, guys named Bong and girls named Bing, grinning hustlers, wheezing bangkas (outrigger boats), crooked politicians, fuzzy carabao (water buffalo), graffiti-splashed jeepneys and cheap beer to enjoy as you take it all in.

Best Beaches

➡ Boracay (p573)

➡ Malapascua (p587)

➡ Sipalay (p579)

➡ Panglao Island (p589)

➡ Port Barton (p595)

Best Places for Culture

➡ Vigan (p567)

➡ Manila (p547)

➡ Banaue (p565)

➡ Siquijor (p580)

➡ Sagada (p564)

When to Go
Manila

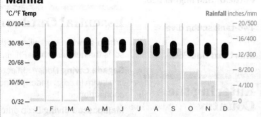

Jan & Feb Cool, pleasant weather and the height of the festival season.

Apr & May Peak time for Donsol whale sharks, and relatively flat seas for boat travel.

Sep Typhoons are a surfer's delight; big low-season discounts on beaches.

AT A GLANCE

Currency Peso (P)

Languages Tagalog (Filipino), English

Money ATMs abound in cities, but are scarce in remote areas

Visas Visa waivers on arrival (30 days) the norm

Mobile phones Prepaid SIM cards are easy to procure

Fast Facts

Area 300,000 sq km

Capital Manila

Emergency ☎117

Exchange Rates

Australia	A$1	P40
Euro	€1	P60
Malaysia	RM1	P15
Thailand	10B	P15
UK	UK£1	P75
US	US$1	P45

Daily Costs

Dorm bed P450

Bottle of San Miguel beer P40

Two-tank scuba dive P2500

Short taxi ride P60

Entering the Country

Entering the country is straightforward and usually done by air through Manila, Cebu, Clark or Kalibo airports.

Don't Miss

Filipinos revel in colourful fiestas, and it's worth scheduling your travels around one. The granddaddy of them all is the Ati-Atihan festival in Kalibo. Cebu's Sinulog Festival sees revelers dancing a unique two-steps-forward, one-step-back shuffle, while Baguio's Panagbenga involves a grand procession of floral floats. The Easter crucifixion ceremony in San Fernando, north of Manila, produces a more macabre tableau, with Catholic devotees being physically nailed to crosses. Every little town holds a fiesta, so your odds of seeing one are pretty good.

The Filipino joie de vivre also manifests itself in other ways – namely, singing. A karaoke night out is essential. Or pay homage to Filipino cover bands worldwide with some live music. Cover-band shows in Malate can be lively, or head up to Quezon City or Makati for more original fare.

ITINERARIES

One Week

Beach bums and divers should select a Visayan island and just fly there. Popular, easy-to-reach picks include Bohol, with its mix of marine and terrestrial attractions; well-rounded Southern Negros; and Cebu island with its thresher sharks and sardines. Kitesurfers and hedonists should plot a course towards Boracay. If mountains are your thing, do the spectacular North Luzon overland loop from Baguio to Sagada to Banaue and back to Manila.

Two Weeks

Spend a day exploring Manila, then complete the North Luzon loop. Fly from Manila to Coron in northern Palawan for some island-hopping, then make the eight-hour sea voyage to El Nido, gateway to cliff-addled Bacuit Bay. Travel overland to Puerto Princesa, taking maximum time to linger on lonely beaches along Palawan's west coast.

Essential Outdoor Activities

Whale sharks Snorkelling with the gentle *butanding* of Donsol is the quintessential Philippine adventure.

Sagada caving Dodge stalactites, slither through crevasses and swim in crisp underground pools on the thrilling cave connection.

Malapascua diving Drop onto Monad Shoal to view thresher sharks by morning and manta rays by day.

Boracay kitesurfing Bulabog Beach's shallow lagoon is perfect for learning, while stiff winds from December to March challenge experts.

Siargao surfing Tackle the Philippines' ultimate wave, Cloud Nine.

LUZON

The Philippines' main island is a vast expanse of misty mountains, sprawling plains, simmering volcanoes and endless coastline – with Manila at the centre of it all. The island's trophy piece is the northern mountainous area known as the Cordillera, where the Ifugao built their world-famous rice terraces in and around Banaue more than 2000 years ago. Along Luzon's northwest coast, historic Vigan is the country's best-preserved Spanish colonial-era town. Explorers can continue north of Vigan to Luzon's wild northern tip, where remote white-sand beaches embrace the coastline and rarely visited islands lurk offshore. Elsewhere, the southeast region of Bicol is home to fiery food and two of the country's top attractions: the whale sharks of Donsol and the perfect cone of Mt Mayon.

Manila

🖉 02 / POP 12 MILLION

Manila's moniker, the 'Pearl of the Orient', couldn't be more apt – its cantankerous shell reveals its jewel only to those resolute enough to pry. The city has endured every disaster both humans and nature could throw at it, and yet today the chaotic 600-sq-km metropolis thrives as a true Asian megacity. Skyscrapers pierce the hazy sky, mushrooming from the grinding poverty of expansive shanty towns, while gleaming malls foreshadow Manila's brave new air-conditioned world.

The determined will discover Manila's tender soul, perhaps among the leafy courtyards and cobbled streets of serene Intramuros, where little has changed since the Spanish left. Or it may be in the eddy of repose arising from the generosity of one of the city's 12 million residents.

History

The Spanish brushed aside a Muslim fort here in 1571 and founded the modern city as the capital of their realm. Spanish residents were concentrated around the walled city of Intramuros until 1898, when the Spanish governor surrendered to the Filipinos at San Agustin Church. After being razed to the ground during WWII, the city grew exponentially during the postwar years as migrants left the countryside in search of new opportunities.

◉ Sights

The main sights are downtown in the old walled city of Intramuros, which lies just south of the Pasig River, and south of Intramuros around Rizal Park (Luneta). You can walk to both of these easily enough from Malate and Ermita.

◉ Intramuros

A spacious borough of wide streets, leafy plazas and lovely colonial-era houses, the old walled city of Intramuros was the centrepiece of Spanish Manila. The Spanish replaced the original wooden fort with stone in 1590, and these walls stand much as they were 400 years ago. They're still studded with bastions and pierced with *puertas* (gates).

At the mouth of the Pasig River you'll find Manila's premier tourist attraction, **Fort Santiago** (Map p554; Santa Clara St; adult/student P75/50; ⊗ 8am-6pm), fronted by a pretty lily pond and the **Intramuros Visitors Center** (Map p554; 🖉 02-527 2961; Fort Santiago; ⊗ 8am-5pm). During WWII the fort was used as a prisoner-of-war camp by the Japanese. Within the fort grounds you'll find the **Rizal Shrine** (Map p554; admission incl with fort entry ticket; ⊗ 9am-6pm Tue-Sun, 1-5pm Mon) in the building where national hero José Rizal was incarcerated as he awaited execution. It contains Rizal's personal effects and a re-creation of his cell and the courtroom trial.

The most interesting building to survive the Battle of Manila is the church and monastery of **San Agustin** (Map p554; 🖉 02-527 4060; General Luna St). The interior is truly opulent and the ceiling, painted in 3-D relief, will make you question your vision. You must visit during a mass, or access it through the interesting **San Agustin Museum** (Map p554; General Luna St; adult/child P100/80; ⊗ 8am-noon & 1-6pm).

Opposite the church, **Casa Manila** (Map p554; 🖉 02-527 4084; Plaza Luis Complex, General Luna St; adult/student P75/50; ⊗ 9am-6pm Tue-Sun) is a beautiful reproduction of a three-storey Spanish colonial-era mansion, filled with priceless antiques.

◉ Rizal Park

Manila's iconic central **park** (Map p554), fondly known to most locals as Luneta, is spread out over some 60 hectares of open lawns, ornamental gardens, and paved walks dotted with monuments to a whole
(Continued on p552)

PHILIPPINES MANILA

Philippines Highlights

1 Drifting among the limestone cathedrals and azure lagoons of the Bacuit Archipelago around **El Nido** (p596).

2 Trekking through the skyscraping rice terraces around Banaue and Bontoc in North Luzon's **Cordillera** (p562).

3 Having a night out in **Manila** (p547), a city that never sleeps.

4 Exploring sunken WWII wrecks and myriad islands around **Coron** (p598).

5 Enjoying sun, sea sports and dancing till dawn on the stunning beaches of **Boracay** (p573).

6 Hopping from natural spring to coral reef to volcano to waterfall around lush

---

200 km
120 miles

PHILIPPINE SEA

SOUTH CHINA SEA

BABUYAN ISLANDS

Claveria

Laoag
Bangued
Vigan
Cordillera
Tuguegarao
Tabuk
Bontoc • Cordillera
Mountains
Sagada
Batad
Cervantes • Banaue
Tagudin • Lagawe
Abatan
Kabayan
Baguio
Solano

San Jose

Cabanatuan
Baler

POLILLO ISLANDS

Dagupan
Tarlac
Clark Airport
Angeles
LUZON
MANILA

Olongapo
Balanga
San Fernando

Alaminos
Hundred Islands National Park

Verde Island Passage
Batangas
Tagaytay • Lucena
Taal Volcano
Puerto Galera
Calapan
MINDORO

Pagsanjan

MARINDUQUE

Lubang Island
Abra de Ilog
Mamburao

Ano Reef Sablayan

Boac

Daet
Caramoan Peninsula
Mt Isarog National Park
Naga
Bicol
Caramoan
CATANDUANES
Virac
Mt Mayon (2462m)
Legazpi • Sorsogon
Donsol
Burias Island

Sorsogon

Legazpi

BURIAS

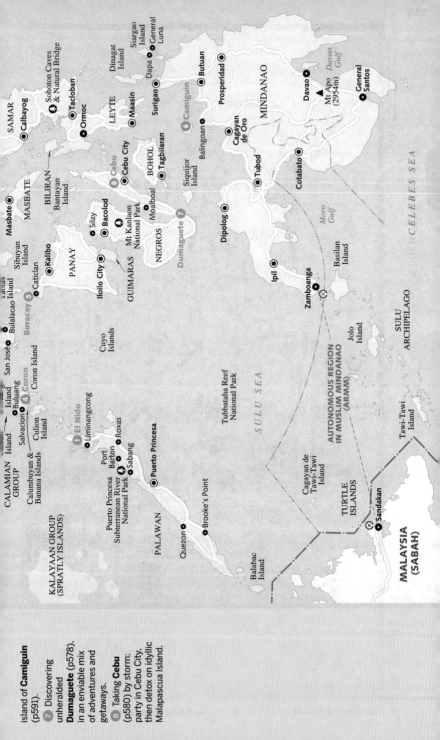

island of **Camiguin** (p591).

7 Discovering unheralded **Dumaguete** (p578), in an enviable mix of adventures and getaways.

8 Taking **Cebu** (p580) by storm: party in Cebu City, then detox on idyllic Malapascua Island.

Metro Manila

PHILIPPINES MANILA

2 km
1 mile

Commonwealth Ave

Katipunan Ave

University Ave
UP Diliman

Maginhawa St

Quezon Memorial Circle

Kalayaan Ave

Visayas Ave

North Ave

QUEZON CITY

North Avenue

Quezon Avenue

West Ave

Timog Ave

Roosevelt Ave

Roosevelt (Muñoz)

Balintawak

BALINTAWAK

Quirino Hwy

North Luzon Expwy

Baguio (180km)

Monumento (North Terminal)

CALOOCAN CITY

GRACE PARK

5th Avenue

MacArthur Hwy

C-3 Rd

MALABON CITY

Mabini Ave

Juan Luna St

Honoratio Lopez Blvd

Velasquez St

Morienes St

C M Recto

NORTH HARBOR DISTRICT

Manila North Harbor Port

28

Tutuban

Jose Abad Santos St

Del Monte Ave

Bonifacio Ave

SANTA MESA HEIGHTS

Mayon St

Blumentritt St

Antipolo St

Blumentritt

Tayuman

Doroteo

José

Bambang

Ave

R Papa

Abad Santos

1

Espana St

E Rodriguez St

Pureza

UST

23

Quezon Blvd

Sampaloc Bus Terminals

Legarda

Recto (Isetan)

Carriedo

2

Central

BINONDO

CITY OF MANILA

SOUTH HARBOR DISTRICT

Quezon Ave

Don Alejandro Roces Ave

21

V Mapa (Araneta)

SAN JUAN

New Panaderos

Ruiz

Gilmore

NEW MANILA

T Morato Ave

Kamuning

GMA

Betty Go Belmonte

EDSA

Kamuning Rd

V Luna Ave

Kamias Rd

Anonas Ave

Anonas

Katipunan

QUIRINO

CUBAO

Cubao

24

19

26

30

Cubao-Araneta Center

Santolan Greenhills

Santolan

People Power Monument

Ortigas Ave

Ortigas

Wack-Wack Golf & Country Club

Shaw Blvd

Ortigas Ave

5

PANDACAN

Malacañang Palace
Malacañang Garden

Malacanang Park

Pandacan

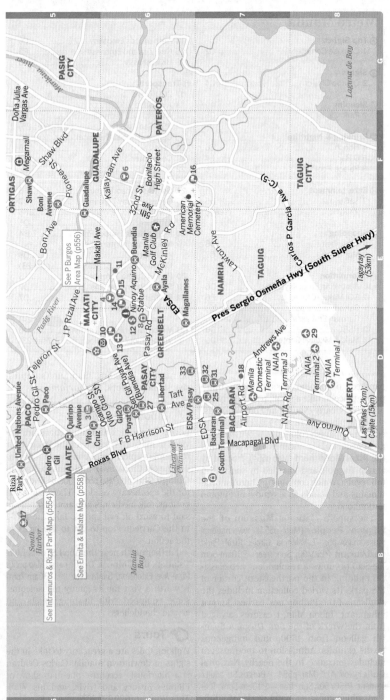

Metro Manila

(Continued from p547)
pantheon of Filipino heroes. It's an atmospheric place to take a stroll, particularly late afternoons, early evening and on weekends.

As the place where José Rizal was executed by the Spanish colonial authorities, it's of great historical significance. Here you'll find the **Rizal Monument** (Map p554), fronted by a 46m flagpole and guarded by sentries in full regalia, which contains the hero's mortal remains and stands as a symbol of Filipino nationhood.

The superb **National Museum of the Filipino People** (Map p554; www.national museum.gov.ph; T Valencia Circle, Rizal Park; adult/student P150/50, Sun free; ⊙10am-5pm Tue-Sun) occupies a resplendent neo-classical building in the northeastern corner of the park. Its varied collection includes the skullcap of the Philippines' earliest known inhabitant, Tabon Man; treasures salvaged from the wreck of the *San Diego,* a Spanish galleon from 1600; and indigenous textile exhibits. Admission to the museum includes entrance to the nearby **National Gallery of Art** (Map p554; P Burgos St; adult/student P150/50, Sun free; ⊙10am-5pm Tue-Sun), which contains many works of Filipino masters, including Juan Luna's impressive signature work, *Spoliarium.*

◎ Binondo & Quiapo

Lovers of markets and utter chaos are advised to make DIY trips over the Pasig River to Manila's epicentre of commerce – Binondo (the old Chinatown) and Quiapo. Around **Quiapo Church** (Map p550; Quezon Blvd) look for the apothecary vendors. They sell herbal potions, folk medicines and amulets that are said to ward off evil spirits. Take the LRT-1 to the Carriedo stop to get to the heart of the action.

Further north near the Abad Santos LRT-1 station, the **Chinese Cemetery** (Map p550; Rizal Ave Extension, Santa Cruz; ⊙7.30am-7pm) is worth a visit for its gaudy mausoleums, some equipped with flushing toilets and crystal chandeliers.

👉 Tours

Walking tours are a great way to take in the sights of downtown Manila. Carlos Celdran is a hilariously eccentric one-man show of Filipino history and trivia, and his **Walk This Way** (0920 909 2021; www.carlosceldran.

com; adults/students P1100/600) tours are highly recommended. **Old Manila Walks** (☎0918 962 6452, 02-711 3823; www.oldmanilawalks.com; tours from P1100) has great all-you-can-eat foodie walking tours in Binondo, as well as tours of the Chinese Cemetery, Corregidor Island and more.

Bambike BICYCLE TOUR
(Map p554; ☎02-525 8289; www.bambike.com; Plaza Luis Complex, General Luna St, Intramuros; 1-/2½hr tour P600/1200; ⊙10am & 3pm) Bambike runs guided cycling tours around Intramuros on handmade bicycles constructed using bamboo frames. Pedalling the laid-back backstreets of the walled city makes for a great way to cover expansive Intramuros, taking in all the main stops plus some less-visited gems. Prices include entrance fees, helmets and water.

Sun Cruises BOAT TOUR
(☎02-831 8140; www.corregidorphilippines.com; CCP Complex jetty, Pasay; ferry only weekday/weekend P1400/1500, excursion incl lunch weekday/weekend P2350/2550, walking tour without lunch P1700) Sun Cruises has the market cornered for trips to infamous Corregidor Island, the last bastion of American resistance during the Japanese invasion of Luzon in 1941. It loads up 100 to 200 passengers every morning at 7.30am; you shall return to Manila by 3.45pm, unless you stay overnight.

Sleeping

Most people stay 'downtown' in Malate or in the business district of Makati. Malate remains a bit blighted but is closer to the sights and is beginning to experience a revival after years of neglect. Makati hostels cost more, but are closer to the best restaurants and nightlife. If you need to be close to the airport, hone in on Pasay.

Malate & Pasay

★**Pink Manila** HOSTEL $
(Map p550; ☎02-484 3145; www.pinkmanilahostel.com; 5th fl, cnr Bautista & San Pedro Sts, Pasay; dm fan/air-con P450/570, d P1600; ❄📶🏊) Floridian owner Crissy pushes all the right buttons with this sociable hostel. It feels like the Big Brother household, where bikini-clad, shirtless backpackers laze poolside around the bar playing guitar. There's a nice mix of dorms with beds swathed in trademark pink linen, a hammock-strewn roof deck, and rocking monthly parties. The somewhat random location is equally convenient to Malate and Makati.

Where 2 Next HOSTEL $
(Map p558; ☎02-354 3533; www.where2nexthostel.com; 1776 Adriatico St; incl breakfast dm with air-con P495, r with fan/air-con P950/1550; ❄@📶) A slick hostel with a sparkling common area full of comfy couches and a glassed-in balcony overlooking Malate's main strip. Well-cleaned rooms are brightened with graffiti murals and there is a full kitchen for self-caterers. It lacks a killer bar but organises bar crawls.

Chill-Out Guesthouse HOSTEL $
(Map p558; ☎02-714 6600; www.chilloutmanila63@gmail.com; 612 Remedios St; dm P350, r P700-1560; ❄@📶) P350 air-con dorms? Works for us. They are plenty clean and livable, too. But what really makes this French-managed guesthouse-hostel hybrid stick out are the private rooms, which are downright roomy and have touches like couches, nightstands and art on the walls. Hang out, cook and eat in the kitchen/common area.

Wanderers Guest House HOSTEL $
(Map p558; ☎02-525 1534; www.wanderersguesthouse.com; 1750 Adriatico St; dm with fan/air-con P300/350, d with fan/air-con from P790/990, tr P1350-1800; ❄@📶) In the heart of Malate, Wanderers knows precisely what backpackers want and delivers beautifully with a mix of clean dorms and private rooms (some with balconies), excellent travel info and cooking facilities. The highlight is its grungy rooftop bar-restaurant–chill-out lounge, perfect for socialising with other travellers over cheap booze.

V Hotel HOTEL $$
(Map p558; ☎02-328 5553; www.vhotelmanila.com; 1766 Adriatico St; d without bathroom P1200,

SPLURGE

With its grey-stone minimalism, **Amélie Hotel** (Map p558; ☎02-875 7888; www.ameliehotelmanila.com; 1667 Bocobo St; r incl breakfast P3900-5100; ⊖❄📶🏊) is the perfect antidote to sweaty, steamy Malate. The throwback art-deco furniture barely fills the immense rectangular space of the rooms. Head up to the rooftop plunge pool for happy hour and dial up drinks from the lobby bar 10 stories below.

Intramuros & Rizal Park

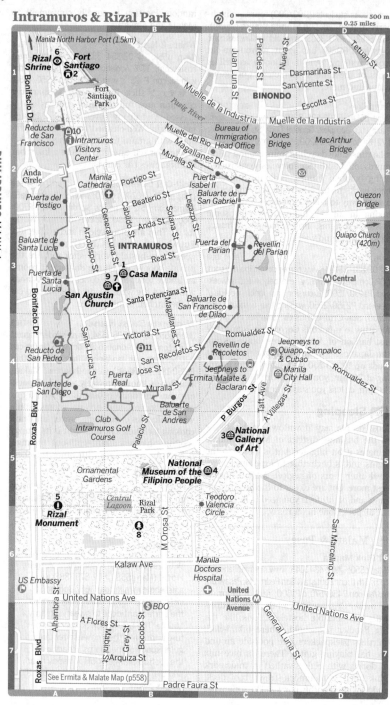

0 — 500 m
0 — 0.25 miles

Manila North Harbor Port (1.5km)

Rizal Shrine 6
Fort Santiago 2
Fort Santiago Park

Tettian St

Juan Luna St
Paredes St
Nueva St

Dasmariñas St
San Vicente St

BINONDO

Escolta St

Muelle de la Industria

Pasig River

Muelle de la Industria

Bonifacio Dr

Reducto de San Francisco 10
Intramuros Visitors Center

Anda Circle

Puerta del Postigo

Manila Cathedral

Bureau of Immigration Head Office

Jones Bridge

MacArthur Bridge

Muelle del Rio
Magallanes Dr
Muralla St

Postigo St

Puerta Isabel II
Baluarte de San Gabriel

Quezon Bridge

Quiapo Church (420m)

Beaterio St

Cabildo St
Anda St
Solana St
Legazpi St

Baluarte de Santa Lucia

Arzobispo St
General Luna St

INTRAMUROS

Real St

Puerta del Parian

Revellin del Parian

Central

Puerta de Santa Lucia

9 7 **Casa Manila** 1
San Agustin Church

Santa Potenciana St

Baluarte de San Francisco de Dilao

Santa Lucia St

Victoria St

Magallanes St

11

San Jose St

Recoletos St

Revellin de Recoletos

Romualdez St

Jeepneys to Quiapo, Sampaloc & Cubao

Reducto de San Pedro

Puerta Real

Jeepneys to Ermita, Malate & Baclaran

Manila City Hall

Romualdez St

Baluarte de San Diego

Muralla St

Baluarte de San Andres

P Burgos

Taft Ave
A Villegas St

Club Intramuros Golf Course

Palacio St

National Gallery of Art 3

Ornamental Gardens

National Museum of the Filipino People 4

M Orosa St

Central Lagoon

Rizal Park

Teodoro Valencia Circle

San Marcelino St

Rizal Monument 5

8

Kalaw Ave

Manila Doctors Hospital

US Embassy

Alhambra St

United Nations Ave

United Nations Avenue

United Nations Ave

BDO 5

A Flores St
Mabini St
Grey St
Bocobo St
Arquiza St

General Luna St

Roxas Blvd

See Ermita & Malate Map (p558)

Padre Faura St

Intramuros & Rizal Park

r with bathroom & incl breakfast P1800-2800; [⚡][🛜][🏊]) A very well-priced designer hotel in downtown Malate with smart (but boxy) rooms, a vibrant cafe and small roof-deck pool. The cheapest rooms have bunk beds and shared bathroom, and are a good budget option over hostels.

🛏 Makati

Hilik Hostel
HOSTEL $

(Map p556; 🕿02-519 5821; www.hilikboutique hostel.ph; Mavenue Bldg, 7844 Makati Ave; incl breakfast dm P500-650, d P1100-1500; [⚡][🛜][🏊]) What separates Hilik from the pack is its downright stylish private rooms, though you'll want to request one off noisy Makati Ave. The air-con dorms at Hilik ('snore' in Tagalog) are cramped but, like the kitchen and common area of this intimate hostel, immaculate.

MNL Boutique Hostel
HOSTEL $

(Map p556; 🕿02-511 7514; www.mnlboutiquehos tel.com; 4688 B Valdez St; dm P500-750, r P1550; [⚡][@][🛜]) Incorporating industrial decor such as polished concrete and colourful plywood doors, arty MNL prides itself on being a creative, comfy backpackers. Space is squashy and lacks natural light, but the beds are quality, unsavoury smells are absent, and the street-level locale makes for a robust Filipino-style happy hour.

Lokal Hostel
HOSTEL $

(Map p556; 🕿02-890 0927; www.lokalhostel. com; 3rd fl, 5023 P Burgos St; dm with fan/air-con

from P400/500, s/d from P800/1300; [⚡][@][🛜]) In the middle of Makati's tacky red-light district, this hostel offers respite from within, and has spacious dorms with big beds, murals and a cool roof-deck hangout. The private rooms are the best value you'll find in Makati.

Z Hostel
HOSTEL $$

(Map p556; 🕿02-856 0851; www.zhostel.com; 5660 Don Pedro St; dm P650-850, d incl breakfast P2430; [⚡][@][🛜]) This is Manila's number-one party address for groovy backpackers thanks to its rocking rooftop bar and chic ground-floor cafe. It's a huge space with 130 beds over seven floors. The airy dorms are all en suite and boast sturdy iron-framed beds with personal charging stations. The private rooms are overpriced. No kitchen.

Junction Hostel
HOSTEL $$

(Map p556; 🕿02-501 6575; www.junctionhostels. com; cnr Gen Luna & Don Pedro Sts; dm P650-850, d without bathroom P1800; [⚡][@][🛜]) Manila's latest 'poshtel', 111-bed Junction has a distinctively urban feel, with murals on the walls, industrial fixtures and boutique dorm rooms in a mix of styles and configurations. In the funky downstairs common area baristas sling boutique coffee and imported beers to patrons hovered over their laptops. It could be Brooklyn.

Clipper Hotel
HOTEL $$

(Map p556; 🕿02-890 8577; www.theclipperho tel.com; 5766 Ebro St; s P1400, d P2300-2500; [⚡][🛜]) The Clipper keeps it classy despite being steps away from seedy P Burgos St. The two quirky, windowless singles resemble boat cabins, with flat-screen TVs built into the beds. The roomy doubles are very white and bright, with parquet floors. For something even classier, target the Clipper's newly opened sister B&B, **La Casita de Mercedes** (Map p556; 🕿02-887 4385; http:// lacasitamercedes.com; cnr Alfonso & Fermina Sts; s P1500, d incl breakfast P2650-2950), in a beautifully restored 1930s house.

Hotel Durban
HOTEL $$

(Map p556; 🕿02-897 1866; www.hoteldurban.net; 4875 Durban St; r P1700-2600; [⚡][🛜]) Makati's best midrange value is a tightly run ship. The immaculate rooms, with faux-wood panelling, are more than adequate for the price. Upgrade to the top-floor 'deluxe' rooms for a window.

P Burgos Area

P Burgos Area

✕ Eating

Food courts in malls such as Robinsons Place (p559) in Ermita are always a good bet for affordable sustenance. For vegetarian food try the dozens of halal restaurants in Malate. Head to Chinatown in Quiapo/Binondo for authentic Chinese food.

✕ Malate & Ermita

★ Shawarma
Snack Center　　　　　MIDDLE EASTERN $
(Map p558; 485 R Salas St; shawarma P60-75, meals P85-300; ⊙24hr) It doesn't sound like much, but his streetside eatery serves the richest and most flavourful falafel, *mutta-bal* (eggplant dip), hummus and kebabs in downtown Manila.

Midtown Diner　　　FILIPINO, AMERICAN $
(Map p558; 551 Padre Faura St; meals P115-180; ⊙7am-8pm Mon-Sat; 🛜) Filipino take on an old-school meat-and-potatoes American

diner. Home in on the budget set meals, which include a soup and iced tea.

Cafe Adriatico
INTERNATIONAL $$

(Map p558; 1790 Adriatico St, Malate; mains P200-400; ⏰7am-5am; 🐾) An old-time Malate favourite, this romantic corner bistro is worth a splurge for original multicultural fare with Spanish, English, American and Italian options, and the people-watching on Remedios Circle. It's open till dawn, so it's great for a late-night meal.

Hap Chan Tea House
CHINESE $$

(Map p558; 561 General Malvar St; mains P200-400; ⏰11am-3am) Delicious, steaming platters of Hong Kong specialities are the name of the game here. It's popular for a reason.

✗ Makati

Felipe St is a great place to browse for chow, with several lively bars and eateries that spill onto the street. The best is **El Chupacabra** (Map p556; 5782 Felipe St; tacos from P95; ⏰8am-midnight Mon-Thu, to 3am Fri-Sun), which serves delicious 'street tacos', often with a Filipino twist, plus margaritas and P45 San Miguel. Opposite are **Tambai** (Map p556; Felipe St; dishes P70-300; 🐾) for quick but highly original Japanese-infused Filipino snacks (try the to-die-for beef-rib *laki-tori* sticks), and sports bar **H&J** (Map p556; 5781 Felipe St; ⏰2pm-7am; 🐾) for pub grub.

For a great Filipino food introduction, try the home-cooked *turu-turò* (point-point) fare at **Friends & Neighbors** (Map p556; 5070 P Burgos St; dishes P70-100; ⏰9am-9pm Mon-Sat), or the open-air **A Venue Food Market** (Hot Asia; Map p556; A Venue Mall, Makati Ave; dishes P75-85; ⏰1pm-midnight) nearby.

Som's Noodle House
THAI $

(Map p556; 5921 A Alger St; mains P120-220; ⏰10.30am-10.30pm) Restaurants in the Philippines generally struggle with Thai food but not Som's, which spices staples such as red curry and *tom yum* to your liking. It's a great deal, and it can deliver to your hotel.

Beni's Falafel
MIDDLE EASTERN $$

(Map p556; A Venue Mall, B Valdez St Entrance; dishes P150-280; ⏰24hr; 🐾) Everything on the menu of this unassuming Yemeni-owned eatery is original and done to perfection. The *shakshuka* (eggs poached in a spicy tomato sauce) and Beni's falafel are our faves.

PHOTOBOMBER EXTRAORDINAIRE

Looming just east of Rizal Park is a half-built 49-storey condo known as Torre de Manila. Its many critics have dubbed it 'Terror de Manila' or the 'Rizal Monument Photobomber' for its tendency to sneak into pictures of Manila's most revered statue. The building's construction was on hold at the time of research, pending the result of lawsuits brought by preservationists who claim that it's an 'eyesore' that damages the country's historical and cultural heritage.

🍷 Drinking & Entertainment

You name it, it's there. That about sums up Manila nightlife. As a rule, Malate has cover bands and karaoke bars; Makati and the Fort are where the nightclubs are; and Quezon City has the best original live music.

Movies (mostly imported blockbusters in English; tickets P150 to P250) are in the malls. Theatres and performing arts troupes are scattered all over the metropolis. See www.clickthecity.com for extensive movie and entertainment listings.

🍷 Malate

Drinking opportunities abound down here. You can quaff cheap suds kerbside just west of Remedios Circle on Remedios St. On this same street are a couple of uni clubs that get going later in the evening.

Erra's Vest Ramen in Town
BAR

(Map p558; 1755 Adriatico St; ⏰24hr) Erra's is your classic Southeast Asian streetside shack luring folk from all corners of the galaxy to quaff cheap San Miguel (P34) and – as its quirky new name implies – slurp the house Ramen (P60 to P90).

Tap Station
BAR

(Map p558; cnr Adriatico & Padre Faura Sts; 330mL beer P120-200; ⏰3pm-2am) Tasty craft beer brewed by next-door neighbour G-Point, served in a more inviting open-air setting festooned with pics of old Manila.

★1951
LIVE MUSIC

(Penguin Cafe; Map p558; 1951 M Adriatico St; ⏰from 6pm Tue-Sat) This legendary bar-cum-gallery is a magnet for bohemian types and lovers of live music, with some of the finest

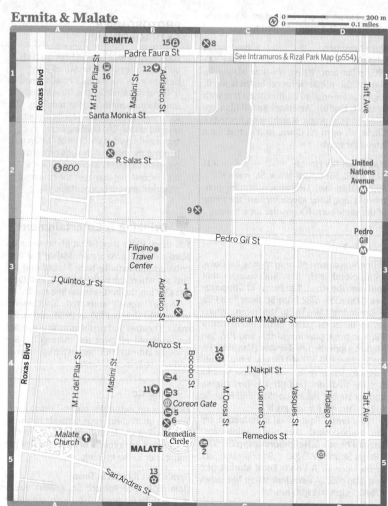

musical talent in the Philippines having graced its stage. The official name is now 1951 but everybody still calls it Penguin Cafe.

🍷 Makati & The Fort

There are several worthy sports bars around P Burgos St, including the fantastic biker bar **Handlebar** (Map p556; www.handlebar.com.ph; 31 Polaris St; ⏰24hr). The club scene changes often. Neighbouring **Valkyrie** (Map p550; http://valkyrie.thepalacemanila.com; 9th Ave cnr 36th St, Fort Bonifacio; admission incl 2 drinks P600-800; ⏰10pm-late Wed-Sat) and **Palace Pool Club** (Map p550; http://poolclub.the

palacemanila.com; 9th Ave cnr 36th St, Fort Bonifacio; 11am-3am) in the Fort were pick of the litter at the time of research. No matter what's hot and what's not, everybody seems to end up at timeless **Time** (Map p556; 7840 Makati Ave; ⏰from 5pm Tue-Sat) when latenight comes.

Z Hostel Roofdeck
BAR

(Map p556; 5660 Don Pedro St; ⏰5pm-late, happy hour 7-9pm) There's no doubt where the top backpacker party spot in Manila is. Z's roof deck draws competent DJs and is popular with locals and expats. Happy hour brings P50 local beers.

Ermita & Malate

⦿ Sleeping
1 Amélie Hotel B3
2 Chill-Out Guesthouse...........................C5
3 V Hotel..B4
4 Wanderers Guest House......................B4
5 Where 2 Next..B4

⊗ Eating
6 Cafe Adriatico..B5
7 Hap Chan Tea House............................B3
8 Midtown Diner.......................................C1
9 Robinsons Place B2
10 Shawarma Snack Center.....................B2

⊜ Drinking & Nightlife
11 Erra's Vest Ramen in Town B4
12 Tap Station B1

⊛ Entertainment
13 1951..B5
14 Library C4

⊜ Shopping
15 Solidaridad Bookshop..........................B1

⊙ Transport
16 Cagsawa Ermita Terminal B1
Isarog Ermita Terminal ....(see 16)

Hooch BAR
(Map p550; 125 Leviste St; ⊙happy hour 2-6pm, to 5pm Sat & Sun; 🛜) A fancy-ish cocktail bar in upscale Salcedo Village, Hooch has a pleasant surprise for budget-conscious beer lovers: P90 pints of decent craft beer at happy hour, easily the best brew value in town.

★**SaGuijo** LIVE MUSIC
(Map p550; ✆02-897 8629; www.saguijo.com; 7612 Guijo St, Makati; admission after 10pm incl a drink P150; ⊙6pm-2am) Wonderfully decrepit dive bar with a packed roster of indie, punk and new wave bands that kick off at 10.30pm.

🛍 Shopping

Worthy souvenir items include wood-carved Ifugao *bulol* (rice guards), *barong* (traditional Filipino shirts), lacquered coconut-shell trinkets and indigenous textiles.

Hulking malls like **Robinsons Place** (Map p558; Pedro Gil St; ⊙10am-9pm), **Mall of Asia** (Map p550; www.smmallofasia.com; Manila Bay; ⊙10am-10pm) and **Greenbelt** (Map p550; Ayala Centre) have plenty of well-stocked bookstores, or check out leftie bookshop **Solidaridad** (Map p558; 531 P Faura St, Ermita; ⊙9am-6pm Mon-Sat) for alternative titles and documentaries on local history and politics.

★**Silahis Arts & Artifacts** SOUVENIRS
(Map p554; www.silahis.com; 744 General Luna St, Intramuros; ⊙10am-7pm) This is almost more of a cultural centre than store. Intricately woven baskets, wooden Ifugao *bulol* (rice guard) statues, textiles and other crafts from around the country are sold next to beautiful antiques.

Manila Collectible Co SOUVENIRS, FOOD
(Map p554; ✆0917 861 3011; Fort Santiago, Intramuros; ⊙10am-6pm; 🛜) This funky shop specialises in handspun textiles and accessories produced by indigenous groups across the Philippines. It also sells fair-trade organic coffee, Filipino cigars, local 'wines', flavoured *pili* nuts and pure cacao.

ⓘ Orientation

Giant Metro Manila is composed of 17 cities. From a tourist perspective, the important ones are the City of Manila ('downtown'), where most sights are; Pasay and Parañaque, where you'll find the airport and many bus terminals; and the business district of Makati. The booming Fort Bonifacio area lies in Taguig but is essentially an extension of Makati. Pleasant, youthful Quezon City is the country's most populous city with almost three million residents.

ⓘ Information

DANGERS & ANNOYANCES
Manila is probably no more dangerous than the next megacity, but it can still be dodgy, especially after dark. The district of Tondo, particularly around the north ports, is one area to avoid walking around solo after dark. The tourist belts

WORTH A TRIP

VOLCANO HOPPING

Besides Corregidor Island, the most popular day tour out of Manila is to **Tagaytay**, 60km south. The town's 15km-long ridge road serves up spectacular views of **Taal Volcano**, which rises out of **Taal Lake** 600m below. You can take a boat to the volcano itself, which can be climbed in just 45 minutes. Many hostels in Manila arrange day tours here.

Another popular tour is a 4WD ride (followed by a two-hour climb) to the stunning emerald crater lake of **Mt Pinatubo**, site of a cataclysmic volcanic eruption in 1991. The mountain is a couple of hours' drive north of Manila and tours leave at around 4.30am.

GAY & LESBIAN MANILA

Manila, like most of the Philippines, is very gay-friendly. The traditional gay-and-lesbian nexus is at the corner of J Nakpil St and M Orosa St in Malate, although the best gay clubs have migrated to Ortigas, Quezon City.

O Bar (Map p550; ☑ 0919 996 4154; Ortigas Home Depot, Julia Vargas Ave, Ortigas; admission incl 3 beers P300-400; ⊙ 10pm-6am Wed-Sun) O Bar expanded from gay bar to gay club upon its move to Ortigas from J Nakpil St in Malate. Raucous parties into the wee hours, plus an infamous drag show.

Library (Map p558; ☑ 02-522 2484; www.thelibrary.com.ph; 1139 M Orosa St; shows P100-500; ⊙ shows from 9pm) In the heart of Malate's gay district, the Library has nightly comedy shows (at 9pm) that are popular with both gay and straight audiences.

in Malate and especially Ermita are rife with street-dwellers. Exercise caution walking around at night, especially south of Remedios Circle.

Pickpocketing is rampant on the MRT, and on major bar strips, where drunk tourists present easy prey.

Traffic is the big annoyance in Manila; you'll probably spend half your time either stuck in it or talking about it. Leave extra time to get to airports, bus stations and dinner dates.

INTERNET ACCESS

Malls such as Robinsons Place have internet cafes, and there are a few along Adriatico St in Malate, and along Makati Ave near the corner of Jupiter St.

MEDICAL SERVICES

Makati Medical Center (Map p550; ☑ 02-888 8999; www.makatimed.net.ph; 2 Amorsolo St, Makati)

Manila Doctors Hospital (Map p554; ☑ 02-558 0888; www.maniladoctors.com.ph; 667 United Nations Ave, Ermita)

MONEY

Malate, Ermita, Makati and malls everywhere are littered with ATMs. Popular banks are BDO, BPI and Metrobank, but all charge P200 for ATM withdrawals and have a P10,000 limit per withdrawal. Along Mabini and Adriatico Sts you'll find some moneychangers but, as always, be careful when using these services.

HSBC (Map p550; 6766 Ayala Ave, Makati) Allows P40,000 withdrawals.

TOURIST INFORMATION

There are tourist information booths in the arrivals area of all four airport terminals. The official website of Philippine tourism is www.visitmyphilippines.com.

TRAVEL AGENCIES

Malate and Ermita are filled with travel agencies that can help with domestic air tickets (for a fee).

Filipino Travel Center (Map p558; ☑ 02-528 4507; www.filipinotravel.com.ph; cnr Adriatico & Pedro Gil Sts, Malate; ⊙ 8am-6pm Mon-Fri, 9am-5pm Sat) Catering to foreign tourists, this helpful and knowledgeable agency organises city tours and day tours around Manila and beyond.

Getting There & Away

AIR

Ninoy Aquino International Airport (NAIA; Map p550; www.miaa.gov.ph) is about 6km south of Malate, in Parañaque. See p606 for information on navigating NAIA's four terminals.

BOAT

The flashy **Manila North Harbor Port** (Map p550; www.mnhport.com.ph; Piers 4 & 6, Tondo), northwest of Binondo, is a beacon of modernity in the capital's hardscrabble Tondo district. All domestic ferry travel uses this port.

2GO Travel (Map p550; ☑ 02-528 7000; http://travel.2go.com.ph; Pier 4, Manila North Harbor Port) is the main shipping line handling inter-island boat trips from Manila. Tickets can be purchased online, through travel agents or at major malls.

BUS

Confusingly, there's no single long-distance bus station in Manila. The terminals are mainly strung along Epifanio de los Santos Ave (EDSA), with a cluster near the intersection of Taft Ave in Pasay City to the south, and in Cubao (part of Quezon City) to the north. Another cluster is north of Quiapo in Sampaloc. Buses heading into Manila will usually just have 'Cubao', 'Pasay' or 'Sampaloc' on the signboard.

Most buses are 40-seat 'air-con' buses with a two-by-two seating arrangement. Comfortable 27-seat 'deluxe' express buses are well worth the extra coin to Baguio, Legazpi and Vigan. Packed 'ordinary' (non-air-con) buses cost 30% less than air-con services but take substantially longer.

Useful Bus Companies

Cagsawa Ermita (Map p558; ☑ 02-525 9756; P Faura Centre, P Faura St); Cubao (Map p550; ☑ 02-998 9050; Araneta Bus Terminal)

Ceres (Map p550; cnr Taft & Sen Gil Puyat Aves, Pasay)

Coda Lines (Map p550; ☏ 0927 559 2197; 277 E Rodriguez Sr Ave, Quezon City)

Dangwa Bus Lines (Map p550; ☏ 02-493 7596; Florida Cubao Terminal, EDSA cnr Kamuning)

Florida Bus Lines (Map p550; ☏ 02-781 5894; cnr Earnshaw St & Lacson Ave, Sampaloc)

Genesis (www.genesistransport.com.ph) Terminals in Pasay (Map p550; ☏ 02-853 3115; Pasay Rotunda) and Cubao (Map p550; ☏ 02-709 0545; cnr New York Ave & EDSA).

Isarog Bus Lines (http://bicolisarog.com) Terminals in Ermita (Map p558; ☏ 02-525 7077; Padre Faura Centre, Padre Faura St) and Cubao (Map p550; ☏ 02-423-2957; 599 EDSA).

Jam Liner (Map p550; ☏ 02-425 5489; www.jam.com.ph; cnr Taft & Sen Gil Puyat Aves, Pasay)

Ohayami (Map p550; ☏ 0927 649 3055; www.ohayamitrans.com; cnr Fajardo St & Lacson Ave, Sampaloc)

Partas Terminals in Cubao (Map p550; ☏ 02-725 1756; cnr Aurora Blvd & Bernadino St) and Pasay (Map p550; ☏ 02-851 4025; Aurora Blvd, Pasay).

Philtranco (Map p550; ☏ 02-851 8077-9; www.philtranco.com.ph; cnr EDSA & Apelo Cruz, Pasay)

BSC San Agustin (Map p550; Pasay Rotunda, cnr Taft Ave & EDSA)

Victory Liner (www.victoryliner.com) Terminals in Cubao (Map p550; ☏ 02-727 4534; cnr EDSA & New York Ave), Pasay (Map p550; ☏ 02-833 5019-20; cnr EDSA & Taft Ave) and Sampaloc (Map p550; ☏ 02-559 7735; www.victoryliner.com; 551 Earnshaw St).

ⓘ Getting Around

EDSA is the main artery, linking Mall of Asia in Pasay with Makati, Ortigas and Quezon City. Iconic Roxas Blvd runs north along Manila Bay from Pasay to Rizal Park via Malate. The MRT line conveniently runs right along EDSA, and links with the LRT-1 line at Taft Ave.

TO/FROM THE AIRPORT, BUS TERMINALS & FERRY PORT

Since there are no direct public-transport routes from any of the four NAIA terminals to the tourist belt in Malate, bite the bullet and take a taxi. Avoid the white, prepaid 'coupon' taxis that charge set rates of more than P400, and look for the yellow airport metered taxis. These have a flag fall of P70 (taxis on the street have a P40 flag fall). Your total bill to Malate should be about P250. To save a few pesos you can walk upstairs to the arrival areas of Terminals 1, 2 or 3 and look for ranks of regular metered taxis on drop-off runs.

If you arrive in Manila by boat, you're also better off catching a taxi into town, as the North Harbor area isn't a place for a foreigner to be wandering around with luggage, and public-transport routes are complicated.

With the number of different bus stations in Manila, if you arrive by bus you could end up pretty much anywhere. Luckily, most terminals are located on or near Manila's major artery, Epifanio de los Santos Ave (EDSA), linked to Malate and Makati by LRT and MRT.

JEEPNEY

Heading south from Ermita/Malate along MH del Pilar St, 'Baclaran' jeepneys end up on EDSA just west of the Pasay bus terminals and just east of Mall of Asia. Going north from Ermita/Malate along Mabini St, jeepneys go to Rizal

BUSES FROM MANILA

DESTINATION	FARE (P)	DURATION (HR)	RECOMMENDED COMPANIES	FREQUENCY
Baguio	air-con/deluxe 450/750	4-6½	Genesis, Victory Liner	frequent
Banaue	450-530	7-8	Dangwa, Ohayami	2-4 night buses
Batangas	160-180	2	Jam Transit, RRCG, Ceres	every 20min
Clark Airport	450	3	Philtranco	3 daily
Legazpi	air-con/deluxe P850/1050	12	Cagsawa, Isarog, Philtranco	frequent
Sagada	720	11	Coda Lines	9pm
Solano (for Banaue)	375	8	Florida, Victory Liner	frequent
Tagaytay	78	2-3	BSC San Agustin	every 20min
Vigan	air-con/deluxe 680/825	7-9	Florida, Partas	hourly

Park before heading off in various directions: 'Santa Cruz' and 'Monumento' jeepneys take the MacArthur Bridge, passing the main post office, while 'Cubao' and 'Espana' jeepneys traverse the Quezon Bridge to Quiapo church before peeling off to, respectively, the Cubao and Sampaloc bus terminals.

TRAIN

There are three elevated railway lines in Manila known as LRT-1, LRT-2 and MRT-3. You'll need a separate ticket for each line. Prices start from P12, and trains run between 4am and midnight. Avoid these trains during rush hour, when they get mosh-pit crowded and huge ticket lines form.

The Cordillera

Most who venture into North Luzon set their sights squarely on the Cordillera, a river-sliced hinterland of lush green forests covering hectare after hectare of jagged earth. Besides numerous rice terraces around Banaue and Bontoc, other draws include stunning hikes, waterfalls and – in hippie-esque Sagada – caving.

The tribespeople of the Cordillera, collectively known as the Igorot, are as compelling as the landscape, and it's worth studying their culture if you're heading up this way. In remote areas you may observe *cañao* (sacrificial ceremonies) and see elders wearing indigenous garb such as loin cloths.

Throw a poncho in your bag, as the Cordillera can get chilly at night. Fog and rain

THE MUMMIES OF KABAYAN

A road heading north out of Baguio for 50 winding kilometres leads to picturesque Kabayan, the site of several caves containing eerie mummies entombed centuries ago by the Ibaloi people. Some of these caves can be visited, while others are known only to Ibaloi elders. After exploring Kabayan for a day or two, you can hire a guide to walk back to the Halsema Hwy (about five hours, straight uphill) via the **Timbac Caves** (admission P100), the spot where the best-preserved mummies are found. The keys are with a caretaker who lives up the hill from the caves. From the caves, it's about a 45-minute walk out to the Halsema Hwy.

are often part of the equation too – the rainy season starts earlier and ends later in the mountains. There are no functioning ATMs outside of Baguio and Sagada, so bring cash.

ⓘ Getting There & Around

The usual way into the Cordillera is via Baguio or Banaue, although more obscure routes exist. Rainy-season landslides often close the roads, so pack patience. The Halsema 'highway' linking Banaue with Bontoc is sealed nowadays. A real engineering feat when it was built in the 1920s, the Halsema snakes along a narrow ridge at altitudes up to 2255m, offering great views of precipitous valleys, green rice terraces and Luzon's highest peak, Mt Pulag (2922m).

Baguio

☏ 074 / POP 319,000 / ELEV 1450M

Vibrant, woodsy and cool by Philippine standards, Baguio (*bah*-gee-oh) is the Cordillera's nerve centre. The Philippines' 'summer capital' was founded as a hill station for the US military in the early 1900s. A university town, Baguio is known for live music, faith healers and funky restaurants. Unfortunately, even without tricycles (which can't climb the hills), Baguio has major air and noise pollution. The city's charm lies well outside the centre, in pine-forested parks such as Camp John Hay.

⊙ Sights & Activities

★ **Tam-awan Village**   ARTS CENTRE
(☏ 074-446 2949, 0921 588 3131; www.tam-awan village.com; Long-Long Rd, Pinsao; adult/student P50/30, workshops per person P450) ✎ Nine traditional Ifugao homes and two Kalinga huts were taken apart then reassembled on the side of a hill at the artist colony Tamawan Village. Spending the night in one of these huts (single/double P500/1000) is a rare treat. You can participate in art workshops, learn dream-catcher or bead making and see indigenous music and dance demonstrations. To get here, take a Quezon Hill–Tam-awan or Tam-awan–Long-Long jeepney from the corner of Kayang and Shagem Sts (P8).

BenCab Museum   MUSEUM
(www.bencabmuseum.org; Km 6, Asin Rd, Tadiangan; adult/student P100/80; ⊙ 9am-6pm Tue-Sun) This superb museum dedicated to the life, times and work of Benedicto Reyes Cabrera (BenCab) is as fascinating as the man who is its subject. The gallery is a mix of high glass

panes slanting light into modern art colon-
nades offset by walls of traditional animist
wood carvings, *bulol* (rice guardians), psychedelic works by Leonard Aguinaldo and
ceremonial *hagabi* (carved wooden benches). Asin Rd jeepneys get you here from Aba-
nao St near City Hall.

🛏 Sleeping

The most unique choice is Tam-awan Village, but it's at least a 15-minute ride from
the centre. For barflies, the **Dreams Tran-
sient House** (📞0933 522 5671; Palispis (Marcos) Hwy, Km 4; d/6-person P1000/3500; ❄) has
clean and spacious rooms under the Baguio
Craft Brewery.

Baguio Village Inn   GUESTHOUSE $
(📞074-442 3901; 355 Magsaysay Ave; s/d from
P400/750; 📶) Beyond the Slaughterhouse
Terminal, this warm and inviting backpacker
special is reminiscent of the cosy pinewood
guesthouses in Sagada. Rooms in the new
annexe at the back are pricier but quieter.

Upstairs Bed & Bath   HOSTEL $
(📞074-446 4687; upstairsbedandbath@gmail.com;
GSP Bldg, Leonard Wood Rd; dm P320, d P800-1200;
@📶) This place just southeast of SM Mall
has 90 beds spread over a variety of spotless
dorm rooms – the four-bed dorms cost the
same as the 20-bed dorms. It would benefit
from a kitchen and better common spaces.

YMCA Hostel   HOSTEL $
(📞074-442 4766; Post Office Loop; dm/d
P390/1300) The 'Y' boasts huge, bright dorm
rooms and colourful private rooms with soft
beds and flat-screen TVs – pretty good value.
It's just off Session Rd, opposite SM Mall.

🍴 Eating

Oh My Gulay!   VEGETARIAN $
(4th fl, La Azotea Bldg, Session Rd; mains P110-140;
⏱11am-8pm Sun-Thu, to 9pm Fri & Sat; 🍴) Step
into an enchanted, multilevel garden, with
wooden carvings, plants, bridges, water
features and little nooks to hide in. The
vego menu tempts with tofu *lumpia* (small
spring rolls) salad, pastas, filled crêpes and
more. Expect some strange flavours.

Volante Pizza   INTERNATIONAL $
(82 Session Rd; 6-/10in pizza from P69/210;
⏱24hr) Catering to night owls, revelers
with post-drinking munchies and a loyal
lunchtime crowd, this informal spot serves
surprisingly good pizza, fried chicken and
heaped po'boy sandwiches.

⭐**Cafe by the Ruins**   FUSION $$
(25 Chuntug St; mains P200-340; ⏱7am-9pm;
📶🍴) The thatched-wood interior of Bagu-
io's most beloved restaurant is awash in fo-
liage and sculpted wood. Its wide-reaching
menu is equally appealing, from the home-
made 'breads and spreads (pâtés)' to organic
salads, imaginative sandwiches and superla-
tive dishes such as the shrimp and mango
curry and Baguio *bagnet* (crispy pork belly).

🍷 Drinking & Entertainment

⭐**18 BC**   BAR
(16 Legarda Rd; ⏱6.30pm-late) In a city where
live music seemingly wafts out of every win-
dow, this dive opposite Prince Plaza Hotel
consistently features Baguio's best original
live music, from jazz and blues to reggae.
Annoyingly, no shorts or flip-flops allowed.

Baguio Craft Brewery   MICROBREWERY
(Palispis (Marcos) Hwy; beers from P160, mains
P300-350; ⏱5pm-2am; 📶) Baguio's entry on
the ever-growing ledger of Philippine craft-
brew houses is worth the mild slog out of
the center. Your reward is about 20 different
types of expertly crafted beers, fine moun-
tain views from the rooftop terrace, and
toothsome wings, fish tacos and other bar
snacks.

Rumours   BAR
(56 Session Rd; cocktails P85-130; ⏱11am-11pm)
A decades-old institution that draws a nice
mix of tourists, expats, local students and
random barflies. Some of the speciality
drinks will, in no uncertain terms, lay you
on your arse.

🛍 Shopping

Baguio is a shopping mecca where you can
find all manner of handicrafts, including
basketwork, textiles, Ifugao woodcarvings
and jewellery (silver is a local speciality).
Bargain hunters and photographers might

check out the lively City Market (Magsaysay Ave; ⊕ 6am-7pm), which sells everything from knock-off handicrafts to discounted Cordillera coffee to fresh-grilled chicken foetus. Didn't realize Baguio was so cold? The Night Market (Harrison Rd) is a great place to find a cheap used hoodie or raincoat.

ⓘ Information

Session Rd hosts several internet cafes and banks. The **Cordillera Regional Tourist Office** (☑ 074-442 7014; Governor Pack Rd; ⊕ 8am-5pm Mon-Fri) arranges guides (P1000 to P1500 per day) and tours throughout the Cordillera.

ⓘ Getting There & Away

Victory Liner (☑ 074-619 0000; Upper Session Rd) and **Genesis** (☑ 074-422 7763; Governor Pack Rd) run a few nonstop 29-seat deluxe buses to/from Manila mostly along new divided highways (P690 to P750, four hours); most Genesis 'Joybus' trips stop at NAIA Terminal 3. Otherwise, regular air-con trips take a much slower route to Manila every 30 minutes (P450, 6½ hours). Vigan-bound **Partas** (☑ 074-444 8431) buses go via San Fernando (P80 to P105, 1½ hours).

GL Lizardo (☑ 074-304 5994) has hourly buses until 1pm to Sagada (P222, 5½ hours) from the **Dangwa Terminal** (Magsaysay Ave), a five-minute walk north of Session Rd. **D'Rising Sun** (☑ 0910 709 9102) buses to Bontoc (P212, 5½ hours) leave hourly until 4pm from the **Slaughterhouse Terminal** (Magsaysay Ave), five minutes by jeepney beyond the Dangwa Terminal. These routes follow the spectacular Halsema Hwy.

Also from the Slaughterhouse Terminal, **NA Liner** has a 10am bus to Kabayan (P135, 4½ hours); or take the more frequent minivans, which leave when full until about 5pm (P150, 3½ hours). Minivans to Solano, where you'll find easy connections to Banaue, leave from the Dangwa Terminal roughly hourly (P250, 4½ hours).

KMS and Ohayami each have at least one night bus to Banaue (P450, 8½ hours) each day. Their terminals are near each other on Shanum St, west of Burnham Park.

Sagada

POP 1550 / ELEV 1477M

The epitome of mountain cool, Sagada is the place to escape from civilisation for a few days – or months. Caves, peaks, waterfalls and hanging coffins beckon the active traveller, while more sedate types can just kick back with a hot drink and a book and revel in Sagada's delightfully earthy ambience and chilly weather. Try to time your visit

for a *begnas* (traditional community celebration), when the hearty Kankanay locals gather in *dap-ay* (outdoor meeting places) to bang gongs, smoke pipes, swill brandy and sacrifice chickens. If possible avoid weekends, when tour vans from Manila arrive en masse. Sagada now has a functioning ATM, in the old Municipal Hall.

Guides are required for any trekking or caving you do around here – even easy ones. Grab one at the **Tourist Information Centre** (⊕ 7am-5pm) in the old Municipal Hall, or at the **Sagada Genuine Guides Association** (☑ 0916 559 9050; www.saggas.org), down the hill a little past Yoghurt House. Our favourite excursion is the thrilling half-day **cave connection** (P400 per person).

Sagada Outdoors (☑ 0919 698 8361; www.luzonoutdoors.com) runs rafting trips on the upper Chico River from September to December and thrilling canyoning trips near Sagada year-round, and is an authority on mountain biking and other adventures in the region.

🛏 Sleeping

Sagada's basic but charming guesthouses, swathed in pinewood and cosy linen, are a delight. Beds fill up on Saturday nights; home in on places (such as the following) that do not work with the invading weekend tour groups.

Misty Lodge & Cafe   LODGE $
(☑ 0926 123 5186; mistylodgeandcafe@rocketmail. com; r without bathroom per person P300; 🛜) It's definitely worth the 15-minute walk east out of town to stay (or just hang out) at this gem. The rooms are sizeable and swathed in radiant blonde wood, while a fireplace crackles in the cafe.

Green House   GUESTHOUSE $
(☑ 0999 903 7675; r per person P200; 🛜) Not only is it about the cheapest guesthouse we found, but it's also one of the warmest and quietest, set up on the hill over the south road. The simple rooms have plenty of rustic charm.

Treasure Rock Inn   GUESTHOUSE $
(☑ 0920 272 5881; r per person P300; 🛜) 'Aunty Mary' runs this spick-and-span guesthouse with killer views of Sagada's famed cliffs from the simple rooms. Its location 1km south of town ensures peace and quiet – except when the nightly videoke ramps up (but only until 9pm). Recently added an annexe with a few en suite rooms.

Davey's Inn & Restaurant GUESTHOUSE **$**
(📞 0939 506 1914; s/d P350/500; 🛜) The simple doubles, better than most in town, are fine value. It overlooks the plaza in the middle of town and has a big fireplace in the downstairs cafe.

✖ Eating

★ Yoghurt House FUSION **$**
(snacks P100, mains P160-240; ⊘ 8am-8.30pm; 🍴) We don't usually rave or fawn, but we can say with absolute certainty that this lovely eatery's tangy yoghurt sauce is the best thing ever to happen to (locally grown, succulent) vegetables. Take your banana pancake out on the balcony for breakfast, get some of the great oatmeal cookies to go, or linger over pasta, chunky sandwiches or beef cutlets.

Gaia Cafe VEGETARIAN **$**
(mains P120-145; ⊘ 7am-7pm Wed-Mon; 🍴) Hidden in the woods 1.6km south of the centre, past the Lumiang Cave entrance, Gaia serves locally sourced vego fare amid pine trees and in view of rice terraces. There are books to browse and a store packed with stuff that hippies like.

Bana's Cafe CAFE **$**
(mains P100-170; ⊘ 6.30am-8pm; 🛜🍴) Oriented toward trekkers, Bana's specialises in coffee, omelettes and delicious homemade yoghurt. Its narrow balcony overlooks a gorge and catches the morning sun.

ℹ Getting There & Away

Jeepneys to Bontoc depart at least every hour until 1pm (P45, 45 minutes). The last bus to Baguio leaves at 1pm.

Coda Lines (📞 0929 521 3247; Sagada Public Mkt) runs a bus to Manila (P720, 11 hours, 3pm).

SPLURGE

The fireplace dining at **Log Cabin** (📞 0915 671 7949; mains P190-290; ⊘ 6-9pm) hits the spot on those chilly Sagada evenings. Treat yourself to the likes of roast meats in delicious sauces, rösti or spicy curries. On Saturdays, there's a wonderful buffet (P390, prepaid reservations only). Upstairs it has one room available (P1500) that is arguably Sagada's best.

Bontoc

📞 074 / POP 3030 / ELEV 900M

This Wild West frontier town is the central Cordillera's transport and market hub. Make a point of visiting the **Bontoc Museum** (admission P60; ⊘ 8am-noon & 1-5pm), which has fascinating exhibits on each of the region's main tribes. Check out the grisly photos of head-hunters and their booty.

There's some awesome trekking to be done around Bontoc, most notably to the stone-walled rice terraces of Maligcong, which rival those in Batad. Secure a guide (P1200 per day) and map at the handy Tourism Information Center. French- and German-speaking **Kinad** (📞 0920 528 1441, 0929 384 1745; kinad139@yahoo.com) is an experienced guide around here.

To really get off the beaten track, head even further north into Kalinga province, where you can hike to remote villages and meet aged former head-hunters. **Francis Pa-In** (📞 0915 769 0843) guides treks in Kalinga province.

If you are staying a night, **Churya-a Hotel & Restaurant** (📞 0999 994 6726; Halsema Hwy; s/d/tr P250/500/800; 🛜) has clean if somewhat dysfunctional rooms, and a pleasant balcony restaurant over Bontoc's main street. If you want air-con and a modicum of comfort, cross the Chico River to the **Archog Hotel** (📞 0917 695 9036, 0918 328 6908; r P600-1200; 🛜).

Jeepneys to Sagada (P45, 45 minutes) leave hourly until 5.30pm. Hourly D'Rising sun buses serve Baguio. For Banaue, there is a jeepney (P150) around 8am, another one around noon, and three morning buses (P120). Minivans (P150) are another option, leaving when full until noon.

For Vigan, take three minivans: Bontoc–Abatan (Bauko; P50, 45 minutes); Abatan–Cervantes (P70, 50 minutes); and Cervantes–Tagudin (P150, two hours). From Tagudin flag down a northbound bus to Vigan (P130, two hours).

Banaue & the Rice Terraces

📞 074 / POP 2600 / ELEV 1200

Banaue is synonymous with the Unesco World Heritage–listed Ifugao rice terraces, hewn out of the hillsides by the Ifugao tribe using primitive tools and an ingenious irrigation system some 2000 years ago. Legend has it that the god Kabunyan used the steps to visit his people on earth.

PHILIPPINES THE CORDILLERA

Banaue proper – a ragged collection of tin-roofed edifices along a ridge – is not the best place to view the terraces. Instead, venture 45 minutes east to Batad, or to even less touristy Ifugao towns like Bangaan, Cambulo, Hapao, Kiangan and Pula. Some of these are accessible on hikes out of Banaue.

If you're short on time, Banaue's own mud-walled terraces are best ogled from a series of viewpoints about 2km north of town; a tricycle there and back costs P220.

🛌 Sleeping & Eating

Most Banaue rooms lack electrical sockets, so prepare to do battle for use of public power outlets. Some guesthouses charge P20 for charging privileges.

⭐ Randy's Brookside Inn GUESTHOUSE $
(📱0917 577 2010; r from P200; 🛜) Not only is Randy a great, knowledgeable host whose brain you may wish to pick about all things Banaue, but he runs a ship-shape guesthouse with the cheapest rooms in town and throws in a free breakfast. A win for backpackers everywhere.

Stairway Lodge & Restaurant GUESTHOUSE $
(📱0916 456 7346; s P250, d P400-600; 🛜) The rooms here are simple delights. They open to cosy common rooms on the 2nd and 3rd floors and come equipped with tables and warm blankets. The cheaper bathroom-less rooms are roadside and, hence, noisier.

People's Lodge GUESTHOUSE $
(📱0935 189 5455; s/d from P300/500; @🛜) This centrally located spot has a huge variety of rooms and a popular restaurant with rice-terrace views and a balcony that most of its neighbours lack.

7th Heaven's GUESTHOUSE $
(📱0908 467 4854; r per person P250; ⊙cafe 7am-8pm) Operating strictly as a cafe when we visited, friendly 7th Heaven's will have rooms open from 2016. Located 500m up the road from the main town, the wonderful cafe has the best views in town, and the rooms promise to have similar allure.

ℹ Information

Pay your environmental fee (P50) at the **Municipal Tourism Center** (📱0906 770 7969; ⊙6am-7pm), up on the ridge road at the bus drop-off point, which also arranges accredited guides (full day P1200), hands out maps and posts a list of prices for private transport. You can change

dollars at the **moneychanger** (Old Banaue Market, 2nd fl; ⊙8am-6pm Mon-Sat, 2-6pm Sun).

ℹ Getting There & Away

Ohayami and more comfortable **Dangwa** (📱0918 522 5049) each run one overnight trip (more in the high season) to/from Manila (seven to eight hours) for P450 and P530, respectively.

If you prefer daytime travel, get to Solano by jeepney (P110, 2½ hours with a transfer in Lagawe) and flag down a frequent Manila-bound bus (P375, eight hours).

KMS and Ohayami night buses to Baguio ply the lowland route via Solano and Rosario (P415, 8½ hours). One or two morning vans do this trip via Solano and the Ambuklao Rd shortcut (P400, six hours).

There's an 8.30am jeepney to Bontoc (P150, 1¾ hours), and a handful of Bontoc-bound buses (P120) pass through Banaue in the late morning.

Batad

POP 1025 / ELEV 1100

Batad sits at the foot of a truly mesmerising amphitheatre of rice fields. Most of the inhabitants still practise traditional tribal customs in what must be one of the most serene, picture-perfect villages to grace the earth. A new sealed road terminating just short of the village means you no longer have to walk 45 minutes in. This will make life easier for locals but will undoubtedly mean more crowds from Manila, especially on weekends and holidays.

If the scene is getting too out of control, hike to nearby Cambulo or Pula, or venture further afield to Mayoyao or to Barlig and Kadaclan in neighbouring Mountain Province. All have simple guesthouses.

A slippery 40-minute walk beyond Batad village itself is the 30m-high **Tappiya Waterfall** and swimming hole. Guides are available through the Batad Environmental Tour Guides Association (P1000 to P1300 per day).

Most guesthouses are up on the 'viewpoint' overlooking Batad village and the amphitheatre, near where you enter the area and pay your heritage fee (P50). Hillside Inn, Batad Guesthouse & Pension, Rita's, Simon's Inn and Ramon's all have restaurants and rooms for about P250 per head. They're all simple, clean and rustic, but Hillside wins our hearts with its good food and all-round charm.

The daily jeepney from Banaue goes most of the way to Batad; you still have to walk the final 15 minutes or so. It departs Banaue at

3pm (P150, 1¼ hours); the return from Batad is at 9am the next morning. A tricycle or motorbike taxi costs P1000 return. Consider exiting Batad via the beautiful two-hour hike down to scenic **Bangaan**, where you can flag down various morning jeepneys to Banaue.

Vigan

📞 077 / POP 49,747

Spanish-era mansions, cobblestone streets and *kalesa* (two-wheeled horse carriages) are the hallmarks of Unesco World Heritage Site Vigan. Miraculously spared bombing in WWII, the city is considered the finest surviving example of a Spanish colonial town. Two of Vigan's finer mansions are the **Crisologo Museum** (Liberation Blvd; entry by donation; ☺ 8.30-11.30am & 1.30-4.30pm) and the **Syquia Mansion Museum** (Quirino Blvd; admission P30; ☺ 9am-noon & 1.30-5pm Wed-Mon).

🛏 Sleeping & Eating

Evening **street stalls** (Plaza Burgos; snacks P50) peddle local snacks such as empanadas (deep-fried tortillas with shrimp, cabbage and egg) and *okoy* (shrimp omelettes).

Henady Inn   HOTEL $
(📞 077-722 8001; National Hwy; dm P250, d P825-1375; 🏵) Out on the highway right where the buses drop you off, the four-bed dorms will please penny pinchers and/or early-morning arrivals looking for a few extra hours of shuteye.

Hem Apartelle   GUESTHOUSE $$
(📞 077-722 2173; 32 Governor A Reyes St; s/d P600/1000; 🏵🛜) No heritage-style lodging here: the Hem is a reliable air-conditioned guesthouse that's relatively easy on the wallet. Rooms are tiled and characterless, but there are TVs, clean sheets, clean floors and clean toilets you can sit on – win!

Cafe Uno   ILOCANO $
(1 Bonifacio St; mains P100-150; ☺ 9am-11.30pm; 🛜) Attached to neighbouring Grandpa's Inn, this cafe has a loyal local clientele, largely thanks to its take on the Vigan *longganisa* (ocal sausage) and *bagnet*. Its shakes and cakes are worth a stop, too.

ℹ Getting There & Away

Many bus companies serve Manila (ordinary/air-con/deluxe P450/680/850, seven to 10 hours). **Partas** (📞 077-722 3369; Alcantara St) and **Dominion** (📞 077-722 2084; cnr Liberation

Blvd & Quezon Ave) have stations near the public market, 1km southwest of the historic centre. Other buses drop you off on the national highway, 500m north of the historic centre.

Partas has about 11 daily air-con trips to Baguio (P330, five hours) via San Fernando.

Legazpi

📞 052 / POP 179,481

Charm is in short supply in the city of Legazpi, but with the towering cone of Mt Mayon hogging the horizon no one seems to notice. The city lies at the centre of Southeast Luzon's Bicol region, an adventure wonderland of sorts known for fiery food and furious volcanoes. Pay extra attention to the news before heading this way lest you waltz into one of the region's patented typhoons.

Legazpi is divided into Albay District, where the provincial government offices and airport are located, and commercial Legazpi City. A steady stream of jeepneys connects the two districts along Rizal St.

Make the vigorous 30-minute climb up **Lignon Hill** (admission P20) near the airport for the best views of Mt Mayon.

🛏 Sleeping

Mayon Backpackers Hostel   HOSTEL $
(📞 052-742 2613; http://mayonbackpackers.wordpress.com; Diego Silang St, Albay District; dm with fan/air-con P250/350, d/q P1000/1200; 🏵@🛜) The only legitimate hostel in Legazpi is the clear top budget choice, with comfy six- and four-bed dorm rooms, a basic common kitchen and a rooftop with hammocks and views to Mt Mayon. Book ahead in the high season as it fills up fast. It's near St Gregory's Cathedral.

Catalina's Lodging House   GUESTHOUSE $
(📞 052-742 0351; 96 Peñaranda Ext; s/d from P200/270) Creaky old wooden standby in the

middle of Legazpi City is cheap, basic and noisy, but who's complaining at these prices. Angle for a room at the back.

★ **Balai Tinay Guesthouse** B&B **$$**
(☑ 052-742 3366; 70 Gapo St; s/d incl breakfast from P1050/1200; ❄ 🛜) Run by the loveliest, most attentive hosts who are happy to assist with planning your Legazpi adventures, this family-run guesthouse sits on a quiet little street in Albay; head right along the riverside path from Albay Central School. The compact en suite rooms are spick and span and guests can help themselves to fruit and drinks in the common area.

✖ Eating & Drinking

Be sure to sample the spicy Bicolano cuisine. Must-try dishes include *pinangat* (taro leaves wrapped around minced fish or pork), '*Bicol exprés*' (spicy minced pork dish), *laing* (a leafy green vegetable) and *pili* nuts mixed with miniscule, red-hot *sili* peppers. Try the nightly **street stalls** along Quezon Ave near the Trylon Monument in Legazpi City for budget Bicolano fare.

For drinking head to **The Boulevard**, a long stretch of seafront restobars beyond the Embarcadero Mall (behind Sleeping Lion Hill).

Seadog Diner FUSION **$**
(The Boulevard; mains P95-150; ⊘ 7am-midnight; 🛜) Good pizzas and Bicol-accented Italian fare. Great spot for a drink, too.

Sibid-Sibid SEAFOOD **$$**
(328 Peñaranda St; mains P100-235; ⊘ 10am-9pm; ☺ 🛜) A wonderful open-air restaurant 1km north of Legazpi City, Sibid-Sibid specialises in highly original, Bicol-inspired seafood concoctions like fish Bicol *express*. Has the best *pinangat* we've had.

❶ Getting There & Away

Cebu Pacific and PAL Express fly several times daily to/from Manila, and Cebu Pacific adds flights to Cebu.

The main bus terminal is at the Satellite Market, just west of Pacific Mall in Legazpi City. **Cagsawa** (☑ 052-235 0381) and **Isarog** (☑ 0908 851 2651) have deluxe 27-seat night buses to the **Araneta Bus Terminal** (Map p550; btwn Times Sq & Gen Romulo Aves) in Cubao (P1050, 12 hours) plus 40-seat air-con buses directly to Ermita in Manila (P850). **Philtranco** (☑ 052-742 0331) has deluxe services to Pasay, and there are loads of air-con and ordinary (P500) services to Cubao.

Air-con minivans zip to Donsol (P75, 1¼ hours) roughly hourly until 5pm, and to Sorsogon (P90, 1¼ hours, frequent), where you can pick up a jeepney to Matnog, departure point of ferries to Samar.

Around Legazpi

Mt Mayon

Bicolanos sure hit the nail on the head when they named this monolith – *magayon* is the local word for 'beautiful'. The impossibly perfect cone rises to a height of 2462m above sea level and emits a constant plume of smoke.

The volcano's summit is closed more often than not because of the risk of eruptions – in 2013 Mayon belched boulders that killed four European climbers and a guide. At the time of research the mountain was at Alert Level 1, meaning you're not meant to climb past Camp 2 (1600m), although many guides (mandatory) will take you higher. The 1½-day trek to Camp 2 costs about P5000 per person for a group of two, including camping equipment, porters, permits, guides, food etc.

The best time of year to climb Mt Mayon is February to April. From May to August it's unbearably hot; from September to January it's wet. Donsol Ecotour (p568) and **Mayon Naturalist Eco-Guides of Albay** (Manega; ☑ 0915 422 4508; pinangat2001@yahoo.com) organise Mt Mayon climbs out of Legazpi. **ATV tours** (P700 to P3000) run by **Bicol Adventure ATV** (☑ 0917 571 4357; www.bicoladventure atv.com) and **Your Brother Travel & Tours** (☑ 052-742 9871; http://mayonatvtour.com) are also popular.

Donsol

POP 4200

Every year between November and June, *butanding* (whale sharks) frolic in the waters off this sleepy fishing village about 50km from Legazpi. It's truly an exhilarating experience swimming along with these silver-spotted leviathans, which can reach 14m in length.

Sightings have become much more unpredictable in recent years. After down years in 2012 and 2013, 2014 and 2015 saw the whale sharks return in decent numbers. We highly recommend contacting **Donsol Ecotour** (☑ 0917 506 3554; www.donsolecotour.

com) in Legazpi or the Donsol Tourist Centre before you visit to see if the whale sharks are in town. If you miss the whale sharks, the manta bowl off nearby Ticao Island is a backup option, albeit one for advanced scuba divers only.

When you arrive in town, head to the **Donsol Tourist Center** (☏0919 707 0394, 0927 483 6735; ◷7am-5pm), 1.5km north of town along the coastal road, to pay your registration fee (P300) and arrange a boat (P3500 for up to six people) for your three-hour tour. Each boat has a spotter and a *butanding* interaction officer on board – tip them a couple of hundred pesos, especially if you've had a good day. Snorkelling equipment is available for hire (P300). Scuba diving is prohibited.

🛏 Sleeping & Eating

There are a couple of homestays in town, the pick of which is super-friendly **Aguluz Homestay** (☏0918 942 0897, 0920 952 8170; razormarilyn@yahoo.com; San José St; r with fan/air-con from P800/1000; ❄🛜). The following are north of town near the tourist centre.

★**Dancalan Beach Resort**　　　　　　RESORT $
(☏0905 218 2973; lyn_amor0122@yahoo.com.ph; dm P500, r P800-2000; ❄🛜) The fan rooms and two-bed dorms at this recently renovated standby are Donsol's best value. The pricier concrete air-con rooms, with shiny white tiles, blonde-wood bed frames and patios, are immaculate. Equally well-maintained sister property **Amor Farm Beach Resort** (☏0909 518 1150; http://amordonsolwhaleshark.com; r P1200-1800; ❄🛜) down the road is another fine option.

Vitton & Woodland Resorts　　　　　　HOTEL $
(☏0917 544 4089; vittonandwoodlandresorts@gmail.com; dm P500, r from P1800; ◷closed Jul-Oct; ❄🛜🏊) Twin resorts a couple of hundred metres away from each other north of the visitors centre. The seven dorm rooms – all of the three-bed variety – are at the older Woodland. The nicer rooms are at Vitton. Each resort has a pool, lovely garden, clean accommodation and friendly service.

❶ Getting There & Away

Air-con minivans (P75, 1¼ hours) and jeepneys (P60, two hours) leave hourly to Legazpi until 4pm.

MINDORO

There are two sides to this large island just south of Luzon: Puerto Galera, and the rest of Mindoro.

Puerto Galera is a dive mecca that lies at the heart of the Verde Island Passage – one of the world's most biologically diverse underwater environments. It's essentially an extension of Luzon.

The rest of Mindoro is an untamed hinterland of virtually impenetrable mountains populated by one of Asia's most primitive tribes, the Mangyan. Those who like to get *way* off the beaten track need look no further. Off the west coast, accessible from the towns of Calintaan and Sablayan, underwater wonderland Apo Reef is populated by sharks and stingrays.

At the south of Mindoro, Roxas is mainly a jumping-off point to Caticlan (for Boracay).

Puerto Galera

☏043 / POP 32,521
It lacks the beautiful beach, classy resorts and hip nightlife of Boracay, but this diving hot spot on the northern tip of Mindoro is conveniently located just a hop, skip and bangka ride from Manila. The name Puerto Galera (PG) typically refers to the town of Puerto Galera and the resort areas surrounding it – namely Sabang Beach, 7km to the east, and White Beach, 7km to the west. The town proper has a breathtakingly beautiful harbour and an ATM, but otherwise is of little interest.

❶ Getting There & Around

Speedy bangka ferries to Puerto Galera town, Sabang Beach and White Beach leave regularly throughout the day from Batangas pier until about 4.30pm or 5pm (P310 including port and environmental fees, 1½ hours). The last trip back to Batangas from Sabang (P230) leaves at 1pm or 2pm (on Sunday and in peak periods there's a later boat); from White Beach it's 3pm, and from Puerto Galera town it's 3.30pm. Be prepared for a rough crossing.

In particularly bad weather, opt for the sturdier 'ROROs' (roll-on-roll-off, or car ferries) and 'fastcraft' boats that connect Batangas and Calapan, 45km south of Puerto Galera.

To reach Roxas, where ferries depart for Caticlan (for Boracay), take a jeepney (P80) or van (P100) to Calapan from the Petron station in PG town (1¼ hours, every 45 minutes), then transfer to a Roxas-bound van (P200, three hours).

PHILIPPINES PUERTO GALERA

Puerto Galera & Around

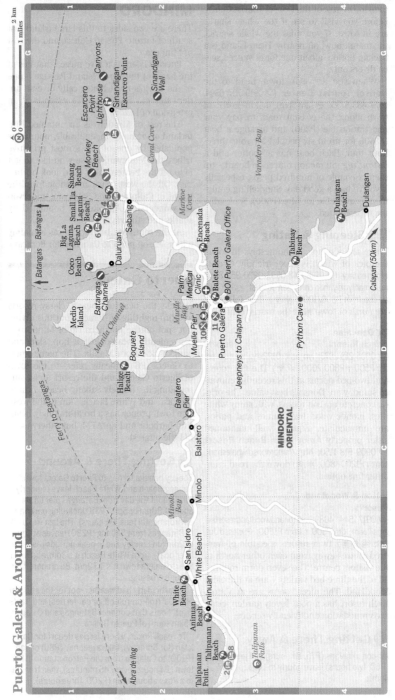

MINDORO ORIENTAL

Calapan (50km)

Python Cave

Dulangan Beach
Dulangan

Tabinay Beach

Encenada Beach
Balete Beach
Palm Medical Clinic
BOI Puerto Galera Office
Puerto Galera
Jeepneys to Calapan

Sabang
Daluruan

Muelle Bay
Muelle Pier

Halige Beach

Boquete Island
Medio Island

Batangas Channel
Manila Channel
Ferry to Batangas

Balatero Pier
Balatero
Minolo
Minolo Bay

San Isidro
White Beach
Aninuan Beach
Aninuan
Talipanan Beach
Talipanan Point
Talipanan Falls

White Beach

Abra de Ilog

Coco Beach
Big La Laguna Beach
Small La Laguna Beach
Sabang Beach
Monkey Beach

Escarcero Point Lighthouse
Escarcero Point
Sinandigan
Canyons
Sinandigan Wall

Varadero Bay
Coral Cove
Marhoe Cove

Puerto Galera & Around

Regular jeepneys connect Sabang and PG town during daylight hours (P20, 20 minutes); a tricycle between the two costs P100 (more at night) and from Sabang to Talipanan a tricycle costs P300. Motorcycle taxis are cheaper.

Sabang & Around

Sabang is where most of the hotels, restaurants and bars are concentrated. Drinking and underwater pursuits are the activities of choice, with plenty of establishments offering variations on these themes.

Sabang's 'beach' is a narrow sliver of brown sand traversed by rivulets of sewage, and its late-night entertainment scene is decidedly less than wholesome. To escape, walk around the headland to cleaner, more laid-back Small La Laguna Beach, where several resorts front a brown strip of sand. Beyond that is prettier Big La Laguna Beach.

Activities

Dive prices vary wildly, so shop around. Tina's Reef Divers (☑0921 205 8578; www.tinasreefdivers.com; Sabang; per dive including equipment P1000) and Big Apple (☑0919 449 8298; per dive P1100) have the best rates, while Octopus Divers (☑0919 379 0811; www.mac-octopusdivers.com; Sabang; per dive P1250)

and Capt'n Gregg's (☑0917 540 4570; www.captngreggs.com; Sabang; per dive P1400) are reliable midrange operators. An open-water course will set you back P14,500 to P20,000.

Sleeping

Expect big discounts in the June-to-October low season. Walk-ins will find some great values up on the hill at the far eastern end of Sabang Beach.

★ **Reynaldo's Upstairs** GUESTHOUSE $
(☑0917 489 5609; rey_purie@yahoo.com; Sabang; r P900-1200; ❈🛜) Run by the nicest family you'll ever meet, Reynaldo's has a splendid mix of more-than-passable budget fan rooms and large 'view' rooms with kitchenettes and private balconies on a hillside. Some rooms even have extras like DVDs and wicker love seats.

★ **Capt'n Gregg's Dive Resort** LODGE $
(☑043-287 3070, 0917 540 4570; www.captngreggs.com; r with fan P800-1200, with air-con P1200-1900; ❈🛜) This Sabang institution has been the best value in town for more than 25 years. The compact but cosy wood-lined 'old' rooms, right over the water, still have the most charm and are also the cheapest.

Cataquis COTTAGE $
(☑0916 297 8455; Big La Laguna Beach; r with fan/air-con from P800/1500; ❈🛜) The tidy concrete cottages here are flush with the beach. A few larger rooms are tucked into the trees at the back. The Filipino restaurant (mains P160 to P350) is excellent value and sits plum on the Sabang area's best beach.

Big Apple Dive Resort RESORT $
(☑043-287 3134; www.divebigapple.com; r P500-2000; ❈🛜🏊) In the middle of Sabang Beach, this is party central, with some noisy and tatty fan rooms to go with swankier digs around the pool out back.

SPLURGE

El Galleon Beach Resort (☑0917 814 5107, 043-287-3205; www.elgalleon.com; Small La Laguna; d incl breakfast US$59-110, villas US$110-315; ❈🛜🏊) features elegant rooms, a fine restaurant and a top technical dive school, not to mention one of the Philippines' best bars in the Point Bar. It's *the* place to stay in Sabang if you want to spend the cash.

Paddy's   GUESTHOUSE $

(☑ 0926 723 1792; Sinandigan; d with fan/air-con P400/500; ☎) About 1.5km east of Sabang (P20 by motorbike), Paddy's is about the closest thing to a hostel in Puerto Galera. It has six boxy doubles and a well-stocked bar overlooking a ravine. Choose from bunk-bed or double-bed configurations.

✖ Eating & Drinking

Restaurants in Sabang are, in a word, expensive. Among the resorts, Cap'n Gregg's and El Galleon Beach Resort are good choices.

Sabang Restaurant   INTERNATIONAL $

(mains P100-465; ⊘7am-11pm) A busy, long-standing restaurant on the main drag in Sabang. It's known for shakes and discount brekkies, but also doles out a surprisingly good range of hearty European fare.

Tina's   GERMAN, FILIPINO $$

(Sabang; mains P200-450; ⊘8am-10pm; ☎) Swiss-tinged Tina's has some of the best food on the beachfront, and the prices are good for PG. Do try the schnitzel.

★ Point Bar   BAR

(El Galleon Beach Resort, Small La Laguna) Our favourite bar. The Point Bar is a mellow sunset-and-beyond meeting place with great views and eclectic music. It's one of the few bars in town where solo women travellers can feel comfortable.

Puerto Galera Town

The town proper boasts a row of restaurants that front the gorgeous harbour at Muelle Pier. Badladz (☑ 043-287 3693; www.badladz.com; Muelle Pier; d/tr P1490/1990; ❄☎) overlooking the harbor is the best place to stay and has a respected dive shop. Around Muelle Pier, Hangout Bar (Muelle Pier; mains P180-280; ⊘7am-10pm; ☎) has pub grub and computers with internet access, while Robby's Cafeteria (Main Rd, opposite Muelle Pier; mains P150-300, pizzas P200-360; ⊘8am-9pm) has harbour views and some of the best Italian food you'll find anywhere.

West Beaches

About 7km west of Puerto Galera are three neighbouring beaches. First up is White Beach. It has a much better beach than Sabang, but accommodation is tacky and overpriced and it fills up with mobs of Mani-leños on weekends. During weekdays it can be quiet and pleasant.

Next up is mellow, clean Aninuan Beach, but an even better option is attractive Talipanan Beach, at the end of the road in the shadow of Mt Malasimbo (1215m). Home in on Amami Beach Resort (☑ 0908 206 8534; www.amamibeachresort.com; Talipanan; r from P1200; ☎). Run with gusto by a hospitable Italian-Filipino family, it has simple but tasteful native-style rooms and an excellent restaurant (mains P180 to P250). Keep an eye out for its periodic full moon parties (see www.fullmoonphilippines.com). Nearby, Mountain Beach Resort (☑ 0906 362 5406; www.mountainbeachresort.com; Talipanan; d with fan/air-con from P1000/2000; ❄@☎) is also good value, with a wide variety of bamboo-infused accommodation.

Roxas

☑ 043 / POP 49,854

Roxas is a dusty little spot with ferry connections to Caticlan from Dangay pier, about 3km from the town centre. If you get stuck, there are several basic hotels at the pier, the most comfortable of which is Tulip Residence Inn (☑ 043-289 3150; Dangay Pier; r 6hr/24hr P1000/1500; ❄@☎).

If you are heading to Caticlan (P400, four hours), call the Ports Authority (☑ 043-289 2813) at Dangay pier to check the schedule, as departures are infrequent during the day. Montenegro Lines (☑ 0909 856 6559) has one fairly reliable afternoon departure at 2pm or 4pm, and a less reliable morning departure at 8am or 10am. Other companies have night trips only.

Vans to Calapan (P200, three hours) leave straight from Dangay pier.

THE VISAYAS

If it's white sand, rum and coconuts you're after, look no further than the jigsaw puzzle of central islands known as the Visayas. From party-mad Boracay and Cebu to mountainous Negros, to dreamy Siquijor and Malapascua, the Visayas have about everything an island nut could ask for. Hopping among paradisiacal, palm-fringed isles, you'll inevitably wonder why you can't go on doing this forever.

Indeed, many foreigners *do* give it all up and live out their years managing this resort

The Visayas

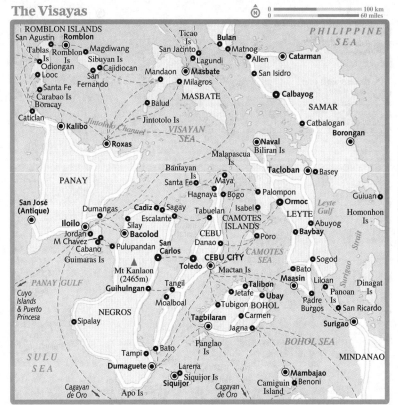

or that dive centre on some exquisite patch of white sand. Others merely end up extending their trip for weeks – or months. This is one area of the country where you can dispense with advanced planning. Just board that first ferry and follow your nose.

Boracay

📞 036 / POP 9800

With a postcard-perfect, 3km-long white beach and the country's best island nightlife, it's not hard to figure out why Boracay is the country's top tourist draw. Overdevelopment has made some old-timers long for the halcyon days of no electricity, but the debate about whether it's better now or was better then won't worry you too much when you're digging your feet into the sand on White Beach and taking in the Philippines' most famous sunset.

Parasails, seabirds, frisbees and *paraw* (small bangka sailboats) cut across the Tech-

nicolor horizon, while palm trees whisper in the breeze and reggae wafts through the air. Oh yeah, and you're in a beachfront bar that's generously serving two-for-one cocktails. Yes, even 'developed' Boracay remains a master mixologist of that mellow island vibe.

Tiny Boracay is a satellite of Panay, the most westerly of the Visayas' six major islands. Panay famously hosts the mother of all Philippine fiestas, Kalibo's Mardi Gras–like Ati-Atihan, around the third week of January. Panay's capital and gateway to the rest of the Visayas is Iloilo, a six-hour bus ride south of Boracay.

🏃 Activities

Beaches

On signature White Beach, three out-of-service 'boat stations' orient visitors. The area south of Station 3, known as Angol, most resembles the less-developed 'old Boracay'. The stretch between Station 3 and

Boracay

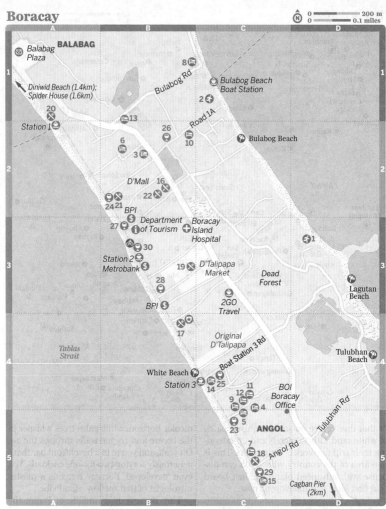

Station 1 is busy and commercial. White Beach's widest, most incredible stretch is north of Station 1 around **Willie's Rock**.

Activities offered on White Beach include paraw rides (per hour P600), diving, stand-up paddleboarding and parasailing. Daily games of football, volleyball and ultimate frisbee kick off in the late afternoon.

North of White Beach, you can find relative solitude on sleepy **Diniwid Beach** (although half of this beach was recently given up to developers), while explorers looking for genuine solitude should seek out **Ilig-Iligan Beach** near Boracay's northeastern tip.

Kitesurfing

During the height of the *amihan* (northeast monsoon, December to March), consistent winds, shallow water and decent prices (P19,000 for a nine- to 12-hour certification course) make **Bulabog Beach** on the east side of the island the perfect place to learn kitesurfing. The action shifts to White Beach during the less consistent May-to-October *habagat* (southwest monsoon). Operators include **Freestyle Academy** (☏ 0915 559 3080; www.freestyle-boracay.com), **Hangin** (☏ 036-288 3766; www.kite-asia.com), and **Habagat** (☏ 036-288 5787; www.kiteboracay.com).

Boracay

PHILIPPINES BORACAY

🛏 Sleeping

Most budget accommodation on White Beach is at Angol. Off White Beach, a backpacker ghetto of sorts is taking shape around Rd 1A toward Bulabog.

Rates everywhere drop 20% to 50% in the low season (June to October). Walking in often nets a discount, and bargaining might bear fruit at any time of year.

🛏 Angol

Walk-in guests are advised to venture south of Station 3 to a cluster of about 10 resorts located up a path behind Arwana Resort. The best deal is **Ocean Breeze Inn** (☑ 036-288 1680; www.oceanbreezeinn.info; r P1100-1900; ❄️🛜), where a couple of elegant rattan-swathed garden cottages complement air-conditioned concrete rooms. Nipa (traditional thatched Filipino hut) colony **Melinda's Garden** (☑ 036-288 3021; www.melindasgarden.com; r with fan P1500, with air-con P2500-3500; ❄️🛜) has the most charm. **Dave's Straw Hat Inn** (☑ 036-288 5465; www.davesstrawhatinn.com; r with fan/air-con P1800/2500; ❄️🛜) is a step up in style and price. Haggle hard at all of these. Other good options here are **Orchids** (☑ 0917 242 0833, 036-288 3313; www.orchidsboracay.com; r P950-2350; ❄️🛜) and **Escurel** (☑ 036-288 3611; escurelinn@yahoo.com; r with fan/air-con P1000/1500; ❄️@🛜).

Tree House Da Mario   RESORT $
(☑ 036-288 3601; littlecornerofitaly@yahoo.com; dm P250-350, d P1400-3800; ❄️🛜) The four-

bed fan dorm rooms here are far from fancy, but they are the island's cheapest crash pads.

Sulu-Plaza   HOTEL $$
(☑ 036-288 3400; www.sulu-plaza.com; r from P1900; ❄️🛜) For a very reasonable price you get a stylish room filled with two bamboo chairs, comfy thick beds and attractive art, plus a beachfront location right at Station 3. Or opt for the spacious corner apartments for two on the upper floor (P3100).

🛏 Central White Beach & Bulabog

⭐ **MNL Hostel**   HOSTEL $
(☑ 0917 702 2160; www.mnlhostels.com; Rd 1a; incl breakfast dm P500-580, d P1550; ❄️@🛜) This high-rise hostel has quickly become the backpacker's choice on Bulabog. Super-clean, intelligently designed (eg private outlets and pull-out lockers at your double-wide dorm bed) and lots of fun, with a rooftop lounge and open-air kitchen, plus karaoke once a week. Hot rain showers and free breakfast don't hurt either.

ℹ SAVINGS IN A BOTTLE

Save the environment – and plenty of money – by refilling plastic water bottles at filling stations dotted along Boracay's main road. Closer to the beach, near Station 3, is **Boracay Nutria Water** (1L refill P7; ⏲ 6.30am-8pm).

> **SPLURGE**
>
> Run by local legend Jude, **Hey! Jude** (☏036-288 2401, 0917 861 6618; www. heyjude-boracay.com; d incl breakfast P2900-5350; ❋🛜) is Boracay's perfect midrange beach hotel. The minimalist style and variety of rooms – the priciest of which open to the sea – are just right. The low-key breakfast by the White Beach path is the ideal start to the day.

Frendz Resort
HOSTEL $

(☏036-288 3801; www.frendzresortboracay.com; Station 1; dm P600, r with fan/air-con P2000/2800; ❋@🛜) A lively bar (open til 11pm) peddling cheap cocktails and teeming with young backpackers makes long-running Frendz the party people's choice. Dedicated beach beds (a two-minute walk) complement your stay. The single-sex dorms are cosy but lack air-con.

Box & Ladder
HOSTEL $

(☏0917 881 0598; www.boxandladder.com; Boracay Midway Bldg; dm incl breakfast P500; ❋🛜) Crawling into bed at this new hostel on the noisy main road feels a bit like crawling into a human-sized cubby hole, but they are nothing if not cosy and all sleeping 'pods' have electrical sockets, lockers and curtains.

Second Wind
GUESTHOUSE $

(☏036-288 1025; www.secondwindbb.com; Bulabog Rd; dm incl breakfast P600-850, d P1750; ❋🛜) The two en suite dorms here feel somewhat like an after-thought. However, they are among the most spacious and well appointed on the island, and the pleasant courtyard restaurant makes up for the lack of a hostel-style common area.

Jeepney Hostel & Boracay Kite Resort
HOSTEL $$

(☏947 777 3551; www.jeepneyhostelboracay.com; Bulabog Rd; incl breakfast dm P700, d P1600-2000; ❋🛜) Canadian-owned Jeepney is Boracay's first all-inclusive backpacker party mecca. On Bulabog Beach, it caters to hard-living kitesurfers with regular parties, a kitesurfing center and the lively Fusion Sports Bar (open 24 hours). Choose from polished bamboo dorm beds in the hostel or the kite resort's clean and colorful private rooms.

Eating

You'll find the best deals on Filipino food along the main road. Of course, it's worth paying a bit more for the ambience of White Beach – just stroll along until you see something that takes your fancy. Self-caterers can shop at two supermarkets in D'Mall, adjacent to the main road.

Nargisa Coffee Shop
JAPANESE $

(Surfside Boracay Hotel, Angol; mains P100-320; ⊙11.30am-3pm & 4.30-11pm) One of several affordable Japanese eateries on Boracay, Nargisa commands the southern end of White Beach, serving up affordable sashimi, okonomiyaki and a big P100 snack menu.

Seagaia
JAPANESE $

(Station 1; meals P70-400; ⊙11.30am-2pm & 6-11pm; 🛜) With all the budget teppanyaki joints on Boracay, you'll think you're turning Japanese. Seagaia is one of the best, with a prime beachfront location to boot. The 'half-size' snacks (from P70) are sizeable enough for a meal. Cut-rate sushi, too.

Smoke
FILIPINO $$

(D'Mall; meals P120-180; ⊙24hr; ☏) Smoke is excellent value, with freshly cooked Filipino food, appetising coconut-milk curries and breakfasts (P80). A second **D'mall branch** (P120-180; ⊙7am-10pm) is closer to the main road.

★ Plato D'Boracay
SEAFOOD $$

(D'Talipapa Market; cook to order P150-250; ⊙8am-9pm) Choose lobster, prawns and other shellfish from the D'Talipapa market, and this family-style grill will cook them for you. The result is prices that substantially undercut the seafood barbecues on the beach.

Crafty's
INDIAN $$

(Main Rd; dishes P250-350; ⊙11am-late) Never mind what's on White Beach, truly the best Indian food on Boracay emerges from the kitchen of this rooftop bar looming over D'Mall. And yes, it's actually spicy. It's also known for burgers and ribs.

🍷 Drinking & Nightlife

Bars range from peaceful, beachfront cocktail affairs, where you can sip a mai tai while watching the sun set, or join throbbing discos on the sand.

Follow thumping beats to find the discos; about five or six of them carry momentum into the wee hours, even in the low season.

Cocomangas (⊙11am-3am) is the rowdiest, followed by **Summer Place** (www.summer-placeboracay.com; Station 2; admission P200; ⊙11am-late). **Epic** (www.epicboracay.com; admission Fri & Sat P300; ⊙10pm-3am) is most chichi. **Bom Bom** (Station 2; ⊙8am-2am) has live reggae on the sand in the early evening, with the beats and fun moving to the back bar after-hours.

★**Red Pirates** PUB
(Angol; ⊙10am-2pm) Way down at the southern end of White Beach, this supremely mellow bar throws funky driftwood furniture onto the sand and best captures the spirit of the 'Old Boracay'.

Nigi Nigi Nu Noos BAR
(⊙10am-midnight) The legendary mason jars of Long Island iced tea (they're two-for-one during happy hour: 5pm to 7pm) more than capably kick-start any evening. And you may just stay for the juicy steaks.

Spider House BAR
On a rocky sunset-facing outcrop at the far end of Diniwid Beach, this is the number one sundowner drinking spot for Boracay's beautiful backpacker set.

Arwana BAR
(Angol; ⊙happy hour 1-10pm) All-day happy hour means Boracay's cheapest San Miguel (P30) and cocktails (P69) on demand.

ⓘ Information

You'll find ATMs galore along the main road near D'Mall, plus a few more along White Beach.
Department of Tourism (DOT; ☑036-288 3689; D'Mall; ⊙8am-5pm Mon-Fri) Has a few brochures and updated ferry schedules out of Caticlan, Kalibo and Iloilo.

SPLURGE

Outstanding traditional Spanish cuisine infused with local flavours – including sophisticated tapas, authentic paella, bean soups and hearty stews – make **Dos Mestizos** (☑036-288 5786; tapas from P300; ⊙10am-11pm) an island treat. Saturdays feature a sinful buffet (6pm to 9.30pm) and agreeable live background music. Amiable owners run the ship.

ⓘ Getting There & Away

To get to Boracay, you must first travel to Caticlan. From Caticlan, bangka ferries shuttle you to Boracay's Cagban pier (or often to Tambisaan pier during the June to October *habagat*). The 15-minute trip costs P215 including terminal and environmental fees.

From Cagban, a tricycle to the White Beach area costs P150, or share a ride for P25 per person.

AIR

Cebu Pacific, PAL Express and Skyjet fly regularly from Manila to Caticlan, with Cebu Pacific adding two daily Cebu flights. Caticlan airport to Caticlan pier is a five-minute walk or a one-minute tricycle ride (P50).

Caticlan airport is being expanded to accommodate bigger planes and more flights, including night flights. Until that happens, flying to nearby Kalibo, which is a cheaper alternative to flying to Caticlan, will remain a popular option. AirAsia, Cebu Pacific and PAL Express fly to Kalibo from Manila. Air-con vans meet flights in Kalibo and run to Caticlan pier (P180, 1½ hours).

International flights land at Kalibo International Airport (p607).

PHILIPPINES BORACAY

MOVING ON FROM BORACAY: OVERLAND OR BY SEA

Domestic flights out of Caticlan and Kalibo are limited to Manila and Cebu. With a little pluck, you can get to the following destinations without taking to the skies.

Puerto Galera This is relatively easy, just take a ferry to Roxas, Mindoro (four hours), then transfer to northbound vans (4½ hours).

Palawan From Iloilo at the south of Panay, Montenegro Lines (P1220, 26 hours, 8am Saturday) and less seaworthy Milagrosa Shipping (P950, 36 hours, 7pm Monday and Thursday) sail to Puerto Princesa, Palawan, via the Cuyo Islands. Another option is to take the ferry to Roxas, Mindoro, then catch a bus or van to San Jose, Mindoro, where you'll find four or five weekly trips to Coron (6½ hours).

Bohol A long one but a fun one. Head down to Iloilo, which is well connected to Bacolod, Negros, by fastcraft (one hour). From Bacolod take a bus to Dumaguete (six hours); go via Sipalay if you wish. Then travel to Bohol by fastcraft (two hours).

From Iloilo at the south of Panay, Cebu Pacific has three weekly flights to Puerto Princesa, Palawan.

BOAT

Caticlan is well connected by ferry to Roxas, Mindoro. In addition, **2GO Travel** (☑ 036-288 1422; Main Rd) has ferries to Batangas (for Manila; from P1000, 10 hours, at least daily).

BUS

Ceres Lines has hourly buses to Iloilo (P350, six hours) via Kalibo (P107, two hours) from Caticlan pier; the last one departs at 4pm.

ⓘ Getting Around

Tricycles ply the main road and cost only P10 provided you steer clear of the disingenuously named 'special trips' offered by stationary tricycles, which cost a not-so-special P50 to P100. Try a silent new E-Trike, whose roominess feels luxurious.

Negros

If any Visayan island can boast to have it all, it is surely Negros. Here you'll find one of the country's top dive spots (Apo Island), one of the top remote beaches (Sipalay) and one of the mellowest provincial towns (Dumaguete). The heavily forested interior, besides being a major biodiversity hotbed, provides a stunning backdrop for drives around the island. Along the west coast, vast, bright-green sugar cane fields abut the shimmering waters of the Sulu Sea.

Dumaguete

☑ 035 / POP 116,000

Dumaguete (doo-ma-*get*-ay) is a perfect base for exploring all that the southern Visayas offer. A huge college campus engulfs much of its centre, saturating the city with youthful energy and attitude. The location – in the shadow of twin-peaked Cuernos de Negros (1903m) and just a few clicks from some marvellous hiking, beaches and diving – takes care of the rest.

Most dining, drinking and strolling happens on and around the attractive waterfront promenade flanking Rizal Blvd.

⚓ Activities

The Dumaguete area boasts top-notch adventures, including diving. Nearby Apo Island is the big draw for underwater breathers. Operators include Harold's Mansion and, in the same building, **Scuba**

Ventures (☑ 035-225 7716; www.dumaguete-dive.com; Hibbard Ave).

Many tour operators offer trips to snorkel with whale sharks in nearby Tan-awan (a barangay of Oslob), Cebu. We do not endorse these as they are essentially captive whale sharks, kept there and disrupted from their normal migratory patterns because locals feed them.

Back on terra firma you'll find caving, rock climbing and trekking on Cuernos de Negros and around the Twin Lakes, north of Dumaguete near Bais.

🛏 Sleeping

Harold's Mansion　　　　　　　HOSTEL **$**
(☑ 0917 302 4455, 035-422 3477; www.haroldsmansion.com; 205 Hibbard Ave; dm/s/d from P250/350/500; ❀@☎) This long-running high-rise hostel has seen better days, but luckily you can escape the dysfunctional rooms and grouchy staff by heading up to the the sociable rooftop bar-restaurant, which remains a good place to quaff beers, play pool and meet fellow travellers.

OK Pensionne House　　　GUESTHOUSE **$**
(☑ 035-225 5702; Santa Rosa St; d P275-770; ❀☎) This massive, sprawling and slightly rundown place is just what it says it is: OK. It has an enormous variety of mostly windowless rooms. But even the cheapies are en suite and have desks.

Island's Leisure　　　BOUTIQUE HOTEL **$$**
(☑ 0915 349 1132; www.islandsleisurehotel.com; Hibbard Ave; d incl breakfast with/without bathroom from P1600/990; ❀☎❄) This alluring property combines Zen modernism with indigenous Philippine elements. Think woven lamps, contemporary art, stone love seats and plasma TVs. Service is hit-or-miss, however. It doubles as a spa and is 1km north of Harold's Mansion.

🍴 Eating & Drinking

Qyosko　　　　　　　　　　FILIPINO **$**
(cnr Santa Rosa & Perdices Sts; mains P60-120; ☺7am-3am; ☎) This local legend serves up sticky ribs and hot Filipino dishes, plus delicious shakes and coffee from its air-conditioned adjoining coffee shop.

La Bella　　　　　　　　　ITALIAN **$$**
(Rizal Blvd; meals P200-300; ☺9am-10pm; ☎) Go ahead, treat yourself to a decent meal; you deserve it. La Bella is an import from Cebu that serves mouth-watering pizzas,

pastas, meaty Italian mains and rich breakfasts like eggs Benedict, all cooked by an Italian chef.

★ **Hayahay**   BAR
(201 Flores Ave; ⊙ 4pm-late) In a cluster of bars and restaurants on the waterfront 2km north of Bethel Guesthouse, Hayahay is known for delicious fresh seafood and rockin' reggae Wednesdays. On weekends the live music continues until 4am.

ℹ️ Getting There & Away

Cebu Pacific and PAL Express each have two daily flights to Manila. Cebu Pacific flies to Cebu thrice weekly.

Oceanjet (☑ 0923 725 3734) fastcraft go to Cebu (P1200, 4½ hours, 3pm) via Tagbilaran (P700, two hours) on Bohol. There are also RORO to Cebu.

From the nearby port of Sibulan, frequent fastcraft (P62) and bangka (P47) alternate trips to Lilo-an (25 minutes) on Cebu island, from where there are buses to Cebu City via Oslob. For Moalboal, cross from Tampi, Negros, to Bato, Cebu, by RORO (every 1½ hours) and pick up a northbound Ceres bus there.

Ceres Bus Lines (Perdices St) connects Dumaguete and Bacolod (ordinary/air-con P275/378, six hours, every 45 minutes) via Kabankalan.

Apo Island

POP 745

For a taste of small-village life on an isolated island, it's hard to beat this coral-fringed charmer, one of the Philippines' best snorkelling and dive spots.

Most people visit on day trips from Dauin or Dumaguete (diving/snorkelling trips from P2800/1000 per person including two dives), but thrifty souls will fare better staying on the island. **Liberty's Lodge & Dive** (☑ 0920 238 5704; www.apoisland.com; dm/s/d incl full board from P900/1650/2100; ❄️ 🛜) has appealingly rustic rooms and a laid-back atmosphere, and transfers guests to the island for P300 per person.

Behind Liberty's, **Mario Scuba** (☑ 0906 361 7254; http://mariosscubadivinghomestay.com; dm P300, d P500-1000; 🛜) has a six-bed dorm and some large, en suite private rooms with polished floors and private balconies.

Around the point from Liberty's, **Apo Island Beach Resort** (☑ 0917 701 7150, in Dumaguete 035-226 3716; www.apoislandresort.com; dm P800, d from P2700) has a lovely secret cove all to itself, but Liberty's and Mario are

better run and better value. There are also **homestays** available on the island for P500 (ask around).

A couple of bangkas depart the island for Malatapay, 18km south of Dumaguete (P20, 40 minutes by bus or jeepney), around 6.30am and return around 3pm (P300, 45 minutes). Chartering a five-passenger bangka costs P1500 to P2000 one way (negotiate).

Sipalay

☑ 034 / POP 11,275

You could get stuck for days – make that months – in this remote fishing town on Negros' southwestern edge. At delicious Sugar Beach a growing cluster of resorts caters to those looking to achieve full Robinson Crusoe effect. It really fills up in the high season these days, so book ahead.

Divers should head 6km south of Sipalay to the pricier resorts of barangay Punta Ballo, which is also a jump-off point for some quality island-hopping to the south. **Kayaking** through the mangroves of the Nauhang River just south of Sugar Beach is another must.

🛏️ Sleeping & Eating

Driftwood Village   BEACH RESORT $
(☑ 0920 900 3663; www.driftwood-village.com; Sugar Beach; dm P250-300, d from P450; 🛜) Offers a classic mellow beach vibe with hammocks and nipa huts of variable quality scattered about its leafy grounds. The kitchen specialises in Thai food, but European classics are also available (dishes around P200). Also has a marvellous pirate pub hidden under a bushy canopy.

Sulu Sunset   BEACH RESORT $
(☑ 0919 716 7182; www.sulusunset.com; Sugar Beach; r P650-1350) The right recipe: nice nipa huts with tile floors, en suite bathrooms, and verandahs with hammocks facing the sea, at very attractive prices. The restaurant serves delicious wood-fired pizza and German specialties. It's at the far end of the beach.

Sugar Rock   INN $$
(☑ 0908 429 8413; r P650-1750; ❄️🛜) Attached to a popular sunset bar perched over an outcrop at the far end of Sugar Beach, Sugar Rock recently added a few stylishly designed rooms. Do come here for sunset. The views are magnificent, and sometimes the party continues on with live music.

ⓘ Getting There & Away

Getting to Dumaguete requires three separate Ceres buses: Sipalay to Hinoba-an (P25, 45 minutes), Hinoba-an to Bayawan (P80, 1½ hours) and Bayawan to Dumaguete (P100, two hours). Connections are easy. Regular Ceres buses also connect Sipalay with Bacolod (ordinary/air-con P189/289, 5½ hours).

Sugar Beach is about 5km north of Sipalay proper, across two rivers. Arrange a boat transfer to your resort from Sipalay proper (P350, 15 minutes), or disembark from the Bacolod–Sipalay bus in barangay Montilla and take a tricycle to barangay Nauhang (P100, 15 minutes), where small paddle boats bring you across the river to Sugar Beach for P15.

Siquijor

📞 035 / POP 87,700

Spooky Siquijor is renowned for its witches and healers, but don't be scared away. It's also a backpacker paradise with lovely scenery and the best-value beachfront accommodation in the Philippines. With your own motorbike you can travel around the island's 72km coastal ring road in a day and explore beaches, colonial-era relics, waterfalls, caves and charming villages. Rent a motorbike at the pier when you arrive (P300).

Sandugan, 15km northeast of Siquijor town, has an end-of-the-earth feel, but the beaches are nicer in **Solangon**, 9km southwest of Siquijor town.

🛏 Sleeping

Kiwi Dive Resort   RESORT $

(📞 0908 889 2283; www.kiwidiveresort.com; Km 16.9, Sandugan; r with fan P450-690, with air-con P990-1190; ❄ @ 🛜) It's a lovely walk down a trellis-covered pathway from the simple and clean hillside rooms to the beach, sitting area and small bar. There's a dive centre, and motorcycles, mountain bikes and kayaks are available for hire.

JJ's Backpackers
Village & Cafe   HOSTEL $

(📞 0918 670 0310; jiesa26@yahoo.com; Km 64.6, Solangon; tent/dm P250/350, d P500-600; @ 🛜) Laid-back JJ's is a throwback to the carefree days when you could camp on a beach, cook your own food and enjoy yourself without any worries. Located on a well-maintained patch of beach, it has only a few rooms; if those are booked you're free to pitch a tent.

Tori's Backpacker's Paradise   HOSTEL $

(📞 0907 132 6666; torisbackpackersparadise@gmail.com; Km 60.8, Tubod; dm/d from P300/500; 🛜) Run by an exceedingly nice couple, this small backpacker crash pad has a handful of basic rooms near the water and a delicious (if slow) restaurant up by the road. It's on a rocky strip of shoreline, but within walking distance of the white-sand beach around Coco Grove Resort.

Casa Miranda   GUESTHOUSE $

(📞 0917 910 6995; Km 64.4, Solangon; dm P250, d P300-500) You won't find beachfront accommodation – en suite, no less – this cheap anywhere in the Philippines. The no-frills rooms and one musty dorm occupy a rambling structure fronting a decent stretch of sand just southeast of JJ's.

Charisma Beach Resort   RESORT $$

(📞 0908 915 3449; www.charisma-resort.com; Km 64.8, Solangon; r P1000-1750; ❄ 🛜) Choose from spacious beachfront fan rooms, air-con rooms abutting a pool set back from the beach, and a single cosy fan cottage at the back. All rooms have private balconies.

ⓘ Getting There & Around

The vast majority of visitors arrive at the pier in Siquijor town via fastcraft from Dumaguete. **GL Shipping** (📞 0915 891 1426; P130, 1½ hours, five trips, none Sat) and **Oceanjet** (p579; P210, 45 minutes, 12.50pm) ply the route. Montenegro Lines and Aleson Lines follow with a few slower ROROs (P100) to both Siquijor town and Larena, 9km northeast of Siquijor town.

At the pier in Larena, you'll find RORO ferries to Cebu (P350, 10½ hours) on Tuesday, Thursday and Sunday nights via Tagbilaran (P270, 3½ hours).

From the pier in Siquijor town, a tricycle costs about P120 to Solangon or Larena, and P170 to Sandugan.

Cebu

Surrounded on all sides by the Philippine isles and dotted with tranquil fishing villages, Cebu is the island heart of the Visayas. Cebuanos are proud of their heritage – it is here that Magellan sowed the seed of Christianity and was pruned for his efforts at the hands of the mighty Chief Lapu-Lapu. The island's booming metropolis, Cebu City, is a transport hub to pretty much anywhere. Pescador Island, near the laid-back town of Moalboal, placed Philippine diving on the world map, while the Malapascua marine scene boasts close encounters of the thresher-shark kind.

Cebu City

☑ 032 / POP 866,000

The island capital is much more laid-back than Manila as a place to arrive in or leave the Philippines. One of the first stops on Spain's conquest agenda, Cebu lays claim to everything old – including the oldest street (Colon St), the oldest university and the oldest fort. By night Cebu turns decidedly hedonistic.

Cebu's downtown district is its mercantile nucleus. Most of the sights are here, but you must wade through exhaust fumes, beggars, prostitutes and block after block of downmarket retail madness to get to them. Uptown is much more pleasant and has better accommodation, mostly near the central Fuente Osmeña roundabout.

◉ Sights

In addition its historic sights, Cebu has a few worthwhile museums, including **Museo Sugbo** (MJ Cuenco Ave; adult/child P75/50; ⊙ 9am-6pm Mon-Sat), with fascinating historical exhibits in the old provincial jail; the archaeology-oriented **University of San Carlos Museum** (Del Rosario St; admission P30; ⊙ 8am-noon & 1.30-5pm Mon-Fri, 8am-noon Sat); and the lovely **Casa Gorordo Museum** (35 L Jaena St; admission P70; ⊙ 9am-5pm Tue-Sun), in a house dating to the mid-1800s.

For a self-guided walking tour of the downtown area, pick up a 'Cebu Heritage Walk' booklet from the **City Tourism Commission** (☑ 032-412 4355; www.cebucitytourism. com; Pres Osmeña Blvd; ⊙ 8am-5pm Mon-Fri).

★ Fort San Pedro FORT

(S Osmeña Blvd; student/adult P20/30; ⊙ 8am-8pm) Built in 1565 under the command of Miguel López de Legazpi, conqueror of the Philippines, Fort San Pedro has served as an army garrison, a rebel stronghold, prison camp and the city zoo. These days it's retired as a peaceful, walled garden and handsomely crumbling ruin. It's a perfect retreat from the chaos and madness of downtown Cebu, especially at sunset.

★ Basilica Minore del Santo Niño CHURCH

(Pres Osmeña Blvd) Cebu's holiest church houses a revered Flemish statuette of the Christ child (Santo Niño) that dates to Magellan's time. The church's belfry came crumbling down in the October 2013 earthquake and is being rebuilt. The church is no stranger to hardship. Established in 1565 (the oldest church in the Philippines) and burnt down three times, it was rebuilt in its present form in 1737.

Tops Lookout VIEWPOINT

(admission P100) Make your way to JY Square Mall in Lahug, where *habal-habal* (motorcycle taxis) depart for the thrilling 20-minute ride (return P300) up a winding road to the Tops lookout point, 600m above Cebu.

🛏 Sleeping

It's worth spending extra to be uptown.

★ Elicon House HOTEL $

(☑ 032-255 0300; www.elicon-house.com; crn Del Rosario & Junquera Sts; s/d P550/800; ✳@🛜)
🖉 The downtown version of its sister Mayflower and West Gorordo hotels. Same idea here – no-nonsense and clean rooms, delightful common spaces loaded with games, great vego-friendly cafe and slogans on permaculture philosophy plastered on the brightly painted walls.

PIGGING OUT IN CEBU

Cebu is *the* place to eat the Filipino delicacy *lechón* (spit-roasted suckling pig). The best places roast dozens of pigs per day and ship their product off to *lechón* addicts in Manila and abroad. Our favourite *lechón* is the spicy variety served at **Rico's Lechon** (www. ricos-lechon.com; F Cabahug St, Mabolo; portions from P135; 🛜). Popular **Zubuchon** (One Mango Pl, Gen Maxilom Ave; meals from P170; ⊙ 10am-10.30pm) has several branches, including one at the airport. Or for a quick fix try the small mall outlets run by **Cora's Lechon** (Robinson's Place Mall, Fuente Osmeña; portions from P115; ⊙ 9am-8pm) or local institution **CnT Lechon** (Ayala Center, 4th fl; portions from P152; ⊙ 10am-9pm).

PHILIPPINES CEBU

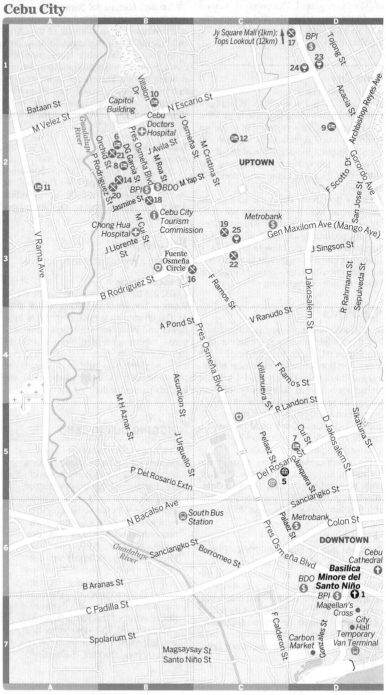

Jy Square Mall (1km);
Tops Lookout (12km)

BPI

PHILIPPINES CEBU

PHILIPPINES CEBU

Map scale: 0 — 500 m / 0 — 0.25 miles, N

Cebu City

Map labels:
Cebu IT Park (1.1km);
Tonyo's Bar & Restaurant (1.3km)
Rico's Lechon (1.1km)
Bohol St
HSBC
Mindanao Ave
Luzon Ave
Cardinal Rosales Ave
HIPPODROMO
McCrew Ville Rd
Cemetery
M Cuenco Ave
Gen Maxilom Ave Extension
SM City Mall (3km);
North (3.5km);
Mactan International (11km)
R Mercad
T Padilla St
A Valle St
Pier 4 (50m);
Pier 5 (70m);
Supercat 2GO (400m);
Weesam Express (500m);
Trans-Asia Shipping Lines (750m)
A Bonifacio St
G Lavilles
Lapu-Lapu St
MJ Cuenco Ave
S Osmeña Blvd
Legaspi St
Quezon Blvd
Pier 3
Pier 2
Pier 1
Fort San Pedro
Cebu Strait

Travelbee Guesthouse   GUESTHOUSE **$**
(www.travelbee.ph; 225 Elizabeth Pond St; d
P900-1200, tr/q P1150/1400; ❋@🐾) The core
rooms at this friendly hotel are essentially
four- and six-bed dorms, but beds cannot
be booked individually so it works best for
small groups. There are nifty doubles as
well, and all rooms are clean and en suite.
It's central but hidden on a quiet side street;
have them call you a cab.

Le Village Hostel   HOSTEL **$**
(📞 0932 413 3978, 032-416 0038; 84 Gorordo Ave; dm with fan/air-con from P400/500, d

without bathroom P900-1500; ⊛ 🖦) Probably the best hostel in Cebu, though that's not saying much. Clean dorm rooms, a big, bright common room and unspectacular common areas both inside and out. A kitchen was in the works at research time.

Tr3ats   HOSTEL $

(📞 032-422 8881; www.tr3ats.com; 785 V Rama Ave; dm/d/q P388/900/1700; ⊛🖦) Cebu's original hostel has three decent six-bed aircon dorms and a few tidy en suite private rooms. However the location isn't perfect. There's not much of a common area; chill in the rooftop bar.

★ Mayflower Inn   HOTEL $$

(📞 032-255 2800; www.mayflower-inn.com; Villalon Dr; s/d/tr/q P850/1150/1400/1750; ⊛🖦) 🖉 The Mayflower bills itself as a 'permaculture' hotel – don't laugh, the green credentials are legit. Besides tidy, meticulously painted rooms you get a feng-shui-friendly garden cafe and a hangout lounge-library with ping pong, foosball, stacks of National Geographic mags and board games.

Gran Tierra Suites   HOTEL $$

(📞 032-253 3575; www.grantierrasuites.com; 207 M Cui St; s/d P790/990; ⊛🖦) Cebu has some terrific values at the midrange, and this is a prime example. Bordering on boutique, rooms are equipped with canvas prints, small flat-screen TVs and ample desk space.

Cebu R Hotel   HOTEL $$

(📞 032-505 7188; www.ceburhotel.com; 101 M Cui St; s/d incl breakfast from P950/1250; ⊛@🖦) Everything is tasteful here, from the smartly uniformed staff to the lime colour scheme. Rooms are kitted out with desks and low-res flat-screen TVs. Deluxe rooms are a jump up in size.

✗ Eating

The residential neighbourhood around parallel Orchid St and M Cui St in the Capitol region is a great place to browse for restaurants. Here you'll find beloved **STK ta Bay! Sa Paolito's Seafood House** (📞 032-256 2700; 6 Orchid St; mains P95-400; ⊙10am-3pm & 5-10pm; 🖦), known for spicy *calamares*, crab and huge, boomerang-like tuna *panga* (jaw); **Bucket Shrimps** (Orchard St; mains P150-300; ⊙9am-10pm), a fun place where you don goofy cling-wrap gloves and attack buckets of Cajun-butter shrimp; and

Yakski Barbecue (M Cui St; skewers P20-70; ⊙11.30am-2.30pm & 5.30pm-midnight), where huge crowds gather to eat five or six varieties of meat on a stick.

Food courts at malls such as the **Ayala Center** (Lahug district; ⊙10am-9pm) are always a good bet for cheap sustenance.

Handuraw Pizza   FILIPINO $$

(📞 032-505 2121; Gorordo Ave; pizzas P300-400; ⊙11am-midnight, to 2am Fri & Sat; 🖦) This Cebu institution adds native twists to its famous thin-crust pizzas. Try the mildly spicy Pizza Cebuana topped with the local chorizo. Sit inside with air-con or outdoors.

Persian Palate   MIDDLE EASTERN $$

(Mango Sq Mall, J Osmeña St; dishes P75-300; ⊙10am-9pm; 🖦🖉) The flagship restaurant of this popular franchise is tucked away behind National Bookstore in Mango Sq. Middle Eastern mains like spinach hummus are complemented by too-mild South Asian and Thai fare. Its menu includes a rarity in Cebu City – a large vegetarian selection.

Joven's Grill   FILIPINO $$

(cnr Pres Osmeña Blvd & Jasmine St; all-you-can-eat buffet P199-260; ⊙11am-9pm) The best place to gorge cheaply after an extended boat journey.

🍷 Drinking & Nightlife

Cebu IT Park (Salinas Dr, Lahug), about a five-minute cab ride northeast of Ayala Center, is a hot spot for bars and clubs. The club names change often so your best bet is to just walk around and pick the most happening spot.

Tonyo's Bar & Restaurant   BAR

(Salinas Dr, Lahug; ⊙24hr) A quintessential Cebu experience, Tonyo's is a huge, always-packed open-air restobar roughly opposite Cebu IT Park. Fill up on a 3L tube of beer (P225) delivered to your table while watching live cover bands croon.

Kukuk's Nest/Turtle's Nest   BAR

(📞 0933 391 3837; 124 Gorordo Ave; ⊙24hr) This bohemian 24-hour restobar is filled with old books and contemporary art inside, and a colourful mix of local arty types outside. If you've had one too many, ask about the budget accommodation on offer (room P600).

Koa   BAR

(157 Gorordo Ave; ⊙9.30am-2.30am Sun-Thu, 24hr Fri & Sat; 🖦) Named after a Hawaiian tree,

Koa has a great outdoor space and live tunes indoors from hump night on. While the beer is cheap and the food is decent, it's the pizzas from on-site La Bella Pizza Bistro that really shine.

Mango Square   BAR, CLUB
(Gen Maxilom Ave; admission per club P50-150) A clubber's heaven attracting a fun, lively crowd, although certain places can get a little sleazy. It gets going around 10pm and the more popular places stay open until sunrise.

ℹ Information

ATMs are everywhere. Internet cafes can be found in the malls.

Cebu Doctors Hospital (☑ 032-255 5555; Pres Osmeña Blvd; ☺ 24hr)

Central Post Office (Quezon Blvd; ☺ 8am-5pm Mon-Sat) A landmark downtown opposite Fort San Pedro.

HSBC (Cardinal Rosales Ave; ☺ 9am-4pm Mon-Fri) Allows P40,000 ATM withdrawals; opposite Ayala Center.

Travellers Lounge (☑ 032-232 0293; ☺ 6am-8.30pm) Located just outside SM City Mall, this handy lounge has a bag-drop (P30, same-day pickup only) and showers (P50), and sells certain ferry tickets.

ℹ Getting There & Away

AIR
AirAsia, Cebu Pacific and PAL have regular flights to Manila and many additional domestic and international destinations.

BOAT
There's rarely a need to purchase tickets ahead for the popular fastcrafts to Tagbilaran (Bohol), Ormoc (Leyte) and Dumaguete. The *Sun Star* daily newspaper runs up-to-date schedules. Buy tickets at the piers.

2GO Travel (☑ 032-233 7000; http://travel.2go.com.ph; Pier 1)

Cokaliong Shipping (☑ 0032-232 7211-18; www.cokaliongshipping.com; Pier 1)

Gabisan Shipping Lines (☑ 0917 791 6618; Pier 3)

George & Peter Lines (☑ 032-254 5154; Pier 2)

Lite Shipping (☑ 032-255 1721; Pier 1)

Oceanjet (☑ 032-255 7560; www.oceanjet. net; Pier 1)

M/V Star Crafts (Pier 1)

Roble Shipping Lines (☑ 032-418 6256; Pier 3)

Super Shuttle Ferry (☑ 032-345 5581; http://supershuttleroro.com; Pier 8)

Supercat 2GO (☑ 032-233 7000; www.2go. com.ph; Pier 4)

PHILIPPINES CEBU

FERRIES FROM CEBU CITY

DESTINATION	DURATION (HR)	FARE (P)	COMPANY	FREQUENCY
Batangas	24	1000-1200	Super Shuttle Ferry	Sun
Cagayan de Oro	8-12	550-980	2GO, Trans-Asia, Super Shuttle Ferry	at least daily
Calbayog, Samar	11	690	Cokaliong	Mon, Wed, Fri
Dumaguete (fastcraft)	4½	950	Oceanjet	8am
Dumaguete (RORO)	6	300-400	Cokaliong, George & Peter Lines	at least daily
Hilongos (Leyte)	3-5	240-280	Gabisan, Roble	several daily
Iloilo	12	600	Trans-Asia	Mon, Wed, Fri 6pm
Larena, Siquijor	10½	350	Lite Shipping	3 weekly
Manila	24	from P1100	2GO	4 weekly
Ormoc (fastcraft)	2½	600-650	Oceanjet, Supercat 2GO, Weesam	several daily
Ormoc (RORO)	5	400	Lite Shipping	daily
Surigao City	7	825	Cokaliong	6 weekly
Tagbilaran (fastcraft)	2¼	400-500	Oceanjet, Supercat 2GO	frequent
Tagbilaran (RORO)	4	230	Lite Shipping	2 daily
Tubigon	1-3	110-220	Lite Shipping, M/V Star Crafts	frequent

Trans-Asia Shipping Lines (☏ 032-254 6491; www.transasiashipping.com; Pier 5)

Weesam Express (☏ 032-231 7737; www. weesam.ph; Pier 1)

BUS

There are two bus stations in Cebu. Ceres Bus Lines services southern and central destinations, such as Bato (P170, four hours, frequent) via Moalboal (P118, three hours) or via Oslob (P155, 3½ hours), from the **South Bus Station** (Bacalso Ave). Quicker air-con vans ('V-hires') leave for Moalboal (P100, 2¼ hours) and Toledo (P100, two hours) from a **temporary terminal** (Quezon Blvd) behind City Hall.

The **North Bus Station** (☏ 032-345 8650/59; M Logarta Ave) is beyond SM City Mall. From here Ceres has buses to Hagnaya (P132, 3½ hours, hourly) for Bantayan Island, and to Maya for Malapascua Island.

❶ Getting Around

You'll find a taxi rank of regular metered taxis (P40 flag fall) on the right as you exit Mactan International Airport. Taking public transport into the centre is complicated but possible; ask the tourist desk in the arrivals hall for directions.

To get uptown from the ports, catch one of the jeepneys that pass by the piers to Pres Osmeña Blvd, then transfer to a jeepney going uptown.

Moalboal

☏ 032 / POP 27,400

The Philippines' original diving hotbed, Moalboal remains a throwback to the days when diving came cheap and minus the attitude. **Panagsama Beach**, where the resorts are, meanders lazily along a sea wall within rock-skipping distance of a stunning diving wall (which can also be snorkelled). In recent years Moalboal has become internationally renowned for the incredible sardine run that delights divers and snorkellers just metres offshore.

⦿ Sights & Activities

Divers can paddle out to the coral-studded wall off Panagsama Beach, or take a 10-minute bangka ride to **Pescador Island**, which swarms with marine life. A single-tank dive costs US$25 to US$30. Freediving with the sardines just off Panagsama Beach is also popular.

While Panagsama Beach is hardly worthy of the name, sand lovers can take a tricycle (P100) 5km north to lovely **White Beach**. Other non-diving pursuits around Moalboal include mountain biking, trekking and can-

yoning at nearby waterfalls. **Cyan Adventures** (☏ 0927 426 6886; www.cyan-adventures. com) and **Planet Action** (☏ 0917 583 0062; www.action-philippines.com) can hook you up.

🛏 Sleeping

Cora's Palm Resort GUESTHOUSE $
(☏ 0998 364 0880; cora_abarquez@yahoo.com; r with fan P500, with air-con P1000-1500; ❄ 🖥) The original Panagsama guesthouse, Cora's is perched right on the waterfront smack dab in the centre. Shoot for the cosy and cheap fan rooms. Pricier rooms have kitchenettes and small fridges.

Moalboal Backpacker Lodge HOSTEL $
(☏ 0917 751 8902; www.moalboal-backpacker lodge.com; dm/s/d/cottage P275/350/550/750; 🖥) This hostel has airy mixed and women's dorms and a couple of semiprivate rooms over a coffee shop, plus two fabulous two-floor cottages that are a steal.

Blue Abyss RESORT $$
(☏ 032-474 3012; www.blueabyssdiving.com; d P850-1350, tr P1500; ❄ 🖥) We prefer the cosy doubles here over the spartan triples, but all rooms are clean and functional. With attractive dive-room packages, it's ideal for divers on a budget. Located a short walk south of the Blue Abyss dive shop.

🍴 Eating & Drinking

Drinking is the national sport of the Moalboal Republic, and there are plenty of eateries where you can secure food to soak up the deluge of beer.

Chilli Bar RESTOBAR $
(mains P150-210; ⊗ 9.30am-last customer) A Panagsama institution known for big pizzas, chilli con carne, Swedish meatballs and a lethal cocktail menu. 'The liver is evil and it must be punished', proclaims a big board by the pool table, where billiard comps take place every Wednesday.

Last Filling Station INTERNATIONAL $$
(meals from P180; ⊗ 7am-10pm; 🖥 🍴) Famous for its energy-boosting breakfasts, replete with yoghurt, muesli, baguettes and protein shakes. Also does decent strong brewed coffee.

❶ Getting There & Around

Frequent Ceres buses pass through town heading south to Bato (for Tampi and Dumaguete; P70, 1½ hours) and north to Cebu's South Bus

Station (P118, three hours). To Cebu, there are also air-con minivans (P100, 2¼ hours).

Habal-habal to Panagsama Beach from Moalboal town cost P50, tricycles double that.

Malapascua Island

POP 3500

A picturesque little island off the northeastern tip of Cebu, Malapascua is the place to view thresher sharks. Divers head out at 5am to **Monad Shoal**, where they park on the seabed at 25m hoping to catch a glimpse of these critters. The chances are pretty good – about 75%. By day Monad Shoal attracts manta rays. Once your dive is over you can relax on signature white-sand **Bounty Beach**, where a string of resorts offer seaside seating in the sand.

Malapascua took a big hit from super-typhoon Yolanda (Haiyan) in 2013. But the little island staged a remarkable recovery, with most resorts reopening within a couple of months.

🛏 Sleeping & Eating

Ask about low-season discounts and dive-accommodation packages.

★ Mike & Diose's Aabana
Beach Resort RESORT $
(🕿 0905 263 2914; www.aabana.de; d incl breakfast P500-2200; ❄ 🛜) Lavish deluxe suites, smart budget rooms, big duplex air-con rooms with kitchens – no matter what you choose, you're in for a treat. Easily Malapascua's best value. And management is as friendly as can be. Bounty Beach feels almost private down here at the extreme eastern end.

Villa Sandra HOSTEL $
(🕿 0977 130 0642; jonjonmalapascua@gmail.com; dm P300; @🛜) Very much a backpacker pad, next to the elementary school in Logan village, with simple shared doubles and quads, a kitchen, a hangout patio and dudes in dreads hanging about. Jonjon is your informative host.

Thresher Cove Resort &
Dive Center RESORT $
(🕿 0908 139 7609; http://www.threshercove.com; dm/s/d without bathroom P350/400/950, r with bathroom incl breakfast P2500; ❄🛜🏊) On a private beach a 10-minute walk north of Bounty Beach, this well-managed operation is an excellent all-rounder. The sea-view dorms and delightfully rustic 'native-style'

cottages will appeal to budget-conscious divers. Free motorbike transfer from the boat drop-off.

Ging-Ging's Restaurant FILIPINO $
(mains P60-100; ⊗ 7am-10pm; 🍴) Inland from the beach, Ging-Ging's serves tasty, cheap, filling vegetarian food and curries.

ℹ Getting There & Away

Bangkas from Maya (P80, 30 minutes) to Malapascua leave when full, roughly every hour until 5.30pm or so (until 2pm from Malapascua). If you miss the last boat, you'll have to charter a bangka for P800 to P2000. At low tide you must pay a barge operator P20 to shuttle you to/from the bangka.

Ceres buses depart Maya pier for Cebu (ordinary/air-con P163/180, 4½ hours) every 30 minutes until mid-evening.

Bohol

It's difficult to reconcile Bohol's bloody history with the relaxed isle of today. It's here that Francisco Dagohoy led the longest revolt in the country against the Spaniards, from 1744 to 1829. These days Bohol is a tourist magnet, with endearing little primates, coral cathedrals off Panglao Island and lush jungle, ripe for exploration. A powerful earthquake rocked the island in October 2013, destroying several centuries-old Spanish churches. The churches remain down, but Bohol as a whole has bounced back nicely and is now thriving. Developers have big plans to turn Panglao Island into a playground for jet-setting international tourists.

ℹ Getting There & Away

Tagbilaran is the main gateway, but ferries to Camiguin leave from Jagna, about 1½ hours east of Tagbilaran. **Super Shuttle Ferry** (🕿 in Jagna 0916 568 2236) has a RORO to Balbagon, Camiguin, on Monday, Wednesday and Friday at 1pm (P425, 3½ hours).

Additional ferries link Cebu and Tubigon in northwest Bohol, and Bato (Leyte) and Ubay in northeast Bohol.

Tagbilaran

📞 038 / POP 97,000

There's no reason to waste much time in traffic-snarled Tagbilaran. Your first port of call should be the **tourist office** (⊘ 8am-6pm) at the ferry dock, which can help with transport arrangements.

If you do need to stay the night, your best bet is homey **Nisa Travellers Hotel** (📞 038-411 3731; www.nisatravellershotel.com; CPG Ave; s/d incl breakfast from P500/600; ❄@🛜) on the main drag. It has simple rooms and great common areas in a maze-like house. **Tr3ats** (📞 0917 888 2069; www.tr3ats.com; 16 Bagong Lipunan St; dm/d P390/950; ❄🛜) is a new hostel with small but tastefully adorned and blissfully air-conditioned five-bed dorm rooms and a few snazzy doubles with flat-screen TVs.

Eat, cool off and escape the tricycle madness at the food court in BQ Mall, opposite Nisa.

The main domestic airlines all serve Tagbilaran from Manila.

Various fastcraft and slowcraft head to Cebu. Oceanjet operates a daily fastcraft to Dumaguete (P680, two hours) that continues to Siquijor town. **Lite Shipping** (📞 038-501 7422) serves Larena and Siquijor on Monday, Wednesday and Saturday at 8pm (P270, 3½ hours). **Trans-Asia** (📞 038-411 3234) has three trips weekly to/from Cagayan de Oro (P670 to P785, 10 hours).

The main bus terminal is next to Island City Mall in Dao, 3km north of the centre.

WARNING

Beware of a for-profit zoo in Loboc disengenuously called the 'Tarsier Conservation Area'. The Philippine Tarsier Foundation, Inc (PTFI), which runs the much more ethical Philippine Tarsier Sanctuary in Corella, has roundly criticised the Loboc facility for inhumane treatment of the animals. Tour vans love to take tourists here because it is conveniently located on the main Chocolate Hills loop. If you end up on one of these tours, insist on detouring to the sanctuary in Corella. If they refuse, go on your own or choose another tour operator.

Here you'll find air-con minivans ('V-hires') to Jagna (P100, 1½ hours, hourly) and frequent buses to Carmen for the Chocolate Hills (P60, 2½ hours).

To avoid expensive private van rentals and slow public transport, consider hiring your own motorbike in Tagbilaran (P500 per day) to explore the rest of Bohol.

Around Tagbilaran

It's just a short drive north of Tagbilaran to two of the Philippines' signature attractions – the Chocolate Hills and that lovable palm-sized primate, the tarsier.

You are unlikely to spot the nocturnal tarsier in the wild, so head to the **Philippine Tarsier Sanctuary** (📞 0927 541 2290; www.tarsierfoundation.org; admission P50; ⊘ 9am-4pm) in barangay Canapnapan, between the towns of Corella and Sikatuna. About 10 saucer-eyed tarsiers hang out in the immediate vicinity of the centre – the guides will bring you right to them. To get to the sanctuary from Tagbilaran catch a jeepney to Sikatuna (P20, one hour) from the Dao terminal and ask to be dropped off at the sanctuary. From Nuts Huts in Loboc, the sanctuary is a 30- to 45-minute motorbike ride, or take a jeepney from Loboc (P25, 45 minutes).

An interesting quirk of nature, the **Chocolate Hills** consist of more than 1200 conical hills, up to 120m high. They were supposedly formed over time by the uplift of coral deposits and the effects of rainwater and erosion. Since this explanation cannot be confirmed, the local belief that they are the tears of a heartbroken giant may one day prove to be correct. From the Dao terminal in Tagbilaran take a bus bound for Carmen (4km north of the Chocolate Hills main viewpoint) and hop off at the viewpoint (P60, two hours, frequent). From Loboc, flag down a Carmen-bound bus. A more invigorating method of seeing the hills is to take a *habal-habal* tour (half-/one hour P250/350) in and around the hills.

You can visit both the Chocolate Hills and the Philippine Tarsier Sanctuary on an excursion from Tagbilaran, but you're much better off basing yourself in Loboc at **Nuts Huts** (📞 0920 846 1559; www.nutshuts.org; dm P400, nipa huts P900-1200), a backpacker Shangri-La in the middle of the jungle. With a sublime location overlooking the emerald-tinged Loboc River, Nuts Huts provides at least as much reason to visit inland Bohol as brown loam lumps or miniature monkeys. The Belgian hosts can tell you everything you need to know about exploring the area, and lead hiking and caving tours in the immediate vicinity. To get to Nuts Huts from Tagbilaran, catch a Carmen-bound bus and get off at the Nuts Huts sign. It's a 15-minute walk from the road. Alternatively, take a bus to Loboc and then a *habal-habal* (P50) or shuttle boat (per person day/evening P150/200) up the river from the Sarimanok landing.

Another excellent option in the Loboc area is the supremely chill riverside guesthouse **Fox & The Firefly Cottages** (☑038-537 9011; www.suptoursphilippines.com; dm/cottage from P450/1200; 🛜). Lodgings are basic but chances are you are here for the guided stand-up paddleboard tours on the Loboc River run by **SUP Tours** (☑0947 893 3022; www.suptoursphilippines.com; Loboc; 1hr/half-day tour per person P950/1450). The nighttime firefly tour is highly recommended.

Panglao Island

☑038

Linked by two bridges to Bohol, Panglao is where divers head to take advantage of the spectacular coral formations and teeming marine life on the nearby islands of Balicasag and Pamilacan. Ground zero for divers is **Alona Beach**, an agreeable stretch of white sand in range of good snorkelling.

🏊 Activities

Stand-up paddleboards can be rented on the beach for P500 per hour, and you can even practice yoga on SUP boards through **Qi Retreats** (www.qiretreats.com; Alona Beach).

Dive prices average a pricey P1250 per dive, not including equipment. Save considerable money with cut-rate operator **Baywatch** (☑038-502-9028; per dive incl equipment P1100). Most dive trips go to **Balicasag Island** (entrance fee snorkellers/divers P150/250).

You can arrange early-morning dolphin-watching tours near **Pamilacan Island** through most resorts and dive centres. Figure on paying P1500 for a four-person boat. A more ecofriendly way to spot dolphins – and if you're really lucky between February and July, whales – is with **Pamilacan Island Dolphin & Whale Watching Tours** (PIDWWT; ☑0919 730 6108, 038-540 9279; http://whales.bohol.ph; group of 1-4 people P3300, lunch per person P300) out of Baclayon near Tagbilaran. These longer tours employ former whalers.

🛏 Sleeping & Eating

Beachfront dining opportunities on Alona Beach are ample but come at a price. Most affordable eateries and bars are off the beach.

Casa-Nova Garden　　　GUESTHOUSE $
(☑038-502 9101; s with shared bathroom P300, d P500-1000; ❄🛜) True shoestring accommodation survives in Alona thanks to this cosy oasis. It's a bit out of the way, however. Turn off the main road 700m beyond (west of) the Alona Beach access road junction.

Peter's House　　　BEACH RESORT $
(☑032-502 9056; www.genesisdivers.com; r non-divers P1200-1400, divers P900-1100; 🛜) A nipa-hut complex with a friendly and laidback communal vibe, Peter's House is a dive resort for those on a budget. There are only a few rooms, all sharing cold-water bathrooms, and unless it's low season is exclusively for divers.

⭐Chill-Out Guesthouse　　GUESTHOUSE $$
(☑0912 926 5557, 038-502 4480; www.chillout-panglao.com; r with fan/air-con P1000/1500; ❄🛜) Spacious, boutique-quality rooms with hardwood floors and roomy private balconies; leafy walkways link the rooms with a delightful open-air common area–restaurant. For this price? Sign us up. It's a 10-minute walk to the beach, or rent a motorbike for P300 per day.

Trudi's Place　　　FILIPINO $$
(mains P150-265; ⊙6.30am-11pm; 🛜) Trudi's qualifies as budget eating on Alona Beach proper. Bonus: P40 San Miguel.

❶ Getting There & Around

From Tagbilaran, buses with 'Tawala Alona' signboards head to Alona Beach roughly hourly until 3pm from the corner of Hontanosas and F Rocha Sts (P25, 45 minutes). An easier option is to hire a *habal-habal* (P150), tricycle (P200) or taxi (P350). You'll pay double those prices from the airport.

MINDANAO

Sprawling Mindanao, the world's 19th-largest island, is known for dazzling scenery, primitive hill tribes and an almost complete lack of tourists because of political unrest and occasional fighting between the government and Muslim separatists. What most don't realise is that the lovely coastal stretch of northern Mindanao between Cagayan de Oro and Siargao Island is Catholic, Cebuano (Visayan) speaking – and quite safe. The area is known for first-rate surfing on Siargao and activities galore on dramatic, dynamic Camiguin. Mainland Mindanao offers up plenty of cherries for the intrepid traveller, including the Philippines' highest mountain, Mt Apo (2954m), accessible from Davao in southern Mindanao. Exercise caution if you are heading south or west of Cagayan de Oro.

Siargao

🏠 086 / POP 70,000

It's best known for having one of the world's great surf breaks, but the island of Siargao is no one-trick pony. Surrounded by idyllic islands and sprinkled with coves and quaint fishing villages, it has plenty to offer non-surfers too. With new sealed roads ringing the island and plans for an expanded airport in place, Siargao is experiencing a boom as new resorts open at a dizzying pace. The time to visit is now.

ℹ️ Getting There & Away

Cebu Pacific flies from Cebu to Siargao three or four times a week.

The other way to Siargao is by boat from Surigao City on mainland Mindanao. Speedy bangka head to Dapa on Siargao from the boulevard area 500m northwest of Surigao's Tavern Hotel (P250, 2½ hours, 5.30am and 6am). In bad weather opt for the daily **Montenegro** (🏠 086-231 6245) RORO (P180, 3½ hours, noon) from Surigao's **main pier** (Borromeo St). Bangka from Dapa to Surigao City depart at 5.30am and 10.30am; the RORO is at 6am.

To get to Surigao City, either fly in from Cebu or Manila, bus in from Butuan or Cagayan de Oro, or sail in from Southern Leyte in the Visayas. There are regular ROROs from the Southern Leyte towns of Lilo-an and San Ricardo to Lipata port, 8km west of Surigao.

ℹ️ Getting Around

Siargao's small airport is in Del Carmen on the western side of the island. An airport van shuttles passengers to/from the resorts around Cloud Nine (P300, 45 minutes).

From the pier in Dapa, a habal-habal costs a negotiable P150 to General Luna ('GL'; 25 minutes), or P200 to Cloud Nine. Habal-habal drivers in Cloud Nine ask more for the reverse trip. Tricycles cost the same but are much slower.

To explore the island, you're best off renting a motorbike (per day P400 to P500).

Cloud Nine & General Luna

The legendary Cloud Nine break off Tuazon Point is what put Siargao on the map. Board rental in the sleepy village of Cloud Nine, a 10-minute habal-habal ride north of GL, is P500 per day or P200 per hour. There are plenty of moderate swells around for beginners; lessons cost P500 per hour including board rental. Peak season for waves is late August to November. Cloud Nine gets overrun in October for the **Siargao International Surfing Cup**.

Hippie's Surf Shop (www.surfshopsiargao. com; ⏱ 6am-6pm) rents boards and holds thrice-weekly yoga classes (P200). Resorts can organise boat transport to offshore surf breaks or island-hopping trips, often with a snorkelling or surfing option.

🛏️ Sleeping

A backpacker oasis of sorts has sprung up 1.5km north of General Luna ('GL') and inland from the main road (turn left at Isla Cabana resort). **Paglaom Hostel** (🏠 0999 990 0308; www.paglaomhostel.com; dm P250; 🛜) is the pick of the bunch, with wide and wonderful open-air dorms, plus a kitchen and a sociable common area. Right next door is hammock-laden **Jing's Place** (🏠 0910 259 6493; www.jingsplace.com; d with/without bathroom from P880/550), with good-value budget rooms in a rambling wood complex. Down the road is **Hangout Siargao** (🏠 0927 611 6117; thehangoutsiargao@gmail.com; Purok 5; dm P250; 🛜), where you sleep in utterly unique, hammock-like mesh beds suspended 3m over the floor.

Ocean 101 Beach Resort   HOTEL **$**
(🏠 0910 848 0893; www.ocean101cloud9.com; r with fan P500-1300, with air-con P1400-2500; ❇️🛜) This is surfing HQ, with a mix of well-maintained budget rooms and pricier beachfront quarters with nice furniture, high ceilings and big bathrooms distributed among two ugly blue concrete edifices on a seawall just north of the Cloud Nine break.

Villa Solaria   HOSTEL **$**
(🏠 0920 407 7730; dm P300, d P1600-2000; ❇️🛜) A great all-rounder just south of Cloud Nine, with a full service kitchen, good-value private rooms and one large outdoor dormitory that fills up fast with shoestring surfers.

Siargao Surfer's Lodge
LODGE $

(📞 0928 374 7947; 2-bed dm P500, d P1000-1500; 🛜) Party people should consider these four immaculately kept rooms at the back of Nine Bar. The cushiony mattresses and – in the dorm room – extra-tall bunk beds really make an impression.

Malijon Siargao
BUNGALOW $$

(📞 0920 507 5793; malijonsiargao@gmail.com; d P1400) The three stand-alone huts at Swedish-run Malijon, just off the main road about halfway between GL and Cloud Nine, are justifiably coveted. They are spacious and attractively designed, with thick mattresses, big bathrooms and glorious balconies.

✗ Eating & Drinking

In GL you'll find cheap eateries and a couple of bars frequented by local surfer dudes and chicks.

★ Mama's Grill
BARBECUE $

(skewers P50-70; 🕑6-9pm) Every evening the surfing herd converges to feed on skewered pork chops, chicken and beef at this modest BBQ shack about 1.5km north of GL. And then, just like that, they're gone...until the next evening.

Cafe Loka
CAFE $$

(🕑6am-6pm; 🛜) Associated with neighbouring Sagana Beach Resort, this place sits under palm trees on a rare (for Cloud Nine) patch of sand, offering healthy snacks, shakes and Aussie-style coffee.

Nine Bar
BAR

(🛜) A handsomely built place on the road between Cloud Nine and GL, Nine Bar is where expats go to swill beer and swap swell tales.

Camiguin

🕑 088 / POP 84,000

With seven volcanoes, various waterfalls, hot springs, cold springs, deserted islands offshore and underwater diversions aplenty, Camiguin is a top adventure-tourism destination. The dramatic landscape makes it a great place to strike out on your own and explore, preferably by motorbike (per day P400 to P500) or mountain bike (per day P250).

Adventure lovers should head to Camiguin Action Geckos or **Johnny's Dive N' Fun** (📞 088-387 9588; www.johnnysdive.com). They both offer a range of trekking, rappelling, mountain-biking and diving tours,

and are happy to dispense advice to do-it-yourselfers. Don't miss world-class diving or snorkelling at splendid **Mantigue Island**, 70m **Kitabawasan Falls**, remote **Binangawan Falls**, or the easy **Stations of the Cross** hike for great views.

White Island, a marooned slick of sand 1km off Agoho, is best visited at midday when intense sun scares off the huge crowds of domestic tourists. Boats to the island dock next to Paras Beach Resort in Yumbing and cost P450 plus P20 per person.

🛏 Sleeping & Eating

Most of Camiguin's resorts are on the black-sand beaches of barangays Bug-Ong, Agoho, Yumbing and Naasag, 5km to 10km west of Mambajao. Several nondescript beach resorts in Yumbing proper rent out rooms from P700, although they raise their rates at the first sign of a crowd. The best by far is lovely **Marianita's Cottages** (📞 0917 276 4199; www.marianitas-cottages.com; National Hwy, Yumbing; r with fan/air-con from P900/1300; ❄🛜).

Camiguin Action Geckos Resort
RESORT $

(📞 088-387 9146; www.camiguin.ph; Agoho; s/d without bathroom P700/900, cottages P2000-2600; 🛜) Every island in the Philippines should have a place just like this. 'Rustic sophistication' says it all – you'll find perfectly constructed, spacious, hardwood cottages with verandahs combined with touches of class and taste. For more value, try one of the small but appealing 'travellers' rooms' upstairs from the open-air restaurant.

Camiguin Souldivers
HOSTEL $

(📞 0947 411 1189; www.camiguinsouldivers.com; Tupsan; dm/s/d/cottage P200/300/350/600) The simple, cave-like dorms and rooms here cater to shoestring divers. It abuts the highway where the road divides about 6km southeast of Mambajao.

WARNING

Most embassies strongly warn tourists against travelling to potential conflict zones such as Maguindanao province (and its notoriously violent capital, Cotabato) and Zamboanga on Mindanao, and the entire Sulu Archipelago. It pays to exercise considerable caution when travelling to these areas. Check local news sources to make sure your destination and travel route are safe.

PHILIPPINES SIARGAO

OFF THE BEATEN TRACK

RIVER RAFTING IN CAGAYAN DE ORO

If you're travelling between Siargao and Camiguin, consider detouring to Cagayan de Oro (CDO) to take on the Class III and IV rapids of the Cagayan River. This is the only place in the country that offers year-round white-water rafting. Tours cost P800 to P1500 per person depending on the length of the trip. Reputable rafting companies in CDO include long-running **1st Rafting Adventure** (☑088-856 3514; 86 Jongko Bldg, Tiano Hayes St).

★ **Casa Roca Inn** GUESTHOUSE **$$**
(☑088-387 9500; www.casarocacamiguin.com; Naasag; r with shared bathroom P1000-1500; ☎) Gnarly tree branches serve as pillars holding up this two-storey home perched on a rocky heading with waves breaking below. There are just three rooms here. The gorgeous sea-facing room, with its sprawling mahogany balcony, is the pick of the island. The two rooms at the back are more modest but terrific value. The international restaurant (mains P200) is highly recommended.

Agohay Villa Forte HOTEL **$$**
(☑0927 805 1050; www.agohayvillaforte.com; Agoho; d P1350-2000, 6-person r P3200; ❉☎❊) Solid all-round choice right on the beach with a variety of garden- and sea-facing rooms, including a large dorm-style room that's perfect for a group of backpackers. Well managed only when owners on property.

Luna Ristorante ITALIAN **$$**
(National Hwy, Yumbing; mains P200-390; ◷7.30am-11pm; ☎) Luna does excellent thin-crust brick-oven pizza, as well as pasta, calzones and a mean mixed-seafood grill. Located on the main road in Yumbing, right after the Checkpoint complex.

ⓘ Getting There & Away

Cebu Pacific has daily flights from Cebu to Camiguin's airport just west of Mambajao. Alternatively, fly to Cagayan de Oro (CDO) and continue to Camiguin by bus/boat via Balingoan, on the mainland 90km northeast of CDO.

RORO from Balingoan leave roughly every 1½ hours until 5.30pm to Benoni port, 17km southeast of Mambajao (P185, 1½ hours). The last reliable ferry back to Balingoan is at 4.15pm.

Additionally, **Super Shuttle Ferry** (☑088-387 4034) has an on again, off again RORO to Jagna, Bohol, from Balbagon port, 2km east of Mambajao (P425, 3½ hours, Monday, Wednesday and Friday at 8am).

From Balingoan, Bachelor buses serve Surigao (ordinary/air-con P300/400, six to seven hours with a transfer in Butuan) and Cagayan de Oro (ordinary/air-con P85/118, two hours) all day and night.

ⓘ Getting Around

Public multicabs (mini-jeepneys) and *motorilla* (oversized tricycles) circle the island; a short ride costs P9. Multicabs meet boats at the pier in Benoni and shuttle people to Mambajao (P23, 30 minutes). A private multicab from Benoni to Mambajao/Agoho costs P350/500.

Motorbike hire is available everywhere, including around Benoni pier, for P400 to P500.

PALAWAN

Drifting on the Philippines' western edge, Palawan is one of the country's last ecological frontiers. Despite becoming something of a travel-media darling in recent years, Thailand-style tourists hordes have yet to arrive and the Amazonian interior remains relatively pristine.

The main attraction is the west coast, which comprises one breathtaking bay after another leading up to the limestone cliffs of El Nido and Bacuit Bay in the north. Eight hours north of mainland Palawan, Coron and the Calamian group of islands offers beaches, unbeatable wreck diving and a number of El Nido–esque cliffs of their own.

Palawan's west coast bears the brunt of the *habagat*, which peaks between mid-June and mid-September, so plan accordingly.

Puerto Princesa

☑048 / POP 45,000
Palawan's bustling capital is mainly a gateway to El Nido and the beaches of the west coast, but 'Puerto' does have enough diversions to warrant a day or two if you're passing through. A decent food scene, some nightlife along main drag Rizal Ave, and a growing number of boutique hotels increase the appeal.

The city is geographically immense. The underground river in Sabang, some 60km away to the northwest, technically lies within municipality limits (hence the official

name: Puerto Princesa Subterranean River).
Many pay a premium for day trips to the underground river out of Puerto. Instead, stay in idyllic Sabang and launch your trip there.

⊙ Sights & Activities

Popular island-hopping tours (P1300 to P1500 for up to six people) in scenic Honda Bay are run out of Sta Lourdes, 11km north of Puerto. Booking these in Puerto costs an exorbitant P1400 or so per person including lunch and various entrance fees.

Palaweño Brewery
BREWERY

(☑ 048-434 0709; www.palawenobrewery.com; 82 Manolo St; 4-beer flight P400; ☺1-9pm Mon-Sat) Producer of Ayahay craft beers, offers free tours and has an attractive tap room for tasting and lounging.

Dolphins & Whale Sharks
WILDLIFE WATCHING

(☑ 0915 263 2105; www.dolphinandwhales.com; whale-shark tours per person P1800, dolphin tours per person P1000; ☺ only Apr-Oct, whale sharks 7am-2pm, dolphins 6.20-10.30am) The effusive Toto Kayabo runs separate tours to spot these creatures in Honda Bay. This is your best chance to spot wild (ie non-hand-fed) whale sharks during the country's southwest monsoon (May to October). Weather permitting, the whale-shark tours (minimum six people) usually only take place within five days of a full moon, while the dolphin tours (minimum 14 people) are daily.

Both tours must be booked in advance and include transport to the jump-off point north of Puerto Princesa. Toto also runs night-time firefly tours that are preferable to the uber-popular Iwahig River firefly tours.

★ Pasyar Developmental Tourism
OUTDOORS

(☑ 048-433 5525; http://pasyarpalawantravel. weebly.com; Gabinete Rd) ⌀ Genuinely dedicated to conservation and community-based tourism, Pasyar can organise Honda Bay island-hopping tours using former illegal fishers, and also arranges seasonal (January to April) coast-to-coast forest treks terminating in Sabang or Simpocan. Also runs an **Environmental Enforcement Museum** (admission P20; ☺ 8am-5pm) ⌀ out of its headquarters, which displays confiscated chainsaws, boats, dynamite and (sometimes) animals such as civets.

🛏 Sleeping

★ Sheebang Hostel
HOSTEL $

(☑ 0915 370 0647, 048-433 0592; judy.sheebang@ gmail.com; 118 Libis Rd; dm P250-350, d P800-960) Sheebang quickly emerged as Puerto's leading hostel after the legendary Banwa Art House burned down in 2014. In a gorgeous wooden house, it has three air-con dorms with sturdy bunk beds and big lockers, plus some basic private rooms. An open-air bar, sprawling garden and competent travel desk make up for the out-of-the-way location.

★ Casa Linda Inn
INN $

(☑ 048-433 2606, 0917 749 6956; casalindainn@ gmail.com; Trinidad Rd; s/d with fan P550/650, with air-con P850/1000; ❄🖥🛜) The meticulously maintained garden courtyard and pergola makes centrally located Casa Linda feel like a country refuge. The surrounding wood-floored rooms are clean and simply furnished, though thin walls mean noise can be a nuisance. Nonetheless, it's easily the best-value hotel in town.

Tree House Inn
HOSTEL $

(☑ 048-434 0005; treehouseinn@yahoo.com; ARL Building, 2nd fl Malvar St; dm P450, d without bathroom P1000; ❄🛜) 'Tree House' is a misnomer given its noisy streetside location in a central office building. It's clean if unspectacular, with a small kitchen and a mix of coed and female dorm rooms.

Dallas Lodge
HOSTEL $

(☑ 0946 392 8818; www.dallas-inn.com; 11 Carandang St; dm/d P300/600; 🛜) A tiny, friendly backpacker crash pad with six grafitti-splashed private rooms and a six-bed dorm, all clad in warm rattan.

🍴 Eating & Drinking

Ima's Vegetarian
VEGETARIAN $

(Fernandez St; dishes P85-140; ☺11am-9pm Sun-Thu, 11am-3pm Fri, 6.30-9pm Sat; 🍴) ⌀ A decidedly healthy and delicious option run by Seventh-Day Adventists. Try the spicy bean burrito or vegan-cheese pizza for *merienda* (a daytime snack).

Bazzo
CAFE $

(cnr Carandang & Lacao Sts; snacks P75-150; ☺9am-11pm; 🛜) Highlights at this arty hole-in-the-wall include all-day breakfasts, cheese-drenched French fries and a killer cookies-and-cream frappe.

Cafe Itoy's   CAFE $
(Rizal Ave; mains P115-230; ⊙7am-11pm; 🛜)
Long-running coffee joint on the main drag with a shady back terrace and an extensive menu of snacks and light bites.

Pham Chaolong   VIETNAMESE $
(Rizal Ave, btwn Valencia & Burgos Sts; dishes P50; ⊙7am-9pm) Good, central option for Vietnamese *chaolong (*a Filipino version of *pho*).

Tiki Restobar   BAR
(cnr Rizal Ave & National Hwy; mains P160; ⊙7pm-2am) A large place in the middle of town, Tiki features bar games, beer buckets and revellers shimmying on the dance floor to live music.

❶ Information

Metrobank, BDO and BPI, all on Rizal Ave, have mainland Palawan's only working ATMs.

The **Subterranean River National Park Office** (☑048-434 2509; City Coliseum, National Hwy; ⊙8am-3.30pm), about 2km north of Rizal Ave, issues Subterranean River permits.

❶ Getting There & Away

AIR

Air Asia, Cebu Pacific and PAL Express each fly at least thrice daily from Puerto Pricesa to Manila, while Cebu Pacific adds one or two daily flights to Cebu, plus three weekly flights to Iloilo, Panay.

BOAT

2GO (☑048-434 9344; Rizal Ave) has a Sunday 1am trip from Puerto Princesa to Manila (from P1300, 30 hours) via Coron.

Milagrosa Shipping (☑048-433 4806; Rizal Ave; P900 to P1500, 36 hours, 3pm Thursday and Sunday) and sturdier **Montenegro Lines** (☑048-434 9344; www.montenegrolines.com.ph; Puerto Princesa Pier; P1220 to P1590, 26

hours, 8pm Saturday and 6pm Monday) serve Iloilo via the Cuyo Islands.

BUS

Buses/jeepneys and/or vans serve Sabang, Port Barton and El Nido. To avoid waiting hours for a van to fill up, steer clear of the touts and take the scheduled vans to El Nido from the bus terminal run by **Lexus Shuttle** (☑0917 585 9613; www.lexusshuttle.com) and others, or pay a premium for advance bookings through **Daytripper** (☑0917 848 8755, 048-723 0533; www.daytripperpalawan.com).

❶ Getting Around

The airport is on Rizal Ave just east of the centre. Airport tricycles cost P50 or walk out and take a public trike for P8.

The main bus terminal is at the San Jose market 6km north of town. To get there grab a tricycle (P50) or multicab (mini-jeepney; P15) from the corner of Rizal Ave and the National Hwy.

You can rent motorbikes (from P450) at various places along Rizal Ave near the airport.

Sabang
☑048

Tiny Sabang has a beautiful beach, huge tracts of pristine jungle and the navigable **Puerto Princesa Subterranean River National Park** (park permit incl paddle boat P250, plus environmental fee P40; ⊙8.30am-3.30pm), which winds through a spectacular cave before emptying into the sea. Trips aboard unmotorised paddle boats proceed about 1.5km upstream into the cave (45 minutes return). When looking up, keep your mouth shut: bats and swiftlets flutter above and are responsible for the guano that 'perfumes' the cave.

Book a bangka (P700 for up to six people, 15 minutes) to the cave entrance through the **Sabang Information Office** (☑048-723 0904; ⊙8am-4pm) at the pier, or walk 5km via the 'jungle trail' (entrance P200 including guide). Important note: unless you can produce an accommodation receipt from a resort in Sabang, Port Barton or points north, you *must* secure your permit in advance from a tour operator or from the national park office in Puerto Princesa.

Other activities in Sabang include waterfall walks, stand-up paddleboarding and body-surfing (when there's swell). Ask around for 'Jungle George', who guides all-day rainforest walks taking in indigenous Batak villages (P500 per person).

🛏 Sleeping & Eating

Most places have electricity only from 6pm to 10pm or 11pm. Two high-end beach resorts have 24-hour electricity and wi-fi.

★ Dab Dab Resort
BUNGALOW $

(☑ 0949 469 9421; cottage with/without bathroom P700/400; 🕲) This place, 200m south of Sabang pier, is an appealing haven. There's no beach here, only a rocky shoreline, but the seven hardwood cottages with nipa roofs are much nicer than those on the beach. Each is equipped with a ceiling fan, private porch and hammock.

Mary's Cottages
BUNGALOW $

(☑ 0936 264 5572; d P500-600, q P1200) Mary's occupies the peaceful northern end of Sabang Beach. The four bungalows are exceedingly basic but have lovely balconies facing the ocean (all you need, really).

Green Verde
COTTAGE $

(☑ 0910 978 4539; d from P800; 🕲) The cramped rooms here are a baby step up on budget accommodation elsewhere on Sabang Beach, and it also has one of Sabang's few decent beachfront restaurants (mains P75 to P300).

Blue Bamboo Cottages
BUNGALOW $

(☑ 0910 797 0038; www.bluebamboo-sabang.com; r P250-700; 🕲) A mix of basic budget rooms and charmingly dilapidated all-bamboo cottages with private porches. It fronts a rocky shoreline around 250m south of Sabang pier.

❶ Getting There & Away

Lexus Shuttle vans connect Sabang and Puerto Princesa five or six times daily in either direction (P200, 1½ hours). Jumbo jeepneys (with/without baggage P150/120, 2½ hours) make four daily trips as well.

Lexus also offers five daily trips to El Nido with a transfer in Salvacion. For Port Barton, the safest bet is to backtrack to Puerto Princesa and grab a van or bus there. Alternatively, flag down the twice-daily Puerto–Port Barton bus from the National Hwy in Salvacion.

Port Barton

☑ 048 / POP 5500

People find themselves unable to leave Port Barton, and only partly because of the town's poor transport links. Set on a small, attractive cove, the area has some fine islands in the bay and good snorkelling. Superb island-hopping excursions (per person including lunch P700) and diving can be easily arranged. Bistro Coron and others rent out sea kayaks (per day P500) for DIY explorers.

🛏 Sleeping & Eating

Demand outstrips supply in the high season so book ahead. Budget-friendly resorts on offshore islands include **Coconut Garden** (☑ 0918 370 2395; www.coconutgarden.palawan. net; Cacnipa Island; s/d P860/995, cottage P1350-1750) and **Blue Cove** (☑ 0908 562 0879; www. bluecoveresort.com; Albaguen Island; cottage with fan/air-con P1500/3000; ❋ 🕲). Expect to pay P1500 or so for the boat transfer. **Thelma & Toby's Island Camping Adventure** (☑ 048-434 8687, 0999 486 3348; www.palawancamping. com; per person incl full board P1600; ☺ mid-Nov–mid-May) offers upscale camping in canopy-covered, fan-cooled tents on a divine mainland beach 20 minutes by boat from Port Barton.

At almost all places electricity runs only from 6pm to midnight.

El Dorado Sunset Resort
COTTAGE $

(☑ 0920 329 9049; lucy_deniega@yahoo.com; d P800-1500; 🕲) The colourful concrete cottages aren't easy on the eyes, but with private porches and clean bathrooms they are reasonably good value. However, the main selling points are the circular bar and the location on the preferable northern end of the beach. Subtract P300 in the low season.

Ausan
COTTAGE $$

(☑ 0929 444 0582; www.ausanbeachfront.com; d/family cottage P1250/2850; ❋ 🕲) Port Barton's best all-around midrange option, centrally located Ausan was the only place in Port Barton with all-day (7am to midnight) electricity at the time of research. Choose from beachfront fan cottages with attractive wood floors and panelling, or larger 'themed' rooms with trippy-looking wall murals, stonework and chintzy furniture.

Barton Bistro
COTTAGE $$

(☑ 0917 884 3301; bartonbistroportbarton@gmail. com; s/d incl breakfast P800/1700; 🕲) It's a bit of a splurge but well worth it for Port Barton's swankiest rooms – in a perfectly central location, no less. A candlelit dinner here is also money well spent (mains P150 to P250). Try the *kinilaw* (crabs in coconut milk), or French toast with wild honey for breakfast.

Jambalaya Cajun Cafe CAFE, INTERNATIONAL **$$**
(☑ 0915 315 3842; mains P240-450; ⊙ 8am-9pm
Mon-Sat; 🛜) A homey and quirky vibe and a
great beachfront location makes Jambalaya
the place to hang in Port Barton. Yes, the sig-
nature seafood jambalaya (P350) and gum-
bo (P300) are expensive, but they just about
feed two. Delicious cocktails too.

ⓘ Information

Jambalaya cafe has a handy booklet with accom-
modation listings and other info; you can leave
your bag there while you prowl the beach looking
for a bed.

ⓘ Getting There & Away

Buses/jeepneys to Puerto Princesa depart at
9am and 1pm (P250, 4½ hours) via Salvacion
(P250, 3½ hours) for Sabang. Departures from
Puerto are at 7.30am and 9am. Vans (P350,
three hours) to Puerto depart at 6am and 1pm.
Trips in the other direction are at 6.30 am and
1pm.

There's an 8am jumbo jeepney to Roxas (P150,
1½ hours); the reverse trip is at noon. Change in
Roxas for El Nido. There's also an 8.30am mini-
van to El Nido (P800, 3½ hours).

El Nido

☑ 048 / POP 8000
El Nido is the primary base for exploring
Palawan's star attraction, the stunning
Bacuit Archipelago. Tiny swiftlets build
edible nests out of saliva in the immense
limestone cliffs that surround the ramshack-
le town – hence the name, El Nido (nest in
Spanish). El Nido has a particularly harsh
rainy season, so check the forecast if head-
ing here between June and September and
be ready to re-route.

⊙ Sights

The El Nido area is blessed with argua-
bly the best beaches in the country. Yeah,
some places have all the luck. The offshore
islands are loaded with postcard-perfect
white beaches. About 5km south of El Nido
proper, **Marimegmeg Beach** (aka Las Caba-
nas Beach) has sunset views and uber-cool
happy-hour spot **Beach Shack**.

Nacpan Beach BEACH
To escape the crowds, head north by tricy-
cle or motorbike to this golden-hued 3km
beach. Development is limited to a few
snack shacks and some basic lodging, but
change is imminent so enjoy the peace while

it lasts. To get here drive 18km north of El
Nido on a paved highway, then another 4km
down a rugged access road.

On the way look for the turn-off to
Nagkalit-kalit Falls just north of the 285km
marker on the highway. It's a 40-minute
hike to the refreshing falls; hire a guide at
the trailhead to avoid getting lost.

🏃 Activities

All-day or overnight island-hopping trips in
Bacuit Bay are *the* thing to do in El Nido.
They are ubiquitously available and cost
P1200 to P1400 per person, including lunch
(four-person minimum). Miniloc Island's
Big Lagoon and **Small Lagoon** are not to
be missed; for full effect get there at dawn
when you'll have them to yourself (pri-
vate boat transport required). Overnight
beach-camping trips average P3500 per per-
son per night.

Sea kayaks are a great way to explore
some of the closer Bacuit Bay attractions
such as **Cadlao Island** and **Seven Com-
mandos Beach**. They are widely available
in El Nido and Corong-Corong, and at Small
Lagoon on Miniloc Isand, for P500 to P1000
per day. It's worth paying up for a non-dodgy
craft; Art Cafe's clear-bottom kayaks are the
best. Art Cafe also hires out stand-up pad-
dleboards (P250/900 per hour/day) and
windsurfers.

There are several scuba-diving operators
in town, plus a range of terrestrial tours of-
fered by myriad tour operators – climbing
the local *taraw* (cliffs) are an option, albeit
not one for the faint of heart.

🛏 Sleeping

Most budget accommodation is off El Nido's
narrow beach. The midrange places that line
the beach east of the pier are generally over-
priced, but do slash rates by up to 60% in the
low season (negotiate).

Head south a couple of kilometres to
Corong-Corong Beach to escape the bustle
of El Nido. For even less bustle, try up-and-
coming Nacpan Beach.

Our Melting Pot Hostel HOSTEL **$**
(OMP; ☑ 0906 412 7861; ourmeltingpotbackpackers
@gmail.com; Real St; dm/s incl breakfast from
P500/600; 🛜) Low-maintenance hardcore
budget travellers who don't mind crowded
sleeping conditions will be happy here. Hot
water and sheets provided, while privacy is
supplied by thin curtains on the bunks.

Where 2 Next HOSTEL $
(📞 0917 804 0434; www.where2nexthostel.com; Nacpan Beach; dm in tent/room P250/400, private tent/room P500/1100; 🛜) Enviably placed just off Nacpan Beach, Where 2 Next is well positioned to ride Nacpan's surging popularity. The communal tent is unique to the Philippines, or opt for a standard dorm or snug private. Solar power, good food and friendly management round out the package.

El Nido Sands Inn GUESTHOUSE $
(📞 0999 452 5843; Sirena St; dm/d without bathroom from P300/600; ❄️🛜) The simple clapboard doubles and dorms here are arguably El Nido's best budget deal. It lacks the services and communal atmosphere of other budget hostels in town, but the four- and six-bed dorms are much roomier and feature wide, sturdy bunk beds.

Lugadia Beach Cottages COTTAGE $
(📞 0946 241 1864; Corong-Corong; cottage P800-1000; 🛜) Old-school nipa huts hidden away down a hill on a razor-thin slice of Corong-Corong beach. The cottages cover little more than the basics – mattress, mozzie net, cold water and private balconies – but have plenty of backpacker appeal.

Bulskamp Inn GUESTHOUSE $$
(📞 0906 552 4624; www.bulskamp-inn.webs.com; Osmeña St; r with fan/air-con P1400/1800; ❄️🛜) Named after the owner's hometown in Belgium, this place gets props for friendly service and a cosy ambience. Rooms have small beds but are spotless. Hot water costs an extra P200.

Jack's Place BUNGALOW $$
(📞 0935 355 3837; Nacpan Beach; d/q cottage P1000/1800; 🛜) Walk toward the north end of Nacpan Beach and you'll encounter this castaway-style gem. It consists of five basic en suite cottages on stilts, all fashioned of wood and equipped with beach-facing balconies. Kayak rental available (per hour/day P150/500).

Spin Hostel HOSTEL $$
(www.spinhostel.com; Balinsasayaw Rd, cnr Calle Real; dm/d from P1000/2500; ❄️@🛜) It remains to be seen whether the eye-popping design of this new luxury hostel can justify the eye-popping prices. Dorms are of the four-bed variety and are comfy enough, but you're paying for the elaborate common areas and regular fun events. Request a room

away from the adjoining field, where frogs produce a deafening chorus by night.

Chislyk Beach Cottages BUNGALOW $$
(📞 0918 243 3780; gladysmisajon@yahoo.com; Hama St; cottage with fan/air-con from P1400/1800; ❄️🛜) Several small bamboo and concrete cottages share a stamp-sized beachfront; however, each does have its own porch – a big amenity in this price range. Consider the prices a starting point for negotiation.

🍴 Eating & Drinking

IBR FILIPINO $
(Hama St; mains P90-200; ⊙24hr) A Filipino greasy spoon where backpackers (often nursing a hangover) and locals chow down on soups and rice and meat dishes. Streetside fan seating and an air-con dining room in back.

Lonesome Carabao MEXICAN $$
(Hama St; mains P200-300; ⊙7am-10pm) The best Mexican food in El Nido, if not Palawan, if not the entire southern Philippines!

Boodle Fight Restaurant FILLIPINO $$
(📞 0928 824 736; National Hwy, Corong-Corong; mains P120-220; ⊙8am-10.30pm) What's a Boodle Fight, you ask? It's a Filipino feast served on a huge banana leaf and eaten communally by hand. A four-person feast here costs P650. Advance bookings recommended.

⭐ Trattoria Altrove ITALIAN $$
(📞 0947 775 8653; Hama St; mains P240-450; ⊙5-10pm) This Slovenian-owned place does the best pizza in El Nido, made with imported mozzarella in the street-level brick oven. A dozen types of pasta from Italy (P230), plus T-bone steak and other meat dishes on the menu.

Pukka Bar BAR
(📞 0908 488 8832; ⊙4pm-4am; 🛜) The most happening bar in El Nido features live reggae, buckets of Red Horse and bands of drunken backpackers spilling onto the beach. It also offers five small, well-kept backpacker rooms (fan/air-con P700/1700).

Lucky Alofa BAR
(Hama St; mains P170-300; ⊙3pm-midnight, closed Jul & Aug; 🛜) Burgers, bar snacks, '90s tunes and quality cocktails are the hallmarks of this buzzing Swedish-owned bar on the main drag.

ℹ Information

All visitors to El Nido must pay a P200 'eco-tourism development fee', good for 10 days, payable to your hotel or tour operator. There are no ATMs so bring cash. The Petron station at the port *may* be able to do cash advances.

El Nido Boutique & Art Café (☑ 0920 902 6317; www.elnidoboutiqueandartcafe.com; Sirena St; ☺ 6.30am-11pm, travel desk 7am-8pm) Run like clockwork by the Swiss owner, this long-running cafe is a repository for information about El Nido. You can buy plane tickets, check boat and bus schedules, change money, browse the library, buy clothes, rent kayaks, eat good food, drink real coffee and listen to live music most nights. It's also as good a place as any to arrange island-hopping trips into Bacuit Bay.

ℹ Getting There & Around

Pricey **Air Swift** (☑ in Manila 02-851 5674; http://air-swift.com) has flights to Manila (low/ high season P4150/6750) and Cebu. The only way to the airport is by tricycle for P200.

All ground transport leaves from the new bus station, about 2km south of town in Corong-Corong (P50 by tricycle). For Puerto Princesa, most people take cramped vans (P600, five hours, frequent until 8pm) booked through their hotel, but the buses (P350 to P450, seven hours, hourly until 10pm) run by Roro Bus and Cherry Bus are more comfortable.

Recardo Transport runs a direct van to Port Barton at 7am (P800, 3½ hours). Alternatively, take a 7am or earlier bus to Roxas (P250, four hours) and catch the noon jumbo jeepney to PB. Lexus Shuttle vans head to Sabang with a van change in Salvacion.

For Coron, one or two large passenger bangkas depart daily at around 8am in either direction (seven to nine hours). Most agents add a couple hundred pesos to the base fare of P1200, so buy straight from the two operators – **Bunso** (☑ 0906 637 4258; El Nido Port) and **Overcomer** (☑ 0999 978 8564; El Nido Port). **M/ Bca Von** (☑ 0910 992 6727; Sirena St) runs this

trip thrice weekly as a van/boat combo via San Fernando (east coast of Palawan) and Linapacan Island. It's pricier (P1500) and less scenic, but might be preferable in bad weather.

Coron

☑ 048 / POP 43,000

Divers know it as a wreck-diving hot spot, but the area known as Coron also has untouched beaches, crystal-clear lagoons and brooding limestone cliffs to tempt non-divers. Coron itself is actually just the sleepy main town of Busuanga Island – not to be confused with Coron Island to the south. Both Busuanga Island and Coron Island are part of the Calamian Group.

🏃 Activities

Wreck Diving

Fifteen Japanese ships sunk by US fighter planes roost on the floor of Coron Bay around Busuanga. Getting to the wrecks from Coron involves a one- to four-hour boat ride, but diving is still affordable – just P2300/2900 for a two-/three-tank dive with **Coron Divers** (☑ 0920 945 7637; www.coron divers.com.ph; Zuric Pension, National Hwy). Most of the wrecks are for advanced divers, although there are a few in less than 25m that are suitable for beginners.

Island Hopping

Coron Town lacks a beach, but you can hire a boat to explore the seemingly infinite supply of islands nearby. A four-person bangka hired from the town dock costs P2000 to P5000, depending on how far you're going, or join a tour for P650 to P1500 per person (P4500 for overnight). Nearby **Coron Island**, with its towering spires of stratified limestone, is the star attraction. Here you can paddle around on a bamboo raft and swim in unspoiled **Lake Kayangan** (admission P250), or go diving in **Barracuda Lake** (admission P100), where the clear water gets scorching hot as you descend.

🛏 Sleeping

The following are in Coron Town.

Krystal Lodge   BUNGALOW **$**
(☑ 0908 357 3309; www.krystallodge.blogspot. com; s/d P400/600, cottage P1200; ☎) Like much of Coron, this bamboo complex is built on stilts over the water. It's a maze of shady walkways ending in rooms that range

---

THE PERFECT BEACH

There's a rumour that the island described in Alex Garland's backpacker classic *The Beach* was somewhere in the Calamian Group. Garland set the book in Thailand, but admits that the real island was somewhere in the Philippines. He lived in the Philippines for a spell and set his second novel, *The Tesseract*, in Manila.

from passable boxes to unique overwater 'apartments' with their own bars and sitting areas.

Patrick & Tezz Guesthouse   GUESTHOUSE **$**
(☑ 0927 953 1407; www.coron.ph; Coastal Rd; s/d from P500/550; ☎) This Swedish-owned place, perched over the water 200m north of the centre, is the very epitome of warm and cosy. The service is suitably hospitable, and there's a small common area and 'dippity' pool for splashing around in. Two-night minimum stay.

Coron Backpacker Guesthouse   HOSTEL **$**
(☑ 0919 388 6028; http://palawan-coron-backpacker.com; d/q P500/750; ☎) This place has nine basic rooms in a shack over the water near the centre of town. The common area is pleasantly rustic, with a kitchen and lots of reading material.

Marley's Guesthouse   GUESTHOUSE **$**
(☑ 0929 539 1133; r without bathroom P400-500; ☎) On the main road near the centre, Marley's is susceptible to street noise, but its arty kitchen and common areas are the best in town.

✖ Eating & Drinking

★ **Bistro Coron**   INTERNATIONAL, FRENCH **$$**
(Coron Town; mains P200-500; ☺8am-11pm) A mouth-watering French bistro on one of the Philippines' most isolated islands? Works for us. The tiger prawns are one of the best meals we've had in the Philippines, and the huge pizzas are top-notch. Pack a fine French-bread sandwich for your day trip.

Blue Moon Restobar   ASIAN **$$**
(National Hwy; mains P150-450; ☺9am-1am) Proprietor mama cooks some of the better Thai food in the country, and will cook Indian food on request. Stay late and enjoy mean cocktails and buckets of San Miguel for P125.

Helldivers   BAR
(Coron Town) Attached to the popular and central Seadive resort and dive shop, Helldivers is a great place to spend sunset and beyond (often well beyond).

❶ Getting There & Away

Cebu Pacific, PAL Express and Skyjet have frequent flights daily between Manila and Coron. Coron's YKR airport is a smooth 30-minute ride north of Coron Town; vans (P150) meet the flights.

OFF THE BEATEN TRACK

THE CORON LOOP

Looking to get off the beaten track? Hire a boat or sea kayak and wade around the untouched beaches and islands off the west coast of Busuanga. Or tackle the rough coastal road – now about half-paved – to Busuanga's northwestern tip by motorcycle (P600 to P800), taking pit stops at beaches along the way (some off-road experience is advised if you do this). You can hire a boat in Concepcion to shuttle you out to Calumbuyan Island (admission P100), which has some of the best snorkelling in the area. One of the more interesting areas in which to kayak is near **Butong**, a mangrove area that cuts through a small peninsula north of Concepcion.

2GO (☑ 0948 126 6445) has weekly ferries to Manila (from P1600, 14 hours) and Puerto Princesa (from P1350, 14 hours). **Bunso Transport** (☑ 0946 263 5838) has bangka ferries to San José, Mindoro (P800, 6½ hours, five weekly, 8am).

All sea transport leaves from the main port, about 1.5km east of the centre. For boats to El Nido, see p598.

UNDERSTAND PHILIPPINES

Philippines Today

All eyes are on the 2016 presidential elections and who will replace Benigno Aquino III, the squeaky-clean son of Corazon Aquino, hero of the 'people power' revolution in 1986.

After being elected in a landslide in 2010, Aquino enjoyed three years of unprecedented popularity as he faced down interest groups, tackled corruption and overcame a decade of staunch opposition by the Catholic Church to sign the Reproductive Health (RH) Act, a national family-planning program that has helped stem the country's explosive population growth.

However, things began to sour around the midpoint of Aquino's six-year term. Several corruption scandals emerged, and while none of them directly implicated Aquino, he came under criticism for unfairly targeting the opposition in the ensuing investigations. Meanwhile, the investigation into the 'Maguindanao Massacre' – which saw 58 people, including 34 journalists, gunned down at a campaign event during gubernatorial elections in South Cotabato, Mindanao – ground to a halt. This further called into question Aquino's ability to crack down on corruption and clean up clan-based regional politics.

Thanks to a humming economy, Aquino remained relatively popular. Whether that popularity would translate into victory for his preferred successor, fellow Liberal Party member Mar Roxas, remained to be seen.

History

In a Nutshell

Ancient Filipinos stuck to their own islands and social groups until the 16th century, when Ferdinand Magellan claimed the islands for Spain and began the bloody process of Christianisation. Filipino's waning acceptance of Spanish rule evaporated after the Spaniards executed national hero José Rizal in 1896. They revolted and won, only to have the Americans take over, whereupon they revolted again and lost.

WWII brought much bloodshed, but out of the war's ashes rose an independent republic, albeit one that would soon elect hardliner Ferdinand Marcos as president. Marcos' declaration of martial law in 1972 and the 1986 'people power' revolution that led to his overthrow are the two defining moments of modern Filipino history. After 'people power', the country's fortunes didn't improve much under a string of leaders who did little to eradicate the paralysing corruption and cronyism of the Marcos years. Only with the election of Benigno Aquino III in 2010 did the country finally begin to shed its reputation as the 'Sick Man of Asia'.

RIZAL'S TOWER OF BABEL

The Philippines' answer to Gandhi and Mandela, writer and gentle revolutionary Dr José Rizal could read and write at the age of two. He grew up to speak more than 20 languages. He was also a doctor of medicine, and a poet, novelist, sculptor, painter, linguist, naturalist and fencing enthusiast. His last words were *consummatum est!* (it is done!).

Spanish Colonialists

In the early 16th century all signs pointed to the archipelago universally adopting Islam, but in 1521 Portuguese explorer Ferdinand Magellan changed the course of Filipino history by landing at Samar and claiming the islands for Spain. Magellan set about converting the islanders to Catholicism and winning over various tribal chiefs before he was killed by Chief Lapu-Lapu on Mactan Island near Cebu City.

In 1565, Miguel de Legazpi returned to the Philippines and, after conquering the local tribes one by one, declared Manila the capital of the new Spanish colony. But outside Manila real power rested with the Catholic friars – the notoriously unenlightened *friarocracia* (friarocracy), who acted as sole rulers over what were essentially rural fiefdoms.

The Philippine Revolution

At the end of the 19th century, as Spain grew weaker and as the friars grew ever more repressive, the Filipino people started to resist. The Spanish sealed their fate in 1896 by executing Rizal for inciting revolution. A brilliant scholar and poet, Rizal had worked for independence by peaceful means. His death galvanised the revolutionary movement.

With aid from the USA, already at war with Spain over Cuba, General Emilio Aguinaldo's revolutionary army drove the Spanish back to Manila. American warships defeated the Spanish fleet in Manila Bay in May 1898, and independence was declared on 12 June 1898.

American Rule

Alas, the Americans had other ideas. They acquired the islands from Spain and made the Philippines an American colony. War inevitably broke out in February 1899. But the expected swift American victory didn't materialise, and as the Philippine–American War dragged on, public opposition mounted in the US. The character of the American home-front debate, and the ensuing drawn-out guerrilla war, would have parallels to the Vietnam and Iraq wars many decades later. It was only on 4 July 1902 that the US finally declared victory in the campaign.

The Americans quickly set about healing the significant wounds their victory had wrought, instituting reforms aimed at improving the Filipinos' lot and promising eventual independence. The first Philippine national government was formed in 1935 with full independence pencilled in for 10 years later.

This schedule was set aside when Japan invaded the islands in WWII. For three years the country endured a brutal Japanese military regime before the Americans defeated the Japanese in the Battle for Manila in February 1945. The battle destroyed a city that had been one of the finest in Asia and resulted in the deaths of over 100,000 civilians.

People Power

The 1983 assassination of Ferdinand Marcos' opponent Benigno 'Ninoy' Aquino pushed opposition to Marcos to new heights. Marcos called elections for early 1986 and the opposition united to support Aquino's widow, Corazon 'Cory' Aquino. Both Marcos and Aquino claimed to have won the election, but 'people power' rallied behind Cory Aquino, and within days Ferdinand and his profligate wife, Imelda, were packed off by the Americans to Hawaii, where the former dictator later died.

Cory Aquino failed to win the backing of the army but managed to hang on through numerous coup attempts. She was followed by Fidel Ramos, Ferdinand Marcos' second cousin. In 1998 Ramos was replaced by B-grade movie actor Joseph 'Erap' Estrada, who promised to redirect government funding towards rural and poor Filipinos. Estrada lasted only 2½ years in office before being ousted over corruption allegations in a second 'people power' revolt and replaced by his diminutive vice-president, Gloria Macapagal Arroyo, who would somehow serve nine years, battling her own corruption allegations and threats of a third 'people power' revolt.

The Moro Problem

Muslim dissent emanating out of Mindanao has been the one constant in the Philippines' roughly 450 years of history as a loosely united territory. The country's largest separatist Muslim group, the Moro Islamic Liberation Front (MILF), has fought the government from its base in the Autonomous Region in Muslim Mindanao (ARMM) since the 1980s, conducting periodic bombings and abductions.

In October 2012 the MILF and the government signed the Bangsamoro Framework Agreement (BFA), a preliminary peace deal meant to hand the MILF more autonomy and end decades of conflict and poverty in Mindanao. The agreement was finally signed by the two parties in 2014.

However, violence has continued apace throughout the peace process, as the agreement excluded the MILF's main rivals, the Moro National Liberation Front (MNLF), as well as other Muslim splinter groups. In 2013 the MNLF orchestrated a siege of the southern city of Zamboanga, resulting in the deaths of more than 200 people. Kidnappings and abductions in Muslim-dominated areas of Mindanao remained common in 2014 and 2015. At the time of writing, peace in Mindanao seemed as tenuous as ever.

People & Culture

Lifestyle

It's impossible to deny it: Filipinos have a zest for life that may be unrivalled on our planet. The national symbol, the jeepney, is an apt metaphor for the nation. Splashed with colour, laden with religious icons and

CULTURE HINTS

➨ Don't lose your temper – Filipinos will think you're *loco loco* (crazy).

➨ When engaged in karaoke (and trust us, you will be), don't insult the guy who sounds like a chicken getting strangled, lest it be taken the wrong way.

➨ Abstain from grabbing that last morsel on the communal food platter – your hosts might think you're a pauper.

festooned with sanguine scribblings, the jeepney flaunts the fact that, at heart, it's a dilapidated pile of scrap metal. No matter their prospects in life, Filipinos face them with a laugh and a wink. Whatever happens…'so be it'. This fatalism has a name: *bahala na,* a phrase that expresses the idea that all things shall pass and in the meantime life is to be lived.

For centuries the two most important influences on the lives of Filipinos have been family and religion. The Filipino family unit extends to distant cousins, multiple godparents and one's *barkada* (gang of friends). Filipino families, especially poor ones, tend to be large. It's not uncommon for a dozen family members to live together in a tiny apartment, shanty or nipa hut.

Filipinos are a superstitious lot. In the hinterland, a villager might be possessed by a wandering spirit, causing them to commit strange acts. In urban areas, faith healers, psychics, fortune tellers, tribal shamans, self-help books and evangelical crusaders can all help cast away ill-fortune.

Another vital thread in the fabric of Filipino society is the Overseas Filipino Worker (OFW) – the nurse in Canada, the construction worker in Qatar, the entertainer in Japan, the cleaner in Singapore. Combined, they send home billions of dollars a year.

Population

A journey from the northern tip of Luzon to the southern tip of the Sulu islands reveals a range of ethnic groups speaking some 170 different dialects. Filipinos are mainly of the Malay race, although there's a sizeable and economically dominant Chinese minority and a fair number of *mestizos* (Filipinos of mixed descent).

The country's population is thought to be about 101 million and expanding at a rapid clip of almost 2% per year – one of the fastest growth rates in Asia. The median age is only 23.2 and almost a quarter of the population lives in or around metro Manila.

Arts

CINEMA

The Philippines has historically been Southeast Asia's most prolific film-making nation. The movie industry's 'golden age' was the 1950s, when Filipino films won countless awards. In the 1980s and '90s the industry surged again thanks to a genre called 'bold' – think sex, violence and dudes with great hair in romantic roles. Today the mainstream studios are in decline, but the quality of films is improving with the proliferation of independent films such as Jeffrey Jeturian's *Kubrador* (2006), *Ekstra* (2013) and Lav Diaz' epic four-hour masterpiece, *Norte, the End of History.* Another important indie director is Brillante Mendoza, who won Best Director at the 2009 Cannes Film Festival for his graphic, controversial film *Kinatay* (Slaughtered).

MUSIC

Filipinos are best known for their ubiquitous cover bands and their love of karaoke, but 'OPM' is wildly popular too. Original Pinoy Music ('Pinoy' is what Filipinos call themselves) encompasses a wide spectrum of rock, folk and New Age genres – plus a subset that includes all three.

The big three of Pinoy rock are slightly grungy eponymous band Bamboo, agreeable trio Rivermaya (formerly fronted by Bamboo), and sometimes sweet, sometimes surly diva Kitchie Nadal, who regularly tours internationally.

One veteran band worth checking out in the bars of Manila is Kalayo, which plays a sometimes-frantic fusion of tribal styles and modern jam-band rock. Alternative rock fans should give quintet Taken by Cars a listen. Two other names to look out for are Mumford & Sons–esque folk rockers Ransom Collective, and jazzy vocalist Jireh Calo.

Food & Drink

Kain na tayo – 'let's eat'. It's the Filipino invitation to eat, and if you travel here, you will hear it over and over again. The phrase reveals two essential aspects of Filipino people: one, that they are hospitable, and two, that they love to, well, eat. Three meals a day isn't enough, so they've added two *merienda*. The term means 'snack', but don't let that fool you – the afternoon *merienda* can include filling *goto* (Filipino congee) or *bibingka* (fluffy rice cakes topped with cheese).

Other favourite Filipino snacks and dishes:

Adobo Chicken, pork or fish in a dark tangy sauce.

Balut Half-developed duck embryo, boiled in the shell.

Crispy pata Deep-fried pork hock or knuckles.

Halo-halo A tall, cold glass of milky crushed ice with fresh fruit and ice cream.

Kare-kare Meat (usually oxtail) cooked in peanut sauce.

Kinilaw Delicious Filipino-style ceviche.

Lumpia Spring rolls filled with meat or vegetables.

Mami Noodle soup, like *mee* soup in Malaysia or Indonesia.

Pancit Stir-fried *bihon* (white) or *canton* (yellow) noodles with meat and vegetables.

Pinakbet Vegetables with shrimp paste, garlic, onions and ginger.

The national brew, San Miguel, is very palatable and, despite being a monopolist, eminently affordable at around P22 (P30 to P55 in bars). Tanduay rum is the national drink and is usually served with cola. Popular nonalcoholic drinks include *buko* juice (young coconut juice with floating pieces of jelly-like flesh) and sweetened *calamansi* (small local lime) juice.

Environment

An assemblage of 7107 tropical isles scattered about like pieces of a giant jigsaw puzzle, the Philippines stubbornly defies geographic generalisation. The typical island boasts a jungle-clad, critter-infested interior and a sandy coastline flanked by aquamarine waters and the requisite coral reef. About 25% of the Philippines is forested, but only a small percentage of that is primary tropical rainforest.

Endangered animal species include the mouse deer, the tamaraw (a species of dwarf buffalo) of Mindoro, the Philippine crocodile of Northeast Luzon, the Palawan bearcat and the flying lemur. As for the country's national bird, there are thought to be about 500 pairs of *haribon* (Philippine eagles), remaining in the rainforests of Mindanao, Luzon, Samar and Leyte.

There's an unbelievable array of fish, shells and corals, as well as dwindling numbers of the *duyong* (dugong, or sea cow). If your timing's right, you can spot wild whale sharks in Donsol, Puerto Princesa and southern Leyte.

National Parks

The Philippines' national parks, natural parks and other protected areas comprise about 10% of the country's total area, but most lack services such as park offices, huts, trail maps and sometimes even trails. The most popular national park is surely Palawan's Subterranean River National Park.

Environmental Issues

The Philippines has strict environmental laws on its books, but they just aren't enforced. Only 1% of the reefs is in a pristine state, according to the World Bank, while more than 50% is unhealthy.

The biggest culprit of reef damage is silt, which is washed down from hills and valleys indiscriminately – and often illegally – cleared of their original forest cover. Deforestation also exacerbates flooding and causes deadly landslides during frequent typhoons and earthquakes. Some lip service is given to the issue by the government, but little is done to combat illegal logging. Incredibly short-sighted techniques for making a few extra bucks include dynamite and cyanide fishing.

SABONG

Heavy male drinking and bonding occur over gambling – on anything from *sabong* (cockfights) to horse racing. But *sabong* are what Filipino men get most excited about. The practice has its critics, but the pastime is ingrained in the culture and as much as P100,000 may be wagered on a big fight. All over the country, every Sunday and public holiday, expensive fighting birds are fitted with three-inch ankle blades and let loose on one another. Fights are short and brutal and the loser usually ends up in the next batch of chicken soup.

SURVIVAL GUIDE

ℹ Directory A–Z

ACCOMMODATION

Rooms in the P250 to P500 range are generally fan-cooled with a shared bathroom, and rooms in the P500 to P700 range usually have fan and private bathroom. Anything higher should have air-conditioning. Prices are higher in Manila and in trendy resort areas such as Boracay and Alona Beach, although Manila and Boracay now have plenty of hostels with affordable dorm beds.

We list high-season (November to May) rates. Prices in tourist hot spots go down by up to 50% in the low season, but may triple or even quadruple during Holy Week (Easter) and around New Year.

Price Ranges

In our listings a hotel qualifies as 'budget' if it has double rooms for less than P1000 and/or double rooms for no more than P500 per bed.

$ less than P1000 (US$22)

$$ P1000 to P3000 (US$22 to US$65)

$$$ more than P3000 (US$65)

CLIMATE

➡ Hot throughout the year, with brief respites possible from December to February.

➡ Typhoons are common from June to early December. Use the website of PAGASA (www.pagasa.dost.gov.ph) or www.typhoon2000.ph to avoid meteorological trouble spots.

➡ For most of the country, the dry season is during the *amihan* (northeast monsoon), roughly November to May. Rains start once the *habagat* (southwest monsoon) arrives in June, peak in August, and taper off in October.

➡ On the country's eastern seaboard, the seasons are flipped. Siargao, Bicol, eastern Samar etc are rainy from December to February and, unless there's a typhoon stirring up trouble, relatively dry when the rest of the country is sopping.

PROSTITUTION

Prostitution and its most insidious form, child prostitution, is unfortunately prevalent in the Philippines. **ECPAT Philippines** (🖉 02-920 8151; www.ecpat philippines.org) in Quezon City works to promote child-safe tourism and end the commercial sexual exploitation of children. To report an incident, contact ECPAT, the **Philippine National Police Women & Children's Division** (🖉 0919 777 7377) or the **Human Trafficking Action Line** (🖉 02-1343).

ELECTRICITY

Philippines uses 225V, 60Hz electricity; power outlets most commonly use two square pins, although variations are found.

EMBASSIES & CONSULATES

Australian Embassy (Map p550; 🖉 02-757 8100; www.philippines.embassy.gov.au; 23rd fl, Tower 2, RCBC Plaza, 6819 Ayala Ave, Makati)

Canadian Embassy (Map p550; 🖉 02-857 9000; www.manila.gc.ca; Levels 6-8, Tower 2, RCBC Plaza, 6819 Ayala Ave, Makati)

French Embassy (Map p556; 🖉 02-857 6900; www.ambafrance-ph.org; 16th fl, Pacific Star Bldg, cnr Gil Puyat & Makati Aves, Makati)

German Embassy (Map p550; 🖉 02-702 3000; 25th fl Tower 2, RCBC Plaza, 6819 Ayala Ave, Makati)

Netherlands Embassy (Map p550; 🖉 02-786 6666; http://philippines.nlembassy.org/; 26th fl, Equitable PCI Bank Tower, 8751 Paseo de Roxas, Makati)

New Zealand Embassy (Map p550; 🖉 02-234 3800; www.nzembassy.com/philippines; 35th fl, Zuellig Building, Makati Ave, Makati City)

UK Embassy (Map p550; 🖉 02-858 2200; 120 Upper McKinley Rd, McKinley Hill, Fort Bonifacio)

US Embassy (Map p554; 🖉 02-301 2000; http://manila.usembassy.gov; 1201 Roxas Blvd, Manila)

FOOD

The following price ranges refer to the average price of a main course.

$ less than P120 (US$2.60)

$$ P120 to P250 (US$2.60 to US$5.50

$$$ more than P250 (US$5.50)

INTERNET ACCESS

Wi-fi is the rule rather than the exception in hotels and coffee shops in large cities and touristy areas, although you shouldn't count on it being reliable or speedy.

LGBT TRAVELLERS

Bakla (gay men) and *binalaki* or *tomboy* (lesbians) are almost universally accepted in the Philippines. There are well-established gay centres in major cities, but foreigners should be wary of hustlers and police harassment.

The Metro Manila Pride March takes place in December, usually in Makati. Online resources include Utopia Asian Gay & Lesbian Resources (www.utopia-asia.com).

MONEY

ATMs

➡ Prevalent in any decent-sized provincial city; dispense pesos.

» Banco de Oro (BDO), Bank of the Philippine Islands (BPI) and Metrobank are common, with functional ATMs.

» Standard ATM charge is P200 per withdrawal. Exception: fee-free HSBC ATMs in Manila and Cebu.

» Standard withdrawal limit per transaction at ATMs: P10,000.

Cash

» Emergency cash in US dollars is a good thing to have in case you get stuck in an area with no working ATM. Other currencies, such as the euro or UK pound, are more difficult to change outside bigger cities.

» 'Sorry, no change' becomes a very familiar line. Stock up on P20, P50 and P100 notes at every opportunity.

Credit Cards

» Major credit cards are accepted by many hotels, restaurants and businesses.

» Outide major cities, many places still charge a bit extra (about 4%) for credit-card transactions.

» Most Philippine banks will let you take a cash advance on your card.

OPENING HOURS

Banks 9am to 4pm Monday to Friday

Bars 6pm to late

Restaurants 7am or 8am to 10pm or 11pm

Shopping malls 10am to 9.30pm

Supermarkets 9am to 7pm or 8pm

PUBLIC HOLIDAYS

Offices and banks are closed on public holidays, although shops and department stores stay open. Maundy Thursday and Good Friday are the only days when the entire country closes down – even most public transport stops running.

New Year's Day 1 January

People Power Day 25 February

Maundy Thursday, Good Friday & Easter Sunday March/April

Araw ng Kagitingan (Bataan Day) 9 April

Labour Day 1 May

Independence Day 12 June

Ninoy Aquino Day 21 August

National Heroes' Day Last Sunday in August

All Saints' Day 1 November

End of Ramadan Varies; depends on Islamic calendar

Bonifacio Day 30 November

Christmas Day 25 December

Rizal Day 30 December

New Year's Eve 31 December

TELEPHONE

The Philippine Long-Distance Telephone Company (PLDT) operates the Philippines' fixed-line network. International calls can be made from any PLDT office for US$0.40 per minute.

Dialling Codes

Dial ✆0 before area codes when calling from a mobile phone or a landline outside that region.

Country code	✆63
Emergency	✆117
International dialling code	✆00
International operator	✆108
PLDT directory assistance	✆187

Mobile Phones

Mobile phones are ubiquitous, and half the country spends much of its time furiously texting the other half.

» Prepaid SIM cards cost as little as P40 and come preloaded with about the same amount of text credits.

» The two companies with the best national coverage are Globe (www.globe.com.ph) and Smart (www.smart.com.ph).

» Text messages on all mobile networks cost P1 to P2 per message; local calls cost P7.50 per minute (less if calling within a mobile network). International text messages cost P15, and international calls cost US$0.40 per minute.

» All Philippine mobile-phone numbers start with 09.

TOILETS

Toilets are commonly called a 'CR', an abbreviation of the delightfully euphemistic 'comfort room'. Public toilets are virtually nonexistent, so aim for one of the ubiquitous fast-food restaurants should you need a room of comfort.

TRAVELLERS WITH DISABILITIES

» Steps up to hotels, tiny cramped toilets and narrow doors are the norm outside of four-star hotels in Manila, Cebu and a handful of larger provincial cities.

» Lifts are often out of order, and boarding any form of rural transport is likely to be fraught with difficulty.

» On the other hand, most Filipinos are more than willing to lend a helping hand, and the cost of hiring a taxi for a day, and possibly an assistant as well, is not excessive.

VISAS

Citizens of nearly all countries do not need a visa to enter the Philippines for stays of less than 31 days. When you arrive, you'll receive a 30-day visa-waiver free of charge. If you overstay your waiver, you face modest fines at the airport upon leaving the country.

Avoid this inconvenience by extending your 30-day waiver to 59 days before it expires. Extensions cost P3030 and are a breeze at Bureau of Immigration (BOI) offices located in all major cities. The process is a bit more painful at the **BOI head office** (BOI; Map p554; ☑02-465 2400; www.immigration.gov.ph; Magallanes Dr, Intramuros; ⊙8am-5.30pm Mon-Fri) in Manila. Dress respectably when applying.

Another option is to secure a three-month visa before you arrive in the Philippines. These cost US$30 to US$45 depending on where you apply.

For a full list of provincial immigration offices, see http://immigration.gov.ph. Useful provincial offices include the following:

BOI Baguio Office (☑074-447 0805; 38 Military Cut Off Rd; ⊙7am-5.30pm Mon-Fri)

BOI Boracay Office (☑036-288 5267; Abrams Compound, Main Rd; ⊙8am-5pm Mon-Fri)

BOI Cebu Branch Office (☑032-340 1473; AS Fortuna St)

BOI Makati Office (Map p550; ☑02-899 3831; 385 Gil Puyat Ave, enter on Jupiter St; ⊙8am-5pm)

BOI Palawan Office (☑048-433 2248; Servando Bldg, Rizal Ave, Puerto Princesa; ⊙8am-4pm Mon-Fri)

BOI Puerto Galera Office (☑043-287 3570; 2nd fl Public Market, Puerto Galera Town; ⊙9am-3pm Mon, Wed & Fri)

Onward Tickets

Be prepared to show the airline at your point of departure to the Philippines a ticket for onward travel. If you don't have one, most airlines make you buy one on the spot.

VOLUNTEERING

Gawad Kalinga (☑in Manila 02-533 2217; www.gk1world.com/ph) GK's mission is building not just homes but entire communities for the poor and homeless. Volunteers can build houses, teach children or get involved in a host of other activities.

Habitat for Humanity (☑02-846 2177; www.habitat.org.ph) Builds houses for the poor all over the country, concentrating on disaster-affected areas.

Hands On Manila (☑02-843 7044; www.handsonmanila.org) This organisation is always looking for volunteers to help with disaster assistance and other projects throughout the Philippines.

Volunteer for the Visayas (☑0917 846 6967; www.visayans.org) Runs various volunteer programs around Tacloban, Leyte.

❶ Getting There & Away

Most people enter the Philippines via one of the three main international airports: Manila, Cebu or Clark. A handful of international flights also go straight to Davao, Mindanao, to Kalibo near Boracay, and to Iloilo on the island of Panay.

Flights and tours can be booked online at www.lonelyplanet.com/bookings.

AIR
Airports

Ninoy Aquino International Airport (NAIA; ☑02-877 1109) All flights into and out of Manila use one of NAIA's four terminals. Shoestring travellers should home in on the cheap flights offered by budget carriers AirAsia, Cebu Pacific and Jetstar Asia.

Clark International Airport (DMIA; ☑045 599 2888; www.clark-airport.com) Clark Airport is near Angeles, a two-hour bus ride north of downtown Manila. Low-cost airlines AirAsia, Cebu Pacific, Jin Air and Tigerair fly here, as do Asiana, Dragonair and Qatar Airways.

Mactan International Airport (CEB; ☑032-340 2486; www.mactan-cebuairport.com.ph) If you're heading to the Visayas, consider flying into Cebu City. Several international and

---

TERMINAL CHAOS

Navigating Manila's convoluted Ninoy Aquino International Airport (NAIA) is a nightmare. NAIA's four terminals share runways, but they are not particularly close to each other and are linked only by busy public roads. A shuttle bus links the four terminals, but it is slow and sporadic, so take a taxi between terminals if you're in a hurry.

Pay close attention to which terminal your airline uses and allow plenty of time between connecting flights if you have to switch terminals. Most international flights use recently upgraded but still dismal Terminal 1 (T1). However, international flights run by Cebu Pacific, ANA, Cathay Pacific, Delta, Emirates Air, KLM and Singapore Airlines use newer Terminal 3 (T3). Most domestic flights run by PAL Express and Cebu Pacific also use T3.

Meanwhile, all Philippine Airlines (PAL) flights use yet another terminal, the Centennial Terminal 2 (T2).

Lastly, all AirAsia and Skyjet flights, and some 'Cebgo'-branded Cebu Pacific flights, use the ancient Manila Domestic Terminal (T4), located near T3.

discount regional airlines fly here, especially Cebu Pacific, which has connections with a large number of Asian cities.

Kalibo International Airport Useful direct flights to Kalibo, near Boracay, from Hong Kong, Singapore and a handful of Korean and Chinese cities.

Airlines

Besides the big national airlines that come up on any internet flight search, the following regional budget and Philippine carriers are worth checking out for flights into and out of the country

AirAsia (☑ 02-722 2742; www.airasia.com)

Cebu Pacific (☑ 02-702 0888; www.cebu pacificair.com)

Jetstar (www.jetstar.com)

Philippine Airlines (PAL; ☑ 02-855 8888; www.philippineairlines.com)

Tigerair (☑ 02-798 4499; www.tigerair.com)

SEA

The only international route open to foreigners is Zamboanga to Sandakan in the Malaysian state of Sabah. **Aleson Shipping Lines** (☑ 062-991 2687; www.aleson-shipping.com; 172 Veterans Ave, Zamboanga) leaves Zamboanga on Monday and (sometimes) Thursday, and departs Sandakan on Tuesday and (sometimes) Friday (economy/cabin P2900/3300, 23 hours). However, travel in the Zamboanga region is considered risky.

❶ Getting Around

AIR

The main domestic carriers are Philippine Airlines (PAL) and low-cost carriers AirAsia and Cebu Pacific. Together they serve most main cities out of Manila and/or Cebu.

PAL's budget subsidiary, PAL Express, competes in the low-cost domestic market, while **Skyjet Airlines** (☑ in Manila 02-863 1333; www.skyjetair.com) operates a few niche routes, including Manila–Caticlan and Manila–Coron.

Air Swift (Map p550; ☑ 02-851 5674; http://air-swift.com; Andrews Ave, Pasay) monopolises the Manila–El Nido and Manila–Cebu routes.

One-way flights cost P1000 to P3000 (including taxes) on most routes, provided you book in advance. Flight times range from 45 minutes for short hops such as Manila to Caticlan, to 1½ hours for flights from Manila to southern Mindanao.

BOAT

If boats are your thing, this is the place for you. The islands of the Philippines are linked by an incredible network of ferry routes and prices are generally affordable. Ferries take the form of motorised outriggers, known locally as bangkas

MOVING ON FROM CLARK AIRPORT

Philtranco has three daily direct 'shuttle' buses from Clark to Manila (P450, 2½ hours). Alternatively take the airport shuttle van (P50) or a fixed-rate taxi (P500) to Angeles' Dau (Mabalacat) bus terminal, where myriad buses serve Manila.

For points north of Clark, get to the Dau terminal, where you'll find plenty of buses going to Baguio, Vigan and elsewhere.

To get to Clark from Manila, take the thrice-daily Philtranco shuttle, or take any northbound bus to the Dau terminal then a taxi to the airport.

(also called pumpboats); speedy 'fastcraft' vessels; car ferries, dubbed RORO, or 'roll-on, roll-off' ferries; or, for long-haul journeys, vast multidecked ships. Fastcraft services are passenger-only and are popular on shorter routes. They can cut travel times by half but usually cost twice as much as slower RORO ferries. Some shipping lines give 20% to 30% off for students.

Booking ahead is essential for long-haul liners and can be done at ticket offices or travel agents in most cities. For fastcraft and bangka ferries, tickets can usually be bought at the pier before departure.

For the most part, ferries are an easy, enjoyable way to island-hop, but accidents are not unknown. In May 2008 a Sulpicio Lines ferry went down off Romblon in Typhoon Frank; fewer than 60 passengers survived and more than 800 perished. A large 2GO Ferry vessel collided with a cargo ship off Cebu in August 2013, resulting in more than 115 deaths. And in 2015 more than 60 people were killed when an overloaded bangka ferry bound for Pilar, Camotes Islands, from Ormoc, Leyte, tipped over in relatively calm seas.

BUS & VAN

Philippine buses come in all shapes and sizes, from rusty boxes on wheels to luxury air-con coaches. Depots are dotted throughout towns and the countryside, and most buses will stop if you wave them down.

Most buses follow a fixed schedule but may leave early if they're full. Night services are common between Manila and major provincial hubs in Luzon. Remote villages may be serviced by only one or two daily buses; generally these leave the village in the morning bound for the regional centre, and return early afternoon.

Speedier but cramped air-con minivans shadow bus routes in many parts of the Philippines and in some cases have replaced buses altogether. However, you may have to play a waiting game until the vehicles are full.

LOCAL TRANSPORT
Jeepney

The first jeepneys were modified army jeeps left behind by the Americans after WWII. They have been customised with Filipino touches such as chrome horses, banks of coloured headlights and neon paintings of everything from the Virgin Mary to scenes from action comic books.

Jeepneys form the main urban transport in most cities and complement the bus services between regional centres. Within towns, the starting fare is usually P8, rising modestly for trips outside of town. Routes are clearly written on the side of the jeepney.

Taxi

Metered taxis are common in Manila and most major provincial hubs. Flag fall is a mere P40, and a 15-minute trip rarely costs more than P150.

Most taxi drivers will turn on the meter; if they don't, politely request that they do. If the meter is 'broken' or your taxi driver says the fare is 'up to you', the best strategy is to get out and find another cab (or offer a low-ball price).

Tricycle

Found in most cities and towns, the tricycle is the Philippine rickshaw – a little, roofed sidecar bolted to a motorcycle. The standard fare for local trips in most provincial towns is P8. Tricycles that wait around in front of malls, restaurants and hotels will attempt to charge five to 10 times that for a 'special trip'. Avoid these by standing roadside and flagging down a passing P8 tricycle. You can also charter tricycles for about P300 per hour or P150 per 10km if you're heading out of town.

Many towns also have nonmotorised push tricycles, alternately known as pedicabs, *put-put* or *padyak,* for shorter trips.

Habal-Habal

Common in many Visayan islands and northern Mindanao, these are simply motorcycle taxis with extended seats (literally translated as 'pigs copulating', after the level of intimacy attained when sharing a seat with four people). *Habal-habal* function like tricycles, only they are a little bit cheaper. Outside of the Visayas (and in the north Visayas) they're known as 'motorcycle taxis' or 'singles'.

Singapore

📱 65 / POP 5.57 MILLION

Best for Regional Specialities

➡ Maxwell Food Centre (p630)

➡ Ya Kun Kaya Toast (p630)

➡ Tekka Centre (p631)

Best Places for Culture

➡ Peranakan Museum (p611)

➡ National Gallery Singapore (p611)

➡ Asian Civilisations Museum (p611)

➡ Little India (p619)

Why Go?

One of Asia's success stories is tiny little Singapore, whose GDP consistently ranks it as one of the wealthiest countries in the world. Along with that wealth comes a rich culture borne of a multiracial population. Get lost in the mad swirl of skyscrapers in the central business district, be transfixed by the Bolly beats in the streets of ramshackle Little India, hike a dense patch of rainforest in Bukit Timah, navigate the air-conditioned retail mayhem of Orchard Rd or rub shoulders with the glamorous crowd at one of the city's rooftop bars.

It's affluent, high-tech and occasionally a little snobbish, but Singapore's great leveller are the hawker centres, the ubiquitous and raucous food markets where everyone mucks in together to indulge the local mania for cheap eating and drinking. In short, Singapore makes for a perfect pit stop to recover from the rough-and-tumble of the rest of Southeast Asia.

When to Go
Singapore

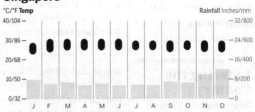

| **Jan & Feb** Chinese New Year and Chingay are the events to catch. | **Apr & May** Lots of events, and just before the local school holidays start. | **Dec** The northeast monsoons bring lashing rains, but they also cool Singapore down. |

AT A GLANCE

Currency Singapore dollar (S$)

Language English (primary), Mandarin, Bahasa Malaysia, Tamil

Money ATMs widely available; credit cards accepted most places

Visas On arrival; generally not needed for stays up to 30 days

Mobile phones SIM cards usually S$18, you'll need your passport for identification

Fast Facts

Area 718 sq km

Emergency ☑ 999

Exchange Rates

Australia	A$1	S$1
Euro	€1	S$1.54
Malaysia	RM10	S$3.26
UK	UK£1	S$2.15
US	US$1	S$1.40

Daily Costs

Dorm bed US$16–40

Hawker meal US$3

Bottle of Tiger US$4.50

Museum entry US$7

Short taxi ride US$4

Entering the Country

Changi Airport is Singapore's main flight hub. Buses link Singapore with Malaysia and Thailand; ferries connect to Malaysia and Indonesia.

Don't Miss

The Colonial District and Marina Bay are the heart of Singapore and the former seat of British power. Today, the cityscape here is evidence of Singapore's ambitions, with gleaming architecture sitting cheek by jowl with preserved heritage buildings and a retro-futuristic conservatory garden. Get to a rooftop bar for a bird's-eye view of the entire area, best enjoyed as the sun sets.

Of course, Singapore is famous for its cuisine. Find a hawker centre or food court (there's one in every mall) and follow your nose or join the longest queues for gastronomic delights.

ITINERARIES

Two Days

Begin your first day taking in the architectural glory of the Colonial District; wander along the Singapore River and through the Quays before getting your culture fix at one of the area's many museums. Head for the impressive Gardens by the Bay before dining at Satay by the Bay. Spend day two immersed in the sights and sounds of Little India and finish with dinner and drinks in Kampong Glam before hitting the dance floor in Clarke Quay.

Five Days

Get back to nature at Singapore Zoo followed by an afternoon stroll through the Botanic Gardens; exiting Tanglin gate, wander down to the retail jungle of Orchard Rd. Spend day four in the entertainment hub of Sentosa Island and enjoy sunset drinks at one of its beachside bars. Finally slow down the pace on Pulau Ubin Island; finish off with dinner and a Tiger beer at Changi Village.

Essential Food & Drink

Hainanese chicken rice Tender poached chicken served on a bed of fragrant rice (cooked in chicken stock) with accompanying garlic chilli sauce.

Char kway teow Flat rice noodles wok-fried with bean sprouts, cockles, prawns and Chinese sausage in dark soy sauce and chilli sauce.

Roti prata Fried flour-based pancake served with chicken or fish curry, variations include mushroom, egg and banana.

Nasi padang Steamed white rice served with your choice of meats and vegetables; just choose and point. Lots of curries available.

Fried carrot cake Not a sweet dessert but steamed rice flour, water and white radish cake stir-fried with eggs and preserved radish. Dark version is cooked in soy sauce.

◉ Sights

◎ Colonial District

The Colonial District is where you'll find many imposing remnants of British rule, including the **Victoria Concert Hall & Theatre**, **Old Parliament House** (now an arts centre), **St Andrew's Cathedral**, **City Hall**, and the **Old Supreme Court**, which are arranged around the **Padang**, a cricket pitch. Rising above them is the spaceship of the Norman Foster–designed **Supreme Court** building.

★**National Gallery Singapore**   GALLERY
(Map p614; www.nationalgallery.sg; St Andrew's Rd; adult/child S$20/15; ◎10am-7pm Sun-Thu, to 10pm Fri & Sat; 🔊; Ⓜ City Hall) Connected by a striking aluminium and glass canopy, Singapore's historic City Hall and Old Supreme Court buildings now form the city's breathtaking National Gallery. Its world-class collection of 19th-century and modern Southeast Asian art is housed in two major spaces, the DBS Singapore Gallery and the UOB Southeast Asia Gallery. The former delivers a comprehensive overview of Singaporean art from the 19th century to today, while the latter focuses on the greater Southeast Asian region.

★**National Museum of Singapore**   MUSEUM
(Map p614; www.nationalmuseum.sg; 93 Stamford Rd; adult/student & senior S$10/5; ◎10am-6pm; Ⓜ Dhoby Ghaut) Imaginative and immersive, Singapore's rebooted National Museum is good enough to warrant two visits. At once cutting-edge and classical, the space ditches staid exhibits for lively multimedia galleries that bring Singapore's jam-packed biography to vivid life. It's a colourful, intimate journey, spanning ancient Malay royalty, wartime occupation, nation-building, food and fashion. Look out for interactive artwork *GoHead/ GoStan: Panorama Singapura*, which offers an audiovisual trip through the city-state's many periods.

★**Asian Civilisations Museum**   MUSEUM
(Map p614; ☑6332 7798; www.acm.org.sg; 1 Empress Pl; adult/child under 6yr S$8/free, 7-9pm Fri half-price; ◎10am-7pm Sat-Thu, to 9pm Fri; Ⓜ Raffles Place) This remarkable museum houses the region's most comprehensive collection of pan-Asian treasures. Recently expanded, its series of thematic galleries explore the history, cultures and religions of Southeast Asia, China, the Asian subcontinent and Islamic West Asia. Exquisite artefacts include glittering Sumatran and Javanese ceremonial jewellery, Thai tribal textiles, Chinese silk tapestries, and astronomical treatises from 14th-century Iran and 16th-century Egypt. Among the more macabre objects is a 17th- or 18th-century Tibetan ritual bone apron, made with human and animal bones.

★**Peranakan Museum**   MUSEUM
(Map p614; ☑6332 7591; www.peranakanmuseum. org.sg; 39 Armenian St; adult/child under 7yr S$6/ free, 7-9pm Fri half-price; ◎10am-7pm Sat-Thu, to 9pm Fri; Ⓜ City Hall) This is the best spot to explore the rich heritage of the Peranakans (Straits Chinese descendants). Thematic galleries cover various aspects of Peranakan culture, from the traditional 12-day wedding ceremony to crafts, spirituality and feasting. Look out for intricately detailed ceremonial costumes and beadwork, beautifully carved wedding beds, and rare dining porcelain. An especially curious example of Peranakan fusion culture is a pair of Victorian bell jars in which statues of Christ and the Madonna are adorned with Chinese-style flowers and vines.

Fort Canning Park   PARK
(Map p614; www.nparks.gov.sg; Ⓜ Dhoby Ghaut) When Raffles rolled into Singapore, locals steered clear of Fort Canning Hill, then called Bukit Larangan (Forbidden Hill) out of respect for the sacred shrine of Sultan Iskandar Shah, ancient Singapura's last ruler. These days, the hill is better known as Fort Canning Park, a lush retreat from the hot streets below. Amble through the spice garden, catch an exhibition at **Singapore Pinacothéque de Paris** (Map p614; ☑6883 1588; www.pinacotheque.com.sg; 5 Cox Tce; Heritage Gallery, Graffiti Walk & Garden Walk free, all galleries adult/student/child under 7yr S$28/19/9; ◎10am-7.30pm Sun-Thu, to 8.30pm Fri & Sat; Ⓜ Dhoby Ghaut) or ponder Singapore's wartime defeat at the **Battle Box Museum** (Map p614; www. battlebox.com.sg; 2 Cox Tce; adult/child S$8/5; ◎10am-6pm, last entry 5pm; Ⓜ Dhoby Ghaut).

Singapore Art Museum   MUSEUM
(SAM; Map p614; ☑6589 9580; www.singapore artmuseum.sg; 71 Bras Basah Rd; adult/student & senior S$10/5, 6-9pm Fri free; ◎10am-7pm Sat-Thu, to 9pm Fri; Ⓜ Bras Basah) Formerly the St Joseph's Institution – a Catholic boys' school – SAM now sings the praises of contemporary Southeast Asian art. Themed

Singapore Highlights

❶ Getting lost in the futuristic green oasis **Gardens by the Bay** (p616), where nature and design collide.

❷ Navigating **Little India** (p619), a jumble of gold,

textiles, temples and cheap eats.

❸ Experiencing the animal magnetism of **Singapore Zoo** (p623), one of three

outstanding open-concept zoos.

❹ Immersing yourself in Southeast Asian art at the newly opened **National Gallery Singapore** (p611).

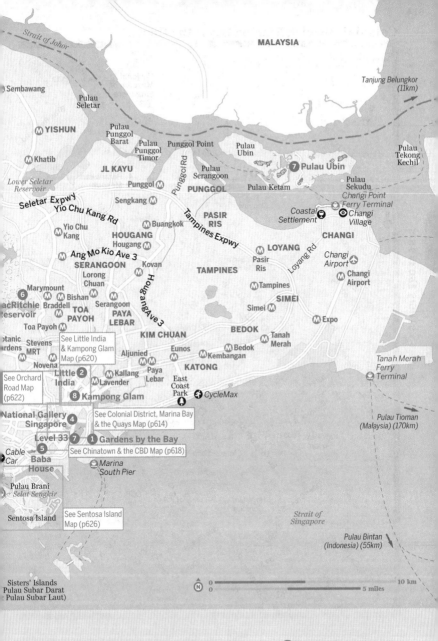

MALAYSIA

Strait of Johor

Sembawang

Pulau Seletar

Ⓜ YISHUN

Pulau Punggol Barat

Ⓜ Khatib

Pulau Punggol Timor

Punggol Point

Pulau Ubin

Tanjung Belungkor (11km)

Pulau Tekong Kechil

JL KAYU

Ⓜ Punggol

PUNGGOL

Pulau Serangoon

❼ Pulau Ubin

Pulau Sekudu

Pulau Tekong Kechil

Lower Seletar Reservoir

Seletar Expwy

Yio Chu Kang Rd

Sengkang Ⓜ

Ⓜ Buangkok

PASIR RIS

Pulau Ketam

Pulau Ketam

Changi Point Ferry Terminal

Ⓜ Yio Chu Kang

HOUGANG

Hougang Ⓜ

Tampines Expwy

Coastal Settlement

Ⓜ Changi Village

Ⓜ Ang Mo Kio Ave 3

SERANGOON

Kovan

TAMPINES

LOYANG

Ⓜ

CHANGI

❻ Marymount

Lorong Chuan

Ⓜ Bishan

Serangoon Ⓜ

Hougang Ave 3

Pasir Ris

Loyang Rd

Changi Airport ✈

ⓂacRitchie Reservoir

Ⓜ Braddell

TOA PAYOH

Ⓜ Tampines

Ⓜ Changi Airport

PAYA LEBAR

SIMEI

Toa Payoh Ⓜ

KIM CHUAN

Simei Ⓜ

BEDOK

Ⓜ Expo

otanic ardens

Stevens MRT

Ⓜ

Aljunied

Eunos

Ⓜ Bedok

Tanah Merah

Ⓜ Novena

See Little India & Kampong Glam Map (p620)

Ⓜ

Ⓜ Kembangan

KATONG

Tanah Merah Ferry Terminal 🚢

See Orchard Road Map (p622)

Little ❷ India

Ⓜ Kallang

Paya Lebar

Ⓜ Lavender

East Coast Park

🚲 CycleMax

❽ Kampong Glam

Pulau Tioman (Malaysia) (170km)

National Gallery Singapore ❹

See Colonial District, Marina Bay & the Quays Map (p614)

Level 33 ❼ ❶ Gardens by the Bay

Cable Car

❺ Baba House

See Chinatown & the CBD Map (p618)

🚢 Marina South Pier

Pulau Brani
Selat Sengkir

Sentosa Island

See Sentosa Island Map (p626)

Strait of Singapore

Pulau Bintan (Indonesia) (55km)

Sisters' Islands
Pulau Subar Darat
: Pulau Subar Laut)

Ⓝ 0 —————————— 10 km
0 —————————— 5 miles

❺ Booking the detailed tour through **Baba House** (p617), a gorgeous restored Peranakan house.

❻ Getting among nature

on the treetop walk at **MacRitchie Reservoir** (p624).

❼ Pulling up a perch at **Level 33** (p633) on Pulau Ubin and enjoy a bird's-eye view of the city as the sun sets.

❽ Joining the night-time buzz in vibrant **Kampong Glam** (p634): start with the eclectic shops then stay for dinner and a drink.

Colonial District, Marina Bay & the Quays

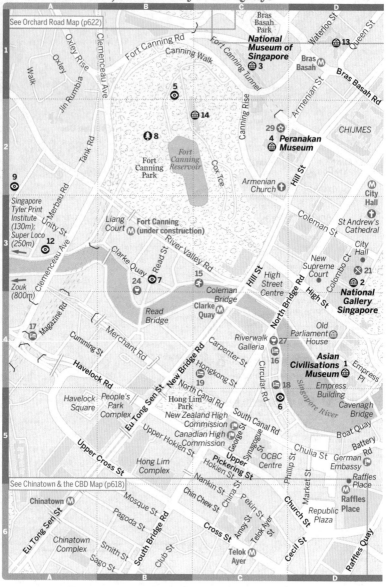

See Orchard Road Map (p622)

See Chinatown & the CBD Map (p618)

SINGAPORE SIGHTS

exhibitions include works from the museum's permanent collection as well as those from private collections, from painting and sculpture to video art and site-specific installations. Free, 45-minute guided tours of the museum are conducted in English two to three times daily; check the website for times.

Raffles Hotel   HISTORIC BUILDING
(Map p614; www.raffleshotel.com; 1 Beach Rd; M City Hall) Although its resplendent lobby is

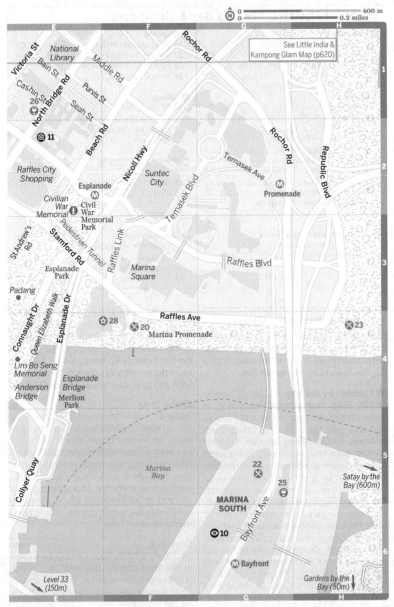

See Little India & Kampong Glam Map (p620)

N
0 — 400 m
0 — 0.2 miles

SINGAPORE SIGHTS

Victoria St
National Library
Middle Rd
Rochor Rd

Bain St
Cashin St
26
North Bridge Rd
Purvis St
Seah St

11
Beach Rd

Raffles City Shopping
Esplanade
Suntec City
Temasek Ave
Rochor Rd
Promenade
Republic Blvd

Civilian War Memorial
Civil War Memorial Park
Nicoll Hwy
Temasek Blvd

St Andrew's Rd
Stamford Rd
Pedestrian Tunnel
Raffles Link
Raffles Blvd

Esplanade Park
Marina Square

Padang
Connaught Dr
Queen Elizabeth Walk
Esplanade Dr
28
20
Marina Promenade
23

Lim Bo Seng Memorial
Esplanade Bridge
Merlion Park
Raffles Ave

Anderson Bridge

Collyer Quay
Marina Bay
22
25
Satay by the Bay (600m)

MARINA SOUTH
Bayfront Ave
10

Level 33 (150m)
Bayfront
Gardens by the Bay (50m)

only accessible to hotel guests and its bars are little more than tourist traps, Singapore's most iconic slumber palace is worth a quick visit for its magnificent ivory frontage, famous Sikh doorman and lush, hushed tropical grounds. The hotel started life in 1887 as a modest 10-room bungalow fronting the beach (long gone thanks to land reclamation), and it still evokes the days when Singapore was a swampy, tiger-tempered outpost of the British Empire.

Colonial District, Marina Bay & the Quays

◉ Marina Bay & the Quays

South of the Colonial District lies Marina Bay, Singapore's glittering new financial district and home to the now-iconic Marina Bay Sands and Gardens by the Bay.

★ Gardens by the Bay
GARDENS

(☏6420 6848; www.gardensbythebay.com.sg; 18 Marina Gardens Dr; gardens free, conservatories adult/child under 13yr S\$28/15; ⊙5am-2am, conservatories & OCBC Skyway 9am-9pm, last ticket sale 8pm; Ⓜ Bayfront) Singapore's 21st-century botanic garden is a S\$1 billion, 101-hectare fantasy-land of space-age biodomes, high-tech Supertrees and whimsical sculptures. The Flower Dome replicates the dry, Mediterranean climates found across the world, while the even more astounding Cloud Forest is a tropical montane affair, complete with waterfall. Connecting two of the Supertrees is the OCBC Skyway, with knockout views of the gardens, city and South China Sea. At 7.45pm and 8.45pm, the Supertrees twinkle and glow for the spectacular Garden Rhapsody show.

Marina Bay Sands
COMPLEX

(Map p614; www.marinabaysands.com; Marina Bay; Ⓜ Bayfront) Designed by Israeli–North American architect Moshe Safdie, Marina Bay Sands is a sprawling hotel, casino, mall, theatre, exhibition and museum complex.

Star of the show is the Marina Bay Sands Hotel, its three 55-storey towers connected by a cantilevered sky park. Head up for a drink and stellar views at Ce La Vie (the sky bar formerly known as Ku De Ta). Each night the complex dazzles with its 13-minute light and laser spectacular, Wonder Full.

Clarke Quay
AREA

(Map p614; www.clarkequay.com.sg; Ⓜ Clarke Quay) Named after Singapore's second colonial governor, Sir Andrew Clarke, this is the busiest and most popular of Singapore's three quays. How much time you spend in its plethora of bars, restaurants and clubs depends upon your taste in aesthetics. This is Singapore at its most hyper-touristy, a kitsch, sprawl of mostly run-of-the-mill eateries and lad-and-ladette drinking holes.

Boat Quay
AREA

(Map p614; Ⓜ Raffles Place, Clarke Quay) Closest to the river mouth, this was once Singapore's centre of commerce, and it remained an important economic area into the 1960s. By the mid-1980s, many of the shophouses were in ruins, businesses having shifted to high-tech cargo centres elsewhere on the island. Declared a conservation zone by the government, the area is now crammed with pubs, touristy eateries and persistent restaurant touts. One bar worth stopping at is rooftop **Southbridge** (Map p614; ☏6877

6965; level 5, 80 Boat Quay; ☺ 5-11.30pm; M Clarke Quay), its skyline and river views are simply jaw-dropping.

Robertson Quay
AREA

(Map p614; 🚌 64, 123, 143, M Clarke Quay) The most remote and least visited of the quays is home to some of the best eateries and bars along the river, including Mexican 'It kid' Super Loco and well-priced wine bar Wine Connection. The precinct is also home to the **Singapore Tyler Print Institute** (🖊6336 3663; www.stpi.com.sg; 41 Robertson Quay; ☺10am-7pm Mon-Fri, 9am-6pm Sat, guided tours 11.30am Tue & Thu, 2.30pm Sat; 🚌51, 64, 123, 186) FREE, which hosts international and local exhibits showcasing the work of resident print- and paper-makers. Close by is the **Hong San See Temple** (Map p614; 31 Mohamed Sultan Rd; ☺7am-6pm; 🚌32, 54, 139, 195) FREE, completed in 1913.

◉ Chinatown & the CBD

Bustling Chinatown is crammed with small shops, eateries and tradition, though some of the tradition has disappeared behind a wave of renovation, some of it good (the restored shophouses), some of it not so good (the Pagoda St tourist market). The CBD is Singapore's financial hub and sits beside Chinatown. The hive of activity during the weekdays stands in stark contrast to the weekends, when it's a proverbial ghost town. Architecture aficionados will enjoy the restored shophouses around the area (Ann Siang Rd and Hill are good places to start).

★ Baba House
MUSEUM

(Map p618; 🖊6227 5731; www.nus.edu.sg/cfa/museum/about.php; 157 Neil Rd; ☺tours 2pm Mon, 6.30pm Tue, 10am Thu, 11am Sat; M Outram Park) FREE Baba House is one of Singapore's best-preserved Peranakan heritage homes. Built in the 1890s, it's a wonderful window into the life of an affluent Peranakan family living in Singapore a century ago. Its loving restoration has seen every detail attended to, from the carved motifs on the blue facade down to the door screens. The only way in is on a one-hour guided tour, held every Monday, Tuesday, Thursday and Saturday; the tour is excellent. Bookings, by phone, are essential.

★ Chinatown Heritage Centre
MUSEUM

(Map p618; 🖊6221 9556; www.singaporechinatown.com.sg; 48 Pagoda St; adult/child S$10/6; ☺9am-8pm; M Chinatown) Delve into Chinatown's gritty, cacophonous backstory at the recently revamped Chinatown Heritage Centre. Occupying several levels of a converted shophouse, its interactive exhibitions shed light on numerous historical chapters, from the treacherous journey of Singapore's early Chinese immigrants to the development of local clan associations to the district's notorious opium dens. It's an evocative place, digging well beneath modern Chinatown's touristy veneer.

Buddha Tooth Relic Temple
BUDDHIST TEMPLE

(Map p618; www.btrts.org.sg; 288 South Bridge Rd; ☺7am-7pm, relic viewing 9am-6pm; M Chinatown) FREE Consecrated in 2008, this hulking, five-story Buddhist temple is home to what is reputedly the left canine tooth of the Buddha, recovered from his funeral pyre in Kushinagar, northern India. While its authenticity is debated, the relic enjoys VIP status inside a 420kg solid-gold stupa in a dazzlingly ornate 4th-floor room. More religious relics await in the 3rd-floor Buddhism museum, while the peaceful rooftop garden features a huge prayer wheel inside a 10,000 Buddha Pavilion.

Sri Mariamman Temple
HINDU TEMPLE

(Map p618; 244 South Bridge Rd; ☺7am-noon & 6-9pm; M Chinatown) FREE Paradoxically in the middle of Chinatown, this is the oldest Hindu temple in Singapore, originally built in 1823, then rebuilt in 1843. You can't miss the fabulously animated, Technicolor 1930s *gopuram* (tower) above the entrance, the key to the temple's South Indian Dravidian style. Sacred cow sculptures grace the boundary

---

SINGAPORE ON THE CHEAP

➡ Stick to eating at hawker centres or food courts.

➡ If you drink at a bar, go during happy hours (for discounted booze or one-for-one specials).

➡ Visit the museums for free (or cheap) after 6pm Friday, and catch free concerts at the Esplanade or Singapore Botanic Gardens.

➡ To cool off, dive into one of Singapore's impressive public pools.

➡ Pack a picnic and spend a day at the beach in East Coast Park or Sentosa.

➡ Hike in Bukit Timah Nature Reserve, around the MacRitchie Reservoir or along the Southern Ridges.

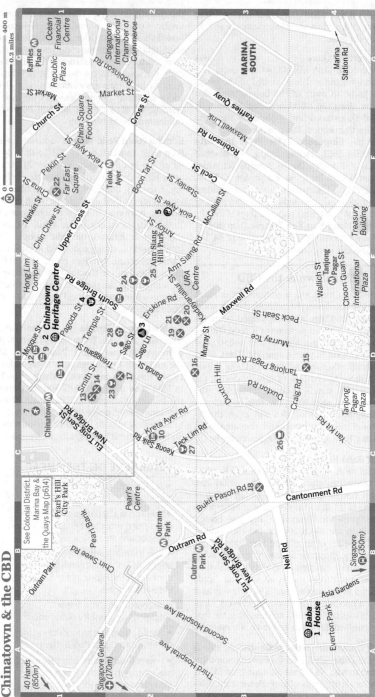

Chinatown & the CBD

SINGAPORE SIGHTS

0   0.2 miles
0   400 m

Raffles Place Ⓜ
Ocean Financial Centre
Republic Plaza
Market St
Singapore International Chamber of Commerce
Robinson Rd
Market St
Church St
Cross St
China Square Food Court
Tevak Ayer St
Far East Square
Pekin St
Chin Chew St
Nankin St
China St
22 Ⓧ
Boon Tat St
Stanley St
Cecil St
Robinson Rd
Maxwell Link
Raffles Quay
MARINA SOUTH
Marina Station Rd
TeIok Ayer Ⓜ
McCallum St
Treasury Building
Upper Cross St
Hong Lim Complex
2 Chinatown Heritage Centre
South Bridge Rd
8 **24**
25 Ann Siang Hill Park
Ann Siang Rd
Amoy St
Telok Ayer St
5
Kadayanallur St
URA Centre
Erskine Rd
Wallich St
Tanjong Pagar Ⓜ
Choon Guan St
International Plaza
Maxwell Rd
Peck Seah St
Mosque St
12 **9**
Pagoda St
Temple St
4
28
6
3
Sago St
Sago Ln
Banda St
21
19 **20**
Murray St
16
Murray Tce
Tanjong Pagar Rd
15 Ⓧ
Tanjong Pagar Plaza
11
Smith St
14 Ⓧ
23 Ⓧ
17
Trengganu St
Duxton Hill
Craig Rd
Yan Kit Rd
Tanjong Pagar Plaza
Chinatown Ⓜ
7
13
Eu Tong Sen St
New Bridge Rd
Kreta Ayer Rd
Keong Saik Rd
Teck Lim Rd
10
27
Duxton Rd
26
Pearl's Centre
Pearl Bank
Pearl's Hill City Park
See Colonial District, Marina Bay & the Quays Map (p614)
Chin Swee Rd
Outram Park
Outram Park Ⓜ
Outram Rd
Eu Tong Sen St
New Bridge Rd
Bukit Pasoh Rd
18 Ⓧ
Cantonment Rd
Neil Rd
Outram Park Ⓜ
Second Hospital Ave
Third Hospital Ave
Singapore General (170m)
40 Hands (850m)
Baba 1 House
Everton Park
Asia Gardens
Singapore Ⓜ (350m)
Singapore Ⓜ (350m)

Chinatown & the CBD

SINGAPORE SIGHTS

walls, while the *gopuram* is covered in kitsch plasterwork images of Brahma the creator, Vishnu the preserver and Shiva the destroyer.

Thian Hock Keng Temple   TAOIST TEMPLE
(Map p618; www.thianhockkeng.com.sg; 158 Telok Ayer St; ⊙7.30am-5.30pm; M Telok Ayer) **FREE**
Surprisingly, Chinatown's oldest and most important Hokkien temple is often a haven of tranquility. Built between 1839 and 1842, it's a beautiful place, and once the favourite landing point of Chinese sailors, before land reclamation pushed the sea far down the road. Typically, the temple's design features are richly symbolic: the stone lions at the entrance ward off evil spirits, while the painted depiction of phoenixes and peonies in the central hall symbolise peace and good tidings, respectively.

◉ Little India & Kampong Glam

Disorderly and pungent, Little India is a world away from the rest of Singapore. Weekends are truly an eye-opener for locals and tourists alike. Produce, spices and trinkets spill onto the streets and crowd the five-foot ways (covered pedestrian walkways). Many businesses operate late into the night (some run 24 hours) and traffic slows to a messy crawl. Southeast of Little India is Kampong Glam, Singapore's Muslim quarter. Here you'll find shops selling clothing, raw cloth and dry goods.

★**Indian Heritage Centre**   MUSEUM
(Map p620; ☑6291 1601; www.indianheritage.org.sg; 5 Campbell Lane; adult/child under 7yr S$4/free; ⊙10am-7pm Tue-Thu, to 8pm Fri & Sat, to 4pm Sun; M Little India, Rochor) Delve into the heritage of Singapore's Indian community at this showpiece museum. Divided into five themes, its hundreds of historical and cultural artefacts explore everything from early interactions between South Asia and Southeast Asia to Indian cultural traditions and the contributions of Indian Singaporeans in the development of the island nation. Among the more extraordinary objects is a 19th-century Chettinad doorway, intricately adorned with 5000 minute carvings.

Malay Heritage Centre   MUSEUM
(Map p620; ☑6391 0450; www.malayheritage.org.sg; 85 Sultan Gate; adult/child under 6yr S$4/free; ⊙10am-6pm Tue-Sun; M Bugis) The Kampong Glam area is the historic seat of Malay royalty, resident here before the arrival of Raffles, and the *istana* (palace) on this site was built for the last sultan of Singapore, Ali Iskander Shah, between 1836 and 1843. It's now a museum, and its recently revamped galleries exploring Malay-Singaporean culture and history, from the early migration of traders to Kampong Glam to the development of Malay-Singaporean film, theatre, music and publishing.

Little India & Kampong Glam

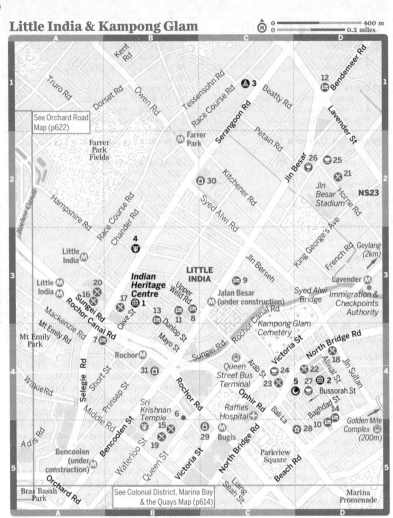

Sultan Mosque

MOSQUE

(Map p620; www.sultanmosque.org.sg; 3 Muscat St; ⊙10am-noon & 2-4pm Sat-Thu, 2.30-4pm Fri; ⓜBugis) **FREE** Seemingly pulled from the pages of the *Arabian Nights,* Singapore's largest mosque is nothing short of enchanting, designed in the Saracenic style and topped by a golden dome. It was originally built in 1825 with the aid of a grant from Raffles and the East India Company, after Raffles' treaty with the Sultan of Singapore allowed the Malay leader to retain sovereignty over the area. In 1928, the original mosque was replaced by the present magnificent building, designed by an Irish architect.

Sri Veeramakaliamman Temple

HINDU TEMPLE

(Map p620; www.sriveeramakaliamman.com; 141 Serangoon Rd; ⊙8am-noon & 6.30-9pm Mon-Thu & Sat, 8am-noon & 6-9pm Fri & Sun; ⓜLittle India) **FREE** Little India's most colourful, visually stunning temple is dedicated to the ferocious goddess Kali, depicted wearing a garland of skulls, ripping out the insides of her victims, and sharing more tranquil family moments with her sons Ganesh and

Little India & Kampong Glam

Murugan. The bloodthirsty consort of Shiva has always been popular in Bengal, the birthplace of the labourers who built the structure in 1881. The temple is at its most evocative during each of the four daily *puja* (prayer) sessions.

Sakya Muni Buddha
Gaya Temple   BUDDHIST TEMPLE
(Temple of 1000 Lights; Map p620; 366 Race Course Rd; ⊙8am-4.30pm; Ⓜ Farrer Park) FREE Dominating this temple is a 15m-tall, 300-tonne Buddha. Keeping him company is an eclectic cast of deities, including Kuan Yin (Guanyin), the Chinese goddess of mercy and, interestingly, the Hindu deities Brahma and Ganesh. The yellow tigers flanking the entrance symbolise protection and vitality, while the huge mother-of-pearl Buddha footprint to your left as you enter is reputedly a replica of the footprint on top of Adam's Peak in Sri Lanka.

◉ Orchard Road

No one visits Orchard Rd for the sights alone, though the Christmas-light displays are breathtaking. The only major historical site is the President's digs, the **Istana** (Map p622; www.istana.gov.sg; Orchard Rd; grounds/palace S$2/4; ⊙8.30am-6pm, open select days only;

Ⓜ Dhoby Ghaut), but it's only open on select public holidays; check the website for details.

★ Singapore Botanic Gardens   GARDENS
(Map p622; ☑6471 7361; www.sbg.org.sg; 1 Cluny Rd; garden admission free, National Orchid Garden adult/child under 12yr $5/free; ⊙5am-midnight, National Orchid Garden 8.30am-7pm, last entry 6pm, Healing Garden 5am-7.30pm Wed-Mon, Jacob Ballas Children's Garden 8am-7pm Tue-Sun, last entry 6.30pm; ☑7, 105, 123, 174, Ⓜ Botanic Gardens) Singapore's 74-hectare botanic wonderland is a Unesco World Heritage Site and one of the city's most arresting attractions. Established in 1860, it's a tropical Valhalla peppered with glassy lakes, rolling lawns and themed gardens. The site is home to the National Orchid Garden, as well as a rare patch of dense primeval rainforest, the latter home to over 300 species of vegetation, over half of which are now (sadly) considered rare in Singapore.

Emerald Hill Road   ARCHITECTURE
(Map p622; Ⓜ Somerset) Take time out from your shopping to wander up frangipani-scented Emerald Hill Rd, graced with some of Singapore's finest terrace houses. Special mentions go to No 56 (built in 1902, and one of the earliest buildings here), Nos 39 to 45 (with unusually wide frontages

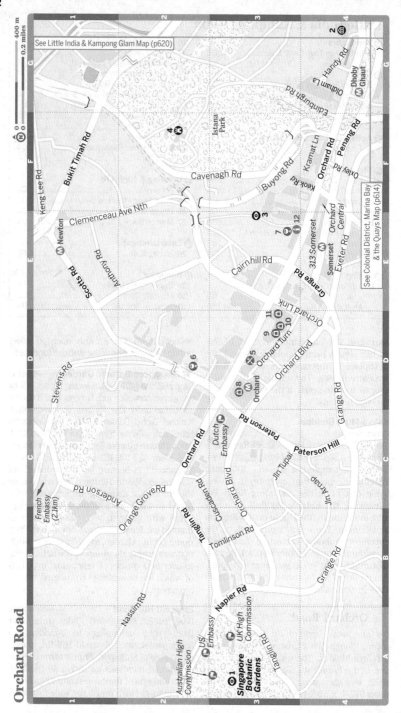

SINGAPORE SIGHTS

Orchard Road

See Little India & Kampong Glam Map (p620)

See Colonial District, Marina Bay & the Quays Map (p614)

Orchard Road

and a grand Chinese-style entrance gate), and Nos 120 to 130 (with art-deco features dating from around 1925). At the Orchard Rd end of the hill is a cluster of popular bars housed in fetching shophouse renovations.

Cathay Gallery   MUSEUM
(Map p622; www.thecathaygallery.com.sg; 2nd fl, The Cathay, 2 Handy Rd; ☉11am-7pm Mon-Sat; Ⓜ Dhoby Ghaut) FREE Film and nostalgia buffs will appreciate this pocket-sized silver-screen museum, housed in Singapore's first high-rise building. The displays trace the history of the Loke family, early pioneers in film production and distribution in Singapore and founders of the Cathay Organisation. Highlights include old movie posters, cameras and programs that capture the golden age of local cinema.

◎ Eastern Singapore

Nowhere else is Singapore's mishmash of food, commerce, religion, culture and sleaze more at ease than in the **Geylang** area. Come nightfall, you might see a crowd spill out onto the streets from evening prayer at a mosque, rubbing shoulders with prostitutes.

Join hordes of people sweating over plates of local food. To get here, take the MRT to Kallang or Aljunied, then cross the road and head south towards all the action.

Katong, a former Peranakan enclave, is rife with food outlets, bars and beautiful shophouse architecture. Take bus 12 or 32 from North Bridge Rd and get off along East Coast Rd.

East Coast Park   PARK
This 15km stretch of seafront park is where Singaporeans come to swim, windsurf, wakeboard, kayak, picnic, bicycle, inline skate, skateboard, and, of course, eat. You'll find swaying coconut palms, patches of bushland, a lagoon, sea-sports clubs, and some excellent eateries.

Renting a bike from kiosks like **CycleMax** (☑ 6445 1147; www.facebook.com/cyclemax.sg; 01-03, 1018 East Coast Parkway; 2hr bike hire S$8; ☉9am-9pm Mon-Fri, to 10pm Sat, 8am-9pm Sun; Ⓜ Bedok, then bus 197 or 401), enjoying the sea breezes, watching the veritable city of container ships out in the strait, and capping it all off with a beachfront meal is one of the most pleasant ways to spend a Singapore afternoon.

Changi Village   AREA
(Ⓜ Tanah Merah, then bus 2) The low-slung buildings are modern, but Changi Village still has a village atmosphere; the lively hawker centre next to the bus terminus is the focal point. Changi Beach (where thousands of Singaporean civilians were executed during WWII), lapped by the polluted waters of the Straits of Johor, is lousy for swimming, but there's a good stretch of sand. The ferry terminal for catching a bumboat to Pulau Ubin is located opposite the hawker centre.

◎ Northern & Central Singapore

★ **Singapore Zoo**   ZOO
(☑ 6269 3411; www.zoo.com.sg; 80 Mandai Lake Rd; adult/child under 13yr S$32/21; ☉8.30am-6pm; ☎; Ⓜ Ang Mo Kio, then bus 138) The line between zoo and botanic oasis blurs at this pulse-slowing sweep of spacious, naturalistic enclosures, freely roaming animals and interactive attractions. Get up close to orangutans, dodge Malaysian flying foxes, even snoop around a replica African village. Then there's *that* setting: 26 soothing hectares on a lush peninsula jutting out into the waters of the Upper Seletar Reservoir.

★ **Night Safari** ZOO
(www.nightsafari.com.sg; 80 Mandai Lake Rd; adult/
child under 13yr S$42/28; ⊙ 7.30pm-midnight, res-
taurants & shops from 5.30pm; 🚇; M Ang Mo Kio,
then bus 138) At Night Safari, electric trams
glide past over 130 species, including tigers
and elephants, with more docile creatures
often passing within inches of the trams.
Walking trails lead to enclosures inaccessi-
ble by tram, though sighting the animals can
be a little hit-and-miss. (In truth, many are
better seen at neighbouring Singapore Zoo.)
If you've got kids in tow, the 20-minute Creatures of the Night show will thrill. Arrive
at the zoo after 9.30pm to avoid the worst
queues.

River Safari ZOO
(www.riversafari.com.sg; 80 Mandai Lake Rd; adult/
child under 13yr S$28/18, boat ride adult/child
S$5/3; ⊙ 9am-6pm; M Ang Mo Kio, then bus 138)
This wildlife park recreates the habitats of
numerous world-famous rivers, including
the Yangtze, Nile and Congo. While most
are underwhelming, the Mekong River and
Amazon Flooded Forest exhibits are impressive, their epic aquariums rippling with giant
catfish and stingrays, electric eels, red-bellied
piranhas, manatees and sea cows. Another
highlight is the Giant Panda Forest enclosure,
home to rare red pandas and the park's famous black-and-whiters, KaiKai and JiaJia.

★ **MacRitchie Reservoir** NATURE RESERVE
(📞1800 471 7300; www.nparks.gov.sg; Lornie
Rd; ⊙ 7am-7pm, TreeTop Walk 9am-5pm Tue-Fri,
8.30am-5pm Sat & Sun; M Toa Payoh, then bus 157)
MacRitchie Reservoir makes for a calming,
evocative jungle escape. Walking trails skirt

ART-DECO HIP: TIONG BAHRU

Hipsters (beards optional!) have been
drawn to the heritage Tiong Bahru
neighbourhood for its unique low-rise
art-deco flats and cluster of bars, cafes
and boutiques. Hit new-school-cool
Yong Siak Street for indie bookstores
and boutiques before heading to the
**Tiong Bahru Market & Food
Centre** for cheap local eats. Sweet
tooths should pop into **Tiong Bahru
Bakery** to sample its signature *kouign
amann* (breton cake). Take the MRT to
Tiong Bahru station, walk east along
Tiong Bahru Rd for 350m, then turn
right onto Kim Pong Rd.

---

the water's edge and snake through the mature secondary rainforest spotted with long-
tailed macaques and huge monitor lizards.
You can rent kayaks at the **Paddle Lodge**
(📞6258 0057; www.scf.org.sg; per hour S$15;
⊙ 9am-noon & 2-6pm Tue-Sun, last hire 4.30pm;
M Toa Payoh, then bus 157), but the highlight
is the excellent 11km walking trail – and
its various well-signposted offshoots. Aim
for the **TreeTop Walk** (⊙ 9am-5pm Tue-Fri,
8.30am-5pm Sat & Sun), the highlight of which
is traversing a 250m-long suspension bridge,
perched 25m up in the forest canopy.

★ **Bukit Timah
Nature Reserve** NATURE RESERVE
(📞1800 471 7300; www.nparks.gov.sg; 177 Hind-
hede Dr; ⊙ 6am-7pm, visitors centre exhibition
8.30am-5pm; 🚌 67, 75, 170, 171, 173, 184, 852, 961,
M Beauty World) Singapore's steamy heart of
darkness is Bukit Timah Nature Reserve, a
163-hectare tract of primary rainforest clinging to Singapore's highest peak, Bukit Timah
(163m). The reserve holds more tree species
than the entire North American continent,
and its unbroken forest canopy shelters
what remains of Singapore's native wildlife,
including long-tailed macaques (monkeys),
pythons and dozens of bird species. Due to
major repair work, only the sealed Summit
Trail was accessible when we visited, and
only on weekends. Check the website for
updates.

◉ Southern & Western
Singapore

For a beautiful view, walk up 116m **Mt Faber**,
then catch the **cable car** (www.singapore
cablecar.com.sg; adult/child return S$29/18, Sen-
tosa Line only S$13/8; ⊙ 8.45am-9.30pm) to the
HarbourFront Centre or across to Sentosa
Island. Mt Faber is connected to Kent Ridge
Park via Telok Blangah Park and HortPark
in a 9km-long chain known as the **Southern Ridges**, arguably Singapore's best walking trail. The walk takes visitors along shady
forested paths and across amazing bridges
that pass through the forest canopy.

Jurong Bird Park BIRD SANCTUARY
(www.birdpark.com.sg; 2 Jurong Hill; adult/child
under 13yr S$28/18; ⊙ 8.30am-6pm; 👶; M Boon
Lay, then bus 194 or 251) Home to some 600
species of feathered friends – including
spectacular macaws – Jurong is a great place
for young kids. Highlights include the wonderful Lory Loft forest enclosure, where you

can feed colourful lories and lorikeets, and the interactive High Flyers (11am and 3pm) and Kings of the Skies (10am and 4pm). We must note, however, that some birds are made to perform for humans, which is discouraged by animal-welfare groups.

NUS Museum MUSEUM
(www.nus.edu.sg/museum; University Cultural Centre, 50 Kent Ridge Cres; ◉10am-7.30pm Tue-Sat, to 6pm Sun; Ⓜ Kent Ridge, then bus A2, the university shuttle bus) FREE Located on the verdant campus of the National University of Singapore (NUS), this museum is one of the city's lesser-known cultural delights. Ancient Chinese ceramics and bronzes, as well as archaeological fragments found in Singapore, dominate the ground-floor Lee Kong Chian Collection; one floor up, the South and Southeast Asian Gallery showcases paintings, sculpture and textiles from the region. The Ng Eng Teng Collection is dedicated to Ng Eng Teng (1934–2001), Singapore's foremost modern artist, best known for his figurative sculptures.

Haw Par Villa MUSEUM, PARK
(☑6872 2780; 262 Pasir Panjang Rd; ◉9am-7pm, Ten Courts of Hell exhibit 9am-5.45pm; Ⓜ Haw Par Villa) FREE The refreshingly weird and kitsch Haw Par Villa was the brainchild of Aw Boon Haw, the creator of the medicinal salve Tiger Balm. After Aw Boon Haw built a villa here in 1937 for his beloved brother and business partner, Aw Boon Par, the siblings began building a Chinese-mythology theme park within the grounds. Top billing goes to the Ten Courts of Hell, a walk-through exhibit depicting the gruesome torments awaiting sinners in the underworld.

◉ Sentosa Island

Epitomised by its star attraction, Universal Studios, Sentosa is essentially a giant theme park. The island itself is packed with rides, activities and shows, most of which cost extra. The beaches, of course, are completely free and very popular with locals and tourists alike.

Universal Studios AMUSEMENT PARK
(Map p626; www.rwsentosa.com; Resorts World; adult/child under 13yr S\$74/54; ◉10am-6pm; Ⓜ Harbourfront, then monorail to Waterfront) Universal Studios is the top-drawer attraction in Resorts World. Shops, shows, restaurants, rides and roller-coasters are all neatly packaged into fantasy-world themes based on

blockbuster Hollywood films. Top draws include Transformers: The Ride, a thrill ride deploying 3D animation, and Battlestar Galactica: Human vs Cylon, the world's tallest duelling roller-coasters. Opening times are subject to slight variations at different times of the year, so always check the website before heading in.

Fort Siloso MUSEUM
(Map p626; www.sentosa.com.sg; Siloso Point; admission free, Surrender Chambers adult/child under 13yr S\$6/4.50; ◉10am-6pm; Ⓜ Harbourfront, then monorail to Beach) Dating from the 1880s, when Sentosa was called Pulau Blakang Mati (Malay for 'the island behind which lies death'), this British coastal fort was famously useless during the Japanese invasion of 1942. Documentaries, artefacts, animatronics and recreated historical scenes talk visitors through the fort's history, and the underground tunnels are fun to explore.

◉ Pulau Ubin

A rural, unkempt expanse of jungle full of fast-moving lizards, strange shrines and cacophonic bird life. Tin-roofed buildings bake in the sun, chickens squawk and panting dogs slump in the dust, while in the forest, families of wild pigs run for cover as visitors pedal past on squeaky rented bicycles. Get to Tanah Merah MRT, then take bus 2 to Changi Village Ferry Terminal. There boats depart for the island (one way S\$3, 10 minutes, sunrise to sunset) whenever there are 12 people aboard.

◉ Southern Islands

Three other islands popular with castaway-fantasising locals are **St John's**, **Lazarus** and **Kusu**. They're quiet and great for fishing, swimming, picnics and guzzling BYO six-packs. The islands have changing rooms and toilets. Kusu Island is culturally interesting; devotees come to pray for health, wealth and fertility at its Taoist temple and Malay *kramat* (shrine). There's nowhere to buy food or drink on any of the islands, so come prepared.

Catch a ferry from the **Marina South Pier** (31 Marina Coastal Dr; Ⓜ Marina South Pier).

🏃 Activities

Though the national pastimes revolve around shopping and eating, there are opportunities for outdoorsy types. The best

Sentosa Island

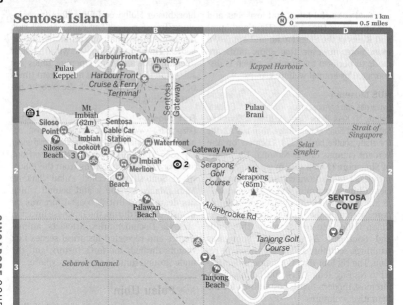

Sentosa Island

spot for **cycling** is definitely East Coast Park. Pulau Ubin has dedicated mountain-biking trails. For **swimming** there are reasonable beaches on Sentosa, the Southern Islands and East Coast Park.

Massages are cheap and readily available, with reflexology a major trade. For a good foot rub check out **People's Park Complex** (Map p618; 1 Park Cres; Ⓜ Chinatown). Most malls have at least one reflexology place.

G-Max Reverse Bungy   ADVENTURE SPORTS
(Map p614; www.gmax.com.sg; 3E River Valley Rd; adult/student per ride S$45/35, incl GX-5 Extreme Swing S$69/50; ⊙ 2pm-late; Ⓜ Clarke Quay) Prepare to be strapped into padded chairs inside a metal cage and propelled skyward to

a height of 60m at speeds of up to 200km/h before being pulled back down by gravity. Though the ride offers spectacular views to those who can keep their eyes open, it's best avoided by people prone to velocity-induced vomiting.

Wave House   SURFING
(Map p626; ☑ 6238 1196; www.wavehousesentosa. com; Siloso Beach; 30min flowbarrel surf session S$30, 1hr double flowrider surf session from S$35; ⊙ 10.30am-10.30pm, Double Flowrider 11am-10pm, FlowBarrel 1-10pm Mon, Tue, Thu & Fri, 11am-10pm Wed, Sat & Sun; Ⓜ HarbourFront, then monorail to Beach) Two specially designed wave pools allow surfer types to practise their gashes and cutbacks at ever-popular Wave House. The non-curling Double Flowrider is good for beginners, while the 3m FlowBarrel is more challenging. Wave House also includes beachside eating and drinking options.

🎓 Courses

Food Playground   COOKING COURSE
(Map p618; ☑ 9452 3669; www.foodplayground. com.sg; 24A Sago St; 3hr class from S$99; ⊙ 9.30am-12.30pm Mon-Sat; Ⓜ Chinatown) You've been gorging on Singapore's famous food, so why not learn to make it? This fantastic hands-on cooking school explores

Singapore's multicultural make-up and sees you cook up classic dishes like laksa, *nasi lemak* (coconut rice) and Hainanese chicken rice. Courses usually run for three hours and can be tailored for budding cooks with dietary restrictions.

☞ Tours

★ Original Singapore Walks WALKING TOUR
(☑ 6325 1631; www.singaporewalks.com; adult S$35-55, child 7-12yr S$15-30) Conducts irreverent but knowledgeable off-the-beaten-track walking tours through Chinatown, Little India, Kampong Glam, the Colonial District, Boat Quay, Haw Par Villa and war-related sites. Rain-or-shine tours last from 2½ to 3½ hours. Bookings are not necessary; check the website for departure times and locations.

SIA Hop-On BUS TOUR
(☑ 6338 6877; www.siahopon.com; 24hr ticket Singapore Airlines passengers adult/child S$8/4, non-passengers S$25/15) Singapore Airlines' tourist bus traverses the main tourist arteries every 20 to 30 minutes daily, starting from Singapore Flyer at 9am, with the last bus leaving at 7.40pm and terminating back at Singapore Flyer at 9.10pm. Buy tickets from the driver; see the website for route details.

Singapore River Cruise BOAT TOUR
(Map p614; ☑ 6336 6111; www.rivercruise.com.sg; bumboat river cruise adult/child S$25/15; M Clarke Quay) Runs 40-minute bumboat tours of the Singapore River and Marina Bay. Boats depart about every 15 minutes from various locations, including Clarke Quay, Boat Quay and Marina Bay. A cheaper option is to catch one of the company's river taxis – commuter boats running a similar route; see the website for stops. River-taxi payment is by EZ-Link transport card only.

★☆ Festivals & Events

Singapore's multicultural population celebrates an amazing number of festivals and events. For a calendar, check out www.yoursingapore.com.

Chinese New Year is the major festival, held in January/February. Look out for parades throughout Chinatown and festive foods in shops. During the **Great Singapore Sale** in June and July, merchants drop prices to boost Singapore's image as a shopping destination.

🛏 Sleeping

Once, budget-room-hunters in Singapore were limited to flea-bitten flophouses (they still exist!), but thankfully these days there are good hostels and guesthouses even in the more expensive parts of the city. Most have female-only dorms. Unless otherwise stated, hostel rates we list are for shared bathrooms.

🛏 Colonial District & the Quays

★ Port by Quarters Hostel HOSTEL $
(Map p614; ☑ 6816 6960; theport.stayquarters. com; 50A Boat Quay; single/queen capsule from S$50/90; @ 🛜; M Clarke Quay) Smack bang on the Singapore River, the Port by Quarters Hostel has raised the bar for capsule hostels in Singapore. The sleek single and queen capsules offer under-bed storage, folding workstation, power points and roll-down privacy screen. The best bit, however, is the views – straight over to Parliament and the skyline beyond.

5Footway.Inn Project Boat Quay HOSTEL $
(Map p614; www.5footwayinn.com; 76 Boat Quay; dm from S$20, tw incl breakfast from S$60; @ 🛜; M Clarke Quay) Right on Boat Quay, the white-washed dorms come in two-, three- and four-bed configurations, and though rooms are small (superior rooms have windows), they're modern and comfortable, with white wooden bunks and handy bedside power sockets. Bathrooms are modern, reception operates round-the-clock, and the cheap-chic breakfast lounge comes with river-view balcony seating.

River City Inn HOSTEL $
(Map p614; ☑ 6532 6091; www.rivercityinn.com; 33 Hong Kong St; dm S$25-35; @ 🛜; M Clarke Quay) Its location, on the 4th floor of a shophouse, hasn't deterred backpackers from booking beds here en masse. The communal areas are well done but the 26-bed dorms get just a bit too cosy...

Holiday Inn Express Clarke Quay HOTEL $$
(Map p614; ☑ 6589 8000; www.hiexpress.com; 2 Magazine Rd; r incl breakfast from S$215; @ 🛜 ▨; M Clarke Quay) This smart newcomer delivers modern, earthy-hued rooms with high ceilings, massive floor-to-ceiling windows and comfortable beds with both soft and firm pillows (embroidered on the pillow slip). Small bathrooms come with decent-size showers. Best of all is the rooftop garden, home to

a tiny gym and impressive glass-sided pool with spectacular city views. The hotel's self-service laundry room is a handy touch.

Discounted online rates can see rooms offered for under S$200.

🛏 Chinatown

★ Adler Hostel   HOSTEL $

(Map p618; ☎6226 0173; www.adlerhostel.com; 265 South Bridge Rd; cabin s/d S$55/110; @ 🛜; Ⓜ Chinatown) Hostelling reaches sophisticated new heights at this self-proclaimed 'poshtel'. Chinese antiques grace the tranquil lobby lounge, fresh towels and feather-down duvets and pillows the beds, and Malin+Goetz products the bathrooms. Airy, air-conditioned dorms consist of custom-made cabins, each with lockable storage and drawable curtain for privacy. Some even feature king-sized beds for couples. Book around three weeks ahead for the best rates.

Wink Hostel   HOSTEL $

(Map p618; ☎6222 2940; www.winkhostel.com; 8 Mosque St; s/d pod S$50/90; @ 🛜; Ⓜ Chinatown) Located in a restored shophouse in the heart of Chinatown, flashbacker favourite Wink merges hostel and capsule-hotel concepts. Instead of bunks, dorms feature private, sound-proof 'pods', each with comfortable mattress, coloured mood lighting, adjacent locker and enough room to sit up in. Communal bathrooms feature rain shower-heads, while the in-house kitchenette, laundry and lounge areas crank up the homely factor.

Rucksack Inn   HOSTEL $

(Map p618; ☎6438 5146; www.rucksackinn.com/temple-st; 52 Temple St; dm incl breakfast from S$34; @ 🛜; Ⓜ Chinatown) Travellers' messages are lovingly scrawled all over the streetside columns of this friendly, two-level hostel. Decked out in white-metal bunk beds and quirky wall murals, the dorms come in four-, six-, eight- and 10-bed configurations, with a female-only room. All are clean, modern and cosy, and the communal showers have rain shower-heads. Tech perks include iMacs, Xboxes and Wii consoles.

Beary Good Hostel   HOSTEL $

(Map p618; ☎6222 4955; www.abearygoodhostel.com; 66 Pagoda St; dm S$27-30; @ 🛜; Ⓜ Chinatown) So popular it has spawned two branches: the Beary Nice Hostel and the Beary Best, both a stone's throw away at 46 Smith St and 16 Upper Cross St. All are fun, brightly painted affairs and the separate bathrooms for boys and girls a beary nice touch.

Hotel 1929   BOUTIQUE HOTEL $$

(Map p618; ☎6347 1929; www.hotel1929.com; 50 Keong Saik Rd; s/d incl breakfast from S$175/200; @ 🛜; Ⓜ Outram Park) Occupying a white-washed heritage building, Hotel 1929 sits on up-and-coming Keong Saik Rd. Rooms are tight, but good use is made of the limited space, and interiors are cheerily festooned with vintage designer furniture (look out for reproduction Eames and Jacobsen) and Technicolor mosaic bathrooms.

🛏 Little India

★ Bunc@Radius   HOSTEL $

(Map p620; ☎6262 2862; www.bunchostel.com; 15 Upper Weld Rd; dm incl breakfast from $20; @ 🛜; Ⓜ Bugis, Little India) Fresh, clean, new-school Bunc@Radius is the coolest flashpacker hostel in town. Concrete floor, art installations and a choice of both iMac and PC computers give the spacious lobby a hip, boutique feel. Dorms – in six-, eight-, 10- and 12-bed configurations – offer both single and double beds, with each thick mattress wrapped in a hygiene cover (no bed bugs!).

InnCrowd   HOSTEL $

(Map p620; ☎6296 9169; www.the-inncrowd.com; 73 Dunlop St; dm from S$20.50; @ 🛜; Ⓜ Rochor, Little India) Wildly popular, the InnCrowd is

---

CAMPING IT UP

The National Parks Board (www.nparks.gov.sg) maintains four campgrounds around Singapore: **East Coast Park**, **West Coast Park** and **Pasir Ris Park**. Permits are free and can be obtained online (www.axs.com.sg) or from several AXS (ATM-like) machines in all malls. There's a small fee to use the barbecue pits and shower facilities. On **Pulau Ubin** you can camp at Jelutong or Maman Beaches. The sites are free, but very basic. There's no drinking water, so bring your own. You can also camp on **Palau Hantu**, one of Singapore's southern islands; permits are free from Sentosa Leisure Group (www.sentosa.com.sg). You'll need to charter a boat from West Coast Pier and BYO drinking water.

ground zero for Singapore's backpackers. Located right in the heart of Little India, this funkily painted hostel has helpful staff and all the facilities you'd expect of a decent hostel (travel advice, free internet, wi-fi, DVDs, laundry), plus a few you might not expect (a Wii console and kick-scooter city tours!). Bookings essential.

Green Kiwi Backpackers Hostel   HOSTEL **$**
(Map p620; ☑ 9695 9331; www.greenkiwi.com. sg; 280A Lavender St; dm S$22-30; @ 🛜; Ⓜ Lavender) An easy walk from the hipster pocket of Jalan Besar is this popular, well-air-conditioned option. Low-frills dorms (which include a female-only room) feature red, wooden bunks; the communal bathrooms are reassuringly clean. Perks include laundry service (S$8 per load, wash and dry) and a leafy rooftop garden. The latter is a good spot to neck a beer, on sale at reception.

Footprints   HOSTEL **$**
(Map p620; ☑ 6295 5134; www.footprintshostel. com.sg; 25A Perak Rd; dm incl breakfast from $25; @ 🛜; Ⓜ Little India) A cheap and friendly hostel in Little India. Dorms – which come in beds of six, 10 and 12 – are narrow but bright and clean, with female-only dorms available to boot. The small communal living area is bright with funky artwork feature walls and random chandeliers that could make royalty blush. Guests have access to computers, wi-fi and a coin-operated laundry.

Central 65   HOSTEL **$**
(Map p620; ☑ 6298 2566; www.central65hostel. com; 134 Jln Besar; dm incl breakfast from S$25; @ 🛜; Ⓜ Bugis, Little India) Walking distance from Little India, Kampong Glam and hipster 'hood Jalan Besar, this five-floor hostel features open-ended 'pod-like' beds. Rooms are small and only one comes with windows, though this is also the noisiest. The lounge and in/outdoor dining area is large, and the cafe is open 24 hours. The icing on the cake is the rooftop terrace with Jacuzzi – nice in the evening.

Albert Court Village Hotel   HOTEL **$$**
(Map p620; ☑ 6339 3939; www.stayfareast.com; 180 Albert St; r from S$200; @ 🛜; Ⓜ Rochor, Little India) A short walk south of Little India is this colonial-era hotel, in a shophouse redevelopment that now shoots up eight storeys. Rooms are classic and spacious, with carved wooden furniture, smallish but spotless bathrooms, and a choice of fan or

air-con. Service is top-notch and there's wi-fi throughout. You'll find the best deals online.

🛏 Kampong Glam

⭐ **Five Stones Hostel**   HOSTEL **$**
(Map p620; ☑ 6535 5607; www.fivestoneshostel. com; 285 Beach Rd; dm S$30-38, tw/d S$100/115; @ 🛜; Ⓜ Bugis, Nicoll Hwy) This upbeat, no-shoes hostel comes with polished-concrete floors and both Wii and DVDs in the common lounge, plus complimentary use of washing machines and dryers. While not all dorms have windows, all feature steel-frame bunks, personal power points and lamps, and bright, mood-lifting murals depicting local themes. There's an all-female floor, plus private rooms with bunks or a queen-sized bed.

Pod   HOSTEL **$**
(Map p620; ☑ 6298 8505; www.thepod.sg; 289 Beach Rd; s/d pod from S$40/75; @ 🛜; Ⓜ Bugis, Nicoll Hwy) Riding the new wave of capsule hotels, the Pod offers sleek accommodation steps from vibrant Kampong Glam. Dorms are modern and sleep 12, in single or double pods; privacy comes in the form of roll-down screens. Each floor has three dorms, a common washroom and three private bathrooms. Extras like free Nespresso coffee, hot breakfast and laundry cement its popularity with the trendy crowd.

🍴 Eating

Singaporean life is best epitomised by the ubiquitous (but wholly unique) hawker centre. Grab a seat, order a super-sweet coffee or a S$6 Tiger beer, join the queue for a local meal and listen to people talk about politics, English Premier League, Hollywood diets and maids. Dishes rarely cost more than S$5 (unless you're eating seafood), and each centre has a huge variety of cuisines, including Malay, South Indian, Cantonese, Hokkien, Teochew and Indonesian. There are also countless excellent restaurants, though costs are going to spiral up to at least S$12 per plate.

🍴 Colonial District

⭐ **Gluttons Bay**   HAWKER **$**
(Map p614; www.makansutra.com; 01-15 Esplanade Mall; dishes from $4; ⏰ 5pm-2am Mon-Thu, to 3am Fri & Sat, 4pm-midnight Sun; Ⓜ Esplanade) Selected by the *Makansutra Food Guide,* this row of alfresco hawker stalls is a great place to start your Singapore food odyssey.

Get indecisive over classics like oyster omelette, satay, barbecue stingray and carrot cake (opt for the black version). Its central, bayside location makes it a huge hit, so head in early or late to avoid the frustrating hunt for a table.

Singapore Food Trail   HAWKER $

(Map p614; www.singaporefoodtrail.com.sg; Singapore Flyer, 30 Raffles Ave; dishes S$5-15; ⊙10.30am-10.30pm Sun-Thu, to 11.30pm Fri & Sat; Ⓜ Promenade) Retro-inspired re-creation of the hawker stalls from 1960s Singapore, except with air-conditioning. A good alternative to Gluttons Bay, located under the shadow of the Singapore Flyer.

National Kitchen by
Violet Oon   PERANAKAN $$

(Map p614; National Gallery Singapore, 1 St Andrew's Rd; S$17-35; ⊙11am-2.30pm & 6-9.30pm; Ⓜ City Hall) Chef Violet Oon is a national treasure, much loved for her faithful Peranakan (Chinese-Malay fusion) dishes – so much so that she was chosen to open her latest venture inside Singapore's showcase National Gallery. Feast on made-from-scratch beauties like sweet, spicy *kueh pie tee* (prawn- and yam bean–stuffed pastry cups), dry laksa and fried turmeric chicken wings with chinchalok sambal.

✕ CBD, Marina Bay & the Quays

★ Satay by the Bay   HAWKER $

(www.gardensbythebay.com.sg; Gardens by the Bay, 18 Marina Gardens Dr; dishes from S$4; ⊙ food stalls vary, drinks stall 24hr; Ⓜ Bayfront) Gardens by the Bay's own hawker centre has an enviable location, alongside Marina Bay and far from the roar of city traffic. Especially evocative at night, it's known for its satay, best devoured under open skies on the spacious wooden deck. As you'd expect, prices are a little higher than at more local hawker centres, with most dishes between S$8 and S$10.

SPLURGE

··

If you're craving breakfast for lunch, head to LoKal (Map p618; ✆ 6423 9918; www.thelokalsingapore.com; 136 Neil Rd; dishes S$5-28; ⊙ 8am-5pm Mon, to 11pm Tue-Sat, 9am-4pm Sun; Ⓜ Outram Park), which serves wholesome homemade dishes until 3.30pm. You can 'pimp' your brunch with a range of add-ons.

★ Ya Kun Kaya Toast   CAFE $

(Map p618; www.yakun.com; 01-01 Far East Sq, 18 China St; kaya toast set S$4.80; ⊙ 7.30am-7pm Mon-Fri, 8.30am-5.30pm Sat & Sun; Ⓜ Telok Ayer) Though it's now part of a chain, this airy, retro coffee shop is an institution, and the best way to start the day the Singaporean way. The speciality is buttery *kaya* (coconut jam) toast, dipped in runny egg (add black pepper and a few drops of soy sauce) and washed down with strong *kopi* (coffee).

Rasapura Masters   HAWKER $

(Map p614; www.rasapura.com.sg; level B2, The Shoppes at Marina Bay Sands, 2 Bayfront Ave; dishes from S$5; Ⓜ Bayfront) If you prefer your hawker grub with a side of air-con, head down to this bustling, gleaming food court in the basement of the Marina Bay Sands mall. Its stalls cover most bases, from Japanese ramen and Korean kimchi to Hong Kong roast meats and local *bak kut teh* (pork-bone tea soup).

Super Loco   MEXICAN $$

(✆ 6235 8900; www.super-loco.com; 01-13, Robertson Quay; tacos S$9-11, quesadillas S$16-18; ⊙5-10.30pm Mon-Fri, 10am-3.30pm & 5-10.30pm Sat & Sun; ▣51, 64, 123, 186) The only thing missing is a beach at this breezy hipster cantina, complete with Mexican party vibe, pink-neon Spanish and playful barkeeps in Cancún-esque shirts. Get the good times rolling with a competent frozen margarita, then lick your lips over the standout ceviche, zingy crab and avocado tostada, and the damn fine *carne asada* (grilled meat) and *pescado* (fish) tacos.

✕ Chinatown

★ Maxwell Food Centre   HAWKER $

(Map p618; cnr Maxwell & South Bridge Rds; dishes from S$2.50; ⊙stalls vary; ✗; Ⓜ Chinatown) One of Chinatown's most accessible hawker centres, Maxwell is a solid spot to savour some of the city's street-food staples. While stalls slip in and out of favour with Singapore's fickle diners, enduring favourites include **Tian Tian Hainanese Chicken Rice** (Map p618; stall 10; chicken rice from S$3.50; ⊙10am-5pm Tue-Sun; Ⓜ Chinatown) and **Rojak, Popiah & Cockle** (Map p618; stall 01-56; popiah S$2.50, rojak from S$3; ⊙noon-10.30pm; Ⓜ Chinatown).

★ Chinatown Complex   HAWKER $

(Map p618; 11 New Bridge Rd; dishes from S$3; ⊙stalls vary; Ⓜ Chinatown) Leave Smith St's revamped 'Chinatown Food Street' to the out-of-towners and join old-timers and foodies at this nearby labyrinth. The 25-minute wait for mixed claypot rice at **Lian He Ben Ji Claypot Rice** (Map p618; Stall 02-198/199; dishes S$2.50-20, claypot rice from S$5; ☺4.30-10pm Fri-Wed) is worth it, while the rich and nutty satay at **Shi Xiang Satay** (Map p618; stall 02-79; satay from S$6; ☺3.30-9pm Fri-Wed;) is insane. For a little TLC, opt for Ten Tonic Ginseng Chicken Soup at **Bonne Soup** (Map p618; stall 02-05; soups from S$3.70; ☺10am-8pm).

Ginza Tendon Itsuki   JAPANESE $
(Map p618; ☑6221 6678; 101 Tanjong Pagar Rd; mains S$12.90-13.90; ☺11.30am-2.30pm & 5.30-10pm; ☑; Ⓜ Tanjong Pagar) Life's few certainties include taxes, death and a queue outside this dedicated *tendon* (tempura served on rice) eatery. Patience is rewarded with cries of *irrashaimase!* (welcome) and generous bowls of Japanese comfort grub. Both the tempura and rice are cooked to perfection, drizzled in sweet and sticky soy sauce, and served with *chawanmushi* (Japanese egg custard), miso soup and pickled vegetables. A cash-only bargain.

Jing Hua   CHINESE $
(Map p618; ☑6221 3060; 21-23 Neil Rd; dishes S$3-10; ☺11.30am-3pm & 5.30-9.30pm Thu-Tue; Ⓜ Chinatown) Locals outnumber out-of-towners at halogen-and-laminex Jing Hua. Tuck into a limited yet satisfying repertoire of northern Chinese classics, among them plump pork dumplings, noodles with minced pork and soya-bean sauce, and red-bean-paste pancake. Skip the lacklustre *xiao long bao* for the moreish Chinese pizza, a hearty, deep-fried pastry packed with minced prawn, pork and crab, and spring onion. Cash only.

✖ Little India

Tekka Centre   HAWKER $
(Map p620; cnr Serangoon & Buffalo Rds; dishes S$3-10; ☺7am-11pm; ☑; Ⓜ Little India, Rochor) There's no shortage of subcontinental spice at this bustling hawker centre, wrapped around the sloshed guts and hacked bones of the wet market. Queue up for real-deal biryani, *dosa* (thin, lentil-flour pancake), *roti prata* and *teh tarik* (pulled tea). Well worth seeking out is **Ah-Rahman Royal Prata** (Map p620; stall 01-248; murtabak S$4-8; ☺7am-10pm, closed alternative Mon; Ⓜ Little India, Rochor), which flips some of Singapore's finest *murtabak* (savoury pancake).

BREAKFAST OF A NATION

Come morning you'll find locals crowded into traditional *kopitiams* (coffee shops) to fuel up on Singapore's quintessential 'breakfast set' comprising char-grilled white toast smothered with butter and *kaya* (coconut jam), two half-boiled eggs and a cup of *kopi* (coffee). To eat, crack the eggs into your bowl, marveling at the just-set whites and creamy yolks, before adding a dash of soy sauce and a shake of ground white pepper. Give it all a good mix and then dunk the toast in, mopping up all the eggy goodness. Recent years has seen this meal enjoyed throughout the day as a quick pick-me-up, so don't worry if you miss the breakfast crowd. Our pick: Ya Kun Kaya Toast.

Ananda Bhavan   INDIAN $
(Map p620; www.anandabhavan.com; block 663, 01-10 Buffalo Rd; dosa S$2.60-4.60, set meals S$6-9; ☺7am-10pm; ☑; Ⓜ Little India) This super-cheap chain restaurant is a top spot to sample South Indian breakfast staples like *idly* (fermented-rice cakes) and *dosa* (thin, lentil-flour pancake; spelt 'thosai' on the menu). It also does great-value thali, some of which are served on banana leaves. Other outlets are at 58 Serangoon Rd, 95 Syed Alwi Rd and Changi Airport's Terminal 2.

Moghul Sweets   SWEETS $
(Map p620; 48 Serangoon Rd; sweets from S$1; ☺9.30am-9.30pm; Ⓜ Rochor, Little India) If you're after a subcontinental sugar rush, tiny Moghul is the place to get it. Bite into luscious *gulab jamun* (syrup-soaked fried dough balls), harder-to-find *rasmalai* (paneer cheese soaked in cardamom-infused clotted cream) and *barfi* (condensed milk and sugar slice) in flavours including pistachio, chocolate and...carrot.

Two Bakers   BAKERY $
(Map p620; ☑6293 0329; www.facebook.com/twobakers; 88 Horne Rd; pastries & cakes S$6.80-10.90; ☺11am-9pm Mon, Wed & Thu, to 11pm Fri & Sat, 9am-7pm Sun; Ⓜ Lavender) The bakers at this light, contemporary bakery-cafe earned their stripes at Paris' Cordon Bleu. The result? Irresistible sweet treats and countless broken diets. Which tart to choose: the crowd favourite yuzu lemon or

the decadent Purple Gold (lavender-infused chocolate ganache, caramel ganache, caramel tuile and roasted almonds)? What the hell: order both!

🍴 Kampong Glam

★ Warong Nasi Pariaman
MALAYSIAN, INDONESIAN $

(Map p620; ✏️6292 2374; 742 North Bridge Rd; dishes from S$4.50; ⊘7.30am-2.30pm Mon-Sat; Ⓜ Bugis) This no-frills corner *nasi padang* (rice with curries) stall is the stuff of legend. Top choices include the *belado* (fried mackerel in a slow-cooked chilli, onion and vinegar sauce), delicate beef *rendang* and *ayam bakar* (grilled chicken with coconut sauce). Get here by 11am to avoid the hordes. And be warned: most of it sells out by 1pm (10am Saturday).

★ Zam Zam
MALAYSIAN $

(Map p620; 699 North Bridge Rd; murtabak from S$5, dishes S$4-20; ⊘7am-11pm; Ⓜ Bugis) These guys have been here since 1908, so they know what they're doing. Tenure hasn't bred complacency, though – the touts still try to herd customers in off the street while frenetic chefs inside whip up delicious *murtabak*, the restaurant's speciality savoury pancakes, filled with succulent mutton, chicken, beef, venison or even sardines.

QS269 Food House
HAWKER $

(Map p620; block 269B, Queen St; ⊘stalls vary; Ⓜ Bugis) This is not so much a 'food house' as a loud, crowded undercover laneway lined with cult-status stalls. Work up a sweat with a bowl of award-winning coconut-curry noodle soup from **Ah Heng Curry Chicken Bee Hoon Mee** (Map p620; stall 01-236; dishes from S$4; ⊘8am-4.30pm Sat-Thu; Ⓜ Bugis) or join the queue at **New Rong Liang Ge Cantonese Roast Duck Boiled Soup** (Map p620; stall 01-235; dishes from S$2.50; ⊘7am-8pm; Ⓜ Bugis), with succulent roast-duck dishes that draw foodies from across the city.

Nan Hwa Chong Fish-Head Steamboat Corner
CHINESE $$

(Map p620; 812-816 North Bridge Rd; fish steamboats from S$28; ⊘4.30pm-12.15am; Ⓜ Lavender) If you only try fish-head steamboat once, do it at this noisy, open-fronted veteran. Cooked on charcoal, the large pot of fish heads is brought to you in steaming *tee po* (dried flat sole fish) spiked broth. One pot is enough for three or four people, and can stretch to more with rice and side dishes.

🍴 Orchard Road

Food Republic
FAST FOOD $

(Map p622; level 4, Wisma Atria, 435 Orchard Rd; dishes S$4-15; ⊘10am-10pm Sun-Thu, to 11pm Fri & Sat; Ⓜ Orchard) A cornucopia of street food in air-conditioned comfort. Muck in with the rest of the crowd for seats before joining the longest queues for dishes spanning Japan, Korea and Thailand, to India, Indonesia and, quite rightly, Singapore.

Takashimaya Food Village
FAST FOOD $

(Map p622; www.takashimaya.com.sg; B2, Takashimaya Department Store, Ngee Ann City, 391 Orchard Rd; dishes S$4-17; ⊘10am-9.30pm; Ⓜ Orchard) In the basement of Japanese department store Takashimaya, this polished, expansive food hall serves up a *Who's Who* of Japanese and other Asian culinary classics. If comfort food is on the agenda, order a fragrant bowl of noodles from the Tsuru-koshi stand. The hall is also home to a large Cold Storage supermarket.

🍷 Drinking & Nightlife

Drinking in Singapore is expensive. The cheapest way to drink is to park yourself in a hawker centre, where beers cost S$6 to S$8 for a large bottle. If you're hitting bars and clubs, start early: happy hours generally finish at 9pm. The main drinking places include Clarke and Boat Quays, and Emerald Hill Rd off Orchard Rd. Most bars open from 5pm daily until at least midnight Sunday to Thursday, and until 2am on Friday and Saturday.

🍷 Colonial District

★ Loof
BAR

(Map p614; ✏️9773 9304; www.loof.com.sg; 03-07 Odeon Towers Bldg, 331 North Bridge Rd; ⊘5pm-1am Mon-Thu, to 2am Fri & Sat; 🛜; Ⓜ City Hall) Red neon warmly declares 'Glad you came up' at upbeat Loof, its name the Singlish mangling of the word 'roof'. Sit on the leafy rooftop deck and look out over the Raffles Hotel and Marina Bay Sands with a calamansi-spiked Singapore sour in hand. The great-value weekday happy hour lasts from 5pm to 8pm, with the cheapest drinks early on.

Orgo
BAR

(Map p614; ☎ 6336 9366; www.orgo.sg; 4th fl, Esplanade Roof Tce, 8 Raffles Ave; ⊙6pm-1.30am; Esplanade, City Hall) It's hard not to feel like the star of a Hollywood rom-com at rooftop Orgo, its view of the skyline so commanding you'll almost feel obliged to play out a tear-jerking scene. Don't. Instead, slip into a wicker armchair, order a vino (you'll get better cocktails elsewhere) and Instagram the view to the sound of soft conversation and sultry tunes.

CBD & the Quays

Clarke Quay is a popular (though very gaudy) nightspot in Singapore. If you don't mind mingling with off-work suits, bars around the CBD area (Raffles Pl) are cheap after 5pm Boat Quay is a popular boozing haunt for expat city workers.

Cé la Vi Club Lounge
BAR

(Map p614; 10 Bayfront Ave; ⊙noon-late) Perched on Marina Bay Sands' cantilevered SkyPark, this bar offers spectacular views of the skyline and beyond. A dress code kicks in from 6pm (no shorts, singlets or flip-flops). Entry is via the lobby of Marina Bay Sands.

Level 33
MICROBREWERY

(www.level33.com.sg; level 33, Marina Bay Financial Tower 1, 8 Marina Blvd; ⊙noon-midnight Sun-Thu, noon-2am Fri & Sat; ☎; ⓂDowntown) In a country obsessed with unique selling points, this one takes the cake – no, keg. Laying claim to being the world's highest 'urban craft brewery', Level 33 brews its own lager, pale ale, stout, porter and wheat beer. It's all yours to slurp alfresco with a jaw-dropping view over Marina Bay. Bargain hunters, take note: beers are cheaper before 8pm.

Attica
CLUB

(Map p614; www.attica.com.sg; 01-03 Clarke Quay, 3A River Valley Rd; ⊙Level One 10.30pm-4am Wed, Fri & Sat, Level Two 11pm-5am Wed, 11pm-5.30am Fri & Sat, outdoor bar 6pm-late Tue-Sat; ⓂClarke Quay) Attica has secured a loyal following among Singapore's fickle clubbers, modelling itself on New York's hippest clubs but losing the attitude somewhere over the Pacific. Locals will tell you it's where the expats go to pick up on the weekends, mostly in the courtyard. Beats span chart hits, house and R&B; check the website for themed nights.

Zouk
CLUB

(www.zoukclub.com; 17 Jiak Kim St; ⊙Zouk & Phuture 11pm-late Wed, Fri & Sat, Velvet Underground 11pm-late Fri & Sat, Wine Bar 6pm-2am Tue, 6pm-3am Wed-Sat; ☐5, 16, 75, 175, 195, 970) Set to move to Clarke Quay (at Block C, The Cannery, River Valley Rd) in May 2016, Singapore's premier club draws some of the world's biggest DJs. Choose between the multilevel main club, the hip-hop-centric Phuture or the plush Velvet Underground, slung with original artworks by Andy Warhol, Frank Stella and Takashi Murakami. Take a taxi, and prepare to queue.

Chinatown

Tanjong Pagar Rd has an active LGBT bar scene but welcomes drinkers regardless of their sexuality. The sophisticated bars of **Club Street** and **Ann Siang Hill** are housed in attractive, restored shophouses (many are closed Sunday).

★Operation Dagger
COCKTAIL BAR

(Map p618; operationdagger.com; 7 Ann Siang Hill; ⊙6pm-late Tue-Sat; ⓂChinatown) From the 'cloud-like' light sculpture to the boundary-pushing cocktails, 'extraordinary' is the keyword here. To encourage experimentation, libations are described by flavour, not spirit, the latter shelved in uniform, apothecary-like bottles. Whether you sample the sesame-infused complexity of the Gomashio, the textural surprise of the Hot & Cold or the bar's raw chocolate–infused vino, prepare to fall deeply in love.

Oxwell & Co
BAR

(Map p618; www.oxwellandco.com; 5 Ann Siang Rd; ⊙11am-midnight; ☎; ⓂChinatown) Laced with cockfighting posters, machinery-turned-furniture and exposed copper pipes, jump-

SINGAPORE DRINKING & NIGHTLIFE

SPLURGE

It's a compulsory and costly cliché to sink a Singapore Sling (S$30) in the Long Bar (open 11am to 12.30am) at Raffles Hotel (p614). However, if you'd like more bang for your buck, perch up at one of Singapore's rooftop bars and catch the skyline sunset, eye-wateringly priced drink in hand. Our picks are Level 33 (p633) and Cé la Vi Club Lounge (p633) for different vistas of the Lion City.

ing Oxwell & Co feels like a saloon crossed with a vintage workshop. Happy-hour deals (4pm to 8pm daily) include S$10 cocktails on tap. If it's on offer, try the brilliant Gin & Chronic, a sprightly blend of clove- and nutmeg-infused gin, soda water and fresh calamansi.

Potato Head Folk COCKTAIL BAR
(Map p618; ☑ 6327 1939; www.pttheadfolk.com; 36 Keong Saik Rd; ⊙ Studio 1939 & rooftop bar 5pm-midnight Tue-Sun; ☎; Ⓜ Outram Park) Offshoot of the legendary Bali bar, this standout, multilevel playground incorporates three spaces, all reached via a chequered stairwell pimped with creepy storybook murals and giant glowing dolls. Skip the Three Buns burger joint and head straight for the dark, plush glamour of cocktail lounge Studio 1939 or the laid back frivolity of the rooftop tiki bar.

Good Beer Company BEER STALL
(Map p618; 02-58, Chinatown Complex, 11 New Bridge Rd; ⊙ 6-10pm Mon-Sat; Ⓜ Chinatown) Injecting Chinatown Complex with a dose of new-school cool, this hawker-centre beer stall has an impressive booty of bottled craft suds, from Japanese Hitachino Nest to Belgian Trappistes Rochefort. A few stalls down is **Smith Street Taps** (Map p618; ⊙ 6.30-10.30pm Tue-Sat; Ⓜ Chinatown), run by a friendly dude and offering a rotating selection of craft and premium beers on tap.

🍷 Little India & Kampong Glam

Druggists BEER HALL
(Map p620; www.facebook.com/DruggistsSG; 119 Tyrwhitt Rd; ⊙ 4pm-midnight Tue-Sun; Ⓜ Lavender) Druggists is indeed addictive for beer

aficionados. Its row of 23 taps pour a rotating selection of craft brews from cognoscenti brewers like Denmark's Mikkeller and Britain's Magic Rock. The week's beers are scribbled on the blackboard, with the option of 250mL or 500mL pours. Sud-friendly grub is also available, though the place is best for drinking, not eating.

Artistry CAFE
(Map p620; ☑ 6298 2420; www.artistryspace. com; 17 Jln Pinang; ⊙ 9am-11pm Tue-Fri, 9.30am-11pm Sat, 9.30am-4pm Sun; ☎; Ⓜ Bugis) Killer coffee, rotating art exhibitions and monthly after-hours events, including singer-songwriter nights: Artistry is a hipster version of the cultural salon. Swig interesting artisanal beers and ciders or tuck into fresh, delicious grub (served till 5pm) like guilt-inducing BRB (blueberry, ricotta and bacon) pancakes or the cross-cultural chilli-crab burger.

🍷 Orchard Road Area

No 5 BAR
(Map p622; 5 Emerald Hill Rd; ⊙ noon-2am Mon-Thu, to 3am Fri & Sat, 5pm-2am Sun; Ⓜ Somerset) Not much imagination went into naming this long-running boozer, set in a 1910 Peranakan shophouse. Happy-hour deals run for much of the day, with specials including two martinis for S$19 between 9pm and 1am. Sure, it's damned touristy around here, but the cool evening ambience is sweet relief from the Orchard Rd madness.

Mezze9 BAR
(Map p622; Grand Hyatt, 10 Scotts Rd; ⊙ noon-midnight Sun-Tue, to 1am Wed-Sat; Ⓜ Orchard) Hankering for a decent martini? Head here

---

GET YOUR (HIPSTER) CAFFEINE FIX

Singaporeans' tastes are heavily driven by 'flavour of the moment', and that flavour has recently been artisanal coffee. A clutch of cafes channels the best of Melbourne, Seattle and London. If you're in need of a latte or pourover fix and fancy cafe grub, head to these places.

Chye Seng Huat Hardware (Map p620; www.cshhcoffee.com; 150 Tyrwhitt Rd; ⊙ 9am-7pm Tue-Fri, to 10pm Sat & Sun; Ⓜ Lavender)

Maison Ikkoku (Map p620; www.maison-ikkoku.net; 20 Kandahar St; ⊙ cafe 9am-10pm Mon-Thu, to midnight Fri & Sat, to 8pm Sun, bar 6pm-1am Mon-Thu, to 2am Fri-Sun; ☎; Ⓜ Bugis)

Plain (Map p618; www.theplain.com.sg; 50 Craig Rd; ⊙ 7.30am-5.30pm Mon-Fri, to 7.30pm Sat & Sun; Ⓜ Tanjong Pagar)

Coastal Settlement (☑ 6475 0200; www.thecoastalsettlement.com; 200 Netheravon Rd; ⊙ 10.30am-midnight Tue-Sun; 🚌 29)

40 Hands (www.40handscoffee.com; 78 Yong Siak St; ⊙ 8am-7pm Tue-Sun; Ⓜ Tiong Bahru)

between 6pm and 8pm Monday to Saturday and toast away at half-price. Drinks are made with the good stuff, meaning smooth, seamless libations, shaken or stirred, briny or sweet. The half-price deal includes other cocktails and house pours too, keeping all palates pleased.

 Sentosa Island

Tanjong Beach Club   BAR
(Map p626; ✆6270 1355; www.facebook.com/tanjongbeachclub; Tanjong Beach; ⊙11am-11pm Tue-Fri, 10am-midnight Sat & Sun; Ⓜ HarbourFront, then monorail to Beach) Generally cooler and scenier than the bars on Siloso beach (especially on weekends), Tanjong Beach Club is an evocative spot, with evening torches on the sand, a small, stylish pool for guests, and a sultry lounge-and-funk soundtrack.

Woobar   BAR
(Map p626; www.wsingaporesentosacove.com; W Singapore, 21 Ocean Way, Sentosa Cove; ⊙11.30am-1am Mon-Fri, 9am-1am Sat & Sun; ☎; Ⓜ HarbourFront, then monorail to Beach) The W Singapore's hotel bar is glam and camp, with suspended egg-shaped pods, gold footrests and floor-to-ceiling windows looking out at palms and pool. The afternoon 'high tea' (weekdays/weekends from S$65/75 for two) is served in dainty birdcages, while the Wednesday ladies night (from S$36) comes with free-pour bubbly between 7.30pm and 9pm, followed by half-price drinks until midnight.

☆ **Entertainment**

Singaporeans love the cinema (a cheap way to dodge the tropical heat; tickets cost S$10 or so). The *Straits Times, I-S Magazine* and *Time Out* have listings for movies, theatre and music. Tickets for most events are available through SISTIC (Map p622; ✆6348 5555; www.sistic.com.sg).

Chinese Theatre Circle   OPERA
(Map p618; ✆6323 4862; www.ctcopera.com; 5 Smith St; show & snacks S$25, show & dinner S$40; ⊙7-9pm Fri & Sat; Ⓜ Chinatown) Teahouse evenings organised by this nonprofit opera company are a wonderful, informal introduction to Chinese opera. Every Friday and Saturday at 8pm there is a brief talk on Chinese opera, followed by a 45-minute excerpt from an opera classic, performed by actors in full costume. You can also opt for a preshow Chinese meal at 7pm. Book ahead.

FREE CONCERTS

The **Esplanade – Theatres on the Bay** (Map p614; ✆6828 8377; www.esplanade.com; 1 Esplanade Dr; Ⓜ Esplanade, City Hall) has free live performances and the **Singapore Symphony Orchestra** (Map p614; www.sso.org.sg; Ⓜ Esplanade) performs free at the Singapore Botanic Gardens monthly. Check the websites for details.

Timbrè @ The Substation   LIVE MUSIC
(Map p614; www.timbre.com.sg; 45 Armenian St; ⊙6pm-1am Sun-Thu, to 2am Fri & Sat; Ⓜ City Hall) Young ones are content to queue for seats at this popular live-music venue, whose daily rotating roster features local bands and singer-songwriters playing anything from pop and rock to folk. Hungry punters can fill up on soups, salads, tapas and passable fried standbys like buffalo wings and truffle fries.

BluJaz Café   JAZZ
(Map p620; www.blujazcafe.net; 11 Bali Lane; admission from $5; ⊙noon-1am Mon-Thu, to 2am Fri & Sat; ☎; Ⓜ Bugis) Bohemian pub BluJaz is one of the best options in town for live music, with regular jazz jams, and other acts playing anything from blues to rockabilly. Check the website for the list of rotating events, which include DJ-spun funk, R&B and retro nights, as well as 'Talk Cock' open-mic comedy nights on Wednesday and Thursday.

🔒 **Shopping**

Once renowned as a bargain paradise, Singapore has been overtaken by other cities in the region, but there are still bargains to be had on items such as clothing, electronics, IT gear and books. Major high-street brands such as Uniqlo and H&M often run sales. Prices are usually fixed, except at markets and in smaller nonchain stores (don't start bargaining if you don't have any real interest in purchasing).

 Orchard Road

Singapore's premier shopping strip; you would need the best part of a week to explore every floor of every mall in the Orchard Rd area.

Ngee Ann City
MALL

(Map p622; www.ngeeanncity.com.sg; 391 Orchard Rd; ⊙10am-9.30pm; Ⓜ Somerset) It might look like a forbidding mausoleum, but this marble-and-granite behemoth promises retail giddiness on its seven floors. International luxury brands compete for space with sprawling bookworm nirvana **Kinokuniya** (Map p622; www.kinokuniya.com.sg; ⊙10am-9.30pm Sun-Fri, to 10pm Sat; Ⓜ Somerset) and upmarket Japanese department store **Takashimaya** (Map p622; www.takashimaya.com.sg; ⊙10am-9.30pm; Ⓜ Somerset), home to Takashimaya Food Village, one of the strip's best food courts.

ION Orchard Mall
MALL

(Map p622; www.ionorchard.com; 430 Orchard Rd; ⊙10am-10pm; Ⓜ Orchard) Rising directly above Orchard MRT station, futuristic ION is the cream of Orchard Rd malls. Basement floors focus on mere-mortal high-street labels like Zara and Uniqlo, while upper-floor tenants read like the index of *Vogue*. Dining options span food-court bites to posher nosh, and the attached 56-storey tower offers a top-floor viewing gallery, **ION Sky** (www.ionorchard.com/en/ion-sky.html; ⊙3-6pm, last entry 5.30pm) `FREE`.

🗎 Little India & Kampong Glam

Little India bursts with handicrafts, gold, saris, incense, Bollywood music and DVDs. In Kampong Glam, wander along **Bussorah Street** and **Arab Street** for handicrafts, raw cloth and tourist trinkets. **Haji Lane** has a series of stores selling up-to-the-minute fashion...assuming they haven't shut down because of soaring rents.

Mustafa Centre
DEPARTMENT STORE

(Map p620; www.mustafa.com.sg; 145 Syed Alwi Rd; ⊙24hr; Ⓜ Farrer Park) Little India's bustling 24-hour Mustafa Centre is a magnet for budget shoppers, most of them from the subcontinent. It's a sprawling place, selling everything from electronics and garish gold jewellery to shoes, bags, luggage and beauty products. There's also a large supermarket with a great range of Indian foodstuffs. If you can't handle crowds, avoid the place on Sunday.

Bugis Street Market
MARKET

(Map p620; www.bugis-street.com; Victoria St; ⊙11am-10pm; Ⓜ Bugis) What was once Singapore's most infamous sleaze pit – packed with foreign servicemen on R&R, gambling dens and 'sisters' (transvestites) – is now its most famous undercover street market, crammed with cheap clothes, shoes, accessories and manicurists especially popular with teens and 20-somethings. In a nod to its past, there's even a sex shop.

Sim Lim Square
ELECTRONICS, MALL

(Map p620; www.simlimsquare.com.sg; 1 Rochor Canal Rd; ⊙10.30am-9pm; Ⓜ Rochor) A byword for all that is cut-price and geeky, Sim Lim is jammed with stalls selling PDAs, laptops, cameras, soundcards and games consoles. If you know what you're doing, there are some deals to be had, but the untutored are likely to be out of their depth. Bargain hard (yet politely) and always check that the warranty is valid in your home country.

ⓘ Orientation

The Singapore River cuts the city in two: south is the CBD and Chinatown, and to the north is the Colonial District. The trendy Clarke and Robertson Quays, and the popular Boat Quay dining areas, hug the riverbanks.

Further north from the Colonial District are Little India and Kampong Glam, the Muslim quarter. Northwest of the Colonial District is Orchard Rd, Singapore's premier shopping strip.

To the west of the island, the predominantly industrial area of Jurong contains a number of tourist attractions. Heading south you'll find the recreational islands of Sentosa, Kusu and St John's.

Eastern Singapore has some historical (and sleazy) suburbs such as Geylang and Katong, and East Coast Park and Changi Airport. The central north of the island has much of Singapore's remaining forest and the zoo.

ⓘ Information

EMERGENCY

Ambulance, Fire (☏ 995)
Police (☏ 999)

INTERNET ACCESS

Hostels offer free internet via PCs or wi-fi. Travellers with wi-fi-enabled devices should sign up for free wireless internet, Wireless@SG, available in most malls and many public buildings. You need a mobile phone with a working SIM (local or global roaming) to register.

MEDIA

Free publications with events information, such as *Juice* and *SG*, are available at tourist offices, most major hotels and several restaurants, cafes and bars. The international listings magazine *Time Out* has a Singapore edition.

English daily newspapers include the pro-government broadsheet the *Straits Times*, the *Business Times* and the tabloid-style *New Paper*. *Today* and *Mypaper* are freebie tabloids that you can pick up at MRT stations.

MEDICAL SERVICES

Raffles Hospital (Map p620; ☑ 6311 1111; www.rafflesmedicalgroup.com.sg; 585 North Bridge Rd; Ⓜ Bugis) Located close to Bugis MRT station.

Singapore General Hospital (☑ 6321 4311; www.sgh.com.sg; block 1, Outram Rd; Ⓜ Outram Park) Also has an emergency room.

TOURIST INFORMATION

Singapore Visitors Centre @ ION Orchard (Map p622; level 1, ION Orchard Mall, 2 Orchard Turn; ⊙10am-10pm; Ⓜ Orchard)

Singapore Visitors Centre @ Orchard (Map p622; ☑ 1800 736 2000; www.yoursingapore.com; 216 Orchard Rd; ⊙ 9.30am-10.30pm; Ⓜ Somerset) Singapore's main tourist-information centre, with brochures, customised itineraries and design-savvy souvenirs.

UNDERSTAND SINGAPORE

Singapore Today

Singapore is undergoing a development boom, gearing up to boost its population to 6.5 million and to position itself as a centre for everything from biomedical research to tourism. Large casino resorts on Sentosa Island and at Marina South were completed in 2011, while the entire Marina Bay area around the Esplanade theatre has been turned into an upmarket commercial, residential, leisure, botanic gardens and water-sports centre (talk about a Swiss army knife of civic planning!). New subway lines are being installed, which, when completed, will rival London's Tube.

In 2015, Singapore celebrated 50 years of independence and dealt with the passing of Lee Kuan Yew, Singapore's first prime minister and who is often referred to as the country's 'founding father'. He is credited with turning Singapore from a tiny fishing port into the financial and cultural hub it is today. Both events have re-instilled national pride throughout the island nation.

Singapore has been named among the most expensive cities to live in recent years, taking out the top spot in 2014 and 2015.

Current Singaporean concerns include the soaring cost of living, overpopulation and the influx of foreign workers.

History

Lion City

Singapore was originally a tiny sea town squeezed between powerful neighbours Sumatra and Melaka. According to Malay legend, a Sumatran prince spotted a lion while visiting the island of Temasek, and on the basis of this good omen he founded a city there called Singapura (Lion City).

Raffles

Sir Thomas Stamford Raffles arrived in 1819 to secure a strategic base for the British Empire in the Strait of Melaka. He decided to transform the sparsely populated, swampy island into a free-trade port. The layout of central Singapore is still as Raffles drew it.

WWII

The glory days of the empire came to an abrupt end on 15 February 1942, when the Japanese invaded Singapore. For the rest of WWII the Japanese ruled the island harshly, jailing Allied prisoners of war at Changi Prison and killing thousands of locals. Although the British were welcomed back after the war, their days in the region were numbered.

Foundation for the Future

The socialist People's Action Party (PAP) was founded in 1954, with Lee Kuan Yew as its secretary general. Lee led the PAP to victory in elections held in 1959, and hung onto power for more than 30 years. Singapore was kicked out of the Malay Federation in 1965, but Lee pushed through an ambitious, strict and successful industrialisation program.

His successor in 1990 was Goh Chok Tong, who loosened things up a little, but maintained Singapore on the path Lee had forged. In 2004 Goh stepped down to make way for Lee's son, Lee Hsien Loong.

Lee the Younger faces the huge challenge of positioning Singapore to succeed in the modern, globalised economy. As manufacturing bleeds away to cheaper competitors, the government is focused on boosting its population, attracting more 'foreign talent' and developing industries such as tourism, financial services, digital media and bio-medical research.

People & Culture

The National Psyche

Affluent Singaporeans live in an apparently constant state of transition, continuously urged by their ever-present government to upgrade, improve and reinvent. On the surface, these are thoroughly modernised people, but many lives are still ruled by old beliefs and customs. There is also a sharp divide between the older generation, who experienced the huge upheavals and relentless graft that built modern Singapore, and the pampered younger generation, who enjoy the fruits of that labour.

Lifestyle

While family and tradition are important, many young people live their lives outside of home, working long hours and staying out late after work.

The majority of the population lives in Housing Development Board flats (you can't miss them). These flats are heavily subsidised by the government (which even dictates the ratio of races living in each block). These subsidies favour married couples, while singles and gay and lesbian couples have to tough it out on the private real-estate market.

Women have equal access to education and employment. Likewise, despite the oft-touted anti-homosexual stance of the government, gay men and lesbians are a visible part of everyday life in Singapore.

Population

The majority of the 5.57 million people are Chinese (74.2% of the population). Next come the Malays (13.3%), Indians (9.2%) and Eurasians and 'others' (3.3%). Western expats are a very visible group. Also visible is the large population of domestic maids and foreign labourers. Contrary to popular belief, English is the first language of Singapore. Many Singaporeans speak a second language or dialect (usually Mandarin, Malay or Tamil).

Religion

The Chinese majority are usually Buddhists or Taoists, and Chinese customs, superstitions and festivals dominate social life.

The Malays embrace Islam as a religion and a way of life. *Adat* (customary law) guides important ceremonies and events, including birth, circumcision and marriage.

More than half the Indians are Hindus and worship the pantheon of gods in various temples across Singapore.

Christianity, including Catholicism, is also popular in Singapore, with both Chinese and Indians pledging their faith to this religion.

Environment

Singapore's chief environmental issue is rubbish disposal. The government has recognised the need to encourage recycling, both industrial and domestic. However, massive government effort doesn't necessarily translate to environmental awareness on the ground level. Locals still love plastic shopping bags, and many get domestic helpers to wash their cars daily. Singaporeans are encouraged to recycle but aren't provided with easy means to do so (all waste in public flats still goes into one central bin).

Air quality is much better than in most large Southeast Asian metropolises, but the annual haze that descends on the island around September and October, generated by slash-and-burn fires in Indonesia, is a serious concern.

Much of Singapore's fresh water is imported from Malaysia but, with large reservoirs, desalination plants and a huge waste-water recycling project called Newater, Singapore hopes to become self-sufficient within the next few decades. Tap water is safe to drink.

Singapore has a proud and well-deserved reputation as a garden city. Parks, often beautifully landscaped, are abundant and the entire centre of the island is a green oasis. However, Singapore loves to build, and large areas of forest are being cleared to make way for residential and infrastructure development.

SURVIVAL GUIDE

ℹ️ Directory A–Z

ACCOMMODATION

Hostels offer competitive prices (S$20 to S$40 for a dorm bed) and facilities such as free internet, breakfast and laundry use. Cheaper en suite hotel rooms (S$50 to S$100) are cramped and often windowless. Most places offer air-con rooms. Establishments usually quote net prices, which include all taxes. If you see ++ after a price, you'll need to add a 10% service charge and 7% GST.

The following price ranges refer to a double room without bathroom in high season. Room prices quoted include all taxes.

$ less than S$100 (US$80)

$$ S$100 to S$250 (US$80 to US$200)

$$$ more than S$250 (US$200)

CUSTOMS REGULATIONS

You can bring in 1L each of wine, beer and spirits duty-free. Alternatively, you are allowed 2L of wine and 1L of beer, or 2L of beer and 1L of wine. Cigarettes are dutiable except for a personal opened pack. Duty-free concessions are not available if you are arriving from Malaysia or if you've been out of Singapore for less than 48 hours.

ELECTRICITY

Electricity is 230V, 50Hz; plugs usually have three flat pins.

EMBASSIES & CONSULATES

For a full list of foreign embassies and consulates in Singapore, check out the Ministry of Foreign Affairs (www.mfa.gov.sg) website.

Australian High Commission (Map p622; ✆6836 4100; www.australia.org.sg; 25 Napier Rd; 🚌7, 75, 77, 105, 106, 123, 174)

Canadian High Commission (Map p614; ✆6854 5900; www.singapore.gc.ca; level 11, 1 George St; Ⓜ Clarke Quay, Raffles Pl)

Dutch Embassy (Map p622; ✆6737 1155; www.mfa.nl/sin; level 13, Liat Towers, 541 Orchard Rd; Ⓜ Orchard)

French Embassy (✆6880 7800; www.ambafrance-sg.org; 101-103 Cluny Park Rd; Ⓜ Botanic Gardens)

German Embassy (Map p614; ✆6533 6002; www.singapur.diplo.de; level 12, Singapore Land Tower, 50 Raffles Pl; Ⓜ Raffles Pl)

New Zealand High Commission (Map p614; ✆6235 9966; www.nzembassy.com/singapore; level 21, 1 George St; Ⓜ Clarke Quay, Raffles Pl)

UK High Commission (Map p622; ✆6424 4200; www.gov.uk/government/world/singapore; 100 Tanglin Rd; 🚌7, 75, 77, 105, 106, 111, 123, 132, 174)

US Embassy (Map p622; ✆6476 9100; http://singapore.usembassy.gov; 27 Napier Rd; 🚌7, 75, 77, 105, 106, 123, 174)

FOOD

Bear in mind that most restaurant prices will have 17% added to them at the end: a 10% service charge plus 7% for GST. You'll see this indicated by ++ on menus.

The following price ranges refer to the all-inclusive price of a single dish or a main course.

$ less than S$10

$$ S$10 to S$30

$$$ over S$30

LGBT TRAVELLERS

Male homosexuality is still technically illegal, but laws have not prevented the emergence of a thriving gay scene. Check out www.utopia-asia.com and www.fridae.asia for coverage of venues and events.

LEGAL MATTERS

The law is extremely tough in Singapore, but also relatively free from corruption. Possession and trafficking of drugs is punishable by death. Smoking in all public places, including bars, restaurants and hawker centres, is banned unless there's an official smoking 'area'.

MAPS

The *Official Map of Singapore*, available free from the STB, the airport and hotels, is excellent.

MONEY

The country's unit of currency is the Singapore dollar, locally referred to as the 'singdollar', which is made up of 100 cents. Singapore uses 5¢, 10¢, 20¢, 50¢ and $1 coins, while notes come in denominations of $2, $5, $10, $50, $100, $500 and $1000. The Singapore dollar is a highly stable and freely convertible currency.

Cirrus-enabled ATMs are widely available at malls, banks, MRT stations and commercial areas.

Moneychangers are easily found in most malls and busy locations; you don't get charged any fees and you can haggle a little if you're changing a large-ish quantity.

OPENING HOURS

Banks 9.30am to 4.30pm Monday to Friday – some branches open at 10am and some close at 6pm or later; Saturday 9.30am to noon or later.

Government offices (Including post offices) Between 8am and 9.30am to between 4pm and 6pm Monday to Friday; between 8am and 9am to 11.30am and 1.30pm Saturday.

GETTING TO MALAYSIA: SINGAPORE TO JOHOR BAHRU OR TANJUNG BELUNGKOR

While you can enter Malaysia via Tanjung Belungkor by boat, the following options provide better onward transport connections.

Getting to the borders The easiest way to reach the border is on the **Causeway Link Express** (www.causewaylink.com.my). Buses run every 15 to 30 minutes between 6am and 11.45pm; fares are S$3.30/RM3.40 one way. There are several routes, with stops including **Queen Street Bus Terminal** (Map p620; cnr Queen & Arab Sts; Ⓜ Bugis), Newton Circus, Jurong East Bus & MRT Interchange, and Kranji MRT station.

At the borders At the Singapore checkpoint, disembark from the bus with your luggage to go through immigration, and reboard the next bus (keep your ticket). After repeating the process on the Malaysian side, it's a quick walk into central JB.

Moving on Most routes also stop at Larkin Bus Terminal (Larkin Sentral), 5km from central JB. From here, long-distance buses depart to numerous Malaysian destinations, including Melaka, Kuala Lumpur and Ipoh.

For information on making this crossing in the opposite direction, see p418.

Restaurants Top restaurants generally open between noon and 2pm for lunch and 6pm till 10pm for dinner. Casual restaurants and food courts are open all day.

Shops 10am to 6pm; larger shops and department stores open till 9.30pm or 10pm. Some smaller shops in Chinatown and Arab St close on Sunday. It's busiest in Little India on Sunday.

POST

Postal delivery in Singapore is very efficient. Call ☏ 1605 to find the nearest branch or check www.singpost.com.sg.

PUBLIC HOLIDAYS

The only holiday that has a major effect on the city is Chinese New Year, when virtually all shops shut down for two days.

New Year's Day 1 January
Chinese New Year Three days in January/February
Good Friday April
Labour Day 1 May
Vesak Day June
Hari Raya Puasa July
National Day 9 August
Hari Raya Haji September
Deepavali November
Christmas Day 25 December

RESPONSIBLE TRAVEL

Modern and cosmopolitan though it appears, Singapore is a little sensitive when it comes to brash behaviour by foreigners – quiet, polite behaviour will win you more respect. Public transport is efficient and you can even call hybrid-fuel taxis.

SAFE TRAVEL

Short-term visitors are unlikely to be troubled by Singapore's notoriously tough laws, which have turned the city into one of the safest in Asia. Street crime is minimal, though pickpockets have been known to operate in Chinatown, Little India and other tourist areas.

TELEPHONE

There are no area codes in Singapore; landline telephone numbers are eight digits unless you are calling toll-free (☏ 1800).

Mobile-phone numbers in Singapore start with 8 or 9.

You can buy a SIM card (usually S$15) with data at local telco stores, post offices and convenience stores; you'll need to show your passport.

TOILETS

Toilets in Singapore are clean and well maintained, though they might vary between the sit-down and rarer squatting types. In some hawker centres you may have to pay S$0.10. You can find toilets in malls, fast-food outlets and large hotels.

TRAVELLERS WITH DISABILITIES

A large government campaign has seen ramps, lifts and other facilities progressively installed around the island. The footpaths in the city are nearly all immaculate, MRT stations all have lifts, and there are some buses and taxis equipped with wheelchair-friendly equipment.

The **Disabled People's Association Singapore** (☏ 6791 1134; www.dpa.org.sg; Jurong Point Shopping Centre) can provide information on accessibility in Singapore.

VISAS

Citizens of most countries are granted 90-day entry on arrival. Citizens of India, Myanmar, the Commonwealth of Independent States and most Middle Eastern countries must obtain a visa before arriving in Singapore. Visa extensions can be applied for at the **Immigration & Checkpoints Authority** (Map p620; ☑ 6391 6100; www.ica.gov.sg; 10 Kallang Rd; Ⓜ Lavender).

VOLUNTEERING

The National Volunteer & Philanthropy Centre (www.nvpc.org.sg) coordinates a number of community groups, including grassroots projects in areas such as education, the environment and multiculturalism.

WOMEN TRAVELLERS

There are few problems for women travelling in Singapore. In Kampong Glam and Little India skimpy clothing may attract unwanted stares. Tampons and pads are widely available across the island, as are over-the-counter medications.

❶ Getting There & Away

AIR

Changi Airport (☑ 6595 6868; www.changi airport.com), 20km northeast of Singapore CBD, is Singapore's main international airport, with three terminals and a fourth opening in 2017.

It's serviced by an abundance of global carriers and has frequent flights to all corners of the globe. You'll find free internet, courtesy phones for local calls, foreign-exchange booths, 24-hour hotel-reservations counters, medical centres, left luggage, hotels, a movie theatre and children's playground, themed gardens, day spas, showers, a gym, a swimming pool and no shortage of shops.

BUS

Numerous private companies run comfortable bus services to many destinations in Malaysia, including Melaka and Kuala Lumpur, as well as Thailand. Many of these services run from the **Golden Mile Complex** (5001 Beach Rd; Ⓜ Nicoll Hwy); shop around or book online at www.bus onlineticket.com.

TRAIN

As of July 2015 it's no longer possible to catch a direct train from Singapore to Kuala Lumpur. Instead Malaysian company Keretapi Tanah Melayu Berhad (p478) operates a shuttle train from **Woodlands Train Checkpoint** (11 Woodlands Crossing; ☐ 170, Causeway Link Express from Queen Street Bus Terminal) to JB Sentral with a connection to Kuala Lumpur. Tickets for the shuttle (S$5) can be bought at the counter. Air-con express trains leave three times daily (sleeper/1st/2nd class RM39/33/18) for the seven-hour run from Johor Bahru to Kuala Lumpur, with connections on to Thailand. You can book tickets at the stations or via the KTM (www. ktmb.com.my) website.

BOAT

There are several main ferry terminals with services to Malaysia and Indonesia:

Changi Point Ferry Terminal (☑ 6545 2305; 51 Lorong Bekukong; Ⓜ Tanah Merah, then bus 2)

HarbourFront Cruise & Ferry Terminal (Map p626; ☑ 6513 2200; www.singaporecruise. com; Ⓜ HarbourFront)

Tanah Merah Ferry Terminal (☑ 6513 2200; www.singaporecruise.com; Ⓜ Tanah Merah, then bus 35)

Indonesia

These are the main ferry operators that travel to Indonesia:

BatamFast (☑ HarbourFront terminal 6270 2228, ☑ Tanah Merah terminal 6542 6310; www.batamfast.com) Ferries to Batam Centre, Sekupang, Harbour Bay and Nongsapura.

SINGAPORE GETTING THERE & AWAY

GETTING TO INDONESIA: SINGAPORE TO THE RIAU ARCHIPELAGO

Getting to the borders Ferries and speedboats run between Singapore and the Riau archipelago islands (including Pulau Batam, Pulau Bintan, Tanjung Balai and Tanjung Batu) in Indonesia. The ferries are modern, fast and air-conditioned. Expect to pay around S$24 for a one-way ticket to Batam, and S$45 to Bintan, Balai or Batu. Ferries to Batam Centre, Sekupang and WaterFront City (all on Batam) depart from the HarbourFront ferry terminal. Ferries to Nongsapura (also Batam) depart from the Tanah Merah terminal.

At the borders The border post at Batam ferry terminal is open during ferry operational hours, and immigration on both sides is straightforward. You'll have to purchase an Indonesian visa (US$35 for 30 days) upon arrival at any of the islands.

Moving on From Pulau Batam, you can find ferries on to Tanjung Buton on the Sumatran mainland, from where it's a three-hour bus ride to Palembang.

For information on making this crossing in the opposite direction, see p253.

ℹ TRANSPORT MADE EZ

If you're going to be using the MRT and buses a lot, it's cheaper and more convenient to buy a S$12 **EZ-Link card** from any MRT station (S$5 nonrefundable deposit). Top up your card using cash or ATM card at station ticket machines or at 7-Elevens.

Alternatively, a **Singapore Tourist Pass** (www.thesingaporetouristpass.com. sg) offers unlimited train and bus travel for one day (S$10), two days (S$16) and three day (S$20).

Bintan Resort Ferries (☑ 6542 4369; www. brf.com.sg) Ferries to Bandar Bintan Telani.

Indo Falcon (☑ 6278 3167; www.indofalcon. com.sg) Ferries to Tanjung Balai.

Sindo Ferries (☑ HarbourFront terminal 6271 4866, Tanah Merah terminal 6542 7105; www. sindoferry.com.sg) Ferries to Batam Centre, Sekupang, Waterfront, Tanjung Balai and Tanjung Pinang.

Malaysia

Limbongan Maju Ferry Services (☑ Tangjung Belungkor 02 827 8001; www.tanjungbelungkor.com) Ferries to Tanjung Belungkor.

ℹ Getting Around

BICYCLE

There is an ever-expanding network of bike paths connecting Singapore's many parks. Search 'Park Connectors' on the website of the National Parks Board (www.nparks.gov.sg) for a map of the bike paths.

The 12km bike path along East Coast Park makes for a good ride; hire a decent mountain bike from S$6 at one of the numerous booths here. You can also get in-line skates.

BUS

Public buses run to every corner of the island. Each bus stop has information on bus numbers and routes. Fares cost S$1.40 to S$2.50 (less with an EZ-Link card). You can pay by cash (you'll need the exact amount, as no change is given), or tap your EZ-Link card or Singapore Tourist Pass on the reader as you board, then again when you get off.

TAXI

The major cab company is Comfort Taxi and CityCab (☑ 6552 1111).

Fares start from S$3 to S$3.90 for the first kilometre, then $0.22 for 400m. There are a raft of surcharges, eg late-night services (50%), peak-hour charges (25%), restricted-zone charges, airport pick-ups and bookings. All taxis are metered. Extra charges are always shown on the meter except for going into a restricted zone during peak hours. You can flag down a taxi any time or use a taxi rank outside hotels and malls. Singapore also has a fast growing Uber tribe.

MASS RAPID TRANSIT (MRT)

The MRT subway system is the easiest, quickest and most comfortable way to get around. The system operates from 5.30am to around midnight, with trains at peak times running every two to three minutes, and off-peak every five to seven minutes. Single-trip tickets cost S$1.60 to S$2.70.

TRISHAW

Bicycle trishaws congregate at popular tourist places, such as Raffles Hotel and outside Chinatown Complex. Agree on the fare beforehand. Expect to pay around S$40 for half an hour. There's also a fixed-price trishaw tour system at **Trishaw Uncle** (Map p620; www.trishawuncle. com.sg; Queen St; 30min tour adult/child from $39/29, 45min tour $49/39; Ⓜ Bugis).

Thailand

📞 66 / POP 68.65 MILLION

Best for Regional Specialities

➡ nahm (p666)

➡ Tong Tem Toh (p694)

➡ Hua Hin Koti (p735)

Best Places for Culture

➡ Cooking courses in Chiang Mai (p689)

➡ Loi Krathong in Ayuthaya (p671)

➡ Trekking in Mae Hong Son (p708)

Why Go?

Thailand is an abundant land with naturally good looks and warm hospitality. A stunning coastline lapped at by cerulean seas invites winter-weary travellers, while the northern mountains that cascade into the misty horizon invite scenic journeys. In between are emerald-coloured rice fields and busy, prosperous cities built around sacred temples. The markets are piled high with pyramids of colourful fruits and tasty treats can be found on every corner.

You'll suffer few travelling hardships, save for a few pushy touts, in this land of comfort and convenience. Bangkok reigns as an Asian superstar, Chiang Mai excels in liveability and the tropical islands are up all night to party. It is relatively cheap to hop around by plane or leapfrog anywhere else in the region, though once you leave you'll miss the fiery curries and simple stir-fries that earn Thai cuisine global acclaim.

When to Go?
Bangkok

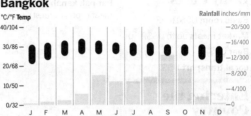

Nov–Feb Cool and dry season; peak tourist season is December to January.

Mar–Jun Hot season is hot but a good shoulder season for the beaches.

Jul–Oct Wet season begins with a drizzle and ends with a downpour; July to August is a mini high season.

AT A GLANCE

Currency Baht (B)

Language Thai

Money ATMs widespread; 150B withdrawal fee on foreign accounts

Visas 30-day free visa for air arrivals; 30- or 15-day free visa (depending on nationality) for land arrivals; pre-arrange 60-day tourist visas

Mobile phones Affordable pre-paid local SIM card on a GMS phone

Fast Facts

Area 513,000 sq km

Capital Bangkok

Country code ☑ 66

Emergency ☑ 191

Exchange Rates

Australia	A$1	26B
Cambodia	10,000r	88B
Euro	€1	39B
Laos	10,000K	44B
Malaysia	RM10	83B
UK	UK£1	55B
US	US$1	35B

Daily Costs

Basic room US$11–28

Market meals up to US$2.50

Beer US$3

Local transport US$1

Entering the Country

Fly to Bangkok's Suvarnabhumi Airport. Land crossings include Poipet/Aranya Prathet (Cambodia), Huay Xai/Chiang Khong (Laos) and Ko Lipe/Langkawi (Malaysia).

Don't Miss

Seeing the early-morning alms route – when barefoot, orange-robed monks walk the streets collecting food from the faithful – is one of the great highlights (made easy when suffering from jet lag) in Thailand. The silent procession transforms Thailand's otherwise deafening cities into calm, meditative spaces.

ITINERARIES

One Week

Get tussled about by Bangkok's chaos, then cruise up to Sukhothai to tour the quiet old ruins. Continue north to Chiang Mai, an easygoing cultural city. Climb up the mountain range to Pai for mountain scenery and bluesy late-nighters.

Two Weeks

From Bangkok, continue south to the Samui islands (Ko Samui, Ko Pha-Ngan, Ko Tao) to become a certified beachaholic and diver. Then hop the peninsula to the Andaman beaches of Railay, Ko Phi-Phi and Ko Lanta.

Essential Food

Pàt gàprow gài Fiery stir-fry of chopped chicken, chillies, garlic and fresh basil.

Kôw pàt Fried rice, you never knew it could be so good; garnish it with ground chillies, sugar, fish sauce and a squirt of lime.

Pàt prík tai krà-thiam gài/mŏo Stir-fried chicken or pork with black pepper and garlic.

Pàt tai Thailand's oh-so-famous dish of rice noodles fried with egg and prawns garnished with bean sprouts, peanuts and chillies; eaten with chopsticks.

Pàt pàk kanáh Stir-fried Chinese greens, often fried with meat (upon request), served over rice; simple but delicious.

BANGKOK

POP 9.6 MILLION

Bored in Bangkok? You've got to be kidding. This high-energy city loves neon and noise, chaos and concrete, fashion and the future. But look beyond the modern behemoth and you'll find an old-fashioned village napping in the shade of a narrow soi (lane). It's an urban connoisseur's dream: a city where the past, present and future are jammed into a humid pressure cooker.

You'll probably pass through Bangkok en route to some place else as it is a convenient transport hub. At first you'll be confounded, then relieved and pampered when you return, and slightly sentimental when you depart for the last time.

◎ Sights

The country's most historic and holy sites are found in Ko Ratanakosin, the former royal district. To soak up Bangkok's urban atmosphere, wander around Chinatown. And to escape the heat and congestion, explore Mae Nam Chao Phraya, especially around sunset.

◎ Ko Ratanakosin & Around

With its royal and religious affiliations, this area hosts many Thai Buddhist pilgrims as well as foreign sightseers.

The temples with royal connections enforce a strict dress code – clothes should cover to the elbows and knees and foreigners should not wear open-toed shoes. Behave respectfully and remove shoes when instructed. Do your touring early in the morning to avoid the heat and the crowds. And ignore anyone who says that the sight is closed.

★Wat Phra Kaew & Grand Palace
BUDDHIST TEMPLE

(วัดพระแก้ว, พระบรมมหาราชวัง; Map p654; Th Na Phra Lan; 500B; ◷8.30am-3.30pm; ⚓Chang Pier, Maharaj Pier, Phra Chan Tai Pier) Also known as the Temple of the Emerald Buddha, Wat Phra Kaew is the colloquial name of the vast, fairy-tale compound that also includes the former residence of the Thai monarch, the Grand Palace.

This ground was consecrated in 1782, the first year of Bangkok rule, and is today Bangkok's biggest tourist attraction and a pilgrimage destination for devout Buddhists and nationalists. The 94.5-hectare grounds encompass more than 100 buildings that

THAILAND BANGKOK

OUTSMARTING THE SCAM ARTISTS

Commit these classic rip-offs to memory and join us in our ongoing crusade to outsmart Bangkok's scam artists.

Closed today Ignore any 'friendly' local who tells you that an attraction is closed for a Buddhist holiday or for cleaning. These are set-ups for trips to a bogus gem sale or shopping.

Túk-túk rides for 10B Say goodbye to your day's itinerary if you climb aboard this ubiquitous scam. These 'tours' bypass the sights and instead cruise to the overpriced tailors and gem shops that pay commissions.

Flat-fare taxi ride Flatly refuse any driver who quotes a flat fare, which will usually be three times more than the meter rate. Head out to the street and flag down a cab. If the driver 'forgets' to turn on the meter, just say, 'Meter, kâ/kráp' (female/male speaker).

Long-distance tourist buses Buy your long-distance bus tickets from the government-run bus stations instead of tourist-centre agents selling private tourist bus tickets. Agents charge commission fees or deliver cut-rate services for VIP rates. Readers have consistently reported thefts from personal bags and stowed luggage from private buses.

Friendly strangers Be wary of smartly dressed locals who approach you asking where you're from and where you're going. Their opening gambit is usually followed with: 'Ah, my son/daughter is studying at university in (your city)'. This sort of behaviour is out of character for Thais and is usually a prelude to the notorious gem scam.

Unset gems Bangkok is no place to be an amateur gem trader. Never accept an invitation to visit a gem shop and refuse to purchase unset stones that can supposedly be resold in your home country.

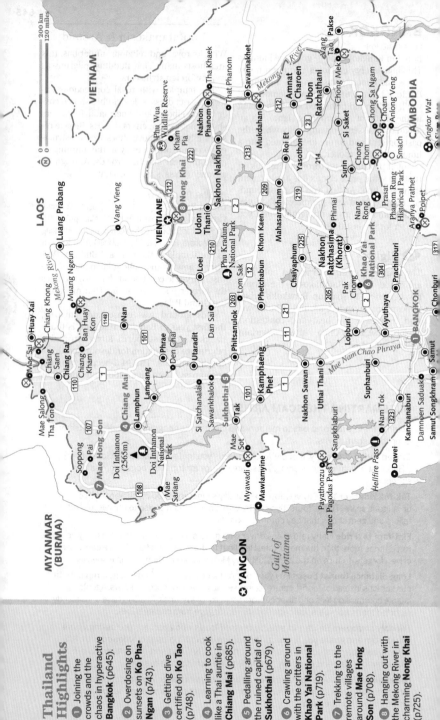

Thailand Highlights

1 Joining the crowds and the chaos in hyperactive **Bangkok** (p645).

2 Overdosing on sunsets on **Ko Pha-Ngan** (p743).

3 Getting dive certified on **Ko Tao** (p748).

4 Learning to cook like a Thai auntie in **Chiang Mai** (p685).

5 Pedalling around the ruined capital of **Sukhothai** (p679).

6 Crawling around with the critters in **Khao Yai National Park** (p719).

7 Trekking to the remote villages around **Mae Hong Son** (p708).

8 Hanging out with the Mekong River in charming **Nong Khai** (p725).

Central Bangkok

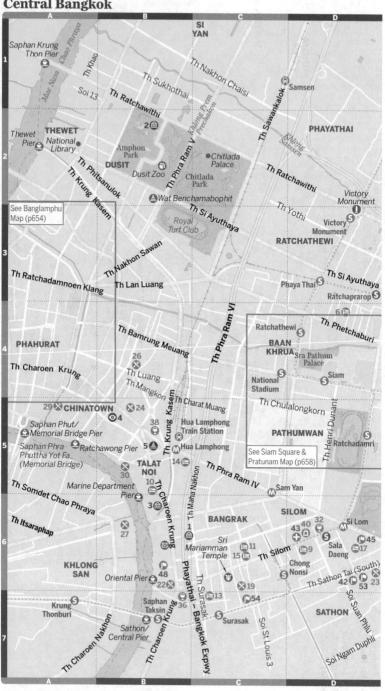

649

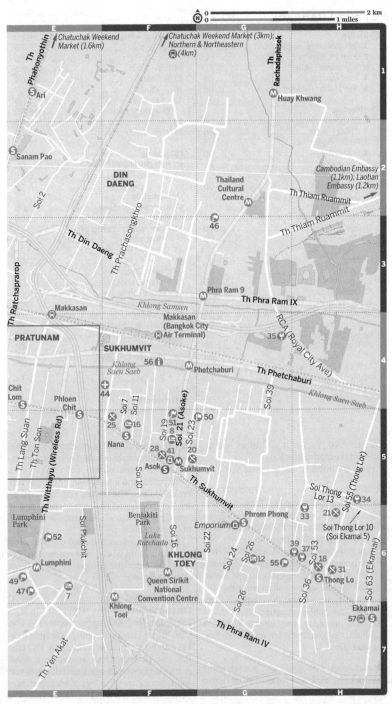

Central Bangkok

represent 200 years of royal history and architectural experimentation.

For more information, see p652.

★ Wat Pho
BUDDHIST TEMPLE

(วัดโพธิ์/วัดพระเชตุพน, Wat Phra Chetuphon; Map p654; Th Sanam Chai; 100B; ◷8.30am-6.30pm; ⛴Tien Pier) You'll find (slightly) fewer tourists here than at Wat Phra Kaew, but Wat Pho is our fave among Bangkok's biggest sights. In fact, the compound incorporates a host of superlatives: the city's largest reclining Buddha, the largest collection of Buddha images in Thailand, and the country's earliest centre for public education.

Almost too big for its shelter is Wat Pho's highlight, the genuinely impressive **Reclining Buddha**.

★ Wat Arun
BUDDHIST TEMPLE

(วัดอรุณฯ; Map p654; www.watarun.net; off Th Arun Amarin; 50B; ◷8am-6pm; ⛴cross-river ferry from Tien Pier) After the fall of Ayuthaya, King Taksin ceremoniously clinched control here on the site of a local shrine and established a royal palace and a temple to house the Emerald Buddha. The temple was renamed after the Indian god of dawn (Aruna) and in honour of the literal and symbolic founding of a new Ayuthaya.

At time of research, the spire of Wat Arun was closed until 2016 due to renovation. Visitors can enter the compound, but cannot climb the tower.

Amulet Market
MARKET

(ตลาดพระเครื่องวัดมหาธาตุ; Map p654; Th Maha Rat; ◷7am-5pm; ⛴Chang Pier, Maharaj Pier, Phra Chan Tai Pier) This arcane and fascinating market claims both the footpaths along Th Maha Rat and Th Phra Chan, as well as a dense network of covered market stalls that run south from Phra Chan Pier; the easiest entry point is clearly marked Trok Maha That. The trade is based around small talismans carefully prized by collectors, monks, taxi drivers and people in dangerous professions.

Museum of Siam
MUSEUM

(สถาบันพิพิธภัณฑ์การเรียนรู้แห่งชาติ; Map p654; www.museumsiam.org; Th Maha Rat; 300B; ⏱10am-6pm Tue-Sun; ♿; ⛴Tien Pier) This fun museum employs a variety of media to explore the origins of the Thai people and their culture. Housed in a European-style 19th-century building that was once the Ministry of Commerce, the exhibits are presented in a contemporary, engaging and interactive fashion not typically found in Thailand's museums. They are also refreshingly balanced and entertaining, with galleries dealing with a range of questions about the origins of the nation and its people.

National Museum
MUSEUM

(พิพิธภัณฑสถานแห่งชาติ; Map p654; 4 Th Na Phra That; 200B; ⏱9am-4pm Wed-Sun; ⛴Chang Pier, Maharaj Pier, Phra Chan Tai Pier) Often touted as Southeast Asia's biggest museum, Thailand's National Museum is home to an impressive, albeit occasionally dusty, collection of items, best appreciated on one of the museum's twice-weekly guided **tours** (Map p654; National Museum, 4 Th Na Phra That; free with museum admission; ⏱9.30am Wed & Thu; ⛴Chang Pier, Maharaj Pier).

Most of the museum's structures were built in 1782 as the palace of Rama I's viceroy, Prince Wang Na. Rama V turned it into a museum in 1874, and today there are three permanent exhibitions spread out over several buildings. At the time of research some of the exhibition halls were being renovated.

⊙ Chinatown & Phahurat

Cramped and crowded Chinatown is a beehive of commercial activity. Th Yaowarat is fun to explore at night when it is lit up like a Christmas tree and filled with food vendors. The area is undergoing a renaissance with an infusion of new and artsy businesses, like the art gallery-hang out spot, **Soy Sauce Factory** (Map p648; www.facebook.com/soysaucefactory; Soi 24, Th Charoen Krung; ⏱10am-7pm Tue-Sun; Ⓜ Hua Lamphong exit 1).

Wat Traimit
(Golden Buddha)
BUDDHIST TEMPLE

(วัดไตรมิตร, Temple of the Golden Buddha; Map p648; Th Mittaphap Thai-China; 40B; ⏱8am-5pm; ⛴Ratchawong Pier, Ⓜ Hua Lamphong exit 1) The attraction at Wat Traimit is undoubtedly the

impressive 3m-tall, 5.5-tonne, **solid-gold Buddha image**, which gleams like, well, gold. Sculpted in the graceful Sukhothai style, the image was 'discovered' some 40 years ago beneath a stucco/plaster exterior, when it fell from a crane while being moved to a new building within the temple compound.

Talat Mai
MARKET

(ตลาดใหม่; Map p648; Soi Yaowarat 6/Charoen Krung 16; ⏱6am-6pm; ⛴Ratchawong Pier, Ⓜ Hua Lamphong exit 1 & taxi) With nearly two centuries of commerce under its belt, New Market is no longer an entirely accurate name for this strip of commerce. Regardless, this is Bangkok's, if not Thailand's, most Chinese market, and the dried goods, seasonings, spices and sauces will be familiar to anyone who's ever spent time in China. Even if you're not interested in food, the hectic atmosphere (be on guard for motorcycles squeezing between shoppers) and exotic sights and smells culminate in something of a surreal sensory experience.

⊙ Other Areas

★Jim Thompson House
HISTORIC BUILDING

(Map p658; www.jimthompsonhouse.com; 6 Soi Kasem San 2; adult/student 150/100B; ⏱9am-6pm, compulsory tours every 20 min; ⛴klorng boat to Sapan Hua Chang Pier, Ⓢ National Stadium exit 1) This jungly compound is the former home of the eponymous American silk entrepreneur and art collector. Born in Delaware in 1906, Thompson briefly served in the Office of Strategic Services (the forerunner of the CIA) in Thailand during WWII. He settled in Bangkok after the war, when his neighbours' handmade silk caught his eye and piqued his business sense; he sent samples to fashion houses in Milan, London and Paris, gradually building a steady worldwide clientele.

Erawan Shrine
MONUMENT

(ศาลพระพรหม; Map p658; cnr Th Ratchadamri & Th Phloen Chit; ⏱6am-11pm; Ⓢ Chit Lom exit 8) FREE The Erawan Shrine was originally built in 1956 as something of a last-ditch effort to end a string of misfortunes that occurred during the construction of a hotel, at that time known as the Erawan Hotel.

Bangkokian Museum
MUSEUM

(พิพิธภัณฑ์ชาวบางกอก; Map p648; 273 Soi 43, Th Charoen Krung; admission by donation; ⏱10am-4pm

(Continued on page 656)

THAILAND BANGKOK

Wat Phra Kaew & Grand Palace

EXPLORE BANGKOK'S PREMIER MONUMENTS TO RELIGION AND REGENCY

The first area tourists enter is the Buddhist temple compound generally referred to as Wat Phra Kaew. A covered walkway surrounds the area, the inner walls of which are decorated with the **murals of the** *Ramakian* ❶ and ❷. Originally painted during the reign of Rama I (r 1782–1809), the murals, which depict the Hindu epic the *Ramayana*, span 178 panels that describe the struggles of Rama to rescue his kidnapped wife, Sita.

After taking in the story, pass through one of the gateways guarded by *yaksha* ❸ to the inner compound. The most important structure here is the *bòht*, or ordination hall ❹, which houses the **Emerald Buddha** ❺.

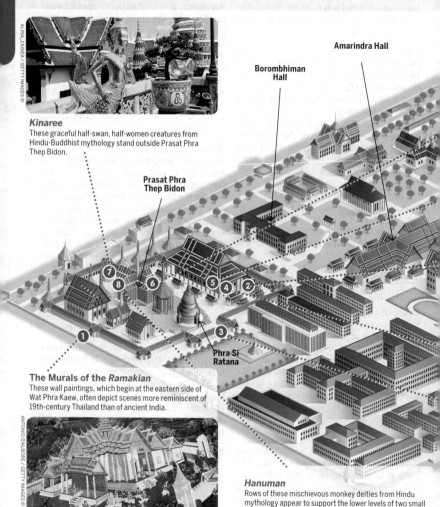

Kinaree
These graceful half-swan, half-women creatures from Hindu-Buddhist mythology stand outside Prasat Phra Thep Bidon.

Amarindra Hall

Borombhiman Hall

Prasat Phra Thep Bidon

❼ ❽ ❻ ❺ ❹ ❷

❶

❸

Phra Si Ratana

The Murals of the *Ramakian*
These wall paintings, which begin at the eastern side of Wat Phra Kaew, often depict scenes more reminiscent of 19th-century Thailand than of ancient India.

Hanuman
Rows of these mischievous monkey deities from Hindu mythology appear to support the lower levels of two small *chedi* near Prasat Phra Thep Bidon.

Head east to the so-called Upper Terrace, an elevated area home to the **spires of the three primary chedi** ⑥. The middle structure, Phra Mondop, is used to house Buddhist manuscripts. This area is also home to several of Wat Phra Kaew's noteworthy mythical beings, including beckoning *kinaree* ⑦ and several grimacing **Hanuman** ⑧.

Proceed through the western gate to the compound known as the Grand Palace. Few of the buildings here are open to the public. The most noteworthy structure is **Chakri Mahaprasat** ⑨. Built in 1882, the exterior of the hall is a unique blend of Western and traditional Thai architecture.

The Three Spires
The elaborate seven-tiered roof of Phra Mondop, the Khmer-style peak of Prasat Phra Thep Bidon, and the gilded Phra Si Ratana *chedi* are the tallest structures in the compound.

Emerald Buddha
Despite the name, this diminutive statue (it's only 66cm tall) is actually carved from nephrite, a type of jade.

The Death of Thotsakan
The panels progress clockwise, culminating at the western edge of the compound with the death of Thotsakan, Sita's kidnapper, and his elaborate funeral procession.

Chakri Mahaprasat
This structure is sometimes referred to as *fa·ràng sài chá·dah* (Westerner in a Thai crown) because each wing is topped by a *mon·dòp*: a spire representing a Thai adaptation of a Hindu shrine.

Dusit Hall

Yaksha
Each entrance to the Wat Phra Kaew compound is watched over by a pair of vigilant and enormous *yaksha*, ogres or giants from Hindu mythology.

Bòht (Ordination Hall)
This structure is an early example of the Ratanakosin school of architecture, which combines traditional stylistic holdovers from Ayuthaya along with more modern touches from China and the West.

Banglamphu

THAILAND BANGKOK

Phra Athit/
Banglamphu Pier

Phra Pin Klao
Bridge Pier

Th Phra Athit

Saphan Phra
Pin Klao

Th Chao Fa

Bangkok
Information
Center

Th Somdet Phra Pin Klao

Soi Ram Buttri

17

Th
Roongmai

Bangkok Noi
(Thonburi)
Train Station

Khlong
Bangkok Noi

25

THONBURI

Thonburi Railway
Station Pier

7

Th Na Phra That

Sanam
Luang

Siriraj
Hospital

Phra Chan
Pier

Thammasat
University

Wang Lang/
Siriraj Pier

Th Phra Chan

Th
Phrannok

4

Th Ratchadamnoen Nai

Soi Tambon
Wanglang 1

Th Maha Rat

Maharaj
Pier

Silpakorn
University

Wat Rakhang Pier

Th Na Phra Lan

5

Th Lak
Meuang

BANGKOK
NOI

Chang Pier

Mae Nam Chao Phraya

Th Sanam Chai

Wat Phra Kaew
& Grand Palace

3

Saranrom
Royal
Garden

Khlong Mon

KO RATANAKOSIN

Th Arun Amarin

Th Thai Wang

Wat Pho

2

Tien Pier

Th Chetuphon

Wat Arun Pier

19

Wat Arun

1

Soi Pratu
Nokyung

6

Banglamphu

(Continued from page 651)

Wed-Sun; 🚤 Si Phraya/River City Pier) A collection of three antique buildings from the early 20th century, the Bangkokian Museum illustrates an often-overlooked period of Bangkok's history.

Dusit Palace Park　　MUSEUM, HISTORIC SITE
(วังสวนดุสิต; Map p648; bounded by Th Ratchawithi, Th U Thong Nai & Th Nakhon Ratchasima; adult/child 100/20B, or free with Grand Palace ticket; ⊙9.30am-4pm Tue-Sun; 🚤Thewet Pier, 🚇Phaya Thai exit 2 & taxi) Following his first European tour in 1897, Rama V (King Chulalongkorn; r 1868–1910) returned with visions of European castles and set about transforming these styles into a uniquely

Thai expression, today's Dusit Palace Park. Today, the current king has yet another home (in Hua Hin) and this complex now holds a house museum and other cultural collections.

Because this is royal property, visitors should wear shirts with sleeves and long pants (no capri pants) or long skirts.

☞ Tours

Bangkok Food Tours　　WALKING TOUR
(☎095 943 9222; www.bangkokfoodtours.com; tours from 1150B) Half-day culinary tours of Bangkok's older neighbourhoods.

Grasshopper Adventures　　BICYCLE TOUR
(Map p654; ☎02 280 0832; www.grasshopper-adventures.com; 57 Th Ratchadamnoen Klang; half-/full-day tours from 1100/1600B; ⊙8.30am-6.30pm; 🚤klorng boat to Phanfa Leelard Pier) This lauded outfit runs a variety of unique bicycle tours in and around Bangkok, including a night tour and a tour of the city's green zones.

✰ Festivals & Events

Chinese New Year　　CULTURAL
(⊙Jan or Feb) Thai-Chinese celebrate the lunar New Year with a week of housecleaning, lion dances and fireworks. Most festivities centre on Chinatown. Dates vary.

Songkran　　CULTURAL
(⊙mid-Apr) The celebration of the Thai New Year has morphed into a water war with high-powered water guns and water balloons being launched at suspecting and unsuspecting participants. The most intense water battles take place on Th Khao San.

Royal Ploughing Ceremony　　CULTURAL
(⊙May) His Majesty the King (or lately the Crown Prince) commences rice-planting season with a ceremony at Sanam Luang. Dates vary.

Vegetarian Festival　　FOOD
(⊙Sep or Oct) A 10-day Chinese-Buddhist festival wheels out yellow-bannered streetside vendors serving meatless meals. The greatest concentration of vendors is found in Chinatown. Dates vary.

Loi Krathong　　CULTURAL
(⊙early Nov) A beautiful festival where, on the night of the full moon, small lotus-shaped boats made of banana leaf and containing a lit candle are set adrift on Mae Nam Chao Phraya.

🛏 Sleeping

Because the city has legendary traffic jams, narrow your search first by the geography then by budget. If you're in the city for a layover, stay as close to your next mode of transport as possible.

🛏 Th Khao San, Banglamphu & Thewet

If you're returning to 'civilisation' and need traveller amenities, then the backpacker ghetto of Th Khao San and surrounding Banglamphu is cheap and convenient. The area is packed with guesthouses and hostels, though the main drag can get rowdy with nightly revelry. Quieter corners can be found in Thewet, the district north of Banglamphu near the National Library.

★ Chern   HOSTEL $

(Map p654; ☑02 621 1133; www.chernbangkok. com; 17 Soi Ratchasak; dm 400B, r 1400-1900B; ❄@🎧; 🚤 klorng boat to Phanfa Leelard Pier) The vast, open spaces and white, overexposed tones of this hostel converge in an almost afterlife-like feel. The eight-bed dorms are above average, but we particularly like the private rooms, which, equipped with attractively minimalist touches, a vast desk, TV, safe, fridge and heaps of space, are a steal at this price.

NapPark Hostel   HOSTEL $

(Map p654; ☑02 282 2324; www.nappark.com; 5 Th Tani; dm 440-650B; ❄@🎧; 🚤 Phra Athit/ Banglamphu Pier) This popular hostel features dorm rooms of various sizes, the smallest and most expensive of which boasts six pod-like beds outfitted with power points, mini-TV, reading lamp and wi-fi. Cultural activities and inviting communal areas ensure that you may not actually get the chance to plug in.

Fortville Guesthouse   HOTEL $

(Map p654; ☑02 282 3932; www.fortvilleguest-house.com; 9 Th Phra Sumen; r 870-1120B; ❄@🎧; 🚤 Phra Athit/Banglamphu Pier) With an exterior that combines elements of a modern church and/or castle, and an interior that relies on mirrors and industrial themes, the design concept of this hotel – undergoing a renovation at the time of research – is tough to pin down. The rooms themselves are stylishly minimal, and the more expensive ones include perks such as a fridge and balcony.

Suneta Hostel Khaosan   HOSTEL $

(Map p654; ☑02 629 0150; www.sunetahostel.com; 209-211 Th Kraisi; dm incl breakfast 490-590B, r incl breakfast 1180B; ❄@🎧; 🚤 Phra Athit/Banglamphu Pier) A pleasant, low-key atmosphere, a unique, retro-themed design (some of the dorm rooms resemble sleeping car carriages), a location just off the main drag and friendly service are what make Suneta stand out.

Penpark Place   HOTEL $

(Map p654; ☑02 628 8896; www.penparkplace.com; 22 Soi 3, Th Samsen; r 330-1650B, ste 2200B; ❄@🎧; 🚤 Thewet Pier) This former factory has been turned into a good-value budget hotel. A room in the original building is little more than a bed and a fan, but an adjacent add-on sees a handful of well-equipped apartment-like rooms and suites.

Sam Sen Sam Place   GUESTHOUSE $$

(Map p654; ☑02 628 7067; www.samsensam.com; 48 Soi 3, Th Samsen; r incl breakfast 590-2400B; ❄@🎧; 🚤 Thewet Pier) One of the homeliest places in this area, if not Bangkok, this colourful, refurbished antique villa gets glowing reports about its friendly service and quiet location. Of the 18 rooms here, all are extremely tidy, and the cheapest are fan-cooled and share a bathroom.

🛏 Chinatown

Hotels near the Hualamphong train station are cheap but not especially interesting and the traffic along Th Phra Ram IV has to be heard to be believed. The surrounding neighbourhood of Chinatown makes for fascinating urban adventures and is sprouting more hip hangouts than before.

BANGKOK BY WATER

You can observe remnants of urban river life by boarding a **Chao Phraya Express boat** at any riverside pier. Women should take care not to accidentally bump into a monk and should not sit next to them or stand in the same area of the boat.

You can also charter a longtail boat to explore **Khlong Bangkok Noi** and other scenic canals in Thonburi. Longtail boats can be arranged from any river pier, including Tha Chang. Just remember to negotiate a price before departure.

Siam Square & Pratunam

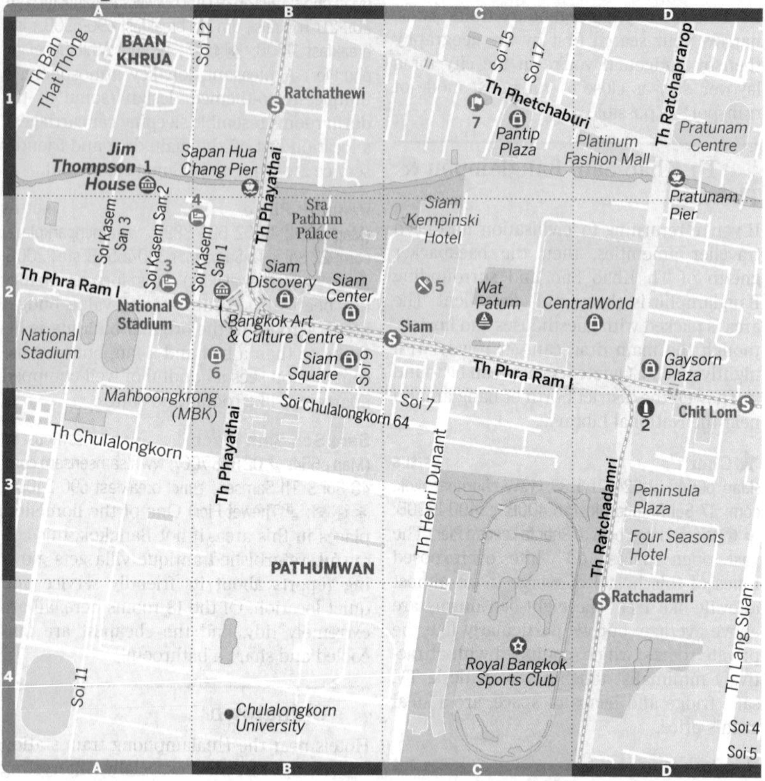

Siam Classic GUESTHOUSE $
(Map p648; ☎02 639 6363; 336/10 Trok Chalong Krung; r incl breakfast 450-1200B; ❄@📶; ⛴Ratchawong Pier, Ⓜ Hua Lamphong exit 1) The rooms here don't include much furniture, and the cheapest don't include air-con or en-suite bathrooms, but an effort has been made at making them feel comfortable, tidy and even a bit stylish. An inviting ground-floor communal area encourages meeting and chatting, and the whole place exudes a welcoming homestay vibe.

Loftel 22 HOSTEL $
(Map p648; www.loftel22bangkok.com; 952 Soi 22, Th Charoen Krung; dm 350B, r 900-1350B; ❄@📶; ⛴Marine Department Pier, Ⓜ Hua Lamphong exit 1) Stylish, inviting dorms and private rooms (all with shared bathrooms) have been coaxed out of these two adjoining shophouses. Friendly service and a location in one of Chinatown's most atmospheric corners round out the package.

Feung Nakorn Balcony HOTEL $$
(Map p654; ☎02 622 1100; www.feungnakorn.com; 125 Th Fuang Nakhon; incl breakfast dm 700B, r 1650B, ste 2100-4700B; ❄@📶; ⛴Saphan Phut/Memorial Bridge Pier, Pak Klong Taladd Pier) Located in a former school, the 42 rooms here surround an inviting garden courtyard and are generally large, bright and cheery. Amenities such as a free minibar, safe and flat-screen TV are standard, and the hotel has a quiet and secluded location away from the strip, with capable staff. A charming and inviting (if not particularly great-value) place to stay.

Siam Square

If you need to be centrally located, opt for Siam Sq, which is on both BTS (Skytrain) lines. Accommodation here is more expensive than Banglamphu but you'll save in cab fares. You can also bypass rush-hour traffic between here and Th Khao San by hopping on the *klorng* boat at Tha Ratchathewi.

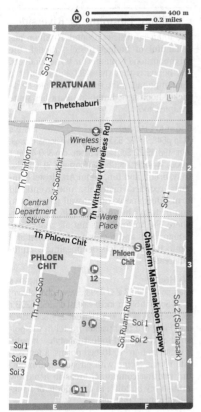

and relatively well equipped (TV, fridge) for this price range.

Boxpackers Hostel HOSTEL $
(Map p648; ☎02 656 2828; www.boxpackershostel.com; 39/3 Soi 15, Th Phetchaburi; incl breakfast dm 500-800B, r 1260-1530B; ❋@☎; ⑤Ratchathewi exit 1 & taxi) A contemporary, sparse hostel with dorms ranging in size from four to 12 double-decker pods – some of which are double beds. Communal areas are inviting, and include a ground-floor cafe and a lounge with pool table. A linked hotel also offers 14 small but similarly attractive private rooms.

⌂ Sukhumvit

Th Sukhumvit is a high-end international neighbourhood that isn't the most budget-friendly crash pad. But it is near the Eastern (Ekamai) bus station and on the BTS and MRT lines; the MRT links to the Hualamphong train station. Be warned that the lower-numbered soi attract sex tourists visiting the nearby go-go bars.

Suk 11 HOSTEL $
(Map p648; ☎02 253 5927; www.suk11.com; 1/33 Soi 11, Th Sukhumvit; r incl breakfast 535-1712B; ❋@☎; ⑤Nana exit 3) Extremely well run and equally popular, this rustic guesthouse is an oasis of woods and greenery in the

THAILAND BANGKOK

★**Lub*d** HOSTEL $
(Map p658; ☎02 634 7999; www.siamsquare.lubd.com; Th Phra Ram I; dm 590B, r 1550-2000B; ❋@☎; ⑤National Stadium exit 1) The title is a play on the Thai *làp dee*, meaning 'sleep well', but the fun atmosphere at this modern-feeling hostel might make you want to stay up all night. Diversions include an inviting communal area stocked with games and a bar, and thoughtful facilities range from washing machines to a theatre room. If this one's full, there's another branch just off **Th Silom** (Map p648; ☎02 634 7999; www.silom.lubd.com; 4 Th Decho; dm 550-600B, r 1250-1900B; ❋@☎; ⑤Chong Nonsi exit 2).

Wendy House HOSTEL $
(Map p658; ☎02 214 1149; www.wendyguesthouse.com; 36/2 Soi Kasem San 1; r incl breakfast 750-2000B; ❋@☎; ⑤National Stadium exit 1) The rooms at this long-standing budget option are small and basic, but are exceedingly clean

urban jungle that is Th Sukhumvit. The rooms are basic, clean and comfy, if a bit dark, while the cheapest of them share bathrooms. Although the building holds nearly 70 rooms, you'll still need to book at least two weeks ahead.

Pause Hostel
HOSTEL $

(Map p648; ☑ 02 108 8855; www.onedaybkk.com; Oneday, 51 Soi 26, Th Sukhumvit; incl breakfast dm 450-550B, r 1300-2000B; ✲ @ ☎; ⑤ Phrom Phong exit 4) Attached to a cafe/co-working space is this modern, open-feeling hostel. Dorms span four to eight beds, and like the private rooms (only some of which have en-suite bathrooms) are united by a handsome industrial-design theme and inviting, sun-soaked communal areas.

Fusion Suites
HOTEL $$

(Map p648; ☑ 02 665 2644; www.fusionbangkok.com; 143/61-62 Soi 21/Asoke, Th Sukhumvit; r incl breakfast 1700-2400B; ✲ @ ☎; Ⓜ Sukhumvit exit 1, ⑤ Asok exit 1) A disproportionately funky hotel for this price range, with unconventional furnishings providing the rooms here with heaps of style, although the cheapest can be a bit dark.

SLEEPING NEAR THE AIRPORT

If you're still in transit and don't want to bed down in central Bangkok, there are more and more options on the eastern outskirts of town within striking distance of the Suvarnabhumi International Airport.

The Cottage (☑ 02 727 5858; www.thecottagesuvarnabhumi.com; 888/8 Th Lad Krabang; r incl breakfast 900-2700B; ✲ @ ☎ ≋; ⑤ Phra Khanong exit 3 & taxi, ℝ Suvarnabhumi Airport & hotel shuttle bus) Near the airport compound and within walking distance of food and shopping is this solid midranger with airport shuttle.

Novotel Suvarnabhumi Airport Hotel (☑ 02 131 1111; www.novotelairportbkk.com; Suvarnabhumi International Airport; incl breakfast r 5613-6200B, ste 8043B; ✲ @ ☎; ⑤ Phra Khanong exit 3 & taxi, ℝ Suvarnabhumi Airport & hotel shuttle bus) Has 600-plus luxurious rooms; located within the Suvarnabhumi International Airport compound.

Silom, Lumphini & Riverside

The financial district around Th Silom has a handful of budget hostels, though the neighbourhood is mainly for bigger budgets. The bonus is that the MRT links with the Hualamphong train station. The old backpacker hood near Lumphini Park has some cheapies, too.

Silom Art Hostel
HOSTEL $

(Map p648; ☑ 02 635 8070; www.silomarthostel.com; 198/19-22 Soi 14, Th Silom; dm 380-450B, r 1200B; ✲ @ ☎; ⑤ Chong Nonsi exit 3) Quirky, artsy, bright and fun, Silom Art Hostel combines recycled materials, unconventional furnishings and colourful wall paintings to culminate in a hostel that's quite unlike anywhere else in town. It's not all about style though: beds and rooms are functional and comfortable, with lots of appealing communal areas.

HQ Hostel
HOSTEL $

(Map p648; ☑ 02 233 1598; www.hqhostel.com; 5/3-4 Soi 3, Th Silom; incl breakfast dm 330-520B, r 890-990B; ✲ @ ☎; Ⓜ Si Lom exit 2, ⑤ Sala Daeng exit 2) HQ is a flashpacker hostel in the polished-concrete-and-industrial-style mould. It includes four- to 10-bed dorms, a few private rooms (some with en suite bathroom) and inviting communal areas in a narrow multistorey building in the middle of Bangkok's financial district.

ETZzz Hostel
HOSTEL $

(Map p648; ☑ 02 286 9424; www.etzhostel.com; 5/3 Soi Ngam Du Phli; dm 250-350B, r 900B; ✲ @ ☎; Ⓜ Lumphini exit 1) This narrow shophouse includes dorms ranging in size from four to 12 beds, and two private rooms (the latter equipped with en suite bathroom), all of which are united by a neat, primary colour theme and a convenient location near the MRT.

Saphaipae
HOSTEL $

(Map p648; ☑ 02 238 2322; www.saphaipae.com; 35 Th Surasak; incl breakfast dm 450B, r 1000-1600B; ✲ @ ☎; ⑤ Surasak exit 1) The bright colours, chunky furnishings and bold murals in the lobby of this hostel give Saphaipae the feel of a day-care centre for travellers – a vibe that continues through to the playful communal areas and rooms. Dorms and rooms are thoughtful and well equipped, and there's heaps of helpful travel resources and facilities.

Urban House   HOTEL $$
(Map p648; ☑081 492 7778; www.urbanh.com;
35/13 Soi Yommarat; incl breakfast r 1200B, ste
1480; ❋❅; Ⓜ Si Lom exit 2, Ⓢ Sala Daeng exit
4) There's nothing showy about this shop-
house with six rooms, but that's exactly
what we like about it. Rooms are subtle,
comfortable and relatively spacious, and
the place boasts a peaceful, homely atmos-
phere, largely due to the kind host and the
quiet residential street it's located on.

✕ Eating

No matter where you go in Bangkok, food
is never far away. Surfing the street stalls is
the cheapest and tastiest culinary pursuit,
but the city's mall food courts combine the
variety of an outdoor market without the
noise and heat.

Bangkok also offers an international
menu thanks to its many immigrant com-
munities. Chinatown is naturally good for
Chinese food; Middle Eastern fare can be
found in Little Arabia, off Th Sukhumvit;
Indian hangs out near the Hindu temple on
Th Silom; and Western cuisine dominates
Th Sukhumvit.

Do note that food vendors do not set up
on Mondays, ostensibly for citywide street
cleaning.

✕ Th Khao San & Banglamphu

Th Khao San is lined with restaurants, but
the prices tend to be high and the quality in-
authentic. Venture deeper into Banglamphu
to find old-school central Thai restaurants.

Pa Aew   CENTRAL THAI $
(Map p654; Th Maha Rat, no roman-script sign;
mains 20-60B; ⊙10am-5pm Tue-Sat; ⑤Tien Pier)
Pull up a plastic stool for some rich, sea-
food-heavy, Bangkok-style fare. It's a bare-
bones, open-air curry stall, but for taste, Pa
Aew is one of our favourite places to eat in
this part of town.

There's no English-language sign; look for
the exposed trays of food directly in front of
the Krung Thai Bank near the corner with
Soi Pratu Nokyung.

Thip Samai   CENTRAL THAI $
(Map p654; 313 Th Mahachai; mains 50-250B;
⊙5pm-2am; ⑤klorng boat to Phanfa Leelard Pier)
Brace yourself – you should be aware that the
fried noodles sold from carts along Th Khao
San have little to do with the dish known as
pàt tai. Luckily, less than a five-minute túk-

túk ride away lies Thip Samai, home to some
of the most legendary fried noodles in town.

Note that Thip Samai is closed on alter-
nate Wednesdays.

Arawy Vegetarian Food   VEGETARIAN, THAI $
(Map p654; 152 Th Din So; mains from 30B;
⊙7am-8pm; ⑤klorng boat to Phanfa Leelard Pier)
Housed in a narrow shophouse, Arawy ('De-
licious') has heaps of prepared meat-free
curries, dips and stir-fries.

Shoshana   ISRAELI $$
(Map p654; 88 Th Chakraphatdi Phong; mains 70-
240B; ⊙10am-midnight; ✐; ⑤Phra Athit/Banglam-
phu Pier) One of Khao San's longest-running
Israeli restaurants, Shoshana resembles your
grandparents' living room right down to the
tacky wall art and plastic placemats. Feel safe
in ordering anything deep-fried – they do an
excellent job of it – and don't miss the deliciously garlicky eggplant dip.

Hemlock   THAI $$
(Map p654; 56 Th Phra Athit; mains 75-280B;
⊙4pm-midnight Mon-Sat; ✐; ⑤Phra Athit/
Banglamphu Pier) Taking full advantage of its
cosy shophouse location, this perennial fa-
vourite has enough style to feel like a spe-
cial night out, but doesn't skimp on flavour
or preparation. And unlike at other similar
places, the eclectic menu here reads like an
ancient literary work, reviving old dishes
from aristocratic kitchens across the coun-
try, not to mention several meat-free items.

★ Jay Fai   CENTRAL THAI $$$
(Map p654; 327 Th Mahachai; mains 180-1000B;
⊙3pm-2am Mon-Sat; ⑤klorng boat to Phanfa
Leelard Pier) You wouldn't think so by looking
at her bare-bones dining room, but Jay Fai
is known far and wide for serving Bangkok's
most expensive *pàt kêe mow* ('drunkard's
noodles'; wide rice noodles fried with seafood and Thai herbs).

Jay Fai is located in a virtually unmarked
shophouse on Th Mahachai, directly across
from a 7-Eleven.

✕ Chinatown

Nay Hong   CHINESE-THAI $
(Map p648; off Th Yukol 2, no roman-script sign;
mains 35-50B; ⊙4-10pm; ⑤Ratchawong Pier,
Ⓜ Hua Lamphong exit 1 & taxi) The reward for lo-
cating this hole-in-the-wall is one of the best
fried noodle dishes in Bangkok. The dish in
question is *gŏo·ay đĕe·o kôo·a gài,* flat rice
noodles fried with garlic oil, chicken and egg.

THAILAND BANGKOK

Food Spotter's Guide

Spanning four distinct regions, influences from China to the Middle East, a multitude of ingredients and a reputation for spice, Thai food can be more than a bit overwhelming. So to point you in the direction of the good stuff, we've put together a shortlist of the country's must-eat dishes.

1. Đôm yam
The 'sour Thai soup' moniker featured on many English-language menus is a feeble description of this mouth-puckeringly tart and intensely spicy herbal broth.

2. Pàt tai
Thin rice noodles fried with egg, tofu and shrimp, and seasoned with fish sauce, tamarind and dried chilli, have emerged as the poster boy for Thai food – and justifiably so.

3. Gaang kĕe·o wăhn
Known outside of Thailand as green curry, this intersection of a piquant, herbal spice paste and rich coconut milk is single-handedly emblematic of Thai cuisine's unique flavours and ingredients.

4. Yam
This family of Thai 'salads' combines meat or seafood with a tart and spicy dressing and fresh herbs.

5. Lâhp
Minced meat seasoned with roasted rice powder, lime, fish sauce and fresh herbs is a one-dish crash course in the strong, rustic flavours of Thailand's northeast.

6. Bà·mèe
Although Chinese in origin, these wheat-and-egg noodles, typically served with roast pork and/or crab, have become a Thai hawker-stall staple.

7. Kôw mòk
The Thai version of *biryani* couples golden rice and tender chicken with a sweet and sour dip and a savoury broth.

8. Sôm·đam
'Papaya salad' hardly does justice to this tear-inducingly spicy dish of strips of crunchy unripe papaya pounded in a mortar and pestle with tomato, long beans, chilli, lime and fish sauce.

9. Kôw soy
Even outside of its home in Thailand's north, there's a cult following for this soup that combines flat egg-and-wheat noodles in a rich, spice-laden, coconut-milk-based broth.

10. Pàt pàk bûng fai daang
'Morning glory', a crunchy green vegetable, flash-fried with heaps of chilli and garlic, is, despite the spice, Thai comfort food.

FLOATING MARKETS

Photographs of Thailand's floating markets – wooden canoes laden with multicoloured fruits and vegetables – have become an iconic image of the kingdom. They are also a sentimental piece of history. Like all good nations do, Thailand has modernised, replacing canals with roads, and boats with vehicles. The floating markets have now crawled ashore with a few enduring throwbacks.

Taling Chan Floating Market (ตลาดน้ำตลิ่งชัน; Khlong Bangkok Noi, Thonburi; ⏰7am-4pm Sat & Sun; ⓢWongwian Yai exit 3 & taxi), located just across the river from Bangkok, is an ordinary produce market with a few floating twists. Vendors in canoes serve food to customers on floating docks. The market can be reached by longtail tours or by air-con bus 79 (16B, 25 minutes) from Ratchadamnoen Klang.

Amphawa Floating Market (ตลาดน้ำอัมพวา; Amphawa; dishes 20-40B; ⏰4-9pm Fri-Sun) is a weekend market popular with Bangkok tourists thanks to its scenic canalside setting. For a cultural immersion, spend the night in one of the village's homestays (250B to 1000B per person) and experience the after-dark firefly display on a canal tour (60B per seat, 500B charter). To get to Amphawa, take a minivan from Bangkok's Victory Monument to Phetchaburi (100B, two hours, every 45 minutes 5.15am to 8pm) or take a bus from Bangkok's Southern Bus Terminal (120B, two hours, frequent).

Damnoen Saduak Floating Market (ตลาดน้ำดำเนินสะดวก; Damnoen Saduak, Ratchaburi; ⏰7am-noon) is the most famous of them all, though it is really a floating souvenir stand catering to tourists, including a surprising number of Thai tourists. You can reach Damnoen Saduak (80B, two hours, frequent) from Bangkok's Southern Bus Terminal. Boats at the market can be hired for 100B per person and make trips into the adjacent residential canals.

To find it, proceed north from the corner of Th Suapa and Th Luang, then turn right into the first side-street; it's at the end of the narrow alleyway.

Nai Mong Hoi Thod CHINESE-THAI $
(Map p648; 539 Th Phlap Phla Chai; mains 50-70B; ⏰5-10pm Tue-Sun; 🚤Ratchawong Pier, Ⓜ Hua Lamphong exit 1 & taxi) A shophouse restaurant renowned for its delicious *or sòo·an* (mussels or oysters fried with egg and a sticky batter) and a decent crab fried rice.

Samsara JAPANESE, THAI $$
(Map p648; Soi Khang Wat Pathum Khongkha; mains 110-320B; ⏰4pm-midnight Tue-Thu, to 1am Fri-Sun; 📷; 🚤Ratchawong Pier, Ⓜ Hua Lamphong exit 1 & taxi) Combining Japanese and Thai dishes, Belgian beers and an artfully ramshackle atmosphere, Samsara is easily Chinatown's most eclectic place to eat. It's also very tasty, and the generous riverside breezes and views simply add to the package.

The restaurant is at the end of tiny Soi Khang Wat Pathum Khongkha, just west of the temple of the same name.

Royal India INDIAN $$
(Map p648; 392/1 Th Chakkraphet; mains 70-?B; ⏰10am-10pm; 📷; 🚤Saphan Phut/Memorial Bridge Pier, Pak Klong Talad Pier) Yes, we're aware that this hole-in-the-wall has been in every edition of our guide since the beginning, but after all these years it's still the most reliable place to eat in Bangkok's Little India. Try any of the delicious breads or rich curries, and don't forget to finish with a homemade Punjabi sweet.

🍴 Siam Square

Mall food courts, which are better than you would expect, are this neighbourhood's primary food troughs.

MBK Food Island THAI $
(Map p658; 6th fl, MBK Center, cnr Th Phra Ram I & Th Phayathai; mains 35-150B; ⏰10am-10pm; 📷; ⓢNational Stadium exit 4) Undergoing a renovation at the time of research, the grandaddy of the genre is set to continue its offer of dozens of vendors selling regional Thai and international dishes.

Gourmet Paradise THAI $
(Map p658; ground fl, Siam Paragon, 991/1 Th Phra Ram I; mains 35-500B; ⏰10am-10pm; 📷; ⓢSiam exits 3 & 5) The perpetually busy Gourmet Paradise unites international fast-food chains, domestic restaurants and food-

court–style stalls, with a particular emphasis on the sweet stuff.

Sukhumvit

Fine dining is Sukhumvit's strong suit. For cheap eats, check out **Pier 21** (Map p648; 5th fl, Terminal 21, cnr Th Sukhumvit & Soi 21/Asoke; mains 39-200B; ☺10am-10pm; ☑; ⓜSukhumvit exit 3, ⓢAsok exit 3), the noisy food court of Terminal 21 mall. A city overrun with mobile meals has embraced the international phenomenon of food trucks. Most food trucks hang out around Sukhumvit and serve Western comfort food (burgers, tacos, hot dogs). Check their Facebook pages for schedules: **Daniel Thaiger** (Map p648; ☑084 549 0995; www.facebook.com/danielthaiger; Soi 23, Th Sukhumvit; mains from 139B; ☺5-10.30pm; ⓜSukhumvit exit 2, ⓢAsok exit 3), **Full Moon Food Truck** (www.facebook.com/fullmoonfood-truckbkk; mains from 150B; ☺5-11.30pm) and **Orn the Road** (☑095 628 0416; www.facebook.com/orntheroadbkk; mains from 160-300B; ☺11am-7pm; ☑).

Gokfayuen   CHINESE $
(Map p648; www.facebook.com/wuntunmeen; 161/7 Soi Thong Lor 9; mains 69-139B; ☺11am-11.30pm; ⓢThong Lo exit 3 & taxi) This new place has gone to great lengths to recreate classic Hong Kong dishes in Bangkok. Couple your (house-made) wheat-and-egg noodles with roasted pork, steamed vegetables with oyster sauce, or the Hong Kong–style milk tea.

Nasir Al-Masri   MIDDLE EASTERN $$$
(Map p648; 4/6 Soi 3/1, Th Sukhumvit; mains 160-370B; ☺24hr; ☑; ⓢNana exit 1) One of several Middle Eastern restaurants on Soi 3/1, Nasir Al-Masri is easily recognisable by its floor-to-ceiling stainless steel 'theme'. Middle Eastern food often means meat, meat and more meat, but the menu here also includes several delicious vegie-based *mezze* (small dishes).

Soul Food Mahanakorn   THAI $$$
(Map p648; ☑02 714 7708; www.soulfoodmahanakorn.com; 56/10 Soi 55/Thong Lor, Th Sukhumvit; mains 140-300B; ☺5.30pm-midnight; ☑; ⓢThong Lo exit 3) Soul Food gets its interminable buzz from its dual nature as both an inviting restaurant – the menu spans tasty interpretations of rustic Thai dishes – and a bar serving deliciously boozy, Thai-influenced cocktails. Reservations recommended.

Bo.lan   THAI $$$
(Map p648; ☑02 260 2962; www.bolan.co.th; 24 Soi 53, Th Sukhumvit; set meals 980-2680B; ☺noon-2.30pm & 7-10.30pm Thu-Sun, 11.30am-10.30pm Tue & Wed; ☑; ⓢThong Lo exit 1) Upscale Thai is often more garnish than flavour, but Bo.lan has proven to be the exception. Bo and Dylan (Bo.lan is a play on words that also means 'ancient') take a scholarly approach to Thai cuisine, and generous set meals featuring full-flavoured Thai dishes are the results of this tuition (à la carte is not available; meat-free meals are). Reservations recommended.

Silom, Lumphini & Riverside

Muslim Restaurant   THAI, HALAL $
(Map p648; 1354-6 Th Charoen Krung; mains 40-140B; ☺6.30am-5.30pm; ⓔOriental Pier, ⓢSaphan Taksin exit 1) Plant yourself in any random wooden booth of this ancient eatery for a glimpse into what restaurants in Bangkok used to be like. The menu, much like the interior design, doesn't appear to have changed much in the restaurant's 70-year history, and the birianis, curries and samosas remain more Indian-influenced than Thai.

Chennai Kitchen   INDIAN $
(Map p648; 107/4 Th Pan; mains 70-150B; ☺10am-3pm & 6-9.30pm; ☑; ⓢSurasak exit 3) This thimble-sized mom-and-pop restaurant puts out some of the best southern Indian vegetarian food in town. Yard-long *dosai* (a crispy southern Indian bread) is always a good choice, but if you're feeling indecisive (or exceptionally famished) go for the banana-leaf *thali* (set meal) that seems to incorporate just about everything in the kitchen.

Never Ending Summer   THAI $$
(Map p648; ☑02 861 0953; www.facebook.com/TheNeverEndingSummer; 41/5 Th Charoen Nakhon; mains 140-350B; ☺11am-2pm & 5-11pm Mon, 11am-11pm Tue-Sun; ⓔriver-crossing ferry from River City Pier) The cheesy name doesn't do justice to this surprisingly sophisticated Thai restaurant located in a former warehouse on the river. Join Bangkok's beautiful crowd for antiquated Thai dishes such as cubes of watermelon served with a dry 'dressing' of fish, sugar and deep-fried shallots, or fragrant green curry with pork and fresh bird's-eye chilli.

THAILAND BANGKOK

★**nahm** THAI $$$

(Map p648; ☑02 625 3388; www.comohotels.com/metropolitanbangkok/dining/nahm; ground fl, Metropolitan Hotel, 27 Th Sathon Tai/South; set lunch/dinner 550-1500/2300B; dishes 280-750B; ⊙noon-2pm Mon-Fri, 7-10.30pm daily; Ⓜ Lumphini exit 2) Australian chef-author David Thompson is the man behind one of Bangkok's – and if you believe the critics, the world's – best Thai restaurants. Using ancient cookbooks as his inspiration, Thompson has given new life to previously extinct dishes with exotic descriptions such as 'smoked fish curry with prawns, chicken livers, cockles, chillies and black pepper'.

Drinking & Nightlife

Most backpackers are pleased to find that the party finds them on Th Khao San, where night-time equals the right time for a drink. If you feel like a wander there are hip watering holes sprinkled throughout the city.

Bangkok's curfew (1am for bars, 2am for clubs) is strictly enforced, though there are always loopholes. Smoking is banned from all indoor bars and clubs and some open-air places as well.

Cover charges for clubs range from 100B to 800B and usually include a drink or two. Most clubs heat up after 11pm; bring your ID.

Bangkok's party people are fickle and dance clubs are used up like tissues. To chase down the crowds check out Dudesweet (www.dudesweet.org) or Paradise Bangkok (www.facebook.com/paradisebangkok), which organise popular monthly parties.

LGBT BANGKOK

Bangkok's LGBT community is loud, proud and knows how to party. A newcomer might want to visit BK (www.bk.asia-city.com) and Bangkok Lesbian (www.bangkoklesbian.com) for nightlife tips.

Bangkok's 'pink alleys' branch off Th Silom. Reliable standards include **Balcony** (Map p648; www.balconypub.com; 86-88 Soi 4, Th Silom; ⊙5.30pm-2am; 🖥; Ⓜ Si Lom exit 2, Ⓢ Sala Daeng exit 1) and **Telephone Pub** (Map p648; www.telephonepub.com; 114/11-13 Soi 4, Th Silom; ⊙6pm-1am; 🖥; Ⓜ Si Lom exit 2, Ⓢ Sala Daeng exit 1), while dance clubs cluster on Soi 2, Th Silom.

★**WTF** BAR

(Map p648; www.wtfbangkok.com; 7 Soi 51, Th Sukhumvit; ⊙6pm-1am Tue-Sun; 🖥; Ⓢ Thong Lo exit 3) Wonderful Thai Friendship (what did you think it stood for?) is a funky and friendly neighbourhood bar that also packs in a gallery space. Arty locals and resident foreigners come for the old-school cocktails, live music and DJ events, poetry readings, art exhibitions and tasty bar snacks. And we, like them, give WTF our vote for Bangkok's best bar.

★**Tep Bar** BAR

(Map p648; www.facebook.com/TEPBAR; 69-71 Soi Nana; ⊙5pm-midnight Tue-Sun; Ⓜ Hua Lamphong exit 1) We never expected to find a bar this sophisticated – yet this fun – in Chinatown. Tep does it with a Thai-tinged, contemporary interior, tasty signature cocktails, Thai drinking snacks, and come Friday to Sunday, raucous live Thai music performances.

Hippie de Bar BAR

(Map p654; www.facebook.com/hippie.debar; 46 Th Khao San; ⊙3pm-2am; 🚢 Phra Athit/Banglamphu Pier) Our vote for Banglamphu's best bar, Hippie boasts a funky retro vibe and indoor and outdoor seating, all set to the type of indie/pop soundtrack that you're unlikely to hear elsewhere in town. Despite being located on Th Khao San, there are surprisingly few foreign faces, and it's a great place to make some new Thai friends.

Iron Fairies BAR

(Map p648; www.theironfairies.com; 394 Soi 55/ Thong Lor, Th Sukhumvit; ⊙6pm-2am; Ⓢ Thong Lo exit 3 & taxi) Imagine, if you can, an abandoned fairy factory in Paris c 1912, and you'll begin to get an idea of the vibe at this popular pub/wine bar. If you manage to wrangle one of the handful of seats, you can test their claim of serving Bangkok's best burgers. There's live music after 9.30pm.

Sky Bar BAR

(Map p648; www.lebua.com/sky-bar; 63rd fl, State Tower, 1055 Th Silom; ⊙6pm-1am; 🚢 Sathon/ Central Pier, Ⓢ Saphan Taksin exit 3) Descend the Hollywood-like staircase to emerge at this bar that juts out over the Bangkok skyline and Chao Phraya River. Scenes from *The Hangover Part II* were filmed here, and the 'hangovertini' cocktail is actually quite drinkable. The views, of course, aren't bad either.

Route 66
CLUB

(Map p648; www.route66club.com; 29/33-48 RCA/ Royal City Ave; 300B; ⊙8pm-2am; Ⓜ Phra Ram 9 exit 3 & taxi) This vast club has been around just about as long as RCA has, but frequent facelifts and expansions have kept it relevant. Top 40 hip hop rules the main space here, although there are several different themed 'levels', featuring anything from Thai pop to live music.

Grease
CLUB

(Map p648; www.greasebangkok.com; 46/12 Soi 49, Th Sukhumvit; ⊙6pm-2am Mon-Sat; Ⓢ Phrom Phong exit 3 & taxi) Bangkok's youngest-feeling, hottest nightclub is also one of its biggest – you could get lost here in the four floors of dining venues, lounges and dance floors.

Studio Lam
BAR

(Map p648; www.facebook.com/studiolambangkok; Soi 51, Th Sukhumvit; ⊙6pm-1am Tue-Sun; Ⓢ Thong Lo exit 3) This new venue is an extension of uberhip record label ZudRangMa, with a Jamaican-style sound system custom-built for world and retro-Thai DJ sets and the occasional live show. Thai-influenced signature drinks bring Studio Lam to the present day.

☆ Entertainment

★ Brick Bar
LIVE MUSIC

(Map p654; www.brickbarkhaosan.com; basement, Buddy Lodge, 265 Th Khao San; 150B Sat & Sun; ⊙8pm-1.30am; ⛴ Phra Athit/Banglamphu Pier) This basement pub, one of our fave destinations in Bangkok for live music, hosts a nightly revolving cast of bands for an almost exclusively Thai crowd – many of whom will end the night dancing on the tables. Brick Bar can get infamously packed, so be sure to get there early.

Ad Here the 13th
LIVE MUSIC

(Map p654; www.facebook.com/adhere13thblues bar; 13 Th Samsen; ⊙6pm-midnight; ⛴ Phra Athit/Banglamphu Pier) Located beside Khlong Banglamphu/Khlong Rob Krung, this closet-sized blues bar is everything a neighbourhood joint should be: lots of regulars, cold beer and heart-warming tunes delivered by a masterful house band (starting at 10pm). Everyone knows each other, so don't be shy about mingling.

Ratchadamnoen Stadium
SPECTATOR SPORT

(Map p654; off Th Ratchadamnoen Nok; tickets 3rd-class/2nd-class/ringside 1000/1500/2000B; ⛴ Thewet Pier, Ⓢ Phaya Thai exit 3 & taxi)

Ratchadamnoen Stadium, Bangkok's oldest and most venerable venue for *moo·ay tai* (Thai boxing; also spelt *muay thai*), hosts matches on Monday, Wednesday and Thursday from 6.30pm to around 11pm, and Sunday at 3pm and 6.30pm. Be sure to buy tickets from the official ticket counter, not from the touts and scalpers who hang around outside the entrance.

Lumpinee Boxing Stadium
SPECTATOR SPORT

(☎02 282 3141; www.muaythailumpinee.net/en; 6 Th Ramintra; tickets 3rd-class/2nd-class/ringside 1000/1500/2000B; Ⓜ Chatuchak Park exit 2 & taxi, Ⓢ Mo Chit exit 3 & taxi) The other of Bangkok's two premier Thai boxing rings has moved to fancy new digs north of town. Matches occur on Tuesdays and Fridays from 6.30pm to 11pm, and on Saturdays at 4pm to 8.30pm and from 9pm to 12.30am. At time of research there were plans underway for a Thai boxing museum and a school for foreign fighters.

🔒 Shopping

Bangkok is a great shopping destination but smart travellers opt for a shopping spree right before their return flight to avoid hauling extra cargo across Southeast Asia.

★ Chatuchak Weekend Market
MARKET

(ตลาดนัดจตุจักร, Talat Nat Jatujak; www.chatuchak. org; Th Phahonyothin; ⊙9am-6pm Sat & Sun; Ⓜ Chatuchak Park exit 1, Kamphaeng Phet exits 1 & 2, Ⓢ Mo Chit exit 1) Among the largest markets in the world, Chatuchak seems to unite everything buyable, from used vintage sneakers to baby squirrels. Plan to spend a full day here, as there's plenty to see, do and buy. But come early, ideally around 10am, to beat the crowds and the heat.

★ MBK Center
SHOPPING CENTRE

(Map p658; www.mbk-center.com; cnr Th Phra Ram I & Th Phayathai; ⊙10am-10pm; Ⓢ National Stadium exit 4) This colossal shopping mall underwent an extensive renovation in 2015 and is set to retain its role as one of Bangkok's top attractions. On any given weekend half of Bangkok's residents (and most of its tourists) can be found here combing through a seemingly inexhaustible range of small stalls and shops that span a whopping eight floors.

Patpong Night Market
SOUVENIRS

(Map p648; Th Phat Phong & Soi Phat Phong 2; ⊙6pm-midnight; Ⓜ Si Lom exit 2, Ⓢ Sala Daeng exit 1) You'll be faced with the competing

HIGH CULTURE, LOW COST

Thai classical dance is typically promoted among package tourists as a dinner-theatre experience, but baht-minded travellers can see performances in free, or nearly free, venues.

➡ **Lak Meuang** (ศาลหลักเมือง; Map p654; cnr Th Sanam Chai & Th Lak Meuang; ⊙ 6.30am-6.30pm; ⊠ Chang Pier, Maharaj Pier, Phra Chan Tai Pier), near Wat Phra Kaew, showcases shrine dances to the guardian spirits by merit-makers whose wishes have been granted.

➡ **Erawan Shrine** (p651), next to Grand Hyatt Erawan hotel, also features shrine dances.

➡ **Artist's House** (บ้านศิลปิน; www.facebook.com/Baansilapin; Khlong Bang Luang; ⊙ 9am-6pm; ⑤ Wongwian Yai exit 2) **FREE** has free traditional Thai puppets shows on weekends at 2pm.

➡ **National Theatre** (Map p654; ☑ 02 224 1342; 2 Th Ratchini; tickets 60-100B; ⊠ Chang Pier, Maharaj Pier, Phra Chan Tai Pier) hosts traditional dance performances on the first and second Sundays of the month; tickets go on sale an hour before the 2pm performance.

---

distractions of strip-clubbing and shopping in this infamous area. And true to the area's illicit leanings, pirated goods (in particular watches) make a prominent appearance even amid a wholesome crowd of families and straight-laced couples. Bargain with determination, as first-quoted prices tend to be astronomically high.

Terminal 21   SHOPPING CENTRE
(Map p648; www.terminal21.co.th; cnr Th Sukhumvit & Soi 21/Asoke; ⊙ 10am-10pm; Ⓜ Sukhumvit exit 3, ⑤ Asok exit 3) Seemingly catering to a Thai need for wacky objects to be photographed in front of, this new mall is worth a visit for the spectacle as much as the shopping. Start at the basement-level 'airport' and proceed upwards through 'Paris', 'Tokyo' and other city-themed floors. Who knows, you might even buy something.

ℹ Information

EMERGENCY

Police (☑ 191) The police contact number functions as the de facto universal emergency number in Thailand, and can also be used to call an ambulance or report a fire.

Tourist Police (☑ 24hr hotline 1155) The best way to deal with most problems requiring police (usually a rip-off or theft) is to contact the tourist police, who are used to dealing with foreigners and can be very helpful in cases of arrest.

MEDICAL SERVICES

There are several outstanding hospitals in Bangkok with English-speaking staff.

Bangkok Christian Hospital (Map p648; ☑ 02 625 9000; www.bch.in.th/en; 124 Th Silom; Ⓜ Si Lom exit 2, ⑤ Sala Daeng exit 1) Modern hospital in central Bangkok.

Bumrungrad International Hospital (Map p648; ☑ 02 667 1000; www.bumrungrad.com/thailandhospital; 33 Soi 3, Th Sukhumvit; ⑤ Phloen Chit exit 3) An internationally accredited hospital.

POST

Main Post Office (Map p648; ☑ 02 233 1050; Th Charoen Krung; ⊙ 8am-8pm Mon-Fri, to 1pm Sat & Sun; ⊠ Oriental Pier) Bangkok's main post office.

TOURIST INFORMATION

Official tourist offices distribute maps, brochures and sightseeing advice. Don't confuse these free services with the licensed travel agents that make bookings on a commission basis. Often, travel agencies incorporate elements of the national tourism organisation name (Tourism Authority of Thailand; TAT) into their business name to confuse tourists.

Bangkok Information Center (Map p654; ☑ 02 225 7612-4; www.bangkoktourist.com; 17/1 Th Phra Athit; ⊙ 9am-7pm Mon-Fri, to 5pm Sat & Sun; ⊠ Phra Athit/Banglamphu Pier) City-specific tourism office providing maps, brochures and directions. Kiosks and booths are found around town; look for the green-on-white symbol of a mahout on an elephant.

Tourism Authority of Thailand (TAT; Map p648; ☑ 02 250 5500, call centre ☑ 1672; www.tourismthailand.org; 1600 Th Phetchaburi Tat Mai; ⊙ 8.30am-4.30pm; Ⓜ Phetchaburi exit 2) This large TAT information service has brochures and maps covering the whole country.

VISAS & IMMIGRATION

Bangkok Immigration Office (☑ 02 141 9889; www.bangkok.immigration.go.th/intro1.html; Bldg B, Government Centre, Soi 7, Th Chaeng Watthana; ⊙ 8.30am-noon & 1-4.30pm Mon-Fri; Ⓜ Chatuchak Park exit 2 & taxi, ⑤ Mo Chit exit 3 & taxi) In Bangkok, visa extensions are filed at this office.

Getting There & Away

AIR

Bangkok is the air-travel hub for Thailand and mainland Southeast Asia. When purchasing tickets, verify which Bangkok airport you'll be using.

Suvarnabhumi International Airport (☑ 02 132 1888; www.suvarnabhumiairport.com), 30km east of Bangkok, handles all international air traffic and most domestic routes. The airport name is pronounced 'sù·wan·ná·poom' and its airport code is BKK.

Don Mueang Airport (☑ 02 535 1253; www. donmueangairportthai.com), 25km north of central Bangkok, handles domestic and some international routes through budget airlines.

BUS

Eastern Bus Terminal (Map p648; ☑ 02 391 2504; Soi 40, Th Sukhumvit; Ⓢ Ekkamai exit 2) The departure point for buses to Pattaya, Rayong, Chanthaburi and other points east, except for Aranya Prathet. Most people call it *sà·tăh·nee èk·gà·mai* (Ekamai station). It's near the Ekkamai BTS station.

Northern & Northeastern Bus Terminal (Mo Chit; ☑ northeastern routes 02 936 2852, ext 602/605, northern routes 02 936 2841, ext 325/614; Th Kamphaeng Phet; Ⓜ Kamphaeng Phet exit 1 & taxi, Ⓢ Mo Chit exit 3 & taxi) Located just north of Chatuchak Park, this hectic bus station is also commonly called *kŏn sòng mŏr chít* (Mo Chit station) – not to be confused with Mo Chit BTS station. Buses depart from here for all northern and northeastern destinations, as well as international destinations including Pakse (Laos), Phnom Penh (Cambodia), Siem Reap (Cambodia) and Vientiane (Laos).

Southern Bus Terminal (Sai Tai Mai; ☑ 02 422 4444, call centre 1490; Th Boromaratchachonanee) The city's southern bus terminal lies a long way west of the centre of Bangkok. Commonly called *săi dâi mài*, it's among the more pleasant and orderly in the country. Besides serving as the departure point for all buses south of Bangkok, transport to Kanchanaburi and western Thailand also departs from here.

Suvarnabhumi Public Transport Centre (☑ 02 132 1888; Suvarnabhumi Airport) Located 3km from Suvarnabhumi International Airport, this terminal has relatively frequent departures to points east and northeast including Aranya Prathet (for the Cambodian border), Chanthaburi, Ko Chang, Nong Khai (for the Lao border), Pattaya, Rayong, Trat and Udon Thani. It can be reached from the airport by a free shuttle bus.

MINIVAN

Privately run minivans (*rót dôo*) are a convenient alternative to buses for neighbouring provinces. In Bangkok, **Victory Monument** (อนุสาวรีย์ชัย; Map p648; cnr Th Ratchawithi & Th Phayathai; ⊙24hr; Ⓢ Victory Monument exit 2) is surrounded by various minivan depots.

TRAIN

Hualamphong Train Station (☑ 02 220 4334, call centre 1690; www.railway.co.th; off Th Phra Ram IV; Ⓜ Hua Lamphong exit 2) Hualamphong is the terminus for the main rail services to the south, north, northeast and east.

Hualamphong has the following services: shower room, mailing centre, luggage storage, cafes and food courts. To get to the station from Sukhumvit take the MRT to the Hua Lamphong stop. From western points (Banglamphu, Thewet), take bus 53.

Bangkok Noi Train Station (☑ 02 418 4310, call centre 1690; www.railway.co.th; off Th Itsaraphap; Ⓢ Thonburi Railway Station, Wang Lang/Siriraj Pier, Ⓢ Wongwian Yai exit 4 & taxi) Also known as Thonburi train station, this station handles infrequent (and overpriced for foreigners) services to Nakhon Pathom, Kanchanaburi and Nam Tok.

Getting Around

Bangkok is nearly always choked with traffic. You will need a good map and a lot of patience to get around.

TO/FROM THE AIRPORTS

Suvarnabhumi International Airport

Airport Rail Link connects the airport to central Bangkok at Makkasan/Bangkok City Air Terminal and at Phaya Thai (45B, 30 minutes, from 6am to midnight). The Makkasan/Bangkok City Air Terminal has access to MRT Phetchaburi, which is convenient for Silom and Sukhumvit. The Airport Rail Link continues to Phaya Thai terminal, with access to the BTS Phaya Thai station.

Local Bus Local buses travel between central Bangkok and the airport's public transport centre, a 3km ride on a free shuttle bus from the airport. There is also a minivan service to Don Muang.

ⓘ TOURIST BUSES FROM TH KHAO SAN

Skip the long-distance bus services that originate out of Bangkok's Th Khao San; these often have hidden costs, commission-generating hassles and a high rate of theft from stowed luggage.

THANON & SOI

....

Thanon (meaning 'street') is abbreviated as 'Th' in our listings. A soi is a small street or lane that runs off a larger street. The address of a site located on a soi will be written as 48/3-5 Soi 1, Th Sukhumvit, meaning off Th Sukhumvit on Soi 1.

⇒ Bus 551 (Victory Monument; 40B, frequent from 5am to 10pm)

⇒ Bus 552 (BTS On Nut station; 20B, frequent from 5am to 10pm)

Intercity Bus The airport's public transport centre has services to other eastern cities within Thailand.

Taxi Public meter taxis (not the 'official airport taxis') queue outside of baggage claim. Taxi lines tend to be long; you can always dodge the line by flagging a cab from the arrivals hall. Touts often offer flat fares (usually inflated), but you can try to bargain for a fare closer to the meter rate. For meter taxis you must also pay a 50B airport surcharge to the driver and toll charges (usually about 75B). Politely insist that the meter is used ('Meter, *kâ/kráp*') if the driver suggests otherwise. Depending on traffic, meter rates should be as follows:

⇒ Banglamphu/Khao San: 350B to 400B

⇒ Th Sukhumvit: 200B to 250B

⇒ Th Silom: 300B to 350B

Don Muang Airport

Airport Bus These services depart from the airport to various points in central Bangkok.

⇒ A1 (BTS Mo Chit; 30B, frequent from 7.30am to 11.30pm)

⇒ A2 (BTS Mo Chit & BTS Victory Monument; 30B, every 30 minutes from 7.30am to 11.30pm)

Local Bus The following air-con buses stop on the highway in front of the airport. Local buses run 24 hours. There is also minivan service to Suvarnabhumi airport.

⇒ Bus 59 (Th Khao San; 23B)

⇒ Bus 29 (BTS Victory Monument and Hualamphong train station; 23B)

Taxi There is a 50B airport surcharge added to the meter fare and tolls are paid by the passenger.

Train Exit Terminal 1 towards the Amari Airport Hotel to connect to Don Muang train station with service to Hualamphong train station (5B to 10B, one hour, roughly every hour from 4am to 11.30am and 2pm to 9.30pm).

BOAT

Chao Phraya Express Boat (☑ 02 623 6001; www.chaophrayaexpressboat.com) is a scenic and efficient way of exploring the sights in Ko Ratanakosin, Banglamphu and parts of Silom. The boats ply a regular route along the Mae Nam Chao Phraya. During rush hour pay close attention to the boat's colour-coded flags to avoid boarding an express line. The company operates the following services:

⇒ **Express** Indicated by an orange flag; from 15B, morning and evening rush hour till about 7pm; travels from Wat Rajsingkorn to Nonthaburi, stopping at major piers only

⇒ **Local** Without a flag; 10B to 14B, morning and evening rush hour till 5.30pm Monday to Friday

⇒ **Tourist** Blue flag; 40B or 150B day pass, every 30 minutes 9.30am to 5pm; travels from Sathon/Central Pier to Phra Athit/Banglamphu piers, stopping at popular sightseeing piers

Klorng boats (9B to 19B, daylight hours) zip up and down Khlong Saen Saep, a narrow waterway connecting eastern and western Bangkok. The canals are something akin to an open sewer so try not to get splashed and take care when boarding and disembarking as the boats stop for mere seconds. Useful piers include the following:

⇒ **Tha Phan Fah** Eastern terminus, Banglamphu

⇒ **Tha Hua Chang** Siam Sq area

⇒ **Tha Pratunam** Interchange pier, BTS Chitlom

BTS & MRT

The elevated **BTS** (☑ 02 617 6000, tourist information 02 617 7341; www.bts.co.th) Skytrain is a slick ride through the modern parts of town. There are two lines: the Sukhumvit and Silom lines. Trains run frequently from 6am to 11.45pm; fares vary from 15B to 52B, or 140B for a one-day pass. Staffed booths provide change for the fare-card machines but do not sell single-fare tickets. You can buy value-stored tickets from the booths.

Trains are labelled with the line and the terminal station (indicating the direction the train is travelling). There are also interchange stations with MRT (Metro).

The underground **MRT** (☑ 02 354 2000; www.bangkokmetro.co.th) (Metro) is most useful if travelling from Silom or Sukhumvit to the Hualamphong train station. Trains operate from 6am to midnight and cost 16B to 42B, or 120B for a one-day pass. The following MRT stations provide interchange to BTS (Skytrain):

⇒ **Chatuchak** (BTS Chatuchak)

⇒ **Sukhumvit** (BTS Asoke)

⇒ **Silom** (BTS Sala Daeng)

BUS

The Bangkok bus service is frequent and frantic and is operated by **Bangkok Mass Transit Authority** (☑ 02 246 0973, call centre ☑ 1348; www.bmta.co.th). Fares for ordinary buses start at 6.50B and air-con buses at 10B. Most buses operate between 5am and 10pm or 11pm; a few run all night.

Bangkok Bus Guide, by thinknet, is the most up-to-date route map available.

TAXI

Most taxis in Bangkok are meter taxis, though some drivers 'forget' to use their meters or prefer to quote a flat (and grossly inflated) fare to tourists. Skip the cabs that park in front of hotels (they operate on a charter basis) and instead flag down a roving cab on one of the main streets. Unless it is a rainy rush hour, cabs are plentiful. Fares should generally run from 60B to 90B, depending on distance.

App-based taxi alternatives have arrived in Bangkok: try Uber or All Thai Taxi.

Motorcycle taxis camp out at the mouth of a soi to shuttle people from the main road to their destinations down the lane. Soi trips cost 10B to 20B; negotiate a fare beforehand. Motorcycle taxis are often used to get somewhere in a hurry because they can weave in and out of traffic, but their accident rates are high and often catastrophic. They are a better alternative on quiet streets where traffic is light and the walk is long.

TÚK-TÚK

The Thai version of a go-kart is Bangkok's most iconic vehicle and its most enduring hassle. Túk-túks chatter like a chainsaw, drivers take corners at an angle and they are relentless in drumming up business. There are so many túk-túk scams that you really need some tenure in the city to know how much your trip should cost before bargaining for a ride and to know when a túk-túk is handier and cheaper than a cab. You must fix fares in advance for all túk-túk rides.

If you climb aboard just for the fun of it, you might end up being taken for a ride, literally. Beware of túk-túk drivers who offer to take you on a sightseeing tour for 10B or 20B – it's a touting scheme designed to pressure you into purchasing overpriced goods.

CENTRAL THAILAND

Thailand's heartland, the central region is a fertile river plain that birthed the country's history-shaping kingdoms of Ayuthaya and Sukhothai, and crafted the culture and language that defines the mainstream Thai identity. The nationally revered river Mae Nam Chao Phraya is the lifeblood of the region and connects the country's interior with the Gulf of Thailand. Geographically, central Thailand is a necessary thoroughfare for any Chiang Mai–bound traveller, but culturally it is a must-see region.

Ayuthaya พระนครศรีอยุธยา

POP 83,217

The fabled city, the fallen city: Ayuthaya crowned the pinnacle of ancient Thai history and defined the country's ascendancy to regional domination. It was built at the confluence of three rivers (Mae Nam Lopburi, Chao Phraya and Pa Sak) on a unique island and was auspiciously named after the home of Rama in the Indian epic *Ramayana*.

The rivers formed both a natural barrier to invasion and an invitation to trade, allowing the city-state to emerge into a fully fledged nation from 1350 to 1767. Though the Thai kings outmanoeuvred Western power plays, it was eventually sacked by the Burmese, ending the city-state's reign and forcing the Thais to re-establish their power centre near present-day Bangkok.

Today, the ruins of the old city survive with many battle scars amid a modern provincial town, a slight distraction for imagining what Ayuthaya once was. To its credit, the kingdom's history is well preserved at local museums. The holiday of Loi Krathong, when tiny votive boats are floated on the rivers as a tribute to the River Goddess, is celebrated with great fanfare in Ayuthaya.

○ Sights

A Unesco World Heritage Site, Ayuthaya's ruins are divided into two geographical areas. Ruins 'on the island' are in the central part of town between Th Chee Kun and the western end of Th U Thong and are best visited by bicycle. Ruins 'off the island', on the other side of the river, are best visited on an evening boat tour or by motorbike.

Most ruins are open from 8am to 4pm; the more famous sites charge an entrance fee. A one-day pass for most sites on the island costs 220B and can be bought at the museums or ruins. The ruins are symbols of royalty and religion, and require utmost respect and proper attire (cover to elbows and knees).

◉ On the Island

★ **Ayutthaya Tourist Center**   MUSEUM
(ศูนย์ท่องเที่ยวอยุธยา; ☑ 035 246076; ☺ 8.30am-4.30pm) FREE A good first stop in Ayuthaya, the excellent upstairs museum puts everything in context with displays about the temples and daily life. Also upstairs is the tiny but interesting Ayutthaya National Art Museum. Downstairs is the tourist information centre.

THAILAND AYUTHAYA

THAILAND AYUTHAYA

Ayuthaya

1 km
0.5 miles

Th Dusit

Main Terminal (5km)

Train Station

Th Watkluay

Chao Phrom Ferry Pier

12

Saphan Pridi Damrong

20

Wat Phanan 3 Choeng

Ko Lai

Th U Thong

18

14 16 23

Soi 2

8

13

Minivans to Bangkok

Th Khlong Makhamriang

Pom Phet Fortress

Mae Nam Chao Phraya

Th Pamaphrao

24

Th Ho Rattanachai

Th Bang Ian

Th Khlong Makhamriang

Th Rotchana

15

17

Th Cheekun

19

Wat Ratchaburana

5

10

Bueng Phra Ram

7

Th Naresuan

Wat Phra Ram

Th Pa Thon

9

Th U Thong

Old Royal Palace

Ayuthaya Historical Park

Wat Phra Si Sanphet

6

Wihan Phra Mongkhon Bophit

1

Ayuthaya Tourist Center

Th Si Sanphet

22

21

Th Khlong Thaw

Mae Nam Lopburi

Th Ayuthaya – Pa Mok

Wat Worachetharam

Wat Lokayasutharam

Queen Suriyothai Memorial Pagoda

11

Mae Nam Chao Phraya

2

Wat Chai Wattanaram

Ayuthaya

★ **Wat Phra Si Sanphet** RUIN
(วัดพระศรีสรรเพชญ์; 50B; ◎8am-6pm) This ruined temple's three magnificent stupas are one of the iconic images of Ayuthaya. Built in the late 15th century, Wat Phra Si Sanphet was a royal temple inside palace grounds, and these were the models for Bangkok's Wat Phra Kaew and Royal Palace. It was Ayuthaya's largest temple and once contained a 16m-high standing Buddha (Phra Si Sanphet) covered with 143kg (or more, depending on the source) of gold, which was later melted down by Burmese conquerors.

★ **Wihan Phra
Mongkhon Bophit** BUDDHIST TEMPLE
(วิหารพระมงคลบพิตร; ◎8am-5pm) FREE Next to Wat Phra Si Sanphet, this sanctuary hall houses one of Thailand's largest bronze Buddha images. The 12.5m-high figure

(17m with the base) was badly damaged by a lightning-induced fire around 1700, and again when the Burmese sacked the city. The Buddha and the building were repaired in the 20th century. In 1956 the Burmese Prime Minister donated 200,000B to restore the building, an act of belated atonement for his country's sacking of the city 200 years before.

Wat Mahathat RUIN
(วัดมหาธาตุ; Th Chee Kun; 50B; ◎8am-6pm) The most photographed image in Ayuthaya is here: a sandstone Buddha head that lies within a bodhi tree's entwined roots. The central *prang* once stood 43m high and it collapsed on its own long before the Burmese sacked the city. It was rebuilt in more recent times, but collapsed again in 1911. Founded in 1374, during the reign of King Borom Rachathirat I, it was the seat of the supreme patriarch and the kingdom's most important temple.

★ **Wat Ratchaburana** RUIN
(วัดราชบูรณะ; 50B; ◎8am-6pm) The *prang* in this temple is one of the best extant in the city, with detailed carvings of lotus and mythical creatures. You can climb inside the *prang* to visit the brightly painted crypt, if you aren't afraid of heights, small spaces or bats. The temple was founded in 1424 by King Borom Rachathirat II, on the cremation site for his two brothers who died while fighting each other for the throne.

**Ayuthaya Historical
Study Centre** MUSEUM
(ศูนย์ศึกษาประวัติศาสตร์อยุธยา; Th Rotchana; adult/child 100/50B; ◎9am-4pm; P) This modern museum funded by Japan features exhibitions on the lives of traditional villagers and the foreign communities during the Ayuthaya kingdom, plus a few dioramas of the city's former glories. You'll have to ask someone to open the downstairs gallery.

**Chantharakasem
National Museum** MUSEUM
(พิพิธภัณฑสถานแห่งชาติจันทรเกษม; Th U Thong; 100B; ◎9am-4pm Wed-Sun) The museum is within the grounds of Wang Chan Kasem (Chan Kasem Palace), built for King Rama IV at the site of a palace used by King Naresuan and seven subsequent Ayuthayan kings. The museum is large, but the collection (Buddhist art, pottery, ancient weapons, lacquered cabinets and original furnishings) isn't – the highly decorated buildings themselves are the main attraction. The tower out back was used for the king's astronomy hobby.

ⓘ TOURING OFF THE ISLAND

A variety of tours around the city and beyond are available. They can be booked through your guesthouse, though you may get more options and flexibility by talking to a travel agent such as **Tour With Thai** (☑ 035 231084; www.tourwiththai.com; Soi 2, Th Naresuan; ◷ 8.30am-6.30pm). The most promoted trip is a two-hour afternoon boat ride (200B per person) making quick stops at Wat Phanan Choeng, Wat Phutthai Sawan and Wat Chai Wattanaram.

Chao Sam Phraya National Museum   MUSEUM
(พิพิธภัณฑสถานแห่งชาติเจ้าสามพระยา; cnr Th Rotchana & Th Si Sanphet; adult/child 150B/free; ◷ 9am-4pm; P) The largest museum in the city displays many of the treasures unearthed during excavations of the ruins, including the golden treasures found in the crypts of Wat Mahathat and Wat Ratchaburana.

◉ Off the Island

★ **Wat Phanan Choeng**   BUDDHIST TEMPLE
(วัดพนัญเชิง; 20B; ◷ dawn-dusk) A bevy of popular merit-making ceremonies makes this a hectic temple on weekends. The signature attraction is the 19m-high Phra Phanan Choeng Buddha, which was created in 1324 and sits inside a soaring *wi-hǎhn* (8am to 5pm) surrounded by 84,000 small Buddha images lining the walls. It's even more imposing than the big Buddha at Wihan Phra Mongkhon Bophit. People come here daily to cover their heads with the end of the big Buddha's robe, a ceremony that other temples normally only do on major holidays.

★ **Wat Chai Wattanaram**   RUIN
(วัดไชยวัฒนาราม; 50B; ◷ 8am-6pm) This is the most impressive off-island site thanks to its 35m-high Khmer-style central *prang* and overall good condition. It was built by King Prasat Thong beginning in 1630 (and taking around 20 years) to honour his mother, and the design's resemblance to Cambodia's Angkor Wat was intentional.

Wat Yai Chai Mongkhon   RUIN
(วัดใหญ่ชัยมงคล; 20B; ◷ 6am-6pm) King U Thong founded this temple in 1357 to house monks returning from ordination in Sri

Lanka, and in 1592 King Naresuan built its fantastic bell-shaped *chedi* after a victory over the Burmese. The landscaped gardens make this one of Ayuthaya's most photogenic ruins. There's a 7m-long reclining Buddha near the entrance and the local belief is that if you can get a coin to stick to the Buddha's feet, good luck will come your way.

🛏 Sleeping

Budget options centre around Soi 2, Th Naresuan, near the bus stop, and around the ferry landings on both sides of the river.

★ **Baan Lotus Guest House**   GUESTHOUSE $
(☑ 035 251988; Th Pamaphrao; dm 200B, s 250B d & tw 350-600B; P ✳ ◈ ❀) Near, but completely separate from, the backpacker strip, this converted teak schoolhouse with a large deck out back is a real treat, and the owner is just as charming as the building. It's so chill that almost nothing happens after 6pm, including check-in.

★ **Ayothaya Riverside House**   GUESTHOUSE $
(081 644 5328; r without bath 400B, r on boat 1500B; ✳ ◈) Across the Chao Phraya on the west side of town, this wonderful guesthouse provides a very different experience from most due to its untouristed neighbourhood setting. Regular rooms are simple shared-bath and fan affairs in an old wooden house, but this is also the only place in town where you can sleep on a boat.

Chantana Guesthouse   GUESTHOUSE $
(☑ 035 323200; chantanahouse@yahoo.com; 12/22 Soi 2, Th Naresuan; r incl breakfast 300-450B; P ✳ ◈) This spic-and-span spot is rather plain, but offers probably the best value on the backpacker strip. Staff are friendly, though English is limited. Splash out an extra 50B for a room with a balcony.

Baan Are Gong   GUESTHOUSE $
(☑ 035 235592; siriporntan@yahoo.com.sg; Soi Satani Rot Fai; r 380-1300B; ✳ ◈) Two minutes from the train station, Baan Are Gong fills a century-old teak building right on the river and is run by a welcoming family. It's not the cheapest lodging in this spot, but it's got the most character. The least-expensive rooms have shared bathrooms.

★ **Tamarind Guesthouse**   GUESTHOUSE $$
(☑ 089 010 0196; tamarindthai2012@gmail; off Th Chee Kun; r incl breakfast 600-1200B; ✳ ◈) There's a creative mix of old and new in this modified

wooden house and the service couldn't be more friendly. Hidden in a little back street directly across from Wat Mahathat, Tamarind manages to be both a peaceful getaway and right in the thick of things.

Tony's Place GUESTHOUSE $$
(☏035 252578; www.tonyplace-ayutthaya.com; Soi 2, Th Naresuan; r 200-1200B; ❄☎☏) Tony's remains the flashpackers' top choice thanks to rooms that are actually attractive, a mini-pool and the chance to swap travel tips with fellow visitors. Cheaper rooms have fans and shared bathrooms.

✕ Eating

The range of restaurants in Ayuthaya can come as a disappointment after living it up in Bangkok. But there is a modest collection of culinary traditions, including Muslim and European fare, that survive from ancient times.

Roti Sai Mai Stalls SWEETS $
(Th U Thong; ⊘8am-8pm) The dessert *roh-dee săi măi* (silk thread roti) was invented in Ayuthaya and is sold all over town, though the shops fronting the hospital are the most famous. Buy a bag then make your own by rolling together thin strands of melted palm sugar and wrapping them inside the roti.

Bang Ian Night Market MARKET $
(Th Bang Ian; ⊘4pm-8.30pm) This big, busy night market at the end of its namesake street is a great noshing destination. It's also ideally situated for a visit either before or after seeing the ruins illuminated at night.

Lung Lek NOODLES $
(Th Chee Kun; mains 30-50B; ⊘8.30am-4pm) Everybody's favourite noodle emporium, Uncle Lek has long served some of the most notable *gŏo·ay đĕe·o reu·a* in town.

★ Bann Kun Pra THAI $$
(☏035 241978; www.bannkunpra.com; Th U Thong; dishes 70-420B; ⊘11am-9.30pm) Far more intimate than most of Ayuthaya's riverside restaurants, this century-old teak house is a great place to sit and watch river life pass by. The inventive menu is loaded with seafood and has several versions of the local river prawn, including grilled with herbs and fried with tamarind sauce. There are some lovely but pricey guestrooms here, too.

★ Pae Krung Gao THAI $$
(Th U Thong; dishes 60-1000B; ⊘10am-9.30pm; ☎) A wonderfully cluttered riverside restaurant serving top-notch Thai food – seemingly half the crowd is here for the grilled river prawns. The English-language menu is limited, so if you know what you like, just ask.

❶ Information

Main Post Office (Th U Thong; ⊘8.30am-4.30pm Mon-Fri, 9am-noon Sat)

THAILAND AYUTHAYA

TRANSPORT FROM AYUTHAYA

Train

DESTINATION	FARE (B)	DURATION (HR)	FREQUENCY
Bangkok (Hualamphong station)	15-66	1½-2½	frequent
Chiang Mai	211-1398	11-14	5 daily
Nong Khai	202-1262	9-11	4 daily
Pak Chong	53-465	2-3	10 daily

Bus & Minivan

DESTINATION	FARE (B)	DURATION (HR)	FREQUENCY
Bangkok (Victory Monument)	60	1½	frequent (minivan)
Bangkok's Northern (Mo Chit) station	50	1	frequent (minivan)
Chiang Mai	419-837	8-10	frequent
Lopburi	80	1½	every 30min (minivan)
Saraburi	45	1½	frequent
Sukhothai	266-342	7	frequent
Suphanburi	45	1½	frequent (minivan)

Phra Nakorn Si Ayuthaya Hospital (☎035 211888; Th U Thong) Has an emergency centre and English-speaking doctors.

Tourism Authority of Thailand (TAT; ☎035 246076; tatyutya@tat.or.th; Th Si Sanphet; ⏱8.30am-4.30pm) Has an information counter with maps and good advice at the **Ayutthaya Tourist Center** (p671).

Tourist Police (☎035 241446; Th Si Sanphet)

ℹ Getting There & Away

BUS

Ayuthaya's minivan bus stop (*đà·làht tâh rót jôw prom*) is just south of the backpacker strip. Minivans to Suphanburi (transfer to Kanchanaburi), Saraburi (transfer to Pak Chong and Khorat) and Bangkok leave from here. There's a second Bangkok departure point one block west.

The main bus terminal is 3km east of the island, off Th Rotchana. You can buy tickets for Chiang Mai and Sukhothai from a **bus ticket office** (⏱6am-5pm) on Th Naresuan. A túk-túk from the terminal to the old city will cost 100B to 150B. Or take the purple *sŏrng·tăa·ou* (passenger pick-up truck; 7B).

TRAIN

Ayuthaya's train station is on the eastern banks of Mae Nam Pa Sak and is an easy walk from the city centre via a short ferry ride (5B). *Sŏrng·tăa·ou* to the guesthouse area should cost 50B. If you're headed to Khao Yai, catch the train to Pak Chong. For Bangkok's Th Khao San, get off at Bang Sue.

ℹ Getting Around

Bikes can be rented at most guesthouses (40B to 50B). Túk-túk can be hired for the day to tour the sites (200B per hour); a single trip within the city should be about 50B.

Lopburi ลพบุรี

POP 161,040

This small, low-key town is a delightful respite from the rigours of the tourist trail. No aggressive túk-túk drivers, no grumpy guesthouse staff and few foreigners making you feel that you flew a long way to be with familiar faces. Lopburi is an ancient town with plenty of old ruins to prove its former occupation by almost every Southeast Asian kingdom: Dvaravati, Khmer and Ayuthaya. The old city is presently occupied by ordinary Thai life: noodle stands, motorcycle stores and, most importantly, a gang of mischief-making monkeys. The city celebrates its resident monkeys with an annual festival in late November.

◉ Sights

Lopburi's historic ruins are easy to walk to from the town centre.

★ Phra Narai Ratchaniwet   MUSEUM

(วังนารายณ์ราชนิเวศน์; entrance Th Sorasak; 150B; ⏱8.30am-4pm Wed-Sun) Plan to spend a few hours at this former royal palace, now home to the Somdet Phra Narai National Museum, which houses excellent displays of local history. Built starting in 1665 with help from French and Italian engineers, the palace was used to welcome foreign dignitaries. It was abandoned after King Narai's death, but reclaimed by King Rama IV. The main displays, covering the 3500 years of the province's known history, are in his former residence.

★ Prang Sam Yot   RUIN

(ปรางค์สามยอด; Th Wichayen; 50B; ⏱6am-6pm) The impressive Prang Sam Yot and its huge resident troop of monkeys are Lopburi's most famous attraction. The three linked towers were built by the Khmer in the 13th century as a Buddhist temple, though it was later converted to Shiva worship. There are two ruined headless Buddha images inside, while a third, more complete Buddha sits photogenically in front of the main *prang*. A heavy metal door keeps the monkeys out, but visitors can go inside.

Wat Phra Si Ratana Mahathat   RUIN

(วัดพระศรีรัตนมหาธาตุ; Th Na Phra Kan; 50B; ⏱8.30am-4.30pm) This Khmer *wát*, built beginning in the 12th century, has been heavily modified over the centuries and makes for a great photo opportunity. The central *prang* is the tallest in Lopburi and it retains a good amount of original stucco, as do many of the surrounding stupas. The northwestern one has U Thong–style angels; their oblong faces and unusual halos are rare.

🛏 Sleeping

In the old town most hotels are old and basic, but they are within walking distance of the ruins.

★ Noom Guesthouse   GUESTHOUSE $

(☎036 427693; www.noomguesthouse.com; Th Phraya Kamjat; dm 150B, r 200-500B; ❉🖥) Easily the most *fa·ràng*-friendly spot in town, Noom's options are either classic shared-bath rooms in the wooden house or cosy little garden bungalows out back.

Nett Hotel HOTEL **$**
(☎036 411738; netthotel@hotmail.com; off Th Ratchadamnoen; r 250-550B; ❉🕾) The Nett remains the best of the old-school hotels near the ruins, since rooms are reasonably clean and have seen some renovation in recent years. Better than the rooms, though, is the caged rooftop, which offers good monkey watching. The cheapest rooms are fan-only and have cold-water showers.

Pee Homestay HOMESTAY **$**
(☎086 164 2184; www.lopburimassage.com; Soi Phromachan; r 200-450B; ❉@🕾) On the wrong side of the tracks...in a good way. Staying with super-friendly Ganaree, a beautician and massage therapist, gives you a very local experience. Her three upstairs rooms are on the shortlist of contenders for cleanest guest rooms in Thailand.

🍴 Eating & Drinking

Best bet for an inexpensive dinner in the old town is the modest **night market** (Th Na Phra Kan; ⊘3-11pm).

★ Naan Stop Curry INDIAN **$**
(Soi Sorasak; dishes 70-180B; ⊘11am-10pm; 🕾🍴) Not your stereotypical stuffy white-linen Indian restaurant. Here you get a small menu of family recipes prepared fresh when you order, along with a sociable owner and a rock-and-roll soundtrack. It doesn't always open for lunch.

Matini INTERNATIONAL, THAI **$**
(Th Phraya Kamjat; dishes 50-350B; ⊘9am-late; 🕾🍴) Free pool, a Blues Brothers' motif on the wall and good food (both Thai and West-

ern) make this Lopburi's chillest backpacker spot. And though the name may look like a typo, 'Matini' means 'come here' in Thai.

Sahai Phanta BAR
(Soi Sorasak) To party with the locals, check out this town-centre venue with its Carabao-style house band.

ℹ️ Information

Muang Narai Hospital (☎036 616300; Th Pahonyohtin)
Post Office (Th Prang Sam Yot)
Tourism Authority of Thailand (TAT; ☎036 770096; tatlobri@tat.or.th; Th Na Phra Kan; ⊘8.30am-4.30pm) Inside the train station.

ℹ️ Getting There & Away

Lopburi's bus station is nearly 2km outside of the old town. Minivans to Bangkok depart from Th Na Phra Kan. The **train station** (Th Na Phra

MONKEY TROUBLE

Lopburi residents are ambivalent about the town's mascot. According to Hindu-Buddhist beliefs, the monkeys have divine connections and should not be harmed. But their behaviour warrants strict punishment. Tourists should exercise caution when visiting San Phra Kan and Prang Sam Yot, the monkeys' favourite hangout. Avoid interacting with the monkeys as they are wild animals and do bite; don't carry bottles of water, cameras, bags or anything that can be grabbed out of your hands.

TRANSPORT FROM LOPBURI

Bus & Minivan

DESTINATION	FARE (B)	DURATION (HR)	FREQUENCY
Ayuthaya	80	1½	every 30min (minivan)
Bangkok (Victory Monument)	110-120	2	frequent (minivan)
Chiang Mai	502-582	9-12	12.30pm, 10.30pm, 11pm, midnight
Pak Chong	70	2	every 30min (minivan)

Train

DESTINATION	FARE (B)	DURATION (HR)	FREQUENCY
Ayuthaya	13-58	45min-1½	18 daily
Bangkok (Hualamphong station)	28-123	2-3½	17 daily
Chiang Mai	212-1353	9-12	5 daily
Phitsanulok	99-1046	3-5	11 daily

Kan) is near the old town and it has luggage storage if you just want to do a brief layover en route to points north.

ℹ️ Getting Around

Săhm·lór (pedicabs) go anywhere in old Lopburi for 20B. *Sŏrng·tăa·ou* run a regular route between the old and new towns for 8B and can be used to travel between the bus station and the old town.

Phitsanulok พิษณุโลก

POP 84,000

Because of its convenient location on an important train route, some travellers use Phitsanulok as a base for visiting the ancient city of Sukhothai. As an attraction in itself, Phitsanulok (often abbreviated as 'Philok') boasts a famous Buddha and a few minor curiosities.

👁 Sights

★ Wat Phra Si Ratana Mahathat
BUDDHIST TEMPLE

(วัดพระศรีรัตนมหาธาตุ; Th Phutta Bucha; ⊙ temple 6am-9pm, museum 9am-5.30pm Wed-Sun) FREE The main *wí·hăhn* (sanctuary) at this temple, known by locals as Wat Yai, appears small from the outside, but houses the Phra Phuttha Chinnarat, one of Thailand's most revered and copied Buddha images. This famous bronze statue is probably second in importance only to the Emerald Buddha in Bangkok's Wat Phra Kaew.

★ Sergeant Major Thawee Folk Museum
MUSEUM

(พิพิธภัณฑ์พื้นบ้านจ่าทวี; 26/38 Th Wisutkasat; adult/child 50/25B; ⊙ 8.30am-4.30pm) This fascinating museum displays a remarkable collection of tools, textiles and photo-graphs from Phitsanulok Province. It's spread throughout five traditional-style Thai buildings with well-groomed gardens, and the displays are all accompanied by informative and legible English descriptions. Those interested in cooking will find much of interest in the display of a traditional Thai kitchen and the various traps used to catch game. Male visitors will feel twinges of empathetic pain upon seeing the display that describes traditional bull castration – a process that apparently involves no sharp tools.

Wat Ratburana
BUDDHIST TEMPLE

(วัดราชบูรณะ; Th Phutta Bucha; ⊙ dawn-dusk) FREE Across the street from Wat Phra Si Ratana Mahathat, Wat Ratburana draws fewer visitors but in some ways is more interesting than its famous neighbour. In addition to a *wí·hăhn* with a 700-year-old gold Buddha, there's a *bòht* (chapel) with beautiful murals thought to date back to the mid-19th century and two wooden *hŏr đrai* (manuscript libraries).

🛌 Sleeping

Lithai Guest House
HOTEL $

(☎ 055 219626; 73/1-5 Th Phayarithai; r incl breakfast 300-580B; ❄️@🛜) The light-filled 60 or so rooms here don't have much character but they are clean. Air-con rooms include perks such as large private bathrooms with hot water, cable TV, fridge and breakfast.

River Homestay
HOTEL $

(☎ 055 249226; off Th Wang Chan; r 550-650B; ❄️@🛜) Reviving a type of accommodation once common in Phitsanulok, the six rooms here are located on a moored houseboat. Rooms are tight but attractive, with semi-open bathrooms and sharing an open TV area.

BUS & MINIVAN TRANSPORT FROM PHITSANULOK

DESTINATION	FARE (B)	DURATION (HR)	FREQUENCY
Bangkok	304-472	5-6	hourly 6.20am-11.30pm
Chiang Mai	232-237	6	frequent 5.40am-12.40pm
Chiang Rai	300	7-8	4 departures 8am-10.30am
Kamphaeng Phet	59-83	3	hourly 5am-6pm
Mae Sot	157-242	4	1am & 2.30am (bus), 4 daily (minivan)
Sukhothai	50-94	1	frequent 7.20am-4.45pm (bus), every 30min 5am-6pm (minivan)
Sukhothai Historical Park	58-70	1½	4 departures 7.15am-12.40pm (bus), every 30min 5am-6pm (minivan)

✕ Eating & Drinking

Night Market   MARKET $
(Th Phra Ong Dam; mains 30-60B; ⊙5pm-
midnight) Lining either side of Th Phra Ong
Dam north of Th Authong, this market has
the usual selection of Thai street foods.

Rim Nan   THAI $
(5/4 Th Phutta Bucha, no roman-script sign; mains
20-35B; ⊙9am-4pm) Just north of Wat Phra
Si Ratana Mahathat, Rim Nan is one of
a few similar restaurants along Th Phutta Bucha that offer *gŏo·ay dĕe·o hôy kàh*
('legs-hanging' noodles) and 'alternative'
seating.

Fah-Ke-Rah   THAI $
(786 Th Phra Ong Dam; mains 20-60B; ⊙7am-
9pm) There are several Thai-Muslim cafes
near the Pakistan Mosque on Th Phra Ong
Dam, and this is probably the best of them.
Thick *roh·đee* (crispy dough 'pancakes') is
served up with rich curries and fresh yoghurt is made daily.

★ Ban Mai   THAI $$
(93/30 Th Authong, no roman-script sign; mains
100-290B; ⊙11am-10pm) Dinner at this local
favourite is like a meal at your grandparents'
place: opinionated conversation resounds,
frumpy furniture abounds and an overfed
cat appears to rule the dining room. The
likewise homey dishes include *gaang pèt
bèt yâhng* (grilled duck curry) and *yam đà
krái* (herbal lemongrass salad). Look for the
yellow compound across from Ayara Grand
Palace Hotel.

Camper   BAR
(Th Baromtrilokanart; ⊙7pm-midnight) An open-
air, ramshackle convocation of falling-apart
retro furniture, local hipsters, draft beer and
live music, Camper is as loose and fun as it
sounds.

ℹ Information

@net (off Th Baromtrilokanart; per hr 8B;
⊙24hr) Twenty-four-hour internet access.
Tourism Authority of Thailand (TAT; ☑055
252742, nationwide ☑1672; tatphlok@
tat.or.th; 209/7-8 Th Baromtrilokanart;
⊙8.30am-4.30pm) Off Th Baromtrilokanart,
with helpful staff who hand out free maps of
the town and a walking-tour sheet. This office
also oversees the provinces of Sukhothai,
Phichit and Phetchabun.
Tourist Police (☑1155; Th Akatossaroth)

ℹ Getting There & Away

Phitsanulok's **airport** (☑055 301002) is
about 5km south of town; a taxi counter can
arrange trips to/from town for 150B. **Air Asia**
(☑Phitsanulok 09 4719 3645, nationwide 02
515 9999; www.airasia.com; Phitsanulok Air-
port; ⊙6am-6.30pm) and **Nok Air** (☑Phitsanu-
lok 055 301051, nationwide ☑1318; www.nokair.
co.th; Phitsanulok Airport; ⊙6am-9pm) con-
duct flights to/from Bangkok's Don Muang In-
ternational Airport (690B to 1100B, 55 minutes,
five daily); and **Kan Air** (☑Phitsanulok 08 6395
0718, nationwide 02 551 6111; www.kanairlines.
com; Phitsanulok Airport; ⊙8am-5pm), to/from
Chiang Mai (1990B, one hour, four weekly).

The city's **bus station** (☑055 212090; Rte
12) is 2km east of town on Hwy 12; túk-túk and
motorcycle taxis to/from town cost 60B. Trans-
port options out of Phitsanulok are good as it's a
junction for several bus and minivan routes.

The **train station** (☑Phitsanulok 055
258005, nationwide ☑1690; www.railway.co.th;
Th Akatossaroth) is within walking distance of
accommodation and virtually every northbound
and southbound train stops here. Destinations
include the following:
Bangkok 69B to 1664B, five to seven hours,
10 daily
Chiang Mai 65B to 1645B, seven to nine hours,
six daily

Sukhothai   สุโขทัย
POP 37,000
The ruins of Sukhothai are a fantastic col-
lection of Angkor-style temple architecture
merged with uniquely Thai flourishes. Con-
sidered the first independent Thai kingdom,
Sukhothai emerged as the Khmer empire
was crumbling in the 13th century and sub-
sequently ruled over parts of the empire's
western frontier for 150 years. This new
Thai kingdom took artistic inspiration from
its former overseers and the resulting city
of temples is now a compact and pleasant
collection of gravity-warped columns, serene
Buddha figures and weed-sprouting towers.

Though Ayuthaya has a more interesting
historical narrative, Sukhothai's ancient city
is better preserved and architecturally more
engaging. No surprise, since Sukhothai
(meaning 'Rising Happiness') is regarded as
the blossoming of a Thai artistic sensibility.

The modern town of Sukhothai (often re-
ferred to as New Sukhothai; 12km from the
ruins) is a standard, somewhat bland, pro-
vincial town but it is a convenient base.

Sukhothai Historical Park

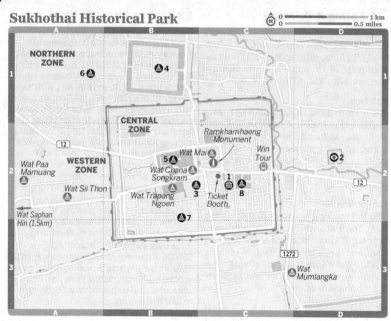

Sukhothai Historical Park

◉ Sights & Activities

Sukhothai Historical Park　　HISTORIC SITE
(อุทยานประวัติศาสตร์สุโขทัย; ☏ 055 697527) The
Sukhothai Historical Park ruins are one of
Thailand's most impressive World Heritage
Sites. The park includes the remains of 21
historical sites and four large ponds within the old walls, with an additional 70 sites
within a 5km radius. The ruins are divided
into five zones, the central, northern and
eastern of which each has a separate 100B
admission fee.

The architecture of Sukhothai temples
is most typified by the classic lotus-bud
chedi, featuring a conical spire topping a
square-sided structure on a three-tiered
base. Some sites exhibit other rich architectural forms introduced and modified during

the period, such as bell-shaped Sinhalese
and double-tiered Srivijaya *chedi*.

Despite the popularity of the park, it's
quite expansive and solitary exploration
is usually possible. Some of the most impressive ruins are outside the city walls, so
a bicycle or motorcycle is essential to fully
appreciate everything.

◉ Central Zone

This is the historical park's main **zone** (100B,
plus per bicycle/motorcycle/car 10/20/50B, audio
guide 150B; ⊘ 6.30am-7pm Sun-Fri, to 9pm Sat)
and is home to the park's most impressive
ruins. An audioguide, available in English,
Japanese or Thai, can be rented at the **ticket booth**. On Saturday night much of the
central zone is illuminated and remains open
until 9pm.

Wat Mahathat　　BUDDHIST TEMPLE
(วัดมหาธาตุ) Completed in the 13th century,
the largest *wát* in Sukhothai is surrounded by
brick walls (206m long and 200m wide) and
a moat that is believed to represent the outer
wall of the universe and the cosmic ocean.

Ramkhamhaeng National Museum　　MUSEUM
(พิพิธภัณฑสถานแห่งชาติรามคำแหง; 150B; ⊘ 9am-
4pm) A good starting point for exploring the

historical park ruins is this museum. A replica of the famous Ramkhamhaeng inscription, said to be the earliest example of Thai writing, is kept here among an impressive collection of Sukhothai artefacts. Admission to the museum is not included in the ticket to the central zone.

Wat Si Sawai   BUDDHIST TEMPLE
(วัดศรีสวาย) Just south of Wat Mahathat, this Buddhist shrine (dating from the 12th and 13th centuries) features three Khmer-style towers and a picturesque moat. It was originally built by the Khmers as a Hindu temple.

Wat Sa Si   BUDDHIST TEMPLE
(วัดสระศรี, Sacred Pond Monastery) Wat Sa Si sits on an island west of the bronze monument of King Ramkhamhaeng (the third Sukhothai king). It's a simple, classic Sukhothai-style wát containing a large Buddha, one *chedi* and the columns of the ruined *wí·hăhn*.

Wat Trapang Thong   BUDDHIST TEMPLE
(วัดตระพังทอง) Next to the Ramkhamhaeng National Museum, this small, still-inhabited wát with fine stucco reliefs is reached by a footbridge across the large lotus-filled pond that surrounds it. This reservoir, the original site of Thailand's Loi Krathong festival, supplies the Sukhothai community with most of its water.

◉ Northern Zone

This zone (100B, plus per bicycle/motorcycle/car 10/20/50B; ⊘6.30am-5.30pm) is located 500m north of the old city walls and is easily reached by bicycle.

Wat Si Chum   BUDDHIST TEMPLE
(วัดศรีชุม; Northern Zone) This wát is northwest of the old city and contains an impressive *mon·dòp* with a 15m, brick-and-stucco seated Buddha. This Buddha's elegant, tapered fingers are much photographed. Archaeologists theorise that this image is the 'Phra Atchana' mentioned in the famous Ramkhamhaeng inscription. A passage in the *mon·dòp* wall that leads to the top has been blocked so that it's no longer possible to view the *Jataka* inscriptions that line the tunnel ceiling.

Wat Phra Phai Luang   BUDDHIST TEMPLE
(วัดพระพายหลวง; Northern Zone) This somewhat isolated wát features three 12th-century Khmer-style towers, bigger than those at Wat Si Sawai in the Central Zone. This may have been the centre of Sukhothai when it was ruled by the Khmers of Angkor prior to the 13th century.

◉ Western Zone

This zone (100B, plus per bicycle/motorcycle/car 10/20/50B; ⊘8am-4.30pm) is 2km west of the old city walls but contains largely featureless ruins. A bicycle or motorcycle is necessary to explore this zone.

Wat Saphan Hin   BUDDHIST TEMPLE
(วัดสะพานหิน; Western Zone) Located on the crest of a hill that rises about 200m above the plain, the name of the wát, which means 'stone bridge', is a reference to the slate path and staircase that leads up to the temple, both of which are still in place.

All that remains of the original temple are a few *chedi* and the ruined *wí·hăhn,* consisting of two rows of laterite columns flanking a 12.5m-high standing Buddha image on a brick terrace. The site is 3km west of the former city wall and gives a good view of the Sukhothai ruins to the southeast and the mountains to the north and south.

⛬ Tours

Cycling Sukhothai   BICYCLE TOUR
(☑055 612519, 08 5083 1864; www.cycling-sukhothai.com; off Th Jarodvithithong; half-day 750B, full day 950-990B, sunset tour 400B) A resident of Sukhothai for nearly 20 years, Belgian cycling enthusiast Ronny Hanquart's rides follow themed itineraries such as the

> **WORTH A TRIP**
>
> ### SANGKHALOK MUSEUM
>
> The small but comprehensive **Sangkhalok Museum** (พิพิธภัณฑ์สังคโลก; Rte 1293; adult/child 100/50B; ⊘8am-5pm) is an excellent introduction to ancient Sukhothai's most famous product and export, its ceramics.
>
> The ground floor displays an impressive collection of original Thai pottery found in the area, plus some pieces traded from Vietnam, Burma and China. The 2nd floor features examples of non-utilitarian pottery made as art, including some beautiful and rare ceramic Buddha statues.
>
> The museum is about 2.5km east of the centre of New Sukhothai; a túk-túk here will run about 100B.

THE EMPIRE'S SUBURBS

The Sukhothai empire expanded its administrative centre and monument-building efforts to Si Satchanalai and Chaliang, two satellite cities about 70km away. Today the remaining temple ruins are set amid rolling hills and offers a more pastoral experience than Old Sukhothai.

An admission fee of 220B allows entry to Si Satchanalai, Wat Chao Chan (at Chaliang) and the Si Satchanalai Centre for Study & Preservation of Sangkhalok Kilns.

Si Satchanalai

This historic **zone** (100B, plus car 50B; ⊘8am-6pm) covers roughly 720 hectares and is surrounded by a 12m-wide moat along the banks of Mae Nam Yom. An information centre distributes maps, and bicycles (30B) can be rented near the entrance gate. **Wat Chang Lom** (วัดช้างล้อม; off Rte 12) **FREE** has a *chedi* (stupa) surrounded by Buddha statues set in niches and guarded by the remains of well-preserved elephant buttresses. Climb to the top of the hill supporting **Wat Khao Phanom Phloeng** (วัดเขาพนมเพลิง) for a view over the town and river. **Wat Chedi Jet Thaew** (วัดเจดีย์เจ็ดแถว) has a group of stupas in classic Sukhothai style.

Chaliang

Chaliang is an older city site, dating to the 11th century, and sits 1km from Si Satchanalai. **Wat Phra Si Ratana Mahathat** (วัดพระศรีรัตนมหาธาตุ; 20B; ⊘8am-4.30pm) contains a bas-relief of the classic walking Buddha, a hallmark of the Sukhothai era. **Wat Chao Chan** (วัดเจ้าจันทร์; 100B; ⊘8am-5pm) has a large Khmer-style tower probably constructed during the reign of Khmer King Jayavarman VII (1181–1297). The roofless *wí·hǎhn* (sanctuary) contains the laterite outlines of a large standing Buddha that has all but melted away from exposure.

Sangkhalok Kilns

This area was famous for its beautiful pottery, much of which was exported to China and Indonesia. **Si Satchanalai Centre for Study & Preservation of Sangkhalok Kilns** (ศูนย์ศึกษาและอนุรักษ์เตาสังคโลก; 100B; ⊘8am-4.30pm), 5km northwest of Si Satchanalai, has large excavated kilns and intact pottery samples documenting the area's pottery traditions.

Getting There & Away

Si Satchanalai-Chaliang Historical Park is off Rte 101 between Sawankhalok and Ban Hat Siaw. From Sukhothai, take a Si Satchanalai bus (49B, 1½ hours, hourly from 6.40am-6pm) and ask to get off at *meu·ang gòw* (old city).

Historical Park Tour, which also includes stops at lesser-seen *wát* and villages. Its office is based about 1.2km west of Mae Nam Yom, in New Sukhothai; free transport can be arranged.

🛏 Sleeping

The accommodation options listed here are in New Sukhothai.

TR Room & Bungalow GUESTHOUSE $
(☑ 055 611663; www.sukhothaibudgetguesthouse.com; 27/5 Th Prawet Nakhon; r 300-450B, bungalows 600B; 🅿 @ 🛜) The rooms here are basic and lack character, but figure among the tidiest we've encountered in northern Thailand. For those needing a bit more leg room, there are five wooden bungalows out back.

Sabaidee House HOTEL $
(☑ 055 616303; www.sabaideehouse.com; 81/7 Th Jarodvithithong; r 200-600B; 🅿 🛜) This cheery guesthouse in a semi-rural setting has seven attractive bungalows and four rooms in the main structure. It's off Th Jarodvithithong about 200m before the intersection with Rte 101; look for the sign.

4T Guesthouse HOTEL $
(☑ 055 614679; fourthouse@yahoo.com; 122 Soi Mae Ramphan; r 300-400B, bungalows 600-800B; 🅿 🛜 🏊) Hardly a leaf is out of place at this expansive budget resort. There's a smorgasbord of bungalows and spacious rooms to

consider, and the swimming pool makes the decision even easier.

At Home Sukhothai
GUESTHOUSE $$

(☑055 610172; www.athomesukhothai.com; 184/1 Th Vichien Chamnong; r 450-900B, bungalows 900B, all incl breakfast; ❋@🛜) Located in the 50-year-old childhood home of the proprietor, the simple but comfortable rooms here – both those fan-cooled in the original structure and the newer air-con ones – really do feel like home. A new addition sees four bungalows overlooking a pond. The only downside is the relative distance from 'downtown' Sukhothai.

J&J Guest House
GUESTHOUSE $$

(☑055 620095; 12 Th Kuhasuwan; bungalows 600-700B; ❋🛜) Located in a manicured garden by the river, the eight bungalows here are attractive, cool and relatively spacious. They're identical, and price depends on whether you go with fan or air-con.

✖️ Eating & Drinking

Jayhae
THAI $

(Th Jarodvithithong; dishes 30-50B; ☺8am-4pm) You haven't been to Sukhothai if you haven't tried the noodles at Jayhae, an extremely popular restaurant that also serves *pàt tai* and tasty coffee drinks.

Tapui
THAI $

(Th Jarodvithithong, no roman-script sign; dishes 30-50B; ☺7am-3pm) Consisting of little more than a brick floor with a tin roof over it, Ta Pui claims to be the first shop in Sukhothai to have sold the city's namesake dish, *gŏo·ay đĕe·o sù·kŏh·tai*. Located about 1.3km west of Mae Nam Yom.

Night Market
MARKET $

(Th Ramkhamhaeng; mains 30-60B; ☺6-11pm) A wise choice for cheap eats is New Suk-

hothai's tiny night market. Most vendors here are accustomed to accommodating foreigners and even provide bilingual menus.

Dream Café
THAI $$

(86/1 Th Singhawat; mains 80-350B; ☺5-11pm; 🍴) A meal at Dream Café is like dining in an antique shop. Eclectic but tasteful furnishings and knick-knackery abound, staff are equal parts competent and friendly, and, most importantly of all, the food is good. Try one of the well-executed *yâhm* (Thai-style 'salads'), or one of the dishes that feature freshwater fish, a local speciality.

Chopper Bar
BAR

(Th Prawet Nakhon; ☺10am-12.30am; 🛜) Both travellers and locals congregate at this restaurant-bar from morning till hangover for food (mains 30B to 150B), drinks and live music. Take advantage of Sukhothai's cool evenings on the rooftop terrace.

ℹ️ Information

Sukhothai Hospital (☑055 610280; Th Jarodvithithong) Located just west of New Sukhothai.

Tourism Authority of Thailand (TAT; ☑055 616228, nationwide ☑1672; Th Jarodvithithong; ☺8.30am-4.30pm) Near the bridge in New Sukhothai, this new office has a pretty good selection of maps and brochures.

ℹ️ Getting There & Away

The airport is an inconvenient 27km from town; **Bangkok Airways** (☑Sukhothai Airport 055 64 7224, nationwide 1771; www.bangkokair.com; Sukhothai Airport; ☺7.30-11.30am & 12.30-5.30pm) operates flights to Bangkok's Suvarnabhumi International Airport.

The **bus station** (☑055 614529; Rte 101) is 1km northwest of the new town centre. A motorcycle taxi between the bus station and New Sukhothai should cost around 50B. Or grab a

BUS & MINIVAN TRANSPORT FROM SUKHOTHAI

DESTINATION	FARE (B)	DURATION (HR)	FREQUENCY
Bangkok	266-342	6-7	every 30min 7.50am-10.40pm
Chiang Mai	214-293	5-6	5 departures 6.20am-2am
Chiang Rai	255	9	4 departures 6.40-11.30am
Kamphaeng Phet	57-72	1½	frequent 7.50am-10.40pm
Mae Sot	130-191	3	4 daily (minivan)
Phitsanulok	40-54	1	hourly 6am-midnight (bus), 3 daily (minivan)
Sawankhalok	28	1	hourly 6.40am-6pm
Si Satchanalai	49	1½	hourly 6.40am-6pm

sŏrng·tǎa·ou bound for Sukhothai Historical Park (20B, 10 minutes, frequent from 6am to 6pm).

Win Tour (Rte 12; ⊘ 6am-9.40pm), located near the historical park, runs buses to Bangkok (342B, six hours, 8.20am, 12.30pm and 9.50pm) and Chiang Mai (222B, five hours, six departures from 6.50am to 2pm).

ⓘ Getting Around

Sŏrng·tǎa·ou run between New Sukhothai and Sukhothai Historical Park (30B, 30 minutes, 6am to 6pm); vehicles leave from Th Jarodvithithong.

Kamphaeng Phet กำแพงเพชร

POP 30,000

An easy detour from the tourist trail, Kamphaeng Phet (Diamond Wall) is a peaceful provincial town known for its whitewashed city walls. Historically it was the first line of defence for the Sukhothai kingdom from attacks from Burma or Lanna armies. Today, it's a nice place to spend a day or so wandering around the ruins and experiencing daily Thai life.

◉ Sights

**Kamphaeng Phet
Historical Park** HISTORICAL PARK
(อุทยานประวัติศาสตร์กำแพงเพชร; ⊘ 8am-6pm) A Unesco World Heritage Site, the Kamphaeng Phet Historical Park features the ruins of structures dating back to the 14th century, roughly the same time as the better-known kingdom of Sukhothai. Kamphaeng Phet's Buddhist monuments continued to be built up until the Ayuthaya period, nearly 200 years later, and thus possess elements of both Sukhothai and Ayuthaya styles, resulting in a school of Buddhist art quite unlike anywhere else in Thailand.

The park consists of two distinct sections: a formerly walled city just north of modern Kamphaeng Phet, and a larger compound about 1.5km farther north.

**Kamphaeng Phet
National Museum** MUSEUM
(พิพิธภัณฑสถานแห่งชาติกำแพงเพชร; Th Pindamri; 100B; ⊘ 9am-4pm Wed-Sun) Kamphaeng Phet's visit-worthy museum has undergone an extensive renovation. It's home to an expansive collection of artefacts from the Kamphaeng Phet area, including an immense Shiva statue that is the largest bronze Hindu sculpture in the country. The image was formerly located at the nearby **Shiva Shrine** until a German missionary stole the idol's hands and head in 1886 (they were later returned). Today a replica stands there in its place.

🛏 Sleeping & Eating

Three J Guest House GUESTHOUSE $
(☑ 055 713129, 08 1887 4189; www.threejguesthouse.com; 79 Soi 1, Soi Ratchavitee; r 250-800B; ✳@🛜) The cheapest bungalows at this welcoming guesthouse are fan-cooled and share a clean bathroom while the more expensive have air-con. There's heaps of local information, and bicycles and motorcycles are available for hire.

Grand View Resort HOTEL $$
(☑ 055 721104; 34/4 Mu 2, Nakhon Chum; r & bungalows incl breakfast 290-890B; ✳🛜) One of a handful of semi-rural 'resorts' on the western bank of Mae Nam Ping, there's a variety of accommodation here, but the highlight is the six floating raft bungalows.

★**Bamee Chakangrao** THAI $
(cnr Soi 9 & Th Rachadumnoen 1, no roman-script sign; mains 30-35B; ⊘ 8.30am-3pm) Thin wheat and egg noodles *(bà·mèe)* are a speciality of Kamphaeng Phet, and this famous restaurant is one of the best places to try them. The noodles are made fresh every

BUS & MINIVAN TRANSPORT FROM KAMPHAENG PHET

DESTINATION	FARE (B)	DURATION (HR)	FREQUENCY
Bangkok	220-330	5	frequent 8am-1.30am
Chiang Mai	218-328	5	8 departures 11.30am-1am
Chiang Rai	291-374	7	5 departures noon-10.30pm
Lampang	161	4	8 departures 11.30am-1am
Mae Sot	120	3	frequent 8am-6pm (minivan)
Phitsanulok	61-85	2½	hourly 5am-6pm
Sukhothai	57-74	1-2	hourly noon-4am (bus), three daily (minivan)

day behind the restaurant, and pork satay is also available. Look for the green banners on the corner.

Night Market
THAI $

(Th Thesa 1; mains 30-60B; ⊘ 4-10pm) For cheap Thai eats, a busy night market sets up every evening near the river just north of the Navarat Hotel.

ⓘ Getting There & Around

The bus station is 1km west of Mae Nam Ping. Motorcycle taxis (50B) and *sŏrng·tăa·ou* (20B, frequent from 7.30am to 3pm) run between the station and town. If coming from Sukhothai or Phitsanulok, get off in the old city or at the roundabout on Th Thesa 1 to save yourself the trouble of backtracking into town.

NORTHERN THAILAND

Forming the crown of the country is a mountainous region loved for its lush forests and unique cultural attractions. This cascade of peaks and valleys unites northern Thailand with the peoples and the cultures of neighbouring Myanmar, Laos and southwestern China. The region's ancient kingdom, known as Lanna Thai (Million Thai Rice Fields), established its capital in Chiang Mai, which retains its connection to the past. Wanderers, such as the autonomous hill-tribe peoples, traversed the range, limited by altitude rather than political boundaries.

Chiang Mai
เชียงใหม่

POP 398,000

Chiang Mai is a cultural darling: it is a cool place to kick back and relax. The streets of the old city are filled with monks (and a ton of Chinese tourists), bookshops outnumber glitzy shopping centres and the region's Lanna heritage is worn with pride. For culture vultures, Chiang Mai is a vibrant classroom to study Thai language, cooking, meditation and massage.

The old city of Chiang Mai is a neat square, bounded by a moat and remnants of a medieval-style wall built 700 years ago to defend against Burmese invaders. A furious stream of traffic flows around the old city, but inside narrow soi lead to a quiet world of family-run guesthouses and leafy gardens. Th Moon Muang, along the east moat, is the primary traveller centre but the tourist business has sprouted up in all corners.

Intersecting with Th Moon Muang, Th Tha Phae runs east from the exterior of the moat towards the Mae Nam Ping. Once it crosses the river, the road is renamed Th Charoen Muang and eventually arrives at the train station.

Finding your way around Chiang Mai is fairly simple. Pick up a copy of Nancy Chandler's *Map Guide to Chiang Mai*, available at bookstores.

⊙ Sights

Chiang Mai's primary attractions are the old city's historic temples that show off distinctive northern Thai architecture. A few standout features include intricate carved teak gables, colourful exterior mosaics, Singha lions guarding the entrances and octagonal high-based *chedi*.

★ Wat Phra Singh
BUDDHIST TEMPLE

(วัดพระสิงห์; Th Singharat; main wí·hăhn 20B; ⊘ 5am-8.30pm) Chiang Mai's most revered temple, Wat Phra Singh is dominated by an enormous, mosaic-inlaid *wí·hăhn* (sanctuary). Its prosperity is plain to see from the lavish monastic buildings and immaculately trimmed grounds, dotted with coffee-stands and massage pavilions. Pilgrims flock here to venerate the famous Buddha image known as **Phra Singh** (Lion Buddha), housed in Wihan Lai Kham, a small chapel immediately south of the *chedi* to the rear of the temple grounds.

★ Wat Chedi Luang
BUDDHIST TEMPLE

(วัดเจดีย์หลวง; Th Phra Pokklao; donations appreciated; ⊘ 6am-6pm) FREE Wat Chedi Luang is not quite as grand as Wat Phra Singh, but its towering, ruined Lanna-style *chedi* (built in 1441) is much taller and the sprawling compound around the stupa is powerfully atmospheric. The famed Phra Kaew (Emerald Buddha), now held in Bangkok's Wat Phra Kaew, resided in the eastern niche until 1475; today, you can view a jade replica, given as a gift from the Thai king in 1995 to celebrate the 600th anniversary of the *chedi*.

★ Lanna Folklife Museum
MUSEUM

(พิพิธภัณฑ์พื้นถิ่นล้านนา; Th Phra Pokklao; adult/child 90/40B; ⊘ 8.30am-5pm Tue-Sun) Set inside the Thai-colonial–style former Provincial Court, dating from 1935, this imaginative museum recreates Lanna village life in a series of life-sized dioramas that explain everything from *lai·krahm* stencilling and

Chiang Mai

THAILAND CHIANG MAI

500 m
0.25 miles

42

Soi 3

Th Charoenrat (Th Faham)

McCormick Hospital (600m);
Arcade (1.6km); 3km):
Payap University (3km)

Th Wat Ket

Th Kaew Nawarat

Th Wat Ket

Th Charoenrat (Th Faham)

Th Praisani

Mae Ping

Th Tha Phae (14km)

49

5

Chinese Welcome Gate

Wat Saen Fang

24

55

Soi 1

Th Muang Samut

Th Ratchawong

Th Chang Moi

Th Tha Phae

Soi 3

Th Atsadathorn

Th Ratanakosin

51

Wat Chomphu

28

Th Moon Muang
Th Chaiyaphum

45

Wat Dokaueng

52

19

58

27

Soi 6

Pratu
Tha Phae

35

Chang Pheuak
Bus Terminal

Th Sanan Kla

Soi 1

15

36

Wat
Lam Chang

Soi 7

Soi 6

Wat
Saen

34

17

Tha Phae

9

23

Phan On

Th Chotana (Th
Chang Pheuak)

Th Ratchaphakhinai

6

20

25

50

Wat
Pan Ping

38

56

Th Mani Nopharat
Th Si Phum

Pratu
Chang
Pheuak

Wat
Hua Khwang

59

Anusawari Sam
Kasat (Three
Kings Monument)

Lanna
Folklife
Museum

1

4

43

Wat
Duang Di

7

Soi 9

Th Jhaban

16

Wat Chai
Phra Kiat

Th Ratchadamnoen

Wat
Chedi Luang

2

Soi 4

29

Former Chiang Mai
Women's Prison

Si Koet

Wat
Thung Yu

47 Wat

11

54

13

Th Singharat

Chiang Mai
Ram Hospital

Wat
Phra
Singh

3

44

Th Inthawarorot

Th Morakot

48

32

Th Hutsadisawee

Pratu
Suan Dok

Th Burneanart
Th Arak

Th Suthep

40

Th Ratchaphuek

Th Huay Kaew

18

Sudsanan (110m);
Burma Study
Center (140m);
Blar Blar
Bar (740m);
Tengoku (770m);
Maya Lifestyle
Shopping Center (800m);
Artel Nimman (870m);
Ristr8to (1km);
Studio Naenna (1km);
Tong Tem Toh (1.1km);
Lanna Muay Thai
Boxing Camp (2.3km);
Wat Phra That Doi
Suthep (16km)

Wat Suan Dok (755m);
Wat Suan Dok Meditation Retreat (1km);
Pun Pun (1.1km);
I-Berry (1.2km);
Warmup Cafe (1.7km)

fon lep (a mystical Lanna dance with false long, metal fingernails) to the intricate symbolism of different elements of Lanna-style monasteries.

★ Wat Phra That Doi Suthep
BUDDHIST TEMPLE

(วัดพระธาตุดอยสุเทพ; Th Huay Kaew, Doi Suthep; 30B; ◷6am-6pm) Overlooking the city from its mountain throne, Wat Phra That Doi Suthep is one of northern Thailand's most sacred temples, and its founding legend is learned by every school kid in Chiang Mai. The wát itself is a beautiful example of northern Thai architecture, reached via a strenuous, 306-step staircase flanked by mosaic *naga* (serpents); the climb is intended to help devotees accrue Buddhist merit, but less energetic pilgrims can take a funicular-style lift for 20B.

Wat Phan Tao
BUDDHIST TEMPLE

(วัดพันเถา; Th Phra Pokklao; donations appreciated; ◷6am-6pm) FREE Without doubt the most atmospheric wát in the old city, this teak marvel sits in the shadow of Wat Chedi Luang. Set in a compound full of fluttering orange flags, the monastery is a monument to the teak trade, with an enormous prayer hall supported by 28 gargantuan teak pillars and lined with dark teak panels, enshrining a particularly graceful gold Buddha image. The juxtaposition of the orange monks' robes against this dark backdrop during evening prayers is particularly sublime.

Wat Chiang Man
BUDDHIST TEMPLE

(วัดเชียงมั่น; Th Ratchaphakhinai; donations appreciated; ◷6am-6pm) FREE Chiang Mai's oldest temple was established by the city's founder, Phaya Mengrai, sometime around 1296. In front of the *ubosot* (ordination hall), a stone slab, engraved in 1581, bears the earliest known reference to the city's founding. The main *wí·hăhn* also contains the oldest known Buddha image created by the Lanna kingdom, cast in 1465.

Chiang Mai City Arts & Cultural Centre
MUSEUM

(หอศิลปวัฒนธรรมเชียงใหม่; www.cmocity.com; Th Phra Pokklao; adult/child 90/40B; ◷8.30am-5pm Tue-Sun) Set in the former Provincial Hall, a handsome Thai-colonial–style building from 1927, this museum provides an excellent primer on Chiang Mai history. Dioramas, photos, artefacts and audiovisual displays walk visitors through the key battles and victories in the Chiang Mai story, from the first

Chiang Mai

settlements to the arrival of the railroad. Upstairs is a charming recreation of a wooden Lanna village.

Chiang Mai
Historical Centre   MUSEUM
(หอประวัติศาสตร์เมืองเชียงใหม่; Th Ratwithi; adult/child 90/40B; ⊙8.30am-5pm Tue-Sun) Housed in an airy Lanna-style building behind the Chiang Mai City Arts & Culture Centre, this appealing museum covers the history of Chiang Mai Province, with displays on the founding of the capital, the Burmese occupation and the modern era of trade and unification with Bangkok. Downstairs is an archaeological dig of an ancient temple wall.

Wat Suan Dok   BUDDHIST TEMPLE
(วัดสวนดอก; Th Suthep; donations appreciated; ⊙6am-10pm) FREE Built on a former flower garden in 1373, this important monastery enshrines the other half of the sacred Buddha relic that was transported by white elephant to Wat Phra That Doi Suthep. The main *chedi* is a gilded, bell-shaped structure that rises dramatically above a sea of immaculate white memorial *chedi* honouring members of the Thai royal family, with the misty ridge of Doi Suthep soaring behind.

🏃 Activities

Chiang Mai is one of the most popular places in Thailand to arrange a hill-tribe trek. Competition for business is fierce, standards fluctuate and most businesses are just booking agents not tour operators.

Most companies offer the same itinerary: about an hour trekking, another hour riding an elephant, some waterfall-spotting then spending the night in a hill-tribe village. Repeat if it is a multiday tour. The tours don't always meet expectations: travellers are often disappointed by the animal welfare standards at the elephant camps and increasing urban migration from hill-tribe villages means that traditional ways are being lost.

We don't advise prebooking in Bangkok. Instead shop around locally to find the lowest commission rates. It is also possible to go trekking in Mae Hong Son and Chiang Rai; the latter has trekking companies with an economic and educational development component.

Elephant Nature Park ELEPHANT INTERACTION
(☑ 053 818754; www.elephantnaturepark.org; 1 Th Ratchamankha; 1-/2-day tour 2500/5800B) 🪝 One of the first sanctuaries for rescued elephants in Chiang Mai, Elephant Nature Park has led the movement to abandon rides and shows and put elephant welfare at the top of the agenda, under the guidance of founder Sangduen (Lek) Chailert. In place of circus routines, visits are focused on interaction – the day is spent wandering with mahouts and their charges, helping feed and wash elephants.

Thai Elephant Care Center ELEPHANT INTERACTION
(☑ 053 206247; www.thaielephantcarecenter.com; Mae Sa; half/full day 2000/3000B) This small centre at Mae Sa, about 25km northwest of Chiang Mai, was set up to provide care for elderly elephants retired from logging camps and elephant shows. There are no rides and visitors feed the old-timers with ground grass, herb balls and bananas and help out at bath-time, as well as visiting the cemetery for elephants who have died of old age.

Chiang Mai Mountain Biking & Kayaking MOUNTAIN BIKING
(☑ 053 814207; www.mountainbikingchiangmai.com; 1 Th Samlan; tours 1250-2300B) This specialist operator offers recommended kayaking trips on Mae Ping and full-day guided mountain-biking tours (using imported bikes) to Doi Suthep-Pui National Park and further afield, including the popular ascent to Wat Phra That Doi Suthep.

Peak Adventure Tour ADVENTURE SPORTS
(☑ 053 800567; www.thepeakadventure.com; 302/4 Th Chiang Mai-Lamphun; tours 900-2500B) The Peak offers a variety of adventure trips, including quad biking, abseiling, trekking, white-water rafting and rock climbing, as well as photography tours of Chiang Mai by sǎhm·lór.

Pooh Eco-Trekking TREKKING
(☑ 053 208538; www.pooh-ecotrekking.com; 59 Th Ratchaphakhinai; 2-day tours per person from 3500B) The owners of this adventure-tour agency take the eco part of their name seriously, offering above-average hill-tribe treks and other adventure tours.

Vocational Training Center of the Chiang Mai Women's Correctional Institution MASSAGE
(☑ 053 122340; 100 Th Ratwithi; foot/traditional massage from 150/180B; ⊙ 8am-4.30pm Mon-Fri, 9am-4.30pm Sat & Sun) Offers fantastic massages performed by female inmates participating in the prison's job-training rehabilitation program. The cafe next door is a nice spot for a post-massage brew.

🎓 Courses

Cooking

Cooking classes typically include a tour of a local market, hands-on cooking instruction and a recipe booklet. Classes are held at either an in-town location for those with limited time or at an out-of-town garden setting for more ambience.

MONK CHAT

If you're curious about Buddhism, many Chiang Mai temples offer 'monk chat', in which monks get to practise their English by fielding questions from visitors.

Wat Suan Dok (p688) has a dedicated room just beyond the main sanctuary hall and holds its chats from 5pm to 7pm, Monday to Friday. **Wat Sisuphan** (วัดศรีสุพรรณ; Soi 2, Th Wualai; donations appreciated) holds its sessions from 5.30pm to 7pm just before its meditation course. **Wat Chedi Luang** (p685) has a table under a shade tree where monks chat from 9am to 6pm daily.

MEDITATION COURSES & RETREATS

The seekers and the curious often come to Thailand to explore the spiritual discipline of meditation.

The sacred city of Chiang Mai is home to **Wat Suan Dok** (☑084 609 1357; www.monkchat.net; Th Suthep, Wat Suan Dok; 2-day retreat 500B; ☺Tue & Wed), which conducts meditation retreats at an affiliated forest temple.

Wat Pa Nanachat (วัดป่านานาชาติ; www.watpahnanachat.org; ☺dawn-dusk) FREE, in Ubon Ratchathani, was founded by renowned forest monk Phra Ajahn Chah. The temple is geared toward serious monastic trainees who speak English.

Thailand's most famous retreat is run by **Wat Suan Mok** (www.suanmokkh-idh.org; Wat Suanmokkh), near the southern town of Chaiya. It is a forest temple founded by Ajahn Buddhadasa Bhikkhu.

You can merge your beach needs with your spiritual needs at Ko Pha-Ngan's **Wat Khao Tham** (Map p744; www.kowtahm.com; ☺dawn-dusk) FREE. Periodic meditation retreats are held by an American-Australian couple.

Gap's Thai Culinary Art School
COOKING COURSE
(☑053 278140; www.gaps-house.com; 3 Soi 4, Th Ratchadamnoen; 1-/2-day course 900/1800B; ☺Mon-Sat) Affiliated with the guesthouse Gap's House, classes are held out of town at the owner's house.

Thai Farm Cooking School
COOKING COURSE
(☑081 288 5989; www.thaifarmcooking.com; 38 Soi 9, Th Moon Muang; course 1300B) Teaches cooking classes at its organic farm, 17km outside of Chiang Mai; the course includes return transport from Chiang Mai.

Language

Being a university town, Chiang Mai fosters continuing education opportunities in Thai language.

Payap University
LANGUAGE COURSE
(☑053 851478; http://ic.payap.ac.th; Th Kaew Nawarat, Kaew Nawarat Campus; Thai courses from 8000B) A private university founded by the Church of Christ of Thailand; offers intensive Thai language courses in 60-hour modules.

American University Alumni
LANGUAGE COURSE
(AUA; ☑053 214120; www.learnthaiinchiangmai.com; 73 Th Ratchadamnoen; group course 4800B) Conducts 60-hour Thai courses, with two hours of classes daily, Monday to Friday. Private instruction is also available.

Thai Massage

Jack Chaiya
MASSAGE
(☑083 154 6877; www.jackchaiya.com; 74/3 Th Wiang Kaew; 3- to 5-day courses from 7000B) Jack

Chaiya was trained by his mother in *jàp sên* (literally 'nerve touch'), a Northern Thai massage technique akin to acupressure, and is passing on the wisdom at this small massage school near Wat Phra Singh.

Old Medicine Hospital
MASSAGE
(OMH; ☑053 201663; www.thaimassageschool.ac.th; 78/1 Soi Siwaka Komarat, Th Wualai; courses 5000-6000B) The government-accredited curriculum is very traditional, with two 10-day massage courses a month, as well as shorter foot and oil massage courses.

Art of Massage
MASSAGE
(☑083 866 2901; www.artofmassage.webs.com; Soi 3, Th Loi Kroh; courses 990-2900B) Khun Wanna gets rave reviews for her practical training sessions, limited to a maximum of two people, lasting two to three days.

Moo·ay Tai (Thai Boxing)

Lanna Muay Thai Boxing Camp
MARTIAL ARTS
(☑053 892102; www.lannamuaythai.com; 161 Soi Chang Khian, Th Huay Kaew; day/week/month 400/2200/8000B) Offers instruction to foreigners and Thais. The gym is famous for having trained the title-winning, transgender boxer Parinya Kiatbusaba.

Chai Yai Muay Thai
MARTIAL ARTS
(☑082 938 1364; Th Sunpiliang, Nong Hoi; day/week/month 450/1700/5000B) This school has been training Thai and foreign fighters of all levels for 30 years. It's southeast of the city, off Rte 11 near the Chiang Mai 700 Years Park.

✨ Festivals & Events

Flower Festival   CULTURAL
(⊙early Feb) A riot of blooms, held over a three-day period in early February. There are flower displays, cultural performances and beauty pageants, plus a floral parade from Nawarat Bridge to Suan Buak Hat.

Songkran   NEW YEAR
(⊙mid-Apr) The traditional Thai New Year (13 to 15 April) is celebrated in Chiang Mai with infectious enthusiasm. Thousands of revellers line up along all sides of the moat to throw water on any passers-by in the city (and each other), while more restrained Songkran rituals are held at Wat Phra Singh.

Loi Krathong   RELIGIOUS
(⊙Oct/Nov) Also known as Yi Peng, this lunar holiday (usually October or November) is celebrated along Mae Ping with the launching of small lotus-shaped boats honouring the spirit of the river, and the release of thousands of lanterns into the night sky.

🛏 Sleeping

Thanks to the boom in Chinese tourists, new accommodation is springing up all over the city. Vacancies disappear during European and Chinese holiday periods.

Most guesthouses make their 'rice and curry' from booking trekking tours and reserve rooms for those customers.

★ Gap's House   GUESTHOUSE $
(☑053 278140; www.gaps-house.com; 3 Soi 4, Th Ratchadamnoen; s/d from 370/470B; ❀🔊) The overgrown garden at this old backpacker favourite is a veritable jungle, providing plenty of privacy in the relaxing communal spaces. Modest budget rooms are set in old-fashioned wooden houses, and the owner runs cooking courses and dishes up a delicious nightly vegetarian buffet. No advance reservations.

★ Diva Guesthouse   GUESTHOUSE $
(☑053 273851; www.divaguesthouse.com; 84/13 Th Ratchaphakhinai; dm 120-180B, r 250-800B; ❀@🔊) An energetic spot on busy Th Ratchaphakhinai, Diva offers the full backpacker deal – dorm beds, budget box rooms, adventure tours, net access, ambient tunes and fried rice and sà-đé (grilled meat with peanut sauce) in the downstairs cafe. Accommodation ranges from dorms to family rooms and come with either fans or air-con. The same owners run **Diva 2** (☑053 224648; Soi 2, Th Ratwithi; s/d from 180/220B; ❀🔊) and **Diva 3** (☑093 171 6078; Soi 3, Th Ratchamankha; dm from 170B; ❀🔊).

Julie Guesthouse   GUESTHOUSE $
(☑053 274355; www.julieguesthouse.com; 7 Soi 5, Th Phra Pokklao; dm from 90B, r without/with bathroom from 150/220B; 🔊) Julie is perennially popular, though this is as much about budget as facilities. For not much more than the price of a fruit smoothie you can get a basic dorm bed, and tiny box rooms cost only a little more. In the evenings travellers congregate on the covered roof terrace.

Shakara Garden   GUESTHOUSE $
(☑053 327535; shakaragarden@gmail.com; 51/1 Soi 4, Th Singharat; dm 150, r with fan/air-con 350/450B; ❀@🔊) The old Aoi Garden Home has been rebranded but it still offers the same old-fashioned backpacker experience at bargain rates. Basic box rooms with mozzie nets are spread across a series of wooden houses, with lots of chilled-out seating areas where travellers sit and chat. Dorms are mixed; private rooms share bathrooms.

MIGRANTS FROM MYANMAR IN CHIANG MAI

Chiang Mai Province hosts an estimated 200,000 people who have fled Myanmar, either as political refugees or economic migrants. Many of these workers are undocumented and are vulnerable to arrest and deportation as well as exploitation by their employers.

The following group works on issues related to displaced peoples, including education and health care.

Burma Study Center (www.burmastudy.org; 302/2 Soi 13, Th Nimmanhaemin; ⊙11.30am-8pm Mon-Fri, 11.30am-6pm Sat) This nonprofit community centre conducts classes in English for migrants from Myanmar living in Thailand. Many of the students are young, low-wage workers whose education has been disrupted by political instability in Myanmar or personal dislocation from their home communities. It also maintains an outreach mission to educate the international community about Myanmar-related issues through its lending library, book discussions and film screenings.

SPLURGE

Mo Rooms (☑053 280789; www.mo-rooms.com; 263/1-2 Th Tha Phae; r from 2800B; ❋@🛜❄) is designed in the urban mould, all exposed concrete and sculptural timbers juxtaposed with natural materials. Each of the Chinese-zodiac-themed rooms was decorated by a different Thai artist, ensuring some unique visions in interior decor – our top picks are 'Monkey' with its woven pod bed and 'Horse' with its surreal bed-tree.

There's a pebble-lined pool out back and an Asian fusion restaurant out front.

Smile House 1 GUESTHOUSE $
(☑053 208661; www.smilehousechiangmai.com; 5 Soi 2, Th Ratchamankha; r with fan/air-con 350/700B; ❋🛜❄🅟) There's a hint of the 1950s motel about this popular and friendly guesthouse, with a splash pool for kids and a bigger pool for grown-ups. It's very relaxed and the simply furnished rooms (with big windows) offer good value for money.

Jonadda Guest House GUESTHOUSE $
(☑053 227281; 23/1 Soi 2, Th Ratwithi; s/d fan-only 200/300B, r with air-con 800B; ❋) This reliable cheapie has spotless, basic rooms, with small communal spaces at the end of each floor where you can sit with a drink of an evening.

Daret's House GUESTHOUSE $
(☑053 235440; 4/5 Th Chaiyaphum; s/d 180/240B) The service at Daret's is as slow and ponderous as the owner's sleepy Pekingese, but you can't fault them on price. Basic rooms come at dorm-bed prices, in a handy location for the Tha Phae city gate. There's a budget restaurant downstairs.

Hostel In Town HOSTEL $
(☑053 234292; www.hit-thapae.com; Soi 2, Th Tha Phae; dm 220B; ❋🛜) One of a cluster of spic-and-span backpacker hostels just east of the old city walls, 'HIT' has neat dorms with lockers, towels and a rooftop cafe. There's a women-only dorm on the 2nd floor.

SoHostel HOSTEL $
(☑053 206360; sohostel.chiangmai@gmail.com; 64/2 Th Loi Kroh; dm from 219B; r from 1500B; ❋🛜) Loi Kroh is better known for girlie bars than backpacker bunks, but this huge modern hostel is a good deal, just an easy stroll from the old city and the Night Bazaar. The two-tone red-and-white dorms (with six to 12 beds) are better value than the somewhat overpriced private rooms.

Spicythai Backpackers HOSTEL $
(☑083 477 9467; www.spicyhostels.com; 14 Th Hutsadisawee; dm 220B; ❋@🛜) Tucked away in the student-y district north of Th Huay Kaew, this old-fashioned backpacker joint follows the classic Southeast Asian model. Beds are in simple single-sex dorms, there's a garden with hammocks and Western movies play all day long in the communal lounge. It closes most summers from June to August to accommodate Thai students.

Bunk Boutique HOSTEL $
(☑091 859 9656; bunkboutique@hotmail.com; 8/7 Th Ratchaphuek; dm 250B, r 900B; ❋🛜) Recently opened Bunk Boutique offers superior accommodation in four-bed dorms in a large apartment block behind Th Huay Kaew. Blonde wood bunks have curtains for privacy and everyone gets a locker. You can rent a dorm as a private room if there's space.

★ **Awanahouse** GUESTHOUSE $$
(☑053 419005; www.awanahouse.com; 7 Soi 1, Th Ratchadamnoen; r with fan/air-con 400/650-875B; ❋@🛜❄🅟) The pick of the guesthouses around Pratu Tha Phae, with rooms for every budget – all kept spotless – and a mini cold-water pool under cover on the ground-floor terrace. Rooms get more comfortable and better decorated as you move up the price scale and there's a rooftop chill-out area with views across old Chiang Mai.

★ **Artel Nimman** BOUTIQUE HOTEL $$
(☑053 213143; Soi 13, Th Nimmanhaemin; r 1350-1850B; ❋🛜) We're suckers for hotels with slides, so the Artel delivers in spades. The modernist building is all round windows, polished concrete, geometric forms and juxtaposed materials, and the rooms are cool, calm, creative spaces. There's a dainty cafe and, as mentioned, a slide from the balcony down to the street.

Nat Len Boutique Guesthouse GUESTHOUSE $$
(www.natlenboutiqueguesthouse.com; 2/4 Soi Wat Chompu, Th Chang Moi; r 650-1200B; ❋🛜❄) Quirky rooms are spread over several colourful houses at this low-key guesthouse just outside the city walls. Our favourite feature is the pale-blue pool with its bubbling

whirlpools, and there are lots of interesting wát in the surrounding alleyways.

Thong Ran's House GUESTHOUSE $$
(☑ 053 277307; www.thongranhouse.com; 105 Th Ratchamankha; r 900-1200B; ❄ 🛜) Cartoon statues of the owners dot the compound at this motel-like guesthouse in a quiet soi off Th Ratchamankha. Rooms have some cute Thai touches, but the sliding doors and coloured bathroom tiles create a lingering 1980s vibe.

🍴 Eating

Dining in Chiang Mai is homey and healthy with an emphasis on vegetarianism. The city is also well known for its covered markets. **Talat Pratu Chiang Mai** (Th Bamrungburi; mains from 40B; ⊙ 4am-noon & 6pm-midnight) is a busy morning market selling fresh fruit, piles of fried food and fistfuls of sticky rice. After its midday siesta, the market caters to the dinner crowd.

★**Pun Pun** VEGETARIAN $
(www.punpunthailand.org; Th Suthep, Wat Suan Dok; mains 40-75B; ⊙ 8am-4pm Thu-Tue; 🖉) 🌱 Tucked away at the back of Wat Suan Dok, this student-y cafe is a great place to sample Thai vegetarian food, which is prepared using little-known herbs and vegetables and lots of healthy whole grains grown on Pun Pun's concept farm, which doubles as an education centre for sustainable living.

There's a branch called **Imm Aim Vegetarian Restaurant** (10 Th Santhitham; mains 40-75B; ⊙ 10am-9pm; 🖉) 🌱 near the International Hotel Chiangmai.

★**Kiat Ocha** CHINESE, THAI $
(Th Inthawarorot; mains 50-90B; ⊙ 6am-3pm) This humble Chinese-style canteen is mobbed daily by locals who can't get enough of the house *kôw man gài* (Hainanese-style boiled chicken). Each plate comes with soup, chilli sauce and blood pudding and the menu also includes wok-fried chicken and pork and *sà-đé*.

★**SP Chicken** NORTHERN THAI $
(9/1 Soi 1, Th Samlan; mains 50-150B; ⊙ 11am-9pm) Chiang Mai's best chicken emerges daily from the broilers at this tiny cafe near Wat Phra Singh. The menu runs to salads and soups, but most people just pick a half (80B) or whole (150B) chicken, and dip the moist meat into the spicy, tangy Northern Thai dipping sauces provided.

Khun Churn VEGETARIAN $
(Th Thiphanet, Old Chiang Mai Cultural Center; buffet 164B; ⊙ 8am-10pm; 🖉) Moved to a slightly inconvenient location in the Old Chiang Mai Cultural Center (about 1km south of the old city walls on Rte 108), Khun Churn is best known for its all-you-can-eat meatless buffet (11am to 2.30pm), with dozens of dishes, salads, herbal drinks and Thai-style desserts.

Angel's Secrets INTERNATIONAL $
(Soi 1, Th Ratchadamnoen; mains 90-150B; ⊙ 7am-4pm Tue-Sun; 🛜🖉) True to its name, this sweet little restaurant is shielded by a fence of greenery from peeping appetites. Inside you'll find creative and wholesome Western breakfasts, including crusty homemade bread, crêpes and omelettes, and made-to-order vegetarian Thai food.

THAILAND CHIANG MAI

WHERE TO EAT KÔW SOY

Showing its Burmese, Chinese and Shan influences, the north prefers curries that are milder and more stewlike than the coconut milk–based curries of southern and central Thailand. Sour notes are enhanced with the addition of pickled cabbage and lime. The most famous example is *kôw soy,* a mild chicken curry with flat egg noodles.

There are several *kôw soy* shops outside of the old city that are mobbed by lunchtime connoisseurs. Our favourites include the following:

Kao Soi Fueng Fah (Soi 1, Th Charoen Phrathet; mains 40-60B; ⊙ 7am-9pm) The best of the Muslim-run *kôw soy* vendors along Halal St, with the choice of beef or chicken with your noodles in curry broth.

Khao Soi Lam Duan Fah Ham (352/22 Th Charoenrat/Th Faham; mains from 40B; ⊙ 9am-4pm) North of the Th Ratanakosin bridge on the east bank, Th Faham is known as Chiang Mai's *kôw soy* ghetto. Khao Soi Lam Duan Fah Ham is the pick of the bunch, serving delicious bowls of *kôw soy* to eager crowds of punters.

AUM Vegetarian Food
VEGETARIAN $

(65 Th Moon Muang; mains 80-150B; ⊙10.30am-8.30pm; ☑) One of the original health-food peddlers, AUM (pronounced 'om') attracts crowds of vegie travellers and a few vegie-curious carnivores. The menu runs from vegetable maki rolls to blue sticky rice and delicious sôm·đam (Isan-style pounded papaya salad) with cashews and carrot. They make their own mushroom-based stock.

Dada Kafe
VEGETARIAN $

(Th Ratchamankha; mains 60-140B; ⊙9am-9pm, to 6pm May & Jun; ☑) A tiny hole in the wall that does a busy trade in vitamin-rich, tasty vegetarian health food and smoothies. Wholesome ingredients like pollen and wheatgrass are whisked into fruit shakes and the food menu includes vegie burgers, omelettes, salads, sandwiches and curries with brown rice.

Blue Diamond
VEGETARIAN $

(35/1 Soi 9, Th Moon Muang; mains 65-140B; ⊙7am-9pm Mon-Sat; ☑) Packed with fresh produce, pre-packaged spice and herb mixes and freshly baked treats, Blue Diamond feels a little like a wholefood store. The cafe offers an adventurous menu of sandwiches, salads, curries, stir-fries and curious fusion dishes such as đôm yam macaroni.

Swan
BURMESE $

(48 Th Chaiyaphum; mains 70-150B; ⊙11am-11pm) This worn-looking restaurant just east of the old city offers a trip across the border, with a menu of tasty Burmese dishes such as gaang hang lay (dry, sour pork curry with tamarind and peanuts). The backyard courtyard provides an escape from the moat traffic.

I-Berry
DESSERTS $

(off Soi 17, Th Nimmanhaemin; ice creams & smoothies from 60B; ⊙10am-10pm; ☎) Mobbed day and night, this shop selling ice-cream and fruit smoothies has star power. I-Berry is owned by Thai comedian Udom Taepanich (nicknamed 'Nose' for his signature feature). When ordering, check the menu signs and order the delicious smoothies, shakes and sundaes using their rather elaborate names.

★ Tong Tem Toh
NORTHERN THAI $$

(Soi 13, Th Nimmamnhaemin; mains 50-170B; ⊙11am-9pm) Set in an old teak house, this trendy cafe serves deliciously authentic Northern Thai cuisine. The menu roams beyond the usual Thai standards to local specialities such as nám prík ong (chilli paste with vegetables for dipping) and gaang hang lay (Burmese-style pork curry with peanut and tamarind).

Huen Phen
NORTHERN THAI $$

(☑053 277103; 112 Th Ratchamankha; lunch dishes 40-60B; evening mains 80-200B; ⊙8am-3pm & 5-10pm) This antique-cluttered restaurant cooks up some true northern magic. By day, meals are served in the canteen out front, but at night, the action moves back to the atmospheric dining room, where you can sample a full range of delicious, highly spiced jungle curries, stir-fries and regional variations on nám prík (chilli sauces with vegetables to dip).

CHIANG MAI CAFES

Chiang Mai is certifiably coffee crazy, with cafes serving locally grown Arabica beans. Here are a few of our faves:

Akha Ama Cafe (www.akhaama.com; 9/1 Soi 3, Th Hutsadisawee, Mata Apartment; coffee from 50B; ⊙9am-9pm; ☎) Probably the best brew in Chiang Mai, Akha Ama specialises in organic, fair-trade coffee, the brainchild of an enterprising Akha who was the first in his village to graduate from college. There's a branch (www.akhaama.com; 175/1 Th Ratchadamnoen; ⊙8am-6pm; ☎) on Th Ratchadamnoen in the old city.

Café de Museum (Th Ratwithi, Lanna Folklife Museum; drinks from 40B; ⊙9am-6pm Mon-Fri, to 7pm Sat & Sun; ☎) The perfect spot to refuel after touring the old-city museums, with a full range of stimulating hot, cold and iced brews. You can sit indoors in comfortable air-conditioning or outside on the terrace in front of the Lanna Folklife Museum.

Ristr8to (153/3 Th Nimmanhaemin; coffee 65-120B; ⊙8am-7pm Wed-Mon) In the midst of the most commercial part of Th Nimmanhaemin, this coffeeshop offers a broader menu than most, with single-origin beans from across the globe and a full range of espresso-based and filtered coffees, supplied with wine-style tasting notes.

Girasole
ITALIAN $$

(☑053 276388; Kad Klang Wiang, Th Ratchadam-noen; mains 90-260B; ⊙11am-9pm) In the tidy little Kad Klang Wiang arcade, Girasole makes a convincing claim to offer the city's best pizzas, prepared using real pepperoni and other hard-to-find ingredients. There are several spaces for eating, both inside and outside, and the menu runs to superior pasta dishes and *secondi piatti,* plus tasty gelato for dessert.

★Tengoku
JAPANESE $$$

(☑053 215801; Soi 5, Th Nimmanhaemin; mains 130-1650B; ⊙11am-2pm & 5.30-10pm; 🛜) Chiang Mai loves Japanese food, but Tengoku leaves everywhere else in town in the shade of Mt Fuji. This sleekly modern restaurant serves superior sushi, yummy yakitori, spectacular sukiyaki and wonderful wagyu steaks, plus cheaper bento box set meals.

🍺 Drinking & Nightlife

The ale flows fast and furious at the tourist bars in the old city. West of the old city, Th Nimmanhaemin is where Thai uni students go bar-hopping.

★Riverside Bar & Restaurant
BAR

(www.theriversidechiangmai.com; 9-11 Th Char-oenrat/Th Faham; mains 130-370B; ⊙10am-1am) Almost everyone ends up at Riverside at some point in their stay. Set in an old teak house, it feels like a boondocks reimagining of a Hard Rock Cafe, and bands play nightly until late. Stake out a claim on the riverside terrace or the upstairs balcony to catch the evening breezes on Mae Ping.

Zoe In Yellow
BAR

(40/12 Th Ratwithi; ⊙11am-2am) Part of a com-plex of open-air bars at the corner of Th Ratchaphakhinai and Th Ratwithi, Zoe is where backpackers come to sink pitchers of cold Chang, sip cocktails from buckets, rock out to cheesy dancefloor-fillers, canoodle and swap travel stories until the wee hours.

Blar Blar Bar
BEER GARDEN

(Soi 5, Th Nimmanhaemin; ⊙6pm-midnight) A big and boozy bar popular with uni students and other youthful punters, with waitresses pro-moting branded beers and live music in the courtyard. Use it as a staging post before mov-ing on to other more intimate drinking spots.

Warmup Cafe
CLUB

(www.facebook.com/warmupcafe1999; 40 Th Nim-manhaemin; ⊙6pm-2am) A Nimmanhaemin survivor, Warmup has been rocking since 1999, attracting a young, trendy and beauti-ful crowd as the evening wears on. Hip-hop spins in the main room, electronic beats reverberate in the lounge, and rock bands squeal out solos in the garden.

☆ Entertainment

★Sudsanan
LIVE MUSIC

(off Th Huay Kaew; ⊙6pm-midnight) A stroll down an unlit dirt track off Th Huay Kaew will take you to a creaky wooden house full of character and music. It's primarily a lo-cal hangout, with Thais of all ages sipping whisky, chewing the fat and nodding appre-ciatively to performers playing tear-jerking *pleng pêu·a chee·wít* (songs for life).

Look for the easy-to-miss signboard just west of Th Ratchaphuek.

Nabé
LIVE MUSIC

(Th Wichayanon; ⊙6pm-1am) A happening spot for Chiang Mai twenty-somethings, with cold beers, hot snacks and rocking live bands who can actually play their instruments, singing Thai songs for a Thai audience.

🛍 Shopping

Chiang Mai has long been an important centre for handicrafts. Th Tha Phae and the small soi near Talat Warorot are filled with interesting antique and textile stores.

★Studio Naenna
CLOTHING, HOMEWARES

(www.studio-naenna.com; 22 Soi 1, Th Nimmanhae-min; ⊙10am-6pm) The colours of the moun-tains have been woven into the naturally dyed silks and cottons here, part of a project to preserve traditional weaving and em-broidery. You can see the whole production process at their main **workshop** (www.stu-dio-naenna.com; 138/8 Soi Chang Khian; ⊙9am-5pm Mon-Fri, also 9am-5pm Sat Oct-Mar), north of Th Huay Kaew.

Kesorn Arts
HANDICRAFTS

(154-156 Th Tha Phae; ⊙9am-6pm) The col-lector's best friend, this cluttered shop has been trading old bric-a-brac from the hills for years. It specialises mainly in textiles, lacquerware and jewellery.

Ethnic Lanna
HANDICRAFTS

(www.ethniclanna.com; Th Singharat; ⊙9am-8pm Mon-Sat) A good selection of tribal bags, trin-kets and textiles, sold on a fair-trade basis.

PEDESTRIAN COMMERCE

Once upon a time Chiang Mai was a destination for itinerant Yunnanese merchants trading goods along an ancient route from China all the way to Burma. Today the city's pedestrian markets tap into this tradition and expertly merge commerce and culture.

Saturday Walking Street (ถนนเดินวันเสาร์; Th Wualai; ⊗ 4pm-midnight Sat) As the sun starts to dip on Saturday afternoon, the **Saturday Walking Street** takes over Th Wualai, running southwest from Pratu Chiang Mai at the southern entrance to the old city. There is barely space to move as locals and tourists from across the world haggle vigorously for carved soaps, novelty dog collars, wood-carvings, Buddha paintings, hill-tribe trinkets, Thai musical instruments, T-shirts, paper lanterns and umbrellas, silver jewellery and herbal remedies.

Sunday Walking Street (ถนนเดินวันอาทิตย์; Th Ratchadamnoen; ⊗ 4pm-midnight Sun) On Sunday afternoon, Thanon Ratchadamnoen is taken over by the boisterous Sunday Walking Street, which feels even more animated than the Saturday Walking Street because of the energetic food markets that open up wát courtyards along the route. If you went to Th Wualai on Saturday, you'll recognise many of the same sellers and buskers that you spotted the night before. The markets are a major source of income for local families and many traders spend the whole week hand-making merchandise to sell on Saturday and Sunday.

Talat Warorot (ตลาดวโรรส; cnr Th Chang Moi & Th Praisani; ⊗ 6am-5pm) Chiang Mai's oldest public market, Warorot (also spelt 'Waroros') is a great place to connect with the city's Thai soul. Alongside souvenir vendors you'll find parades of stalls selling must-have items for ordinary Thai households: woks, toys, fishermen's nets, pickled tea leaves, wigs, sticky-rice steamers, Thai-style sausages, *kâap mŏo* (pork rinds), live catfish and tiny statues for spirit houses. It's easy to spend half a day wandering the covered walkways, watching locals browsing, and haggling for goods that actually have a practical use back home.

Chiang Mai Night Bazaar (Th Chang Khlan; ⊗ 7pm-midnight) Chiang Mai Night Bazaar is one of the city's main night-time attractions, especially for families, and is the modern legacy of the original Yunnanese trading caravans that stopped here along the ancient trade route between Simao (in China) and Mawlamyaing (on Myanmar's Gulf of Martaban coast). Today the night bazaar sells the usual tourist souvenirs, similar to what you'll find at Bangkok's street markets.

Backstreet Books BOOKS
(2/8 Th Chang Moi Kao; ⊗ 8am-8pm) Backstreet, a rambling shop along 'book alley' (Th Chang Moi Kao), has a good selection of guidebooks and stacks of crime and thriller novels.

Maya Lifestyle Shopping Center SHOPPING CENTRE
(www.mayashoppingcenter.com; Th Huay Kaew; ⊗ 11am-10pm Mon-Fri, from 10am Sat & Sun) Chiang Mai's flashiest shopping centre hides behind a geometric facade, with all the big international brands, a whole floor of electronics, a good supermarket, multiscreen cinema and excellent eating options on the 4th floor.

ℹ Information

DANGERS & ANNOYANCES

The majority of guesthouses in town subsidise their cheap room rates through commissions on booking trekking tours. For this reason, they might limit nontrekkers to a three-day stay, but ask at check-in.

Avoid the private bus and minivan services from Bangkok's Th Khao San to Chiang Mai because they are full of commission-generating schemes to subsidise the cut-rate fares.

Dengue has become a major concern in Chiang Mai province, especially during the wet season. Use DEET-insect repellent throughout the day and night to avoid mosquito bites.

EMERGENCY

Immigration Office (☑ 053 201755; http://chiangmaiimm.com; off Rte 1141/Th Mahidol;

⊘8.30am-4.30pm Mon-Fri) By the airport; handles visa extensions.

Tourist Police (☑053 247318, 24hr emergency ☑1155; 608 Rimping Plaza, Th Charoenraj; ⊘6am-midnight) Volunteer staff speak a variety of languages.

MEDICAL SERVICES

Chiang Mai Ram Hospital (☑053 920300; www.chiangmairam.com; 8 Th Bunreuangrit) The most modern hospital in town.

McCormick Hospital (☑053 921777; www.mccormick.in.th; 133 Th Kaew Nawarat) Former missionary hospital; good for minor treatments.

MONEY

All major Thai banks have branches and ATMs throughout Chiang Mai; many are along Th Tha Phae and Th Moon Muang.

TOURIST INFORMATION

Tourism Authority of Thailand (TAT; ☑053 248604; www.tourismthailand.org; Th Chiang Mai-Lamphun; ⊘8.30am-4.30pm) English-speaking staff provide maps, and advice on travel across Thailand.

ⓘ Getting There & Away

AIR

Domestic and international flights arrive and depart from **Chiang Mai International Airport** (☑053 270222; www.chiangmaiairportthai.com), 3km southwest of the old city.

Schedules vary with the seasons and tourist demand. **Thai Airways** (THAI; ☑053 211044, 023 561111; www.thaiair.com; 240 Th Phra Pokklao; ⊘8.30am-4.30pm Mon-Fri) has the widest range of domestic routes, but **Air Asia** (☑053 234645; www.airasia.com; 416 Th Tha Phae; ⊘10am-8pm) and other budget carriers are rapidly expanding domestic and international routes.

Destinations include Bangkok (1800B to 2200B), Phuket (2350B), Yangon (from 4950B), Luang Prabang (from 5000B) and Kuala Lumpur (3340B).

BUS

There are two bus stations in Chiang Mai. **Arcade bus terminal** (Th Kaew Nawarat), 3km northeast of town, covers long-distance destinations. From the town centre, a túk-túk should cost 80B to 100B; *rót daang*, about 60B. **Chang Pheuak bus terminal** (Th Chang Pheuak), north of the old city, handles buses to nearby provincial towns (Tha Ton); to reach the bus station catch a *rót daang* (20B).

TRAIN

The train station is 2.5km east of the old city. With the rise of budget airfares and a series of derailments in 2013, the once popular overnight trains from Bangkok's Hualamphong station are less attractive. At the time of research, fares to/from Bangkok were as follows:

2nd-class sleeper berth 531B to 581B fan, 791B to 881B air-con

1st-class sleeper cabin 1253B to 1953B air-con

Transport to the station should cost 40B to 60B.

ⓘ Getting Around

Red *sŏrng·tăa·ou* (called *rót daang*) circulate around the city operating as shared taxis. Flag one down and tell them your destination; if they are going that way, they'll nod and pick up other passengers along the way. The starting fare is 20B, with longer trips 40B. Túk-túk rides around town cost about 60B to 80B; negotiate the fare beforehand.

You can rent bicycles (100B to 150B a day) or 100cc motorcycles (from 200B) to explore Chiang Mai. Bicycles are a great way to get around the city.

THAILAND CHIANG MAI

BUS TRANSPORT FROM CHIANG MAI

DESTINATION	PRICE (B)	DURATION (HR)	FREQUENCY
Bangkok	420-840	9-10	frequent
Chiang Khong	280-430	6½	3 daily
Chiang Rai	140-280	3-4	hourly
Khorat (Nakhon Ratchasima)	580-680	12	11 daily
Mae Hong Son	140-185	6	every 1½hr
Mae Hong Son (minivan)	250	5	hourly
Mae Sai	175-350	5	7 daily
Mae Sot	320	6	2 daily
Pai	from 75	4	hourly
Pai (minivan)	150	3	hourly
Sukhothai	from 230B	5-6	10 daily

Around Chiang Mai

Doi Inthanon
National Park
อุทยานแห่งชาติดอยอินทนนท์

Thailand's highest peak – Doi Inthanon (often abbreviated to Doi In) – soars to 2565m above sea level, an impressive altitude for the kingdom, but a tad diminutive compared to its cousins in the Himalaya. Surrounding this granite massif is a 1000-sq-km **national park** (☑053 286730; adult/child 300/150B, car/motorcycle 30/20B; ☺4am-6pm), dotted with hiking trails and waterfalls and enveloped in an impenetrable curtain of jungle. When the heat of Chiang Mai gets too much, locals decamp to Doi Inthanon for day trips, especially during the New Year holiday when there's the rarely seen phenomenon of frost at the summit.

Most visitors come with private transport or on a tour from Chiang Mai; if coming by motorcycle from Chiang Mai allow 2½ hours each way.

Mae Sa Valley Loop   แม่สา

One of the easiest mountain escapes, the Mae Sa valley loop travels from the lowlands' concrete expanse into the highlands' forested frontier. The 100km route makes a good day trip with private transport.

Head north of Chiang Mai on Rte 107 (Th Chang Pheuak) toward Mae Rim, then left onto Rte 1096. The road becomes more rural but there's a steady supply of tour-bus attractions: orchid farms, butterfly parks, snake farms, you name it.

The road eventually starts to climb and twist into the fertile **Mae Sa Valley**, once a high-altitude basin for growing opium poppies. Now the valley's hill-tribe farmers have re-seeded their terraced fields with sweet peppers, cabbage, flowers and fruits – which are then sold to the royal agriculture projects under the Doi Kham label.

On the outskirts of the valley, the road swings around the mountain ridge and starts to rise and dip until it reaches the conifer zone. Beyond, the landscape unfolds in a cascade of mountains and eventually the road spirals down into **Samoeng**, a pretty Thai town, and then arcs back into Chiang Mai.

Chiang Rai   เชียงราย

POP 70,000

Leafy and well groomed, Chiang Rai is more liveable than visitable. The town itself is a convenient base for touring the Golden Triangle and an alternative to Chiang Mai for arranging hill-tribe treks. Don't assume you'll be the only foreigner in town; Chiang Rai is well loved by well-heeled package tourists.

◉ Sights

Wat Phra Kaew   BUDDHIST TEMPLE
(วัดพระแก้ว; Th Trairat; ☺temple 7am-7pm, museum 9am-5pm) **FREE** Originally called Wat Pa Yia (Bamboo Forest Monastery) in the local dialect, this is the city's most revered

---

SLOW BOATS TO CHIANG RAI

Escape the daredevil highway antics of Thailand's bus drivers with a slow ride on Mae Nam Kok departing from Tha Ton, north of Chiang Mai. The river ride is a big hit with tourists and includes stops at hill-tribe villages that specialise in Coca-Colas and souvenirs. This isn't uncharted territory but it is scenic and relaxing.

Chiang Rai–bound boats (☑053 053727; ticket 350B; ☺departs 12.30pm) leave from Tha Ton and make stops along the way at Mae Salak, a large Lahu village, and Ban Ruam Mit, a village of mixed hill-tribe groups. The trip takes three to five hours; the boat carries 12 passengers.

In order to catch the boat on time, you'll need to overnight in Tha Ton; there are several pretty riverside guesthouses, including **Apple Resort** (☑053 373144; applethaton@ yahoo.com; r 500-1200B; ❋ 🖘). Buses from Chiang Mai to Tha Ton leave from Chang Pheuak bus station.

You can also do the trip in reverse (from Chiang Rai to Tha Ton), a less popular option because it takes much longer. Boats disembark from Chiang Rai's **CR Pier** (☑053 750009; ☺7am-4pm) in the northwest corner of town at 7am.

Adding to your indecision, you could skip the river and backdoor to Chiang Rai via the ridgetop village of Mae Salong.

WAT RONG KHUN & BAAN DUM

Modern art meets religious symbolism in two of Chiang Rai's bizarre but beloved attractions.

Wat Rong Khun (White Temple, วัดร่องขุ่น; off Rte 1/AH2; ⊘8am-5pm Mon-Fri, to 5.30pm Sat & Sun) Whereas most of Thailand's Buddhist temples have centuries of history, Wat Rong Khun's construction began in 1997 by noted Thai painter-turned-architect Chalermchai Kositpipat. Seen from a distance, the temple appears to be made of glittering porcelain; a closer look reveals that the appearance is due to a combination of whitewash and clear-mirrored chips. It's located about 13km south of Chiang Rai. To get here, hop on one of the regular buses that run from Chiang Rai to Chiang Mai or Phayao (20B).

Baan Dum (บ้านดำ, Black House; off Rte 1/AH2; ⊘9am-noon & 1-5pm) The bizarre brainchild of Thai National Artist Thawan Duchanee, and a rather sinister counterpoint to Wat Rong Khun, Baan Dum unites several structures, most of which are stained black and ominously decked out with animal pelts and bones. It's located 13km north of Chiang Rai in Nang Lae; any Mae Sai–bound bus will drop you off here for around 20B.

Buddhist temple. The main prayer hall is a medium-sized, well-preserved wooden structure. The octagonal *chedi* behind it dates from the late 14th century and is in typical Lanna style. The adjacent two-storey wooden building is a museum housing various Lanna artefacts.

Oub Kham Museum MUSEUM
(พิพิธภัณฑ์อูบคำ; www.oubkhammuseum.com; Th Nakhai; adult/child 300/100B; ⊘8am-5pm) This slightly zany museum houses an impressive collection of paraphernalia from virtually every corner of the former Lanna kingdom. The items, some of which truly are one of a kind, range from a monkey-bone food taster used by Lanna royalty to an impressive carved throne from Chiang Tung, Myanmar. It's located 2km west of the town centre and can be a bit tricky to find; túk-túk will go here for about 60B.

Hilltribe Museum & Education Center MUSEUM
(พิพิธภัณฑ์และศูนย์การศึกษาชาวเขา; www.pdacr. org; 3rd fl, 620/25 Th Thanalai; 50B; ⊘8.30am-6pm Mon-Fri, 10am-6pm Sat & Sun) This museum and cultural centre is a good place to visit before undertaking any hill-tribe trek. Run by the nonprofit Population & Community Development Association (PDA), the displays are underwhelming in their visual presentation, but contain a wealth of information on Thailand's various tribes and the issues that face them.

Mae Fah Luang Art & Culture Park MUSEUM
(ไร่แม่ฟ้าหลวง; www.maefahluang.org/rmfl; 313 Mu 7, Ban Pa Ngiw; adult/child 200B/free; ⊘8am-5pm Tue-Sun) In addition to a museum that houses one of Thailand's biggest collections of Lanna artefacts, this vast, meticulously landscaped compound includes antique and contemporary art, Buddhist temples and other structures. It's located about 4km west of the centre of Chiang Rai; a túk-túk or taxi here will run to around 100B.

Tham Tu Pu & Buddha Cave BUDDHIST TEMPLE
(ถ้ำตูปู่/ถ้ำพระ; ⊘dawn-dusk) **FREE** Cross the Mae Fah Luang Bridge (located just northwest of the city centre) to the northern side of Mae Nam Kok and you'll come to a turn-off for both Tham Tu Pu and the Buddha Cave. Neither attraction is particularly amazing on its own, but the surrounding country is beautiful and would make an ideal destination for a lazy bike or motorcycle ride.

🏃 Activities

Most two-day tours (starting at 2900B) typically cover the areas of Doi Tung, Doi Mae Salong or Chiang Khong. The following are primarily nonprofit community development organisations working in hill-tribe communities that use trekking as an awareness campaign and fundraiser.

Mirror Foundation TREKKING
(☏053 737 616; www.thailandecotour.org) Although its rates are higher, trekking with this nonprofit NGO helps support the training of its local guides. Treks range from one to three days and traverse the Akha, Karen and Lahu villages of Mae Yao District, north of Chiang Rai.

Chiang Rai

PDA Tours & Travel
TREKKING

(☎053 740 088; www.pda.or.th/chiangrai/package_tour.htm; Hilltribe Museum & Education Center, 3rd fl, 620/25 Th Thanalai; ⊘8.30am-6pm Mon-Fri, 10am-6pm Sat & Sun) One- to three-day treks are available through this NGO. Profits go back into community projects that include HIV/AIDS education, mobile health clinics, education scholarships and the establishment of village-owned banks.

Rai Pian Karuna
TREKKING

(☎082 195 5645; www.facebook.com/raipiankaruna) This new, community-based social enterprise conducts one- and multiday treks and homestays at Akha, Lahu and Lua villages in Mae Chan, which is north of Chiang Rai. Other activities, from weeklong volunteering stints to cooking courses, are also on offer.

🛏 Sleeping

Baan Bua Guest House
GUESTHOUSE $

(☎053 718 880; www.baanbua-guesthouse.com; 879/2 Th Jetyod; r 250-550B; ❀@🤙) This quiet guesthouse consists of a strip of 11 bright green rooms surrounding an inviting garden. Rooms are simple, but unanimously clean and cosy.

FUN-D Hostel
HOSTEL $

(☎053 712 123; www.facebook.com/FunDHostelChiangRai; 753 Th Phahonyothin; dm 260-290B, r 800B, all incl breakfast; ❀@🤙) A lively-feeling hostel located, appropriately, above a restaurant-bar-cafe. Dorms are spacious and bright, and range from six to eight beds, the more expensive of which have semi-private, en-suite bathroom facilities.

The North
HOTEL $

(☎053 719 873; www.thenorth.co.th; 612/100-101 Sirikon Market; dm 200B, r 390-490B; ❀@🤙)

Chiang Rai

◎ Sights
1 Hilltribe Museum & Education
   Center..C2
2 Wat Phra Kaew.....................................A1

⊕ Activities, Courses & Tours
PDA Tours & Travel.....................(see 1)

⊜ Sleeping
3 Baan Bua Guest House.......................B4
4 Baan Warabordee...............................C4
5 FUN-D Hostel.......................................D3
6 Moon & Sun Hotel...............................C2
7 The North...B3

⊗ Eating
8 Khao Soi Phor Jai................................B3
9 Phu Lae...C2

⊜ Drinking & Nightlife
10 BaanChivitMai Bakery.........................B4
11 Cat Bar..B4
12 Easy House..B3

⊜ Shopping
13 Night Bazaar...B3
14 Walking Street......................................B2

⊕ Transport
15 Interprovincial Bus Station.................C4

This hotel has provided the drab market/bus station area with a bit of colour. The 15 rooms here combine both Thai and modern design, some attached to inviting chill-out areas.

Baan Warabordee　　　　　　　HOTEL $
(☏053 754 488; baanwarabordee@hotmail.com; 59/1 Th Sanpanard; r 500-600B; ❋🛜) A handsome, good-value hotel has been made from this three-storey Thai villa. Rooms are decked out in dark woods and light cloths, and are equipped with air-con, fridge and hot water.

Moon & Sun Hotel　　　　　　　HOTEL $
(☏053 719 279; 632 Th Singhaclai; r 500-600B, ste 800B; ❋🛜) Bright and sparkling clean, this little hotel offers large, modern, terrific-value rooms. Some feature four-poster beds, while all come with desk, cable TV and refrigerator. Suites have a separate, spacious sitting area.

**★ Bamboo Nest
de Chiang Rai**　　　　　　GUESTHOUSE $$
(☏09 5686 4755, 08 9953 2330; www.bamboo nest-chiangrai.com; bungalows incl breakfast 800-1800B) The Lahu village that's home to this unique accommodation is only 23km from Chiang Rai but feels a world away. Bamboo Nest takes the form of simple but spacious bamboo huts perched on a hill overlooking tiered rice fields. The only electricity is provided by solar panels, so leave your laptops in town and instead take part in activities that range from birdwatching to hiking.

Bamboo Nest is located about 2km from the headquarters of Lamnamkok National Park; free transport to/from Chiang Rai is available for those staying two nights or more.

✖ Eating

★ Lung Eed　　　　　　NORTHERN THAI $
(Th Watpranorn; mains 40-100B; ⊕11.30am-9pm Mon-Sat) One of Chiang Rai's most delicious dishes is available at this simple shophouse restaurant. There's an English-language menu on the wall, but don't miss the sublime *lap kai* (minced chicken fried with local spices and topped with crispy deep-fried chicken skin, shallots and garlic). The restaurant is on Th Watpranorn about 150m east of Rte 1/AH2.

Paa Suk　　　　　　NORTHERN THAI $
(Th Sankhongnoi, no roman-script sign; mains 10-25B; ⊕8.30am-3pm) Paa Suk does big, rich bowls of *kà·nǒm jeen nám ngée·o* (a broth of pork or beef and tomatoes served over fresh rice noodles). The restaurant is between Soi 4 and Soi 5 of Th Sankhongnoi (the street is called Th Sathanpayabarn where it intersects with the southern end Th Phahonyothin); look for the yellow sign.

Khao Soi Phor Jai　　　　　　THAI $
(Th Jetyod, no roman-script sign; mains 35-60B; ⊕7.30am-5pm) Phor Jai serves mild but tasty bowls of the eponymous curry noodle dish, as well as a few other northern Thai staples. Look for the open-air shophouse with the blue interior.

Phu Lae　　　　　　THAI $
(673/1 Th Thanalai; mains 80-320B; ⊕11.30am-3pm & 5.30-11pm) This air-conditioned restaurant is popular with Thai tourists for its tasty but somewhat gentrified northern Thai fare. Recommended local dishes include the *gaang hang·lair* (pork belly in a rich Burmese-style curry) served with cloves of pickled garlic and *sâi òo·a* (herb-packed pork sausages).

THAILAND CHIANG RAI

🍷 Drinking

Th Jetyod is Chiang Rai's bar strip thanks to popular **Cat Bar** (1013/1 Th Jetyod; ⊙5pm-1am) and **Easy House** (cnr Th Jetyod & Th Pemavipat; ⊙5pm-midnight).

BaanChivitMai Bakery CAFE
(www.baanchivitmai.com; Th Prasopsook; ⊙8am-7pm Mon-Fri, to 6pm Sat & Sun; 🛜) In addition to a proper cup of joe made from local beans, you can snack on surprisingly authentic Swedish-style sweets and Western-style meals and sandwiches at this popular bakery. Profits go to BaanChivitMai, an organisation that runs homes and education projects for vulnerable, orphaned or AIDS-affected children.

🛍 Shopping

★ Walking Street MARKET
(Th Thanalai; ⊙4-10pm Sat) If you're in town on a Saturday evening be sure not to miss the open-air Walking Street, an expansive street market focusing on all things Chiang Rai, from handicrafts to local dishes. The market spans Th Thanalai from the Hilltribe Museum to the morning market.

Night Bazaar MARKET
(off Th Phahonyothin; ⊙6-11pm) Adjacent to the bus station off Th Phahonyothin is Chiang Rai's night market. On a much smaller scale than the one in Chiang Mai, it is nevertheless an OK place to find an assortment of handicrafts and touristy souvenirs.

Thanon Khon Muan MARKET
(Th Sankhongnoi; ⊙6-9pm Sun) Come Sunday evening, the stretch of Th Sankhongnoi from Soi 2 heading west is closed to traffic, and in its place are vendors selling clothes, handicrafts and local food. Th Sankhongnoi is called Th Sathanpayabarn where it intersects with the southern end of Th Phahonyothin.

ℹ Information

Banks can be found along Th Thanalai and along Th Phahonyothin. Internet access is readily available for about 30B.

Overbrook Hospital (☑053 711 366; www.overbrook-hospital.com; Th Singhaclai) English is spoken at this modern hospital.

Tourism Authority of Thailand (TAT; ☑053 744 674, nationwide ☑1672; tatchrai@tat.or.th; Th Singhaclai; ⊙8.30am-4.30pm) English is limited, but staff here do their best to give advice and can provide a small selection of maps and brochures.

Tourist Police (☑053 740 249, nationwide ☑1155; Th Uttarakit; ⊙24hr) English is spoken and police are on stand-by around the clock.

ℹ Getting There & Away

Chiang Rai International Airport (Mae Fah Luang International Airport; ☑053 798000; www.chiangraiairportonline.com) is 8km north of town. **Air Asia** (☑053 793 543, nationwide 02 515 9999; www.airasia.com; Chiang Rai International Airport; ⊙8am-9pm), **Nok Air** (☑053 793000, nationwide 1318; www.nokair.co.th; Chiang Rai International Airport; ⊙8am-

---

TRANSPORT FROM CHIANG RAI

DESTINATION	AIR	BUS	MINIVAN
Bangkok	2135-3590B, 1¼hr, 5 daily	493-935B, 13hr, frequent 7am-7pm	
Chiang Khong		65B, 2hr, frequent 6am-5pm	
Chiang Mai		144-288B, 3-7hr, hourly 6.30am-7.30pm	
Chiang Saen		39B, 1½hr; frequent 6.20am-7pm	45B, 1½hr, hourly
Kunming (China)	7500B, 1hr, 3 weekly		
Nakhon Ratchasima (Khorat)		514-771B, 12-13hr, 6 daily	
Luang Prabang (Laos)		950B, 16hr, 1pm	
Mae Sai		39B, 1½hr, frequent 6am-8pm	46B, 1½hr, frequent 6.30am-6pm
Mae Sot		384-493B, 12hr, 8.15am & 8.45am	
Phitsanulok		273-410B, 6-7hr, hourly 6.30am-10.30pm	
Sukhothai		300B, 8hr, hourly 7.30am-2.30pm	

GETTING TO LAOS: NORTHERN BORDERS

Chiang Rai to Huay Xai

The Chiang Khong/Huay Xai crossing is the most popular crossing for Chiang Mai–Luang Prabang (Laos) travellers. Since the completion of the Thai-Lao Friendship Bridge 4, the boat crossing is only for locals.

Getting to the border The bridge is 10km south of Chiang Khong, a 150B sǎhm·lór ride from town.

At the border After passing through the **Thai immigration office** (☑ 053 792824; ⊙ 7am-8.30pm), board the shuttle bus (from 20B) to Lao immigration, where visas are available on arrival.

Moving on On the Lao side, sǎhm·lór charge 100B (25,000K) per person to Huay Xai. Destinations from Huay Xai's bus station include the major Laos destinations as well as southern China (though Chinese visas need to be arranged beforehand).

There is also a slow boat (1000B/250,000K, two days, departs around 10.30am) to Luang Prabang and a noisy fast boat (350,000K, six to seven hours, frequent departures from 9am to 11am). There have been reports of accidents. Ticket agents in Chiang Khong can make bookings and arrange transport.

For information on doing this crossing in reverse, see p352.

Phrae/Nan to Hongsa

The Ban Huay Kon/Muang Ngeun border crossing is 140km north of Nan, which is somewhat off the beaten track. Transport originates in Phrae, which is a little less off the track.

Getting to the border To Ban Huay Kon, minivans start in Phrae and stop in Nan (100B, three hours, five daily from 5am to 9.30am).

At the border After passing the Thai immigration booth, foreigners can purchase a 30-day visa for Laos; prices are based on nationality and surcharges may apply.

Moving on Proceed 2.5km to the Lao village of Muang Ngeun. Sǒrng·tǎa·ou leave from the passenger car station beside the market for Hongsa (40,000K, 1½ hours, between 2pm and 4pm).

For information on doing this crossing in reverse, see p352.

7pm) and **Thai Lion Air** (☑ nationwide 02 529 9999; www.lionairthai.com; Chiang Rai International Airport; ⊙ 8am-8pm) fly to Bangkok's Don Muang and **Thai Airways International** (THAI; ☑ 053 798202, nationwide 02 356 1111; www.thaiair.com; ⊙ 8am-8pm) and **Thai Smile** (☑ 053 798200, nationwide 02 118 8888; www.thaismileair.com; Chiang Rai International Airport; ⊙ 8am-8pm) fly to Suvarnabhumi. **China Eastern** (☑ nationwide 02 636 6980; www.flychinaeastern.com; ⊙ 8.30am-5pm) flies to Kunming. From town, a metered taxi will cost 120B.

Chiang Rai's **inter-provincial bus station** (☑ 053 715952; Th Prasopsook) is in the heart of town; it also has ordinary (fan) buses and minivans. The **long-distance bus station** (☑ 053 773989) is 5km south of town on Hwy 1. Sǒrng·tǎa·ou link the two stations (15B).

Chiang Rai is accessible by boat along Mae Nam Kok from Tha Ton, the northern tip of Chiang Mai Province.

Golden Triangle

The three-country border between Thailand, Myanmar and Laos forms the legendary Golden Triangle, once a mountainous frontier where the opium poppy was a cash crop for the region's ethnic minorities. Thailand has successfully stamped out its cultivation through infrastructure projects, crop-substitution programs and aggressive law enforcement. But the porous border and lawless areas of the neighbouring countries have switched production to the next generation's drug of choice: methamphetamine and, to a lesser extent, heroin. Much of this illicit activity is invisible to the average visitor and the region's heyday as the leading opium producer is now marketed as a tourist attraction.

Mae Sai
แม่สาย

POP 22,000

Thailand's northernmost town is a busy trading post for gems, jewellery, cashews and lacquerware, and is also a legal border crossing into Myanmar. Many travellers make the trek here to extend their Thai visa or to dip their toes into Myanmar. The town is also a convenient base for exploring the surrounding Golden Triangle area.

Most guesthouses line the street along the Mae Nam Sai to the left of the border checkpoint. **Maesai Guest House** (☑053 732021; 688 Th Wiengpangkam; bungalows 200-600B; �) has a collection of A-frame bungalows with varying amenities. **Afterglow** (☑053 734188; www.afterglowhostel.com; 139/5 Th Phahonyothin; r 500-800B, bungalows 500B, all incl breakfast; ✱�) is injecting Mae Sai with a hipster scene. **Mom Home** (☑053 731537; haritchayahana@gmail.com; off Th Sailomjoy; r 300-500B; ✱�) is a shiny newcomer.

Mae Sai has a **night market** (Th Phahonyothin; mains 30-60B; ⊙5-11pm) with an excellent mix of Thai and Chinese dishes. **Bismillah Halal Food** (Soi 4, Th Phahonyothin; mains 30-100B; ⊙5am-5pm) does an excellent biryani.

The **bus station** (☑053 646403; Rte 110) is 4km from the immigration office. Destinations include Bangkok (519B to 980B, 12 hours, frequent), Chiang Mai (144B to 288B, five hours, nine departures), Chiang Rai (39B, 1½ hours, frequent) and Tha Ton (92B, two hours, 8am and 2pm).

On Th Phahonyothin by Soi 8 there's a bus stop from which *sŏrng·tăa·ou* run to Sop Ruak (50B, frequent) and terminate in Chiang Saen (50B). *Sŏrng·tăa·ou* around town cost 15B.

Mae Salong
แม่ สลอง

POP 20,000

Built along the spine of a mountain, Mae Salong is more like a remote Chinese village in Yunnan than a Thai town. It was originally settled by the 93rd Regiment of the Kuomintang Nationalist Party (KMT), which fled from China after the 1949 revolution. The ex-soldiers and political exiles initially settled in Myanmar but later were forced to Thailand, where they supported themselves as middlemen between the opium growers and the opium warlords. The modern-day descendants still carry on the language and traditions (minus the profession) of their

GETTING TO MYANMAR: MAE SAI TO TACHILEIK

Getting to the border The **Thai immigration office** (☑053 733261; Th Phahonyothin; ⊙6.30am-9pm) at the Mae Sai/Tachileik border is just before the bridge over the Mae Nam Sai in the centre of town. Travellers have reported that the duration of Thai visa exemptions are subject to the discretion of the immigration official.

At the border If you're approaching from Thailand and haven't already obtained a Myanmar visa, it's relatively straightforward to cross to Tachileik for the day and slightly more complicated to get a two-week visa and permission to visit Kyaingtong and/or Mong La.

Proceed through the Thai immigration office and on to the Myanmar immigration office, where you will receive a day pass (500B). Your passport will be kept at the office. The border town of Tachileik looks a lot like Mae Sai, except with more teashops and Burmese restaurants (go figure).

Moving on If you are headed to Kyaingtong and/or Mong La, on the Chinese border, proceed directly to the Myanmar Travels & Tours (MTT) office. There, you'll inform the authorities exactly where you're headed and provide three photos and US$10 or 500B for a border pass valid for 14 days. Your passport will be kept at the border, and you're expected to exit Myanmar at Tachileik. It's also obligatory to hire a guide (1000B per day plus 400B guiding fee) and to provide for their accommodation and food. If you haven't already arranged a guide beforehand, you'll be assigned one by MTT. Recommended guides include **Leng** (☑+95 9490 31470; sairoctor.htunleng@gmail.com) and **Freddie** (Sai Yot; ☑+95 9490 31934; yotkham@gmail.com).

Buses bound for Kyaingtong (K10,000, five hours, 8am to 8.30am and 11.30am to 12.30pm) depart from Tachileik's bus station. Or charter a taxi (K65,000) or catch a share taxi (K15,000 or K20,000).

For information on doing this crossing in reverse, see p509.

forefathers: Chinese is more frequently spoken here than Thai and the land's severe incline boasts tidy terraces of tea and coffee plantations.

An **all-day market**, at the southern end of town, provides the bustling entertainment of commerce. Local guesthouses organise hill-tribe treks.

Shin Sane Guest House (☎053 765026; www.maesalong-shinsane.blogspot.com; r 100B, bungalows 300B; @☏) is Mae Salong's original guesthouse, boasting the standards and prices of decades past. **Little Home Guesthouse** (☎053 765389; www.maesalonglittle home.com; bungalows 800B; @☏) has a nice collection of bungalows near the market intersection. Local Yunnanese restaurants, such as **Salema Restaurant** (mains 30-250B; ⊙7am-8pm), attract plenty of Thai tourists.

Probably the easiest way to get to Mae Salong is to take a bus to Mae Chan and catch a green *sŏrng·tăa·ou* to Mae Salong (60B, half-hourly from 7.30am to 4.30pm). You can charter one for around 700B. It's also possible to take a Mae Sai–bound bus to Ban Pasang, from where blue *sŏrng·tăa·ou* head up the mountain to Mae Salong only when full (60B, one hour, 6am to 5pm).

You can also reach Mae Salong by road from Tha Ton (60B, one hour, every two hours from 8am to 2pm).

Chiang Saen เชียงแสน

POP 11,000

A sedate river town, Chiang Saen is famous in the Thai history books as the 7th-century birthplace of the Lanna kingdom, which later moved to Chiang Mai. Today, huge river barges from China moor in town, reviving an old interior Asian trade route.

You can wander around the kingdom's ruins at **Wat Pa Sak** (วัดป่าสัก; off Rte 1290; historical park 50B; ⊙8.30am-4.30pm Wed-Sun) **FREE**, about 200m from Pratu Chiang Saen, along with other ruins scattered throughout town. Or survey the artefacts at **Chiang Saen National Museum** (พิพิธภัณฑสถานแห่งชาติ เชียงแสน; 702 Th Phahonyothin; 100B; ⊙8.30am-4.30pm Wed-Sun).

An easy day trip from Chiang Saen is the 'official' centre of the Golden Triangle, **Sop Ruak**, an odd souvenir and museum stop for package tourists. The **House of Opium** (บ้าน ฝิ่น; Rte 1290; 50B; ⊙7am-7pm), across from the giant Buddha statue known as Phra Chiang Saen Si Phaendin, has historical displays pertaining to opium culture. Another drug-themed museum is the **Hall of Opium** (หอ ฝิ่น; Rte 1290; adult/child 200B/free; ⊙8.30am-4pm Tue-Sun), 1km south of town opposite the Anantara Resort & Spa. Sop Ruak is accessible from Chiang Saen via **Mekong River Trips** (☎08 5392 4701; Th Rimkhong; ⊙8am-5pm), for 600/700B one way/return per boat (five passengers). Or you can catch a *sŏrng·tăa·ou* (20B, frequent 8am to 1pm).

Sleeping options in Chiang Saen include **Jay Nay** (☎08 1960 7551; Th Nhongmoon, no roman-script sign; r 350-400B; ❋☏) and **Sa Nae Charn Guest House** (☎053 651138; 641 Th Nhongmoon; r 250-450B; ❋☏). **Riverside Food Vendors** (Th Rimkhong; mains 30-60B; ⊙4-11pm) set up in the dry months. There are also **evening food vendors** (Th Phahonyothin; mains 30-60B; ⊙4-10pm) and a **Walking Street** (Th Rimkhong; mains 20-60B; ⊙4-9pm Sat).

Chiang Saen has a covered bus terminal at the eastern end of Th Phahonyothin. Destinations include Chiang Rai (37B, 1½ hours, frequent) and Chiang Mai (222B, five hours, 9am). *Sŏrng·tăa·ou* go to Mae Sai (50B) and Hat Bai (50B), where you'll transfer to Chiang Khong).

Chiang Khong เชียงของ

POP 12,000

Remote yet lively Chiang Khong is historically important as a market town for local hill tribes and for trade with northern Laos. Travellers pass through en route to Laos and southern China.

🛏 Sleeping

Funky Box HOSTEL $
(☎08 2765 1839; Soi 2, Th Sai Klang; dm 100B; ❋☏) Pretty much what the name suggests: a box-like structure holding 16 dorm beds. And rest assured that it's funky in the good sense of the word.

Namkhong Resort HOTEL $
(☎053 791055; 94/2 Th Sai Klang; r 200-1000B; ❋☏☲) Just off the main drag is this semi-secluded compound of tropical plants and handsome wooden structures. Even the fan-cooled, shared-bathroom cheapies are charming, and the swimming pool is an added bonus.

Baan-Fai Guest House GUESTHOUSE $
(☎053 791394; 108 Th Sai Klang; r 200-800B; ❋☏) A renovation has this inviting wooden house looking better than ever. The eight

rooms in the main structure have air-con and en suite bathrooms, while the newer rooms are fan-cooled and share bathroom facilities; all are linked to an attached cafe.

🍴 Eating

Street eats can be found at the twice-weekly **Walking Street** (Th Sai Klang; mains 30-60B; ⊙6-10pm Wed & Sat, Nov-May).

Khao Soi Pa Orn   THAI $
(Soi 6, Th Sai Klang, no roman-script sign; mains 30-40B; ⊙8am-4pm) You may think you know *kôw soy,* the famous northern curry noodle soup, but the version served in Chiang Khong forgoes the curry broth and replaces it with clear soup topped with a rich, spicy minced pork mixture. Several non-noodle dishes are also available.

Bamboo Mexican House   INTERNATIONAL $$
(Th Sai Klang; mains 70-250B; ⊙7.30am-8.30pm; ✍) Run by the manager of a now-defunct guesthouse who learned to make Mexican dishes from her American and Mexican guests. To be honest, though, we never got past the coffee and tasty homemade breads and cakes. Opens early, and boxed lunches can be assembled for the boat ride to Luang Prabang.

❶ Getting There & Away

Chiang Khong has no central bus terminal; buses stop at various points near the market, south of the town centre. If you're going to Bangkok, buy tickets at **Sombat Tour** (☑ 053 791644; Rte 1020). If you're bound for Chiang Saen, take a *sŏrng·tăa·ou* to Ban Hat Bai (50B, one hour, around 8am) from a stall on Th Sai Klang.
Nok Air (p702) offers minivan transfer to/from Chiang Khong via the airport in Chiang Rai, about two hours away.

Pai   ปาย
POP 2000
This cool corner of the northern mountains started out as a hippie enclave for Chiang Mai bohos, who would come to hang out beside the rambling river and strum out blues tunes at night. Word spread and the dusty little town now does a thriving trade in mountain scenery and laid-back living. Urban Thais crowd into Pai for its stress-reducing setting and the oddity of 'winter' (from December to January). The town itself – a modest mixture of Shan, Thai and Muslim-Chinese residents – can be explored in a matter of minutes, but the real adventure is in the hills beyond.

◎ Sights & Activities

Since Pai is more of a 'state of mind', it is lean on fully fledged tourist attractions. For an outing, head to **Wat Phra That Mae Yen** (วัดพระธาตุแม่เย็น; ⊙dawn-dusk) FREE, 1km east of town, for its hilltop vista. **Tha Pai Hot Springs** (บ่อน้ำร้อนท่าปาย; adult/child 300/150B; ⊙7am-6pm) is a well-kept park featuring a scenic stream and pleasant hot-spring bathing pools. The park is 7km southeast of town across Mae Nam Pai.

The rest of your time will be spent on various wanderings or pamperings (traditional massage is big here). All the guesthouses in town can provide information on **trekking**.

Thai Adventure Rafting   RAFTING
(☑053 699111; www.thairafting.com; Th Chaisongkhram; ⊙8am-5pm) This French-run outfit leads one- and two-day rafting excursions. On the way, rafters visit a waterfall, a fossil reef and hot springs; one night is spent at the company's permanent riverside camp.

Pai Traditional Thai Massage   MASSAGE
(PTTM; ☑08 3577 0498; www.pttm_2001@hotmail.com; 68/3 Soi 1, Th Wiang Tai; massage per 1/1½/2hr 180/270/350B, sauna per visit 100B, 3-day massage course 2500B; ⊙9am-9pm) This long-standing and locally owned outfit offers very good northern Thai massage, as well as a sauna (cool season only) where you can steam yourself in medicinal herbs. Three-day massage courses begin every Monday and Friday and last three hours per day. The friendly couple who do the massages and teach the course are accredited and are graduates of Chiang Mai's Old Medicine Hospital.

BUS TRANSPORT FROM CHIANG KHONG

DESTINATION	FARE (B)	DURATION (HR)	FREQUENCY
Bangkok	650-1019	13	7am, 7.25am & frequent departures 3pm-4pm
Chiang Mai	279-434	6-7	7.15am, 9.45am & 10.30am
Chiang Rai	65-126	2½	hourly 5am-3pm

THAILAND PAI

Thom's Pai
Elephant Camp ELEPHANT INTERACTION
(☑ 053 699286; www.thomelephant.com; Th Rang-siyanon; elephant rides per person 800-1200B; ⏱ 8am-9pm) Pai's most established elephant outfitter has an office in town. You can choose between riding bareback or in a seat, and some rides include swimming with the elephants. Rides include a soak in the hot-spring-fed tubs afterwards.

It's worth nothing that animal welfare experts claim elephant rides can be harmful for these gentle giants, with arguments in favour of admiring elephants instead of clambering all over them.

🛏 Sleeping

Pai has a huge range of options, both in town and outside of town in a more rural setting. During the cool season (November to April) it can be difficult to find a room and prices increase with demand.

Pai Country Hut HOTEL $
(☑ 08 7779 6541; www.paicountryhut.com; Ban Mae Hi; bungalows incl breakfast 300-800B; 🛜) The bamboo bungalows here are utterly simple, but are tidy and most have bathrooms and inviting hammocks. Although it's not exactly riverside, it's the most appealing of several similar budget places close to the water.

★ Pairadise HOTEL $$
(☑ 053 698065; www.pairadise.com; Ban Mae Hi; bungalows 900-1500B; 🐾🛜📶) This neat resort looks over the Pai Valley from atop a ridge just outside of town. The bungalows are stylish, spacious and include gold leaf lotus murals, beautiful rustic bathrooms and terraces with hammocks. All surround a spring-fed pond that is suitable for swimming. You'll find it about 750m east of Mae Nam Pai; look for the sign just after the bridge.

Tayai's Guest House GUESTHOUSE $$
(☑ 053 699 579; off Th Raddamrong; r & bungalows 800-1200B; 🐾🛜) Simple but clean fan and air-con rooms and bungalows in a quiet, leafy compound just off the main drag.

Baankanoon GUESTHOUSE $$
(☑ 053 699 453; www.baankanoonpai.com; 33 Soi Wanchalerm; bungalows 500-1200B; 🛜) Consisting of 14 bright duplex and free-standing bungalows around a 100 year-old kà·nǔn (jackfruit) tree, this locally owned place is quiet, clean and cosy.

✖ Eating

During the morning there's takeaway food at **Saengthongaram market** (Th Khetkelang; mains 30-60B; ⏱ 6-11am). For tasty local eats, try the **evening market** (Th Raddamrong; mains 30-60B; ⏱ 3-7pm). Night vendors turn Th Chaisongkhram and Th Rangsiyanon into an open-air buffet during tourist season.

★ Larp Khom Huay Poo NORTHERN THAI $
(Ban Huay Pu; mains 50-80B; ⏱ 9am-8pm) Escape the wheat-grass-and-tofu crowd and get your meat on at this unabashedly carnivorous local eatery. The house special (and the dish you must order) is *larp moo kua,* northern-style *lâhp,* minced pork fried with local herbs and spices. Accompanied by a basket of sticky rice, a plate of bitter herbs and an ice-cold Singha, it's the best meal in Pai. The restaurant is about 1km north of town, on the road to Mae Hong Son.

★ Yunnanese Restaurants CHINESE $
(no Roman-script sign; mains 30-250B; ⏱ 7am-8pm) Several open-air restaurants in Ban Santichon, 4km west of Pai, serve the traditional dishes of the town's Yunnanese residents. Choices include *màntŏ* (steamed buns), here served with pork leg stewed with Chinese herbs, hand-pulled noodles and several dishes using unique local crops and exotic ingredients such as black chicken.

Good Life INTERNATIONAL $
(Th Wiang Tai; mains 35-190B; ⏱ 8am-11pm; 🛜🥗) Kefir, kombucha, beet juice and wheat grass are indicators of the vibe of this eclectic and popular cafe. But don't fear: soft drinks are available, as is a thick menu of Thai and international dishes, many of which are meat-free.

Mama Falafel ISRAELI $
(Soi Wanchalerm; set meals 100-110B; ⏱ 2.30-10pm Mon-Sat; 🛜🥗) This friendly native of Pai has been cooking up tasty felafel, hummus, schnitzel and other Israeli faves since 2002; the set meals win in both quality and quantity.

⏻ Drinking & Entertainment

Check out the tourist season **Walking Street** (Th Chaisongkhram & Th Rangsiyanon; ⏱ 6-10pm) for evening entertainment. Go drinking at the VW van cocktail bars along Th Chaisongkhram. Or imbibe with a reggae beat at the bars along Th Wiang Tai.

THAILAND PAI

Edible Jazz LIVE MUSIC
(www.ediblejazz.com; Soi Wat Pa Kham; ⊙4-11pm)
Stroke a cat and nurse a beer while listening to acoustic guitar performances, every night around 8.30pm. Depending on who's in town, the open-mic night on Sunday can be surprisingly good.

Bebop LIVE MUSIC
(Th Rangsiyanon; ⊙8pm-1am) This legendary box is popular with both locals and travellers and has live music nightly (from about 10pm), emphasising blues, R&B and rock.

ⓘ Getting There & Around

Pai's airport is 1.5km north of town and offers flights to Chiang Mai through **Kan Air** (☑053 699955, nationwide 025 516111; www.kanair-lines.com; Pai Airport; ⊙8.30am-5.30pm).

Pai's tiny **bus station** (Th Chaisongkhram) is the place to catch slow, fan-cooled buses and more efficient minivans. The road from Chiang Mai to Pai and on to Mae Hong Son is savagely steep.

Chiang Mai 80B, three to four hours, noon (bus); 150B, three hours, hourly from 7am to 5pm (minivan)

Mae Hong Son 80B, three to four hours, 11am (bus); 150B, 2½ hours, 8.30am (minivan)

Aya Service (☑053 699888; www.ayaservice.com; 22/1 Th Chaisongkhram; motorcycles per 24hr 100-1800B; ⊙7am-10pm) and **Duan-Den** (☑053 699966; 20/1 Th Chaisongkhram; per 24hr 100-250B; ⊙7am-9pm) also run air-con minivan buses to Chiang Mai (from 150B to 200B, three hours, hourly from 7am to 5.30pm).

Mae Hong Son แม่ฮ่องสอน

POP 7000

Northern Thai aficionados prefer the far-flung border feel of Mae Hong Son to that of Pai. Mae Hong Son is a quiet provincial capital that practically peers into Myanmar and is skirted by forested mountains. The local trekking scene in Mae Hong Son is the primary draw but the daily market and local eats further impress its fan base. November to February are cool and pleasant times to visit.

◉ Sights & Activities

Mae Hong Son's temples are surviving monuments to their Burmese and Shan artisans and benefactors and hint at the town's past as a logging and elephant-training centre. **Wat Jong Klang** (วัดจองกลาง; Th Chamnansatit; ⊙dawn-dusk) FREE and **Wat Jong Kham** (วัด

จองคำ; Th Chamnansatit; ⊙dawn-dusk) FREE boast whitewashed stupas and glittering zinc fretwork. The temples are often lit up at night, reflecting in the still waters of Nong Jong Kham (Jong Kham Lake).

Glimpse the morning fog from **Wat Phra That Doi Kong Mu** (วัดพระธาตุดอยกองมู; ⊙dawn-dusk) FREE, which sits on a hilltop west of town.

The **Poi Sang Long Festival** in March takes place at Wat Jong Klang and Wat Jong Kham. It's a Shan custom in which young boys entering the monastery as novice monks are dressed in ornate costumes and paraded around the temple under festive parasols.

Treks to nearby hill-tribe villages and **longtail boat trips** on Mae Nam Pai are all popular pastimes. Guesthouses can handle bookings for outdoor trips, which start at around 1000B for the day.

Friend Tour TREKKING
(☑053 611647, 08 6180 7031; PA Motor, 21 Th Pradit Jong Kham; ⊙8am-6.30pm) With nearly 20 years' experience, this recommended outfit offers trekking and rafting excursions, as well as day tours.

Nature Walks TREKKING
(☑08 9552 6899; www.naturewalksthai-myanmar.com) Treks here might cost more than elsewhere, but John, a native of Mae Hong Son, is the best guide in town. Hikes range from day-long nature walks to multiday journeys across the province. John can also arrange custom nature-based tours, such as the orchid-viewing tours he conducts from March to May. Email or call John for info.

🛏 Sleeping

Friend House GUESTHOUSE $
(☑053 620119; 20 Th Pradit Jong Kham; r 200-500B; ⊛) The super clean though characterless rooms here run from the ultra basic, which share hot-water bathrooms, to larger rooms with private bathrooms.

Palm House GUESTHOUSE $
(☑053 614022; 22/1 Th Chamnansatit; r 400-1000B; ⊛⊛) This two-storey cement building offers several characterless but large, clean rooms with TV, fridge, hot water and fan/air-con. A new annexe was being built when we were in town. The helpful owner speaks English and can arrange transport when he's not napping.

Piya Guesthouse HOTEL $$

(☑053 611260; piyaguesthouse@hotmail.com; 1/1 Th Khunlumprapas; bungalows 700B; ※ 🛜 🌊) Steps from Mae Hong Son's central lake is this compound of bungalows ringing a garden and a tiny pool. Rooms come equipped with air-con, fridge, TV and hot showers. It's all clean and inviting, and couldn't be more conveniently located.

★**Fern Resort** RESORT $$$

(☑053 686110; www.fernresort.info; off Rte 108; bungalows incl breakfast 2500-3500B; ※ @ 🛜 🌊) This long-standing ecofriendly resort is one of the pleasanter places to stay in northern Thailand. The 35 wooden bungalows are set among tiered rice paddies and streams, and feature stylishly decorated interiors. There's no TV, but dogs, a pool, pétanque area and the nearby nature trails at the adjacent Mae Surin National Park are more than enough to keep you occupied.

🍴 Eating & Drinking

Mae Hong Son's morning market (off Th Phanich Wattana; mains 10-30B; ⏲6-9am) is a cultural and culinary adventure. Several vendors at the north end of the market sell *tòo·a poo ùn*, a Burmese noodle dish with thick chickpea porridge. Others sell a local version of *kà·nŏm jeen nám ngée·o* (thin white noodles) topped with Shan-style deep-fried vegetables.

There are two night markets: the one near the airport is mostly takeaway northern Thai food, while the market on Th Khunlumprapas has seating and serves standard Thai food. There is also an evening Walking Street (Th Pradit Jong Kham; ⏲5-10pm Oct-Feb) with eats and more.

Maesribua NORTHERN THAI $

(cnr Th Pradit Jong Kham & Th Singha-nat Barm Rung; mains 20-40B; ⏲8am-1pm) Like the Shan grandma you never had, Auntie Bua prepares a generous spread of local-style curries, soups and dips on a daily basis.

Chom Mai Restaurant THAI $

(off Rte 108, no roman-script sign; mains 40-290B; ⏲8.30am-3.30pm; 🛜🍴) The English-language menu here is limited, but don't miss the deliciously rich *kôw soy* (northern-style curry noodle soup) or *kôw mòk gài* (the Thai version of biryani). Chom Mai is located about 4km south of Mae Hong Son, along the road that leads to Tha Pong Daeng – look for the Doi Chaang coffee sign.

Salween River Restaurant & Bar INTERNATIONAL, THAI $

(www.salweenriver.com; 23 Th Pradit Jong Kham; mains 60-330B; ⏲8am-10pm; 🛜🍴) Salween is your typical traveller's cafe: a few old guidebooks, free wi-fi and a menu ranging from burgers to Burmese. Yet unlike most traveller's cafes, the food here is good; don't miss the Burmese green-tea salad.

Ban Din Coffee CHINESE $

(Th Pradit Jong Kham, no roman-script sign; mains 30B; ⏲7am-9pm) If you didn't make it up to Mae Aw (Ban Rak Thai), be sure to stop by this open-air restaurant selling delicious and unique noodle dishes, dried fruit, tea and other specialities of Mae Hong Son's Chinese/Yunnanese residents.

Sunflower INTERNATIONAL, THAI

(Th Pradit Jong Kham; ⏲7.30am-10pm) Technically a restaurant (mains 50B to 320B), Sunflower's draught beer, live lounge music, views of the lake and tacky artificial waterfall also make it a decent bar.

ℹ️ Information

Most of the banks on Th Khunlum Praphat have ATMs.

Maehongson Living Museum (27 Th Singha-nat Barm Rung; ⏲7am-5pm) An attractive wooden building – actually Mae Hong Son's former bus depot – has been turned into a museum on local culture, food and architecture, though the bulk of information is only in Thai. There are a few maps and brochures

THAILAND MAE HONG SON

BUS & MINIVAN TRANSPORT FROM MAE HONG SON

DESTINATION	FARE (B)	DURATION (HR)	FREQUENCY
Bangkok	742-865	15	3pm & 4pm
Chiang Mai (bus)	118-333	8-9	8.30am (northern route), 4 daily (southern route)
Chiang Mai (minivan)	250	6	hourly 7am-5pm
Pai (bus)	66	4½	8.30am
Pai (minivan)	150	2½	hourly 7am-5pm

in English, and there's also free wi-fi and bike rental for only 15B per day.

Tourism Authority of Thailand (TAT; ☎053 612982, nationwide ☎1672; www.tourismthai land.org/Mae-Hong-Son; Th Ni-wet Pi-sarn; ⊘8.30am-4.30pm) Basic tourist brochures and maps can be picked up here.

Tourist Police (☎053 611812, nationwide ☎1155; Th Singha-nat Barm Rung; ⊘8.30am-4.30pm)

ⓘ Getting There & Around

Mae Hong Son is 368km from Chiang Mai, but the terrain is so rugged that the trip takes at least eight long, but scenic, hours. For this reason many people opt for the 35-minute flight to/from Chiang Mai (1490B to 1590B, 35 minutes, seven daily) with **Kan Air** (☎0 5361 3188, nationwide 02 551 6111; www.kanairlines.com; Mae Hong Son Airport; ⊘7.30am-5pm). The airport is near the town centre.

Mae Hong Son's bus station is 1km south of the city. A túk-túk or motorcycle ride into town costs 60B. The centre of Mae Hong Son can be covered on foot. Motorbike rental is available from **PA Motor** (☎053 611647, 08 6180 7031; 21 Th Pradit Jong Kham; per day motorbike 150-250B, car 1500-3000B; ⊘8am-6.30pm), opposite Friend House.

Mae Sariang   แม่สะเรียง

Little-visited Mae Sariang is well known by adventurous travellers. There's natural beauty, ethnic and cultural diversity as well as community-based trekking outfits.

Dragon Sabaii Tours (☎08 5548 0884; www.thailandhilltribeholidays.com; Th Mongkol-chai), **Mae Sariang Tours** (☎08 8404 8402; www.facebook.com/maesariang.man) and **Piak Private Tours** (☎09 3179 9786; piak1003@hotmail.com) are all recommended for their ecoconscious and culturally sensitive tours.

⌨ Sleeping

Northwest Guest House   GUESTHOUSE $
(☎08 9700 9928; patiat_1@hotmail.com; 81 Th Laeng Phanit; r 250-350B; ❋@☎) The eight

rooms in this cosy wooden house are mattress-on-the-floor simple, but get natural light and are relatively spacious. Trekking and other excursions can be arranged here.

Pang Sariang   GUESTHOUSE $
(☎053 682333; 2 Th Laeng Phanit, no roman-script sign; r 250-300B; ❋@☎) A villa with four homey-feeling, simple rooms. Look for the sign that says Guest House & Restaurant.

✗ Eating & Drinking

Local eats can be found at the **Sunday Market** (Th Wiang Mai; mains 20-60B; ⊘3-8pm).

★ **Muu Thup**   NORTHERN THAI $
(Th Wiang Mai, no roman-script sign; mains 50-80B; ⊘8am-7pm) An authentic – and delicious – northern Thai–style grilled meat shack. You can't go wrong with the eponymous *mŏo đúp* (pork that's been grilled then tenderised with a mallet). Muu Thup is located roughly across from Mae Sariang Museum; look for the grill.

Intira Restaurant   THAI $
(Th Wiang Mai; mains 50-200B; ⊘8am-10pm) Probably the town's best all-around restaurant, this place features a thick menu of dishes using unusual ingredients such as locally grown shiitake mushrooms and fish from Mae Nam Moei.

WESTERN THAILAND

Tall rugged mountains rise up from the central plains to meet Thailand's western border with Myanmar. Though the distances from population centres are minor, much of the region remains remote and undeveloped with an undercurrent of border intrigue. Kanchanaburi, just a few hours' bus ride from Bangkok, is a convenient and historical gateway to the region.

BUS & MINIVAN TRANSPORT FROM MAE SARIANG

DESTINATION	FARE (B)	DURATION (HR)	FREQUENCY
Bangkok	590-689	12	7pm & 7.30pm
Chiang Mai (bus)	100-180	4-5	4 daily
Chiang Mai (minivan)	200	3½	6 daily
Mae Hong Son	100-200	3-4	7 departures 12.30pm-4am
Mae Sot (sŏrng·tăa·ou)	250	6	frequent

WHY BRIDGE THE RIVER KWAI?

Japan's construction of the 'Death Railway' was an astonishing feat of engineering. Allied prisoners of war and conscripted workers were forced to conquer rugged terrain with brute strength rather than modern machines. Over 12,000 POWs and as many as 90,000 labourers died due to the brutal working conditions, disease and inadequate supplies of food and medicine.

The 415km railway was built during the WWII-era Japanese occupation of Thailand (1941–45) and its objective was to secure an overland supply route to Burma (Myanmar) for the Japanese conquest of other west Asian countries. The bridge that spans the 'River Kwai' near Kanchanaburi city (dubbed the **Death Railway Bridge**) was the only steel bridge built in Thailand at the time. It was bombed several times by the Allies, but the POWs were sent to rebuild it.

When the war's tide turned, the railway became an escape path for Japanese troops. After the war the British took control of the railway on the Burmese side, and ripped up 4km of the tracks leading to Three Pagodas Pass for fear of the route being used by Karen separatists.

On the Thai side, the State Railway of Thailand (SRT) assumed control and continues to operate trains on 130km of the original route between Nong Pladuk, south of Kanchanaburi, and Nam Tok.

Kanchanaburi กาญจนบุรี

POP 94,602

Short on time but long on must-dos? Kanchanaburi is the short-termers' answer to doing it all. It has a healthy soft-adventure scene that rivals Chiang Mai's but it is much closer to Bangkok and the beaches than the northern mountains. The town lounges quietly alongside Mae Nam Khwae (known in English as Kwai River) and offers a peaceful respite from Bangkok's hyperactivity. It also has an unlikely claim on WWII history as the site of a Japanese-operated WWII prisoner-of-war camp made famous by the movie *The Bridge Over the River Kwai*. Today visitors come to pay their respects to fallen Allied soldiers or to learn more about this chapter of the war.

⊙ Sights

★ **Death Railway Bridge**   HISTORIC SITE
(สะพานข้ามแม่น้ำแคว, Bridge Over the River Kwai) The famous 300m railway bridge still retains its power and symbolism, especially if you visit early or late enough in the day to bypass the tourist scrum. Its centre was destroyed by Allied bombs in 1945, so only the outer curved spans are original. Nothing remains of a second (wooden) bridge the Japanese built 100m downstream. You're free to roam over the bridge. Stand in one of the safety points along the bridge if a train appears.

★ **Thailand–Burma Railway Centre**   MUSEUM
(ศูนย์รถไฟไทย-พม่า; www.tbrconline.com; 73 Th Jaokannun; adult/child 140/60B; ⊙9am-5pm) This modern, informative museum explains Kanchanaburi's role in WWII and ensures that the deaths are understood as a tragedy, not a statistic. The galleries tell the history of the railway, how prisoners were treated and what happened after the line was completed. Upstairs is a display of wartime artefacts, including one POW's darts fashioned from old razors, and a diorama showing how Hellfire Pass got its name. Be sure to take time to watch the poignant video from POW survivors.

★ **Kanchanaburi War Cemetery**   CEMETERY
(สุสานทหารพันธมิตรดอนรัก; Th Saengchuto; ⊙24hr) The largest of Kanchanaburi's two war cemeteries, immaculately maintained by the Commonwealth War Graves Commission, is right in town. Of the 6981 soldiers buried here, nearly half were British; the rest came mainly from Australia and the Netherlands. As you stand at the cemetery entrance, the entire right-hand side contains British victims, the front-left area holds Australian graves, the rear left honours Dutch soldiers, and unknown soldiers and those who were cremated lie at the furthest spot to the left.

Kanchanaburi

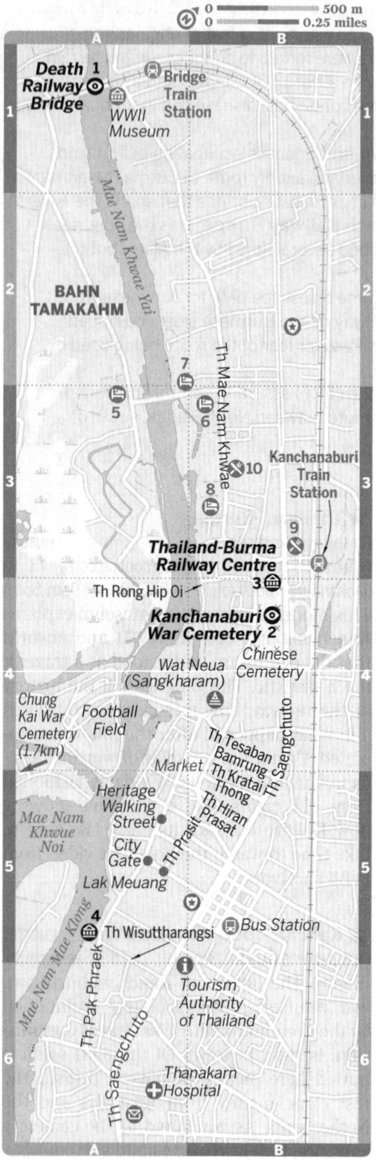

Kanchanaburi

Top Sights

1 Death Railway Bridge A1
2 Kanchanaburi War Cemetery B4
3 Thailand–Burma Railway Centre B4

Sights

4 Jeath War Museum A5

Sleeping

5 Apple's Retreat A3
6 Blue Star Guest House B3
7 Good Times Resort A2
8 Jolly Frog B3

Eating

Blue Rice .... (see 5)
9 JJ Market B3
10 On's Thai-Issan B3

Jeath War Museum MUSEUM
(พิพิธภัณฑ์สงคราม; Th Wisuttharangsi; 50B; ⏲8am-5pm) This small museum contains correspondence and artwork from former POWs that detail their harsh living conditions, plus various personal effects and war relics, including an Allied bomb dropped to destroy the bridge that didn't explode. The main reason to come, however, is that one of the three galleries is built from bamboo in the style of the shelters (called *attap*) that the POWs lived in.

Chung Kai War Cemetery CEMETERY
(สุสานทหารพันธมิตรช่องไก่; ⏲7am-6pm) FREE Chung Kai was the site one of the biggest Allied prisoner-of-war camp during WWII and prisoners built their own hospital and church close to here. Smaller and less visited, but just as well maintained, as the cemetery in town, 1400 Commonwealth and 300 Dutch soldiers are honoured here. The cemetery is near the river, 2.5km southwest of the Wat Neua bridge and can easily be reached by bicycle.

Sleeping

The most atmospheric places to stay are along the river. The further north you go, the quieter it gets.

Blue Star Guest House GUESTHOUSE $
(☎034 624733; www.bluestar-guesthouse.com; 241 Th Mae Nam Khwae; r 200-750B; P❄📶) Nature wraps itself around Blue Star's super-basic but fairly priced waterside huts, creating a jungly vibe. Better, more modern rooms sit up on solid land. Overall, one of the best budget choices in town.

Jolly Frog GUESTHOUSE $
(☎034 514579; 28 Soi China; s 100B, d 180-320B, f 400B; P❄📶) The Jolly Frog's heyday has long passed, but since the grungy rooms

are among the cheapest in town, it remains popular with backpackers. The communal atmosphere and hammocks in the garden are other selling points.

★ Good Times Resort HOTEL $$
(☑087 162 4949; www.good-times-resort.com; r incl breakfast 1150-2700B; P❄🅰️🏊) Although the road to the resort doesn't inspire confidence, get past the car park and you'll find a little riverside oasis with large, attractive rooms plus good service and dining.

Apple's Retreat GUESTHOUSE $$
(☑034 512017; www.applesguesthouse.com; 153/4 Mu 4, Ban Tamakham; r incl breakfast 990B; P❄🅰️) Almost like a chic homestay, Apple and Noi offer simple but stylish rooms, a friendly welcome and bags of local knowledge in a quiet part of town. While the restaurant is on the river, the rooms are across the road. Unlike most places at this price, rooms lack a TV and fridge.

✖ Eating

Riverside restaurants abound on Th Mae Nam Khwae. **JJ Market** (Th Saengchuto; ⊙5.30-10pm), near the train station, has tasty takaway options.

★ Blue Rice THAI $
(www.applesguesthouse.com; 153/4 Mu 4 Ban Tamakahm; dishes 135B; ⊙11am-2pm & 6-10pm; 🅰️☑) A perfect riverside setting, brilliant menu and fantastic flavours make this a winner. Chef Apple puts a fresh, gourmet spin on Thai classics such as the eponymous rice, *yam sôm oh* (grapefruit salad) and chicken-coconut soup with banana plant.

On's Thai-Issan VEGETARIAN $
(☑087 364 2264; www.onsthaiissan.com; Th Mae Nam Khwae; dishes 50B; ⊙10am-10pm; ☑) The Thai (and a little Isan) vegetarian and vegan food on offer here is so good that there are many carnivorous diners. Friendly On will even be happy to teach you how to make it. A two-hour, three-dish cookery course costs 600B.

ℹ️ Information

Main Post Office (Th Saengchuto; ⊙8.30am-4.30pm Mon-Fri, 9am-noon Sat & Sun)

Thanakarn Hospital (☑034 622370; Th Saengchuto) This is the best-equipped hospital to deal with foreign visitors.

Tourism Authority of Thailand (TAT; ☑034 511200; tatkan@tat.or.th; Th Saengchuto; ⊙8.30am-4.30pm) Provides free maps of the town and province, along with advice on activities to do.

Tourist Police (☑034 512795; Th Saengchuto)

ℹ️ Getting There & Away

BUS
Kanchanaburi's **bus and minivan station** (☑034 515907) is just off of Th Saengchuto. If you're heading to Hua Hin, transfer at Ratchaburi. If you're headed to Ayuthaya, transfer at Suphanburi.

TRAIN
Kanchanaburi's train station is 500m from the river, near the guesthouse area. Kanchanaburi is on the Bangkok Noi–Nam Tok rail line, which includes a portion of the historic Death Railway. The SRT promotes this as a historic route, and charges foreigners 100B for any one-way journey, regardless of the distance.

BUS & MINIVAN TRANSPORT FROM KANCHANABURI

DESTINATION	FARE (B)	DURATION (HR)	FREQUENCY
Bangkok's Khao San Rd (minivan)	120	2½	frequent
Bangkok's Northern (Mo Chit) bus terminal (minivan)	120	2½	frequent
Bangkok's Southern (Sai Tai Mai) bus terminal (bus/minivan)	110/100	2½/2	every 30min/ frequent
Bangkok's Victory Monument (minivan)	120	2½	frequent
Chiang Mai	594	10-11	9am, 7pm
Ratchaburi	50	2	frequent
Sangkhlaburi (bus/minivan)	130/175	5/3½	6 daily 6am-1.30pm/ frequent
Suphanburi	50-65	2	every 40min

SIGHTS OUTSIDE KANCHANABURI

Head out of town to explore Kanchanaburi's forests and rivers. Most of the guesthouses will book minivan tours that do a little bit of everything in a hurry.

Erawan National Park (อุทยานแห่งชาติเอราวัณ; ☎ 034 574222; adult/child 300/200B) is the home of the seven-tiered **Erawan Falls**, which makes for a refreshing day swimming in pools and climbing around the trails. Go early as this is a popular tour spot. Buses from Kanchanaburi stop at the visitor centre (50B, 1½ hours, eight daily from 8am to 5.40pm). The last bus back to Kanchanaburi leaves at 4pm.

Hellfire Pass Memorial (ช่องเขาขาด; ☎ 034 919605; Rte 323; ☺ museum 9am-4pm, grounds 7.30am-6pm) FREE curates a section of the Death Railway that was carved out of unforgiving mountain terrain at breakneck speed. The pass was so named for the fire-light shadows cast by the night-labouring POWs. A portion of the walking trail follows the old railbed. Located near the Km 66 marker on the Sai Yok–Thong Pha Phum road, the memorial can be reached by a Sangkhlaburi-bound bus (55B to 65B, 1½ hours, every 30 minutes); the last bus back is at 5pm. Inform the attendant of your destination so that the bus stops en route.

Destinations include the following:
Bangkok Noi station (three hours, departs 7.19am, 2.48pm and 5.41pm) Located in Thonburi, across the river from Bangkok.
Nam Tok (two hours, departs 6.07am, 10.35am and 4.26pm) Terminus station.

ⓘ Getting Around

Motorcycle taxis haul travellers and their luggage from the bus station to the guesthouses for about 50B. Regular *sŏrng·tăa·ou* ply Th Saengchuto for 10B, but be careful you don't accidentally 'charter' one. There are plenty of places hiring motorbikes (200B) and bicycles (50B) along Th Mae Nam Khwae.

Sangkhlaburi สังขละบุรี

Few tourists know the scenic but small town of Sangkhlaburi, but for international aid workers this is one of many remote outposts for refugee relief work. Many displaced people, whether they be Mon, Karen or Burmese, arrive in Thailand with few belongings and fewer rights.

The town itself consists of just a few paved roads overlooking the enormous Kheuan Khao Laem (Khao Laem Reservoir). The surrounding wilderness is a vast natural attraction boasting one of the largest conservation areas in Southeast Asia.

Guesthouses in town can arrange outdoor jaunts.

⊙ Sights & Activities

Tap into the town's ethnic diversity with a visit to the iconic **Saphan Mon** (สะพาน มอญ) (Mon Bridge), a 440m wooden bridge that connects the main town with the Mon settlement. A 70m section of the bridge collapsed during the 2013 rains and the floating replacement structure will not be rebuilt. For a brief glimpse into local ways, check out **Sangkhlaburi Cultural Center** (ศูนย์ วัฒนธรรม อำเภอสังขละบุรี; ☎ 086 178 4096; Th Sangkhlaburi; ☺ 8am-4pm Mon-Fri, to noon Sat & Sun) FREE, at the east side of town near Soi 7. **Scenns** (☎ 080 602 3184; www.scenns.com) offers Thai cookery, dance and language classes.

Sangkhlaburi Jungle Trekking (☎ 085 425 4434; jarunsaksri1@gmail.com) explores the surrounding forest along the Myanmar border, staying at Karen villages along the way.

Baan Dada (☎ 084 412 5443; www.baandada. org; Sangkhlaburi) runs a children's home and is the one of the few local organisations that takes volunteers on a short-term basis.

🛏 Sleeping & Eating

The day market is across from the bus stop and is good for sampling Mon-style curries (look for the large metal pots). The **night market** (☺ 4.30-9.30pm) is next door and the **Walking Street** (☺ 5-10pm Sat) is in front of the hospital.

★ **P Guesthouse**　　　　　　GUESTHOUSE **$**
(☎ 034 595061; www.p-guesthouse.com; Th Sri Sukwankiri; r 300-950B; P ❋ ☎) You don't normally get views like this for 300B. Stone and log-built rooms gaze upon the scenic waters at this family-run spot. There are two choices: fan rooms share cold-water, squat-toilet

bathrooms, while air-con rooms have the best views (especially room 7). Both are good value for Sangkhlaburi. The restaurant is expensive, but it's a fantastic place to lounge.

J Family Homestay
HOMESTAY $

(☑034 595511; per person 150B; ☎) This is a great little spot if you want a very local experience. Rooms are just mattresses on the floor with a shared bathroom. The family is a great source of local info. It's signed one road east of Th Sri Sukwankiri.

Baan Unrak Bakery
BAKERY $

(Th Sri Sukwankiri; snacks 25-90B; ☺8am-7.30pm Mon-Sat; ☑) Vegetarians will love this meatless (mostly vegan) cafe, which is part of the Baan Unrak organisation.

★ Suanmagmai Resort
THAI $$

(dishes 40-450B; ☺10am-9.30pm; ☎) The English part of the menu will leave you scratching your head (the deep-fried 'platypus' is really duck bills) – the pictures can help out some – but you can be sure whatever you get will be perfectly prepared. It's a great place to try something new since there are several local specialities like the fern salad and 'spicy soup with (cat)fish'.

It's 300m directly north of the Mon Bridge.

ⓘ Getting There & Away

A parking lot on the west edge of the town has old buses bound for Kanchanaburi (130B, four hours, 6.30am, 8am, 9.30am and 1pm). Air-con buses to Bangkok's Mo Chit terminal (238B to 306B, seven hours, 7.45am and 9.30am) leave from nearby. Minivans to Kanchanaburi (175B, 3½ hours, frequent) go from the other side of town, just two blocks from the bus station.

Mae Sot
แม่สอด

POP 52,000

Mae Sot is a scruffy border town preoccupied with the jade and gem trade and cross-border traffic. But it's the population's diversity that is most striking – Burmese, Chinese, Karen, Hmong and Thai – the ethnic mix that makes border towns so intriguing. The town also hosts a relatively large population of foreign doctors and NGO aid workers, dealing with the consequences of the clashes between Myanmar's central government and ethnic minorities.

There aren't a lot of official sights to lure tourists this far west, but Mae Sot is one of the most convenient land entries into Myanmar. Other selling points include underdeveloped nature preserves, diverse hill-tribe communities and being off the well-trodden path.

⊙ Sights & Activities

Border Market
MARKET

(ตลาดริมน้ำเมย; Rte 105; ☺7am-7pm) Alongside Mae Nam Moei on the Thai side is an expansive market that sells a mixture of workaday Burmese goods, black-market clothes, cheap Chinese electronics and food, among other things. It's 5km west of Mae Sot; *sŏrng·tǎa·ou* depart from a spot on Th Chid Lom between approximately 6am and 6pm (20B).

Herbal Sauna
SAUNA

(Wat Mani, Th Intharakhiri; 20B; ☺3-7pm) Wat Mani has separate herbal sauna facilities for men and women. The sauna is towards the back of the monastery grounds, past the monks' *gù·dì* (living quarters).

GETTING TO MYANMAR: PHU NAM RON TO HTEKE

This crossing is new and still something of an adventure. Myanmar visas are not available at the border. If you leave early you can make it to Dawei in a day, though there are guesthouses in Phu Nam Ron if you need them.

Getting to the border There are buses (70B, two hours, 9am) and minivans (100B, 1½ hours, 9am) from Kanchanaburi's bus station to the border.

At the border After getting stamped out of Thailand wait for the shuttle bus (50B) or take a motorcycle taxi to Myanmar immigration. Formalities are hassle-free, though a bit slow, on both sides.

Moving on Not far from immigration are minivan drivers who will take you to Dawei (800B per person, five hours; the price is sometimes negotiable). You can also do it for less if you find a truck driver willing to take you. The drive is through beautiful mountains but the road is still rough.

🛏 Sleeping

Phan Nu House GUESTHOUSE $
(🖉08 1972 4467; 563/3 Th Intharakhiri; r 250-500B; ❈ 🛜) This place consists of 29 large rooms in a residential strip just off the street. Most rooms are equipped with air-con, TV, fridge and hot water, making them a good deal.

Picturebook Guesthouse HOTEL $$
(🖉09 0459 6990; www.picturebookthailand.org; 125/4-6 Soi 19, Th Intharakihiri; r incl breakfast 600-800B; ❈ 🛜) Located in an attractive garden, the 10 rooms here, with their smooth concrete, artsy details and custom wood furniture, call to mind trendy dorms. Staff are friendly and keen to help, and are part of a not-for-profit training program. You'll find the hotel in unmarked Soi 19, directly behind the J2 hotel, about 1km east of Mae Sot.

🍴 Eating & Drinking

Mae Sot is a culinary crossroads. For breakfast head to the area south of the mosque where several **Muslim restaurants** serve sweet tea, roti and *nanbya* (a tandoori-style bread). Mae Sot's **night market** (Th Prasatwithi; mains 30-60B; ⊘6-11pm), at the eastern end of Th Prasawithi, features mostly Thai-Chinese dishes. For a night on the town, head to the bars at the western end of Th Intharakhiri.

Lucky Tea Garden BURMESE $
(Th Suksri Rat-Uthit; mains 10-50B; ⊘6am-6pm) For the authentic Burmese teashop experience without crossing over to Myawaddy, visit this friendly cafe equipped with sweet tea, tasty snacks and, of course, bad Myanmar pop music.

Khrua Canadian INTERNATIONAL, THAI $$
(3 Th Sri Phanit; dishes 40-280B; ⊘7am-10pm; 🛜🖉) This is the place to go if you want to forget you're in Asia for one meal. Dave, the titular Canadian, brews his own coffee and also offers homemade bagels, deli meats and cheeses. The servings are large, the menu is varied, and when you finally remember you're in Thailand again, local information is also available.

🛍 Shopping

Borderline Shop HANDICRAFTS
(www.borderlinecollective.org; 674/14 Th Intharakhiri; ⊘9am-7pm Tue-Sun) Selling arts and crafts made by refugee women, the profits from this shop go back into a women's collective and a child-assistance foundation. The upstairs gallery sells paintings and the house is also home to a tea garden and cookery course.

Municipal Market MARKET
(off Th Prasatwithi; ⊘6am-6pm) Mae Sot's municipal market is among the largest and most vibrant we've encountered anywhere in Thailand. There's heaps of exotic stuff from Myanmar, including Burmese book shops, sticks of *thanaka* (the source of the yellow powder you see on many faces), bags of pickled tea leaves and velvet thong slippers from Mandalay.

Walking Street MARKET
(Soi Rong Chak; ⊘5-9pm Sat) Every Saturday evening the small street by the police station is closed to traffic, and in its place are vendors selling handicrafts, clothes and food.

ℹ Information

Tourist Police (🖉1155; 738/1 Th Intharakhiri) Located east of the centre of town.

ℹ Getting There & Away

Mae Sot has air service to Bangkok's Don Muang airport via **Kan Air** (🖉Mae Sot 09 0907 1817,

BUS & MINIVAN TRANSPORT FROM MAE SOT

DESTINATION	FARE (B)	DURATION (HR)	FREQUENCY
Bangkok	333-666	7-8	frequent 8am-9.50pm
Chiang Mai	259-333	5-6	6am & 10am
Chiang Rai	488	9	6am & 10am
Kamphaeng Phet (bus/minivan)	120/140	3	4 departures 10am-8.30pm/ hourly
Mae Sai	583	12	3 departures 6am-10am
Phitsanulok	158	4	4 departures 7am-1pm
Sukhothai	120	3	4 departures 7am-1pm

GETTING TO MYANMAR: MAE SOT TO HPA-AN

The 420m Friendship Bridge links Mae Sot and Myawaddy in Myanmar's Kayin State.

Getting to the border *Sŏrng·tăa·ou* make the 5km trip to the border (20B, frequent 6am to 6pm) from Mae Sot.

At the border The **Thai immigration booth** (☑055 563004; ⊘5.30am-8.30pm) sits at the foot of the Friendship Bridge. If you have a pre-arranged visa, you can proceed through to the **Myanmar immigration booth** (☑95 0585 0100; ⊘5am-8pm, Myanmar time) and on to your next destination. Without a visa, you can buy a 500B temporary ID, which allows you to stay in Myawaddy until 6pm the same day; your passport will be held at the border and returned upon departure.

Moving on About 200m from the border crossing are white share taxis that depart when full on even-numbered days to the following destinations: Mawlamyine (10,000K to 15,000K, six hours), Hpa-an (7,500K to 10,000K, six hours) and Yangon (12,000K, 16 hours). There's also a bus to Yangon (12,000K, 16 hours, 5am).

For information on doing this crossing in reverse, see p502.

---

nationwide 02 551 6111; www.kanairlines.com; Mae Sot Airport, Th Asia) and **Nok Air** (☑Mae Sot 055 563883, nationwide ☑1318; www.nokair.co.th; Mae Sot Airport, Th Asia; ⊘8am-5pm). Nok Air also connects to Yangon. Mae Sot's **bus station** (☑055 563435; Th Asia) is 1.5km west of town; transport there costs 50B.

NORTHEASTERN THAILAND

Thailand's other regions are known for parties and scenery, but the northeast has soul. The main event in this undervisited region is the people: friendly, hard-working folks who cradle a traditional culture influenced by nearby Laos and Cambodia.

Also referred to as Isan, the northeast is one of Thailand's most rural and agricultural regions. The mighty Mekong River carves out a muddy path between Thailand's international neighbours and Isan's sister cultures of Laos and Cambodia. Local festivals display the region's unique fusion of cultures, and magnificent mini-Angkor Wats were left behind by the great Khmer empire. And the the flat, sun-beaten landscape of rice fields punctuated by shade trees and lonely water buffaloes spring to life when the wet season bears tender green rice shoots.

Rice is more than just a staple dish here; the holy trinity of Isan cuisine – *gài yâhng* (grilled chicken), *sôm·đam* (papaya salad) and *kôw něe·o* (sticky rice) – is integral to the identity of hard-working farmers and a de facto official dish for the region. Everything is eaten with the hands, using sticky rice as a 'spoon', and a plate of fresh vegetables helps offset the *sôm·đam*'s chilli burn (warning: Isan cuisine is hot!)

There's little in the way of guesthouse culture and English speakers aren't widespread. Indeed, this is the end of the tourist trail and the beginning of the Thailand trail.

Nakhon Ratchasima (Khorat) นครราชสีมา (โคราช)

POP 151,450

To most shoestringers, Nakhon Ratchasima (more commonly known as 'Khorat') is just a transit hub. Bland concrete development has buried much of its history, and its status as Thailand's second-largest city puts it unfairly in league with Bangkok. But if you're curious, Khorat is a part of the urban Isan puzzle, where village kids grew up to be educated bureaucrats living comfortable middle-class lives – an economic success story that has defined the Thai experience for several generations.

Sitting in the center of the city is the **Thao Suranari Monument** (อนุสาวรีย์ท้าวสุรนารี; Th Rajadamnern), dedicated to the wife of a city leader during Rama III's reign. Affectionately called Ya Mo (Grandma Mo), she helped save the city from a Lao invasion.

🛏 Sleeping

⭐ **Sansabai House** HOTEL $
(☑044 255144; www.sansabai-korat.com; Th Suranaree; r 300-450B; [P][⚟][🖧]) This place is hidden beside the Tokyo hotel, which does a

Nakhon Ratchasima (Khorat)

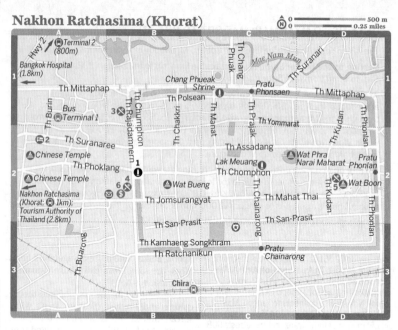

Nakhon Ratchasima (Khorat)

much better job of advertising itself, but the obscurity fits its understated ambience. The lobby is welcoming and the rooms are constantly being refitted. There are fan rooms as well as air-con rooms.

🍴 Eating

Khorat is famous for *pàt mèe khorâht*, a local twist on the ubiquitous *pàt tai*. **Wat Boon Night Bazaar** (Th Chompon; ⊙5-9.30pm) has great northeastern eats.

Ming Ter VEGAN $
(Th Rajadamnern; dishes 40-80B; ⊙7.30am-6pm; 🍃) There's little English at this homely vegan affair, but since it does mock-meat versions of Thai and Chinese standards, you can just order your favourites and the message will get through. Or just point to something in the buffet tray.

Gai Yang Saang Thai THAI $
(Th Rajadamnern; whole free-range chicken 140B; ⊙7.30am-8pm) Has served some of the best *gài yâhng* (grilled chicken) in Khorat for half a century.

ℹ Information

Bangkok Hospital (🕿044 429999; Th Mittaphap)

Bangkok Bank (Th Jomsurangyat; ⊙10.30am-7pm) Bank inside Klang Plaza. There's also an AEON ATM outside by the alley entrance.

Post Office (Th Jomsurangyat; ⊙8.30am-10.30pm Mon-Fri, 9am-noon & 4-10.30pm Sat, 4-10.30pm Sun & holidays)

Tourism Authority of Thailand (TAT; 🕿044 213666; tatsima@tat.or.th; 2102-2104 Th Mittaphap; ⊙8.30am-4.30pm) Next to Sima Thani Hotel.

ⓘ Getting There & Away

Khorat has two bus stations: **Bus Terminal 1** (☑ 044 242899; Th Burin) in the city centre serves Bangkok and towns within Nakhon Ratchasima Province. **Bus Terminal 2** (bor kŏr sŏr sŏrng; ☑ 044 295271; Hwy 2), known locally as *bor kŏr sŏr sŏrng*, is north of downtown and serves all other destinations. White No 15 *sŏrng·tăa·ou* goes to Terminal 2.

Khorat Train Station (☑ 044 242044) sees a lot of traffic but buses are faster. The smaller **Chira Train Station** (☑ 044 242363) is closer to town. Destinations include the following:

Bangkok (50B to 425B, five to seven hours)

Ubon Ratchathani (58B to 453B, five to six hours)

ⓘ Getting Around

Sŏrng·tăa·ou (8B) run fixed routes through the city, but even locals complain about how difficult it is to figure out the numbers and colours assigned to the routes. Most pass down Th Suranaree near the market, which is a good place to start. Heading west on Th Suranaree, the yellow *sŏrng·tăa·ou* No 1 with white and green stripes will take you to the train station and the Mall.

Túk-túk and motorcycle taxis cost between 40B and 70B around town.

Khao Yai National Park
อุทยานแห่งชาติเขาใหญ่

Thailand's oldest and most remarkable national park, **Khao Yai** (อุทยานแห่งชาติเขาใหญ่; ☑ 086 092 6529; adult/child 400/200B, plus car 50B; ⊙ 6am-6pm) is a vast wilderness astonishingly close to the country's major population centres. This is one of the largest intact monsoon forests in mainland Asia and, along with neighbouring forest complexes, it is now a Unesco World Heritage Site.

The park is surrounds a 1351m-high mountain on the western edge of the Dangrek range, which forms a natural boundary between Thailand and Cambodia. There are more than 50km of trekking trails (many of them formed by the movement of wildlife), some wild elephant herds, majestic waterfalls (for part of the year) and impressive bird life.

The most beautiful time to visit is just after the monsoon rains in November through to the start of the hot season (around April), when the landscape is green and the waterfalls are full. But – this is also when leeches are at their fiercest.

The park headquarters has some general trail information. For the major highlights it is easy enough to visit on your own but you'll need a guide for minor trails and to spot wildlife. The guesthouses in Pak Chong can arrange transport and day tours. Greenleaf Guesthouse has long enjoined enthusiastic praise and **Bobby's Apartments & Jungle Tours** (☑ 086 262 7006; www.bobbysjungletourkhaoyai.com) earns high marks, too.

🛏 Sleeping & Eating

Staying within the park cuts out your commute, though access to food and transport is limited. **Campsites** (per person with own tent 30B, 3-person tent 225B) and **lodging** (☑ 02 562 0760; www.dnp.go.th/parkreserve; r & bungalows 800-9000B, 30% discount Mon-Thu) can be booked online. Park restaurants at the visitor centre close at 7pm. Most backpackers base themselves in the nearby town of Pak Chong.

Greenleaf Guesthouse   GUESTHOUSE **$**
(☑ 044 365073; www.greenleaftour.com; Th Thanarat, Km 7.5; r 200-300B; P) The common areas are chaotic and the rooms basic at best at this long-running family-owned place. But there's flexibility with families to share rooms at no extra cost, and a family bungalow that's excellent value (500B). Wi-fi only

BUS & MINIVAN TRANSPORT FROM NAKHON RATCHASIMA (KHORAT)

DESTINATION	FARE (B)	DURATION (HR)	FREQUENCY
Aranya Prathet (bus/minivan)	165/132	4	5 daily/frequent
Chiang Mai	473	12-13	11 daily
Lopburi	120	3½	every 30min 6am-7pm
Nang Rong (bus/minivan)	75-95/75	2/1½	frequent
Nong Khai	220-435	6	hourly
Surin	136-175	4	every 30min
Trat	324	8	1am
Ubon Ratchathani	288-445	5-6	14 daily

PHIMAI พิมาย

Of the many Khmer temples that pepper the Isan countryside, **Phimai Historical Park** (อุทยานประวัติศาสตร์พิมาย; ☏044 471568; Th Ananthajinda; 100B; ☺7.30am-6pm) is picturesque and easily accessible.

The temple was built a century before its strikingly similar cousin Angkor Wat and marked one of the westernmost outposts of the Khmer empire's holy highway of laterite temples. The site was originally started by King Jayavarman V in the late 10th century and finished by King Suryavarman I (r 1002–49). The majestic structure boasts a 28m-tall main shrine of cruciform design and made of white sandstone, while the adjunct shrines are of pink sandstone and laterite. The sculptures over the doorways to the main shrine depict Hindu gods and scenes from the *Ramayana*.

Phimai National Museum (พิพิธภัณฑสถานแห่งชาติพิมาย; Th Tha Songkhran; 100B; ☺9am-4pm Wed-Sun), outside the main complex, has a fine collection of Khmer sculpture, including temple lintels and other architectural ruins.

Sai Ngam (ไทรงาม; ☺dawn-dusk) is a 350-plus-year-old tree that blankets an island east of town where food vendors serve *pàt phimai*, which is basically *pàt mèe khorâht*, which is basically *pàt tai*.

All buses to Phimai leave from Khorat's Bus Terminal 2 (50B, 1½ hours, frequent departures).

extends to the common areas. With a limited number of rooms, preference is given to guests who are taking the wildlife tours.

Khaoyai Garden Lodge HOTEL $
(☏044 365178; www.khaoyaigardenlodgekm7. com; Th Thanarat, Km 7; r with fan 350B, with air-con 2000-3200B, f 2800B; P❄@🛜🏊) This friendly, family-run place offers a variety of rooms (the cheapest are large, have shared hot-water bathrooms and fans and are better value than other cheapies in the area), all spread out around an attractive garden. It's great value and the restaurant-lounge in front encourages interaction with fellow guests.

❶ Getting There & Around

Pak Chong, the primary base town for the park, is served by buses and minivans from the following destinations:

Bangkok (Mo Chit) Northern and Northeastern bus terminal 128B to 150B, 2½ to three hours

Bangkok Victory Monument 180B, 2½ hours, hourly (minivans)

Nakhon Ratchasima (Khorat) 80B, one hour

Pak Chong is also on the rail line, but this is only a good option if you're coming from Ayuthaya (23B to 363B, two to three hours, nine daily).

Sŏrng·tăa·ou travel the 30km from Pak Chong to the park's northern gate (40B, 45 minutes, every 30 minutes from 6am to 5pm); hop aboard on Th Thanarat in front of the 7-Eleven

and hop off at the ticket gate. From here it is another 14km to the visitor centre; hitchhiking this stretch is quite common. There are also motorcycle rentals at the gate (500B) and in Pak Chong town (300B).

Phanom Rung Historical Park อุทยานประวัติศาสตร์เขาพนมรุ้ง

Spectacularly located atop an extinct volcano, **Phanom Rung Historical Park** (อุทยานประวัติศาสตร์เขาพนมรุ้ง; ☏044 666251; 100B, combined ticket with Prasat Muang Tam 150B; ☺6am-6pm) is the largest and best restored of the ancient Khmer sanctuaries in Thailand. Dating from the 10th to 13th centuries, the complex faces east towards the sacred capital of Angkor in Cambodia. It was first built as a Hindu monument and features sculpture relating to Vishnu and Shiva. Later it was converted into a Buddhist temple.

One of the most striking design features is the promenade, an avenue sealed with laterite and sandstone blocks and flanked by sandstone pillars with lotus-bud tops. It leads to the first and largest of three *naga* bridges, which are the only surviving architectural features of their kind in Thailand.

If you can, plan your visit for one of the four times of the year when the sun shines through all 15 sanctuary doorways. This solar alignment happens during sunrise on 3 to 5 April and 8 to 10 September, and sunset on 5 to 7 March and 5 to 7 October (one day earlier in leap years).

Phanom Rung is a day trip from Nakhon Ratchasima (Khorat) and Surin, but some people spend the night in Nang Rong, the nearest town to the temple. **P California Inter Hostel** (☑081 808 3347; www.pcaliforniananangrong.webs.com; Th Sangkakrit; r with fan 250B, with air-con 350-600B; P ❖ ☎) and **Honey Inn** (☑044 622825; www.honeyinn.com; Soi Si Kun; r with fan/air-con 250/350B; ❖ @ ☎) are two local and helpful lodging options.

To get to Phanom Rung from Nakhon Ratchasima (Khorat; 75B to 95B, two hours, hourly) or Surin (80B, two hours, every 30 minutes), take a bus to Ban Tako, a well-marked turn-off 14km east of Nang Rong. From here, hire a motorcycle taxi (300B return).

Nang Rong can be reached via bus from Khorat and Pak Chong. Guesthouses in Nang Rong can arrange transport to Phanom Rung.

Worth visiting for its remote ambience, **Prasat Muang Tam** (ปราสาทเมืองต่ำ; 100B; ◷6am-6pm) was once a shrine to Shiva and dates to the 10th or 11th century. Motorcycle taxis will make the trip from Phanom Rung for another 150B.

Surin

POP 41,200

There's not a lot to see in sleepy Surin until the annual Elephant Round-up comes to town in November. The rest of the year, a few travellers trickle through en route to the Khmer temples that line the Cambodian border. Culturally, Surin has a strong Khmer influence, and the province is renowned for its silk-weaving traditions.

Surin is also a launching point for a border-crossing point for Siem Reap–bound travellers.

◎ Sights & Activities

Surin's cultural highlights are outside of town and are best visited by private transport. View Surin's distinctive silk-weaving skills at the **Queen Sirikit Sericulture Center** (ศูนย์หม่อนไหมเฉลิมพระเกียรติสมเด็จพระนางเจ้าสิริกิติ์ พระบรมราชินีนาถ (สุรินทร์); ☑044 511393; Rte 226; ◷8am-4.30pm) FREE, 4km outside of town; the silk makers harness their looms on weekdays only. Take a trip into the countryside en route to **Prasat Ta Meuan** (ปราสาทตาเมือน; ◷dawn-3pm) FREE, which is an atmospheric Khmer ruin along the Cambodian border. The **Elephant Study Centre** (☑044 145050; 100B; ◷8.30am-4pm) is based in Ban Tha Klang, a traditional elephant herding village of the Suai people. Performers from Ban Tha Klang come to Surin town in November for the annual **Elephant Round-up** (◷Nov), which showcases mock battles and feats of strength and dexterity – activities that are now viewed as dangerous and inhumane to the animals.

🛏 Sleeping & Eating

During the Elephant Round-up, every hotel in town is booked and rates can triple; reserve well in advance.

Baan Chang Ton HOMESTAY $
(☑087 459 8962; www.baanchangton.com; Th Suriyarart; r 400-500B; P ❖ @ ☎) This old wooden house has lovely dark timbers and will give you a good feel for Thai home life. The friendly owners make it a great place to stay. It's quite simple (shared bathrooms, mattresses on the floor and air-conditioning in only one room) but the atmosphere makes it special.

Maneerote Hotel HOTEL $
(☑044 539477; www.maneerotehotel.com; Soi Poi Tunggor, Th Krungsri Nai; s 450B, d 450-500B; P ❖ @ ☎) This quiet hotel southwest of the fresh market is hands down the best-value place in town. Rooms are clean and modern and there's an attached restaurant and coffee shop. The optional breakfast is an extra 100B.

Night Market THAI $
(Th Krungsri Nai; ◷5-10pm) A block south of the fountain, this good night market whips up a wide selection of Thai and Isan dishes.

BUS TRANSPORT FROM SURIN

DESTINATION	FARE (B)	DURATION (HR)	FREQUENCY
Bangkok	272-389	6-7	9 daily
Khorat	125-175	4	every 30min
Ubon Ratchathani	105-200	3	every 2hr

VOLUNTEERING IN SURIN

The **Surin Project** (☑ 084 482 1210; www.surinproject.org), based in Ban Tha Klang, offers volunteering opportunities for visitors who would like to spend quality time with elephants in a traditional elephant-herding village.

Petmanee 2   THAI $

(Th Murasart; dishes 20-80B; ☺9am-3pm) This simple spot south of Ruampaet Hospital by Wat Salaloi (look for the large chicken grill) is Surin's most famous purveyor of *sôm·đam* and *gài yâhng*. The *súp nòr mái* (bamboo-shoot curry) is good, too. There's little English, spoken or written, but the food is so good it's worth stumbling through an order.

ⓘ Getting There & Away

The **bus terminal** (☑ 044 511756; Th Jitbumrung) is one block from the **train station** (☑ 045 511295); both are centrally located. The best service is **Nakhonchai Air** (☑ 044 515151), which has its own terminal 1km north of the train station.

Train destinations include the following:

Bangkok (73B to 489B, seven to nine hours, nine daily)

Ubon Ratchathani (31B to 382B, two to four hours, 10 daily)

Saren Travel and Surin Chai Kit restaurant hire cars, and some of the *fa·ràng* bars on the soi behind the bus station hire motorcycles.

Ubon Ratchathani   อุบลราชธานี

POP 86,800

Although it is one of the bigger cities in the region, Ubon still retains a small-town feel thanks to the relaxing nature of Mae Nam Mun, Thailand's second-longest river, and the town's palpable Lao heritage. It is easily traversed by foot and easily appreciated by aimless wandering.

Ubon doesn't see a lot of foreign visitors because it is in an odd corner of the country, but the annual Candle Parade is a true spectacle in religious art and culture. The nearby Thai–Lao border crossing provides an alternative route into southern Laos.

◉ Sights

A trip to the provinces means a trip to the temples. **Wat Thung Si Meuang** (วัดทุ่ง

ศรีเมือง; Th Luang; ☺dawn-dusk) 𝗙𝗥𝗘𝗘 and **Wat Si Ubon Rattanaram** (วัดศรีอุบลรัตนาราม; Th Uparat; ☺dawn-dusk) 𝗙𝗥𝗘𝗘 are the city's premiere spots; the latter contains a 7cm-tall topaz Buddha regarded as the city's holiest possession. The most prized possession of **Ubon Ratchathani National Museum** (พิพิธภัณฑสถานแห่งชาติอุบลราชธานี; Th Kheuan Thani; 100B; ☺9am-4pm Wed-Sun) is a 9th-century statue combining Shiva and his consort Uma into one being.

⚒ Festivals

Candle Parade   CULTURAL

(Kabuan Hae Tian) In preparation for Khao Phansaa (the start of Buddhist Lent, usually in July) it was customary to offer candles to the temples as a source of light. Ubon took the tradition and supersized it into huge wax sculptures depicting Buddhist iconography. The creations are then paraded through town during this annual festival.

🛏 Sleeping & Eating

Rates shoot up and availability goes down during the Candle Parade. The **Night Market** (Th Kheuan Thani; ☺4-11pm) is a small affair but is augmented by the weekend **Walking Street** (Th Ratchabut; ☺6pm-11pm Fri-Sun).

Phadaeng Hotel   HOTEL $

(☑045 254600; www.thephadaeng.com; Th Phadaeng; r 500-800B; 🅿❄@🛜) One of the best-value hotels in Ubon, the Phadaeng has newish, well-maintained rooms with good furnishings (including large TVs and desks) just minutes from Thung Si Meuang park. It has a large parking area that separates the rooms from the street noise. The hotel is livened up with copies of classic paintings. Bike hire costs 50B per day.

★Outside Inn   GUESTHOUSE $$

(☑088 581 2069; www.theoutsideinnubon.com; 11 Th Suriyat; r incl breakfast 650-790B; 🅿❄🛜) A nice little garden lounge area sets the relaxed, communal vibe here. Rooms are large, comfy and fitted with tastefully designed reclaimed timber furnishings. The Thai-American owners are great hosts and cook good Thai and Mexican food.

★Rung Roj   THAI $

(☑045 263155; Th Nakhonban; dishes 45-150B; ☺9.30am-8.30pm Mon-Sat; 🛜) It's surprising the prices are so low at this upmarket-looking establishment. It's an Ubon institution serving excellent food using family recipes and fresh ingredients. From the outside it looks more like a well-to-do house than a restaurant. Look for the plate, fork and spoon sign.

★ **Jumpa-Hom**   THAI **$$**
(☑045 260398; Th Phichitrangsan; dishes from 100B; ☺5pm-midnight; 🖘) One of the loveliest and most delicious restaurants in Isan, Jumpa-Hom has a large menu featuring some less-common dishes. You can dine on a water-and-plant-filled wooden deck or in the air-con dining room, which offers a choice of tables and chairs or cushions for floor seating. On the premises is the bakery **U-Bake** (cake from 50B; ☺9am-11pm; 🖘).

ℹ Information

Tourism Authority of Thailand (TAT; ☑045 243770; tatubon@tat.or.th; 264/1 Th Kheuan Thani; ☺8.30am-4.30pm) Has helpful staff.

Ubonrak Thonburi Hospital (☑045 260285; Th Phalorangrit) Has a 24-hour casualty department.

ℹ Getting There & Around

Ubon has an airport serviced by **Air Asia** (☑02 515 9999; www.airasia.com) and **Nok Air** (☑02 900 9955; www.nokair.com) with flights to Bangkok's Don Muang Airport (1400B, two to seven daily); **Thai Airways** (THAI; ☑045 313340; www.thaiairways.com) flies to Bangkok's Suvarnabhumi Airport. Kan Air flies to Chiang Mai (1200B).

Ubon's **bus terminal** (☑045 316085) is north of town; take *sŏrng·tăa·ou* 2, 3 or 10. The top Bangkok services are **999 VIP** (☑045 314299) and **Nakhonchai Air** (☑045 269777).

The train station is in Warin Chamrap, south of central Ubon, accessible via *sŏrng·tăa·ou* 2.

Numbered *sŏrng·tăa·ou* (10B) run throughout town. A túk-túk trip will cost 30B to 50B.

Mukdahan   มุกดาหาร
POP 34,300

Mukdahan is linked to Savannakhet in Laos by the Thai-Lao Friendship Bridge 2, part of the ambitious Trans-Asia Hwy that continues all the way to the Vietnamese port town of Danang.

If you need to overnight here, **Ban Rim Suan** (☑042 632980; www.banrimsuan.weebly.com; Th Samut Sakdarak; s/d 350/450B; P✳🖘) is the best budget deal in the city. **Wine Wild Why?** (Th Samran Chaikhongtai; dishes 40-150B; ☺9am-10pm; 🖘) is an atmospheric eatery for Thai and Isan food. **Goodmook*** (☑042 612091; Th Song Nang Sathit; dishes 70-450B; ☺9am-10pm Tue-Sun; 🖘) has all the ingredients of a travellers' cafe: an international menu and actual decor. The **night market** (Th Song Nang Sathit; ☺4-9pm) provides plenty of Vietnamese food along with the usual suspects.

ℹ Getting There & Away

Mukdahan's bus terminal is on Rte 212, west of town. Take a yellow *sŏrng·tăa·ou* (10B, 6am to 5pm) from Th Phitak Phanomkhet near the fountain. Destinations include the following:

Bangkok's Northern & Northeastern (Mo Chit) terminal 420B to 829B, 10 hours, evening departures

Nakhon Phanom 80B, two hours, frequent

That Phanom 40B, 45 minutes

Ubon Ratchathani 105B, 2½ hours, frequent

Nakhon Phanom   นครพนม
POP 31,700

This tidy provincial capital has a picturesque setting beside the Mekong River overlooking the asymmetrical peaks of Laos. With its French colonial buildings and Vietnamese influences, this is an unexpected slice of Indochina on the northeastern fringes of Siam. There's also a legal border crossing into Laos should you be looking for an escape hatch.

BUS TRANSPORT FROM UBON

DESTINATION	FARE (B)	DURATION (HR)	FREQUENCY
Bangkok	420-767	10	frequent
Chiang Mai	872	12	6pm
Mukdahan	75-135	3½	every 30min
Nakhon Ratchasima (Khorat)	286-445	5-6	14 daily
Pakse (Laos)	200	3	9.30am & 3.30pm
Surin	105-200	3	every 2hr

GETTING TO LAOS: EASTERN BORDERS

Ubon Ratchathani to Pakse

The busy Chong Mek/Vang Tao border crossing connects to Laos' Si Phan Don (Four Thousand Islands) region via Pakse; it is also the only Thai–Lao border where you don't have to cross the Mekong.

Getting to the border Direct Ubon Ratchathani–Pakse buses stop at the border for visa formalities.

At the border The border is open 6am to 8pm and is largely hassle-free, save for the occasional practice of a 'stamping' levy by Lao officials. Lao visas are available on arrival.

Moving on The southern Lao city of Pakse is about an hour away.

For information on doing this crossing in reverse, see p364.

Mukdahan to Savannakhet

The Thai–Lao Friendship Bridge links Mukdahan and Savannakhet, where transport continues to the Vietnamese coast.

Getting to the border From Mukdahan, buses to Savannakhet (50B to 55B, one to two hours, hourly from 7.30am to 7pm) leave from the bus station.

At the border Border formalities are handled on the bridge.

Moving on On the Lao side there are long-distance buses to Vietnam, a journey of about seven hours.

For information on doing this crossing in reverse, see p364.

GETTING TO LAOS: REMOTE BORDERS

Nakhon Phanom to Tha Khaek

Though not the most convenient crossing, Nakhon Phanom feeds into the Lao town of Tha Khaek.

At the border Buses cross the Thai–Lao Friendship Bridge 3 to Tha Khaek (70B to 75B, eight daily from 8am to 5pm). Lao visas are available at the border; bring a passport photo.

Moving on Savannakhet is a two-hour bus ride from Tha Khaek.

For information on doing this crossing in reverse, see p357.

Bueng Kan to Paksan

Although it's very rarely done, you can cross the border here to Paksan, but only if you already have your Lao visa.

Getting to the border Buses to Bueng Kan leave from Nong Khai (100B to 150B, 3½ hours, eight daily) and Nakhon Phanom (140B, 3½ hours, four daily). The border crossing is 2.5km northwest of town; a túk-túk costs 60B.

At the border You'll need a pre-arranged Lao visa in order to cross.

Moving on Boats cross the river to Paksan (60B, 8.30am to noon and 1pm to 4.30pm).

For information on doing this crossing in reverse, see p357.

Tha Li to Kaen Thao

Foreigners can get Lao visas at the seldom-used Tha–Lao Nam Heuang Friendship Bridge at the Tha Li/Kaen Thao border crossing, 60km northwest of Loei. A VIP bus service goes all the way from Loei to Luang Prabang (700B, 10 hours). Loei is accessible by bus from all major Thai towns.

For information on doing this crossing in reverse, see p352.

The neighbouring village of Ban Na Chok, 3km west of town, gave refuge to Vietnamese liberator Ho Chi Minh and remembers his life at **Ho Chi Minh's House** (บ้านโฮจิมินห์; ☑ 042 522430; entry by donation; ☺ dawn-dusk).

The city runs an hour-long **sunset cruise** (☑ 086 230 5560; per person 50B) along the Mekong on *Thesaban,* which docks across from the Indochina Market.

Nakhon Phanom is famous for its **Lai Reua Fai** (☺ late Oct/early Nov) (Illuminated Boat Procession) in October. It is a modern twist on the ancient tradition of floating offerings to the Mekong *naga,* a mythical serpent.

SP Hotel (☑ 042 513505; Th Nittayo; s/d 450/500B; P❋@☎) has plain but modern rooms and **777 Hometel** (☑ 042 514777; Th Tamrongprasit; r with breakfast 590-790B; P❋@☎), known as *dorng jet* in Thai, has stylish rooms and helpful staff. The outdoor terrace at the **Indochina Market** (Th Sunthon Wijit; ☺ 7am-7pm) has choice mountain-view seats.

The **bus terminal** (☑ 042 513444; Th Fuang Nakhon) is west of the town centre. Destinations include Nong Khai (200B, 6½ hours, four daily), Mukdahan (80B, 2½ hours), That Phanom (40B, one hour) and Bangkok (477B to 614B, 12 hours, three daily).

That Phanom ธาตุพนม

This drowsy hamlet is a little piece of Laos on the wrong side of the Mekong River. It is a lovely detour if you're headed to Nong Khai from Mukdahan. The highlight is **Wat Phra That Phanom** (วัดพระธาตุพนม; Th Chayangkun; ☺ 5am-8pm), crowned by a Lao-style *chedi* that is loudly celebrated during the **That Phanom Festival** in late January or early February.

Kritsada Rimkhong Hotel (☑ 042 540088; www.ksdrimkhong-resort.com; Th Rimkhong; r 500-600B; P❋@☎) has rooms that range from plain to attractive and **Baan-Ing-Oon Guesthouse** (☑ 042 540111; Th Phanom Phana-

rak; r 490-590B; ❋☎) supplies much-needed guesthouse culture. There's a small **night market** (☺ 4pm-10pm) for dinner.

That Phanom's bus station is west of town with services to Mukdahan (47B to 50B, one hour), Nakhon Phanom (40B to 50B, one hour, seven daily) and Ubon Ratchathani (168B to 185B, 4½ hours, frequent). There are also *sŏrng·tăa·ou* to Nakhon Phanom (40B, 1½ hours).

Nong Khai หนองคาย

POP 61,500

Adorable Nong Khai has a winning recipe: a sleepy setting beside the Mekong River, enough tourist amenities to dispel isolation and enough local attractions to fill a day with sightseeing. It's an easy overnight train ride from Bangkok and sits right on a convenient border crossing into Vientiane, Laos.

☉ Sights

★ **Sala Kaew Ku** SCULPTURE PARK
(ศาลาแก้วกู่; 20B; ☺ 8am-6pm) Yes, it's cheesy, but the sheer size of the sculptures here can't fail to impress. Built over a period of 20 years by Luang Pu Boun Leua Sourirat, a mystic who died in 1996, the park features a weird and wonderful array of gigantic sculptures ablaze with Hindu-Buddhist imagery.

Tha Sadet Market MARKET
(ตลาดท่าเสด็จ; Th Rimkhong; ☺ 8.30am-6pm) It is the most popular destination in town and almost everyone loves a stroll through this covered market. It offers the usual mix of clothes, electronic equipment, food and assorted bric-a-brac, most of it imported from Laos and China, but there are also a few shops selling quirky quality stuff.

✪✪ Festivals

Like many northeastern towns, Nong Khai has a Rocket Festival, which begins on Visakha Bucha day in late May/early June.

THAILAND THAT PHANOM

BUSES FROM NONG KHAI

DESTINATION	FARE (B)	DURATION (HR)	FREQUENCY
Bangkok's Northern & Northeastern (Mo Chit) station	380-760	11	afternoon & evening departures
Bangkok's Suvarnabhumi (Airport) bus station	495	9	8pm
Nakhon Phanom	200	6½	2 daily
Udon Thani	50	1	frequent

The end of Buddhist Lent (*Ork Phansaa*) in late October/early November ushers in a variety of river-based events, including **longtail boat races** and the mysterious **naga fireballs** (when illuminated gaseous balls rise out of the river on the night of the full moon).

🛌 Sleeping

Nong Khai is the only Isan town with a fully fledged backpacker scene, so enjoy it while you can.

⭐Mut Mee Garden
Guest House   GUESTHOUSE $
(☑ 042 460717; www.mutmee.com; 1111/4 Th Kaew Worawut; s & d without bathroom 200-300B, d 300-420B, d with air-con 600-1400B; ❄️🛜) Occupying a sleepy stretch of the Mekong, Nong Khai's budget classic has a garden so relaxing it's intoxicating, and most nights it's packed with travellers. Mut Mee caters to many budgets, with a huge variety of rooms (the cheapest with shared bathroom, the most expensive with an awesome balcony) clustered around a thatched-roof restaurant with expansive views of the Mekong.

Ruan Thai Guesthouse   GUESTHOUSE $
(☑ 042 412519; Th Rimkhong; r with fan/air-con 300/400B; P❄️@🛜) Popular for its good prices, convenient location, regular maintenance and friendly vibe. There's a mix of fan and air-con rooms, plus one wooden cottage and some flower-filled garden greenery.

Sawasdee Guesthouse   GUESTHOUSE $
(☑ 042 420259; www.sawasdeeguesthouse.com; 402 Th Meechai; r with fan & shared bathroom 200-220B, with air-con 450-650B; P❄️@🛜) If you could judge a hotel by its cover, this charismatic guesthouse in an old Franco-Chinese shophouse would come up trumps. The tidy rooms mostly lack the old-school veneer of the exterior and lobby, but they're tidy and fairly priced. Rooms are set around an open courtyard that's great for lounging. Bicycles are 40B per day, motorbikes 250B.

WEIRD & WONDERFUL ISAN

From ghosts to gunpowder, Isan dominates in the bizarre attractions category.

Dan Sai's Spirit Festival
The raucous **Phi Ta Khon Festival** is a cross between the revelry of Carnival and the ghoulishness of Halloween. The festival coincides with the subdued Buddhist holy day of Bun Phra Wet (Phra Wet Festival), honouring the penultimate life of Buddha. But in Dan Sai the main event is a rice-whisky-fuelled parade in which villagers don masks to transform themselves into the spirits who welcomed Phra Wet's return. Dan Sai **homestay** (☑ 086 862 4812, 042 892339; dm/tw or d 170/550B, with air-con 650B) arranges lodging with local families. The shop **Kawinthip Hattakham** (กวินทิพย์หัตถกรรม; ☑ 042 892339; Th Kaew Asa; ⊙ 8am-7pm) is a good local resource. Dan Sai sits between Loei (65B to 70B, 1½ hours) and Phitsanulok (73B to 102B, three hours) and the festival usually occurs in June.

Yasothon's Kaboom Fest
Rocket festivals are held across Isan in May and June to tell Phaya Thaen, a pre-Buddhist rain god, that it's time for him to send down the wet stuff; but no place celebrates as fervently as Yasothon, where the largest rockets, called *bâng fai síp láhn*, are 3m long and packed with 500kg of gunpowder. The festival is held on the second weekend of May. **BM Grand** (☑ 045 714262; Th Rattanakhet; s/d 400/450B; P❄️🛜) has cheap sleeps in the city centre. Yasothon can be reached by bus from Ubon Ratchathani (90B to 105B, 1½ hours) and Mukdahan (80B to 103B).

Si Saket's Glass Temple
Before recycling was in vogue, the idea for **Wat Lan Khuat** (วัดล้านขวด; ⊙ dawn-dusk) **FREE**, better known as the Million Bottle Temple, was a religious, rather than environmental, vision. In 1982 the abbot dreamt of a sanctuary in heaven made of diamonds and gems. Wishing to replicate this divine splendour he covered the temple buildings in the most sparkly material he could find: green bottles. The temple sits outside of Si Saket in Khun Han, 11km south of Hwy 24 via Rte 2111. Public transport is limited so you'll have to rent a motorbike in Surin.

GETTING TO LAOS: NONG KHAI TO VIENTIANE

The Nong Khai/Tha Na Long crossing is one of the most popular Thai–Lao border crossings.

Getting to the border If you already have your Lao visa, a direct bus from Nong Khai to Vientiane (55B to 60B, one hour, six daily) and Vang Vieng (270B to 275B, four hours, 10am) leaves from the bus station. If you're getting a visa at the border, take a túk-túk (50B) from the town centre to the bridge. Don't let the driver take you to a visa-service agency.

At the border After getting stamped out of Thailand, take a minivan (20B to 30B) across the bridge. Lao visas are available upon arrival; bring a passport photo.

Moving on It is 20km to Vientiane, via buses, túk-túk and taxis.

For information on doing this crossing in reverse, see p328.

✗ Eating

★ Dee Dee Pohchanah   THAI $
(Th Prajak; dishes 45-250B; ⊙10.30am-2am)
How good is Dee Dee? Just look at the dinnertime crowds. Despite having a full house every night, this simple place is a well-oiled machine and you won't be waiting long.

★ Saap Lah   THAI $
(Th Meechai; dishes 25-150B; ⊙ 7am-8pm) For excellent *gài yâhng, sôm·đam* and other Isan foods, follow your nose to this no-frills shop.

Daeng Namnuang   VIETNAMESE $
(Th Rimkhong; dishes 60-130B; ⊙8am-8pm; 🕾)
This massive river restaurant is an Isan institution, and hordes of out-of-towners head home with car boots and carry-on bags (there's an outlet at Udon Thani's airport) stuffed with *năam neu·ang* (pork spring rolls).

Nagarina   THAI $$
(☑ 042 412211; Th Rimkhong; dishes around 100B, meals 200B; ⊙10am-9pm; 🕾🍴) Mut Mee Garden Guesthouse's floating restaurant, which specialises in fish, turns out the real deal. There's a sunset cruise most nights (100B; at least 10 guests needed before the cruise will go ahead) around 5pm; order food at least 30 minutes before departure.

🛍 Shopping

Nong Khai
Walking Street Market   MARKET
(⊙4pm-10pm Sat) This street festival featuring music, handmade items and food takes over the promenade every Saturday night.

Hornbill Books   BOOKS
(Soi Mut Mee; ⊙10am-7pm Mon-Sat) Buys, sells and trades books in English, French and other languages. Also sells coffee and has internet access.

Village Weaver
Handicrafts   HANDICRAFTS
(1020 Th Prajak) This place sells high-quality, handwoven fabrics and clothing (readymade or made to order) that help fund development projects around Nong Khai. The *mát·mèe* cotton is particularly good here.

ℹ Information

Nongkhai Hospital (☑ 042 413461; Th Meechai) Has a 24-hour casualty department.
Tourism Authority of Thailand (TAT; ☑ 042 421326; tat_nongkhai@yahoo.com; Hwy 2; ⊙8.30am-4.30pm) Inconveniently located outside of town.

ℹ Getting There & Away

Nong Khai's main **bus terminal** (☑ 042 412679) is just off Th Prajak, about 1.5km from the riverfront guesthouses. Nearby is Udon Thani, a major bus hub with more transport options.

The **train station** (☑ 042 411637) is 2km west of town. Two express trains connect to Bangkok (seat 103B to 498B, sleeper 117B to 1317B, 11 to 12 hours, one morning and one afternoon departure).

EASTERN GULF COAST

Thailand's east coast isn't as stunning as the postcard-famous southern coast, but it is an ideal beach jaunt from jostling Bangkok if you're pinched for time or travelling overland to/from Cambodia. While your friends are still packed into buses en route to Ko Pha-Ngan, you'll be sun-kissed and sandy-toed.

THAILAND EASTERN GULF COAST

Ko Samet

เกาะเสม็ด

Bangkok's beachy backyard, Ko Samet is close enough for a weekend escape, yet worlds away from the urban bustle. Traffic-weary Thais, Russian and Chinese package tourists, and Bangkok expats are Samet's steady clientele – and everyone squeezes into the petite east-coast beaches. It's been a national park (adult/child 200/100B) since 1981 and is still surprisingly rustic considering Thailand's penchant for urban makeovers of its seaside parks. Walking trails connect the beaches and the rocky headlands.

🛏 Sleeping & Eating

Most resorts and bungalows have restaurants offering mixed menus of Thai and traveller food. Rates skyrocket on weekends and holidays. Hat Sai Kaew, Ao Hin Khok, Ao Phai and Ao Wong Deuan are popular party beaches.

Mossman House　　　　　GUESTHOUSE $
(☑038 644017; Hat Sai Kaew; r 800-1300B; ❄🛜) On the main street, before the national park ticket office, is this sound guesthouse, with large, comfortable rooms and leafy grounds. Choose a spot at the back for some quiet.

Apache　　　　　　　　　GUESTHOUSE $
(☑081 452 9472; Ao Thian; r 800-1500B; ❄) Apache's eclectic, quirky decorations add character to this super-chilled spot. Bungalows are basic but adequate. Apache's restaurant-on-stilts is worth a look.

Nice & Easy　　　　　　　　HOTEL $$
(☑038 644370; www.niceandeasysamed.com; Ao Wong Deuan; r 1200-2500B; ❄🛜) As the name suggests, this is a very amiable place, with comfortable, modern bungalows set around a garden behind the beach. A great deal for this beach.

❶ Information

ATMs and internet cafes can be found in Na Dan and Ao Wong Deuan.

Ko Samet Health Centre (☑038 644123; ⊙24hr) On the main road between Na Dan and Hat Sai Kaew.

❶ Getting There & Around

Ko Samet is reached by boat from the mainland town of Ban Phe (one way/return 70/100B, 40 minutes, hourly 8am to 5pm). Na Dan is the primary port on the island.

Sŏrng·tăa·ou on the island cost from 200B to 500B, depending on your destination and the number of passengers.

Buses and minivans fan out from Ban Phe and the nearby town of Rayong has more transport options; *sŏrng·tăa·ou* make the trip between Ban Phe and Rayong (25B, frequent).

Chanthaburi & Trat

จันทบุรี / ตราด

Surrounded by palm trees and fruit plantations, Chanthaburi and Trat are mainly transit points for travellers headed to Ko Chang or the Cambodian border. If you stop to catch your breath, you'll find that Chanthaburi dazzles with its weekend gem market, and sleepy Trat is filled with old teak shophouses and genuine small-town living.

🛏 Sleeping & Eating

🛏 Chanthaburi

You're unlikely to need a bed in Chanthaburi, but just in case...

River Guest House　　　　　　HOTEL $
(☑039 328211; 3/5-8 Th Si Chan; r 190-490B; ❄@🛜) Rooms are tiny and the beds are basic but the riverside seating area compensates for this. The cheapest rooms have a shared bathroom.

Muslim Restaurant　　　　INDIAN, THAI $
(☑081 353 5174; cnr Soi 4, Th Si Chan; dishes 50-80B; ⊙9.30am-6pm) Run by Thai Muslims, this tiny place has excellent *paratha, biryani,* curries and chai.

BUSES & MINIVANS FROM BAN PHE

DESTINATION	FARE (B)	DURATION (HR)	FREQUENCY
Bangkok's Eastern (Ekamai) bus station	166	4	every 2hr 7am-6pm
Bangkok's Victory Monument	200	4	every 40min
Laem Ngop (mainland pier for Ko Chang boats)	250	3	3 daily

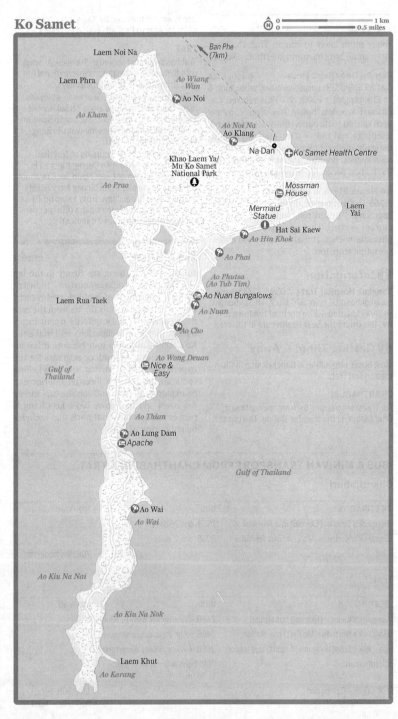

Ko Samet

0 — 1 km
0 — 0.5 miles

Laem Noi Na

Laem Phra

Ban Phe (7km)

Ao Wiang Wan

Ao Noi

Ao Kham

Ao Noi Na
Ao Klang

Na Dan

Ko Samet Health Centre

Khao Laem Ya/
Mu Ko Samet
National Park

Mossman
House

Ao Prao

Mermaid
Statue

Laem
Yai

Hat Sai Kaew

Ao Hin Khok

Ao Phai

Ao Phutsa
(Ao Tub Tim)

Ao Nuan Bungalows

Laem Rua Taek

Ao Nuan

Ao Cho

Gulf of
Thailand

Ao Wong Deuan

Nice &
Easy

Ao Thian

Ao Lung Dam

Apache

Gulf of Thailand

Ao Wai

Ao Wai

Ao Kiu Na Nai

Ao Kiu Na Nok

Laem Khut

Ao Karang

Trat

You're more likely to stay in Trat; the town has a small but charming guesthouse scene.

Ban Jai Dee Guest House   GUESTHOUSE $
(📱083 589 0839; banjaideehouse@yahoo.com; 6 Th Chaimongkol; r 200B; 🖥) This relaxed traditional wooden house has simple rooms with shared bathrooms (hot-water showers). Paintings and objets d'art made by the artistically inclined owners decorate the common spaces. Booking ahead is essential. Ask the owner, Serge, for travel advice.

No Name Steak & Pasta   INTERNATIONAL, THAI $
(61-65 Th Chaimongkol; dishes 50-120B; 🕐8am-9pm Sun-Fri) Bright red, white and blue restaurant serving Thai and Western classics, plus sandwiches. It makes for a good coffee/smoothie stop, too.

❶ Information

Bangkok Hospital Trat (📱039 532735; www.bangkokhospital.com; 376 Mu 2, Th Sukhumvit; 🕐24hr) Located 400m north of the town centre, this offers the best health care in the area.

❶ Getting There & Away

Most buses originating in Bangkok stop in Chanthaburi and Trat.

CHANTHABURI

For travellers heading to/from the northeast, Chanthaburi is the transfer station. The bus station is west of the river. Sa Kaew is the transfer point for Aranya Prathet–bound travellers.

TRAT

Trat has an airport served by Bangkok Airways with flights to Suvarnabhumi International Airport (from 2090B, three times daily).

The bus station is outside of town. Minivans leave from various stops along Th Sukhumvit. **Family Tour** (📱081 940 7380; cnr Th Sukhumvit & Th Lak Meuang) runs minivans to Bangkok's Victory Monument.

There are three piers outside of Trat that handle ferries to/from Ko Chang; the area is collectively known as Laem Ngop. Inquire about transfers to the pier when buying ferry tickets in Trat. *Sŏrng·tăa·ou* leave from a stop on Th Sukhumvit to Laem Ngop's piers (60B per person for six passengers, 40 minutes).

Ko Chang   เกาะช้าง

Jungle-clad Ko Chang sits firmly in the lap of Thailand's package-tourism industry, with an assortment of sophisticated resorts, tonnes of bars and daily flights from the capital to nearby Trat. Despite its recent incarnation, plenty of backpackers still make the Ko Chang–Cambodia tour because it has an appealing array of outdoor activities for the hyperactive visitor. Diving and snorkelling spots are nearby, the forested interior can be explored by foot, and kayaks can survey sea coves and mangrove bays. Ko Chang is part of a larger **national park** that includes neighbouring islands.

BUS & MINIVAN TRANSPORT FROM CHANTHABURI & TRAT

Chanthaburi

DESTINATION	BUS	MINIVAN
Bangkok's Eastern (Ekamai) Bus Terminal	198B, 4hr, 25 daily	
Bangkok's Northern (Mo Chit) Bus Terminal	205B, 4hr, 2 daily	
Trat		70B, 1hr, frequent

Trat

DESTINATION	BUS	MINIVAN
Bangkok's Eastern (Ekamai) bus station	248B, 4½hr, hourly 6am-11.30pm	
Bangkok's Northern (Mo Chit) bus station	248B, 5½hr, 2 morning departures	
Bangkok's Suvarnabhumi (Airport) bus station	248B, 4-4½hr, 5 daily departures	
Chanthaburi	70B, 1½hr, every 1½hr 6.30am-11.30pm	
Hat Lek (for Cambodia)		120-150B, 1½hr, hourly 5am-6pm

GETTING TO CAMBODIA: COASTAL BORDERS

Trat to Koh Kong

The Hat Lek/Cham Yeam crossing is the most convenient border crossing between Ko Chang and Sihanoukville in coastal Cambodia.

Getting to the border Take a minivan from Trat's bus station to the border at Hat Lek (120B, 1½ hours, hourly from 5am to 6pm).

At the border Cambodian tourist visas are available at the border for 1200B (as opposed to the standard US$20); payment is only accepted in baht. Bring a passport photo and avoid the runner boys who want to issue a health certificate or other 'medical' paperwork. The border closes at 8pm.

Moving on From the Cambodian border, take a taxi (US$10) or moto (US$3) to Koh Kong, where you can catch onward transport to Sihanoukville (four hours, one or two departures per day) and Phnom Penh (five hours, two or three departures until 11.30am).

For information on doing this crossing in reverse, see p111.

Chanthaburi to Pailin

If you're heading to Siem Reap (or Battambang) from Ko Chang, you don't have to schlep up to Aranya Prathet/Poipet border. The Ban Pakard/Psar Pruhm crossing isn't crowded and shaves some travel time.

Getting to the border Take a minivan from Chanthaburi to Ban Pakard/Pong Nam Ron (150B, 1½ hours, 10am, 11am and 6.30pm); the Chanthaburi minivan stop is across the river from River Guesthouse.

At the border Cross the border with the usual formalities (a passport photo and US$20 visa fee) to Psar Pruhm.

Moving on Arrange a motorbike taxi to Pailin, which has connections to Battambang (US$5, 1½ hours) and from there to Siem Reap.

For information on doing this crossing in reverse, see p111.

◎ Sights & Activities

Mainly the west coast has been developed for tourism. **Hat Sai Khao** is by far the biggest, busiest and brashest beach. The backpacker fave is **Lonely Beach**, which is lonely no more, especially at night. An old-fashioned fishing community in **Bang Bao** has become a bustling tourist market. The east coast is less developed.

In a forested setting in the northern interior, **Ban Kwan Chang** (บ้านควาญช้าง; ☑087 811 3599; chaitientong@yahoo.com; tours 800-1300B; ◎8am-5pm) offers a quiet experience with its nine resident elephants.

Ko Chang cuts an impressive and heroic profile when viewed from the sea aboard a kayak. **KayakChang** (☑087 673 1753; www.kayakchang.com; Emerald Cove Resort, Khlong Prao; kayak per day from 2000B) rents closed-top kayaks and leads day and multiday trips. On the east side of the island, explore the mangrove swamps of Ao Salak Kok while supporting an award-winning ecotour program. The

Salak Kok Kayak Station (☑087 748 9497; kayak rental per hr 200B) rents self-guided kayaks and is a village work project designed to protect the traditional way of life. The kayak station can also arrange hiking tours.

The **dive sites** near Ko Chang offer a variety of coral, fish and beginner-friendly shallow waters on par with other Gulf of Thailand dive sites.

🛏 Sleeping

Accommodation prices on Ko Chang are higher than the quality because of the package-tour industry. Prices and crowds increase around the Christmas holiday.

★**BB World of Tapas**　　　HOSTEL **$**
(☑089 504 0543; www.bbworldoftapas.com; dm 200B, r with fan 500-600B; 🛜🗷) Much like tapas, you get a little taste of everything here. The on-site dive school, gym, eclectic tapas menu and a chill-out zone make it a great spot to meet fellow travellers. One of the only dorms within reach of the beach.

Independent Bo's GUESTHOUSE $
(r 300-800B; 🛜) The closest this beach gets to bohemian is this eclectic range of rooms that cling to the cliff. Quirky signs and a wi-fi ban in the communal bar add to the hippie feel. All the fan-only bungalows are different so prices vary. No reservations (and no children).

Porn's Bungalows BUNGALOW $
(📋080 613 9266; www.pornsbungalows-kohchang. com; r 600-1500B) Very chilled spot at the far western end of the beach, with a popular on-site restaurant. All of the wooden bungalows are fan-only. The 1000B beachfront bunga-lows are a great deal.

Little Eden GUESTHOUSE $
(📋084 867 7459; www.littleedenkohchang.com; r 700-1100B; ❄@🛜) There are 15 bungalows here, all connected by an intricate series of wooden walkways. Rooms are quite spa-cious with surprisingly good bathrooms. Pleasant communal area and staff.

GETTING TO CAMBODIA

Many travellers undertaking the Angkor pilgrimage take the direct bus from Bangkok through the Aranya Prathet/Poipet border. There are also other remote and little-used crossings with access to Siem Reap. We do not recommend the tourist buses that leave from Th Khao San road.

Bangkok to Siem Reap

Getting to the border Buses from Bangkok's Northern and Northeastern (Mo Chit) bus terminal travel through the Aranya Prathe/Poipet border. There are also buses to Aranya Prathet from Suvarnabhumi (Airport) bus station and minivans to Aranya Prathet from Bangkok's Victory Monument.

Aranya Prathet is also accessible by bus from Chanthaburi and Nakhon Ratchasima (Khorat). Most buses and minivans go all the way to the Rong Kluea Market at the bor-der, sparing you the hassle of transferring to local transport in Aranya Prathet town.

There are also daily trains from Bangkok's Hualamphong station to Aranya Prathet town.

At the border Thai immigration is open 7am to 8pm. It is advisable to reach the border as early as possible, especially on weekends when casino-bound Thais and guest workers clog the immigration lines. Cambodian visas are available on arrival from Cambodian immigra-tion with the usual formalities. Ignore any touts or money-exchange services on both sides of the border, watch out for pickpockets and interact directly with immigration officials.

Moving on If you didn't opt for the direct Bangkok–Siem Reap bus, the best way to con-tinue to Siem Reap is by share taxi departing from the main bus station in Poipet, 1km from the border near the main market. A motorcycle taxi from the border to the main bus station should cost 2000r. Don't go to the international bus station, 9km east of town, where prices are double.

For information on doing this crossing in reverse, see p100.

Surin to Anlong Veng

Surin has public transport options to Anlong Veng, a transfer point to Siem Reap, via the **Chong Chom/O Smach border**. Another nearby crossing (Chang Sa-Ngam to Cho-am) doesn't have public transport options.

Getting to the border Cambodian casinos run minivans to this border from Surin's bus terminal (60B, 1½ hours, frequent).

At the border The border is open from 7am to 8pm. When entering Cambodia, note that they charge a premium for visas on arrival – US$25 instead of the normal US$20. Try to talk them down to the normal rate.

Moving on Share taxis on the Cambodian side will take you to Anlong Veng (350B to 500B); prices depend on your bargaining skills. If you arrive after 9am, you might have to charter the whole vehicle (1500B to 1800B). In Anlong Veng you can arrange transport to Siem Reap.

For information on doing this crossing in reverse, see p105.

Paradise Cottage HOTEL $
(☑081 773 9337; y_yinggg@hotmail.com; r fan/air-con 500/800-1200B; ❄🛜) With house music as a backdrop, hammock-clad pavilions facing the sea and comfy rooms, Paradise Cottage is tailor-made for flashpackers. At low tide a sandbank just beyond the rocks can be reached.

Siam Hut GUESTHOUSE $
(☑039 619012; www.siamhutkohchang.com; r 480-680B; ❄🛜🍽) Part Ibiza and part Full Moon, Siam Hut is party central on Lonely Beach. Backpackers are attracted by the cheap wooden huts that sit next to one of the few sandy strips around here. Wi-fi is available by reception.

Jungle Way GUESTHOUSE $
(☑089 247 3161; Khlong Son Valley; r 200-500B) Set deep in the forest, accessible via a rope bridge, is this wonderful jungle hideaway. Owner and local expert Khun Ann can arrange treks from here. The fan-only bungalows are simple but adequate and the on-site restaurant is good.

Arunee Resort GUESTHOUSE $$
(☑086 111 9600; aruneeresorttour@hotmail.com; r incl breakfast fan/air-con 500/1500B; ❄🛜) Recent renovations mean the super-cheap rooms have been replaced by bright and breezy ones. Arunee is set back from the main road and is a 50m-walk to the beach.

Apple Beachfront Resort HOTEL $$
(☑039 551228; applebeachfrontresort@gmail.com; r incl breakfast 2800B; ❄🛜🍽) Employing lots of natural materials, Apple has neat, simple rooms facing the sea or a large terraced pool area.

Blue Lagoon Bungalows GUESTHOUSE $$
(☑039 557243; www.kohchang-bungalows-blue lagoon.com; r 500-1800B; ❄🛒) Set beside a scenic estuary, Blue Lagoon has a variety of bungalows and rooms, or you can rent a tent (250B). A wooden walkway leads to the beach. Check out the larger family room, which was made using elephant dung. The staff, who are excellent, provide numerous activities, including yoga and cookery classes.

✗ Eating

Nid's Kitchen THAI $
(nidkitchen@hotmail.com; Khlong Prao; dishes 50-150B; ☯6-10pm) Nid's creates all the Thai standards like a wok wizard in a hut festooned with rasta imagery. Equally fine for a drink or three.

★Phu-Talay SEAFOOD $$
(☑039 551300; Khlong Prao; dishes 100-320B; ☯10am-10pm) Cute, homely feel at this wooden-floored, blue-and-white-decorated place perched over the lagoon. There's a sensible menu of Ko Chang classics (lots of fish) and it's far more reasonably priced than many other seafood places.

★Barrio Bonito MEXICAN $$
(Hat Kaibae; dishes 160-250B; ☯5-10.30pm) Fab fajitas and cracking cocktails are served by a charming French/Mexican couple at this roadside spot in the middle of Kaibae. Authentic food and stylish surroundings.

KaTi Culinary THAI $$
(☑081 903 0408; Khlong Prao; dishes 130-290B; ☯11am-3pm & 6-10pm) Seafood, a few Isan dishes and their famous, homemade curry sauce are the best bets here. The menu features creative smoothies, featuring lychee, lemon and peppermint, and there's a children's menu.

Magic Garden THAI $$
(☑039 558027; Lonely Beach; dishes 100-220B; ☯9am-midnight; 🛜) The hippest place on Lonely Beach to have a smoothie or vodka bucket, as travellers swap tales or catch up on some reading. The menu covers Thai and Western standards.

❶ Information

Ko Chang Hospital (☑039 586096; Ban Dan Mai) Public hospital with a good reputation and affordably priced care; south of the ferry terminal.

Tourist Police Office (☑1155) Based north of Ban Khlong Prao. Also has smaller police boxes in Hat Sai Khao and Hat Kaibae.

❶ Getting There & Away

Beware of the cheap minibus tickets from Siem Reap to Ko Chang; these usually involve some sort of time- and money-wasting commission scam.

Ko Chang–bound boats depart from the mainland piers collectively referred to as Laem Ngop, southwest of Trat. You'll arrive in Ko Chang at either Tha Sapparot or Tha Centrepoint, depending on which pier and boat company you used on the mainland. The ferry prices are the same at both piers (80B, 30 to 45 minutes, frequent 6am to 7pm).

THAILAND KO CHANG

ⓘ BYPASSING BANGKOK: U-TAPAO AIRPORT

Pattaya's airport was once just an airfield and only handled charter flights. It has since expanded and has been rechristened the U-Tapao-Rayong-Pattaya International Airport. With flights to Chiang Mai, Ko Samui, Kuala Lumpur, Phuket and a few Chinese cities, Pattaya is now a feasible alternative to Bangkok for an onward journey from Ko Chang and other eastern gulf coast destinations. Presently Bangkok Airways, Air Asia and Kan Air operate out of U-Tapao. Minivans connect to Pattaya from almost everywhere.

Tha Sapparot is the closest to the west-coast beaches and receives vehicle ferries from the mainland pier of Tha Thammachat. **Koh Chang Ferry** (☑ 039 555188) runs this service.

Tha Centrepoint is further from the west-coast beaches and is served by a mainland pier of the same name by the **Centrepoint Ferry** (☑ 039 538196) company.

Tha Bang Bao is at the southern end of the island and **Bang Bao Boats** (☑ 039 558046; www.kohchangbangbaoboat.com) runs to nearby islands.

A direct bus from Bangkok's Eastern (Ekamai) bus station goes all the way to a mainland pier on Laem Ngop (263B, six hours, two daily); this route includes a stop at Suvarnabhumi (Airport) bus station as well as Trat's bus station.

ⓘ Getting Around

Sŏrng·tǎa·ou on the island will shuttle you from the pier to the various beaches (100B to 200B).

It is not recommended to drive a motorcycle between Ban Khlong Son south to Hat Sai Khao as the road is steep and treacherous with several hairpin turns and occasional mudslides during storms. If you do rent a motorbike, stick to the west-coast beaches, and wear protective clothing.

SOUTHERN GULF COAST

Palm-fringed beaches, warm lazy days, jewel-toned seas: the southern gulf coast pours an intoxicating draught of paradise that attracts a steady crowd of sun worshippers. Most are bound for one or more of the islands in the Samui archipelago: resort-y Ko Samui, hippie Ko Pha-Ngan and dive-centric Ko Tao.

If the Vitamin D treatments have you recharged, stop off at the mild-mannered provincial capitals for a glimpse at the rhythms of coastal Thailand. Even further south, Thailand starts to merge with Malaysia: onion-domed mosques peep over the treeline; the diction is fast and furious, as southern Thais are legendary speed talkers; a roti seller can be found on every corner.

The best time to visit Thailand's southern reaches is from February to June, when the rest of the country is practically melting from the angry sun.

Hua Hin

หัวหิน

POP 42,000

Within reach of Bangkok, Hua Hin is considered the elegant alternative to seedy Pattaya. It is a city by the sea long favoured by older Europeans and hi-so Bangkok Thais, and oft neglected by backpackers searching for rustic island living. It is time to reconsider Hua Hin and its old fishing port charm, lively seafood night market and long silky sand beaches.

Hua Hin's best **beaches** are south of town heading towards Khao Takiab (Chopstick Mountain; accessible by green *sŏrng·tǎa·ou* leaving from the market) and Khao Tao (Turtle Mountain; accessible by Pranburi bus, transfer to motorcycle taxi).

🛌 Sleeping

Most of the budget options are in town, an atmospheric location but you'll have to 'commute' to the beach.

Victor Guest House   GUESTHOUSE $
(☑ 032 511564; victorguesthouse@gmail.com; 60 Th Naresdamri; r 390-1290B; ❋ @ 🅢) Popular with both Thais and foreigners, this efficient guesthouse has solid rooms, a small garden and a central location. Helpful staff and a good source of travel tips.

★Pattana Guest House   GUESTHOUSE $$
(☑ 032 513393; 52 Th Naresdamri; r 990B; ❋ 🅢) Located in a simple teak house tucked away down a soi, this recently remodelled guesthouse features a lovely, peaceful garden. All rooms are two-storey, with bathrooms and a small living room downstairs.

Mod   GUESTHOUSE $$
(☑ 032 512296; www.modguesthouse.com; Th Naresdamri; r 600-800B; ❋ 🅢) Refurbished and now more comfortable (better beds) than

most pier guesthouses, the more expensive rooms here come with air-con and sea views. A few cheaper rooms lack windows and are fan-only.

Tong-Mee House GUESTHOUSE $$
(☑032 530725; tongmeehuahin@hotmail.com; 1 Soi Raumpown, Th Naebkehardt; r 600-1000B; ❋@🛜) Hidden away in a quiet residential soi, this long-running guesthouse has cosy and clean rooms with balconies. Book ahead.

Rahmahyah Hotel GUESTHOUSE $$
(☑032 532106; rahmahyah@yahoo.co.uk; 113/10 Soi Hua Hin 67, Th Phetkasem, South Hua Hin; r 800-1300B; ❋🛜🏊) Across the street from Market Village, about 1km south of town, is a small guesthouse enclave tucked between the high-end resorts, with beach access. The Rahmahyah is the best of the bunch with clean, functional rooms. Guests can use the communal swimming pool opposite. Book ahead here.

★**Baan Bayan** HOTEL $$$
(☑032 533540; www.baanbayanresort.com; 119 Th Phetkasem, South Hua Hin; r 3500-21,000B; ❋🛜🏊🐕) A beautiful teak house built in the early 20th century, Baan Bayan is perfect for travellers seeking a luxury experience without the overkill of a big resort. Airy, high-ceilinged rooms, attentive staff and the location is absolute beachfront.

🍴 Eating

Night Market MARKET $
(Th Dechanuchit btwn Th Phetkasem & Th Sasong; dishes from 50B; ⊙5pm-midnight) An attraction that rivals the beach, Hua Hin's night market mixes food and clothes, and draws in both locals and visitors. Ice-packed lobsters and king prawns appeal to the big spenders but the fare at simple stir-fry stalls is just as tasty. Try *pàt pŏng gà·rèe Ƃoo* (crab curry), *gûng tôrt* (fried shrimp) and *hŏy tôrt* (fried mussel omelette).

Thanon Chomsin Food Stalls FOOD STALL $
(cnr Th Chomsin & Th Naebkehardt; dishes 35-45B; ⊙9am-9pm) If you're after 100% authentic eats, check out the food stalls congregated at this popular lunch corner. Though the setting is humble, Thais are fastidious eaters and use a fork (or their fingers with a pinch of *kôw nĕe·o*) to remove the meat from the bones of *gài tôrt* (fried chicken) rather than putting teeth directly to flesh.

Chatchai Market MARKET $
(Th Phetkasem; dishes from 35B; ⊙dawn-dusk) The city's day market resides in an historic building from 1926, with a distinctive seven-eaved roof in honour of Rama VII. There are the usual market refreshments: morning vendors selling *Ƃah·tôrng·gŏh* (Chinese-style doughnuts) and *gah·faa bohrahn* (ancient-style coffee spiked with modern sweetened condensed milk); as well as all-day noodles with freshly made wontons, and the full assortment of fresh fruit.

★**Hua Hin Koti** CHINESE, THAI $$
(☑032 511252; 16/1 Th Dechanuchit; dishes from 120B; ⊙noon-10pm) Across from the night market, this Thai-Chinese restaurant is a national culinary luminary. Thais adore the fried crab balls, while foreigners swoon over *dôm yam gûng* (shrimp soup with lemon grass). And everyone loves the spicy seafood

THAILAND HUA HIN

TRANSPORT FROM HUA HIN

DESTINATION	BUS	MINIVAN	TRAIN
Bangkok Hualamphong			44-622B, 4-6hr, 13 daily 12.45am-4.01pm
Bangkok Southern (Sai Tai Mai) Bus Terminal	180B, 4½hr, 8 daily 3am-9pm		
Bangkok Suvarnabhumi International Airport	294B, 5hr, 7 daily 6am-6pm		
Bangkok Victory Monument		180B, 4hr, every 30min 6am-7pm	
Chiang Mai	813B, 12hr, 8am, 5.30pm & 6pm		
Phuket	1011B, 9-10hr, 10am & 9pm		
Surat Thani	787B, 7-8hr, 10am & 10pm		

salad *(yam tá-lair)* and deep-fried fish with ginger. Be prepared to wait for a table.

ℹ Information

Hospital San Paolo (☑ 032 532576; 222 Th Phetkasem) Just south of town with emergency facilities.

Municipal Tourist Information Office (☑ 032 511047; cnr Th Phetkasem & Th Damnoen Kasem; ☉ 8.30am-4.30pm Mon-Fri) Provides maps and information about Hua Hin. There's another branch (☑ 032 522797; Th Naebkehardt; ☉ 9am-7.30pm Mon-Fri, 9.30am-5pm Sat & Sun) near the clock tower.

Tourism Authority of Thailand (TAT; ☑ 032 513885; 39/4 Th Phetkasem; ☉ 8.30am-4.30pm) Staff here speak English and are quite helpful; the office is north of town near Soi Hua Hin 70.

Tourist Police (☑ 032 515995; Th Damnoen Kasem) At the eastern end of the street.

ℹ Getting There & Around

Hua Hin's **long-distance bus station** (Th Phetkasem btwn Soi Hua Hin 94 & 98) is south of town. Buses to Bangkok's Southern bus station (Sai Tai Mai) leave from a bus company's in-town **office** (Th Sasong), near the night market. Minivans to Bangkok's Victory Monument leave from an office at the corner of Th Phetkasem and Th Chomsin. Ordinary buses depart from north of the market on Th Phetkasem.

Hua Hin's historic train station is on Th Phrapokklao. **Lomprayah** (☑ 0 3253 3739; Th Narasdamri) offers a bus-boat combination from Hua Hin to Ko Tao.

ℹ Getting Around

Green *sŏrng·tăa·ou* depart from the corner of Th Sasong and Th Dechanuchit, near the night market, and travel south on Th Phetkasem to Khao Takiab (20B). Túk-túk fares in Hua Hin are outrageous (starting at 100B). Motorcycle taxis are much more reasonable (40B to 50B) for short hops.

Prachuap Khiri Khan
ประจวบคีรีขันธ์

POP 86,870

A prettier-than-average seaside town, Prachuap Khiri Khan is relaxed and not-too-touristed with only a few minor attractions, a draw in itself if you're looking to escape 'Khao San' culture.

At the base of town is a sparkling blue bay sprinkled with brightly coloured fishing boats. To the north is **Khao Chong Krajok** (Mirror Tunnel Mountain), topped by a wát with spectacular views; the hill is claimed by a clan of monkeys who supposedly hitched a ride into town on a bus from Bangkok to pick up some mangoes. There isn't much else to do except walk along the waterfront promenade or rent a motorcycle and explore the northern bays, fishing villages and the cave temple at **Wat Ao Noi**. You'll find a swimming beach at **Ao Manao**, 6km south of the city within the grounds of a Thai airforce base. It is popular with local Thais who swim fully clothed.

🛏 Sleeping & Eating

There are many oceanfront accommodations but as Prachuap becomes more popular, it is worth booking ahead. The **night market** (Th Kong Kiat; ☉ 5-9pm) has evening meals.

Thur Hostel HOSTEL $
(☑ 096 047 5622; thurhostel@gmail.com; 58 Th Chai Thaleh; dm 350B, r 600-1000B; ❊ ⓢ) A hostel right on the oceanfront that has small but well-maintained dorms with good, thick mattresses. The most expensive rooms have terraces with fine sea views.

Maggie's Homestay GUESTHOUSE $
(☑ 087 597 9720; 5 Soi Tampramuk; r 180-550B; ❊ @ ⓢ) In the old-school backpacker tradition, owner Maggie oversees an eclectic collection of travellers who call her house

TRANSPORT FROM PRACHUAP KHIRI KHAN

DESTINATION	BUS	MINIVAN	TRAIN
Bangkok Hualamphong			168-455B, 7-8hr, 12.14am-11.35pm
Bangkok Southern (Sai Tai Mai) Bus Terminal	200B, 6-7hr, 9am, 12.30pm & 1am	220B, 5-6hr, hourly 7am-5pm	
Bangkok Victory Monument		220B, 6hr, hourly 6am-5pm	
Hua Hin		80B, 1½hr, hourly 6am-5pm	19B, 1hr, 8 daily

ANG THONG MARINE NATIONAL PARK

The 40-some jagged jungle islands of Ang Thong Marine National Park stretch across the cerulean sea like a shattered emerald necklace – each piece a virgin realm featuring sheer limestone cliffs, hidden lagoons and perfect peach-coloured sands. These dream-inducing islets inspired Alex Garland's cult classic *The Beach*, about dope-dabbling backpackers.

The best way to reach the park is to catch a private day-tour from Ko Samui, such as **Blue Stars** (☑077 300615; www.bluestars.info; Hat Chaweng; kayak & snorkelling tours adult/child 2500/1600B). The park officially has an admission fee, although it should be included in the price of every tour (verify this when buying tickets).

February, March and April are the best months; crashing monsoon waves means that the park is almost always closed during November and December.

home. Rooms in a converted traditional house mostly have shared bathrooms and range from the very basic to the comfortable, and there's a shady garden and shared kitchen facilities.

★**House 73** GUESTHOUSE $$
(☑086 046 3923; www.facebook.com/house-73prachuab/info; 73 Th Suseuk; r 800-1300B; ❈⍩) Lovingly designed to within an inch of its life, this modernist boutique guesthouse is the most eye-catching building in town. There are only four (big) rooms here, all painted in pastel colours, with huge beds. There's a communal lounge and, best of all, a fantastic roof terrace with commanding views across the bay.

★**In Town** THAI $$
(118 Th Chai Thaleh; dishes from 80B; ⊙3-10pm) Now the go-to place for discerning locals, here you can eat outside while gazing at the bay. Great range of fresh seafood on display – barracuda, tuna, crab and shellfish – so you can point and pick, and they will tone down the spices if you ask.

Rim Lom SEAFOOD $$
(5 Th Suanson; dishes 90-190B; ⊙10am-10pm) Popular with the locals, the *pàt pŏng gà·rèe boo* (crab curry) comes with big chunks of sweet crab meat and the *yam tá·lair* (seafood salad) is spicy and zesty. It's 200m past the bridge on the left and right opposite Ao Prachuap beach.

❶ Getting There & Around

Prachuap's bus station is 2km northwest of town on the main highway; motorcycle taxis make the trip for 40B to 50B. Buses to Bangkok use an in-town office on Th Phitak Chat. Minivans to Bangkok leave from the corner of Th Thetsaban

Bamrung and Th Phitak Chat. There is also a train station on Th Maharat.

Prachuap is small enough to get around on foot but a motorcycle (250B) is handy for exploring the nearby beaches, and traffic is minimal so it is safer to drive here than in other places.

Chumphon ชุมพร
POP 55,835

Chumphon is a jumping-off point for boats to Ko Tao. The transition from bus to boat is fairly painless, and travel agencies can help with onward travel to the Andaman coast plus provide all sorts of day-use amenities (such as luggage storage, shower and toilet).

If you need to spend the night, try **Suda Guest House** (☑080 144 2079; 8 Soi Sala Daeng 3; r 200-650B; ❈@⍩), **Fame Guest House** (☑077 571077; www.chumphon-kohtao.com; 188/20-21 Th Sala Daeng; r 150-300B; @⍩) or **Salsa Hostel** (☑077 505005; www.salsa-chumphon.com; 25/42 Th Krom Luang Chumphon; dm 280-300B, d 650-750B; ❈@⍩). The **night market** (Th Krom Luang Chumphon; ⊙4-11pm) is a good spot for meals and entertainment.

❶ Getting There & Away

AIR
Chumphon's airport is served by Nok Air to/from Bangkok's Don Muang airport (1720B, 1 hour, two daily).

BOAT
You have a number of boat options for getting to Ko Tao, though departure times are mainly limited to morning and night. Most ticket prices include pier transfer. If you buy a combination ticket, make sure you have a ticket for both the bus and the boat.

Car Ferry A comfortable ride with bunk or mattress options available on board.

Songserm (☏ 077 506205; www.songserm-
expressboat.com; ⏰ 9am-8pm) Faster, morning
option leaving from Tha Talaysub, 10km from
town. Recent complaints about the company
includes not providing promised free transport into town from the islands. Book tickets
through guesthouses.

Lomprayah (☏ 077 558214; www.lomprayah.
com; ⏰ 5am-9pm) The best and most popular
bus-boat combination; it leaves from Tha
Tummakam, 25km from town. The ticket office
is beside Chumphon train station.

BUS

The main bus terminal is on the highway, an
inconvenient 16km from Chumphon. To get there
you can catch a *sŏrng·tăa·ou* (50B) from Th
Nawamin Ruamjai. You'll have to haggle with the
taxi drivers for night transit to/from the station;
it shouldn't cost more than 200B.

There are several in-town bus stops. **Choke
Anan Tour** (☏ 077 511757; soi off Th Pracha
Uthit), in the centre of town, has departures
to Bangkok, Phuket and Ranong. **Suwannatee
Tour** (☏ 077 504901) serves Bangkok and Pra-

chuap Khiri Khan. Buses to Hat Yai depart from
near the petrol station on Th Nawamin Ruamjai.
Minivans to Surat Thani and Prachuap Khiri
Khan leave from the no-name soi opposite Salsa
Guesthouse.

TRAIN

The **train station** (Th Krom Luang Chumphon) is
within walking distance of the centre of town.

Ko Samui เกาะสมุย
POP 50,000

One of the original backpacker islands, Ko
Samui has matured into an all-purpose
beach resort. The hotels have international
standards, the guests are mainly package
tourists and the transition from home to
deck chair involves little culture shock. Families and honeymooners put Ko Samui at the
top of their lists for its conveniences and impressive stoles of sand.

Despite its international conveniences,
Samui still retains its island vibe and a

TRANSPORT FROM CHUMPHON

DESTINATION	BOAT	BUS	MINIVAN	TRAIN
Bangkok Hualamphong				192-690B, 8hr, 11 daily
Bangkok Southern (Sai Tai Mai) bus terminal		300-591B, 8hr, 11 daily		
Hat Yai		400B, 7hr, 4 daily		269-652B, 6hr, 7 daily
Ko Pha-Ngan (Lomprayah)	1000B, 3¼hr, 7am & 1pm			
Ko Pha-Ngan (Songserm)	900B, 5½hr, 7am			
Ko Samui (Lomprayah)	1100B, 4½hr, 7am & 1pm			
Ko Samui (Songserm)	1000B, 6hr, 7am			
Ko Tao (car ferry)	400B, 6hr, 11pm Mon-Sat			
Ko Tao (Lomprayah)	600B, 1½hr; 2 daily; 7am & 1pm			
Ko Tao (Songserm)	500B, 3hr, 7am			
Phuket		350B, 3½hr, 2 daily		
Prachuap Khiri Khan			180B, 4hr, 3pm	84B, 3-4hr, 10 daily
Ranong		120B, 2½hr, 4 daily	120B, 2hr, frequent	
Surat Thani			170B, 3hr, hourly 6am-5pm	100B, 2-3hr, 12 daily

thriving local community where you can nosh at roadside curry shacks and morning markets. It is a unique hybrid for beach people who also want to see Thailand.

◎ Sights

Ko Samui is quite large – the island's ring road is almost 100km in total length. **Chaweng** is the longest and most beautiful beach on the island, and everyone knows it. At the south end of **Lamai**, the second-largest beach, you'll find the infamous **Hin-Ta** and **Hin-Yai** stone formations providing endless mirth to giggling tourists. **Hua Thanon**, just beyond, is home to a Muslim fishing community.

Although the **northern beaches** have coarser sand, they have a laid-back vibe and stellar views of Ko Pha-Ngan. **Bo Phut** stands out with its charming Fisherman's Village.

🛏 Sleeping

🛏 Chaweng

Lucky Mother GUESTHOUSE $
(☑ 077 230931; 60 Moo 2; r & bungalows 800-1500B; ❄️🛜) The action-filled beachfront location, clean, bright rooms and popular bar out front that's prime for mingling with your toes in the sand all get thumbs up. If you want a Chaweng beach location, it's a great deal (though some staff members could be friendlier).

P Chaweng HOTEL $
(☑ 077 230684; r from 600B, f 1000B; ❄️@🛜) At the end of a road off the main drag, this vine-covered cheapie has clean, pink-tiled rooms and wood-floored family rooms in two blocks, all decked out with air-con, hot water, TVs and fridges. It's a 10-minute walk to the bar zone and not particularly hip, but good luck finding a better room in the area for this price.

Pott Guesthouse GUESTHOUSE $
(r with fan 300-400B, with air-con 500-600B; ❄️🛜) The big, bright cement rooms all with attached hot-water bathrooms and balcony in this nondescript apartment block are a steal. Reception is at an unnamed restaurant on the main drag right opposite across the alley.

Samui Hostel HOSTEL $
(☑ 089 874 3737; dm 200-300B, d 850B; ❄️@) It doesn't look like much from the front, but this very neat, tidy and friendly place has clean fan and air-con dorm rooms and

WALKING STREETS

Dine, shop and people-watch at the weekly Walking Streets (4pm to 11pm or midnight), which occupy the centre of each beach's main village. Check with your guesthouse about the walking street schedules.

spruce air-con doubles. Service is a cut above the rest and there's a popular room at the front with wooden tables for lounging and chatting.

★ **Jungle Club** BUNGALOW $$
(☑ 081 894 2327; www.jungleclubsamui.com; huts 800-1800B, houses 2700-4500B; ❄️@🛜🏊) The perilous drive up the slithering road is totally worthwhile once you take in the incredible views from the top. With a relaxed back-to-nature vibe, this isolated mountain getaway is a huge hit among locals and tourists alike. Guests chill around the stunning horizon pool or catnap under the canopied roofs of an open-air *săh·lah* (often spelt as *sala*).

Call ahead for a pick-up (from the Chaweng area only) – you don't want to spend your precious jungle vacation in a body cast.

🛏 Lamai

New Hut BUNGALOW $
(☑ 077 230437; newhutlamai@yahoo.co.th; Lamai North; huts 300-800B; 🛜) A-frame huts right on the beach all share a big, clean block of bathrooms. There's a lively restaurant, friendly-enough staff and one of the most simple and a happy backpacker vibes.

Amarina Residence HOTEL $
(☑ 077 418073; www.amarinaresidence.com; r 1200-1800B; ❄️🛜) A two-minute walk to the beach, this excellent-value small hotel has two storeys of big, tastefully furnished, tiled rooms encircling the lobby and an incongruous dipping pool.

Spa Resort BUNGALOW $$
(☑ 077 230855; www.spasamui.com; Lamai North; bungalows 720-1200B; ❄️🛜🏊) Programs at this friendly, practical and simple spa include colonics, massage, aqua detox, hypnotherapy and yoga, just to name a few. With rattan furniture, traditional wall art and balconies, rooms are comfortable and excellent value, but book up quickly. Nonguests are

Ko Samui

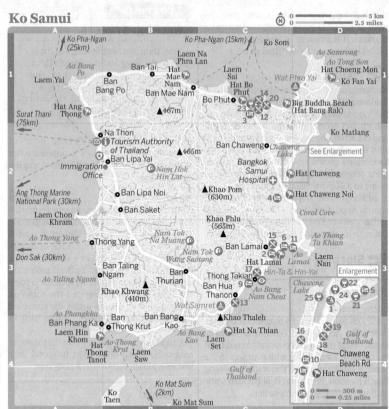

welcome to partake in the spa programs and dine at the excellent (and healthy) open-air restaurant by the beach.

⭐ **Rocky Resort** RESORT $$$
(☏ 077 418367; www.rockyresort.com; Hua Thanon; r 8000-20,000B; ❄ 🛜 🏊) With a supremely calm reception area and two swimming pools, Rocky effortlessly finds the right balance between an upmarket ambience and an unpretentious, sociable vibe. During quieter months prices are a steal, since ocean views abound and each room (some with pool) has been furnished with beautiful Thai-inspired furniture that seamlessly incorporates a modern twist.

🛏 Northern Beaches

Castaway Guesthouse GUESTHOUSE $$
(☏ 098 464 6562; r with fan/air-con 650-1500B; ❄ 🛜) A block away from the beach, right in the Fisherman's Village, the newly renovated Castaway's 15 rooms are all clean, bright and cheery.

Shangri-la BUNGALOW $
(☏ 077 425189; Mae Nam; bungalows with fan/air-con from 500/1300B; ❄ 🛜) A backpacker's Shangri La indeed – these are some of the cheapest huts around and they're on a sublime part of the beach. Grounds are sparsely landscaped but the basic concrete bungalows, all with attached bathrooms (only air-con rooms have hot water), are well-kept and the staff is pleasant.

🍴 Eating & Drinking

🍴 Chaweng

Dozens of the restaurants on the 'strip' serve a mixed bag of local bites, international cuisine and greasy fast food. Market oglers should not miss **Laem Din Market** (dishes from 35B; ⏱ 4am-6pm, night market 6pm-2am).

Ko Samui

Ninja Crepes THAI **$**
(dishes from 75B; ⊙11am-midnight) Rammed nightly, with flaming woks at the heart of things working double-time to keep the pace, this lively warehouse-sized restaurant serves Thai seafood, curries, crêpes, soups and sticky desserts to throngs of patrons.

★**Stacked** STEAK **$$**
(www.stacked-samui.com; mains from 295B; ⊙noon-midnight; 🛜) All sharp lines, open kitchen/grill, a team of busy and super-efficient staff plus a cracker of a menu, this awesome burger restaurant is a visual and culinary feast. Burgers and steaks – bursting with flavour – are served up on slate slabs in generous portions. Go with a sizeable hunger as the inclination is to simply keep ordering.

Bar Solo BAR
(Hat Chaweng) Bar Solo's bubbly party mood, decent DJs and evening drink specials lure in front-loaders preparing for a late, late night at the dance clubs on Soi Solo and Soi Green Mango.

Ark Bar BAR
(⏱7am-2am; www.ark-bar.com; Hat Chaweng) Drinks are dispensed from the multi-coloured bar to an effusive crowd, guests recline on loungers on the beach, and the party is on day and night.

Green Mango BAR
(ww.thegreenmangoclub.com; Hat Chaweng) This place is so popular it has an entire soi named after it. Samui's favourite power drinking house is very big, very loud and very *fa·ràng*. Green Mango has blazing lights, expensive drinks and masses of sweaty bodies swaying to dance music.

Reggae Pub BAR
(Hat Chaweng; ⊙6pm-3am) This fortress of fun sports an open-air dance floor with music spun by foreign DJs. It's a towering two-storey affair with long bars, pool tables and a live-music stage. The whole place doubles as a shrine to Bob Marley; it's often empty early in the evening, getting going around midnight. The long road up to Reggae Pub is ladyboy central.

Lamai

The **Lamai Day Market** (dishes from 30B; ⊙6am-8pm) and the Muslim **Hua Thanon Market** (dishes from 30B; ⊙6am-6pm) both have local eats.

★**La Fabrique** BAKERY **$$**
(set breakfasts from 120B; ⊙6.30am-10.30pm; 🛜) Ceiling fans chop the air and service is snappy and helpful at this roomy French-styled boulangerie/patisserie away from the main drag, near Wat Lamai on Rte 4169. Choose from fresh bread, croissants, gratins, baguettes, meringues, yoghurts, pastries or unusually good set breakfasts that include fresh fruit and well-cooked eggs. Wash down with a selection of coffees or teas.

Northern Beaches

The Hut THAI **$**
(mains 60-550B; ⊙1-10pm) Basic, reasonably priced Thai specialities share space with more expensive fresh seafood and Western

THAILAND KO SAMUI

treats here, but the dozen or so tables fill fast so get here early or late if you don't want to wait. If you're a fisher, this is the place to get your own catch cooked up. Staff can be a bit surly.

Karma Sutra INTERNATIONAL **$$**
(mains 180-700B; ◉8am-2am; 🛜) A haze of purples and pillows, beanbags and low tables, this charming chow spot straddles the heart of Bo Phut's Fisherman's Village and serves up very good international and Thai eats, with al fresco seating by the wayside.

★ Chez François FRENCH **$$$**
(www.facebook.com/chezporte; 33/2 Moo 1 Fisherman's Village; set meal 1700B; ◉6-11pm Tue-Sat) With no à la carte menu, but a reputation for outstanding cuisine that has sent waves across the culinary map of Ko Samui, Chez François serves a three-course surprise meal. Book ahead using the Facebook page and if you're only on Ko Samui for a few days, book early to get a table. It's tiny (and cash only).
    Chez François is hidden away behind a wooden door near a pharmacy.

Coco Tam's BAR
(Bo Phut; shisha pipes 500B; ◉5pm-1am) Plop yourself on a beanbag on the sand, order a giant cocktail served in a jar and take a toke on a shisha (water pipe). It's a bit pricey, but this boho, beach bum–chic spot oozes relaxation. There are fire dancers most nights.

🍴 West Coast

The quiet west coast features some of the best seafood on Samui. Na Thon has a giant **day market** on Th Thawi Ratchaphakdi where you can grab snacks before your ferry ride.

★ Ging Pagarang SEAFOOD **$**
(Thong Tanote; meals from 50B; ◉11.30am-8pm) Locals know this is one of the island's best beachside places to sample authentic Samui-style seafood. It's simple and family-run, but the food and views are extraordinary. Try the sea algae salad with crab, fried dried octopus with coconut or the spectacular fried fish or prawns with lemon grass.

ℹ️ Information

Road accidents and fatalities in Samui are high, in part because inexperienced motorcycle drivers take to the crowded and poorly maintained roads. If you've never driven a motorbike before, don't learn on Samui. If you do rent a

motorcycle, do the customary inspection with the rental associate and document (with photos) any pre-existing damage to avoid incurring responsibility.
    A car bomb exploded in the new Central Festival shopping centre in 2015, wounding six people; the prime suspects in the case had ties to Thailand's restive Deep South.

Bangkok Samui Hospital (☑077 429500, emergency 077 429555) Your best bet for just about any medical problem.

Immigration Office (☑077 421069; ◉8.30am-noon & 1-4.30pm Mon-Fri) Offers seven-day tourist visa extensions. Located about 2km south of Na Thon.

Main Post Office Near the TAT office; not always reliable.

Tourism Authority of Thailand (TAT; ☑077 420504; Na Thon; ◉8.30am-4.30pm)

Tourist Police (☑077 421281, emergency ☑1155) Based at the south of Na Thon.

🚍 Getting There & Away

AIR

Samui's airport is in the northeast of the island near Big Buddha Beach. Bangkok Airways operates direct flights to Bangkok's Suvarnabhumi Airport (from 3400B, 50 minutes, frequent), Phuket and Chiang Mai; there are also direct flights to Singapore and Hong Kong. **Firefly** (http://www.fireflyz.com.my) flies to Kuala Lumpur's Subang airport.
    If Samui flights are full, check out flights to Surat Thani on the mainland.

BOAT

Between Samui and the mainland, there are frequent boat services, including the high-speed **Lomprayah** (☑077 4277 656; www.lomprayah.com) (450B) and the slower, stinkier **Raja** (☑022 768 2112; www.rajaferryport.com) car ferry (120B). Ferries take one to five hours, depending on the boat. There is also a slow night boat to Samui (300B, six hours, 11pm) from Surat Thani. It returns at 9pm, arriving at around 3am. Watch your bags on this boat.
    There are combination ticket options that arrange transport all the way to Bangkok either by bus or by train. Lomprayah has the best bus-boat combination. Phum Phin is the closest train station to the mainland pier in Surat Thani.
    Boats to Ko Pha-Ngan (200B to 300B, 20 minutes to one hour, frequent) and Ko Tao depart from various piers across Samui. When booking tickets, tell the agent where you're staying on Samui and where you'll be staying on Ko Pha-Ngan to reduce transit time to the various piers.
    The *Haad Rin Queen* is a handy service during Full Moon parties; it travels from Big Buddha

Beach (Ko Samui) to Hat Rin (Ko Pha-Ngan, 200B, 50 minutes) with sailing times to accommodate demand. The last boat leaves at 6.30pm.

ⓘ Getting Around

You can rent motorcycles (150B to 200B) from almost every resort on the island. *Sŏrng·tǎa·ou* (50B to 100B) run a loop between the popular beaches during daylight hours. Taxis typically charge around 500B for an airport transfer.

Ko Pha-Ngan   เกาะพะงัน

POP 12,500

Swaying coconut trees, brooding mountains, ribbons of turquoise water: Ko Pha-Ngan has held fast to its title as favourite backpacker idyll despite modernisation and an impending airport. The island's legendary Full Moon parties re-create a college campus of drunken abandon with some 30,000 people cramming the shores. The rest of the time, it is a delightful place to be. For divers, Ko Pha-Ngan is a fun-dives alternative to Ko Tao's certificate-focused industry.

🏃 Activities

The favourite snorkelling spot is **Ko Ma**, a small island in the northwest connected to Ko Pha-Ngan by a charming sandbar. A major perk of diving from Ko Pha-Ngan is the proximity to **Sail Rock** (Hin Bai), the best dive site in the Gulf of Thailand and a veritable beacon for whale sharks.

Two-dive trips cost 2500B to 2800B.

Chaloklum Diving   DIVING
(☏077 374025; www.chaloklum-diving.com; ☺6am-8pm) One of the more established dive shops on the island, these guys (based on the main drag in Ban Chalok Lam) have quality equipment and high standards in all that they do.

Haad Yao Divers   DIVING
(☏086 279 3085; www.haadyaodivers.com; Hat Yao) Established in 1997, this dive operator has garnered a strong reputation by maintaining European standards of safety and customer service.

🛏 Sleeping

🛏 Hat Rin

During Full Moon events, bungalow operations in Hat Rin expect you to stay for a minimum of five nights. Advanced bookings are obligatory. New budget hostels have sprung up to accommodate demand.

Lighthouse Bungalows   BUNGALOW **$**
(Map p744; ☏077 375075; www.lighthousebunga-lows.com; Hat Seekantang; bungalows 400-1000B; ✳️📶) This outpost perched on the rocks has simple fan options and newer spacious air-con bungalows, all great value and with sweeping views of the sea; plus there's a cushion-clad restaurant/common area and high-season yoga classes. To get there, follow the wooden boardwalk southeast from Hat Leela or take the high road (motorbike). Beware the monthly techno parties (check), unless that's on your wishlist.

Seaview Sunrise   BUNGALOW **$**
(Map p746; www.seaviewsunrise.com; Hat Rin Nok; r 500-1400B; ✳️📶) Budget Full Moon revellers who want to sleep inches from the tide: apply here. Some of the options back in the jungle are sombre and musty, but the solid, beachfront models have bright, polished wooden interiors facing onto a line of coconut palms and the sea.

Blue Marine   BUNGALOW **$$**
(Map p746; ☏077 375079; www.bluemarinephang-an.com; Hat Rin Nai; bungalows 1000-1200B; ✳️📶) This cluster of identical concrete bungalows with blue tiled roofs surrounds a manicured green lawn; the best have dreamy views over the whitest and cleanest part of quiet Sunset Beach. Every unit is spacious, clean and has air-con, fridge, hot water and TV.

Delight   GUESTHOUSE **$$**
(Map p746; ☏077 375527; www.delightresort. com; Ban Hat Rin; r 800-6400B; ✳️📶🏊) In the

---

ⓘ DANGERS & ANNOYANCES

There is a lot of trouble mixed up with all of Ko Pha-Ngan's fun. Don't buy drugs on the street: usually this is an extortion set-up (or worse, a sting operation) with the local police. Beware of broken glass on the beach and watch out for strong ocean currents. No drunken swimming.

Women travellers should be very, very cautious about travelling alone during the Full Moon parties or when they've been out drinking. Reports of rapes and assaults by motorcycle drivers are common.

Don't drive here if you don't have motorcycle skills.

Ko Pha-Ngan

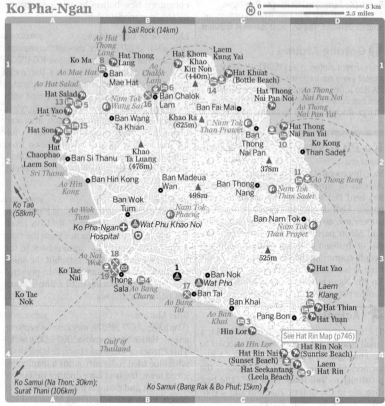

THAILAND KO PHA-NGAN

Ko Pha-Ngan

◉ Sights
1 Wat Khao Tham	B3

🛏 Sleeping
2 Bamboo Hut	D4
3 Boom's Cafe Bungalows	C4
4 Coco Garden	B3
5 Cookies Salad	A1
6 Fantasea	B1
7 High Life	A2
8 Island View Cabana	B1
9 Lighthouse Bungalows	D4
10 Longtail Beach Resort	C2
11 Mai Pen Rai	D2
12 Sanctuary	D3
13 Shiralea	A1
14 Smile Bungalows	C1
15 Tantawan Bungalows	A2

🍴 Eating
16 Cucina Italiana	B1
17 Fisherman's Restaurant	B3
18 Night Market	B3
19 Nira's	B3

centre of Hat Rin, friendly Delight offers some of the best lodging around. Spick-and-span rooms in a Thai-style building come with subtle designer details (such as peacock murals) and are sandwiched between an inviting swimming pool and a lazy lagoon peppered with lily pads.

🏖 Southern Beaches

The southern beaches are nothing special but they host copy-cat moon parties and are a close and cheap alternative to Hat Rin.

★ **Coco Garden** BUNGALOW **$**
(Map p744; ☑ 086 073 1147, 077 377721; www.co-cogardens.com; Thong Sala; bungalows 550-1100B; ❄🗢) The best budget hang-out along the southern coast, fantastic Coco Garden one-ups the nearby resorts with well-manicured grounds and 25 neat bungalows and an excellent beach bar. Super popular with the backpacker set, it's a fun and enjoyable scene.

Boom's Cafe Bungalows BUNGALOW **$**
(Map p744; ☑ 077 238318; www.boomscafe.com; Ban Khai; bungalows 600-1000B; ❄) Staying at Boom's is like visiting the Thai family you never knew you had. Super friendly and helpful owner Nok takes care of all her guests and keeps things looking good. No one seems to mind that there's no swimming pool, since the curling tide rolls right up to your doorstep. Boom's is at the far eastern corner of Ban Khai, near Hat Rin.

West Coast Beaches

The west coast is an upmarket outpost, though there are a few cheapies in the mix. The atmosphere is a middle ground between the seclusion of the east coast and hyper-social Hat Rin.

Tantawan Bungalows BUNGALOW **$**
(Map p744; ☑ 077 349108; www.tantawanbunga-low.com; Hat Son; bungalows 900-3300B; ❄⊠) This relaxed, chilled out and recently renovated 11-bungalow (fan and air-con) teak nest, tucked among jungle frond has fantastic views and a fine pool but it's a bit of a steep climb with luggage.

High Life BUNGALOW **$**
(Map p744; ☑ 077 349114; www.haadyaohighlife.com; Hat Yao; air-con bungalows 1200-3500B; ❄🗢⊠) We can't decide what's more conspicuous: the dramatic ocean views from the infinity-edged swimming pool, or the blatant double entendre in the resort's name. True to its moniker, the 25 bungalows, of various shapes and sizes, sit on a palmed outcropping of granite soaring high above the cerulean sea. Staff are polite and responsive.

Shiralea BUNGALOW **$**
(Map p744; ☑ 080 719 9256; www.shiralea.com; Hat Yao; dm 250B, bungalows 600-1300B; ❄🗢⊠) The fresh-faced poolside bungalows are simple but the new air-con dorms are great and the ambience, with an on-site bar with

draught beer, is convivial. It's about 100m away from the beach and it fills up every few weeks with Contiki student tour groups.

Northern Beaches

Hat Salad is a slim stretch of sand with many rustic charms. Ao Mae Hat has ocean vistas, plenty of sand and access to petite Ko Ma. The fishing village of Ban Chalok Lam is transforming slowly into a tourist enclave due to the new road. Hat Khuat (Bottle Beach) is still a far-flung dune that fills up fast in the high season. On the northeast of the island, Thong Nai Pan has beautiful beaches that are now more accessible with the new road.

Island View Cabana BUNGALOW **$**
(Map p744; ☑ 077 374173; islandviewcabana@gmail.com; Ao Mae Hat; bungalows 400-1500B; 🗢) Well-positioned for sunsets, the bungalows here are really big, though not that new, but this is a lovely spot at the end of the beach right at the isthmus to Ko Ma. Cheaper fan bungalows are at the rear.

Fantasea BUNGALOW **$**
(Map p744; ☑ 089 443 0785; www.fantasea.asia; Chalok Lam; bungalows with fan/air-con 500/800B; 🗢) This friendly place is one of the better of a string of family-run bungalow operations along the quiet, eastern part of Chalok Lam. There's a thin beach out front with OK swimming and an elevated Thai-style restaurant area to chill out in.

Smile Bungalows BUNGALOW **$**
(Map p744; ☑ 085 429 4995; www.smilebunga-lows.com; Bottle Beach/Hat Khuat; bungalows 520-920B; ⊗ closed Nov) At the far western corner of the beach, family-run Smile features an assortment of all-fan wooden huts climbing up a forested hill. The two-storey bungalows (920B) are our favourite.

Longtail Beach Resort BUNGALOW **$**
(Map p744; ☑ 077 445018; www.longtailbeach-resort.com; Thong Nai Pan; bungalows with fan/air-con from 550/2590B; ❄🗢) Tucked away at the lovely, southern end of the beach by the forest, Longtail offers backpackers charming thatch-and-bamboo abodes that wind up a lush garden path. The sand is fantastic and the green, lush setting is adorable.

Cookies Salad RESORT **$$**
(Map p744; ☑ 083 181 7125, 077 349125; www.cookies-phangan.com; bungalows 1800-3300B; 🗢⊠) Sling out on a hammock at this resort

Hat Rin

with private Balinese-styled bungalows on a steep hill, orbiting a two-tiered lap pool tiled in various shades of blue. Shaggy thatching and dense tropical foliage give the realm a certain rustic quality, although you won't want for creature comforts. It's super friendly and books up fast.

East Coast Beaches

The new road connects all the way to Than Sadet and its lovely bay. Hat Thian and Hat Yuan remain secluded, for now; the two beaches are accessible via long-tail boat (300B to 400B) from Hat Rin.

Mai Pen Rai   BUNGALOW $
(Map p744; ☎ 081 894 5076, 077 445090; www.thansadet.com; Than Sadet; bungalows 550-1200B; 🖥️) This quiet, beachy bay elicits nothing but sedate smiles. Trek up to Nam Tok Than Sadet falls, hike an hour to Thong Nai Pan or explore by sea with a rented kayak. Bungalows mingle with Plaa's next door on the hilly headland, and sport panels of straw weaving with gabled roofs. Family bungalows are available for 900B and there's a friendly on-site restaurant.

Bamboo Hut   BUNGALOW $
(Map p744; ☎ 087 888 8592; Hat Yuan; bungalows 400-1000B; 🖥️) Beautifully lodged up on the bouldery outcrops that overlook Hat Yuan and back into the jungle, groovy, hippie village, Bamboo Hut is a favourite for yoga retreats and meditative relaxation. Dark wood bungalows are small and have terraces and the patrons all float around the property high on fasting.

★**Sanctuary**   BUNGALOW $$
(Map p744; ☎ 081 271 3614; www.thesanctuarythailand.com; Hat Thian; dm 220B, bungalows 770-6000B) A friendly forested enclave of relaxed smiles, the Sanctuary is a haven of splendid lodgings, yoga classes and detox sessions. Accommodation, in various manifestations of twigs, is scattered along a tangle of hillside jungle paths while Hat Thian is wonderfully quiet and is great for swimming. Note that payment is cash only.

🍴 Eating

🍴 Hat Rin

The infamous **Chicken Corner** is a popular intersection stocked with munchie cure-alls, be it noon or midnight.

Lazy House   INTERNATIONAL $$
(Map p746; Hat Rin Nai; dishes 90-270B; ⊙ lunch & dinner) Back in the day, this joint was the owner's apartment – everyone liked his cooking so much that he decided to turn the place into a restaurant and hang-out spot. Today, Lazy House is easily one of Hat Rin's best places to veg out in front of a movie with a scrumptious shepherd's pie.

🍴 Southern Beaches

A **Walking Street** (4pm to 10pm Saturday) sets up on a side street in the eastern part of Thong Sala. The **Night Market** (Map p744; Thong Sala; dishes 25-180B; ⊙2-11pm) has a bevy of snacks and people-watching.

Nira's   BAKERY $
(Map p744; snacks from 80B; ⊙7am-7pm) With outstanding service, a big and bright

interconnected two room interior, scrummy baked goodies, tip-top coffee (and exotic rarities such as Marmite) and trendy furniture, Nira's is second to none in Thong Sala, and perhaps the entire island. This is *the* place for breakfast. Music is of the Grover Washington school.

★ **Fisherman's Restaurant** SEAFOOD $$
(Map p744; ☑ 084 454 7240; Ban Tai; dishes 50-600B; ☺1-10pm) Sit in a long-tail boat looking out over the sunset and a rocky pier. Lit up at night it's one of the island's nicest settings and the food, from the addictive yellow curry crab to the massive seafood platter to share, is as wonderful as the ambience. Reserve ahead, especially during party time.

 Other Beaches

★ **Cucina Italiana** ITALIAN $$
(Jenny's; Map p744; Chalok Lam; pizzas 180-200B; ☺5-10pm) If it weren't for the sand between your toes and the long-tail boats whizzing by, you might think you had been transported to the Italian countryside. The friendly Italian chef is passionate about his food, and creates everything from his pasta to his tiramisu daily, from scratch. The rustic, thin-crust pizzas are out-of-this-world good.

🍷 **Drinking & Nightlife**

Hat Rin is the beating heart of the legendary Full Moon fun, and the area can get pretty wound up even without the lunar influence.

Rock (Map p746), Drop-In (Map p746) and Sunrise (Map p746) are a few party venues that flank Hat Rin's infamous Sunrise Beach.

 Information

Backpackers Information Centre (Map p746; ☑ 077 375535; www.backpackersthailand.com; Hat Rin; ☺11am-8pm) A must for travellers looking to book high-quality tours (diving, live-aboards, jungle safaris etc) and transport. Not just for backpackers, it's an expat-run travel agency that offers peace of mind with every purchase – travellers are provided with the mobile phone number of the owners should any problems arise. Service is first rate and staff are forever helpful. It also runs the Crystal Dive shop next door.

Ko Pha-Ngan Hospital (Map p744; ☑ 077 377034; Thong Sala; ☺24hr) About 2.5km north of Thong Sala; offers 24-hour emergency services.

Main Police Station (Map p744; ☑ 077 377114, 191) Located about 2km north of Thong Sala. Come here to file a report. You might be charged between 110B and 200B to file the report, which is for insurance and refusing to pay may lead to complications. If you are arrested you have the right to an embassy phone call; you don't have to accept the 'interpreter' you are offered.

Main Post Office (Map p744; ☺8.30am-4.30pm Mon-Fri, 9am-noon Sat) In Thong Sala; there's a smaller office (Map p746) right near the pier in Hat Rin.

THAILAND KO PHA-NGAN

THE 10 COMMANDMENTS OF FULL-MOON FUN

On the eve of every full moon, tens of thousands of bodies converge on Sunrise Beach for an epic trance-a-thon. Though people come for fun, having a good time is serious business. There is a 100B entrance fee for much-needed beach clean-up and security.

➡ Thou shalt arrive in Hat Rin at least three days early to nail down accommodation.

➡ Thou shalt double-check the party dates as sometimes they are rescheduled.

➡ Thou shalt secure all valuables, especially when staying in budget bungalows.

➡ Thou shalt savour some delicious fried fare in Chicken Corner before the revelry begins.

➡ Thou shalt wear protective shoes, unless thou wants a tetanus shot.

➡ Thou shalt cover thyself with swirling patterns of neon body paint.

➡ Thou shalt visit the Rock for killer views of the heathens below.

➡ Thou shalt not sample the drug buffet, nor shall thou swim in the ocean under the influence.

➡ Thou shalt stay in a group of two or more people, especially if thou art a woman.

➡ Thou shalt party until the sun comes up and have a great time.

ℹ Getting There & Away

Ko Pha-Ngan's airport missed its 2014 opening and has no rescheduled date at the time of writing; once open, Kan Air will service the airport with flights to Bangkok.

The main pier on Ko Pha-Ngan is Thong Sala, though some companies run boats to Hat Rin and the east coast from northern piers on Samui (200B to 400B, 20 minutes to one hour, frequently 7am to 6pm). Bus-boat combinations connect all the way to Bangkok (1300B, 17 hours).

The **Haad Rin Queen** (☑ 077 484668) goes back and forth between Hat Rin and Big Buddha Beach on Ko Samui (200B, 50 minutes, four times a day). Service increases during the Full Moon parties. The wobbly *Thong Nai Pan Express* connects Hat Rin and east coast beaches, including Thong Nai Pan, to Mae Hat on Ko Samui (200B to 400B, once a day). The boat won't run in bad weather.

ℹ Getting Around

Motorbike rental is widely available for 150B to 250B. It is not recommended to rent a motorbike on the island if you're a novice.

Sŏrng·tăa·ou chug along the island's major roads, charging 100B between Thong Sala to Hat Rin and 150B to 200B for other beaches. Rates double after sunset. Ask your accommodation about free or discount transfers when you leave the island.

Longtail-boats depart from Thong Sala to various beaches throughout the day. Rates range from 50B to 300B.

Ko Tao

เกาะเต่า

POP 1500

The smallest of the Samui islands, Ko Tao has long attracted visitors for its near-shore reefs, cheap dive certificates and jungle-clad coves. It has firmly moved into upscale territory but it still remains one of the cheapest places to learn how to scuba.

◉ Sights & Activities

Diving & Snorkelling

The shallow bays scalloping the island are perfect for beginners. Over 40 dive centres are ready to saddle you up with some gear and teach you the ropes in a 3½-day Open Water certification course. Stiff competition means prices are low and standards are high.

Expect large crowds and booked-out beds throughout the months of December, January, June, July and August, and a monthly glut of wannabe divers after every Full Moon Party on Ko Pha-Ngan next door.

Dive schools typically have affiliated accommodation with discounted rates for diving guests.

Most snorkellers hire a long-tail boat to putter around the various bays. Equipment can be rented for 100B to 200B per day from guesthouses, though the quality is not superb.

Ban's Diving School   DIVING
(Map p750; ☑ 077 456466; www.bansdivingresort.com; Sairee Beach) A well-oiled diving machine that's relentlessly expanding, Ban's is one of the world's most prolific diver certification schools yet it retains a five-star feel. Classroom sessions tend to be conducted in large groups, but there's a reasonable amount of individual attention in the water. A range of international instructors means that students can learn to dive in their native tongue.

Big Blue Diving   DIVING
(Map p750; ☑ 077 456050; www.bigbluediving.com; Sairee Beach) If Goldilocks were picking a dive school, she'd probably pick Big Blue – this mid-size operation (not too big, not too small) gets props for fostering a sociable vibe while maintaining a high standard of service. Divers of every ilk can score dirt-cheap accommodation at Big Blue's resort.

Buddha View   DIVING
(☑077 456074; www.buddhaview-diving.com; Chalok Ban Kao) One of several big dive operations on Ko Tao, Buddha View offers the standard fare of certification and special programs for technical diving (venturing beyond the usual parameters of recreational underwater exploration). Discounted accommodation is available at its friendly resort.

🛏 Sleeping

🛏 Sairee Beach

Tao's longest strip of sand is its dive training zone coupled with decompression bars and restaurants.

Blue Wind   BUNGALOW $
(Map p750; ☑077 456116; bluewind_wa@yahoo.com; bungalows 350-1400B; ❋ 🛜) Blue Wind is a great rustic but relaxing alternative to the high-intensity dive resorts strung

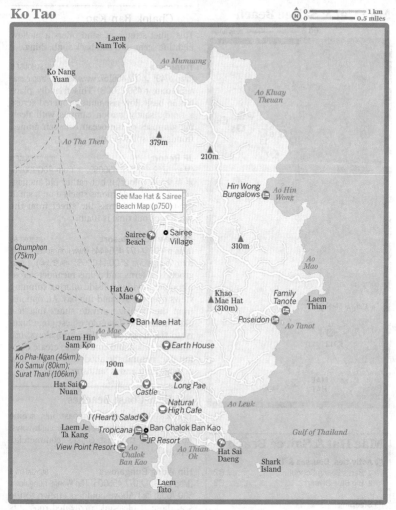

along Sairee Beach. Sturdy bamboo huts are peppered along a dirt trail behind the beachside bakery. Large, tiled air-conditioned cabins and attractive rooms in blocks with balcony boast hot showers and TVs. Reception is shut in the evenings and wi-fi is limited to the beach area.

Spicytao Backpackers   HOSTEL **$**
(Map p750; ☑ 082 278 7115; www.spicyhostels. com/Home.html; dm 200-250B; ❄ 🛜) Like your own super-social country hang-out, Spicytao is hidden off the main drag in a rustic garden setting. Backpackers rave about the am-

bience and staff who are always organising activities. Book in advance!

Ban's Diving Resort   RESORT **$$**
(Map p750; ☑ 077 456466; www.bansdivingresort. com; r 600-10,000B; ❄ @ 🛜 ⚊) This dive-centric party palace offers a wide range of quality accommodation from basic backpacker digs to sleek hillside villas, and it's growing all the time. Post-scuba chill sessions take place on Ban's prime slice of beach or at one of the two swimming pools tucked within the strip of jungle between the two-storey, pillared and terraced white hotel blocks.

Mae Hat & Sairee Beach

Mae Hat & Sairee Beach

Mae Hat & Sairee Beach

🛏 Chalok Ban Kao

This quiet stretch of sand offers a mellow nightlife scene and laid-back sunbathing.

Tropicana GUESTHOUSE $

(Map p749; ☑ 077 456167; www.koh-tao-tropicana-resort.com; r 450-2500B) This friendly place has 56 basic, low-rise units peppered across a sandy, shady garden campus with fleeting glimpses of the ocean between fanned fronds and spiky palms.

JP Resort GUESTHOUSE $

(Map p749; ☑ 077 456099; r from 700-1300B; ❋@🛜) A colourful but rather old menagerie of motel-style rooms stacked on a small scrap of jungle across the street from the sea. Check out time is 10am.

★View Point Resort RESORT $$

(Map p749; ☑ 077 456444; www.kohtaoviewpoint. com; bungalows 2500-14,000B; ❋🛜🏊) Lush grounds of ferns and palms meander across a boulder-studded hillside offering stunning views over the sea and the bay. All options, from the exquisite private suites that feel like Tarzan and Jane's love nest gone luxury to the huge, view-filled bungalows, use boulders, wood and concrete to create comfortable, naturalistic abodes. It's under new management and is fantastic value.

🛏 East-Coast Beaches

The less-developed east coast has scenic boulder-strewn coves perfect for castaways. Ao Tanot is the east coast's 'commercial' centre.

Hin Wong Bungalows BUNGALOW $

(Map p749; ☑ 077 456006; Hin Wong; bungalows 500-700B; 🛜) Above boulders strewn to the sea, these 11 pleasant corrugated roof huts are scattered across a lot of untamed tropical terrain – it all feels a bit like *Gilligan's Island*. A rickety dock, jutting out just beyond the breezy restaurant, is the perfect place to dangle your legs and watch schools of black sardines slide through the cerulean water.

Poseidon BUNGALOW $

(Map p749; ☑ 077 456735; poseidonkohtao@hotmail.com; Ao Tanot; bungalows 800-1500B; 🛜) Poseidon keeps the tradition of the budget bamboo bungalow alive with 150 or so basic-but-sleepable fan huts scattered near the sand. Wi-fi in restaurant.

Family Tanote BUNGALOW $$
(Map p749; ☑ 077 456757; Ao Tanot; bungalows 800-3500B; ❄@☎) This family-run scatter of hillside bungalows is a good choice for solitude seekers. Strap on a snorkel mask and swim around with the fish at your doorstep, or climb up to the restaurant for a tasty meal and beautiful views of the bay.

🍴 Eating

🍴 Sairee Beach

★**995 Roasted Duck** CHINESE $
(Map p750; mains from 70B; ⊙9am-9pm) You may have to queue a while to get a seat at this glorified shack and wonder what all the fuss is about. The fuss is excellent roast duck, from 70B for a steaming bowl of roasted waterfowl with noodles to 700B for a whole bird. Fantastic.

Su Chili THAI $
(Map p750; dishes 85-225B; ⊙10am-10.30pm) Inviting and bustling, Su Chili serves fresh and tasty Thai dishes, with friendly staff always asking how spicy you want your food and somehow getting it right. Try the delicious northern Thai specialities or Penang curries. There's a smattering of Western comfort food for homesick diners.

Los Pollos Hermanos BARBECUE $
(Map p750; www.lospolloshermanos-kohtao.com; mains from 140B; ⊙8am-midnight) No, there's no Nandos on Ko Tao. But there's Los Pollos Hermanos, which does a mighty fine job of grilling up peri-peri chicken with sauces arriving in three different grades of spiciness. We hope they lose the wooden plates though. It's tucked away along an alley off the main drag.

★**Barracuda Restaurant & Bar** ASIAN FUSION $$
(Map p750; ☑080 146 3267; mains 240-590B; ⊙6-10.30pm) Chef Ed Jones caters for the Thai princess when she's in town, but you can sample his exquisite cuisine for mere pennies in comparison to her budget. Locally sourced ingredients are sourced for creative, fresh, fusion masterpieces. Try the seafood platter, sesame-seared tuna fillet or braised lamb shank – then wash it down with a lemon grass and ginger mojito.

Chopper's Bar & Grill INTERNATIONAL $$
(Map p750; www.choppers-kohtao.com; mains 160-300B; ⊙9am-midnight) Frequently rammed and a fixture on the Ko Tao pub crawl, Chopper's is a riotously popular two-storey hang-out with live music, sports on the TVs, billiards, a cinema room and decent pub grub. Happy hour is 5pm to 8pm.

🍴 Mae Hat

Pranee's Kitchen THAI $
(Map p750; dishes 50-150B; ⊙7am-10pm; ☎) An old Mae Hat fave, Pranee's serves scrumptious curries and other Thai treats in an open-air pavilion sprinkled with lounging pillows, wooden tables and TVs. English language movies are shown nightly at 6pm.

Food Centre THAI $
(Map p750; mains from 30B; ⊙breakfast, lunch & dinner) An unceremonious gathering of hot-tin food stalls, Food Centre – as it's come to be known – lures lunching locals with veritable smoke signals rising up from the concrete parking lot abutting Mae Hat's petrol station. You'll find some of the island's best papaya salad here.

★**Whitening** INTERNATIONAL $$
(Map p750; dishes 150-400B; ⊙1pm-1am; ☎) This starched, white, beachy spot falls somewhere between being a restaurant and a chic seaside bar – foodies will appreciate the tasty twists on indigenous and international dishes. Dine amid dangling white Christmas lights while keeping your bare feet tucked into the sand. And the best part? It's comparatively easy on the wallet.

🍴 Chalok Ban Kao

I (Heart) Salad CAFE $$
(Map p749; mains from 120B; ⊙8am-9pm; ☎) This rustic choice offers a healthy array of salads using fresh ingredients, with a good supply of vegetarian and vegan dishes and sticky desserts to follow. There are also real fruit juices and healthy egg white–only breakfasts.

Long Pae STEAK $$$
(Map p749; mains from 160B; ⊙10am-midnight) Ensconced off the radar from most of the island's tourist traffic, 'Uncle Pae' sits on a terrace in hilly jungle with distant views of the sea down below. The speciality here is steak, which goes well with a generous smattering of pan-Asian appetisers. If the weather's clear, try to tie in sunset, but if the winds blow, hold on to your napkins.

THAILAND KO TAO

Drinking & Entertainment

After diving, Ko Tao's favourite pastime is drinking, and there's definitely no shortage of places to get tanked. In fact, the island's three biggest dive centres each have bumpin' bars: **Fishbowl Beach Bar**, **Crystal Bar** and **Buddha on the Beach**. Stop in even if you aren't a diver. Chopper's (p751) and **Safety Stop Pub** (Map p750; mains 60-250B; ⊙7am-11pm; 🛜) are great grub pubs.

⭐ **Earth House**   BEER GARDEN
(Map p749; www.theearthhousekohtao.com; ⊙noon-midnight Mon-Sat) Run by Kelly from Worcester, this relaxing, secluded and rustic spot serves up a global selection of 40 beers, craft labels and ciders in a dreamy garden setting. With it's own relaxing treehouse, there's also a restaurant for bites (9am to noon and 1pm to 6pm Monday to Saturday) and bungalows for going prone if you overdo it on the Green Goblin (cider).

Earth House is on the road to Ao Tanot, just before the turn off for Ao Leuk.

⭐ **Fizz**   BAR
(Map p750; Sairee Beach) Sink into a bean bag, order up a designer cocktail and let the hypnotic surf roll in amid a symphony of ambient sounds. Fantastic.

Castle   CLUB
(Map p749; www.thecastlekohtao.com; Mae Hat) Located along the main road between Mae Hat and Chalok Ban Kao, the three-floor Castle is the top hip-hop, garage, electro and funk party venue on the island, luring an array of local and international DJs to its limited number of parties each month.

Natural High Cafe   CAFE
(Map p749; ⊙10.30am-midnight) With a fine elevated open air terrace and ranging views in all directions over the profuse island greenery, hammocks for lying around in, ambient chill-out sounds and coffee served up in enamel cups, this cafe is ideal for zoning out, but there's pool for fidgets. It's on a hill on the road to Hat Sai Daeng, look out for the signs.

ℹ Dangers & Annoyances

The island's roads are not safe enough for novice motorbike drivers. Dengue is a problem on the island, so use mosquito repellent day and night. Avoid arguing with Thais in bars after too much to drink; an unsolved, brutal murder of two foreigners in 2014 possibly had links to an argument with a well-connected Thai.

ℹ Information

Police Station (Map p750; 📞077 456631) Between Mae Hat and Sairee Beach along the rutted portion of the beachside road.

Post Office (Map p750; 📞077 456170; ⊙9am-5pm Mon-Fri, 9am-noon Sat) A 10- to 15-minute walk from the pier; at the corner of Ko Tao's main inner-island road and Mae Hat's 'down road'.

ℹ Getting There & Away

Chumphon is the mainland jumping-off point for Ko Tao. Inter-island ferries connect Tao to its neighbours and on to Surat Thani. Mae Hat is the island's primary pier. Book your tickets in advance around Ko Pha-Ngan's Full Moon parties. Pier transfer costs should be included in the price of the ticket.

Services to Ko Pha-Ngan include Lomprayah (500B to 600B, one hour, three daily), Seatran Discovery Ferry (430B, one hour, three daily) and Songserm (350B, two hours). Services to Samui include Lomprayah (600B, two hours, twice daily), Seatran Discovery Ferry (600B, three daily) and Songserm (450B, 3½ hours, once daily).

ℹ Getting Around

Sŏrng·tǎa·ou and motorbikes haul passengers from the pier in Mae Hat to their hotels. Rates to Sairee Beach and Chalok Ban Kao cost 100B to 200B per person, depending on the number of passengers; try to hook up with other travellers to keep the transfer inexpensive. Water taxis leave from Mae Hat to Chalok Ban Kao to the northern part of Sairee Beach for about 100B. Chartered boats start at 1500B per day.

Surat Thani   อำเภอเมืองสุราษฎร์ธานี
POP 128,990

Surat Thani was once the seat of the ancient Srivijaya empire, which ruled much of southern Thailand, Malaysia and Sumatra. Today it is an important transport hub that indiscriminately moves cargo and people around the country. Travellers rarely linger here as they make their way to the Samui archipelago and the Andaman coast.

If you need to stay the night, **My Place @ Surat Hotel** (📞077 272288; 247/5 Th Na Meuang; d 490-590B, f 620B; ✴🛜) is central and clean and **Wangtai Hotel** (📞077 283020; 1 Th Talad Mai; r 790-2000B; ✴@🛜✳) has smart options.

Go to the **night market** (Sarn Chao Ma; Th Ton Pho; dishes from 35B; ⊙6-11pm) for fried, steamed, grilled or sautéed delicacies. There are additional evening food stalls near the departure docks for the night boats to the islands, and a **Sunday market** (⊙4-9pm) near the TAT office. During the day many food stalls near the downtown bus terminal sell *kôw gài òp* (marinated baked chicken on rice).

❶ Information

Taksin Hospital (☑077 273239; Th Talat Mai) The most professional of Surat's three hospitals. Just beyond the Talat Mai Market in the northeast part of downtown.

Tourism Authority of Thailand (TAT; ☑077 288818; 5 Th Talat Mai; ⊙8.30am-4.30pm) This friendly office southwest of town has useful brochures and maps, and staff speak good English.

❶ Getting There & Away

In general, if you are departing from points north (such as Bangkok or Hua Hin) for the Samui islands, use Chumphon rather than Surat as a jumping-off point to the islands.

AIR

Use Surat Thani's airport as an alternative to flying to/from Bangkok, if you can't get a flight to Samui. Transferring from Surat's airport to the pier adds significant time and hassle to the trip. Surat's airport is serviced by Air Asia, which has transfer shuttles to the boat pier, Nok Air and Thai Airways International.

BOAT

Lomprayah (p742), **Seatran Discovery** (☑077 275063; www.seatrandiscovery.com) and **Songserm** (☑077 377704; www.songserm-expressboat.com) have frequent and reliable boat service to the islands. Night ferries to Ko Samui (300B, six hours, 11pm departure) leave from the centre of town; these are simple cargo ships so bring supplies.

TRAIN

Surat's train station is in Phun Phin, 14km west of town. From Phun Phin there are buses to Phuket, Phang-Nga and Krabi, some via Takua Pa, the stopping point for Khao Sok National Park. There are also train-boat combinations that connect arriving train passengers to the Samui islands.

BUS & MINIVAN

Frequent buses and minivans depart from two main locations in town: Talat Kaset 1, on the north side of Th Talat Mai (the city's main drag), and Talat Kaset 2, on the south side of Th Talat Mai.

The long-distance bus terminal is located 7km south of town and serves Bangkok (380B to 800B, 11 to 14 hours).

Buses from Surat Thani centre:

DESTINATION	FARE (B)	DURATION (HR)
Bangkok	421-856	10
Hat Yai	160-290	5
Krabi	150	2½
Phuket	250	6

❶ Getting Around

Airport minivans will drop you off at your hotel for 100B per person. *Sŏrng·tăa·ou* around town cost 10B to 30B. Orange ordinary buses run from Phun Phin train station to Surat Thani (15B, 25 minutes). Taxis from the train station charge 200B for a maximum of four people.

Hat Yai   หาดใหญ่

POP 191,696

Welcome to southern Thailand's urban hub. In addition to its shopping malls and modern amenities, it is also a favourite weekend trip for Malaysian men looking for prostitutes, giving it a slightly rough border-town image. Occasionally the low-scale insurgent war in Thailand's nearby Deep South provinces spills over to Hat Yai with bomb attacks on high-profile targets (such as shopping malls, hotels and the airport). The most recent bombing occurred in 2014, injuring eight people. However, these violent attacks do not mean that Hat Yai is off-limits to foreign tourists, but do exercise caution if transiting through.

Hat Yai has dozens of hotels within walking distance of the train station. The city is the unofficial capital of southern Thailand's cuisine, offering Muslim roti and curries, Chinese noodles and dim sum, and fresh Thai-style seafood from both the Gulf and Andaman coasts.

❶ Information

Immigration Office (Th Phetkasem) Near the railway bridge, it handles visa extensions.

Tourism Authority of Thailand (TAT; call centre ☑1672; www.tourismthailand.org/hatyai; 1/1 Soi 2, Th Niphat Uthit 3; ⊙8.30am-4.30pm) The very helpful staff here speak excellent English and have loads of info on the entire region.

Tourist Police (Th Niphat Uthit 3; ⊙24hr) Near the TAT office.

GETTING TO MALAYSIA: SUNGAI KOLOK TO KOTA BHARU

This border is within Thailand's Deep South, an area that has had a small-scale insurgent war for more than a decade. Exercise caution when travelling overland through here. Tak Bai, also in Narathiwat Province, and Betong, further south in Yala, are also legal crossing points for foreigners, but Sungai Kolok is by far the most convenient place to cross the border.

Getting to the border The Thai immigration post (open 5am to 9pm) at the Sungai Kolok/Rantau Panjang border is about 1.5km from the centre of Sungai Kolok or the train station. Motorbike taxis charge 30B.

At the border This is a hassle-free, straightforward border crossing. After completing formalities, walk across the Harmony Bridge to the Malaysian border post.

Moving on Shared taxis (RM$10/90B) and buses (RM$5.10/45B) to Kota Bharu can be caught 200m beyond the Malaysian border post. You can charter a car for RM$50 (450B).

For information on doing this crossing in reverse, see p429.

ⓘ Getting There & Away

AIR

Thai Airways International (THAI; www.thai-airways.com; 182 Th Niphat Uthit 1), Air Asia and Nok Air operate flights to Bangkok. Air Asia also has flights to Kuala Lumpur.

BUS

Most provincial buses and south-bound minivans leave from the bus terminal, 2km southeast of the town centre. Most northbound minivans leave from a minivan terminal 5km west of town at Talat Kaset, a 60B túk-túk ride from the centre of town. **Prasert Tour** (Th Niphat Uthit 1) and **Cathay Tour** (93/1 Th Niphat Uthit 2) run minivans to many destinations in the south.

Buses from Hat Yai:

DESTINATION	FARE (B)	DURATION (HR)
Bangkok	688-1126	15
Krabi	182-535	5
Phuket	360	7
Sungai Kolok	200	4
Surat Thani	235	5

TRAIN

Hat Yai is a convenient place to catch the train south to Butterworth (Malaysia), and then transfer to Penang. The train station is centrally located.

ⓘ Getting Around

Airport Taxi Service (182 Th Niphat Uthit 1; 100B per person; ☉ 6.30am-6.45pm) makes the run to the airport six times daily. A private taxi for this run costs 320B.

Sŏrng·tăa·ou run along Th Phetkasem (10B per person). Túk-túk and motorcycle taxis around town cost 20B to 40B per person.

THE ANDAMAN COAST

The Andaman is Thailand's turquoise coast, that place on a 'Travel to Paradise' poster that makes you want to leave your job and live in flipflops. White beaches, cathedral-like limestone cliffs, neon corals and hundreds of jungle-covered isles extend down the Andaman Sea from the border of Myanmar to Malaysia. It is a postcard-perfect destination thoroughly serviced by the package-tourist industry, and finding budget spots takes some searching.

Ranong   ระนอง

POP 29,096

On the eastern bank of the Sompaen River's turbid, tea-brown estuary, Ranong is a short boat ride – or a filthy swim – from Myanmar. This border town *par excellence* (frenetic, slightly seedy) has a multi-culti mix of people from Myanmar, tremendous street food and an emerging expat scene.

The town is a transit point to Ko Phayam, a popular southern visa run and border into Myanmar. Meanwhile, dive operators specialising in live-aboard trips to the Surin or Similan Islands and Burma Banks are establishing themselves here. Try **A-One-Diving** (☏ 077 832984; www.a-one-diving.com; 256 Th Ruangrat; 3-day live-aboard 17,900-18,900B; ☉ Oct-Apr) or **Andaman International Dive**

Center (📞 089 814 1092; www.aidcdive.com; Bus Terminal, Th Phetkasem; 4-day live-aboard 19,000B; 🕐 Oct-Apr).

🛏 Sleeping & Eating

If you are doing a visa run through an agency, they'll ship you in and out of town without having to sleep over. If you decide to spend the night, try the remodelled **Luang Poj** (📞 077 833377, 087 266 6333; www.facebook.com/luangpojhostel; 225 Th Ruangrat; r 500B; ✳ 🖥).

For some grub, there's a **night market** (Th Kamlangsap, off Hwy 4; dishes 30-50B; 🕐 2-7pm) and a **day market** (Th Ruangrat; dishes 40-50B; 🕐 5am-midnight) offering inexpensive Thai and Burmese meals. **Pon's Place** (📞 081 597 4549; www.ponplace-ranong.com; Th Ruangrat; 🕐 7.30am-7pm) is Ranong's one-stop shop for food, tourist information and everything in between. Expats hang out at **Ranong Hideaway** (📞 077 832730; www.ranonghideaway.com; 323/7 Th Ruangrat; mains 90-300B; 🕐 10am-11pm; 🖥), which has a bit of everything, including a pool table, pizza and a well-stocked bar.

ℹ Information

Post Office (Th Chonrau; 🕐 8.30am-4.30pm Mon-Fri, 9am-noon Sat & Sun)

Ranong Immigration Office (Th Chalermprakiat; 🕐 8.30am-5pm) Main immigration office, 4km southwest of town; handles visa extensions.

Ranong Immigration Post (Tha Saphan Plaa; 🕐 8am-5pm) If you're just popping in and out of Myanmar's Kawthoung, visiting this small immigration post, 5km southwest of town, is sufficient.

ℹ Getting There & Away

AIR

The airport is 22km south of town. **Nok Air** (📞 02 900 9955; www.nokair.com) flies Bangkok's Don Muang airport twice daily.

BUS

The bus terminal is on Th Petchkasem 1km from town, sŏrng·tăa·ou 2 passes the terminal. Minivans travel to the Gulf Coast towns of Chumphon and Surat Thani.

ℹ Getting Around

Motorcycle taxis will take you almost anywhere in town for 50B. Sŏrng·tăa·ou 4 goes to the piers.

Ko Chang
เกาะช้าง

If you're looking for the big Ko Chang, you've come to the wrong place. But if you're seeking a lonely stretch of sand, then you've chosen the right Chang.

Unlike most of the Andaman's islands, Ko Chang enjoys its back-to-basics lifestyle – there are no ATMs, no 24-hour electricity and no cars.

🛏 Sleeping & Eating

⭐**Crocodile Rock** GUESTHOUSE $
(📞 080 533 4138; tonn1970@yahoo.com; Ao Yai; bungalow 400-700B) Outstanding bamboo bungalows perched on Ao Yai's serene southern headland with superb bay views. The classy kitchen turns out homemade yoghurt, breads, cookies, good espresso, and a variety of vegie and seafood dishes. It's popular, so book ahead.

Sawadee BUNGALOW $
(📞 086 906 0900; www.sawadeekohchang.com; Ao Yai; bungalow 350-950B; 🕐 Nov–mid-Apr) A-frame wooden bungalows have vented walls to keep things cool and are equipped with sunken bathrooms painted bright colours and hammocks on terraces. Sawadee is located at the southern end of Ao Yai.

THAILAND KO CHANG

BUS & MINIVAN TRANSPORT FROM RANONG

DESTINATION	FARE (B)	DURATION (HR)	FREQUENCY
Bangkok	445-692	9-10	hourly 7am-1pm, 3pm, 5pm, 7pm & 8pm (VIP)
Chumphon	120	2	hourly 7am-5pm
Hat Yai	420	7	6am, 10am & 8pm
Khao Lak	180	3½	hourly 6.30am-5.45pm
Krabi	197	6	7.30am, 10.15am & 2pm
Phang-Nga	190	5	7.30am, 10.15am & 2pm
Phuket	250	5-6	hourly 6.30am-5.45pm
Surat Thani	190	4-5	6am & 2pm

GETTING TO MYANMAR: RANONG TO KAWTHOUNG (VICTORIA POINT)

Since 2014, Thai authorities have been cracking down on visa runs at this border, aimed at curtailing beach-bumming foreigners from working illegally in Thailand. Most travellers opt for the organised 'visa trips' (from 1000B per person including visa fees) offered by travel agencies in Ranong. But the trip could just as easily be arranged independently. Do note that Myanmar is 30 minutes behind Thailand.

This border now also allows land entry into Myanmar (with a pre-arranged visa) or you could visit the tumbledown port city of Kawthoung as a day trip.

Getting to the border Boats to Kawthoung leave from the Saphan Plaa pier, 5km from Ranong. Red *sŏrng·tăa·ou* from Ranong go to the pier (20B).

At the border Long-tail boat drivers will meet you at the pier and negotiate a fare; trips to Myanmar should cost 125/250B one way/return. Get photocopies of your passport at the pier for 5B. You'll get stamped through **Thai immigration** (p755), board the boat to the other side and go through Myanmar's checkpoint.

Upon arriving at the Myanmar immigration office, you'll most likely be greeted by an English-speaking tout who insists on 'helping' in return for tips; it's your choice as to whether or not you engage their services.

As a day visitor, you will pay a US$10 fee (crisp, untorn bills) for a border pass; your passport will be kept at the border. There are some well-meaning border 'helpers' who will carry your bag and collect forms for a tip. As a visa-runner the whole process should take two hours.

Moving on You can tour Kawthoung for the day or continue into Myanmar with a pre-arranged visa.

For information on doing this crossing in reverse, see p502.

ⓘ Getting There & Away

From Ranong, *sŏrng·tăa·ou* (20B) or motorcycle taxis (50B) go from Th Ruangrat to **Tha Ko Phayam** near Saphan Plaa.

Long-tail taxi boats (150B, two hours, 9.30am and 1pm) leave for Ko Chang. In high season they stop at the west-coast beaches, returning to the mainland at approximately 8.30am and 1.30pm. During the monsoon, only morning long-tails make the crossing (weather permitting) from the northeast's main pier.

During the November-to-April high season, speedboats (350B, 30 minutes, 8am to 4.30pm) run between Ranong's Tha Ko Phayam and Ko Chang's northeast-coast pier.

Motorcycle taxis meet boats, charging 100B to Ao Yai.

Ko Phayam   เกาะพยาม

Little Ko Phayam, part of the Laem Son National Park, is a beach-laden isle that has gone mainstream without selling out. It is rustic compared to Thailand's high-flyer resort islands with simple beachside lodging, barefoot beach bars and a barely developed jungle interior crisscrossed by dirt and concrete paths.

The main drawback of Ko Phayam is that the snorkelling isn't great, but the Surin Islands are relatively close by. For dive trips and PADI courses try **Phayam Divers** (☑ 086 995 2598; www.phayamlodge.com; Ao Yai; 2 dives 6400B, 3-day live-aboard 16,000-17,000B; ☉Nov-Apr). There are no ATMs on the island.

🛏 Sleeping & Eating

★ **PP Land**   BUNGALOW $
(☑ 081 678 4310; www.ppland-heavenbeach.com; Ao Hin Khow; bungalow 700-1400B; �☀) ☘ A stunning Thai-Belgian–owned ecolodge, just north of the pier on the little-visited east coast. Beautifully designed concrete bungalows are powered by wind and sun, with 24-hour electricity and hammocks on terraces overlooking the sea. The knowledgeable owners bake cakes, run an organic garden, treat sewage and make their own all-natural laundry detergent. Excellent value.

Aow Yai Bungalows   BUNGALOW $
(☑ 083 389 8688; www.aowyai.com; southeast end of Ao Yai; bungalow 400-800B; �) This French-Thai operation is the thatched bamboo bungalow pioneer that kicked it all off two decades ago. Choose between decent, rustic

small wooden-and-bamboo bungalows amid towering palms and pines, and larger beach-front wood models or concrete bungalows. Electricity 10am to 3am.

ⓘ Getting There & Around

From Ranong, ferries go to Ko Phayam's main pier (200B, two hours, 10am); the return trip is at 3pm. During the high season, speedboats go to Ko Phayam (350B, 35 minutes, hourly from 7.45am to 4.30pm); they make eight return trips.

A motorcycle taxi from the pier to the main beaches costs 50B to 80B per person. Motorcycle and bicycle rentals are available in the village and from most of the larger resorts.

Khao Sok National Park

อุทยานแห่งชาติเขาสก

If your leg muscles have atrophied after too much beach-bumming, consider venturing inland to the wondrous **Khao Sok National Park** (อุทยานแห่งชาติเขาสก; ☑077 395154; www.khaosok.com; adult/child 300/150B; ☉8am-5pm). Many believe this lowland jungle – the wettest spot in Thailand – to be over 160 million years old, making it one of the oldest rainforests on the globe. It features dramatic limestone formations and waterfalls that cascade through thickets drenched with rain. A network of dirt trails snakes through the quiet park, allowing visitors to spy on the exciting array of indigenous creatures.

🛏 Sleeping

We recommend the two-day, one-night trips (2500B per person) to Chiaw Lan, where you sleep in floating huts on the lake and go on a variety of canoeing excursions.

Jungle Huts BUNGALOW $
(☑077 395160; www.khaosokjunglehuts.com; 242 Mu 6; r fan 300-700B, air-con 1000B; ❇🛜) This popular budget hang-out, 1km northeast off Rte 401, contains an ever-growing collection of decent, individually styled bungalows, all with bathrooms and porches. Choose from plain stilted bamboo huts, bigger wooden editions, pink-washed concrete bungalows, or air-con rooms along vertiginous walkways.

Art's Riverview
Jungle Lodge GUESTHOUSE $$
(☑098 826 6967, 090 167 6818; www.facebook.com/Arts-Riverview-Lodge-Travel-15620901807 32965; 54/3 Mu 6; bungalow fan 650-1000B, air-con 1200-1500B; ❇🛜🐾) In a monkey-filled jungle bordering a rushing river with a limestone cliff-framed swimming hole, Art's enjoys Khao Sok's prettiest setting. Stilted brick, shingled and all-wood bungalows are spacious and comfy, many with river views, though the bungalows could use a refresh. There's a variety of rooms, including family-sized options, and a host of family-friendly activities. It's signposted 1.5km northeast off Rte 401.

ⓘ Information

Khao Sok National Park Headquarters
(☑077 395154; www.khaosok.com; ☉8am-5pm) About 1.8km northeast off Rte 401, exiting near the Km 109 marker; helpful maps and information.

ⓘ Getting There & Around

From Surat Thani catch a bus going towards Takua Pa; from the Andaman coast, take a Surat Thani-bound bus. Buses stop on Rte 401, 1.8km southwest of the visitors centre. If touts don't meet you, you'll have to walk to your chosen guesthouse (50m to 2km).

Daily minivans include the following destinations: Bangkok (850B, 11 hours), Krabi (1100B, eight hours), Surat Thani (250B, one hour) and Khao Lak (150B, 1¼ hours).

Hat Khao Lak & Around

Hat Khao Lak is a beach for folks who shun the glitzy resorts of Phuket, but still crave civilisation (comfort, shopping and amenities). With warm waves to frolic in, long stretches of golden sand backed by forested hills, and easy day trips to nearby national parks, the area is a central base for exploring the North Andaman – above and below the water.

🏃 Activities

Diving or snorkelling day excursions to the Similan and Surin islands are immensely popular, but if you can, opt for a live-aboard trip since the islands are around 60km offshore (about three hours by boat). All dive shops offer live-aboard trips from around 19,000/35,000B for three-/six-day packages and day trips for 5000B to 6000B.

The following offer live-aboard trips: **Wicked Diving** (☑076 485868; www.wickeddiving.com; Th Phetkasem, Khao Lak; 2 dives 5700B, snorkelling day/overnight trip 2900/8100B; ☉Oct-May), **Fantastic** (☑076 485998; www.fantasticsimilan.com; adult/child 2300/1700B; ☉mid-Oct–mid-May) and **Sea Dragon Dive Centre**

(☑076 485420; www.seadragondivecenter.com; Th Phetkasem, Khao Lak; 2 dives 5100B, snorkelling day trip 2700B; ☉Oct-May).

🛏 Sleeping

Tiffy's   HOSTEL $

(☑076 485440; www.tiffyscafekhaolak.com; 5/15 Mu 6, Khao Lak; dm 180-250B, d 400B; 🛜) At the northern end of Khao Lak proper, this simple choice attached to a Thai-German cafe offers small, clean, fan-cooled six- and -three bed dorms and shared-bathroom doubles.

Walker's Inn   GUESTHOUSE $

(☑084 840 2689; www.walkersinn.com; 26/61 Mu 7, Th Phetkasem, Khao Lak; dm/r 200/600B; ❋🛜) A long-running backpacker fave and classic old-school guesthouse that features bright, spacious air-con rooms, decent single-sex dorms, and a popular downstairs pub dishing up full English breakfasts. It also does laundry and hire motorbikes (per day 200B).

Fasai House   GUESTHOUSE $

(☑076 485867; www.fasaihouse.com; 5/54 Mu 7, Khao Lak; r 650-900B; ❋@☲) Arguably Khao Lak's top budget choice, Fasai wins us over with its delightful staff and immaculate, motel-style air-con rooms set in a warm yellow-washed block framing a little pool. It's signposted west off Hwy 4 towards the northern end of Khao Lak.

🍴 Eating & Drinking

Early-morning divers will be hard-pressed to find a place to grab a bite before 8.30am.

Go Pong   THAI $

(Th Phetkasem, Khao Lak; dishes 40-120B; ☉10am-11pm) Get a real taste of local flavours at this terrific streetside diner where they stir-fry noodles and sensational spicy rice dishes, and simmer aromatic noodle soups that attract a loyal lunch following. Dishes are packed full of flavour.

Jumbo Steak & Pasta   ITALIAN $$

(☑098 059 8293; Th Phetkasem, Ban Khukkhuk; mains 70-280B; ☉noon-10.30pm Thu-Tue) A hole-in-the-wall joint on the west side of Hwy 4, 6km north of Khao Lak proper, launched by a former Le Meridien line chef who does beautiful pasta dishes in all kinds of flavours: penne arrabiata, hot-and-spicy seafood spaghetti, creamy spinach tagliatelle, a host of pizzas and terrific steaks. Dishes are great value in terms of quality, though portions aren't huge.

ℹ Information

For emergencies (included dive-related ones) call the **SSS Ambulance** (☑076 209 347, emergency 081 081 9000), which rushes injured persons to Phuket.

There are numerous travel agencies, including **Khao Lak Land Discoveries** (☑076 485411; www.khaolaklanddiscovery.com; 21/5 Mu 7, Th Phetkasem, Khao Lak; ☉9am-8pm).

ℹ Getting There & Away

Any bus running along Hwy 4 will stop at Hat Khao Lak en route to Takua Pa (55B, 45 minutes) or Phuket (100B, two hours); let the driver know you're getting out at Khao Lak.

Khao Lak Discoveries runs minivans to/from Phuket International Airport (600B, 1¼ hours). Alternatively you can take a Phuket-bound bus and ask for the airport; you'll be dropped off at an intersection where motorcycle taxis will complete the journey (10 minutes, 100B). It works, we promise.

Surin Islands Marine National Park

อุทยานแห่ง ชาติหมู่ เกาะสุรินทร์

The five gorgeous islands that make up this **national park** (อุทยานแห่งชาติหมู่เกาะ สุรินทร์; ☑076 472145; www.dnp.go.th; adult/child 500/300B; ☉mid-Oct–mid-May) sit about 60km offshore and 5km from the Thai–Myanmar marine border. Healthy rainforests, pockets of white-sand beach in sheltered bays and rocky headlands that jut into the ocean characterise these granite-outcrop islands. The clearest of water makes for great marine life, with underwater visibility often up to 20m. Park headquarters and all visitor facilities are on Ko Surin Neua, near the jetty.

Khuraburi, on the mainland, is the jumping-off point for the park. The pier is 9km north of town, as is the **national park office** (☑076 472145; www.dnp.go.th; Tha Khuraburi; ☉8.30am-4.30pm mid-Oct–mid-May).

⦿ Sights & Activities

Dive sites in the park include **Ko Surin Tai** and **HQ Channel**. **Richelieu Rock** (a seamount 14km southeast) is also technically in the park and happens to be one of the best, if not the best, dive site on the Andaman Coast. There's no dive facility in the park itself, so dive trips must be booked from the mainland. Bleaching has damaged some of the hard corals but you'll see plenty of fish and soft corals.

Snorkelling trips (150B per person, two hours, 9am and 2pm) leave from the park headquarters, or contact **Greenview** (☑076 472070; greenviewtour99@gmail.com; Tha Khuraburi; adult/child one-day tour 3500/2100B; ☺7.30am-9pm).

After the tsunami in 2004, a community of *chow lair* (sea gypsies; also spelled *chao leh*) settled in a sheltered bay on Ko Surin Tai. Their village is called **Ban Moken**, 'moken' being the local term for these nomadic seafarers. The national park runs trips from Ko Surin Neua to Ban Moken (150B, minimum five people, two hours). A major ancestral worship ceremony (Loi Reua) takes place in April.

🛏 Sleeping & Eating

Decent **park accommodation** (☑076 472145; www.dnp.go.th; Ko Surin Neua; d/q 2000/3000B, camping site per person 80B, with tent hire 300B; ☺mid-Oct–mid-May; ❄) includes bungalows and a campground, but because of the island's short, narrow beaches it can feel seriously crowded when full (around 300 people).

❶ Getting There & Away

Tour operators use speedboats (1700B roundtrip, 1¼ hours, 9am). Several tour operators run day trips from Khao Lak. The Surin Islands are also accessible via live-aboard boats that depart from the mainland.

Similan Islands Marine National Park

อุทยานแห่งชาติหมู่ เกาะสิมิลัน

Known to divers the world over, beautiful **Similan Islands Marine National Park** (อุทยานแห่งชาติหมู่เกาะสิมิลัน; ☑076 453272; www. dnp.go.th; adult/child 500/300B; ☺mid-Oct–mid-May) is 70km offshore. Its smooth granite islands are as impressive above water as below, topped with rainforests, edged with white-sand beaches and fringed with coral reefs.

Two of the nine islands, Island 4 (Ko Miang) and Island 8 (Ko Similan), have ranger stations and accommodation; park headquarters and most visitor activity centres are on Island 4.

Khao Lak is the jumping-off point for the park. The pier is at Thap Lamu, about 10km south of town.

⊙ Sights & Activities

The Similans offer diving for all levels of experience, at depths 2m to 30m. No facilities for divers exist in the national park itself, so you'll need to take a dive tour from Hat Khao Lak. Day trippers from Khao Lak usually visit three or four different snorkelling sites (trips from 1900B).

The islands also have some lovely walking trails where you can spot a variety of bird life.

Coral bleaching has affected many of the reefs and unregulated tourism is taking a toll on the natural beauty of the islands. There are often queues to climb viewpoints and some snorkelling outfitters feed the fish, an ecological no-no.

🛏 Sleeping & Eating

Park accommodation (☑076 453272, in Bangkok 02 562 0760; www.dnp.go.th; r fan/aircon 1100/2000B, camping with tent hire 570B; ☺mid-Oct–mid-May; ❄) can be booked online or through the national park office at Thap Laum pier in Hat Khao Lak. Ko Miang has bungalows, longhouses and camp sites; there's electricity from 6pm to 6am. There is also a restaurant on Ko Miang.

❶ Getting There & Away

There's no public transport to the park so you'll have to join a tour; most tours spend the night in the park so it is almost like you did it yourself.

Phuket

ภูเก็ต

POP 94,325

The island of Phuket has long been misunderstood. First of all, the 'h' is silent. Ahem. And second, Phuket doesn't feel like an island at all. It's so huge (the biggest in the country) that one can never really get the sense that they're surrounded by water. Dubbed the 'pearl of the Andaman' by savvy marketing execs, this is Thailand's original tailor-made fun-in-the-sun resort.

Phuket's beating heart can be found in Patong, a 'sin city' that is the ultimate gong show where podgy beachaholics sizzle like rotisserie chickens and go-go girls play ping-pong – without paddles...

These days, however, Phuket's affinity for luxury far outshines any of its old-school hedonism. Jet-setters touch down in droves, getting pummelled at swanky spas and swigging sundowners at fashion-forward nightspots.

Phuket Province

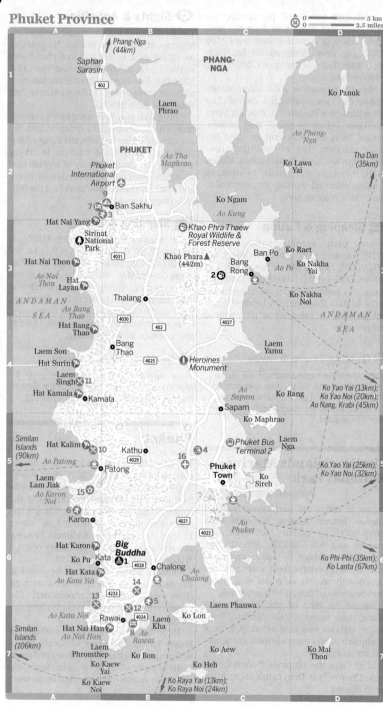

Phang-Nga
(44km)

PHANG-
NGA

Saphan
Sarasin

402

Laem
Phrao

Ko Panuk

PHUKET

Ao Tha
Maphrao

Ao Phang-
Nga

Tha Dan
(35km)

Phuket
International
Airport

Ko Lawa
Yai

9

7

3

Ban Sakhu

Ko Ngam

Hat Nai Yang

Ao Kung

Sirinat
National
Park

4031

Khao Phra Thaew
Royal Wildlife &
Forest Reserve

Ko Raet

Ban Po

Hat Nai Thon

Khao Phara
(442m)

Bang
Rong

Ko Nakha
Yai

Ao Po

Ao Nai
Thon

Hat
Layan

2

Ko Nakha
Noi

ANDAMAN
SEA

Ao Bang
Thao

Thalang

ANDAMAN

SEA

Hat Bang
Thao

4030

402

4027

Laem Son

Bang
Thao

4025

Laem
Yamu

Hat Surin

Heroines
Monument

Laem
Singh

11

Ao
Sapam

Ko Rang

Ko Yao Yai (13km);
Ko Yao Noi (20km);
Ao Nang, Krabi (45km)

Hat Kamala

Kamala

Sapam

Ko Maphrao

Similan
Islands
(90km)

Hat Kalim

10

Kathu

4029

16

4

Phuket Bus
Terminal 2

Laem
Nga

Ao Patong

Patong

Phuket
Town

Ko
Sireh

Ko Yao Yai (25km);
Ko Yao Noi (32km)

Laem
Lam Jiak

15

Ao Karon
Noi

6

Karon

4021

4023

Ao
Phuket

Hat Karon

Big
Buddha

1

Ko Phi-Phi (35km);
Ko Lanta (67km)

Ko Pu

Kata

4028

Chalong

Ao
Chalong

Hat Kata

14

Ao Kata Yai

Laem Phanwa

13

4233

12

5

Ao Kata Noi

Rawai

4024

Laem
Kha

Ko Lon

Similan
Islands
(106km)

Hat Nai Han
Ao Nai Han

8

Ao
Rawai

Laem
Phromthep

Ko Bon

Ko Aew

Ko Heh

Ko Mai
Thon

Ko Kaew
Yai

Ko Kaew
Noi

Ko Raya Yai (13km);
Ko Raya Noi (24km)

0   5 km
0   2.5 miles

Phuket Province

Shoestringers should treat Phuket as a splurge for its seaside setting and high-end dining.

◎ Sights

Phuket's stunning west coast, scalloped by sandy bays, faces the crystal Andaman Sea. **Patong** is the eye of the tourist storm, with **Kata** and **Karon** – Patong's little brothers – to the south. **Phuket Town** is the provincial capital and home to wonderful Sino-Portuguese architecture, dating back to the island's shipping days; many of these stately buildings have been revitalised by artsy entrepreneurs, making Phuket Town a hip, cultural venue.

★ **Big Buddha**   BUDDHIST
(พระใหญ่; www.mingmongkolphuket.com; off Rte 4021; ⊙6am-7pm; Ⓟ) FREE High atop the Nakkerd Hills, northwest of Chalong circle, and visible from half of the island, the 45m-high Big Buddha sits grandly on Phuket's finest viewpoint. Though it's a tad touristy, tinkling bells and flapping flags give this space

an energetic pulse. Pay your respects at the tented golden shrine, then step up to Big Buddha's glorious plateau, where you can peer into Kata's perfect bay, glimpse the shimmering Karon strand and, to the southeast, survey the pebble-sized channel islands of Chalong Bay.

Phuket Gibbon Rehabilitation Project   WILDLIFE SANCTUARY
(โครงการคืนชะนีสู่ป่า; ☑076 260492; www.gibbonproject.org; off Rte 4027; admission by donation; ⊙9am-4.30pm, to 3pm Thu; Ⓟ) ✎ Financed by donations (1800B cares for a gibbon for a year), this tiny sanctuary adopts gibbons that have been kept in captivity in the hope that they can be reintroduced to the wild. The centre has volunteer opportunities that include providing educational information to visitors, cleaning cages, feeding and tracking released gibbons. Swing by around 9am to hear the gibbons' morning song. Note that you can't get too close to them, which may disappoint kids, but the volunteer work done here is outstanding.

🏃 Activities

Diving & Snorkelling
Phuket isn't the cheapest place to dive but it is centrally located to many renowned sites in the Andaman. Decent snorkelling spots can be found in Hat Nai Yang and Hat Kamala or it's possible to day-trip to nearby islands.

Sea Fun Divers   DIVING
(☑076 340480; www.seafundivers.com; 29 Soi Karon Nui; 2/3 dives 4100/4500B, Open Water certification 18,400B; ⊙9am-6pm) An outstanding, very professional diving operation, with high standards, impeccable service and keen, knowledgeable instructors. They're based at Le Meridien resort at the southern end of Patong; there's a **second location** (☑076 330124; www.seafundivers.com; Katathani, 14 Th Kata Noi; ⊙9am-6pm) in Kata Noi.

Sea Kayaking

★ **John Gray's Seacanoe**   KAYAKING
(☑076 254505; www.johngray-seacanoe.com; 86 Soi 2/3, Th Yaowarat; adult/child from 3950/1975B) ✎ The original, the most reputable and by far the most ecologically sensitive kayaking company on Phuket. The Hong by Starlight trip dodges the crowds, involves sunset paddling and will introduce you to Ao Phang-Nga's famed after-dark bioluminescence. Like any good brand in Thailand, John

THAILAND PHUKET

DON'T MISS

PHUKET TOWN'S SINO-PORTUGUESE ARCHITECTURE

Stroll along Ths Thalang, Dibuk, Yaowarat, Ranong, Phang-Nga, Rassada and Krabi for a glimpse of Phuket Town's Sino-Portuguese architectural treasures. The most magnificent examples are the **Standard Chartered Bank** (Th Phang-Nga), Thailand's oldest foreign bank and the old post office building, which now houses the **Phuket Philatelic Museum** (Th Montri; ⊘10am-5pm Mon-Sat) FREE. Some of the most colourfully revamped buildings line Soi Romanee, off Th Thalang, once home to brothels, gamblers and opium dens.

Stop in at the **Phuket Thaihua Museum** (พิพิธภัณฑ์ภูเก็ตไทยหัว; ☑076 211224; 28 Th Krabi; 200B; ⊘9am-5pm) for a dose of Phuket's multicultural history.

The best-restored residential properties lie along Ths Thalang, Dibuk and Krabi. The fabulous 1903 Phra Phitak Chyn Pracha Mansion has been refurbished into the upscale **Blue Elephant restaurant** (☑076 354355; www.blueelephant.com; 96 Th Krabi; mains 670-1000B, set menus 1350-2400B; ⊘11.30am-2.30pm & 6.30-10.30pm; 🖥🖉) and **culinary school** (☑076 354355; www.blueelephant.com; 96 Th Krabi; half-day class 3270B).

Gray's 'Seacanoe' name and itineraries have been frequently copied. He's 3.5km north of Phuket Town.

Surfing

Decent surfing occurs from June to September. **Phuket Surf** (☑087 889 7308; www.phuketsurfing.com; Hat Kata Yai; lesson 1500B, board rental per hr/day 150/500B; ⊘8am-7pm Apr–late Oct) is a good spot for rentals and information.

Kiteboarding

The best spots are in Hat Nai Yang, Karon and Rawai (ideal for beginners). Phuket's kiteboarding operators – **Kiteboarding Asia** (☑081 591 4594; www.kiteboardingasia.com; Hat Nai Yang; 1hr lesson 1300B, 3-day course 11,000B; ⊘Apr-Oct), **Kite Zone** (☑083 395 2005; www.kitesurfthailand.com; Hat Friendship; 1hr lesson 1100B, 3-day course 10,000-15,000B) and **Bob's Kite School Phuket** (☑092 459 4191; www.kiteschoolphuket.com; Hat Nai Yang; 1hr lesson 1500B, 3hr course 3500B; ⊘May–mid-Oct) – are affiliated with the International Kiteboarding Organization.

☞ Tours

Amazing Bike Tours　　CYCLING
(☑087 263 2031; www.amazingbiketoursthailand.asia; 191 Th Patak East, Hat Kata; day trip adult/child 2900/2500B) This highly popular Kata-based adventure outfitter leads small groups on half-day bicycle tours through Khao Phra Thaew Royal Wildlife & Forest Reserve. It also runs terrific day trips around Ko Yao Noi and more challenging three-day adventures rides around Khao Sok National Park (14,900B) and Krabi Province (15,900B).

Prices include bikes, helmets, meals, water and national park entry fees.

✿ Festivals

The annual **Vegetarian Festival** (www.phuketvegetarian.com; ⊘late Sep–Oct) takes place in late September or October and is a cacophonous and colourful street procession of trancelike worshippers performing acts of self-mortification.

🛏 Sleeping

🛏 Phuket Town

Phuket Town has a healthy assortment of budget-friendly options, but you'll have to commute to the beach.

Ai Phuket Hostel　　HOSTEL $
(☑076 212881; www.aiphukethostel.com; 88 Th Yaowarat; dm 259B, d 650-850B; 🕸@🛜) Doubles are tight but full of character with wood floors, black-and-white photos, muralled ceilings and, for some, private bathrooms. Dorms are bright, colourful and clean, sleeping six (girls only) to eight. All share polished-concrete hot-water bathrooms and a cramped downstairs hangout lounge.

Best Stay Hostel　　HOSTEL $
(☑099 301 9499; www.beststayhostel.com; 88 Th Phang-Nga; dm/r 250/600B; 🕸🛜) Another fresh Phuket Town hostel, featuring shiny-white eight- to 10-person dorms with gleaming green floors and chunky-framed bunks with individual lamps and white duvets, plus boxy doubles. It's friendly and has a cute tile-floored cafe downstairs.

★ **The RomManee** BOUTIQUE HOTEL **$$**
(☑089 728 9871; www.therommanee.com; Th Romanee; r 1200B; ❄️🛜) On Phuket Town's prettiest street, this 'boutique guesthouse' definitely packs in plenty of style with its turquoise-toned exterior, varnished-concrete floors and wood-block reception bar. The four spacious rooms have an arty modern feel with wood floors, flat screens, colour feature walls, neon-washed chairs and tasteful lighting. Stairs are steep and there's no lift. There's another comfy, less-friendly **branch** (☑076 355488; www.therommanee.com; 4-6 Th Krabi; r 1000-1200B; ❄️🛜) a block away.

🛏 Patong

Patong is crammed with tourists and tourist schlock – you'll either love it or hate it. Budget digs are disappearing but rates drop in the low season.

★ **Lupta Hostel** HOSTEL **$**
(☑076 602462, 092 934 6453; www.luptahostel.com; 138 Th Tawiwong; dm 490-590B, d 1200B; @🛜) Just 100m from Th Bangla, this wonderful, warm, modern newcomer feels more European posh-tel than Patong crashpad. Small, comfy four- to eight-person dorms in light woods and whites share smartish bathrooms. Each bed gets its own locker, plug socket and tiny shelf. Enjoy light breakfast in the social lobby loaded with cushions, high stools and rattan lamps. There's a girls-only dorm.

Patong Backpacker Hostel HOSTEL **$**
(☑076 341196; 140 Th Thawiwong; dm 250-450B; ❄️🛜) This busy budget spot has a great location across the road from the beach and a welcoming communal lounge. Colour-walled dorms sleep three to 10. The top floor is brightest, but dorms on the lower floors have their own attached bathroom.

Red Planet HOTEL **$$**
(☑076 341936; www.redplanethotels.com; 56 Th Rat Uthit; r 1200-2500B; 🅿️❄️🛜) Part of a budding Southeast Asian brand, this red-and-white block offers no-frills, tidy, three-star living. And it works. Rooms are a tight fight, but smart, cushy and well-equipped with wood floors, hairdryers and plush linens.

🛏 Southern Beaches

South of Patong, the vibe mellows out in increments. Hat Karon is the most hyperactive of the bunch. Hat Kata is more well-heeled yet still social, and Hat Nai Han is a beautiful beach, best for a day's ocean frolic rather than a budget sleep. Way down south, Rawai is carved out of lush rolling hills.

Rumblefish Adventure HOSTEL **$**
(☑076 330315; www.rumblefishadventure.com; 98/79 Th Kata, Hat Kata; dm 250-300B, d 800B; ❄️🛜) A water-sports flop house offering reasonably clean doubles with private bathrooms, hot water and air-con. Dorms sleep three to six and are airy with turquoise accent walls. The priciest are girls-only and come with air-con and their own bathroom. It's one of many guesthouses in the Beach Centre complex.

Fantasy Hill Bungalow BUNGALOW **$**
(☑076 330106; fantasyhill@hotmail.com; 8/1 Th Kata, Hat Kata; r fan 500-650B, air-con 900-1200B; 🅿️❄️🛜) Tucked into a lush garden on a low-rise hill, longstanding Fantasy Hill is peaceful and central. The ageing but well-maintained bungalows offer great value and staff are super sweet. Go for a corner air-con room with views across Kata and beyond.

Pineapple Guesthouse GUESTHOUSE **$**
(☑076 396223; www.pineapplephuket.com; 291/4 Karon Plaza, Hat Karon; dm 280B, r fan/air-con 500/1100B; ❄️🛜) Pocketed away 400m inland from Hat Karon, Pineapple is an excellent budget choice under warm Thai-English management. It's full of brilliantly kept, bright hot-water rooms adorned with colourful feature walls, fridges and, in some cases, small balconies, and there's a simple, clean 10-bed dorm.

Good 9 at Home GUESTHOUSE **$**
(☑088 457 6969; www.facebook.com/good9athome; 62 Mu 6, Soi Wassana, Hat Rawai; r incl breakfast 900B; ❄️🛜) Beside a cute patio, these seven small but wonderfully fresh, gleaming contemporary-style rooms spiced

THAILAND PHUKET

ℹ️ **PHUKET TAXIS**

Once run by a notorious mafia that charged outrageous rates, Phuket's taxis have been reined in with maximum fare limits and drivers who actually use the meters. If you find a reliable taxi driver, get their phone number and use them for on-call service. Uber and GrabTaxi are providing some much-needed competition, too.

up with colour feature walls, tiled bathrooms and the odd bit of artwork make for good-value digs, 300m up the street from Hat Rawai. The lime-green-and-grey house is kept clean, cosy and friendly, with a thoughtful little coffee corner thrown into the mix.

★ **Bazoom Haus** GUESTHOUSE $$
(☑076 396414; www.bazoomhostel.com; 269/5 Mu 3, Karon Plaza, Hat Karon; dm 400B, r 2300-3500B; ❄️☂️) The bold modern exterior suggests something special. Fabulous doubles have wood floors and furnishings, concrete walls, recessed lighting, mosaic showers and, for some, private terraces. There are DJ decks and colourful art in the polished-concrete, in-house Korean restaurant (the helpful young owners are Korean), plus a dive shop. Dorms sleep six. Up to 60% off in low season.

🛏 Northern Beaches

The northern beaches are sublime and so are the luxury rates. Hike up past the resorts to the Sirinat National Park for beauty on a budget.

Sirinat National Park Accommodation CAMPGROUND, BUNGALOW $
(☑076 327152, in Bangkok 02 562 0760; www.dnp.go.th; Hat Nai Yang; camping per person 30B, bungalow 700-1000B) At the park headquarters at the north end of Hat Nai Yang you'll find campsites (bring your own tent) and large, concrete, air-con bungalows just back from the beach on a gorgeous, shady, white-sand bluff. Book ahead online or by phone.

Discovery Beach Resort GUESTHOUSE $
(☑082 497 7500; discovery-phuket@hotmail.com; 90/34 Mu 5, Hat Nai Yang; r fan/air-con 800/1500B; ❄️☂️) With wooden Thai accents on the facade, lacquered timber handrails and furnishings, and fridges in the rooms, this spotless budget place is a perfectly decent choice. It's nothing fancy, but the location – right on the beach – makes it great value.

✖ Eating

✖ Phuket Town

There's great, local food in Phuket Town, and meals cost a lot less than those at the beach.

Kopitiam by Wilai THAI $
(☑083 606 9776; www.facebook.com/kopitiambywilai; 18 Th Thalang; mains 80-120B; ☺11am-10pm Mon-Sat; ☂️) Kopitiam serves Phuket soul food. It does Phuketian *pàt tai* (thin rice noodles with egg, tofu and/or shrimp) with a kick, and a fantastic *mee sua*: noodles sautéed with egg, greens, prawns, chunks of sea bass, and squid. Wash it all down with fresh chrysanthemum or passionfruit juice.

The Cook THAI, FUSION $
(☑076 258375; 101 Th Phang-Nga; mains 65-240B; ☺8am-9.30pm Tue-Sun) The Thai owner-chef used to cook Italian at a mega-resort, so when he opened this ludicrously inexpensive Old Town restaurant he successfully fused the two cultures. Try one of the sensational green chicken curry or *dôm yam* (spicy Thai soup) pizzas, or a classic pasta plate, and you'll see what the fuss is about.

★ **Suay** INTERNATIONAL, THAI $$
(☑081 797 4135; www.suayrestaurant.com; 50/2 Th Takua Pa; mains 15-400B; ☺5pm-midnight) Fabulous fusion at this converted house, just south of old town proper, means mouth-melting glass noodle salad, bright pomelo salad with salmon carpaccio and roasted chilli dressing, lamb-chop massaman curry, turmeric-infused sea bass wrapped in banana leaf, smoked eggplant with chilli-coconut dressing and crab meat, and an innovative *sôm-đam* (spicy green papaya salad) featuring flavour-popping mangosteen.

✖ Patong

Bargain seafood and noodle stalls pop up across town at night – try the lanes on and around Th Bangla, or venture over to the **Patong Food Park** (Th Rat Uthit; dishes 50-200B; ☺4.30pm-midnight) once the sun drops.

Chicken Rice Briley THAI $
(☑081 597 8380; Patong Food Park, Th Rat Uthit; meals 50-60B; ☺6am-9pm) One of few diners in Patong Food Park to offer sustenance while the sun shines. Steamed chicken breast is served on a bed of rice with a bowl of chicken broth with crumbled bits of meat; dip it in the fantastic chili sauce. They do a popular stewed pork on rice, plus mango with sticky rice. There's a reason it's perennially packed.

Kaab Gluay
THAI **$**

(☑076 346832; 58/3 Th Phra Barami; dishes 60-165B; ⊙11am-2am; 🛜) It's hardly Patong's most peaceful spot, but this easygoing roadside eatery is a hit for its authentic, affordable Thai food, with switched-on staff and well-spelt (!) English menus to match. Unpretentious dining happens under a huge tin roof. Expect red-curry prawns, chicken satay, sweet-and-sour fish, deep-fried honeyed chicken, classic noodles and stir-fries, and 30-plus takes on spicy Thai salads.

★Home Kitchen
INTERNATIONAL **$$$**

(☑093 764 6753; www.facebook.com/HOME.kitchen.bar.bed; 314 Th Phra Barami, Hat Kalim; mains 300-800B; ⊙5am-1am; 🛜) White leather, faded tables, floaty fabrics, burning lanterns and neon lighting crash together with Mediterranean flair. This crazily beautiful, quirky-chic dining room/cocktail bar shaped like a ship's hull is a stunning work of art. And the creative Thai-Mediterranean food is fab, too. Try avocado and crabmeat salad, squid-ink pasta with salmon, massaman Wagyu beef, deep-fried *pá·naang*-curry sea bass and perfectly crispy Parmesan-coated chips.

🍴 Southern Beaches

★Pad Thai Shop
THAI **$**

(Th Patak East, Hat Karon; dishes 50B; ⊙9am-6pm) This glorified roadside food shack does rich, savoury chicken stew and absurdly good *kôw pàt bòo* (crab fried rice), *pàt see·éw* (fried noodles) and noodle soup. It also serves up some of the best *pàt tai* we've ever tasted: spicy and sweet, packed with tofu, egg and peanuts, and plated with a side of spring onions, beansprouts and lime. Don't miss the house-made chilli sauces.

Kata Mama
THAI **$**

(Hat Kata Yai; mains 50-400B; ⊙8am-9pm) Our pick of several cheapie seafood huts hidden at the southern end of Hat Kata Yai, Kata Mama keeps busy thanks to its charming management, reliably tasty Thai standards and low-key beachside setting.

Mama Noi's
THAI, ITALIAN **$**

(Karon Plaza, Hat Karon; mains 90-185B; ⊙9am-10pm; 🛜) This simple tile-floored cafe with faded photos of Italy, a good local vibe and dangling pot-plants has been feeding the expat masses for a generation. They do fantastic versions of all the Thai dishes plus a huge list of popular pastas – anyone for red-curry spaghetti? Cheap, tasty and friendly.

Som Tum Lanna
THAI **$**

(☑081 597 0569; 3/7 Th Sai Yuan, Hat Rawai; mains 80-150B; ⊙9am-5pm Tue-Sun) When it comes to *sôm·đam*, order it mild – it'll still bring some serious heat. And while the fish at this Isan soul-food shack is good, its equal exists elsewhere. The chicken, on the other hand, is outstanding.

★Sabai Corner
INTERNATIONAL, THAI **$$**

(☑089 875 5525; www.facebook.com/Sabai-Corner-150517525037992; Hat Kata, off Rte 4233; mains 100-400B; ⊙10am-10pm; 🛜) There's no better Phuket view than the one you'll glimpse from this wide deck: all the way to Karon in one direction and an endless horizon of blue ocean wrapping around the island in the other. It's rare that a location like this gets the restaurant it deserves, but this popular Thai-Swiss-American–owned indoor-outdoor eatery is a stellar nature-fringed find frequented by local expats.

★Rum Jungle
INTERNATIONAL **$$$**

(☑076 388153; www.facebook.com/Rum-Jungle-Cafe-Rawai-Phuket-173738946050909; 69/8 Mu 1, Th Sai Yuan; mains 240-620B; ⊙11.30am-2pm & 6-10.30pm; 🚗) One of Rawai's finest, this semi-open thatched-roof restaurant with an exceptional world-beat soundtrack is family-run and spearheaded by a terrific Aussie chef. The New Zealand lamb shank is divine, as are the steamed clams, and the pasta sauces are all made from scratch. Tempting vegie choices include aubergine parmigiana and pasta Gorgonzola.

★Boathouse Wine & Grill
INTERNATIONAL **$$$**

(☑076 330015; www.boathousephuket.com; 182 Th Koktanod, Hat Kata; mains 470-1750B; tasting menu 1800-2200B; ⊙11am-10.30pm) The perfect place to wow a special date, this is the pick of the bunch for many a local foodie. The atmosphere can feel a little old-school stuffy, but it's all very glam – plus the Thai and Mediterranean food (think: tiger prawn risotto and lobster soufflé) is fabulous, the wine list famously expansive and the sea views sublime. Special sharing platters are prepared at your table.

🍴 Northern Beaches

Meena Restaurant
THAI **$**

(Hat Kamala; mains 80-150B; ⊙9am-5pm) This family-run beachside shack with rainbow-striped and leopard-print sarongs for tableclothes is a real find. The owners couldn't be more welcoming. The tasty authentic Thai food is exceptional and so are the fresh fruit shakes. The rustic setting is exactly what you (most likely) came to Kamala for. It's at the north end of the beach.

 Drinking & Entertainment

 Phuket Town

Ka Jok See　　　　　　　　　　CLUB
(☑076 217903; kajoksee@hotmail.com; 26 Th Takua Pa; buffet per person 2500B; ☺8pm-1am Nov-Apr, reduced hours May-Oct) Dripping with Old Phuket charm and the owner's fabulous trinket collection, this intimate century-old house has two identities: half glamorous eatery, half crazy party venue. There's good Thai food, but once the tables are cleared it becomes a bohemian madhouse party with top-notch music and – if you're lucky – some sensationally extravagant cabaret. Book a month or two ahead. There's no sign.

Timber Hut　　　　　　　　　　CLUB
(☑076 211839; 118/1 Th Yaowarat; ☺6pm-2am) Thai and expat locals have been packing out this two-floor pub-club nightly for 25 years, swilling whiskey and swaying to live bands that swing from hard rock to pure pop to hip-hop. No cover charge.

Patong

Th Bangla is Patong's beer and bar-girl mecca and features a number of spectacular go-go extravaganzas, where you can expect the usual mix of gyrating Thai girls and often red-faced Western men.

★**Seduction**　　　　　　　　　　CLUB
(www.facebook.com/seductiondisco; 70/3 Th Bangla; ☺10pm-5am) International DJs, professional-grade sound system and forever the best dance party on Phuket, without question.

Sole Mio　　　　　　　　　　　　BAR
(☑081 5378116; Th Thawiwong; ☺10am-midnight; 🛜) A whimsically decorated Caribbean-feel bar, crafted from reused corrugated tin, strings of shells and reclaimed pastel-washed wood. It's right by the beach, pulses with pop songs and is fuelled by middling cocktails and Chang draught. There are worse ways to spend an afternoon.

Phuket Simon Cabaret　　　　CABARET
(☑076 342114; www.phuket-simoncabaret.com; 8 Th Sirirach; adult 700-800B, child 500-600B;

☺shows 6pm, 7.45pm & 9.30pm) About 500m south of town, Simon puts on fun, colourful trans cabarets. The 600-seat theatre is grand, the costumes are glittery, feathery extravaganzas and the ladyboys are convincing. It's noticeably geared towards an Asian audience and the house is usually full – book ahead.

Bangla Boxing Stadium　　SPECTATOR SPORT
(☑076 273416; www.banglaboxingstadiumpatong.com; Th Pangmuang Sai Kor; admission 1700-2500B; ☺9pm Wed, Fri & Sun) Old name, same game: a packed line-up of competitive *moo·ay tai* bouts featuring Thai and foreign fighters.

 Southern Beaches

★**Ska Bar**　　　　　　　　　　　BAR
(www.skabar-phuket.com; 186/12 Th Koktanod; ☺noon-late) Tucked into rocks on the southernmost curl of Hat Kata Yai and seemingly intertwined with the trunk of a grand old banyan tree, Ska is our choice for seaside sundowners. The Thai bartenders add to the laid-back Rasta vibe, and buoys, paper lanterns and flags dangle from the canopy. Hang around if there's a fire show.

ℹ **Dangers & Annoyances**

During May to October, large waves and fierce undertows make it too dangerous to swim, especially at certain beaches; red-flag warnings are posted when conditions are rough.

Phuket's roads are congested with erratic road rules. It is not advised to rent a motorcycle, especially for inexperienced drivers, as vehicle accidents and fatalities are common. If you do drive a motorbike, wear a helmet and protective clothing and keep your belongings on your person, not in the basket. Do not drink and drive.

ℹ **Information**

The English-language *Phuket Gazette* (www.phuketgazette.net) is a news and lifestyle weekly.

Phuket International Hospital (☑076 361818, 076 249400; www.phuketinternationalhospital.com; 44 Th Chalermprakiat) International doctors rate this hospital as the island's best.

Post Office (Th Montri; ☺8.30am-4.30pm Mon-Fri, 9am-noon Sat & Sun)

Tourism Authority of Thailand (TAT; ☑076 211036; www.tourismthailand.org/Phuket; 191 Th Thalang; ☺8.30am-4.30pm) Has maps, brochures, transport advice and info on boat trips to nearby islands.

Tourist Police (☑1669, 076 342719; cnr Th Thawiwong & Th Bangla)

❶ Getting There & Away

AIR

Phuket International Airport (☑076 327230; www.phuketairportthai.com) is 30km north-west of Phuket Town; it takes around 45 minutes to an hour to reach the southern beaches from here. An orange government airport bus runs between the airport and Phuket Town (100B, one hour, from 6.30am to 8.30pm); taxis to the airport start at 550B.

Flights to Bangkok are handled by Air Asia, Bangkok Airways and Thai Airways International. Direct international destinations, in Asia, are also served; frequencies and destinations often increase during high season.

BOAT

Tha Rasada, 3km southeast of Phuket Town, is the main pier for boats to Ko Phi-Phi and other southern Andaman islands. Boats to Krabi and Ao Nang via the Ko Yao Islands leave from Tha Bang Bong, 26km north of Tha Rasada.

BUS & MINIVAN

Phuket Bus Terminal 2 (Th Thepkrasattri) is 4km north of Phuket Town. Minivans to the Gulf Coast and the southern Andaman coast leave from nearby.

❶ Getting Around

Large *sŏrng·tăa·ou* run from Th Ranong near Phuket Town's day market to the beaches (25B to 40B, regularly 7am to 6pm).

Túk-túk and taxis should cost about 400B to 600B from Phuket Town to the beaches. Motorcycle rentals (300B) are widely available but are not recommended for novice riders.

Krabi Town กระบี่

POP 30,882

Krabi Town is the jumping-off point to the karst-studded Krabi peninsula. The town is well stocked for transiting travellers with lodging, amenities and transport.

🛏 Sleeping

Krabi has an exceptional and ever-improving guesthouse scene; flashpackers should head to Ao Nang.

★Pak-Up Hostel HOSTEL $
(☑075 611955; www.pakuphostel.com; 87 Th Utarakit; dm 280-390B, d 400-500B; ❉@🛜) This snazzy hostel features super-contemporary, polished-cement four- to 10-bed air-con dorms with big wooden bunks built into the wall, each with its own locker. Massive, modern shared bathrooms have cold-water stalls and hot-water rain showers. The two doubles share bathrooms and women-only dorms are available. There are two on-site bars and a young, fun-loving, club-like vibe; you'll never want to leave.

Chan Cha Lay GUESTHOUSE $
(☑075 620952; www.lovechanchalay.com; 55 Th Utarakit; r fan 350-600B, air-con 450-800B; ❉@🛜) The en-suite, air-con rooms at ever-busy Chan Cha Lay, done up in Mediterranean blues and whites with white-pebble and polished-concrete open-air bathrooms, are among Krabi's most comfortable and full of character. Shared-bathroom, fan-only rooms are plainer but spotless, with firm beds. Service ranges from rude to delightful.

Hometel GUESTHOUSE $
(☑075 622301; hometel_2012@hotmail.com; 7 Soi 10, Th Maharat; r 750B; ❉🛜) A modern,

THAILAND KRABI TOWN

BUS TRANSPORT FROM PHUKET

DESTINATION	BUS TYPE	FARE (B)	DURATION (HR)	FREQUENCY
Bangkok	VIP/air-con	1011/650	13	5 evening departures/hourly 3.30pm-7pm
Chiang Mai	VIP	1826	22	3pm
Hat Yai	VIP/air-con	560/360	7/7	9.45pm/hourly 7.30am-12.30pm, 7.30pm & 9.30pm
Ko Samui	air-con	450	8 (bus/boat)	9am
Ko Pha-Ngan	air-con	550	9½ (bus/boat)	9am
Krabi	air-con/minivan	155/140	3½/3	hourly 6.20am-7pm
Ranong	air-con	250	6	hourly 5.30am-6.10pm
Surat Thani	air-con/minivan	195/200	5/4	8am, 10am, noon & 2pm

friendly boutique sleep with 10 rooms on three floors crafted entirely from polished concrete. Abstract art brings colour, some rooms have two terraces and all have rain showers and high ceilings. The lack of windows might not suit everyone. There's a tour/transport desk plus a sunny cafe serving international breakfasts.

Eating & Drinking

Krabi Town has great market eats. Try the **night market** (Th Khong Kha; meals 30-60B; ☺4-10pm) near the Khong Kha pier. **Playground** (www.facebook.com/krabiplaygroundbar; 87 Th Utarakit; ☺5.30pm-2am; ☎) is Pak-Up's cool courtyard bar.

ⓘ Information

Krabi Immigration Office (☎075 611097; 382 Mu 7, Saithai; ☺8.30am-4.30pm Mon-Fri) Handles visa extensions; 4km southwest of Krabi.

Post Office (Th Utarakit; ☺8.30am-4.30pm Mon-Fri, 9am-noon Sat & Sun)

ⓘ Getting There & Away

AIR

The airport is 14km northeast of Krabi. Most domestic carriers offer flights to/from Bangkok. Bangkok Air has a daily service to Ko Samui, and Air Asia to Chiang Mai. To get to/from the airport, a taxi will cost 350B. A tourist airport bus costs 130B.

BOAT

Boats to Ko Phi-Phi (250B to 300B, 1½ to two hours, four daily) and Ko Lanta (400B, two hours, one daily) leave from the passenger pier at Khlong Chilat, about 4km southwest of Krabi. Travel agencies will arrange free transfers. Schedules vary in the low season.

Take a long-tail boat from Krabi's Khong Kha pier to Hat Raily (150B, 45 minutes, between 7.45am to 6pm).

BUS & MINIVAN

The **Krabi bus terminal** (☎075 663503; cnr Th Utarakit & Hwy 4) is in nearby Talat Kao, about 5km north of Krabi. *Sŏrng·tăa·ou* run from the bus station to central Krabi (50B, frequently 6am to 6.30pm).

Travel agencies run minivans run to popular tourist destinations in southern Thailand but they tend to be uncomfortably overcrowded. The cheaper minivans that leave from the bus terminal are a better deal.

Railay ไร่เลย์

Krabi's fairytale limestone crags come to a dramatic climax at Railay, the ultimate jungle gym for rock-climbing fanatics. Towering karst poke out of the azure waters and from the forested interior. In between are quiet sandy patches from which to view the splendour.

◉ Sights

The picturesque limestone towers are beautiful from land and sea. Hike to **Tham Phra Nang** (Princess Cave), an important shrine for local fishermen. About halfway along the path from Hat Railay East to Hat Phra Nang, a crude path leads up the jungle-cloaked cliff wall to a hidden lagoon known as **Sa Phra Nang** (Holy Princess Pool) with a killer viewpoint. **Tham Phra Nang Nai** (Inner Princess Cave, Diamond Cave; adult/child 200B/free; ☺9am-4.30pm) is another large cave above Hat Railay East.

🏃 Activities

Railay is one of the most scenic spots to go **rock climbing**, with nearly 700 bolted routes, ranging from beginner to challenging advanced climbs, all with unparalleled cliff-top vistas of a marine karst garden. The going rate for climbing courses is 800B to

BUS & MINIVAN TRANSPORT FROM KRABI TOWN

DESTINATION	FARE (B)	DURATION (HR)	FREQUENCY
Bangkok	955-650	12	morning & evening departures
Hat Yai	230	4½	hourly 9am-3.20pm
Ko Lanta	250-300	2½	
Phuket	150	3	every 30min 7.30am-5.30pm
Ranong	210	5	8.30am & noon
Satun	234	5	11am, 1pm & 3pm
Surat Thani	150	2½	hourly 4.30am-4.30pm
Trang	120	2	hourly 9am-3.20pm

1000B for a half-day and 1500B to 2000B for a full day.

Snorkelling trips and overnight kayaking trips to deserted islands can also be arranged.

★ Basecamp Tonsai   ROCK CLIMBING
(✆081 149 9745; www.tonsaibasecamp.com; Hat Ton Sai; half/full day 800/1500B, 3-day course 6000B; ⊘8am-5pm & 7-9pm) Arguably Railay's most professional outfit and big on deep-water soloing (700B).

Highland Rock Climbing   ROCK CLIMBING
(✆084 443 9539; http://highlandrockclimbingthailand.weebly.com; Railay Highlands; half/full day 1000/1800B, 3-day course 6000B; ⊘8am-10pm) If you're sleeping on the mountain, Mr Chao is the man to climb with.

Hot Rock   ROCK CLIMBING
(✆085 641 9842; www.railayadventure.com; Hat Railay East; half/full day 1000/2000B, 3-day course 6000B; ⊘9am-8pm) Owned by one of the granddaddies of Railay climbing, Hot Rock has a good reputation.

King Climbers   ROCK CLIMBING
(✆081 797 8923; www.railay.com; Walking St; half/full day 1000/1800B, 3-day course 6000B; ⊘8.30am-9pm Mon-Fri, to 6pm Sat & Sun) One of the biggest, oldest, most reputable and commercial schools.

🛏 Sleeping & Eating

Midrange and top-end resorts occupy Railay's three primary beaches (Hat Railay West, Hat Railay East and Hat Tham Phra Nang). Budget spots occupy Railay Highlands (500m up the hills from Hat Railay East) and nearby Hat Ton Sai (the next cove over from Hat Railay West).

Rapala Rockwood Resort   BUNGALOW $
(✆075 622586; Hat Railay East; bungalow 800-900B; ☎) These ramshackle wooden bungalows have been spruced up with gleaming paint and hammocks on verandas. Within lie colourful linens, cold-water bathrooms, mosquito nets and fans. There's a teensy paddling pool beside a couple of sun loungers. The hilltop location means breezes, sea panoramas and some steep steps. Walk-ins only.

Railay Cabana   BUNGALOW $
(✆075 621733, 084 534 1928; Railay Highlands; bungalow 500B) Superbly located in a bowl of karst cliffs, this is your tropical hip-

pie mountain hideaway. Creaky yet clean thatched-bamboo bungalows with 24-hour electricity are surrounded by mango, mangosteen, banana and guava groves. It's just north of Tham Phra Nang Nai, inland from Hat Railay East.

Paasook   BUNGALOW $
(✆081 893 9220; juaaup@gmail.com; Hat Ton Sai; bungalow 600-900B) Cheaper, concrete-floored cells are clean and just about do-able, but wooden cottages are huge, with floor-to-ceiling windows and tiled bathrooms. The gardens are lush and management is friendly.

Railay Garden View   BUNGALOW $$
(✆085 888 5143; www.railaygardenview.com; Hat Railay East; bungalow incl breakfast 1450-1950B; ☎) A collection of tin-roof, woven-bamboo and shiny-wood bungalows, stilted between tropical gardens high above the mangroves at the northeastern end of the beach. Some look weather-beaten from outside, but all are spacious and decently lit, graced with Thai fabrics, creative concrete bathrooms and floor cushions. Bring mosquito repellent and a torch for after-dark walks.

Mama's Chicken   THAI $
(Hat Ton Sai; 70-100B; ⊘7am-10pm; 🖉) Relocated to the jungle path leading inland to Hat Railay East and West, Mama's remains one of Ton Sai's favourite food stops for its international breakfasts, fruit smoothies and extensive range of cheap Thai dishes, including a rare massaman tofu and other vegetarian-friendly adaptations.

❶ Getting There & Around

Long-tail boats to Railay run from Khong Kha pier in Krabi (150B, 45 minutes, 7.45am to 6pm) when full (eight passengers). The *Ao Nang Princess* stops at Hat Railay West en route to Ko Phi-Phi (450B, two hours, daily November to April); service is less frequent from May to October).

The next bay over from Railay is Ao Nang, which has land access to Krabi Town. Ao Nang is accessible by boat from Hat Railay West and Hat Ton Sai (100/150B day/night, 15 minutes, with eight passengers). From Ao Nang, *sŏrng·tăa·ou* and buses go to Krabi Town (50B, 20 minutes) and Krabi airport (150B, hourly from 9am to 5pm). There are also minivans to other southern Thai locations from Ao Nang.

North of Ao Nang is Hat Noppharat, a national park with speedboat access to Phuket (1200B, 1¼ hours, 11am from November to April).

Ko Phi-Phi

เกาะพีพีดอน

With movie-star good looks, Ko Phi-Phi lives life in the fast lane with hedonistic parties and a drunken abandon. The island is still a stunner: craggy cliffs, curvy, blonde beaches and bodacious jungles. But it isn't a peaceful idyll: boats unload tons of package tourists and bars terrorise the night's slumber. On the plus side there are still cheap places to stay and the carless island isn't nearly as chaotic as Thailand's paved beaches.

🏃 Activities

Diving & Snorkelling

Crystal-clear Andaman water and abundant marine life make the perfect recipe for top-notch scuba. An Open Water certification course costs around 13,800B, while the standard two-dive trips cost from 2500B to 3500B. Snorkelling day trips start at 700B and there are good spots on Ko Mai Phai.

Adventure Club   DIVING

(☏ 081 895 1334; www.diving-in-thailand.net; Ton Sai Village; 2 dives 2500B, Open Water certification 13,800B; ⊙ 8am-10pm) 🤿 Our favourite Phi-Phi diving operation runs an excellent assortment of educational, responsible diving and snorkelling tours. You won't mind getting up at 6am for the popular shark-watching snorkel trips (800B) on which you're guaranteed to cavort with at least one reef shark.

Rock Climbing

There are some good rock-climbing outfitters on the island. Try **Ibex Climbing & Tours** (☏ 075 601370, 084 309 0445; www.ibex climbingandtours.com; Ton Sai Village; half/full day 1100/1950B).

👉 Tours

Ever since Leo smoked a spliff in the movie adaptation of Alex Garland's novel *The Beach,* uninhabited **Ko Phi-Phi Leh,** with

Ko Phi-Phi Don

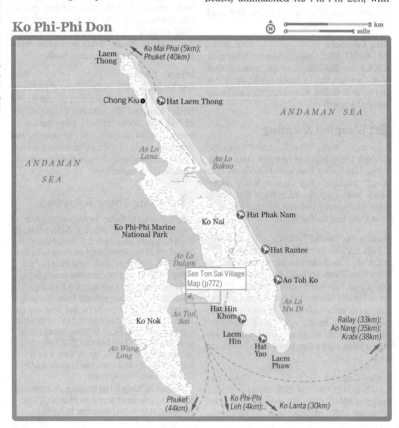

0 ————————— 2 km
0 ————————— 1 mile

Ko Mai Phai (5km);
Phuket (40km)

Laem Thong

Chong Kiu ● ○ Hat Laem Thong

ANDAMAN SEA

Ao Lo Lana

Ao Lo Bakao

ANDAMAN SEA

Ko Phi-Phi Marine National Park

Ko Nai

🐾 Hat Phak Nam

🐾 Hat Rantee

Ao Lo Dalam

See Ton Sai Village Map (p772)

🐾 Ao Toh Ko

Ao Lo Mu Di

Hat Hin Khom 🐾

Railay (33km);
Ao Nang (35km);
Krabi (38km)

Ao Ton Sai

Ko Nok

Laem Hin

Hat Yao 🐾

Laem Phaw

Ao Wang Long

Phuket (44km)

Ko Phi-Phi Leh (4km);

Ko Lanta (30km)

its scenic lagoons, has become a pilgrimage site. Most visitors come on a day trip with snorkelling stops. **Maya Bay Sleepaboard** (www.mayabaytours.com; per person 3000B) puts you as close to a Phi-Phi Leh overnight as regulations allow: aboard a boat moored offshore. Or you could forgo all the over-rated athletic torture in favour of **Captain Bob's Booze Cruise** (☑ 084 848 6970; www.phiphiboozecruise.com; women/men 2500/3000B; ⊙ tour 1pm), where you sail around and drink.

🛏 Sleeping

Book in advance during holiday periods and secure your windows and doors to deter break-ins. More and more dorm options are popping up around Ao Lo Dalam.

Blanco HOSTEL $
(☑ 093 638 3781; Ao Lo Dalam; dm 470-625B; ❄ 🛜) This bare-bones (bring your own top sheet!) but modern party hostel offers four- to eight-bed dorms in concrete-floor bamboo chalets. Digs are cramped, there's usually sand on the floor and mattresses are gym-mat hard, but this is where the hard-core revellers stay, thanks to the fun-loving vibe and super-sociable beach bar with cushioned lounges and a pool table.

Ibiza House HOSTEL, HOTEL $
(☑ 075 601274, 080 537 1868; ibizahouseppth@gmail.com; Ao Lo Dalam; dm 450-700B, r incl breakfast 2000-5500B; ❄ 🛜 ⊠) Ibiza House stacks up points for its popular, well-kept (slightly sandy) 10-bed air-con dorms with hot showers, safes, and wi-fi, and lively party atmosphere, and also has a collection of shiny white doubles and 'villas'. All guests can use the pool – which hosts regular Sunday parties.

Rock Backpacker HOSTEL $
(☑ 081 607 3897; Ton Sai Village; dm 300B; r fan/air-con 800/1600B; ❄ 🛜) A proper hostel on the village hill, with clean dorms lined with bunk beds, tiny private rooms, an inviting restaurant-bar and a rugged, graffiti-scrawled exterior. It's still one of Ton Sai's cheaper pads and there's a buzzing backpacker scene – just don't expect a friendly welcome. Walk-ins only.

Oasis Guesthouse GUESTHOUSE $
(☑ 075 601207; 115 Mu 7, Ton Sai Village; r 700-800B; ❄ 🛜) Up the side road east of central Ton Sai you'll find this cute, simple guesthouse with wooden shutters, surrounded by trees. Staff can be surly, but freshly painted rooms have gleaming bathrooms. No reservations: it's first-come, first-served.

JJ Residence HOTEL $$
(☑ 075 601098; www.jjresidence.com; 95 Mu 7, Ton Sai Village; r 2500B; ❄ 🛜 ⊠) Spacious tiled rooms with smart wood panelling, beamed ceilings, duvets, mini fridges, built-in desks and wardrobes and private terraces make this one of Ton Sai's better choices. Rooms on the first floor spill out onto the pool with its feature waterfall. A new, similar-style accommodation block directly opposite should be ready by the time you read this.

Up Hill Cottage BUNGALOW $$
(☑ 075 601124; www.phiphiuphillcottage.com; 140 Mu 7, Ton Sai Village; r fan 1200B, air-con 2000-2500B; ❄ 🛜) These newly renovated, cream-painted wood-panelled bungalows come in cute pastels offset by colourful bed runners and snazzily tiled bathrooms. Most enjoy island views (of varying beauty) from private balconies. Cheaper fan rooms are simple but still clean. It's *slightly* beyond the madness, at the eastern end of the main street heading north from Ton Sai Village. Beware the hundreds of stairs.

🍴 Eating & Drinking

All of your partying needs will be met at **Slinky** (Ao Lo Dalam; ⊙ 9pm-2am), **Ibiza** (Ao Lo

BOATS TO/FROM KO PHI-PHI

DESTINATION	FARE (B)	DURATION (HR)	TO KO PHI-PHI	FROM KO PHI-PHI
Ao Nang	350	1¾	9.30am	3.30pm
Ko Lanta	250-700	1½	8am, 12.30pm, 1pm & 4pm	11.30am & 3pm
Krabi	250-300	1½-2	9am, 10.30am, 1.30pm & 3pm	9am, 10.30am, 1.30pm & 3.30pm
Phuket	250-300	1¼-2	9am, 11am & 3pm	9am, 2pm, 2.30pm & 3.30pm
Railay	350-400	1¼	9.45am	3.30pm

Ton Sai Village

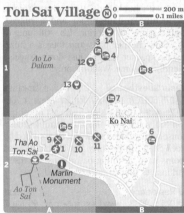

0 — 200 m
0 — 0.1 miles

Ao Lo Dalam

Ko Nai

Tha Ao Ton Sai

Marlin Monument

Ao Ton Sai

Dalam; ⊙9pm-2am) or the mellow **Sunflower Bar** (Ao Lo Dalam; ⊙11am-2am; 🐾).

Local Food Market   MARKET, THAI **$**
(Ton Sai Village; meals 60-80B; ⊙7am-10pm) Phi-Phi's cheapest, most authentic eats are at the market (which was being renovated at research time), on the narrowest sliver of the isthmus. A handful of enthusiastic local stalls serve up scrumptious *pàt tai*, fried rice, *sôm·đam* and smoked catfish.

Papaya Restaurant   THAI **$**
(📋087 280 1719; Ton Sai Village; dishes 100-350B; ⊙10am-10.30pm) Cheap, tasty and spicy.

Here's some real-deal Thai food served in heaping portions. It has your basil and chilli, all the curries, *sôm·đam* and *đôm yam*, too. There's a second branch, **Papaya 2** (📋087 280 1719; Ton Sai Village; dishes 100-350B; ⊙10am-10pm), a block away.

🛈 Getting There & Away

Boats moor at Ao Ton Sai, though a few Phuket boats use the northern pier at Laem Thong. To get to Railay, use the boat bound for Ao Nang.

🛈 Getting Around

There are no roads on Phi-Phi Don so transport on the island is mostly by foot. Long-tails can be chartered from Ao Ton Sai pier to the different beaches for 100B to 600B, depending on distance.

Ko Lanta   เกาะลันตา

POP 20,000

Once the domain of backpackers and *chow lair* (sea gypsies), Lanta has morphed into a midrange, package-tour getaway. But it is infinitely more relaxed than party-hard Ko Phi-Phi and there are still a few cheapies sprinkled across the island.

Ko Lanta is relatively flat compared to the karst formations of its neighbours, so the island can be easily explored by motorbike. A quick trip around reveals a colourful crucible of cultures – fried-chicken stalls sit below slender minarets, creaking *chow lair* villages dangle off the island's side, and small Thai *wát* hide within green-brown tangles of mangroves. Don't miss a visit to **Ban Si Raya** (Old Town), the original port and commercial centre for the island, that retains many 100-year-old wooden stilt houses.

Ko Lanta Marine National Park (อุทยานแห่งชาติหมู่เกาะลันตา; 📋075 660711, in Bangkok 02 561 4292; www.dnp.go.th; adult/child/motorbike 200/100/20B; ⊙8am-6pm) – which protects 15 islands in the Ko Lanta group – can be explored on sea-kayak tours.

Just off-shore are some of Thailand's top diving and snorkelling spots, including the undersea pinnacles of Hin Muang and Hin Daeng. Dive trips cost 3400B to 4500B. **Scubafish** (📋075 665095; www.scubafish.com; Ao Kantiang; 2 dives 3500B; ⊙8am-8pm) is a recommended dive operator.

Time for Lime (📋075 684590; www.timeforlime.net; Hat Khlong Dao; class 1800B; ⊙class 4pm) is a cooking school on Hat Khlong Dao, which funds Lanta Animal Welfare with its profits.

🛌 Sleeping

Some resorts close for the May-to-October low season; others drop rates by 50%. Hat Phra Ae is a large travellers' village and Hat Khlong Khong is a Thai-Rasta enclave. Both have thinning beaches, a problem on much of northern Lanta. White-sand Hat Khlong Nin has lots of small, flashpacker guesthouses. Ao Mai Pai is a lush nearly forgotten cove with one of Lanta's finest beaches. The southern tip of the island at Laem Tanod is a wild and precipitous cliff. Ban Si Raya is an oft-ignored, wonderfully dated village.

★ Bee Bee Bungalows   BUNGALOW $
(📞081 537 9932; Hat Khlong Khong; bungalow 600-900B; ⊗Oct-Apr; 🛜) One of Lanta's best budget spots, Bee Bee's is comprised of a dozen creative bamboo cabins managed by super-friendly staff. Each bungalow is unique; a few are stilted in the trees. The on-site restaurant has a library of tattered paperbacks to keep you occupied while you wait for your delicious Thai staples.

Hutyee Boat   BUNGALOW $
(📞083 633 9723; Hat Phra Ae; bungalow 500-700B) A hidden, hippie paradise of big, solid bungalows on stilts with tiled bathrooms, mini fridges and swinging hammocks in a forest of palms and bamboo. It's just back from the beach (behind Nautilus Resort) and run by a friendly Muslim family.

Andaman Sunflower   BUNGALOW $
(📞089 969 2610, 075 684668; Hat Phra Ae; bungalow 750-1350B; ⊗Oct-Mar; 🛜) Hidden amid bougainvillea- and palm-filled gardens, this is a terrific set of wood and bamboo bungalows with built-in platform beds, high palm-leaf ceilings, polished-wood floors, glass-bowl bathroom sinks and hammock-laden verandas. Set back from the beach, these are some of the best upper-budget bungalows around Hat Phra Ae.

Mu Ko Lanta National Park Accommodation   BUNGALOW, CAMPGROUND $
(📞075 660711, in Bangkok 02 561 4292; www.dnp.go.th; Laem Tanod; bungalow 1500-3000B, camp site per person 40B, with tent hire 300B) Engulfed by craggy outcrops and the sound of crashing waves, the secluded national park headquarters grounds are a gloriously serene place to stay, in simple four- to eight-person bungalows or tents. There are toilets, running water and a shop, but bring your own food. You can also get permission for camping on Ko Rok here.

Sriraya   GUESTHOUSE $
(📞075 697045; punpun_3377@hotmail.com; Ban Si Raya; r with shared bathroom 500B) Sleep in a simple but beautifully restored, thick-beamed Chinese shophouse with plenty of style and a friendly welcome. Walls are brushed in earth tones and sheets are bright. Go for the street-front balcony room overlooking the old town's character-rich centre.

Round House   GUESTHOUSE $$
(📞086 950 9424; www.lantaroundhouse.com; Hat Khlong Nin; r 1600B, bungalow without/with bathroom 600/1500B, house 3000B; ❄🛜) A cute multi-option find on the north end of the beach. Stilted bamboo and wood fan bungalows are simply styled with (mostly) shared hot-water bathrooms, and are just behind the breezy beachfront restaurant. Also available is a cool two-person adobe round house, concrete rooms fronted by porches and an air-con beach house perfect for families. Good low-season and solo-traveller discounts.

Baan Phu Lae   BUNGALOW $$
(📞075 665100, 085 474 0265; www.baanphulae-resort.com; Ao Mai Pai; bungalow fan 1800B, air-con 2000-2400B; ❄🛜) Set on secluded rocks at the northern end of the final beach before Lanta's southern cape, this collection of cute, canary-yellow concrete fan and air-con bungalows have thatched roofs, colourful art, bamboo beds and private porches. Just behind stand stilted, wooden, air-con bungalows. It also arranges diving and snorkelling trips, cooking classes, massages and transport.

✖ Eating

Don't miss the seafood restaurants, like **Lanta Seafood** (Ban Sala Dan; mains 80-250B; ⊗11am-9pm), along the northern edge of Ban Sala Dan. In Ban Ko Lanta, try **Beautiful Restaurant** (📞086 282 1777; Ban Si Raya; mains 100-350B; ⊗10am-9pm; 🛜), where tables are scattered on four piers that extend into the sea.

🍷 Drinking & Nightlife

If you're looking for roaring discotheques, pick another island. If you want a low-key bar scene, head to Hat Phra Ae.

ⓘ Information

Ban Sala Dan has the usual traveller amenities.
Ko Lanta Hospital (📞075 697017; Ban Si Raya) About 1km south of the Ban Si Raya Old Town.
Police Station (📞075 668192; Ban Sala Dan)

ⓘ Getting There & Away

There are two piers at Ban Sala Dan. The passenger jetty is about 300m from the main strip of shops; vehicle ferries leave from a second jetty several kilometres further east. Ferry service varies with the weather and the tourist season; services provided here are for high season only. Minivans are your best option for year-round travel.

DESTINATION	MINIVAN	BOAT
Ko Phi-Phi		250B, 1½hr, 2 daily
Ko Lipe		1700B, 5hr
Krabi (Khlong Chilat pier)		400B, 2hr, 2 daily
Krabi Town/ Airport	300B, 2½/3hr, hourly 7am-4pm	

ⓘ Getting Around

Most resorts provide transfer from the piers. In the opposite direction expect to pay 100B to 400B. Alternatively, you can take a motorcycle taxi from opposite the 7-Eleven in Ban Sala Dan; fares vary from 50B to 400B depending on distance.

Motorcycles (250B per day) can be rented all over the island.

Ko Tarutao Marine National Park

อุทยานแห่ง ชาติหมู่ เกาะตะรุเตา

One of the most exquisite and unspoilt regions in all of Thailand, **Ko Tarutao Marine National Park** (☑ 074 783485; www.dnp.go.th; adult/child 200/100B; ⊙ mid-Oct–mid-May) encompasses 51 barely developed islands surrounded by healthy coral reefs and radiant beaches. The drawback to the lack of civilisation is a lack of infrastructure, especially rubbish removal, which is a problem.

Ko Tarutao is the biggest island in the group but it is still rustic. The national park headquarters and government accommodation are here. Bookings can be made at the **park office** (☑ 074 783485; Pak Bara Pier; ⊙ 8am-5pm) or online. The island closes from the end of May to 15 September. There are no foreign-exchange facilities on the islands – the mainland pier of Pak Bara has services.

Ko Lipe is the marine park's most popular island, having morphed from a hippie backwater to a paved resort in recent years. Budget accommodations are lean. Some of the cheapest options are **Koh Lipe Backpackers Hostel** (☑ 085 361 7923; www.kohlipebackpackers.com; Hat Pattaya; dm 400-500B, r 2500-3000B; ❊ ☎), **The Box** (☑ 086 957 2480; www.theboxliperesort.com; Walking St; r incl breakfast with fan 1200-1900B, air-con 1600-2900B; ❊ ☎) and **Forra Dive** (☑ 084 407 5691; www.forradiving.com; Hat Sunrise; bungalow 1000-1400B; ☎).

ⓘ Getting There & Away

Boats from Pak Bara stop at Ko Tarutao (450B, four daily) and Ko Lipe (650B, 1½ hours). Service runs from 21 October to mid-May with four daily trips.

Tigerline (☑ 081 358 0808, 089 737 0552; www.tigerlinetravel.com) runs high-season (November to late April) ferries from Phuket to Ko Lipe (2400B, eight hours) with stops in Ko Lanta (1700B) and Ko Phi-Phi (1950B). **Satun Pak Bara Speedboat Club** (☑ 099 404 0409, 099 414 4994; www.tarutaolipeisland.com) and **Bundhaya Speedboat** (☑ 081 678 2826, 074 7503889; www.bundhayaspeedboat.com) run from Ko Lanta to Ko Lipe (1900B, three hours, one daily).

GETTING TO MALAYSIA: KO LIPE TO PULAU LANGKAWI

It is easy to island-hop from Ko Lipe to the Malaysian island of Pulau Langkaw. Note: Malaysia is one hour ahead of Thailand.

Getting to the border From Ko Lipe, ferries travel to Pulau Langkawi (1000B to 1400B, 1½ hours, four daily from mid-October to mid-April).

At the border Before departing on the boat, get stamped out of Thailand from the **immigration office** (⊙ 8am-6pm) at the Bundhaya Resort in Ko Lipe. Border formalities on Pulau Langkawi are straightforward and most European nationals receive a visa on arrival.

Moving on Pulau Langkawi has transport connections to the mainland and to Penang.

For information on doing this crossing in reverse, see p415.

UNDERSTAND THAILAND

Thailand Today

Thailand's political situation continues to simmer after nearly a decade of in-fighting over the now-deposed and self-exiled prime minister Thaksin Shinawatra, his self-appointed replacements and the power shift that his tenure ushered in.

On 22 May 2014, the military took control of the country after an all-too familiar popular protest movement occupied the streets of Bangkok. Under the leadership of General Prayut Chan-o-cha, the military-led government (called the National Council for Peace and Order, NCPO) repealed the 2007 constitution, suspended elections with no further notice and suppressed press freedoms and social-media dissent. A slowing economy, weakening currency and several high-profile migrant abuse cases have dogged the 'return to happiness' that the military dictatorship promised. Tourism, however, still carries on, with increasing numbers of visitors, especially from China.

The military junta has forced a much-needed truce between the two political camps – primarily the urban elite and middle classes who want to exorcise the country of all of Thaksin's influences and are comfortable with a suspension of democracy, against the predominately rural and working classes, who support Thaksin and the political power and voice he brought to this under-represented sector of Thai society. Currently the government is working on a new constitution intended to settle the long-standing debate over how much popular representation will exist in the parliament. The first draft was rejected by the National Reform Council, in part because of provisions for an unelected prime minister and for more than half of all senators in parliament to be appointed rather than elected. The elites are clearly coming out ahead lately.

Few observers believe that an election is likely before 2017, and even fewer are confident that the new constitution will end Thailand's political divisions. NCPO appears to be following the model of the country's previous military rulers who dominated the post–Cold War era.

History

Rise of Thai Kingdoms

It is believed that the first Thais migrated southwest from modern-day Yúnnán and Guangxi, China, to what is today known as Thailand. They settled along river valleys and formed small farming communities that eventually fell under the dominion of the expansionist Khmer empire of present-day Cambodia. What is now southern Thailand, along the Malay peninsula, was under the sway of the Srivijaya empire based in Sumatra.

By the 13th and 14th centuries, what is considered to be the first Thai kingdom – Sukhothai (meaning 'Rising Happiness') – emerged and began to chip away at the crumbling Khmer empire. The Sukhothai kingdom is regarded as the cultural and artistic kernel of the modern Thai state.

Sukhothai was soon eclipsed by another Thai power, Ayuthaya, established by King U Thong in 1350. This new centre developed into a cosmopolitan port on the Asian trade route, courted by various European nations. The small nation managed to thwart foreign takeovers, including one orchestrated by a Thai court official – a Greek man named Constantine Phaulkon – to advance French interests. For 400 years and 34 successive reigns, Ayuthaya dominated Thailand until the Burmese led a successful invasion in 1765, ousting the monarch and destroying the capital.

The Thais eventually rebuilt their capital in present-day Bangkok, established by the Chakri dynasty, which continues to occupy the throne today. As Western imperialism marched across the region, King Mongkut (Rama IV, r 1851–68) and his son and successor, King Chulalongkorn (Rama V, r 1868–1910), successfully steered the country into the modern age without becoming a colonial vassal. In return for the country's continued independence, King Chulalongkorn ceded huge tracts of Laos and Cambodia to French-controlled Indochina – an unprecedented territorial loss in Thai history.

A Struggling Democracy

In 1932 a peaceful coup converted the country into a constitutional monarchy, loosely based on the British model. What has followed has been a near-continuous cycle of power struggles among three factions – the elected government, military leaders and the monarchy backed by the aristocrats. These groups occasionally form tenuous allegiances based on mutual dislike for the opposition, and the resulting power grab is often a peaceful military takeover sometimes dubbed the 'smooth as silk' coup.

During the mid-20th century the military dominated the political sphere with an anti-communist position that is widely regarded as being ineffectual except in the suppression of democratic representation and civil rights. In 1973 student activists staged demonstrations calling for a real constitution and the release of political dissidents. A brief respite came, with reinstated voting rights and relaxed censorship. But in October 1976 a demonstration on the campus of Thammasat University in Bangkok was brutally quashed, resulting in hundreds of casualties and the reinstatement of authoritarian rule. Many activists went underground to join armed communist insurgency groups hiding in the northeast.

In the 1980s, as the regional threat of communism subsided, the military-backed Prime Minister Prem Tinsulanonda stabilised the country and moved towards a representative democracy. The military reemerged in 1991 to overthrow the democratically elected government; this was the country's 10th successful coup since 1932. In May 1992, huge demonstrations led by Bangkok's charismatic governor Chamlong Srimuang erupted throughout the city and the larger provincial capitals. The bloodiest confrontation occurred at Bangkok's Democracy Monument, resulting in nearly 50 deaths, but it eventually led to the reinstatement of a civilian government.

Same, Same But Different

Straddling the new millennium, Thailand seemed to have entered an age of democracy. Elected governments oversaw the 1997 enactment of Thailand's 16th constitution, commonly called the 'people's constitution' because it was the first charter in the nation's history not written under military order. The country pulled through the 1997 Asian currency crisis and entered a stable period of prosperity in the early 2000s. Telecommunications tycoon Thaksin Shinawatra and his populist Thai Rak Thai party were elected into power in 2001 and over the next five years effectively engineered one-party rule. With little political opposition, Thaksin consolidated power in all ranks of government, stifling press criticism and scrutiny of his administration.

In 2006 Thaksin was accused of abusing his powers and conflicts of interest, most notably in his family's sale of their Shin Corporation to the Singaporean government for 73 billion baht (US$1.88 billion), a tax-free gain thanks to telecommunications legislation that he helped craft. Meanwhile Thaksin's working-class and rural base rallied behind him, spotlighting longstanding class divides within Thai society.

Behind the scenes the military and the aristocrats forged an allegiance that resulted in the 2006 coup of the Thaksin government. At first the military takeover was heralded as a necessary step in ridding the country of an elected cleptocracy. The military banned Thaksin's political party (Thai Rak Thai), only to have the regenerated (and re-christened) party win the 2007 re-

ERAWAN SHRINE BOMBING

Bangkok has seen its fair share of street protests and violence, but the bomb that detonated in front of the popular and beloved Erawan Shrine on 17 August 2015 was an unfamiliar and unprecedented act of terrorism. The blast killed 20 people, including five Chinese tourists, and wounded 100 more. No group has claimed responsibility for the bombing, but the Thai police offered to the public a very tidy narrative that the attack was retaliation for Thailand's July 2015 deportation of 109 Uighur Muslims back to China. Within two weeks, police arrested suspects who were Turkish nationals or had ties to Turkey, and found in their residences bomb-making supplies and fake Turkish passports – evidence of an international human-trafficking network. (Turkey has cultural and political ties with the Uighurs, who have sought refuge there since clashes with the Chinese government.) According to the police, the alleged mastermind of the Erawan bombing is believed to be a Chinese national who is still at large.

DON'T GET TIED UP BY THAI ETIQUETTE

Master this simple list of dos and don'ts (mainly don'ts) and you'll be an honoured guest.

➡ The king's anthem is played before every movie in a theatre and the national anthem is played twice a day (in the morning and evening) in public places. You are expected to stand respectfully during both.

➡ Thailand is a nonconfrontational culture. Don't get angry; keep your cool and things will work out.

➡ Feet are the lowest and 'dirtiest' part of the body. Keep your feet on the floor, not on a chair. Never touch anyone or point with your foot; never step over someone (or something) sitting on the ground. Take your shoes off when you enter a home or temple.

➡ Dress modestly (cover shoulders and knees) and don't sunbathe topless.

➡ Women aren't allowed to touch or sit next to a monk or his belongings. The very back seat of the bus and the last row on public boats are reserved for monks.

➡ A neat and clean appearance complements Thais' persistent regard for beauty. Frequent daily showers provide natural air-conditioning and a pleasing scent to your neighbours.

➡ Traditionally, Thais greet each other with a *wâi*, a prayerlike gesture. In general, if someone *wâi* you, then return the *wâi* (unless *wâi*-ed by a child or a service person). The placement of the fingertips in relation to the facial features varies with the recipient's social rank and age. The safest, least offensive spot is to place the tips of your fingers to nose level and slightly bow your head.

➡ All images of the king (on money and coins) are treated like holy objects.

THAILAND HISTORY

instatement of elections. In response, the aristocrats staged massive protests in Bangkok that took over the parliament building and closed down the city's two airports for a week in November 2008. This dealt a blow to Thailand's economy just as the US financial crisis was morphing into a global recession.

The Constitutional Court sided with the elites and dissolved the ruling (and popularly elected) party due to a technicality. This decision by the courts was viewed by pro-Thaksin factions as a silent coup. A new coalition was formed in December 2008, led by Oxford-educated Abhisit Vejjajiva, leader of the Democrat party and Thailand's fourth prime minister for the year.

The pro-Thaksin faction (known as 'Red Shirts') retaliated with a crippling, two-month demonstration in Bangkok's central shopping district that was ended in May 2010 through military force. The crackdown resulted in 91 deaths and US$1.5 billion in arson damage.

In an effort to avoid future civilian–military showdowns, elections were held in 2011 and the party that Thaksin had an affiliation with won a clear majority. His sister, Yingluck Shinawatra, became Thailand's first female prime minister. She fulfilled her campaign promise of raising the minimum wage to 300B per day and introduced a populist rice-pledging scheme intended to boost farmers' incomes. The rice-pledging scheme was an expensive flop that bruised the Thai economy. But it was her government's attempt to introduce an amnesty bill that would have allowed Thaksin's return that earned her the infamous title of being the second member of the Shinawatra clan to be removed from office by military coup. On 7 May 2014 Yingluck stepped down and the military junta remains in place today.

The Monarchy

Revered King Bhumibol Adulyadej (Rama IX, r 1946–) defined the contemporary monarch role as a paternal figure who acted with perceived wisdom in times of political crisis. Now 88 years old, the king is the world's longest-serving monarch but as his health has declined, his role in the society at large has diminished. The heir apparent is Crown Prince Vajiralongkorn, the king's son. The king's eldest daughter, Princess Srindhorn, enjoys much public support and carries on many of her father's philanthropic projects.

People & Culture

Thais are laid-back, good-natured people whose legendary hospitality has earned their country a permanent place on the global travel map.

The National Psyche

Paramount to the Thai philosophy of life is sà·nùk (fun) – each day is celebrated with food and conversation, foreign festivals are readily adopted as an excuse for a party and every task is measured on the sà·nùk meter.

The social dynamics of Thai culture can be perplexing. The ideals of the culture are based on Buddhist principles and include humility, gratitude and filial piety. These golden rules are translated into such social conventions as saving face (nâa), in which confrontation is avoided and people endeavour not to embarrass themselves or other people.

An important component of saving face is knowing one's place in society: all relationships in Thai society are governed by conventions of social rank defined by age, wealth, status, and personal and political power. Thais 'size up' a Westerner's social status with a list of common questions: Where are you from? How old are you? Are you married? These questions to a Thai are matters of public record and aren't considered impolite.

Religion and the monarchy, which is still regarded by many as divine, are the culture's sacred cows. Whatever you do, don't insult the king or disrespect his image, especially in this new era of ultra-sensitivity towards the institution of the monarchy.

Lifestyle

Thailand straddles the divide between the highly Westernised urban life in major cities and the traditional rhythms of rural, agricultural life. But several persisting customs offer a rough snapshot of daily life. Thais wake up early, thanks in part to the roosters that start crowing sometime after sunrise. In the grey stillness of early morning, barefoot monks carrying large round bowls travel through the town to collect their daily meals from the faithful. The housewives are already awake steaming rice and sweeping their front porches with stiff bristled brooms. Soon business is in full swing: the vendors have arrived at their favourite corner to feed the uniformed masses, be they khaki-clad civil servants or white-and-black-wearing university students.

Eating appears to make up the rest of the day. Notice the shop girls, ticket vendors or even the office workers: they can be found in a tight circle swapping gossip and snacking (or gin lên, literally 'eat for fun'). Then there is dinner and after-dinner and the whole seemingly chaotic, yet highly ordered, affair starts all over again.

Population

About 75% of citizens are ethnic Thais, further divided by geography (north, central, south and northeast). Each group speaks its own Thai dialect and to a certain extent

---

MODERN MIGRANTS

Refugees from Myanmar first crossed into Thailand in 1984, when Myanmar's army penetrated the ethnic Karen state and began a campaign of forced relocation. Today there are refugee camps around Mae Sot and elsewhere along the two countries' border, and the UN High Commissioner for Refugees (UNHCR) estimates that about 57,000 people from Myanmar, mainly ethnic Karen, live in these camps, and a total of 130,238 refugees live in Thailand. Refugees are assured protection from the military, but have little opportunity to gain an education, employment or an independent life because the Thai government does not recognise them as citizens or residents. Some have lived in this limbo state for decades.

Since 2012, conflict between the Myanmar military and armed ethnic groups has declined but instability still exists in Myanmar's Rakhine state, causing the Rohingya people to seek asylum across the sea in Thailand; once they land in Thailand they are held in detention centres.

In addition to refugees there are also approximately three million economic migrants, predominately from Myanmar, working in Thailand; a minority of them have work permits and legal protection from exploitation.

PARTS OF A WÁT

Planning to conquer Thailand's temples and ruins? With this handy guide, you'll be able to sort out your wát (Thai temple complex) from your what's that:

Chedi Large bell-shaped tower usually containing five structural elements symbolising (from bottom to top) earth, water, fire, wind and void; relics of Buddha or a Thai king are housed inside the *chedi;* also known as a stupa.

Prang Towering phallic spire of Khmer origin serving the same religious purpose as a *chedi.*

Wí·hǎhn Main sanctuary for the temple's Buddha sculpture and where laypeople come to make offerings; sometimes it is translated as the 'assembly hall'; typically the building has a three-tiered roofline representing the triple gems (Buddha, the teacher; Dharma, the teaching; and Sangha, the followers).

practises customs unique to its region or influenced by neighbouring countries. Politically and economically, the central Thais are the dominant group. People of Chinese ancestry make up roughly 14% of the population, many of whom have been in Thailand for generations. Other large minority groups include the Malays in the far south, the Khmers in the northeast and the Lao, spread throughout the north and east. Smaller non–Thai-speaking groups include the hill tribes living in the northern mountains. An increasing community of economic migrants, predominately from Myanmar, are changing the racial and cultural demographics of Thailand.

Religion

Alongside the Thai national flag flies the yellow flag of Buddhism – Theravada Buddhism (as opposed to the Mahayana schools found in East Asia and the Himalaya). Country, family and daily life are all married to religion. Every Thai male is expected to become a monk for a short period in his life, since a family earns great merit when a son 'takes robe and bowl'.

More evident than the philosophical aspects of Buddhism is the everyday fusion with animist rituals. Monks are consulted to determine an auspicious date for a wedding or the likelihood of success for a business. Spirit houses *(phrá phuum)* are constructed outside buildings and homes to encourage the spirits to live independently from the family but to remain comfortable so as to bring good fortune to the site.

Roughly 95% of the population practises Buddhism, but in southern Thailand there is a significant Muslim minority community.

Arts

Music

Classical Thai music was developed for the royal court as an accompaniment to classical dance-drama and other forms of theatre. Traditional instruments have more pedestrian applications and can often be heard at temple fairs or provincial festivals. Whether used in the high or low arts, traditional Thai music has an incredible array of textures and subtleties, hair-raising tempos and pastoral melodies.

In the north and northeast there are several popular wind instruments with multiple reed pipes, which function like a mouth organ. Chief among these is the *kaan,* which originated in Laos; when played by an adept musician it sounds like a calliope organ. It is used chiefly in *mŏr lam* music, a rural folk tradition often likened to the American blues. A near cousin to *mŏr lam* is *lôok tûng* (literally 'children of the fields'), which enjoys a working-class fan base much like country music does in the US.

Popular Thai music has borrowed rock-and-roll's instruments to create perky teeny-bop hits, hippie protest ballads and even urban indie anthems. It is an easy courtship with Thai classic rock, like the decades-old group Carabao and the folk style known as *pleng pêu·a chee·wít* (songs for life). Alternative rock groups such as Modern Dog and Aparment Khunpa have defined Thailand's new millennial sound and a host of new-indie bands carry on the tradition.

Sculpture & Architecture

Thailand's most famous sculptural output has been its bronze Buddha images, coveted the world over for their originality and grace. Traditional architecture is more visible as it is applied to simple homes and famous temples. Ancient Thai homes consisted of a single-room teak structure raised on stilts, since most Thais once lived along river banks or canals. The space underneath also served as the living room, kitchen, garage and barn. Rooflines in Thailand are steeply pitched and often decorated at the corners

---

THAILAND'S HILL-TRIBE COMMUNITIES

Thailand's hill-tribe communities (referred to in Thai as *chao khao,* literally 'mountain people') are ethnic minorities who have traditionally lived in the country's mountainous frontier. Most tribes migrated from Tibet and parts of China some 200 years ago and settled along Southeast Asia's mountain belt from Myanmar to Vietnam. The Tribal Research Institute in Chiang Mai recognises 10 different hill tribes, but there may be up to 20 in Thailand. Increasing urban migration has significantly altered the hill tribes' cultural independence.

Hill-Tribe Groups

The **Karen** are the largest hill-tribe group in Thailand and number about 47% of the total tribal population. They tend to live in lowland valleys and practise crop rotation rather than swidden agriculture. Their numbers and proximity to the mainstream society have made them the most integrated and financially successful of the hill-tribe groups. Thickly woven V-neck tunics of various colours are their traditional dress.

The **Hmong** are Thailand's second-largest hill-tribe group and are especially numerous in Chiang Mai Province. They usually live on mountain peaks or plateaus above 1000m. Traditional dress is a simple black jacket and indigo or black baggy trousers. Sashes may be worn around the waist, and embroidered aprons draped front and back.

The **Akha** are among the poorest of Thailand's ethnic minorities and live mainly in Chiang Mai and Chiang Rai Provinces, along mountain ridges or steep slopes 1000m to 1400m in altitude. They are regarded as skilled farmers but are often displaced from arable land by government intervention. Their traditional garb includes a headdress of beads, feathers and dangling silver ornaments.

Other minority groups include the Lisu, Lahu and Mien.

Village Etiquette

If you're planning on visiting hill-tribe villages, talk to your guide about dos and don'ts. Here are some general guidelines.

➡ Always ask permission before taking photos, especially at private moments inside dwellings. Many traditional belief systems view photography with suspicion. Some tribespeople will ask for money in exchange for a photo; honour their request.

➡ Show respect for religious symbols and rituals. Don't touch totems at village entrances or sacred items. Don't participate in ceremonies unless invited to join.

➡ Avoid cultivating a tradition of begging, especially among children. Instead talk to your guide about donating to a local school.

➡ Avoid public nudity and be careful not to undress near an open window where village children might be able to peep in.

➡ Don't flirt with members of the opposite sex unless you plan to marry them. Don't drink or do drugs with the villagers; altered states sometimes lead to culture clashes.

➡ Smile at villagers even if they stare at you; ask your guide how to say 'hello' in the tribal language.

➡ Avoid public displays of affection, which in some traditional systems are viewed as offensive to the spirit world.

➡ Don't interact with the villagers' livestock; these creatures are valuable possessions, not curiosities. Avoid interacting with jungle animals, which may be viewed as visiting spirits.

➡ Adhere to the same feet taboos of Thai culture.

or along the gables with motifs related to the *naga* (mythical sea serpent), long believed to be a spiritual protector. Temple buildings demonstrate more formal aspects of traditional architecture and artistic styles.

Theatre & Dance

Traditional Thai theatre consists of six dramatic forms, including *kŏhn,* a formal masked dance-drama depicting scenes from the *Ramakian* (the Thai version of India's *Ramayana*) that were originally performed only for the royal court. Popular in rural villages, *lí·gair* is a partly improvised, often bawdy folk play featuring dancing, comedy, melodrama and music. The southern Thai equivalent is *má·noh·rah,* which is based on a 2000-year-old Indian story. Shadow puppet plays (*năng*) found in southern Thailand demonstrate that region's shared cultural heritage with Malaysia and Indonesia.

Food & Drink

Food

Thai food is a complex balance of spicy, salty, sweet and sour. The ingredients are fresh and zesty with lots of lemongrass, basil, coriander and mint. Chilli peppers pack a nose-running, tongue-searing burn. And pungent *nám blah* (fish sauce; generally made from anchovies) adds a touch of the sea. Throw in a little lime and a pinch of sugar and you've got the true taste of Thailand.

Day and night markets, pushcart vendors, makeshift stalls, open-air restaurants – Thais eat most of their meals outside of the home as prices are relatively low and local cooks are famous for a particular dish. No self-respecting shoestringer would shy away from the push-carts in Thailand for fear of stomach troubles.

For breakfast and late-night snacks, Thais nosh on *gŏo·ay děe·o,* a noodle soup with chicken or pork and vegetables. There are two major types of noodles: *sên lék* (thin) and *sên yài* (wide and flat). Before you dig into your steaming bowl, first use the chopsticks and a spoon to cut the noodles into smaller segments so they are easier to pick up. Then add to taste a few teaspoonfuls of the provided spices: dried red chilli, sugar, fish sauce and vinegar. It's a combination that is pure Thai. The weapons of choice when eating noodles are chopsticks and a rounded soup spoon.

Thais are social eaters: meals are rarely taken alone and dishes are meant to be shared. Usually a small army of plates will be placed in the centre of the table, with individual servings of rice for each diner. The protocol goes like this – ladle a spoonful of food at a time on to your plate of rice. Dishes aren't passed in Thailand; instead you reach across the table to the different items. When you are full, leave a little rice on your plate (an empty plate is a silent request for more rice) and place your fork so that it is cradled by the spoon in the centre of the plate.

Even when eating with *fa·ràng,* it is wise to order 'family style', as dishes are rarely synchronised. Ordering individually will leave one person staring politely at a hot plate and another staring wistfully at the kitchen.

Drink

Water purified for drinking is simply called *náam dèum* (drinking water), whether boiled or filtered. All water offered in restaurants, offices or homes will be purified. Ice is generally safe in Thailand. *Châa* (tea) and *gah·faa* (coffee) are prepared strong, milky and sweet – an instant morning buzz.

Thanks to the tropical bounty, fruit juices are sold on every corner. Thais prefer a little salt to cut the sweetness of the juice; the salt also has some mystical power to make a hot day tolerable.

Cheap beer appears hand-in-hand with backpacker ghettos. Beer Chang, Beer Singha (pronounced 'sing', not 'sing-ha') and Beer Leo are a few local brands. Thais have created yet another innovative method for beating the heat; they drink their beer with ice to keep the beverage cool and crisp.

More of a ritual than a beverage, Thai whisky usually runs with a distinct crowd – soda water, Coke and ice. Fill the short glass with ice cubes, two-thirds whisky, one-third soda and a splash of Coke. Thai tradition dictates the youngest in the crowd is responsible for filling the other drinkers' glasses. Many travellers prefer to go straight to the ice bucket with shared straws, not forgetting a dash of Red Bull in cocktails to keep them going.

Environment

Thailand's shape on the map has been likened to the head of an elephant, with its trunk extending down the Malay peninsula. The country covers 517,000 sq km, which is slightly smaller than the US state of Texas. The centre of the country, Bangkok, sits at about 14° north latitude – level with Madras, Manila, Guatemala City and Khartoum. Because the north–south reach spans roughly 16 latitudinal degrees, Thailand has perhaps the most diverse climate in Southeast Asia.

The Land

The country stretches from dense mountain jungles in the north to the flat central plains to the southern tropical rainforests. Covering the majority of the country, monsoon forests are filled with a sparse canopy of deciduous trees that shed their leaves during the dry season to conserve water. The landscape becomes dusty and brown until the rains (from July to November) transform everything into a fecund green. As the rains cease, Thailand enters its 'winter', a period of cooler temperatures, virtually unnoticeable to a recent arrival except in the north, where night-time temperatures can drop to 13°C. By March, the hot season begins and the mercury climbs to 40°C or more at its highest, plus humidity.

In the south, the wet season lasts until January, with months of unrelenting showers and floods. Thanks to the rains, the south supports the dense rainforests more indicative of a 'tropical' region. Along the coastline, mangrove forests anchor themselves wherever water dominates.

Thailand's national flower, the orchid, is one of the world's most beautiful air plants.

Wildlife

Thailand is particularly rich in bird life: more than 1000 resident and migrating species have been recorded and approximately 10% of all world bird species dwell here. Thailand's most revered indigenous mammal, the elephant, once ran wild in the country's dense virgin forests. Since ancient times, annual parties led by the king would round up young elephants from the wild to train them as workers and fighters. Integral to Thai culture, the elephant symbolises wisdom, strength and good fortune. White elephants are even more auspicious and by tradition are donated to the king. Sadly, elephants, both wild and domesticated, are now endangered, having lost their traditional role in society and much of their habitat.

Environmental Issues

Like all countries with a high population density, there is enormous pressure on Thailand's ecosystems: in the middle of last century about 70% of the countryside was forest; by 2000 an estimated 20% of the natural forest cover remained.

In response to environmental degradation, the Thai government created protected natural areas and outlawed logging. Thailand designated its first national park (Khao Yai) in the 1960s and has added over 100 parks, including marine environments, to the list since. Together these cover 15% of the country's land and sea area, one of the highest ratios of protected to unprotected areas of any nation in the world. Since the turn of the millennium, forest loss has slowed to about 0.2% per year (according to the World Bank).

Though the conservation efforts are laudable, Thailand's national parks are poorly funded and poorly protected from commercial development, illegal hunting and logging, and swidden agriculture. The passing of the 1992 Environmental Act was an encouraging move by the government, but standards still lag behind Western nations. Thailand is a signatory to the UN Convention on International Trade in Endangered Species (CITES). Forty of Thailand's 300 mammal species are on the International Union for Conservation of Nature (IUCN) list of endangered species.

SURVIVAL GUIDE

 **Directory A–Z**

ACCOMMODATION

There is a healthy selection of budget accommodation in Thailand, starting at around 250B to 400B for a dorm bed and 400B for a bed-in-a-box single with fan and shared (cold water) bathroom. Rates, starting around 700B, are higher in Bangkok and on the beaches.

Guesthouses are the primary budget options. These converted family homes or multistorey apartment-style buildings usually subsidise their low room rates with an attached restaurant and travel agency. Small, boutique hotels offer style and comfort with less socialising.

During Thailand's peak season (December to February and June to August) prices increase and availability decreases, especially on the island and beach resorts.

Unless otherwise noted, reservations at the guesthouses are not recommended as standards vary from room to room and year to year. It is recommended to inspect the room beforehand since refunds are not a common practice. Advance payment to secure a reservation is also discouraged.

In our listings, high-season prices have been quoted. Enquiries for discounts can be made during low seasons.

Price Ranges

In big cities and beach resorts, the following prices ranges refer to a double room.

$ less than 1000B (US$28)

$$ 1000B to 3000B (US$28 to US$85)

$$$ more than 3000B (US$85)

In small towns, the following prices ranges are used:

$ less than 600B (US$17)

$$ 600B to 1500B (US$17 to US$42)

$$$ more than 1500B (US$42)

CUSTOMS REGULATIONS

Thailand allows a reasonable amount of personal effects, professional instruments, 200 cigarettes and 1L of wine or spirits to enter the country without duty; see www.customs.go.th for more regulations. Thailand prohibits import of the following: firearms and ammunition (unless preregistered with the police department), illegal drugs and pornographic media.

Licenses are required for exporting religious images and other antiquities.

ELECTRICITY

Thailand uses 220V AC electricity; power outlets most commonly feature two-pronged round or flat sockets.

EMBASSIES & CONSULATES

Foreign embassies are located in Bangkok; some nations also have consulates in Chiang Mai, Phuket or Pattaya.

Australian Embassy (Map p648; ☑ 02 344 6300; www.thailand.embassy.gov.au; 37 Th Sathon Tai/South, Bangkok; ☺ 8.30am-4.30pm Mon-Fri; M Lumphini exit 2)

Cambodian Embassy (☑ 02 957 5851; 518/4 Th Pracha Uthit/Soi Ramkhamhaeng 39,

Bangkok; ☺ 9am-noon Mon-Fri; M Phra Ram 9 exit 3 & taxi)

Canadian Embassy (Map p648; ☑ 02 646 4300; www.thailand.gc.ca; 15th fl, Abdulrahim Pl, 990 Th Phra Ram IV, Bangkok; ☺ 7.30am-12.15pm & 1-4.15pm Mon-Thu, to 1pm Fri; M Si Lom exit 2, S Sala Daeng exit 4)

Canadian Consulate (☑ 053 850147; 151 Superhighway, Tambon Tahsala, Chiang Mai; ☺ 9am-noon Mon-Fri)

Chinese Embassy (Map p648; ☑ 02 245 0888; www.chinaembassy.or.th/eng; 57 Th Ratchadaphisek, Bangkok; ☺ 9am-noon & 3-4pm Mon-Fri)

Danish Embassy (Map p648; ☑ 02 343 1100; http://thailand.um.dk; 10 Soi 1, Th Sathon Tai, Bangkok; ☺ 10am-noon & 1-3pm Mon-Thu)

French Embassy (Map p648; ☑ 02 657 5100; www.ambafrance-th.org; 35 Soi 36, Th Charoen Krung, Bangkok; ☺ 8.30am-noon Mon-Fri; ☻ Oriental Pier) With consulates in Chiang Mai, Chiang Rai, Ko Samui, Pattaya and Phuket.

French Consulate (☑ 053 281466; 138 Th Charoen Prathet, Chiang Mai; ☺ 10am-noon Mon-Fri)

German Embassy (Map p648; ☑ 02 287 9000; www.bangkok.diplo.de; 9 Th Sathon Tai/South, Bangkok; ☺ 8.30-11.30am Mon-Fri; M Lumphini exit 2)

Indian Embassy (Map p648; ☑ 02 258 0300; www.indianembassy.in.th; 46 Soi 23, Th Sukhumvit, Bangkok; ☺ 9am-noon & 3-4.30pm Mon-Fri)

Indonesian Embassy (Map p658; ☑ 02 252 3135; www.kemlu.go.id/bangkok; 600-602 Th Phetchaburi, Bangkok; ☺ 9am-noon & 2-4pm Mon-Fri)

Israeli Embassy (Map p648; ☑ 02 204 9200; http://embassies.gov.il/bangkok-en; 25th fl, Ocean Tower 2, 75 Soi 19, Th Sukhumvit, Bangkok; ☺ 9am-noon)

Irish Embassy (Map p658; ☑ 02 632 6720; www.irelandinthailand.com; 12th fl, 208 Th Witthayu/Wireless Rd, Bangkok; ☺ 8.30am-12.30pm Mon-Fri; S Phloen Chit exit 1)

Japanese Embassy (Map p648; ☑ 02 207 8500; www.th.emb-japan.go.jp; 177 Th Witthayu/Wireless Rd; ☺ 8.30am-noon & 1.30-4pm Mon-Fri)

Japanese Consulate (☑ 053 203367; Airport Business Park, 90 Th Mahidol, Chiang Mai)

Laotian Embassy (☑ 02 539 6667; www.laoembassybkk.gov.la/index.php/en; 502/1-3 Soi Sahakarnpramoon, Th Pracha Uthit/Soi Ramkhamhaeng 39, Bangkok; ☺ 8am-noon & 1-4pm Mon-Fri; M Phra Ram 9 exit 3 & taxi)

Malaysian Embassy (Map p648; ☑ 02 629 6800; www.kln.gov.my/web/tha_bangkok/home; 33-35 Th Sathon Tai/South, Bangkok;

THAILAND DIRECTORY A-Z

⊗ 8am-4pm Mon-Fri; Ⓜ Lumphini exit 2) With consulate in Songkhla.

Myanmar Embassy (Map p648; ☑ 02 233 7250; www.myanmarembassybkk.com; 132 Th Sathon Neua/North, Bangkok; ⊗ 9am-noon & 1-3pm Mon-Fri; Ⓢ Surasak exit 3)

New Zealand Embassy (Map p658; ☑ 02 254 2530; www.nzembassy.com/thailand; 14th fl, M Thai Tower, All Seasons Pl, 87 Th Witthayu/ Wireless Rd, Bangkok; ⊗ 9am-noon & 1-2.30pm Mon-Fri; Ⓢ Phloen Chit exit 5)

Philippine Embassy (Map p648; ☑ 02 259 0139; www.bangkokpe.dfa.gov.ph; 760 Th Sukhumvit, Bangkok; ⊗ 9am-noon & 1-6pm Mon-Fri)

UK Embassy (Map p658; ☑ 02 305 8333; www.gov.uk/government/world/organisations/ british-embassy-bangkok; 14 Th Witthayu/ Wireless Rd, Bangkok; ⊗ 8am-4.30pm Mon-Thu, to 1pm Fri; Ⓢ Phloen Chit exit 5) UK Embassy in Bangkok.

US Embassy (Map p658; ☑ 02 205 4000; http://bangkok.usembassy.gov; 120-122 Th Witthayu/Wireless Rd, Bangkok; ⊗ 7am-4pm Mon-Fri; Ⓢ Phloen Chit exit 5) US Embassy in Bangkok; additional consulate in Chiang Mai.

Vietnamese Embassy (Map p658; ☑ 02 251 3552; www.vietnamembassy-thailand.org; 83/1 Th Witthayu/Wireless Rd, Bangkok; ⊗ 9-11.30am & 2-4.30pm Mon-Fri)

FESTIVALS & EVENTS

Many Thai festivals are linked to Buddhist holy days and follow the lunar calendar. Thus they fall on different dates each year. Many provinces hold annual festivals or fairs to promote their agricultural specialities.

Businesses typically close and transport becomes difficult preceding any public holiday or national festival. The following are popular national festivals:

Songkran Festival From 12 to 14 April, Buddha images are 'bathed', monks and elders have their hands respectfully sprinkled with water and a lot of water is wildly tossed about on everyone else. Bangkok and Chiang Mai are major battlegrounds.

Loi Krathong On the night of the full moon in November, small lotus-shaped boats made of banana leaves and decorated with flowers and candles are floated on waterways in honour of the river goddess.

FOOD

The following price ranges refer to the cost of a main dish:

$	less than 150B (US$4.25)
$$	150B to 350B (US$4.25 to US$10)
$$$	more than 350B (US$10)

INTERNET ACCESS

Internet cafes are on the decline as smartphones become more prolific. Free wi-fi is available in guesthouses, restaurants and some hot spots. Mobile 3G networks are available, mainly in urban centres.

LEGAL MATTERS

In general, Thai police don't hassle foreigners, especially tourists. One major exception is in regard to drugs – there are strict drug laws for possession and trafficking of narcotics.

If you are arrested for any offence, the police will allow you the opportunity to make a phone call to your embassy or consulate in Thailand, if you have one, or to a friend or relative if not. Thai law does not presume an indicted detainee to be either 'guilty' or 'innocent' but rather a 'suspect', whose guilt or innocence will be decided in court. Trials are usually speedy.

LGBT TRAVELLERS

LGBT travellers won't have a problem travelling through Thailand as long as they are respectful of the culture and remain somewhat discreet. Prominent gay communities exist in large cities such as Bangkok, Chiang Mai, Pattaya and Phuket. Although public displays of affection are common between members of the same sex (and are usually platonic), you should refrain from anything beyond friendly hand-holding. The same goes for hetero couples, too.

Gay, lesbian and transsexual Thais are generally tolerated in day-to-day life, though they face institutional discrimination and are often labelled as 'sexual deviants' and barred from studying to become teachers or from joining the military.

MONEY

The Thai baht (B) is divided into colour-coded notes as well as coins of various sizes.

Coins come in 1B, 2B (gold-coloured), 5B and 10B denominations. There are 100 satang to 1B and occasionally you'll see 25 and 50 satang coins at department stores or supermarkets.

Notes are denominations of 20B, 50B, 100B, 500B and 1000B. In the dark it can be easy to mix up a 50B note with a 500B note so take care to segregate your bills by denomination. ATM withdrawals dispense cash in 1000B notes, which can be impossible for a taxi driver or market vendor to change. Break your big bills at 7-Elevens.

POST

The Thai postal system is relatively efficient and few travellers complain about undelivered mail or lost parcels. Never send cash or small valuable objects through the postal system, even if the items are insured.

PUBLIC HOLIDAYS

Government offices and banks close on the following public holidays.

1 January New Year's Day

February (date varies) Makha Bucha Day, Buddhist holy day

6 April Chakri Day, commemorating the founder of the Chakri dynasty, Rama I

13–14 April Songkran Festival, traditional Thai New Year and water festival

1 May Labour Day

5 May Coronation Day, commemorating the 1946 coronation of the king and queen

May/June (date varies) Visakha Bucha, Buddhist holy day

July (date varies) Asahna Bucha, Buddhist holy day

12 August Queen's Birthday

23 October Chulalongkorn Day

October/November (date varies) Ork Phansa, the end of Buddhist 'lent'

5 December King's Birthday/Father's Day

10 December Constitution Day

31 December New Year's Eve

SAFE TRAVEL

Although Thailand is not a dangerous country, it's wise to be cautious, particularly if travelling alone. Most tourist-oriented towns will have a **tourist police office** (⏀1155), with officers who can speak English and liaise with the Thai police. The tourist police can also issue official documentation for insurance purposes if valuables are stolen.

It is not recommended to travel into Thailand's southernmost provinces of Yala, Narathiwat, Pattani and remote corners of Songkhla because of a low-level war between the national government and ethnic separatists.

Here are a few pointers to avoid problems:

➡ Avoid arguments with Thais (especially about money or matters of the heart and if alcohol is involved). Thais who feel that they've been embarrassed occasionally retaliate with violence. Periodically, there are stories of backpackers being murdered after a drunken altercation with a well-connected Thai.

➡ Don't wander around alone at night intoxicated; this is especially the case for women and especially on Ko Samui and Ko Pha-Ngan.

➡ Don't buy, sell or possess drugs (opium, heroin, amphetamines, hallucinogenic mushrooms and marijuana); there are strict punishments for drug possession and trafficking that are not relaxed for foreigners.

➡ Don't accept an invitation to go shopping or play cards with a stranger you've met on the street. This is the lead-up to a well-rehearsed scam.

➡ Carry your personal effects (money, credit cards, passport) on your person to avoid theft or loss, especially during long-distance travel when stowed luggage can be accessed by thieves.

TELEPHONE

The telephone numbers in listings are written for domestic dialling; to call a Thai telephone number from outside the country, omit the initial '0'.

If you want to call an international number from Thailand, dial an international access code then the country code then the subscriber number. There are various international access codes with different rates per minute. Do

OPENING HOURS

The following are standard business hours in Thailand. Government offices and banks are closed public holidays.

TYPE OF BUSINESS	OPENING HOURS	EXCEPTIONS
Bars	6pm-1am (officially)	Closing times vary due to local enforcement of curfew laws; bars close during elections and certain religious public holidays.
Banks	9.30am-3.30pm Mon-Fri	ATMs accessible 24hrs.
Nightclubs	6pm-2am	Closing times vary due to local enforcement of curfew laws; clubs close during elections and certain religious public holidays.
Government offices	8.30am-4.30pm Mon-Fri	Some close for lunch (noon-1pm), while others are open Saturday (9am-3pm).
Restaurants	8am-10pm	Some shops specialise in morning meals and close by 3pm.
Stores	local stores 10am-6pm; department stores 10am-8pm	In some small towns, local stores close on Sunday.

an internet search to find out the promotional codes associated with your wireless provider.

TOILETS

Increasingly, the Asian-style squat toilet is less of the norm in Thailand. There are still specimens in provincial bus stations, older homes and modest restaurants. Some modern toilets also come with a small spray hose – Thailand's version of the bidet.

TOURIST INFORMATION

The Tourism Authority of Thailand (TAT) has offices throughout the country that distribute maps and sightseeing advice. TAT offices do not book accommodation, transport or tours.

TRAVELLERS WITH DISABILITIES

Thailand presents one large, ongoing obstacle course for the mobility-impaired. The following organisations might be useful:

Asia Pacific Development Centre on Disability (www.apcdfoundation.org)

Society for Accessible Travel & Hospitality (www.sath.org)

Wheelchair Holidays @ Thailand (www.wheelchairtours.com)

VISAS

The Ministry of Foreign Affairs oversees immigration and visa issues. Check the Thai embassy or consulate for application procedures and costs. Changes to visa requirements are often monitored by Thaivisa (www.thaivisa.com).

Visa Exemptions & Tourist Visas

The Thai government allows citizens from most of Europe, Australia, New Zealand and the USA to enter the country without a prearranged visa. Arrivals by air receive a 30-day visa. Arrivals by land receive either a 30- or 15-day visa, depending on your nationality.

Technically, without proof of an onward ticket and sufficient funds, any visitor can be denied entry but this is rarely enforced.

If you plan to stay in Thailand longer than your arrival visa allows, you should apply for the 60-day tourist visa from a Thai consulate or embassy before entering the country.

Visa Extensions

If you have already arrived in Thailand and wish to stay longer than your visa allows, you have two options. You can cross a land border and receive a new 30-/15-day visa, depending on your nationality, upon re-entry (at no charge); or you can apply for a visa extension at a Thai immigration office for 30 days with a fee of 1900B. Bring two passport-sized photos and one copy each of the photo and visa pages of your passport. Dress neatly and do not hire a third-party proxy.

If you overstay your visa, the penalty is 500B per day, with a 20,000B limit. Fines can be paid at the airport or in advance at an immigration office. If you've overstayed only one day, you don't have to pay.

There are immigration offices in Bangkok, Chiang Mai, Ko Samui and Krabi Town, among other Thai cities and border towns.

VOLUNTEERING

Volunteer Work Thailand (www.volunteerworkthailand.org) maintains a database of opportunities with grassroots organisations. It is essential to do your homework about the organisation and its work. Lonely Planet does not endorse any organisations that we do not work with directly.

WORKING

Teaching English is one of the easiest ways to immerse yourself in a Thai community. Those with academic credentials, such as teaching certificates or degrees in English as a second language (ESL) or English as a foreign language (EFL), get first crack at the better-paying jobs at universities and international schools. But there are hundreds of language schools for every variety of native English speaker. The site www.ajarn.com has job listings and tips on teaching. TEFL certificate programs are increasingly popular, especially in tourist towns like Chiang Mai.

ⓘ Getting There & Away

AIR

Thailand has one primary international airport (Suvarnabhumi International Airport) plus a budget carrier airport (Don Muang Airport) with some international connections in Bangkok. Chiang Mai and Phuket also have some international flights from nearby countries, especially China.

Most major carriers fly in and out of Bangkok.

LAND

Thailand enjoys open and safe border relations with all of its neighbours. Improved highways and bridges have made it easier to travel overland to/from China. Visas on arrival are available for land-crossings into Cambodia, Laos and Malaysia. Pre-arranged visas are required for land entry into Myanmar. A passport photo and visa fee are typical requirements but each country has its own regulations and there can be variations at different border posts.

ⓘ Getting Around

AIR

Every year provincial routes through budget air carriers increase and become cheaper, making long-distance bus travel less convenient.

BICYCLE

Bikes are an ideal form of local transport because they're cheap, nonpolluting and keep you moving slowly enough to see everything. Carefully note the condition of the bike before hiring; most have dodgy brakes.

BOAT

Being a riverine people, Thais have colourful boats of traditional design. With a long graceful breast that barely skims the water and an elongated propeller, longtail boats are used as island-hoppers, canal coasters and river ferries. Small wooden fishing boats sometimes shuttle tourists out to nearby islands. Cargo boats and high-speed ferries make the island voyage as well. Boat services are often suspended during wet season and schedules are subject to weather conditions.

BUS & MINIVAN

The Thai bus service is widespread, convenient and phenomenally fast – nail-bitingly so. Reputable companies operate out of the government bus stations, not the tourist centres. Starting at the top, VIP buses are the closest you will come to a rock star's tour bus. The seats recline, the air-con is frosty and an 'air hostess' dispenses refreshments. Various diminishing classes of air-con buses strip away the extras until you're left with a fairly beat-up bus with an asthmatic cooling system.

For trips to nearby cities, minivans are a convenient option. They depart from the market instead of an out-of-town bus station and, in some cases, offer hotel drop-off.

For long-distance trips, check out schedules and/or purchase tickets the day before.

CAR & MOTORCYCLE

Cars and motorcycles can be rented in most tourist towns. Inspect the vehicle beforehand as fleets are often poorly maintained and document any existing damage to avoid being charged for it. Always verify that the vehicle is insured for liability before signing a rental contract, and ask to see the dated insurance documents.

Motorcycle travel is a popular way to do local sightseeing. Motorcycle rental usually requires that you leave your passport as a deposit.

Thais drive on the left-hand side of the road – most of the time. Every two-lane road has an invisible third lane in the middle that all drivers use as a passing lane. The main rule to be aware of is that 'might makes right' and smaller vehicles always yield to bigger ones. Drivers usually use their horns to indicate that they are passing.

An International Driving Permit is necessary to drive vehicles in Thailand, but this is rarely enforced for motorcycle hire.

HITCHING

It is uncommon to see people hitching, since bus travel is inexpensive and reliable. Hitching becomes an option where public transport isn't available. In this case you can usually catch a ride, but remember to use the Asian style of beckoning: hold your arm out towards the road, palm-side down and wave towards the ground.

That said, hitching is never entirely safe, and travellers who do so should understand that they are taking a small but potentially serious risk.

TRAIN

The **State Railway of Thailand** (053 242094, 1690; www.railway.co.th; Th Charoen Muang; ticket office 5am-10pm) operates comfortable and moderately priced, but rather slow, services. All rail travel originates in Bangkok and radiates north, south and northeast. Trains are convenient for overnight travel between Bangkok and Chiang Mai and south to Chumphon or Surat Thani. The train can also dodge Bangkok traffic to Ayuthaya.

The SRT operates passenger trains in three classes – 1st, 2nd and 3rd – but each class varies depending on the train type (ordinary,

---

ROAD SAFETY

Thailand rates as one of the most dangerous places to be on the road and many Western nations issue travel advisories for highway safety.

Fatal bus crashes make headlines, but more than 80% of vehicle accidents in Thailand involve motorcycles. Many tourists are injured riding motorcycles because they don't know how to handle the vehicles and are unfamiliar with local driving conventions.

If you are a novice motorcyclists, familiarise yourself with the vehicle in an uncongested area of town and stick to the smaller 100cc automatic bikes. Drive slowly, especially when roads are slick or when there is loose gravel. Remember to distribute weight as evenly as possible across the frame of the bike to improve handling. And don't expect that other vehicles will look out for you. Wear a helmet and protective clothing.

It is not advised for novice motorcyclists to drive in Ko Samui, Ko Pha-Ngan and other places where road conditions are poor.

rapid or express). Rapid and express trains make fewer stops than ordinary trains.

Fares are calculated from a base price with surcharges added for distance, class and train type. Extra charges are added for air-con and for sleeping berths (either upper or lower).

Advance bookings can be made from one to 60 days before your intended date of departure. You can make bookings in person from any train station. Train tickets can also be purchased at travel agencies, which usually add a service charge to the ticket price. If you are planning long-distance train travel from outside the country, you should email the State Railway of Thailand at least two weeks before your journey. You will receive an email confirming the booking. Pick up and pay for tickets an hour before leaving at the scheduled departure train station.

LOCAL TRANSPORT
Sǎhm-lór & Túk-Túk

Sǎhm-lór (also spelt 'sǎamláw'), meaning 'three wheels', are pedal rickshaws found mainly in small towns for short hops. Their modern replacements are the motorised túk-túk, named for the throaty cough of their two-stroke engines. In Bangkok, túk-túk drivers give all local transport a bad name. In other towns they tend to be more reliable.

You must bargain and agree on a fare before accepting a ride.

Sǒrng·tǎa·ou

Sǒrng·tǎa·ou (literally, 'two benches') are small pick-up trucks with a row of seats down each side. In some towns, sǒrng·tǎa·ou serve as public buses running regular, fixed-fare routes. But in tourist towns, they act as shared taxis or private charter; in this case agree on a fare beforehand.

Timor-Leste

♪ 670 / POP 1,167,242

Best Colonial Relics

➡ Pousada de Baucau (p799)

➡ Balibo Fort Hotel (p801)

➡ Pousada de Maubisse (p802)

➡ Prisão do Apelo (p801)

➡ Escola do Reino de Venilale (p800)

Best Places for Culture

➡ Resistance Museum (p792)

➡ Balibo Flag House (p801)

➡ Santa Cruz Cemetery (p792)

➡ Chega! Exhibition (p792)

➡ Lospalos Cultural Centre (p801)

Why Go?

With mountains to climb, untouched reefs to dive, and ancient traditions that have survived the ravages of war, Asia's newest country offers some of the world's last great off-the-beaten-track adventures. Get an insight into Timor-Leste's dark history in Dili's museums, then venture out of the capital for wild cultural experiences. Head for the hills to hike to jungle caves, wander misty mountain village markets, and sip local coffee on the terrace of a grand Portuguese *pousada*. Bump along diabolical roads in search of your own perfect beach, stopping for photos of the stunning seascapes as you grip the rugged cliffs along the north coast road. Strap on a snorkel and marvel at the pristine reefs that fringe the north coast and Atauro Island, or delve deeper with Dili-based dive companies, which have spent the past decade discovering world-class sites. Trailblaze your way through this amazing country, and find out what everyone else has been missing.

When to Go

Dili

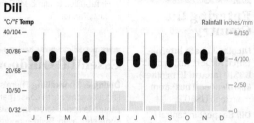

May–Nov (Dry Season) There's little rainfall and good weather, though it can get very dusty.

Sep–Nov It's whale-watching season as pods of whales migrate through the Wetar Strait.

Dec–Apr (Wet Season) Heavy rain makes the landscape lush; some roads are impassable in the districts.

DON'T MISS

One of the world's highest concentrations of dolphins and whales ply the deep channels off Timor-Leste's north coast; keep your eyes peeled for cetaceans during the boat trip to Atauro Island.

Fast Facts

Area 14,870 sq km

Capital Dili

Emergency police ☎ 333 1283
fire and ambulance ☎ 115

Exchange Rates

Australia	A$1	US$0.70
Euro	€1	US$1.12
Singapore	S$1	US$0.79
UK	UK£1	US$1.53

Daily Costs

Dorm bed US$12–15

Local restaurant meal US$3–12

Single dive US$45–50

Entering the Country

Nicolau Lobato International Airport Taxi to centre US$10 (around 10 minutes). *Mikrolet* (local bus) from main road US$0.25.

Dili Seaport In central Dili, taxis around the city US$2.

At a Glance

Currency US dollars (US$). Anything under US$1 can be paid in East Timorese Centavos (cv).

Language Portuguese and Tetun (official languages), Bahasa Indonesia, local dialects.

Money International ATMs very scarce outside Dili. Expensive hotels take credit cards.

Visas Visa on arrival at Dili airport or seaport; US$30 for 30 days. Most nationalities need a visa in advance for land border arrivals.

Mobile Phones Good coverage throughout major population centres. Timor Telecom, Telkomsel and Telemor SIM cards can be used in unlocked phones.

ITINERARIES

One Week

From Dili it's off to the island's east, stopping for photos along the spectacular coast before overnighting in Baucau. Head to Ossu and hike Mt Mundo Perdido (Lost World) or take on a smaller hike to Fretilin cave hideouts before spending the night by the river at Hotel Wailakurini. Next, to Com for lunch then onto Tutuala, from where you can reach the sacred Jaco Island for magnificent snorkelling. Return to Dili to explore museums and markets, and cap off your trip by heading out to Atauro Island for at least one night.

One Month

Complete the one-week itinerary then return to Dili for some diving and head west to Liquiçá for luxury camping at Caimeo Beach. Continue toward the Indonesian border, stopping at Maubara Fort for lunch. Overnight at the new Balibo Fort Hotel (opposite Balibo Flag House), before heading south via Marobo and Bobonaro to Suai, with its traditional villages and beach, then turn east and head back into the mountains via Ainaro or Same to Hatubuilico to climb Mt Ramelau. Head back to Dili via misty Maubisse.

Essential Outdoor Activities

Diving & Snorkelling There's excellent diving and snorkelling along the north coast (particularly east of Dili) and off Atauro Island. Sacred Jaco Island's turquoise waters are snorkel-heaven. Diving conditions are best (with up to 30m visibility) during the dry season.

Hiking Timor-Leste offers tempting terrain for hikers from casual to serious; 10-day north-to-south coast hikes are not unheard of. Popular day hikes include Mt Ramelau, the nation's highest peak, while Mt Manucoco on Atauro offers a diversion from beach-bumming. Mt Matebian beckons more serious hikers. Check www.trekkingeasttimor.org for info on routes.

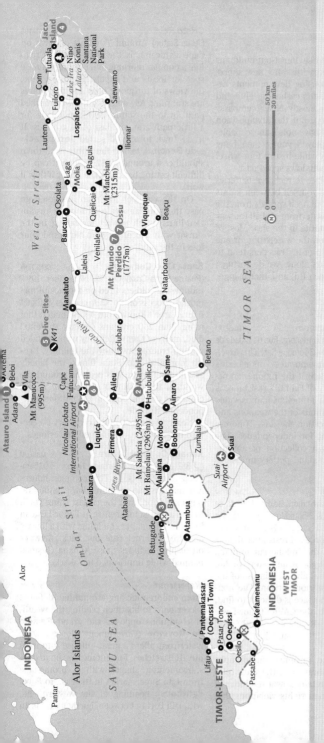

Timor-Leste Highlights

1 Escaping the 'bustle' of Dili for the rugged serenity of **Atauro Island** (p798).

2 Venturing to an *uma lulik* (sacred house) near the misty mountain village of **Maubisse** (p802) after scaling the mighty **Mt Ramelau** (p802).

3 Making the pilgrimage to **Balibó** (p801), where five Australia-based journalists were killed in 1975.

4 Relaxing on the powder-white sands of sacred **Jaco Island** (p800), with dazzling snorkelling just offshore.

5 Ticking off one of Timor–

Leste's top **dive sites** (p793), such as the epic K41.

6 Getting a dose of history at its powerful museums then kicking back with a beer by the seaside in **Dili** (p792).

7 Relaxing in a riverside bungalow in jungly **Ossu** (p800) or trekking to **Mt Mundo Perdido** (p800) ('Lost World').

DILI

POP 252,884

Dili is a city on the rise. Burnt-out buildings have been replaced with shiny new shops, restaurants and housing developments catering to Timor-Leste's cashed-up elite and expat community (mostly NGOs, embassy staff and engineers). But the juxtaposition between haves and have-nots is inescapable: throngs of unemployed young men hang around the streets while luxury four-wheel drives with tinted windows speed past.

Dili is a good place to recharge batteries (literally) and base yourself between jaunts into the districts. Dili itself spreads from the airport, along the waterfront and all the way to the Cristo Rei statue in the east. Most of the action occurs on the waterfront, or one or two blocks south of it. Travellers tend to hang out in the bars along Ave de Portugal (also known as Beach Rd) and, increasingly, at Areia Branca.

◉ Sights

★ **Resistance Museum**   MUSEUM

(☑ 333 1159; www.amrtimor.org; Rua de Cidade de Lisboa; US$1; ⊘ 9am-4.30pm Tue-Sat) This excellent museum commemorates Timor-Leste's 24-year struggle against the Indonesian occupation. The story of Falintil's resistance is brought to life with a timeline, photos, video recordings and exhibits of the weapons and tools of communication the East Timorese used in their fight for independence. The last room houses a collection of antique textiles, woven mats and pottery unique to various districts.

Chega! Exhibition   MUSEUM

(☑ 331 0315; www.cavr-timorleste.org; Estrada de Balide; ⊘ 9am-noon & 2-5pm Mon-Fri) FREE Set in the buildings and cells of a Portuguese-era prison where hundreds of resistance figures were interned by the Indonesian military, the exhibition (*chega* means 'stop' or 'no more' in Portuguese) gives a glimpse of the realities of the notorious prison. The non-descript exhibition space is difficult to find; direct taxi drivers to the 'CAVR (Timor-Leste Commission for Reception, Truth and Reconciliation) building' and just walk in through the gate.

Don't miss the gripping photographs displayed in the library, and the 'dark cells' which have been retained as a reminder of the countless human rights violations that occurred here.

Cristo Rei   STATUE

(Jesus Statue) Around 7km east of town on Cape Fatucama is the hard-to-miss Cristo Rei, a popular morning and evening exercise spot for locals and expats. From the cape, the views of turquoise bays and mountains are stunning. As you climb the well-marked path up to the statue (590 steps), look for a little path after the last of 14 grottoes. It leads down to often-deserted **Jesus Backside Beach**. A taxi to the statue from town should cost around US$7, though it can be difficult getting back (ask the driver if they'll wait).

On the way out to Cristo Rei you'll go past the popular **Areia Branca**, a restaurant-lined beach perfect for taking in the sunset with a beer in your hand and your toes in the sand.

Santa Cruz Cemetery   CEMETERY

(Rua de Santa Cruz) On 12 November 1991, Indonesian soldiers fired on a peaceful memorial procession to this cemetery. Exact figures aren't known, but it's estimated that more than 250 civilians (mostly students) died, many of them after they were rounded up and trucked away by the military. British journalist Max Stahl filmed the bloody attack; his footage was beamed around the world in the documentary *In Cold Blood*, cited as a turning point in the nation's independence struggle.

Nearly every inch of the cemetery is occupied by elaborate, pastel-hued gravestones.

Xanana Cultural Centre   MUSEUM

(☑ 331 2890; Rua Belarmino Lobo; ⊘ 9.15am-5.30pm Mon-Sat) FREE This complex houses Xanana Gusmão memorabilia, a photography exhibition, and the closest thing you'll find to a tourist info centre in Timor-Leste in its main, colonial-era building, with a library and free internet cafe out back. Artwork on display includes those Xanana Gusmão painted while imprisoned in Jakarta.

Waterfront   AREA

From children kicking around half-deflated soccer balls to boatmen reading the weather conditions opposite the grand **Palácio do Governo** (Government House), Dili's waterfront offers a great glimpse into local life. It stretches for kilometres in a quasi-boomerang shape, with a promenade from Lita Supermarket in the east, to **Farol lighthouse** beaming at the western end, with Dili Port in between. Further west is an esplanade dotted with gigantic embassies and expat bars offering excellent sunset views.

Arte Moris   GALLERY
(Av dos Mártires de Pátria, Comoro; ⊙ 9am-6pm Mon-Sat) FREE 'Quirky' is one way to describe this art space housed in the grounds of Dili's domed, Indonesian-era museum. Beyond the oddball outdoor sculptures, you'll find a collection of modern works, from woodcarvings to paintings sprayed onto *tais* (woven cloth) housed on the ground floor. The compound is just west of the Comoro bridge, before the airport turn-off.

🏃 Activities

The reef fringing Timor-Leste's north coast provides spectacular **diving** and **snorkelling** opportunities. Many sites, including the legendary K41 (41km east of Dili), are easily accessed by walking in from the beach, with dramatic drop-offs just 10m offshore in parts.

All dive shops we list offer a full range of PADI certification courses, and can also arrange snorkelling tours.

Aquatica Dive Resort   DIVING
(☑7803 8885; www.aquaticadiveresort.com; Aldeia Metin, Comoro) This professional Aussie-run outfit has top-notch gear, a comfortable car for dive trips along the bumpy north coast road, and one of Dili's better dive boats. Offers US$50 local dives, two-dive coast trips for $US120, and two-dive excursions to Atauro Island for US$170. It's behind the Ocean View Beach Hotel, just east of the Comoro River.

Dive Timor Lorosae   DIVING
(☑7723 7092; www.divetimor.com; Av de Portugal) Located underneath Castaway Bar, this long-running dive centre offers shore dives (US$45), two-dive day-trips to sites along the north coast (US$110) and two-dive trips to sites around Atauro Island (US$165). Has its own training pool.

Compass Charters   DIVING
(☑7723 0965; www.compassadventuretours.com; Av dos Mártires de Pátria) Specialises in multiday trips to Atauro Island's spectacular north coast sites (US$250 for two nights at its Adara beach camp; add US$35 for each dive). Two-dive Atauro day trips start at US$180. Also offers local and coast dives. It's next to Tiger Fuel.

👉 Tours

A tour can allow you to visit places not easily accessible by public transport (hint: most destinations outside Dili), and a guide can bridge the language barrier.

★ Eco Discovery   TOUR
(☑332 2454; www.ecodiscovery-easttimor.com; Landmark Plaza, Av dos Mártires de Pátria; ⊙ 9am-5pm) 🤿 This local operator can organise custom 4WD tours to corners of Timor-Leste even most locals don't know about, with some of the country's best guides/drivers (it won't take long to realise why the driving part is important).

Timor Adventures   TOUR
(☑7726 1059; www.timoradventures.com.au; Dili Beach Hotel, Av de Portugal) 🤿 This reputable Australian-run outfit specialises in motorcycle and 4WD tours of Timor-Leste. Slightly more expensive than Eco Discovery.

🎉 Festivals & Events

Tour de Timor   CYCLING
(www.tourdetimorlorosae.com; registration US$600; ⊙ Sep) Cheer on the several hundred hardy cyclists who embark on this five-day race around Timor-Leste's gnarly roads, or join in the challenge yourself.

DUGONGS OF TIMOR-LESTE

Located in the Coral Triangle, Timor-Leste boasts some of Southeast Asia's best untapped diving. Just metres from the shore lie pristine reefs filled with small colourful marine life, with the odd turtle or reef shark swinging by. But if there's one thing to really keep your eye out for, it's a dugong. While sightings are never guaranteed, these huge placid beasts are often spotted by divers and snorkellers at various sites along the coast east of Dili such as Secret Garden, and muck diving hot spot Tasi Tolu, just west of Dili's airport. You'll need luck on your side, of course, but if you head to Tasi Tolu with your snorkel at around noon, you have a good chance of seeing a dugong affectionately known as Douglas, who seems to favour the sea grass just offshore at lunchtime. Local dive operators can show you where to point your GoPro.

Dili

Map legend / locations:

Esplanada (200m);
'Fish on a Stick' Stalls (3km);
Aquatica Dive Resort (3.5km)

The Cove (2km);
Caz Bar (2.5km);
Beachside Hotel (2.6km);
Cristo Rei (4.6km)

Becora (2km)

Bémori River

Santana River

WETAR STRAIT

Dili Harbour

To Atauro Island

To Oecussi

Av de Portugal (Beach Rd)

Av dos Mártires da Pátria

Landmark Plaza (600m);
Timor Plaza (2.1km);
Arte Moris (4.4km)

Santana River

Estrada de Bidau

Av Liberdade Emprensa

Hospital Nacional Guido Valadares

LECIDERE

Largo de Lecidere

Av dos Direitos Humanos

Rua Cidade Viana do Castelo

Rua Belarmino Lobo

Rua Cidade de Lisboa

Palácio do Governo

Av Bispo de Medeiros

Rua de Cidade

Av José Maria Marques

Av Alves Aldeia

Ferries to Atauro Island & Oecussi

Nakroma Ferry Office

Resistance Museum

Rua Jacinto de Candido

Western Union

Stamford Medical Clinic

Clock Tower Roundabout

Santa Cruz Massacre Memorial Monument

Farol Lighthouse

MOTAEL

Australian Embassy Clinic

Timor-Leste Immigration Service

UN House

COLMERA

MATADOURO

CAICOLI

Rua Caicoli

Rua Colmera

Rua Quinze de Outubro

Timor Tour & Travel

National Stadium

Rua Circunvalação

Taibessi Bus Terminal

Av Circunvalação

Estrada de Balide

BAIRO PITE

N

0   1 km
0   0.5 miles

Numbered locations: 1, 2, 3, 4, 5, 6, 8, 9, 10, 11, 12, 13, 14, 15, 16, 17, 18, 19, 20, 21, 22, 23, 24, 25

Dili

Dili Marathon   RUNNING
(☺May) Running is huge in Timor-Leste, and locals hope this popular full (42km) and half (21km) marathon will be revived after taking something of a hiatus in recent years. In July there's the 10km First Lady's Cup charity run.

🛏 Sleeping

Cheap beds are rare in Dili; more so following the early-2016 closure of East Timor Backpackers (at press time the owner was considering reopening in a new location). While the big UN crowds have long gone, prices remain high for what you get. Rates are often negotiable.

The Cove   HOSTEL $
(☏7725 1289; www.dtceasttimor.com; Meituit; dm US$15; ☎) Just south of Areia Branca, this new spot's four- and six-bed dorms are disappointingly cramped and characterless; doubles with mod cons (US$65 to US$85) are also available.

Rocella   HOTEL $$
(☏7723 7993; Rua Presidente Nicolau Lobato 18; d incl breakfast US$45; ❄☎) The comfortable and clean rooms here are Dili's best in this price range. There's a pleasant shaded bar-dining area (Portuguese-style mains around US$7) downstairs. Offers free laundry.

**Dive Timor Lorosae
Guest House & Apartments**   GUESTHOUSE $$
(☏7723 7092; www.divetimor.com; Av de Portugal; s US$30, d US$60-100; ❄🌐❄) This well-equipped guesthouse has a share-house vibe: rooms come with a shared bathroom, kitchen and lounge. The stylish apartments are set around the pool and are good value if shared. Breakfast isn't included, but you can grab a pre-dive feed at Castaway Bar upstairs.

Dili Beach Hotel   HOTEL $$
(☏331 0493; www.dilibeachhotel.com; Av de Portugal; incl breakfast d US$45-90; ❄🌐❄) The rooms are a little dark and the lime-green walls don't do it any favours, but the pool is a bonus and the sports bar–restaurant upstairs has a great range of pub-style meals (US$7 to US$14). There's free laundry, and a good secondhand book shop/swap at reception.

Beachside Hotel   HOTEL $$
(☏7754 9681; www.beachsidehoteldili.com; Areia Branca; d from US$85; ☎) Opposite Areia Branca beach, this is one of Dili's best options under $100/night. Tastefully decorated rooms have kitchenettes; more expensive ones overlook the beach. There's a great on-site cafe (7.30am to 7pm). Also offers a 'backpacker' rate of US$30 per person for groups of two to nine.

SPLURGE

The Hotel Timor has historic value and the Novo Turismo is shiny and new, but if you're going to fork out for a Dili hotel we say opt for the **Esplanada** (☑ 331 3088; www.hotelesplanada.com; Av de Portugal; d incl breakfast US$115; ❄ ☎ ☲). It has a great ocean-facing location on Av de Portugal and a good bar-restaurant that makes the most of the views. Two-storey blocks surround a palm-tree-shaded pool at this modern compound; the perfect place to relax after an excursion to the districts.

🍴 Eating

Most of Dili's eateries are concentrated along Av de Portugal (Beach Rd) and along Rua Presidente Nicolau Lobato, with another cluster at Metiaut, about 2km east of the centre towards Cristo Rei.

Starco INDONESIAN, CHINESE $
(Rua Presidente Nicolau Lobato; meals US$3-5; ⊙11am-2pm & 5-9pm) Point at the pre-prepared dishes or order off the small menu for a quick and tasty Indo-Chinese meal. Next to the Plaza Hotel.

'Fish on a Stick' Stalls HAWKER $
(Bebonuk Beach; skewers US$0.25-4; ⊙dinner) From around 4pm every day, the row of blue-roofed beach huts about 300m west of Pertamina Pier are a-smokin' with skewered hunks of chicken, fish and other seafood being cooked over open fires. Your bowels may not thank you for indulging, but it's an interesting sight – just ask permission before taking photos.

Coffee Nook BAKERY, CAFE $
(Rua Presidente Nicolau Lobato; gourmet meat pie US$4.50; ⊙8.30am-6pm Mon-Sat) Dili's answer to the Aussie-style bakery/cafe does decent toasted sandwiches, reheated imported pies, pastries, smoothies, and fresh Maubere Mountain Coffee. In the Central Hotel arcade.

Lita Supermarket SUPERMARKET $
(Av dos Direitos Humanos; ⊙9am-8pm) Sells a wide range of groceries and homewares, and there's a fresh fruit-and-veg market across the road. Good for grabbing supplies before trips to the districts.

★**Castaway Bar** INTERNATIONAL $$
(Av de Portugal; mains US$6-16; ⊙6am-midnight) Crowds enjoy Aussie comfort food staples (salt 'n' pepper calamari, homemade pies) as well as steaks, pizzas and Asian fare at this popular two-storey joint overlooking the waterfront. Check the blackboard for lunch and dinner specials. Stays open until 1am Friday and Saturday if there's a live band.

Windmill CHINESE $$
(Av Marginal, Metiaut; mains US$6-22; ⊙11am-10.30pm) Expats claim this spacious, newer restaurant along the Metiaut beachfront does Dili's best Chinese. Next door, rough 'n' ready **Victoria Restaurante** (Av Marginal, Metiaut; fish with sides per person around $15) does good local BBQ seafood.

Diya INTERNATIONAL $$$
(☑ 331 1111; www.discoveryinntimorleste.com; Rua Presidente Nicolau Lobato; mains US$12-22; ⊙11.30am-10.30pm Mon-Sat, 5.30pm-10.30pm Sun; ❄ ☲) The extensive menu at Timor-Leste's fanciest restaurant ranges from homemade ravioli to grilled chicken with wasabi mash, with some good Indian-style veg options thrown in. It's behind the Discovery Inn (which has a nice bar).

🍷 Drinking & Nightlife

★**Letefoho Specialty Coffee Roaster** COFFEE
(Av de Portugal; ⊙7am-7pm Mon-Fri, 9am-5pm Sat & Sun) The super-friendly, Australian-trained baristas at Timor-Leste's first speciality coffee shop transform house-roasted Timorese beans into perfect flat whites, iced lattes, or whichever way you like it. Located in the Hotel Royal Beach building.

★**Di Za** BAR
(☑ 7808 9877; Av Marginal, Metiaut; ⊙10am-midnight Tue-Sun) Battle it out with Dili's expat crowd for the best seats to watch the sun set over the harbour – passionfruit mojito (US$6) in hand – at this beautifully appointed, Balinese-inspired beachside bar. The Portuguese-style food is good, if pricey (book ahead at the weekend).

Caz Bar BAR
(Areia Branca; ⊙7am-9pm Mon-Fri, to 10pm Sat & Sun) Sink back in your chair on the sand at this popular place that tops the line-up of beachside joints in Aeria Branca. At sunset, it's a toss-up between a beer and a fresh

coconut water. The food menu charts the backpacker favourites; the pancakes hit the spot.

Shopping

Alola Foundation HANDICRAFTS
(www.alolafoundation.org; Av Bispo de Medeiros; ⊙8.45am-5.30pm Mon-Fri, 10am-3pm Sat) Sells *tais* (woven cloth), sculptures, soaps and other crafts from around the country to support its work with the women and children of Timor-Leste.

Tais Market HANDICRAFTS
(Rua Sebastião da Costa; ⊙vary) Each region in Timor-Leste possesses its own distinctive style of *tais*. This daily market has *tais* of varying quality from across the country. Bargain hard.

ⓘ Information

There's no proper tourist office, but the tourism websites www.turismo.gov.tl and www.visiteast-timor.com are handy sources of info.

DANGERS & ANNOYANCES

Be aware that violent outbreaks can and do occur quickly, so stay clear of simmering trouble. Theft can be a problem. The city is all but deserted after dark, when you should take extra care.

INTERNET ACCESS

For free internet, head to the Xanana Cultural Centre. Those staying in Timor-Leste longer (or travelling around) may want to purchase a 3G USB dongle (US$25 to US$65) from one of three internet providers. Expect to pay about $10 for 650MB of data.

Timor Telecom (☑330 3357; www.timor telecom.tp; Hotel Timor; ⊙8am-6pm Mon-Fri, 9am-3pm Sat) Timor-Leste's largest phone and internet provider has the best network coverage in most regions. The Hotel Timor office is usually most convenient; branches in Timor Plaza and at Dili's airport open on Sunday.

Telemor (☑7551 1555; www.telmor.tl; Landmark Plaza; ⊙8am-8pm)

Telkomsel (☑7373 7373; www.telkomcel.tl; Timor Plaza; ⊙9am-7pm)

MEDICAL SERVICES

Medical services in Timor-Leste are limited; serious cases may require evacuation to Australia or Singapore. Check with your embassy for other options.

Australian Embassy Clinic (☑331 1555; Av de Portugal; ⊙Mon-Fri, hours vary) You don't have to be Australian to see the doctor at this fee-per-service clinic located in the Australian Residential Compound.

Hospital Nacional Guido Valadares (☑331 1008; Bidau) A cadre of Western volunteers assists locals at this busy hospital (formerly known as Dili National Hospital) just east of Estrada de Bidau.

Stamford Medical Clinic (☑emergencies 7772 1111, 331 0141; Av dos Mártires de Pátria; ⊙9am-6pm Mon-Fri; 9am-1pm Sat) This spotless, Western clinic also opens after hours for emergencies.

MONEY

ANZ (☑330 6100; www.anz.com/timorleste; Timor Plaza, Comoro; ⊙8am-5pm Mon-Fri) The ATM dispenses US dollars. Also has ATMs at the airport, Tiger Fuel and outside Hotel Dili.

Western Union (☑332 1586; wunionet@yahoo. com.au; Rua José Maria Marques; ⊙9am-4.30pm Mon-Fri, 9am-noon Sat) Transfers funds internationally.

GETTING TO INDONESIA: DILI TO KUPANG

Getting to the border Catch a direct daily Dili–Kupang minibus (US$23, 12 hours) through **Timor Tour & Travel** (☑7723 5093, Kupang office +62 8123 794 199; Rua Quinze de Outubro 17). **Paradise Tour & Travel** (☑728 6673, Kupang office +62 813 3916 1593; Av Presidente Nicolau Lobato) offers the same service to West Timor. Buses depart each morning; book several days in advance.

It's slightly cheaper but harder work to catch a local bus to Batugade (US$5). Walk through both border checkpoints and catch local transport on the other side (US$3 to Atambua, then US$7 Kupang; eight hours). Start early, and expect to wait for transport connections.

At the border You'll need an Indonesian visa, available from the Indonesian Embassy (p809) in Dili. Usual business hours apply.

Moving on To head through to Oecussi you'll need to have a multi-entry visa for Timor-Leste.

For information on doing this crossing in reverse, see p250.

POST

Central Post Office (Av Bispo de Medeiros; ⊙ 9am-noon Mon-Sat, plus 2-5pm Mon-Fri) The only place you can receive/send mail in Dili (aside from DHL in Colmera Plaza) is opposite the Alola Foundation.

ⓘ Getting There & Away

The **Nakroma ferry office** (☑ 331 7264; Av de Portugal; ⊙ 8.30am-5.30pm) is in the large building at the port. When the Nakroma is running (it occasionally takes a maintenance break), ferries for Oecussi (12 hours, US$8) leave at 5pm Monday and Thursday, returning Tuesday and Friday. At the time of writing new operator **Dragon Star Shipping** (☑ 7302 2288, 7302 2266) had just launched a fast service (4½ hours) to Oecussi (tourist class US$45, Monday to Saturday at 8am) and **Beloi Beach Hotel** (p798) was set to add its own Oecussi service. The Nakroma and Beloi Beach Hotel, along with **Compass Charters** (☑ 7723 0965; www.compassadventuretours.com; Av dos Mártires de Pátria), run ferry services to Atauro Island, with Dragon Star Shipping likely to add its own.

Dili's bus 'terminals' (more like shabby shelters) are served by taxis and *mikrolet* (small minibuses). Buses are more frequent in the morning.

Tasitolu Terminal, west of the airport, is the hub for destinations to the west of the country (Ermera, Maliana and Liquiçá). Buses travelling to the east (Baucau, Lospalos, Viqueque) leave from Becora Terminal, about 1.5km east of the Bemori River. The Taibessi Terminal, next to the huge Taibessi market, is the stop for transport to Maubisse, Same and Suai.

ⓘ Getting Around

Mikrolet (US$0.25) buzz about on designated routes during daylight hours. They stop frequently over relatively short distances, so a taxi is usually quicker.

Cars are useful for night travel, but walking and using taxis should suffice otherwise.

Decrepit yellow (unmetered) taxis abound in Dili, and if you negotiate before you get in, most trips cost US$2. If you find a good driver, ask for their mobile number and see if they'll be your night driver, as streets are usually taxi-free by 9pm.

ATAURO ISLAND

After busy Dili, Atauro Island seems positively deserted. Located 30km from Dili over a section of sea 3km deep in parts, it was used as a jail by both the Portuguese and Indonesian governments.

Atauro's sandy beaches are gateways to broad fringing reefs and there's great snorkelling all around the island. Walking trails lead through traditional villages, savannah, and remnants of tropical forest.

🏃 Activities

Dili's dive shops arrange underwater tours of the island's technicolour coral drop-offs (there are no dive shops based on Atauro yet); guesthouses and local fishermen can arrange boat transport for snorkelling the outer reef from US$10 per boat, or stick to the reefs just offshore.

Hike across the island's hilly interior to reach a pristine white-sand beach at **Adara** (three to four hours), where you'll find some of the best snorkelling on the island. Barry's Place and Beloi Beach Hotel can organise lunch and a fishing boat (from US$80/ boat) to get you back to **Beloi**. Both guesthouses can also organise a boat to stunning **Akrema** beach (boat from US$60). You can also hike to **Mt Manucoco** (995m, around three hours up from **Vila**), the island's highest peak.

🛏 Sleeping

Manukoko-Rek Guesthouse   GUESTHOUSE $ (☑ 7748 7301; r per person incl breakfast US$15) Opposite the Bonecas de Atauro doll workshop in Vila, this guesthouse has basic, clean bungalow-style rooms (most with shared bathrooms) and the island's only Italian restaurant (homemade gnocchi US$12 to US$15). Flag down a motorbike or a truck for the 6km drive from the ferry dock (offer US$2).

★ **Beloi Beach Hotel**   GUESTHOUSE $$ (☑ 7558 3421; www.beloibeachhoteltimorleste.com; Beloi; r per person incl meals with/without boat transfers US$160/$80; ❄ ⓦ 🛗) 𝄐 Arguably Timor-Leste's best guesthouse, this lovingly furnished new spot set on a hill just back from Beloi's beach is the ultimate retreat from Dili. Its lovely terrace has great sea views, meals are organic and hearty, and Dili-born owner Neyl – who offers an exhaustive list of activities – makes a mean cocktail.

It's the only guesthouse on the island with its own boat (plus a massage hut and kids play area; a pool was also being built when we passed through). Kids under five stay free, with discounts for under 14s.

Barry's Place
BUNGALOW $$

(☑ 7723 6084; www.barrys-place-atauro.com; Beloi Beach; per person incl meals tent US$30, r US$45) 🏄 Just north of the ferry dock in Beloi, this collection of sun-drenched thatched bungalows, each with its own hammock, is Atauro's original castaway HQ; owner Barry works hard to minimise its footprint on the island. Book ahead.

ℹ Getting There & Away

Compass Charters (p798) and **Beloi Beach Hotel** (p798) both run a daily water-taxi service to Atauro Island (US$45 one way, 90/60 minutes). Boats depart from opposite the European Commission at around 8am.

The **Nakroma ferry** (p798) departs from Dili port every Saturday at 9am and returns at 3pm, taking two hours each way. Fares for foreigners are US$5 each way.

EAST OF DILI

With your own wheels (or on painfully slow public transport) you'll stumble across lime-green rice paddies, mangroves and idyllic beaches where buffalos (and the occasional crocodile) roam. Some of the best diving in the country is just offshore. About 19km east of Manatuto, look out for Laleia's pink 1933 church, arguably Timor-Leste's loveliest.

Baucau

POP 124,061

Perched on a steep hillside 123km east of Dili, Baucau is a tale of two cities (or, rather, large towns): the Old Town with its sea views and Portuguese-era relics, and the bland, Indonesian-built New Town (Kota Baru), 2km uphill. A road leads downhill from the *pousada* thorough a lush ravine to the palm-fringed seaside village of Osolata.

◎ Sights

Old Town
AREA

The colonial buildings in Baucau's Old Town have fared better than those in other villages. Its grand, canary-yellow *mercado municipal* (municipal market) was recently renovated, but is now a government office, and so can only be admired from the outside. The Old Town market has been relegated to the roadside; head to the *pousada*, and the picturesque swimming pool (entry US$0.50), fed by a clear natural spring.

🛏 Sleeping & Eating

Melita Guesthouse
GUESTHOUSE $

(☑ 7725 0267; menobruno@yahoo.com; Rua Vao Redi Bahu, Old Town; s/d fan US$20/30; ❄) With clean rooms, friendly staff and a huge open-air balcony, Melita is one of Baucau's best budget options. To find it, take a left downhill at the Pousada roundabout. Add US$5 per night per room for air-con, and an extra US$2.50 for a good breakfast. Often books out with school groups and aid workers.

Baucau Beach Bungalow
BUNGALOW $

(☑ 7739 7467; Osolata; r per person inc breakfast US$15) Choose from a simple thatched bungalow that sleeps five, or one of three rooms in a neighbouring Indonesian-style house (with shared kitchen and lounge) down on the beach. Good meals can be arranged for US$8, with fish sourced from the local fishing boats. You may need to charter a *mikrolet* from Baucau for a few dollars if you don't have your own wheels for the 6km slog.

Pousada de Baucau
HOTEL $$

(☑ 7724 1111; www.pousadadebaucau.com; Rua de Catedral, Old Town; s/d incl breakfast US$70/75; ❄) Despite its eerie history as a torture centre during the Indonesian occupation, this large, salmon-pink building is one of Timor-Leste's nicest hotels, with *tais* bedheads, timber floorboards and antique furniture. A big block of new rooms behind the main building was going up when we stopped by. The restaurant has good Portuguese food (meals from US$6).

★ Restaurante Amalia
PORTUGUESE $

(☑ 7723 8983; Old Town; mains US$4-7; ☺noon-10pm) Take a shady spot on the outdoor terrace and enjoy the sea views, or pull up a chair inside and admire the wonderfully decorated altar along with hearty Portuguese-style meals (try the coffee beef) served with a smile. It's just off the main road on the block before the *mercado*.

ℹ Information

On the road linking the two parts of town, Timor Telecom has internet access (9am to 5pm, US$1 per hour) and there's a currency exchange next door.

ℹ Getting There & Away

Numerous buses each day drive the 123km between Dili and Baucau (US$5, four hours). Buses also head to Viqueque (US$3, three hours, via Venilale) and Lospalos (US$5, four hours).

South of Baucau

South of Baucau are the lush hills where Fretilin members hid during the Indonesian occupation.

After 28km of rugged road you come to the crumbling colonial buildings of **Venilale**, a town wedged between Mt Matebian in the east and Mt Mundo Perdido (Lost World; 1775m) in the west. Almost halfway, look for the caves tunneled out of the hillside by Japanese forces in WWII. The blue building at the entrance to Venilale houses a tourist information centre; don't miss the 1933 Escola do Reino de Venilale, one of the nation's prettiest colonial relics.

The road deteriorates along the 16km to the misty village of **Ossu**. About 8km south of here take a sharp left at the sign for **Hotel Wailakurini** (📞7832 6687; hotelcomunitariawailakurini@gmail.com; Loi Hunu; d incl breakfast US$40), a friendly guesthouse set up on a picturesque hillside near a river (great for swimming when it's not surging). The meals (US$7) are delicious and staff can arrange guides to take you to Fretilin jungle cave hideouts. Stump an extra US$10 to stay in the fabulous traditional wooden 'hut'.

Travel past roadside waterfalls for another 20-odd minutes to the sprawling town of **Viqueque**. The new town has a market and an abundance of Indonesian monuments. Stay at the newer **Borala Guesthouse** (📞7701 0281; r incl breakfast US$35) (behind the petrol station) or **Luminar Guesthouse** (📞7727 6422; r incl breakfast from US$15). **Finlos Restaurant & Guesthouse** (📞7725 2827; r incl breakfast US$15) is also good for meals.

Buses and *mikrolet* run daily between Viqueque and Baucau (US$3, three hours) and on to Dili (US$5, four hours).

Southeast of Baucau

Southeast of Baucau is **Mt Matebian** (2315m). Topped with a statue of Christ and known as 'Mountain of the Dead', this holy place attracts thousands of pilgrims annually for All Souls Day (2 November). After 19km along the coast road east of Baucau you'll hit peaceful **Laga**. Turn off past the village's pale blue church for the relaxed hill town of **Baguia** (38km), the best base for climbing Matebian. Bed down at **Vila Rabilai** (📞7737 6137; r from US$10), which offers meals and can help organise a guide if you're keen to attempt the tough slog up the mountain (about six hours each way). The town has an abandoned fort dating from 1915; 2km before Baguia you'll also spot the ruins of a Portuguese-era school.

At the time of research, a landslide, along with the closure of the Matebian Guesthouse (the owner hopes to reopen when tourist numbers increase), had detracted from the ease of using **Quelicai** as an alternate hiking base. Watch this space...

East of Baucau

Com

You're literally at the end of the road in Com, a tiny town focused on fishing and tourism. There's decent snorkelling and a good, long beach. At low tide, watch pigs snuffle along the sand for crustaceans.

There are daily *angguna* from Lospalos to Com (US$2, 1½ hours).

🛏 Sleeping & Eating

Simple guesthouses line Com's one and only road parallel to the beach. All can provide simple but hearty meals (ideally with advance notice).

Kati Guesthouse GUESTHOUSE **$$**
(📞7732 4294; d US$20-$25) This brightly painted, *uma lulik*–styled guesthouse right on the beach is Com's best budget option. Its 10 small rooms share bathrooms. Add US$3 for a simple breakfast.

Com Beach Resort HOTEL **$$**
(📞7728 3311; camping $8; r US$25-130; ❄ 🗭) The popularity of this shell-studded 're-sort' has waned since it changed hands a few years ago. Rooms are comfortable (if dated), but the cheapest are cell-like. Has Com's only proper **restaurant** (mains US$8-12; ☉7am-10am, 12pm-2pm, 6.30pm-9.30pm) if you don't fancy eating at your guesthouse.

Tutuala & Jaco Island

The 50km of road from Lautem to Tutuala ventures past the shimmering waters of Lake Ira Lalaro, a few stilted Fataluku houses and through Nino Konis Santana National Park. The road ends on a bluff in Tutuala village, where there are sweeping views out to sea from a renovated Portuguese **pousada** (📞7724 9880; r incl breakfast US$35-55). You'll need a 4WD to tackle the steep 8km track

BALIBÓ

Inland from Batugade is the mountain town of Balibó, where five Australia-based journalists were killed by Indonesian soldiers in October 1975.

The Australian flag the journalists painted for protection is (just) still visible on **Balibo Flag House** (www.balibohouse.com; ⊗8am-noon & 2pm-5pm Mon-Sat, 10am-12noon & 2pm-5pm Sun) **FREE**, which is now a community centre with a memorial inside – press play on the DVD player to watch Greg Shackleton's final, chilling broadcast. The Australian film *Balibo* (1999) was based on these tragic events.

A restored 18th-century Portuguese fort stands on the hill opposite, housing a visitor centre, and the excellent **Balibo Fort Hotel** (☑7709 1555; www.baliboforthotel.com; opposite Balibo Flag House; d/tw incl breakfast US$85/95; ❋🏵) ⌖, which opened in 2015. Its eight spacious, tastefully furnished rooms are set along the path to the restored 18th-century *pousada,* and the food is excellent. At the very least, stop by for a cocktail in the lovely garden bar and enjoy the exquisite ocean views.

down to **Walu**, a picturesque, rocky beach. Turn left after the descent to find thatched cabins at the community-run **Walu Sere** (☑7724 0647; camping own/rented tent US$5/$10, r US$20) ⌖. Fall asleep listening to waves lapping and wake to the stunning vision of Jaco Island, just offshore across the turquoise waters. Development (and overnight stays) is prohibited on this sacred isle, but fishermen will take you across for US$10. Once you arrive, it's like being on a deserted tropical island. The water is crystal clear and there's excellent snorkelling along the coral drop-off.

Staff at Walu Sere can organise tours of the local rock-art caves nearby.

You can take a daily *mikrolet* from Lospalos to Tutuala (US$3, three hours), or you can charter one from Com for about US$20, but you'll have to walk the last 8km down to the beach.

Lospalos

Lospalos, home to the Fataluku-language speakers, is mostly of interest for its market, nearby caves and Fataluku houses. About 3km from the centre, the **Residencia Madre ADM** (7728 2967; dm/s/d incl breakfast US$10/25/40) is the best budget sleeping option. Turn left off the main road to Fuiloro after the excellent Indonesian **restaurant** (nasi goreng US$1.75) run by the Residencia's Catholic sisters.

The **Lospalos Cultural Centre** (☑7799 7661; www.manyhands.org.au) opened its doors in 2014 with a small gallery and cultural presentations available on request. It's in the centre of town next to the old market.

Buses and *mikrolet* run between Lospalos and Baucau (US$5, four hours).

WEST OF DILI

The border with Indonesian West Timor is almost four hours west of Dili along a coast-gripping road punctuated by small villages selling differing wares.

A few kilometres before **Liquiçá**, you'll spot the picturesque seaside ruins of the Portuguese-era **Prisão do Apelo**. Liquiçá itself (34km from Dili) has some grand old buildings; its church was the site of one of the worst massacres of 1999. Just west of town, **Caimeo Beach Camping** (☑7798 8305; www.caimeobeach.com; per tent US$30-65) is *the* best place to stay west of Dili. Located right on the beach, the luxurious tents come with ready-made beds, fans, lights and hot showers. The attached Black Rock Restaurant (meals US$4.50 to US$18.50, 8am to 8pm) has tasty food and daybeds to lounge on.

At beachside **Maubara**, 49km from Dili, there's a Portuguese restaurant (mains US$4 to US$7, 9.30am to 4.30pm Monday to Friday, until 5.30pm Saturday and Sunday) in the rejuvenated 17th-century Dutch **fort** and a handicraft market. *Mikrolet* from Dili stop at both villages (US$1 to US$2). Buses from Dili pass through the tiny border town of **Batugade** (113km from Dili).

The hills of West Timor are in plain view over the rice fields adjoining **Maliana**, 26km inland from **Balibó**. Stay at the clean and modern **Câmara Eclesiástica** (☑7803 9630, 7737 7489; s/d incl breakfast US$30/40), attached to a seminary, and eat at Restaurante Maliana, opposite the market. From Maliana head east to **Marobo** and follow the signs to the *bee manas* (hot springs). You'll need a 4WD for the steep 6km track down. Once a former

Portuguese mountain resort, the hot springs flow into an old pool surrounded by aqueducts covered in lime-green algae. There is no formal accommodation here (yet), but Eco Discovery (p793) in Dili can house you with a local family who can lead hikes to the traditional villages in the hills once inhabited by their elders. Do not hike to this sacred village without permission and a guide.

Continue on to Suai (though roads can be impassable during the wet season). You can also do a round trip to Same and Maubisse from here.

SOUTH OF DILI

From bare winding passes to rainforest canopies that shade coffee beans, the area south of Dili shows how diverse this country is. Coffee-country grabs you in Aileu before you hit the mountain town of Maubisse.

Maubisse

ELEV 1400M

Waking up in chilly Maubisse, 70km from Dili, and watching clouds rising, uncovering the village below, is a highlight of travelling in Timor-Leste.

Buses depart from Dili for Maubisse (US$5, three-odd hours) each morning.

🛌 Sleeping & Eating

★Hakmatek Cooperative   GUESTHOUSE $
(☑7771 4410; turismo_etico@yahoo.com; tw per person US$20) 🍴 Choose from three basic thatched huts with sweeping views at this stunning spot in Tartehi, just south of Maubisse. Don't miss a guided visit to the *uma lulik* (sacred house) on the hill behind it, where some villagers live traditionally. Add US$2.50 for an egg roll breakfast. Proceeds support the local community who runs the cooperative.

Café Maubisse   GUESTHOUSE $
(☑7727 4756; per person US$20) Opposite Maubisse's large church, this simple guesthouse now conveniently has a restaurant.

Pousada de Maubisse   HOTEL $$
(☑7734 5321; r Sun-Thu US$20, Fri & Sat US$56) This historic hilltop *pousada* was formerly the governor's residence. It has gorgeous grounds and views, and good food (mains US$7), but the rooms are in dire need of an upgrade.

Luciano Bar & Restaurant   TIMORESE, INTERNATIONAL $
(☑7839 8948; www.santanatimorleste.com; sandwich US$3.50, buffet for 4 people from US$95; ⊙lunch & dinner) 🍴 This organic restaurant, part of a new 'green school' for local youth, is the best new place to eat in the area (call ahead to order). An ecoresort was also under construction when we stopped by.

Hatubuilico & Mt Ramelau

Wild roses grow by the road and mountain streams trickle through the teeny town of Hatubuilico, located at the base of Mt Ramelau (2963m). Stay at the eight-room Pousada Alecrim Namrau (☑7730 4366; Rua Gruta Ramelau Hun 1; r per person incl breakfast US$15); staff can arrange meals. The uniquely decorated guesthouse is run by the village chief, who can arrange a guide (per person from US$10) to get you up the mountain; most hikers set off in the wee hours to summit before sunrise.

Hiking from the village to the Virgin Mary statue at the top of Mt Ramelau takes up to three hours; with a 4WD you can drive 2.5km to a meadow from where it's a two-hour walk to the top. The trail is a wide walking path, with plenty of evidence of use by horses, and is very easy to follow (though hiring a guide helps to support the community). An open-air church sits on a plateau at the 2700m mark. From the peak both the south and north coasts are visible. Dress adequately, as the summit temperature averages 5°C.

From Maubisse, the Hatubuilico turn-off is at the 81km post; you'll reach the village after 18km (around two hours in your own vehicle). If the road is passable, *angguna* (tray trucks) travel from Maubisse to Hatubuilico on Wednesdays and Saturdays. The price depends on the number of passengers, but the trip should cost around US$4 and take three hours.

Same & Betano

Same (sar-may), 43km south of Maubisse, is a lush town at the base of a picturesque valley. There's a great little handicrafts market in the centre and a couple of good places to stay.

If you've made it this far, it is worth making the simple 45-minute *mikrolet* journey to the quiet black-sand beach at Betano

(27km). From here, in dry season, you can journey east over narrow tracks through crocodile-infested mangroves to Viqueque (this takes five or more hours by 4WD).

Mikrolet run frequently between Maubisse and Same (US$5, three hours) and between Same and Betano (US$1.50, 45 minutes).

🛏 Sleeping

Hotel Umaliurai   GUESTHOUSE **$$**
(☑ 7725 3849; bmonagh@yahoo.com; r incl breakfast s US$35-60, d US$50-75; ❄ ❄) The best rooms in the Same area have teak furniture, air-con, satellite TV and fridges. Meals (US$6 to US$12) are delicious. Rates include laundry.

Suai

Suai, the south coast's main town, sprawls 5km inland and is a confusing collection of villages. The main town, Debos, is dominated by a recently rebuilt cathedral, where, in September 1999, locals were pushed to their deaths from the balcony by Indonesian forces. Look for the memorial to 'Black September' at the nearby Our Lady of Fatima Church, also the scene of the grizzly massacre of around 200 locals, including three priests.

By the sea, the traditional fishing village of Suai Loro still feels a world away from the oil supply base under construction a few kilometres east.

Angguna run between Suai and Maubisse (around US$4, at least five hours), via Ainaro (with its colourful church) or Same. You can also get here via Maliana.

🛏 Sleeping & Eating

Fronteria Guesthouse   GUESTHOUSE **$$**
(s/d incl breakfast US$25/35) This bare-bones guesthouse will do the job for budgeteers. The guesthouse is located down the hill behind Our Lady of Fatima Church in Debos.

Eastern Dragon   CHINESE **$**
(☑ 223 0047; easterndragondet@yahoo.com; mains US$4-6; ⊗ 10am-2pm & 6-10pm) This Chinese restaurant on the main road into Suai (near the petrol station) is the best place to eat in the area. It's attached to the characterless and pricey but comfortable hotel (single/double including breakfast US$52/65) of the same name. Also has a small supermarket.

OECUSSI

POP 64,025 / AREA 814 SQ KM

The remote enclave of Oecussi is a Cinderella-in-waiting. Surrounded on all sides by Indonesian West Timor, Oecussi can be tricky to get to (although a new fast ferry helps). But if you make the journey, you'll be rewarded with long stretches of beach and reef and absolute quiet and isolation, although this could change as the central government has targeted Oecussi for economic development. There is talk of a Macau-backed casino and a hotel.

Pantemakassar, aka Oecussi Town, is (literally) a one-taxi town. It's a flat, spread-out town with so little going on that any movement seems surprising. There are frequent sightings of dugongs in the waters here, and the sheer coral drop-off about 20m offshore augurs well for snorkelling, though a 'croc watch' is essential. Just 1.5km to its south you can climb up to the rapidly disappearing remains of old Portuguese fort Fatusuba. Travel 5km along the coast west of Pantemakassar and you'll find Lifau, the site of the original Portuguese settlement. A rock-studded monument commemorates the first landing. The best beach begins 2km east of town on Pantai Mahata, which ends at a stunning red-rock headland.

The newer rooms at Rao Hotel & Restaurant (☑ 7755 6255; r US$20-45; ❄) are clean and have all the basics. Book ahead. Oecussi Amasat (☑ 7732 9755; oe-cusseamasat@hotmail.com; r incl breakfast from US$55), a homestay run by an Australian owner and his wife from Oecussi, is comfortable.

Transport to/from Dili is much improved with the introduction of the Dragon Star Shipping fast ferry (☑ 7302 2288, 7302 2266; one way tourist class US$45) (around four hours), departing Dili in the morning and returning in the afternoon.

The often-crowded Nakroma ferry (☑ Dili office 331 7264) travels from Dili to Oecussi (12 hours) on Monday and Thursday evenings. The return departure is around 5.30pm on Tuesday and Friday. In Pantemakassar the office is opposite the dock.

You'll need an Indonesian visa to get from Oecussi to West Timor overland (available in Dili). *Ojek* (motorbikes that take passengers) can give you a lift from the border to town for a few dollars.

UNDERSTAND TIMOR-LESTE

Timor-Leste Today

Life after independence was turbulent, with a series of violent events (communal conflict, violence between the army and police and an assumed attempted coup) leaving many wondering: when do the good times start?

Well, finally, for many, the good times *have* started. The nation is playing host to international events and petroleum revenues are (slowly) flowing from the Timor Sea. Plenty of Timorese-owned businesses are in operation. The international presence is still here and newcomers arrive daily.

Fretilin, which led the struggle for independence during the Indonesian occupation, suffered from divisions in 2005. Prime Minister Mari Alkatiri sacked one third of the army in March 2006 and, in the ensuing months of rioting, more than 150,000 people fled their homes. Relative peace only returned after public demonstrations forced Alkatiri to resign, and the UN force was beefed up again. In 2007, after a year as acting prime minister, José Ramos-Horta was elected president of Timor-Leste with 70% of the vote. The vote for prime minister was not as clear-cut. Xanana Gusmão's Council of National Congress for Timorese Reconstruction (CNRT) came second to Fretilin, winning 24% of the votes to Fretilin's 29%. However, CNRT quickly formed a coalition with other parties and Gusmão was sworn in as prime minister. Angry Fretilin supporters rioted, causing damage around the country and boosting the numbers of the more than 100,000 people already living in crowded internally displaced persons camps.

In February 2008, Ramos-Horta was shot and injured near his home during an alleged attempted coup led by former naval commander and Timor-Leste Defence Force (F-FDTL) Major Alfreido Reinado. Reinado, who had been playing a cat-and-mouse game with Australian forces since escaping from jail in 2006, was killed at the scene by Ramos-Horta's security. Since 2008 Timor-Leste has been a safer and more stable country. Elections in 2012 were peaceful and the UN and International Stabilisation Force (Australian and New Zealand forces) both withdrew without any problems. The nation's focus is now on development rather than security, with new Prime Minister Rui Maria de Araújo (inaugurated in February 2015 following Gusmão's retirement) looking to tourism, agriculture and fisheries to diversify the nation's economy from oil and gas.

History

Portugal Settles In

Little is known of Timor before AD 1500, although Chinese and Javanese traders visited the island from at least the 13th century, and possibly as early as the 7th century. These traders searched the coastal settlements for aromatic sandalwood and beeswax. Portuguese traders arrived between 1509 and 1511, and in 1556 a handful of Dominican friars established the first Portuguese settlement at Lifau in Oecussi and set about converting the Timorese to Catholicism.

To counter the Portuguese, the Dutch established a base at Kupang in western Timor in 1653. The Portuguese appointed an administrator to Lifau in 1656, but the Topasses (people from the region who claimed Portuguese ancestry and/or identified with the culture) went on to become a law unto themselves, driving out the Portuguese governor in 1705.

By 1749 the Topasses controlled central Timor and marched on Kupang, but the Dutch won the ensuing battle, expanding their control of western Timor in the process. On the Portuguese side, after more attacks from the Topasses in Lifau, the colonial base was moved east to Dili in 1769.

The 1859 Treaty of Lisbon divided Timor, giving Portugal the eastern half, together with the north-coast pocket of Oecussi; this was formalised in 1904. Portuguese Timor was a sleepy and neglected outpost ruled through a traditional system of *liurai* (local chiefs). Control outside Dili was limited and it wasn't until the 20th century that the Portuguese intervened in a major way in the interior.

World War II

In 1941 Australia sent a small commando force (known as Sparrow Force) into Portuguese Timor to counter the Japanese. Although the military initiative angered neutral Portugal and dragged the colony into the Pacific War, it slowed the Japanese expansion. In February 1942 the Japanese forced the surrender of the Allies following the bloody Battle of Timor, but several hundred commandos stayed on for another year, waging many successful raids on Japanese forces with the help of locals, including *creados* (Timorese boys who assisted Australian servicemen during WWII). The Japanese retaliated by razing villages, seizing food and killing Timorese in areas where Australians were operating. By the end of the war, up to 60,000 Timorese had died.

Portugal Pulls Out, Indonesia Invades

After WWII the colony reverted to Portuguese rule. Following the Carnation Revolution in Portugal on 25 April 1974, Lisbon set about discarding its colonial empire. Within a few weeks political parties had formed in Timor-Leste, and the Timorese Democratic Union (UDT) attempted to seize power in August 1975. A brief but brutal civil war saw UDT's rival Fretilin (previously known as the Association of Timorese Social Democrats) come out on top, and it urgently declared the independent existence of the Democratic Republic of East Timor on 28 November, amid an undeclared invasion by Indonesia. On 7 December, Indonesia officially launched its full-scale attack on Dili after months of incursions (including at Balibó, where five Australia-based journalists were killed on 16 October).

Anti-communist Indonesia feared an independent East Timor governed by a left-leaning Fretilin would bring communism to its door, and commenced its invasion of East Timor just a day after Henry Kissinger and Gerald Ford departed Jakarta, having tacitly given their assent. (Indeed, the Americans urged the Indonesians to conduct a swift campaign so that the world wouldn't see them using weapons the US had provided). Australia and Britain also sided with Indonesia.

Falintil, the military wing of Fretilin, fought a guerrilla war against Indonesian troops (which numbered 35,000 by 1976) with marked success in the first few years. It weakened considerably thereafter, though the resistance continued. The cost of the takeover to the Timorese was huge; it's estimated that up to 183,000 died in the hostilities, and the ensuing disease and famine.

By 1989 Indonesia had things firmly under control and opened East Timor to limited controlled tourism. On 12 November 1991, Indonesian troops fired on protesters who'd gathered at the Santa Cruz Cemetery in Dili to commemorate the killing of an independence activist. With the event captured on film and aired around the world, the Indonesian government admitted to 19 killings (later increased to more than 50), although it's estimated that over 250 died in the massacre. While Indonesia introduced a civilian administration, the military remained in control. Aided by secret police and civilian pro-Indonesian militia to crush dissent, reports of arrest, torture and murder were commonplace.

CAST OF CHARACTERS

Two men form the face of modern-day Timor-Leste.

Xanana Gusmão is Timor-Leste's charismatic former prime minister. Gusmão was a leader of guerrilla forces from 1978 until 1992, when he was captured and imprisoned in Jakarta. He became the first president of the country, and earned the enmity of many of his old Fretilin brethren by breaking with the party after independence. Following the troubled 2007 parliamentary elections, Gusmão was named prime minister, leading the National Congress for Timorese Reconstruction (CNRT) party. His former wife, Australian-born Kirsty Sword Gusmão, runs prominent charity the Alola Foundation. Gusmão retired in February 2015, though, passing the prime ministerial baton to the Minister for Health, Rui Maria de Araújo, though, remains heavily involved in strategic planning and economic development.

José Ramos-Horta is the magnetic Nobel Prize winner who spent 20 years in exile during the Indonesian occupation. He took over as prime minister after Alkatiri was forced from office in 2006, and was elected president in 2007 with a huge margin. In 2008 he was shot during an alleged assassination attempt and recovered in Darwin, Australia. In 2012 the widely respected Taur Matan Ruak, a former leader of the resistance army Falintil, defeated him at the polls. Ramos-Horta now works as the UN secretary general's special envoy to Guinea-Bissau, but can often be seen hooning around Timor-Leste in his navy-blue convertible hot rod.

Independence

After Indonesia's President Soeharto resigned in May 1998, his replacement BJ Habibie unexpectedly announced a referendum for autonomy in East Timor. January 1999 marked the commencement of attacks by Indonesian military-backed militias, who began terrorising the population to coerce them to reject independence.

Attacks peaked in April 1999, just prior to the arrival of the UN Electoral Mission, when, according to a report commissioned by the UN Office of the High Commissioner for Human Rights, up to 60 people were massacred near Liquiçá church. Other attacks occurred in Dili and Maliana while Indonesian authorities watched on. Attacks escalated in the weeks prior to the vote, with thousands seeking refuge in the hills away from the reach of the Indonesian army and militia.

Despite threats, intimidation and brutality, on 30 August 1999 East Timor voted overwhelmingly (78.5%) for independence from, rather than autonomy within, Indonesia. Though the Indonesian government promised to respect the results of the UN-sponsored vote, militias and Indonesian forces went on a rampage, killing people, burning and looting buildings and destroying infrastructure.

While the world watched in horror, the UN was attacked and forced to evacuate, leaving the East Timorese defenceless. On 20 September, weeks after the main massacres in Suai, Dili, Maliana and Oecussi, the Australian-led International Force for East Timor (Interfet) arrived in Dili. The Indonesian forces and their militia supporters left for West Timor, leaving behind an incomprehensible scene of destruction. Half a million people had been displaced, and telecommunications, power installations, bridges, government buildings, shops and houses were destroyed. More than 15 years on, many of these physical scars remain.

The UN set up a temporary administration during the transition to independence, and aid and foreign workers flooded into the country. As well as physically rebuilding the country, Timor-Leste has had to create a civil service, police, judiciary, education, health system and so on, with staff recruited and trained from scratch.

The UN handed over government to Timor-Leste on 20 May 2002. Falintil leader Xanana Gusmão was elected president of the new nation, and the long-time leader of Fretilin, Mari Alkatiri, who ran the party from exile in Mozambique, was chosen as prime minister.

Birth Pangs

In December 2002 Dili was the scene of riots, as years of poverty and frustration proved too much for the nascent democracy. The economy was in a shambles, and without any viable industry or employment potential, Timor-Leste was reliant almost entirely on foreign aid.

Only a small UN contingent remained in Timor-Leste by mid-2005. As the number of outsiders shrank, the challenges of creating a new nation from the ground up became all too apparent. Parliamentary factions squabbled while the enormous needs of the people festered.

The Future

Timor-Leste continues to rely partly on foreign money, and proceeds from its petroleum fields are filtering through.

In 2006 Australia and Timor-Leste signed an agreement to give US$10 billion in oil revenue to each country over the next 40 years, but Timor-Leste is attempting to annul the treaty, claiming Australian intelligence agencies bugged Timor's cabinet room during negotiations. During the negotiations, Australia's Howard government was accused of using bullying tactics to deny the struggling and poor country its fair share of the money (initially offering only 20%, later

---

WHICH LANGUAGE?

Most East Timorese speak several languages. On the street you'll hear Tetun (also known as Tetum), one of two official languages, and most people also speak a regional dialect (16 are officially recognised, but there are thought to be 32 surviving dialects). Most folks educated before and after the Indonesian occupation speak Portuguese (the other official language), while those who were educated or working between 1975 and 1999 are likely to be more fluent in Bahasa Indonesia. Any attempt to communicate in Tetun will be greeted with big smiles. Lonely Planet's *East Timor Phrasebook* is a handy introduction.

agreeing on a 50/50 split). The arbitration case is an ongoing David and Goliath battle, and one that could monumentally impact Timor-Leste's oil revenues.

High in the hills outside Dili is another natural resource: coffee. Some 100,000 people work seasonally to produce arabica beans, noted for their cocoa and vanilla character. Shade-grown and organic, Timorese coffee is prized by companies such as Starbucks, and production is increasing.

Timor-Leste's tourism industry has great potential, although there needs to be a perception of stability (and more developed infrastructure) for numbers to grow beyond the 9600 or so tourists who currently visit each year.

People & Culture

The National Psyche

Timor-Leste's identity is firmly rooted in its survival of extreme hardship and foreign occupation. As a consequence of the long and difficult struggle for independence, the people of Timor-Leste are profoundly politically aware – not to mention proud and loyal. While there is great respect for elders and church and community leaders, there lurks a residual suspicion surrounding foreign occupiers, most recently in the form of the UN (not to mention Australian oil bosses). Religious beliefs (Catholic and animist) also greatly inform the national consciousness.

Lifestyle

Most East Timorese lead a subsistence lifestyle: what is farmed (or caught) is eaten. While the birth rate continues to decline, large families (with an average of 5.7 children per mother) are still common, and infant mortality remains high. Malnutrition and food insecurity is widespread. Infrastructure remains limited; only a few towns have 24-hour electricity and running water. Most roads are dismal.

Family life exists in simple thatched huts, though rising wages have meant that satellite dishes are appearing beside even the most basic huts, beaming Indonesian TV into homes. NGOs and aid projects have helped to create self sufficiency, but the ability to rise above poverty is a huge challenge for many as bad roads and drought or floods play havoc. Motorised vehicles remain rare; on weekends, buses are packed with those heading to the family events that form the backbone of Timorese life.

Population

Timor-Leste has at least a dozen indigenous groups, the largest being the Tetun, who live around Suai, Dili and Viqueque. The next largest group is the Mambai, who live in the mountains of Maubisse, Ainaro and Same. The Kemak live in the Ermera and Bobonaro districts; the Bunak also live in Bobonaro, and their territory extends into West Timor and the Suai area. The Baikeno live in the area around Pantemakassar, and the Fataluku people are famous for their high-peaked houses in the area around Lospalos. More groups are scattered among the interior mountains.

Religion

Religion is an integral part of daily life for most Timorese. Recent estimates indicate 98% of Timor-Leste's population is Catholic (though many observe the faith alongside animist beliefs), 1% Protestant and less than 1% Muslim.

Indigenous beliefs revolve around an earth mother, from whom all humans are born and shall return after death, and her male counterpart, the god of the sky or sun. These are accompanied by a complex web of spirits from ancestors and nature. The *matan d'ok* (medicine man) is the village mediator with the spirits; he can divine the future and cure illness. Many people believe in various forms of black magic.

Arts

MUSIC & DANCE

The East Timorese love a party, and celebrate with *tebe* (dancing) and singing. Music has been passed down through the years and changed little during Indonesian times. Traditional trancelike drumming is used in ceremonies, while local rock and hip-hop groups are popular. Country-and-western style is popular, too, and features plenty of guitar use and the usual lovelorn themes.

TEXTILES

Each region has its own style of *tais* (woven by women using small back-strap looms) and they're usually used as skirts or shawls for men *(tais mane)* or sewn up to form a tube skirt/dress for women *(tais feto)*. Some are made with organic dyes.

TIMOR-LESTE PEOPLE & CULTURE

Environment

The Land

Timor-Leste consists of the eastern half of the island of Timor, Atauro and Jaco Islands, and the enclave of Oecussi on the north coast, 70km to the west and surrounded by Indonesian West Timor.

Once part of the Australian continental shelf, Timor fully emerged from the ocean only four million years ago, and is therefore composed mainly of marine sediment, principally limestone. Rugged mountains, a product of the collision with the Banda Trench to the north, run the length of the country, the highest of which is Mt Ramelau (2963m).

Wildlife

Timor-Leste is squarely in the area known as Wallacea, a kind of crossover zone between Asian and Australian plants and animals, and one of the most biologically distinctive areas on earth.

Timor-Leste's north coast is a global hot spot of whale and dolphin activity, and its coral reefs are home to a diverse range of marine life. Species spotted include dugongs, blue whales and dolphins. More than 260 species of bird have been recorded in its skies. The eastern fringe of the nation was declared a national park partly because of its rich bird life: it's home to honeyeaters, critically endangered lesser sulfur-crested cockatoos and endangered *wetar* ground-doves. The number of mammals and reptiles in the wild is limited, though monkeys, civets, crocodiles and snakes make appearances.

Environmental Issues

Timor-Leste's first national park, the Nino Konis Santana National Park, was declared in 2008 – a 123,000-hectare parcel of land (including some tropical forest) and sea at the country's eastern tip, also incorporating Jaco Island and Tutuala. Most of the country, however, is suffering from centuries of deforestation, and erosion is a huge problem: roads and even villages have been known to slip away. Quarries popping up on roadsides near offshore dive sites are a concern.

SURVIVAL GUIDE

ⓘ Directory A–Z

ACCOMMODATION

Dili's accommodation is nothing to write home about: expect sit-down loos and air-conditioning and not a lot more. Accommodation with adjoining restaurants/bars is a good idea for those who'd prefer not to travel around at night. Elsewhere, don't expect anything swank – if you get a clean room with good mosquito nets and a few hours of electricity for reading and a fan, you're doing well.

In most places you'll be able to find some sort of accommodation, even if it is a homestay (offer at least US$10 a night). Washing facilities are likely to be Indonesian *mandi*-style (a tub from which you scoop water in a small bucket to wash yourself).

The following price ranges refer to the price of a room:

$ less than US$25

$$ US$25 to US$100

$$$ more than US$100

CUSTOMS REGULATIONS

You can bring the following into Timor-Leste:

Alcohol 1.5L of any type

Cigarettes 200

Money Up to US$10,000 per person, but amounts over US$5000 must be declared. No restrictions on taking cash out of the country.

DANGERS & ANNOYANCES

Malaria and dengue are a concern; take precautions. Stick to bottled water. Antibiotics and other pharmaceuticals are easily bought in Dili but are hard to find elsewhere.

Cases of theft occur most frequently from cars, with mobile phones a prime target. Be aware of personal security issues, particularly in Dili. Walking around or taking taxis after dark, unless you're in a group, is risky. There have been attacks on tourists in isolated spots. Given the bouts of political instability that can occur in Timor-Leste, check the current situation before you visit (although government travel advisories are usually cautious in the extreme).

Drive with extreme caution on the nation's notoriously bad roads; hiring a driver is recommended.

ELECTRICITY

At hotels you can often plug in Australian flat three-pin plugs (type I), in other places two-pin (round) plugs are used.

EMBASSIES & CONSULATES

More than two dozen countries have embassies, consulates or representative offices in Dili.

Australian Embassy (📞 332 2111; www.
timorleste.embassy.gov.au; Av dos Mártires de
Pátria) Also assists Canadian citizens.

French Representative Office (📞 731 4081;
frcoopedili@gmail.com; Casa Europa, Av Presidente Nicolau Loboto)

Indonesian Embassy (📞 331 7107; www.kemlu.
go.id/dili; Rua Gov. Maria de Serpa Rosa, Farol)

Irish Representative Office (📞 332 4880; www.
irishaid.gov.ie; Rua Alferes Duarte Arbiro 12)

New Zealand Embassy (📞 331 0087; dili@
mfat.govt.nz; Rua Geremias do Amaral, Motael)
Also assists British citizens.

Portuguese Embassy (📞 331 2531; embaix
ador@embaixadaportugal.tl; Av Presidente
Nicolau Loboto)

US Embassy (📞 332 4684; www.timor-leste.
usembassy.gov; Av de Portugal) At the western
end of Av de Portugal.

FOOD

As an approximate guide, the following price
ranges refer to the price of a main course.

$ less than US$5
$$ US$5 to US$10
$$$ more than US$10

INSURANCE

Travel insurance is vital in Timor-Leste. Medical
facilities outside Dili are limited and any serious
cases generally get evacuated from the country
to Darwin or Singapore. Accordingly, travellers
need to ensure that they have full evacuation
coverage.

INTERNET ACCESS

Many hotels in Dili have decent (if slow) wi-fi
access, but there are a couple of internet cafes
in Dili. All Timor Telecom offices in the district
capitals have access (US$1 an hour), as do high-
er-end hotels attracting foreigners outside of
Dili, such as the Pousada Baucau.

LEGAL MATTERS

If you are the victim of a serious crime, go to the
nearest police station and notify your embassy.
If arrested, you have the right to a phone call and
legal representation, which your embassy can
help locate.

LGBT TRAVELLERS

There's no organised network for the LGBT
community in Timor-Leste, but it's also unlikely
that there will be any overt discrimination. While
there is no law against homosexuality, it's wise
to be less demonstrative in the more conservative rural areas outside of Dili.

OPENING HOURS

In Dili most of the budget and midrange eateries are open from morning until late, with the
high-end restaurants only doing lunch (noon

to 2pm) and dinner (6pm to 10pm). Expect
smaller shops to be open from 9am to 6pm
and closed on Sundays. Larger supermarkets
are generally open 8am to 8pm everyday.
Outside Dili, there are only a handful of places
that keep business hours, typically 9am to
6pm Monday to Friday, sometimes with a
long lunchtime siesta as a reminder of the old
Portuguese influence, and maybe with a few
Saturday hours to keep busy.

PUBLIC HOLIDAYS

Timor-Leste has a large list of public holidays;
many special days of commemoration are declared each year.

New Year's Day 1 January

Good Friday March/April (date varies)

World Labour Day 1 May

Restoration of Independence Day 20 May
(the day in 2002 when sovereignty was transferred from the UN)

Corpus Christi Day May/June (date varies)

Popular Consultation Day 30 August (marks
the start of independence in 1999)

Idul Fitri End of Ramadan (date varies)

All Saints' Day 1 November

All Souls' Day 2 November

Idul Adha Muslim day of sacrifice (date varies,
usually September)

National Youth Day 12 November (commemorates the Santa Cruz Cemetery massacre)

Proclamation of Independence Day 28
November

National Heroes' Day 7 December

**Day of Our Lady of Immaculate Conception
and Timor-Leste Patroness** 8 December

Christmas Day 25 December

TELEPHONE
Phone Codes

International access code 📞 0011

International country code 📞 670

Landline numbers 7 digits starting with a 2,
3 or 4

Mobile numbers 8 digits starting with a 7

Mobile Phones

Bring an unlocked handset with you and buy a
SIM card from **Timor Telecom** (p797), **Telemor**
(p797), or **Telkomsel** (p797) in Dili or a regional
office.

TOILETS

Hotels and restaurants have toilet facilities
ranging from modern Western flush toilets down
to *mandi*-style (a hole in the ground with a bucket of water to flush).

TOURIST INFORMATION

Timor-Leste doesn't have a central tourist office, but you can pick up a Dili map at the Xanana Cultural Centre. Dili's expat community is especially generous with information. Language barriers aside, locals are also very happy to help.

VISAS

Dili International Airport & Dili Seaport Arrivals

An entry visa (US$30 for 30 days) is granted to holders of a valid passport on arrival. Always ask for a 30-day visa, even if you don't plan on staying that long. Tourist visas can be extended for 30 days (US$35) or 60 days (US$75) with a Timorese sponsor. If needing a multiple-entry visa or to stay between 30 and 90 days, you can apply for the Visa Application Authorisation before arrival.

Land-Border Arrivals From Indonesia

All nationalities (other than Indonesian and Portuguese nationals) must apply for a Visa Application Authorisation prior to their arrival at the border – apply in person at a consulate (there's one in Kupang) or via the Immigration Service's website (http://migracao.gov.tl) and they'll email you a printable authorisation letter in about 10 working days. You need to present this and the US$30 fee at the border.

VOLUNTEERING

Many NGOs and local organisations take on volunteers to assist in a wide variety of roles. Visit www.unofficialeasttimor.com and the links page at www.etan.org for voluminous listings.

It is essential to do your homework about the organisations and their work. Lonely Planet does not endorse any organisations that we do not work with directly.

WOMEN TRAVELLERS

Sanitary products are available in Dili, but can be scarce in the districts.

Getting There & Away

There are no passenger boat services to Timor-Leste from other countries.

AIR
Airports & Airlines

You can fly to Dili from Denpasar (Bali) and Jakarta (Indonesia), Darwin (Australia) and Singapore. Dili's Nicolau Lobato International Airport is a 10-minute drive from town. The 24-hour

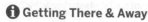

DEPARTURE TAX

There's a departure tax of US$10 when leaving Dili's airport.

Flybus airport shuttle (☑7750 8585; kijoli@ bigpond.com) can pick up and drop off for US$10 per person, or you can share a taxi for US$10. Mikrolet (small minibuses) charge $US0.25 from the main road into town.

Air Timor (☑331 2777; www.air-timor.com; Timor Paza, Rua Presidente Nicolau Lobato, Comoro; ☺8am-5pm Mon-Sat, to noon Sun) Flies daily between Dili and Denpasar (Bali) and Singapore on Tuesdays, Thursdays and Saturdays.

Sriwijaya Air (☑331 1355; www.sriwijayaair. co.id; Timor Paza, Rua Presidente Nicolau Lobato, Comoro; ☺9am-4pm) Flies daily between Dili and Denpasar (Bali) and Jakarta.

Air North (☑+61 8 8920 4001; www.airnorth. com.au) Flies at least twice daily between Dili and Darwin (Australia). At the time of writing Air North did not have an office in Dili, but you can book online.

Getting Around

BICYCLE

New bikes can be purchased in Dili from around US$150 (United, opposite the Presidential Palace, has cheaper bikes; for serious rigs/repairs try Benefika, opposite the Resistance Museum). Road conditions away from the north coast call for proper mountain bikes.

BOAT

Ferry transport is available between Dili and Oecussi on the **Nakroma ferry** (p798) and **Dragon Star Shipping** (p798). **Beloi Beach Hotel** (p798) and **Compass Charters** (p798) run daily water-taxi services to/from Atauro Island; the Nakroma services Atauro on Saturdays.

BUS

Mikrolet operate around Dili and other large towns. Crowded buses do the main routes from Dili to Lospalos, Viqueque, Maliana and Suai. More rugged routes are covered by anguna (tray trucks where passengers, including the odd buffalo or goat, all pile into the back). If anguna aren't covering their usual turf you can be assured the road conditions are exceptionally dire. Trip times are a rough guide only – times depend on how bad the roads are and the whim of the driver when it comes to the frequency and length of stops.

CAR & MOTORCYCLE

Timor-Leste's notoriously bad roads are a minefield of animals and school children. Dips, ditches and entire missing sections of road are common, as are very fast karetta estadu (government car) drivers. There are plenty of blind corners. Fortunately, upgrades are afoot – works on the Dili–Batugade and Dili–Maubisse stretches were nearing completion as of late 2015.

While conventional cars can handle Dili, a 4WD is still recommended for the roads elsewhere. Small 4WDs can be rented in Dili for around US$95 per day; try **eSilva** (☑ 332 5055; www. esilvacarrentals.com; Av dos Mártires de Pátria, Comoro; ☉ 8am-5pm Mon-Sat, 8am-noon Sun), **RentLo** (☑ 7741 6982; www.rentlocarhire.com; Av dos Mártires de Pátria, Comoro; ☉ 8am-5pm Mon-Sat) or **EDS** (☑ 7723 0880; www. eds-timorleste.com) (all can organise a driver, which is recommended). For motorbikes, head to **Taltabi Motor** (☑ 7795 7364; Av dos Mártires de Pátria, Comoro) ($35 per day). As well as the stretches listed above, the only other 'good' road runs from Dili to Com via Baucau. The International Drivers Permit is not technically valid in Timor-Leste, but most foreign license cards are accepted for visitors on tourist visas who are pulled over.

Fuel

Petrol (gasoline) in Portuguese is *bensin*, diesel fuel is *solar;* expect to pay from US$1.20 to US$1.60 per litre. **Tiger Fuel** (☑ 7723 1200; Av dos Mártires de Pátria, Comoro) is the best place to fill up in Dili.

HITCHING

Locals on long walks into towns may ask for a ride. Waiting for a lift may be the only option if you're leaving Oecussi and heading into Kefamenanu in West Timor. However, hitchhiking is never entirely safe, so we don't recommend it.

Vietnam

📞 84 / POP 94.3 MILLION

Best Places to Eat

➡ Minh Thuy's (p826)
➡ Hill Station Signature Restaurant (p841)
➡ Nu Eatery (p867)
➡ The Racha Room (p889)
➡ Lac Canh Restaurant (p873)

Best Beaches

➡ Phu Quoc (p897)
➡ An Bang (p868)
➡ Mui Ne (p875)
➡ Phu Thuan (p859)
➡ Bai Dai (p874)

Why Go?

A kaleidoscope of dazzling colours and subtle shades, limestone highlands and endless rice paddies, full-on cities and laid-back beach resorts, deeply moving war sites and grand colonial-era architecture – Vietnam has a unique appeal.

The nation is a budget traveller's dream, with inexpensive transport, outstanding street food, good-value accommodation and *bia hoi* – perhaps the world's cheapest beer.

Nature has gifted Vietnam soaring mountains in the north, tropical islands in the south and a sensational, curvaceous coastline of ravishing sandy beaches. Travelling here you'll witness children riding buffalo, see the impossibly intricate textiles of hill-tribe communities, taste the super-fresh and incredibly subtle flavours of Vietnamese cuisine and hear the buzz of a million motorbikes.

This is a dynamic nation on the move, where life is lived at pace. Prepare yourself for the ride of your life.

When to Go
Hanoi

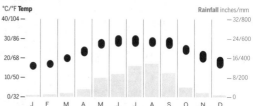

Dec–Mar Expect cool weather north of Hue as the winter monsoon brings cloud, mist and drizzle.

Apr Danang's riverfront explodes with colour and noise during the city's fireworks festival.

Jul & Aug Perfect beach time on the central coastline, with balmy sea and air temperatures.

Don't Miss

Northern Vietnam comprises one of the world's most impressive limestone landmasses, a vast swathe of spectacular scenery that has been eroded into ethereal rock formations. The myriad pinnacle-like islands of Halong Bay are one superb example of this spectacular karst scenery, or head to neighbouring Lan Ha Bay for less crowds.

Near Ninh Binh, the jagged limestone mountains of Tam Coc are a surreal sight, while further south the extraordinary Phong Nha-Ke Bang National Park is home to three gargantuan cave systems (including the world's largest cave) set in tropical forest studded with towering peaks.

ITINERARIES

One Week

Begin in Hanoi, immerse yourself in Old Quarter life and tour the capital's sights. Then it's a day trip to Halong Bay to lap up the surreal karst scenery. Move down to Hue to explore the imperial citadel and then shift to Hoi An for two days of foodie treats, old-world ambience and beach time. Finish off with a night in Ho Chi Minh City.

One Month

Check out the capital, seeing the sights and experiencing Hanoi's unique street life. Tour incomparable Halong Bay, followed by more epic scenery in the highlands around Sapa and Bac Ha. Then it's the extraordinary caves of Phong Nha. Hue, city of pagodas and tombs, beckons next, followed by booming Danang and charming Hoi An. Continue south via the beach resort of Nha Trang, genteel Dalat and kitesurfing capital Mui Ne before hitting high-energy Ho Chi Minh City. After a tour of the Mekong Delta, enjoy some beach bliss in lovely Phu Quoc before returning to HCMC.

Essential Food & Drink

White rose An incredibly delicate, subtly flavoured shrimp dumpling topped with crispy onions.

Pho Rice-noodle soup. A good *pho bo* (beef noodle soup) hinges on the broth, which is made from beef bones boiled for hours in water with shallots, ginger, fish sauce, black cardamom, star anise and cassia.

Banh xeo This giant crispy, chewy rice crêpe is made in 12in or 14in skillets or woks and amply filled with pork, shrimp, mung beans and bean sprouts.

Bia hoi 'Fresh' or draught beer brewed daily, without additives or preservatives, to be drunk within hours.

Vietnamese coffee Often served iced, with condensed milk.

AT A GLANCE

Currency Dong (d)

Language Vietnamese

Money ATMs are widespread

Visas Complicated, see p910

Mobile phones Prepay SIM cards available for a few dollars

VIETNAM

Fast Facts

Area 329,566 sq km

Capital Hanoi

Emergency Police ☑113

Exchange Rates

Australia	A$1	16,041d
Cambodia	10,000r	55,829d
Euro	€1	24,495d
Laos	10,000K	27,528d
UK	UK£1	34,341d
US	US$1	22,316d

Daily Costs

Budget room US$8–20

Filling meal US$2–4

Beer from US$0.30

Short taxi ride US$2

Entering the Country

Fly into Hanoi or Ho Chi Minh City, or cross at one of the many land borders with Cambodia, China and Laos.

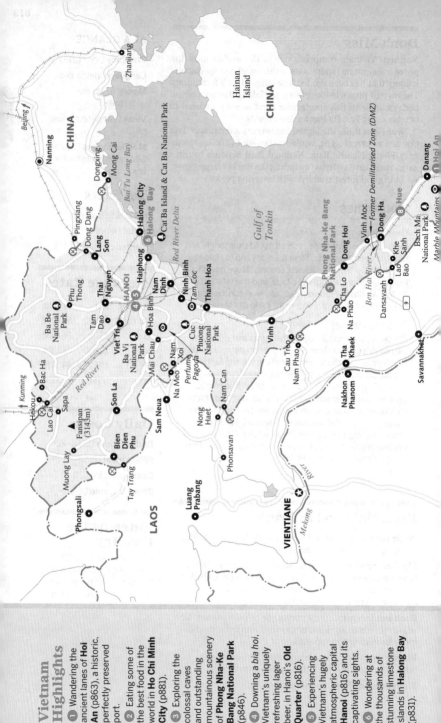

Vietnam Highlights

1 Wandering the ancient lanes of **Hoi An** (p863), a historic, perfectly preserved port.

2 Eating some of the best food in the world in **Ho Chi Minh City** (p881).

3 Exploring the colossal caves and outstanding mountainous scenery of **Phong Nha-Ke Bang National Park** (p846).

4 Downing a *bia hoi*, Vietnam's uniquely refreshing lager beer, in Hanoi's **Old Quarter** (p816).

5 Experiencing Vietnam's hugely atmospheric capital **Hanoi** (p816) and its captivating sights.

6 Wondering at the thousands of stunning limestone islands in **Halong Bay** (p831).

7 Searching for the perfect white-sand beach on tropical **Phu Quoc Island** (p897).

8 Marvelling at **Hue** (p849), a majestic former imperial capital of temples, tombs and palaces.

9 Chilling in **Mui Ne** (p875), a cosmopolitan beach and water-sports resort.

HANOI

☑ 04 / POP 7.1 MILLION

Showcasing sweeping boulevards, tree-fringed lakes and ancient pagodas, Hanoi is Asia's most atmospheric capital. Just don't expect a sleepy ambience: it's an energetic city on the move, and Hanoi's ambitious citizens are determined to make up for lost time.

A mass of motorbikes swarms through the tangled web of streets that is the Old Quarter, a cauldron of commerce for almost 1000 years and still the best place to check the pulse of this resurgent city. Hanoi has it all: ancient history, a colonial legacy and a modern outlook. There is no better place to untangle the paradox that is contemporary Vietnam.

◉ Sights

Note that some museums are closed on Mondays and take a two-hour lunch break on other days of the week. Check opening hours carefully before setting off.

◉ Old Quarter

Steeped in history, pulsating with life, bubbling with commerce, buzzing with motorbikes and rich in exotic scents, the Old Quarter is Hanoi's historic heart and soul. Hawkers pound the streets bearing sizzling, smoking baskets that hide a cheap meal. *Pho* (noodle soup) stalls and *bia hoi* (draught beer) dens hug every corner, resonant with the sound of gossip and laughter. Take your time and experience this captivating warren of lanes – this is Asian street life at its purest and most atmospheric.

The flip side is that it's also a notoriously chaotic and polluted enclave, and tough to explore on foot, as you pick your way through an urban assault course of motorbikes (parked and speeding) and cracked pavements. One day the authorities will get round to a pedestrianisation program, but for now enjoy the anarchy.

⭐ **Bach Ma Temple**   BUDDHIST TEMPLE
(Den Bach Ma; Map p818; cnr P Hang Buom & P Hang Giay; ⊙8-11am & 2-5pm Tue-Sun) **FREE** In the heart of the Old Quarter, the small Bach Ma Temple is said to be the oldest temple in the city, though much of the current structure dates from the 18th century and a shrine to Confucius was added in 1839. It was originally built by Emperor Ly Thai To

in the 11th century to honour a white horse that guided him to this site, where he chose to construct his city walls.

Memorial House   HISTORIC BUILDING
(Ngoi Nha; Map p818; 87 P Ma May; admission 5000d; ⊙9am-noon & 1-5pm) One of the Old Quarter's best-restored properties, this traditional merchants' house is sparsely but beautifully decorated, with rooms set around two courtyards and filled with fine furniture. Note the high steps between rooms, a traditional design incorporated to stop the flow of bad energy around the property.

◉ Around Hoan Kiem Lake

⭐ **Hoan Kiem Lake**   LAKE
(Map p820) Legend claims that in the mid-15th century Heaven sent Emperor Ly Thai To a magical sword, which he used to drive the Chinese from Vietnam. After the war a giant golden turtle grabbed the sword and disappeared into the depths of this lake to restore the sword to its divine owners, inspiring the name Ho Hoan Kiem (Lake of the Restored Sword). Every morning at around 6am local residents practise traditional t'ai chi on the shore.

⭐ **National Museum of Vietnamese History**   MUSEUM
(Bao Tang Lich Su Quoc Gia; Map p820; ☑04-3824 2433; baotanglichsu.vn; 1 P Trang Tien; adult/student 40,000/15,000d; ⊙8am-noon & 1.30-5pm, closed 1st Mon of the month) Built between 1925 and 1932, this architecturally impressive museum was formerly home to the École Française d'Extrême Orient. Its architect, Ernest Hebrard, was among the first in Vietnam to incorporate a blend of Chinese and French design elements. Exhibit highlights include bronzes from the Dong Son culture (3rd century BC to 3rd century AD), Hindu statuary from the Khmer and Champa kingdoms, jewellery from imperial Vietnam, and displays relating to the French occupation and the Communist Party.

Hoa Lo Prison Museum   HISTORIC BUILDING
(Map p820; ☑04-3824 6358; cnr P Hoa Lo & P Hai Ba Trung; admission 30,000d; ⊙8am-5pm) This thought-provoking site is all that remains of the former Hoa Lo Prison, ironically nicknamed the 'Hanoi Hilton' by US POWs during the American War. Most exhibits relate to the prison's use up to the mid-1950s, focusing on the Vietnamese struggle for

Greater Hanoi

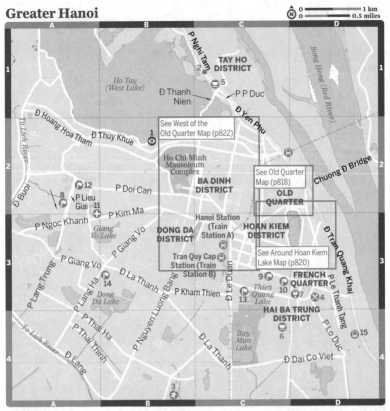

Greater Hanoi

independence from France. A gruesome relic is the ominous French guillotine, used to behead Vietnamese revolutionaries. There are also displays focusing on the American pilots who were incarcerated at Hoa Lo during the American War.

Vietnamese Women's Museum MUSEUM
(Map p820; ☎ 04-3825 9936; www.baotangphunu.org.vn; 36 P Ly Thuong Kiet; admission 30,000d; ⊗8am-5pm) This excellent, modern museum showcases women's role in Vietnamese society and culture. Labelled in English and French, it's the memories of the wartime

Old Quarter

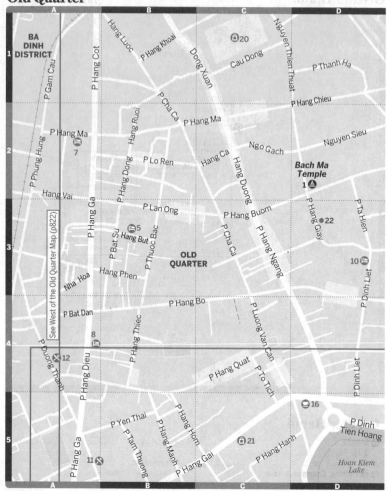

contribution by individual heroic women that are most poignant. There is a stunning collection of propaganda posters, as well as costumes, tribal basketware and fabric motifs from Vietnam's ethnic minority groups. Check the website for special exhibitions.

Ngoc Son Temple BUDDHIST TEMPLE
(Den Ngoc Son; Map p820; Hoan Kiem Lake; adult/student 20,000/10,000d; ⊘7.30am-5.30pm) Meaning 'Temple of the Jade Mountain', Hanoi's most visited temple sits on a small island in the northern part of Hoan Kiem Lake, connected to the lakeshore by an el-

egant scarlet bridge, constructed in classical Vietnamese style. The temple is dedicated to General Tran Hung Dao (who defeated the Mongols in the 13th century), La To (patron saint of physicians) and the scholar Van Xuong.

St Joseph Cathedral CHURCH
(Nha To Lon Ha Noi; Map p820; P Nha Tho; ⊘8am-noon & 2-6pm) Hanoi's neo-Gothic St Joseph Cathedral was inaugurated in 1886, and boasts a soaring facade that faces a little plaza. Its most noteworthy features are its twin bell towers, elaborate altar and fine stained-

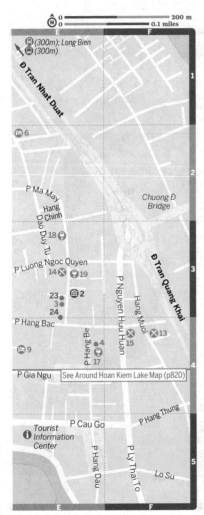

See Around Hoan Kiem Lake Map (p820)

Old Quarter

glass windows. Entrance via the main gate is only permitted during Mass: times are listed on a sign on the gates to the left of the cathedral.

◎ West of the Old Quarter

★ **Temple of Literature**   CONFUCIAN TEMPLE
(Van Mieu Quoc Tu Giam; Map p822; ☏ 04-3845 2917; P Quoc Tu Giam; adult/student 30,000/15,000d; ⊙ 8am-5pm) Founded in 1070 by Emperor Ly Thanh Tong, the Temple of Literature is dedicated to Confucius (Khong Tu). Inside you'll find a pond known as the 'Well of Heavenly Clarity', a low-slung pagoda and statues of Confucius and his disciples. A rare example of well-preserved traditional Vietnamese architecture, the complex honours Vietnam's finest scholars and men of literary accomplishment. It is the site of Vietnam's first university, established here in 1076, when entrance was only granted to those of noble birth.

★ **Ho Chi Minh's Mausoleum**   MONUMENT
(Lang Chu Tich Ho Chi Minh; Map p822; ☏ 04-3845 5128; www.bqllang.gov.vn; ⊙ 8-11am Tue-Thu, Sat & Sun Dec-Sep, last entry 10.15am, closed 4 Sep-4 Nov) **FREE** In the tradition of Lenin, Stalin and Mao, Ho Chi Minh's Mausoleum is a monumental marble edifice. Contrary to his desire for a simple cremation, the mausoleum was constructed from materials

Around Hoan Kiem Lake

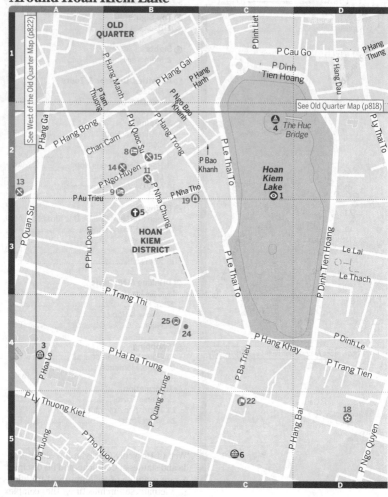

gathered from all over Vietnam between 1973 and 1975. Set deep in the bowels of the building in a glass sarcophagus is the frail, pale body of Ho Chi Minh. The mausoleum is usually closed from 4 Sep to 4 Nov while his embalmed body goes to Russia for maintenance.

Vietnam Military History Museum   MUSEUM
(Bao Tang Lich Su Quan Su Viet Nam; Map p822; ☑04-733 6453; www.btlsqsvn.org.vn; 28a P Dien Bien Phu; admission 30,000d, camera fee 20,000d; ⊗8-11.30am daily & 2-4pm Tue-Thu, Sat & Sun)

Easy to spot thanks to a large collection of weaponry at the front, the Military Museum displays Soviet and Chinese equipment alongside French- and US-made weapons captured during years of warfare. The centrepiece is a Soviet-built MiG-21 jet fighter, triumphant amid the wreckage of French aircraft downed at Dien Bien Phu, and a US F-111.

Fine Arts Museum of Vietnam   MUSEUM
(Bao Tang My Thuat Viet Nam; Map p822; ☑04-3733 2131; www.vnfam.vn; 66 P Nguyen Thai Hoc; adult/concession 30,000/15,000d; ⊗8.30am-5pm) This

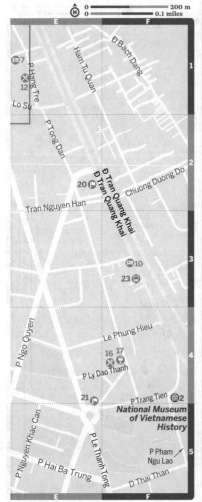

excellent Fine Arts Museum is housed in two buildings that were once the French Ministry of Information. Treasures abound, including ancient Champa stone carvings and some astonishing effigies of Guan Yin, the thousand-eyed, thousand-armed goddess of compassion. Look out for the lacquered statues of Buddhist monks from the Tay Son dynasty and the substantial collection of contemporary art and folk-naive paintings. Guided tours are available for 150,000d.

Ho Chi Minh's Stilt House HISTORIC SITE
(Nha San Bac Ho & Phu Chu Tich Tai; Map p822; admission 25,000d; ⊙8-11.30am daily & 2-4pm Tue-Thu, Sat & Sun) This humble, traditional stilt house where Ho lived intermittently from 1958 to 1969 is set in a well-tended garden adjacent a carp-filled pond and has been preserved just as Ho left it. From here, you look out on to Hanoi's most opulent building, the beautiful, beaux-arts, **Presidential Palace** (Map p822), constructed in 1906 for the Governor General of Indochina. It's now used for official receptions and isn't open to the public. Visitors may wander the grounds if you stick to the paths.

West of the Old Quarter

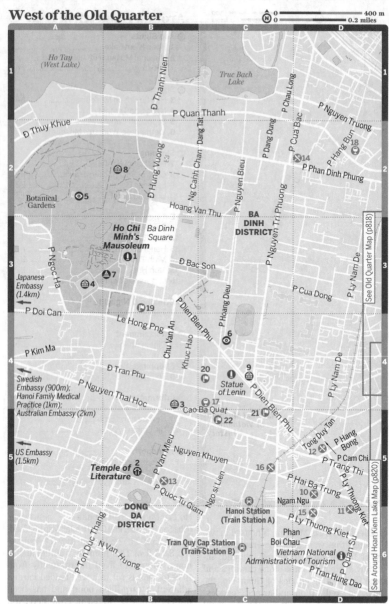

Ho Chi Minh Museum MUSEUM
(Bao Tang Ho Chi Minh; Map p822; ☑ 04-3845
5435; www.baotanghochiminh.vn; admission
25,000d; ☺ 8-11.30am daily & 2-4pm Tue-Thu, Sat
& Sun) The huge concrete Soviet-style Ho Chi
Minh Museum is a triumphalist monument
dedicated to the life of the founder of modern Vietnam and to the onward march of
revolutionary socialism. Mementos of Ho's
life are showcased, and there are some fascinating photos and dusty official documents
relating to the overthrow of the French and

West of the Old Quarter

the rise of communism. Photography is forbidden and you may be asked to check your bag at reception.

One Pillar Pagoda　　　BUDDHIST TEMPLE
(Chua Mot Cot; Map p822; P Ong Ich Kiem; admission 25,000d; ☉8-11.30am daily & 2-4pm Tue-Thu, Sat & Sun) The One Pillar Pagoda was originally built by the Emperor Ly Thai Tong who ruled from 1028 to 1054. According to the annals, the heirless emperor dreamed that he met Quan The Am Bo Tat, the Goddess of Mercy, who handed him a male child. Ly Thai Tong then married a young peasant girl and had a son and heir by her. As a way of expressing his gratitude for this event, he constructed a pagoda here in 1049.

Imperial Citadel of Thang Long HISTORIC SITE
(Hoang Thanh Thang Long; Map p822; www.hoangthanhthanglong.vn; 19c P Hoang Dieu; admission 30,000d; ☉8-11.30am daily & 2-4pm Tue-Thu, Sat & Sun) Added to Unesco's World Heritage List in 2010 and reopened in 2012, Hanoi's Imperial Citadel was the hub of Vietnamese military power for over 1000 years. Ongoing archaeological digs of ancient palaces, grandiose pavilions and imperial gates are complemented by fascinating military command bunkers from the American War – complete with maps and 1960s communications equipment – used by the legendary Vietnamese General Vo Nguyen Giap.

◉ Greater Hanoi

★**Vietnam Museum of Ethnology**　MUSEUM
(☎04-3756 2193; www.vme.org.vn; Đ Nguyen Van Huyen; adult/concession 40,000/15,000d; guide 100,000d; ☉8.30am-5.30pm Tue-Sun) This fabulous collection relating to Vietnam's ethnic minorities features well-presented tribal art, artefacts and everyday objects gathered from across the nation, and examples of traditional village houses. Displays are well labelled in Vietnamese, French and English. If you're into anthropology, it's well worth the approximately 200,000d each-way taxi fares to the Cau Giay district, about 7km from the city centre, where the museum is located.

Ho Tay　　　LAKE
(West Lake; Map p817) The city's largest lake, known as both Hay To and West Lake, is 15km in circumference and ringed by upmarket suburbs, including the predominantly expat Tay Ho district. On the southern side, along Đ Thuy Khue, are seafood restaurants, and to the east, the Xuan Dieu strip is lined with restaurants, cafes, boutiques and luxury hotels. A pathway circles the lake, making for a great bicycle ride.

🏆 Courses & Tours

★**Hanoi Free Tour Guides**　WALKING TOUR
(☎0974 596 895; hanoifreetourguides.com) There's no better way to experience the real Hanoi than with this not-for-profit social organisation run by a team of over 400 volunteer staff and guides comprising students and ex-students, speaking a multitude of languages. A variety of suggested tours are available, or work with your guide to tailor your own itinerary. Book online.

Vietnam Awesome Travel　WALKING TOUR
(Map p818; ☎04-3990 1733; www.vietnam awesometravel.com; 19b P Hang Be; tours from US$15) A wide range of good-value walking tours, including the popular Food on Foot (US$25) street-food walking tours around the Old Quarter. A wide range of day trips and longer guided tours are available. See the website for details.

Hidden Hanoi COOKING, LANGUAGE COURSE
(Map p817; ☑0912-254 045; www.hiddenhanoi.
com.vn; 147 P Nghi Tam, Tay Ho; per class with/
without market tour US$55/45; ⊙11am-2pm Mon-
Sat) Offers cooking classes from its kitchen
near the eastern side of Ho Tay (West Lake).
Options include seafood and village-food
menus. Walking tours (per person US$20 to
US$25) exploring the Old Quarter and Ha-
noi street food are available.

Hidden Hanoi also offers a language-study
program (per person from $US200), includ-
ing two field trips.

🛏 Sleeping

Most good budget places are in the Old
Quarter or neighbouring Hoan Kiem Lake
area.

🛏 Old Quarter

May De Ville Backpackers HOSTEL $
(Map p818; ☑04-3935 2468; www.maydeville
backpackershostel.com; 1 Hai Tuong, P Ta Hien;
dm/d from US$6/25; ❄@🛜) A short walk
from Ta Hien's bars, May De Ville is one of
Hanoi's best hostels. Dorms are spotless and
there's also a movie room. Doubles are also
good value.

Hanoi Hostel HOSTEL $
(Map p818; ☑0972 844 804; www.vietnam-hostel.
com; 91c P Hang Ma; dm/d/tr US$6/16/21; 🛜)

This small, quiet, privately owned hostel is
nicely located away from Hanoi's conglomeration of hostels. It's well run and clean,
with tours on tap and plenty of information
about onward travel to China or Laos.

Hanoi Rendezvous Hotel HOTEL $
(Map p818; ☑04-3828 5777; www.hanoirendez
voushotel.com; 31 P Hang Dieu; dm/s/d/tr
US$8/25/30/40; ❄@🛜) Deliciously close
to several brilliant street-food places, Hanoi Rendezvous features spacious rooms,
friendly staff, and organises well-run tours
to Halong Bay, Cat Ba Island and Sapa.

Camel City Hotel GUESTHOUSE $
(Map p818; ☑04-3935 2024; www.camelcity
hotel.com; 8/50 Dao Duy Tu; d/tw US$17/30;
❄@🛜) A family owned operation in a quiet
lane just a short walk from the after-dark attractions on P Ta Hien. Rooms are trimmed
with Asian design touches and service is
friendly.

★La Beaute de Hanoi HOTEL $$
(Map p818; ☑04-3935 1626; la-beautehanoihotel.
com; 15 Ngo Trung Yen; d from US$40; ❄🛜)
Opened in 2014, this 18-room hotel has
a fresh white and cream palette with red
accents, cable TV, fast wi-fi, and the larger
suites and family rooms have small private
balconies. It's in an excellent location on a
quiet lane just a hop, skip and a jump from
all the action on P Ma May.

SCAM ALERT!

Hanoi is a very safe city on the whole and crimes against tourists are extremely rare.
That said, the city certainly has its share of scams. Make sure you report any to the
Vietnam National Administration of Tourism (Map p822; ☑04-3942 3760; www.
vietnamtourism.gov.vn; 80 Quan Su), who might well pressure the cowboys into cleaning up
their act.

Fake hotels The taxi and minibus mafia at the airport take unwitting tourists to the
wrong hotel. Invariably, the hotel has appropriated the name of another popular property
and will then attempt to swindle as much of your money as possible. Check out a room
before you check in. And walk on if you have any suspicions.

Hotel tours Some budget hotel staff have been verbally aggressive and threatened
physical violence towards guests who've declined to book tours through their in-house
tour agency. Don't feel pressured, and if it persists, find another place to stay.

After midnight Walking alone at night is generally safe in the Old Quarter, but you
should always be aware of your surroundings. Hailing a taxi is a good idea if it's late and
you have a long walk home.

The kindness of strangers There's a scam going on around Hoan Kiem Lake where a
friendly local approaches you, offering to take you out. You end up at a karaoke bar or a
restaurant, where the bill is upwards of US$100. Gay men have been targeted in this way.
Exercise caution and follow your instincts.

⭐ **Art Trendy Hotel**   HOTEL **$$**
(Map p818; ☑04-3923 4294; www.arttrendyho
tel.com; 6 Hang But; d/tw US$30/70; ❸❇@❂)
Art Trendy enjoys a quiet location on the
western edge of the Old Quarter. Rooms are
stylish and relatively spacious, and there's
a real can-do attitude from the exceptional
and friendly staff. Each room has a laptop,
and breakfast includes warm baguettes,
omelettes and fresh fruit.

🛏 Around Hoan Kiem Lake

Especen Hotel   HOTEL **$**
(Map p820; ☑04-3824 4401; www.especen.vn; 28
P Tho Xuong; d US$12-22; ❇@❂) This budget
hotel near St Joseph Cathedral has spa-
cious and light rooms, excellent rates and
an almost tranquil location (by Old Quarter
standards). There are two annexes within
walking distance.

B&B Hanoi Hostel   HOSTEL **$**
(Map p820; ☑04-3935 2266; www.bbhanoihos
tel.com; 16 Hang Trung; d from US$20; ❇❂) This
clean hostel has friendly, hard-working staff
and is located a short walk to the northeast-
ern shore of Hoan Kiem Lake. Fresh flowers,
fruit and Vietnamese coffee give the place a
homey feel.

Central Backpackers Hanoi   HOSTEL **$**
(Map p820; ☑04-3938 1849; www.centralback
packershostel.com; 16 P Ly Quoc Su; dm US$5;
@❂) This well-run hostel is in close prox-
imity to good cafes and street eats. Not for
the withdrawn, reclusive traveller, it's an
easily excitable, social spot, with a nightly
free beer happy hour from 7pm. Note that
this operator has similarly named hotels at
three locations.

🍴 Eating

Hanoi offers cuisine from all over the world,
but as the capital's grub is so tasty, fragrantly
spiced and inexpensive you're best sticking
to local fare. Don't miss the street food either.

🍴 Old Quarter

New Day   VIETNAMESE **$**
(Map p818; ☑04-3828 0315; newdayrestaurant.
com; 72 P Ma May; meals 50,000-100,000d; ⊙8am-
late) Clean and tidy New Day attracts locals,
expats and travellers with its broad menu.
The eager staff always find space for new din-
ers, so look forward to sharing a table with
some like-minded fans of Vietnamese food.

SPLURGE

La Badiane (Map p822; ☑04-3942
4509; www.labadiane-hanoi.com; 10 Nam
Ngu; meals from 265,000d; ⊙noon-11pm)
is a stylish bistro set in a restored white-
washed French villa. French cuisine
underpins the menu but Asian and Med-
iterranean flavours also feature. Menu
highlights include sea bass tagliatelle
with smoked paprika, and prawn bisque
with wasabi tomato bruschetta. Three-
course lunches from 325,000d are
excellent value.

Mon Hue   VIETNAMESE **$**
(Map p820; ☑0986 981 369; 37 P Ly Quoc Su;
meals 40,000-80,000d; ⊙10am-10pm; ❂) While
this simple, somewhat grubby little restau-
rant is by no means a member of the famous
Ho Chi Minh–based chain whose name it
has appropriated, it does have genuinely
friendly staff, good food in the style of Hue
(adopted by a Hanoian family to local tastes)
and a picture menu to ease you in to the
almost-street-food experience.

Namaste   INDIAN **$$**
(Map p822; ☑04-3935 2400; www.namasteha
noi.com; 46 P Nuom; meals 85,000-225,000d;
⊙11am-2.30pm & 6-10pm Mon-Sun; ❂🍴) This
sprawling restaurant serves delicious Indian cuisine from a huge menu with a decent
selection of vegetarian options. Thali (set
meals; 105,000d to 225,000d) are filling and
excellent value. There's also free wi-fi!

Highway 4   VIETNAMESE **$$**
(Map p818; ☑04-3926 0639; www.highway4.com;
3 P Hang Tre; meals 120,000-275,000d; ⊙noon-
late) This is the original location of a restau-
rant family famed for adapting Vietnamese
cuisine for Western palates, although with
increasing popularity it beccomes harder to
please everybody. There are now four other
branches in Hanoi: check the website for lo-
cations. Come for small plates to share, cold
beer and funky decor.

Cha Ca Thang Long   VIETNAMESE **$$**
(Map p818; ☑04-3824 5115; www.chaca
thanglong.com; 19-31 P Duong Thanh; cha ca fish
180,000d; ⊙10am-3pm & 5-10pm) Bring along
your DIY cooking skills and grill your own
succulent fish with a little shrimp paste
and plenty of herbs. *Cha ca* is an iconic Hanoi dish, and while another nearby

more-famous *cha ca* eatery gets all the tour-bus traffic, the food here is better.

Around Hoan Kiem Lake

★**Minh Thuy's**   VIETNAMESE $
(Map p820; ☑04-3200 7893; 2a Duong Thanh; meals 45,000-155,000d; ☺11am-10pm; ☑) Masterchef Vietnam contestant Minh Thuy's eponymous restaurant is tucked away in backpacker central and worth your attention. It's cheap, clean and serves mouthwatering Vietnamese food with some very original European twists and plenty of vegetarian options. Highly recommended.

Hanoi Social Club   CAFE $$
(Map p820; ☑04-3938 2117; www.facebook.com/TheHanoiSocialClub; 6 Hoi Vu; meals 95,000-175,000d; ☺8am-11pm) On three funky levels with retro furniture, the Hanoi Social Club is the city's most cosmopolitan cafe. Dishes include potato fritters with chorizo for breakfast, and pasta, burgers and wraps for lunch or dinner. Vegetarian options feature a tasty mango curry, and the quiet laneway location is a good spot for a coffee, beer or wine.

West of the Old Quarter

Ray Quan   VIETNAMESE $
(Map p822; ☑0913 578 588; 8a Nguyen Khuyen; dishes from 30,000-120,000d) Popular with expats in the know, this quirky spot directly on the train tracks won't be for everyone, but those who like it, will love it. A wide range of delicious Vietnamese cuisine is cooked to order by the eccentric owner-chef who ferments her own rice wine: it's strong and delicious.

Net Hue   VIETNAMESE $
(Map p822; ☑04-3938 1795; nethue.com.vn; cnr P Hang Bong & P Cam Chi; snacks & meals from 35,000d; ☺11am-9pm) One of a small chain, Net Hue is well priced for such comfortable surroundings. Head to the top floor for the nicest ambience and enjoy Hue-style dishes like *banh nam* (steamed rice pancake with minced shrimp).

Quan An Ngon   VIETNAMESE $
(Map p822; ☑04-3942 8162; www.ngonhanoi.com. vn; 18 Phan Boi Chau; dishes 70,000-150,000d; ☺7am-11pm) This branch of a number of small same-named kitchens turns out streetfood specialities from across Vietnam. Try and visit just outside the busy lunch and dinner periods, or consider Quan An Ngon's newest branch in a lovely French villa just north of the Old Quarter (Map p822; ☑04-3734 9777; www.ngonhanoi.com.vn; 34 P Phan Đinh Phung; dishes 70,000-150,000d; ☺11am-11pm).

★**Nha Hang Koto Van Mieu**   CAFE $$
(Map p822; ☑04-3747 0338; www.koto.com. au; 59 P Van Mieu; meals 120,000-160,000d; ☺7.30am-10pm, closed dinner Mon; ☻) Stunning four-storey modernist cafe-bar-restaurant overlooking the Temple of Literature, where

---

HANOI STREET EATS

When in Hanoi, chow down with the masses. Most of these stalls specialise in just one dish and have somewhat flexible opening hours.

Bun Rieu Cua (Map p820; 40 P Hang Tre; ☺7-10:30am) Get to this incredibly popular spot early, as its sole dish of *bun rieu cua* (noodle soup with beef in a spicy crab broth) is only served for a couple of hours. A Hanoi classic.

Bun Cha Nem Cua Be Dac Kim (Map p818; 67 P Duong Thanh; ☺11am-7pm) Visiting Hanoi and not eating *bun cha* (barbecued pork with rice vermicelli) with a side of *nem cua be* (sea-crab spring rolls) should be classed as a capital offence. This is an excellent spot to try this street-food classic.

Pho Thin (Map p817; 13 P Lo Duc; ☺6am-3pm) Negotiate your way to the rear of this narrow, rustic establishment and sit down to some excellent *pho bo* (beef noodle soup). A classic Hanoi experience that hasn't changed in decades.

Banh Ghoi (Map p820; 52 P Ly Quoc Su; ☺10am-7pm) Nestled under a banyan tree near St Joseph Cathedral, this humble stall turns out *banh ghoi*, moreish deep-fried pastries crammed with pork, vermicelli and mushrooms.

Xoi Yen (Map p818; cnr P Nguyen Huu Huan & P Hang Mam; ☺7am-11pm) Equally good for breakfast or as a hangover cure, Xoi Yen specialises in sticky rice topped with goodies, including sweet Asian sausage, gooey fried egg and slow-cooked pork.

the interior design has been taken very seriously, from the stylish seating to the fresh flowers by the till. Daily specials are chalked up on a blackboard, and the short menu has everything from excellent Vietnamese food to yummy pita wraps and beer-battered fish and chips.

Other Areas

★ **Moto-san Uber Noodle**   NOODLES $
(Map p820; ☑04-6680 9124; 4 Ly Dao Thanh; meals 45,000-70,000d) Brainchild of Hanoi artist, journalist and designer Nguyen Qui Duc (of Tadioto fame), this wonderful noodle stall seats eight eager eaters. The menu is simple: miso, shōyu (soy) or *shio* (salty) ramen, and spicy *banh my thit ko* (stewed pork) sandwiches with killer hot sauce (optional) *a la* central Vietnam. Sake and beer are, of course, readily available.

 Drinking & Nightlife

With dive bars, congenial pubs, sleek lounges and clubs and *bia hoi* joints by the barrel-load you won't go thirsty in Hanoi. Ha Tien in the Old Quarter has a choice of bars and is a good starting or finishing point for a crawl. Cafes come in every persuasion too. Coffee meccas include P Trieu Viet Vuong, around 1km south of Hoan Kiem Lake, which has scores of cafes.

Tadioto   BAR
(Map p820; ☑04-6680 9124; www.tadioto.com; 24b P Tong Dan; ⊙7am-midnight) Nguyen Qui Duc's unofficial clubhouse for the underground arts scene's latest incarnation is this dark and quirky colonial-era bar in the French Quarter. Obligatory red accents (seat covers, wrought-iron grill on the doors), reworkings of art-deco furniture and recycled ironwork feature heavily. The highlight of the cool cocktail list is the sweet mojito.

Moose & Roo   PUB
(Map p818; ☑04-3200 1289; www.mooseandroo. com; 42b P Ma May; ⊙11am-midnight) This jovial Canadian-Aussie-themed pub and grill serves excellent home-style comfort food (burgers, pulled pork, wings, fish and chips) in a fun and friendly environment. One for the homesick or those looking to hook up with fellow travellers.

Nola   BAR
(Map p818; 89 P Ma May; ⊙9am-midnight) Retro furniture is mixed and matched in this bohe-

HANOI ON THE WEB

Hanoi has some great online resources:

TNH Vietnam (tnhvietnam.xemzi.com) Premier resource with useful restaurant reviews.

Hanoi Grapevine (www.hanoigrape vine.com) What's on in Hanoi.

Sticky Rice (www.stickyrice.typepad. com) Brilliant foodie website.

The Word (www.wordhanoi.com) Great articles.

And Of Other Things (www.andofother things.com) All things arty.

mian labyrinth tucked away from Ma May's tourist bustle. Pop in for a coffee and banana bread, or return after dark for one of Hanoi's best little bars.

Bar Betta   BAR
(Map p822; ☑0165 897 9073; www.facebook.com/ barbetta34; 34 Cao Ba Quat; ⊙9am-midnight) Retro decor and a jazz-age vibe combine with good cocktails, coffee and cool music in this breezy French colonial-era villa. Two-for-one beers are available from 3pm to 7pm, and the rooftop terrace (from 8pm) is essential on a sultry Hanoi night.

Manzi Art Space   BAR
(Map p822; ☑04-3716 3397; www.facebook.com/ manzihanoi; 14 Phan Huy Ich; ⊙cafe 9am-midnight, shop 10am-6pm) Part cool art gallery, part chic cafe and bar, Manzi is worth seeking out north of the Old Quarter. A restored French villa hosts diverse exhibitions of painting, sculpture and photography, and the compact courtyard garden is perfect for a coffee or glass of wine. There's also a small shop selling works by contemporary Vietnamese artists.

Quan Ly   BAR
(Map p817; 82 P Le Van Hu; ⊙10am-9pm) Owner Pham Xuan Ly has lived on this block since 1950, and now runs one of Hanoi's most traditional *ruou* (Vietnamese liquor) bars. Kick off with the ginseng one, and work your way up. An English-language menu makes it easy to choose, and there's also cheap beer and good Vietnamese food on offer.

Le Pub   PUB
(Map p818; ☑04-3926 2104; 25 P Hang Be; ⊙7am-late) Le Pub is a great place to hook up with others, as there's always a good

mix of travellers and Hanoi expats. There's a cosy, tavern-like interior (with big screens for sports fans), a street-facing terrace and a rear courtyard. Bar snacks are served, the service is slick and the music usually includes tunes you can sing along to.

Café Duy Tri   CAFE
(Map p817; ☑04-3829 1386; 43a P Yen Phu) In the same location since 1936, this caffeine-infused labyrinth is a Hanoi classic. You'll feel like Gulliver as you negotiate the tiny ladders and stairways to reach the 3rd-floor balcony. Order the delicious *caphe sua chua* (iced coffee with yoghurt), and you may have discovered your new favourite summertime drink. You'll find P Yen Phu a couple of blocks east of Truc Bach Lake, north of the Old Quarter.

Cafe Pho Co   CAFE
(Map p818; 4th fl, 11 P Hang Gai) One of Hanoi's best-kept secrets, this place has plum views over Hoan Kiem Lake. Enter through the silk shop, and continue through the antique-bedecked courtyard up to the top floor for the mother of all vistas. You'll need to order coffee and snacks before tackling the final winding staircase. For something deliciously different, try the *caphe trung da* (coffee topped with a silky-smooth beaten egg white).

Cong Caphe   CAFE
(Map p817; congcaphe.com; 152 P Trieu Viet Vuong) Settle in to the eclectic beats and kitsch Communist memorabilia at Cong Caphe with a *caphe sua da* (iced coffee with condensed milk). You'll notice a bunch of branches around the city – a full list appears on its website.

☆ Entertainment

Cinematheque   CINEMA
(Map p820; ☑04-3936 2648; 22a P Hai Ba Trung) This Hanoi institution is a hub for art-house film lovers, and there's a great little cafe-bar here too. It's nominally 'members only', but a 50,000d one-off membership usually secures visitors an always-interesting themed double bill.

Hanoi Rock City   LIVE MUSIC
(www.hanoirockcity.com; 27/52 To Ngoc Van, Tay Ho) Hanoi Rock City is tucked away down a residential lane about 7km north of the city near Tay Ho, but it's a journey well worth taking for an eclectic mix, including reggae, Hanoi punk and electronica nights. A few interna-

tional acts swing by; check the website or www.newhanoian.xemzi.com for listings.

🛍 Shopping

The Old Quarter is brimming with temptations: fake sunglasses, T-shirts, musical instruments, herbal medicines, jewellery, spices, propaganda art, fake English Premier League football kits and much, much more.

For ethnic minority garb and handicrafts P Hang Bac and P To Tich are good hunting grounds. North and northwest of Hoan Kiem Lake around P Hang Gai, P To Tich, P Hang Khai and P Cau Go are dozens of shops offering handicrafts, artwork and antiques.

Dong Xuan Market   MARKET
(Map p818; Dong Xuan; ⊙6am-7pm) A large, nontouristy market in the Old Quarter of Hanoi, 900m north of Hoan Kiem Lake. There are hundreds of stalls here, and it's a fascinating place to explore if you want to catch a flavour of Hanoian street life. The area around it also has loads of bustling shops.

Hanoi Moment   HANDICRAFTS
(Map p818; ☑04-3926 3630; www.hanoimoment.vn; 101 P Hang Gai; ⊙8am-9pm) An oasis of classier Vietnamese souvenirs, including lacquerware and jewellery, amid the T-shirt overkill of nearby stores. Bamboo, stone and porcelain are also used to great effect.

Things of Substance   CLOTHING
(Map p820; ☑04-3828 6965; 5 P Nha Tho; ⊙9am-6pm) Tailored fashions and some off-the-rack items at moderate prices. The staff are professional and speak decent English.

ℹ Information

INTERNET ACCESS
Virtually all budget and midrange hotels offer free internet access, with computers in the lobby and wi-fi. You'll find several cybercafes on P Hang Bac in the Old Quarter; rates start at 5000d per hour.

MEDICAL SERVICES
Hanoi Family Medical Practice (Map p817; ☑04-3843 0748; www.vietnammedical practice.com; Van Phuc Diplomatic Compound, 298 P Kim Ma; ⊙24hr) Located a few hundred metres west of the Ho Chi Minh Mausoleum Complex, this practice includes a team of well-respected international physicians and dentists, and has 24-hour emergency cover. Prices are high, so check that your medical travel insurance is in order.

MONEY

Hanoi has many ATMs, and around Hoan Kiem Lake are international banks where you can change money and get cash advances on credit cards.

TOURIST INFORMATION

In the cafes and bars of the Old Quarter, look for the excellent local magazine *The Word*.

Tourist Information Center (Map p818; ☑ 04-3926 3366; P Dinh Tien Hoang; ⊙ 9am-7pm) City maps and brochures, but privately run with an emphasis on selling tours.

TRAVEL AGENCIES

Hanoi has hundreds of budget travel agencies. It's not advisable to book trips or tickets through guesthouses and hotels.

Ethnic Travel (Map p818; ☑ 04-3926 1951; www.ethnictravel.com.vn; 35 P Hang Giay; ⊙ 9am-6pm Mon-Sat, 10am-5pm Sun) Off-the-beaten-track trips across the north in small groups. Some trips are low-impact using public transport and homestays, others are activity-based (including hiking, cycling and cooking). Offers Bai Tu Long Bay tours and also has an office in Sapa.

BUSES FROM HANOI

Gia Lam Bus Station

DESTINATION	FARE (D)	DURATION (HR)	FREQUENCY
Ba Be	150,000	5	noon
Bai Chay (Halong City)	120,000	3½	every 30min
Haiphong	70,000	2	frequent
Lang Son	90,000	5	every 45min
Lao Cai	300,000	4-8	frequent
Mong Cai	230,000	9	hourly (approx)
Sapa	250,000	10	6.30pm, 7pm (sleeper)

Luong Yen Bus Station

DESTINATION	FARE (D)	DURATION (HR)	FREQUENCY
Cat Ba Island	240,000	5	5.20am, 7.20am, 11.20am, 1.20pm
Haiphong	70,000	2	frequent
Lang Son	80,000	4	frequent

My Dinh Bus Station

DESTINATION	FARE (D)	DURATION (HR)	FREQUENCY
Cao Bang	120,000	10	Every 45min
Dien Bien Phu	350,000	8	11am, 6pm
Hoa Binh	40,000	2	frequent
Son La	190,000	7	frequent

Giap Bat Bus Station

DESTINATION	FARE (D)	DURATION (HR)	FREQUENCY
Danang	365,000	12	frequent sleepers noon-6.30pm
Dong Ha	380,000	8	frequent sleepers noon-6.30pm
Dong Hoi	380,000	8	frequent sleepers noon-6.30pm
Hue	380,000	10	frequent sleepers noon-6.30pm
Nha Trang	700,000	32	10am, 3pm, 6pm
Ninh Binh	70,000	2	frequent 7am-6pm

Handspan Adventure Travel (Map p818; ☑ 04-3926 2828; www.handspan.com; 78 P Ma May; ⊗ 9am-8pm) Sea-kayaking trips in Halong Bay and around Cat Ba Island, plus 4WD tours, mountain biking and trekking. Other options include remote areas such as Moc Chau and Ba Be National Park, community-based tourism projects in northern Vietnam, and the *Treasure Junk*, the only true sailing craft cruising Halong Bay. Handspan also has offices in Sapa and Ho Chi Minh City.

Vega Travel (Map p818; ☑ 04-3926 2092; www.vegatravel.vn; cnr P Ma May & 24a P Hang Bac; ⊗ 8am-8pm) Family-owned-and-operated company offering well-run tours around the north and throughout Vietnam. Has excellent guides and drivers, and also financially supports ethnic minority kindergartens and schools around Sapa and Bac Ha. Halong Bay tours on a private boat are excellent value and bespoke touring is available.

ⓘ Getting There & Away

AIR

Hanoi has a growing number of international connections. **Vietnam Airlines** (Map p820; ☑ 1900 545 486; www.vietnamair.com.vn; 25 P Trang Thi; ⊗ 8am-5pm Mon-Fri), **Jetstar Airways** (☑ 1900 1550; www.jetstar.com) and **VietJet Air** (☑ 1900 1886; www.vietjetair.com) fly to most domestic airports in Vietnam.

BUS

Hanoi has four long-distance bus stations, each serving a particular area. The stations are pretty well organised with ticket offices, displayed schedules and fixed prices.

Gia Lam Bus Station (☑ 04-3827 1569; Đ Ngoc Lam) Located 3km northeast of the centre, this is the place for buses to points east and northeast of Hanoi.

Luong Yen Bus Station (Map p817; ☑ 04-3942 0477; cnr Tran Quang Khai & Nguyen Khoai) Located 3km southeast of the Old Quarter, serving destinations to the south and the east, including sleeper buses to Hue, Dalat, Nha Trang and transport to Cat Ba Island.

My Dinh Bus Station (☑ 04-3768 5549; Đ Pham Hung) Located 7km west of the city, provides services to the west and the north, including sleeper buses to Dien Bien Phu.

Giap Bat Bus Station (☑ 04-3864 1467; Đ Giai Phong) Located 7km south of the Hanoi train station; it is used by some buses from Ninh Binh and the south.

Most travellers prefer the convenience of open-tour buses (hop-on, hop-off bus services that connect the capital with HCMC). From Hanoi, these services stop at all main destinations heading south, including Hue.

Tourist-style minibuses also run to Halong Bay and Sapa. Prices include a hotel pick-up.

Buses also connect Hanoi with Nanning in China. Two daily services (at 7.30am and 9.30am) to Nanning (480,000d, nine hours) leave from the private terminal of **Hong Ha Tourism** (Map p820; ☑ 04-3824 7339; 204 Đ Tran Quang Khai). Tickets should be purchased in advance and you may be asked to show your Chinese visa.

CAR & MOTORCYCLE

Car hire is best arranged via a travel agency or tour operator. The roads in the north are in pretty good shape but expect an average speed

TRAINS FROM HANOI

Eastbound & Northbound Trains

DESTINATION	STATION	HARD SEAT/ SLEEPER	SOFT SEAT/ SLEEPER	DURATION (HR)	FREQUENCY
Beijing (China)	Tran Quy Cap	US$240	US$352	18	6.30pm Tue & Fri
Haiphong	Gia Lam	60,000d	70,000d	2	6am
Haiphong	Long Bien	60,000d	70,000d	2½-3	9.20am, 3.30pm, 6.10pm
Nanning (China)	Gia Lam	US$28	US$42	12	9.40pm

Southbound Trains

These all leave from Hanoi Train Station.

DESTINATION	HARD SEAT	SOFT SEAT	HARD SLEEPER	SOFT SLEEPER
Danang	From 430,000d	From 630,000d	From 782,000d	From 954,000d
HCMC	From 790,000d	From 1,160,000d	From 1,340,000d	From 1,692,000d
Hue	From 374,000d	From 545,000d	From 675,000d	From 894,000d
Nha Trang	From 692,000d	From 998,000d	From 1,240,000d	From 1,647,000d

of 35km to 40km per hour. You'll definitely need a 4WD. Daily rates start at about US$110 a day (including driver and petrol).

TRAIN

The main **Hanoi Train Station** (Ga Hang Co; Train Station A; ☑ 04-3825 3949; 120 Đ Le Duan; ☺ ticket office 7.30am-12.30pm & 1.30-7.30pm) is at the western end of P Tran Hung Dao. Trains from here go to destinations south.

To the right of the main entrance of the train station is a separate ticket office for northbound trains to Lao Cai (for Sapa) and China. Note that all northbound trains leave from a separate station (just behind the main station) called **Tran Quy Cap Station** (Train Station B; ☑ 04-3825 2628; P Tran Quy Cap; ☺ ticket office 4-6am & 4-10pm).

To make things even more complicated, some northbound (Lao Cai and Lang Son included) and eastbound (Haiphong) trains depart from Gia Lam on the eastern side of the Song Hong (Red River), and Long Bien on the western (city) side of the river. Be sure to ask just where you need to go to catch your train.

Schedules, fares, information and advance bookings are available at Bau Lau (www.baolau.vn). Travel agents will also book train tickets for a commission.

It's best to buy tickets at least one day before departure to ensure a seat or sleeper.

ⓘ Getting Around

TO/FROM THE AIRPORT

Hanoi's Noi Bai International Airport is 35km north of the city. Don't use freelance taxi drivers touting for business – the chances of a rip-off are too high. Here are the transport options:

Airport Taxi (☑ 04-3873 3333) US$20 for a door-to-door taxi ride.

Jetstar Airport bus (Map p820; 206 Đ Tran Quang Khai) (40,000d, hourly)

Public bus 17 (5000d, 1½ hours) To/from Long Bien bus station.

Vietjet minibus (40,000d, hourly) To/from 67-69 Tran Nhan Tong.

Vietnam Airlines minibus (Map p820; every 45min, 40,000d) To/from the Vietnam Airlines office.

BICYCLE

Many Old Quarter guesthouses and cafes rent bikes for about US$2 per day.

BUS

Plenty of local buses (fares from 3000d) serve routes around Hanoi but very few tourists bother with them.

CYCLO

A few *cyclo* (pedicab) drivers still frequent the Old Quarter but they tend to charge more than taxis, around 50,000d for a shortish journey.

MOTORCYCLE

Offers for *xe om* (motorbike taxi) rides are incessant. A short ride should be about 20,000d, about 5km around 70,000d.

TAXI

Taxis are everywhere. Flag fall is around 20,000d, which takes you 1km or 2km; every kilometre thereafter costs around 15,000d. Some dodgy operators have high-speed meters, so use the following reliable companies:

Mai Linh (☑ 04-3822 2666)

Thanh Nga Taxi (☑ 04-3821 5215)

NORTHERN VIETNAM

Vistas. This is Vietnam's big-sky country; a place of rippling mountains, cascading rice terraces and karst topography. Halong Bay's seascape of limestone towers are the view everyone's here to see, but the karst connection continues inland to Ba Be's sprawling lakes until it segues into the evergreen hills of the northwest highlands. Not to be outdone by the scenery, northern Vietnam's cultural kaleidoscope is just as diverse. In this heartland of hill-tribe culture, villages snuggle between paddy field patchworks outside of Sapa and the scarlet headdresses of the Dzao and the Black Hmong's indigo fabrics add dizzying colour to chaotic highland markets. If you're up for some road-tripping, this is the place to do it.

Halong Bay

Majestic and mysterious, inspiring and imperious, Halong Bay's 3000 or more incredible islands rise from the emerald waters of the Gulf of Tonkin. A Unesco World Heritage Site, this mystical seascape of limestone islets is a vision of breathtaking beauty.

The islands are dotted with wind- and wave-eroded grottoes, many now illuminated with technicolour lighting effects. Sadly, litter and trinket-touting vendors are also part of the experience.

From February until April the weather is often cold and drizzly, and the ensuing fog can cause low visibility, although the temperature rarely falls below 10°C. Tropical storms are frequent during the summer months (July to September).

Most visitors sensibly opt for tours that include sleeping on a boat in the bay. Some dodge the humdrum gateway Halong City completely and head independently for Cat Ba Town, from where trips to the less-visited, equally alluring Lan Ha Bay are easily set up.

Boat trips leave from Bai Chai wharf, 2km west of Halong City. You can hook up with others here to share a boat; rates are 100,000/150,000d for a four-/six-hour cruise.

As Halong Bay is a national park there's an entrance ticket (120,000d) and also separate admission tickets for caves and fishing villages (30,000d to 50,000d). Most admission fees are included with organised cruises.

Halong City

📞 033 / POP 203,000

Halong City is the main gateway to Halong Bay. Its seafront is blighted by high-rise hotels, but you will find good budget accommodation here.

An elegant suspension bridge connects the western, touristy side of town (known as Bai Chay) with the much more Vietnamese entity (Hon Gai) to the east.

🛏 Sleeping & Eating

The 'hotel alley' of Đ Vuon Dao has more than 50 mini-hotels, most of them almost identical and costing US$15 for a double room. For cheap, filling food there are modest places with English menus at the bottom of Đ Vuon Dao.

The Light Hotel   HOTEL $
(📞 033-384 8518; www.thelighthalong.vn; 108a Đ Vuon Dao; 350,000d; ✳🕸) The good-sized, modern and super-clean rooms here are excellent value. Chuck in the fact that some of the helpful staff speak English and you've got Halong City's best budget find.

Halong Backpacker Hostel   HOSTEL $
(📞 033-361 9333; www.halongbackpackerhostel. com; 41 Đ Anh Dao; dm US$5; ✳🕸) This new hostel (don't confuse it with the 'Halong Backpacker's Hostel' on Đ Vuon Dao) has small, light-filled six-bed dorms and a lively downstairs bar.

❶ Getting There & Away

The bus station is 6km south of central Bai Chay, just off Hwy 18.

From Tuan Chau ferry pier, 13km southwest of Bai Chay, there are two car ferries to Cat Ba Island's Gia Luan Harbour at 8am and 3pm (per person/motorbike 70,000/10,000d, one hour) throughout the year with hourly services during the peak period of June to early August.

Cat Ba Island

📞 031 / POP 14,500

Rugged, craggy and jungle-clad, Cat Ba is northern Vietnam's adventure sport and eco-tourism mecca. There's a terrific roll-call of activities here – sailing trips, birdwatching, biking, hiking and rock climbing – and some fine tour operators organising them.

Lan Ha Bay, off the southeastern side of the island, is especially scenic and offers numerous beaches to explore. You could spend a year here discovering a different islet every day while swimming and snorkelling the bay's turquoise waters. Cat Ba Island has a few fishing villages, as well as a fast-growing town.

Much of Cat Ba Island was declared a national park in 1986 to protect the island's diverse ecosystems and wildlife, including the endangered golden-headed langur, the world's rarest primate. There are beautiful beaches, numerous lakes, waterfalls and grottoes in the spectacular limestone hills.

In recent years Cat Ba Town has experienced a hotel boom, and a chain of ugly concrete hotels now frames a once-lovely bay. That said, its ugliness is skin deep, as the rest of the island and Lan Ha Bay are so alluring.

BUSES FROM HALONG CITY

DESTINATION	FARE (D)	DURATION (HR)	FREQUENCY
Hanoi	90,000	3½	every 15min
Haiphong	60,000	2	every 20min
Mong Cai	80,000	4	every 40min till 3pm
Ninh Binh	100,000	4	5.30am, 11.30am
Lao Cai	400,000	12	7am, 6pm

CRUISING THE KARSTS: TOURS TO HALONG BAY

Halong Bay tours sold out of Hanoi start from US$60 per person for a dodgy day trip, rising to around US$220 for two nights on the bay with kayaking. For around US$110 to US$130 you should get a worthwhile overnight cruise. Some tips:

➡ We get many complaints about poor service, bad food and rats running around on the boats, but these tend to be on the ultra-budget tours.

➡ Most tours include transport, meals and, sometimes, island hikes or kayaking.

➡ Cruises tend to follow a strict itinerary, with stops at touristy caves. On an overnight trip there's simply not time to stray far from Halong City.

➡ Boat tours are sometimes cancelled in bad weather – ascertain in advance what a refund will be.

➡ Take care with your valuables on day trips; most overnight cruises have lockable cabins.

If you want to experience Halong Bay without the crowds, consider heading to Cat Ba Island. From there, tour operators concentrate on Lan Ha Bay, which is relatively untouched and has sublime sandy beaches.

◎ Sights

★ Lan Ha Bay   BAY
(admission 30,000d) Lying south and east of Cat Ba Town, the 300 or so karst islands and limestone outcrops of Lan Ha are just as beautiful as those of Halong Bay and have the additional attraction of numerous white-sand beaches.

Due to being a fair way from Halong City, not so many tourist boats venture here, meaning Lan Ha Bay has a more isolated appeal. Sailing and kayak trips here are best organised in Cat Ba Town.

Cat Ba National Park   NATIONAL PARK
(☑ 031-216 350; admission 30,000d; ☺ sunrise-sunset) Cat Ba's beautiful national park is home to 32 types of mammal, including most of the world's 65 remaining golden-headed langur, the world's most endangered primate. There are some good hiking trails here, including a hardcore 18km route up to a mountain summit.

To reach the park headquarters at Trung Trang, hop on the green QH public bus from the docks at Cat Ba Town, hire a *xe om* (around 80,000d one way), or rent a motorbike for the day.

Hospital Cave   HISTORIC SITE
(☑ 031-368 8215; admission 15,000d; ☺ 7am-4.30pm) Hospital Cave served both as a secret, bomb-proof hospital during the American War and as a safe house for VC leaders. Built between 1963 and 1965 (with assistance from China), this incredibly well-constructed three-storey feat of engi-

neering was in constant use until 1975. The cave is about 10km north of Cat Ba Town on the road to Cat Ba National Park entrance.

Cat Co Cove   BEACH
A 10-minute walk southeast from Cat Ba Town, the three Cat Co Cove beaches boast the nearest sand to town, although rubbish in the water can be problematic some days. Cat Co 3 is the closest, with a blink-and-you-miss-it sliver of sand. From there a walking trail, cut into the cliff, offering gorgeous sea views, winds its way to Cat Co 1 dominated by a rather ugly resort, then onwards to the pretty white-sand swath of Cat Co 2.

🏃 Activities

Cat Ba is a superb base for adventure sports.

Mountain Biking
Hotels can arrange Chinese mountain bikes (around US$6 per day), and Blue Swimmer (p834) rents Trek bikes for US$15 per day.

One possible route traverses the heart of the island, past Hospital Cave down to the west coast's mangroves and crab farms.

Rock Climbing
Cat Ba Island and Lan Ha Bay's spectacular limestone cliffs make for world-class rock climbing amid stunning scenery. Asia Outdoors (p834) uses fully licensed and certified instructors and is the absolute authority.

Half-day climbing trips including instruction, transport, lunch and gear start at US$66 per person. Climbing and boat trips incorporate kayaking, beach stops and exploring the amazing karst landscape.

VIETNAM CAT BA ISLAND

BAI TU LONG BAY

The area immediately northeast of Halong Bay is part of **Bai Tu Long National Park** (admission 100,000d), which is blessed with spectacular limestone islands every bit as beautiful as its more famous neighbour Halong.

Hanoi travel agencies including Ethnic Travel (p829) run trips into the Bai Tu Long area. Or for more flexibility head overland to Cai Rong and visit the outlying islands by boat from there.

Sailing, Kayaking & SUP

Plenty of places in Cat Ba Town rent kayaks (half-day around US$8) that are ideal for exploring the coastline independently. SUP (stand-up paddle-boarding) trips are run by Asia Outdoors.

Blue Swimmer offers sailing excursions to myriad islands around Cat Ba, often including kayaking and sleeping on a private beach.

Trekking

Most of Cat Ba Island consists of protected tropical forest; the national park has some good treks. Asia Outdoors offers a great hike in Butterfly Valley.

🐦 Tours

Tours of the island and boat trips around Halong Bay are offered by nearly every hotel in Cat Ba, costing around US$20 for day trips and US$80 for two-day, one-night tours.

We have received unfavourable feedback – cramped conditions and dodgy food – about some of these trips. The following adventure tour operators will steer you to really special areas of Cat Ba, Lan Ha Bay and beyond.

Asia Outdoors ROCK CLIMBING
(☑031-368 8450; www.asiaoutdoors.com.vn; Noble House, Đ 1-4, Cat Ba Town; half-/full-day climbing US$66/84; ⊙8am-7.30pm) Expert climbing instruction, climbing and kayaking packages (overnight US$130) and stand-up paddle-boarding (SUP) trips (US$36).

Cat Ba Ventures BOAT TOUR
(☑031-388 8755, 0912 467 016; www.catbaventures.com; 223 Đ 1-4, Cat Ba Town; overnight boat tour per person US$128; ⊙8am-7pm) Boat trips around Lan Ha and Halong bays, one-day

kayaking trips (US$29) and guided hikes in Cat Ba National Park.

Blue Swimmer ADVENTURE TOUR
(☑031-368 8237, 0915 063 737; www.blueswimmersailing.com; Ben Beo Harbour; overnight sailing trip per person from US$161; ⊙8am-6pm) Superb sailing and kayaking trips, trekking and mountain-biking excursions.

🛏 Sleeping

Most hotels are in Cat Ba Town. Room rates fluctuate greatly between high-season summertime and the slower winter months. The following are low-season prices.

🛌 Cat Ba Town

Cat Ba Sea View HOTEL $
(☑031-388 8201; www.catbaseaviewhotel.com; 220 Đ 1-4; r US$15, with sea view US$25; ❋🛜) Neat-as-a-pin, light-coloured rooms are further spruced up by snazzy fake-flower decor. All are good-sized, though the seafront ones are by far the most spacious. Each floor has a teensy communal balcony so you can take in the harbour vistas without shelling out extra for your room.

Cat Ba Central Hostel HOSTEL $
(☑0913 311 006; www.catbacentralhostel.com; 240 Đ 1-4; dm US$5; ⊖❋🛜) Owner Kong is your host at this friendly hostel that's fast becoming the heart of Cat Ba's backpacker action. Beds in dorms (one 28-bed, 14-bed; and two six-bed, including a female-only room) come with individual storage locker and power point.

Cat Ba Dream HOTEL $
(☑031-388 8274; www.catbadream.com.vn; 226 Đ 1-4; r US$12, with sea view US$15; ❋🛜) Service may be a bit lacklustre, but Cat Ba Dream has smart, small rooms at the back, and larger sea-facing ones with killer views of the bay (room 606 is the best).

Thu Ha HOTEL $
(☑031-388 8343; Đ 1-4, Cat Ba Town; r US$12-15; ❋🛜) This small family-run place has basically furnished, clean rooms. Negotiate hard for a front room and wake up to sea views.

Sea Pearl Hotel HOTEL $$
(☑031-368 8567; www.seapearlcatbahotel.com.vn; 219 Đ 1-4; r 730,000-1030,000d; ❋🛜) Although we'd like to see the bathrooms refurbished at this price, the Sea Pearl is a solid choice. Classically styled rooms are decent-sized

and comfortable, and staff are professional and helpful.

Around Cat Ba Island

Cat Ba Mountain View
Guesthouse
BUNGALOW **$**

(📞 031-368 8641; 452 Đ Ha Sen, Ang Soi village; d US$15, dm US$5) One step removed from the hustle of town, this new hostel has a collection of cute bungalows (both private and dorm options), backed by a cliff. The spacious, thatch-roofed restaurant area is a great social spot for hanging out and meeting fellow travellers. It's on the main road, 3km from Cat Ba Town.

Ancient House Homestay
HOMESTAY **$**

(📞 0915 063 737, 0916 645 858; www.catba-homestay.com; Ang Soi village; shared house per person US$15, private house per 2 people US$50; 📶) Located around 3km from Cat Ba Town, down an unmarked alley in the village of Ang Soi, this heritage house was carefully moved here from the outskirts of Hanoi. Antiques fill the high-ceilinged interior and outside are well-tended gardens. It's not set up to receive independent travellers and is best booked through Blue Swimmer.

Eating & Drinking

For a cheap feed, head to the food stalls in front of the market. You'll find bia hoi stalls (Đ 1-4) near the entrance to the fishing harbour.

Green Bamboo Forest
VIETNAMESE **$**

(Đ 1-4; meals 50,000-150,000d; ⏰7am-11pm; 📶) Friendly and well-run waterfront eatery that also acts as a booking office for Blue Swimmer. There's some good seafood on offer and a myriad of rice and noodle dishes. The quieter location is also a bonus.

Buddha Belly
VEGETARIAN **$**

(Đ 1-4; meals 30,000-80,000d; ⏰10am-9pm; 📶) Right next to Cat Ba market, this bamboo-clad place serves up lots of vegetable and tofu goodness, and doesn't use any dairy or eggs so is a top choice for vegans as well. Its 30,000d daily-changing set menu is excellent value.

Family Bakery
BAKERY **$**

(196 Đ 1-4, Cat Ba Town; pastries 10,000-15,000d, sandwiches 30,000-40,000d; ⏰7am-4pm) Friendly spot that opens early for goodies like pain au chocolat and almond pastries. Pop in for a coffee, crème caramel or

croissant before the bus-ferry-bus combo back to Hanoi.

Phuong Nhung
VIETNAMESE **$**

(184 Đ 1-4, Cat Ba Town; meals 45,000d; ⏰7-10am) Bustling breakfast spot that's a popular place for a hearty bowl of *pho bo* (beef noodle soup) – just the thing you need before a day of climbing or kayaking.

Rose Bar
BAR

(15 Đ Nui Ngoc; ⏰noon-3am; 📶) With cheap cocktails (US$2), loads of happy-hour specials and *shisha* (water pipes), Rose Bar ticks all the boxes for backpacker fun a long way from home. It often stays open after midnight in the busy season.

Oasis Bar
BAR

(Đ 1-4; ⏰noon-11pm; 📶) A pool table, smiley staff and a location slap in the centre of the seafront strip make Oasis a popular spot to plonk yourself down for a beer or two. The menu is pretty decent if you're feeling peckish.

ℹ️ Information

There are internet cafes and an **Agribank** (📞 031-388 8227; ⏰24hr) ATM on the harbourfront. The best impartial travel information is at Asia Outdoors.

ℹ️ Getting There & Away

Cat Ba Island is 45km east of Haiphong and 50km south of Halong City. Various boat and bus combinations make the journey, starting in either Hanoi or Haiphong.

The easiest way to Hanoi is via the city's Luong Yen bus station. **Hoang Long** (📞 031-268 8008; Đ 1-4) offers a combined bus-boat-bus ticket (250,000d, five hours). Buses depart Cat Ba Town at 7.15am, 9.15am, 1.15pm and 3.15pm. From October to April buses leave at 9.15am and 1.15pm.

Haiphong-bound hydrofoils depart Cat Ba Town Pier at 8am, 10am, 2pm and 4pm.

Ferries from Halong City's **Tuan Chau Ferry Pier** (Tuan Chau Island) terminate at Cat Ba Island's Gia Luan harbour on the northern side of the island, which means you're still 40km from Cat Ba Town. The local QH Green bus links Gia Luan with and Cat Ba Town. For years this ferry route was blighted by a taxi mini-mafia who did their best to make sure you couldn't catch this bus, but a recent crackdown has made it more doable.

From Gia Luan Harbour to Halong City, car ferries (per person/motorbike 70,000/10,000d, one hour) leave at 9am and 4pm. Catch the

7.40am or 3pm QH Green bus from Cat Ba Town to connect with the boat. There are usually hourly sailings from late May to early August.

ℹ Getting Around

Rented bicycles are a good way to explore the island. Motorbike rentals (with or without driver) are available from most of the hotels from US$5 per day.

Haiphong

📞031 / POP 1.90 MILLION

Vietnam's third-largest city, Haiphong has a graceful air, and its verdant tree-lined boulevards conceal some classic colonial-era structures. It's an important seaport, industrial centre and transport hub, but very few visitors linger long.

◉ Sights & Activities

★ **Haiphong Museum** MUSEUM
(66 P Dien Bien Phu; admission 5000d; ⊙8-11am Tue-Sun & 7.30-9.30pm Wed & Sun) In a splendid colonial-era building, this small museum concentrates on the city's history with English translations on displays. The front hall's taxidermy collection is rather creepy but there are good exhibits of finds from the Trang Kenh and Viet Khe Tombs archaeological sites and some beautiful ceramic pieces. The museum's garden harbours a diverse collection of war detritus.

🛏 Sleeping & Eating

Bao Anh Hotel HOTEL $
(📞031-382 3406; www.hotelbaoanh.com; 20 P Minh Khai; r incl breakfast 400,000-600,000d; ✱🖙) Refurbished with lots of white paint and new white linen, the Bao Anh has a great location in a leafy street framed by plane trees and buzzy cafes. It's a short walk to good beer places if you're after something stronger. The friendly English-speaking reception is definitely open to negotiation.

Com Vietnam VIETNAMESE $
(📞031-384 1698; 4a P Hoang Van Thu; meals 40,000-60,000d; ⊙11am-9pm) This restaurant hits the spot for its affordable local seafood and Vietnamese specialities. Diminutive, unpretentious and with a small patio.

ℹ Information

There are internet cafes on P Dien Bien Phu; many cafes have free wi-fi. ATMs dot the city centre.

ℹ Getting There & Away

Vietnam Airlines (📞031-3810 890; www.vietnamair.com.vn; 30 P Hoang Van Thu), **Jetstar Pacific** (📞1900 1550; www.jetstar.com) and **VietJet** (📞1900 1886; www.vietjetair.com) all offer flights to cities across the nation.

Buses for Hanoi (70,000d, two hours, every 10 minutes) leave from the **Tam Bac Bus Station** (P Tam Bac), 4km from the waterfront. Buses heading to points south, including Ninh Binh (120,000d, 3½ hours, every 30 minutes), leave from **Niem Nghia Bus Station** (Đ Tran Nguyen Han). **Lac Long Bus Station** (P Cu Chinh Lan) also has buses to Hanoi and points north and is close to the harbour for Cat Ba boats.

There are four trains a day to Hanoi (from 70,000d, 2½ hours) from Haiphong Train Station.

Ba Be National Park

📞0281 / ELEV 145M

Boasting mountains high, rivers deep, and waterfalls, lakes and caves, **Ba Be National Park** (📞0281-389 4014; admission per person 25,000d) is an incredibly scenic spot. The region is surrounded by steep peaks (up to 1554m) while the park contains tropical rainforest with more than 550 plant species. Wildlife in the forest includes bears, monkeys, bats and lots of butterflies. Surrounding the park are Tay minority villages.

Ba Be (Three Bays) is in fact three linked lakes, with a total length of 8km and a width of about 400m. The Nang River is navigable for 23km between a point 4km above Cho Ra and the **Dau Dang Waterfall** (Thac Dau Dang), which is a series of spectacular cascades between sheer walls of rock. River cave **Puong Cave** (Hang Puong) is about 30m high and 300m long.

Park staff can organise tours, starting at about US$35 per day for solo travellers, less for a group. Boat trips (650,000d per boat) take around seven hours to take in most sights. Tay-owned **Ba Be Tourism Centre** (📞0989 587 400; www.babenationalpark.com.vn; Bo Lu village) arranges homestays, boat trips, trekking, cycling and kayaking (or a combo of all four) from US$30 per day.

Homestays in Pac Ngoi village are very popular with travellers; there's also accommodation near the national park entrance. **Mr Linh's Homestay** (📞0989 587 400; www.mrlinhhomestay.com; dm/s/d incl breakfast US$5/20/25; ✱🖙) in Coc Toc village is a step up from most and has kayaks for hire.

Ba Be National Park is 240km from Hanoi and 18km from Cho Ra. Most travellers come on prearranged tours from Hanoi. A noon bus (180,000d, six hours) leaves Hanoi's Gia Lam bus station for Cho Ra, where you'll have to overnight before continuing to Ba Be by *xe om* (around 100,000d).

Mai Chau

🎵 0218 / POP 47,500

In an idyllic valley, Mai Chau is surrounded by lush paddy fields and the rural soundtrack is defined by gurgling irrigation streams and birdsong.

Dozens of local families have signed up to a highly successful homestay initiative, and for visitors the chance to sleep in a traditional stilt house is a real appeal – though note that the villages are on the tour-group agenda.

◎ Sights & Activities

You can walk or cycle past rice fields and trek to minority villages; a local guide costs about US$10. Many travel agencies in Hanoi run inexpensive trips to Mai Chau.

🛏 Sleeping & Eating

Most visitors stay in **Thai stilt houses** (per person 80,000-200,000d) in the villages of Lac or Pom Coong. All homestays have electricity, running water, hot showers, mosquito nets and roll-up mattresses. **Mai Chau Nature Lodge** (🎵 0946 888 804; www.maichaunatureplace.com; dm US$5, d with fan US$30; 🛜) in Lac village offers dorms, private bungalows with bamboo furniture and free bikes.

Most people eat where they stay; note that some families charge up to 200,000d for dinner.

❶ Getting There & Around

Direct buses to Mai Chau leave Hanoi's My Dinh bus station at 6am, 8.30am and 11am (100,000d, 3¾ hours). Heading back to Hanoi, buses leave at 9am, 11am and 1pm. Homestay owners can book these buses for you and arrange for you to be picked up from the village.

Lao Cai

🎵 020 / POP 47,000

One of the gateways to the north, Lao Cai lies at the end of the train line, 3km from the Chinese border. The town has no sights but is a major hub for travellers journeying between Hanoi, Sapa and the Chinese city of Kunming. There are hotels and ATMs next to the train station.

GETTING TO CHINA: LAO CAI TO KUNMING

Getting to the border The Lao Cai/Hekou crossing connects northern Vietnam with Yunnan Province in China. The border is about 3km from the Lao Cai train station; *xe om* charge 25,000d.

At the border The border crossing is open from 7am to 10pm. Visas must be arranged in advance.

Moving on There are four daily trains between Hekou to Kunming, plus several sleeper buses.

❶ Getting There & Around

Frequent buses ply the Hanoi–Lao Cai route. There are four daily Lao Cai–Hanoi trains, the cheapest is the LC4 (hard/soft seat 130,000/215,000d, 10 hours), the others are sleepers (425,000d, eight hours).

Minibuses for Sapa (30,000d, 30 minutes) wait by the train station, while services to Bac Ha (70,000d, 2½ hours, seven daily) leave from a terminal next to the Red River bridge.

Bac Ha

🎵 020 / POP 7400

An unhurried and friendly town, Bac Ha makes a relaxed base to explore the northern highlands and hill-tribe villages. The climate here is also noticeably warmer than in Sapa.

Bac Ha has a certain charm, though its stock of traditional old adobe houses is dwindling and being replaced by concrete structures. Wood smoke fills the morning air and chickens and pigs poke around the back lanes. For six days a week Bac Ha slumbers, but its lanes fill up to choking point each Sunday when tourists and Flower Hmong flood in for the weekly market.

◎ Sights

Bac Ha's Sunday market is a riot of colour and commerce, with an entire area devoted to *ruoc* (corn hooch).

While you're here, check out the outlandish **Vua Meo** ('Cat King' House; ⊙7.30-11.30am & 1.30-5pm; FREE), a palace that has been built in a kind of bizarre 'oriental baroque' architectural style.

Beyond town lie several interesting markets; tour operators in Bac Ha can arrange day trips to surrounding markets in villages including Can Cau (Saturday), Co Ly (Tuesday) and Lung Phin (Sunday).

Activities

There's great hiking to hill-tribe villages around Bac Ha. The Nung village of Sin Chai and Hmong village Phec Bung are only a short stroll from town. Visits to rural schools as part of a motorbiking or trekking day trip can be arranged.

Contact **Green Sapa Tour** (0912 005 952; www.bachatourist.com; Đ Tran Bac; 8am-6pm), operated by English-speaking Mr Nghe, for tours.

Sleeping & Eating

Room rates increase on weekends.

Ngan Nga Bac Ha HOTEL $
(0203-880 286; www.nganngabachahotel.com; 117 P Ngoc Uyen; r incl breakfast US$15-20;) This friendly place is above a popular restaurant that does a roaring trade in tasty *lau*. Rooms here are the best budget deal in town; decent-sized and decked out with a few homey touches that give them some character. Bag a front room for a balcony.

Toan Thang Hotel HOTEL $
(0962 255 410; Đ 20-9; r 150,000-300,000d;) This rickety wooden house has barebones basic rooms with fan, while at the front more expensive, rather plain rooms run past a pot-plant-festooned terrace. There's no English spoken, but the lovely lady who owns the place tries hard to help.

Restaurant 36 VIETNAMESE $
(P Ngoc Uyen; meals 30,000-100,000d; 9am-9.30pm) This cute place dishes up lots of *pho* and barbecue options, as well as hotpots for two (from 300,000d). Most travellers come for the great-value set menu of five dishes for 100,000d.

Information

There's an ATM at the Agribank and virtually all hotels have wi-fi.

Getting There & Away

Tours to Bac Ha from Sapa cost from US$20 per person; on the way back you can bail out in Lao Cai and catch the train back to Hanoi.

A motorbike/taxi to Lao Cai costs US$25/70, or to Sapa US$30/80.

Sapa

020 / POP 38,600 / ELEV 1650M

Sapa overlooks a plunging valley of cascading rice terraces, with mountains towering above the town on all sides. Founded as a French hill station in 1922, it's the premier tourist destination in northern Vietnam. Views of this epic scenery are often subdued by thick mist rolling across the peaks, but even if it's cloudy, Sapa is still a fascinating place. Local hill-tribe people fill the town with colour and are canny (and persistent) traders of handicrafts.

The town's colonial-era villas fell into disrepair during successive wars, but Sapa has experienced a recent renaissance – the downside of which is a hotel-building boom.

Sapa is known for its cold, foggy winters (down to 0°C). The dry season for Sapa is approximately January to the end of June.

Sights & Activities

Surrounding Sapa are the Hoang Lien Mountains, including **Fansipan**, which at 3143m is Vietnam's highest peak. The trek from Sapa to the summit and back can take several days (though a cable car is also under construction). Some of the better-known sights around Sapa include the epic **Tram Ton Pass**; the pretty **Thac Bac** (Silver Falls); and **Cau May** (Cloud Bridge), which spans the Muong Hoa River.

Treks can be arranged at many guesthouses and tour operators. **Sapa O'Chau** (020-377 1166; www.sapaochau.com; 8 Đ Thac Bac; 6.30am-6.30pm) is one excellent outfit which benefits Hmong children, and Hmong-owned **Sapa Sisters** (0203-773 388; www.sapasisters.com; Sapa Graceful Hotel, 9 Đ Phan Si; 8am-5pm) is another good operator.

BUSES FROM BAC HA

DESTINATION	FARE (D)	DURATION (HR)	FREQUENCY
Hanoi	300,000	11	3 daily
Lao Cai	70,000	2½	hourly

GETTING TO CHINA: NORTHEASTERN BORDERS

Huu Nghi Quan to Youyi Guan

Getting to the border This border post is at Huu Nghi Quan (Friendship Gate), 3km north of Dong Dang. Take a bus from Hanoi to Dong Dang (160,000d, 3¼ hours) and a *xe om* (30,000d) to the border. International trains that run direct from Hanoi to Nanning and Beijing also pass through this border, but it's not possible to jump aboard these services in Lang Son or Dong Dang.

At the border Open 24 hours. Chinese visas must be arranged in advance.

Moving on On the Chinese side, it's a 20-minute drive to Pingxiang by bus or shared taxi. Pingxiang is connected by train and bus to Nanning.

Mong Cai to Dongxing

Getting to the border Rarely used by travellers, the Chinese border at the Mong Cai/Dongxing border crossing is around 3km from the Mong Cai bus station; around 20,000d on a *xe om* or 40,000d in a taxi.

At the border The border is open daily between 7am and 10pm, Vietnam time. Note that China is one hour ahead of Vietnam. You'll need to have a prearranged visa for China.

Moving on Across the border in Dongxing, frequent buses run to Nanning in China's Guangxi province.

★**Sapa Market**　　　　MARKET
(Đ Ngu Chi Son; ⊙6am-2pm) Unfortunately turfed out of central Sapa, and now in a purpose-built modern building near the bus station, Sapa Market is still a hive of activity with fresh produce, a butcher's section not for the squeamish and hill-tribe people from surrounding villages heading here most days to sell handicrafts. Saturday is the busiest day.

Sapa Museum　　　　MUSEUM
(103 Đ Xuan Vien; ⊙7.30-11.30am & 1.30-5pm) FREE Excellent showcase of the history and ethnology of the Sapa area, including the colonial times of the French. Exhibitions demonstrate the differences between the various ethnic minority people of the area, so it's definitely worth visiting the museum when you first arrive in town.

🛏 Sleeping

Sapa Graceful Hotel　　　　HOSTEL $
(☑0203-773 388; www.gracefulhotel.com; 9 Đ Phan Si; dm US$5, d US$18; 🛜) This bijoux hostel has bags of homey charm and knows how to pull backpackers in, with two-for-one beer happy hours every evening. The dorm is a squeeze, but the foyer has comfy sofas and stacks of books, and as it's the base for Sapa Sisters, there's a ton of trekking info on offer.

Go Sapa Hostel　　　　HOSTEL $
(☑0203-871 198; www.gosapahostel.com; 25 Đ Thac Bac; dm 110,000-150,000d, d 400,000d;

@🛜) Up the hill from central Sapa, this set-up has a multitude of eight-bed dorms (with lockers) set around a communal courtyard. More expensive dorm options come with private bathroom and some have tiny balconies. There are washing machines, free computers and bike rentals.

Luong Thuy
Family Guesthouse　　　　GUESTHOUSE $
(☑0203-872 310; www.familysapa.com; 28 Đ Muong Hoa; dm US$5, d US$15-20, tw US$25; @🛜) This friendly guesthouse has a decent, though dark, dorm and snug private rooms. Motorcycles and bikes can be rented, trekking and transport arranged, and there are valley views from the front balconies.

★**Nam Cang**
Riverside House　　　　HOMESTAY $$
(www.namcangriversidelodge.com; Nam Cang village; d US$60) Located in a valley, on the outskirts of teensy Nam Cang village, 36km from Sapa, this stylish wooden house with nine rooms is a collaboration between a Red Dzao family and Topas Travel. This is a Sapa-stay replete with stunning scenery and local hill-tribe life. The house is right beside a trickling river and backed by lush green forest.

🍴 Eating & Drinking

For cheap eats check out Sapa market and the night-market stalls south of the church for *bun cha* (barbecued pork).

Sapa

VIETNAM SAPA

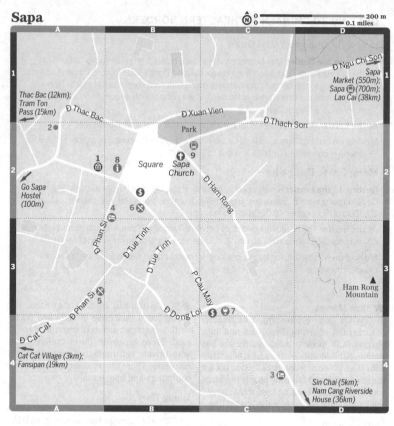

Sapa

◉ Sights
1 Sapa Museum A2

⊕ Activities, Courses & Tours
2 Sapa O'Chau A2
   Sapa Sisters .... (see 4)

⊜ Sleeping
3 Luong Thuy Family Guesthouse C4
4 Sapa Graceful Hotel B2

⊗ Eating
5 Hill Station Signature Restaurant A3

6 Little Sapa B2
   Sapa O'Chau .... (see 2)

⊙ Drinking & Nightlife
7 Mountain Bar & Pub C3

ℹ Information
8 Sapa Tourism B2

ℹ Transport
9 Minibuses to Lao Cai B2

Little Sapa VIETNAMESE **$**
(18 P Cau May; meals 50,000-80,000đ; ⊙8am-10pm) One of the better-value eateries along touristy P Cau May, Little Sapa also lures in locals. Steer clear of the largely mediocre European dishes and concentrate on the Vietnamese menu.

Sapa O'Chau CAFE **$**
(www.sapaochau.org; 8 Đ Thac Bac; snacks from 20,000đ; ⊙6.30am-6.30pm; 🕿) 🖉 Don't miss warming up with a cup of ginger tea sweetened with Sapa mountain honey at this simple cafe attached to the Sapa O'Chau tour

company. Also does good breakfasts and a few simple snacks.

★ Hill Station Signature
Restaurant VIETNAMESE **$$**
(www.thehillstation.com; 37 Đ Phan Si; meals 90,000-180,000đ; ⊘7am-11pm; ?) A showcase of Hmong cuisine with cool Zen decor and superb views. Dishes include flash-cooked pork with lime, ash-baked trout in banana leaves, and traditional Hmong-style black pudding. Tasting sets of local rice and corn wine are also of interest to curious travelling foodies. Don't miss the delicate rainbow-trout rolls; think of them as 'Sapa sushi'.

Mountain Bar & Pub BAR
(2 Đ Muong Hoa; ⊘noon-11pm; ?) Dangerously strong cocktails, cold beer and ultra-competitive games of table-football conspire to make this Sapa's go-to place for a great night out. Even if it's freezing outside, a *shisha* beside the open fire will soon perk up the chilliest of travellers. Try the warm apple wine for some highland bliss.

ⓘ Information

Wi-fi is commonplace in hotels and many restaurants and cafes. There are several ATMs in town including **Agribank** (P Cau May; ⊘8am-3pm Mon-Fri, ATM 24hr). **Sapa Tourism** (⊘020-387 3239; www.sapa-tourism.com; 103 Đ Xuan Vien; ⊘7.30-11.30am & 1.30-5pm) has helpful English-speaking staff offering details about transport, trekking and weather.

ⓘ Getting There & Away

The gateway to Sapa is Lao Cai, 38km away to the west. Minibuses (30,000đ, 30 minutes, every 30 minutes) run between 6am and 6pm.

Hotels and travel agents offer minibus tours to Bac Ha (from US$20 return) for the Sunday market, or you can travel by public minibus, via Lao Cai.

From Sapa bus station, buses run to Hanoi (250,000đ to 300,000đ, six to 10 hours, six daily). From a stop near Sapa Church minibuses

head to Lai Chau (75,000đ, three hours, 10 daily). For Dien Bien Phu change in Lai Chau.

Most hotels and travel agencies can book train tickets from Lao Cai to Hanoi.

Dien Bien Phu

☑0230 / POP 72,700

On 7 May 1954 French colonial forces were defeated by the Viet Minh in a decisive battle at Dien Bien Phu (DBP), and the days of their Indochine empire were numbered.

Previously just a minor settlement, DBP has recently boomed. Boulevards and civic buildings have been constructed and the airport has daily flights from Hanoi.

⊙ Sights

★ Dien Bien Phu Museum MUSEUM
(☑0230-382 4971; Đ 7-5; admission 15,000đ; ⊘7-11am & 1.30-4.30pm) This well-laid-out museum, contained in a space-agey modern structure, features an eclectic collection that commemorates the 1954 battle. Alongside weaponry and guns, there's a bath tub that belonged to the French commander Colonel Christian de Castries, a bicycle capable of carrying 330kg of ordnance, and photographs and documents, some with English translations.

Bunker of
Colonel de Castries MONUMENT
(admission 5000đ; ⊘7-11am & 1.30-5pm) Across the Ron River, the command bunker of Colonel Christian de Castries has been recreated. A few discarded tanks linger nearby, and you'll probably see Vietnamese tourists mounting the bunker and waving the Vietnamese flag, re-enacting an iconic photograph taken at the battle's conclusion.

A1 Hill MONUMENT
(Đ 7-5; admission 3000đ; ⊘7-11am & 1.30-5pm) There are tanks and a monument to Viet Minh casualties on this former French

VIETNAM DIEN BIEN PHU

BUSES FROM DIEN BIEN PHU

DESTINATION	FARE (D)	DURATION (HR)	FREQUENCY
Hanoi	270,000-300,000	11½	frequent 4.30am-9pm
Lai Chau	130,000	6-7	6.15am, 7am, 8am, 9am, 10am, 12.30pm, 1.15pm
Muang Khua (Laos)	110,000	7-8	5.30am
Muong Lay	62,000	3-4	2.30pm, 3pm, 4pm
Son La	105,000	4	4.30am, 8am, noon, 2pm

GETTING TO LAOS: DIEN BIEN PHU TO MUANG KHUA

Getting to the border Buses from Dien Bien Phu to Muang Khua (110,000d, seven to eight hours) leave daily at 5.30am, crossing at the Tay Trang/Sop Hun border. Other destinations in Laos from DBP include Luang Prabang (495,000d, 6am), Nam Tha (350,000d, 6.30am) and Udomxai (230,000d, 7.30am).

At the border Open daily from 7am to 7pm. Most travellers can get a 30-day visa on arrival (US$20 to US$42, depending on your nationality). Have photo ID and additional cash (around US$5) on hand for local 'administrative' fees.

Moving on From Muang Khua there are buses to Udomxai.

For information on doing this crossing in the opposite direction, see p346.

---

position, known to the French as Eliane and to the Vietnamese as A1 Hill. The elaborate trenches at the heart of the French defenses have also been recreated.

🛏 Sleeping & Eating

Dining options are limited in DBP. You'll find *pho* stalls and simple restaurants opposite the bus station.

★ Ruby Hotel HOTEL $
(☑091 365 5793; www.rubyhoteldienbien. com; off Đ Nguyen Chi Thanh; s/d/tr 400,000/500,000/600,000d) The best deal in Dien Bien Phu is this friendly hotel, down a signposted alleyway. Rooms are comfortably fitted out with new beds, flat-screen TVs and bathrooms featuring rain shower heads. If you're travelling solo, treat yourself to a double room as the singles are quite small.

Binh Long Hotel GUESTHOUSE $
(☑0230-382 4345; 429 Đ Muong Thanh; d 200,000d; ❀🗟) This small, family-run place is squeezed between shops, right in the thick of things on the main road. The small rooms are very worn, but kept in better shape than the rest of DBP's cheapies.

Yen Ninh VIETNAMESE $
(P Be Van Dan; meals 50,000-80,000d; ☉11am-9pm; 🖉) This modest fully vegetarian diner dishes up tasty noodle and rice plates with plenty of tofu.

ℹ Information

Internet cafes are on Đ Hoang Van Thai. DBP has many ATMs.

ℹ Getting There & Away

Vietnam Airlines (☑0230-382 4948; www. vietnamairlines.com; Đ Nguyen Huu Tho; ☉7.30-11.30am & 1.30-4.30pm) operates two flights daily between Dien Bien Phu and Hanoi. The office is near the airport, about 1.5km from the town centre, along the road to Muong Lay.

NORTH-CENTRAL VIETNAM

With ancient history, compelling culture, incredible food and terrific beaches, north-central Vietnam has real allure. This is an area that packs in the serene city of Hue (Vietnam's former imperial capital), DMZ battle sites, booming Danang, and Hoi An, an exquisite architectural gem that time forgot. Chuck in the ruins of My Son, the extraordinary cave systems of Phong Nha, the karst scenery around Ninh Binh and numerous nature reserves and the region's appeal is overwhelming.

Ninh Binh

☑030 / POP 158,000
The city of Ninh Binh isn't a destination in itself, but it's a good base for exploring some quintessentially Vietnamese karst scenery and bucolic countryside (including Tam Coc and Cuc Phuong National Park). However, many attractions are heavily commercialised.

🛏 Sleeping & Eating

Accommodation is excellent value. Restaurant choices are limited, try the local speciality, *de* (goat meat).

Xuan Hoa Hotel 1 HOTEL $
(☑030-388 0970; www.xuanhoahotel.com; 31D P Minh Kai; r US$15-30; ❀@🗟) A friendly operation with rooms across two buildings. The original Xuan Hoa Hotel 1 has a room where guests can leave their luggage or

have a free shower after checkout. Nearby **Xuan Hoa Hotel 2** (☑030-388 0970; www.xuanhoahotel.com; 3D Minh Khai; r US$6-12; ➦🅿@🛈) has balconies overlooking a quiet neighbourhood. Before dining at the Xuan Hoa Hotel 1, have a beer on the edge of the compact lake.

Thanh Thuy's Guest House & New Hotel GUESTHOUSE **$**
(☑030-387 1811; www.hotelthanhthuy.com; 53 Đ Le Hong Phong; dm US$6, r US$12-30; 🅿@🛈) This guesthouse's courtyard and restaurant are a great place to meet other travellers. Offers good-value, clean rooms, some with balcony, and also books tours. Cheaper rooms are fan-only.

Trung Tuyet VIETNAMESE **$**
(14 Đ Hoang Hoa Tham; meals 40,000-75,000d; ☉7am-9.45pm) Expect filling portions and a warm welcome from the host family at this busy little place which is popular with travellers. They'll even drop you off at the nearby train station if you're kicking on after your meal.

❶ Information

Internet cafes are on Đ Luong Van Tuy and ATMs on Đ Tran Hung Dao.

❶ Getting There & Away

The city is connected by very regular buses from Giap Bat and Luong Yen bus stations in Hanoi (from 65,000d, 2½ hours).

Ninh Binh is a scheduled stop for both open-tour buses and some trains travelling between Hanoi and HCMC.

Around Ninh Binh

Guesthouses in Ninh Binh can arrange transport and tours to all the sights around town.

Tam Coc

Famed for huge limestone rock formations that loom over rice paddies, this famous, though touristy, site is 9km southwest of Ninh Binh. **Tam Coc Boat Trips** (adult/child 120,000/60,000d, boat 150,000d, maximum 2 per boat; ☉7am-3.30pm) take in some breathtaking scenery, passing through karst caves on the beautiful two-hour tour. Boats seat two passengers (and have no shade). Prepare yourself for pushy vendors.

Chua Bai Dinh

A vast (modern) Buddhist temple complex, **Chua Bai Dinh** (☉7am-5.45pm) FREE attracts thousands of Vietnamese visitors.

Cloister-like walkways pass 500 stone *arhats* (statues of enlightened Buddhists). They line the route up to the triple-roofed Phap Chu pagoda, which contains a 10m, 100-tonne bronze buddha.

Chua Bai Dinh is 11km northwest of Ninh Binh. An electric train (per person 30,000d) shuttles between the car park and the main entrance.

Hoa Lu

Hoa Lu was the capital of Vietnam under the Dinh (968–980) and Le dynasties (980–1009). The **ancient citadel**, most of which, sadly, has been destroyed, once covered an area of about 3 sq km.

Hoa Lu is 12km north of Ninh Binh.

Cuc Phuong National Park

☑030 / ELEV 150-648M

This impressive **national park** (☑030-384 8006; www.cucphuongtourism.com; adult/child 40,000/20,000d) was declared the nation's first national park in 1963 and is home to 307 bird, 133 mammal and 122 reptile species, plus more than 2000 different plants. However, due to illegal poaching, little wildlife is encountered.

Trekking opportunities are good, including a hike (8km return) to an enormous 1000-year-old tree (*Tetrameles nudiflora*, for botany geeks), and to a Muong village, where you can also go rafting. A guide is mandatory for longer treks.

The **Endangered Primate Rescue Center** (☑030-384 8002; admission 30,000d; ☉9-11am & 1.30-4pm) is home to around 150 rare monkeys bred in captivity or confiscated from illegal traders. These gibbons, langurs and lorises are rehabilitated, studied and, whenever possible, released into semi-wild protected areas.

There's also a **Turtle Conservation Center** (☑030-384 8090; www.asianturtle program.org; ☉9-11am & 2-4.45pm). You'll find excellent information displays, and there are incubation and hatchling viewing areas. The centre successfully breeds and releases turtles of 11 different species.

MATT MUNRO/LONELY PLANET ©

1. Pho Bo
This beef noodle soup is flavoured with shallots, ginger, fish sauce, black cardamom, star anise and cassia.

2. Japanese Covered Bridge (p863)
Hoi An's iconic bridge was constructed in the 1590s by the town's Japanese community.

3. Market-stall dining, Hoi An (p863)
Stopping for a meal at a market restaurant is a good way to try local specialities.

4. Tet celebrations (p27), Ho Chi Minh City
The lunar New Year is marked by street parades, gift giving and family get-togethers.

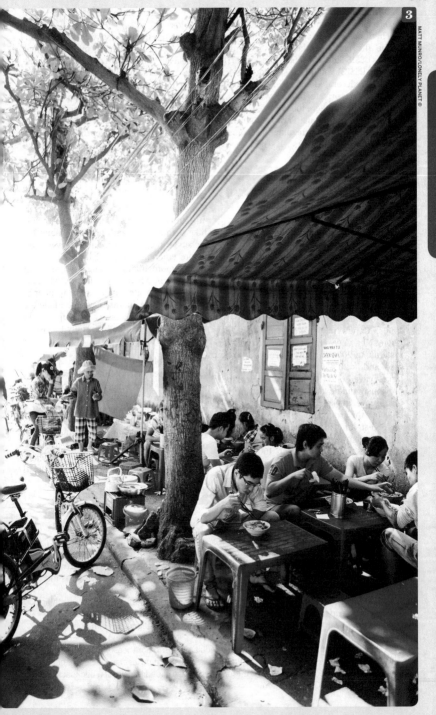

During the rainy season (July to September) leeches are common in Cuc Phuong.

There are several accommodation areas inside the park. At the **park headquarters** (s US$16-35, d US$27-50, stilt house US$14, bungalow US$23) you'll find standard rooms, recently redecorated 'deluxe' rooms, a stilt house and a private bungalow. There's a simple restaurant here too.

Cuc Phuong National Park is 45km west of Ninh Binh, with irregular bus connections (28,000d, 1½ hours). It's best visited with your own wheels.

Phong Nha-Ke Bang National Park

A Unesco World Heritage Site, the remarkable **Phong Nha-Ke Bang National Park** FREE contains the oldest karst mountains in Asia and is riddled with hundreds of cave systems. Its collection of stunning dry caves, terraced caves, towering stalagmites and glistening crystal-edged stalactites represent nature on a very grand scale indeed.

Serious exploration only began in the 1990s. Cavers first penetrated deep into Phong Nha Cave, one of the world's longest systems. In 2005 Paradise Cave was discovered, and in 2009 a team found the world's largest cave – Son Doong. Huge caverns and previously unknown cave networks are being discovered each year.

Above the ground, most of this mountainous 885-sq-km national park is near-pristine tropical evergreen jungle, over 90% of which is primary forest. More than 100 types of mammal (including 10 species of primate, tigers, elephants and the saola, a rare Asian antelope), 81 types of reptile and amphibian, and more than 300 varieties of bird have been logged.

Until recently, access was strictly controlled by the Vietnamese military. Things are relaxing, but remain quite tight: officially you are not allowed to hike here without a licensed tour operator.

The Phong Nha region is changing fast, with more and more accommodation options opening. **Son Trach** village (population 3000) is the main centre, but it's tiny and transport connections (though improving) are still infrequent.

⊙ Sights & Activities

★**Tu Lan Cave**   CAVE
(www.oxalis.com.vn; 2-day tour 5,500,000d) The Tu Lan cave trip begins with a countryside hike then a swim (with headlamps and life jackets) through two spectacular river caves before emerging in an idyllic valley. Then there's more hiking through dense forest to a 'beach' where rivers merge, which is an ideal camp site. There's more wonderful swimming here in vast caverns. Moderate fitness levels are necessary. Tu Lan is 65km north of Son Trach and can only be visited on a guided tour.

★**Hang Toi**   CAVE
(Dark Cave; per person 350,000d) Incorporating an above-water zipline, followed by a swim into the cave, and then exploration of a pitch-black passageway of oozing mud, it's little wonder Hang Toi is the cave experience you may have already heard about from other travellers. Upon exiting the cave, a leisurely kayak paddle heads to a jetty where there's more into-the-water zipline thrills to be had.

HANG SON DOONG

Ho Khanh, a hunter, stumbled across gargantuan **Hang Son Doong** (Mountain River Cave) in the early 1990s, but the sheer scale and majesty of the principal cavern (more than 5km long, 200m high and, in some places, 150m wide) was only confirmed as the world's biggest cave when British explorers returned with him in 2009.

Sections of the cave are pierced by skylights that reveal formations of ethereal stalagmites (some up to 80m high) that cavers have called the Cactus Garden. Colossal cave pearls have been discovered, measuring 10cm in diameter. Magnificent rimstone pools are present too.

Hang Son Doong is one of the most spectacular sights in Southeast Asia, and the only specialist operator permitted (by the Vietnamese president no less) to lead tours here is Son Trach–based Oxalis Adventure Tours. Seven-day expeditions cost a backpacking blowout of US$3000 per person.

Paradise Cave   CAVE

(Thien Dong; adult/child under 1.3m 250,000/125,000d; ⊙7.30am-4.30pm) Surrounded by forested karst peaks, this remarkable cave system extends for 31km, though most people only visit the first kilometre. The scale is breathtaking, as wooden staircases descend into a cathedral-like space with colossal stalagmites and glimmering stalactites. Get here early to beat the crowds, as during peak times (early afternoon), tour guides shepherd groups using megaphones. Paradise Cave is about 14km southwest of Son Trach. Electric buggies (per person one-way/return 15,000/25,000d) ferry visitors from the car park to the entrance.

Phong Nha Caves   CAVE

(adult/child under 1.3m 150,000/25,000d, boat up to 14 people 320,000d; ⊙7am-4pm) The spectacular boat trip through Phong Nha Cave is a enjoyable, though touristy, experience beginning in Son Trach village. Boats cruise along past buffalo, limestone peaks and church steeples to the cave's gaping mouth. The engine is then cut and the boats are negotiated silently through cavern after garishly illuminated cavern. On the return leg there's the option to climb (via 330 steps) up to the mountainside Tien Son Cave (80,000d) with the remains of 9th-century Cham altars.

Hang Va   CAVE

(per person 9,000,000d) Discovered in 2012, and opened to visitors in 2015, Hang Va is explored on a two-day/one-night excursion which travels firstly along an underground river in Hang Nuoc Nut. Tours overnight in a jungle camp at the entrance to Hang Va, where the cave's highlight is a spectacular stalagmite field partly submerged in crystalline waters. Ropes and harnesses are used extensively. Tours can be booked via Oxalis.

Hang En   CAVE

(per person 6,000,000d) This gigantic cave is very close to Hang Son Doong, and featured in the same *National Geographic* photographic spread in 2011. Getting here involves a trek through dense jungle, valleys and the Ban Doong minority village, a very remote tribal settlement (with no electricity or roads). You stay overnight in the cave or a minority village. Tours can be booked via Oxalis or Phong Nha Farmstay Tours.

⟨⟩ Tours

★**Oxalis Adventure Tours**   TOUR

(⌧091 990 0423; www.oxalis.com.vn; Son Trach) Oxalis are unquestionably *the* experts in caving and trekking expeditions, and are the only outfit licensed to conduct tours to Hang Son Doong. Staff are all fluent English speakers, and trained by world-renowned British cavers Howard and Deb Limbert. All excursions, from day trips to Tu Lan to week-long expeditions to the world's largest cave, are meticulously planned and employ local guides and porters, so the wider community benefits. You can discuss trips at its riverside Expedition Cafe.

Phong Nha Farmstay Tours   ADVENTURE TOUR

(⌧052-367 5135; www.phong-nha-cave.com; Cu Nam) The Farmstay can book cave tours – in conjunction with Oxalis – but equally interesting is bouncing in a US jeep or Russian Ural motorbike and sidecar exploring the area's scenery and war history. The Farmstay's popular National Park Tour (per person 1,450,000d) travels by minibus to incorporate the Ho Chi Minh Trail with Paradise Cave and Hang Toi.

Jungle Boss Trekking   HIKING

(⌧094 374 8041; www.junglebosshomestay.com; per person US$75) Originally from the DMZ, Dzung – aka 'Jungle Boss' – has been in Phong Nha for eight years, and is an experienced guide to the area. He speaks excellent English and runs an exciting one-day tour around the Ho Chi Minh Trail and the remote Abandoned Valley area of the national park. You'll need moderate to high fitness levels.

⟨⟩ Sleeping

There are also a dozen or so guesthouses (all 350,000d) in Son Trach village.

Easy Tiger   HOSTEL $

(⌧052-367 7844; www.easytigerphongnha.com; Son Trach; dm 160,000d; ❄@🛜☀) In Son Trach town, this hostel has four-bed dorms, a great bar-restaurant area, pool table and excellent travel information. A swimming pool and beer garden make it ideal for relaxation after trekking and caving. And yes, the bedspreads are actually faux leopard skin. Don't ask. Do ask about free bicycles and a map to explore the interesting Bong Lai valley.

GETTING TO LAOS: CENTRAL BORDERS

Vinh to Lak Sao

Getting to the border The Cau Treo/Nam Phao border (96km west of Vinh and 30km from Lak Sao in Laos) has a dodgy reputation with independent travellers. Chronic overcharging on local buses is the norm; stick to direct services. Buses leave Vinh at 6am on Monday, Wednesday, Friday and Saturday for Vieng Khan in Laos (280,000d).

At the border The border is open from 7am to 6pm; 30-day Laos visas (US$30 to US$40) are available on arrival.

Moving on On the Laos side, a jumbo or *sŏrngtǎaou* (small pick-up truck) between the border and Lak Sao costs about 50,000K (bargain hard).

For information on doing this crossing in the opposite direction, see p358.

Vinh to Phonsavan

Getting to the border The Nam Can/Nong Haet border crossing is 250km northwest of Vinh. Buses leave at 6am Monday, Wednesday, Friday and Saturday for Luang Prabang (700,000d, 22 hours) via Phonsavan (410,000d, 12 hours).

At the border Lao visas are available for most nationalities for between US$30 and US$40.

Moving on Transport on the Laos side to Nong Haet is erratic, but once you get there you can pick up a bus to Phonsavan.

For information on doing this crossing in the opposite direction, see p346.

Dong Hoi to Tha Khaek

Daily buses leave Dong Hoi for Vientiane (400,000d) and for Tha Khek from Tuesday to Sunday (300,000d). Both nine-hour services run via the Cha Lo–Na Phao border crossing where Lao visas are available. For all up-to-date transport information, see Sy at the **Nam Long Hotel** (091 892 3595; www.namlonghotels.com) in Dong Hoi.

For information on doing this crossing in the opposite direction, see p358.

★ **Phong Nha Farmstay** GUESTHOUSE $$
(052-367 5135; www.phong-nha-cave.com; Cu Nam; r 900,000-1,200,000d, f 1,300,000-2,000,000d;) The place that really put Phong Nha on the map, the Farmstay has peaceful views overlooking an ocean of rice paddies. Rooms are smallish but neat, with high ceilings and shared balconies. The bar-restaurant serves up Asian and Western meals, and there's a social vibe and occasional movies and live music. Local tours are excellent and there's free bicycle hire.

Phong Nha Lake House Resort HOTEL $$
(052-367 5999; www.phongnhalakehouse.com; Khuong Ha; dm $10, d $42-60, f $70;) Impressive lakeside resort owned by an Australian-Vietnamese couple with an excellent dorm (with quality beds, mozzie nets, en suite bathroom and high ceilings), and spacious and stylish villas. A pool and newer lake view bungalows are more proof this is the area's most comfortable place to stay. The wooden restaurant is a traditional structure from Ha Giang province in northern Vietnam.

Pepper House GUESTHOUSE $$
(016 7873 1560; www.facebook.com/Pepper HouseHomestay; Khuong Ha; dm 200,000d, villas 1,400,000d;) Run by long-term Aussie expat Dave (aka 'Multi') and his local wife Diem, this welcoming place combines a rural setting and new double rooms in villas arrayed around a compact swimming pool. There are also simpler dorms inside the main house. Look forward to good food and cold beer as well.

✕ Eating & Drinking

Bamboo Cafe CAFE $
(www.phong-nha-bamboo-cafe.com; Son Trach; meals 35,000-70,000d; 7am-10.30pm;) This laid-back haven on Son Trach's main drag has colourful decor, a cool outside deck, and well-priced food and drink, including excel-

lent fresh fruit smoothies. It's also where you'll usually find the friendly Hai who runs **eco conservation tours** (☑096 260 6844; www.phong-nha-bamboo-cafe.com; per person 1,000,000d).

The Best Spit Roast Pork & Noodle Shop in the World (probably...) VIETNAMESE $
(Son Trach; meals 30,000-50,000d; ⊙7am-4pm) Also probably the longest name of any restaurant in Vietnam, and excellent grilled pork paired with noodles, baguettes or rice. Get ready to smell this place well before you see it as you're wandering Son Trach's sleepy main street.

★ **Jungle Bar** BAR
(Son Trach; ⊙7am-midnight; 🛜) The on-site bar/cafe at Easy Tiger (p847) is the most happening place in Son Trach, with cheap beer, pool tables, and live music four nights a week. Add to the growing display of national flags if you're feeling patriotic. There's loads of local information on hand, even if you're not staying at Easy Tiger.

ⓘ Information

Hai at the Bamboo Cafe is a superb source of independent travel information, and the helpful staff at the Phong Nha Farmstay and Easy Tiger can assist with tours, information and transport.

There are two ATMs in Son Trach.

ⓘ Getting There & Around

The coastal city of Dong Hoi, 166km north of Hue on Hwy 1 and on the north-south train line, is the main gateway to Phong Nha. The national park abuts Son Trach village, which is 50km northwest of Dong Hoi.

Hotels can organise lifts in private cars to Dong Hoi (500,000d); they work together so rides can be shared between travellers to cut costs.

Regular local buses (35,000d, 1½ hours, 6am to 5pm) shuttle between Dong Hoi's bus station and Son Trach. There's also a bus from Hue.

Coming from Danang or Hoi An, a local bus (250,000d, seven hours) leaves the Danang bus station for Phong Nha around 1pm. This service has been haphazard so check the Easy Tiger or Oxalis websites for the latest status.

It's possible to rent a bike and explore the region yourself, though road signs are lacking. But with a sense of adventure, some wheels and a map (ask at Jungle Bar or Easy Rider) it's perfectly doable. **Thang's Phong Nha Riders** (www.easytigerhostel.com/thangs-phong-nha-riders; beside Easy Tiger) charge around 400,000d for a day's hire of a bike and driver.

Hue

☑054 / POP 361,000

Palaces and pagodas, tombs and temples, culture and cuisine, history and heartbreak – there's no shortage of poetic pairings to describe the graceful city of Hue. A World Heritage Site, the capital of the Nguyen emperors is where tourists come to see opulent royal tombs and the grand, crumbling Citadel. Most of these architectural attractions lie along the northern side of the Song Huong (Perfume River). For rest and recreation the south bank is where it's at.

The city hosts a biennial arts festival, the **Festival of Hue** (www.huefestival.com; ⊙late Apr-early May 2018), every even-numbered year, featuring local and international artists and performers.

⊙ Sights & Activities

Most of Hue's principal sights reside within the moats of its Citadel, including the Imperial Enclosure. Other museums and pagodas are dotted around the city. All the principal royal tombs are some distance south of Hue.

GETTING TO LAOS: DONG HA TO SAVANNAKHET

Getting to the border The Lao Bao/Dansavanh border crossing is one of the most popular and least problematic border crossings between Laos and Vietnam. Buses to Savannakhet in Laos run from Hue via Dong Ha and Lao Bao. From Hue, there's a 7am air-con bus (350,000d, 9½ hours), on odd days only, that stops in Dong Ha at the Sepon Travel office around 8.30am to pick up more passengers. It's also easy to cross the border on your own; Dong Ha is the gateway. Buses leave the town to Lao Bao (55,000d, two hours) roughly every 15 minutes. From here *xe om* charge 15,000d to the border.

At the border The border is open 7am to 6pm. Lao visas are available on arrival.

Moving on *Sŏrngtǎaou* head regularly to Sepon, from where you can get a bus or another *sŏrngtǎaou* to Savannakhet.

For information on doing this crossing in the opposite direction, see p360.

Hue

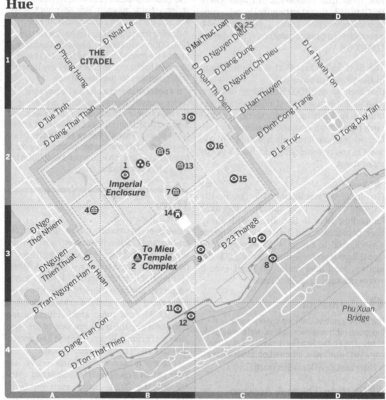

Inside the Citadel

Built between 1804 and 1833, the **Citadel** (Kinh Thanh) is still the heart of Hue. Heavily fortified, it consists of 2m-thick, 10km-long walls, a moat (30m across and 4m deep), and 10 gateways.

The Citadel has distinct sections. The Imperial Enclosure and Forbidden Purple City formed the epicentre of Vietnamese royal life. On the southwestern side were temple compounds. There were residences in the northwest, gardens in the northeast and, in the north, the Mang Ca Fortress (still a military base).

For more information about the Citadel, see p854.

★ Imperial Enclosure
HISTORIC SITE

(adult/child 150,000/30,000d; ⏷7am-5.30pm) The Imperial Enclosure is a citadel-within-a-citadel, housing the emperor's residence, temples and palaces and the main buildings of state within 6m-high, 2.5km-long walls. What's left is only a fraction of the original – the enclosure was badly bombed during the French and American wars, and only 20 of its 148 buildings survived. This is a fascinating site that is easily worth half a day, but poor signage can make navigation a bit difficult. Restoration and reconstruction are ongoing.

Ngo Mon Gate
GATE

The principal entrance to the Imperial Enclosure is Ngo Mon Gate, which faces the Flag Tower. The central passageway with its yellow doors was reserved for the use of the emperor, as was the bridge across the lotus pond. Others had to use the gates to either side and the paths around the pond. On top of the gate is Ngu Phung (Belvedere of the Five Phoenixes); on its upper level is a huge drum and bell.

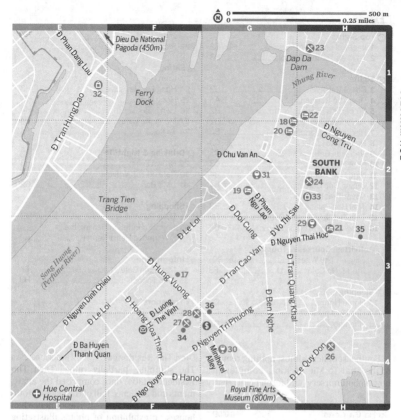

Thai Hoa Palace
PALACE

This palace (Palace of Supreme Harmony; 1803) is a spacious hall with an ornate timber roof supported by 80 carved and lacquered columns. It was used for the emperor's official receptions and important ceremonies. On state occasions the emperor sat on his elevated throne, facing visitors entering via the Ngo Mon Gate. No photos are permitted, but be sure to see the impressive audio-visual display, which gives an excellent overview of the entire Citadel, its architecture and the historical context.

Halls of the Mandarins
HISTORIC BUILDING

Located immediately behind Thai Hoa Palace, on either side of a courtyard, these halls were used by mandarins as offices and to prepare for court ceremonies. The hall on the right showcases fascinating old photographs (including boy-king Vua Duya Tan's coronation), gilded Buddha statues and assorted imperial curios. Behind the courtyard are the ruins of the Can Chanh Palace, where two wonderful long galleries, painted in gleaming scarlet lacquer have been reconstructed.

Emperor's Reading Room
HISTORIC BUILDING

(Thai Binh Lau) The exquisite (though crumbling) little two-storey Emperor's Reading Room was the only part of the Forbidden Purple City to escape damage during the French reoccupation of Hue in 1947. It's currently being renovated and so it's not open to visitors, but it's worth checking out the Gaudi-esque roof mosaics.

Royal Theatre
HISTORIC BUILDING

(Duyen Thi Duong; ☏ 054-351 4989; www.nhan hac.com.vn; performances 50,000-100,000d; ⊙ performances 9am, 10am, 2.30pm & 3.30pm) The Royal Theatre, begun in 1826 and later home to the National Conservatory of Music, has been rebuilt on its former foundations. Cultural performances here last 45 minutes.

Hue

Southeast of here almost nothing remains of the **Thai To Mieu temple complex** (it's now a plant nursery) and former **University of Arts**.

Co Ha Gardens   GARDENS
Occupying the northeastern corner of the Imperial Enclosure, these delightful gardens were developed by the first four emperors of the Nguyen dynasty but fell into disrepair. They've been beautifully recreated in the last few years, and are dotted with little gazebo-style pavilions and ponds. This is one of the most peaceful spots in the entire Citadel, and was undergoing further careful renovation when we last visited.

Forbidden Purple City   RUIN
(Tu Cam Thanh) In the very centre of the Imperial Enclosure, there's almost nothing left of the once-magnificent Forbidden Purple City. This was a citadel-within-a-citadel-within-a-citadel and was reserved solely for the personal use of the emperor – the only servants allowed into this compound were eunuchs who would pose no threat to the royal concubines. The Forbidden Purple City was almost entirely destroyed in the wars, and its crumbling remains are now overgrown with weeds.

Dien Tho Residence   HISTORIC BUILDING
The stunning, partially ruined Dien Tho Residence (1804) once comprised the apartments and audience hall of the Queen Mothers of the Nguyen dynasty. The audience hall houses an exhibition of photos illustrating its former use, and there is a display of embroidered royal garments. Just outside a pleasure pavilion above a lily pond has been transformed into a cafe worthy of a refreshment stop.

★ **To Mieu**
Temple Complex   BUDDHIST TEMPLE
Taking up the southwestern corner of the Imperial Enclosure, this highly impressive walled complex has been beautifully restored. The imposing three-tiered **Hien Lam Pavilion** sits on the southern side of the complex; it dates from 1824. On the other side of a courtyard is the solemn **To Mieu Temple**, housing shrines to each of the emperors, topped by their photos. Between these two temples are **Nine Dynastic Urns** *(dinh)*, cast between 1835 and 1836, each dedicated to one Nguyen sovereign.

Nine Holy Cannons   HISTORIC SITE
Located just inside the Citadel ramparts, near the gates to either side of the Flag Tow-

er, are the Nine Holy Cannons (1804), symbolic protectors of the palace and kingdom. Commissioned by Emperor Gia Long, they were never intended to be fired. The **four cannons** near **Ngan Gate** represent the four seasons, while the **five cannons** next to **Quang Duc Gate** represent the five elements: metal, wood, water, fire and earth.

Outside the Citadel

★ Thien Mu Pagoda
BUDDHIST TEMPLE

FREE Built on a hill overlooking the Perfume River, 4km southwest of the Citadel, this pagoda is an icon of Vietnam and as potent a symbol of Hue as the Citadel. The 21m-high octagonal tower, **Thap Phuoc Duyen**, was constructed under the reign of Emperor Thieu Tri in 1844. Each of its seven storeys is dedicated to a *manushi-buddha* (a Buddha that appeared in human form). Visit in the morning before tour groups show up.

Dieu De National Pagoda
BUDDHIST TEMPLE

(Quoc Tu Dieu De; 102 Đ Bach Dang) **FREE** Overlooking Dong Ba Canal, this pagoda was built under Emperor Thieu Tri's rule (1841–47) and is famous for its four low towers, one either side of the gate, and two flanking the sanctuary. The pavilions on either side of the main sanctuary entrance contain the 18 La Ha, whose rank is just below that of Bodhisattva, and the eight Kim Cang, protectors of Buddha. In the back row of the main dais is Thich Ca Buddha, flanked by two assistants.

Royal Fine Arts Museum
MUSEUM

(150 Đ Nguyen Hue; ☉ 6.30am-5.30pm summer, 7am-5pm winter) **FREE** This recently renovated museum is located in the baroque-influenced An Dinh Palace, commissioned by Emperor Khai Dinh in 1918 and full of elaborate murals, floral motifs and trompe l'œil details. Emperor Bao Dai lived here with his family after abdicating in 1945. Inside, you'll find some outstanding ceramics, paintings, furniture, silverware, porcelain and royal clothing, though information is a little lacking.

👉 Tours

Most hotels and travellers' cafes offer shared tours covering the main sights (from as little as US$5 to around US$20 per person). There are many different itineraries; some of the better ones start with a morning river cruise, stopping at pagodas and temples, then after lunch you transfer to a minibus to hit the main tombs and then return to Hue by road. On the cheaper options you'll often have to hire a motorbike to get from the moorings to the tombs, or walk (in the intense heat of the day).

It's perfectly possible to rent a *xe om* or your own bike and do a DIY tour.

Stop & Go Café
TOUR

(☑ 054-382 7051; www.stopandgo-hue.com; 3 Đ Hung Vuong) A full-day DMZ car tour guided by a Vietnamese vet costs around US$27 per person for four people, representing a good deal. Guided trips to Hoi An stopping at beaches are also recommended.

Cafe on Thu Wheels
TOUR

(☑ 054-383 2241; minhthuhue@yahoo.com; 10/2 Đ Nguyen Tri Phuong) Inexpensive bike hire, plus motorbike, minibus and car tours around Hue and the DMZ. Can also arrange transfers to Hoi An by motorbike (US$45) or car (US$55)

Hue Flavor
TOUR

(☑ 0905 937 006; www.hueflavor.com; per person US$45) Excellent street food tours exploring the delights of Hue cuisine. Transport is by *cyclo* and around 15 different dishes are sampled across four hours.

🛏 Sleeping

★ Home Hotel
HOTEL **$**

(☑ 054-383 0014; www.huehomehotel.com; 8 Đ Nguyen Cong Tru; r US$16-25; ❋ @ 🛜) Run by a really friendly team, the welcoming Home Hotel has a young, hip vibe and spacious rooms arrayed across several levels. Ask to book a room looking over Đ Nguyen Cong Tru for a compact balcony, French doors and views of the river. No lift.

SPLURGE

Around 6km from Hue in Long Ha village, **Tam Tinh Vien** (☑ 054-3519 990; www.huehomestay.wevina.vn; r US$40; ❋ @ 🛜 ⛱) is called a homestay but is really a delightful boutique guesthouse. Arrayed around a small pool and verdant garden, spacious villas with four-poster beds are imbued with a chic Asian aesthetic. Borrow a bike to make the 30-minute journey into Hue – a taxi is 100,000d.

Hué's Imperial Enclosure

EXPLORING THE SITE

An incongruous combination of meticulously restored palaces and pagodas, ruins and rubble, the Imperial Enclosure is approached from the south through the outer walls of the Citadel. It's best to tackle the site as a walking tour, winding your way around the structures in an anticlockwise direction.

You'll pass directly through the monumental **Ngo Mon Gateway** ❶ where the ticket office is located. This dramatic approach quickens the pulse and adds to the sense of occasion as you enter this citadel-within-a-citadel. Directly ahead is the **Thai Hoa Palace** ❷ where the emperor would greet offical visitors from his elevated throne. Continuing north you'll step across a small courtyard to the twin **Halls of the Mandarins** ❸, where mandarins once had their offices and prepared for ceremonial occasions.

To the northeast is the Royal Theatre, where traditional dance performances are held several times daily. Next you'll be able to get a glimpse of the Emperor's Reading Room built by Thieu Tri and used as a place of retreat. Just east of here are the lovely Co Ha Gardens. Wander their pathways, dotted with hundreds of bonsai trees and potted plants, which have been recently restored.

Guarding the far north of the complex is the Tu Vo Phuong Pavilion, from where you can follow a moat to the Truong San residence and then loop back south via the **Dien Tho Residence** ❹ and finally view the beautifully restored temple compound of To Mieu, perhaps the most rewarding part of the entire enclosure to visit, including its fabulous **Nine Dynastic Urns** ❺.

TOP TIPS

Allow half a day to explore the Citadel. Drink vendors are dotted around the site, but the best places to take a break are the delightful Co Ha Gardens, the Tu Vo Phuong Pavilion and the Dien Tho Residence (the latter two also serve food).

Dien Tho Residence
This pretty corner of the complex, with its low structures and pond, was the residence of many Queen Mothers. The earliest structures here date from 1804.

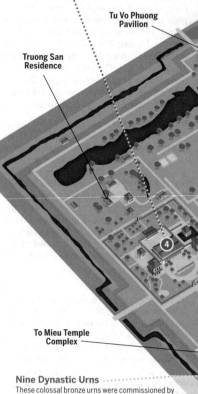

Tu Vo Phuong Pavilion

Truong San Residence

To Mieu Temple Complex

Nine Dynastic Urns
These colossal bronze urns were commissioned by Emperor Minh Mang and cast between 1835 and 1836. They're embellished with decorative elements including landscapes, rivers, flowers and animals.

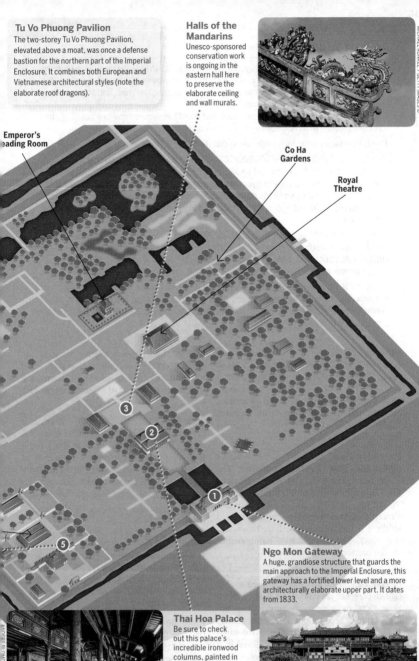

Tu Vo Phuong Pavilion
The two-storey Tu Vo Phuong Pavilion, elevated above a moat, was once a defense bastion for the northern part of the Imperial Enclosure. It combines both European and Vietnamese architectural styles (note the elaborate roof dragons).

Halls of the Mandarins
Unesco-sponsored conservation work is ongoing in the eastern hall here to preserve the elaborate ceiling and wall murals.

MICHAEL RUNKEL / GETTY IMAGES ©

Emperor's eading Room

Co Ha Gardens

Royal Theatre

Ngo Mon Gateway
A huge, grandiose structure that guards the main approach to the Imperial Enclosure, this gateway has a fortified lower level and a more architecturally elaborate upper part. It dates from 1833.

Thai Hoa Palace
Be sure to check out this palace's incredible ironwood columns, painted in 12 coats of brilliant scarlet and gold lacquer. The structure was saved from collapse by restoration work in the 1990s.

SAMI SARKIS / GETTY IMAGES ©

DON'T MISS

ROYAL TOMBS

The tombs of the rulers of the Nguyen dynasty (1802–1945) are extravagant mausoleums, spread out along the banks of the Perfume River between 2km and 16km south of Hue. Almost all were planned by the emperors during their lifetimes, and some were even used as residences while they were still alive.

Some tombs are included in boat tours, but you'll have more time to enjoy them by renting a bicycle, motorbike or *xe om* for the day.

These three are particularly impressive, but there are many more:

Tomb of Tu Duc (adult/child 100,000/20,000d) This tomb, constructed between 1864 and 1867, is the most popular and impressive of the royal mausoleums. Emperor Tu Duc designed it himself to use before and after his death. The enormous expense of the tomb and the forced labour used in its construction spawned a coup plot that was discovered and suppressed. Tu Duc's tomb is 5km south of Hue on Van Nien Hill in Duong Xuan Thuong village.

Tomb of Minh Mang (adult/child 100,000/20,000d) A majestic tomb renowned for its architecture and sublime forest setting. The tomb was planned during Minh Mang's reign (1820–1840) but built by his successor, Thieu Tri. Minh Mang's tomb is in An Bang village, on the west bank of the Perfume River, 12km from Hue.

Tomb of Khai Dinh (adult/child 100,000/20,000d) This hillside monument is a synthesis of Vietnamese and European elements. Most of the tomb's grandiose exterior is covered in blackened concrete, creating an unexpectedly gothic air, while the interiors resemble an explosion of colourful mosaic.

Huenino GUESTHOUSE $
(☑054-625 2171; www.hueninohotel.com; 14 Đ Nguyen Cong Tru; r US$18-25; ☀❄@🖥) Family-owned, this warm, welcoming guesthouse has an artistic flavour with stylish furniture, artwork and smallish rooms with minibar, cable TV and good-quality beds. A generous breakfast is included.

Beach Bar Hue HOTEL $
(☑090 899 3584; www.beachbarhue.com; Phu Thuan beach; dm US$12; ❄🖥) At glorious Phu Thuan beach (about 7km southeast of Thuan An), the Beach Bar Hue has excellent shared four-bed bungalows and sits on a sublime stretch of sand (with no hawkers... for now). There's a funky bamboo-and-thatch bar for drinks and snacks.

Stay Hotel HOTEL $
(☑054-3823 999; www.stayhotelhue.com; 7 Đ Nguyen Cong Tru; dm US$7, d US$14-24; ❄@🖥) Stay Hotel is a new opening in the up-and-coming accommodation scene along Đ Nguyen Cong Tru. Rooms are decorated with colourful art, breakfast is offered in a stylish dining area, and some rooms have river views.

Hue Backpackers HOSTEL $
(☑054-382 6567; www.vietnambackpackerhostels. com; 10 Đ Pham Ngu Lao; dm US$8-12, r US$18; ❄@🖥) Backpacker mecca thanks to its central location, eager-to-please staff, good info and sociable bar-restaurant. Dorms are well designed and have air-conditioning and lockers.

Jade Hotel GUESTHOUSE $
(☑054-393 8849; http://jadehotelhue.com; 17 Đ Nguyen Thai Hoc; r US$17-30; ❄❄@🖥) You'll find simply excellent service standards at this fine place; staff are very sweet and welcoming. Rooms enjoy soft comfy mattresses and there's a nice lobby-lounge for hanging out.

✗ Eating

Hue's culinary variety is amazing, with many unique local dishes, including lots of veggie creations. Royal rice cakes, the most common of which is *banh khoai,* are well worth seeking out.

Hang Me Me VIETNAMESE $
(16 Đ Vo Thi Sau; snacks from 20,000d) A top spot to try Hue's dizzying menu of royal rice cakes. Serving portions are pretty big, so rustle up a few friends to try the different variations. Our favourite is the *banh beo,* perfect little mouthfuls topped with scallions and dried shrimp.

Com Hen
VIETNAMESE $

(17 Đ Han Mac Tu; meals from 10,000d; ⊘7am-11pm) Tuck into bowls of rice *(com hen)* or noodles *(bun hen)* combining fresh herbs and tasty local clams from a nearby island in the middle of the Perfume River. Servings are fairly small, so maybe have a bowl of each.

Lien Hoa
VEGETARIAN $

(3 Đ Le Quy Don; meals 50,000-75,000d; ⊘6.30am-9.30pm;) No nonsense Viet vegetarian restaurant renowned for filling food at bargain prices. Fresh *banh beo*, noodle dishes, crispy fried jackfruit and aubergine with ginger all deliver. The menu has very rough English translations to help you order (staff speak little or no English).

Hong Mai
VIETNAMESE $

(110 Đ Dinh Tien Toang; snacks from 20,000d; ⊘11am-8pm) After you've admired the Citadel, make your way to this excellent Vietnamese eatery for superior versions of two street food classics. The *banh khoai* (rice crêpes filled with pork and shrimp) are light and crammed with bean sprouts, and the *nem lui* (minced pork grilled on lemongrass sticks) go perfectly with a chilled Huda lager.

Mandarin Café
VIETNAMESE $

(054-382 1281; www.mrcumandarin.com; 24 Đ Tran Cao Van; meals from 25,000d; ⊘6am-10pm;) Owner-photographer Mr Cu, whose inspirational pictures adorn the walls, has been hosting backpackers for years, and his relaxed restaurant has lots of vegetarian and breakfast choices. Also operates as a tour agency.

Ta.ke
JAPANESE $$

(34 Đ Tran Cao Van; meals 60,000-140,000d; ⊘10am-10pm) An authentic Japanese restaurant with tasteful furnishings including lanterns and calligraphy, and a winsome menu with sushi, tempura and yakitori dishes. The interior is a calming haven away from Hue's increasingly busy streets.

🍷 Drinking & Nightlife

DMZ Bar
BAR

(www.dmz.com.vn; 60 Đ Le Loi; ⊘7am-1am;) Ever-popular riverside bar with a free pool table, cold Huda beer, cocktails (try a watermelon mojito) and a good vibe most nights. Also serves Western and local food till midnight, smoothies and juices. Happy hour is 3pm till 8pm. Check out the upside-down map of the DMZ – complete with a US chopper – on the ceiling of the bar.

Brown Eyes
BAR

(Đ Chu Van An; ⊘5pm-late;) The most popular late-night bar in town, with a good blend of locals and traveller-revellers and a party vibe. DJs drive the dance floor with r 'n' b, hip-hop and house anthems, and staff rally the troops with free shots.

Café on Thu Wheels
BAR

(10/2 Đ Nguyen Tri Phuong; ⊘6.30am-11pm;) Graffiti-splattered walls, a sociable vibe, excellent food and smoothies all combine at this welcoming spot owned by a friendly family. They also offer good tours, serve cheap meals and have books and mags to browse.

🛍 Shopping

Hue produces the finest conical hats in Vietnam and is renowned for rice paper and silk paintings. As ever, bargain hard.

Spiral Foundation Healing the Wounded Heart Center
HANDICRAFTS

(054-383 3694; www.spiralfoundation.org; 23 Đ Vo Thi Sau; ⊘8am-6pm) Generating cash from trash, this store stocks lovely handicrafts – such as quirky bags from plastic, and picture frames from recycled beer cans – made by artists with disabilities. Profits aid heart surgery for children in need.

WORTH A TRIP

BACH MA NATIONAL PARK

A French-era hill station known for its cool weather, **Bach Ma National Park** (Vuon Quoc Gia Bach Ma; 054-387 1330; www.bachmapark.com.vn; adult/child 40,000/20,000d) is 45km southeast of Hue.

There's some decent trekking in the lower levels through subtropical forest to villages on the fringes of the park. You can book village and birdwatching tours and English- or French-speaking guides (300,000d to 500,000d per day) at the visitors centre. A new **zipline** (two to five people 800,000d) is proving popular. Unexploded ordnance is still in the area, so stick to the trails.

There's a **guesthouse** (054-387 1330; www.bachmapark.com.vn; campsite per person 20,000d, r 300,000d) at the park entrance.

Dong Ba Market MARKET
(Đ Tran Hung Dao; ⊙6.30am-8pm) Just north of Trang Tien Bridge, this is Hue's largest market, selling anything and everything.

ⓘ Information

Wi-fi is very widespread and internet cafes abound on Đ Hung Vuong and Đ Le Loi.

Hue Central Hospital (Benh Vien Trung Uong Hue; ☑054-382 2325; 16 Đ Le Loi; ⊙6am-10pm) Well-regarded local hospital.

Mandarin Café (☑054-382 1281; www. mrcumandarin.com; 24 Đ Tran Cao Van) Mr Cu offers great information, transport and tours around Hue and beyond.

Post Office (8 Đ Hoang Hoa Tham; ⊙7am-5.30pm Mon-Sat) Main post office.

Sinh Tourist (☑054-384 5022; www.thesinh tourist.vn; 37 Đ Nguyen Thai Hoc; ⊙6.30am-10pm) Books open-tour buses and buses to Laos.

Vietin Bank ATM (12 Đ Hung Vuong) Centrally-located ATM.

ⓘ Getting There & Away

AIR

Vietnam Airlines (☑054-382 4709; 23 Đ Nguyen Van Cu; ⊙closed Sun) flies to/from Hanoi and HCMC. **Jetstar** (☑1900 1550; Đ Hung Vuong; ⊙closed Sun) and **VietJet** (☑1900 1886; www.vietjetair.com) connect with HCMC.

Hue's Phu Bai Airport is 14km south of the city. Taxis cost about 220,000d to the centre, or use the minibus services for 50,000d. Vietnam Airlines also runs an airport shuttle.

BUS

The **main bus station**, 4km southeast of the centre, has connections to Danang and south to HCMC. **An Hoa bus station** (Hwy 1), northwest of the Citadel, serves northern destinations,
including Dong Ha (44,000d, two hours, every 30 minutes).

For Phong Nha (around 120,000d, five hours), the Hung Thanh open-tour bus leaves 49 Đ Chu Van An at 4.30pm, and the Tan Nha bus leaves from the Why Not? bar on Đ Vo Thi Sau around 6.30am. One daily bus (look for 'Phuc Vu' in the windscreen) heads for Phong Nha and Son Trach at 11.15am (150,000d, four hours) from Hue's An Hoa bus station.

Mandarin, Sinh and Stop & Go Café can arrange bookings for buses to Savannakhet, Laos.

TRAIN

Hue Train Station (☑054-382 2175; 2 Đ Phan Chu Trinh) is at the southwestern end of Đ Le Loi.

ⓘ Getting Around

Bicycles (US$1 to US$3), motorbikes (US$5 to US$10) and cars (from US$50 per day) can be hired through hotels all over town. **Mai Linh** (☑054-389 8989) has taxis with meters. Cyclos and xe om will find you whether you need them or not.

Around Hue

Demilitarised Zone (DMZ)

From 1954 until 1975 the Ben Hai River served as the dividing line between South Vietnam and North Vietnam. The DMZ, 90km north of Hue, consisted of the area 5km on either side of the line.

Many of the 'sights' around the DMZ may not be worthwhile unless you're into war history. To make sense of it all, and to avoid areas where there's still unexploded ordnance, a guide is essential. Group day tours from Hue cost from US$15 for a budget bus trip to as much as US$120 for a specialised car tour with a Viet vet.

TRANSPORT FROM HUE

DESTINATION	AIR	BUS	CAR/MOTORBIKE	TRAIN
Danang		60,000d, 3hr, frequent	2½-4hr	US$3.50-6, 2½-4hr, 7 daily
Dong Hoi		85,000d, 4hr, frequent	3½hr	US$5-11, 3-5½hr, 7 daily
Hanoi	from 1,000,000d, 1hr, 3 daily	260,000d, 13-16hr, 9 daily	16hr	US$24-42, 12-15½hr, 6 daily
HCMC	from 480,000d, 1¼hr, 4 daily	490,000d, 19-24hr, 9 daily	22hr	US$32-55, 19½-23hr, 5 daily
Ninh Binh		250,000d, 10½-12hr, 8 daily	11hr	US$19-35, 10-13hr, 5 daily

TOMBS & DUNES

From the centre of Hue it's only 15km north to the sands of **Thuan An Beach** where there's a large resort hotel. If you continue southeast from here there's a beautiful, quiet coastal road to follow with very light traffic (so it's ideal for bikers). The route actually traverses a narrow coastal island, with views of the Tam Giang-Cau Hai lagoon on the inland side and simply stunning sandy beaches and dunes on the other. This wonderful coastal strip is virtually undeveloped, but between September and March the water's often too rough for swimming.

From Thuan An the road winds past villages alternating with shrimp lagoons and vegetable gardens. Thousands and thousands of garishly colourful and opulent graves and family temples line the beach, most the final resting places of Viet Kieu (overseas Vietnamese). Little tracks cut through the tombs and sand dunes to the ocean. Just pick a spot and the chances are you'll have a beach to yourself.

At glorious **Phu Thuan beach** (about 7km southeast of Thuan An) you pass the lovely **Beach Bar Hue** (p856), then 8km from there are the remains of **Phu Dien**, a small Cham temple half-buried in a sand dune.

Continuing southeast a narrow but paved road weaves past fishing villages, shrimp farms, more giant sand dunes and the settlement of Vinh Hung until you reach the mouth of another river estuary at Thuon Phu An, where there's a row of seafood restaurants. This spot is 40km from Thuan An. Cross the Tu Hien bridge here and you can continue around the eastern lip of the huge Cau Hai lagoon and link up with Hwy 1.

◎ Sights

Vinh Moc Tunnels　　　　HISTORIC SITE
(admission 20,000d; ⊙7am-4.30pm) A highly impressive complex of tunnels, Vinh Moc is the remains of a coastal North Vietnamese village that literally went underground in response to unremitting American bombing. More than 90 families disappeared into three levels of tunnels running for almost 2km, and continued to live and work while bombs rained down around them. Most of the tunnels are open to visitors, and are kept in their original form (except for electric lights, a recent addition).

Khe Sanh Combat Base　　　HISTORIC SITE
(museum 20,000d; ⊙museum 7am-5pm) The site of the most famous siege of the American War, the USA's Khe Sanh Combat Base was never overrun, but saw the bloodiest battle of the war. About 500 Americans, 10,000 North Vietnamese troops and uncounted civilian bystanders died around this remote highland base. It's eerily peaceful today, but in 1968 the hillsides trembled with the impact of 1000kg bombs, white phosphorus shells, napalm, mortars and endless artillery rounds, as American forces sought to repel the NVA.

Truong Son National Cemetery　　CEMETERY
An evocative memorial to the legions of North Vietnamese soldiers who died along the Ho Chi Minh Trail, this cemetery is a sobering sight. More than 10,000 graves dot these hillsides, each marked by a simple white tombstone headed by the inscription *liet si* (martyr). Many graves lie empty, simply bearing names, representing a fraction of Vietnam's 300,000 soldiers missing in action. It's 27km northwest of Dong Ha; the turn-off from Hwy 1 is close to Doc Mieu.

Danang

📞 0511 / POP 1,070,000
Nowhere in Vietnam is changing as fast as Danang. For decades it had a reputation as a slightly mundane provincial backwater, but big changes are ongoing. The Han riverfront is resplendent with gleaming new modernist hotels and restaurants and spectacular new bridges. Beachside, five-star hotel developments are emerging. Oh, and a revamped international airport opened in 2012.

That said, the city itself still has few conventional sightseeing spots except for a decent museum. For most travellers, a day or two is probably enough.

◎ Sights

★ **Museum of Cham Sculpture**　　MUSEUM
(Bao Tang; 1 Đ Trung Nu Vuong; admission 40,000d; ⊙7am-5pm) This fine museum has the world's largest collection of Cham artefacts,

Danang

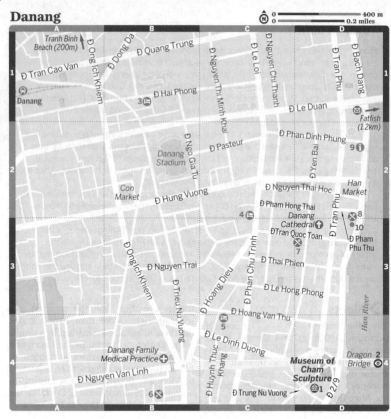

housed in buildings marrying French-colonial-era architecture with Cham elements. Founded in 1915 by the École Française d'Extrême Orient, it displays more than 300 pieces including altars, lingas, garudas, apsaras, Ganeshas and images of Shiva, Brahma and Vishnu – all dating from the 5th to 15th centuries. To hire an MP3 audioguide (20,000d), you'll need to show ID – passport or drivers licence – or leave a refundable US$50 bond.

Dragon Bridge BRIDGE
(Cau Rong) Welcome to the biggest show in town every Saturday and Sunday night. At 9pm, this graceful golden-hued bridge spouts fire and water from the dragon's head near the Han River's eastern bank. The best places to observe are the various cafes lining the eastern bank to the north of the bridge. Boat trips also depart from Đ Bach Dang on

the river's western bank to make the most of Danang's after-dark, neon-lit splendour.

Tours

Several excellent Danang tours are available.

Danang Food Tour FOOD
(www.danangfoodtour.com; per person US$45) Excellent explorations of the local food scene by a passionate expat.

Funtastic Tours TOUR
(090 356 1777; www.funtasticdanang.com; per person US$45) Tours including street food and sightseeing. Transport is by car.

Meet My Danang TOUR
(www.meetmydanang.com; per person US$8-40) From after-dark river cruises to bar-hopping and the city's spooky past.

Danang

🛏 Sleeping

Good budget places are tough to find, but there are some excellent midrange mini-hotels close to the river.

Funtastic Beach Hostel　　HOSTEL $
(☎ 0511-392 8789; www.funtasticdanag.com; K02/5 Ha Bong; dm US$8, d US$24, apt US$36; ❄ @ 🛜) In the rapidly developing accommodation scene across the river near China Beach, Funtastic Beach Hostel is brightly decorated, has a good rooftop terrace, and has a range of rooms from dorms through to a small self-contained apartment that's good for families or friends. Breakfast is included and there's a good chill-out area with DVDs and video games on tap.

Funtastic Danang Hostel　　HOSTEL $
(☎ 0511-389 2024; www.funtasticdanang.com; 115 Đ Hai Phong; dm US$9, d & tw US$19; ❄ @ 🛜) Danang's first specialist hostel is a goodie, with young and energetic owners, colourful rooms and dorms, and a comfortable lounge area when all you want to do is chill and watch a DVD. Ask about the street food tours.

Zion Hotel　　HOTEL $
(☎ 0511-382 8333; http://sion.com.vn; 121/7 Đ Hoang Van Thu; s US$15, d US$20-25; ❄ @ 🛜) There's a scarlet theme running through this excellent-value hotel from the lobby to the inviting, modern rooms. Boasts a convenient location and staff are eager to please.

Sanouva　　BOUTIQUE HOTEL $$
(☎ 0511-382 3468; www.sanouvadanag.com; 68 Đ Phan Chau Trinh; d from US$40; ❄ @ 🛜) Boutique meets business at the stylish Sanouva, located in a bustling commercial street just a few blocks from Danang's riverfront. An Asian chic lobby is the introduction to relatively compact but modern rooms, and the on-site S'Spa and S'Ngon restaurant are two good reasons to linger within the Sanouva's chic interior.

🍴 Eating & Drinking

Quan Com Hue Ngon　　VIETNAMESE $
(65 Đ Tran Quoc Toan; meals 45,000-80,000d; ⏱ 3-9pm) Fab barbecue place, all charcoal smoke and sizzling meats, where you grill your own. There's a street terrace, and the welcoming English-speaking owner will help with the menu.

Com Tay Cam Cung Dinh　　VIETNAMESE $
(K254/2 Đ Hoang Dieu; meals 20,000-50,000d; ⏱ 11am-8pm) This simple place is good for local dishes, including *hoanh thanh* – a wonton-like combination of minced pork and shrimp. It's down a little alley.

★ **Fatfish**　　FUSION, PIZZA $$
(www.fatfishdanang.com; 439 Đ Tran Hung Dao; meals 70,000-285,000d; ⏱ 9am-11pm; 🛜) This stylish restaurant and lounge bar is leading the eating and drinking charge across the river on the Han's eastern shore. Innovative Asian fusion dishes, pizza and wood-fired barbecue all partner with flavour-packed craft beers from Saigon's Pasteur St Brewing. Fatfish is good for a few snacks or a more leisurely full meal.

SPLURGE

Waterfront (☎ 0511-384 3373; www.waterfrontdanang.com; 150-152 Đ Bach Dang; meals 95,000-360,000d; ⏱ 10am-11pm; 🛜) is a riverfront lounge-cum-restaurant that gets everything right on every level. It works as a stylish bar for a chilled glass of NZ Sauvignon Blanc and also as a destination restaurant for a memorable meal (book the terrace deck for a stunning river vista). The menu features imported meats, Asian seafood and also terrific 'gourmet' sandwiches.

ℹ Information

There are internet cafes and ATMs scattered all over Danang. Consult the website www.in danang.com for reviews and information.

Danang Family Medical Practice (☏ 0511-358 2700; www.vietnammedicalpractice.com; 50-52 Đ Nguyen Van Linh; ⊗7am-6pm) With in-patient facilities; run by an Australian doctor.

Danang Visitor Centre (☏ 0511-3863 595; www.tourism.danang.vn; 32A Đ Phan Dinh Phung; ⊗7.30am-9pm) Really helpful, with English spoken, and good maps and brochures. Danang's official tourism website is one of Vietnam's best.

Main Post Office (64 Đ Bach Dang; ⊗7am-5.30pm) Near the Song Han Bridge.

Sinh Tourist (☏ 0511-384 3258; www.thesinh tourist.vn; 154 Đ Bach Dang; ⊗7am-10pm) Books open-tour buses and tours, and offers currency exchange.

ℹ Getting There & Away

AIR

Danang's busy airport, 2km west of the city centre, has international flights to cities including Kuala Lumpur, Hong Kong and Singapore.

Domestic services to HCMC, Hanoi, Dalat, Nha Trang, Can Tho and Haiphong are operated by Vietnam Airlines, VietJet Air and Jetstar.

BUS

Danang's **intercity bus station** (☏ 0511-382 1265; Đ Dien Bien Phu) is 3km west of the city centre. A metered taxi to the riverside will cost around 70,000d.

Buses leave for all major centres, including Quy Nhon (130,000d, six hours, six daily).

For Laos, there are daily buses to both Savanna-khet at 8pm (from 300,000d, 14 hours) and Pakse at 6.30am (from 340,000d, 13 hours). Buses to the Lao Bao border alone are 150,000d (six hours); you may have to change buses at Dong Ha.

Yellow public buses to Hoi An (18,000d, one hour, every 30 minutes until 6pm) travel along Đ Bach Dang. The price is usually posted inside the door, if any bus drivers attempt to overcharge.

Sinh Tourist open-tour buses operate from the company office twice daily to both Hue (89,000d, 2½ hours) and Hoi An (79,000d, one hour).

TAXI & MOTORBIKE

A taxi to Hoi An officially costs around 500,000d, but most will drop to around 400,000d, while *xe om* charge 150,000d. Call **Mai Linh** (☏ 0511-356 5656) for a cab.

TRAIN

Danang's **train station** (202 Đ Hai Phong) has services to all destinations on the north–south main line.

The train ride to Hue is one of the best in the country – it's worth taking as an excursion in itself.

Around Danang

About 10km south of Danang are the striking **Marble Mountains**, which consist of five craggy marble outcrops topped with jungle and pagodas. With natural caves sheltering small Hindu and Buddhist sanctuaries and stunning views of the ocean and surrounding countryside, they're worth taking the time to explore. **Thuy Son** (admission 15,000d; ⊗7am-5pm) is the largest and most famous of the five mountains.

China Beach (Bai Non Nuoc), once an R'n'R hangout for US soldiers during the war, is actually a series of beaches stretching 30km between Hoi An and Danang.

For surfers, China Beach's break gets a decent swell from mid-September to December. There's a mean undertow, so take care.

TRANSPORT FROM DANANG

DESTINATION	AIR	BUS	CAR/MOTORBIKE	TRAIN
Dong Hoi		120,000d, 6½hr, 7 daily	6-7hr	US$12-20, 5½-8½hr, 6 daily
Hanoi	from US$42, 1hr 10min, 9 daily	365,000d, 16-19hr, 7 daily	19hr	US$35-50, 14½-18hr, 6 daily
HCMC	from US$47, 1hr 15min, 18 daily	380,000d, 19-25hr, 9 daily	18hr	US$35-55, 17-22hr, 5 daily
Hue		55,000d, 3hr, every 20min	2½-4hr	US$4-7, 2½-4hr, 6 daily
Nha Trang	from US$45, 30min, 2 daily	230,000d, 10-13hr, 8 daily	13hr	US$20-35, 9-12hr, 5 daily

Hoi An

📞 0510 / POP 134,000

Graceful, historic Hoi An is Vietnam's most atmospheric and delightful town. Once a major port, it boasts the grand architecture and beguiling riverside setting that befits its heritage, and the 21st-century curses of traffic and pollution are largely absent.

In the Old Town, an incredible legacy of tottering Japanese merchant houses, Chinese temples and ancient tea warehouses has been preserved and converted into stylish restaurants, wine bars and a glut of tailor shops. And yet down by the market and over in neighbouring An Hoi, peninsula life has changed little.

Travel a few kilometres further – you'll find some superb bicycle, motorbike and boat trips – and some of central Vietnam's most enticing bucolic scenery and beaches are within easy reach.

⊙ Sights

⊙ Hoi An Old Town

A Unesco World Heritage Site, Hoi An Old Town levies an admission fee to most of its historic buildings, which goes towards funding the preservation of the town's architecture. Buying the ticket (120,000d) gives you a choice of five heritage sites to visit – Chinese Assembly Halls, pagodas and temples, historic houses and museums. Booths dotted around the Old Town sell tickets.

★ **Japanese Covered Bridge**   BRIDGE
(Cau Nhat Ban) `FREE` This beautiful little bridge is emblematic of Hoi An. A bridge was first constructed here in the 1590s by the Japanese community to link them with the Chinese quarters. Over the centuries the ornamentation has remained relatively faithful to the original Japanese design. The French flattened out the roadway for cars, but the original arched shape was restored in 1986.

★ **Assembly Hall of the Fujian Chinese Congregation**   TEMPLE
(Phuc Kien Hoi Quan; opposite 35 Đ Tran Phu; admission with Old Town ticket; ⊘7am-5.30pm) Originally a traditional assembly hall, this structure was later transformed into a temple for the worship of Thien Hau, a deity from Fujian province. The green-tiled triple gateway dates from 1975. The mural on the right-hand wall depicts Thien Hau, her way lit by lantern light as she crosses a stormy sea to rescue a foundering ship. Opposite is a mural of the heads of the six Fujian families who fled from China to Hoi An in the 17th century.

★ **Tan Ky House**   HISTORIC BUILDING
(101 Đ Nguyen Thai Hoc; admission by Old Town ticket; ⊘8am-noon & 2-4.30pm) Built two centuries ago by an ethnically Vietnamese family, this gem of a house has been lovingly preserved through seven generations. Look out for signs of Japanese and Chinese influences on the architecture. Japanese elements include the ceiling (in the sitting area), which is supported by three progressively shorter beams, one on top of the other. Under the crab-shell ceiling are carvings of crossed sabres wrapped in silk ribbon. The sabres symbolise force, the silk represents flexibility.

Tran Family Chapel   HISTORIC BUILDING
(21 Đ Le Loi; admission by Old Town ticket; ⊘7.30am-noon & 2-5.30pm) Built for worshipping family ancestors, this chapel dates back to 1802. It was commissioned by Tran Tu, one of the clan who ascended to the rank of mandarin and served as an ambassador to China. His picture is to the right of the chapel. The architecture of the building reflects the influence of Chinese (the 'turtle' style roof), Japanese (triple beam) and vernacular (look out for the bow-and-arrow detailing) styles.

Quan Cong Temple   CONFUCIAN TEMPLE
(Chua Ong; 24 Đ Tran Phu; admission by Old Town ticket) Founded in 1653, this small temple is dedicated to Quan Cong, an esteemed Chinese general who is worshipped as a symbol of loyalty, sincerity, integrity and justice. His partially gilded statue, made of papiermâché on a wooden frame, is on the central altar at the back of the sanctuary. When someone makes an offering to the portly looking Quan Cong, the caretaker solemnly strikes a bronze bowl that makes a bell-like sound.

ℹ️ OLD TOWN ENTRANCE TICKETS

Officially all visitors need a ticket just to enter Hoi An Old Town. Tickets are valid for 10 days. You won't normally be checked if you're just dining or shopping in the area, but keep your ticket with you just in case.

VIETNAM HOI AN

Hoi An

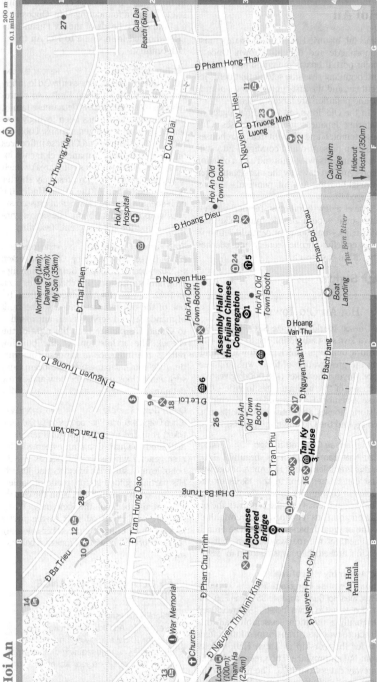

G
27

Cua Dai
Beach (6km)

Đ Pham Hong Thai

11

23 Đ Truong Minh
Luong

22

Cam Nam
Bridge
Hideout
Hostel (350m)

Đ Cua Dai

Hoi An Hospital

Đ Ly Thuong Kiet

Đ Thai Phien

Northern (1km);
Danang (30km);
My Son (35km)

Đ Nguyen Duy Hieu

Hoi An Old
Town Booth

Đ Hoang Dieu

19

24

17 5

Đ Nguyen Hue

Assembly Hall of
the Fujian Chinese
Congregation

Hoi An Old
Town Booth

1

Hoi An Old
Town Booth

Đ Phan Boi Chau

Thu Bon River

Boat
Landing

Đ Hoang
Van Thu

4

Đ Nguyen Truong To

$

9

18

6

Đ Le Loi

26

Hoi An
Old Town
Booth

Đ Nguyen Thai Hoc

8

17

7

Đ Bach Dang

Đ Tran Cao Van

Đ Tran Phu

20

16

Tan Ky
3 House

Đ Hai Ba Trung

25

Japanese
Covered
Bridge

2

Đ Tran Hung Dao

28

12

10

Đ Ba Trieu

21

Đ Phan Chu Trinh

Đ Nguyen Phuc Chu

An Hoi
Peninsula

War Memorial

Church

14

13

Local (100m);
Thanh Ha
(2.5km)

Đ Nguyen Thi Minh Khai

200 m
0.1 miles

Hoi An

Museum of Trading Ceramics   MUSEUM
(80 Đ Tran Phu; admission by Old Town ticket; ☺7am-5.30pm) Occupies a restored wooden house and contains artefacts from all over Asia, with oddities from as far afield as Egypt. While this reveals that Hoi An had some rather impressive trading links, it takes an expert's eye to appreciate the display. The exhibition on the restoration of Hoi An's old houses provides a useful crash course in Old Town architecture.

Arts & Crafts Villages

All those neat fake antiques sold in Hoi An's shops are manufactured in nearby villages. Cross the An Hoi footbridge to reach the **An Hoi Peninsula**, noted for boat building and mat weaving. **Cam Kim Island** is renowned for its woodcarvers. Cross the Cam Nam bridge to **Cam Nam** village, a lovely spot also noted for arts and crafts.

🏃 Activities

Two reputable dive schools, **Cham Island Diving Center** (☑0510-391 0782; www.vietnamscubadiving.com; 88 Đ Nguyen Thai Hoc) and **Blue Coral Diving** (☑0510-627 9297; www.divehoian.com; 77 Đ Nguyen Thai Hoc), offer trips to the Cham Islands. Both charge almost exactly the same rates: two fun dives are US$80. The diving is not world class, but can be intriguing, with good macro life – and the day trip to the Cham Islands is superb.

Snorkellers pay about US$40. Trips only leave between February and September; conditions are best in June, July and August.

★ **Palmarosa**   SPA
(☑0510-393 3999; www.palmarosaspa.vn; 90 Đ Ba Trieu; massages & treatments from 220,000d; ☺10am-9pm) This highly professional spa offers massages (including Thai and Swedish), scrubs, facials as well as hand and foot care.

📖 Courses

Vietnamese cooking classes are offered all over Hoi An.

Green Bamboo Cooking School   COOKING
(☑090 581 5600; www.greenbamboo-hoian.com; 21 Đ Truong Minh Hung, Cam An; per person US$40) Groups are limited to a maximum of 10, and take place in course director Van's spacious kitchen.

Herbs and Spices   COOKING
(☑0510-393 6868; www.herbsandspicesvn.com; 2/6 Đ Le Loi; per person US$35-59; ☺10.30am, 4.30pm & 8pm) Offers three different menu options and small classes.

Morning Glory Cooking School   COOKING
(☑0510-2241 555; www.msvy-tastevietnam.com; 106 Đ Nguyen Thai Hoc; half-day course US$25-32) The original. Directed by Vy, owner of several restaurants in town, or one of her protégés.

🛏 Sleeping

Hoi An has an excellent selection of accommodation.

Hideout Hostel
HOSTEL $

(☑0510-3927 359; www.vietnamhideouthostels.com; To 5, Thon Xuyen Trung, Cam Nam; dm US$9-11, d US$25; ✳@🛜🏊) Across the Thu Bon river on Can Nam island, the Hideout is an excellent recent addition to Hoi An's accommodation scene. Dorms and rooms are colourful and spacious, rates include a free beer or soft drink every night, and the centre of town is a 10-minute walk away. Other highlights include a small swimming pool and the popular Hideout Bar.

Hoi An Backpackers Hostel
HOSTEL $

(☑0510-391 4400; www.vietnambackpackerhostels.com; 252 Đ Cua Dai; dm/s/tw/d US$7/18/36/36; ✳@🛜) Offering loads of backpacker-friendly attractions, this is the new Hoi An location for a hostel empire spanning Vietnam. Bikes, breakfast and the occasional beer are all free, and accommodation ranges from dorms through to private rooms with en suite bathrooms. Regular tours take in Hoi An's street food scene, and there's an exceedingly social bar with regular happy hour deals.

Phuong Dong Hotel
HOTEL $

(☑0510-391 6477; www.phuongdonghoian.com; 42 Đ Ba Trieu; s/d/tr US$13/16/20; ✳@🛜) It's nothing fancy, but a safe budget bet: plain, good-value rooms with comfortable mattresses, reading lights, fridge and air-con. The owners rent motorbikes at fair rates too.

Hoang Trinh Hotel
HOTEL $

(☑0510-391 6579; www.hoianhoangtrinhhotel.com; 45 Đ Le Quy Don; r US$22-35; ✳@🛜) Well-run hotel with helpful, friendly staff where travellers are made to feel welcome. Rooms are quite 'old school' Vietnamese but spacious and clean. A generous breakfast and pick-up from bus stations are included.

Hoa Binh Hotel
HOTEL $

(☑0510-391 6838; www.hoabinhhotelhoian.com; 696 Đ Hai Ba Trung; dm US$8, r US$16-20; ✳@🛜🏊) A good selection of modern rooms, all with minibar, cable TV and air-con, and a reasonable dorm. The inclusive breakfast is good, but the pool is covered by a roof.

Ha An Hotel
HISTORIC HOTEL $$

(☑0510-386 3126; www.haanhotel.com; 6-8 Đ Phan Boi Chau; r US$60-109; ✳@🛜) Elegant and refined, the Ha An feels more like a colonial-era mansion than a hotel. All rooms have nice individual touches – a textile wall

hanging or painting – and views over a gorgeous central garden. The helpful, well-trained staff make staying here a very special experience. It's about a 10-minute walk from the centre in the French Quarter.

🍴 Eating

Hoi An offers a culinary tour de force, including several amazing local specialities. Be sure to try *banh bao* ('white rose'), an incredibly delicate dish of steamed dumplings stuffed with minced shrimp. *Cao lau* – doughy flat noodles mixed with croutons, bean sprouts and greens, topped with pork slices and served in a savoury broth – is also delicious. The other two culinary treats are fried *hoanh thanh* (won ton) and *banh xeo* (crispy savoury pancakes rolled with herbs in fresh rice paper).

★Mermaid Restaurant
VIETNAMESE $

(☑0510-386 1527; www.restaurant-hoian.com; 2 Đ Tran Phu; meals 45,000-115,000d; ⊘10.30am-10pm) For local specialities, you can't beat this modest little restaurant, owned by local legend Vy, who chose the location because it was close to the market, ensuring the freshest produce was directly at hand. Hoi An's holy culinary trinity (*cao lau, banh bao* and *banh xeo*) are all superb, as are the special fried wontons.

Cocobox
CAFE $

(www.cocoboxvietnam.com; 94 Đ Le Loi; juices & smoothies 60,000-75,000d; ⊘9am-9pm Mon-Sat) Refreshing cold-press juices are the standout at this compact combo of cafe and deli. Our favourite is the Watermelon Man juice combining watermelon, passion fruit, lime and mint. Coffee, salads and snacks are also good – try the chicken pesto sandwich. The attached 'farm shop' sells Vietnamese artisanal produce including local honey and cider from Saigon.

Bale Well
VIETNAMESE $

(45-51 Đ Tran Cao Van; meals 100,000d; ⊘11.30am-10pm) Down a little alley near the famous well, this local place is renowned for one dish: barbecued pork, served up satay-style, which you then combine with fresh greens and herbs to create your own fresh spring roll. A global reputation means it can get busy.

Little Menu
VIETNAMESE $

(www.thelittlemenu.com; 12 Đ Le Loi; meals 45,000-115,000d; ⊘9.30am-11pm; 🛜) English-speaking owner Son is a fantastic host at this great little restaurant with an open kitchen and short menu – try the fish in banana leaf or duck spring rolls.

★ **Nu Eatery** FUSION $$
(www.facebook.com/NuEateryHoiAn; 10A Đ Nguyen Thi Minh Khai; mains 80,000d; ☺noon-9pm Mon-Sat) Don't be deceived by the humble decor at this compact eatery tucked away near the Japanese Bridge. There's a real wow factor to the seasonal small plates at our new favourite Hoi An restaurant. Combine the pork belly steamed buns with a salad of grilled pineapple, coconut and pomelo, and don't miss the homemade lemongrass, ginger or chilli ice cream.

★ **Cargo Club** INTERNATIONAL, VIETNAMESE $$
(☎0510-3911 227; www.msvy-tastevietnam.com/cargo-club; 107 Đ Nguyen Thai Hoc; meals 60,000-150,000d; ☺8am-11pm; ☎) This is a remarkable cafe-restaurant, serving Vietnamese and Western food, with a terrific riverside location (the upper terrace has stunning views). A relaxing day here munching your way around the menu would be a day well spent. The breakfasts are legendary (try the eggs Benedict), the patisserie and cakes are superb, and the fine dining dishes and good cocktails also deliver.

Morning Glory Restaurant VIETNAMESE $$
(☎0510-2241 555; www.msvy-tastevietnam.com/morning-glory; 106 Đ Nguyen Thai Hoc; meals 60,000-160,000d; ☺8am-11pm; ☎⌨) An outstanding restaurant in historic premises that concentrates on street food and traditionally prepared dishes (primarily from central Vietnam). Highlights include the pork-stuffed squid, and shrimp mousse on sugarcane skewers. There's an excellent vegetarian selection (try the smoked eggplant), including many wonderful salads. Prices are reasonable given the surrounds, ambience and flavours.

🍷 Drinking & Nightlife

★ **Dive Bar** BAR
(88 Đ Nguyen Thai Hoc; ☺8am-midnight; ☎) The best bar in town, with a great vibe thanks to the welcoming service, contemporary electronic tunes and sofas for lounging. There's also a cocktail garden and bar at the rear, a pool table and pub grub.

Mia Coffee House CAFE
(www.facebook.com/miacoffeehouse; 20 Đ Phan Boi Chau; ☺8am-5pm) Our favourite spot for an espresso, latte or cappuccino features a shaded corner location and good food, including grilled panini sandwiches and hearty baguettes. Its own coffee blend sourced from Dalat Arabica beans is the standout brew, and be sure to try the coffee *affogato*, a delicious blend of dessert and hot beverage.

3 Dragons PUB
(51 Đ Phan Boi Chau; ☺7.30am-midnight; ☎) Half sports bar (where you can watch everything from Aussie Rules to Indian cricket), half restauran t (burgers, steaks and local food).

🛍 Shopping

Tailor-made clothing is one of Hoi An's best trades, and there are more than 200 tailor shops in town that can whip up suits, shirts, dresses and much more.

Couleurs D'Asie Gallery PHOTOGRAPHY, BOOKS
(www.facebook.com/couleurs.asie; 7 Đ Nguyen Hue; ☺9am-9pm) Superb images for sale of Vietnam and Asia by Hoi An–based photographer Réhahn. His portraits are particularly stunning, and the best of his images are collected in books also for sale.

★ **Metiseko** CLOTHING
(www.metiseko.com; 86 Đ Nguyen Thai Hoc; ☺9am-9.30pm) 🍃 Winners of a Sustainable Development award, this eco-minded store stocks gorgeous clothing (including kids' wear), accessories, and homewares such as cushions using natural silk and organic cotton. It is certified to use the Organic Contents Standards label.

★ **Reaching Out** SOUVENIRS, CLOTHING
(www.reachingoutvietnam.com; 103 Đ Nguyen Thai Hoc; ☺8.30am-9pm Mon-Fri, 9.30am-8pm Sat & Sun) 🍃 Excellent fair-trade gift shop that stocks good-quality silk scarfs, clothes, jewellery, hand-painted Vietnamese hats, handmade toys and teddy bears. The shop

---

ⓘ STAY SAFE

Hoi An is one of Vietnam's safer towns, but there infrequent stories of late-night bag-snatching, pickpockets and, very occasionally, assaults on women. If you are a lone female, walk home with somebody. There have also been reports of drinks being spiked in some bars, so keep a close eye on your glass.

employs and supports artisans with disabilities, and staff are happy to show visitors through the workshop.

❶ Information

The website www.livehoianmagazine.com is excellent for cultural content, features and reviews. Virtually all hotels have lobby computers and free wi-fi.

Hoi An Hospital (☑ 0510-386 1364; 4 Đ Tran Hung Dao; ⊙ 6am-10pm) For serious problems, go to Danang.

Rose Travel Service (☑ 0510-391 7567; www.rosetravelservice.com; 37-39 Đ Ly Thai To; ⊙ 7.30am-5.30pm) Tours around the area and Vietnam, plus car rental and buses.

Sinh Tourist (☑ 0510-386 3948; www.thesinhtourist.vn; 587 Đ Hai Ba Trung; ⊙ 6am-10pm) Books reputable open-tour buses.

❶ Getting There & Away

Most north–south bus services do not stop at Hoi An, but you can head for Vinh Dien (10km to the west) and catch one there.

More convenient open-tour buses offer regular connections for Hue (US$12, four hours) and Nha Trang (regular/sleeper US$14/19, 11 to 12 hours).

Buses to Danang (18,000d, one hour) leave from the **northern bus station** (Đ Le Hong Phong). Note the last bus back from Danang leaves around 6pm.

The nearest airport and train station are both in Danang. **Go Travel Vietnam** (☑ 0510-392 9115; www.gotravel-vietnam.com; 61A Đ Phan Chau Trinh; ⊙ 9am-9pm) offers shuttle bus transfers between Hoi An and Danang airport and train station five times per day (80,000d, one hour).

❶ Getting Around

Metered taxis and motorbike drivers wait for business over the footbridge in An Hoi. Call **Hoi An Taxi** (☑ 0510-391 9919) or **Mai Linh** (☑ 0510-392 5925) for a pick-up.

Many hotels offer bicycles/motorbikes for rent from 20,000/100,000d per day.

Around Hoi An

Beaches

The nearest beach to Hoi An, **Cua Dai** has been so badly affected by coastal erosion that little sand remains.

Just 3km north of Cua Dai, **An Bang** is one of Vietnam's most happening and enjoyable beaches. It's easy to see what all the fuss is about – you're greeted with a wonderful stretch of fine sand, a huge empty ocean and an enormous horizon, with only the distant Cham Islands interrupting the seaside symmetry. **Under the Coconut Tree** (☑ 0168-245 5666; www.underthecoconuttreehoian.com; dm US$9, d US$30-40; 🛜) is the funkiest place to stay. Cool bar-restaurants serving European and Vietnamese cuisine line the shore and the lane behind including **K'Tu Market & Coffee** (meals from 60,000d; ⊙ 8am-6pm), **Soul Kitchen** (☑ 0906 440 320; www.soulkitchen.sitew.com; meals 90,000-180,000d; ⊙ 10am-10pm Tue-Sun, 10am-6pm Mon; 🛜) and **La Plage** (☑ 0510-392 8244; www.laplagebeachbar.wordpress.com; meals 80,000-140,000d; ⊙ 8am-10pm; 🛜), which are all quite pricey but worth a splurge.

The coastline immediately to the north of An Bang remains pristine, a glorious broad beach lined with casuarina and pandan trees and dotted with the curious coracles of local fisher-folk.

Cham Islands

☑ 0510 / POP 2750

A breathtaking cluster of granite islands offshore from Hoi An, the beautiful **Cham Islands** make a wonderful excursion. It'll have to be between March to September, as the ocean is usually too rough at other times. And if possible avoid weekends and holidays when day-trippers flood the place.

The best trips include diving or snorkelling at Cham's (modest) coral reefs, and a visit to the main island of **Hon Lao**. The islands are protected as a marine park; the underwater environment includes 135 species of soft and hard coral and varied macro life.

Bai Lang, Hon Lao's pretty little port, is the only real settlement. Drop by the curious temple **Ong Ngu**, which is dedicated to whales (locals worshipped them as oceanic deities). **Thu Trang** (☑ 0510-393 0007; r with shared bathroom 300,000d; ⊙ Bai Lang village) is a good simple guesthouse.

A dirt track heads southwest from Hon Lao for 2km past coves to a fine, sheltered beach, home to **Cham Restaurant** (☑ 0510-224 1108; meals 50,000-120,000d; ⊙ 10am-5pm).

Tiny **Bai Huong**, a fishing village 5km southeast of Bai Lang, is an idyllic but isolated spot where there's an excellent **homestay** (www.homestaybaihuong.com; per person 120,000d, meals 30,000-70,000d) program. Facilities are basic and little or no English is spoken by locals, but it's certainly the perfect place to get away from it all.

ⓘ Getting There & Away

Most visitors arrive on tours (US$25 to US$40) organised in Hoi An; those run by the dive schools are recommended. There's also a scheduled daily boat connection from the boat landing on Đ Bach Dang in Hoi An (150,000d for foreigners, two hours, 7am daily). Boats do not sail during heavy seas. Bring a copy of your passport and visa.

My Son

Set under the shadow of Cat's Tooth Mountain are the enigmatic ruins of **My Son** (admission 100,000d; ⏱6.30am-4pm), the most important remains of the ancient Cham empire and a Unesco World Heritage Site. Although Vietnam has better-preserved Cham sites, none are as extensive and few have such beautiful surroundings, with brooding mountains and clear streams running between the temples.

The ruins are 55km southwest of Hoi An. Day tours to My Son can be arranged in Hoi An for between US$5 and US$10, not including admission, and some trips return to Hoi An by boat. Independent travellers can hire a motorbike, *xe om* or car. Get here early in order to beat the tour groups, or later in the afternoon.

SOUTHEAST COAST

Vietnam has an incredibly curvaceous coastline and on this coast it's defined by sweeping sands, towering cliffs and concealed bays.

Nha Trang and Mui Ne are key destinations, but the beach breaks come thick and fast here. If your idea of paradise is reclining in front of turquoise waters, weighing up the merits of a massage or a mojito, then you have come to the right place.

On hand to complement the sedentary delights are activities to set the pulse racing, including scuba diving, snorkelling, surfing, windsurfing and kitesurfing. Action or inaction, this coast bubbles with opportunities.

Nha Trang

📞 058 / POP 397,000

Welcome to the beach capital of Vietnam. Loud and proud (say it!), the high-rise, high-energy resort of Nha Trang enjoys a stunning setting – ringed by a necklace of

> **MUDFEST**
> ⋯⋯⋯⋯⋯⋯⋯⋯⋯⋯⋯⋯⋯⋯⋯⋯⋯⋯⋯⋯
> Of the three thermal baths around town, **I Resort** (☑ 383 8838; 19 Xuan Ngoc, Vinh Ngoc; packages from 250,000d; ⏱ 7am-8pm) is the most attractive, with hot mineral mud baths and lovely bathing pools. Budget spending at least half a day here – it's well worth it. All kinds of mud/spa packages are available. Call for a shuttle (20,000d one way) from your hotel.

hills, with a sweeping crescent beach and turquoise bay dotted with tropical islands.

Nha Trang is a party town at heart, like any self-respecting resort should be. Forget the curfews of the capital; people play late here. Or if cocktail buckets and shooters aren't your flavour, try the natural mud baths or visit the imposing Cham towers.

⊙ Sights

⭐**Nha Trang Beach**   BEACH

Forming a magnificent sweeping arc, Nha Trang's 6km-long golden-sand beach is the city's trump card. Various sections are roped off and designated for swimmers (where you won't be bothered by jet-skis or boats). The turquoise water is fabulously inviting, and the promenade a delight to stroll.

Two popular lounging spots are the Sailing Club and Louisiane Brewhouse. If you head south of here, the beach gets quieter and it's possible to find a stretch of sand to yourself.

⭐**Po Nagar Cham Towers**   BUDDHIST TEMPLE

(Thap Ba, Lady of the City; admission 22,000d, guide 50,000d; ⏱6am-6pm) Built between the 7th and 12th centuries, these four Cham Towers are still actively used for worship by Cham, Chinese and Vietnamese Buddhists. Originally the complex had seven or eight towers, but only four towers remain, of which the 28m-high North Tower (Thap Chinh), which dates from AD 817, with its terraced pyramidal roof, vaulted interior masonry and vestibule, is the most magnificent.

The towers stand on a granite knoll 2km north of central Nha Trang, on the banks of the Cai River.

Long Son Pagoda   BUDDHIST TEMPLE

(⏱7.30-11.30am & 1.30-5.30pm) `FREE` This striking pagoda was founded in the late 19th

Central Nha Trang

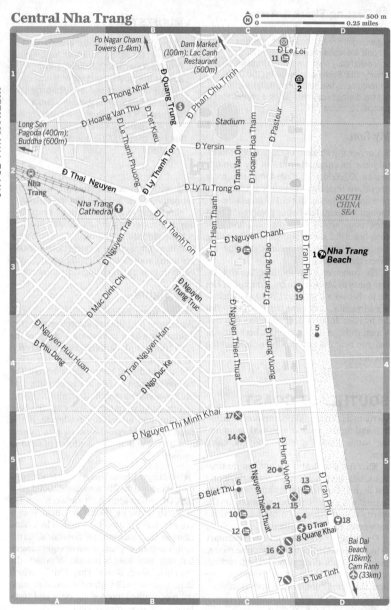

century. The entrance and roofs are decorated with mosaic dragons constructed of glass and ceramic tiles, while the main sanctuary is a hall adorned with modern interpretations of traditional motifs.

Behind the pagoda is a huge white **Buddha** (Kim Than Phat To) seated on a lotus blossom. Around the statue's base are fire-ringed relief busts of Thich Quang Duc and six other Buddhist monks who died in self-immolations in 1963.

Central Nha Trang

Alexandre Yersin Museum   MUSEUM
(☑ 058-382 2355; 10 Đ Tran Phu; admission 26,000d; ⊙ 7.30-11am & 2-4.30pm Mon-Fri, 8-11am Sat) Highly popular in Vietnam, Dr Alexandre Yersin (1863–1943) founded Nha Trang's Pasteur Institute in 1895. He learned to speak Vietnamese fluently, introduced rubber- and quinine-producing trees to Vietnam, and discovered the rat-borne microbe that causes bubonic plague.

You can see Yersin's library and office at this small, interesting museum; displays include laboratory equipment (such as astronomical instruments) and a fascinating 3D photo viewer.

Tours are conducted in French, English and Vietnamese, and a short film on Yersin's life is shown.

🏃 Activities

Diving

Nha Trang is Vietnam's most popular scuba-diving centre. February to September is considered the best time to dive, while October to December is the worst time of year.

There are around 25 dive sites in the area. Some sites have good drop-offs and there are small underwater caves to explore. It's not world-class diving, but the waters support a reasonable number of small reef fish.

A two-dive boat trip costs between US$60 and US$85; snorkellers typically pay US$15 to US$20.

Most dive operators also offer a range of dive courses. Watch out for dodgy dive shops

not following responsible diving practices and even using fake PADI/SSI accreditation – stick to reputable operators.

Oceans 5   DIVING
(☑ 058-381 1969, 058-352 2012; www.oceans5.co; 78 Tue Tinh) SSI school run by two Australian instructors, providing professionally run training courses and well-organised fun dives. Gear is in good condition and it also does dive training inside the protected marine area. Two dives are US$75.

Angel Dive   DIVING
(☑ 058-352 2461; www.angeldivevietnam.info; 1/27 Đ Tran Quang Khai) Reliable, experienced SSI operator with English, French and German instruction, with good courses for kids. Snorkelling trips cost US$20 per person.

Other Activities

Vietnam Active   ADVENTURE SPORTS
(☑ 058-351 5821; www.vietnamactive.com; 115 Đ Hung Vuong) Offers a diverse range of excellent activities including rafting, kayaking, mountain-biking trips and scuba diving (SSI and PADI accredited). Exact prices depend upon numbers. Stretch those aching limbs afterwards at one of the Hatha or Ashtanga yoga classes. It also rents quality bikes (from US$5 per day).

Shamrock Adventures   RAFTING
(☑ 058-352 7548; www.shamrockadventures.vn; Đ Tran Quang Khai; trips per person incl lunch from US$40) This outfit runs white-water rafting excursions (which can be combined with

TRIPPING THE BAY BY BOAT

The 71 offshore islands around Nha Trang are renowned for their remarkably clear water. Boat trips to these islands – booze cruises and snorkelling excursions from just 180,000d – are wildly popular with young backpackers.

Frankly, most of these trips are extremely touristy, involving whistle-stop visits to the **Tri Nguyen Aquarium** (Ho Ca Tri Nguyen; admission 90,000d), some snorkelling on a degraded reef, and a bit of beach time (beach admission 30,000d). The booze cruises feature (very) organised entertainment with a DJ on the deck (or a cheesy boy band) and lots of drinking games.

Keep the following tips in mind:

➡ Choose the right tour. Some are geared towards Asian families, others are booze cruises.

➡ Remember sunscreen and drink plenty of water.

➡ Entrance charges are not usually included.

➡ If you're more interested in snorkelling than drinking, the dive schools' trips will be more appropriate.

Some decent boat-trip operators include the following:

Funky Monkey (☑ 091 3458 950, 058-352 2426; http://funkymonkeytour.com; 75A Đ Hung Vuong; cruise incl pick-up 200,000d) A party-hard, backpacker-geared trip that kicks off at 8.30am. Features live 'entertainment' from the Funky Monkey boy band, as well as the usual stops.

Nha Trang Tours (☑ 058-352 4471; www.nhatrangtour.com.vn; 29 Đ Biet Thu) Budget party-themed booze cruises for 200,000d or snorkelling trips for 320,000d.

Khanh Hoa Tourist Information (☑ 058-352 8000; khtourism@dng.vnn.vn; Đ Tran Phu; cruise incl lunch 380,000d) For something a little different, consider a far-flung boat trip to beautiful Van Phong Bay. The two-hour trip there puts many off, but the remote, secluded bays certainly help compensate. Contact the tourist office for details and bookings.

some mountain biking). Kayaking, snorkelling and fishing trips are also on offer.

🛏 Sleeping

★ **Sunny Sea** HOTEL **$**
(☑ 058-352 2286; sunnyseahotel@gmail.com; 64B/9 Đ Tran Phu; r US$10-15; ※ @ 🛜 📶) A class above the others on 'budget alley' just off the beach, this exceptional place is run by a welcoming local couple (a doctor and nurse) and their super-helpful staff. The rooms are kept very clean and are in fine shape, with good-quality mattresses, minibar and modern bathrooms; some have a balcony.

Mojzo Inn HOSTEL **$**
(☑ 0988 879 069; www.facebook.com/MojzoInn; 120/36 Đ Nguyen Thien Thuat; dm US$8, r US$16-20; ※ @ 🛜) OK, the name is more cocktail list than hotel bed, but this funky hostel gets most things right, with well-designed dorms and a lovely cushion-scattered lounge area. Staff really go the extra mile to help here.

Carpe DM Hotel HOTEL **$**
(☑ 058-352 7868; www.carpedmhotel.com; 120/62 Đ Nguyen Thien Thuat; r US$16-22; ※ 🛜) This likeable, well-managed place has excellent, well-scrubbed, bright rooms with a contemporary touch, all very well equipped and attractively furnished with large flat-screen TV. The more expensive options have a balcony. It's a no-smoking hotel.

Binh An Hotel GUESTHOUSE **$**
(www.binhanhotel.com; 28H Đ Hoang Hoa Tham; r 350,000-380,000d; ※ @ 🛜) A welcoming place run by an accommodating couple who look after guests with pride. Rooms are spotless, spacious and boast good air-con and fast wi-fi. Say hi to Zon, the pet chihuahua dog, while you're here.

Michelia Hotel HOTEL **$$**
(☑ 058-382 0820; www.michelia.vn; 4 Đ Pasteur; r/ste incl breakfast from 1,150,000/2,550,000d; ※ @ 🛜 ♨) One block from the beach towards the northern end of the centre, the

Michelia has sleek, modern accommodation, helpful staff and the breakfast buffet is excellent. The pool is big enough for laps.

✗ Eating

For inexpensive, authentic Vietnamese food, head to **Dam Market** (Đ Trang Nu Vuong; ⊘6am-4pm), which has good stalls and lots of veggie choices.

Tasty   CAFE $
(30 Đ Nguyen Thien Thuat; snacks/meals from 22,000/40,000d; ⊘6.30am-10.30pm; 🛜🍴) A hip, bustling cafe with real appeal thanks to the bold retro murals (camper vans and Vespas), kitsch touches and mismatched seating. You'll find plenty of interest on the menu too, including good *banh mi,* Vietnamese salads, cheap breakfasts, juices and coffee. There's an open kitchen.

Nha Hang Yen's   VIETNAMESE $
(📲 093 3766 205; http://yensrestaurantnhatrang.com; 3/2a Đ Tran Quang Khai; dishes 55,000-120,000d; ⊘7am-9.30pm; 🛜) Stylish restaurant with a hospitable atmosphere and a winning line-up of flavoursome claypot, curry, noodle, rice and stir-fry dishes. Lilting traditional music and waitresses in *ao dai* add to the vibe.

Au Lac   VEGETARIAN $
(28C Đ Hoang Hoa Tham; meals 15,000-30,000d; ⊘10am-7pm; 📲) Long-running, no-frills vegan/vegetarian restaurant near the corner of Đ Nguyen Chanh. A mixed plate (15,000d) is just about the best value meal you can find in Nha Trang.

★Lac Canh Restaurant   VIETNAMESE $$
(44 Đ Nguyen Binh Khiem; dishes 30,000-150,000d; ⊘11am-8.45pm) This bustling, smoky, scruffy and highly enjoyable place is crammed most nights with groups firing up the table-top barbecues (beef, richly marinated with spices, is the speciality, but there are other meats and seafood, too). Closes quite early.

★Mix   GREEK $$
(77 Đ Hung Vuong; meals 80,000-150,000d; ⊘11am-10pm) Somehow Christos, the affable, kind-hearted Greek owner, manages to keep the quality high and prices moderate at his ever-busy restaurant – a Herculean effort. Everything is freshly prepared and beautifully presented. Highlights include the seafood and meat platters, salads and souvlaki. Book ahead.

Lanterns   VIETNAMESE $$
(www.lanternsvietnam.com; 34/6 Đ Nguyen Thien Thuat; dishes 48,000-117,000d; ⊘7.30am-9.30pm; 😊🛜📲🍴) 🍴 This restaurant supports local orphanages and provides scholarship programs. Flavours are predominantly Vietnamese, with specials including curries, claypots and steaming hotpots (210,000d for two). The 'street food' items are not bad and international offerings include pasta. Cooking classes and tours get good feedback. Eat between 2pm and 4pm and 20% is knocked off your bill.

🍸 Drinking & Nightlife

Sailing Club   BAR, CLUB
(www.sailingclubnhatrang.com; 72-74 Đ Tran Phu; ⊘7am-2am; 🛜) This Nha Trang beach club is a city institution with DJs and bands, and draws a beautiful, up-for-it crowd. On Thursday, Friday and Saturday a bonfire is lit and the action moves to the sand (weather permitting!). Attracts a good mix of locals and foreigners.

Skylight Bar   BAR
(http://skylightnhatrang.com; Best Western Premier Havana Nha Trang, 38 Đ Tran Phu; admission incl drink 100,000d; ⊘4.30-11pm; 🛜) Soaring above the city on the 43rd floor, this bombastic new place set up by a team from LA boasts mile-high vistas from its rooftop perch, a killer cocktail list (120,000d to 150,000d), shishas, cigars, DJs and pool parties. The only question: is it too ahead of the curve? Is Nha Trang ready for it?

❶ Information

Though Nha Trang is generally a safe place, be very careful on the beach during the day (theft) and at night (robbery). Pickpocketing is a perennial problem. Bags with valuables left behind bars for 'safekeeping' are regularly relieved of

---

❶ DRINK SPIKING

There have been a number of reports of laced cocktail buckets doing the rounds in popular night spots. This might mean staff using homemade moonshine instead of legal spirits or could mean the addition of drugs of some sort by other punters. While buckets are fun and communal, take care in Nha Trang and try to keep an eye on what goes into the bucket. You don't want your night to end in paranoia or robbery.

WORTH A TRIP

BAI DAI BEACH

South of Nha Trang, a spectacular coastal road leads to the Cam Ranh Bay, a gorgeous natural harbour and the airport. Virtually the entire shoreline south of Mia Resort (which is 18km from central Nha Trang) forms Bai Dai (Long Beach), a breathtaking sandy coast.

Until very recently, the Vietnamese military controlled the entire area, restricting access to the odd fishing boat. However, times are a-changing and now the entire strip has been earmarked for development. Dozens of giant resort hotels are planned and giant advertising billboards now line the coastal road.

As of late 2015, only a few hotels had been completed, so it should still be possible to find a virgin stretch of sand. Some of the best surf breaks in Vietnam are found along here.

At the northern tip of Bai Dai, **Shack Vietnam** (www.shackvietnam.com) offers surf instruction for 600,000d per hour (board rental is 180,000d per hour). It also offers kayak hire and great fish tacos (40,000d each).

A one-way journey in a *xe om*/taxi to the northern end of Bai Dai costs around 130,000/260,000d. There's no public transport along Bai Dai road. As traffic is very light, this is a region that's ideal to explore on a motorbike.

cash and phones. And note the warning about spiked cocktail buckets (p873).

Most hotels and bars have free wi-fi. ATMs are widespread.

Main Post Office (4 Đ Le Loi; ⊙6.30am-8pm Mon-Fri, 6.30am-1pm Sat)

Pasteur Institute (☑058-382 2355; www. pasteur-nhatrang.org.vn; 8-10 Đ Tran Phu; ⊙7-11am & 1-4.30pm) Offers medical consultations and vaccinations. Located inside the Alexandre Yersin Museum.

Sinh Tourist (☑058-352 2982; www.thesinhtourist.vn; 90C Đ Hung Vuong; ⊙6am-10pm) A reliable, professional company for inexpensive local trips, including a city tour for 259,000d (excluding entrance fees) and island boat cruises, as well as open-tour buses.

Vietcombank (17 Đ Quang Trung; ⊙7.30am-4pm Mon-Fri) Has an ATM.

❶ Getting There & Away

AIR

Vietnam Airlines (☑058-352 6768; www. vietnamairlines.com; 91 Đ Nguyen Thien Thuat)

connects Nha Trang with Hanoi (three daily), and HCMC and Danang daily. VietJet Air (p912) flies to both Hanoi and HCMC daily. Jetstar (www.jetstar.com) has good connections with both Hanoi and HCMC.

BUS

Phia Nam Nha Trang Bus Station (Đ 23 Thang 10) has services to Danang. Heading south, there are sleeper buses to HCMC from 7pm. Open-bus tours are the best option for Mui Ne (four to five hours). Open buses also head to Dalat (five hours) and Hoi An (11 hours).

TRAIN

Nha Trang Train Station (☑058-382 2113; Đ Thai Nguyen; ⊙ticket office 7-11.30am, 1.30-6pm & 7-9pm) is in the middle of town.

❶ Getting Around

Cam Ranh international airport is 35km south of the city. A shuttle bus runs the route (65,000d), leaving from the old airport (86 Đ Tran Phu) two hours before scheduled departure

TRANSPORT FROM NHA TRANG

DESTINATION	AIR	BUS	CAR/MOTORBIKE	TRAIN
Dalat		US$7, 5hr, 15 daily	4hr	
Danang	from US$31, 1hr, 1 daily	US$11-15, 12hr, 13-15 daily	11hr	US$15-21, 9-11hr, 6 daily
HCMC	from US$21, 1hr, 8 daily	US$10-15, 11hr, 13 daily	10hr	US$11-16, 7-9hr, 7 daily
Mui Ne		US$7, 5hr 30min, open-tour buses only	5hr	

times, taking about 40 minutes. Taxis cost 380,000/300,000d to/from the airport.

Cyclos and *xe om* cost 20,000d for a short ride. Hotels and cafes rent bicycles from 30,000d per day. **Mai Linh** (☑058-382 2266) taxis are safe and reliable.

Mui Ne

☑062 / POP 15,000

Once upon a time, Mui Ne was an isolated stretch of sand, but it was too beautiful to be ignored – now it's a string of resorts spread along a 10km stretch of highway. Mercifully, most of these are low-rise and set amid pretty gardens by the sea.

Windsurfing and kitesurfing are huge here – surf's up from August to December. It's also the 'Sahara' of Vietnam, with the most dramatic sand dunes in the region looming large.

◉ Sights

Sand Dunes BEACH

Mui Ne is famous for its enormous red and white sand dunes. The white dunes are the more impressive, the near-constant oceanic winds sculpting the sands into wonderful Saharaesque formations. But as this is Vietnam (not deepest Mali) there's little chance of experiencing the silence of the desert.

Prepare yourself for the hard-sell as children press you to hire a plastic sledge to ride the dunes. Unless you weigh next to nothing, it can be tricky to travel for more than a few meters this way.

✦ Activities

Surfpoint Kiteboarding School KITESURFING, SURFING

(☑0167 3422 136; www.surfpoint-vietnam.com; 52A Đ Nguyen Dinh Chieu; 3hr course incl all gear US$150; ☉7am-6pm) With well-trained instructors and a friendly vibe, it's no surprise Surfpoint is one of the best-regarded kite schools in town. A five-hour course costs US$250. Surfing lessons on softboards are also offered (from US$50) when waves permit and there are short boards for rent.

Jibes KITESURFING

(☑062-384 7405; www.windsurf-vietnam.com; 84-90 Đ Nguyen Dinh Chieu; ☉7.30am-6pm) Mui Ne's original kitesurfing school, Jibes provides safety-conscious and patient instruction (US$60 per hour) and rents gear including windsurfs (US$35 per half-day), SUPs, surfboards, kitesurfs and kayaks.

Manta Sail Training Centre SAILING

(☑0908 400 108; http://mantasailing.org; 108 Đ Huynh Thuc Khang; sailing instruction per hour US$60) Excellent new sailing school offering International Sailing Federation training (from beginner to advanced racing), wakeboarding (US$100/hour including boat) and SUP rentals. Staff are very professional and they also have budget rooms available.

⌸ Sleeping

★**Mui Ne Backpacker Village** HOSTEL

(☑062-374 1047; www.muinebackpackervillage. com; 137 Đ Nguyen Dinh Chieu; dm/r from US$7/25; ⊜✳️🛜🏊) Cornering the backpacker market, this ambitious, well-designed new construction is proving wildly popular thanks to its inviting pool, bar-restaurant and social vibe. All dorms have air-con, individual beds (no bunks!) and lockers, while the 18 private rooms all have a balcony or patio.

Coco Sand Hotel GUESTHOUSE $

(☑0127 364 3446; http://cocosandhotel.com; 119 Đ Nguyen Dinh Chieu; r US$13-16; ✳️🛜) Excellent-value rooms are grouped around a shady courtyard garden (with hammocks) at this very hospitable place. It's off the just main drag, down a little lane so it's quiet. The owners rent out motorbikes at fair rates.

Seaflower Guesthouse GUESTHOUSE $

(Hoa Bien; 86 Đ Huynh Thuc Khang; r 250,000-350,000d; ✳️🛜🏊) At the eastern end of the Mui Ne bay, this two-storey place is run by a friendly Vietnamese couple. Rooms are at the rear of a compound that stretches down to the shore.

Mui Ne Hills Budget Hotel HOTEL $

(☑062-374 1707; www.muinehills.com; 69 Đ Nguyen Dinh Chieu; dm/r from US$5/15; ✳️🛜🏊)

SPLURGE

An outstanding hotel-restaurant, **Sandals** (www.miamuine.com/dine; 24 Đ Nguyen Dinh Chieu, Mia Resort; meals 120,000-370,000d; ☉7am-10pm; 🛜) has tables set around a shoreside pool. Staff are knowledgeable, attentive and welcoming. The menu is superb with everything from pasta dishes to Vietnamese claypots executed beautifully. Consider visiting for the breakfast buffet, which is also wonderful.

Mui Ne Beach

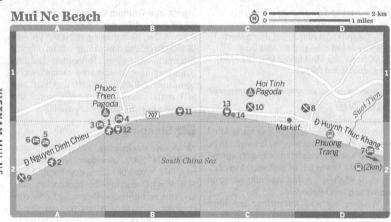

VIETNAM MUI NE

This place offers a good bed for your buck, with several air-con dorms that have en suites, while the rooms have quality furnishings and contemporary design touches. Around 300m north of the main strip, via an incredibly steep access road.

Mui Ne Hills Villa Hotel　　　BOUTIQUE HOTEL **$$**
(☎062-374 1707; www.muinehills.com; 69 Đ Nguyen Dinh Chieu; r US$35-55; ❇@🛰🏊) Formerly Mui Ne Hills 1, this fine villa-style hotel has wonderful vistas from its pool. Rooms are superb value, all with contemporary design touches and full facilities, but

it's the personal touch from staff and owners that makes a real difference. It's located up a dusty, very steep lane (but is close to the best section of beach).

🍴 Eating

★**Com Chay Vi Dieu**　　　VEGETARIAN **$**
(15B Đ Huynh Thuc Khang; meals 25,000-40,000đ; ⏱7am-9pm; 🥗) This simple roadside place scores strongly for inexpensive Vietnamese vegetarian dishes, and serves up great smoothies (20,000đ). It's right opposite the Eiffel Tower of the Little Paris resort.

Sindbad　　　MIDDLE EASTERN **$**
(www.sindbad.vn; 233 Đ Nguyen Dinh Chieu; mains 50,000-85,000đ; ⏱11am-1am; 🍴) A kind of kebab shack par excellence. Come here for inexpensive shawarma and shish kebabs and other Med favourites like greek salads. Very inexpensive, portions are generous; opens late.

Nhu Bao　　　SEAFOOD **$**
(146 Đ Nguyen Dinh Chieu; mains 50,000-180,000đ; ⏱9am-9.30pm) A classic, no-nonsense Vietnamese seafood place: step past the bubbling tanks and there's a huge covered terrace which stretches down to the ocean. It's renowned for its crab.

🍸 Drinking & Nightlife

★**PoGo**　　　BAR
(www.thepogobar.com; 138 Đ Nguyen Dinh Chieu; ⏱8.30am-2pm, Tue-Thu) A mighty fine bar with a prime beach location, daybeds for lounging, DJs on weekends and regular

movie nights. Staff are very friendly and there's a full menu too.

Joe's Café
BAR

(www.joescafegardenresort.com; 86 Đ Nguyen Dinh Chieu; ⊘7am-1am; 🛜) If bangin' techno is not your bag, Joe's is worth a try with live music (every night at 7.30pm) and a pub-like vibe. During the day it's a good place to hang too, with a sociable bar area, lots of drinks specials and an extensive food menu.

Dragon Beach
BAR, CLUB

(120-121 Đ Nguyen Dinh Chieu; ⊘4pm-2am) Western and local DJs play EDM, bass, house and techno at this shoreside bar-club. There's a chill-out deck with cushions to one side and shishas for puffing. Happy hour is 8pm to 10pm.

Information

Internet and wi-fi are widely available and there are numerous ATMs.

Main Post Office (348 Đ Huynh Thuc Khang; ⊘7am-5pm) In Mui Ne village.

Sinh Tourist (www.thesinhtourist.vn; 144 Đ Nguyen Dinh Chieu; ⊘7am-10pm) Ever-reliable and trustworthy agency for open-tour buses, trips around Mui Ne and credit-card cash advances.

Getting There & Around

Few regular buses serve Mui Ne.

WORTH A TRIP

CAT TIEN NATIONAL PARK

Unesco-listed **Cat Tien National Park** (☑061-366 9228; www.cattiennationalpark.vn; adult/child 50,000/20,000d; ⊘7am-10pm) 🍃 comprises an amazingly biodiverse area of lowland tropical rainforest. The hiking, mountain biking and birdwatching are outstanding.

Fauna in the park includes 326 bird species, 100 mammals (including elephants) and 79 reptiles, though the last rhino was killed by poachers in 2010.

Call ahead for reservations, as the park can accommodate only a limited number of visitors.

Sights & Activities

Cat Tien National Park can be explored on foot, by mountain bike, by 4WD and also by boat. There are 14 well-established hiking trails in the park. A guide (from 1,200,000d per group) is only mandatory for three difficult trails.

Trips to the **Crocodile Lake** (Bau Sau; admission 200,000d, guide fee 500,000d, boat trip 450,000d), taking in a three-hour jungle trek, are popular.

Dao Tien Endangered Primate Species Centre (www.go-east.org; adult/child incl boat ride 300,000/150,000d; ⊘tours 8.30am & 2pm) is located on an island in the Dong Nai River. This rehabilitation centre hosts gibbons, langurs and lorises. The **Bear & Wild Cat Rescue Station** (admission 150,000d; ⊘7.30am-4pm) is also worth a visit.

Wild Gibbon Trek (ecotourism@cattiennationalpark.vn; per person US$60, maximum 4 people) involves a 4am start to hear the gibbons' dawn chorus and a fully guided tour of the Primate Species Centre. Book ahead.

Sleeping & Eating

Cat Tien National Park (☑061-366 9228; cattienvietnam@gmail.com; dm/d/tr from 80,000/200,000/680,000d, 2-person tents 200,000d; 🌀🛜) offers basic bungalow rooms and tented accommodation close to the park headquarters. **River Lodge** (☑0973 346 345; r US$12; 🌀🛜) is better value, while **Ta Lai Long House** (☑0935 160 730; www.talai-adventure.vn; dm 315,000d; 🌀🛜🚹) is another goodie, but 12km away. There are two small restaurants near the park HQ.

Getting There & Around

Cat Tien is 175km south of Dalat; turn off Hwy 20 at Tan Phu and it's another 24km up a paved access road to the entrance.

Buses between Dalat and HCMC pass the access road. Waiting motorbikes (around 170,000d) will then take you to the park entrance.

Guesthouses either rent or provide bicycles free of charge.

Open-tour buses are the most convenient option. Several companies have daily services to/from HCMC (99,000d to 150,000d, six hours), Nha Trang (from 122,000d, 5½ hours) and Dalat (100,000d, four hours).

Phuong Trang (https://futabus.vn; 97 Đ Nguyen Dinh Chieu) has four comfortable buses a day running between Mui Ne and HCMC (135,000d).

SOUTHWEST HIGHLANDS

There's a rugged charm to this distinctly rural region, with pine-studded hilltops soaring over intensively farmed fields and remote, bumpy roads meandering through coffee plantations.

Looking for big nature? Check out Cat Tien National Park, where there are gibbons, crocodiles and elusive tigers.

Dalat, a former French hill station that still boasts plenty of colonial-era charm, makes a great base.

Dalat

☑ 063 / POP 208,000 / ELEV 1475M

Dalat is the alter-ego of lowland Vietnam. The weather is spring-like cool instead of tropical hot. The town is dotted with elegant French-colonial villas, and farms are thick with strawberries and flowers, not rice.

Dalat is small enough to remain charming, and the surrounding countryside is blessed with lakes, waterfalls, evergreen forests and gardens.

The town is a big draw for domestic tourists. For travellers, the moderate climate is ideal for adrenalin-fuelled activities – mountain biking, forest hiking, canyoning and climbing.

◉ Sights

Perhaps there's something in the cool mountain air that fosters the distinctly artistic vibe that veers towards cute kitsch in Dalat.

Hang Nga Crazy House   ARCHITECTURE
(☑ 063-382 2070; 3 Đ Huynh Thuc Khang; admission 40,000d; ⊘ 8.30am-7pm Mon-Fri) A free-wheeling architectural exploration of

---

OFF THE BEATEN TRACK

MOTORBIKE RIDES IN THE CENTRAL HIGHLANDS

It's easy to get off the beaten track in the wonderfully scenic highlands. This is a great part of the country to see from the back of a motorbike. Indeed, for many travellers, the highlight of their central highlands trip is a motorcycle tour with an Easy Rider (driver-guide). The flip side to the popularity of the Easy Riders is that now everyone claims to be one. In central Dalat, you can't walk down the street without being invited (sometimes harassed) for a tour.

Rider-guides can be found in hotels and cafes in Dalat. Read testimonials from past clients. Check the bike over. Test-drive a rider first before committing to a longer trip. Then discuss the route in detail – for scenery, the new coastal highways that link Dalat to Mui Ne and Nha Trang, plus the old road to the coast via Phan Rang, are wonderful. Rates start at US$25 for a day tour, or US$60 to US$75 per day for longer journeys.

Here are some tips for exploring :

➡ The upgrading of the historic **Ho Chi Minh Trail** has made it easier to visit out-of-the-way places such as **Kon Tum**, one of the friendliest cities in Vietnam.

➡ Buon Ma Thuot is the major city in the region, but the biggest buzz you'll get is from the coffee beans. Nearby **Yok Don National Park** (☑ 0500-378 3049; www.yokdonnationalpark.vn; admission 40,000d) is home to 38 endangered mammal species, including plenty of elephants. Stunning waterfalls in this area include **Dray Sap, Gia Long & Dray Nur Falls** (☑ 0500-321 3194; admission 30,000d; ⊘ 8am-6pm) along the Krong Ana River.

➡ Northeast of Dalat, the **high road to Nha Trang** offers spectacular views, hitting 1700m at Hon Giao mountain, following a breathtaking 33km pass.

➡ And 43km southeast of Dalat, it's possible to see the ocean from the spectacular **Ngoan Muc Pass**.

surrealism, Hang Nga Crazy House is a joyously designed, outrageously artistic private home. Imagine sculptured rooms connected by super-slim bridges rising out of a tangle of greenery, an excess of cascading lava-flow-like shapes, wild colours, spider-web windows and an almost organic quality to it all, with the swooping hand rails resembling jungle vines. Think Gaudí meeting Tolkien and dropping acid together.

King Palace   PALACE

(Dinh 1; www.dinh1dalat.com; Hung Vuong; adult/child 20,000/10,000d; ⊙7.30am-5pm) Tastefully revamped, the main palace of Bao Dai, Vietnam's last emperor, beckons visitors with its beautiful tree-lined avenue and a surprisingly modest royal residence. Its peach-coloured rooms were once home to him, his wife and their five children before being taken over by Prime Minister Ngo Dinh Diem once Bao Dai went into exile in France in 1954.

Highlights are the family photos: Bao Dai playing with a dog, riding a horse, and well-scrubbed royal children with serious faces.

Crémaillère Railway Station   HISTORIC BUILDING

(Ga Da Lat; 1 Đ Quang Trung; ⊙6.30am-5pm) FREE From Dalat's wonderful art-deco train station you can ride one of the five scheduled trains that run to Trai Mat (return 124,000d, 30 minutes) daily between 7.45am and 4pm; a minimum of 20 passengers required.

A crémaillère (cog railway) linking Dalat and Thap Cham from 1928 to 1964 was closed due to VC attacks. A Japanese steam train is on display, and the classy waiting room retains a colonial-era feel.

🏃 Activities

★Phat Tire Ventures   ADVENTURE TOUR

(☑063-382 9422; www.ptv-vietnam.com; 109 Đ Nguyen Van Troi; ⊙8am-7pm) A highly professional and experienced operator with mountain-biking trips from US$49, trekking from US$39, kayaking from US$39, canyoning (US$75), rapelling (US$57) and white-water rafting (US$67) in the rainy season. Multi-day cycling trips are available and it also ventures into Cat Tien National Park.

Groovy Gecko
Adventure Tours   ADVENTURE TOUR

(☑063-383 6521; www.groovygeckotours.net; 65 Đ Truong Cong Dinh; ⊙8am-7pm) Experienced agency operated by a lively young team with prices starting at US$38 for rock climbing,

---

GETTING TO CAMBODIA: PLEIKU TO BAN LUNG

Getting to the border Remote and rarely used by foreigners, the Le Thanh/O Yadaw border crossing links Pleiku with Ban Lung, Cambodia. From Pleiku there's a daily Noi Thinh bus at 7am (65,000d, two hours) from the main marketplace on Đ Tran Phu direct to Le Thanh.

At the border Open 7am to 5pm. Visas are available on arrival in Cambodia.

Moving on From O Yadaw, on the Cambodia side of the border, local buses (US$10) or motorbikes (around US$25) head to Ban Lung. There are far fewer transport options in the afternoon.

For information on doing this crossing in the opposite direction, see p135.

canyoning or mountain biking, day treks from US$25 and two-day treks from US$65.

🛏 Sleeping

★Ken's House   HOSTEL $

(☑063-383 7119; www.kenhousedalat.com; D59 Hoang Van Thu; r US$12-22; ☀🛜) With walls covered with creeping vines, Parisian scenes and jungle imagery and patterned quilts on beds, this is by far Dalat's most colourful hostel. Join an impromptu hotpot party/communal dinner with the friendly staff.

Sleep In Dalat Hostel   HOSTEL $

(☑0913 923 379; www.sleepindalathostel.com; 83/5B Đ Nguyen Van Troi; dm US$7, d US$20-35; 🛜) Haunted by Ben the sausage dog, this welcoming hostel is tucked away down a narrow alleyway, insulating you from main street noise. Owner Linh cooks communal dinners so that you can get to know your fellow travellers, and the canyoning tours get rave reviews. Private rooms have their own bathrooms; dorms share (clean) facilities.

Dalat Cozy Nook Hostel   HOSTEL $

(☑0949 691 553; 45/5a Đ Phan Dinh Phung; dm US$5; ❄🛜) Two spotless mixed dorms with the most comfortable bunks in Dalat attract a constant crowd of international backpackers, and the lively group dinners, organised by helpful owners, give you the perfect opportunity to swap traveller tales.

Central Dalat

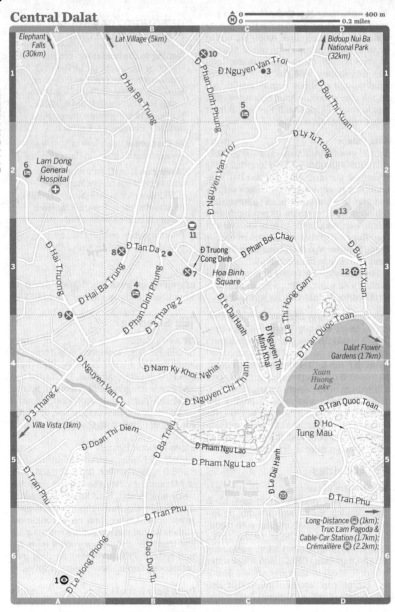

Villa Pink House HOTEL **$**
(☎063-381 5667; ahomeawayfromhome_dalat@
yahoo.com; 7 Đ Hai Thuong; s/d/tr US$16/20/30;
@🛜) A well-run family-owned place, where
many rooms have great views. It's managed
by the affable Mr Rot, who can arrange motorbike tours in the surrounding countryside.

★Villa Vista BOUTIQUE HOTEL **$$**
(☎063-351 2468; huongdo_82@yahoo.com; 93
Ngo Thi Sy, Phuong 4; r from US$60; 🌀🛜) Look
down from this mansion on the hill and the
whole of Dalat opens up in the valley below
you. There are only four exquisite rooms
here, decorated in the 19th-century French

Central Dalat

fashion (albeit with flat-screen TVs and rain showers). Delightful owners Tim and Huong prepare remarkable breakfasts, hook you up with Easy Riders and share their Dalat knowledge.

✕ Eating

There are vegetarian food stalls and cheap eats in the market area.

★ Trong Dong   VIETNAMESE $
(☎ 063-382 1889; 220 Đ Phan Dinh Phung; meals 80,000-120,000d; ⊙ 11.30am-3pm & 5.30-9.30pm; ☏) Intimate restaurant run by a very hospitable team where the creative menu includes such delights as shrimp paste on a sugar cane stick, beef wrapped in *la lut* leaf, and fiery lemongrass and chilli squid.

One More Cafe   CAFE $
(77 Đ Hai Ba Trung; cake 25,000d; ⊙ 8am-9pm Thu-Tue; ☺☏♪) Comfy chairs to sink into, eclectic-lined peach walls and a glass display full of cakes greet you at this cosy, Aussie-run cafe. Linger over an array of teas, an espresso, an all-day breakfast or a smoothie.

Da Quy   VIETNAMESE $
(Wild Sunflower; 49 Đ Truong Cong Dinh; meals from 50,000d; ⊙ 8am-10pm) Run by Loc, a friendly English speaker, this place has a sophisticated ambience but unsophisticated prices. The traditional claypot dishes and hotpots are more exciting than the Western menu.

★ Restaurant Ichi   JAPANESE $$
(☎ 063-355 5098; 1 Đ Hoang Dieu; meals 100,000-300,000d; ⊙ 5.30-10pm Tue-Sun) Dalat's only truly genuine Japanese restaurant is compact, with subdued lighting and jazz in the background. Spicy tuna rolls, chicken yakitori and tempura are all fantastic, the

bento boxes are a bargain and there's even *natto* for aficionados. Perch in front of the bar (with extensive whisky offerings from around the world) to watch sushi master Tommo at work.

♿ Drinking & Entertainment

La Viet   COFFEE
(82 Đ Truong Cong Dinh; ⊙ 7am-10pm) Is it an antique store? Is it a cafe? This cosy corner beguiles with its riot of plants, old bicycle parts, bird cages, vintage telephones and antique pianos. Find a corner to perch in to sip some seriously good coffee.

★ Escape Bar   LIVE MUSIC
(www.escapebardalat.com; basement, Muong Thanh Hotel, 4 Đ Phan Boi Chau; ⊙ 4pm-midnight; ☏) Outstanding live-music bar, owned by blues guitarist Curtis King who performs here nightly with a rotating band (from 9pm). Expect covers of Hendrix, The Eagles, The Doors and other classics, but the improvisation is such that each tune takes on a life of its own; travelling musicians are welcome to jam. The bar's decor, all 1970s chic, suits the sonics perfectly.

🛍 Shopping

Hoa Binh Sq and the market building adjacent to it are the places to purchase ethnic handicrafts, including Lat rush baskets that roll up when empty.

ℹ Information

Dalat has numerous ATMs and internet cafes; wi-fi is widely available.

Lam Dong General Hospital (☎ 063-382 1369; 4 Đ Pham Ngoc Thach; ⊙ 24hr) Emergency medical care.

Main Post Office (14 Đ Tran Phu; ⊙7am-6pm)

Sinh Tourist (☑063-382 2663; www.thesinh tourist.vn; 22 Đ Bui Thi Xuan; ⊙8am-7pm) Tours, including city sightseeing trips, and open-tour bus bookings.

Vietcombank (6 Đ Nguyen Thi Minh Khai; ⊙7.30am-3pm Mon-Fri, to 1pm Sat) Changes travellers cheques and foreign currencies.

🛈 Getting There & Around

There are regular flights with Vietnam Airlines, VietJet Air and Jetstar, including a daily service to Danang and four daily to Hanoi and HCMC. Lien Khuong Airport is 30km south of the city.

Dalat's modern **long-distance bus station** (Ben Xe Lien Tinh Da Lat; Đ 3 Thang 4) is 1.5km south of Xuan Huong Lake and has express buses to HCMC and other cities in the highlands, Danang and Nha Trang. Phuong Trang operates smart double-decker buses, including several sleeper services, to HCMC (230,000d, seven to eight hours, roughly hourly).

Dalat is a major stop for open-tour buses. Sinh Tourist has daily buses to Mui Ne (from 99,000d, four hours), Nha Trang (from 99,000d, five hours) and HCMC (from 159,000d, eight hours).

Full-day tours with motorbike guides (from US$20) are a great way to see the area. Many hotels offer bicycle and motorbike hire. For a taxi call **Mai Linh** (☑063-352 1111).

Around Dalat

Truc Lam
Pagoda & Cable Car
BUDDHIST TEMPLE

(Ho Tuyen Lam; cable car one way/return adult 50,000/70,000d, child 30,000/40,000d; ⊙cable car 7.30-11.30am & 1.30-5pm) The Truc Lam Pagoda enjoys a hilltop setting and has splendid gardens. It's an active monastery, though the grounds frequently teem with tour groups. Be sure to arrive by cable car (the terminus is 3km south of the centre), which soars over majestic pine forests.

The pagoda can be reached by road via turn-offs from Hwy 20.

HO CHI MINH CITY (SAIGON)

📞08 / POP POP 7.4 MILLION

Ho Chi Minh City (HCMC) is Vietnam at its most dizzying: a high-octane city of commerce and culture. A chaotic whirl, the city breathes life and vitality into all who settle here – visitors cannot help but be hauled along for the ride.

Wander through alleys to ancient pagodas or teeming markets, past ramshackle wooden shops selling silk and spices, before fast-forwarding into the future beneath skyscrapers and mammoth malls. The ghosts of the past live on in the churches, temples, former GI hotels and government buildings that one generation ago witnessed a city in turmoil. Put simply, there's nowhere else quite like it. Saigon has it all.

◉ Sights

◉ Dong Khoi Area

This well-heeled area, immediately west of the Saigon River, is a swish enclave of designer stores and fashionable restaurants, concrete towers and tree-lined boulevards.

★**Notre Dame Cathedral**   CHURCH

(Map p884; Đ Han Thuyen; ⊙Mass 9.30am Sun) Built between 1877 and 1883, Notre Dame Cathedral enlivens the heart of Ho Chi Minh City's government quarter, facing Đ Dong Khoi. A brick, neo-Romanesque church with 40m-high square towers tipped with iron spires, the Catholic cathedral is named after the Virgin Mary. Interior walls are inlaid with devotional tablets and some stained glass survives. English-speaking staff dispense tourist information from 9am to 11am Monday to Saturday. If the front gates are locked, try the door on the side facing the Reunification Palace.

HCMC Museum   MUSEUM

(Bao Tang Thanh Pho Ho Chi Minh; Map p884; www. hcmc-museum.edu.vn; 65 Đ Ly Tu Trong; admission 15,000d; ⊙8am-5pm) A grand, neo-classical structure built in 1885 and once known as Gia Long Palace (and later the Revolutionary Museum), HCMC's city museum is a singularly beautiful and impressive building, telling the story of the city through archaeological artefacts, ceramics, old city maps and displays on the marriage traditions of its various ethnicities. The struggle for independence is extensively covered, with most of the upper floor devoted to it.

Central Post Office   HISTORIC BUILDING

(Map p884; 2 Cong Xa Paris) Right across the way from Notre Dame Cathedral, Ho Chi Minh City's striking French post office is a period classic, designed by Gustave Eiffel and built between 1886 and 1891. Painted on the walls of its grand concourse are

Ho Chi Minh City

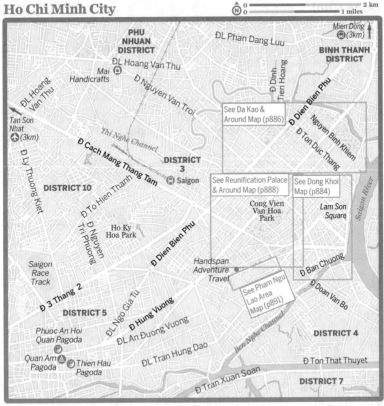

fascinating historic maps of South Vietnam, Saigon and Cholon, while a mosaic of Ho Chi Minh takes pride of place at the end of its barrel-vaulted hall. Note the magnificent tiled floor of the interior and the copious green-painted wrought iron.

◉ Da Kao & Around

★ Jade Emperor Pagoda   TAOIST TEMPLE
(Phuoc Hai Tu, Chua Ngoc Hoang; Map p886; 73 Đ Mai Thi Luu; ⊙7am-6pm, on 1st & 15th of lunar month 5am-7pm) **FREE** Built in 1909 in honour of the supreme Taoist god (the Jade Emperor or King of Heaven, Ngoc Hoang), this is one of the most spectacularly atmospheric temples in Ho Chi Minh City, stuffed with statues of phantasmal divinities and grotesque heroes. The pungent smoke of *huong* (incense) fills the air, obscuring the exquisite woodcarvings. Its roof encrusted with elaborate tile work, the temple's statues, depicting characters from both Buddhist and Taoist lore, are made from reinforced papier mâché.

★ History Museum   MUSEUM
(Bao Tang Lich Su; Map p886; Đ Nguyen Binh Khiem; admission 15,000d; ⊙8-11.30am & 1.30-5pm Tue-Sun) Built in 1929 by the Société des Études Indochinoises, this notable Sino-French museum houses a rewarding collection of artefacts illustrating the evolution of the cultures of Vietnam, from the Bronze Age Dong Son civilisation (which emerged in 2000 BC) and the Funan civilisation (1st to 6th centuries AD), to the Cham, Khmer and Vietnamese. The museum is just inside the main gate to the city's botanic gardens and zoo.

Botanic Gardens   GARDENS
(Thao Cam Vien; Map p886; 2 Đ Nguyen Binh Khiem; 50,000d incl entry to zoo; ⊙7am-7pm) One of the first projects undertaken by the French after establishing Cochinchina as a colony was founding these fantastic, lush gardens.

Dong Khoi

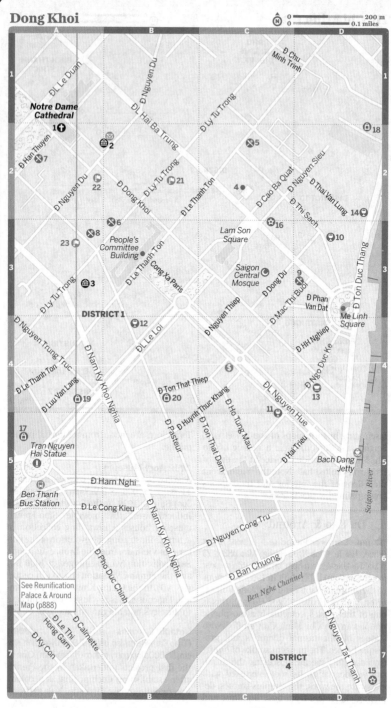

Dong Khoi

Once one of the finest such gardens in Asia, they're very agreeable for strolling beneath giant tropical trees, including towering Tung and So Khi trees. Also equipped with a miserable zoo, the gardens are next to the History Museum.

◎ Reunification Palace & Around

★ **War Remnants Museum** MUSEUM
(Bao Tang Chung Tich Chien Tranh; Map p888; ☑08-3930 5587; www.baotangchungtichchientranh.vn; 28 Đ Vo Van Tan, cnr Đ Le Quy Don; admission 15,000d; ⊙7.30am-noon & 1.30-5pm) Formerly the Museum of Chinese and American War Crimes, the War Remnants Museum is consistently popular with Western tourists. Few museums anywhere convey the brutality of war and its civilian victims. Many of the atrocities documented here were well publicised but rarely do Westerners hear the victims of US military action tell their own stories. While some displays are one-sided, many of the most disturbing photographs illustrating US atrocities are from US sources, including those of the infamous My Lai Massacre.

★ **Reunification Palace** HISTORIC BUILDING
(Dinh Thong Nhat; Map p888; ☑08-3829 4117; www.dinhdoclap.gov.vn; Đ Nam Ky Khoi Nghia; adult/child 30,000/5000d; ⊙7.30-11am & 1-4pm) Surrounded by royal palm trees, the dissonant 1960s architecture of this government building and the eerie mood that accompa-

nies a walk through its deserted halls make it an intriguing spectacle. The first Communist tanks to arrive in Saigon rumbled here on 30 April 1975 and it's as if time has stood still since then. The building is deeply associated with the fall of the city in 1975, yet it's the kitsch detailing and period motifs that steal the show.

Mariamman Hindu Temple HINDU TEMPLE
(Chua Ba Mariamman; Map p888; 45 Đ Truong Dinh; ⊙7.30am-7.30pm) Only a small number of Hindus live in HCMC, but this colourful slice of southern India is also considered sacred by many ethnic Vietnamese and Chinese. Reputed to have miraculous powers, the temple was built at the end of the 19th century and dedicated to the Hindu goddess Mariamman. Remove your shoes before stepping onto the slightly raised platform and ignore any demands to buy joss sticks and jasmine. The temple is three blocks west of Ben Thanh Market.

◎ Cholon

Cholon, 5km southwest of the centre, forms the city's Chinatown. The district has a wealth of wonderful Chinese temples including **Thien Hau Pagoda** (Ba Mieu, Pho Mieu, Chua Ba Thien Hau; Map p883; 710 Đ Nguyen Trai) **FREE**, dedicated to Thien Hau (Tianhou), the Chinese goddess of the sea, and the fabulously ornamental **Phuoc An Hoi Quan Pagoda** (Map p883; 184 Đ Hong Bang) **FREE**, built in 1902 by the Fujian Chinese congregation.

Da Kao & Around

Quan Am Pagoda (Chua Quan Am; Map p883; 12 Đ Lao Tu) FREE has a roof decorated with fantastic scenes, rendered in ceramic, from traditional Chinese plays and stories.

🍴 Courses

Saigon Cooking Class COOKING COURSE
(Map p884; ☑ 08-3825 8485; www.saigoncook ingclass.com; 74/7 ĐL Hai Ba Trung; per adult/child under 12yr US$39/25; ⊙ 10am & 2pm Tue-Sun) Watch and learn from the chefs at Hoa Tuc as they prepare three mains (including *pho bo* – beef noodle soup – and some of their signature dishes) and one dessert. A mar-
ket visit is optional (per adult/child under 12 years US$45/28, including a three-hour class).

Cyclo Resto COOKING COURSE
(Map p888; ☑ 0975 513 011; www.cycloresto.com; 6/28 Đ Cach Mang Thang Tam; per person US$29) Fun and informative three-hour cooking class, including a *cyclo* trip to the Thai Binh Market near Pham Ngu Lao.

🧭 Tours

HCMC has some excellent quirky tours, with themes as diverse as street food and the city's art scene.

XO Tours CULTURAL TOUR
(☑ 0933 083 727; www.xotours.vn; from US$45) Wearing *ao-dai* (traditional dress), these girls run scooter/motorbike foodie, sights and Saigon by night tours: super hospitable and fantastic fun.

Saigon Unseen TOUR
(www.saigonunseen.com; from US$25) Motorbike tours around local markets and off-the-beaten path parts of HCMC and around.

🛏 Sleeping

Virtually all budget travellers head straight to the Pham Ngu Lao area. Saigon's backpacker precinct has more than 100 places to stay, most with rooms between US$10 and US$35, and even the odd dorm. Some hotels with Đ Pham Ngu Lao or Đ Bui Vien addresses are located in alleys off those main streets.

★ **Lily's Hostel**   HOSTEL **$**
(Map p891; ☑ 0948 213 181; lilyhostel.hcm@gmail.
com; 35/5 Đ Bui Vien; dm/d US$8/26; ✿✲@🖤)
One of the new breed of modern hostels popping up in Pham Ngu Lao, Lily's has a warm
and welcoming ambience courtesy of the elegant and soothing decor. Located in a quiet
lane just off bustling Đ Bui Vien, Lily's easily
bridges the gap between hostel and boutique
guesthouse. Some private rooms have flat-
screen TV and a minibar.

★ **Madame Cuc 127**   GUESTHOUSE **$**
(Map p891; ☑ 08-3836 8761; www.madamcuc
hotels.com; 127 Đ Cong Quynh; US$20-30; ✲@🖤)
The original and by far the best of the three
hotels run by the welcoming Madame Cuc
and her friendly and fantastic staff. Rooms
are clean and spacious.

The Hideout Hostel   HOSTEL **$**
(Map p891; ☑ 08-3838 9147; www.vietnamhide
outhostels.com; 281 Đ Pham Ngu Lao; dm US$8;
✲@🖤) A new PNL hostel, this time with
an emphasis on good times and meeting
other travellers. Dorms are spick and span
with bright colours, two free beers per day
are on offer at the Hideout Bar next door,
and the hostel also runs pub crawls three
times a week that are free for guests (US$2
for nonguests).

Diep Anh   GUESTHOUSE **$**
(Map p891; ☑ 08-3836 7920; dieptheanh@hcm.vnn.
vn; 241/31 Đ Pham Ngu Lao; r US$20-25; ✲@🖤)
A step above most PNL guesthouses, figuratively and literally (think thousand-yard
stairs), Diep Anh's tall and narrow shape
makes for light and airy upper rooms. The
gracious staff ensure they're kept in good
nick.

Giang Son   GUESTHOUSE **$**
(Map p891; ☑ 08-3837 7547; www.guesthouse.
com.vn; 283/14 Đ Pham Ngu Lao; r US$20-30;
✲@🖤) Tall and thin, with three rooms on
each floor, a roof terrace and charming service, Giang Son's sole downer is that there's
no lift. Consider upgrading to a room with
window.

Town House 50   GUESTHOUSE, HOSTEL **$**
(Map p888; ☑ 08-3925 0210; www.townhouse
saigon.com; 50e Đ Bui Thi Xuan; dm $US11, s/d/
tr US$20/35/45; ✿✲@🖤) Part guesthouse
and part boutique hotel, Town House 50
offers stylish accommodation down a quiet
laneway on a street with good restaurants
and cafes. All dorms and rooms are non-

smoking, and the decor is clean and modern. Rates include a cooked breakfast, and
the team at reception have loads of local
information on offer.

Hong Han Hotel   GUESTHOUSE **$**
(Map p891; ☑ 08-3836 1927; www.honghan
hotel.com.vn; 238 Đ Bui Vien; r US$18-30; ✲@🖤)
A corker guesthouse (seven floors, no lift),
Hong Han has front rooms with ace views
and smaller, quieter and cheaper rear
rooms, plus free breakfast served on the 1st-
floor terrace.

PP Backpackers   HOSTEL **$**
(Map p891; ☑ 0930 815 799; www.ppbackpackers.
com.vn; Đ 283/41 Đ Pham Ngu Lao; dm US$7, d
US$16-18; ✲@🖤) Very helpful, friendly and
efficient staff at this cheap and welcoming
hostel where you can nab a dorm bed or
fork out a bit more for an affordable double
room.

Liberty Hotel Saigon Greenview   HOTEL **$$**
(Map p888; ☑ 08-3836 9522; www.odyssea
hotels.com/saigongreenview; 187 Đ Pham Ngu Lao;
r from US$47; ✲@🖤) Recently refurbished
in a cool and classy mix of soothing neutral
colours and natural wood, Liberty's Saigon
Greenview is one of Pham Ngu Lao's flasher
accommodation options. Rooms at the front
have views of the 23/9 park on the northern
edge of Saigon's backpacker district.

✖ Eating

HCMC is the reigning culinary king of Viet-
nam. Restaurants here range from dirt-cheap
sidewalk stalls to atmospheric villas. Besides
brilliant Vietnamese fare, Saigon offers world
cuisine, with Indian, Japanese, Thai, French,
Spanish and Korean all on offer.

The Dong Khoi area has many top-quality
restaurants. Pham Ngu Lao's eateries are
generally less memorable, though there are
exceptions.

To really discover more of the city's great
street food, a tour is an excellent option.

✖ Dong Khoi Area

Secret Garden   VIETNAMESE **$**
(Map p884; 8th fl, 158 Đ Pasteur; meals 55,000-
80,000d; ⊙ 8am-10pm; ☑) Negotiate the stairs
in this faded Saigon apartment building to
arrive at Secret Garden's wonderful roof-
top restaurant. Rogue chickens peck away
in the herb garden, Buddhist statues add
Asian ambience, and delicious homestyle

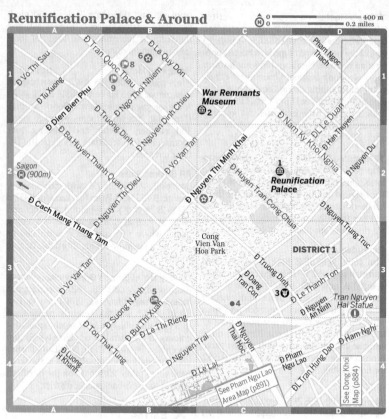

Reunification Palace & Around

dishes are served up with city views. Service can sometimes be a little *too* casual, but it's worth persevering for the great flavours.

5Ku Station BARBECUE **$**
(Map p884; 29 Đ Le Thanh Thon; meals around 100,000d; ☺4pm-late) Hopping with evening diners, this chain of makeshift-looking alfresco barbecue restaurants is fun, bois-terous, outgoing and tasty. Grab yourself a wooden box seat, a cold beer and chow down on BBQ and hotpot alongside a mix of locals, travellers and expats.

Huong Lai VIETNAMESE **$**
(Map p884; ☑08-3822 6814; www.huonglai 2001saigon.com; 38 Đ Ly Tu Trong; meals 55,000-160,000d; ☺noon-3pm & 6-10pm) A must for

finely presented, traditional Vietnamese food, the airy and high-ceilinged loft of an old French-era shophouse is the setting for dining with a difference. Staff are from disadvantaged families or are former street children and receive on-the-job training, education and a place to stay.

Propaganda   VIETNAMESE $$

(Map p884; ☑08-3822 9048; www.propaganda saigon.com; Đ 21 Han Thuyen; meals 95,000-185,000d; ☺7.30am-10.30pm) Colourful murals and retro Socialist posters brighten up this popular bistro with park views. The menu focuses on street-food classics from around Vietnam, all enjoyed with a bustling and energetic ambience. Salads are particularly good – try the wild pepper and green mango salad with BBQ chicken – and retreat to the 1st floor if downstairs is too crowded.

✖ Da Kao & Around

Pho Hoa   VIETNAMESE $

(Map p886; 260c Đ Pasteur; meals 60,000-75,000d; ☺6am-midnight) This long-running establishment is more upmarket than most but is definitely the real deal – as evidenced by its popularity with regular local patrons. Tables come laden with herbs, chilli and lime, as well as *gio chao quay* (fried Chinese bread), *banh xu xe* (glutinous coconut cakes with mung-bean paste) and *cha lua* (pork-paste sausages wrapped in banana leaves).

Banh Xeo 46A   VIETNAMESE $

(Map p886; ☑08-3824 1110; 46a Đ Dinh Cong Trang; regular/extra large 70,000/110,000d; ☺10am-9pm; ☑) Locals will always hit the restaurants that specialise in a single dish and this renowned spot serves some of the best *banh xeo* in town. These Vietnamese rice-flour pancakes stuffed with bean sprouts, prawns and pork (vegetarian versions available) are legendary. Other dishes available include excellent *goi cuon* (fresh summer rolls with pork and prawn).

✖ Pham Ngu Lao Area

Five Oysters   VIETNAMESE $

(Map p891; www.fiveoysters.com; 234 Đ Bui Vien; meals from 35,000d; ☺9am-11pm) With a strong seafood slant and friendly service, light and bright Five Oysters in backpack-erland is frequently packed with travellers feasting on oysters (30,000d), grilled octopus, seafood soup, snail pie, *pho,* fried noodles, grilled mackerel with chilli oil and

more. Bargain-priced beer also makes it a popular spot along the PNL strip.

An Lac Chay   VEGETARIAN $

(Map p888; Upstairs, 175/1 Đ Pham Ngu Lao; meals 35,000-100,000d; ☺8am-10pm; ☑) Head upstairs at the rear of the Margherita restaurant to An Lac Chay, a purely vegetarian restaurant offering an eclectic range of tasty choices, from Vietnamese sour soup through to four-cheese pizzas and Mexican dishes.

Coriander   THAI $

(Map p891; 16 Đ Bui Vien; meals 50,000-180,000d; ☺11am-2pm & 5-11pm) The blonde-wood furniture and cheap bamboo wallpaper do Coriander few favours, but the menu is stuffed with authentic Siamese delights. The lovely fried *doufu* (tofu) is almost a meal in itself, the green curry is zesty, and the claypot seafood fried rice is excellent.

Dinh Y   VEGETARIAN $

(Map p891; 171b Đ Cong Quynh; meals from 30,000d; ☺6am-9pm; ☑) Run by a friendly Cao Dai family, this humble eatery is in a very 'local' part of PNL near Thai Binh Market. The food is delicious and cheap.

🍷 Drinking & Nightlife

Action is concentrated around the Dong Khoi area, with everything from dives to designer bars. However, places in this zone generally close around 1am while Pham Ngu Lao rumbles on into the wee hours.

HCMC's hippest club nights include the semi-regular **Everyone's a DJ** (www.face book.com/everyonesadj) loft party and **Beats Saigon** (www.facebook.com/pages/The-Beats-Saigon/207148399324751).

SPLURGE

The **Racha Room** (Map p884; ☑0908 791 412; www.facebook.com/theracha room; 12-14 Đ Mac Thi Buoi; shared plates 195,000-320,000d; ☺11.30am-midnight) is one of the city's most hip eateries. Thai street food underpins the diverse menu of bar snacks (40,000d to 150,000d) and shared plates, but effortlessly stretches to include neighbouring countries as well. Asian-inspired cocktails ensure the Racha Room is also one of the city's best bars. Pop in for happy hour from 5pm to 7.30pm.

Dong Khoi Area

★Pasteur Street
Brewing Company   CRAFT BEER
(Map p884; www.pasteurstreet.com; 144 Đ Pasteur; small/large beer from 45,000/95,000d; ⊙11am-10pm; 🛜) Proving there's hoppy life beyond 333 lager, Pasteur Street Brewing turns out a fine selection of excellent craft beer. Brews utilise local ingredients, including lemongrass, rambutan and jasmine, and up to six different beers are always available. Great bar snacks – try the spicy Nashville fried chicken – are also served in Pasteur Street's hip upstairs tasting room.

The Workshop   COFFEE
(Map p884; www.facebook.com/the.workshop. coffee; 10 Đ Ngo Duc Ke; coffee from 45,000d; ⊙8am-8pm; 🛜) Coffee-geek culture comes to HCMC at this spacious upstairs warehouse space that's also perfect if you need to do some writing or other work. Single-origin fair-trade roasts from Dalat feature, and there's a great display of B&W photos of old Saigon to peruse while you're waiting for your Chemex or cold brew.

Vesper   BAR
(Map p884; www.facebook.com/vespersaigon; ground fl, Landmark Bldg, 5b Đ Ton Duc Thang; ⊙11am-late Mon-Sat) From the sinuous curve of the hardwood bar to the smoothly arranged bottles on the shelves, soft chill-out rhythms, funky caramel leather furniture and fine tapas menu, Vesper is a cool spot by the river. There's a roadside terrace, but traffic noise is epic.

Apocalypse Now   CLUB
(Map p884; ☑08-3824 1463; www.facebook.com/ apocalypsenowsaigon; 2c Đ Thi Sach; ⊙7pm-2am) 'Apo' has been around since 1991 and remains one of the must-visit clubs. A sprawling place with a big dance floor and an outdoor courtyard, the bar's eclectic cast combines travellers, expats, Vietnamese movers and shakers, plus the odd working girl. The music is thumping and it's apocalyptically rowdy. The 150,000d weekend charge gets you a free drink.

Broma: Not a Bar   BAR
(Map p884; www.facebook.com/bromabar; 41 Đ Nguyen Hue; ⊙5pm-2am) Compact and bohemian rooftop bar overlooking the busy pedestrian mall of Đ Nguyen Hue. Look forward to a good selection of international beers, live gigs, and DJs with a funk, hip-hop and electronica edge.

Pham Ngu Lao Area

The View   BAR
(Map p891; www.theviewrooftopbar.com; 8th fl, Duc Vuong Hotel, 195 Đ Bui Vien; ⊙10am-midnight Mon-Fri, to 2am Sat & Sun) Not as elevated as other rooftop bars around town, but less pretentious, and a whole lot easier on the wallet. It's still a good escape to look down on the heaving backpacker bustle of Pham Ngu Lao, and the food menu is also good value.

Le Pub   PUB
(Map p888; ☑08-3837 7679; www.lepub.org; 175/22 Đ Pham Ngu Lao; ⊙9am-2am; 🛜) The name says it all – British pub meets French cafe-bar – and the pomegranate-coloured result, ranging over three floors, is a hit. An extensive beer list, nightly promotions, cocktail jugs and pub grub draw in the crowds. The surrounding lane is becoming popular with a local after-dark crowd.

☆ Entertainment

Pick up the *Word HCMC*, *Asialife HCMC* or the *Guide* to find out what's on during your stay in Saigon, or log onto www.anyarena. com or www.thewordhcmc.com.

★Acoustic   LIVE MUSIC
(Map p888; ☑08-3930 2239; www.facebook.com/ acousticbarpage; 6e1 Đ Ngo Thoi Nhiem; ⊙7pm-midnight; 🛜) Don't be misled by the name: most of the musicians are fully plugged and dangerous when they take to the intimate stage of the city's leading live-music venue. And judging by the numbers that pack in, the crowd just can't get enough. It's at the end of the alley by the up-ended VW Beetle, and the cocktails are deceptively strong.

★Cargo   LIVE MUSIC
(Map p884; www.facebook.com/cargosaigon; Đ 7 Nguyen Tat Thanh; ⊙3pm-midnight Wed-Sun) Hugely popular spacious warehouse venue for up-and-coming local acts, regional bands and DJ events backed up by a great sound system; it's across the river in District 4.

Saigon Ranger   LIVE MUSIC
(Map p884; www.facebook.com/saigonranger; 5/7 Đ Nguyen Sieu; ⊙3pm-late Tue-Sun) Centrally located just a short stroll from Lam Son Park, Saigon Ranger is a raffish live music and performance venue with different acts from Tuesday to Sunday. Look forward to an eclectic roster of performers – including rock, blues and Latin sounds – with most gigs kicking off around 9pm.

Pham Ngu Lao Area

Golden Dragon Water Puppet Theatre WATER PUPPETS

(Map p888; ☑ 08-3930 2196; 55b Đ Nguyen Thi Minh Khai; ticket US$7.50) Saigon's main water-puppet venue, with shows starting at 5pm, 6.30pm and 7.45pm and lasting about 50 minutes.

🔒 Shopping

Among the tempting wares to be found in Saigon are embroidered silk shoes, miniature *cyclos* and fake Zippos engraved with GI philosophy. Boutiques along Đ Le Thanh Ton and Đ Pasteur sell handmade ready-to-wear fashion. In Pham Ngu Lao, shops sell ethnic-minority fabrics, handicrafts, T-shirts and various appealing accessories.

Ben Thanh Market (Cho Ben Thanh; Map p884; ĐL Le Loi, ĐL Ham Nghi, ĐL Tran Hung Dao & Đ Le Lai) has both everyday items and a lucrative tourist trade.

Mekong Quilts HANDICRAFTS

(Map p884; ☑ 08-2210 3110; www.mekong-quilts. org; 1st fl, 68 ĐL Le Loi; ☺ 9am-7pm) 🖋 For beautiful handmade silk quilts, sewn by the rural poor in support of a sustainable income.

Giant Step Urban Art Gallery ARTS

(Map p884; ☑ 0126 415 4338; 3a Đ Ton Duc Thang; ⊙ 11am-6pm Mon-Sat) Excellent gallery and retail outlet focusing on street art. Find it on Facebook to see what exhibitions are scheduled. The surrounding laneways are also packed with street art.

Saigon Kitsch SOUVENIRS

(Map p884; 33 Đ Ton That Thiep; ⊙ 9am-10pm) This colourful store specialises in reproduction propaganda posters, emblazoning its revolutionary motifs on coffee mugs, coasters, jigsaws and T-shirts. Also cool laptop and tablet covers fashioned from recycled Vietnamese packaging.

Orange CLOTHING, ACCESSORIES

(Map p891; 180 Đ Bui Vien; ⊙ 9am-10pm) Funky T-shirts and bags.

Mai Handicrafts HANDICRAFTS

(Map p883; ☑ 08-3844 0988; www.facebook.com/maivietnamesehandicrafts; 298 Đ Nguyen Trong Tuyen, Tan Binh District; ⊙ 9am-5pm Mon-Sat) 🌿 A fair-trade shop dealing in ceramics, ethnic fabrics and other gift items that, in turn, support disadvantaged families and street children. To get here, head northwest on Đl Hai Ba Trung, which becomes Đ Phan Dinh Phung and turn left on Đ Nguyen Trong Tuyen.

🛈 Information

DANGERS & ANNOYANCES

Be careful in the Dong Khoi area and along the Saigon riverfront, where motorbike 'cowboys' operate and specialise in bag, phone, tablet and camera snatching.

INTERNET ACCESS

Most hotels, cafes, restaurants and bars have free wi-fi. Internet cafes are everywhere.

MEDICAL SERVICES

International SOS (Map p886; ☑ 08-3829 8520; www.internationalsos.com; 167a Đ Nam Ky Khoi Nghia; ⊙ 24hr) Has an international team of doctors who speak English, French, Japanese and Vietnamese.

MONEY

Citibank (Map p884; 115 Đl Nguyen Hue) Citibank in the foyer of the Sun Wah Tower dispenses 8,000,000d, but only for Citibank cards (2,000,000d for other cards).

POST

Central Post Office (Map p884; 2 Cong Xa Paris; ⊙ 7am-9.30pm) Right across from Notre Dame Cathedral is the city's magnificent central post office.

TRAVEL AGENCIES

Dozens of travel agents offer tours of the Mekong Delta and other jaunts beyond HCMC. Some of the better ones include the following:

Handspan Adventure Travel (Map p883; ☑ 08-3925 7605; www.handspan.com; 10th fl, Central Park Bldg, 208 Nguyen Trai) Excellent, high-quality tours from this HCMC branch of the Hanoi-based travel agency.

Sinh Tourist (Map p888; ☑ 08-3838 9593; www.thesinhtourist.vn; 246 Đ De Tham; ⊙ 6.30am-10.30pm) Budget travel agency.

🛈 Getting There & Away

AIR

Jetstar Pacific Airlines (☑ 1900 1550; www.jetstar.com/vn/en/home) Flies to/from Hanoi, Hai Phong, Vinh, Hue, Phu Quoc, Nha Trang, Buon Ma Thuot, Dong Hoi and Danang.

VietJet Air (☑ 1900 1886; www.vietjetair.com) Flies to/from Hanoi, Haiphong, Vinh, Dong Hoi, Hue, Danang, Quy Nhon, Nha Trang, Dalat, Buon Ma Thuot and Phu Quoc Island.

Vietnam Air Service Company (VASCO; ☑ 08-3845 8017; www.vasco.com.vn) Flies to/from Rach Gia, Con Dao Islands and Ca Mau.

Vietnam Airlines (☑ 08-3832 0320; www.vietnamairlines.com) Flies to/from Hanoi, Hai Phong, Vinh, Dong Hoi, Hue, Danang, Quy Nhon, Nha Trang, Dalat, Buon Ma Thuot, Pleiku, Rach Gia and Phu Quoc Island.

BUS

Intercity buses operate from two main bus stations around HCMC. Local buses (from 4000d) travelling to the intercity bus stations leave from the local bus station opposite Ben Thanh Market.

TRANSPORT FROM HCMC

DESTINATION	AIR	BUS	TRAIN
Dalat	50min, from US$41	7hr, US$11-15	
Nha Trang	55min, from US$22	12hr, US$10-20	6½hr, US$14-32
Hue	80min, from US$48	29hr, US$26-37	18hr, US$17-44
Hanoi	2hr, from US$62	41hr, US$39-49	30hr, US$47-69

Open-tour buses conveniently depart and arrive in the Pham Ngu Lao area and are used by most backpackers. Many travellers buy a ticket to Hanoi (from US$45 to US$70), but you can also do short hops to destinations including Mui Ne, Nha Trang and Dalat. Sinh Tourist (p913) is a good company.

Plenty of international bus services connect HCMC and Cambodia, most with departures from the Pham Ngu Lao area. **Sapaco** (Map p891; ☑ 08-3920 3623; www.sapacotourist. vn; 325 Đ Pham Ngu Lao) has nine direct daily services to Phnom Penh (230,000d, six hours, departing between 6am and 3pm), as well as one to Siem Reap (450,000d, 12 hours, 6am).

Mien Dong Bus Station (Ben Xe Mien Dong; ☑ 08-3829 4056) Buses to locations north of HCMC leave from the immensely huge and busy Mien Dong bus station, in Binh Thanh District, about 5km from central HCMC on Hwy 13 (Quoc Lo 13; the continuation of Đ Xo Viet Nghe Tinh). The station is just under 2km north of the intersection of Đ Xo Viet Nghe Tinh and Đ Dien Bien Phu. Note that express buses depart from the eastern side, and local buses connect with the western side of the complex.

Mien Tay Bus Station (Ben Xe Mien Tay; ☑ 08-3825 5955; Đ Kinh Duong Vuong) This bus station serves all areas south of HCMC, which basically means the Mekong Delta. This huge station is about 10km west of HCMC in An Lac, a part of Binh Chanh District (Huyen Binh Chanh). Buses and minibuses from Mien Tay serve most towns in the Mekong Delta, using air-conditioned express buses and premium minibuses.

CAR

Hotels and travellers' cafes can arrange car rentals (from US$50 per day).

TRAIN

Trains from **Saigon Train Station** (Ga Sai Gon; ☑ 08-3823 0105; 1 Đ Nguyen Thong, District 3; ☺ ticket office 7.15-11am & 1-3pm) head north to many destinations. Purchase tickets from travel agents for a small booking fee at the train station.

ℹ Getting Around

TO/FROM THE AIRPORT

Tan Son Nhat Airport is 7km northwest of central HCMC. Metered taxis cost around 180,000d to/from the centre. Stick to either Mai Linh or Vinasun taxis.

Air-conditioned buses (route 152; 6000d, every 15 minutes 6am to 6pm) also run to and from the international airport terminal. These make regular stops along Đ De Tham (Pham Ngu Lao area) and at international hotels along Đ Dong Khoi.

GETTING TO CAMBODIA: HCMC TO PHNOM PENH

Getting to the border The busy Moc Bai/Bavet border crossing is the fastest land route between HCMC and Phnom Penh. Reliable bus companies to the Cambodian capital include Mekong Express (www.catmekongexpress.com) and Sapaco (www.sapacotourist.vn). Allow six hours for the trip.

At the border Cambodian visas (US$30) are issued at the border (you'll need a passport-sized photo).

Moving on Most travellers have a through ticket.

For information on doing this crossing in the opposite direction, see p85.

CYCLO

Cyclos are an interesting way to get around, but overcharging tourists is the norm. Short hops are 30,000d to 40,000d.

MOTORBIKE TAXI

Short hops are 30,000d.

TAXI

Metered taxis are very affordable; a 2km ride is about 25,000d. **Mai Linh Taxi** (☑ 08-3838 3838) and **Vinasun Taxi** (☑ 08-3827 2727) are reliable.

AROUND HO CHI MINH CITY

Cu Chi

If the tenacious spirit of the Vietnamese could be symbolised by a single place, then Cu Chi might be it. Its fame is such that it's become a place of pilgrimage for many Vietnamese, and a must-see for travellers.

⊙ Sights

Cu Chi Tunnels   HISTORIC SITE
(adult/child 110,000/30,000d) Two sections of this remarkable tunnel network (which are enlarged and upgraded versions of the real thing) are open to the public. One is near the village of Ben Dinh and the other is 15km beyond at Ben Duoc. Most tourists visiting the tunnels end up at Ben Dinh, as it's easier for

tour buses to reach. Even if you stay above ground, it's still an interesting experience learning about the region's ingenious and brave resistance activities.

**Cu Chi Wildlife
Rescue Station** WILDLIFE
(www.wildlifeatrisk.org; adult/child US$5/free; ⊘ 7.30-11.30am & 1-4.30pm) Just a few kilometres from the Ben Dinh tunnels, Cu Chi Wildlife Rescue Station is dedicated to the protection of wildlife that has been confiscated from owners or illegal traders. Animals include bears, otters and gibbons. There is an informative display on the rather depressing state of wildlife in Vietnam, including the 'room of death' featuring traps and baits.

Note that it's tough to navigate these back roads solo, so talk to a travel agent about incorporating a visit into a Cu Chi Tunnels trip.

Tay Ninh
☑ 066 / POP 127,000
Tay Ninh town serves as the headquarters of Cao Dai, one of Vietnam's most interesting indigenous religions. The **Cao Dai Great Temple** was built between 1933 and 1955. Victor Hugo is among the Westerners especially revered by the Cao Dai; look for his likeness at the Great Temple.

Tay Ninh is 96km northwest of HCMC. The Cao Dai Holy See complex is 4km east of Tay Ninh. One-day tours from Saigon, including Tay Ninh and the Cu Chi Tunnels, cost from US$7.

MEKONG DELTA

The 'rice bowl' of Vietnam, the Mekong Delta is a landscape carpeted in a dizzying variety of greens. It's also a water world where boats, houses, restaurants and even markets float upon the innumerable rivers, canals and streams that flow through like arteries.

Visitors can experience southern charm in riverside homestays, while Phu Quoc is a tropical island lined with white-sand beaches.

Delta tours are very convenient (book through travel agencies in Ho Chi Minh City) but independent travel is perfectly feasible, if sometimes time-consuming.

Vinh Long
☑ 070 / POP 151,000
Vinh Long is a noisy, chaotic transit hub, but the riverfront has plenty of cafes and restaurants. Close by are several worthwhile sites including the Cai Be floating market, beautiful islands, abundant orchards and atmospheric homestays.

Cuu Long Tourist (☑ 070-382 3616; www.cuulongtourist.com; 2 Đ Phan B Chau; ⊘ 7am-5pm) offers boat tours ranging from three hours (from US$15 per person) to three days.

Bustling **Cai Be Floating Market** (⊘ 5am-noon) is worth including on a boat tour from Vinh Long. Arrive early in the morning to see huge boats packed with tropical fruit and vegetables.

We suggest you don't stay in town; instead opt for a homestay.

Frequent buses go to HCMC (105,000d, three hours) and Can Tho (50,000d) from a bus station 2.5km south of town.

Can Tho
☑ 071 / POP 1.25 MILLION
Can Tho is the political, economic, cultural and transportation epicentre of the Mekong Delta. It's a buzzing city with a waterfront lined with sculpted gardens and an appealing blend of narrow backstreets and wide boulevards.

English-speaking **Hieu** (☑ 093 966 6156; www.hieutour.com; 27a Đ Le Thanh Ton) offers excellent trips to floating markets (from US$23), cycling excursions and food tours.

Cai Rang is the biggest floating market in the Mekong Delta, 6km from Can Tho; it's a morning affair. You can hire boats (about 120,000d per hour) on the river near the Can Tho market. Cai Rang is one hour away by boat, or you can drive to Cau Dau Sau boat landing, where you can get a rowing boat (per hour around 100,000d) to the market, 10 minutes away.

Less crowded and less motorised is the **Phong Dien Market**, 20km from Can Tho by road, which has more stand-up rowboats. It's best between 6am and 8am. You can hire a boat on arrival.

🛏 Sleeping & Eating
★ **Xoai Hotel** HOTEL $
(☑ 0907 652 927; http://hotelxoai.com; 93 Đ Mau Than; s/d 235,000/293,000d; ❄ @ 🛜) Fantastic

Mekong Delta

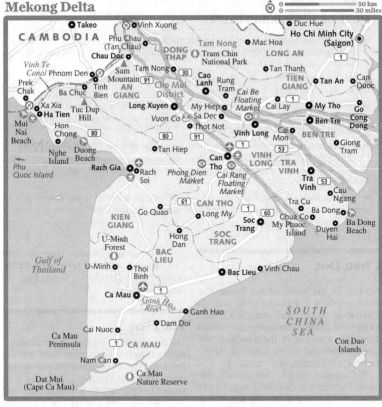

value at this friendly, efficient hotel with bright, mango-coloured (the hotel name means 'Mango Hotel'), airy rooms. Helpful staff speak excellent English and there's a roof terrace with hammocks.

Thanh Ha   GUESTHOUSE $
(📱0918 183 522; mshaguesthouse@gmail.com; 118/14 Đ Phan Dinh Phung; r US$12; ❉🛜) You'll find this guesthouse with a clutch of large, sparkling white rooms down a narrow alleyway that bustles quietly with local life. Ms Ha – the proprietress – is a character, and she can help arrange tours and rent you a bicycle or motorbike.

★ Nem Nuong Thanh Van   VIETNAMESE $
(cnr Nam Ky Khoi Nghia & 30 Thang 4; meals 45,000d; ⊗8am-9pm) The only dish this locally acclaimed little spot does is the best *nem nuong* in town. Roll your own rice rolls using the ingredients provided: pork sausage, rice paper, green banana, starfruit, cucum-

ber and a riot of fresh herbs, then dip into the peanut-and-something-else sauce, its secret jealously guarded. Simple and fantastic!

ℹ Getting There & Around

AIR

Can Tho's airport, 10km northwest of the centre, is served by Vietnam Airlines, Vietjet Air and Vasco with daily flights to Phu Quoc, Danang, HCMC and Hanoi and also Dalat (two weekly) and Con Dao (four weekly).

BOAT

Boat services include hydrofoils to Ca Mau (300,000d, three to four hours), passing through Phung Hiep.

BUS

All buses depart from a new bus station in the southwest of town. Destinations include HCMC Mien Tay terminal (110,000d, 3½ hours, every 30 minutes) and Chau Doc (from 105,000d, 3¼ hours, hourly).

OFF THE BEATEN TRACK

MORE OF THE MEKONG DELTA

Most tourists are on hit-and-run day trips from HCMC or passing through on their way to or from Cambodia, but it's not hard to get off the beaten track in the Mekong Delta. Here are some lesser-known regional gems:

➡ Check out some Khmer culture in **Tra Vinh**, home to a significant population of Cambodians and their beautiful temples.

➡ The Khmer kingdom of Funan once held sway over much of the lower Mekong; its principal port was at **Oc-Eo**, located near Long Xuyen. Archaeologists have found ancient Persian and Roman artefacts here.

➡ Birdwatching enthusiasts will want to make a diversion to **Tram Chin National Park** (◷7am-4pm) near Cao Lanh, a habitat for the rare eastern sarus crane. These huge birds are depicted on the bas-reliefs at Angkor and are only found here and in northwest Cambodia.

➡ The small and secluded beach resort of **Hon Chong** has the most scenic stretch of coastline on the Mekong Delta mainland. The big attractions here are Chua Hang Grotto, Duong Beach and Nghe Island.

Chau Doc

☑ 076 / POP 112,000

Perched on the banks of the Bassac River, Chau Doc is a charming town near the Cambodian border, with sizeable Chinese, Khmer and Cham communities. Its cultural diversity – apparent in the mosques, temples, churches and nearby pilgrimage sites – makes it a fascinating place to explore.

The popular nearby river crossing between Vietnam and Cambodia means many travellers pass through. Nearby Sam Mountain is a local beauty spot with terrific views over Cambodia.

War remnants near Chau Doc include Ba Chuc, the site of a Khmer Rouge massacre with a bone pagoda, and Tuc Dup Hill, where an expensive American bombing campaign in 1963 earned it the nickname Two Million Dollar Hill.

It's also possible to visit fish farms set up underneath floating houses on the river.

Mekong Tours (☑076-386 7817; www.mekongvietnam.com; 14 Đ Nguyen Huu Canh; ◷8am-8pm) is a reliable travel agent offering boat or bus transport to Phnom Penh, car rentals and boat trips on the Mekong.

Good budget places to stay include **Trung Nguyen Hotel** (☑076-356 1561; www.trungnguyenhotel.com.vn; 86 Đ Bach Dang; s/d US$15/17; ❀❅) and **Hai Chau** (☑076-626 0066; www.haichauhotel.com; 63 Đ Suong Nguyet Anh; s US$15, d US$18-28; ❀❅), while **Bay Bong** (22 Đ Thuong Dang Le; meals 50,000-100,000d; ◷9am-8pm) has excellent hotpots and soups.

There are very regular buses to both Can Tho (245,000d, 3½ hours) and HCMC (150,000d to 350,000d, 3½ hours) from the main bus station.

Ha Tien

Ha Tien's location on the Gulf of Thailand makes it feels a world away from the rice fields and rivers that typify the region. Dramatic limestone formations define the area, pepper tree plantations dot the hillsides and the town itself has a sleepy tropical charm. It's a transport hub for road links to the Cambodia border at Xa Xia/Prek Chak and boats to Phu Quoc.

As for hotels, family-run **Hai Yen** (☑077-385 1580; www.kshaiyen.com; 15 Đ To Chau; d/tr/q 300,000/370,000/450,000d; ❀❅) is good value, while for a real cheapie **Hai Van** (☑077-385 2872; www.khachsanhaivan.com; 55 Đ Lam Son; s/d from 200,000/250,000d; ❀❅) fits the bill. For cheap grub the **night market** (Đ Lam Son; meals from 20,000d; ◷5-9pm) can't be beat, while **Oasis** (☑077-370 1553; www.oasisbarhatien.com; Đ Tran Hau; meals 60,000-150,000; ◷9am-9pm; ❅) is a popular expat-run bar-restaurant; the owner provides good travel advice.

❶ Getting There & Away

Buses connect HCMC (200,000d, 10 hours) and Ha Tien; they also run to destinations including Chau Doc (130,000d to 200,000d), Rach Gia (60,000d) and Can Tho (from 180,000d). At the time of writing, the bus station was due to relocate to a large, purpose-built facility 1.5km south of the bridge by early 2016.

Phu Quoc Island

🎵 077 / POP 108,000

Fringed with idyllic beaches and with large tracts still covered in dense, tropical jungle, Phu Quoc has morphed from a sleepy backwater into a favoured escape. Beyond the resorts lining Long Beach there's still ample room for exploration and escaping. Dive the reefs, kayak the bays, eat up back-road miles on a motorbike, dine on fresh seafood or just lounge on the beach.

Despite increasing development (including a new international airport), close to 70% of the island is protected as Phu Quoc National Park.

Phu Quoc's rainy season is from late May to October; the peak season for tourism is between December and March.

⊙ Sights

Deserted white-sand beaches ring Phu Quoc.

Duong Dong   TOWN
The island's main town and chief fishing port on the central west coast is a tangle of budget hotels catering to domestic tourists, streetside stalls, bars and shops. The old bridge in town is a great vantage point to photograph the island's scruffy fishing fleet crammed into the narrow channel, and the filthy, bustling produce market makes for an interesting stroll.

Long Beach   BEACH
(Bai Truong) Long Beach is draped invitingly along the west coast from Duong Dong almost to An Thoi port. Development concentrates in the north near Duong Dong, where the recliners and rattan umbrellas of the various resorts rule; these are the only stretches that are kept garbage-free. With its west-facing aspect, sunsets here can be stupendous.

A motorbike or bicycle is necessary to reach some of the remote stretches flung out towards the southern end of the island.

An Thoi Islands   ISLAND
(Quan Dao An Thoi) Just off the southern tip of Phu Quoc, these 15 islands and islets can be visited by chartered boat. It's a fine area for sightseeing, fishing, swimming and snorkelling. **Hon Thom** (Pineapple Island) is about 3km in length and is the largest island in the group.

Most boats depart from An Thoi on Phu Quoc, but you can make arrangements through hotels on Long Beach, as well as dive operators. Boat trips generally do not run during the rainy season.

Sao Beach   BEACH
(Bai Sao) With picture-perfect white sand, the delightful curve of beautiful Sao Beach bends out alongside a sea of mineral-water clarity just a few kilometres from An Thoi, the main shipping port at the southern tip of the island. There are a couple of beachfront restaurants, where you can settle into

---

A NIGHT ON THE MEKONG

For many travellers, the chance to experience river life and to share a home-cooked meal with a local family is a highlight of a Mekong visit. Vinh Long offers many homestay options.

Ngoc Sang (🎵 070-385 8694; 95/8 Binh Luong, An Binh; per person 250,000d; ✽ 🛜) Most travellers love this friendly, canal-facing rustic homestay. The grandmother cooks up some wonderful local dishes, free bikes are available, the owner runs decent early-morning boat tours and there's a languid atmosphere about the place. The family seems shy when it comes to hanging out with the guests, though.

Phuong Thao Homestay (🎵 070-3836 854; en.phuongthaohomestay.com; An Binh; dm/d US$10/32; ✽ 🛜) Tucked away by the river, around 1.5km from the An Binh boat landing, this rustic guesthouse is run by the friendly Mr Phu, who speaks very good English and who can lend you bicycles and motorbikes to explore the island. Stay in the large, thatch-walled dorms with mozzie nets or the two concrete doubles; good ratio of guests per bathroom.

Ba Linh Homestay (🎵 070-385 8683, 0939 138 142; balinhhomestay@gmail.com; 95 An Thanh, An Binh; r 500,000d) Run by friendly Mr Truong, this traditional-looking and popular place has six simple, high-roofed, partitioned rooms in a line, all with fan. Breakfast and dinner is included in the price and you may get to try such local specialities as rice-field rat.

GETTING TO CAMBODIA: SOUTHERN BORDERS

Chau Doc to Phnom Penh

Getting to the border The Vinh Xuong/Kaam Samnor border crossing is located north-west of Chau Doc along the Mekong River. Several companies in Chau Doc sell boat journeys to Phnom Penh via the Vinh Xuong border. **Hang Chau** (☑ Chau Doc 076-356 2771, Phnom Penh 855-12-883 542; www.hangchautourist.com.vn; per person US$25) boats depart Chau Doc at 7.30am from a pier at 18 Đ Tran Hung Dao, arriving at 12.30pm.

At the border Cambodian visas are available, but minor overcharging is common.

For information on doing this crossing in the opposite direction, see p85.

Ha Tien to Kep

Getting to the border The Xa Xia/Prek Chak border crossing connects Ha Tien with Kep and Kampot on Cambodia's south coast. Several minibus companies leave Ha Tien for Cambodia at around 1pm, heading to Kep (US$9, one hour), Kampot (US$12, 1½ hours), Sihanoukville (US$15, four hours) and Phnom Penh (US$15, four hours). Book via Ha Tien Tourism.

At the border Cambodian visas are available at the border.

Moving on Most travellers opt for a through minibus ticket.

For information on doing this crossing in the opposite direction, see p128.

Chau Doc to Takeo

Getting to the border The Tinh Bien/Phnom Den border crossing is rarely used by travellers. A bus to Phnom Penh (US$25, five to six hours) passes through Chau Doc at around 7.30am; book through Mekong Tours (p896) in Chau Doc.

At the border Cambodian visas can be obtained here, although it's not uncommon to be charged US$35, several dollars more than the official rate.

Moving on Most travellers opt for a through bus ticket from Chau Doc.

For information on doing this crossing in the opposite direction, see p85.

---

a deckchair or partake in water sports. If heading down to Sao Beach by motorbike, fill up with petrol before the trip.

Phu Quoc National Park   NATURE RESERVE
About 90% of Phu Quoc is forested and the trees and adjoining marine environment enjoy official protection. This is the last large stand of forest in the south, and in 2010 the park was declared a Unesco Biosphere Reserve. The forest is densest in northern Phu Quoc, in the Khu Rung Nguyen Sinh forest reserve; you'll need a motorbike or mountain bike to tackle the bumpy dirt roads that cut through it. There are no real hiking trails.

🏃 Activities

Jerry's Jungle Tours (☑ 0938 226 021; www.jerrystours.wix.com; 112 Đ Tran Hung Dao; day trips from US$30) and **John's Tours** (☑ 0918 939 111; www.johnsislandtours.com; 4 Đ Tran Hung Dao; tours per person US$15-35) offer boat trips, snorkelling, fishing, motorbike tours, bouldering, birdwatching, hiking and cultural tours around Phu Quoc.

There's good scuba diving around Phu Quoc, but only during the dry months (from November to May). Two fun dives cost from US$70 to US$80; four-day PADI open water certification starts at US$340 and snorkelling trips cost around US$30. **Flipper Diving Club** (☑ 077-3994 924; www.flipperdiving.com; 60 Đ Tran Hung Dao; ⊙ 9am-9pm) and **Rainbow Divers** (☑ 0913 400 964; www.divevietnam.com; 11 Đ Tran Hung Dao; ⊙ 9am-6pm) are two good dive schools in the Duong Dong area.

There are several places to rent kayaks (around 80,000d per hour) on Sao Beach.

🛏 Sleeping

Most beachside accommodation options are at Long Beach. Expect to pay more here than elsewhere in Vietnam; accommodation prices also yo-yo depending on the season.

Long Beach

★**Langchia Hostel**   HOSTEL $
(☑0939 132 613; www.langchia-village.com; 84
Đ Tran Hung Dao; dm/d US$6/15; ❈☎☀) A fa-
vourite with solo travellers, this hostel gets
plenty of praise for the friendliness and
helpfulness of its staff, the lively bar with
pool table and the swimming pool to cool
down in. Dorm beds come with mozzie nets
and individual fans and it's worth paying extra for the decent breakfast.

**Mush'rooms
Backpacker Hostel**   HOSTEL $
(☑0937 942 017; www.mushroomsphuquoc.com;
170 Đ Tran Hung Dao; dm US$7, d US$12-15; ❈☎)
Pros? This colourful hostel is a great place to
meet fellow backpackers. Cons? The grungy
charm wears off when staff forget to clean
the rooms and bathrooms and veer between
being uncooperative and surly, the plug-in
fans struggle to cool the rooms and there's
not mush'room to move in the dorms.

Beach Club   RESORT $$
(☑077-398 0998; Ap Cua Lap, Xa Duong To; r US$25-
45; ❈☎) Run by an English-Vietnamese
couple, this is a great escape from the main-
drag bustle, with tightly grouped and well-
kept rooms and bungalows on a small plot,
plus a breezy beachside restaurant.

**Lan Anh
Garden Resort**   RESORT $$
(☑077-398 5985; www.lananhphuquoc.com.vn;
KP7 Tran Hung Dao; d US$58-75, f US$115; ❈☎☀)
Enticing little resort hotel with friendly, professional staff, a clutch of rooms arranged
around a small pool and motorbikes for
rent. Nab an upstairs room if you can for the
breezy verandahs.

Around the Island

Mango Garden   B&B $$
(☑077-629 1339; mangogarden.inn@gmail.com;
r US$38-55; ☉Oct-Mar; ❈@☎) Best suited
to those with their own (two) wheels, this
isolated B&B is reached by a bumpy dirt
road (turn left just before Sao Beach and
look for the signs) away from the beach.
Run by a Vietnamese-Canadian couple, the
Western-style, generator-powered B&B is
surrounded by gorgeous flower and mango
gardens, with solar showers and fishing and
snorkelling trips. Book ahead.

Freedomland   HOMESTAY $$
(☑077-399 4891; www.freedomlandphuquoc.com;
2 Ap Ong Lang, Xa Cua Duong; bungalow US$30-60;
☉Oct-Jun; ☎) With an emphasis on switching
off (no TV) and socialising – fun, communal
dinners are a mainstay – Freedomland has
11 basic bungalows (mozzie nets, fans,
solar-heated showers) scattered around a
shady plot. The beach is a five-minute walk
away, or you can slump in the hammocks
strung between the trees. Popular with solo
budget travellers; call ahead. Shut in the
rainy season.

✕ Eating & Drinking

Most hotels have on-site cafes or restaurants. The seafood restaurants in the fishing
village of Ham Ninh also offer an authentic
local experience.

✕ Duong Dong

Dinh Cau Night Market (Đ Vo Thi Sau; meals
from 70,000đ; ☉5pm-midnight) is one of the
most atmospheric (and affordable) places to
dine with a delicious range of Vietnamese
seafood, grills and vegetarian options.

Buddy Ice Cream   INTERNATIONAL $$
(www.visitphuquoc.info; 6 Đ Bach Dang; meals
80,000-180,000đ; ☉8am-10pm; ☎) With the
coolest music in town, this cafe is excellent
for sides of tourist info with its New Zealand
ice-cream combos, toasted sandwiches, fish
'n' chips, thirst-busting fruit juices, shakes,
smoothies, all-day breakfasts, comfy sofas
and book exchange.

✕ Long Beach

Rory's Beach Bar (118/10 Đ Tran Hung Dao;
☉9am-late) is the liveliest bar on the island,
with bonfires on the beach and great happy
hour specials.

Winston's Burgers & Beer   BURGERS $
(121 Đ Tran Hung Dao; burgers from 70,000đ;
☉1-9pm) The name says it all: this bar is all
about (really good) burgers, beer and a large
selection of cocktails, mixed by the epon-
ymous Winston. Linger for a chat or chal-
lenge your drinking companions to a game
of Connect 4.

Alanis Deli   CAFE $
(98 Đ Tran Hung Dao; pancakes from 80,000đ;
☉8am-10pm; ☎) Fab caramel pancakes, Amer-
ican breakfast combos, plus good (if pricey)
coffees and wonderfully friendly service.

★**Spice House at**
Cassia Cottage   VIETNAMESE $$
(www.cassiacottage.com; 100C Đ Tran Hung Dao; meals 180,000-300,000d; ⊘7-10am & 11am-10pm) Nab a beachside high-table, order a papaya salad, grilled garlic prawns, a cinnamon-infused okra, a delectable fish curry, or grilled beef skewers wrapped in betel leaves and time dinner to catch the sunset at this excellent restaurant.

ℹ Information

There are ATMs in Duong Dong and in many resorts on Long Beach. Buddy Ice Cream (p899) offers free internet and wi-fi.

ℹ Getting There & Away

AIR

There are international flights to Singapore and Siem Reap. Vietnam Airlines, VietJet Air and Jetstar between them offer daily flights to Can Tho, Hanoi, HCMC and Rach Gia.

Demand can be high in peak season, so book ahead

BOAT

Fast boats connect Phu Quoc to both Ha Tien (1½ hours) and Rach Gia (2½ hours). Five virtually identical operators, including **Duong Dong Express** (⌨ Phu Quoc 077-399 0747, Rach Gia 077-387 9765) and **Superdong** (⌨ 077-387 7742), run several daily fast boats from Rach Gia to Bai Vong (per passenger 250,000d).

Three daily fast ferries (230,000d) from Ha Tien arrive at the Ham Ninh port, just north of Bai Vong. There are also car ferries to/from Ha Tien and Phu Quoc's Da Chong port.

ℹ Getting Around

The island's airport is 10km from Duong Dong; a taxi costs around 100,000d to Long Beach.

Bicycles/motorbikes are available through most hotels from 70,000/120,000d per day.

There is a skeletal bus service (every hour or two) between An Thoi and Duong Dong. A bus (20,000d) waits for the ferry at Bai Vong to take passengers to Duong Dong.

Motorbike taxis are everywhere. Short hops cost 20,000d; figure on around 50,000d for about 5km.

Call **Mai Linh** (⌨ 077-397 9797) for a reliable taxi.

UNDERSTAND VIETNAM

Vietnam Today

Two decades of rising, sustained growth has transformed Vietnam. Change is most apparent in the big cities, where steel-and-glass highrises define skylines and a burgeoning middle class now has the spending power to enjoy air-conditioned living and overseas travel. Yet in rural areas the nation's new-found prosperity is less evident, and up in the highlands, life remains a day-to-day struggle for millions of minority people.

The Big Picture

In the 40 years since the end of the American War, Vietnam has made giant strides. A victorious, though bankrupt, nation has worked around the clock, grafting its way forward, overcoming a series of formidable hurdles (including a 19-year US trade embargo). Per capita income has grown from US$98 in 1993 to over US$2000 by 2015, and today Vietnam is one of the 10 fastest-growing economies in the world, boosted by strong manufacturing. Startup business numbers are booming. And yet this rapid development is disjointed. The state sector remains huge, controlling around two-fifths of the economy – 100 of the 200 biggest Vietnamese companies are state-owned (including oil production, shipbuilding, cement and coal). Many of these operations haemorrhage money.

The spectre of corruption casts a shadow over development every step of the way. Transparency International ranked Vietnam the lowest of all the Asia-Pacific countries it measured in 2014. Corruption scandals emerge on a daily basis, such as the nine Vinashin shipbuilding execs jailed following the company's near-collapse under US$4.5 billion of debt. For most Vietnamese people corruption is simply a part of day-to-day life, as they have to pay backhanders for everything from securing a civil service job to an internet connection.

North & South

The Vietnamese economy has been buoyant for 20 years, but some areas are more buoyant than others. In 2015 Ho Chi Minh City's economy was growing at 8.6%, well above that in the North. It's the South that's benefited most from inward investment as Viet Kieu (overseas Vietnamese, the vast majority of whom are southerners) have returned and invested in the region.

The government is aware of these divisions and tries to balance the offices of state, so if the prime minister is from the South, the head of the Communist Party is from the North.

When it comes to the older generation, the South has never forgiven the North for bulldozing their war cemeteries, imposing communism and blackballing whole families. The North has never forgiven the South for siding with the Americans against their own people. Luckily for Vietnam, the new generation seems to have less interest in the country's harrowing history.

Uneasy Neighbours

On the surface Vietnam and its northern neighbour China have much in common, with a shared heritage, common frontier and all-powerful ruling Communist parties. But for the Vietnamese, China represents something of an overbearing big brother (and 1000 years of subordination). The nations fought a recent on-off border war which rumbled on for years, only ending in 1990. In a 2014 survey over 80% of Vietnamese were concerned that another conflict could erupt over offshore islands in the South China Sea (always the 'East Sea' in Vietnam). China claims virtually the whole area, and is busy constructing port facilities and airstrips. In May 2014 anti-Chinese riots erupted in several provinces, resulting in at least 21 deaths, in response to China deploying an oil rig in the Paracel Islands. Thousands of Chinese nationals fled the country. By November 2015 tensions remained but the situation had calmed enough for President Xi Jinping to visit Hanoi as the countries sought to repair ties.

The two nations have plenty of common ground. Trade has continued to boom (though it is more one way than the Vietnamese would like), reaching US$58 billion in 2014, and Chinese is the second most popular foreign language studied in Vietnam. Ultimately, Presidents Trong and Xi signed various cooperation agreements concerning investment and infrastructure but little progress was evident over territorial disputes.

History

Early Vietnam

The Vietnamese trace their roots back to the Red River Delta where farmers first cultivated rice. Millennia of struggle against the Chinese then followed. Vietnam only became a united state in the 19th century, but quickly faced the ignominy of French colonialism and then the devastation of the American intervention. The Vietnamese nation has survived tempestuous, troubled times, but its strength of character has served it well. Today the signs are it's continuing to grow with some promise.

The sophisticated Indianised kingdom of Funan flourished from the 1st to 6th centuries AD in the Mekong Delta area. Archaeological evidence reveals that Funan's busy trading port of Oc-Eo had contact with China, India, Persia and even the Mediterranean. Between the mid-6th century and the 9th century, the Funan empire was absorbed by the pre-Angkorian kingdom of Chenla.

Meanwhile, around present-day Danang, the Hindu kingdom of Champa emerged in the late 2nd century AD. Like Funan, it adopted Sanskrit as a sacred language and borrowed heavily from Indian art and culture. By the 8th century Champa had expanded to include what is now Nha Trang and Phan Rang. The Cham warred constantly with the Vietnamese to the north and the

BEST FILMS

Apocalypse Now (1979) The American War depicted as an epic 'heart of darkness' adventure.

The Deer Hunter (1978) Examines the psychological breakdown suffered by small-town servicemen.

Platoon (1986) Based on the first-hand experiences of the director, it follows idealistic volunteer Charlie Sheen to 'Nam.

Cyclo (1995) Visually stunning masterpiece that cuts to the core of HCMC's underworld.

The Quiet American (2002) Atmospherically set in Saigon during the French colonial period, with rebellion in the air.

THE WAY IT IS

Vietnam's political system could not be simpler: the Communist Party is the sole source of power. Officially, according to the Vietnamese constitution, the National Assembly (or parliament) is the country's supreme authority, but in practice it's a tool of the party and carefully controlled elections ensure 90% of delegates are Communist Party members.

Khmers to the south and ultimately found themselves squeezed between these two great powers.

Chinese Occupation

The Chinese conquered the Red River Delta in the 2nd century BC and over the following centuries attempted to impress a centralised state system on the Vietnamese. There were numerous small-scale rebellions against Chinese rule – which was characterised by tyranny, forced labour and insatiable demands for tribute – between the 3rd and 6th centuries, but all were defeated.

However, the early Viets learned much from the Chinese, including advanced irrigation for rice cultivation and medical knowledge as well as Confucianism, Taoism and Mahayana Buddhism. Much of the 1000-year period of Chinese occupation was typified by both Vietnamese resistance and the adoption of many Chinese cultural traits.

In AD 938 Ngo Quyen destroyed Chinese forces on the Bach Dang River, winning independence and signalling the start of a dynastic tradition. During subsequent centuries the Vietnamese successfully repulsed foreign invaders, including the Mongols, and absorbed the kingdom of Champa in 1471 as they expanded south.

Contact with the West

In 1858 a joint military force from France and the Spanish colony of the Philippines stormed Danang after several missionaries were killed. Early the next year, Saigon was seized. By 1883 the French had imposed a Treaty of Protectorate on Vietnam. French rule often proved cruel and arbitrary. Ultimately, the most successful resistance came

from the communists, first organised by Ho Chi Minh in 1925.

During WWII the only group that significantly resisted the Japanese occupation was the communist-dominated Viet Minh. When WWII ended, Ho Chi Minh – whose Viet Minh forces already controlled large parts of the country – declared Vietnam independent. French efforts to reassert control soon led to violent confrontations and full-scale war. In May 1954 Viet Minh forces overran the French garrison at Dien Bien Phu.

The Geneva Accords of mid-1954 provided for a temporary division of Vietnam at the Ben Hai River. When Ngo Dinh Diem, the anti-communist, Catholic leader of the southern zone, refused to hold the 1956 elections, the Ben Hai line became the border between North and South Vietnam.

The War in Vietnam

Around 1960 the Hanoi government changed its policy of opposition to the Diem regime from one of 'political struggle' to one of 'armed struggle'. The National Liberation Front (NLF), a communist guerrilla group better known as the Viet Cong (VC), was founded to fight against Diem.

An unpopular ruler, Diem was assassinated in 1963 by his own troops. When the Hanoi government ordered North Vietnamese Army (NVA) units to infiltrate the South in 1964, the situation for the Saigon regime became desperate. In 1965 the USA committed its first combat troops, soon joined by soldiers from South Korea, Australia, Thailand and New Zealand in an effort to bring global legitimacy to the conflict.

As Vietnam celebrated the Lunar New Year in 1968, the VC launched a surprise attack, known as the Tet Offensive, marking a crucial turning point in the war. Many Americans, who had for years believed their government's insistence that the USA was winning, started demanding a negotiated end to the war. The Paris Agreements, signed in 1973, provided for a ceasefire, the total withdrawal of US combat forces and the release of American prisoners of war.

Reunification

Saigon surrendered to the NVA on 30 April 1975. Vietnam's reunification by the communists meant liberation from more than a century of colonial oppression, but was soon followed by large-scale internal repression.

Hundreds of thousands of southerners fled Vietnam, creating a flood of refugees for the next 15 years.

Vietnam's campaign of repression against the ethnic Chinese, plus its invasion of Cambodia at the end of 1978, prompted China to attack Vietnam in 1979. The war lasted only 17 days, but Chinese-Vietnamese mistrust lasted for well over a decade.

Post-Cold War

After the collapse of the Soviet Union in 1991, Vietnam and Western nations sought rapprochement. The 1990s brought foreign investment and Association of Southeast Asian Nations (Asean) membership. The US established diplomatic relations with Vietnam in 1995, and Bill Clinton and George W Bush visited Hanoi. Vietnam was welcomed into the World Trade Organization (WTO) in 2007.

In recent years friction has grown between Vietnam and China over territorial claims in the South China Sea, and there were anti-Chinese riots in 2014. Conversely, relations between the USA and Vietnam have become much warmer, with booming bilateral trade.

People & Culture

The Vietnamese are battle-hardened, proud and nationalist, as they have earned their stripes in successive skirmishes with the world's mightiest powers. But that's the older generation, who remember every inch of the territory for which they fought. For the new generation, Vietnam is a place to succeed, a place to ignore the staid structures set in stone by the communists, and a place to go out and have some fun.

As in other parts of Asia, life revolves around the family; there are often several generations living under one roof. Poverty, and the transition from a largely agricultural society to that of a more industrialised nation, sends many people seeking their fortune to the bigger cities, and is changing the structure of the modern family unit. Women make up 52% of the nation's workforce but are not well represented in positions of power.

Vietnam's population is 84% ethnic Vietnamese (Kinh) and 2% ethnic Chinese; the rest is made up of Khmers, Chams and members of more than 50 minority peoples, who mainly live in highland areas.

VIETNAM PEOPLE & CULTURE

UNCLE OF THE PEOPLE

Father of the nation, Ho Chi Minh (Bringer of Light) was the son of a fiercely nationalistic scholar-official. Born Nguyen Tat Thanh near Vinh in 1890, he was educated in Hue and adopted many pseudonyms during his momentous life. Many Vietnamese affectionately refer to him as Bac Ho (Uncle Ho) today.

In 1911 he signed up as a cook's apprentice on a French ship, sailing the seas to North America, Africa and Europe. While odd-jobbing in England and France as a gardener, snow sweeper, waiter, photo-retoucher and stoker, his political consciousness developed.

Ho Chi Minh moved to Paris, where he mastered languages including English, French, German and Mandarin and began to promote the issue of Indochinese independence. He was a founding member of the French Communist Party in 1920.

In 1941 Ho Chi Minh returned to Vietnam for the first time in 30 years, and established the Viet Minh (whose goal was independence from France). As Japan prepared to surrender in August 1945, Ho Chi Minh led the August Revolution, and his forces then established control throughout much of Vietnam.

The return of the French compelled the Viet Minh to conduct a guerrilla war, which ultimately led to victory against the colonists at Dien Bien Phu in 1954. Ho then led North Vietnam until his death in September 1969 – he never lived to see the North's victory over the South.

Since then the party has worked hard to preserve the image and reputation of Bac Ho. His image dominates contemporary Vietnam. This cult of personality is in stark contrast to the simplicity with which Ho lived his life. For more Ho, check out *Ho Chi Minh*, the excellent biography by William J Duiker.

VIETNAM PEOPLE & CULTURE

Religion

Over the centuries, Confucianism, Taoism and Buddhism have fused with popular Chinese beliefs and ancient Vietnamese animism to form what's collectively known as the Triple Religion (Tam Giao). Most Vietnamese people identify with this belief system, but if asked, they'll usually say they're Buddhist. Vietnam also has a significant percentage of Catholics (8% to 10% of the total population).

Cao Daism is a unique and colourful Vietnamese sect that was founded in the 1920s. It combines secular and religious philosophies of the East and West, and is based on seance messages revealed to the group's founder, Ngo Minh Chieu.

There are also small numbers of Muslims (around 65,000) and Hindus (50,000).

Etiquette

Take your time to learn a little about the local culture in Vietnam.

➡ Respect local dress standards: shorts to the knees, women's tops covering the shoulders, particularly at religious sites. Remove your shoes before entering a temple. Topless or nude sunbathing is totally inappropriate.

➡ Exchanging business cards is an important part of even the smallest transaction or business contact. Hand them out like confetti.

➡ Leaving a pair of chopsticks sitting vertically in a rice bowl looks very much like the incense sticks that are burned for the dead. This is not appreciated anywhere in Asia.

➡ Remove shoes when entering somebody's home. Don't point the bottom of your feet towards other people. Never, ever point your feet towards anything sacred, such as a Buddha image.

➡ As a form of respect to elderly or other esteemed people, such as monks, take off your hat and bow your head politely when addressing them. The head is the symbolic highest point – never pat or touch a person on the head.

Arts

CONTEMPORARY ART & MUSIC

It is possible to catch modern dance, classical ballet and stage plays in Hanoi and Ho Chi Minh City.

The work of contemporary painters and photographers covers a wide swathe of styles and gives a glimpse into the modern Vietnamese psyche; there are good galleries in Hanoi, HCMC and Hoi An.

Youth culture is most vibrant in HCMC and Hanoi, where there's more freedom for musicians and artists. There's a small but growing hip-hop scene, with HCMC-born Suboi acknowledged as Vietnam's leading female artist; she raps to eclectic beats including dubstep rhythms. Hot bands include rock band Microwave, metal merchants Black Infinity, punk band Giao Chi and alt-roots band 6789.

ARCHITECTURE

The Vietnamese were not great builders like their neighbours the Khmer. Early Vietnamese structures were made of wood and other materials that proved highly vulnerable in the tropical climate. The grand exceptions are the stunning towers built by Vietnam's ancient Cham culture. These are most numerous in central Vietnam. The Cham ruins at My Son are a major draw.

SCULPTURE

Vietnamese sculpture has traditionally centred on religious themes and has functioned as an adjunct to architecture, especially that of pagodas, temples and tombs.

The Cham civilisation produced exquisite carved sandstone figures for its Hindu and Buddhist sanctuaries. The largest single collection of Cham sculpture is at the Museum of Cham Sculpture in Danang.

WATER PUPPETRY

Vietnam's ancient art of *roi nuoc* (water puppetry) originated in northern Vietnam at least 1000 years ago. Developed by rice farmers, the wooden puppets were manipulated by puppeteers using water-flooded rice paddies as their stage. Hanoi is the best place to see water-puppetry performances, which are accompanied by music played on traditional instruments.

Food & Drink

Food

Vietnamese food is one of the world's greatest cuisines; there are said to be nearly 500 traditional dishes. It varies a lot between North, centre and South. Soy sauce, Chinese influence and hearty soups like *pho* typify northern cuisine. Central Vietnamese food is known for its prodigious use of fresh herbs and intricate flavours; Hue imperial cuisine and Hoi An specialities are key to this area. Southern food is sweet, spicy and tropical – its curries will be familiar to lovers of Thai and Cambodian food. Everywhere you'll find that Vietnamese meals are superbly prepared and excellent value.

Most restaurants trade seven days a week, opening around 7am or 8am and closing around 9pm, often later in the big cities.

FRUIT

Aside from the usual delightful Southeast Asian fruits, Vietnam has its own unique *trai thanh long* (green dragon fruit), a bright fuchsia-coloured fruit with green scales. Grown mainly in the coastal region near Nha Trang, it has white flesh flecked with edible black seeds, and tastes something like a mild kiwifruit.

MEALS

Pho is the noodle soup that built a nation and is eaten at all hours of the day, but especially for breakfast. *Com* are rice dishes. You'll see signs saying *pho* and *com* everywhere. Other noodle soups to try are *bun bo Hue* and *hu tieu*.

Spring rolls (*nem* in the North, *cha gio* in the South) are a speciality. These are normally dipped in *nuoc mam* (fish sauce), though many foreigners prefer soy sauce (*xi dau* in the North, *nuoc tuong* in the South).

Because Buddhist monks of the Mahayana tradition are strict vegetarians, *an chay* (vegetarian cooking) is an integral part of Vietnamese cuisine.

SNACKS

Street stalls or roaming vendors are everywhere, selling steamed sweet potatoes, rice porridge and ice-cream bars even in the wee hours.

There are also many other Vietnamese nibbles to try, including the following:

Bap xao Made from stir-fried fresh corn, chillies and tiny shrimp.

Bo bia Nearly microscopic shrimp, fresh lettuce and thin slices of Vietnamese sausage rolled up in rice paper and dipped in a spicy-sweet peanut sauce.

Sinh to Shakes made with milk and sugar or yoghurt, and fresh tropical fruit.

VIETNAMESE COFFEE CULTURE

Enjoying a Vietnamese coffee is a tradition that can't be rushed. A glass tumbler with a curious aluminium top is placed before you while you crouch on a tiny plastic chair. A layer of condensed milk on the bottom of the glass is gradually infused with coffee lazily drop, drop, dropping from the aluminium top. Minutes pass, and eventually a darker caffeine-laden layer floats atop the condensed milk. Stir it together purposefully – maybe pouring it over ice in a separate glass – and it's definitely an energising ritual worth waiting for. While you're waiting, consider the *caphe* variations usually on offer in a Vietnamese cafe.

Caphe sua da Iced coffee with condensed milk.

Caphe da Iced coffee without milk.

Caphe den Black coffee.

Caphe sua chua Iced coffee with yoghurt.

Caphe trung da Coffee topped with a beaten egg white.

THERE'S SOMETHING FISHY AROUND HERE...

Nuoc mam (fish sauce) is the one ingredient that is quintessentially Vietnamese, and it lends a distinctive character to Vietnamese cooking. The sauce is made by fermenting highly salted fish in large ceramic vats for four to 12 months. Connoisseurs insist high-grade sauce has a much milder aroma than the cheaper variety. Dissenters insist it is a chemical weapon. It's very often used as a dipping sauce, and takes the place occupied by salt on a Western table.

SWEETS

Many sticky confections are made from sticky rice, like *banh it nhan dau,* which also contains sugar and bean paste and is sold wrapped in banana leaf.

Most foreigners prefer *kem* (ice cream) or *yaourt* (yoghurt), which is generally of good quality.

Try *che,* a cold, refreshing sweet soup made with sweetened black bean, green bean or corn. It's served in a glass with ice and sweet coconut cream on top.

Drink

ALCOHOLIC DRINKS

Memorise the words *bia hoi,* which mean 'draught beer'. Probably the cheapest beer in the world, *bia hoi* starts at around 5000d a glass, so anyone can afford a round. Places that serve *bia hoi* usually also serve cheap food.

Several foreign labels brewed in Vietnam under licence include Tiger, Carlsberg and Heineken.

National and regional brands include Halida and Hanoi in the North, Huda and Larue in the centre, and BGI and 333 *(ba ba ba)* in the South.

Wine and spirits are available but at higher prices. Local brews are cheaper but not always drinkable.

NONALCOHOLIC DRINKS

Whatever you drink, make sure that it's been boiled or bottled. Ice is generally safe on the tourist trail, but may not be elsewhere.

Vietnamese *cà phê* (coffee) is fine stuff and there is no shortage of cafes in which to sample it. See p905 for more information.

Foreign soft drinks are widely available in Vietnam. An excellent local treat is *soda chanh* (carbonated mineral water with lemon and sugar) or *nuoc chanh nong* (hot, sweetened lemon juice).

Environment

Environmental consciousness is low in Vietnam. Rapid industrialisation, deforestation and pollution are major problems facing the country.

Unsustainable logging and farming practices, as well as the extensive spraying of defoliants by the US during the war, have contributed to deforestation. This has resulted not only in significant loss of biological diversity, but also in a harder existence for many minority people.

The country's rapid economic and population growth over the last decade – demonstrated by the dramatic increase in industrial production, motorbike numbers and helter-skelter construction – has put additional pressure on the already-stressed environment.

The Land

Vietnam stretches more than 1600km along the east coast of the Indochinese peninsula. The country's land area is 329,566 sq km, making it slightly larger than Italy and a bit smaller than Japan.

As the Vietnamese are quick to point out, it resembles a *don ganh,* or the ubiquitous bamboo pole with a basket of rice slung from each end. The baskets represent the main rice-growing regions of the Red River Delta in the north and the Mekong Delta in the south.

Of several interesting geological features found in Vietnam, the most striking are its spectacular karst formations (limestone peaks with caves and underground streams). The northern half of Vietnam has a spectacular array of karst areas, particularly around Halong Bay and Phong Nha.

Wildlife

We'll start with the good news. Despite some disastrous bouts of deforestation, Vietnam's flora and fauna is still incredibly exotic and varied. The nation has an estimated 12,000 plant species, only 7000 of which have been identified; more than 275 species of mammal; 800 species of bird; 180 species of reptile; and 80 species of amphibian. The other side of the story is that despite this outstanding diversity, the threat to Vietnam's remaining wildlife has never been greater due to poaching, hunting and habitat loss. Three of the nation's iconic animals – the elephant, the saola and the tiger – are on the brink. It's virtually certain that the last wild Vietnamese rhino was killed inside Cat Tien National Park in 2010. And for every trophy animal there are hundreds of other less 'headline' species that are being cleared from forests and reserves for the sake of profit (or hunger).

Many officials still turn a blind eye to the trade in wildlife for export and domestic consumption, though laws are now in place to protect the animals. Poachers continue to profit from meeting the demand for exotic animals for pets and traditional medicines.

National Parks

There are 31 national parks and over 150 nature reserves; officially, 9% of the nation's territory is protected. In the North the most interesting and accessible include Cat Ba, Bai Tu Long, Ba Be and Cuc Phuong. Heading south Phong Nha-Ke Bang, Bach Ma National Park, Yok Don National Park and Cat Tien National Park are well worth investigating.

SURVIVAL GUIDE

ℹ Directory A–Z

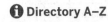

ACCOMMODATION

In general, accommodation in Vietnam offers superb value for money and excellent facilities. In big cities and the main tourism centres you'll find everything from hostel dorm beds to luxe hotels. Cleanliness is generally good and there are very few real dumps.

Most hotels in Vietnam quote prices in Vietnamese dong and/or US dollars.

Hostel dorm beds (around US$5 to US$10) are usually the cheapest options, but these only exist in the main backpacker centres. Guesthouses are the next level up, and rooms here often have private bathrooms and cost from around US$9 to US$20. A class above guesthouses, mini-hotels typically come with more amenities, such as satellite TV.

When it comes to midrange places, flash a bit more cash and three-star touches are available, such as chic decor or access to a swimming pool. Be aware that some hotels apply a 10% sales tax.

Accommodation is at a premium during Tet (late January or early February), when the whole country is on the move and overseas Vietnamese flood back into the country. Prices can rise by 25% or more. Christmas and New Year represent another high season.

Price Ranges

The following price ranges refer to a double room with bathroom in high season.

$ less than 560,000d (US$25)

$$ 560,000d to 1,680,000d (US$25 to US$75)

$$$ more than 1,680,000d (US$75)

POLLUTION WOES

Vietnam has a serious pollution problem. In Ho Chi Minh City the air quality is punishing, while Hanoi is the most contaminated city in Southeast Asia. Vehicles discharge such toxic substances as sulphur dioxide and nitrogen oxide. Motorbikes are the main culprits, all running on low-quality fuel that has choking levels of benzene, sulphur and microscopic dust (PM10). Particulate (dust, grime) matter in Hanoi is around 150 micrograms per cu metre, whereas the World Health Organization recommends a limit of 20.

Water pollution affects many regions, particularly the cities and coastal areas (where groundwater has become saline due to over-exploitation). Manufacturers have flooded into Vietnam to build clothing, footwear and food-processing plants, but most industrial parks have no waste-water treatment plants. The result is that discharge has caused biological death for rivers like the Thi Van. Nationwide only 14% of all city waste water is treated.

Toxic and industrial waste is illegally imported along with scrap for use as raw materials for production and for re-export. Enforcement is lax, though some violators have been fined.

HOMESTAYS

Homestays are popular in parts of Vietnam. These are usually well organised in specific villages, including several minority areas. Often the accommodation is in a longhouse or communal space with people sleeping on roll-up mattresses.

Areas that are well set up include Vinh Long in the Mekong Delta, the Cham islands, Mai Chau and Ba Be National Park.

CHILDREN

Children get to have a good time in Vietnam. There are some great beaches, but pay close attention to any playtime in the sea.

Kids generally enjoy local cuisine, which is rarely too spicy; the range of fruit is staggering. Comfort food from home (pizzas, pasta, burgers and ice cream) is available in most places too.

With babies and infants, the main worry is keeping an eye on what they're putting in their mouths: dysentery, typhoid and hepatitis are common.

Keep hydration levels up, and slap on the sunscreen.

ELECTRICITY

Voltage is 220V, 50 cycles. Sockets are two pin, round head.

EMBASSIES & CONSULATES

Australian Embassy (Map p817; ☑ 04-3774 0100; www.vietnam.embassy.gov.au; 8 Đ Dao Tan, Ba Dinh District, Hanoi)

Australian Consulate (Map p884; ☑ 08-3521 8100; www.hcmc.vietnam.embassy.gov.au; 20th fl, Đ 47 Ly Tu Truong, Vincom Center, Ho Chi Minh City)

Cambodian Embassy (Map p817; camemb. vnm@mfa.gov.kh; 71A P Tran Hung Dao, Hanoi)

Cambodian Consulate (Map p886; ☑ 08-3829 2751; camcg.hcm@mfa.gov.kh; 41 Đ Phung Khac Khoan, HCMC)

Canadian Embassy (Map p822; www.canada international.gc.ca/vietnam; 31 Đ Hung Vuong, Hanoi)

Canadian Consulate (Map p884; ☑ 08-3827 9899; hochi@international.gc.ca; 10th fl, 235 Đ Dong Khoi, HCMC)

Chinese Embassy (Map p822; ☑ 04-8845 3736; http://vn.china-embassy.org/chn; 46 P Hoang Dieu, Hanoi)

Chinese Consulate (Map p886; ☑ 08-3829 2457; http://hcmc.chineseconsulate.org; 175 Đ Hai Ba Trung, HCMC)

French Embassy (Map p817; ☑ 04-3944 5700; www.ambafrance-vn.org; P Tran Hung Dao, Hanoi)

French Consulate (Map p886; www.consul-france-hcm.org; 27 Đ Nguyen Thi Minh Khai, HCMC)

German Embassy (Map p822; ☑ 04-3845 3836; www.hanoi.diplo.de; 29 Đ Tran Phu, Hanoi)

German Consulate (Map p886; ☑ 08-3829 1967; www.ho-chi-minh-stadt.diplo.de; 126 Đ Nguyen Dinh Chieu, HCMC)

Japanese Embassy (Map p817; ☑ 04-3846 3000; www.vn.emb-japan.go.jp; 27 P Lieu Giai, Ba Dinh District, Hanoi)

Japanese Consulate (Map p888; ☑ 08-3933 3510; www.hcmcgj.vn.emb-japan.go.jp; 261 Đ Dien Bien Phu, HCMC)

Laotian Embassy (Map p817; ☑ 04-3942 4576; www.embalaohanoi.gov.la; 22 P Tran Binh Trong, Hanoi)

Laotian Consulate (Map p884; ☑ 08-3829 7667; 93 Đ Pasteur, HCMC)

Netherlands Embassy (Map p820; ☑ 04-3831 5650; www.hollandinvietnam.org; 7th fl, BIDV Tower, 194 Đ Tran Quang Khai, Hanoi)

Netherlands Consulate (Map p886; ☑ 08-3823 5932; www.hollandinvietnam.org; Saigon Tower, 29 ĐL Le Duan, HCMC)

New Zealand Embassy (Map p820; ☑ 04-3824 1481; www.nzembassy.com/viet-nam; Level 5, 63 P Ly Thai To, Hanoi)

New Zealand Consulate (Map p884; ☑ 08-3822 6907; www.nzembassy.com; 8th fl, The Metropolitan, 235 Đ Dong Khoi, HCMC)

Thai Embassy (Map p822; ☑ 04-3823 5092; www.thaiembassy.org; 3-65 P Hoang Dieu, Hanoi)

Thai Consulate (Map p888; ☑ 08-3932 7637; www.thaiembassy.org/hochiminh; 77 Đ Tran Quoc Thao, HCMC)

UK Embassy (Map p820; ☑ 04-3936 0500; http://ukinvietnam.fco.gov.uk; 4th fl, Central Bldg, 31 P Hai Ba Trung, Hanoi)

UK Consulate (Map p886; ☑ 08-3829 8433; consularenquiries.vietnam@fco.gov.uk; 25 ĐL Le Duan, HCMC)

US Embassy (Map p817; ☑ 04-3850 5000; http://vietnam.usembassy.gov; 7 P Lang Ha, Ba Dinh District, Hanoi)

US Consulate (Map p886; ☑ 08-3822 9433; http://hochiminh.usconsulate.gov; 4 ĐL Le Duan, HCMC)

FOOD

The following price ranges are based on a typical meal, excluding drinks.

$ less than 112,000d (US$5)

$$ 112,000d to 337,000d (US$5 to US$15)

$$$ more than 337,000d (US$15)

INSURANCE

Travel insurance is a *must* for Vietnam, as the cost of major medical treatment is prohibitive. A policy to cover theft, loss and medical problems is the best bet.

If you're driving a vehicle you'll need a Vietnamese insurance policy.

Worldwide travel insurance is available at www.lonelyplanet.com/travel-insurance. You can buy, extend or claim anytime – even if you're already on the road.

INTERNET ACCESS

Internet and wi-fi is very widely available throughout Vietnam. Connection speeds in towns and cities are normally quite good.

Something like 98% of hotels and guesthouses have wi-fi; it's almost always free of charge. Cybercafes charge from 3000d per hour for internet access.

LEGAL MATTERS

Very few foreigners experience any hassle from police. If you lose something really valuable such as your passport or visa, you'll need to contact them. Note you may face imprisonment and/or large fines for drug offences, and drug trafficking can be punishable by death.

LGBT TRAVELLERS

Vietnam is pretty hassle-free for gay travellers. There's not much in the way of harassment, nor are there official laws on same-sex relationships. VietPride (www.vietpride.com) marches have been held in Hanoi and HCMC since 2012. Gay weddings were officially authorised in 2015 (though their legal status has not yet been recognised). Checking into hotels as a same-sex couple is perfectly OK. But be discreet – public displays of affection are not socially acceptable whatever your sexual orientation.

Check out Utopia (www.utopia-asia.com) for contacts and useful travel information.

MONEY

The Vietnamese currency is the dong (abbreviated to 'd'). US dollars are also widely used.

For the last few years the dong has been fairly stable at around 22,000d to the dollar.

ATMs are widespread and present in virtually every town in the country.

Tipping is not expected, but is appreciated.

Credit & Debit Cards

Visa and MasterCard are accepted in many tourist centres, but don't expect noodle bars to take plastic. Commission charges (around 3%) sometimes apply.

For cash advances, try branches of Vietcombank in cities or Sinh Tourist travel agencies. Expect at least a 3% commission for this service.

OPENING HOURS

Vietnamese people rise early and consider sleeping in to be a sure indication of illness. Lunch is taken very seriously and many government offices close between 11.30am and 2pm.

Banks 8am to 3pm weekdays, to 11.30am Saturday

Offices and museums 7am or 8am to 5pm or 6pm; museums generally close on Monday

Restaurants 11.30am to 9pm

Shops 8am to 6pm

Temples and pagodas 5am to 9pm

PUBLIC HOLIDAYS

If a Vietnamese public holiday falls on a weekend, it is observed on the following Monday.

New Year's Day (Tet Duong Lich) 1 January

Vietnamese New Year (Tet) A three-day national holiday; late January or February

Founding of the Vietnamese Communist Party (Thanh Lap Dang CSVN) 3 February

Hung Kings Commemorations (Hung Vuong) 10th day of the 3rd lunar month; late March or April

Liberation Day (Saigon Giai Phong) 30 April

International Workers' Day (Quoc Te Lao Dong) 1 May

Ho Chi Minh's Birthday (Sinh Nhat Bac Ho) 19 May

Buddha's Birthday (Phat Dan) Eighth day of the fourth lunar month (usually June)

National Day (Quoc Khanh) 2 September

SAFE TRAVEL

All in all, Vietnam is an extremely safe country to travel. Sure, there are scams and hassles in some cities, particularly in Hanoi (p824) and Nha Trang. But overall the police keep a pretty tight grip on social order and we very rarely receive reports about muggings, armed robberies and sexual assaults.

Watch out for petty theft. Drive-by bag snatchers on motorbikes are not uncommon, and thieves patrol buses, trains and boats. Don't be flash with cameras and jewellery.

Since 1975 many thousands of Vietnamese have been maimed or killed by rockets, artillery shells, mortars, mines and other ordnance left over from the war. Stick to defined paths and *never* touch any suspicious war relic you might come across.

TIME

Vietnam is seven hours ahead of Greenwich Mean Time/Universal Time Coordinated (GMT/UTC). There's no daylight-saving or summer time.

TOILETS

Western-style sit-down toilets are the norm, but the odd squat bog still survives in some cheap hotels and bus stations.

TOURIST INFORMATION

Tourist offices in Vietnam have a different philosophy from the majority of tourist offices worldwide. Most are really travel agencies whose primary interests are booking tours and turning a profit.

Travellers' cafes, travel agencies and your fellow travellers are a much better source of information than most of the so-called tourist offices.

TRAVELLERS WITH DISABILITIES

Vietnam is not the easiest of places for travellers with disabilities. Tactical problems include the chaotic traffic, a lack of lifts in smaller hotels, and pavements (sidewalks) that are routinely blocked by parked motorbikes and food stalls.

That said, with some careful planning it is possible to enjoy your trip. Find a reliable company to make the travel arrangements. Many hotels in the midrange and above category have elevators, and disabled access is improving. Bus and train travel is tough, but rent a private vehicle with a driver and almost anywhere becomes instantly accessible.

The hazards for blind travellers in Vietnam are acute, with traffic coming at you from all directions, so you'll definitely need a sighted companion.

The Travellers with Disabilities forum on Lonely Planet's Thorn Tree (www.lonelyplanet.com) is a good place to seek advice.

You might also try contacting the following organisations:

Mobility International USA www.miusa.org

Royal Association for Disability Rights http://disabilityrightsuk.org

Society for AccessibleTravel & Hospitality www.sath.org

USEFUL WEBSITES

Vietnam Coracle (http://vietnamcoracle.com) Excellent independent travel advice.

The Word (www.wordhcmc.com) Comprehensive Vietnam coverage and excellent features.

Thanh Nien News (www.thanhniennews.com) Government-approved news, but includes diverse and interesting content.

Lonely Planet (www.lonelyplanet.com/vietnam) Destination information, hotel bookings, traveller forum and more.

Vietnam Online (www.vietnamonline.com) Good all-rounder.

VISAS

The (very complicated) visa situation is fluid – always check the latest regulations.

Firstly, if you are staying more than 15 days and are from a Western country you'll still need a visa (or approval letter from an agent). If your visit is under 15 days, some nationalities are now visa exempt.

Note that travellers using a visa exemption *cannot* extend their stay at the end of the visa exemption period and must leave Vietnam, and cannot return again using a visa exemption within 30 days.

If you are from a non-visa-exempted country (say the USA, Australia or New Zealand) or you wish to stay longer in Vietnam than your permitted period, or you wish to enter and leave Vietnam multiple times, you will need to apply for a visa in advance.

Tourist visas are valid for either 30 days or 90 days. A single-entry 30-day visa costs US$25, a three-month multiple entry visa is US$50.

There are two methods of applying for a visa: via online visa agents, or via a Vietnamese embassy or consulate.

Vietnam Visa Agents

This is now the preferred method for most travellers arriving by air, since it's cheaper, faster and you don't have to part with your passport

VISA EXEMPTED NATIONALITIES

Citizens of the following countries do not need a Vietnamese visa if staying less than the permitted period (when arriving by either air or land). Always double-check visa requirements before you travel as policies change regularly.

COUNTRY	DAYS
Brunei, Myanmar (Burma)	14
Cambodia, Indonesia, Laos, Malaysia, Singapore, Thailand	30
Philippines	21
Belarus, Denmark, Finland , France, Germany, Italy, Japan, South Korea, Norway, Russia, Spain, Sweden, UK	15

by posting it to an embassy. It can only be used if you are flying into any of Vietnam's five international airports, not at land crossings. The process is straightforward: you fill out an online application form and pay the agency fee (around US$20). You'll then receive by email a Visa on Arrival approval letter signed by Vietnamese immigration which you print out and show on arrival (and then pay your visa fee). There are many visa agents, but we recommend you stick to well-established companies; these two are professional and efficient:

Vietnam Visa Choice (www.vietnamvisachoice. com) Online support from native English speakers and they guarantee your visa will be issued within the time specified.

Vietnam Visa Center (www.vietnamvisacenter. org) Competent all-rounder which offers a two-hour express service for last-minute trips.

Visas via an Embassy or Consulate

You can also obtain visas through Vietnamese embassies and consulates around the world but fees are normally higher than using a visa agent, and (depending on the country) the process can be slow. In Asia, Vietnamese visas tend to be issued in two to three working days in Cambodia; in Europe and North America, it takes around a week.

Multiple-Entry Visas

It's possible to enter Cambodia or Laos from Vietnam and then re-enter without having to apply for another visa. However, you must hold a multiple-entry visa.

If you arrived in Vietnam on a single-entry visa, multiple-entry visas are easiest to arrange in Hanoi or HCMC, but you will have to ask a visa or travel agent to do the paperwork for you. Agents charge about US$50 and the procedure takes up to seven days.

Visa Extensions

Tourist visa extensions officially cost as little as US$10, and have to be organised via agents. The procedure can take seven days and you can only extend the visa for 30 or 90 days, depending on the visa you hold.

You can extend your visa in big cities, but if it's done in a different city from the one you arrived in it'll cost you around US$30. In practice, extensions work most smoothly in HCMC, Hanoi, Danang and Hue.

VOLUNTEERING

Opportunities for voluntary work are quite limited in Vietnam.

The **NGO Resource Centre** (Map p817; ☑ 04-3832 8570; www.ngocentre.org.vn; Room 201, Building E3, 6 Dang Van Ngu, Trung Tu Diplomatic Compound, Dong Da, Hanoi) keeps a database of all of the NGOs assisting Vietnam.

KOTO (www.koto.com.au) helps give street children career opportunities in its restaurants in Hanoi and HCMC; volunteers need a three-month minimum commitment.

WORK

At least 90% of foreign travellers seeking work in Vietnam end up teaching English, though some dive centres and hostels need workers.

ⓘ Getting There & Away

Most travellers enter Vietnam by plane or bus, but there are also train links from China and boat connections from Cambodia via the Mekong River.

ENTERING VIETNAM

Formalities at Vietnam's international airports are generally smoother than at land borders. Crossing the border between Vietnam and Laos can be particularly slow.

Passport

Your passport must be valid for six months upon arrival in Vietnam. Many nationalities have to arrange a visa in advance.

AIR
Airports

There are three main international airports in Vietnam. Phu Quoc also has flights to Cambodia and Singapore.

Tan Son Nhat International Airport (☑ 08-3848 5383; www.tsnairport.hochiminhcity.gov. vn/vn; Tan Binh District) For Ho Chi Minh CIty.

Noi Bai Airport (☑ 04-3827 1513; www.hanoi airportonline.com)

Danang Airport (☑ 0511-383 0339) International flights to Nanning (China) with China Southern Airlines; to Hong Kong with Dragonair; to Siem Riep (Cambodia) and Singapore with Silk Air; and to Pakse, Savannakhet and Vientiane (all in Laos) with Lao Airlines.

BORDER CROSSINGS

Vietnam shares land border crossings with Cambodia, China and Laos. For those nationalities that qualify, visa exemptions are now available at land borders. Officials at border crossings occasionally ask for an 'immigration fee' of a dollar or two.

Cambodia

Cambodia and Vietnam share a long frontier with seven border crossings. One-month Cambodian visas are issued on arrival at all border crossings for US$30, but overcharging is common at all borders except Bavet.

Cambodian border crossings are officially open daily between 8am and 8pm.

China

There are three borders where foreigners are permitted to cross between Vietnam and China: Huu Nghi Quan (the Friendship Pass), Lao Cai and Mong Cai. It is necessary to arrange a Chinese visa in advance.

China time is one hour ahead.

Laos

There are seven overland crossings between Vietnam and Laos. Thirty-day Lao visas are available at all borders.

The golden rule is to try to use direct city-to-city bus connections between the two countries, as potential hassle will be greatly reduced. If you decide to travel step-by-step using local buses, you can expect hassle and transport scams (eg serious overcharging) on the Vietnamese side.

Transport links on both sides of the border can be hit and miss, so don't use the more remote borders unless you have plenty of time, and patience, to spare.

❶ Getting Around

AIR

Vietnam has good domestic flight connections, and very affordable prices (if you book early). Airlines accept bookings on international credit or debit cards. However, note that cancellations are not unknown.

Jetstar Airways (☑ 1900 1550; www.jetstar.com) Serves 16 airports in Vietnam.

Vasco (☑ 038 422 790; www.vasco.com.vn) Connects HCMC with the Con Dao Islands and the Mekong Delta.

Vietjet Air (☑ 1900 1886; www.vietjetair.com) Serves 15 domestic airports.

Vietnam Airlines (www.vietnamairlines.com.vn) Comprehensive coverage of the entire nation.

BICYCLE

Bikes are a great way to get around Vietnam, particularly when you get off the main highways.

The main hazard is the traffic, and it's wise to avoid certain areas (notably Hwy 1). Some of the best cycling is along quiet coastal roads in Central Vietnam, in the Southwest Highlands and up in the northern mountains (although you'll have to cope with some big hills here). The Mekong Delta is a rewarding option for those who like it flat.

Bicycles can be rented from guesthouses from US$1 per day, while good-quality mountain bikes cost from US$10.

BOAT

In the North, cruises on Halong Bay or Lan Ha Bay area are extremely popular and should not be missed. Hydrofoils also connect Haiphong with Cat Ba Island (near Halong Bay). Day trips by boat to islands off the coast of Nha Trang and to the Chams off Hoi An are also worthwhile.

The extensive network of canals in the Mekong Delta makes getting around by boat feasible. Travellers to Phu Quoc Island can catch ferries from Ha Tien or Rach Gia.

BUS

Vietnam has an extensive network of buses that reach the far-flung corners of the country. Modern buses, operated by myriad companies, run on all the main highways.

Many travellers (perhaps the majority) never actually visit a Vietnamese bus station at all, preferring to stick to the convenient, tourist-friendly open-tour bus network.

Whichever class of bus you're on, bus travel in Vietnam is never speedy; reckon on just 50km/h on major routes including Hwy 1.

Bus Stations

Many cities have several bus stations – make sure you go to the right one! Bus stations all look chaotic, but many now have ticket offices with official prices and departure times displayed.

Reservations & Costs

Always buy a ticket from the office, as bus drivers are notorious for overcharging. Reservations aren't usually required for most of the frequent, popular services between towns and cities.

On rural runs foreigners are typically charged anywhere from twice to 10 times the going rate. As a benchmark, a typical 100km ride should be between US$2 and US$3.

Bus Types

On most popular routes, modern air-conditioned buses offer comfortable reclining seats, while sleeper buses have flat beds for really long trips.

Deluxe buses are nonsmoking. On the flip side, most of them are equipped with blaring TVs and even karaoke.

Connecting backpacker haunts across the nation, open-tour buses are wildly popular in Vietnam. These air-con buses use convenient, centrally located departure points and allow you to hop on and hop off at any major city along the main north to south route. Prices are reasonable. An open-tour ticket from Ho Chi Minh City to Hanoi costs between US$30 and US$75; the more stops you add, the higher the price. **Sinh Tourist** (☑ 08-3838 9597; www.thesinhtourist.com) has a good reputation, with computerised seat reservations and comfortable buses.

Local buses in the countryside are slow and stop frequently. Conductors tend to routinely overcharge foreigners on these local services.

CAR & MOTORCYCLE

Having your own set of wheels gives you maximum flexibility to visit remote regions and stop when and where you please. Car hire always includes a driver. Motorbike hire is good value and this can be self-drive or with a driver.

Driving Licence

Foreigners are now permitted to drive in Vietnam with an International Drivers' Permit (IDP). However, this must be combined with local insurance for it to be valid. The reality on the ground has always been that foreigners are never asked for IDPs by police, and no rental places ever ask to see one. However, this may change with the new law.

Car & Minibus

Renting a vehicle with a driver is a realistic option (even for budget travellers) if you share the cost.

Costs per day:

Standard model US$50 to US$100
4WD/minibus US$100 to US$130

Motorbike

Motorbikes can be rented from virtually anywhere, including cafes, hotels and travel agencies. Some places will ask to keep your passport as security. Ask for a signed agreement stating what you are renting, how much it costs, the extent of compensation and so on.

It is compulsory to wear a helmet when riding a motorbike in Vietnam, even when travelling as a passenger.

Costs per day:

Moped US$5 to US$10
Trail and road bikes US$15 to US$30

Plenty of local drivers will be willing to act as a chauffeur and guide for about US$20 per day.

Insurance

If you're using a rental bike the owners should have insurance. If you're considering buying a vehicle, Baoviet (www.baoviet.com.vn) has a third-party fire and theft coverage policy which includes liability for 87,000d.

Many rental places will make you sign a contract agreeing to a valuation for the bike if it is stolen. Make sure you always leave it in guarded parking where available.

Road Conditions & Hazards

Road safety is definitely not one of Vietnam's strong points. Vehicles drive on the right-hand side (in theory). Size matters and small vehicles get out of the way of big vehicles. Accidents are common.

In general, the major highways are hard-surfaced and reasonably well maintained, but seasonal flooding can be a problem. Nonpaved roads are best tackled with a 4WD vehicle or motorbike. Mountain roads are particularly dangerous: landslides, falling rocks and runaway vehicles can add an unwelcome edge to your journey.

LOCAL TRANSPORT

Cyclos

These are bicycle rickshaws. Drivers hang out in touristy areas and some speak broken English. Bargaining is imperative; settle on a fare before going anywhere. A short ride should be 10,000d to 20,000d.

Taxis

Metered taxis are found in all cities and are very, very cheap by international standards and a safe way to travel around at night. Average tariffs are about 12,000d to 15,000d per kilometre. Mai Linh (www.mailinh.vn) and Vinasun (www.vinasuntaxi.com) are two excellent nationwide firms.

Xe Om

Motorbike taxis are everywhere. Fares should be about half that of a taxi. Drivers usually hang around street corners, markets, hotels and bus stations.

TOURS

These Vietnam-based travel agencies offer great tours:

Handspan Travel Indochina (✆04-3926 2828; www.handspan.com) A wide range of innovative, interesting tours to seldom-visited regions.

Ocean Tours (✆04-3926 0463; www.ocean tours.com.vn) Heads to Ba Be National Park and has a great Thousand Island tour of Halong Bay.

Buffalo Tours (Map p818; www.buffalotours.com) Offers diverse and customised trips.

TRAIN

The railway system, operated by **Vietnam Railways** (Duong Sat Viet Nam; ✆04-3747 0308; www.vr.com.vn), is an ageing, slow, but pretty dependable service, and offers a relaxing way to get around the nation. Travelling in an air-con sleeping berth sure beats a hairy overnight bus journey along Hwy 1. And there's spectacular scenery to lap up too.

Routes

The main line connects HCMC with Hanoi. Three rail-spur lines link Hanoi with other parts of northern Vietnam: Haiphong, Lang Son and Lao Cai.

'Fast' trains between Hanoi and HCMC take between 32 and 36 hours.

Classes & Costs

Trains classified as SE are the smartest and fastest. There are four main ticket classes: hard seat, soft seat, hard sleeper and soft sleeper. These classes are further split according to whether or not they have air-conditioning. Presently, air-con is only available on the faster express trains. Hard-seat class is usually packed. It's tolerable for day travel, but expect plenty of cigarette smoke.

Ticket prices vary depending on the train; the fastest trains are the most expensive.

Reservations

You can buy tickets in advance from the Vietnam Railways bookings site (http://dsvn.vn), but at the time of research only Vietnamese credit cards were accepted. However, you can book online using the travel agency Bao Lau (www.baolau.vn), which has an efficient website, details seat and sleeper berth availability and accepts international cards. E-tickets are emailed to you; there's a 40,000d commission per ticket.

You can reserve seats/berths on long trips 60 to 90 days in advance (less on shorter trips). Most of the time you can book train tickets a day or two ahead without a problem, except during peak holiday times. But for sleeping berths, it's wise to book a week or more before the date of departure.

Many travel agencies, hotels and cafes will also buy you train tickets for a small commission.

Understand Southeast Asia

Southeast Asia Today

From democracies to dictatorships, the political landscape of Southeast Asia is far from simple. Myanmar is the new poster child for democracy, while other players in the region revert to bad habits such as military coups in Thailand and political repression in Cambodia. China casts a long shadow over the region with its ambitious claims to the South China Sea. But a booming economy continues to deliver better lives to a growing population.

Best in Print

Burmese Days (1934) George Orwell's classic tale of close-minded colonials living in Burma.

Phaic Tăn: Sunstroke on a Shoe-string (2004) Ultimate spoof guide-book pokes fun at locals, travellers and guidebook authors.

The Beach (1998) Alex Garland's now-legendary tale about a backpacker utopia in southern Thailand.

The Quiet American (1955) Graham Greene's classic novel about intrigues in Saigon as the US slowly descends into war in Vietnam.

Best on Film

Apocalypse Now (1979) Set in Vietnam, filmed in the Philippines, this is the ultimate anti-war film.

The Killing Fields (1984) Oscar-winning classic based on a true story of survival during the Khmer Rouge takeover.

The Lady (2011) A French-directed biopic about Myanmar's democracy leader Aung San Suu Kyi.

The Look of Silence (2014) Acclaimed follow-up to *The Act of Killing* in which an optician confronts his brother's killers.

Metro Manila (2013) Filipino film showing the harsh realities of adjusting from a simple rural life to an edgy urban life.

A New Myanmar

The headline news in 2015 was the birth of democracy in Myanmar. The Aung San Suu Kyi–led National League for Democracy won a landslide victory in the historic 2015 election, but Myanmar's powerful military continues to play an influential role with 25% of seats in parliament. Myanmar remains a work in progress, even if the country is heading in the right direction.

Same Old Thailand

With the military in charge again and no real prospect of elections before 2017, the country remains divided politically between the rural poor at one end and the traditional elite and urban middle classes at the other. A poor human-rights record has tarnished Thailand's image as an oasis of relative stability in Southeast Asia, yet tourism hasn't taken much of a hit, with visitors still arriving in droves.

The Political Jungle

Malaysia is stumbling along, with opposition leader Anwar Ibrahim in prison once again and allegations of corruption against Prime Minister Najib Razak. By comparison, the democracies in Indonesia, the Philippines and Timor-Leste appear somewhat healthier. Joko Widodo, nicknamed Jokowi, has grand plans to redefine Indonesia, but has riled international allies by resuming the execution of foreigners on death row for drug offences. Indonesia has also angered near neighbours, as the smoke from forest fires cloaks Singapore, Malaysia and Thailand in a polluting haze. Brunei, meanwhile, made international headlines with the phasing in of sharia Islamic laws from April 2014. It mainly applies to Muslims, however non-Muslims can also be charged for offences including drinking alcohol in public, adultery and homosexual acts. The application of rules regarding Friday prayers and fasting during Ramadan have also been toughened up and will affect visitors.

Cambodia has been slipping towards authoritarianism again after a promising year of detente. All eyes are on the countdown to the 2018 election and the prospects for freedom of expression. It's business as usual across the border in neighbouring Laos and Vietnam, where communist parties remain firmly entrenched in power, refusing to hold elections, but allowing the population to enjoy the fruits of economic freedom.

Economies United

The new Asean Economic Community (AEC) unites the 10 Southeast Asian countries into a liberalised marketplace to increase competitiveness. The AEC removes restrictions on the movement of goods, services and skilled workers, and streamlines customs.

What remains uncertain is how the AEC will impact on the movement of labour. Economic disparity between the richer and poorer members of the community remains extreme, so the lure of a better life in Bangkok, Kuala Lumpur or Singapore may prove irresistible to citizens of Cambodia, Laos or Myanmar at the other end of the scale.

The economies of Southeast Asia remain in good shape, posting above-average growth of around 5%. Indonesia is the biggest economy in the region with a GDP approaching US$1 trillion, but Thailand, Malaysia, Singapore and the Philippines are significant players. The smaller economies of Cambodia, Laos and Myanmar are posting off-the-scale growth rates from a lowly base.

Big Brother China

As the Southeast Asian nations move closer together, the whale in the pond is China. The big issue impacting on relations between the Asean countries and China is control over the South China Sea and the remote Spratly and Paracel Islands, both potentially awash with oil. To Vietnam, this is the 'East Sea' and has been a recent flashpoint in historically tense relations with the mighty northern neighbour.

Throw in competing claims from the Philippines and Malaysia and you have a complex geopolitical situation. The US, meanwhile, has conducted 'freedom of navigation' naval patrols and flyovers in the area.

Beijing exerts political and economic influence as it invests in the region. A number of Chinese-led infrastructure projects are underway, including sensitive hydroelectric dams in countries such as Cambodia (Lower Sesan II Dam) and Laos (Don Sahong Dam), and these projects have raised concerns among NGOs about their environmental and cultural impact.

POPULATION: **618 MILLION**

COMBINED GDP: **US$2.46 TRILLION**

GDP PER CAPITA: **SINGAPORE US$53,224; CAMBODIA US$1139**

UNEMPLOYMENT: **CAMBODIA 0.3%; PHILIPPINES 7.3%**

INFLATION: **SINGAPORE 1.0%; MYANMAR 5.9%**

if South East Asia were 100 people

39 would be Muslim
36 would be Buddhist
18 would be other
7 would be Christian

economy
(% of GDP)

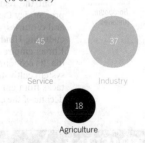

Service 45

Industry 37

Agriculture 18

population per sq km

SOUTH EAST ASIA   USA   UK

≈ 30 people

History

Sitting at the crossroads of land and sea routes, the Southeast Asian nations share unifying historic themes: they have traded, adopted religions, paid tribute, repulsed invaders, endured colonialism and declared independence. The mainland is united by religious associations and historic empires, while the island nations struggle with diversity within their respective archipelagos. Today they are dynamic economies transitioning at various speeds from subsistence farming into modern and prosperous nations with expanding tourism sectors.

Early Kingdoms

The mainland Southeast Asian countries owe much of their early historical happenings to the dominant civilisations of China and India. As early as 150 BC, China and India interacted with the scattered Southeast Asian communities for trade and tribute. Vietnam, within short reach of China, was a subject, student and reluctant offspring of its more powerful neighbour for more than 1000 years. India, on the other hand, conquered by spiritual means, spreading Hinduism, Buddhism and later Islam across the region, and influencing art and architecture.

Ancient Capitals

....

Angkor
(Cambodia)

....

Sukhothai
(Thailand)

....

Bagan (Myanmar)

My Son (Vietnam)

....

Borobodur
(Indonesia)

Several highly organised states emerged in the region as a result of contact with India. From the 7th to the 9th centuries AD, the Srivijaya empire controlled all shipping through the Java Sea from its capital at Palembang in southeast Sumatra. The Srivijaya capital was also a religious centre for Mahayana Buddhism and attracted scholars as well as merchants.

But the region's most powerful empire emerged in the interior of present-day Cambodia. The Khmer empire ruled the mainland for several centuries, absorbing territory and labour to build unparalleled and enduring Hindu-Buddhist monuments to its god-kings. Eventually the Khmer empire included most of what is now Thailand, Laos and Cambodia. Its economy was based on agriculture, and a sophisticated irrigation system cultivated vast tracts of land around Tonlé Sap (Great Lake). Attacks from emerging city-states on the Thai frontier contributed to the decline of the empire and the abandonment of the Angkor capital.

TIMELINE	2800–100 BC	7th century	AD 802
	Ancestors of modern Southeast Asians begin to migrate south from China and Tibet, populating river valleys and coastal areas and organising small city-states.	A Buddhist empire, Srivijaya, emerges in present-day Malaysia and Sumatra (Indonesia) as a coastal shipping interest on the India–China trade route.	King Jayavarman consolidates the Khmer empire in parts of present-day Cambodia, Thailand, Myanmar and Vietnam that supplants the local Funan state.

The Classical & Colonial Period

As the larger powers waned, Southeast Asia entered an age of cultural definition and international influence. Regional kingdoms created distinctive works of art and literature, and put themselves on the emerging global map as important ports. The Thais expanded into the dying Khmer empire and exerted control over parts of Cambodia, Laos and Myanmar. Starting around 1331, the Hindu kingdom of Majapahit united the Indonesian archipelago from Sumatra to New Guinea and dominated the trade routes between India and China. The kingdom's dominance continued until the advent of Islamic kingdoms and the emergence of the port town of Melaka on the Malay Peninsula in 1402. Melaka's prosperity soon attracted European interest, and it fell first to the Portuguese in 1511, then the Dutch and finally the English.

Initially these European nations were only interested in controlling shipping in the region, usually brokering agreements and alliances with local authorities. Centred on Java and Sumatra, the Dutch monopolised European commerce with Asia for 200 years. The Spanish, French and later the English had civilisation and proselytising on their minds. Spain occupied the Philippines archipelago; Britain steadily rolled through India, Myanmar and the Malay Peninsula; the Dutch grasped Indonesia to cement a presence in the region; and France, with a foothold in Vietnam, usurped Cambodia and Laos to form Indochina.

Although its sphere of influence was diminished, Thailand was the only Southeast Asian nation to remain independent. One reason for this was that England and France agreed to leave Thailand as a 'buffer' between their two colonies. Credit is also frequently given to the Thai kings who Westernised the country and played competing European powers against each other.

Independence Movements

The 20th century and WWII signalled an end to European domination in Southeast Asia. As European power receded, the Japanese expanded control throughout the region, invading Thailand, Malaysia and Indonesia. After the war, the power vacuums in formerly colonised countries provided leverage for a region-wide independence movement. Vietnam clamoured most violently for freedom, resulting in almost uninterrupted conflicts against foreign powers. After the French were defeated by communist nationals, Vietnam faced civil war and the intervention of the USA, which hoped to contain the spread of communism within the region. Cambodia's civil war ended in one of the worst nightmares of modern times, with the ascension of the Khmer Rouge. The revolutionary army evacuated the cities, separated families into labour camps and

European Hill Stations

Sapa (Vietnam)

Cameron Highlands (Malaysia)

Pyin Oo Lwin (Myanmar)

Bokor National Park (Cambodia)

HISTORY THE CLASSICAL & COLONIAL PERIOD

AD 938	13th century	1511	1939–45
The Chinese are kicked out of Vietnam after a 1000-year occupation.	The beginning of the decline of the Khmer empire and rise of powerful states in modern-day Thailand and Vietnam.	Melaka falls to the Portuguese and marks the beginning of colonial expansion in the region by European powers including the Dutch, Spanish, French and British.	WWII; Japan occupies much of Southeast Asia using Thailand as a cooperative base and Malaysia and Indonesia as a source of conscripts.

Born in 1967, the Association of Southeast Asian Nations (Asean) is a regional cooperation organisation that includes 10 member countries (excluding Timor-Leste).

closed the country off from the rest of the world. An estimated 1.7 million people were killed by the regime during its four-year rule (1975–79).

Many of the newly liberated countries struggled to unite a land mass that shared only a colonial legacy. Dictatorships in Myanmar, Indonesia and the Philippines thwarted the populace's hopes for representative governments and civil liberties. Civilian rioters, minority insurgents and communist guerrillas further provoked the unstable governments, and the internal chaos was usually agitated by the major superpowers: China, the Soviet Union and the USA.

The Era of Boom & Bust

Near the turn of the current millennium, the region entered a period of unprecedented economic growth. Singapore, along with Hong Kong and South Korea, was classified as an 'Asian Tiger' economy – export-driven countries experiencing as much as 7% annual growth in GDP. Emerging tigers included Thailand, Malaysia, Indonesia and the Philippines. These countries were rapidly industrialising and beginning to dominate sophisticated manufacturing sectors such as automobile, machinery and electronics production.

In 1997 the upward trend was derailed by a currency crisis. Thailand's baht was the first currency to crash and neighbouring currencies soon followed. A period of economic retraction and financial austerity restored these developing economies to a more sustainable footing. More than a decade after the economic crash of 1997, many of the former tigers enjoy a respectable GDP growth of about 5%, foreign investment, and an increasingly affluent and educated population.

The closed countries of Vietnam, Laos and Cambodia began to open up in the mid- to late 1990s and have experienced various degrees of economic success and industrialisation. Vietnam continues to be a determined capitalist engine with an ever-expanding economy and a youthful optimism that counteracts government inefficiencies.

Laos woke up from its backwater slumber to find that China needed it for natural resources; the landlocked country is quickly becoming a trading crossroads with neighbouring markets. Increased infrastructure is helping Laos and Cambodia develop a thriving tourism sector that has matured from low-budget adventurers to high-end jet-setters. In addition to tourism, the two countries still depend largely on small-scale agriculture with a real focus on the textile industry in Cambodia. Both economies are much smaller than their regional neighbours, but have experienced some dramatic growth in recent years. The standard of living remains low for many and they are still classified by the UN as being among the poorest countries in Asia.

1946–65 ⟩	1965 ⟩	1955–75 ⟩	1999 ⟩
Post-war Europe withdraws from the region, ushering in independence movements. First, the Philippines gains independence, followed by Myanmar, Indonesia, the countries of Indochina, Malaysia and Singapore.	Singapore splits from Malaysia and forms an independent country, which goes on to become the most successful economy in the region.	The US becomes involved in Vietnam's civil war as an anti-communism effort. Laos and Cambodia are sucked into the melee. The US withdraws after the fall of Saigon to North Vietnamese troops.	Timor-Leste votes for independence from Indonesian occupiers. An international peacekeeping force enters the country to prevent violence.

Indonesia and the Philippines rode the first wave of post-colonial development, stalled during the 1997 economic crisis and then became the region's classic underachievers. Both have incredible natural resource wealth but are hampered by ethnic conflicts, corruption, political instability, vast geography and a diverse populace. The Philippines has emerged as the world's new call centre, while Indonesia nervously monitors the Chinese and Australian economies and their slowing demand for minerals.

Myanmar, long shunned by international investors due to the political climate, has opened up its economy and foreign capital is flowing in. This process is only likely to accelerate now Suu Kyi and the NLD are in power.

Trouble Spots

In general, Southeast Asia is safer now than it was during the communist era of the mid-20th century or during the jihadist terror attacks in the early 2000s.

Between 2002 and 2005, Indonesia suffered civilian-targeted, allegedly Jemaah Islamiyah (JI)–linked bombings on an annual basis. The militant Islamic group JI, which was formed in the 1990s with a mission to establish a pan-Islamic state, was believed to have links with Al Qaeda and its global jihad. The group turned to civilian terror tactics in the 2000s and allegedly orchestrated multiple bombing attacks in Indonesia and the Philippines.

The worst event occurred in October 2002 on the island of Bali where suicide bombers targeted crowded nightspots, killing 202 people and injuring hundreds more, mostly Australian tourists. In 2010 Abu Bakar Bashir, alleged to be the spiritual leader of JI, was sentenced to 15 years in jail for his involvement in a terror-training camp in Aceh. Today, Indonesia is on high alert from terrorist activity linked to Isis, which claimed responsibility for a January 2016 attack in Jakarta that killed four civilians.

In the southern Philippines, mainly the island of Mindanao and the Sulu Archipelago, there are several active Islamic insurgency groups. In 2012 the Filipino government reached a preliminary peace deal with one of the nationalist groups, but rival factions who oppose government negotiations continue to destabilise the region with indiscriminate bombs and targeted kidnaps of tourists.

Since 2004 the Muslim-dominated areas of southern Thailand (Narathiwat, Pattani, Yala and parts of Songkhla) have waged an ethno-nationalist struggle. Thousands have died in the region, but it has rarely impacted on the tourism industry in Thailand. However, terrorism came to the capital in 2015 with a major bomb attack near the Erawan Shrine in Bangkok, which Thai authorities have linked to the Uighur insurgency in western China, following the forced deportation of 100 Uighurs in the summer.

Historical Reads

Southeast Asia: An Introductory History (Milton Osborne)

In Search of Southeast Asia: A Modern History (David P Chandler, et al)

Southeast Asia: Past and Present (DR SarDesai)

2004	2008	2009	2015
An Indian Ocean earthquake with its epicentre near Sumatra (Indonesia) triggers a giant tsunami that kills thousands in Indonesia and Thailand.	Cyclone Nargis kills 138,000 people and causes US$10 billion in damages, qualifying as Myanmar's worst natural disaster.	Tribunals of surviving members of Cambodia's Khmer Rouge's senior leadership begins, 30 years after their genocidal reign was toppled.	The Asean Economic Community (AEC) goes into effect, uniting the region into a common marketplace. Myanmar holds historic elections ushering Suu Kyi and the NLD into power.

People & Culture

Southeast Asia is a culturally rich region that encompasses most of the world's religions with a unique tropical flair. Colourful artistic traditions date back to a period of regional empires, when kings and sultans were cultural patrons. Akin to the region's personality, each country's culture chest is generously shared with curious outsiders. There is also a fascinating dynamic between ancient traditions and modern sensibilities in the rural villages and dense urban cities that add up to a region that is going places.

People

Top Flicks

Balibo (2009, East Timor)

Heneral Luna (2015, Philippines)

The Act of Killing (2012, Indonesia)

The Last Reel (2014, Cambodia)

The Island Funeral (2015, Thailand)

Within the dominant cultures of Southeast Asia are minority groups that remain in isolated pockets or cultural islands. Regarded as the Jews of Asia, ethnic Chinese have long filtered into the region as merchants and labourers, establishing distinct neighbourhoods within their host communities and perpetuating their mother country's language and customs.

Every small town has a Chinatown (typically the main business district). In places like Malaysia and Singapore, the Chinese diaspora has morphed into a distinct entity, termed Straits Chinese, which refers to the inter-marrying of Chinese and Malay couples. This union is most obvious in the kitchen, where traditional Chinese dishes have a distinctly Malay flair. Lunar Chinese festivals are celebrated throughout the region and Chinese temples appear alongside the dominant religious buildings. While most countries derive cultural and commercial strength from Chinese immigrants, in times of economic hardship, especially in Malaysia and Indonesia, ethnic Chinese have been targets of abuse for their prosperity and ethnic differences. Ethnic Indians from the southern provinces of Tamil Nadu have also settled along the Malay Peninsula and Bangkok.

High up in the mountains that run through Myanmar, Laos, Thailand and Vietnam, a diverse mix of minority groups, collectively referred to as hill tribes, maintain ancient customs, speak their own tribal languages and wear traditional clothing. Believed to have migrated from the Himalaya or southern China, hill-tribe communities such as the Akha, Karen and Hmong were isolated from the dominant culture until the latter half of the 20th century. They were often considered nuisances by the central governments because of their cultural non-conformity, their involvement in illicit poppy cultivation (used to make opium and heroin) and their political opposition, which was leveraged by outsiders during the war in Vietnam. Myanmar has the largest concentration of hill tribes and until recently many of these groups were engaged in a long-standing resistance war against the central government.

A host of minority tribes occupies the diverse archipelago nations of Indonesia and the Philippines. On some islands, a bus ride to the next town places the visitor in an entirely new cultural context. Maintaining a cohesive identity from such diversity is crucial to the character of these two countries.

Lifestyle

The diverse countries of Southeast Asia share the unifying characteristics of developing nations. Foreign visitors have varying reactions to the sometimes low standard of living and the great disparity that exists between the haves and the have-nots.

In the rural areas, life is still tied to the agricultural clock with deep roots in a home village. In these communities multi-generational households are the norm and distinct animistic customs are ingrained in daily life. Rice farming, especially with crude tools such as ploughs drawn by water buffalo, is difficult work that typically affords only a subsistence lifestyle.

Increasingly, though, the region is moving towards a more urban and industrialised way of life. Southeast Asian cities, with the exception of Singapore, are studies in disorder and dysfunction, and are fascinating places for their faults. In the cities, the rich live modern air-conditioned lives while the poor huddle in makeshift slums on abandoned land that lacks proper sewage or water treatment. In between is the middle class, usually educated government workers who can afford terrace house apartments.

Thailand and Vietnam, Malaysia, and Singapore are considered lower-middle, upper-middle and high-income countries, respectively. In real terms, these countries have enjoyed half a millennium of stable governments and relatively prosperous economies. Laos and Cambodia are still tipped toward the poorer end of the scale.

Indonesia and the Philippines are both lower-middle economies but they are stories unto themselves because of their diverse geography and ethnic make-up. Certain islands are prosperous and modern while others are remote and undeveloped. Myanmar is just beginning its voyage into the global economy as it emerges from its decades-long isolation.

Bayanihan is a Filipino term meaning 'communal work', a beloved term evoked during the relief efforts following super-typhoon Yolanda (Haiyan).

PEOPLE & CULTURE PEOPLE

Identity

Like a symphony orchestra, Southeast Asian society focuses on group identity rather than the independent self-determination favoured by Western cultures. Social harmony is ensured by the concept of 'face' – avoiding embarrassing yourself or others by being non-confrontational. This translates into everyday life by not showing anger or frustration and avoiding serious debates that could cause offence. Keeping calm in stressful situations is a cultural ideal. Once you've spent time in the region you will appreciate the undercurrent of peace that this approach provides to an otherwise chaotic landscape.

INVASION OF PERSONAL SPACE

Southeast Asia might be known for its easy-going nature but it is a pressure cooker when it comes to personal space. Tight quarters are everywhere – public transport, city streets and markets – and people are always squeezing into spaces that already seem filled to capacity. You might think that the minivan is full but the driver will shoehorn in three more sweaty bodies before he careens off towards the horizon.

There are no queues. Customers crowd around the vendor, handing over money or barking orders. And they think Westerners are dim for standing around wide-eyed waiting for someone to pay attention to them. Southeast Asians fill empty spaces like flowing water, never leaving a gap, and they exhibit a Zen-like calm on cheek-to-jowl bus rides.

Religion

Religion is a fundamental component of the national and ethnic identities of the people in Southeast Asia. Buddhism and Islam are the region's dominant religions and both have absorbed many of the traditional animistic beliefs of spirit and ancestor worship that predate the region's conversions. Christianity is present in former colonies of Catholic European countries and among ethnic minorities converted by missionaries.

Animist beliefs were absorbed into Buddhism and comprise many religious rituals, from tending family altars and spirit houses to consulting monk astrologers.

Buddhism

Buddhism is the majority religion in most of mainland Southeast Asia, and because many of these countries are cultural cousins the religion has a specific regional identity. Outside of the Buddhist majority countries, there are also minority Buddhist populations, mainly ethnic Chinese, in the Philippines, Indonesia, Malaysia and Brunei.

History & Fundamentals of Buddhism

Buddhism begins with the story of an Indian prince named Siddhartha Gautama in the 6th century BC, who left his life of privilege at the age of 29 on a quest to find the truth. After years of experimentation and ascetic practices, he meditated under a bodhi tree for 49 days, reaching final emancipation and breaking the cycle of birth, death and rebirth. He returned as Buddha, the 'Awakened One', to teach the 'middle way' between extremes. Passion, desire, love and hate are regarded as extremes, so Buddhism counsels that constant patience, detachment, and renouncing desire for worldly pleasures and expectations brings peace and liberation from suffering.

The ultimate end of Buddhism is nirvana, which literally means the 'blowing out' or extinction of all grasping and thus of all suffering (*dukkha*). Effectively, nirvana is also an end to the cycle of rebirths (both moment-to-moment and life-to-life) that is existence.

Conversion to Buddhism

The adoption of Buddhism followed the same route into Southeast Asia as Hinduism – through traders and missionaries from India and Sri Lanka. The Khmer empire's adoption of Buddhism during King Jayavarman's reign in the 12th century marked the beginning of the religion's dominance. The subsequent Thai and Lao kings promoted the religion and were often viewed as divine religious figures as well as national leaders. Most of the monarchies did not survive into the modern era but the religion did, with 90% or more of the population in each mainland Southeast Asian country identifying as Buddhist.

BUDDHA IMAGES

Buddha images are visual sermons. Elongated earlobes, no evidence of bone or muscle, arms that reach to the knees, a third eye: these non-human elements express Buddha's divine nature. Periods within Buddha's life are also depicted in the figure's 'posture' or pose:

Reclining Exact moment of Buddha's enlightenment and death.

Sitting Buddha teaching or meditating. If the right hand is pointed towards the earth, Buddha is shown subduing the demons of desire; if the hands are folded in the lap, Buddha is turning the wheel of law.

Standing Buddha bestowing blessings or taming evil forces.

Walking Buddha after his return to earth from heaven.

PRINCELY TALES

The literary epic of the Ramayana serves as cultural fodder for traditional art, dance and shadow puppetry throughout the region. In this fantastic tale, Prince Rama (an incarnation of the Hindu god Vishnu) falls in love with beautiful Sita and wins her hand in marriage by completing the challenge of stringing a magic bow. Before the couple can live in peace, Rama is banished from his kingdom and his wife is kidnapped by Ravana. With the help of the monkey king, Hanuman, Sita is rescued, but a great battle ensues. Rama and his allies defeat Ravana and restore peace and goodness to the land.

Thailand, Cambodia, Laos and Myanmar practise Theravada Buddhism (Teaching of the Elders), which travelled to the region via Sri Lanka. Vietnam adopted Mahayana Buddhism (Greater Vehicle), which took a northern route through Tibet, China and Japan. Though in practice, most Vietnamese practise a fusion of Confucianism, Taoism and Buddhism, collectively known as Tam Giao or the Triple Religion.

One of the major theological differences between the two types of Buddhism lies in the outcome of a devout life. In Theravada, followers strive to obtain nirvana (release from the cycle of existence) over the course of many reincarnations, the final one of which is as a member of the monastic order. The emphasis is on self-enlightenment. But in Mahayana tradition, nirvana can be achieved within a single lifetime and emphasis is on helping others become enlightened. With this emphasis on teaching, more attention is given to bodhisattva, one who has almost reached nirvana but renounces it in order to help others attain it.

This doctrinal difference and country of origin can be viewed in the two schools' places of worship. Theravada temples typically have one central hall of worship containing a central (Gautama) Buddha image. Hindu elements inherited from South Asia infuse the Theravada religious art and architecture. Mahayana temples conform more to inherited aesthetics from China. Temples contain a hall dedicated to the three Buddhas (including modern incarnations Amitabha and Medicine Buddha) and another hall to the three important bodhisattvas.

Buddhist Monuu ments

Temples of Angkor (Cambodia)

Borobudur (Indonesia)

Bagan (Myanmar)

Sukhothai Historical Park (Thailand)

Islam

Islam in Southeast Asia is characterised by the region's unique cultural, historical and philosophical landscape. For this reason, many Westerners notice a vast difference between the way Islam is practised in Southeast Asia compared with the way it is practised in other parts of the Muslim world, such as the Middle East.

History & Fundamentals of Islam

Islam is a monotheistic religion that originated in Arabia in the 7th century. The religion's primary prophet is Mohammed, who received and promoted the word of God (the Quran, the holy book of the faith). Islam means 'submission' in Arabic, and it is the duty of every Muslim to submit to Allah (God). This profession of faith is the first of the five pillars of Islam; the other four are to pray five times a day, give alms to the poor, fast during Ramadan and make the pilgrimage to Mecca.

Conversion to Islam

Trade played an important role in the introduction of the religion. Many Southeast Asian communities converted to Islam in order to join a brotherhood of merchants (Muslim Arabs, Indians and Chinese) and to escape the inflexible caste system of the Srivijaya kingdom, a Hindu-Buddhist empire that controlled the Malay Peninsula and parts of

THE FACE OF MODERN ISLAM

Just going by the numbers, modern Islam is a lot more Asian than Arab. In fact only 15% of the world's Muslims are Arab, while the majority are South and Southeast Asians. If the media were looking for a model citizen, they could choose Indonesia, which has the largest population of Muslims in the world (it's home to 12% of the world's Muslims). It is a devout country and sends the largest national delegation of pilgrims to Mecca every year. But it is also a multi-national, multi-ethnic and multi-religious democratic country – more like Turkey than Saudi Arabia.

Indonesia. It is believed that Muslim conversions and settlements first occurred in northern Sumatra's Aceh province and then spread to the port cities, including the important trade and cultural centre of Melaka (Malaysia). Starting around the 12th century, Islam gained in popularity, spreading through Malaysia to southern Thailand, Indonesia and parts of the Philippines.

The mystical traditions of Sufism are often credited for this widespread adoption of Islam. Sufis were itinerant holy men ('suf' is an Arabic word for the 'coarse wool' worn by a religious ascetic) who were believed to have magic abilities and encouraged a personal expression of the religion instead of a strict orthodoxy and adherence to the law. Scholars believe that Sufis helped mould traditional beliefs and folk practices stemming from the region's Hindu-Buddhist past around an Islamic core, instead of forcing local communities to abandon pre-Islamic practices. Chanting and drumming remain a component of Southeast Asia's Islamic prayer tradition; shadow puppetry adopted Arabic and Islamic stories as well as the original Hindu myths; the ideas of the annihilation of the ego and of nirvana were tweaked to fit Islamic theology. Women were never cloistered and retained their traditional roles outside the home. In the past, the older generation did not wear headscarves, but the younger generation has adopted the practice, much to the concern of non-Muslim observers who fear an increased regional fundamentalism.

Political Islam

The practice of Islam in Southeast Asia has been characterised by many of the same tensions that have emerged in Muslim communities around the world. Debates continue to rage about the interpretation of various passages in the Quran, and their implications for legal, social and financial institutions. As the region's colonial era was waning, the reform movement of Wahhabism became a popular political tool. Wahhabism promoted a literal interpretation of the Quran and intended to purge the religion of its pagan practices. It also emphasised the development of an Islamic political state.

Integral to an Islamic political state is sharia (Islamic law or God's law), which regulates criminal, civil and personal conduct. There are debates within the Muslim world as to the exact extents of sharia and how to overlap contradictory elements within a modern pluralistic state. A few indisputable components are the abstinence from pork products, drinking and gambling, as well as modesty in dress, though the last is also subject to local and generational interpretation.

Within Southeast Asia, sharia justice systems are on the rise. Malaysia has long maintained a parallel sharia system applied to Muslim Malays only, though there are censorship rules that often cross over into mainstream film and print media. Indonesia does not have national sharia, but it does allow the province of Aceh to enforce partial sharia under the terms of the 2005 peace deal. The Philippines government has proposed

Violent low-scale wars exist in the Muslim-majority region of southern Thailand and the southern Philippines. These conflicts are considered to be ethnic independence struggles rather than jihad.

a similar agreement with the Moro people on the southern island of Mindanao as part of its 2013 peace agreement.

Most of Brunei's criminal system is based on a British model, but over the last five years it has increasingly adopted Islamic laws and punishments, including hand amputation for thefts and public stoning.

Christianity

Catholicism was introduced to Vietnam by the French, to the Philippines by the Spanish and to Timor-Leste by the Portuguese. Parts of Indonesia are Christian, mainly Protestant, due to the efforts of Western missionary groups. In each of these converted groups there are remnants of the original animistic beliefs and an almost personal emphasis on preferred aspects of the liturgy or the ideology. The local adaptations can often be so pronounced that Westerners of the same faith might still observe the practice as foreign.

Hinduism

Hinduism ruled the spiritual lives of Southeast Asians more than 1500 years ago, and the great Hindu empires of Angkor and Srivijaya built grand monuments to their pantheon of gods. The primary representations of the multiple faces of the one omnipresent god are Brahma (the creator), Vishnu (the preserver) and Shiva (the destroyer or reproducer). All three gods are usually shown with four arms, but Brahma has the added advantage of four heads to represent his all-seeing presence.

Although Buddhism and Islam have filtered across the continent, Hinduism has filtered through these mainstream religions and Buddhism regards the Hindu deities with respect. Also, the Hindu island of Bali is a spiritual anomaly in the region. Within the last 100 years, the influx of Indian labourers to Southeast Asia has bolstered the religion's followers.

Arts & Architecture

Southeast Asia's most notable artistic endeavours are religious in nature. The Buddhist countries have distinctive artistic depictions of the Hindu deities and symbols of Buddhism. Both an artistic and architectural wonder, the temples of Angkor in Cambodia defined much of mainland Southeast Asia's artistic interpretation of religious iconography. The temples' elaborate sculptured murals pay homage to Hindu gods Vishnu (represented as a four-armed figure) and Shiva (styled either in an embrace with his consort or as an ascetic), while also recording historical events and creation myths. Angkor-inspired monuments were built by the Khmers in neighbouring countries and were adopted by later regional empires, such as the Thai kingdoms of Sukhothai and Ayuthaya.

Statues of Buddha reflect an individual country's artistic interpretations of an art form governed by highly symbolic strictures. Buddha is depicted sitting, standing and reclining – all representations of historic moments in his life. In Vietnam, representations of the Buddha are more akin to Chinese religious art, rather than India or Angkor. Also found decorating many temple railings is the mythical water serpent, known as *naga*, which represents the life-giving power of water.

In Indonesia, Malaysia, Brunei and the Philippines, Islamic art and architecture intermingled with animist traditions. Every town in Malaysia has a grand fortressed mosque with an Arabic minaret and Moorish tile work. Indonesia is home to the region's biggest mosque (Istiqlal Mosque in central Jakarta, designed by a Christian architect), as well as stunning mosques that incorporate palace-like features from international inspirations.

PEOPLE & CULTURE ARTS & ARCHITECTURE

Religious Reads

Living Faith: Inside the Muslim World of Southeast Asia by Steve Raymer

Buddhism for Beginners by Thubten Chodron

Top Museums

Asian Civilisations Museum (Singapore)

Islamic Arts Museum (Malaysia)

Jim Thompson House (Thailand)

National Museum (Cambodia)

Vietnam Museum of Ethnology (Vietnam)

Food

Top Noodle Dishes

laksa (Malaysia)

pho (Vietnam)

pàt tai (Thailand)

mie goreng (Indonesia)

nam ben choc (Cambodia)

lard na (Laos)

pancit bihon (Philippines)

char kway teow (Singapore)

Southeast Asia is foodie heaven. While the culinary heavyweights of Thailand and Vietnam hog the headlines, all the countries of the region boast a rich and varied cuisine.

Southeast Asia's tropical climate creates a year-round bounty. Food is central to every cultural celebration. Many traditional holidays revolve around the region's staple, rice. Village festivals mark the beginning of rice-planting season, with rituals and customs designed to ensure a bountiful harvest. Even the invisible spirits who guide good luck in the Buddhist countries require daily offerings of food to sate their mischievous nature.

Traces of Southeast Asia's cultural parents – India and China – can be detected in the individual nations' cuisines. In Myanmar, Malaysia and southern Thailand, Indian-style flatbreads accompany curries as the meal's staple, instead of rice. Throughout the region, the Indian creation of curry receives much reinvention, drawing on such local ingredients as coconut milk and a penchant for chillies. As the centre of the ancient spice trade, Indonesia became a global kitchen, adopting recipes from India, Arabia, Europe and China, and fashioning them into such dishes as buffalo curries and peanut sauces for satay (peanuts were brought by Spanish and Portuguese traders).

Among many other dishes, the Chinese donated noodles, which are fried, drowned in broth or tossed in salads. Noodle soups are the quintessential comfort food, eaten in the morning, after a night carousing or at midday when pressed for time. Much of the Chinese cuisine that has become comfortably settled in Southeast Asia is from southern China, but it has been reinvented, imported to neighbouring countries and reproduced so many times that some dishes' pedigrees are totally obscured.

Thailand and Laos share many common dishes, often competing for the honour of spiciest cuisine (Laos wins in our humble opinion). Green papaya salad is a mainstay of both – the Thais like theirs with ground peanuts, fresh tomatoes and dried shrimp; the Lao version uses fermented fish sauce, field crabs and lots of chillies (it is more delicious than it sounds). In Laos and neighbouring Thai provinces, the local people eat 'sticky rice' (a shorter grain than the standard fluffy jasmine rice). This kind of rice is eaten with the hands and usually rolled up into balls and dipped into spicy sauces.

Spicy food is beloved by Southeast Asian cultures and each country has a spicy condiment, consisting of ground chillies, lime juice and sometimes, but not always, fish sauce or paste. The Spanish are often credited for introducing chillies to the region.

As dictated by the strictures of Islam, Muslim communities throughout the region don't eat pork, creating a culinary culture clash with their Chinese neighbours who adore pork dishes.

Survival Guide

Responsible Travel

In Southeast Asia, tourism brings blessings and curses. Small-scale tourism fosters family-owned businesses and one-on-one cultural exchanges that broaden people's perspectives, and helps preserve cultural and environmental assets. But tourism also puts environmental and cultural pressures on the host country. To ensure that your trip is a gift, not a burden, mind your manners, be green, learn everything you can about the host country and be a conscientious consumer.

ENVIRONMENTAL CONCERNS

Southeast Asia has some of the greatest biodiversity on the planet, containing species that do not exist anywhere else, particularly in mega-diverse countries such as Indonesia, Malaysia and the Philippines. Environmental superlatives include: reefs regarded as the world's most abundant (75% of the world's coral species are found here), including the 6-million-sq-km Coral Triangle, which stretches all the way from Malaysia to the Solomon Islands; the Mekong River, which rivals the Amazon for biodiversity; the world's largest lizard (the Komodo dragon); and numerous endemic bird species (the region is also an important stopover for migratory species).

But the region is also densely populated and environmental degradation is immediately tangible. Smoke fills the air as the forests are cleared for beach bungalows, small-scale farms, palm-oil plantations or logging. Major cities are choked with smog and pollution from vehicle emissions. The waterways are clogged with trash, and raw sewage is dumped into turquoise waters because of inadequate waste treatment facilities.

Deforestation

Due to deforestation and associated forest fires, Indonesia is the world's third-largest greenhouse gas emitter. Smoke from Indonesian forest fires regularly cloaks Singapore and parts of Malaysia in a choking haze. Destruction of the mangrove forests, which act as tidal buffer zones, has resulted in coastal storms which have a disastrous effect on the local population, contributing to the death toll of the 2004 Boxing Day tsunami and 2013 typhoon Yolanda (Haiyan).

Water Systems

Water systems are suffering as well. Environmental degradation of coral reefs is caused by overfishing and sediment run-off from coastal development, as well

as climate change. Along the Mekong River, hydroelectric dams are significantly altering the river's ecosystem, from sediment movement to fish migration, as well as water levels downstream.

Habitat Loss

Habitat loss is a serious threat to the region's indigenous wildlife. The few remaining natural areas are also subject to poaching. Thailand is one of the primary conduits through which live wildlife and harvested wildlife parts travel to overseas markets.

Solutions

Though the environmental problems are apparent, obvious answers are not. Conserving wild lands requires political convictions undeterred by moneyed interests, a tall order in a region with limited national budgets and a culture of corruption. Of all of the Southeast Asian nations, Brunei leads the conservationist charge with approximately 70% of its original forest cover still intact, but its oil wealth allows it to overlook the profits of undeveloped lands.

What You Can Do

There are many environmental problems that the average tourist has zero control over, but on a local level visitors can strive to reduce their individual 'footprint' by putting as little pressure on the natural environment and the local infrastructure as possible. Here are some modest steps:

➡ Live like a local: opt for a fan instead of an air-con room; shower with cold water instead of hot.

➡ Use biodegradable soap to reduce water pollution.

➡ Eat locally sourced meals instead of imported products.

➡ Dispose of plastic packaging before leaving home so that it doesn't end up in overburdened refuse systems.

➡ Dispose of cigarette butts in rubbish bins not on the beach or into the water.

➡ Choose unplugged modes of transit (walking tour over minivan tour, bicycle over motorbike, kayak over jet ski).

➡ Volunteer with a local conservation or animal-welfare group.

➡ Be a responsible diver.

➡ Dispose of your rubbish in a proper receptacle, even if the locals don't.

➡ Don't eat or drink food products made from endangered animals or plants.

➡ Avoid plastic bottles: take a reusable water bottle and treat water.

➡ Patronise businesses that promote sustainable tourism, responsible tourism and ecotourism.

WILDLIFE ENCOUNTERS

Southeast Asia offers some incredible opportunities for wildlife encounters and animal interaction. Walk with elephants, zipline through the jungle canopy with gibbons, dive with whale sharks and spot the world's largest

lizard, the Komodo dragon. However, it is crucial to remember these are wild animals in their natural habitat, so it is important to behave in an appropriate manner. Some tips:

➡ Do not leave any litter in the natural environment in case it enters the food chain, particularly in a marine location.

➡ Do not smoke anywhere near wild animals.

➡ Do not use flash photography near animals in case it disturbs them.

➡ Do listen to rangers and guides and keep a safe and respectful distance from the animal at all times.

➡ Do choose responsible wildlife encounters such as walking with an elephant herd instead of taking a typical tourist elephant ride. Organisations promoting responsible wildlife encounters in the region:

Conservation International (CI; www.conservation.org)

Elephant Asia Rescue and Survival Foundation (http://earsasia.org)

Wildlife Alliance (www.wildlifealliance.org)

Wildlife Conservation Society (WCS; www.wcs.org)

WWF International (www.panda.org)

CULTURAL & SOCIAL CONCERNS

Most Southeast Asians don't expect tourists to know very much about them and for this reason they overlook innocent breaches of social etiquette. But each culture has a host of taboos and sacred beliefs that should not be disrespected. Before arriving, figure out the touchy subjects and tread cautiously.

Tourists also encounter problems when they show anger over money disputes or miscommunication and during drunken escapades. Being polite and patient is better than being right and belligerent.

USEFUL WEBSITES

Responsible Travel (www.responsible-travel.org) Tips on how to be a 'better' tourist regarding environmental issues, begging and bargaining, as well as ethical holidays.

Mekong Responsible Tourism (www.mekongresponsibletourism.org) Online guide promoting community-based and socially responsible tourism in the Mekong region, including homestays and eco-lodges.

WWF International (www.panda.org) Read up on WWF's environmental campaigns to protect Southeast Asia's threatened species and landscapes.

Mongabay (www.mongabay.com) Environmental science and conservation news site with a focus on tropical rainforests, including Indonesia.

Ecology Asia (www.ecologyasia.com) Facts and figures about Southeast Asia's flora and fauna.

Sealang Projects (www.sealang.net) Academic resource for learning Southeast Asian languages.

Travelers Against Plastic (www.travelersagainstplastic.org) Promotes the use of reusable water bottles to help the environment.

What You Can Do

Here are some pointers to keep you on everyone's good side:

➡ Respect local dress standards, particularly at religious sites. Remove shoes and hat before entering a religious building.

➡ Always ask for permission before you take a picture of someone, especially during private moments; asking in the local language is even better.

➡ Take a language course or at least learn the local greetings in each country.

➡ Treat religious objects, no matter how old or decrepit, with the utmost respect; don't clamber on temple ruins or pose behind headless Buddha statues.

➡ Share your snacks or cigarettes with your neighbour on long bus rides.

➡ Tip fairly where possible, as daily wages are very low.

➡ Smile while bargaining; your beauty will distract them from opportunistic pricing.

➡ Do not raise your voice or show signs of aggression as this will lead to a 'loss of face' for locals and could have serious repercussions.

POVERTY & ECONOMIC DISPARITY

The disparity between rich and poor is one of Southeast Asia's most pressing social concerns. Only a few of the region's countries have well-developed social safety nets to catch people left homeless or jobless by debt mismanagement, rapid industrialisation or institutionalised discrimination.

Remote villagers, including ethnic minorities, often live precarious subsistence lives without access to health care, economic opportunity or basic education. In some cases, their traditional lifestyles are incompatible with the modern marketplace, and many villages lose their young people to jobs in the cities. Urban migrants often do menial labour for menial wages; some turn to more profitable enterprises, such as prostitution or other illicit ventures. When a family is financially compromised, children are often expected to work, either formally in a factory or informally as a street hawker. They often don't have the luxury of time or money to receive an education.

There is also an ongoing problem of human trafficking, mainly economic migrants who are lured to a neighbouring country for work to find that they are vulnerable to exploitation.

Begging is common in many of the major cities of the region and that tug on the shirtsleeve can become tiresome after a time. However, try to remember that many of these countries have little in the way of a social security net to catch people when they fall. It is best to keep denominations small to avoid foreigners becoming more of a target than they already are. Cambodia has a large number of amputee beggars, a legacy of landmines and civil war.

Avoid giving money to children, as this is more likely to go directly to a begging 'pimp' or human trafficker than to the child. Food is an option for children as at least they are likely to benefit directly. However, child welfare organisations would counsel against giving to children altogether to avoid creating a culture of dependency from a young age. Instead, consider making a donation to one of the many local organisations assisting in the battle against poverty.

PROSTITUTION

Prostitution is technically illegal but common and tolerated in many parts of Southeast Asia. While some sex workers are adults, others are minors who have been sold or recruited by family members and are exploited by the business owner through intimidation and abuse. Unicef estimates that there are close to one million child prostitutes in all of Asia – one of the highest figures in the world.

Sex with minors is a serious offence that is enforced with severe penalties by Southeast Asian countries. Many Western countries also prosecute and punish citizens for paedophile offences committed abroad. For more information contact **End Child Prostitution & Trafficking** (Ecpat; www.ecpat.net), a global network that works to stop child prostitution, child pornography and the trafficking of children for sexual purposes. **Childsafe International** (www.childsafe-international. org) aims to educate businesses and individuals to be on the lookout for children in vulnerable situations.

What You Can Do

➡ Support businesses with a social-justice mission, such as fair-trade weaving cooperatives or job-skills development sites.

➡ Stay at village homestays to support traditional lifestyles.

➡ Discourage child labour by not patronising child vendors or hawkers.

➡ Make a donation to a local school or charity instead of handing out money or gifts to beggars, especially children.

➡ Hire local guides to encourage village-based employment opportunities.

➡ Avoid all-inclusive purchases (lodging, transport, tours, food); instead, spread your spending so that more local people benefit.

VOLUNTEERING & VOLUNTOURISM

Voluntourism is a booming business in Southeast Asia, with travel companies co-opting the idea as a new marketing angle. To avoid the bulk of your placement fees going into the pockets of third-party agencies, it's important to do your research on the hundreds of organisations that now offer volunteer work and find a suitable one that supports your skills. For any organisation working with children, child protection is a serious concern; organisations that do not conduct background checks on volunteers should be regarded with extreme caution.

Lonely Planet does not endorse any organisations that we do not work with directly, so it is essential that you do your own thorough research before agreeing to volunteer with or donate to any organisation.

Orphanage Tourism

In recent years, visiting orphanages has become a popular activity, but is it always good for the children and the host country in the longer run? Orphanage tourism and all the connotations that come with it are a disturbing development that can draw some unscrupulous elements into the world of childcare. Some orphanages have been established based on a business model and in other cases the 'orphans' are not orphans at all, but have a living parent or have been 'rented' from a local school.

Many orphanages in the region are doing a good job in difficult circumstances. Some are world class, enjoy funding and support from wealthy benefactors and don't need visitors. Others are desperate places that need all the help they can get. However, if a place is promoting orphanage visits, then proceed with caution,

as the adults may not always have the best interests of the children at heart.

Friends International and Unicef joined forces to launch the 'Think Before Visiting' campaign. Learn more at www.thinkchildsafe.org/thinkbeforevisiting before you inadvertently contribute to the problem. Some dos and don'ts:

➡ Do think about volunteering for a minimum of a month or longer rather than a short-term stay.

➡ Do think carefully about what skills you have that will make a difference to the children.

➡ Do work with the local staff rather than directly with the children. Teach the local staff how to speak English for a sustainable impact.

➡ Don't under any circumstances visit orphanages as part of a brief tour or go to any that actively solicit tourists.

➡ Don't hand over large fees for a placement without checking where the money goes.

➡ Don't volunteer at any orphanage without thoroughly researching it. Is it regulated? Do they require background checks on volunteers?

Directory A–Z

Accommodation

The accommodation listed in reviews occupies the low end of the price and amenities scale. Basic rooms typically have four walls, a bed and a fan (handy for keeping mosquitoes at bay). In the cheapest instances, the bathroom is shared. Most places geared to foreigners have Western-style toilets, but hotels that cater to locals usually have Asian squat toilets. Air-con and private bathrooms cost more. Camping is not a widespread option due to the tropical heat, but dorms are becoming a more economical option – especially in the Philippines, Singapore and Thailand, where accommodation tends to be more expensive.

Be a smart shopper when looking for a room. Always ask for the price first, then ask to see a room to inspect it for cleanliness, comfort and quiet. Don't feel obligated to take a room just because the place is mentioned in Lonely Planet.

Each hotel or guesthouse has its own convention for payment. Some require payment in advance; others collect the money upon check out. Before you pay for numerous nights in advance, make sure that you find the accommodation acceptable, as getting a refund will be impossible.

Bathing

In remote corners or basic accommodation, you'll meet the Southeast Asian version of a shower: a large basin that holds water for bathing. Water should be scooped out of the basin with a smaller bowl and poured over the body. Resist the urge to climb in like a bathtub and avoid washing directly over the basin, as this is your source for clean water.

Modern facilities usually have a cold-water shower. More expensive accommodation, large cities and colder regions will offer hot-water showers at a higher price.

Many rural people bathe in rivers or streams. If you choose to do the same, be aware that public nudity is not acceptable. Do as the locals do and bathe while wearing a sarong.

Customs Regulations

Customs regulations vary little around the region. Drugs and arms are strictly prohibited – death or a lengthy stay in prison are common sentences. Pornography is also a no-no.

Discount Cards

The International Student Identity Card (ISIC) is moderately useful in Southeast Asia, with limited success in gaining the holder discounts. Some domestic and international airlines provide discounts to ISIC cardholders, but the cards carry little bargaining power because knock-offs are available in Bangkok.

Discrimination

Skin colour may be a factor in Southeast Asia. White foreigners stand out in a crowd. Children will often point, prices may double and a handful of presumptions may precede your arrival. In general, these will seem either minor nuisances or exotic elements of travel. If you are a Westerner of Asian descent, some Southeast Asians will assume that you are a local until the language barrier proves otherwise.

BOOK YOUR STAY ONLINE

For more accommodation reviews by Lonely Planet authors, check out www.lonelyplanet.com/hotels/. You'll find independent reviews, as well as recommendations on the best places to stay. Best of all, you can book online.

With the colour barrier removed, many Westerners with Asian heritage are treated like family and sometimes get charged local prices. People with darker complexions will be regarded to be as foreign as white visitors, but may sometimes be the victim of local prejudices.

Electricity

Most countries work on a voltage of 220V to 240V at 50Hz (cycles); note that 240V appliances will happily run on 220V. You should be able to pick up adapters in electrical shops in most Southeast Asian cities.

Embassies & Consulates

It's important to realise what your own embassy – the embassy of the country of which you are a citizen – can and can't do to help you if you get into trouble.

Generally speaking, it won't be much help in emergencies if the trouble you're in is remotely your own fault. You are bound by the laws of the country you are in. Your embassy will not be sympathetic if you end up in jail after committing a crime locally, even if such actions are legal in your own country.

In genuine emergencies you might get some assistance if other channels have been exhausted. If you need to get home urgently, a free ticket home is exceedingly unlikely – the embassy would expect you to have insurance. If you have all your money and documents stolen, it might assist with getting a new passport, but a loan for onward travel is out of the question.

Most travellers should have no need to contact their embassy while in Southeast Asia, although if you're travelling in unstable regions or going into uncharted territory, it may be worth letting your embassy know upon departure and return. In this way valuable time, effort and money won't be wasted looking for you while you're relaxing on a beach somewhere.

LGBT Travellers

Parts of Southeast Asia could easily be ranked as some of the most progressive regions regarding homosexuality outside the Western world. In general most urban centres have gay communities, and attitudes towards same-sex relationships are tolerant, though travellers should still mind the region-wide prescription of refraining from public displays of affection. However, the situation is less relaxed in more conservative Muslim countries such as Brunei and Malaysia.

Utopia Asian Gay & Lesbian Resources (www.utopia-asia.com) has an excellent profile of each country's record on acceptance, as well as short reviews on gay nightspots and handy travel guides to the various Southeast Asian countries.

Insurance

A travel-insurance policy to cover theft, loss and medical problems is a necessity. There's a wide variety of policies available, so check the small print. For more information about the ins and outs of travel insurance, contact a travel agent or travel insurer.

Some policies specifically exclude 'dangerous activities', which can include scuba diving, motorcycling and even trekking. A locally acquired motorcycle licence is also not valid under some policies. Check that the policy covers ambulance rides, emergency flights home and, in the case of death, repatriation of a body.

Worldwide travel insurance is available at www.lonelyplanet.com/travel-insurance.

You can buy, extend and claim online anytime – even if you're already on the road.

Internet Access

In metropolitan areas, Southeast Asia is incredibly well wired, with abundant wi-fi access, internet cafes, fast connections and low prices. Outside the big cities, things start to vary. Good internet connections are usually commensurate with a destination's road system: well-sealed highways usually mean speedy travel through the information superhighway as well. 3G and even 4G mobile access is available in large urban centres.

Censorship of some sites is in effect across the region, particularly in Vietnam.

Legal Matters

Be sure to know the national laws so that you don't unwittingly commit a crime.

If you are a victim of a crime, contact the tourist police, if available; they are usually better trained to deal with foreigners and foreign languages than the regular police force.

Drugs

The risks associated with recreational drug use and distribution are serious even in places with illicit reputations. Just down the road from Kuta Beach in Bali is a jail where travellers are staying much longer than they had intended. In Indonesia, you can be jailed because your travel companions had dope and you didn't report them. In Malaysia and Singapore, possession of certain quantities of dope can lead to hanging. Even laid-back Laos seriously prosecutes drug trafficking. With heightened airport security, customs officials are zealous in their screening of both luggage and passengers.

The death penalty, prison sentences and huge fines are given as liberally to foreigners as to locals; no one has evaded punishment because of ignorance of local laws. In Indonesia in 2005, nine Australians (dubbed the 'Bali Nine') were arrested on charges of heroin possession: seven received life sentences, while the other two were executed by firing squad in 2015.

Recreational drug use is often viewed in the same league as drug trafficking and can result in prison terms. In Thailand, sometimes the drug dealers are in cahoots with the police and use a drug transaction as an opportunity to extract a huge bribe.

Money

Check www.xe.com for current exchange rates. Refer to the specific destination chapters for the availability of ATMs and any other pre-arrival concerns about money.

Bargaining

Most Southeast Asian countries practise the art of bargaining. Remember that it is an art, not a test of wills, and the trick is to find a price that makes everyone happy.

Bargaining is acceptable in markets and in shops where the prices aren't displayed. Here are some basic 'dance moves' for bargaining for goods. First ask the price and then ask for a discount. If the discount isn't acceptable offer something slightly lower but be prepared to accept an amount in between. Once you counter, you can't lower your price. Don't start to haggle unless you're serious about buying. If you become angry or visibly frustrated, you've lost the game.

It is also customary (and mandatory) to bargain for chartered transport as tourists are often taken advantage of by local taxi drivers. Ask at your guesthouse how much a trip should cost

before chartering a vehicle. Then head out to the street and start negotiations with a driver, counter with your own offer and accept something in between. If the driver won't budge, then politely decline the service and move on. Don't fight with the driver, as they are famous for their tempers.

Passports

To enter most countries your passport must be valid for at least six months from your date of entry, even if you're only staying for a few days. It's probably best to have at least a year left on your passport if you are heading off on a big trip around Southeast Asia.

Testy border guards may refuse entry if your passport doesn't have enough blank pages available. Before leaving get more pages added to a valid passport (if this is a service offered by your home country). Once on the road, you can apply for a new passport in most major Southeast Asian cities from your home embassy or consulate.

Photography

Before leaving home, determine whether your battery charger will require a power adapter by visiting the website of the World Electric Guide (www.kropla.com/electric.htm).

The best places to buy camera equipment or have repairs done are Singapore, Bangkok and Kuala Lumpur. Remember that the more equipment you travel with, the more vulnerable you are to theft.

You should always ask permission before taking a person's photograph. Many hill-tribe villagers seriously object to being photographed, or they may ask for money in exchange; if you want the photo, you should honour the price. Also respect people's privacy even if they

are in public; guesthouses and small restaurants serve double-duty as the owner's living space and they deserve to have family time without being a photo-opportunity.

Post

Postal services are generally reliable across the region. There's always an element of risk in sending parcels home by sea, though as a rule they eventually reach their destination. If it's something of value, you're better off mailing home your dirty clothes to make room in your luggage for precious keepsakes. Don't send cash or valuables through government-run postal systems.

Poste restante is widely available, although infrequently used, and is the best way of receiving mail.

Safe Travel

It is safer in Southeast Asia than you might think. But you still need to keep your wits about you to avoid scams, injury and assault.

Assaults

Violent assaults in Southeast Asia are not common, but instances of attacks on foreigners generate media attention and corresponding anxiety. Travellers should exercise basic street smarts: avoid quiet areas at night, excessive drinking or angering locals. Police enforcement of local laws and investigations into crimes are often inadequate so don't assume that a country's general friendliness equals a crime-free zone.

Avoid confrontations with locals, in general, but especially when alcohol is involved. What might seem like harmless verbal sparring to you might be regarded as injurious by the local and might provoke disproportionately violent acts of retribution thanks to the complicated concept of 'saving face'.

Special caution should be exercised at big parties like Thailand's Full Moon raves, where criminal gangs with political connections take advantage of intoxicated revellers. Other party places, such as Sihanoukville and Bali, both have seedy underbellies that should be avoided.

Drugs

When it comes to drugs, you never really know what you're getting. In Cambodia, what is sold as methamphetamine or MDMA is often a homemade concoction of cheap and toxic chemicals and what is sold as cocaine is heavy-duty heroin that is easily consumed in overdose levels.

Political Unrest

Avoid all political demonstrations, no matter how benign or celebratory they may appear. Mass rallies can quickly turn into violent clashes between rival factions or the military. With that said, just because there are rallies in one corner of a massive city, like Bangkok, doesn't mean that the whole country, or even the whole city, is off limits. Your home country's embassy will issue the safest possible travel warnings, which should be balanced with coverage in the local press in order to gauge the political temperature. No-go zones experiencing low-scale independence wars exist in parts of eastern Myanmar, southern Thailand and the Philippines.

Scams

Every year we get emails from travellers reporting that they've been scammed in Southeast Asia. In most cases the scams are petty rip-offs, in which a naive traveller pays too much for a ride to the bus station, to exchange money, buy souvenirs and so on. Rip-offs are in full force at border crossings, popular tourist attractions, bus and rail stations and wherever travellers might get confused.

Here are some tips for avoiding scams:

➡ Be diplomatically suspicious of over-friendly locals.

➡ Avoid super-cheap, inclusive transport packages, which often include extra commission-generating fees.

➡ Don't accept invitations to play cards or go shopping with a friendly stranger; this is a prelude to a well-rehearsed and expensive scam.

➡ Understand that commissions are common business practices in the region and are levied wherever there is a third party.

Theft

Theft in Southeast Asia is usually by stealth rather than by force. Violent theft is rare but can occur late at night and often after the victim has been drinking. Be sure that you are with people you trust if you are going to drink your weight in Thailand's famous booze buckets or Vietnam's endless supply of draught beer. Travel in groups late at night, especially after a night of carousing, to ensure safety in numbers. Women should be especially careful about returning home late at night from a bar.

Clandestine theft is a concern, especially on overnight buses, in communal dorms or in lodging with inadequate locks on windows and dorms. In Malaysia, petty thieves have been known to check into a guesthouse and then rob the other guests in the middle of the night.

Snatch thieves are an increasing problem, especially in Vietnam and Cambodia. Typically the thieves aboard a motorcycle pull up alongside a tourist just long enough to grab a bag or camera and then they speed away. This can happen when the tourist is walking along the street or riding in a vehicle like a moto or túk-túk.

Here are some tips for keeping your stuff safe:

➡ Keep your money and valuables in a money belt (worn underneath your clothes).

➡ Don't carry valuables in a bag that can be grabbed by snatch thieves and don't carry your camera by its strap.

➡ Place your bag in between you and the driver when riding on a motorcycle or between your legs when riding in a tuk-tuk to prevent snatch thieves.

➡ Don't store valuables in easily accessible places such as backpack pockets or packs that are stored in the luggage compartment of buses.

➡ Don't put valuables in the baskets of a motorcycle or bicycle, easy pickings for snatch thieves.

➡ Be especially careful about your belongings when sleeping in dorms.

Unexploded Ordnance & Landmines

The legacy of war lingers on in Cambodia, Laos and Vietnam. Laos suffers the fate of being the most heavily bombed country per capita in the world, while all three countries were on the receiving end of more bombs than were dropped by all sides during WWII. There are still many undetonated bombs and explosives out there, so be careful walking off the trail in areas near the Laos–Vietnam border or around the Demilitarised Zone (DMZ). Cambodia suffers the additional affliction of landmines, some four to six million of them according to surveys. It pays to stick to marked paths anywhere in Cambodia.

Toilets

As tourism continues to grow in the region, Western-style sit-down toilets are increasingly common. However, in rural areas squat toilets are widespread.

If you encounter a squat, here's what you should do. Straddle the two footpads and face the door. To flush use the plastic bowl to scoop water out of the adjacent basin and pour into the toilet bowl. Some places supply a small pack of toilet paper available for purchase at the entrance; otherwise bring your own stash or wipe the old-fashioned way with water.

Even in places where sit-down toilets are installed, the septic system may not be designed to take toilet paper. In such cases there will be a waste basket where you're supposed to place used toilet paper and feminine hygiene products.

Tourist Information

Most of the Southeast Asian countries have government-funded tourist offices of varying usefulness. Better information is sometimes available through guesthouses and from fellow travellers. Do be aware that official tourist offices don't make accommodation and transport bookings. If a so-called tourist office provides this service, then they are a travel agency that charges a commission.

Travellers with Disabilities

Travellers with serious disabilities will likely find Southeast Asia to be a challenging place to travel. Even the more modern cities are very difficult to navigate for mobility- or vision-impaired people. Generally speaking, infrastructure is often inadequate for those with disabilities.

International organisations that can provide information on mobility-impaired travel include the following:

Mobility International USA www.miusa.org

Disability Alliance www.disabilityrightsuk.org

Society for Accessible Travel & Hospitality (SATH) www.sath.org

Lonely Planet's free Accessible Travel guide can be downloaded here: http://lptravel.to/AccessibleTravel

Visas

Before arriving in a country (either by air, land or sea), find out if you need to pre-arrange a visa or if one is available for your nationality upon arrival. Here are some additional visa tips:

➡ Plan your trip around the length of stay mandated by the visa.

➡ If you plan on staying longer than the typical allotment, apply for a longer visa from the embassy in your home country or from an embassy in a neighbouring country or investigate the ease of extending a visa within the country.

➡ Stock up on passport photos, as you'll probably need at least two pictures each time you apply for a visa.

➡ Have the correct amount of local currency (or US dollars) to pay the on-arrival visa fee.

➡ Dress smartly when you're visiting embassies, consulates and borders; Southeast Asians appreciate appearance.

Women Travellers

While travel in Southeast Asia for women is generally safe, solo women should exercise caution when travelling at night or returning home by themselves from a bar or a party. While physical assault is rare, local men often consider foreign women to be exempt from their own society's rules of conduct.

Be especially careful in party towns, especially the Thai islands and Bali, where drunken abandon may be exploited by opportunists.

Travelling in Muslim areas introduces some challenges for women. In conservative areas, local women rarely go out unaccompanied and are usually modestly dressed. Foreign women doing the exact opposite are observed firstly as strange and secondly as searching for a local boyfriend. While the region is very friendly, be careful about teaming up with young men who may not respect certain boundaries.

Keep in mind that modesty in dress (covering the shoulders and past the knees) is the cultural norm right across Southeast Asia.

Finally, you can reduce hassles by travelling with other backpackers you meet along the way.

Work

Teaching English is the easiest way to support yourself in Southeast Asia. For short-term gigs, Bangkok, Ho Chi Minh City (Saigon), Jakarta and Phnom Penh have language schools and a high turnover of staff. In the Philippines, English speakers are often needed as language trainers for call centres. In Indonesia and Thailand you may be able to find some dive-school work. TEFL programs, especially in Thailand, are popular ways to prepare for an international job and live in a foreign country.

Payaway (www.payaway.co.uk) provides a handy online list of language schools and volunteer groups looking for recruits for its Southeast Asian programs.

Transitions Abroad (www.transitionsabroad.com) is a web portal that covers all aspects of overseas life, including landing a job in a variety of fields.

For information on volunteering, see p933.

Transport

GETTING THERE & AWAY

Step one is to get to Southeast Asia; flying is the easiest option. The only overland possibilities from outside the region are from China into Vietnam or Laos; from Papua New Guinea into Indonesia; or from India into Myanmar, although this requires a special permit. Flights, cars and tours can be booked online at lonelyplanet.com/bookings.

Air

The major Asian gateways for cheap flights are Bangkok, Kuala Lumpur, Singapore, Denpasar (Bali) and Manila. Thanks to the proliferation of budget carriers, there are often cheap fares between China and Southeast Asian cities or beach resorts.

When pricing flights compare the cost of flying to an East Asian city (such as Hong Kong) from your home country and then connecting to a budget carrier to the cost of flying directly to your destination on a long-haul airline. Fares on budget carriers don't usually factor into online search engines, but if you have more time than money, the budget forces may be with you.

Also be flexible with travel dates and know when to buy a ticket. Trips longer than two weeks tend to be more expensive. Buying a ticket too early or too close to your departure will affect the price as well. The ticket-purchasing sweet spot is 28 to 15 days before departure. When researching airline fares, clear out your web browser's cookies: these track your online activity and can sometimes result in a higher fare upon subsequent searches.

Round-the-World & Circle Asia Tickets

If Asia is one of many stops on a worldwide tour, consider a round-the-world (RTW) ticket, which allows a certain number of stops within a set time period (as long as you don't backtrack). Circle Asia passes are offered by various airline alliances for a circular route that originates in the USA, Europe or Australia and travels to certain destinations in Asia.

Before committing to purchase, check the fares offered by the budget regional carriers to see if either of these multi-stop tickets offer enough of a savings over à la carte fares. Contact airlines or a travel agent for more information or try Air Treks (www.airtreks.com).

Land

The land borders between Southeast Asia and the rest of Asia include those between Myanmar and India and Bangladesh, and the Chinese border with Myanmar, Laos and Vietnam. Of these, it is possible to travel overland from China into Laos and Vietnam. The Mu-Se–Ruili border between Myanmar and China and the Tamu–Moreh border between Myanmar and India are both open but currently require special permits that take one month to issue.

Another international crossing is between Indonesia and Papua New Guinea, although this isn't a feasible international gateway.

Adventurous travellers with plenty of time might consider the Trans-Manchurian or Trans-Mongolian express trains that connect Europe with China by rail.

Sea

Ocean approaches to Southeast Asia can be made aboard cargo ships plying routes around the world. Ridiculously expensive and hopelessly romantic, a trip aboard a cargo ship is the perfect chance for you to write that novel that never writes itself. Some freighter ships have space for a few noncrew members, who have their own rooms but eat meals with the crew. Prices vary depending on your departure point, but costs start at around US$150 a day plus additional fees.

GETTING AROUND

Border Crossings

It is easier than ever to travel overland (or over water) between neighbouring Southeast Asian countries. There are some well-trodden routes, especially within mainland Southeast Asia, that have straightforward public transport options and plenty of migrating travellers to share the road with. In some cases overland travel is the cheapest (though not always the fastest) route between major destinations. However, with the increasing affordability of flights, sometimes an airfare is equivalent to a long-distance bus ticket.

With the inception of the Asean Economic Community (AEC), border relations between most countries have normalised, but there are still visa regulations and minor scams to be prepared for.

Do be aware that some border crossings are not recommended due to political violence and instability in the region. Areas to avoid include the west coast of Thailand crossing to Malaysia (Sungai Kolok to Rantau Panjang) and boat crossings from Malaysian Borneo to the southern Philippines' port of Zamboanga.

Ask around or check the Lonely Planet Thorn Tree forum (lonelyplanet.com/thorntree) for border-crossing trip reports for further information and transport recommendations.

Other considerations when planning the border crossings for your trip include the following:

➡ Know which borders offer visas on arrival and which require prearranged visas.

➡ When arriving at borders that do issue visas upon arrival, be prepared with two passport photos and enough cash in the required currency to pay the visa fee and complete border formalities.

➡ Plan your trip so that you arrive at the border during opening hours to avoid being stranded overnight or needing to make last-minute arrangements in a small border town.

➡ There are few legal money-changing facilities at some border crossings (even at crossings that do not seem remote, such as Cambodia's Poipet crossing with Thailand) so be sure to have some small-denomination US dollars handy.

➡ The black-market money changers are an option for local currencies, but remember that black marketeers have a well-deserved reputation for short-changing customers and offering unfavourable exchange rates.

➡ Be aware of border-crossing scams, like dodgy transport schemes and pesky runner boys (see p937).

➡ At some border crossings staff may request or demand extra processing fees, like overtime surcharges, in addition to the legitimate visa-issuing fees. Resisting might result in some savings but it will not make the crossing speedier or smoother. Whatever approach you take, stay calm and don't get angry.

➡ See p942 for a list of border crossings detailed in this book.

Air

Air travel can be a bargain within the region, especially from transit hubs such as Bangkok, Singapore and Kuala Lumpur. No-frills regional carriers have made travelling between capital cities cheaper than taking land transport in some cases. Some airports in Southeast Asia charge a departure tax, so make sure you have a bit of local currency left. The following airlines often have affordable fares between cities and capitals:

Air Asia (www.airasia.com) Leading regional budget airline with hubs in Bangkok, Kuala Lumpur and Manila.

Cebu Pacific Air (www.cebupacificair.com) Popular Filipino budget carrier flying in and out of Manila.

Jetstar (www.jetstar.com) Big player with hubs in Singapore and Vietnam.

Lion Air (www.lionair.co.id) Indonesia's leading budget carrier.

Tigerair (www.tigerair.com) Low-cost carrier based out of Singapore.

CLIMATE CHANGE & TRAVEL

Every form of transport that relies on carbon-based fuel generates CO_2, the main cause of human-induced climate change. Modern travel is dependent on aeroplanes, which might use less fuel per kilometre per person than most cars but travel much greater distances. The altitude at which aircraft emit gases (including CO_2) and particles also contributes to their climate change impact. Many websites offer 'carbon calculators' that allow people to estimate the carbon emissions generated by their journey and, for those who wish to do so, to offset the impact of the greenhouse gases emitted with contributions to portfolios of climate-friendly initiatives throughout the world. Lonely Planet offsets the carbon footprint of all staff and author travel.

MOTORCYCLE SAFETY

Traffic accidents are a leading cause of death in Southeast Asia, especially in Thailand, and motorcycles are among the most vulnerable vehicles on the road, in part because of no (or unenforced) helmet laws, reckless driving, poor road conditions and inadequate emergency response systems. The World Health Organization has begun a region-wide campaign trying to reduce these accidental deaths.

Foreigners who rent motorbikes in the region expose themselves to greater risk because they don't have prior experience driving motorcycles and don't understand the local road rules (or lack of rules). Foreign consulates in Indonesia and Thailand are often inundated with requests to assist nationals injured in motorcycling accidents.

If you accept the risks, be sure to take the following precautions:

➡ Wear a helmet and protective clothing (long pants and long shirts).

➡ Drive carefully and defensively.

➡ Yield to bigger vehicles; 'might makes right' here.

➡ Slow down in rainy conditions, around curves or where there is loose gravel.

➡ Get in the habit of climbing off a moto to your left, stepping clear of the scorching exhaust pipe. Singed flesh doesn't smell very nice, and in tropical humidity takes a long time to heal.

Most Asians are so adept at riding motorcycles that they can balance the whole family on the front bumper or even take a quick nap as a passenger. Foreigners unaccustomed to motorcycles are not as graceful. If you're riding on the back of a motorcycle, remember to relax so that the driver can balance your body. Tall people should keep long legs tucked in as most drivers are used to shorter passengers. Women wearing skirts should collect loose material so it doesn't catch in the wheel or chain.

Air Passes

National airlines of Southeast Asian countries frequently run promotional deals from select Western cities or for regional travel. Airline alliances also offer regional air passes. You'll have to do a generic web search for 'air passes' to find the most up-to-date information, as monitoring sites aren't always current.

Bicycle

Touring Southeast Asia on a bicycle has long had many supporters. Long-distance cyclists typically start in Thailand and head south through Malaysia to Singapore. Road conditions are good enough for long-haul touring in most places, but mountain bikes are definitely recommended for forays off the beaten track.

Vietnam is a great place to travel by bicycle – you can take bikes on buses, and the entire coastal route is feasible. If flat-land cycling is not your style, then Indonesia might be the challenge you're looking for. Roads here are rough and inclines steep, but the scenery is stunning. In Laos and Cambodia, road conditions are improving and the traffic is still light.

Top-quality bicycles and components can be bought in major cities such as Bangkok, but fittings are hard to find. Bicycles can travel by air; check with the airline about charges and specifications.

Boat

Ferries and boats travel between Singapore and Indonesia, Malaysia and Indonesia, Thailand and Malaysia, and the Philippines and Malaysia. You also have the option of crossing the Mekong River from Thailand to Laos and from Cambodia to Vietnam. Guesthouses or travel agents sell tickets and provide travellers with updated departure times. Check visa regulations at port cities: some don't issue visas on arrival.

Bus

In most cases, land borders are crossed via bus. In some cases, direct buses connect two major towns with a stop for border formalities, while in other cases buses terminate at the border towns and you'll need to negotiate onward travel on the other side. Bus travellers will enjoy a higher standard of luxury in Thailand, the Philippines and Malaysia, where roads are well paved and reliable schedules exist. Be aware that theft does occur on some long-distance buses – keep all valuables on your person, not in a stowed locked bag.

Car & Motorcycle

What is the sound of freedom in Southeast Asia? The 'put-put' noise of a motorcycle. For visitors, motorcycles are convenient for getting around the beaches or touring the

SOUTHEAST ASIAN BORDER CROSSINGS

From Brunei Darussalam

TO	BORDER CROSSING	CONNECTING TOWNS	SEE MORE
Malaysia	Kuala Berait (B)/Miri (M)	Bandar Seri Begawan (B)/Miri (M)	p63
Malaysia	Muara (B)/Bandar Labuan (M)	Bandar Seri Begawan (B)/Kota Kinabalu (M)	p63

From Cambodia

TO	BORDER CROSSING	CONNECTING TOWNS	SEE MORE
Laos	Trapeang Kriel (C)/Nong Nok Khiene (L)	Stung Treng (C)/Si Phan Don (L)	p133
Thailand	Cham Yeam (C)/Hat Lek (T)	Koh Kong (C)/Trat (T)	p111
Thailand	Choam (C)/Chong Sa-Ngam (T)	Anlong Veng (C)/Chong Sa-Ngam (T)	p105
Thailand	O Smach (C)/Chong Chom (T)	Samraong (C)/Surin (T)	p105
Thailand	Poipet (C)/Aranya Prathet (T)	Siem Reap (C)/Bangkok (T)	p100
Thailand	Psar Pruhm (C)/Ban Pakard (T)	Pailin (C)/Chanthaburi (T)	p111
Vietnam	Bavet (C)/Moc Bai (V)	Phnom Penh (C)/Ho Chi Minh City (V)	p86
Vietnam	Kaam Samnor (C)/Vinh Xuong (V)	Phnom Penh (C)/Chau Doc (V)	p86
Vietnam	Phnom Den (C)/Tinh Bien (V)	Takeo (C)/Chau Doc (V)	p86
Vietnam	Prek Chak (C)/Xa Xia (V)	Kep (C)/Ha Tien (V)	p128
Vietnam	O Yadaw (C)/Le Thanh (V)	Ban Lung (C)/Pleiku (V)	p135
Vietnam	Trapeang Plong (C)/Xa Mat (V)	Kompong Cham (C)/Tay Ninh (V)	p135
Vietnam	Trapeang Sre (C)/Loc Ninh (V)	Snuol (C)/Binh Long (V)	p135

From Indonesia

TO	BORDER CROSSING	CONNECTING TOWNS	SEE MORE
Malaysia	Dumai (I)/Melaka (M)	Bukittinggi (I)/Melaka (M)	p272
Malaysia	Entikong (I)/Tebedu (M)	Pontianak (I)/Kuching (M)	p277
Malaysia	Riau Islands (I)/Johor Bahru (M)	Riau Islands (I)/Johor Bahru (M)	p417
Malaysia	Tarakan & Nunukan (I)/Tawau (M)	Tarakan & Nunukan (I)/Tawau (M)	p447
Papua New Guinea	Skouw (I)/Wutung (P)	Jayapura (I)/Vanimo (P)	p297
Singapore	Riau Islands (I)/Singapore	Riau Islands (I)/Singapore	p253
Timor-Leste	Kupang (I)/Dili (T)	Kupang (I)/Dili (T)	p250

From Laos

TO	BORDER CROSSING	CONNECTING TOWNS	SEE MORE
Cambodia	Nong Nok Khiene (L)/Trapeang Kriel (C)	Si Phan Don (L)/Stung Treng (C)	p370
China	Boten (L)/Mohan (Ch)	Luang Namtha (L)/Mengla (Ch)	p351
Thailand	Huay Xai (L)/Chiang Khong (T)	Huay Xai (L)/Chiang Rai (T)	p352

Thailand	Kaen Thao (L)/Tha Li (T)	Pak Lai (L)/Loei (T)	p352
Thailand	Muang Ngeun (L)/Ban Huay Kon (T)	Hongsa (L)/Phrae (T)	p352
Thailand	Paksan (L)/Bueng Kan (T)	Paksan (L)/Bueng Kan (T)	p357
Thailand	Savannakhet (L)/Mukdahan (T)	Savannakhet (L)/Mukdahan (T)	p364
Thailand	Tha Khaek (L)/Nakhon Phanom (T)	Tha Khaek (L)/Nakhon Phanom (T)	p357
Thailand	Tha Na Long (L)/Nong Khai (T)	Vientiane (L)/Nong Khai (T)	p328
Thailand	Vang Tao (L)/Chong Mek (T)	Pakse (L)/Ubon Ratchathani (T)	p364
Vietnam	Dansavanh (L)/Lao Bao (V)	Savannakhet (L)/Dong Ha (V)	p360
Vietnam	Na Phao (L)/Cha Lo (V)	Tha Khaek (L)/Dong Hoi (V)	p358
Vietnam	Nam Phao (L)/Cau Treo (V)	Lak Sao (L)/Vinh (V)	p358
Vietnam	Nam Soi (L)/Na Meo (V)	Sam Neua (L)/Thanh Hoa (V)	p346
Vietnam	Nong Haet (L)/Nam Can (V)	Phonsavan (L)/Vinh (V)	p346
Vietnam	Sop Hun (L)/Tay Trang (V)	Muang Khua (L)/Dien Bien Phu (V)	p346

From Malaysia

TO	BORDER CROSSING	CONNECTING TOWNS	SEE MORE
Brunei Darussalam	Bandar Labuan (M)/Muara (B)	Pulau Labuan (M)/Bandar Seri Begawan (B)	p449
Brunei Darussalam	Miri (M)/Kuala Berait (B)	Miri (M)/Bandar Seri Begawan (B)	p465
Indonesia	Johor Bahru (M)/Riau Islands (I)	Johor Bahru (M)/Riau Islands (I)	p417
Indonesia	Melaka (M)/Dumai (I)	Melaka (M)/Bukittinggi (I)	p400
Indonesia	Tawau (M)/Tarakan & Nunukan (I)	Tawau (M)/Tarakan & Nunukan (I)	p447
Indonesia	Tebedu (M)/Entikong (I)	Kuching (M)/Pontianak (I)	p455
Philippines	Sandakan (M)/Zamboanga (P)	Sandakan (M)/Zamboanga (P)	p443
Singapore	Johor Bahru (M)/Singapore	Johor Bahru (M)/Singapore	p418
Thailand	Bukit Kayu Hitam (M)/Sadao (T)	Alor Setar (M)/Hat Yai (T)	p413
Thailand	Padang Besar (M)/Hat Yai (T)	Kangar (M)/Hat Yai (T)	p413
Thailand	Pulau Langkawi (M)/Ko Lipe & Satun (T)	Pulau Langkawi (M)/Ko Lipe & Satun (T)	p415
Thailand	Rantau Panjang (M)/Sungai Kolok (T)	Kota Bharu (M)/Bangkok (T)	p429

From Myanmar

TO	BORDER CROSSING	CONNECTING TOWNS	SEE MORE
China	Mu-Se (My)/Ruili (Ch)	Mu-Se (My)/Ruili (Ch)	p521
India	Tamu (My)/Moreh (India)	Mawlaik (My)/Imphal (India)	p939
Thailand	Hteke (My)/Phu Nam Ron (T)	Dawei (My)/Kanchanaburi (T)	p715
Thailand	Kawthoung (My)/Saphan Pla Pier (T)	Kawthoung (My)/Ranong (T)	p502
Thailand	Myawaddy (My)/Mae Sot (T)	Hpa-an (My)/Mae Sot (T)	p502
Thailand	Tachileik (My)/Mae Sai (T)	Kyaingtong (My)/Mae Sai (T)	p509

From Thailand

TO	BORDER CROSSING	CONNECTING TOWNS	SEE MORE
Cambodia	Aranya Prathet (T)/Poipet (C)	Bangkok (T)/Siem Reap (C)	p732
Cambodia	Ban Pakard (T)/Psar Pruhm (C)	Chanthaburi (T)/Pailin (C)	p731
Cambodia	Chong Chom (T)/O Smach (C)	Surin (T)/Samraong (C)	p732
Cambodia	Chong Sa-Ngam (T)/Choam (C)	Chong Sa-Ngam (T)/Anlong Veng (C)	p732
Cambodia	Hat Lek (T)/Cham Yeam (C)	Trat (T)/Koh Kong (C)	p731
Laos	Ban Huay Kon (T)/Muang Ngeun (L)	Phrae (T)/Hongsa (L)	p703
Laos	Bueng Kan (T)/Paksan (L)	Bueng Kan (T)/Paksan (L)	p724
Laos	Chiang Khong (T)/Huay Xai (L)	Chiang Rai (T)/Huay Xai (L)	p703
Laos	Chong Mek (T)/Vang Tao (L)	Ubon Ratchathani (T)/Pakse (L)	p724
Laos	Mukdahan (T)/Savannakhet (L)	Mukdahan (T)/Savannakhet (L)	p724
Laos	Nakhon Phanom (T)/Tha Khaek (L)	Nakhon Phanom (T)/Tha Khaek (L)	p724
Laos	Nong Khai (T)/Tha Na Long (L)	Nong Khai (T)/Vientiane (L)	p727
Laos	Tha Li (T)/Kaen Thao (L)	Loei (T)/Pak Lai (L)	p724
Malaysia	Hat Yai (T)/Padang Besar (M)	Hat Yai (T)/Kangar (M)	p413
Malaysia	Ko Lipe & Satun (T)/Pulau Langkawi (M)	Ko Lipe & Satun (T)/Pulau Langkawi (M)	p774
Malaysia	Sadao (T)/Bukit Kayu Hitam (M)	Hat Yai (T)/Alor Setar (M)	p413
Malaysia	Sungai Kolok (T)/Rantau Panjang (M)	Sungai Kolok (T)/Kota Bharu (M)	p754
Myanmar	Mae Sai (T)/Tachileik (My)	Mae Sai (T)/Kyaingtong (My)	p704
Myanmar	Mae Sot (T)/Myawaddy (My)	Mae Sot (T)/Hpa-an (My)	p717
Myanmar	Phu Nam Rom (T)/Hteke (My)	Kanchanaburi (T)/Dawei (My)	p715
Myanmar	Saphan Pla Pier (T)/Kawthoung (My)	Ranong (T)/Kawthoung (My)	p755

From Vietnam

TO	BORDER CROSSING	CONNECTING TOWNS	SEE MORE
Cambodia	Le Thanh (V)/O Yadaw (C)	Pleiku (V)/Ban Lung (C)	p881
Cambodia	Loc Ninh (V)/Trapeang Sre (C)	Binh Long (V)/Snuol (C)	p135
Cambodia	Moc Bai (V)/Bavet (C)	Ho Chi Minh City (V)/Phnom Penh (C)	p893
Cambodia	Tinh Bien (V)/Phnom Den (C)	Chau Doc (V)/Takeo (C)	p898
Cambodia	Vinh Xuong (V)/Kaam Samnor (C)	Chau Doc (V)/Phnom Penh (C)	p898
Cambodia	Xa Mat (V)/Trapeang Plong (C)	Tay Ninh (V)/Kompong Cham (C)	p135
Cambodia	Xa Xia (V)/Prek Chak (C)	Ha Tien (V)/Kep (C)	p898
China	Huu Nghi Quan (V)/Youyi Guan (Ch)	Dong Dang (V)/Pingxiang (Ch)	p839
China	Lao Cai (V)/Hekou (Ch)	Hanoi (V)/Kunming (Ch)	p837
China	Mong Cai (V)/Dongxing (Ch)	Mong Cai (V)/Dongxing (Ch)	p839
Laos	Cau Treo (V)/Nam Phao (L)	Vinh (V)/Lak Sao (L)	p842
Laos	Lao Bao (V)/Dansavanh (L)	Dong Ha (V)/Savannakhet (L)	p849
Laos	Cha Lo (V)/Na Phao (L)	Dong Hoi (V)/Tha Khaek (L)	p842
Laos	Nam Can (V)/Nong Haet (L)	Vinh (V)/Phonsavan (L)	p842
Laos	Nam Soi (V)/Na Meo (L)	Thanh Hoa (V)/Sam Neua (L)	p346
Laos	Tay Trang (V)/Sop Hun (L)	Dien Bien Phu (V)/Muang Khua (L)	p842

countryside. Car hire, also available in most countries, is handy for local sightseeing or long-haul trips. You can hit Thailand and Malaysia by car pretty easily, enjoying well-signposted, well-paved roads. Road conditions in Cambodia, Laos and Myanmar vary, although sealed roads are becoming the norm. Indonesia and the Philippines have roads that vary between islands, but most are in need of repair. Vietnam's major highways are in relatively good health.

Driving Licences

Parts of Southeast Asia, including Malaysia, Indonesia and Thailand, are good spots for exploring by car and motorcycle. If you plan to do any driving, get an International Driving Permit (IDP) from your local automobile association before you leave your home country; IDPs are inexpensive and valid for one year. Read up on road safety as road accidents are a serious concern in Southeast Asia.

Insurance

Get insurance with a motorcycle if at all possible. The more reputable motorcycle-rental places insure all their motorcycles; some will do it for an extra charge. Without insurance, you're responsible for anything that happens to the bike. To be absolutely clear about your liability, ask for a written estimate of the replacement cost for a similar bike – and take photos as a guarantee. Some agencies will accept only the replacement cost of a new motorcycle.

Insurance for a rented car is also necessary. Be sure to ask the car-rental agent about liability and damage coverage.

Rental

Western car-rental chains camp out at Southeast Asian airports, capitals and major tourist destinations. Local shops also rent motorcycles and cars, but these fleets are often poorly maintained. Before renting a vehicle, take a walk around it with the proprietor, noting any existing damage so you won't be charged for old knocks. Taking pictures of the vehicle before driving it off the premises is another safeguard. Check the tyre treads and brakes to make sure that the vehicle is in good working order.

Road Rules & Safety

Drive carefully and defensively. Remember that smaller vehicles yield to bigger vehicles regardless of the circumstances. The middle of the road is used as a passing lane, even in oncoming traffic. Use your horn to notify other vehicles that you intend to pass.

Hitching

Hitching is never entirely safe and we don't recommend it. Travellers who hitch should understand that they are taking a small but potentially serious risk. People who do choose to hitch will be safer if they travel in pairs and let someone know where they are planning to go.

Local Transport

Local transport keeps cities on the move. For the right price, drivers will haul you from the bus station to town, around town, around the corner or around in circles. The bicycle rickshaw still survives in the region, assuming such aliases as săhm·lór in Thailand and *cyclo* in Vietnam. Anything motorised is often modified to carry passengers, from Thailand's obnoxious three-wheeled chariot, the túk-túk, to the Philippines' altered US Army jeeps.

In large cities, extensive bus systems either travel on fixed routes or do informal loops around the city, picking up passengers on the way.

Bangkok, Kuala Lumpur and Singapore boast state-of-the-art light-rail systems that make zipping around town feel like time travel.

Train

The International Express train runs from Bangkok all the way through the Malay Peninsula, ending its journey in Singapore. Trains also serve the Lao capital, Vientiane, and Aranya Prathet, on the Thailand–Cambodia border. Thailand and Malaysia have the most extensive rail systems, although trains rarely run on time.

Health

Health issues and the quality of medical facilities vary enormously depending on where you travel in Southeast Asia.

Travellers tend to worry about contracting infectious diseases when in the tropics, but infections are a rare cause of serious illness or death in travellers.

Accidental injury (such as traffic accidents) and pre-existing medical conditions account for most life-threatening problems. Becoming ill in some way, however, is relatively common and may include respiratory infections, diarrhoea and dengue fever. Fortunately, most common illnesses can be either prevented or treated.

BEFORE YOU GO

Pack medications in their original, clearly labelled containers. A signed, dated letter from your physician describing your medical conditions and medications, including generic names, is recommended. If carrying syringes or needles, have a physician's letter stating their medical necessity. If you have a heart condition, bring a copy of your ECG.

If you take any regular medication, bring a double supply in case of loss or theft. In most Southeast Asian countries, excluding Singapore, you can buy many medications over the counter, but it can be difficult to find some of the newer drugs, particularly the latest antidepressants, blood-pressure medications and contraceptive pills.

Insurance

Even if you are fit and healthy, don't travel without health insurance – accidents do happen. Adventure activities, such as rock climbing, often require extra coverage. If your existing health insurance doesn't cover you for medical expenses abroad, consider purchasing travel insurance that includes emergency evacuation.

Find out in advance if your insurance plan will make payments directly to providers or reimburse you later for overseas health expenditures. (In many countries doctors expect payment in cash.) If you have to claim later, make sure you keep all documentation. Some policies ask you to call a centre in your home country, where an immediate assessment of your problem is made.

Divers should ensure their insurance covers them for decompression illness – get specialised dive insurance through an organisation such as Divers Alert Network (www.diversalert-network.org). Have a dive medical before you leave your home country; there are certain medical conditions that are incompatible with diving.

Recommended Vaccinations

Specialised travel-medicine clinics can advise on which vaccines are recommended for your trip. Some vaccines require multiple injections spaced out over a certain period of time; start the process six weeks prior to departure.

The World Health Organization (WHO) recommends the following vaccinations for travellers to Southeast Asia:

➡ Adult diphtheria and tetanus

➡ Hepatitis A

➡ Hepatitis B

➡ Measles, mumps and rubella (MMR)

➡ Polio

➡ Typhoid

➡ Varicella

The following immunisations are recommended for long-term travellers (more than one month) or those at special risk:

➡ Japanese B Encephalitis

➡ Meningitis

➡ Rabies

➡ Tuberculosis (TB)

Required Vaccinations

The only vaccine required by international regulations is for yellow fever. Proof of vaccination will be required only if you have visited a country in the yellow-fever zone within the six days before entering Southeast Asia. If you are travelling to Southeast Asia from Africa or South America you should check to see if you require proof of vaccination.

IN SOUTHEAST ASIA

Availability of Health Care

Most capital cities in Southeast Asia have clinics that cater specifically to travellers and expats. These clinics are more expensive than local medical facilities but offer a superior standard of care and the staff speak English.

It is difficult to find reliable medical care in rural areas. Your embassy and insurance company are good contacts.

The standard of care in Southeast Asia varies from country to country:

Brunei Darussalam General care is reasonable. There is no local medical university, so expats and foreign-trained locals run the health-care system. Serious or complex cases are better managed in Singapore.

Cambodia There are international clinics in Phnom Penh and Siem Reap and an NGO-run surgical hospital in Battambang that provide primary care and emergency stabilisation. Elsewhere, government hospitals should be avoided. For more serious conditions, it is advisable to be evacuated to Bangkok.

MEDICAL CHECKLIST

Recommended items for a personal medical kit:

☐ antibacterial cream (eg mupirocin)

☐ antibiotic for skin infections (eg amoxicillin/clavulanate or cephalexin)

☐ antibiotics for diarrhoea (eg norfloxacin or ciprofloxacin; azithromycin for bacterial diarrhoea; tinidazole for giardiasis or amoebic dysentery)

☐ antifungal cream (eg clotrimazole)

☐ antihistamine (eg cetirizine for daytime and promethazine for night)

☐ anti-inflammatory (eg ibuprofen)

☐ antiseptic (eg Betadine)

☐ antispasmodic for stomach cramps (eg Buscopan)

☐ contraceptives

☐ decongestant (eg pseudoephedrine)

☐ DEET-based insect repellent

☐ diarrhoea treatment, including an oral rehydration solution (eg Gastrolyte), diarrhoea 'stopper' (eg loperamide) and antinausea medication (eg prochlorperazine)

☐ first-aid items such as scissors, plasters, bandages, gauze, thermometer (but not one with mercury), sterile needles and syringes, safety pins and tweezers

☐ indigestion medication (eg Quick-Eze or Mylanta)

☐ iodine tablets to purify water

☐ laxative (eg Coloxyl)

☐ paracetamol

☐ permethrin to impregnate clothing and mosquito nets

☐ steroid cream for allergic or itchy rashes (eg 1% to 2% hydrocortisone)

☐ sunscreen and hat

☐ throat lozenges

☐ thrush (vaginal yeast infection) treatment (eg Clotrimazole pessaries or Diflucan tablet)

☐ Ural or equivalent if you're prone to urine infections

Divers and surfers should seek specialised advice on stocking medical kits for coral cuts and tropical ear infection treatments.

Indonesia Local medical care in general is not yet up to international standards. Foreign doctors are not allowed to work in Indonesia, but some clinics catering to foreigners have 'international advisers'. Almost all Indonesian doctors work at government hospitals during the day and in private practices at night. This means that private hospitals often don't have their best staff available during the day. Serious cases are evacuated to Australia or Singapore.

Laos There are no good facilities in Laos; the nearest acceptable facilities are in northern Thailand. The Australian Embassy Clinic in Vientiane treats citizens of Commonwealth countries.

Malaysia Medical care in the major centres is good and most problems can be adequately dealt with in Kuala Lumpur.

Myanmar (Burma) Local medical care is dismal and local hospitals should be used only in desperation. There is an international medical clinic in Yangon.

Philippines Good medical care is available in most major cities.

Singapore Excellent medical facilities and referral centre for most of Southeast Asia.

Thailand After Singapore, Bangkok is the city of choice for expats living in Southeast Asia who require specialised care.

Timor-Leste Private clinics available in Dili. The government hospital is basic and should be avoided.

Vietnam Government hospitals are overcrowded and basic. To treat foreigners, the facility needs to obtain a special licence, and so far only a few have been provided. The private clinics in Hanoi, Ho Chi Minh City and Danang should be your first choice.

Infectious Diseases

Cutaneous Larva Migrans

Risk areas All countries except Singapore.

This disease, caused by dog hookworm, is particularly common on the beaches of Thailand. The rash starts as a small lump then slowly spreads in a linear fashion. It is intensely itchy, especially at night. It is easily treated with medications and should not be cut out or frozen.

Dengue

Risk areas All countries.

This mosquito-borne disease is increasingly problematic throughout Southeast Asia, especially in the cities. There is no vaccine, only preven-

tion. The mosquito that carries dengue bites day and night, so use DEET-mosquito cream periodically throughout the day. Symptoms include high fever, severe headache and body ache (dengue used to be known as breakbone fever). Some people develop a rash and experience diarrhoea. There is no specific treatment, just rest and paracetamol – do not take aspirin as it increases the likelihood of haemorrhaging. See a doctor to be diagnosed and monitored.

Don't assume this is a rural issue: Southeast Asia's cities, such as Bangkok and Singapore, as well as Thailand's southern islands and Chiang Mai province are high-risk areas.

Hepatitis A

Risk areas All countries.

A problem throughout the region, this food- and water-borne virus infects the liver, causing jaundice (yellow skin and eyes), nausea and lethargy. There is no specific treatment for hepatitis A; you just need to allow time for the liver to heal. All travellers to Southeast Asia should be vaccinated against hepatitis A.

Hepatitis B

Risk areas All countries.

The only serious sexually transmitted disease that can be prevented by vaccination, hepatitis B is spread by body fluids. In some parts of Southeast Asia, up to 20% of the population carry hepatitis B, and usually are unaware of it. The long-term consequences can include liver cancer and cirrhosis.

Hepatitis E

Risk areas All countries.

Hepatitis E is transmitted through contaminated food and water, and has similar symptoms to hepatitis A but is far less common. It is a severe problem in pregnant women, and can result in the death of both mother and baby. There is currently

---

FOOD & WATER

Food and water contamination are the biggest risk factor for contracting traveller's diarrhoea. Here are some safety considerations:

➡ Eat only freshly cooked food and fruit that can be peeled.

➡ Avoid food that has been sitting around for hours.

➡ Eat in busy restaurants with a high turnover of customers.

➡ Never drink tap water; opt for bottled or filtered water instead.

➡ Avoid ice.

➡ Avoid fresh juices that may have been watered down.

➡ Boil water or use iodine tablets as a means of purification; pregnant women or those with thyroid problems should avoid iodine use.

no vaccine; prevention is by following safe eating and drinking guidelines.

HIV

Risk areas All countries.

HIV is now one of the most common causes of death in people under the age of 50 in Thailand. The Southeast Asian countries with the worst and most rapidly increasing HIV problem are Myanmar, Thailand and Vietnam. Heterosexual sex is now the main method of transmission in these countries.

Influenza

Risk areas All countries.

Present year-round in the tropics, influenza (flu) symptoms include high fever, muscle aches, runny nose, cough and sore throat. It can be very severe in people over the age of 65, and in those with underlying medical conditions such as heart disease or diabetes; vaccination is recommended for these individuals. There is no specific treatment, just rest and paracetamol.

Leptospirosis

Risk areas Thailand and Malaysia.

Leptospirosis is most commonly contracted after river rafting or canyoning. Early symptoms are very similar to the flu, and include headache and fever. The disease can vary from very mild to fatal. Diagnosis is through blood tests and it is easily treated with doxycycline.

Malaria

Risk areas All countries except Singapore and Brunei.

Many parts of Southeast Asia, particularly city and resort areas, have minimal to no risk of malaria, and the risk of side effects from the prevention tablets may outweigh the risk of getting the disease.

For most rural areas, however, the risk of contracting the disease is increased and malaria can be fatal. Before you travel, seek medical advice on the right medication and dosage.

Malaria is caused by a parasite transmitted by the bite of an infected mosquito. The most important symptom of malaria is fever, but general symptoms such as headache, diarrhoea, cough or chills may also occur. Diagnosis can only be made by taking a blood sample.

Two strategies are combined to prevent malaria – mosquito avoidance and antimalarial medications.

Travellers are advised to prevent mosquito bites by taking the following steps:

➡ Use an insect repellent containing DEET on exposed skin.

➡ Sleep under a mosquito net that is impregnated with permethrin.

➡ Choose accommodation with screens and fans (if not air-conditioned).

➡ Impregnate clothing with permethrin when in high-risk areas.

➡ Wear long sleeves and trousers in light colours.

➡ Use mosquito coils.

➡ Spray your room with insect repellent before going out for your evening meal.

Measles

Risk areas All countries except Singapore and Brunei.

Measles remains a problem in some parts of Southeast Asia. This highly contagious bacterial infection is spread via coughing and sneezing. Most people born before 1966 are immune as they had the disease during childhood. Measles starts with a high fever and rash, and can be complicated by pneumonia and brain disease. There is no specific treatment.

Rabies

Risk areas All countries except Singapore and Brunei.

Still a common problem in most parts of Southeast Asia, this uniformly fatal disease is spread by the bite or lick of an infected animal, most commonly a dog or monkey. You should seek medical advice immediately after any animal bite and commence post-exposure treatment. Having a pre-travel vaccination means the post-bite treatment is greatly simplified. If an animal bites you, gently wash the wound with soap and water, and apply iodine-based antiseptic. If you are not pre-vaccinated you will need to receive rabies immunoglobulin as soon as possible.

Schistosomiasis

Risk areas Laos, Philippines, Vietnam and Sulawesi (Indonesia).

Schistosomiasis is a tiny parasite that enters your skin after you've been swimming in contaminated water. Travellers usually only get a light infection and hence develop no symptoms. On rare occasions, travellers may develop 'Katayama fever'. This occurs some weeks after exposure, as the parasite passes through the lungs and causes an allergic reaction; symptoms are coughing and fever. Schistosomiasis is easily treated with medications.

STDs

Risk areas All countries.

Sexually transmitted diseases most commonly found in Southeast Asia include herpes, warts, syphilis, gonorrhoea and chlamydia. People carrying these diseases often have no signs of infection. Condoms will prevent gonorrhoea and chlamydia but not warts or herpes. If after a sexual encounter you develop any rash, lumps, discharge or pain when passing urine, seek immediate medical attention. If you have been sexually active during your travels, have an STD check on your return home.

Strongyloides

Risk areas Cambodia, Myanmar and Thailand.

This parasite, transmitted by skin-contact with soil, is

common in travellers but rarely affects them. It is characterised by an unusual skin rash called larva currens – a linear rash on the trunk that comes and goes. Most people don't have other symptoms until their immune system becomes severely suppressed, when the parasite can cause an overwhelming infection. It can be treated with medications.

Typhoid

Risk areas All countries except Singapore.

This serious bacterial infection is spread via food and water. It gives a high and slowly progressive fever and a headache, and may be accompanied by a dry cough and stomach pain. It is diagnosed by blood tests and treated with antibiotics. Vaccination is recommended for all travellers spending more than a week in Southeast Asia, or travelling outside the major cities. Vaccination is not 100% effective so you must still be careful about what you eat and drink.

Traveller's Diarrhoea

Traveller's diarrhoea is by far the most common problem that affects travellers – between 30% and 50% of people will suffer from it within two weeks of starting their trip. In over 80% of cases, traveller's diarrhoea is caused by bacteria (there are numerous potential culprits), and therefore responds promptly to treatment with antibiotics. Treatment will depend on your situation – how sick you are, how quickly you need to get better and so on.

Traveller's diarrhoea is defined as the passage of more than three watery bowel actions within 24 hours, plus at least one other symptom such as fever, cramps, nausea, vomiting or feeling generally unwell.

Treatment consists of staying well hydrated; rehydration solutions such as Gastrolyte are the best for this. Antibiotics such as

norfloxacin, ciprofloxacin or azithromycin will kill the bacteria quickly.

Loperamide is just a 'stopper'. It can be helpful if you have to go on a long bus ride. Don't take loperamide if you have a fever, or blood in your stools. Seek medical attention quickly if you do not respond to an appropriate antibiotic.

Amoebic Dysentery

Amoebic dysentery is very rare in travellers but is often misdiagnosed by poorquality labs in Southeast Asia. Symptoms are similar to bacterial diarrhoea – fever, bloody diarrhoea and generally feeling unwell. You should always seek reliable medical care if you have blood in your diarrhoea. Treatment involves two drugs: tinidazole or metronidazole to kill the parasite in your gut, and then a second drug to kill the cysts. If left untreated, complications such as liver or gut abscesses can occur.

Giardiasis

Giardia lamblia is a relatively common parasite in travellers. Symptoms include nausea, bloating, excess gas, fatigue and intermittent diarrhoea. 'Eggy' burps are often attributed solely to giardiasis, but work in Nepal has shown that they are not specific to this infection. The parasite will eventually go away if left untreated but this can take months. The treatment of choice is tinidazole, with metronidazole being a second option.

Environmental Hazards

Heat

Many parts of Southeast Asia are hot and humid. For most people it takes at least two weeks to adapt to the climate. Swelling of the feet and ankles is common, as are muscle cramps caused by excessive sweating. You can

---

RARE BUT BE AWARE

The following diseases are common in the local population (in all countries except Singapore) but rare in travellers:

Filariasis A mosquito-borne disease prevented by mosquito-avoidance measures.

Typhus Murine typhus is spread by the bite of a flea and scrub typhus is spread via a mite; symptoms include fever, muscle pains and a rash. Prevention is through general insect-avoidance measures or doxycycline.

Tuberculosis Medical and aid workers and long-term travellers should take precautions and consider pre- and post-travel testing; symptoms are fever, cough, weight loss and tiredness.

Meliodosis (Thailand only) An infection contracted by skin contact with soil; symptoms are similar to tuberculosis.

Japanese B Encephalitis (Vietnam, Thailand and Indonesia are highest risk areas) A viral disease, transmitted by mosquitoes; most cases occur in rural areas and vaccination is recommended for travellers spending more than one month outside cities.

prevent these by avoiding dehydration and excessive activity; you should also take it easy when you first arrive. Treat cramps by stopping activity, resting, rehydrating with double-strength rehydration solution and gently stretching.

Dehydration is the main contributor to heat exhaustion. Symptoms include weakness, headache, irritability, nausea or vomiting, sweaty skin, a fast pulse, and a slightly elevated body temperature. Treatment involves getting out of the heat, fanning and applying cool wet cloths to the skin, lying flat with legs raised, and rehydrating with water containing a quarter of a teaspoon of salt per litre. Recovery is usually rapid, though it is common to feel weak afterwards.

Heat stroke is a serious medical emergency. Symptoms come on suddenly and include weakness, nausea, a hot dry body with a body temperature of over 41°C, dizziness, confusion, loss of coordination, seizures, and eventually collapse and loss of consciousness. Seek medical help and commence cooling by getting out of the heat, removing clothes, fanning and applying cool wet cloths or ice to the body, especially to the groin and armpits.

Prickly heat is a common skin rash in the tropics caused by sweat being trapped under the skin. The result is an itchy rash of tiny lumps. Treat by moving out of the heat and into an air-conditioned area for a few hours and by having cool showers. Creams and ointments clog the skin so they should be avoided. Locally bought prickly-heat powder can be helpful.

Insect Bites & Stings

Bedbugs don't carry disease but their bites are very itchy. They live in the cracks of furniture and walls, and then migrate to the bed at night to feed on you. You can treat the itch with an antihistamine.

Lice inhabit various parts of your body, but most commonly your head and pubic area. Transmission is via close contact with an infected person. Lice can be difficult to treat and you may need numerous applications of an anti-lice shampoo. Pubic lice are usually contracted from sexual contact.

Ticks are contracted after walking in rural areas. They are commonly found behind the ears, on the belly and in armpits. If you have had a tick bite and experience symptoms such as a rash at the site of the bite or elsewhere, or fever or muscle aches, you should see a doctor. Doxycycline prevents tick-borne diseases.

Leeches are found in humid rainforest areas. They do not transmit any disease but their bites are often intensely itchy for weeks afterwards and can easily become infected. Apply an iodine-based antiseptic to any leech bite to help prevent infection.

Bee and wasp stings mainly cause problems for people who are allergic to them. Anyone with a serious bee or wasp allergy should carry an injection of adrenaline (eg an Epipen) for emergency treatment. For others, pain is the main problem – apply ice to the sting and take painkillers.

Most jellyfish in Southeast Asian waters are not dangerous, just irritating. First aid for jellyfish stings involves pouring vinegar onto the affected area to neutralise the poison. Do not rub sand or water onto the stings. Take painkillers, and if you feel ill in any way after being stung seek medical advice. Take local advice if there are dangerous jellyfish around and keep out of the water.

Sandflies inhabit beaches (usually the more remote ones) across Southeast Asia. They have a nasty bite that is extremely itchy and can easily become infected. Use an antihistamine to quell the itching, and, if you have to itch, use the palm of your hand and not your nails or infection may follow.

Parasites

Numerous parasites are common in local populations in Southeast Asia; however, most of these are rare in travellers. The two rules for avoiding parasitic infections are to wear shoes and to avoid eating raw food, especially fish, pork and vegetables. A number of parasites are transmitted via the skin by walking barefoot, including *Strongyloides*, hookworm and cutaneous larva migrans.

Skin Problems

Fungal rashes are common in humid climates. There are two common fungal rashes that tend to affect travellers. The first occurs in moist areas that get less air, such as the groin, armpits and between the toes. It starts as a red patch that slowly spreads and is usually itchy. Treatment involves keeping the skin dry, avoiding chafing and using an antifungal cream such as clotrimazole or Lamisil. *Tinea versicolor* is also common – this fungus causes small, light-coloured patches, most commonly on the back, chest and shoulders. Consult a doctor.

Cuts and scratches become easily infected in humid climates. Take meticulous care of them to prevent complications such as abscesses. Immediately wash all wounds in clean water and apply antiseptic. If you develop signs of infection (increasing pain and redness), see a doctor. Divers and surfers should be particularly careful with coral cuts as they can be easily infected.

Snakes

Southeast Asia is home to many species of both poisonous and harmless snakes. Assume that all snakes are poisonous and never try to catch one. Wear boots and

FURABLE READING

Centers for Disease Control & Prevention (www.cdc.gov) Country-specific advice.

International Travel & Health (www.who.int/ith) Health guide published by the World Health Organization (WHO).

MD Travel Health (www.mdtravelhealth.com) Travel-health recommendations for every country.

long pants if walking in an area that may have snakes. First aid in the event of a snakebite involves pressure immobilisation using an elastic bandage firmly wrapped around the affected limb, starting at the bite site and working up towards the chest. The bandage should not be so tight that the circulation is cut off, and the fingers or toes should be kept free so the circulation can be checked. Immobilise the limb with a splint and carry the victim to medical attention. Do not use tourniquets or try to suck the venom out. Antivenin is available for most species, but not necessarily in rural areas of less-developed countries such as Cambodia, Laos and Myanmar.

Sunburn

Even on a cloudy day sunburn can occur rapidly. Always use a strong sunscreen (at least factor 30), making sure to reapply after a swim, and always wear a wide-brimmed hat and sunglasses outdoors. Avoid lying in the sun during the hottest part of the day (10am to 2pm). If you become sunburnt, stay out of the sun until you have recovered, apply cool compresses and take painkillers for the discomfort. One per cent hydrocortisone cream applied twice daily is also helpful.

Women's Health

In the urban areas of Southeast Asia, supplies of sanitary products are readily available. Birth-control options may be limited so bring adequate supplies of your own form of contraception. Heat, humidity and antibiotics can all contribute to thrush. Treatment is with antifungal creams and pessaries such as clotrimazole. A practical alternative is a single tablet of fluconazole (Diflucan). Urinary tract infections can be precipitated by dehydration or long bus journeys without toilet stops; bring suitable antibiotics.

Pregnant women should receive specialised advice before travelling. The ideal time to travel is in the second trimester (between 16 and 28 weeks), when the risk of pregnancy-related problems is at its lowest and women generally feel at their best. During the first trimester there is a risk of miscarriage and in the third trimester complications such as premature labour and high blood pressure are possible. It's wise to travel with a companion. Always carry a list of quality medical facilities available at your destination and ensure you continue your standard antenatal care at these facilities. Avoid rural travel in areas with poor transport and medical facilities. Most importantly of all, ensure travel insurance covers all pregnancy-related possibilities.

Malaria is a high-risk disease during pregnancy. WHO recommends that pregnant women do *not* travel to areas with chloroquine-resistant malaria. None of the more effective antimalarial drugs are completely safe in pregnancy.

Traveller's diarrhoea can quickly lead to dehydration and result in inadequate blood flow to the placenta. Many of the drugs used to treat various diarrhoea bugs are not recommended in pregnancy. Azithromycin is considered safe.

Language

This chapter offers basic vocabulary to help you get around Southeast Asia. Read our coloured pronunciation guides as if they were English, and you'll be understood. The stressed syllables are in italics. The polite and informal forms are indicated by the abbreviations 'pol' and 'inf' where needed. The abbreviations 'm' and 'f' indicate masculine and feminine gender respectively.

BURMESE

In Burmese, there's a difference between aspirated consonants (pronounced with a puff of air) and unaspirated ones. These consonants are said with a puff of air after the sound: ch (as in 'church'), k (as in 'kite'), ş (as in 'sick'), t (as in 'talk'); the following ones are pronounced with a puff of air before the sound: hl (as in 'life'), hm (as in 'me'), hn (as in 'not'), hng (as in 'sing'), hny (as in 'canyon'). Note also that the apostrophe (') represents the sound heard between 'uh-oh', th is pronounced as in 'thin' and ţh as in 'their'.

There are three distinct tones in Burmese (the raising and lowering of pitch on certain syllables). They are indicated in our pronunciation guides by the accent mark above the vowel: high creaky tone, as in 'heart' (á), plain high tone, as in 'car' (à), and the low tone (a). Note also that ai is pronounced as in 'aisle', aw as in 'law', and au as in 'brown'.

WANT MORE?

For in-depth language information and handy phrases, check out Lonely Planet's *Southeast Asia Phrasebook*. You'll find it at **shop.lonelyplanet.com**, or you can buy Lonely Planet's iPhone phrasebooks at the Apple App Store.

Basics

Hello.	မင်္ဂလာပါ။	ming·guh·la·ba
Goodbye.	သွားမယ်နော်။	thwà·me·naw
Excuse me.	ဆောရီးနော်။	sàw·rì·naw
Sorry.	ဆောရီးနော်။	sàw·rì·naw
Please.	တဆိတ်လောက်။	duh·şay'·lau'
Thank you.	ကျေးဇူး တင်ပါတယ်။	jày·zù ding·ba·de
Yes.	ဟုတ်ကဲ့။	hoh'·gé
No.	ဟင့်အင်း။	híng·ìn
Help!	ကယ်ပါ။	ge·ba

NUMBERS – BURMESE

1	တစ်	di'
2	နှစ်	hni'
3	သုံး	thòhng
4	လေး	là,
5	ငါး	ngà
6	ခြောက်	chau'
7	ခုနစ်	kung·ni'
8	ရှစ်	shi'
9	ကိုး	gòh
10	တစ်ဆယ်	duh·şe

What's your name?

နာမည် ဘယ်လို	nang·me be·loh
ခေါ်သလဲ။	kaw·ţhuh·lè

My name is ...

ကျနော်/ကျမ	juh·náw/juh·má
နာမည်က - - - ပါ။	nang·me·gá ... ba (m/f)

Do you speak English?

| အင်္ဂလိပ်လို | ìng·guh·lay'·loh |

ပြောတတ်သလား။		byàw·da'·thuh·là
I don't understand.		
နားမလည်ဘူး။		nà·muh·le·bòo
How much is it?		
ဒါဘယ်လောက်လဲ။		da be·lau'·lè
Where are the toilets?		
အိမ်သာ ဘယ်မှာလဲ။		ayng·ṭha be·hma·lè
I'd like the ..., please.	- - - ပေးပါ။	... bày·ba
bill	ဘောက်ချာ	bau'·cha
menu	မီးနူး	mì·nù
Call ...	- - - ခေါ်ပေးပါ။	... kaw·bày·ba
a doctor	ဆရာဝန်	ṣuh·ya·wung
the police	ရဲ	yèh

FILIPINO

Filipino is easy to pronounce and most sounds are familiar to English speakers. In addition, the relationship between Filipino sounds and their spelling is straightforward and consistent, meaning that each letter is always pronounced the same way. Note that ai is pronounced as in 'aisle', ay as in 'say', ew like ee with rounded lips, oh as the 'o' in 'go', ow as in 'how' and ooy as the 'wea' in 'tweak'. The r sound is stronger than in English and rolled. The glottal stop, pronounced like the pause between the two syllables in 'uh-oh', is indicated in our pronunciation guides by an apostrophe (').

Basics

Good day.	Magandáng araw pô. (pol)	ma·gan·dang a·row po'
	Magandáng araw. (inf)	ma·gan·dang a·row
Goodbye.	Paalam na pô. (pol)	pa·a·lam na po'
	Babay. (inf)	ba·bai

NUMBERS – FILIPINO

1	isá	ee·sa
2	dalawá	da·la·wa
3	tatló	tat·lo
4	apat	a·pat
5	limá	lee·ma
6	anim	a·neem
7	pitó	pee·to
8	waló	wa·lo
9	siyám	see·yam
10	sampû	sam·poo'

Yes.	Opò. (pol)	o·po'
	Oo. (inf)	o·o
No.	Hindí pô. (pol)	heen·dee' po'
	Hindî. (inf)	heen·dee'
Thank you.	Salamat pô. (pol)	sa·la·mat po'
	Salamat. (inf)	sa·la·mat
Help!	Saklolo!	sak·lo·lo

What's your name?
Anó pô ang pangalan ninyó? — a·no po' ang pa·nga·lan neen·yo

My name is ...
Ang pangalan ko pô ay ... — ang pa·nga·lan ko po' ai ...

Do you speak English?
Marunong ka ba ng Inglés? — ma·roo·nong ka ba nang eeng·gles

I don't understand.
Hindí ko náiintindihán. — heen·dee ko na·ee·een·teen·dee·han

How much is it?
Magkano? — mag·ka·no

Where are the toilets?
Násaán ang kubeta? — na·sa·an ang koo·be·ta

I'd like the menu.
Gustó ko ng menú. — goos·to ko nang me·noo

Please bring the bill.
Pakidalá ang tsit. — pa·kee·da·la ang tseet

Call ...!	Tumawag ka ng ...!	too·ma·wag ka nang ...
a doctor	doktór	dok·tor
the police	pulís	poo·lees

INDONESIAN & MALAY

Indonesian and Malay are very similar, so in this section we've provided translations in both languages – indicated by (I) and (M) respectively – only where the differences are significant enough to cause confusion. Most letters are pronounced more or less the same as their English counterparts, except for the letter c which is always pronounced as the 'ch' in 'chair'. Nearly all syllables carry equal emphasis, but a good approximation is to lightly stress the second-last syllable.

Basics

Hello.	Salam./Helo. (I/M)
Goodbye.	Selamat tinggal/jalan. (by person leaving/staying)
Excuse me.	Maaf.
Sorry.	Maaf.
Please.	Silakan.
Thank you.	Terima kasih.
Yes.	Ya.

NUMBERS – INDONESIAN/MALAY

1	satu
2	dua
3	tiga
4	empat
5	lima
6	enam
7	tujuh
8	delapan (I)
	lapan (M)
9	sembilan
10	sepuluh

No.	Tidak.
Help!	Tolong!
What's your name?	Siapa nama anda/kamu? (I/M)
My name is ...	Nama saya ...
Do you speak English?	Anda bisa Bahasa Inggris? (I) Adakah anda berbahasa Inggeris? (M)
I don't understand.	Saya tidak mengerti. (I) Saya tidak faham. (M)
How much is it?	Berapa harganya?
Where are the toilets?	Kamar kecil di mana? (I) Tandas di mana? (M)
I'd like the menu.	Saya minta daftar makanan.
Bring the bill, please.	Tolong bawa kuitansi/bil. (I/M)
Call a doctor!	Panggil doktor!
Call the police!	Panggil polis!

KHMER

In our pronunciation guides, vowels and vowel combinations with an h at the end are pronounced hard and aspirated (with a puff of air). The symbols for vowels are read as follows: aa as the 'a' in 'father'; a and ah shorter and harder than aa; i as in 'kit'; uh as the 'u' in 'but'; ii as the 'ee' in 'feet'; eu like 'oo' (with the lips spread flat); euh as eu (short and hard); oh as the 'o' in 'hose' (short and hard); ow as in 'glow'; u as the 'u' in 'flute' (short and hard); uu as the 'oo' in 'zoo'; ua as the 'ou' in 'tour'; uah as ua (short and hard); œ as 'er' in 'her' (more open); ia as the 'ee' in 'beer' (without the 'r'); e as in 'they'; ai as in 'aisle'; ae as the 'a' in 'cat'; ay as ai (slightly more nasal); ey as in 'prey'; o as the 'ow' in 'cow'; av like a nasal ao (without the 'v'); euv like a nasal eu (without the 'v'); ohm as the 'ome' in 'home'; am as the 'um' in 'glum'; ih as the 'ee'

in 'teeth' (short and hard); eh as the 'a' in 'date' (short and hard); awh as the 'aw' in 'jaw' (short and hard); and aw as the 'aw' in 'jaw'.

Some consonant combinations in our pronunciation guides are separated with an apostrophe for ease of pronunciation, eg 'j-r' in j'rook and 'ch-ng' in ch'ngain. Also note that k is pronounced as the 'g' in 'go'; kh as the 'k' in 'kind'; p as the final 'p' in 'puppy'; ph as the 'p' in 'pond'; r as in 'rum' but hard and rolling; t as the 't' in 'stand'; and th as the 't' in 'two'.

Basics

Hello.	ជម្រាបសួរ	johm riab sua
Goodbye.	លាសិនហើយ	lia suhn hao-y
Excuse me.	សុមទោស	sohm toh
Sorry.	សុមទោស	sohm toh
Please.	សុម	sohm
Thank you.	អរគុណ	aw kohn
Yes.	បាទ/ចាស	baat/jaa (m/f)
No.	ទេ	te
Help!	ជួយខ្ញុំផង!	juay kh'nyohm phawng

What's your name?
អ្នកឈ្មោះអ្វី? — niak ch'muah ei

My name is ...
ខ្ញុំឈ្មោះ... — kh'nyohm ch'muah ...

Does anyone speak English?
ទីនេះមានអ្នកចេះ — tii nih mian niak jeh
ភាសាអង់គ្លេសទេ? — phiasaa awngle te

I don't understand.
ខ្ញុំមិនយល់ទេ — kh'nyohm muhn yuhl te

How much is it?
នេះថ្លៃប៉ុន្មាន? — nih th'lay pohnmaan

NUMBERS – KHMER

1	មួយ	muy
2	ពីរ	pii
3	បី	bei
4	បួន	buan
5	ប្រាំ	bram
6	ប្រាំមួយ	bram muy
7	ប្រាំពីរ	bram pii
8	ប្រាំបី	bram bei
9	ប្រាំបួន	bram buan
10	ដប់	dawp

Where are the toilets?

ບ່ອນໃນໄປໄຂໃໄນ? bawngkohn neuv ai naa

Do you have a menu in English?

ມານມຸ່ໃນຸຈາ mien menui jea

ພາສາອໃໄຊ່ເກິສ່ເທ? piasaa awnglay te

The bill, please.

ສ່ມຕິຄ່ລຸຍ sohm kuht lui

Call a doctor!

ຊູຍເຫໃຄ່ເຊພ່ເທ່ມ່ມກ! juay hav kruu paet mok

Call the police!

ຊູຍເຫໃປ່ໃໄລ່ໃສນ່ມກ! juay hav police mok

LAO

Lao is a tonal language, meaning that many identical sounds are differentiated only by changes in the pitch of a speaker's voice. Pitch variations are relative to the speaker's natural vocal range, so that one person's low tone isn't necessarily the same pitch as another person's. There are six tones in Lao, indicated in our pronunciation guides by accent marks on letters: low tone (eg ḍẹe), high (eg héu·a), rising (eg sǎhm), high falling (eg sôw) and low falling (eg kòw). Note that no accent mark is used for the mid tone (eg het).

The pronunciation of vowels goes like this: i as in 'it'; ee as in 'feet'; ai as in 'aisle'; ah as the 'a' in 'father'; a as the short 'a' in 'about'; aa as in 'bad'; air as in 'air'; er as in 'fur'; eu as in 'sir'; u as in 'put'; oo as in 'food'; ow as in 'now'; or as in 'jaw'; o as in 'phone'; oh as in 'toe'; ee·a as in 'lan'; oo·a as in 'tour'; ew as in 'yew'; and oy as in 'boy'. Most consonants correspond to their English counterparts. The exceptions are đ (a hard 't' sound, a bit like 'dt') and ɓ (a hard 'p' sound, a bit like 'bp').

In our pronunciation guides, the hyphens indicate syllable breaks, eg àng·gìt (English). Some syllables are divided with a dot to help pronounce compound vowels, eg kěe·an (write).

Basics

Hello.	ສະບາຍດີ	sábại-děe
Goodbye.	ສະບາຍດີ	sábại-děe
Excuse me.	ຂໍໂທດ	kǒr tôht
Sorry.	ຂໍໂທດ	kǒr tôht
Please.	ກະລຸນາ	ga-lú-náh
Thank you.	ຂອບໃຈ	kòrp jại
Yes.	ແມນ	maan
No.	ບໍ່	bor
Help!	ຊ່ວຍແດ່	soo·ay daa

NUMBERS – LAO

1	ໜຶ່ງ	neung
2	ສອງ	sǒrng
3	ສາມ	sǎhm
4	ສີ່	see
5	ຫ້າ	hàh
6	ຫກ	hók
7	ເຈັດ	jét
8	ແປດ	ɓàat
9	ເກົ້າ	gôw
10	ສິບ	síp

What's your name?

ເຈົ້າຂື່ຫຍັງ jôw seu nyǎng

My name is ...

ຂ້ອຍຂື່ ... kòy seu ...

Do you speak English?

ເຈົ້າປາກ jôw ɓàhk

ພາສາອັງກິດໄດ້ບໍ່ páh-sǎh ạng·kít dâi bor

I don't understand.

ບໍ່ເຂົ້າໃຈ bor kòw jại

How much (for) ...?

... ເທົ່າໃດ ... tow dại

Where are the toilets?

ຫ້ອງນໍ້າຢູ່ໃສ hòrng nâm yoo sǎii

Menu

ລາຍການອາຫານ lái-gạhn ạh-hǎhn

Please bring the bill.

ຂໍແຊ້ກແດ່ kǒr saak daa

Call a doctor!

ຊ່ວຍຕາມຫາໝໍ soo·ay đạhm hǎh mǒr

ໃຫ້ແດ່ hài daa

Call the police!

ຊ່ວຍເອີ້ນຕໍາລວດແດ່ soo·ay êrn đam-lòo·at daa

TETUN

Tetun pronunciation is pretty straightforward. Letters always have the same sound value, and are generally pronounced just like in English, with the following exceptions: *j* is pronounced as the 's' in 'pleasure' (and sometimes as the 'z' in 'zebra'), *x* is pronounced as the 'sh' in 'ship' (sometimes as the 's' in 'summer'), while *lh* and *nh* are pronounced as the 'ly' in 'million' and the 'ny' in 'canyon' respectively (and outside Dili they are often reduced to *l* and *n* respectively).

Word stress is fairly regular and usually falls on the second-last syllable of a word; if it falls on another syllable, we've indicated this with an accent mark on the vowel (eg *polísia*).

Basics

Hello.	Haló./Olá. (pol/inf)
Goodbye.	Adeus.
Excuse me.	Kolisensa.
Sorry.	Disculpa.
Please.	Favór ida./Faz favór.
Thank you.	Obrigadu/a. (m/f)
Yes.	Sin./Diak./Los.
No.	Lae.
Help!	Ajuda!

NUMBERS – TETUN

1	ida
2	rua
3	tolu
4	hat
5	lima
6	nen
7	hitu
8	ualu
9	sia
10	sanulu

What's your name?	Ita-nia naran saida?
My name is ...	Hau-nia naran ...
Do you speak English?	Ita koalia Inglés?
I don't understand.	Hau la kompriende.
How much is it?	Folin hira?
Where are the toilets?	Sintina iha nebé?
Please bring the menu/bill.	Favór ida lori hela menu/konta mai.
Call a doctor!	Bolu dotór!
Call the police!	Bolu polísia!

THAI

In Thai the meaning of a syllable may be altered by means of tones. In standard Thai there are five tones: low (eg *bàht*), mid (eg *dee*), falling (eg *mâi*), high (eg *máh*) and rising (eg *sǎhm*). The range of all tones is relative

to each speaker's vocal range, so there is no fixed 'pitch' intrinsic to the language.

In our pronunciation guides, the hyphens indicate syllable breaks within words, and for ease of pronunciation some compound vowels are divided with a dot (eg *mêu·a·rai*).

The vowel a is pronounced as in 'about', aa as the 'a' in 'bad', ah as the 'a' in 'father', ai as in 'aisle', air as in 'flair' (without the 'r'), eu as the 'er' in 'her' (without the 'r'), ew as in 'new' (with rounded lips), oh as the 'o' in 'toe', or as in 'torn' (without the 'r') and ow as in 'now'.

Note also the pronunciation of the following consonants: b (a hard 'p' sound, almost like a 'b', eg in 'hip-bag'); d (a hard 't' sound, like a sharp 'd', eg in 'mid-tone'); and r (as in 'run' but flapped; often pronounced like 'l').

Basics

Hello.	สวัสดี	sà-wàt-dee
Goodbye.	ลาก่อน	lah gòrn
Excuse me.	ขออภัย	kǒr à-pai
Sorry.	ขอโทษ	kǒr tôht
Please.	ขอ	kǒr
Thank you.	ขอบคุณ	kòrp kun
Yes.	ใช่	châi
No.	ไม่	mâi
Help!	ช่วยด้วย	chôo·ay dôo·ay
What's your name?		
คุณชื่ออะไร		kun chêu à-rai
My name is ...		
ผม/ดิฉัน		pǒm/dì-chǎn
ชื่อ...		chêu ... (m/f)

NUMBERS – THAI

1	หนึ่ง	nèung
2	สอง	sǒrng
3	สาม	sǎhm
4	สี่	sèe
5	ห้า	hâh
6	หก	hòk
7	เจ็ด	jèt
8	แปด	bàat
9	เก้า	gôw
10	สิบ	sìp

Do you speak English?

คุณพูดภาษา	kun pôot pah-săh
อังกฤษได้ไหม	ang-grìt dâi măi

I don't understand.

ผม/ดิฉันไม่	pŏm/dì-chăn mâi
เข้าใจ	kôw jai (m/f)

How much is it?

เท่าไร	tôw-rai

Where are the toilets?

ห้องน้ำอยู่ที่ไหน	hôrng nám yòo têe năi

I'd like the menu, please.

ขอรายการ	kŏr rai gahn
อาหารหน่อย	ah-hăhn nòy

Please bring the bill.

ขอบิลหน่อย	kŏr bin nòy

Call a doctor!

เรียกหมอหน่อย	rêe·ak mŏr nòy

Call the police!

เรียกตำรวจหน่อย	rêe·ak đam·ròo·at nòy

VIETNAMESE

Vietnamese is written in a Latin-based phonetic alphabet, which was declared the official written form in 1910.

In our pronunciation guides, a is pronounced as in 'at', aa as in 'father', aw as in 'law', er as in 'her', oh as in 'doh!', ow as in 'cow', u as in 'book', uh as in 'but' and uhr as in 'fur' (without the 'r'). We've used dots (eg dee·úhng) to separate the combined vowel sounds. Note also that d is pronounced as in 'stop', đ as in 'dog', and ğ as in 'skill'.

Vietnamese uses a system of tones to make distinctions between words – so some vowels are pronounced with a high or low pitch. There are six tones in Vietnamese, indicated in the written language (and in our pronunciation guides) by accent marks on the vowel: mid (ma), low falling (mà), low rising (mả), high broken (mã), high rising (má) and low broken (mạ). The mid tone is flat.

The variation in vocabulary between the Vietnamese of the north and the south is indicated by (N) and (S) respectively.

Basics

Hello.	Xin chào.	sin jòw
Goodbye.	Tạm biệt.	daạm bee·ụht

NUMBERS – VIETNAMESE

1	một	mạwt
2	hai	hai
3	ba	baa
4	bốn	báwn
5	năm	nuhm
6	sáu	sóh
7	bảy	bảy
8	tám	dúhm
9	chín	jín
10	mười	muhr·eè

Excuse me.	Xin lỗi.	sin lõy
Sorry.	Xin lỗi.	sin lõy
Please.	Làm ơn.	laàm ern
Thank you.	Cảm ơn.	ğaảm ern
Yes.	Vâng./Dạ. (N/S)	vuhng/yạ
No.	Không.	kawm
Help!	Cứu tôi!	ğuhr·oó doy

What's your name?

Tên là gì?	den laà zeè

My name is ...

Tên tôi là ...	den doy laà ...

Do you speak English?

Bạn có nói tiếng	baạn ğó nóy dee·úhng
Anh không?	aang kawm

I don't understand.

Tôi không hiểu.	doy kawm heé·oo

How much is this?

Cái này giá bao nhiêu?	ğaí này zaá bow nyee·oo

Where is the toilet?

Nhà vệ sinh ở đâu?	nyaà vẹ sing ẻr đoh

I'd like the menu.

Tôi muốn thực đơn.	doy moo·úhn tụhrk đern

The bill, please.

Xin tính tiền.	sin díng dee·ùhn

Please call a doctor.

Làm ơn gọi bác sĩ.	laàm ern goỵ baák seẽ

Please call the police.

Làm ơn gọi công an.	laàm ern goỵ ğawm aan

Behind the Scenes

SEND US YOUR FEEDBACK

We love to hear from travellers – your comments keep us on our toes and help make our books better. Our well-travelled team reads every word on what you loved or loathed about this book. Although we cannot reply individually to your submissions, we always guarantee that your feedback goes straight to the appropriate authors, in time for the next edition. Each person who sends us information is thanked in the next edition – the most useful submissions are rewarded with a selection of digital PDF chapters.

Visit **lonelyplanet.com/contact** to submit your updates and suggestions or to ask for help. Our award-winning website also features inspirational travel stories, news and discussions.

Note: We may edit, reproduce and incorporate your comments in Lonely Planet products such as guidebooks, websites and digital products, so let us know if you don't want your comments reproduced or your name acknowledged. For a copy of our privacy policy visit lonelyplanet.com/privacy.

OUR READERS

Many thanks to the travellers who used the last edition and wrote to us with helpful hints, useful advice and interesting anecdotes:

A Anna Meisser, Anne Fortin **B** Billy Allen, Bonnie Cheung, Brittney Laver **C** Carla Giustozzi, Christopher Sadler, Colin Pischke **D** Daniel Cox **E** Eduard Ringe, Erica Wijarnako **F** Florian Reichert **G** George Bloomfield **H** Heather Adams, Hendriekje Decorte **J** Johann Schelesnak, Johannes Wölfel, John Roberts **K** Katarzyna Jaklewicz, Katie Ingham **L** Lauren Marinigh, Laurie Collard, Leorah McGinnis, Lucie Samohylova **M** Manon van der Steen, Matias Rivera, Michelle Biggs, Miriam Ganem-Rosen, Moritz Laux **N** Nadia Muttalib, Nadine Timm **O** Ola Wawrzon, Oliver Heard, Omar Risk **P** Pam Gould **R** Rick Beunk, Romuald Chasseur, Ruth Obando **S** Sam Hoagland, Sander Jansen, Sandro Ferrari, Sarah Anthony **T** Thomas Wiser **V** Viktoria Jokisch

AUTHOR THANKS

Nick Ray

As always a huge and heartfelt thanks to the people of Southeast Asia, whose warmth and humour, stoicism and spirit make it a happy yet humbling place to be. Biggest thanks are reserved for my lovely wife, Kulikar Sotho, as without her support and encouragement the adventures would not be possible. And to our young children, Julian and Belle, for enlivening our lives immeasurably. Many thanks to my mum and dad for giving me the freedom to travel and their many visits to this part of the world. Thanks to fellow travellers and residents, friends and contacts in Southeast Asia who have helped to shape my knowledge and experience in this region. Thanks also to my co-authors for going the extra mile to ensure this is a worthy new edition. Finally, thanks to the Lonely Planet team who have worked on this title. The authors may be the public face, but a huge amount of work goes into making this a better book behind the scenes and I thank you all for your hard work.

Isabel Albiston

Thanks to everyone who helped out along the way, especially Mrs Lee, Stephen Baya and Tine Hjetting, Mado in Pa Lungan, Dina Bailey, Chongteah Lim, Leslie Chiang, Anthony Chieng, Polycarp Teo Sebum and Louise, Jacqueline Fong and Jo-Lynn Liao. Cheers also to Stefan Arestis and Sebastien Chaneac for making me laugh and to my friends and family for their love and support. Lastly, huge thanks to Sarah.

Greg Bloom

A huge thanks to my dedicated research assistant, Windi, for toughing it out with me in various locales. Being an RA is a tough job but somebody has to do it. The cumulative knowledge of my *barkada* (gang of friends) in Manila was elemental as usual. Thanks as always to Anna for her sanity-inducing sweetness on deadline. Thank you Alan in Sagada, and thanks to the gentlemen of the Mabanlay *dap-ay* (outdoor meeting place) in Dagdag for inviting me to your *begnas* (traditional community celebration).

Ria de Jong

Thank you to Destination Editor Sarah Reid for holding my hand through my first Lonely Planet adventure, and to Cristian Bonetto who trod the path before me. To my parents and sister who nurtured my love of the road less travelled and to Craig, Cisca and William who are my travelling circus tribe.

David Eimer

Much gratitude to Htwe Htwe in Hsipaw for tips and transport and Samara and Yu Yu for Yangon guidance. Thanks to Laura Crawford and the rest of the Lonely Planet team in London. As ever, thanks to everyone who passed on advice along the way, whether knowingly or unwittingly.

Sarah Reid

Thank you to my managers at Lonely Planet for supporting my amazing Timor-Leste adventure; to my brilliant local guide Luis for your careful driving, infinite patience and wealth of local knowledge; to all the other kind, helpful people I met in Timor-Leste (shout-outs to Des, Neyl, Megan and Dan) and finally to Timmy, my partner in travel and in life.

Simon Richmond

Terima kasih (thank you) to the following: Nozara Yusof, Alex Yong, Andrew Sebastian, Narelle McMurtrie, Gregers Reimann and Scott Dunn.

Iain Stewart

Thanks to Nick Ray, Laura Crawford and the Lonely Planet editorial and production staff. On the ground we benefited from a fine team of authors: Anna, Brett, Jess and Ben. Hi to Slo and Mark in HCMC, Caroline and Neil, Vinh Vu, Ben and Bich, Howard and Deb, Mark and Dzung in Hoi An.

Ryan Ver Berkmoes

Many thanks to friends like the extraordinary Amy Brenneman, Romy and Lola; the incomparable Hanafi; Patticakes, Ibu Cat, Stuart, Rucina and Kerry and Milt Turner. Off-Bali: Amber Clifton, Paul Landgraver, Ilham, Saripa, Philip, Edwin and many, many more were generous with time, ideas and expertise. And Alexis Averbuck, who I once met in Bali and who I married while writing this book.

Richard Waters

My sincere thanks to the people of Laos who welcome me like an old friend every time I'm lucky enough to visit, and to my editor, Laura, for sending me back there again. In no particular order my thanks also to Eliz V, Dennis, Mr Saly, Harp, Marcus, Michel S, Ivan, Matt V, Basile and finally my wife and kids who allow me to disappear to strange places.

China Williams

Thanks to my children, Felix and Phoebe, and my husband, Matt, for being my best travelling companions. And thanks to my beloved Thai friends and former students who I get to hang out with on a daily basis on Facebook. Thanks to Sarah Reid for making room for me on this project, and finally to all of Lonely Planet's other Thailand writers who assisted on the project.

ACKNOWLEDGEMENTS

Climate map data adapted from Peel MC, Finlayson BL & McMahon TA (2007) 'Updated World Map of the Köppen-Geiger Climate Classification', Hydrology and Earth System Sciences, 11, 163344.

Illustrations p94-5, p652-3 and p854-5 by Michael Weldon.

Cover photograph: Temple detail, Angkor, Cambodia/Csilla Zelko 500px ©

THIS BOOK

This 18th edition of Lonely Planet's *Southeast Asia on a Shoestring* guidebook was researched and written by Nick Ray, Isabel Albiston, Greg Bloom, Ria de Jong, David Eimer, Sarah Reid, Simon Richmond, Iain Stewart, Ryan Ver Berkmoes, Richard Waters and China Williams. Additional research for Cambodia was provided by Jessica Lee. Additional research for Indonesia was provided by Loren Bell, Stuart Butler, Trent Holden, Anna Kaminski, Hugh McNaughten, Adam Skolnick and Iain Stewart. Additional research for Malaysia was provided by Greg Benchwick, Anita Isalska, Robert Scott Kelly and Brett Stewart. Original research for Myanmar was provided by David Eimer. Additional research for Singapore was provided by Cristian Bonetto. Additional research for Thailand was provided by Mark Beales, Tim Bewer, Joe Bindloss, Austin Bush, David Eimer, Bruce Evans, Damian Harper and Isabella Noble. Additional research for Vietnam was provided by Brett Atkinson, Anna Kaminski, Jessica Lee and Benedict Walker. This guidebook was commissioned and produced by the following:

Destination Editors Laura Crawford, Sarah Reid

Coordinating Editor Andrea Dobbin

Product Editors Kate Mathews, Luna Soo

Senior Cartographer Diana Von Holdt

Book Designer Wendy Wright

Assisting Editors Carolyn Bain, Carolyn Boicos, Paul Harding, Gabrielle Innes, Ali Lemer, Jodie Martire, Susan Paterson, Ross Taylor, Amanda Williamson

Cartographers Julie Dodkins, Michael Garrett, Valentina Kremenchuskaya, Alison Lyall, Julie Sheridan

Cover Researcher Campbell McKenzie

Thanks to Anita Banh, Grace Dobell, Bruce Evans, Mao Monkolransey, Catherine Naghten, Stephen Nolan, Kirsten Rawlings, Juan Winata

Index

INDEX S–T

Map Legend

Sights
- Beach
- Bird Sanctuary
- Buddhist
- Castle/Palace
- Christian
- Confucian
- Hindu
- Islamic
- Jain
- Jewish
- Monument
- Museum/Gallery/Historic Building
- Ruin
- Shinto
- Sikh
- Taoist
- Winery/Vineyard
- Zoo/Wildlife Sanctuary
- Other Sight

Activities, Courses & Tours
- Bodysurfing
- Diving
- Canoeing/Kayaking
- Course/Tour
- Sento Hot Baths/Onsen
- Skiing
- Snorkelling
- Surfing
- Swimming/Pool
- Walking
- Windsurfing
- Other Activity

Sleeping
- Sleeping
- Camping

Eating
- Eating

Drinking & Nightlife
- Drinking & Nightlife
- Cafe

Entertainment
- Entertainment

Shopping
- Shopping

Information
- Bank
- Embassy/Consulate
- Hospital/Medical
- Internet
- Police
- Post Office
- Telephone
- Toilet
- Tourist Information
- Other Information

Geographic
- Beach
- Gate
- Hut/Shelter
- Lighthouse
- Lookout
- Mountain/Volcano
- Oasis
- Park
- Pass
- Picnic Area
- Waterfall

Population
- Capital (National)
- Capital (State/Province)
- City/Large Town
- Town/Village

Transport
- Airport
- Border crossing
- Bus
- Cable car/Funicular
- Cycling
- Ferry
- Metro/MRT/MTR station
- Monorail
- Parking
- Petrol station
- Skytrain/Subway station
- Taxi
- Train station/Railway
- Tram
- Underground station
- Other Transport

Note: Not all symbols displayed above appear on the maps in this book

Routes
- Tollway
- Freeway
- Primary
- Secondary
- Tertiary
- Lane
- Unsealed road
- Road under construction
- Plaza/Mall
- Steps
- Tunnel
- Pedestrian overpass
- Walking Tour
- Walking Tour detour
- Path/Walking Trail

Boundaries
- International
- State/Province
- Disputed
- Regional/Suburb
- Marine Park
- Cliff
- Wall

Hydrography
- River, Creek
- Intermittent River
- Canal
- Water
- Dry/Salt/Intermittent Lake
- Reef

Areas
- Airport/Runway
- Beach/Desert
- Cemetery (Christian)
- Cemetery (Other)
- Glacier
- Mudflat
- Park/Forest
- Sight (Building)
- Sportsground
- Swamp/Mangrove

David Eimer

Myanmar David first travelled to Myanmar back in the days of the military junta. Since then he's made repeated visits that have taken him throughout the country. When not travelling, David lives in Bangkok and works as a journalist for several newspapers and magazines. Originally from London, he was previously based in Beijing and LA. He has contributed to over a dozen Lonely Planet books.

Sarah Reid

Timor-Leste Lonely Planet Destination Editor and travel writer Sarah Reid added Timor-Leste to her travel wish list after interviewing the cast of *Balibo* in her past life as an entertainment journalist in Sydney. Getting the chance to visit this poor but wonderful country for the first time six years later (on the 40th anniversary of the events that inspired the film) to research this guide was a great privilege. Originally hailing from Byron Bay, Australia, Sarah has lived on three continents, and visited more than 80 countries in between.

Simon Richmond

Peninsular Malaysia Simon first travelled in the region back in the early 1990s. A lot has changed since, but Malaysia remains among Simon's favourite destinations for its easily accessible mix of cultures, landscapes, adventures and, crucially, delicious food. An award-winning travel writer and photographer, Simon has helmed Lonely Planet's *Malaysia, Singapore & Brunei* guide for five editions. He's also the author of Lonely Planet's *Kuala Lumpur, Melaka & Penang* guide as well as a shelf-load of other titles for this and other publishers. Read more about Simon's travels at www.simonrichmond.com and on Twitter and Instagram @simonrichmond.

Iain Stewart

Vietnam Iain has been visiting Vietnam since 1991 and has explored virtually every province in the country in search of the perfect *bia hoi* and *ca phe sua*. On this trip he travelled the coastal road between Vung Tau and Hoi An taking in some stunning coastal scenery and numerous memorable meals.

Ryan Ver Berkmoes

Indonesia Ryan first visited Indonesia in 1993. On his visits since he has criss-crossed the archipelago, trying to make a dent in those 17,000 islands. Recent thrills included the ancient villages of West Timor and finding his new favourite beach on Flores (it's near Paga). Off-island, Ryan travels the world writing and calls New York City home. Read more at ryanverberkmoes.com and at @ryanvb.

Richard Waters

Laos Richard's first night in Laos was back in '99 when he broke down in a speedboat on the Mekong and, while marooned on the riverbank, twilight sent a body floating past. Since then it got a lot better (that very night he eventually saw Luang Prabang for the first time). As a Lonely Planet author he's also written about Malawi, Transylvania, Greece and Borneo; while as a journalist he regularly works for the *Daily Telegraph,* the *Sunday Times* and the *Independent,* and has won the odd international writing award. He lives with his wife and kids in the Cotswolds. He also writes a wellbeing blog called Soul Tonic.

China Williams

Thailand China first travelled to Thailand in 1997 to teach English in the rural northeast. Since then she has filled two passport books and has inaugurated both of her children's passports with Thai entry and exit stamps. Before children she wandered all over the US but is now firmly planted in the suburbs of Baltimore, MD, USA.

OUR STORY

A beat-up old car, a few dollars in the pocket and a sense of adventure. In 1972 that's all Tony and Maureen Wheeler needed for the trip of a lifetime – across Europe and Asia overland to Australia. It took several months, and at the end – broke but inspired – they sat at their kitchen table writing and stapling together their first travel guide, *Across Asia on the Cheap*. Within a week they'd sold 1500 copies. Lonely Planet was born.

Today, Lonely Planet has offices in Franklin, London, Melbourne, Oakland, Beijing and Delhi, with more than 600 staff and writers. We share Tony's belief that 'a great guidebook should do three things: inform, educate and amuse'.

OUR WRITERS

Nick Ray

Coordinating author, Cambodia A Londoner of sorts, Nick comes from Watford, the sort of town that makes you want to travel. He lives in Phnom Penh with his wife, Kulikar, and children, Julian and Belle. He has written for numerous guidebooks covering Southeast Asia, including Lonely Planet's *Cambodia, Indonesia, Laos, Myanmar* and *Vietnam* as well as *Vietnam, Cambodia, Laos & Northern Thailand*. When not writing, he is often out exploring the remote parts of the Mekong region as a location scout and manager for the world of television and film, including projects from *Tomb Raider* to *Top Gear Vietnam*. Motorbikes are a part-time passion (riding them a passion, maintaining them part-time) and he has travelled through most of Indochina on two wheels.

Isabel Albiston

Brunei, Malaysian Borneo Since her first trip to Malaysia six years ago, Isabel has grown to love clambering up slippery trails on sweaty jungle hikes. After three months exploring Borneo's forests and longhouses, feasting on Sarawak laksa, downing shots of *tuak*, dancing at the Rainforest World Music Festival and dropping in on the sultan at his palace in Brunei, the temptation to stay nearly won out. Isabel is a journalist who has written for a number of newspapers and magazines including the UK's *Daily Telegraph*.

Greg Bloom

Philippines Greg has lived in Southeast Asia for more than a decade, dividing his time between Cambodia and his current home of Manila. This is his fifth straight stint on Lonely Planet's *Southeast Asia*. His latest assignment brought plenty of highs (*ginebra*-fueled *begnas* in Ifugao and Sagada) as well as the occasional low (losing a money-filled wallet mid-typhoon Ineng in Bontoc). When not writing about Southeast Asia, Greg might be found snouting around Russia or patrolling Asia's ultimate frisbee fields.

Ria de Jong

Singapore Ria started life in Asia, born in Sri Lanka to Dutch/Australian parents; she has always relished the hustle and excitement of this continent of contrasts. After growing up in Townsville, Australia, Ria moved to Sydney to work as a features writer before packing her bags for a five-year stint in the Philippines. Having moved to Singapore in 2015 with her husband and two small children, Ria is loving discovering every nook and cranny of this tiny city-country-nation. This is Ria's first Lonely Planet title.

OVER MORE
PAGE WRITERS

Published by Lonely Planet Global Limited
CRN 554153
18th edition – October 2016
ISBN 978 1 78657 119 9
© Lonely Planet 2016   Photographs © as indicated 2016
10 9 8 7 6 5 4 3 2 1
Printed in Singapore